D0971527

Also by Myra MacPherson

The Power Lovers:
An Intimate Look at Politicians and Their Marriages

Long Time Passing:
Vietnam and the Haunted Generation

She Came to Live Out Loud

An Inspiring Family Journey Through Illness, Loss, and Grief

Myra MacPherson

A Lisa Drew Book
SCRIBNER

A LISA DREW BOOK/SCRIBNER
1230 Avenue of the Americas
New York, NY 10020

Copyright © 1999 by Myra MacPherson

All rights reserved, including the right of reproduction in whole or in part in any form.

SCRIBNER and design are trademarks of Simon & Schuster Inc.

Set in Adobe Garamond

DESIGNED BY ERICH HOBBING

Manufactured in the United States of America

1 3 5 7 9 10 8 6 4 2

Library of Congress Cataloging-in-Publication Data

MacPherson, Myra.
She came to live out loud: an inspiring family journey through illness, loss, and grief/Myra MacPherson.
p. cm.
"A Lisa Drew Book."
Includes bibliographical references and index.

1. Death—Psychological aspects. 2. Johannessen, Anna Margaret, 1952–1997. 3. Cancer—Patients—United States. 4. Terminally ill—Psychology. 5. Terminally ill—Family relationships. 6. Loss (Psychology). 7. Grief. I. Title.
BF789.D4M33 1999
155.9'37'0922—dc21
[B] 98-28125
CIP

ISBN 684-82264-4

For Anna,

Jan, Ellery, Lindsay, and

their extended family and friends

and

for Jack and

our extended family and friends

and

in memory of my mother

If you asked me what I came into this world to do,
I will tell you: I came to live out loud.

Émile Zola

Contents

PART III
A New Level of Existence

PART IV
Grieving: Our Common Bond

Introduction

In *Living with Life-Threatening Illness,* I emphasize that even in the midst of a struggle with a disease that threatens existence, persons still continue to live. They work, raise children, argue with spouses, make love, enjoy friends, and otherwise engage in the sublime and mundane facets of life. They do this as they cope with anxieties and treatments. Even in the face of illness, they *live.*

But Anna's story illustrates that point far more eloquently in this new book by Myra MacPherson, *She Came to Live Out Loud.* The book is subtitled *An Inspiring Family Journey Through Illness, Loss, and Grief.* And it is. Part of the reason for that is that it is Anna's story, powerfully told.

As MacPherson recounts in this book, I met Anna toward the end of her struggle with cancer. It was to be one of her last "good" days. And it wasn't that great a day. Despite the wonderfully prepared and presented dinner, Anna did not have much of an appetite. No matter, she still sparkled. She had a way of engaging each and any person she encountered. Any sense of sorrow, even pity, fell to her enchantment. Only later did reality remind me that this rare individual might not be alive in a few weeks.

Yet this is more than the story of a special person, of even an unusual family's struggle with cancer. It is much more universal than that. In a sense, every story of a life-threatening illness is the story of how one person, and one family, cope. These cases are the building blocks of the theories we have about how we react to illness, loss, and grief. Those theories are merely abstractions of that individual reality. Moreover, Anna's story reminds us never to lose sight of the individual in our theorizing but instead to focus on how that person copes, on his or her strengths, on the uniquely individual sources of hope and sustenance.

MacPherson shares with us Anna's story, her up-and-down struggle with the disease, her decisions, and her strengths and weaknesses. And in telling that story, we learn another truth, that every disease affects those around—spouse, children, family, and friends. And so we see how they cope with Anna's illness as well as her death. We learn from them as well.

This book will touch us in very different ways. For some of us, it may remind us of the struggles we have experienced or witnessed. For others, it may reaffirm, help us rediscover—or, even, discover—our own strategies and strengths as we confront illness or loss. And I believe for all of us, it will allow us to acknowledge the very quiet yet special heroism that allows us to live fully even as we die.

KENNETH J. DOKA, PH.D.,
Professor of Gerontology, College of New Rochelle; Lutheran minister;
Senior Adviser to the Hospice Foundation of America;
Chair of the International Work Group on Death, Dying, and Bereavement;
Past President of the Association for Death Education
and Counseling

PROLOGUE

Learning

THE ELEPHANT IN THE ROOM

> There's an elephant in the room. It is large and squatting, so it is hard to get around it. Yet we squeeze by with "How are you?" and "I'm fine" . . . and a thousand other forms of trivial chatter. We talk about the weather. We talk about work. We talk about everything else—except the elephant in the room. There's an elephant in the room. We all know it's there. We are thinking about the elephant as we talk together. It is constantly on our minds. For, you see, it is a very big elephant. It has hurt us all. But we do not talk about the elephant in the room. Oh, please say her name. Oh, please say "Barbara" again. Oh, please, let's talk about the elephant in the room. For if we talk about her death, perhaps we can talk about her life. Can I say "Barbara" to you and not have you look away? For if I cannot, then you are leaving me. Alone . . . in a room . . . with an elephant.
>
> TERRY KETTERING

I kiss her forehead. It is as cold as an ice sculpture. I involuntarily reach up to touch my mouth, tingling now with that ice-burn feeling. It conjures up a remembrance of times past, childhood mittens beaded with snow lifted to mouth, cold fabric sticking to warm lips.

I look down at my mother, who is no longer my mother. I had not been able to get there in time, while her eyes were open, while she could say hello, while I could hold her. At eighty-one, she looks as young in death as she had in life, a round full face saved by high cheekbones. But her arresting dark brown eyes are closed forever. My mother is unpainted in death, thank God. Unlike the rituals of funereal viewing, the urn would not need such cosmetic totems as rouge and lipstick and silk-lined caskets.

When I stumbled off the plane from the East Coast that Saturday morning, I picked up my father and soon we entered this tiny funeral home in Indio, an undistinguished hamlet in the windswept California desert. The funeral home had gone all out, one could say, by opening its doors even though my father and I had not requested an appointment—which, we were assured by the young man in the T-shirt and Bermuda shorts, was protocol.

"You are here to arrange the final details?" he asked, in a tone not far removed from that of an elementary teacher talking to the class. Nothing could be more final, I felt like saying, anger rising. This was an indifferent man among the dead, with his pressing concern, no doubt, an afternoon tennis game. His calculator clicked away: the cost of embalming, for having picked mother up at the hospital, for putting a notice in the newspaper. I said that I would like to see my mother. The young man informed me that they hadn't prepared her "to receive guests," as if she were a grande dame in her mansion. "I am not a guest," I said. "She is my mother and I would like to see her."

"Very well," he said, flipping his calculator open again. "It will take a few minutes to prepare her."

"What do you mean 'prepare'?"

"Well, we have to make her look presentable."

I found out that preparation meant putting my mother's body on a table and covering her with a pink blanket; pink, of course, to cast color.

"To see her," he said, "will be an additional fifty dollars."

He was not conditioned for the explosion that came from me and my father. The Uriah Heep of Funeral Homes mysteriously and quickly summoned the owner, who entered from a back door. He was apologetic about the appearance of his assistant. "Normally, he would have received you in a coat and tie, but since you didn't call for an appointment . . ." he said, his voice trailing off.

Appearances weren't the problem, I said. What mattered was a basic lack of consideration for feelings, the concern for their precious fifty dollars. The voice of the owner glided along: "Had you requested viewing of the body, it would have, of course, been itemized in the initial billing, but since this was a last-minute request, we could do nothing but to add it."

"Why does it cost fifty dollars?" I asked.

"Well, it just *does.* It is so itemized," he said, bringing out his list much like a clerk at the dry cleaners: $3.75 to iron a shirt with French cuffs, $4.50 for a suit jacket.

The desire to see my mother took precedence over the principle of refusing to pay their fee. After my moments with Mom, a whispered "I love you" to that stilled body beneath the pink blanket, I returned to the outer office with its brown fake-wood paneling, fake orange flowers, fake sentiments (at least to this funeral home) hung on the walls: "Show me the manner in which a nation or community cares for its dead and I will measure with mathematical exactness the tender sympathies of its people, their respect for the laws of the land and their loyalty to high ideals." The funeral home's notepaper had placed its most ironic message in italics above the telephone number: "In Your Hour of Need."

Flying home, I read a newspaper item that sent me into hysterical laughter—dark, macabre humor that inexplicably relieves tension and sorrow. A funeral home and a customer had quarreled over a bill, the customer saying that it had been paid in full, the funeral home disagreeing. The home settled the argument by dumping the dead body on the doorstep of the survivors. I read it to my dad on the phone, saying, "Well, it could have been worse!" This image, despite the grimness for those involved, caused both of us to laugh. It was the only laugh in a week that had jangled and jarred its way to an end. No sooner had we walked back inside my parents' bungalow from the funeral home than I was quickly erasing all traces of my mother. My father had instructed me to.

"This was not the way it was supposed to be," I thought, taking jackets and golf skirts and slacks off the rack, folding up nightgowns, grown larger over the years. No good-byes and no warning. Mom was never seriously sick a day in her life. Nor did we ever say good-bye as a family. Dad felt that he could not get through it and said no to a memorial service.

* * *

The jangle of the phone broke into the quiet of the cabin in the North Carolina mountains. My father, stumbling over his words, told me that Mom was in the hospital and may have had a slight heart attack. I had never heard such frailness in his voice. My hands trembled as I called the hospital three thousand miles away. Mom was in intensive care but resting well. I walked through the woods with my dog to reach the clearing and my private place of serenity. Sun shone over mountains misting into rounded humps. Insects buzzed. "Please, God," I said.

The next call from the hospital was noncommittal. It appeared as if mother had had a mild heart attack. If tests showed no complications, she might go home within days. I fastened on to that part of the message. I could not catch a plane until early next morning. That would be fine, they assured me. (Later I learned that my mother, like countless others who feel something is wrong, had avoided rather than sought help; only when my father saw her reading up on angina did she go to the hospital.)

Relief overwhelmed me as I threw clothes into a bag, planning to care for my father first and then Mom when she got home. I had such a longing to talk to Mom, but there are no phones in ICU. The nurse assured me that Mom knew I was coming tomorrow and that the news made my mother "very happy." Forty-five minutes later I was completing last-minute details in my office. The phone rang. It was a call I will remember all of my life. I heard my father's strangled words. "Things are worse. They don't think she is going to make it." I felt nauseous; a tingling shot through my body. Suddenly I was shrieking. Six years later I still remember that raw, banshee wail, echoing through the trees as I raced up to the house. My husband, Jack, caught me in his arms in the living room. "They think Mom is dying," I sobbed.

In that instant, my husband, there for me as always, decided to fly with me to California. The two-and-a-half-hour drive to Charlotte, North Carolina, was silent. My husband's quiet manner, sometimes a soothing balm, sometimes an irritant, seemed in keeping with my own stunned silence. I did not want so-called reassuring platitudes. Nor did I want practical advice on how to handle things. We pulled into the driveway of my daughter, Leah's, apartment; she was starting her television career in Charlotte. I raced to the phone. Dad's line was busy, so was my brother's. I knew without speaking to anyone that Mom had died, even as she was wired and monitored in the intensive care unit. My brother confirmed this when I broke in on the call.

Leah set about making stiff drinks, and I downed them quickly as tears and storming anger fought for supremacy: anger at the hospital and the airlines and for the circumstance of living in rural mountains in the summer that made it impossible to catch a plane immediately; anger at myself for not having called Mom the week before, for believing those nurses and doctors and their positive reports.

And there was guilt: Why had it taken me so long to understand my mother? I asked myself many times. There were encroaching family dynamics. My daughter was concerned for me, not for a distant grandmother who had died on the West Coast. "You never got a chance to really know her," I wailed. Such secondary losses, as they are termed, were already entering my thoughts. At dawn, eyes bloodshot, with a fiercely pounding head, I started on a journey—a long journey as I collapsed into grief and the shock of sudden and unexpected death. It lingers to this day. But this led to a journey of discovery as I determined to learn how to ease the inevitable grief of this inevitable end of living we all face, for us and for our friends and families—a determination that led me to this book.

If there was any reward to this knifelike shock of Mom's death, it was sensitizing me to the full weight of grief. As I sought answers to help people through this time, I found myself facing an American paradox of insane proportions. We encounter loss and sorrow daily. And yet we collude in a pathological dance of denial that merely heightens the pain of grieving. I am no stranger to this disease of denial myself—that ostrich-head-in-the-sand this-won't-happen-to-me-or-people-I-love syndrome, an avoidance of what is so real and constant. Frantic activity, "burying yourself in work," are distractions, but they won't cause grief to disappear. We grieve for everything, the small and the large—the end of a summer's vacation, the end of youth (and that can mean anything from turning thirty to turning eighty!), lost friendships and lost loves, divorces and downsizing, not getting into the college of our choice, dwindling careers or power, moving away from family or friends, and on to the deepest losses, illness and death. Being alive automatically means experiencing grief. It is *normal*—our common bond. If we are capable of love, we are capable of grief; that's all there is to it.

Death has been the fascinating core of plays, books, poetry, song, comedies, and romance since antiquity. It is constant fare in the movies and in *New Yorker* cartoons, an endless television staple, either in love stories and violent dramas or in the nightly news. Perhaps this is how we can deal with it, at a remove. But in some cultures death is a healthier presence, as in the Mexican celebration of the dead, All Saints' Day, where the dead are honored in wakelike abundance.

Denying death, which is a natural part of living, is as destructive as denying grief. In the United States alone, some 2.4 million people die each year; they are the top of an ever-widening pyramid as additional millions of friends and family remain behind to grieve. And, as I found out, to face illness, death, and grieving without guidelines or help can be perilous.

It has been said that teachers teach what they most need to learn. Perhaps writers write about what they most need to learn. I fell apart in my grief, unable to find the fierce concentration needed to complete a book, not knowing that there were people out there who could help me, not fathoming why I was so unable to function, not understanding why the arsenal of bromides from well-meaning friends and acquaintances offended me, especially as I realized I too had been just as guilty as they. Those same stumbling, helpless mumbles had come forth when I had tried to console grieving friends in the days before I had felt its full weight myself: "You had her a long time," "You're lucky that you were not young; when *my* mother died I was in my thirties . . . ," "At least she didn't suffer." All I could think of was that they had no understanding of how I felt. Nor of the loneliness that comes with the relative indifference an adult child faces with the "expected" loss of an elderly parent. To me, the most insensitive of platitudes is the one so popularized by President Clinton—"I feel your pain"—followed by "I understand how you feel." One can empathize, but no one can understand what another is feeling in times of desolation and grief.

At the same time, my children were trying to cope with a different face of death—the long-term illness of their father, my ex-husband, Morrie Siegel. "It was May 1994 as I stared down at my father, resting in the hospital," wrote my son, Michael. "Dad's seven-year battle with cancer had brought him to this anesthetized state of recovery twice before. My father was a sportswriter. He had been in the business for over fifty years. His most memorable assignment remained the night he covered Rocky Marciano's victory over Jersey Joe Walcott to retain the world heavyweight boxing title at Philadelphia's Shibe Park in 1962. My most memorable moment with him remains the week I watched as he recovered from six hours of surgery at Washington's Georgetown University Hospital in November 1989. The operation was a success, but my life changed forever that day, at the age of twenty-two. I realized that I had a limited amount of time to be all I could be to my father.

"Now I want to seal away every detail of these past seven years. Not that I hope to pass them on as anecdotes to my children, family, or friends. Hospital stories would hardly do justice to him. Dad, like most people, hated hospitals and although his grace and wit distinguished him from most of the cancer patients I met, his life was too large to be eclipsed by a seven-year illness. Years from now, I am certain he will not be remembered as a patient. But his hospital days will always be important to me. Important because, above all else, these stays gave me a chance to see the private side of a man who lived to be public." Morrie died a few days later.

The twenty-nine-year-old son was a picture of grace and eloquence later at a memorial service large on laughter, merciful laughter, as one story after another rolled off the tongues of Morrie's buddies—satirist Mark Russell; the *Washington Post*'s Ben Bradlee; Morrie's mentor, Shirley Povich; The Palm restaurateur Tommy Jacomo; *Washington Post* sports editor, George Solomon. The synagogue rocked with laughter as on flowed the stories about bookmakers and card sharks, of sportswriting in the days when it was a quirky art, stories certainly never heard in a synagogue before—a fact that registered in the eyebrows of the cantor as they rose sharply as each testifier seemed bent on topping the other.

At the end, it was my son's turn: "Dad battled the odds with courage and a selfless grace many of us will never know. . . . Dad has left us all with endless memories and an eternal friendship. He also gave me and my sister something that we will carry with pride for the rest of our lives—and that is that we are Morrie Siegel's children."

* * *

All too soon the support that comes immediately following a death fades into the realities of everyday life, although for the survivors, that is when depression and mourning really take hold. My children and I learned, as have all too many of us, that grieving involves many complex emotions—among them anger, guilt, relief, sadness, anxiety, depression, and loneliness. The feeling that nobody understands heightens one's isolation. Few of my son's friends, for example, had shared his experience of losing a father. My daughter had a less complicated relationship with her father and also a less complicated grief. She also had had more experience with death, having worked at a home for AIDS victims. I fell into the category of disenfranchised grief. I was an "adult child" in my fifties when my mother died, and I came under the heading of "developmentally expected loss." Translating the jargon, this meant "At your age it shouldn't be so difficult." But it can be terribly difficult for us who, as one friend said, "found myself an orphan at age sixty-three." Yet our grief is treated with relative indifference. Adult children themselves tend to fight their own deep emotions when it comes to an expected loss. "My mother is dying—she's ninety-five—that's what she's *supposed* to do," said a friend of mine, Ginny Thornburgh. "So *why* am I feeling so terrible?" I helped her recognize what I had to be taught—that the loss of a long, close relationship can be as unsettling as an earlier death of a parent.

I joined the disenfranchised again when I grieved for my ex-husband and memories past, even though I was happily remarried. The former spouse, the lover, the good friend, the business colleague, very young children, distant relatives—all are among those seldom considered as socially accepted deep grievers. Yet who is to say that the loss for these people is any less heartbreaking than that of the immediate family?

In such shattering times, it is important to remember that there is no one way—and no "correct" way—to grieve. Emotional expression may not be your style, or you may collapse in tears for months or years at some remembrance. You may retreat or you may race back to work; you may seek frenetic activity or champion a cause to honor the dead. Because it is *your* grief, it is happening for the first time, it is the hardest time, the most searing. Give yourself permission to grieve the way you want to and for as long, or as short, as you need and not be driven by friends and family who urge you to "get on with life" or to "get over it." Grief is a process, not an obstacle course to "get over."

Grief can be disorienting—judgment, thinking, coherent action, concentration can vanish, and grievers can think they are going crazy. One can drive a car and forget where one is going, conversations can blur in an instant, nothing can be retained. The diagnostic manual of the American Psychiatric Association now agrees that "thinking that [a survivor] hears the voice of or transiently sees the image of the deceased person" is not abnormal grieving. This can come in the form of astonishingly real dreams or premonitions, including uncanny knowledge of the exact time of death.

Physically, grief can cause stomachaches, headaches, arms that ache for a loved one, and serious illnesses. One woman, living through anticipatory grief when her father was diagnosed with cancer, ground her teeth so much that she deadened the nerve in a tooth and had to have a root canal operation. When a spouse dies, the losses are great at any age—not only the intense loneliness of losing one's closest companion but such secondary losses as social and/or financial support and a defined role in the community. The hole in one's heart when a child dies is immeasurable.

In our culture, however, where people race from meeting to meeting, zap the instant E-mail, everything and every emotion has the shelf life of fresh shrimp. We are not kind to grievers. We expect drive-through grieving—as if one's feelings can be deposited at a window with efficient haste like one deposits checks in the drive-through lane of a bank. Many people do not recognize, for example, that grieving begins at the moment of diagnosis. Even if one gets better or beats the odds, the precariousness of life is there, a knowledge that, paradoxically, often coincides with a heightened appreciation of life and living for each moment.

We are used to thinking of mortality as the province of the aged, but it strikes children and adolescents and the middle aged, rich and poor, good and bad. One hundred years ago, the death of a child was a terrifying probability. Then came the wonders of vaccines and sanitation, and a child dying before a parent became considered as a horrible, unnatural occurrence. Unfortunately, this cannot be said today. The AIDS pandemic, for one, has changed the equation enormously as entire countries, families, and friends bear witness to a young generation annihilated the world over. A man in Key West told me, "I've just turned forty—and I have been to seventy-five funerals. I've stopped counting." Pain borne when children die is for many parents heartbreakingly unavoidable; gunshot wounds are the second leading cause of death for adolescents aged seventeen to twenty-five, following vehicular deaths. Adolescence is a peak period for suicides, while cancer and other illnesses claim them even younger. In the same month last year, two couples I know lost their sons—one to a long battle with cancer, the other in a bizarre accident.

My involvement with illness, end-of-life issues, and bereavement coincided with a cataclysmic, volatile time of exploration. Both overtreatment (technical measures) and undertreatment (not providing pain-free care) were under attack. Living wills became talk-show fare; one television participant revealed the lengths she went to in order to make her wishes understood—her living will was tattooed on her stomach. Rebellion surfaced in citizens who tired of the horrors of HMOs and insurance companies, hospitals where 180,000 people died annually from errors, the medical profession's indifference to humane pain management. Everything from AIDS quilts to the Kevorkian battle awakened a nation to the need to honor both the dying and the bereaved, and spawned the question, Who's death is it anyway? In 1997, Oregon's voters pushed us into a new stage of medical ethics; it became the first state to uphold an assisted suicide law. The fierce debate prompted deep examination of end-of-life alternatives. As a result, Oregon leads the country in at-home hospice care as opposed to hospitals for the dying. Assisted dying, in my opinion, is a far more accurate description.

Studies indicate that the vast majority of Americans—90 percent—wish to die at home, but most die in hospitals. A burgeoning movement toward hospice—where the goal is to have patients die at home with pain-free palliative care—is changing those odds. Of the 2.4 million who died in the United States in 1996, nearly half a million died in hospice care—a fair number if one rules out those deaths that would not fall into hospice categories: homicides; auto accidents; suicides; and deaths resulting from short, acute illnesses or accidents; or for those who live alone. A longing to return to spiritual and emotional succor for the dying has been the backbone of the 3,000-member Association for Death Education and Counseling (ADEC), comprised of social workers and sociologists, psychiatrists and psychologists, doctors and hospice leaders throughout the world. Courses are now taught that are aimed at changing American attitudes on death and dying. A vivid example of personal sorrow turned positive is financier philanthropist George Soros, who set aside $15 million of his institute's money for Project Death in America following his experience with the death of his mother. The medical profession has been forced to police itself with committees that expose drastic deficiencies and offer solutions in the education, training, and performance of doctors, nurses, and other medical personnel in humane end-of-life practices.

A shockingly small amount of time is spent in med school on how to deal with patients, which should be a prominent part of the curriculum. Says Dr. William Lamers, an internationally known hospice doctor, "There is much we doctors could do to ease the pain, the anxieties, and concerns of dying persons and their families." Like many young medical professionals, Mary Jo Devine, a Washington, D.C., nurse, was rebelling against the inhumane warehousing of the dying in many hospitals. "A hospital nurse is not able to have an emotional connection with patients," she remarked. "The most I'm able to spend with a patient is thirty minutes before they're gone." She was taking courses on bereavement. "I hope to balance this out and provide the emotional connection missing in my work. To be more 'natural' in dealing with emotionally charged situations. For example, my roommate's father died. We haven't even spoken about it!"

When my husband became the president of the Hospice Foundation of America and I later began my book, I said that we would be the two most unpopular people at any party. Not so. People who had never talked about anything more personal than the president's budget began revealing their own encounters with death—family suicides, losing parents and children to accidents and illness, and a desire to express their hospice experiences and how to get through mourning. Try bringing up the subject. You may find a level of rewarding communication. A sign of changing times was the public display of understanding the Knicks coach and teammates showed for the player John Starks, whose performance suffered the effects of his grieving for the beloved grandmother, who raised him, as she lay dying in the final stages of cancer in 1998. During his slump, said one teammate, "We're all for him. She means a lot to him."[1] Perhaps the final days of the twentieth century may become known as a time when death was allowed to come out of the closet.

Along the way, I made the decision to tell the story of one family—to explore their interior lives, hopes, dreams, and fears in all its richness—rather than recite disjointed and disembodied case histories to prove a point. In my random search, I was given an inexpressible gift. I found Anna and Jan Johannessen and their circle of family and friends, with whom I spent more than two years. Like one-third of all Americans, the Johannessens are part of the baby-boom generation who are now facing their own or their friends' illnesses and deaths as well as that of their parents'. I had not thought of writing about a specific disease. The wounds are as deep for a family coping with any illness, dying, and bereavement. Given that three out of four families will be touched by cancer and that breast cancer is the number one killer of women between the ages of thirty-five and fifty-four, however, it was not surprising that I found Anna, who faced the fear that all women face.[2] But what is amazing was this magical woman, her family, and those who cared for her.

Hers is an intimate story of coping writ large, a personal tale woven into a larger mosaic of the universal concerns of us all—living and loving, dying and death, family tragedies and joys, dealing with children in positive ways when the news is so bad, grief and learning to live again. Anna's story is uplifting in its humor and compassion, its wisdom and its caring. She teaches us all how to live out loud.

Dr. Kenneth Doka opens speeches with a line that ensures immediate attention: "I know how you are all going to die." He then goes on to say that most of us will die as we live. If you are a crank and a grouse, thinking only of yourself, that's probably how you will go. One can hope that being forearmed is being forewarned. Anna always said she was just an ordinary person. In the world of instant celebrity hype, the jillion-dollar basketball star, the latest microtalent out of Hollywood, perhaps she was right. But in the ways that matter, Anna was extraordinary—and she was not alone. Her story, an exaltation of the human spirit in adversity, is replicated daily throughout this land. Beyond the klieg lights are ordinary people just like Anna, whose lives are founded on courage and compassion, determination and dreams, humor and humanity.

Well, maybe not *just* like Anna. No one could be just like Anna. She remains one of the greatest gifts of my lifetime. It is my privilege to pass that gift on to you.

JUNE 1998

PART I

A Charmed Life

Those who bring sunshine to others cannot keep it from themselves.

SIR JAMES BARRIE

Jan and Anna (1980)

Anna and Lockie Fuller (Richmond, 1978)

CHAPTER ONE

Meeting Anna

October 18, 1995 She is in the front yard, halfway up from the mailbox, in active combat with two restless five-month-old puppies. Part Akita and part retriever, they look as unalike as their mixed parentage could fashion: Peaches is ginger colored with long hair and curled-up tail; Cream is black and white. They are united in their passion to disobey. Somehow she thinks she can also look at the envelopes she has retrieved from the mailbox as she tugs her way up the lawn toward the front door. In her sweatshirt and jeans, with small diamond studs in each pierced ear, she could be an androgynous teenager, making a statement. Her head is completely bald. Up close, however, one sees the fine features of a woman who looks to be in her midthirties but has just turned forty-three. Smooth, tanned skin, not even one fine hair on her face. The tops of the black rims of her glasses fit exactly where eyebrows should be; it takes time to realize she does not have any.

"Hi! I'm Anna," she says with a quick grin. "Don't mind me, I just have to get the puppies in." Intense moments of hauling and tugging ensue. Finally the puppies are skidded, shoved, and pushed into the kitchen. "Whewwwww," says Anna. Then the talk begins. Talk, talk, talk. Gatling-gun energy. "Where do you want to go for lunch? Been out to Olney before? Just let me get my things and we're outta here." She pats herself, the eternal mental checklist of us all. "Let's see, keys, wallet . . ." Then Anna pats her head and the right side of her chest as if she has forgotten something else. "No boob, no hat, what the heck, let's just go."

She is out the door and through the carport, where a huge and heavy yellow aluminum store sign leans against the wall. It says "Happy Feet," a logo of smiling feet, toes wiggling. Until recently, it beckoned young children and their parents to Anna's shoe store in a nearby mall. It is just one of her many careers that she can no longer do. This realization gnaws away inside, but to the outside world, Anna says little.

Anna Johannessen, her two children, Lindsay and Ellery, and her husband, Jan Johannessen (pronounced Yon Yohannessen), live in Olney, Maryland, a middle- to upper-middle-class suburb of Washington, D.C. There are rolling hills, a good local theater, malls, of course. Tract houses are spacious bungalows, softened by oak trees and willows and flower gardens. Yet behind those doors in suburbs so similar to Olney throughout the United States, all is not fairy-tale happiness; entire families are mourning the death or illness of friends or relatives. Some have suffered strokes or heart attacks or been disabled or killed in automobile accidents. And some are coping with prolonged anxiety and stalled grief—an in-limbo, roller-coaster stage, soaring into hope and plunging into despair, sometimes for months and years—as they endure and bear witness to a family member's battle with cancer or AIDS or Alzheimer's or emphysema or kidney or heart failure.

At this time, Anna is a long-term cancer survivor, but her breast cancer has spread, an indication that she may die from it. And yet there is more mirth than mournfulness, more fiery determination than tepid acceptance. It is the first meeting with the author, a sizing up, a concern about whether this will work. It is not unlike a first date, except that two women are talking and before long rapport is set. They talk about the feminine losses that "no one tells you about when you have cancer and take chemo." Hair for one. "Do you know the pubic hair goes too?" says Anna. "I'm barer than my ten-year-old daughter." The lack of libido, pain of intercourse, eternal hot flashes, excruciating side effects of chemotherapy are glossed over for now. This is basic to Anna's personality. Only occasionally does her effervescence fizzle.

She mostly repeats what is by now an effortless litany, brushing the surface of her life, medical history, and concerns she feels for herself and her family. Later she will tell it all, with anguish and humor, tears and laughter, amazing pragmatism at times and equally amazing moments of courage. Halfway through lunch, the flow slows down. She emphasizes every word, leaning forward. "Every decision you make from the moment you find out you have cancer . . ." She pauses, then speaks with intensity. "*It's all your decision.* It's *not* the doctor's decision. Whether to take this chemo. Whether to not. Whether to try for a bone marrow transplant. Whether to not. Whether to get more opinions. Whether to try something new. That's what is so hard." Anna puts down her sandwich. "I *know* what I'm dealing with and I can't change it. That's what is so terrible." Tears well. "I have my days, believe me."

In the next breath, optimism reappears. "I am so *lucky* that my husband and I are able to absorb the information. My husband is in the biomedical field [previously at the National Institutes of Mental Health and now at the Food and Drug Administration]. He is able to ask the questions. I'm so appreciative that he understands more than ninety-nine percent of the men out there." Anna later reveals that his knowledge does not help him avoid a typical male response, silent grieving and an ineptitude at discussing with her or anybody how he feels about Anna's illness and the uncertainty of their life.

Anna howls with laughter when she is shown a cartoon of a man in the waiting room of a doctor's office, being approached by the nurse, who says, "The doctor will kill you now." Anna has developed a curdled contempt for doctors who are unable to provide emotional comfort or to explain medical situations succinctly, and who, conversely, can badly botch diagnoses. Anna is no stranger to technical errors—misread X rays and MRIs and bumbled reports. Once she even had the wrong rib operated on.

Anna is like every patient caught in today's world of highly charged and controversial scientific research. Anxiety collides with hope, often false hope. Today the intense speculation on genetic factors ignores a frightening statistic for all women: more than 70 percent of those who develop breast cancer have no high-risk factors at all, including genetic. In fact, only 5 to 10 percent of breast cancers are due to heredity.[1] Just being female is a high-risk factor.

The drumroll of ceaseless scientific studies sounds out new doubts as well as new hopes. "Being a human guinea pig, not in a program, just out there in society, can be extremely frustrating. Take tamoxifen—which I took for nearly five years. Now they're saying that it's dangerous to take this 'wonder drug' for any longer than that!" The most widely used estrogen blocker to help prevent the recurrence of cancer, tamoxifen was used by more than 1 million women in 1995, an estimated 20 percent of whom had been on the drug for more than five years. Anna was referring to the National Cancer Institute (NCI) "clinical alert" sent just that month to cancer physicians—only the fourth time the institute has issued such an alert—advising that tamoxifen should not be taken for any longer than five years. Females by the thousands were thrown into panic after studies showed a trend toward higher death rates in women whose use exceeded that period.[2] "The only reason I stopped," says Anna dryly, "is that my cancer had already come back."

Despite positive advances in treatment to prolong the lives of people with cancer, AIDS, and other diseases, the sad but unassailable truth is that some people will fall into the percentile of those for whom the results are not favorable. Even if there were but a 5 percent chance of an illness recurring, someone has to be among that 5 percent. Unfortunately, doctors cannot divine who will win out and who won't.

Anna had a mammogram early because her sister had breast cancer. A benign fibroid tumor was found in Anna's right breast. A year and a half later, another lump was biopsied. This time, the doctor told Anna, "I don't know what to say. It's cancer."

Anna leans forward. "This was the hardest thing a human being can go through. When they told me I had cancer, it was so terrible." Her eyes fill with tears.

Her right breast was cut away. Anna was thirty-seven. Her son, Ellery, was five; her daughter, Lindsay, had just turned four.

The mood changes abruptly as Anna looks at her watch. "Oh, my God, I'm late to pick up Lindsay." In her maroon Chevy blazer, Anna talks about her various careers. She has taught high school English and drama, performed in local theatrical productions, served as creative media director for major companies, owned the children's shoe store. Anna held down two jobs following her mastectomy, while the children were growing from toddlers to preteens. "Now," says Anna, as she approaches Lindsay's school, "I'm using my energies to be with the family." The laugh is filled with some regret. "I am now 'gracefully' accepting that."

A lot of anger grows within this stage, however, often called anticipatory grief, a term more misunderstood than not. It is not only a stage in which one anticipates a final grief. It concerns the daily anger and grief that comes with unwanted change, with loss of control, with having to accept limitations that for someone like Anna would have been unheard of a year ago. Anna will mourn her loss of a career for many months.

"One of my friends said, 'Anna, you're somebody who used to go at the speed of light. Now you're finally going at the pace of everyone else.' "

Anna spots her daughter, the tallest in a cluster of talking girls. Lindsay separates herself from the pack and heads for the car. She has arresting features, large eyes, a wide mouth, all framed in a cascade of chestnut hair, so long she can sit on it. She looks much older than ten.

"Hi, honey!"

"Hi, Mom." They talk easily. "Hey, Ma-om, I'm gonna be late for ballet!" "No you're not," says Anna, coolly ignoring the complaint in Lindsay's voice. "We'll go home, walk the dogs quickly, grab your things, and go." Lindsay calms down. In a matter of minutes, Anna pulls up to their brick bungalow and parks in the driveway. They walk into the carport, past the Happy Feet sign, and as Anna opens the side door into the kitchen, all is madness as they try to keep the puppies from bolting out.

It is a cold evening, January, 28, 1997—a year and three months after Anna began recording her life in October of 1995. Jan and Anna are now forty-four. Anna sits in the rounded corner of their living room sectional. "Would you look at this?" she says in disgust, running her hand over her hair, removing it in tufts. For many weeks, Anna had a "drug holiday," her term for no chemotherapy, and a glorious Anna with a wide smile and lush black hair was captured in stunning photos by a photographer friend and cancer patient, Linda Suarez. Now she is back on chemo and is shedding like a Saint Bernard in August. "Ya better get pictures fast," she cracks. "I'm *really* having a bad hair day." Joking with Lindsay, Anna shakes her head over her homework. "Oh, gross," says Lindsay, laughing as she brushes off the falling hair. "We're buzzing this head!" says Anna, talking to her daughter as if she were one of her friends. "Oh, God, I woke up this morning and turned my head and got a mouthful of hair, yuck."

The dogs set up a mighty howl when the pizza man comes with his delivery. Munching his pizza on the couch, Jan launches into his day, an interesting experiment with rats at the Food and Drug Administration, and Anna makes jokes about his "rat world." Then she leans over and calls Jan by her pet name. "Nilsie [for his middle name Nils], can't you shave my head tonight? Please? I can't stand it falling out all over the place. I had to clean the shower drain out three times it was so clogged this morning. Honestly. I'll feel much better."

Soon the night has a name, the "Beer, Pizza, and Head-Shaving Party." Anna drags out a kitchen chair and centers it in the kitchen on the yellow-and-white vinyl floor. Jan brings in a towel and long shears, the kind used to shear lab animals. Very tenderly, Jan starts up the back of Anna's head. Knowing that this is difficult for Anna, no matter how much she jokes, Jan remarks gently, "You look cute with a bald head." When he finishes, Jan softly rubs it and bends down to quietly give her a kiss on the top of her head. Anna's snapping dark eyes glow as she looks at him. And Jan smiles, locking his eyes with hers.

Then she is on a search for the wigs she bought years ago, when chemotherapy followed her mastectomy. They are crushed under books on a shelf in her bedroom. "These suckers are just too damn hot and uncomfortable to wear." They look terrible and unnatural on her, except the short one. Anna pokes and pushes and pats hard to press this wig down on the sides and sits on the sofa, giggling. "Let's see if Lindsay notices." Jan has gone to pick up Lindsay from ballet class. She is now eleven and is five feet four inches and walks with a dancer's grace. Jan enters the room first, and Anna whispers, "Don't tell Lindsay." Jan says, "I already did." Anna makes a face, but when Lindsay rounds the corner, she stares at her mother for a second and says, "I thought Dad shaved it off!" Then she sees it's the wig. Anna yanks it off her head—"Ta-da!"—throws it to her daughter, who laughs loudly along with her.

On another day, Anna reflects on Jan's reaction to her cancer. "I know that I physically would drive most men away in quiet yet guilty disgust. But I smile and look at Jan and know I have the best marriage there is. This man loves me because of who I am. The fact that he has seen me get fat from medication, bear a huge scar on my right side, with only one left breast now dangling, lose my raven tresses and become totally hairless all over my body, hobble along daily from permanent nerve damage to my feet and legs, and, despite all of this, still adores me is more than most people can claim as a test of their love and commitment to marriage. And after several years of chemotherapy, I have become essentially a sexual nothing, but Nils doesn't care. We used to love it, but he assures me that priorities have changed. I've even said he could find someone for sex, but he says that's not important. He just wants me around. He knows we are both losing certain former aspects of our marriage that were important at the time, but now we both cherish other aspects—being together, sharing a sunny day, laughing over a funny cartoon in the newspaper, getting a good report from the doctor, taking a walk hand in hand. This is our love."

For many women, the mutilation of their bodies causes traumatic grieving. "I have met too many women whose husbands were uncomfortable and ashamed by the scars and physical damage from their disease. These men demanded that their wives endure more physical suffering to 'grow another boob through surgery,' to make them look 'normal.' I don't know that the women, themselves, wanted to go through more surgery, but they did for the sake of their husbands. Nils just wanted me. Me, alive, as I was and as I was comfortable being."

For the past few months, Anna's life has revolved around the curved center of her cream leather sectional, phone at hand, pale blue–and-white plaid blanket draped over her sweatpants and sweatshirt. One afternoon, Anna's deep-throated laugh echoes as she talks with friends on the phone. She clucks in shared misery for a friend who has to have a root canal operation, another whose mother is diabetic and still eats sweets. Anna sympathizes with her angry friend; if the mother doesn't stop, gangrene could set in. Anna expounds on the selfishness and stubbornness of some who are seriously ill, thus becoming burdens upon their families and friends.

Anna waves at Lindsay, who comes home from school and sits cross-legged in the blue chair by the window across from the sofa, doing math homework, listening to her mom's conversations, which are blunt, direct, and honest. When Anna hangs up, she goes over to hug Lindsay. Ellery, now twelve, comes home, so tired that he walks robotlike. Ellery is in a magnet school where he takes accelerated courses that include eighth- and even ninth-grade math—complicated, time-consuming work. He has a major midsemester math test tomorrow plus "so much homework, I don't know where to start." Anna is in the bedroom floating on the hunter green sea of a down comforter. Ellery leans against his mother and she puts her arm around his waist. Ellery's growth spurts have been phenomenal; now at five feet seven inches, he takes great pleasure in calling his mother Shorty. "Can we have pizza to help study for my test?"

"No, we're having chicken. I already took it out from the freezer to defrost." Then Anna brightens as if she has just thought of the most exciting plan in the world. "How 'bout we'll have pizza tomorrow night to *celebrate* having finished your test?"

Anna has sensed her son's panic, his overwhelming sense of defeat and hopelessness about the looming test and an avalanche of homework. "You know more than you think you do about your math. Why don't you start with the math problems and see how that goes? That'll give you a head start on the test. Get some food first." Lindsay pokes her head around the corner. "Who is the Jell-O pudding for?"

"You guys can have it." Lindsay grins and heads for the refrigerator, then returns to poke her head into the bedroom again and say hesitantly, "There'll only be one left after we take two, is that okay?" Her children are extra solicitous about Anna these days, aware of how little she feels like eating. "Sure, honey," Anna reassures her.

The Johannessens are living a life of abnormal normalcy and it is hard to fathom how they can function so well, and yet this is a life lived, with varying degrees of success, by hundreds of thousands daily in a world where medical advances have made prolonged illness common. The daily minutiae continues, except for knifelike moments of panic or sorrow or pain; groceries to buy, dinners to fix, dogs to walk, laundry and homework and house repairs to do, bills to pay, school and jobs to attend, PTA and school athletics and ballet. Abnormal normalcy.

There are moments of laughter—vacation, video games or movies on TV, reading, eating pizza in the downstairs rec room by the fireplace. And yet, there are certain books, tossed on the piano—*What You Need to Know About Breast Cancer*—and in the bedroom, hidden in a manila envelope—*Dying Well.* And when the children are asleep, Anna and Jan hold each other in bed, thinking thoughts that Anna has become comfortable with but that Jan would rather avoid. Anna won't let him, insisting that he face a very possible reality. One night, Anna asks Jan to prepare for a possible future without her by asking, "What do you think life would be like without me?"

Tears coarse down Jan's cheek and he can only choke out a one-word sentence—"Difficult."

CHAPTER TWO

Starting Out

When people experience prolonged or life-threatening illness, writing or videotaping their lives and reflections can provide a catharsis and give meaning to their existence. This taking stock, reviewing family history, reliving the best of times, provides a comforting sense that they are imbuing their loved ones with a part of themselves and leaving something for posterity. (This process of recording one's thoughts and remembrances of loved ones is also recommended for the bereaved.) Over the months, Anna eagerly delves into her life, in writing and in conversations.

Anna Margaret Megregian, born in Washington, D.C., on October 2, 1952, began life seeking attention. Her first memory: "I would sit at the top of the stairs and cry, working my con job. Somebody would come up and say, 'Oooh, what's the matter, honey?' And I got what I wanted. Until the day my dad caught on, came up, and paddled my rump instead. That ended my stair-warming nights."

Boys and girls were equally drawn to Anna—the tomboy who swung on tree vines and played male roles in backyard theatrics, the teenager who lied to school officials that she had not been drinking, in order to protect the other girls, the high school actress who carried a live pig onstage as Moonbeam McSwine in *Li'l Abner,* the gifted musician who turned down a scholarship to the Eastman Academy of Music in order to live a more normal life.

"Anna spelled trouble—very aggressive and into everything," says her sister, Roseann, twelve years older. "But she was very creative and always very bubbly. She's very much like our aunt, who was a character." Anna inherited her aunt's mischievous spirit, which included storming in every Thanksgiving dressed in turkey feathers. When Anna had to clean the kitchen in the bakery where she worked one summer, she and a girlfriend would throw stale pies and cakes on the walls and, like culinary Jackson Pollocks, watch the dripping collage of blueberry, strawberry, lemon, chocolate. Then they would clean up to spotless perfection. Later, when Anna became a top advertising executive, she and a friend designed a huge three-foot birthday card for her female boss. "One of the words of our poem on the card was 'but' and I couldn't resist." The letter *B* on her card became a huge photocopied rear end, turned sideways. "We screamed with laughter as I sat buck naked on the Xerox machine." Some would stare at the *B* on the well-circulated card, but no one guessed at Anna's contribution.

Anna's favorite topic is Jan, her lifelong love. Anna was sixteen when she met Johannessen—"a very cute French horn player with wire-rimmed glasses, a wonderful laugh and brilliant wit, and his own way of doing things. He was a quiet nonconformist who was systematically late by five minutes every day for school." "Sparkling" is the adjective that came to Jan's mind when he first saw Anna, possessed of whirlwind energy, a wide smile, a quick laugh, and dark hair that cascaded down to her waist. They played in the band and as they marched on the field one autumn afternoon, the sun glinted on her hair. "It sparkled, like her personality."

Anna was curious about Jan before she met him. The whole school was talking about the new student who had gotten into trouble for wearing shorts to school. Jan and Anna were coming of age during the Vietnam War and although youthful rebellion had toppled establishment rituals everywhere, their suburban school still clung to dress codes. Jan had the full support of his mother, born and reared in England where shorts were the norm, and continued to wear shorts. Soon others followed. Anna laughs. "Jan was clueless that he'd started a fashion trend." Anna, who thrived on the offbeat, made it a point to meet Jan. In the fall of 1995, as they reflect on their long life together, Jan, forty-two, still looks like the round-faced boy of sixteen; a guileless smile reveals dimples, his sandy hair is thick, his five-foot-seven-inch frame is slender despite a slight adult spread.

Unlike most high school romances, the instant click between Jan and

Anna has lasted a lifetime. Anna remembers their first date—"We saw *Butch Cassidy and the Sundance Kid*"—our first kiss! From that point, we were hooked. I never questioned whether I loved him or how much, all those weird questions one asks oneself when delving into a serious relationship. I knew that this was for life. I had found my soul mate." Jan nods agreement. "Jan and I are and have always been profoundly happy," Anna says with unwavering certitude. "Oh, there have been times of boredom, of curiosity about others, but I could never imagine us apart."

Anna fervently says yes to life. In a list of clichés regarding optimism versus pessimism, Anna wins: the bottle is always half full not half empty; she always finds the pony. Her lightning enthusiasms and passions have an intensity all but lost in adults. Methodical Jan complements her. On the surface, they are opposites—Anna the impulsive up-for-fun character, Jan the solid rock. She wanted high drama. He chose science. Yet looks can deceive. Anna is the disciplined, organized spark plug. Jan is the ivory-tower dreamer. Beneath the surface, they are guided by the same principles—to live an honest life, deep commitment to work, and devotion to friends and family.

Remarkable childhood similarities shaped and defined Jan and Anna. They were like two army brats, endlessly uprooted in childhood. Both learned early about loss—Anna often sobbing undying fidelity to pals as she moved on again and again. Yet they also found strength in their adaptability and an easy ability to make friends. By the time they met, Anna had lived in six cities and four states as the family followed her father's career as a government expert in water pollution. Jan had lived in four cities in three states until his meteorologist father returned to Washington as President Lyndon Johnson's deputy director of the National Weather Service.

Both reaped the benefits of being the youngest of four siblings. As babies, they were adored. As adolescents, they were reared with more ease and freedom than their brothers and sisters. This helped Anna and Jan to grow into secure, happy, contented adults. "We were very strict when we first came to this country," recalls Jan's mother, Phoebe, "but the American way rubbed off on us. Nils got away with murder!" Anna was known as the "wild one" in her family, with an impish need to rebel.

Although their families came from different parts of the world, Anna and Jan also shared exotic backgrounds; three out of four parents immigrated to the United States.

The Johannessen story unfolds in Anna and Jan's home the day after Thanksgiving, 1995. The scene is a modern-day version of Currier and Ives, Hans Christian Andersen, and Norman Rockwell rolled into one. Anna's in-laws are visiting from their home on an island off Seattle. Jan and his seventy-eight-year-old father, Jo, are in the backyard, chopping wood. Snow mists the ground and their breath frosts the air. Tea steams on the stove and turkey bones simmer into a rich broth for soup.

Phoebe, a tanned, stunning woman, with a button nose, deep blue eyes, and short snow white hair, curls up in a corner of the sectional. At seventy-three, the former ballet instructor carries herself like a woman years younger. Artistic talent runs in the Johannessen family and Anna's house is filled with impressive paintings by Phoebe; her brother, John; and Jan's sister, Sissel.

Jan's Norwegian father was a student at Oslo University and when the Nazis invaded Norway in 1940, Johannessen literally skied to safety, with help from friends in the underground who hid him on his way until he reached the Swedish border. Short and burly, Jo still carries himself like a former athlete as he comes in from the cold, peeling off his jacket and joining the family for tea. There is a resemblance to his son. With thinning hair, turned silver, close cut, he looks something like the actor E. G. Marshall, ruddy faced, a pleasant twinkle in his eye, but a no-nonsense reserve and formality. A slight accent remains.

The courtship of Johannessen and Phoebe Frith was filled with the romance and tumult of war-torn England, where they were stationed, plotting the weather's course for British Air Force maneuvers, including the invasion of D day. "Phoebe was a sergeant," Jo says with a smile. "But you outranked me," says Phoebe, laughing. As a meteorologist and member of the Norwegian air force working in Sweden, Jo was soon on loan to the British air force and became an instant attraction when he entered England's meteorology headquarters. "Here was this good-looking Norwegian in our midst and all the girls were after him—and I got him." Phoebe's laugh bubbles over.

They married at war's end. Phoebe's eldest was born in England.

Then they settled in Norway, where two more children were born, and moved to Washington in 1951, when Jo was hired by the U.S. government weather service. Jan was born four months after Anna, in January of 1953.

"I had a charmed childhood," says Jan. "I had lots and lots of friends, especially in O'Fallon, Illinois, where we moved after Chicago, where I was a toddler." For six years, Jan's life was proscribed by small-town pleasures. "Now you hear about kids knifing each other on playgrounds. I can't remember even one fistfight at school." In summer, Jan would be gone from sunup until dinner; his mother never knew where he was but never worried. Phoebe loved her ballet studio there, teaching her daughters and on occasion dragooning Jan onstage. She says, "Nils was the lead in *The Emperor's New Clothes,* and he marched in his underwear quite undeterred." Anna loves the picture of Jan, then six, standing in imperial splendor in braided jacket and black tights. "I was forced out by peer pressure," says Jan with a laugh.

Religion played no important part in either the Megregian or the Johannessen household. "In O'Fallon, we lived just down from a church and so I got packed off to Sunday school, probably because we were new in town and our parents wanted to make a good showing," says Jan. "I got bored to tears with that, so it didn't last long."

At the end of the sixth grade, the family moved again and Jan spent his preteen years in Freeport, Long Island, loving independent pursuits, often heading out to Jones Beach by himself in an old aluminum fishing boat. When Jan's father joined the National Weather Service, and they moved back to Washington, D.C., Jan went to the same junior high school where his son now attends an accelerated magnet program. On parents night, Jan found his science class, frozen in time. "I dragged Anna in and made her sit in my old seat."

Jan's parents knew Anna as one of the crowd that hung around the house. Anna must have seemed like a tornado in their midst. "She *was* a bit loud," remembers Phoebe with a laugh. "The girls seemed to be chasing Nils, but Anna was it for him. Anna had a much more open family life. The English are all very uptight. She's able to express herself to everybody about what she feels, and I think that's just so great. I wish I could do that." A fondness grew between Anna and Phoebe. "Anna is truly remarkable," she says. "The marriage has been a huge success."

Her sad face indicates that she has allowed the present to intrude in her reverie. Anna manages a duality—she lives with considerable contentment in the present yet refuses to deceive anyone about the progression of her illness. Such direct, open communication is applauded by experts who study prolonged illness and dying. "I do not know how Anna does it," her mother-in-law remarks. "She really is a philosopher. She faces the facts and says, 'This is how it is,' and then goes on, as if she has the flu! I so admire the way she has been so open with Ellery and Lindsay, telling them everything about her treatment, what's happening. She is so 'right there.' It is so hard for us to be like that. I can't understand how anybody can have that much courage!" continues Phoebe. "She's so positive and drags everybody along with her. You can't be depressed around Anna. I'm sure she has her moments—when my children were at the beach with her, they all had a little cry—but apart from that, she's just amazing."

Anna has confided some of her concerns to Phoebe. "She has talked quite a lot to Nils about what he should do. She's worried that he would just get too much involved with work and the frightfully busy job of caring for the kids to have any fun. He's not a person who goes out and seeks other people's company and goes to parties and things; it's Anna who does that. So she has instructed her friends to bug him a bit."

How does Phoebe handle this terrible time? There is a pause. "I just try to hold on to Anna's spirit. She makes it easy for all of us." Still, the horrible possibility of her son being alone "concerns me greatly. They are so intertwined and Anna is so incredibly vibrant that Nils's life would be a hollow shell compared to what it is."

An attempt to talk to Jan's father about Anna illustrates the Johannessen reluctance to express personal feelings; he offers few comments. Anna laughs heartily. "That's so typical. When we told him we were going to get married, he just said, 'Oh.' " Anna imitates the absent-minded nod of the head, as if they had just said they were going to the movies. "That's Jo."

Anna and Jo have tangled more than once. "They are both very forceful personalities," says Phoebe. "Anna is very sure of herself when she believes in something—and so is Jo," she says, indicating that neither is quick to back down. Jan says he never felt the need to interfere with Anna and Jo. "Anna can take care of herself. In families, everybody has trouble getting along with someone, at one time or another. But Dad has great respect for Anna, certainly as much, if not more, than for his kids and other in-laws. He always sees her as pragmatic, business-minded, and aggressive; to an immigrant, that kind of 'can do' get-up-and-go is very important."

That same "can do" spirit made it possible for Anna to exist. Her grandparents grew up in Armenian enclaves, had arranged marriages, and lived with the specter of mass murder by the Turks. Anna's father, Stephen, was six years old when he heard his widowed mother talking fearfully with her friends about a Turkish invasion in their beautiful seacoast town of Izmir, south of Istanbul. She and Stephen and his three-year-old brother quickly set sail for the United States. "I just marvel at the guts those people had," says Stephen. "My mother travels eight thousand miles with two little kids to a country where the only soul she knows is a sister." Such fierce survival instincts perpetuated Anna's lineage. Stephen says, "I was the lucky recipient, believe me." The lives of Anna's grandparents and parents were a mixture of Old Country edicts and customs and the hustling modernity of Detroit, the car capital of the world.

Now, seventy-five years later, in January 1996, Anna's eighty-one-year-old father nestles into his favorite leather chair in his home in Cocoa Beach, Florida, and talks about their escape as if it were yesterday. His mother had come from wealth, was well educated, knew French, Turkish, and Greek, besides Armenian. None of these languages helped her, however, when she was robbed of everything she owned in the sleeping car from New York to Detroit. Her son woke up to her screaming in every language but English. All that was left of the money she had saved, their papers, and her jewelry were two 24-karat-gold bracelets. Those delicately woven bracelets, worn by their grandmother that fateful night, are cherished possessions of Anna and Roseann.

Anna walks through the room and her father's deep brown eyes, so like Anna's, light up. His smile is kind in his craggy tanned face, even though he is seldom free of the pain of a crippling back injury. He is expressive, volatile, and intense as he brags about Anna. "I love all my kids, but there's nobody like Anna for exuberance, zip, always on the go, challenging people all the time." Anna's formative years included the urban (Chicago) and the bucolic (Ames, Iowa—where Anna was first viewed as a wild "Chicago gangster"). Once Anna's willful teenage years were over, Anna's rapport with her father became total. "Dad had a philosophy that after we became adults, which was about eighteen in his mind, he would give us advice only when we solicited it. I have so much respect for him for that. When I really wanted to, I could talk to him about anything—and I still can. But he never started making arbitrary judgments or decisions. If you ever wanted a true cheerleader, there he was."

He waves her off with a smile as he continues his tale of growing up. His mother had remarried, again an arranged union, but this one, says Stephen, "must have been made in heaven." He adored his stepfather Megregian. The depression had cloaked Detroit in fear, panic, and hunger and they lived on Megregian's four-dollar-a-day factory job. Stephen worked any odd job, discovering a lifelong talent for golf when he caddied for the rich who had not lost it all in the crash. A chemistry major, Stephen worked his way through college, acing exams—"I could cite things back verbatim."

By his freshman year, Stephen had picked his mate, an example his daughter would emulate years later. When he first met Audrie Torosian, however, he thought she was "strictly a pest." She was eight years old—"and a girl!" Their parents were friends in a large, clannish Armenian colony that held summer picnics overflowing with shish kebabs and Armenian music and dancing. At one outing, Stephen noticed a fifteen-year-old who had filled out a bathing suit and had become a "good-looking *woman*!" It was Audrie, the pest of yesteryear. Like her daughter, she was a few months older than her husband and, like Anna, a grade ahead. After Stephen graduated from college in 1938, they were wed. With her degree in psychology, Anna's mother became a social worker for the Detroit welfare department. In 1940, their first child was born, Roseann. Simultaneously, Anna's father began a wandering career as a U.S. Public Health Service expert on pollution and sanitation. His son, Stephen, was born in 1942. Eight years later, a second family was begun. "One day we found out Audrie was pregnant. We said, 'Let's have the baby.' We didn't want this one, Marty, to be alone, so we said, 'Let's have another.' After that, Audrie got her tubes tied."

Audrie was nearing forty when her last child was born, the girl they named Anna.

Anna fondly recollects an extended household that included two grandparents. "I remember going to get ice cream with my grandfather. Grandmother and I played gin and cribbage for hours. Even after she went blind, she could still crochet by feel. She was a soft, genteel, aristocratic old woman." Roseann did not share her sister's joyous memories, remembering instead that she never had a chance to be a free spirit like Anna. Ro saw mostly the duties of caring for the sick and elderly, her mother's father and her father's mother. "A lot of Mom's time was spent running them to doctors and taking care of them."

Their mother, a caregiver by profession and choice, also worked long hours. Anna's earliest memories are of her mother helping others. "She would plop me in the car as she would ferry children from orphanages to foster homes," recalls Anna. "One time, we picked up a little boy who had ringworm and his head was all shaved. This poor little weird guy sat there and bawled. I thought, 'I can't believe I'm riding in the car with this kid who's bald!' I was mad because I wanted to do something else, but she had to take care of him."

Roseann became a "mini-mother"—"I would take over with Marty and Anna as soon as I came home from school. By the time I was eight, I could bake a cake and cook a meal for six because I had to. I didn't resent all that work, but, sure, it was tough. When I got married, you betcha I didn't want any kids. I wanted to do my own thing, have my own life and my own career, which I did. I didn't want to go from kids *to* kids."

As carefree teenagers, Anna and Jan thought their luck would never end. Then in her first year in college, Anna was traumatized by a near rape. After all these years, Anna still recalls the incident with intensity, rushing her sentences, switching from past to present tense and back again. "I was eighteen years old and was taking drama and one of my classmates was this huge, tall kid. I was hardly a sexual statement—baggy jeans, an Israeli army shirt. I was your basic hippie."

The student lured Anna to his room on the pretext of needing help with his mime project. "Then he locks the door! I turn around, and see a guy who looks really scary. I knew I was in trouble. And he began saying, 'You want it—all women want it,' and he started to unzip. I just thought, 'Chain-smoke your brains out and think about what the hell you're going to do.' He had a psychological need to think I wanted to be raped. And I used that to my advantage because at the time I hadn't even had sex. I kept chain-smoking and saying"—Anna revs up her speed to demonstrate—" 'I've never done this in my life, I'm not ready to have sex, you've been misinformed, we are friends, let's be friends.' And I kept talking and smoking like mad. Meanwhile he took his member out and proceeded to jack off in front of my face." Anna holds her hand eight inches from her face. "I couldn't move and just kept talking and smoking. He ejaculated right in front of me, then walked me to my bike and let me go!"

"I got back to the dorm room and then I lost it. That's typical in my family. We can manage through the crisis—I have great survival instincts—then after, we fall apart. I was babbling on the phone to Jan, 'Come over, come over.' As soon as he walked in the room, I said, 'Don't come near me.' My hackles went up and that poor man, my wonderful husband-to-be, sat there, forever, it seems." The rape attempt could have scarred Anna psychologically had it not been for Jan. "He supported me while I tried to get perspective and made me enjoy the blessing that I was alive. The attempted rape was a small price to pay for my life.

"Mom went nuts. Dad said, 'You can quit school,' and I said, 'I don't want to quit school.' For a month, I was escorted to classes. I found out that an instructor had known this guy was having problems! I was very angry at him for not turning that guy over to a place to get help before some student got raped or killed." The episode changed Anna's career direction. "I buckled under to my parents' request." They urged her to quit drama, reasoning that a mainstream curriculum would not draw misfits. Anna became an English major. "I figured, 'Hey, I can be theatrical in class.' "

In her senior year, 1973, Anna faced a terrible crisis that overshadowed the attempted rape. Anna was studying in her dorm when she got the phone call. Anna plodded past music and laughter and talk emerging from rooms, and picked up the dangling phone. Anna's mother was on the line, trying to choke out a message while sobbing. "She told me that Ro had breast cancer and that it was really bad and had spread and doctors said she had three months to live. She was only thirty-two."

Anna slid down the wall onto the floor, sobbing. The surrogate mother while Anna was a toddler and then a distant sister when Roseann left home for college was now a friend. "It was devastating. I was potentially losing a sister who meant everything to me." Roseann had met her husband, Clifford Beutell, at Case Western Reserve University in Ohio. Cliff was an editor for the *Wall Street Journal* and Roseann was a department store buyer in Cincinnati. Anna marveled at her sister's fashion flair; at that time, Roseann looked like a young Anna Magnani, five feet eight inches, with a gorgeous full figure.

Now Anna and her family experienced the full weight of anticipatory grief. College pressures, Anna's graduation and pending marriage, were eclipsed by a cold clutch of panic. Anna's thoughts were of Ro. She would have angry imaginary conversations with her—"Dammit, you're not going to die." Then: "Mom will never recover, I can't live without my sister, Oh, my God, will I get this? How did Ro get it?"

"Cancer had erupted through her skin and gone into the lymph glands," recalls Anna. "She had estrogen-dependent cancer. Well, they pulled out *every estrogen source in her body*—full mastectomy, the lymph nodes, ovaries—and she had an adrenalectomy!" Such drastic surgery meant that Roseann would be dependent forever on cortisone, a steroid with severe side effects. But no doctors could tell her how long "forever" was. Anna smiles. "Well, Ro's still living! That was more than twenty-one years ago."

Roseann's recovery after the complete removal of her body's estrogen-making system was one of the cases that inspired research toward creating tamoxifen, a chemical that prevents the body from actively using estrogen. "Instead of taking the ovaries, the adrenals, etcetera, they have created a marvelous drug," says Anna dryly. "The ironic series of events is that Ro's cancer led to the research—and now those drugs aren't helping her sister, me. Ro gets very angry. Says they should have taken everything out like they did with her, but I keep telling her they don't *do* that anymore."

Roseann's cancer occurred the year before First Lady Betty Ford had the courage to bring breast cancer out of the closet. Following her radical mastectomy in the fall of 1974, the first lady broke through taboos to talk openly and frankly about the words "breast" and "cancer," until then barely acknowledged in polite company. Her fearlessness gave hope to countless women who had suffered in silence and sent thousands more in search of mammograms. Little research had been done by the mostly male medical and scientific professions. Roseann's surgery was a major crapshoot. "It's the only time in my life I ever gambled," she recalls. "Within forty-eight hours, the abscess started to shrink!" Daily X rays were astounding. "The tumors went away, totally." The doctor published his miraculous trial operation on estrogen-based breast cancer in a "32-year-old female." Anna's sister now belonged to medical history.

Roseann's constant, massive doses of cortisone have caused her to "lose bone mass. I've shrunk two inches and gained all this weight." She waves her hand over her plump body. Emergencies are life-threatening; Roseann carries a med alert note with her always. "But it's been twenty-plus years and I'm very happy to be walking around," says Roseann, "so side effects I deal with. That's less important than the fact that I'm here."

By the day of Anna's wedding, August 17, 1974, the family had two reasons to celebrate. Roseann was going to be fine. Anna, svelte but busty, sighed when she looked at her baby-faced bridegroom-to-be. "The wedding dresses I really liked would make me look like his mother, so I changed to an ethereal 'princessy' style to accent youthfulness rather than fashion flair. It had short sleeves and I walked down the aisle with poison ivy all over my arms and Jan had strep throat and was sick as a dog." But all of that was forgotten when Jan slipped the simple band—that her dentist brother, Marty, had fashioned out of dental gold—on Anna's finger. Jan was a senior at the University of Maryland; Anna had graduated but had yet to find a job. "But what a way to start out," Anna recalls. "Two cars brand new and totally paid for as wedding gifts from our parents! Boy, I have had the life of Riley."

Although Anna matured into a young woman of talent and wisdom, nothing altered her exuberance, not even five disillusioning years of teaching junior and senior high school, first in Maryland and then in Richmond, where Jan attended graduate school. Within a few weeks of the wedding, Anna found a teaching job that covered their $143-per-month rent, food, and electricity. Jan joked that he was being kept by an older woman. They found a cheap apartment with old lovely rooms, and a modern division of labor was soon in place. Jan did the cooking.

"I am just an uninspired cook on a daily basis," says Anna, "while Jan can glance into the fridge, ponder this and that for a moment, and the next instant, I am eating a fabulous concoction of his invention. I don't envy this talent—I cherish the fact that I am married to it!"

While Jan finished his senior year as a biochemistry major at the University of Maryland, he worked part-time at AFRRI, the Armed Forces Radiobiology Research Institute. Meanwhile, Anna was getting the education of her life teaching in a Prince George's County Junior High. "Along with English, I taught everything from the next step above remedial reading to honors classes! I was clueless—red meat to that class." Her dream that "I would have my own stage and audience in class" gave way to grim reality. "The seventies was a very frustrating era of 'students' right,' and teachers had lost control, were at the whim of the students' lies and abuses, the faculty's fear of lawsuits." One day Anna heard incessant pounding through her wall. She raced to the adjoining classroom and found a teacher, battered, on the floor. A student had purposely grabbed and ripped a stack of papers the teacher was grading. As the teacher placed his hand on the student's shoulder, the boy grabbed the teacher and slammed him repeatedly into the blackboard. "This teacher was a timid, gentle fellow and he quit his job, defeated and disheartened. I felt terrible. He blamed himself for having touched the boy. *Touched!?* I would have collared the kid."

Anna made up her mind to make classes fun but rule with toughness. "We goofed off doing participles or nouns or gerunds—cracking up and coming up with gibberish—but the academic points were made. I was determined that learning did not have to be boring." The quid pro quo was that "they had better learn the material, study for their tests, and do their homework or *else.*" Her biggest accolade was her nickname—"The Fail Queen." One boy she did not pass—"He had a thirty-three average!"—leaped up and choked her in class. It took four others to drag him off. "The system opted to give him his diploma anyway—'Let him become someone else's problem'—and let him enter the army. God, imagine giving this boy a weapon!"

Jan bypassed his master's and in 1976 was accepted directly into a Ph.D. program at the Medical College of Virginia. Anna found few discipline problems in Richmond, where students called her "ma'am," but was disheartened when she saw the special favors athletes and coaches were given while schools scrimped on money for education. Anna's classroom career came to an end when she was commanded to teach a restricting, unimaginative sentence structure. "I was being forced to teach completely useless things. To me, the education system is bent on squeezing out your enthusiasm by continually pushing 'ordinariness' until you must either go through the motions for a paycheck or quit. Jan and I decided I would go crazy if I stayed. I quit with no job in the wings." Characteristically, Anna saw the half-full bottle, facing the end of one career with high spirits and a sense that new opportunity awaited.

Life in Richmond, 120 miles south of the nation's capital, is captured in magical memories. "It was the happiest time of our lives," recalls Anna. "We discovered a cultural world full of people our age with inspiration, ambitions, and dreams." When Jan and Anna left a decade later, Anna would mourn that loss for the rest of her life.

With her always through sorrows and triumphs, then and now, was a young woman who lived across the street, Lockard—"That's her full name, but no one calls her that." Anna and Jan became inseparable from Lockie and her then-husband, Wayne Westbrook. One weekend, Anna visits Lockie in Richmond. Anna's closest friend for more than twenty years retains her arresting good looks. She is a tall, slim brunette with eyes that change from deep green-blue to hazel, depending on the lighting. "Men flock to Lockie," says Anna, "always have." Sitting in Lockie's cozy living room, Anna says, "Do you remember when someone did a tarot card read—and we were told that in former lifetimes we had been brothers, and another time we had been married? I do think there was an old soul connection."

Lockie nods. "When we met, we couldn't talk fast enough. We had all this stuff to get out." Anna was twenty-six and Lockie twenty-nine. Lockie, the beautiful art teacher, and Anna, the wild and attractive English teacher, fresh and in their twenties, were too radical for their older, conservative teaching colleagues, so their comradeship grew daily at work. "And then Anna goes into advertising and I go into advertising and she hires Wayne and me. She was responsible for us getting on our feet in the business." Lockie and Wayne have long been divorced, but they remain friends and partners in a successful audiovisual production company, Mainstreet Productions.

Lockie eagerly says, "Anna's never met a stranger and is so full of humor and so terrific to be around that everyone wants to be her friend." Lockie jumps up off her living room sofa to demonstrate Anna in her twenties, hopping back and forth, as if playing basketball. " 'So what are we going to do now? Okay, okay, want to watch television? You want to listen to music?' Literally she was going *boinngg!*" says Lockie, leaping up. "She had so much vitality, passion, and animation."

Anna rocks with laughter. "I was tiring to be around." In those days, Anna drank coffee, downed chocolate by the gulpfuls, and chain-smoked, lighting another cigarette as one smoldered in the ashtray. "The worst argument Jan and I ever had was over my smoking. Jan thought that I had quit—and I *never* said those words. I told him I'd *try* and that I wasn't going to *buy* any. And I didn't—I bummed them." Both guffaw. "He just went berserk. Locked me out of the house! I had had both kids by then, but there wasn't secondary smoke because I never smoked around the kids or in the house."

"Jan is such a dear, sweet man," comments Lockie. "And so bright. He always comes up with something that makes you think a little harder. Always that twist—'Yes, but, what if . . . ?' It's the scientific mind, I guess. You two have always been 'content,' " reflects Lockie. "It used to piss me off. I would be pacing the floor saying, 'Life has got to be more,' and you were such happy campers, and I'd say, 'Oh, *God.*' "

Anna rests her head back in the car, warming herself in the welcoming sun, as Lockie and Anna head across town to their haunts of yesteryear. They pass the James River, where a wildlife sanctuary skirts the lake, just minutes from downtown. "This is what kept us sane," says Lockie. "Oh, look at our spot!" exclaims Anna. Down below, water swirls around huge flat slabs of rock, forming small whirlpools. There they would float on inner tubes, their dogs racing along beside the river. Lockie's car glides down Monument Boulevard, where DAR memorabilia and a Jefferson Davis monument coexist with a statue of Arthur Ashe. ""We just rode past the country club where he was not allowed to play," Lockie notes with irony.

The streets grow smaller, the houses closer together, as Lockie approaches their old South Side neighborhood. "People on the North Side used to say you needed shots to come over here. Most of us were so poor, we qualified for low-income housing. It was just us hippie teachers, musicians, arty crowd," says Lockie. The two couples were the hub: Wayne was the lead guitarist and songwriter; Jan played drums, sax, and French horn; Anna bass; and both women sang. Anna points to her former home. Friends would join them, swinging on the front-porch swings and singing until two A.M. "No neighbors complained because we were all involved," says Anna, savoring her memories before they leave for brunch with Wayne, Anna's closest male friend.

Westbrook is tall, with a small gold earring in one ear, and a sharp dresser, wearing slim-legged black pants, black boots, black jacket, blue-green plaid scarf around the neck. Many women note that he looks not unlike Paul McCartney. "Sir Paul," Lockie says. It is fitting that Wayne is a Beatles fan. Anna snuggles fondly against Wayne. "We were famous for movie marathons," she says. "We saw five in one day. We got stoned between movies." In Richmond, Anna finally got her theatrical chance and she recalls her most memorable performances. "I was Ariel in *The Tempest* at the huge amphitheater, with audiences of three to four thousand. The critic thought I had ballet training!" Anna and Jan were known for the best party of the year, the Annual Post–Income Tax Backyard Champagne Brunchfest, which grew to a crowd of about 300 and lasted into the next day. "There was always a surprise event," Anna recalls. "One year, accidentally, it was the birth of puppies. Another, Jan drove our white Olds Cutlass into the yard and everyone painted the car." For many, as the partaking of pleasures increased, the rainbow-colored car took on a shimmering psychedelic glow.

As they drive back to Lockie's house, Anna says, "I'll never forget the day that Hershel got it." Anna, the child who was not allowed to have pets, made up for that loss in adulthood by surrounding herself with animals. Her devotion to Hershel, their English springer spaniel, was obsessive. "That driver was so reckless that she had her young baby on her lap, not even in the seat belt. The minute she hit Hershel, I went crazy. I knelt in the middle of the street screaming." The dog lingered for three months. Anna cried all night when they finally made the decision to put her to sleep.

The death of a pet can engender deep mourning in adults as well as children, and Hershel's death precipitated one of the worst crises in their marriage. The next day, Anna returned from work to a deadly still house. "There was no trace. No Hershel, no Nils, no note, *nothing!* I sat on the kitchen floor, sobbing and raging." Then Jan called. "He had gone ahead and put Hershel to sleep! His note had been covered up."

That moment provides an abstract lesson on how people can misconstrue the needs of others in marriage and in death, in sorrow and in mourning. Anna felt cheated. "I was furious because I didn't get to ease Hershel's pain and be with her when she died." Jan, on the other hand, felt he was saving his wife from that ordeal. He couldn't stand to see either the dog or Anna in pain any longer. "I know he bore the burden of it by himself—but he took away the ability for us to be together, to comfort each other." This was no small matter and Anna brought it up repeatedly. "He let me rant and rave. After, I felt very self-indulgent and foolish." Later Anna realized that, as a childless woman, she had transferred her maternal love to the dog, which intensified the trauma. Still, from then on, Anna and Jan kept a vow to face the tough moments in life together.

When Anna quit teaching, she found creativity in advertising. "After only three months in the field, I had a management position—'in-house advertising manager' for a bank." When the bank merged nine months later and the Richmond-based group lost their jobs, Anna was outraged. "They did not care; this was politics." Characteristically, she had not lost her voice. "I marched into my boss's office and told him that he had no dignity or character for allowing a perfect stranger to fire us. Then I went down to the main branch, withdrew every cent, vowing in a loud voice, so customers could hear, never to set foot in there again." She laughs. "What an asshole I was."

As Anna downed drinks in a bar that night with other fired colleagues, panic set in. She and Jan had signed a contract to have their house renovated—at a cost larger than their original purchase. "I kept thinking, 'Where am I going to get a job?' We scrimped and took money out of savings." Anna's voice grows intense. "It was incredibly scary. My shoes would echo as I walked from empty room to empty room. There was nothing familiar or cozy. I would dig clothes out of a wardrobe box to get dressed and look for jobs. For almost half a year, I searched for work."

Then it dawned on Anna that she wanted to work where there were no openings—for the advertising director at Best Products Company, Helen Lloyd, "a dynamo role model." Anna hounded Lloyd until she hired her as a copywriter. Anna quickly advanced to ad manager, then creative director, handling print, radio, and TV ads for 300 stores nationwide.

Despite Anna's galloping career, life in Richmond collapsed when Jan, doctoral degree in hand, found a job at the National Institute of Mental Health, in Bethesda, Maryland, in 1982. He was soon immersed in riveting research on Parkinson's disease, but was gone all week for the next three and a half years, which put a strain on the marriage. Then, after ten years, Anna became pregnant. Their freewheeling decade was over. Although Anna and Jan were blissfully happy, the timing was terrible. Ellery was born May 15, 1984, when Anna was thirty-two. "Ellery was such a delightful baby, inquisitive and happy, but I began to resent single-handedly caring for the little guy—getting him up, feeding and bathing him, hauling him to day care, working all day, fetching him, feeding him and the two dogs, and falling into bed exhausted."

Meanwhile, Anna, the dramatist, invented a rosy life for Jan. "Jan drives up to D.C.—okay, the drive is hell, but, hey?—then he works at something he loves and goes home to a nice dinner made by his mom. 'So where was the stress in that?' I would think." Yet Jan was as battered as Anna, squeezing five days of work into four so that he could have a longer weekend with Anna.

Then Lindsay was born on October 9, 1985, a week shy of seventeen months after Ellery. This baby was not easy. "She threw tantrums in the womb." Anna was in a single-working-mother quandary. She found a day care center in a woman's home that took infants. "I nursed them each for about four months; I would pump my breasts, run over from work at lunch with it. When Lindsay was two and a half months old, on Christmas Day, 1985, I threw in the towel. I announced that our Christmas present to each other was to decide where we were to live and work together, set a date, and *do* it. We picked Washington for the obvious reason—that is where the science work is. Jan's work opportunities were geographically limited. I worked right to the end. On March 1, 1986, we moved back, lugging all our possessions, and, against my better judgment, lived with Jan's parents while we looked for a house to buy."

CHAPTER THREE

A New Stage

Despite Anna's fervent warnings that living with her in-laws once more would be disastrous, "they talked me into the worst seven months of our married lives—theirs too, no doubt. The Johannessens are such optimists," she recalls with a laugh. "In family dynamics, I am the realist. Jan wants to believe we are not capable of being small and petty, and we all are, all families are when it comes to invaded space."

The six-bedroom home became too small under the onslaught of two more adults, one toddler, one infant, and two dogs. Anna always had a hard time accepting generosity that could not be reciprocated and hated the situation. She held her breath when toddler Ellery would leave toys around for his grandfather to trip over. Jan and Anna feverishly searched for a house in what was then a seller's market, settling in Olney, twenty miles outside Washington. They still live in the same house, but Anna was never to know the joys of Richmond, on this, her third return to the D.C. area. "Nils and I both hate it. No offense to those who love it, but we find it impersonal and extremely pretentious. Like Los Angeles, who you know is what dictates life here."

Anna plunged into her new life as primary breadwinner and Supermom. In August of 1986, Anna became director of advertising in the Washington area for Creative Hairdressers (The Hair Cuttery), a chain of 250 budget hair salons. With sublime confidence, Anna became a leader as she moved from one career to another. They found a good day care center, the house was shaping up, life seemed radiant.

* * *

In May of 1988, Anna was only thirty-five when she had a mammogram. In light of Roseann's cancer, doctors had suggested Anna start mammograms at forty, but she decided not to wait. The mammogram showed a questionable spot on her right breast. It turned out to be a benign fibroid. Anna merrily forgot about the incident, certain that her guardian angel was watching out for her. "Mom told me that my birth date, October 2, 1952, was known as Guardian Angel Day. I've never been sure if there is such a thing—but my life sure seemed as though there is. Terrible things always seemed to happen to others. I seemed to be able to cope, find that silver lining, see a new opportunity and forge ahead. Especially in my twenties, I felt guilty for having it so good, and felt that I should shoulder some of the burden. Ro had to struggle for everything, not me. Mom had a terrible childhood, not me. My brother Marty had a horrible first marriage and Steve, the older one, had years of marital and financial difficulty, not me. I just went along, with my guardian angel watching over me." Anna continued her routine exams and mammograms and as the months stretched to over a year, with perfect checkup after perfect checkup, she forgot all about it.

About that time, Anna quit The Hair Cuttery to join the mostly male world of Jiffy Lube as an executive. Anna achieved a record-breaking 1993 sales year and won National Franchise Association honors as director of marketing for Jiffy Lube Washington Area Co-op—an advertising cooperative comprised of thirty-nine Washington-area franchised Jiffy Lube centers.

On Halloween night, 1989—eighteen months after the discovery of the nonmalignant fibroid—Anna found a lump near the scar tissue that had formed following the needle biopsy. "I was giving out candy to kids, when my bosom started to itch. The surgeon had warned me that I might be a fibroid tumor grower and I assumed I had grown another [benign] fibroid. I had no panic, but Jan urged me to see the doctor right away."

The surgeon probed the lump; it was not a fluid-filled cyst that could be drained. The itching stopped, and Anna agreed to wait until the bruising went away to decide whether a lumpectomy was necessary. The Johannessens went on vacation. Says Anna, "I firmly was in my optimistic mode." Five weeks later, on Pearl Harbor Day, December 7, 1989, a lumpectomy was performed. As Anna came out of anesthesia, still groggy, the doctor told her, "You have cancer; we could tell that from the section we removed. I am sorry."

"I should never have let her wait," Jan says years later. "*No one* can tell you what it is until they slice it up and look at it under a microscope. The first thing the doctor said to me was 'Well, a month wouldn't make any difference,' so I knew he was thinking about that. I didn't know if he was covering his ass, but no one can put a time on when a cancer cell breaks away. That should be a lesson for everyone."

Anna lay dazed, stunned, frightened, as the doctor turned around and walked out. Like so many patients, Anna had been socked in the stomach with a terrifying truth, then left alone to absorb it. "That was one of the few times Anna was totally vulnerable," says Jan, remembering her forlornness. "She sobbed and I cried." In a follow-up visit, the doctor gave a terse recital of Anna's surgical and postsurgical options. "My surgeon was a perfectionist," she remembers, caustically. "Other doctors complimented me on the quality of my mastectomy scar. But obviously he had taken no classes in dealing with human beings. The scary point is that my situation is not the exception. I am a typical patient."

Only in the last few years of this century has there been a concerted effort—led by caregivers and some compassionate doctors—to humanize the care of patients. Unfortunately, Anna's story is far too common. Start a conversation at any gathering and one will find more incidents than can be imagined. Here are just three: Ten years ago, Herbert Bloom, a gentle Miami Talmudic scholar with heart problems, was given bad news by his longtime doctor and friend, who then clapped him on the back and said, "Well, we all have to go sometime." The man lived for years. A Washington businessman, Aaron Woloshin, and his wife, Deirdre Pierce, endured numbing fear and anguish when the doctor abruptly broke the news, with great certitude, that Woloshin had acute leukemia and would die. The man took his illness to another doctor and found out, after days of torturous mental pain, that the first doctor was wrong. It was a form of chronic leukemia; most people with it can live an almost normal, if not normal, life for a long time. Years later, Woloshin is still healthily alive. Thirty years ago, a pregnant young woman named Mary Esty woke up in the hospital minus a breast. The exploratory surgery had turned into a mastectomy without her knowledge. (Her husband had signed for the operation, convinced by the surgeon of the necessity to act quickly. In those days, women having exploratory surgery often woke to the shocking reality that their breast was removed. If it was nighttime, it meant that the operation had been long enough for a mastectomy.) The surgeon came to her bed and told her, "You have only three months to live and I suggest that you have an abortion." Esty had her child and is now a Washington psychologist doing important work in the field of alternative medicine. Esty's experience spurred her search for better ways to treat cancer survivors with nonchemotherapy alternative measures.

Heavy emotions assault the stunned patient, including grieving, which begins with the moment of diagnosis. Whether one survives or the illness is transient, whether there is later cause for rejoicing, no one can understand the patient's depth of sorrow for what might happen and a loss for what has been. An irreversible altering takes place.

"Learning the surgical skill seems to harden surgeons," says Anna. "They have no heart. When ordinary people are told they have cancer, technical information is thrown at them by the surgeon—who then removes himself from any responsibility by citing he only cuts you up! Where is the surgeon who talks slowly, calmly, reassuringly to the patient? Nonexistent! This information must be given slowly and again and again because the patient is in shock. The patient cannot comprehend it all and only thinks, 'My God, I have cancer. I am going to die!' It takes a while for that panic and loss of control to abate before the patient can start making cogent decisions. I dare any person to give a patient a memory test two hours later and see how much information he or she has absorbed following one of those sessions when the news is so bad. Luckily I have a husband who could absorb the technical jargon that flowed out of the surgeon's mouth. I learned the hard way and I make my doctors *work* for *me*! They are only people and often wrong. There is no critical thinking unless the patient demands it."

As Anna began to face the facts, she knew she wanted a modified radical mastectomy. "After my sister's breast cancer, I said, 'Let's do it! I want this gone forever.' " The mastectomy was performed on December 14, 1989, a week after the lumpectomy. Her breast and lymph nodes under the arm were removed by the surgeon who made such beautiful scars. Anna had made an appointment to see an oncologist in Olney, Dr. Ken Miller, following surgery. She was surprised to see Miller at her bedside as she recovered. He stayed more than an hour, discussing her cancer. "That amazed me. We had immediate rapport. He had all the empathy lacking in other doctors but was very straightforward." From then on, Anna called him Ken.

Anna had to wait seven days to learn if the cancer had spread to the lymph nodes. This time, the surgeon had good news—the cancer had not spread, he assured Anna. "Every single one of twenty-four lymph nodes they took out was negative. So the opinion was that, once they took that breast off, I was cured. I didn't need chemotherapy, but I said, 'Hey, guys, not with my family history. Give me all you've got.' "

Anna was thirty-seven years old and her youngest child had yet to see kindergarten. Ellery was five, and Lindsay, four, was in day care. Now Anna had to explain the inexplicable to her toddlers. They came into the hospital room, eyes wide, unused to seeing their mother sick and in bed. Anna grinned and acted as if it were a normal everyday occurrence. Soon they were sampling the fruit and candy gifts, smelling the flowers, pushing the buttons to see how the bed went up and down.

Anna looked at her children as she patted her flat right chest. " 'There was something bad growing in my breast and we had to take it off to protect me,' " she explained. "Jan and I didn't make a big deal of it and, as a result, they didn't. But they knew all the facts. I won't say it was easy, but it was amazing how accepting they were. After the operation, you really can't raise your arm from the shoulder. They move those muscles and take the lymph nodes out under your arm. They tell you it takes about six weeks and give you exercises. I had my range of motion back in three weeks. I just couldn't stand it and I exercised like crazy. I was determined that the cancer would not control me, I would control it!" In two weeks, she was back at Jiffy Lube part-time.

Still, Anna entered a survival phase that took some psychological effort. She worked hard at "staying myself around the kids; I would take the time and build my energy up, and when they were around, I was trying to be relatively normal. They knew, of course, that things were different. They saw the tubes, the fluid bags hanging out. They had lots of questions and wanted to see everything. I told them, 'You guys, right now I've got staples in me; can you imagine being all stapled up?' and I described how staples clip things together. And I said, 'I want it to look a little prettier before you see it.' When the staples were out, I let them see it, touch the scar tissue, and ask questions. Lindsay, barely four, asked her father one night, "Daddy, am I going to get what Mommy got?" Jan hugged her and smoothed back her hair. "Honey, it's not contagious. That means Mommy can't give it to you or anybody." Rather than plunge into concern, Anna treated this as a normal, typical question of a curious child, a view with which experts in child behavior agree.

Two weeks after the surgery, Anna and Jan walked into Dr. Miller's office, five minutes from home. They brought with them all the documents concerning Ro's cancer. "I want every piece of heavy artillery you can throw at me," said Anna. Miller agreed; at the time, NCI had begun recommending adjunct chemo after node-negative breast cancer. Anna began chemotherapy two days after Christmas. "I told the kids that these drugs would stop me from getting sick again and I showed them the life port, where the intravenous drip would go." It looks like a slightly raised scar on the left side of her chest, above the remaining breast. A fine membrane of skin covers the opening, which is easily primed when the tube is inserted to draw blood or drip in medicines. The treatment consisted of one-month cycles. "It was a cumulative effect and by the third week, I would collapse, exhausted. As I started building my strength back up in the fourth week, the cycle would begin all over again."

For those six months, Anna retained an amazing schedule, rushing the children to kindergarten and day care before going to work at Jiffy Lube. "When I said it was Mommy's 'tired time,' they knew I had to rest. I explained that the chemo was attacking any bad cells inside me, sort of like Pac Man gobbling up the bad guys, and that that sometimes meant that the good parts hurt too." As soon as the chemo treatments ended in July 1990, Anna started tamoxifen. The medical profession had moved on to a new world of chemo cocktails—adrenalectomies belonged to the past.

"Like Ro, my cancer was estrogen dependent. Tamoxifen helps inhibit estrogen from being the catalyst for cancer again. The chemo and tamoxifen caused me to go through menopause just like that," says Anna, snapping her fingers. "I had the hot flashes from hell. Even Ken is surprised that they have not abated. Often I have to sit down because I fear that I will pass out. Once my body is about to burst, I break out in gushing sweat from head to toe. Droplets of sweat fall from my face and people stare with curious amazement. Then I become very cold and clammy from the damp perspiration. On very good days, this happens only once every two hours. I have yet to meet another breast cancer patient who suffers hot flashes to this extreme." After years of this daily soaking, Anna learned to dress in layers so that outer clothing stays dry enough to protect her from the chills that follow. After a sudden drenching, Anna's face and head are as wet as if she had just walked in a thunderstorm. Sleeping is a special nightmare; Anna drenches the bedclothes, hunts for a fresh spot until that one gets drenched, and on and on, into the night.

Dr. Miller, Anna's slim, mustached oncologist, is near Anna's age. "We're both Star Trekkies," says Anna, referring to one of the instant-rapport litmus tests among baby boomers who spent their adolescence glued to the TV series *Star Trek.* Miller received his medical degree from Tufts University, interned at the Yale University School of Medicine, was a Fellow in Hematology at the National Institutes of Health, and a Clinical Fellow in Oncology at Johns Hopkins Oncology Center.

One afternoon in 1995, between constant phone interruptions, he talks about breast cancer. When Anna first came to him in 1989, the number of affected women in their thirties was low. Now he is among the many oncologists who call breast cancer an epidemic. "It used to be one in fourteen, then one in ten; now it is one in eight women who will develop breast cancer." Some of this boost is caused by early detection and by sheer numbers; women in that huge pig-in-the-python bulge of baby boomers. Other high-risk theories—from later pregnancies to pesticide exposure to genetics to fatty-food diets or smoking—are considerations, but no one knows how and why one gets breast cancer.

Anna kept to a rigid schedule of doctor's visits, starting every three months, then every four months after two years, and every six months after three years. There was a never a hint of anything wrong. Anna also went to her gynecologist for endometrial biopsies because tamoxifen can cause endometrial cancer. These biopsies were always negative. By 1994, Anna's checkups were as routine as going to the dentist.

Anna stayed with Jiffy Lube for three more years, but the situation had turned sour. Anna was reluctant to lose such a good position and salary—$76,000 a year. Like many, however, who are faced with the shock of a serious illness or the death of a loved one, Anna was soberly reexamining her life. "Getting sick rocked me enough to ask, 'What is it you really want to do?' What I wanted was to open a cute shoe store for children. I did my research, put the money together, and in July of 1992 opened up Happy Feet Shoes in the oldest mall in Olney." The framed dollar bill from Anna's first sale hangs on the dining room wall. Anna was putting every other Jiffy Lube paycheck into the store and needed her job more than ever.

"At first, I made every stupid mistake known to man." Anna jokes that if "something is in style, give it two years before it hits Olney." Yet she could not resist buying as if the store were on Fifth Avenue. "Purple shoes for five-year-old girls," she says, rolling her eyes. She had to sell stock at a steep markdown. A blizzard piled up twenty-seven inches of snow. It took a week for the snow-removal trucks to get to her side of the mall, even though county law required removal within three days. Anna told her partner, Connie Giordano, "Call 'em and tell them somebody just slipped in front of my store." Her walks were shoveled within hours. For Anna, there was always a solution.

At year's end, Anna's partner left for a better-paying job. Determined not to lose the store, Anna quit Jiffy Lube to run it by herself. "I was burning the candle at both ends and was tired of the ugliness and squabbling that was going on among the franchisees. That store was my little baby and I was going to make it go." Her decision was a financial blow—"We took a good sixty percent hit in income. But I was so exhausted that Jan was just glad to see me choose one or the other." Anna made her store so intriguing that business picked up. Wallpaper featured Day-Glo sneakers. A play area contained TV videos, a pink flamingo rocking chair and toys, hats and costumes for dress-up. Parents rejoiced that one child could play while another tried on shoes.

The only children who hated the store were her own. No longer able to afford sitters, every afternoon Anna closed the store, raced to pick them up at school, and hurried back. Ellery and Lindsay did homework on a stockroom table until closing time. "It was hard," recalls Anna. "They had to be on their best behavior." Anna told herself that soon she would be able to afford help with her children and the store. "It was starting to turn. I didn't pay myself a salary, but I didn't have to put money in anymore."

As Anna faced the public daily, she adamantly refused breast reconstruction. "I wore the damn prosthesis when I was the center of attention, like at the store, so that what I was doing took precedence over my physical appearance. They're making boobs out of this fine latex," Anna says one day, drawing out a breast mold that has the texture of raw chicken breast. The fake bosom became an object of fun; the family tossed the "rubber chicken" around like a ball. Then it settled, forgotten, tucked away in a drawer.

During those financial hard times, Jan, a respected scientist, made about $55,000 a year, typical for researchers who do not opt for big-money pharmaceutical companies. Anna and Jan give each other total support for their career moves. "Only once did I ask Jan about a job he was considering with a company," recalls Anna. "It would have paid a lot and been a fast-track job. As he talked, I could tell that it wasn't for him. I realized it was too important that Jan find an environment in which he can mentally prosper. Private research companies don't give you the freedom to pursue scientific curiosity. It's a trade-off. Government perks made up for less pay. Our insurance company pays a huge part of our medical benefits."

Anna and Jan saw sunny days ahead, with Anna the happy entrepreneur, Jan the contented researcher, the children growing into fun-loving companions. For years, cancer was a distant specter. Nothing but the life of Riley and guardian angels were on the horizon.

In 1993, however, Anna was felled by a major loss. Anna was nearing forty-one when her mother died after being ill for only three months. She had been a profound, confounding influence in her daughter's life. Anna mourned deeply. The death of a parent at any age is a special grief. By the time children have become adults, myriad emotions accompany that grieving—from relief to rancor, conciliation to unfinished business, abiding love to ambivalence. Feelings are not just of that moment but reach into the past and extend into the future. Sometimes one feels freed up or compelled to change one's own life, to divorce or get married, as one's mortality is realized. One's life is forever changed.

For solace, survivors often gather possessions of the dead. This can take the form of wearing clothing and jewelry or placing pictures and treasured trinkets nearby. Sometimes closeness comes with tactile remembrances. One woman kept and used her mother's powder puff, conjuring up her mother's soft skin as she had applied powder to her face. Anna remembered her mother's caregiving gesture—holding a person's hand, softly touching it with the other in a rhythm of three taps.

Audrie Megregian was a tiny, five-foot-two-inch bundle of complexities. Her remarkable creation of a rape crisis center—Anna's near rape in college was the catalyst—catapulted Audrie into the White House for honors and lunch with then-president Ronald Reagan. Her public persona was the picture of self-assurance—gregarious, every hair in place, exquisitely neat in suits and heels and nylons, never slacks, a gentle smile that did not hide the firmness in her voice when speaking about her work. Yet she was driven by personal demons of self-doubt stemming from a bruising childhood.

"Mom was one of the neediest people I ever knew," recalls Anna. "As much as she was able to do, I've always wondered what heights she could have reached had she been motivated by confidence instead of by terrible insecurity and need. To the day she died, Mom was seeking approval. Her whole existence was knowing that people needed her." Her work—her mother termed it her "calling"—was a direct response to a childhood "that would today be called child abuse," says Anna. "She was still trying to get approval from her mother. It killed me to watch her fighting ghosts." Anna's father concurs. "Her mother pushed Audrie around like she was dirt—chattel, a slave." Anna gasps, "My mother was forbidden to speak by her mother! Commanded to be silent! Once she got out from under her mother's grasp, she talked twenty-four hours a day. *Never stopped talking.* That drove people away." In a laudatory article about her mother, the author, Jim Ash, could not resist mentioning this trait: Audrie "is a 74-year-old perpetual motion machine, admired as much for her bottomless well of compassion and 18-hour days as she is sometimes feared for her marathon conversations."[1]

Like many children who have been abused, Audrie felt it was her fault—and lavishly praised her mother until her husband would remind her of reality. "Finally the dam would break," says Anna. "She would slowly work herself up to 'no one will keep me down anymore.' " That was when Anna heard bizarre stories, such as the day her grandmother ripped off Audrie's blouse in a jealous rage because Audrie and Stephen were going to a picnic attended by a woman she detested. Anna's father's anger flashes and he slams his palm on a leather chair. "I tried to get her to forget about it all, but I never could. It just stays with you."

The fascinating enigma that was Audrie contained a sad irony. Her social worker gifts were stunning. "Strangers in airports were drawn to Audrie like a magnet," recalls her husband. "Casual acquaintances came to live with us for four or five weeks at a time because of Audrie. A colleague of mine died of a brain tumor and Audrey took his widow in, quieted her down, got her a job." In her private life, however, those skills disappeared when dealing with family members.

Audrie became a feminist role model regarding Anna's careers. "She gave us a lot of strength and a lot of guts—but when it came to working with her children, she dealt with the family completely differently," says her daughter. "She could not tolerate criticism at all." This created a barrier to intimacy. Anna's attempts to "try to explain how she made me feel" were met by a deeply hurt and defensive "Wasn't I a good mother?"

Anna loved her and embraced many of her qualities, yet deliberately eschewed others. Although she vehemently rejected her mother's wish that she become a social worker, Anna absorbed that same empathy and generosity, applying it to her daily interaction with friends, relatives, acquaintances, coworkers. Disavowing other traits, Anna endeared herself to others with her directness, ability to take criticism and to laugh at herself. "I've worked very hard to let my kids know when I screw up. I say, 'I'm sorry, I screwed up.' We don't play the parent-is-always-right game—that's just not correct."

The pretty, petite, "life of the party" square dancer taught her daughters nothing about what it meant to be female. "It was tough. Ro got her period in the middle of camp and thought she was dying. Luckily, my sister was able to tell me all about it." Anna still guffaws at the conversation she had with her mother the night before her marriage. "*Finally* she told me the facts of life, at age twenty-one! 'It's okay, honey, if it hurts the first time.' And I'm going, 'Right, Mom. No problem,' ready to fall over in hysterics in the bathtub. For God's sake, Jan and I had been all over England together! The only person I ever was really intimate with. Hello-oh. She never wanted to see it."

When Anna and Roseann became adults, Audrie's desire to help could overwhelm, although in retrospect they tell their special "Audrie stories" with fondness. The night of Ellery's birth, Anna went into serious labor at midnight. "Mom had gone to sleep, but the next thing I know, she was down the stairs, dressed in a neat blue suit, nylon hose with garter belt—she never wore panty hose—even had a necklace on, her hair done and lipstick on . . . oh, I forgot, and in high heels!"

It was a difficult birth and the gasping baby was raced to the incubator. "Man, that was Mom's big claim to fame—that she was right there making those nurses run along with that cart, doing everything right. In her high heels. She went nuts when Ro got sick," says Anna. "She came with great intentions and then she'd get in your kitchen *and she'd clean.* Rearrange cupboards, everything." Ro laughs. "We lost a bowl for five years. I teased her about it, but she couldn't take the joke."

In retrospect, Anna admires her mother, the fierce lioness with her cubs. "She never had a mean bone in her body." Audrie's criticisms were always oblique, yet she aggressively urged her children to succeed, often in goals that she had chosen. Audrie's beautiful, lilting voice would fill the house—"In a different era, she could have had a singing career," says son Steve. For her children, music was a must and piano lessons a requirement. Anna is glad for that today, but other traits produced lasting rebellion, among them her mother's compulsive neatness. "We were not allowed to be messy kids! I had a white fancy bedspread and I had better pull it back to sit on the bed or I was in trouble." Today Anna uses furniture until it wears out and turns her king-size bed into a cozy island for the kids, her, Jan, and the dogs.

Although Anna's father spends most of his time in the den off the pool in his Florida home, his wife's presence lives on in the ornate living and dining room untouched since her death in 1993. French-style furniture upholstered in pale blues and pinks sit in pristine readiness. Silk flowers forever bloom in Audrie's vases. Porcelain knickknacks abound along with Oriental vases, Japanese and Chinese paintings.

As a teenager, Anna's rebellious independence, her smoking and drinking, created strife. Those days were long forgotten in later pleasures shared by mother and daughter. However, Audrie endured painful discord and alienation with her daughters-in-law until her death. Audrie was never obviously critical. For example, says Anna, "there was the time Jan grew a beard. Mom looked at him and didn't say a thing. Then she calmly said, 'You know, the district attorney in Florida had a beard.' Pause. 'He shaved it off.' Boom. Jan just laughed." She didn't boss her sons' wives, "but if you were insecure, her every word would bother you. I think she intimidated my sisters-in-law."

Adds Roseann, "Mom was not *allowed* to participate in the joys of being a grandmother to my brothers' kids." Anna says, "Oh, man, it really hurt to see Mom so torn up. I wanted to say to my brothers, 'This is your mom. This is your wife. Have some gonads, boys; sit them down and get this solved.' But I never did." Nor was her mother helpful in fence mending. After watching this impasse, Anna made sure that Audrie and Stephen visited with her children and created a lasting bond. Ellery and Lindsay have loving memories of their grandmother. Says Ellery, "She was always singing."

Family dynamics can frequently be puzzling. Grudges can fester into feuds of mystifying proportions and duration. Says Anna, "We're no different. I look at others and I shake my head and say, 'Everybody reacts to somebody in a very unusual way,' and when you're on the outside, you say, 'Huh? What? You're kidding me!' "

Audrie's continuing isolation from her Florida grandchildren propelled her into long hours with her baby, CASA. Audrie founded CASA—Commission Against Sexual Assault—after she moved to Cocoa Beach in 1975 for a so-called retirement. Audrie single-handedly carved out the volunteer organization that brought national accolades. One wall in the Megregian Cocoa Beach den is a shrine to Audrie. In her picture with President Reagan, the petite Audrie seems weighted down with the large sterling silver medal, worn on a wide red, white, and blue sash, as she clasps the president's hand in her customary two-handed greeting. Audrie was one of 20 culled from 40,000 nationwide volunteers to receive a 1983 President's Volunteers Action Award. More plaques and awards are on display, along with a July 1, 1984, cover story from *Parade* magazine, "What Happens to Heroes?" by Jack Anderson, featuring Audrie.

Audrie became a messenger of enlightenment. She started rape-trauma support groups, held child abuse seminars, and dealt with as many as 100 rape victims a year. Well into her seventies, Audrie would be, as she phrased it, "on the street" all night. "I didn't like that at all," says Anna's dad, "but I couldn't stop her." Sometimes Audrie's ventures sounded like the stuff of X-rated movies. She coaxed a reluctant nineteen-year-old rape victim to give a police report that resulted in the capture and imprisonment of the man called the Vampire Rapist, who had drained more than 50 percent of the girl's blood, then drank it from a beaker. For Audrie, there was never any hesitation. Once, she rose from a hospital bed, walked out, catheter trailing, and showed up at the courthouse to stand by one of her "children."[2] Not only did she comfort victims, Audrie was determined to put rapists behind bars. One time, Audrie was not allowed in the courtroom to guide a child, only eleven years old. "I get goose bumps just thinking about this," recalled Audrie. She told the girl, "Sweetheart . . . I'm in your brain. . . . I know you can do it."[3] After that ordeal, the child drew a picture of Audrie—with a halo.

Audrie's unrelenting devotion to CASA—she never took a cent in salary and used some of her own money to keep it afloat—was rewarded with a terse dismissal; it was never explained by Brevard County health authorities, even after local newspapers probed what seemed an astonishingly cruel act for someone so respected and honored. When CASA finally had the potential as a government-funded agency, "they kicked Mom out. They didn't want a seventy-plus grandmother running it," says Anna. Audrie called it the "rape of my soul."[4] Anna's mother was nearly destroyed; she mourned her loss, her weight dipping below eighty-five pounds.

A year later, she was back in the public eye, however, enthusiastically plugging her new job, which she termed the first of its kind in the country, counseling families of prison inmates. Still, Anna says, losing CASA was a mortal blow. "I do think that stress is a cancer inducer and after those people did such a horrible thing to her, Mom was never the same. It ate her away." Nearly four years into that job, Audrie started constantly clearing her throat. She was diagnosed as having stomach ulcers. The doctor switched medication often, but nothing helped. After treating Audrie for three months, he reexamined her. This time the doctor told the stunned couple, "I'm sorry, I can't do anything more for her. She's got cancer." Her husband recalls, "In all that time, nobody said anything about cancer!" The horror is replayed in his face.

In the spring of 1993, Audrie's stomach was removed, but the cancer had spread. She lived for only three months and was in severe pain. Had they known the results, no one in the family would have considered the operation. A belief remains that Audrie might have lived longer had she been properly diagnosed earlier. Stephen's eyes fill as he fights off tears. "I get so damn mad when I think of that doctor."

In those swift final months, Anna recalls, the roles were reversed. The daughter remembers "tapping her hand, talking to her, just like she used to for me." The task of caring for her mother fell to Roseann, who was out of a job then. Says Roseann, "Anna once said, 'She's getting even with you for not having kids, because now she's your kid.' At the end, it was like taking care of a baby and changing diapers."

Stephen refused a hospital bed; after more than half a century of sleeping together, he wanted to remain at her side. Near the end, however, he moved to another room; he could not take seeing his wife, who was no longer the Audrie he had known. He recalls hospice as "the greatest support you can get." Not in Roseann's mind. The emotional and spiritual aspects of the hospice team—social worker, chaplain, and volunteer—were declined. The team consisted of two, a nurse and an aide. For Roseann, with her weakened back, the aide who daily washed her mother was a "great help." But, says Roseann, "I was angry that I wasn't trained." Instead, a nurse friend showed her how to "pillow her in bed so that it would not hurt, how to turn her so as not to have bedsores. Nobody from hospice prepared me for what to look out for."

Roseann's anger was not only at hospice. "The whole time I was there, neither of my brothers or their wives offered to help. One night, Marty and his wife came over and she took me out and he stayed with Mom. One time! Over three solid months." Stephen asserts that "Mom didn't want their help. She would have tolerated only Anna and Ro. No one else."

Audrie gave her last speech at a retirement party less than three weeks before she died. Reed-thin but still pretty, Audrie was hugged by family, present and former coworkers, and victims she had helped. She heard the words that made her feel needed; she was "irreplaceable and we love you very much." Her last words were about giving. "Something I've tried to raise my children with—and that is that all of you, in some way, give five minutes a day for somebody else."

Audrie Megregian died on July 21, 1993. She was seventy-nine. Anna had already written her mother's obituary. "I sat down in tears one day and wrote the thing." At a memorial service, some of those who had been instrumental in Audrie's dismissal from CASA showed up. The infuriated but gracious Megregians said nothing. Then Anna, with a fury as strong as any of those times when her mother felt the need to fight for her children, marched up to their flower arrangement and, after making sure that they had seen her, threw it in the canal out back.

PART II

A Rage to Live

Do not go gentle into that good night,

. . . .

Rage, rage against the dying of the light.

Dylan Thomas

Anna's oncologist, Ken Miller, with family. (Back row) Cara, Joan, Kimberly, and Dr. Miller (Front row) Caramel, Julie

Child bereavement counselor Dottie Ward-Wimmer with a blind patient, at a camp for children with cancer.

CHAPTER FOUR

"The Return of the Big C," Insurance Companies, and Other Snafus

The death of her mother was an incomparable blow to Anna. For so many people in the first stages of mourning, never being able to talk to the loved one again, never to hear the voice again, never to see the person walk through the door again, is a torturous reality that nullifies any wistful denial of death. For years, Anna and her mother had talked on Sunday nights, a connection now irrevocably broken. Anna sobs on Sunday nights now, even though she maintains the ritual phone call with her father. She worries about her father, terribly alone, for the first time in fifty-five years. And she is learning that one misses a departed loved one forever. The ache is physical as well as emotional and is often described as feeling like there is a hole in one's heart. As time continues, for most, the emptiness of loss becomes more manageable.

A half year later, Anna's personal life, as the New Year of 1994 arrives, is positive. Still struggling with her Happy Feet shoe store, Anna finds that ownership, even an in-debt one, is exciting. "It was so nice to be my own master." Her children are growing by the day and, for the most part, happily, although they miss their hardworking mother. And the best news is that her January routine six-month checkup—four years after her mastectomy—shows that Anna remains cancer free.

Suddenly that summer, a year to the month of her mother's death,

Anna learned a terrible truth. Her cancer had metastasized and was spreading through her body.

"I knew then that cancer would kill me. I just didn't know when."

Anna had noticed a bump on a bone in her right chest. She thought she may have pulled a muscle while working vigorously in the garden, not an unusual possibility. Anna was just weeks away from her semiannual cancer checkup and decided to wait. Later Jan says, "The lesson on this is 'One, you know your own body and, two, don't wait!" Anna admits that "I was waking up at night in agony but kept thinking that the tamoxifen hot flashes were causing it." Miller did his blood work and suggested that a surgeon examine Anna. The surgeon suggested ibuprofen "to see if the swelling went down." Within days, the situation changed dramatically. "Ken called and said, 'Get a bone scan right away!' Blood work results showed that my cancer marker—the test that checks for a certain protein associated with breast cancer—was way off the scale. Normal is from zero to thirty and mine was up to nearly two hundred eighty-five." The next day, Anna had the bone scan. "To Ken's credit, he came down and sat with me." They looked at the results. Anna said, "I'm supposed to be worried, aren't I?" Miller choked as he said yes. Anna burst into tears. "He held me as I cried."

When Anna could stop crying, they reviewed what she should get done while Miller was on vacation. "He apologized profusely because he wouldn't be here for me." An absolute must was a bone biopsy. Afterward, the surgeon announced that the results were negative and that Anna was cancer free. The surgeon had operated on the *wrong* rib. As Anna came out of the operating room, recalls Jan, "I took one look—the bandages were way down here!" He points to his chest. "A good three inches below where it should have been." Anna and Jan raced to Miller's new assistant, Joe Kaplan. "We're in Joe's face. 'This is not right. I am sick! You can see it with the naked eye!' " recalls Anna. Kaplan instantly ordered a CAT scan–assisted biopsy on the right spot. "It showed, of course, that it was malignant and obviously that I still had cancer."

In fact, the cancer recurred with swift, thorough, heartbreaking fury. An MRI, taken immediately after the correct bone biopsy, revealed that "there was cancer running amok in the liver, my neck, the bone, and my chest."

Anna and Jan were thankful for only one thing. The children were visiting his parents in Seattle. They had a little time to face up to this terrible moment before breaking the bad news.

What happened to cause, as Anna terms it, "the return of the Big C" lies in the unknown. She was a victim of what doctors call the "monster" or "evil" disease. There are over 100 different types of cancer. How and why one gets cancer is still a mystery, although there are high-risk facts and theories (smoking, high-fat diets, environmental causes, and for breast cancer, early menses, child-bearing after thirty, among them). After decades of scientific trials, there remains no cure, although there have been successes in extending patients' lives—so much so in some types of cancer that one can live productively into old age. Still, most everyone will experience the sorrow of cancer, either for themselves or for family or friends.

When Anna discovered at the time of her mastectomy in 1989 that the lymph nodes in the armpit and surrounding area were cancer free, she felt a gush of relief. Her early-stage diagnosis made Anna a primary candidate for long-term survival. This diagnosis—and the fact that she was but five months away from what is popularly termed the "five-year cure," the widespread opinion that if you reached five years, you were cancer free—brought complacency. But Anna was wrong on both counts. All of her nodes were not checked and, alas, the accepted wisdom of the five-year cure does not apply to breast cancer, which can recur at any time as the years pass.[1]

In two frenetic, anxious weeks of tests, Anna went from a carefree "almost cured" survivor to a woman facing death. It is true that those twenty-four biopsied lymph nodes taken from Anna's armpit area were all negative. However, few women know that there are lymph nodes nearer the center of the chest as well as in the armpit area. Anna's breast cancer tumor was very central—and could have infected the mammary nodes close to the breastbone. Biopsies are not done; to reach nodes in that area would be extremely dangerous and difficult. "You don't open a woman's chest up to do a biopsy," explains Miller. "The risk outweighs the very small benefit. When her breast cancer was found, there must have been some cells that were outside of the breast. The problem was that at that time, they were too small to see on CAT scans and X rays. Even if you could remove those nodes, you may not have seen an individual cancer cell or two." Anna had used the one accepted method for killing cells in that area, chemotherapy, but, as Miller says, they could have been lying dormant, like some diabolical alien.

Dr. Miller is asked if he was surprised when Anna's cancer recurred. He sighs. "Yes. The feeling is a mixture of a lot of things. On one hand, the scientific part of me says that this is the nature of breast cancer. It's a rotten disease." A certain percentage of cancers will recur, but doctors cannot gauge which of their patients will be so stricken. "The personal part of me says, 'This is sad, it's shocking, it's demoralizing.' And I rack my brain and say, 'What could we have done? Why did this come back?' If I detach myself, I can say that's the nature of cancer. But it doesn't prevent me from saying, 'Jeez, I wish things were different,' and being angry."

As Anna faced her future in 1994, she knew that, unless medical science produced a miraculous cure, metastatic breast cancer was considered unsurvivable. Yet Anna was determined to fight to the last possible moment. And hope for that miracle cure. "*I* was going to control the cancer—not have *it* control me. By the time Ken returned, I already had my life port put in. I said, 'Let's get this sucker in here.' I was ready to combat this disease." She immediately went back on chemotherapy, but even as these poisons coursed through Anna's body, Anna and Jan feverishly searched for the newest treatment possible. Instead of help, they found terrifying nightmares.

Their big plunge was a frenzied race for an autologous bone marrow transplant (ABMT). In 1994, bone transplants were so new that many insurance companies labeled them experimental and refused to pay for them, including most federal insurance plans. Without insurance, the whopping bill (well into six figures) for a bone marrow transplant fell to the patient and family. Anna called the National Cancer Institute to see if she would be eligible for their transplant clinical trial. Anna's hopes soared after she spoke to the NCI coordinator and was repeatedly told that she was not disqualified for having had one chemotherapy treatment. "The point was made very clear to Ken and me that a second would definitely disqualify me, so I held off." She pinned all her hopes on the trial treatment, which included high-dose chemotherapy combined with the bone marrow transplant, and which was being heralded as a miracle breakthrough in cancer treatment.

She contacted one of the medical centers participating in the project on Long Island, and was scheduled for a September 19 appointment. Anna slept little in anticipation, then flew to New York with Jan. The National Cancer Institute had sent its records, stating that Anna was eligible. As they rented a car and drove to Long Island, Jan and Anna fell into their old pattern of thinking positively. After an examination and lab work, the doctor told Anna that she met the criteria, but that he was concerned that Anna had taken a first dose of chemotherapy. Anna assured him that NCI had given her a green light. "So I signed the consent form." The form spelled out the drastic treatment, which had even caused death, but Anna flew home to her children and the dogs "feeling there was hope" for the first time since July.

She had read the consent form meticulously before signing. It is a combination of graphic risks and phrases that sound as if the doctors were merely farming a field crop: "The harvested cells will be frozen and stored." These stem cells and bone marrow would be reintroduced later into her body. Massive amounts of chemotherapy "will totally destroy the bone marrow [left in the body], placing me at risk of infection and bleeding complications. . . . I may die from the complications of this treatment or if the reinfused bone marrow fails to function normally." A grim litany of possible lesser side effects—from vomiting to reversible abnormalities of liver and kidney function—filled two single-spaced pages. The list of possible benefits was only one paragraph and did not mention cure: "further tumor shrinkage, longer duration of disease remission, prolongation of life." Anna felt she had nothing to lose and possibly years to gain.

The next day, Anna called the doctor, anxious to get started. Her stomach churned, first with panic, then rage, as Anna heard him explain that she was not eligible after all. The criteria had been changed and her one chemotherapy dosage now disqualified her. Anna demanded to know why the NCI coordinators for bone marrow transplants—those who pass on the information to cancer patients—did not know there had been a change. Anna's voice became icy as she asked the doctor, "*If and when* do you plan on informing the NCI coordinators?!" After a sobbing phone conversation with Jan, Anna called NCI and "blasted the poor young volunteer on the telephone for the fact that something so important as life and death is treated so lackadaisically." The change became well known "*after* my discussion with the doctor. It was *my* situation that enlightened them. Until then, coordinators were completely unaware that the criteria had changed in any way whatsoever!"

The following day, a front-page article in the *Washington Post* carried great news for federal employees. The Office of Personnel Management (OPM) announced that effective immediately (September 21, 1994), bone marrow transplants would be covered by all government insurance policies. "Oh, happy day," thought Anna. That week, Ken Miller told Anna to contact Johns Hopkins Breast Cancer Institute; if her liver tumors decreased sufficiently, she might be eligible for a bone marrow transplant. Then came another blow. Anna was told by the insurance company that prestigious Johns Hopkins was a nondesignated facility and they would not pay for a bone transplant. Anna fired off letters of complaint regarding these policies and her searing encounter with government incompetence. In a letter to the Office of Insurance Programs, Anna termed the bone marrow clinical trial snafu an "unconscionable" error for patients whose lives hung in the balance. Her request for financial reimbursement for her futile New York trip was tersely refused. Anna sat for hours composing letters that outlined both situations, catastrophes to her. Form letters came back from female congressional members whose inquiries to the insurance company and NCI were ineffective. President Clinton's form reply never mentioned Anna's problems as he pushed health care reform: "At some point each year, 58 million Americans lack health insurance, and each month, two million lose their coverage."

Anna's frustrations point up the widespread disillusionment of millions of Americans, victimized by a crumbling health system. The current medical state transcends the Big Scare, so fiercely orchestrated by insurance companies in their massive and costly ad campaign to defeat Clinton's national health insurance in his first term. As insurance-run HMOs and PPOs (Preferred Provider Organizations) took hold, the dire predictions happened anyway—narrowed choice of doctors, hospitals, treatments, humane care—thanks to those very same insurance companies. Instead of the government setting the agenda, money-making insurance companies are in charge. Now cost-counting accountants, not doctors, decide what procedures should be done on an outpatient basis, where, and for how long, and for what procedure a patient can be admitted to the hospital. Major complications can set in with an office procedure that used to be performed in hospitals or if patients are forced to leave hospitals early. Many doctors are as angered as their patients about the present and future demolition of health care. As insurance company CEOs get rich while slashing the amount they pay for services, doctors are forced to reduce fees or quality of service or hope that patients can pick up the tab.

Anna's fury returns as she sounds a universal alarm. "Our horrible insurance company, I hated them. All of a sudden, doctors I'd gone to forever weren't in their plan and we were paying a higher percentage! You don't realize what's happened until you're sick. You're a prisoner of the damn insurance and drug companies. The only reason bone marrow transplants finally got approved was because they were sued for seventy-five million dollars in California. That made insurance companies go, 'Whooops, we'd better do something.' " Luckily Jan was able to switch to an insurance company that surpassed their expectation. "You have a certain amount of out-of-pocket fees for an entire year. By January, the first month, I already hit the maximum, one thousand dollars. From then on, Jan's insurance foots the bill. Between all of the medical tests, weekly blood counts, drugs that keep my white and red cells operable, plus the chemo and all, I cost about ten grand a month. I told Jan, 'I'm not a cheap date.' "

How can any one of Clinton's estimated 58 million annually uninsured afford cancer? "They *can't.* Nobody understands that. I can sure relate to people with HIV. Every couple of days, something new happens [in clinical studies or FDA approval of new drugs] and I'm like, 'Wow!' Then I think about those who don't have insurance to get these new drugs. Or there's some company with a gun to your head saying, 'Here's your bill. Whomp! We're going to keep your family in debt forever.' The thought of doing that to your family is so burdensome." And for millions in the United States there is no choice. A Washington nurse watched her family collapse in anguish when they could not afford a $350,000 bone marrow transplant hospital down payment for her brother after he reached the limit on his between-jobs coverage. He died of leukemia.

That fall, Anna's joy in knowing that the insurance company would finally pay for her bone marrow transplant is fleeting. She has too many liver tumors to be eligible. No one can understand the incredible emotional stress the terminally ill endure as they ride the roller coaster of hope and despair. Anna now returns to a conventional chemotherapy, Adriamycin, in hopes that this will shrink her tumors enough for the transplant. Exhausted and demoralized by her fruitless battles with the government and insurance companies, Anna now experiences the side effects of chemotherapy, the poison that kills good cells as well as cancerous cells. She is sapped of energy by low blood counts and loss of iron, and in pain. "I kept saying that it was good pain—'Go, you buddies, go'—because chemo was attacking the bad guys. The pain was actually quite bearable," she recalls, then describes a condition that makes medieval torture sound pleasurable. "My guts were on fire—I would compare the pain to getting a bad sunburn and peeling the skin early, exposing it to the elements before its time." Except that the fiery feeling was on the inside, in Anna's stomach and intestines, as the drug worked through her body, killing the lining cells.

"I lost my hair, of course, but they don't tell you that you have tufts left. Not all the hair comes out and it is much better to shave off the remainder, or you really look stupid." Nor do they tell one that the loss can be total. "When your eyelashes go, you have no protection." It is like having no windshield wipers when it rains. Although shielded slightly by her eyeglasses, everything—dust, rain, snow, wind, and, especially, sweat—pours into Anna's eyes. Her soaking hot flashes continue unabated.

At this time, however, Anna feels that she might win this race for survival. This is no denial of reality, because Anna is clinging to a possibility—the cure-all concept of a bone marrow transplant. At Miller's suggestion, Anna visits Dr. Nancy Davidson, a breast cancer oncology specialist at Johns Hopkins, to get another opinion on her chances for a bone marrow transplant.

"She's very nice," says Jan, "but most people that Ken sends up there don't like her because she's very straightforward and a lot of people want to be coddled, don't want to hear bad news. But Anna's like, 'Whatever it is, give it to me straight.' The first thing that Nancy said was that metastatic breast cancer is not considered a curable disease. That was her *starting* point. You go from there. The name of the game, medically, is to stretch it out as long as you can."

They had blocked such reality; while never denying it, Miller had not stressed that "you don't survive metastatic breast cancer," says Jan. Davidson's bluntness left no doubt. "It was two days before Christmas," recalls Anna. Davidson told Anna that she had to have a 50 percent reduction in her tumors to be eligible. In the darkened lab, the doctor held up Anna's X rays to the light and pointed one by one to the opaque markings. They were tumors. Ten of them. Two huge tumors literally stopped Anna in her tracks. "I had been told that one was eleven centimeters, but I had never seen the pictures, and I was just absolutely flabbergasted at how many there were. One was monstrous—six inches!" She gulped for air. Jan steadied her, his arm around her.

They stumbled out of Hopkins and said nothing, a horrible panic setting in as Jan wheeled the car out of the parking lot and drove through the old district of Baltimore and past Camden Yard Baseball Stadium. That cold December day seemed grayer and colder during the long ride home. Both began to sob and sob. She kept repeating to Jan, "Oh, my God, did you see the size of those?" Even through her tears, Anna could not resist a play on words. She repeated over and over, "I've got sausages in my liver!" Anna recalls, "At one point, Jan said the only thing that ever made my breath go away. He didn't yell, didn't shout. He said it gently but forcefully—'If you don't spend time with the kids, I will never forgive you.' Anna said, 'I hear you.' "

Both of them had entered a new zone of anticipatory grief, experiencing daily blips of sorrow—for the past, for the present, for the future. Eventually the shock wore off, but there was that undercurrent of waiting, wondering, trying to gauge a lifetime and how much of it was left and how and when it would vanish. No longer "if."

At home, the couple was thrown into a staggering paradox of duties—wrapping presents, decorating the house, and preparing for visiting relatives, as they wondered if this was the last Christmas Anna would see.

Viewing those tumors had brought thundering certainty. "Being a fighter, Anna could deal with the pain, but she hadn't dealt with the sense of time and the unpredictability of her illness," recalls Jan. Now she moved to another plane—vowing to fight, to stretch life out, for as long as she could.

Anna, the woman of countless careers, knew what Jan was telling her about spending time with the children. She would have to give up the store. "I decided to finish the chemo series because earlier tests showed some improvement. Then I would decide." Anna was borrowing time, trying to avoid those sausages in her liver. Anna finished her Adriamycin cycle. "If anything, I had more cancer in the liver. So it had not worked. I said to Jan, 'That's all I need. I'm closing the business.' " Anna immediately started a chemotherapy drug just on the market, Taxol, which was touted as miraculously shrinking tumors. "And that was the clincher. Taxol creates the neuropathy [affects the nervous system] in my hands and my feet. All of a sudden, walking back and forth and sitting on the floor and then getting up to get shoes—I couldn't do it. I realized that the Taxol was going to take me down if nothing else. But Taxol was really shrinking those tumors, and I was so happy with the results that I asked Ken what we could do to really kick some butt with it."

Anna is so different from most of his patients; her animated imagination—a necessary component for her upbeat survival—causes Miller to smile. "I reminded him of the Borg episode on *Star Trek: The Next Generation,* where they kept changing their defensive field frequency so that the Borg couldn't lock on and wouldn't know what was coming at them next. I asked if we could do the same—confuse the little cancer buggers. So we doubled my Taxol dosage. The effects on the tumors were excellent: many shrunk; some *disappeared.*

"At that dose, I suffered ridiculous side effects, totally losing my nerves in my feet, legs, and fingers, as well as the ability to regulate my body temperature. I would be freezing, then the next instant become Hot-Flash Woman. Two days after taking the Taxol infusion, every nerve ending in my body was on fire. My fingers curled up into my hands and I would lie in bed not moving, fearing the act of breathing because it sent waves of nerve spasms. But it was working—so who's to complain?" Anna cautions, "No two people have the same kind or depth of pain. The same chemo can be a comparative snap for someone, while another is tortured by it."

*   *   *

In the winter and spring of 1995, Anna is dealing with the emotional and physical trauma of saying good-bye to what she knows might be her last career. When Anna finally made the decision to close the store, she did it "literally in a month," but she mourned the loss of her pride and joy forever. Like her mother before her, this career loss cut deep, especially since Anna could see progress. "If I could have gone through this fall, I would have had a great season!" Anna's eyes fill with tears. "I still get notes from customers saying, 'There's no store like yours. We really miss you.' "

Anna refuses to call the closing of her store the death of a dream. "I don't look at it that way because part of the dream was just being able to *do* it. Something I'd never done before." Her smile flashes in remembrance. Yet the first month was "very hard" on Anna. A shadow of sorrow touches her eyes. Then comes her upbeat response. "We decided, 'Okay, we're going to Florida for Easter and we're all meeting at the beach for July,' and all of a sudden, I had things to look forward to. And I had a couple of freelance marketing jobs that filled in the gaps until I could settle into, as I called it, my retirement. And that took a while."

During this period, the double dose of Taxol "did me in. I would walk with no feeling from the knee down, no feeling in my fingers or feet, but the rest of me felt shooting nerve pain. Some days, I couldn't get out of bed—the pain of moving was blinding. I felt guilty because my poor kids could not even hop up on the bed with me without causing extreme agony. Then the children felt guilty. It is so horrible to think that the simple act of snuggling with Mom can become a negative if I react to the pain without remembering to let them know it is not their fault."

On better days, she turned up for her spring softball team, cheering them on even though she couldn't run. By the end of the summer, her toes wouldn't move. "I was in chronic pain, walked like a cripple, had no control over my balance, and was taking two Percocets every four hours for pain. Hardly a day at the beach."

Still Anna managed to visit her father at Easter, to share the summer with Jan and the children and friends. One golden beach day is captured in a photo that rests on the piano. A group of Anna's Richmond friends sit in a row on beach chairs, young, fit, good-looking baby boomers. Anna's bald head is tanned in perfect harmony with her face and lithe young body. A glistening turquoise bathing suit cannot compete with her even more glistening smile.

The jolts and losses, the pain and fear, the shock and struggling acceptance of limitations—all of those horrors that Anna experienced for more than a year since the summer of 1994—are nowhere reflected in that photo taken in the summer of 1995. With just a slight sigh, Anna says of her period of hard transition, "Well, so that's the end of *that* chapter in my life." A slight pause. "Hey, look at it this way. I'm still alive!"

CHAPTER FIVE

Resilience, Anger, and Humor

"I hate the fact that so much regarding the treatment of this disease is a big crapshoot!" says Anna. "Again, this is a control issue for me. As we make decisions, I still wonder if these are the right ones, but there is no data to support or refute them. I feel unconsolable regarding my treatment and Jan and I are constantly searching for options that make scientific sense."

Fired by righteous anger, Anna makes an impassioned plea for the media to think of the millions of ill people in their audience. "I wish I could shoot every single news anchor and reporter who starts their ten-second teaser with 'A new breakthrough in the cure for breast cancer, the story at eleven.' Nils gets furious when he hears things like this, knowing that so often experiments in animals do not pan out for humans. The false hopes and wild-goose chases that this reckless reporting creates in terminal cancer patients is flagrantly irresponsible and cruel. Think of the thousands of men, women, and children who are sent into a tizzy of futile hope. There may be the few on the bell curve for whom so-called miracles have worked, but these are hyped out of proportion. I have known people to follow irrational treatment courses—which, in essence, killed them faster—from bits of information they heard on the news about claims of curing cancer. The wish to stay alive and fight cancer causes many people to do desperate things—and there are enough quacks around, bleeding them of funds, offering futile hope. And the media does the same damn thing! Advancements have come from scientists finally identifying things about cancer cells and proteins. But the breakthroughs so far are not about *curing* cancer but about developing drugs to slow the process *down*. That is a far cry from a cure!"

Nevertheless, some breakthroughs have added time to Anna's life, such as the newly marketed Taxol, which she took for nine months. Now, in the autumn of 1995, Anna learns that Taxol is no longer working. "I got a lot of time out of it, so I'm not complaining." In October, Dr. Miller imposes what Anna terms a "drug holiday," to build up her immune system. A zest for life returns. "I was amazed at how badly I needed it until I began to really feel strong, whole. Only when you feel good do you realize how poorly you felt, how little energy you had, and how depressed you were!"

It is rare to hear Anna admit that she had been depressed. Her friend Lockie laughed when she once related how Anna, in a telephone call with another friend, Tina, admitted that things were a little hard and that she didn't feel well. "Tina just died laughing and started clapping over the phone and shouted, 'Yea! Anna's depressed; this is something I can finally understand!' " Another time, Anna called a friend who complained that her fighting optimism was too good to be true. "You're going to be pleased," said Anna. "I got depressed today!"

Her sister, Roseann, explains, "That's part of her personality, the way she deals with it, because she has a family and she has children and, to her, whatever time is with that family and those children is precious. She's not going to change. That gives her her joy and her happiness. I don't think she feels she can do much about the other."

"Depression?" says Anna. "I can't do that. I get bored with it. This really sounds dumb, but even when I try, I can't stay depressed for long. Like now; I went for my MRI on Monday and I'm back in trouble. The liver has more tumors in it. Next week, I'm getting a stomach and a brain CAT scan. Ken just wants to make sure—" She doesn't finish the sentence. "When I learned that the tumors were growing again, I was only able to be depressed for about half a day. There's too much going on, I don't want to mope. I've never been one to sit around and wait for things to happen to me. Anger? Yes! Depression? No." She will start her new chemo treatment in November. "So we're about to boldly go again into some new uncharted waters. Not the best of news, but, like I said, if that miracle's out there, hey, I'll take it. But if not—" Anna shrugs.

* * *

Anna speaks to a strong universal emotion when she mentions the word "anger." "Anger is almost always present in every significant loss," explains Kenneth J. Doka, Lutheran minister and leading death educator. "If you are angry, you can't *not* be angry. The question is how to use your anger." For the person who is dying, anger, lots of it, is validated by the professionals who advise caregivers that it can take forms of unpleasant ferocity at everything and everyone around them or it can be a more compassionate venting that seeks no target.

"They are angry because of the losses they are experiencing, and they are angry because others—apparently for no justifiable reason—are enjoying happy, healthy, and satisfying lives," write Charles and Donna Corr and Clyde Nabe in *Death and Dying, Life and Living.* These authors instruct caregivers to expect such strong feelings and to learn to listen empathetically.[1]

"Anger is a natural response to situations where we are faced with more and more limitations and fewer and fewer options," write Ronna Fay Jevne and Alexander Levitan in *No Time for Nonsense,* a book that Anna has underlined, which emphasizes that getting out one's anger leaves more room and time for joy and caring. The importance is "where you target it." Among their suggestions, Anna marked the following: "Hang an old duffel bag stuffed with old linens or clothes where you will go by it often. Put a tennis racket beside it and enjoy smashing the duffel bag when you go by." "When having a 'mad,' hang up a sign that says, 'If you are intending to cheer me up, go home.' " "Go to the mirror and say all the things you fantasize saying to whomever you are angry with." "Have a 'getting even' price list. What is any given frustration worth? One hour of tolerating George may be worth an uninterrupted bubble bath."[2]

Anna felt a certain kinship with such helpful but humorous suggestions. For many who are ill, humor is one way of venting anger in a nonconfronting fashion. Today humor is recognized for its healing and painkilling power; it is the subject of conferences. It relaxes the body, which helps resting and healing. Quite simply, it makes life more bearable. "It distances us from the indignities of diagnosis and treatment. It helps restore our common humanity. It dispels fear."[3]

A joke to deflect anger comes to mind: "I understood most of your message, but would you mind repeating that last scream?"[4] And Woody Allen expresses a common thought, "I don't mind dying, I just don't want to be there when it happens." Unfortunately, humor is not universal. Although it may sound tasteless or cruel to those who weren't there, humor's shock value in a tensely serious moment among the ill and the dying can create invaluable levity. One nurse studying to be a bereavement counselor recalls the humor of her Irish family. When her mother accidentally tripped on a cord that disconnected her dying uncle's IV tube, he joked, "So what's the rush—you aren't even in my will!" When a young man who had terminal cancer received one of those annoying phone calls soliciting life insurance, he replied, "Buddy, do *you* have the wrong number!"

Gallows humor among hospitalized Vietnam veterans was a stinging antidote to self-pity. Men remember the crucial bonding of black humor—such as dedicating "You'll Never Walk Alone" to a double amputee. Said one veteran with no legs, "That lack of pity is the only thing that saved me."[5] Along those lines, a heavyset woman with an amputated leg was sitting in a waiting room, feeling shy and self-conscious in her wheelchair. When one of the office staff asked, "How are you doing?" the woman said, "Fine." The aide then said, "How are the ballet lessons going?" The woman gasped, then laughed so hard, she almost fell out of the wheelchair and the other patients joined in. Then the woman topped the aide with "Wait until you see my tutu!"[6] It was a great icebreaker in a gloomy situation. Maryln Schwartz, a witty *Dallas Morning News* columnist much in demand as a speaker, joked as she saved for breast reconstruction surgery following a mastectomy. In a takeoff on Walking for Dollars, Race for the Cure, and so forth, she told friends. "I'm Talking for Tits." During a time of remission, Anna, the former copywriter, cracked about the book in progress, "This may be the first time that I've missed a *dead*line."

Anger and macabre humor, of course, are not reserved for patients alone. Caregivers and family members can experience plenty of both. Often their anger is compounded by a sense of helplessness. It is not uncommon for them to rail at doctors, hospitals, insurance companies, hospices, or anyone else in the medical system who is not curing the person they love. "It's perfectly legitimate to complain to everyone around you about your anger at the doctors or why somebody didn't do this or that, or find fault with the manner in which someone dealt with his or her illness," comments Ken Doka, "but the question is how you use that anger, whether it's destructive or constructive. When you take your criticisms to the *patient,* who is really struggling with 'Did I make the right decision?,' you are not being helpful."

Much of Anna's anger is directed in general at medical incompetence and the frustrating state of medical science. One passage she underlined in *No Time for Nonsense* fits her feelings: "Institutions don't like anger. . . . Angry people often say what they think, feel and want." The horror of her wrong-rib surgery, her insurance and medical travails, generated Anna's never-ending crusade to warn any sick person that he or she cannot be too vigilant regarding doctors, records, treatment, procedures, tests, results. "SWITCH DOCTORS IMMEDIATELY IF YOU REALIZE THAT YOU ARE NOT BEING LISTENED TO NOR GIVEN THE TIME AND ATTENTION THAT YOU DESERVE AND HAVE PAID FOR!" she writes in capital letters.

Newspapers contain far too many stories of surgeons operating on the wrong leg or arm or breast, for example, to say nothing of errors that cause a scandalous number of hospital deaths. A Harvard School of Public Health study bears repeating—hospital-related errors in treatment kill 180,000 Americans each year.[7] Only when doctors experience the same disasters as their patients do they get exercised enough to write about it. *How to Get Out of the Hospital Alive* was written by Dr. Sheldon Blau after he developed a life-threatening infection in his bloodstream following surgery, an all-too-common occurrence. In writing about hospital-caused errors in medication, in surgery, in laboratory tests, and just in admitting patients, Blau offers a nostrum known to any hospital patient. It can be expressed in the form of a riddle: "How many people does it take to be sick?" Answer: "At least two—one to be sick and one to run interference." Only after his own experience did the doctor write, almost in wonderment, that "the most important thing a hospitalized patient can do is to bring in a relative or close friend who will observe all and question everything being done."[8] He suggests what should be a given when undergoing an operation—mark with indelible ink the area or limb to be cut.

Yet, despite horror stories, a patient mentality still exists, that "the hospital is 'Mama' and they're going to take care of me," writes Blau. Anna concurs. "Our society still suffers under an almost castelike behavior when it comes to assuming instant respect for doctors who, as yet, still live in the safety of that myth. I have had too many medical errors to believe that doctors are infallible."

When Anna was a child, the dentist nearly drilled the wrong tooth because he read her brother's chart instead, another doctor removed the surrounding skin on the wrong side of a gangrenous toenail. "I am like everyone else, an ordinary person for whom things sometimes go wrong—I suspect that what makes me different is that I catch the mistakes," she says. "Most patients don't even know to be on 'error watch.' I've decided that the two worst doctors are radiologists and anesthesiologists," complains Anna, "because they rarely deal with their patients. Even though I am paying for their services, they only communicate with my referring physician. You are not informed about how much the anesthesiologist charges. There you are, woozy from presurgical relaxers, and a perfect stranger waltzes up, announces that he is your anesthesiologist, asks you a few questions, and shoots you up! Why does the patient have no choice in what is a very important part of a surgical procedure? What if he has a bad track record? How can a patient help control insurance costs when these facts are completely hidden? *I have had several general anesthesia surgeries and only once was I informed (in my prerelaxed state) of what would happen.* I have even awakened on the operating table—I ask you, Is this supposed to happen?!"

Anna emphasizes a "need for change" list. "Listening to a patient describe his body symptoms, really listening, is something that doctors should initiate. Patients have the right to learn about all doctors and to discuss their case with anyone who is a part of their diagnosis or treatment—radiologists, anesthesiologists, and so forth. Doctors have too many patients, crowd their appointments, run all over in too many hospitals, and that causes errors." Also there is the problem of the system as doctors rely on clerks to pull the right files or keep accurate records. "How many times have you witnessed your doctor telling you what is going on while he is reading your chart to get up to date? There you have it. That is all the time he spends on you. Enough said."

* * *

The week before she resumes chemotherapy, Anna flies to Rye Brook, New York, for a visit with her sister, Roseann. Anna whoops it up with Cliff in the kitchen, sampling his exotic beers; he is an aficionado from his days overseas with the *Wall Street Journal.* Anna is at home in their house with its high-cathedral-ceiling living room, sweeping windows, huge modern black-and-glass cabinet holding the Ming vase that belonged to her mother. Many of Audrie's jewelry pieces went to Ro—"Mom and Ro are jewelry junkies," jokes Anna. Ro designed striking rings out of gold and semiprecious stones and wears many at a time, calling attention to her attractive hands.

Upstairs in her bedroom, Roseann's eyes flood with tears when she talks of Anna. She continues to grieve deeply for what might have been. "My feeling is, it didn't have to be," Ro says angrily. Over the years, her argument remains the same, that Anna should have had an adrenalectomy and her ovaries removed, as she had. "She's still got that damn estrogen supply." When Anna comes upstairs, the evening takes on aspects of a slumber party. They laugh at "rubber chicken" inserts for bras. "The insurance companies don't pay for wigs, but they pay for bras every two years," says Anna. "How I've grown! I started with a size four and am now a size eight."

But soon the old debate surfaces, as always. Surgical removal was the only answer, says Ro. Anna reiterates that this is no longer done and that tamoxifen is supposed to do the same thing chemically. "Why did this happen? Who knows? Every six months I was checked and I was fine." Ro says, "With your history, they should have checked you more than every six months!" Anna recalls her sister's prodding talks over the years as she kept asking if Anna thought tamoxifen was working. " 'Man, I don't know if it's working,' I'd say. 'Something's weird with these hot flashes.' " Ro vehemently interjects, saying that Anna's doctor did not monitor her enough. "When something falls out of the norm, you start treating it *out* of the norm! You watch it more closely so if something's going to go wrong, you have a better shot at catching it."

Anna sighs and repeats that tests revealed no problems. Usually she defends Miller, with whom she has a special rapport, but Anna's anger and ambivalence builds as her sister forces her to rethink the tamoxifen route. "It's fucking killing me," Anna finally storms irrationally. She says to her sister, "The irony is that your success with the adrenalectomy helped them create the medicine that is now killing me." Perhaps an adrenalectomy at the beginning would have helped, says Anna, but it is too late now that cancer has spread. Ro stubbornly reiterates, "Get the goddamn estrogen out!"

Anna says, "The problem is, you get locked into a protocol, based on a numerical average for a huge group of people." Her expletives punctuate her sentences as Anna revs up. "They're not going to waste their effing time on one person in a billion who doesn't fit their 'protocol.' "

Later, Dr. Miller addresses the sisters' discussion. "Unfortunately, even though Anna and her sister's breast cancers were both hormonally responsive, that doesn't mean they would necessarily act the same," he says, justifying the disuse of adrenalectomies and why the procedure would not have been done in 1989. "I have never heard of an instance where they were done. Twenty years ago, a lot of the therapies we have now weren't available, and so perhaps the only thing that could have been done with Anna's sister is hormonal ablation [surgical removal]. They used to sometimes remove the ovaries, the adrenals, and the pituitary gland. That's a terribly painful, difficult way to have to live the rest of your life."

He defends his initial course of treatment for Anna. "A woman who had negative nodes, like Anna, and a small cancer, the overall statistics would say that approximately eighty percent of them—it depends on what study you read—are cured or long-term survivors. Unfortunately, for unknown reasons, a significant portion of breast cancers—that twenty percent—will recur.

"Oncologists for the most part, and I speak for myself, are not creative. There are books and books of protocols and we tend to use other people's protocols for two reasons. One is you know what efficacy to expect and, two, you also know what are the side effects. Therefore you can give very specific dosages." If one doesn't work, oncologists try a second and third regimen, in hopes of confusing the cancer cells with new poisons. "And if they don't work? You don't throw up your hands and say, 'Sorry, tough luck.' Sometimes it's fair to say to people who've been through several regimens that the chance of success with the next is potentially low and here's what side effects to expect, which may be severe, and do you want to do this? At each step there has to be the option of saying, 'No, I don't want this.' And Anna's never been like that."

Ken is aware that Anna knows the truth, that "most of the time when a woman has a recurrence of breast cancer, it is terminal," but he also knows that she will not give up. In some ways, Miller is as optimistic as Anna. "Perhaps she can have a bone marrow transplant later, and perhaps with super-high-dose therapy, she would stay in remission. If we're going to do these things, we always should aim for a home run even though we may not get there. For women who have recurrence of breast cancer, there is some prolongation of and improvement in the quality of life with treatment. Taxol, while not a home run for Anna, did keep the disease stable for a long time."

Miller is asked about Ro's view that Anna should have been checked more frequently than six months. "It makes me sad that Anna's sister is upset." His voice takes on a defensive, hurt tone. "I try to do the very best job I can. I think Anna feels that way and Anna is a wonderful person whom I care about deeply and I feel very comfortable that we've done everything that can be done. The problem is not *when* it recurred, it's *that* it recurred." Anna cannot put to rest her suspicion—"I have no proof that the cancer might have been detectable earlier because my tumor marker reports are missing in my January 1994 file—yet to go from cancer free to a tumor marker of two hundred eighty-five was a huge leap for a six-month period." Miller has no idea what happened to those long-ago records. He sighs. "Unfortunately, studies show, diagnosing the recurrence early does not portend a longer survival. Sadly, finding it a month or two earlier I don't think would have changed anything. It's one thing when it's primary cancer, but when a breast cancer has *recurred,* it's a different issue."

Doctors are always on the front line when it comes to the frustrating ire of patients and family. Sometimes the anger is legitimate; sometimes it is based on a shoot-the-messenger fury; sometimes doctors are scapegoats for viciously unfair diseases that destroy one's body. Miller is among many who agonize when things go bad. Oncologist E. Roy Berger describes the "great fear and anxiety" he feels about telling the truth to patients: "It seemed so difficult to get this right . . . for each patient, to say it the right way, to do it without destroying all hope, yet without lying, so that . . . the patient would believe me when I said I would and could keep them comfortable in the end. . . ." If he fudged the facts, he might avoid the lashing anger of the moment. But, he asks, "If I told the whole truth would I avert the inevitable anger that is oftentimes aimed at me for holding out too long?"[9]

Miller sees adult men and women with cancer, about half of whom are breast cancer patients. A third of his patients are receiving adjutant chemo and radiation therapy and are doing well, another third are on more minimal therapy, and a final third are in advanced stages. Among those in advanced stages, "there is this sense for all of my patients who have done exceptionally well—and Anna's one of them—and for me too, that it should continue that way. For large-cell lymphoma, the cure rate today is around seventy percent. Unfortunately, some of my patients are part of the thirty percent. And you think, 'Oh, my God, what did I do? What could I have done differently? Should I have given *x* instead of *y*?' The problem is that cancer can be a deadly disease." Miller adds as vehemently as he is capable, "A rotten, *rotten* disease."

How do you comfort yourself?

Ken answers slowly. "When the outcomes are not good, I do try to say I've done the best I can to fight this cancer, to give someone a better quality of life, a longer life, I hope, and to respect their wishes. By giving people a choice and wanting them to participate, at least I feel like I've tried to be supportive of their wishes. There are days where I wonder if I could have done a better job. What that reflects is that I'm not perfect. But I feel I do the best job I can do."

Despite advances, Miller is concerned that he sees more young women with breast cancer now than when Anna's occurred in 1989. "I don't think it's simply a matter of detection or that there are more women demographically in that age group. Why? Nobody knows." In 1995, the public battle over whether to do mammograms under age fifty is raging. Miller rails against those who argue that women do not need them before fifty. "That's crazy! Insurance companies don't want to, but when you talk about an individual's health, this whole concept of cost-effectiveness is irrelevant. The forty-two-year-old woman who has a mammogram and we find a lesion, it may save her life. They should be done and paid for by insurance companies annually by age forty."

Miller approves of Anna's need to be on top of every test, every examination, every drug. "I think people do need to be involved." Miller is a proponent of positive thinking and feels strongly that Anna, with her upbeat approach, will continue to do better, both with the disease and in dealing with impending death, than those who hold out little hope. He is bolstered by many in the health field who see the same results. "I tell people when they start on chemotherapy there are two choices. One choice is where you come in and say, 'Oh, my God, I can't believe I'm doing this, this is the worst thing. This is horrible. And it's not going to help me.' And then there are the others who say, 'You know what? I plan on doing well and I'm going to picture those cancer cells actually melting, shriveling, and deteriorating and being floated away out of my body.' They're less likely to have side effects and more likely to have benefit.

"Cancer is a disease that is out of people's control, and so taking the reins, adopting a positive approach, is an attempt to bring life back in the person's control. Even if it doesn't include quantity of life—I think it does—it improves quality of life. My best case for Anna would be that her tumors respond with continued treatment and she goes into remission. Then we do a bone marrow transplant and she stays in remission.

"Much of my work is based on the patient's goals. A lot of it becomes their choice. Often I'll say, 'You know you've got a serious cancer. We have these choices.' Sometimes people say, 'Doctor, give me everything you have, I want to plug away and I really don't care about the side effects.' Other times people say, 'Doc, don't give me all this toxic chemotherapy unless there's almost a one hundred percent guarantee I'm going to get better.' Someone who's thirty and has lymphoma may say, 'You bet I want absolutely everything done, I plan on getting well.' And someone who's ninety and has colon cancer says, 'Absolutely not.' For him, it's a quality-of-life issue. Most cases are not that clear-cut and fall in the middle: 'Do some chemo and see what happens.' Many difficult issues go into the decisions that people help make about their care."

"Hey there!" announces Anna as she enters Dr. Miller's waiting room. Everyone in the office brightens. Anna sticks her face up to the admitting window, lifts her eyebrows like Groucho Marx, and says, "Without chemo—see how my eyebrows are growing back?" One of the women says, "Yea!" They cluster around Anna and her flow of conversation: "What are you doing for Thanksgiving?" "Are you going away?" "Families coming? Oh, neat." A pretty blonde assistant tells her she is tired and going home early. "Got a cold?" "No, I'm pregnant. Starting my sixth month." "Gosh," says Anna. "All the time I've been coming in and you didn't show—and you didn't tell. You look great. Listen, if you want a place to stretch out and rest during the day, I'm just five minutes away. You can nap, put your feet up." The woman smiles gratefully.

Other patients flip absentmindedly through magazines or simply stare, waiting for checkups or chemotherapy treatment or dreading answers from tests. Not a person is smiling. Two women, obviously together, do not speak. An older man sits next to Anna. She admires his multicolored tam-o'-shanter. "I have a reason to wear it," he says, with a smile, doffing his hat to show a bald head. "So do I," says Anna, whipping off her green turban with perfect timing—"only you have more hair than I!" The man chortles, but the others, caught in their own circle of worry, fear, and depression, just look at them. This is not a joking matter, they seem to say.

As Anna walks down the hall for her treatment, she says, "Did you see how gloomy those people are? It gives me the creeps. That's why I try to lighten it up. Those people in the office hear only complaints, complaints. Can you think of how grim that must be?" Anna's steady patter is partly pure Anna and partly a conscious attempt to quiet her anxiety. There is always that flutter of nerves, the sweat, the stomach flip-flops, before she starts another treatment.

Anna sits in a tiny room, barely large enough for two chairs, a small TV on a table. Autumn sunshine and a few dried leaves dangling on spiky branches are visible through the half-slanted Venetian blinds. Anna comes prepared in a sweat top with a convenient zipper. She unzips it and bares her life port, above her left breast. "This shunt is built into my chest. It gets to the bloodstream, zap! So it can be a real rush."

Dr. Miller's head nurse, Suzanne, brings in the two drugs she has prepared. Once again, Anna's joking imagery is a therapeutic force. Doctors in many fields encourage positive imagery, feeling that attitude plays a vital role in how patients respond to medication. Some suggest, for example, that their patients picture their medication as white knights, bringing help.

Some of Miller's patients view their drugs as Rambo-like characters kicking out the bad guys, others as gentle swans carrying their pain and cancer away. Anna needs no encouragement. She chuckles at the names of the two drugs she is taking, Mitomycin and Vinblastine. "They sound like cartoon characters." She lowers her voice as an announcer might in a TV cartoon—"Mighty My Sin meets Vin *Blast* Teen! Picture that any minute the little green alien creatures from another planet will zap us with deadly poisons as they begin their attack on Earth cancers. . . ."

As Suzanne attaches the opening of the plastic packet of blue liquid to Anna's life port, Anna says, "Oh, this is interesting. I've never had blue before," as if she were buying a dress. Suzanne says, "Let's see, you've had red, yellow. . . ." "Yeah," says Anna, "gotta be fair to the color spectrum."

Just then, Anna gets a taste of the medication. Oncologists have candy on hand like psychiatrists have Kleenex. In anticipation, Anna had grabbed a fistful of multicolored candy balls on her way in. "Ohhhh," she says, pressing her head back on the chair. Her face flushes. "Oh, this really has a horrible taste to it." She grabs a candy and sucks on it. Suzanne dilutes the blue drug with the second drug, which eases the taste. "At first, it makes my heart pound," describes Anna. "And there's a very chemical smell; it's almost like tasting metal." Soon Anna is rattling on as always. As the chemo bag empties into Anna's body, she says, "This is so much easier! I used to sit here for hours, the bag was so huge. Most patients take a drug that makes them fall asleep." She points to the VCR. "I'm probably the only one who sat here and watched movies."

Dr. Miller comes in and Anna greets him enthusiastically. "This drug is too wonderful! It's short, quick." Miller smiles at her enthusiasm. He tells Anna that the medicine "stays in the cancer cells," employing positive suggestion; "every minute, they will be shrinking." Anna outlines her four-week cycle. "And then—wheeee!" she says, in mock pleasure. "We start over again."

A giddiness takes over as Anna leaves the office, as if she had been let out of school early. She drives through the mall. "My shoe store was right over there," she says, pointing. At the deli, she attacks fried onion rings and a chocolate biscotti and decaffeinated cappuccino. "I'm really going to test the old stomach."

Lights are glowing in Anna's house as she gets out of the car and walks toward her family. She is still elated that the day went well, but she has no illusions. "At best, this is borrowing time. Even the bone marrow transplant, I think, would be borrowing time. It's so very new, they don't have much history on it."

A few days later, Anna writes, "As strange as it seems, I find that the more I know about my disease and its progression, the less I feel panicked by it." Studies support Anna's view. Those with a positive proactive involvement often fare better than those who leave it all to the doctors. Some sense of control over an uncontrollable disease is the key. "The more I can feel some control with respect to my treatment, the easier I can cope with knowing I will die of this disease. If I were to blindly put my faith in a doctor, asking no questions, not participating in the treatment, I am quite sure that by now I would have given up hope and I would be dead because my mind would not be caught up in a struggle for the preservation of my being."

CHAPTER SIX

Coping Day by Day

Throughout October and November of 1995—the drug holiday months before Anna's new chemotherapy—she revels in the physical strength flowing back into her body. Emotionally, the roller coaster of the inevitable but wrenching redirecting of her life produces upbeat moments for Anna as well as those of hopelessness and, yes, depression. Her despairing moods are fostered by waves of sorrow about all that she would miss if she died, particularly Jan and the children. More often, Anna's optimism takes over. "Hey, I'm *living* with cancer, not dying from it—yet. I may beat this sucker!"

No one can observe her pain as Anna walks as forcefully as she can, or when she stands, straight and tall—as she does one autumn afternoon in the foyer of one of her favorite haunts, The Cheesecake Factory, near Bloomingdale's in Maryland's White Flint Shopping Mall. She orders a cheeseburger and a beer and talks a mile a minute—about her children's homework ("I really have to sit on 'em to get it done") and about the Olney Ballet, where Lindsay has been dancing since she was four and Anna has been a helping mom. "Two weeks ago, they said, 'These kids need a parent adviser and it's you.' I said [dryly], 'How *did* you know?' Now I'm doing everything—using my marketing skills. Nothing had been done. I said, 'We don't have time for this.' "

Once again, Anna finds the pony. "I've had this setback piece of news about the tumors and yet here I am, working with great kids once again. Part of me still wants to be an owner. I've been too long in the corporate world. But I'm a fast one to put regrets behind me. Mine is not a coulda, woulda, shoulda life. I don't live in the past and I can't see the future." Anna cannot always keep to this maxim; emotional nosedives occur when she obsesses about her children or reflects on a lost career.

Anna's major recreation is her family; now more than ever she hordes her moments. She almost reluctantly lets a friend take Ellery and Lindsay to a movie and for pizza one day. She is happier with them around and having adult friends come to the house. "They know all of my friends. I was that way with my parents. A lot of kids are totally separated from their parents' friends and lives. I think that's a shame."

Kaleidoscopic scenes of Anna that fall and early winter: Anna clowning with her friends from Richmond, who surprise her with a visit to celebrate her forty-third birthday on October 2, treating her normally, with the same irreverent humor of days gone by, which is so important for those who are ill . . . Halloween glitter gunk all over the glass coffee table as Anna helps, but mostly observes, Lindsay's wild creativity . . . An afternoon in a nearby suburban indoor pool—a state-of-the-art gymnasium with high ceilings of glass, lit with sun. Anna in the Jacuzzi, bald, no prosthesis in her bathing suit, talking away to a friend, letting the jets bubble onto her back, unconscious of a man who stares at her wordlessly . . . Anna working the sound system to coordinate records to the flight of lithe little bodies as Lindsay and her friends twirl as Candy Canes to an audience of toddlers in a nearby school. "We're takin' this show on the road," says Anna, with a grin.

Anna curled up with the phone, an eternal appendage now that she is home, talking to a friend about how she hated to give up the store, then moving out of her personal sorrows to talk about the shattering international horror and grief over the assassination of Israel's Yitzhak Rabin: "It was just horrible! I feel like we all did when Anwar Sadat got shot at the time when peace seemed to be rolling along. After all the grief and the fighting, the land will still be there. What are they fighting over? One flood and it's over. It seems so pointless for them [the extremists] to cling to it so." . . . Anna yanking her suitcase with the ease of a truck driver, no matter her pain, as she gets off the plane in New York . . . Anna collapsing on the bed with laughter at her sister Ro's house in Rye Brook in Westchester until two A.M., then catching an early-morning ride into Manhattan to meet her book editor for the first time.

Michael's literary haunt on West Fifty-fifth Street is an annex for editors, agents, and authors who ply their wares over power lunches. The maître d' greets everyone with an enthusiasm that manages to be genuine and practiced at the same time (who knows where the next best-seller will come from?). Anna takes the two steps down into the dining room. Her easy style melds with the editor's and they are soon talking like old friends. Late into lunch, as a hot flash comes on, Anna says, "Do you mind if I take my cap off?" "Certainly not," says the editor. Anna peels off her green cotton turban, and breathes easier as the heat exits from her glistening, bared head. Everyone is so busy making deals that no one even glances at Anna. Not so that night at the theater. A woman in the row in front of Anna turns back often to stare disapprovingly, as if Anna had suddenly lit up a cigar in a no-smoking area.

Months later, at a breast cancer function, a famous TV commentator looked at Anna, whose hair was beginning to come back in tufts and looked like sprouts of grass peeking out during a spring thaw. "Isn't that a little 'in your face'?" questioned the woman, who lived by her looks in a narcissistic profession. Why people feel such effrontery is hard to fathom. Is the raw reminder of an obvious illness and treatment so fearful that people disregard the person as being human? Anna says, "That's their problem." And then there are such times as the day a leather-garbed teenager in a 7-11 asked in awe, "Man, are you a skinhead?!" Anna gave him a mock glare. "Yeah."

One of Lindsay's most vivid memories is painting her mother's bald head, just another insightful concept of Anna's to normalize the illness as much as possible. Those days are captured in photos showing multi-colored swirls, stars, circles on the head of a grinning Anna. A colleague of Jan's recalls: "Anna had this idea to paint the heads of children who lose their hair from chemo so that it would not become such a social stigma. What a woman!" says Tom Sobotka. "Anyone else flat on her back after chemo would not have an idea in her head about anyone else. And she's also an entrepreneur, thinking about making a buck—'How can I turn this terrible thing into an advantage?' "

Anna is sensitive to her children's concerns. Like everything about her illness, she approaches the question of her looks by talking to them. "It's hard for them having to explain *any* mom at that age. It's very embarrassing—this parent with the big bald head." Anna's dynamic personality always draws attention—"You're a nut," someone wrote in her yearbook years ago. Her children are at an age when most are grateful to have parents fade into the background, as any parent who has tried to dance to hard rock around their children can attest. On the other hand, sometimes "their friends say, 'Your mom's really cool,' and *that's* embarrassing." Lindsay disagrees. "I like her that way. Mom's fun. I think she's different. Other moms are more, you know, like parents."

Says Anna, "I used to ask them, 'Do you want me to wear the wig?' and at first, they said, '*Maybe*'—so I knew there were times. But now they want me to just go bald." Ellery and Lindsay snuggle up to her one-breasted body with ease. Love has nothing to do with how she looks. One day, Lindsay, who had just turned ten on October 9, talks about her feelings regarding Anna's not wearing wigs. "Well, like, I only care if it's at school, because then I get into fights because kids make fun of her. I just tell 'em, 'If your mom had cancer, how would you feel?' But if she does it in the grocery store or around other people and my friends, then that's okay."

Two rooms that seem off-limits to anyone over the age of eleven are Lindsay's and Ellery's bedrooms—refuges at times from reminders of their mother's illness. They are cluttered with toys and books and choked with clothes on the floor. Anna, the child who was not allowed to sit on her pristine white bedspread, now says as a mom, "I'm not going to have a place where they have to worry about every little thing."

One day, they are asked, If you had to write an essay on what you like about your mom and dad, what would you say? Or what don't you like?

"Oh, boy. Let's see," starts Ellery. Both know what they don't like. "Making us do our homework. Nonstop." "Mom can be uptight about things, not cleaning our rooms, and we have chores," says Lindsay. "If you look at some of the kids in my school, they are very bossy and spoiled and mean. It's actually rather sad, seeing these kids with nothing to do. Like my mom says, 'When kids are spoiled and get everything, when they want more, there's nothing left to get.' "

Both Lindsay and Ellery, in separate conversations, say that the trait they admire most in their mother is her humor. The children feel a sense of privilege in being brought up in what they feel is an unusual household. "I think we're brought up a lot differently than any other kids because we're very open with adults," says Ellery. "It's not just 'Hi' and try to kiss up to adults. How can I put this? We're communicative. Like their friends in Richmond, we just have a good old time with them."

One Sunday night just before Halloween, Anna and Jan entertain a couple. They enter the blue-gray-shuttered brick bungalow through the kitchen door. Only strangers use the front. Anna and Jan greet them with warm smiles in their crowded but cozy center of activity, filled with the smells of Jan's cooking. The dining room table usually holds a laptop computer and an avalanche of papers, but tonight they have been replaced with place settings. The living room is dominated by a bone-colored leather sectional and a glass-topped coffee table often buried in homework. Since Anna's strength has returned, paintings that sat on the floor waiting rearranging have been hung. Phoebe, Jan's mother, had painted one, of the North Carolina Outer Banks. "My favorite place in the whole world," says Anna. By the unused front door is a hall rack filled with Anna's hats, including one with a stuffed alligator on top. Another has a price tag still on it. ("Just call me Minnie Pearl.")

"This house needs work now, and I'm frustrated. There's a lot of stuff I want to do—Lindsay's room is way too small, for example—but I don't have the energy and it all costs a fortune." Anna's independence can be exasperating; she turns away offers from family and friends to get help in the house, feeling she must do it all, along with Jan. Part of this is her intense desire to retain her normal style of living as long as possible.

While Anna is in the kitchen cleaning up after dinner, the phone rings. "That'll be Dad," she says, looking at the clock. "Hi there!" booms Anna into the phone enthusiastically, making the routine weekly call seem special. First they talk about Ro and her job. "She's really angry. Oh, I don't know, some pup coming in and trying to take over everything. I tell her, who needs it?" Anna listens for a minute or two, then says, "Now for the bad news . . . Yeah, some bad news," sounding as if she is going to tell her father something as trivial as that the dogs peed on the carpet. "Well, the MRI, they found that stuff is not being contained, stuff's growing in the liver. [Anna avoids the word "cancer."]

So now I'm going in for a CAT scan to check the brain and other places to see if it's spread." Her father fumbles with something to say, then asks if they will still visit in January. "You bet. No way in hell I'm going to miss it. . . . The good news is that I'm on a drug holiday. . . . So how's everything? Playing golf? Seeing your woman?" says Anna, encouraging him about a female companion.

As she hangs up the phone, Lindsay comes in with glitter glue drawings and cutouts. Anna gives her a hug. "Those are great!" As she turns back to the dishes, her eyes fill with tears. She leans her hands on the sink ledge. "The worst thing is the thought of leaving the kids." Her voice gets high as she tries to talk over the tears streaming down an anguished face. "Jan can take care of himself, I just know that, but I want to be there for the kids—and I just can't stand that. That little girl *needs* me." As Lindsay returns with another glitter glue offering, she sees her mother wiping tears from her face. After she leaves, Anna says, "That's okay. She knows I've been talking about my mother to Dad and that always makes me cry." Anna feels some release talking about the emotional pain she feels. "I want to see Ellery graduate. I want to see Lindsay's prom dress." The tears cascade again. "I don't think that's going to happen."

Dealing with her children is by far the most difficult emotional problem now. "I play it by ear. My concept is that whatever happens to children happens in such enlarged proportions at these ages—and therefore they're dealing with enough at this point. They've got worry. Concern. Fears. But to point-blank tell them that something is or isn't going to happen when even the doctors can't really tell us, I don't see a point to that." One day, Lindsay asked her mother if she thought she was going to die. Anna answered truthfully, "I'm not planning on it."

Yet Anna is seeing enough changes to consider getting some help for the children. "When we go to parents' night at school and I pick up one of their journals, I see that I'm the topic of conversation, 'Mom has cancer,' and so on. So I know it's on their minds." There was further evidence when Anna looked at Lindsay's work for a drug abuse program and noted that "on at least three of these drugs, Lindsay's first answer was that it causes cancer. It wasn't in the book, but there it was on her paper.

"Lindsay's afraid she's going to get it and we talked about proactive things she can do to make sure she doesn't. I said to her, 'I don't know that you will necessarily. If breast cancer does skip generations, well, it skipped my mother. She had a whole different kind of cancer. And look at Aunt Ro—she survived it.' I explained what it meant about skipping generations and said, 'If in fact it does, you have to watch your daughter like a hawk if you have a daughter, make sure she does certain things.' And then I talked about the advantage of time and medical science and told her about how they've cured polio, as an example. 'You take a vaccine now. Cancer is another one of these diseases that's being fought, and eventually they're going to come up with a cure.' I absolutely believe that. It's just a matter of time. So I told her she's got time on her side and she shouldn't assume anything. But when she is older, she should go to the doctor and make sure she's okay." Lindsay listened but said nothing in reply.

"I think both of them are a little clingy. Not regressive at all. They are very mature for their ages. With Ellery, it's hysterical. He wants to be part of every conversation we have. He's a little old man sometimes." Ellery says the way his mom handles her cancer makes it easier for him. "The demonstration of her being open about her cancer is her giving nicknames for each drug. Like Mighty Mouse for Mitomycin. Her cartoon cocktails, as she calls them."

Lindsay pulls back in denial and avoidance. "She's still a little girl, but she has matured so much physically—God, she's five feet three-quarter inches now—that sometimes I start talking about something and I can see I've totally lost her." Barely ten years old, Lindsay keenly feels this burden. "I'm the tallest person in my class. Everybody thinks I am twelve or thirteen. Adults always expect me to do things that I'm not capable of yet."

Sometimes Anna can't tell if Lindsay's overreaction to incidences is simply par for her volatile age or an indication of deeper concerns about her mother. Anna wisely assumes it's mostly her age. One day, Anna utters without thinking when she sees Lindsay's class pictures, "Ohhhh, honey! You covered your face with your hair. I wish you had put it back like I said." Lindsay bursts into tears and slams out of the kitchen into the living room. A friend who came home from school to do homework with Lindsay sits at the dining room table. Anna immediately says to Lindsay, "Oh, honey, I didn't mean to hurt your feelings . . ." but Lindsay won't listen. She goes in her room and shuts the door. Anna feels terrible, knowing that she has committed the sin of saying something critical in front of a friend of her daughter's, who is now making a quick exit for home.

That night, Anna goes into Lindsay's room and talks quietly, then gently asks, "What's bothering you?" Lindsay bursts into tears and says she hated the pictures too. Anna's frankness made her all the more aware of how much she despised the pictures; her mother had rubbed her the wrong way with honesty. "Well, sweetie, if you don't like the pictures, we'll get them done again," says Anna. Lindsay brightens and says, "Cool." Anna says, "Promise me you will smile and pull your hair off your face." The bald mother is hugging her daughter with hair so long she can sit on it. Lindsay feels even closer as Anna confides to her, "I had hair that long too, and there were days when I didn't feel so good about myself. I used to throw that hair in front of my face."

Another day, Lindsay comes home from ballet, puts her head on her mom's shoulder, and sobs as if her world had ended. Anna instantly knew the reason. The ballet director and close friend, Jane Bittner, will not let Lindsay dance on pointe. Anna calms her down, explaining that toe shoes are not good while her feet are still growing and that next year she will dance on pointe. Anna makes a puppy dog face and pants and Lindsay starts laughing in spite of herself.

But Anna is human and there are days when her positiveness fades. One December day, Anna simply gives in to her "feel-sorry-for-myself day." It is just after she had chemo and the chemical changes in her body produce a natural depression. This, combined with her thoughts, brings Anna down. Although she feels it is self-indulgent, she also recognizes the need to release these emotions. Anna says to herself, "Well, if you're going to cry, then, God dammit, turn on some music that will *really* make you cry." Today there would be no favorites played when she feels upbeat, no stirring drums and rhythms from the African group Ladysmith Black Mambazo, no nostalgia time with the Rolling Stones or the Beatles, no sweeping Chopin. Anna turns on Enya, the popular Irish singer who blends her haunting voice with ancient instruments.

Anna curls up on the sofa and stares out the window and listens and weeps. Her thoughts turn to her mother. How she was not seeing this day. And Anna conjures up everything she would never see if she dies—a beautiful day, Jan, the kids—the whole world. How she wouldn't be experiencing anything. She thinks, "You can't stop the big steamroller and everything will just keep right on going after I'm gone."

Tears flood her face as she sees the impotence in death, the total loss of control. Her mother had written an addendum to her will while she was mad at her sons, which was, in Anna's words, "pretty nasty." The family decided that she really didn't mean it and, after her death, omitted the addendum. Anna starts thinking, "Obviously I won't be there, so whatever decisions I make can be rescinded." She wasn't thinking about her will, in which everything goes to Jan and then to the children if he should die. She weeps as she thinks, "Gee, what are my opinions going to mean? On anything!" Then she feels guilty. "Hey, look what I did to my own mother! I blew off her opinion, even though I feel that we could have sat down and talked to her about it and said, 'You're being too severe.' But we didn't try."

Anna turns, as always, to Lindsay and Ellery, who figure strongly in her blue day. "What will this experience of watching me and then having me gone, if that's what happens, do to *how* they grow up?" Fear that she will not be remembered grips Anna as eerie music wafts through the room. Later she explains, "When I find out that someone had a parent that died young and when they were young, I ask, 'Tell me about your mom.' Well, she died, you know, and I don't remember that much.' So many people that I know just don't have any strong recollections even of parents who were very active with them. Look at myself. I kind of blissfully went along through childhood and I really have to think hard about what I remember; it's amazing what it takes to jog my memory. So I really worry about that with my kids. 'Oh, my God, I'm not going be here. They're not going to remember me.' And then I like my area of control in my own right too, and I get sad thinking that I will have no say in how they grow up."

As she races through these thoughts on her blue day, the tears never stop. After she can cry no more and her eyes are swollen, Anna experiences a deep anger at her fate. On the phone, she screams at her sister, "God dammit, why were you the lucky one? You don't have kids. Why am I not the lucky one?" Anna has formed her own reasons. "I've always lived a charmed life and I've always known that sooner or later something bad was going to have to happen to me." Not that Anna lives in puritanical fear, waiting for that shoe to drop. "I feel that I am a simple person, philosophically, and am not as complicated as those who have had extensive problems and dissatisfactions. I'm happy with what I have, and if I'm not, I change it. I've been the little engine that could and I really stupidly believe in that philosophy because I've done it."

Now she is fighting something that doesn't pay the least bit of attention to her drives, desires, or dreams. "I'm waiting more now for the shoe to drop than I ever have in my life."

In a matter of hours, Anna is back to her more typical operating spirit. "You really cannot dwell on it or you'll go crazy."

Asked what advice she has for others to keep from obsessing about their plight, Anna offers her solution. "Think about other people. *Do* things for other people. Involve yourself with other people. I have friends who say to me, 'I can't believe it, here you are in your situation, and I've just spent two hours complaining about some trivial matter and you're listening and giving *me* support and advice.' " Little do they know that they are giving Anna a gift by treating her as one of them.

"If you're involved with people, you're not thinking about yourself all the time, you're thinking about them. It's very rewarding. Find things to do that make you feel good," says Anna. "You can still have a very fulfilling life and a very good time."

And if you're like Anna, even on a blue day, you hatch a plot to make life better. The next step was one of the most rewarding that she would ever take.

CHAPTER SEVEN

The Clay Wall

Thwack! A wad of clay hits the wall with a satisfactory slap that echoes in the room. More clay wads find their mark. *Thwack! Thwack!* Giggles follow from the adults who are thrilled by the sheer childish pleasure of it all. The instructor tells them to think of something or someone that is causing them anger. *Thwack! Thwack!* A wonderful surge, starting deep in the stomach, flows through the body as pain and anger is released as each smack of clay shakes the wall. Grown-ups have taken over the playroom as they study the complexities of how to help grieving children.

Ten adults are surrounded by the childhood magic that fills the world of children's counselor Dottie Ward-Wimmer at the St. Francis Bereavement Center in Washington, D.C. Anna has called to make an appointment with Ward-Wimmer, who will come that week to the Johannessen's home for an initial conference.

But today, Ward-Wimmer is hard at work training prospective volunteers how to work with children. Which is why they are pummeling the clay wall. Originally, Ward-Wimmer had children tackle their immense anger by pounding the clay on a board. Then one day a boy with tears streaming down his face picked up a handful of clay and threw it at the wall. That gave the center an idea. Plexiglas was affixed to the entire wall and children found great relief, as well as fun, in throwing at the wall instead.

Some years ago, an angry teenage client had refused to even talk to Ward-Wimmer for weeks. His first verbal contact was to command that Ward-Wimmer stand in front of the wall. Then he aimed handfuls of clay all around her body. She tried not to flinch as each new round of clay whizzed close to her with terrifying velocity. When the boy stopped, Ward-Wimmer knew they could finally start therapy. "I had to show that I could trust him before he could possibly trust me with his huge awful feelings." His father had shot himself to death in front of the child.

Ward-Wimmer has a remarkable ability to get close to children of all ages. An aura of the long ago '60s flower child remains inside this plump, comforting earth mother with curly, wild blond hair. "I do this work because I love it," she says. "I help make sense out of what is senseless. I give this [knowledge] to others and they, in turn, pass it on. It is easier for me to sit with children who are in pain than it is to walk away and worry about them. I know this is going to take time for them. Their life is a mess. But at least we have done for them everything that could get done that will help them get through it."

What Ward-Wimmer demonstrates and says about listening to children, especially with the heart, is invaluable for any parent. Children face losses every day of their young lives and they face them without the maturity to understand their feelings. A beloved kindergarten teacher disappears forever when one goes on to a scary first grade; Daddy has to move on account of business and guess who has to go too, and has to give away the dog; Grandma gets sick or a favorite gerbil dies; Mommy and Daddy aren't going to live together anymore and they are going to share me, whatever that means; adolescence descends, along with acne, heartbreak, a voice one can't depend on—and a loss of what was and a fear of what is going to be. Friends move. New schools lurk. All of the grieving of saying good-bye is a part of their lives, and so is death—the dog who gets run over, the friend who drowns or, more so today, is violently killed in a car wreck, the father who drops dead of a heart attack, the mother who lingers through months of cancer. This happens daily—and it is a terrible load. And yet there are those who persist in thinking that children do not grieve, that their attention span will not hold that emotion.

Unfortunately for parents who could learn so much from her, Ward-Wimmer's classes are for professionals who have worked with children but who feel that they need to learn more. "I work with people who have AIDS, including children, and I'm here to learn about anger and grief—how it can be expressed," says one. A male D.C. superior court family counselor says, "I see children taken from their fathers and I want to learn more about how to handle the grief that I see." A young woman comes in late, nearly in shock. "I work at a special education treatment facility with children, and most have been involved in a violent incident." Pause. "I just found out a few minutes ago on the news that a boy I worked with got arrested. [The media would cover in major detail the story of this boy, a gang leader, who had allegedly set up someone to kill a member of another gang.] I'm probably in grief myself right now," she says.

A social worker at the Hospital for Sick Children explains, "I came here to be able to help kids I work with and also to help their siblings. Children *die.* A lot of times, their healthy siblings are neglected terribly." And a Fairfax County school counselor, who observes healthy, average children, wants to learn more about how to work with children trying to cope with the trauma of parents, siblings, or grandparents dying. "Also, being removed from the home, if the parent is abusive or cannot afford to keep them, is a different kind of grief." A nurse practitioner for a pediatric oncologist says, "I want to learn how to listen and try not to intervene as much. That's kind of the opposite from my feelings." An artist and art therapist who works with adolescents says, "I am interested in how grief touches adolescents and what I can do to help in a world that does not acknowledge grief, even when it's all around us."

Ward-Wimmer nods. "Yes, it is all around us. All of us have experienced what seems like the mother of all griefs. Grief is *normal.* Grief is part of every day. It is universal, but what I must stress," says Ward-Wimmer, "is that *grief is healing and necessary to healing*!" She pauses and looks around the room, making sure the point is absorbed. "Grief is natural, normal, very very functional. NOTHING WRONG WITH IT," she shouts. "The problem is, we all want to make it 'better.' " She emphasizes her point, hitting one hand on the other and speaking in a rhythm. "It's not about fixing grief—because we *can't.* We have to give it room." It applies as much, if not more so, to children. "We're the support system so their healing can occur."

The first thing to remember is that children don't talk about emotions. For adolescents, it is too scary to speak of them. For younger children, there is no concept of what their feelings even mean. The attention span of a four-year-old to understand the sad feeling when someone close dies may be fleeting, but that child will revisit grief in more depth and with more understanding at different ages during his or her life. And as adults, we relive and often reshape those childhood losses with deep emotions, triggered by new losses and current bereavement. If not handled well in childhood, those emotions can resound with incredible pain.

Ward-Wimmer is adamant about one point. A child needs to know the truth. "Because children still have this wonderful magical thing, which is part of childhood, they can misconstrue things if they are not given information or are given lies or evasions instead. So children can often look like they don't know what's going on and yet they are aware and they're frequently blaming themselves because nobody's talking to them, so they figure this means that they did something wrong. Children need to have information given to them in a way that is clear, correct, and age appropriate.

"Some say that, from a psychological perspective, children can't grieve the way we do. Well, if you're old enough to have feelings, you're old enough to respond to change or loss. In order to work those changes through, you have to know what's going on. Otherwise you're just shadowboxing. What you need to do with little children—as with adults—is to give clear information. If I said to you as adults that so-and-so got sick, you'd want to know, 'What do you mean sick? How sick? What kind of sickness?' So that you can process and make sense of it.

"Children need that too. They don't need things like [she imitates a kind but vague tone] 'Oh, don't worry about it, it's just a sickness, now you just go out and play.' They don't need, when someone has died, 'Well, God loved Mommy so much and He needed another angel, so He took Mommy to heaven.' Sweet things like that only confuse children. The child would just get mad at God. Or desperately try to find a way to join Mommy. If you just tell a child, 'Well, Grandma went away,' a child would think that she did something bad to make Grandma mad, so she went away and will never come back. They can't possibly begin to process what's going on.

"It is important to help take away the fear of the unknown. If you're making the assumption that they don't or shouldn't know, then you're making the assumption that they don't need to be comforted, and that's wrong. Oh, they get noticed, people hugging them and saying, 'Oh, poor baby'; they get a toy and then are told to go and play. The child likes the attention, but at night, he or she is still wondering, 'What's going on?' 'What's going to happen to me?' 'Why is everybody crying?' 'What did I do?' The child has been *distracted* but hasn't been *comforted.* Certainly sometimes that's appropriate, but you need to know that the child deserves to be comforted as well.

"When the whole family is grieving, it's hard for the parent to be really emotionally available," continues Ward-Wimmer. "So it's wonderful to have friends or more distant relatives who aren't as intensely grieving. They have some free energy to be able to give to the kids, because kids will sometimes try to be quiet and not upset Mommy or Daddy, who's already an emotional basket case. Those extra people are really useful. The whole-village concept.

"But we as grown-ups have to ask ourselves a tough question. When we reach out to comfort a child or another person, are we reaching out with a willingness to hear and to witness their pain? Or are we reaching out to say, 'Don't cry, because I can't take feeling the pain'? Are we really shutting them down? This is a habit we can get into. If a child is asking questions or is crying, just take a breath. Just take a breath. Watch the child cry. *Allow* that child to cry. That says to the child, 'You have a right to cry. This is sad. This is really tough stuff.' Give them that moment. Then you reach out to the child and say, 'May I hug you?' "

Sometimes people don't want to be hugged, Ward-Wimmer is told. She laughs. "I've learned that by making lots of mistakes, by hugging people who don't want to be hugged, because it may not be the right time. It might be better to say out loud or to think, 'I'm just going to sit here with you, because this is sad and people need to cry.' " She expands the topic to include adults. "Some people feel that crying makes them more vulnerable. They are conditioned to think they might feel worse—'I'll look like an English muffin, all red in the face, and it's not going to do any good.' People have a *right*—children and adults—to have their feelings in whatever way feels good for them!" she emphasizes. "It's not our job as helpers, whether it be therapists, neighbors, friends, family, ministers, to make somebody cry. It is not our job to make somebody laugh and cheer up. If we honestly wish to support somebody in grief, it is our job to be willing to hear what's happening inside of them and to be able to respect it and to honor them and to ask *them* what they need.

"Certainly we need to be able to reassure children and adults, but we must do it carefully. It's nice to be able to reassure them that this feeling will not last forever. You can allow somebody to be in their sadness and then at some point in time offer the hope that 'thank goodness these bad feelings don't last forever.' There is a big difference between that and, as soon as you see the child or adult, running over and patting a shoulder and saying, 'Oh, you'll get over it. This will take time, but you've got to get back into life and you'll get over it.' "

Meaningless, often offensive, platitudes are ways to stop conversation with grieving adults and children—"You had her a long time," "He lived a full life," "God has his reasons," "You're young, you'll get married again," "I know what you're going through." Ward-Wimmer says, "A lot of what we say to other people we're saying because we don't want to sit and feel that pain. So we say something 'nice.' We give them an emotional cookie to make them feel better. And you *can't* make them feel better. They need to feel grief so that they can feel better."

Ward-Wimmer walks over on her knees to one adult, pretending to be a four-year-old, puts a finger in her mouth, and lisps, "What is dead?" The startled adult tries to answer. "Um, ah, dead is ah, um, well, not living." Ward-Wimmer doesn't let her off the hook. "What is not living?" As the woman squirms, Ward-Wimmer says, "It's important to be literal." She demonstrates an answer to the child. "When things are dead, they don't breathe, they don't drink, they don't eat, they don't smile, they don't laugh, they don't talk. Their body is dead. It is not alive anymore. Dead means not alive." Do they absorb that? she is asked. "They absorb it in a small way. It's important to know that they are not going to grasp it with the same permanence as adults or older children. But you're giving them a beginning, something to think about. It's not just important that you are telling them what dead is. More important, you are conveying, 'I respect you. You deserve to have your questions answered. You are not going to be left alone in this. You're part of this family and this process.'

"It is wrong to make blanket assumptions, such as the death of a grandparent is the biggest loss, or the death of the mother or father is the biggest loss. Each relationship with a child is unique. We can't know what the impact of a loss is until we find out from the child what that relationship meant." How do you know you are getting through? she is asked. "Sometimes you don't know. Sometimes you have to kind of go on faith. Sometimes what you need to look at is 'What are the behaviors that are happening outside of your conversation?' Is this a child who is brought to you because he's not sleeping well? Some kind of behavior is going on that is different. And even though you haven't addressed that correctly, if the behavior is diminishing, then you know if the inner adjustment, the healing process, is taking place.

"A major mistake," says Ward-Wimmer, "is that we expect children to talk to us in the same way we talk to each other. It's like expecting an infant to get up and walk to us. Developmentally they're just learning what these feelings are, just learning what names go with these feelings. Their egos are not yet fully developed. It takes a strong ego to be able to hold on to some of these feelings and then be able to own them and share them.

"How many times do you not want to talk about how you feel? For kids, it's the same. Especially prepubescent kids. They're in a place—and all of us have been there—where 'I know something but I don't want to know it.' " Anna's children are of that age group. "For a kid this age to be willing to talk about how they feel, first they have to trust you implicitly, second they're coming into an age where peers are the most important thing in their world. These things are *private.* 'Talking about Mom being sick makes Mom really be sick. I can no longer on any level pretend that my mom is fine and she's at home, just taking a little chemotherapy, but things are really better. I can't, if I'm talking about how sick she is. That opens the door for the fear sitting in my gut that says, My God, Mom could die, and then I can feel it and I don't want to. So I don't want to talk about it.'

"Now there are lots of kids who are very articulate and very verbal—and they can be real good at knowing how to say what *you* want them to say. But to articulate what they're really feeling is extremely difficult. That's why we use games, artwork. 'I can't find the words sometimes to say how angry or how scared I am, but give me a choice of colors and I can tell you what color I feel.' " Unlike some child therapists, Ward-Wimmer does not set as much store on the colors children chose (red for anger, yellow for sunny thoughts, for example) as much as the manner in which they are used. "If a child picks up a yellow crayon and balls it up in his little hand and rips that paper with that crayon, that tells me more than looking at the color."

Now the adults in her class are laughing self-consciously as they sample her games and artwork. They draw happy scenes, as instructed, on blank white puzzle pasteboard. When they finish, Ward-Wimmer tells them to pull apart their puzzles of rainbows, sunshine, lakes, forests, families standing together. There are some groans as their artwork lies in pieces. Then they are told to put them back again. There are bumps and cracks where the puzzle pieces have been fitted back together. "A child in grief learns with the puzzle that nothing will ever go back as absolutely as it was—but you can put your life together. It will be different. It can be solid, but it will have some edges and marks it didn't have before."

Another favorite tool is the picture box filled with sand. All sorts of toy objects are available to place in the box—people, animals, birds, trees, water, cannons, houses, graves. "Sometimes kids will make a general picture. If they've lost a mother they may put a family in—and the mother figure is left out. Sometimes you can be very specific [again more indirectly—not 'How do you feel about your daddy having cancer?']. You can ask, 'Do you think you could make a scene in the sand that would help me understand how you feel about what it's like to have a dad who has cancer?' It's amazing what they will do. They will put cannons in the box. They want to shoot that cancer away. They will put the whole family in a corner and cover them up with rocks, to protect them, so that nothing will happen to the family, including the sick father, so the whole family can stay together. That's their way of pretending that nothing's wrong. That the cancer can't get them; there *is* no cancer. I have some little graves and they will put graves in there—that's what it's like to worry about a dad with cancer. They might have a baseball player at one end and a grave in the other—'Sometimes we can play Little League and sometimes he might as well be dead he's that sick.' "

Ward-Wimmer warns that there are no absolutes with children's grief, any more than there are with adults. "I've worked with kids who literally every week all they do is go to the sand trays. Some kids use more clay. Some love to dress up and play out the funeral. They have funerals for each other because they're afraid they'll get shot too."

And sometimes Ward-Wimmer uncovers horrible secrets. "One kid was brought in to grieve. Couldn't cry. Never cared. Had terrible temper tantrums. As I worked with him, I realized he had been sexually abused. He asked me for a horsey ride and then he started humping me. Kids don't hump grown-ups. That's behavior he learned." Slowly the awareness and healing process began. "He used the puppets a lot, in terms of making sense out of this. This child would *never* converse about this. It was all done in the metaphor—puppets to puppets. He used the shark, the alligator. And he used a soft, nonthreatening puppet, a bunny. These are little kids. They emotionally can't process it yet, can't own it. So they have to do it 'out there' in the world of animals, not people, because it's safer. Then, bit by bit, they take it into their own lives and start healing. He'd take a doll and pull its head off with the shark puppet. I'd sew the head back on and the following week the shark would pull its head off again.

"I had to get involved in that play with him and eventually begin to find some protection for the doll. And then he would say, as the shark, 'Oh, you can really trust me,' and I would say, as the doll, 'Okay, I think I can trust you,' and the shark would come again and bite its head off. Then I would say—not in the doll's voice but in my adult voice—'I *hate* it when I think I can trust somebody and they hurt me. It's a horrible feeling. I hate it.' What I was doing was voicing for him some of the emotions he was feeling inside but was not able to put words to.

"It turned out that the father who died was the perpetrator. And that's why he couldn't grieve. He was so glad that this man was dead and yet he did miss 'a dad' because everybody wants a dad. But he didn't feel guilty that he wasn't grieving for him. He felt guilty for all the reasons abused children feel guilty: that somehow he deserved it, that it was his fault. It was a very complicated case. He was grieving because what he wanted was a real dad who didn't hurt him. And he needed to hear someone saying to the soft doll whose head was being pulled off, 'It's *never* your fault. Never the doll's fault. Grown-ups know better, but sometimes grown-ups make bad choices and they do the wrong thing.'

"The issue with abuse is not just what happens to the genitals or with hitting the body, it's the misuse of power. What kids have to grapple with is that misuse of power, that trust which was destroyed and that god-awful feeling of helplessness and waiting for someone to protect them. They don't believe that somebody is going to protect them. And so we had to play it out."

How did he turn out? "Great. It took the better part of three years. He was eight when he started and eleven when he left." She hasn't heard from him in a few years and Ward-Wimmer feels this is as it should be. "When it's done, it's done. But kids do regrieve. Sometimes you'll get a call six months, two years, later. 'Can I bring him back here?' He's having nightmares or he's having trouble in school or it's just that he wants to come. And I'll say, 'Fine.' They're rethinking it, they're reprocessing it. When they come back, it's not usually for a long period of time."

Ward-Wimmer regrets that there is not enough space or staff to handle more children, including those trying to cope with anticipatory grief "If we could work with children who are dealing with cancer, we could help a lot more, but our specific group is for children who are dealing with somebody who has AIDS." (For those without insurance or in need, the center provides counseling on a sliding scale and pro-bono basis for both adults and children.)

The anxieties and fears and sorrows of children who are coping with the possibility of death, such as Lindsay and Ellery, are different from those who have lost someone. "They're still holding on. They're still hoping that it won't happen. You give it room. Once they're allowed to say that they're scared, once they're allowed to say that word 'die'—'I'm afraid he is going to die'—and they discover that their tongues didn't fall out and Mom and Dad did not drop dead just because they said they're afraid, then they can put it in a more realistic context. Again, we have to pull it out from that magical thinking place which says, 'If I am really good, and if I don't make any stress in Daddy's life, he's not going to have another heart attack.'

"This carries over to adults. How many people do you know who will not write a will because they're afraid that as soon as they do, they'll die? Better to avoid, but, of course, it's really not. With children, we have to help them try to discover that they are not to blame and not as powerful [to cause death or illness] as they think they are.

"Some of it is having to work with them, to figure how they are going to live with it. 'I can't make all of your anxieties go away. Your mom is being treated for a real severe kind of cancer. That's scary. But how are we going to balance it? Do we need to be afraid all of the time? Do we need to be afraid some of the time?' Sometimes I just say it, we talk about the truth. You don't manipulate them. You empower them. If they know what you're thinking and why you're doing some of the things you do, you're giving them the tools to do it on their own. What good is it for a kid to come in, talk to you or play with you, go home, and not have a clue what's happened? All you've done is make them dependent on you. You have to teach them as they go.

"Part of therapy is to help children learn that it's okay to talk to Mom and Dad, to tell them what they're thinking about death and dying. They don't deal with that because they don't want to upset their parents. All they can think is 'I just want my mom to get well.' When they play with the sand tray, part of the action is to separate themselves *out* of the picture, separate from this 'other family' that has all these problems." With work, trust, and time, Ward-Wimmer helps them integrate their feelings.

"Initially I usually see them once a month just to check in. The kid might say, 'Hey, I feel fine,' and off she goes and you might not see her until the parent is really sick and about to die. But there is wonderful groundwork because the child doesn't have to go to a stranger at this so vulnerable time. Sometimes they never have to use it—because knowing that the therapist is there gives them the courage to try."

One of the hardest situations is to know when a child is acting out or failing in school, for example, just because of being a child, who may be bullied at the playground or experiencing hormonal changes, rather than suffering through life-threatening illnesses or deaths in the home. "We try to tease out, with the kids and with the family, what part of this is due to the illness, and we respond to that when we can, and what part of it is, well, 'He's a kid. These things kids do.' Sometimes you can't separate them. So you just bite the bullet. If a kid's grades are dropping, sometimes you just have to do things that you would normally do anyway, which is to say, for example, 'Hey, we have to institute a study period in this house.' Sometimes understanding the psychodynamics isn't the most important thing. You can analyze it to death, but meanwhile the grades are plummeting. 'So we're going to cut out the telephone time, cut out TV, and at the same time that we're doing these practical, tutoring kind of things, we're going to make sure you have somebody to talk to, be it the school counselor, whatever.' "

Ward-Wimmer is asked what advice she can give parents to help them better understand and to help their children with everyday losses.

"Pets are a big thing," says Ward-Wimmer. "Often we tend to dismiss pet losses. It's a perfect place for kids to learn about mourning and funerals and to have a funeral, a ritual to allow the child to say good-bye. You're teaching them that their feelings are worthwhile, that there are ways that they can say good-bye, and you're also teaching them that they will get over it someday. They have gone through this little practice ritual of crying for their goldfish. They get to ask questions about what happens when you put something into the ground.

"If Mommy says, 'Are you feeling bad about leaving school?' and the kid says, 'I don't know, mumble mumble,' how does one say this in a comforting way that leaves it open-ended for a kid to accept or maybe not? We don't have to pathologize everything and think the kid is going to be traumatized every June—because he's not. But if there has been a favorite teacher, you can put it this way [again, Ward-Wimmer does not confront with a direct response, but asks for a child's permission to suggest], 'This has been a very special year, you really like Miss Jones. You might find you will miss her a lot at the end of the year. Is there anything special we can do to say good-bye?' You don't have to buy something. Far better to spend the time on the floor making something. If the child is not writing yet, he can dictate it to you. 'Let's write her a special letter and tell her what she meant to you.' This is saying, 'You have a sad feeling, let's acknowledge it. Close it and move on.'

"A child comes home and tells you the old lady down the street died. You've seen her twice. No big deal to you. Frequently we just brush it off. But if the child is telling you the lady died, it's clearly an issue. You can sit down and say, 'Tell me about her. I didn't realize you knew her that well,' and then your child can acknowledge that she talked to her on the way to or from school. 'Sounds like you're going to miss her a lot. We might wind up going to the funeral or driving past her house and waving good-bye if you'd like.' Or it could be simpler, say, the first time he or she has known anybody who has died, so they are really asking questions about what this dead thing is. You could start by saying, 'Oh, what happened?' 'I don't know, I just heard she died.' 'Okay, well, if you have any questions or want to talk about it, I'll sure listen.' Or the child might say, 'Are you going to die?' 'You sound scared; well, that's an important thing to ask. And it gives me great pleasure to tell you that Mommy is very healthy.' "

A true story is told about a famous artist whose son came home from kindergarten with drawings that used only brown, black, and gray crayons. As this continued, his parents became worried enough to wonder if he should see a psychiatrist. Surely such somber work indicated something was wrong. "Don't you like bright colors—like blue and green and red and purple?" the artist father asked. "Sure," said the child, "but Bobby keeps taking all my good colors."

Ward-Wimmer laughs. "That's a perfect example of why we can't make assumptions. We are not infallible." In fact, experts have to weed out questionable would-be counselors and therapists who are drawn to this work because of their own needs. "We're in this business because we all have our stories and we use our stories a lot when we teach. But when doing therapy, it's very important that we have some very clear supervision so it's not our stuff that is being worked on," says Ward-Wimmer, who had her own childhood demons. "If something is triggered in me, then I have to go talk to somebody and process that through."

And sometimes, says Ward-Wimmer, you have to admit a mistake, have to say "I'm sorry" to a child. Early in her career, Ward-Wimmer worked with a seven-year-old who was dying. He had reached a placid acceptance and looked forward to going to heaven. One day, he asked Ward-Wimmer how one goes about getting to heaven. She fancifully answered that the boy's mother and she would hold on to the corners of his sheet and toss him way up in the air and he would land smack on a cloud in heaven. A few days later, the mother called and asked, "What have you said to my son? He's hysterical and won't sleep. He keeps saying, 'What if they don't throw me far enough and I land on a telephone pole and never get to heaven!?' A mortified Ward-Wimmer told her the story. The next morning, she was by the boy's side. "You know that story about going to heaven?" she said. "I lied. I lied because I really don't know how someone gets to heaven. I'm so sorry."

The boy sighed in relief and told her, "That's okay. I think I have it figured out. Jesus comes down and takes me by the hand and leads me there." Ward-Wimmer nodded, a lump in her throat, and this time she gave no opinions. "That's a wonderful way to think about it."

Redefining the family pattern during a life-threatening illness or after death is often another grueling experience, especially if family members are not forewarned. For example, adult children who feel torn because they cannot leave their own responsibilities to care for a parent may feel deep guilt, while an adult sibling who has taken up the burden may feel deep resentment and anger at the rest. In some instances, the terrible anger that comes with the death of a loved one may be dissipated irrationally. The surviving parent, for example, can become the scapegoat as grieving children, including adults, elevate the dead father or mother to sainthood. This is particularly true if the parents are divorced or have cobbled together a family that includes children from previous marriages.

An adult male, made aware of his own mortality by his father's death, may leap headlong into a romance or even divorce his wife to obtain a new, "younger" life. Others who have held off on becoming fathers can suddenly see the virtue of preserving their own mortality by having children of their own. Unmarried adult children of both sexes may shy away from intimacy during their long period of mourning.

And the entire family pattern is changed, sometimes shattered, when a widowed mother or father or the surviving in-law comes to live with their adult children, particularly if the adult child and spouse have not come to grips with their own grieving over the loss of the parent.

For adolescents, such as Ellery and Lindsay, there are special pitfalls. A developmental challenge—turmoil in its own right—is balancing one's desire for independence with the security of childhood. A prolonged illness and death of a parent greatly interfere with how preteens and teenagers face this challenge. They desperately want life to be as it was.

"Not thinking about it helps teenagers quell their fears about living in the future without their parent," writes Betty Davies, a nurse specializing in death, dying, and bereavement.[1] Shielding themselves from such horror becomes a major goal. "A seriously ill parent disrupts the normal process of breaking away from the family, shatters their security and draws them back into the family." They often hide it from parents, but they resent the changes and long for the normalcy of their other friends. They may cling out of their own needs, but, on the other hand, since they lack the ability to see into the future and the inevitability of death, "they do not feel the need to make the most of the time they have with their parent."[2]

Intuitively understanding, Jan and Anna welcome and do not discourage this aspect. Anna never makes her children feel they have to stay with her, never complains about her illness in order to make them do something, such as attacking household chores, when they balk. She is relieved when they express themselves in such normal lazy teenage ways and treats it on that level, getting after her children as any mother would. Sowing the seed for such guilt trips is abhorrent to both Jan and Anna. Her concern now is for finding professional help to ease the way for her children.

Guidelines to grieving and mourning are always useful, just as preconceptions can often mean misconceptions and absolutes spell disaster. As Ward-Wimmer and other experts in the field of death and dying continually emphasize, no two people, children or adults, grieve the same; no two people carry the same baggage or pleasant memories into the grieving process.

At this point, a saying by Carl Jung, hung on the wall in one of the rooms at St. Francis, seems applicable: "Learn your theories as best as you can, but put them aside when you touch the miracle of the human soul."

CHAPTER EIGHT

Paving the Way

Brilliant winter sun pouring in through the living room window belies the whipping coldness of outdoors. A red-faced Dottie Ward-Wimmer takes off her parka and blows onto cold hands before extending one to Jan and Anna. The dogs sniff; Ward-Wimmer pets. Hot tea is served and, as easy chitchat fills the room, Anna feels instantly comfortable with Ward-Wimmer.

"First of all," says Ward-Wimmer, "call me Dottie." Anna slips onto the sofa and Dottie sits next to her, while Jan perches nearby on the arm of the chair underneath the window. Anna is low-keyed today. As the conversation sprawls over a couple of hours, Dottie guides Anna and Jan back always to the children—finding out what they are like, how their lives and Anna's illness affects them. Dottie does this with the ease of a neighbor just in for a chat—all the while extrapolating vital information. She lets Anna talk at length about her illness, knowing that she must, that it is necessary.

"I want to thank you so much for coming," begins Anna. "We're starting to notice particularly my daughter is becoming a lot clingier. One day this month, she said, 'Mom, I'm going to get cancer.' She felt absolutely certain. She's just turned ten in October. She looks like me, although she's more slender. She's already had her first period, just like I did—I was nine and I think my sister was nine also and Lindsay got hers at ten."

Dottie asks about the history of Anna's cancer and how old the children were at the beginning. They were four and five. "How did you explain the loss of your breast?" she asks. "I told them that there was something bad growing in my breast and we had to take it off to protect me. And we just didn't make a big deal of it and, as a result, they didn't either, but they knew all the facts." She repeats the often-told details of making the children comfortable with her mastectomy. Dottie cuts through Anna's upbeat reprise and moves into deeper waters. "Did you ever cry?" "Yes, oh, yes. I told them I hurt and I explained it all and they even came with me and saw me get chemo. I didn't hide the illness from them at all. I'm just not naturally a person who gets real depressed. I get bored. I can't stay depressed. Sad? Sure."

"How long does the sadness last?"

"Hmm, I'll have a day here and there and then I say, 'Well, what are you going to do about that?' And I'm still sad, but I say, 'Let's enjoy *now.*' I can't go, 'Zap! The cancer's gone.' So I'm just staying happy and positive and enjoying my family and the kids."

Anna recites her cancer history and its frustrating course after it returned in 1994. Jan says, "Fortunately the kids were away, at my folks' home in Seattle for two weeks." Anna interrupts. "To me that was a miracle because I was completely out of control. I was on the phone screaming at people. I just couldn't believe how stupid everyone was." "Can we go back to the kids coming back from Seattle?" continues Dottie. "They were jet-lagged and we waited until the next day. We sat them down, told them I had cancer again and that it was going to be hard work—that I was going to probably go through chemotherapy—and I told them, 'I'm going to lose my hair and I'm going to have periods when I'm really tired and I'm not going to be able to do the things that normally I can do.' I said this is a time for all of us to pitch in and help each other. They were ten and eight; Lindsay was two months from her ninth birthday. Later that day, Lindsay snuggled up and said, 'Mommy, are you going to die?' And I said, 'Honey, I don't plan on it.' [Later, Dottie said it was a perfectly fine and truthful answer, but thought that Anna could have then used the question to draw out Lindsay's feelings, the scariness of the situation.] She went to her dad, however, and said, 'Am I going to get cancer?' She couldn't ask me." Jan explains, "She's not at the level where she understands genetics. I think she was more asking, 'Can I catch it?' like a cold."

Anna starts to cry. "But now, things are getting muddier. And I don't know how . . . I mean, I don't know the right thing to say. . . . But I sensed it was time. Last night, we told Lindsay to go to bed and I was down watching the fire until it was safe to leave it and she came down to be with me. She just wanted to be there, with her mother. So I know something's going on. I just can tell. I think the realities and fears are becoming more evident. And you know I don't hide it. If I'm talking to somebody and they say, 'How are you feeling,' I don't sneak off to another phone to protect them. If I have bad days, they can—they should—know that. Overall we're really open. But now it's getting harder. I'm on my third drug and I don't know that I'm going to get this bone marrow transplant."

Anna sobs as she relates how Jan insisted she spend more time with the children, how she gave up the shoe store. Dottie asks, "What did you tell the kids about why you were retired?" "So that I could focus on getting well. I said I can't run a business and drag myself down. I have to concentrate on being with you guys, staying as healthy as I can—" Dottie asks a vital question that had never occurred to Anna. "They don't blame themselves that you had to quit to be home with them or anything like that?" Anna pauses. "I don't believe so. No, I was really clear it had nothing to do with them."

As Jan enters into the conversation, Dottie asks pleasantly, "Do you work at home all the time?" Anna answers, "No, he's here because I wanted him to be part of it. He's a very internalizing person." There is silence as the women wait for Jan to speak. "Well, it's difficult to put—probably a typical male thing—to put your finger on emotions," Jan says. "If somebody asks me, 'How do you feel about something?' I don't know why it's difficult. Maybe it's just that it's difficult to describe. It's like if you taste something and you say, 'This is really good,' and somebody says, 'Well, what does that taste like?' You know what it tastes like, but it's just difficult to describe."

Dottie nods reassuringly at Jan, letting him know she understands, and then steers back. "I want to know—who are your children?" Anna begins with Lindsay, who is concerning her more at this time. Intuitively, Anna is on target again. Adolescent girls are particularly at risk for psychological problems when a parent has cancer, according to a study of 117 families. In addition, Lindsay is dealing with a double whammy. In general, more symptoms of stress, anxiety, and depression occur in children who are of the same sex as the parent who develops cancer.[1]

"Lindsay is very sensitive, very artistic. She's insecure about it, she's not really sure that she's as smart as she really is. Her insecurities are coming out now, I think, possibly because I'm sick, possibly because her hormones are kicking in. I say, 'Honey, it's hormones. Your body is going wild right now.' So I try to calm her down with thinking about hormones sometimes. She's a very generally happy kid. She has her moments; her temper is like mine. She gets very, very mad and then two seconds later, she'll be laughing. It's gone. So she's able, I think, pretty well to work through things."

"When she's very, very mad, what is she doing?"

"She'll stomp into her room, slam the door."

"Screaming?" "No." "She doesn't scream?" "She threw tantrums when she was young. She loves to hug and kiss and touch and so do I, so we do a lot of that. And she's fighting growing up. She's afraid of it, and that she's going to get cancer." Jan adds, "She's sensitive, but she's also tough. She will stand up to people. When her best friend gets teased at school because she's the smartest in the class, Lindsay sticks up for her." Anna adds, "She forges strong friendships. A very sweet, loving, generous person." Anna's tears begin to fall and she brushes at them with the back of her hand.

Dottie asks, "So if you had three adjectives, what would they be?" After much discussion, they come up with creative first. Jan adds, "I think if you could make a cross between loving and giving . . ." Anna laughs through her tears. " 'Gliving.' Yes, gliving actually works." Jan continues, "She'll almost always share anything with someone—except her brother. And even usually then, she'll lend him money." Jan provides the third attribute, "a strong sense of justice."

"Are the kids named after anybody?"

"No" says Anna. "We picked names we like so that nobody in the family would be mad." Jan nods. "We're fairly unconventional." He then introduces his son into the conversation. "I think that Ellery's fairly unconventional." Anna adds enthusiastically, "Ellery also is very loving and warm. We're very lucky. He is eleven years old and that boy still will come and give me hugs and kisses. Half the time at night, the four of us are on the bed with the two dogs, watching TV, talking and playing and goofing. He still likes to be held and cuddled." The parents continue with their Ellery list. "A real independent thinker," says Anna. "Like Jan, he also does not show as much internal emotion. Lindsay will let it out more, but he's also starting to ask things in a very scientific manner"—Anna laughs as she looks at Jan—"emulating somebody we know. He's wonderfully curious, as is Lindsay." And they are both musical, says Jan.

Anna addresses the fact that "both have been diagnosed as having attention deficit disorder [ADD]. They both take Ritalin. We went through a battery of tests and he fit in every way. However, the tests also said his memory was at postgraduate level. He has an incredible mind, but all of this stuff in there couldn't come out. Ritalin changed completely how he viewed himself. Ellery went from hating school, feeling bad about himself, to being relaxed; he realized how smart he was.

"He's very creative and there's a cleverness too. He and Jan one day went to the store to get a prescription for me—" Jan tells the story. "We were back in the car and he asked about the prescription, 'What's this?' And I said Dexamethasone. And he said, 'What's that?' And I said it's an anti-inflammatory. And he looked at me and said, 'Dad, Mom is in no danger of spontaneous combustion.' And I had to explain to him what an anti-inflammatory was."

Anna laughs. "Isn't that great? His mind is just wonderful."

Dottie says, "Your kids are so lucky to have you." Anna beams. The conversation has been very cathartic for her. "I've said to the kids, 'We are the luckiest family there is.' You know, I kind of say, 'Forget about my cancer.' We talk about everything. The four of us are so happy together and we do things together and we really are good communicators with our kids—I think. With what's coming up, though, I want to be as good a communicator as I can be."

Dottie asks Jan if he has always been active with the children. Both nod yes. "We went into this marriage absolutely dead equal," says Anna. "Anna's always worked," says Jan, who was used to helping with the children from the very beginning. "Anna nursed with both Ellery and Lindsay. I would get up in the middle of the night, bring them in and put 'em down in the bed, and then take 'em back." Anna says, "I think Jan has really great mothering instincts for a father. A lot of men don't have that."

Anna returns to her fears if she should die. "What I'm concerned with—and he knows it—is his inability to talk about things. The one fight we've had during all of this is when I said to him, 'Stop treating me like a patient!' Because that's a safe haven for him. That's how he can express how he feels—in a medical way. [Anna also sometimes hides behind the technical.] He's comfortable there, but it's removing himself a bit too.

"And that's got to be the wrong way, I think, of dealing with the kids. The three of them need to be able to have a good dialogue. I just start in—blah blah blah—and cry and the kids know it and we hug. And he doesn't do that. It's going to be harder for them to express themselves because he's not easy at doing that." For the first time, Jan protests, a bit defensively. "I talk to the kids pretty well." "Yeaaahhh, you do, but it's going to be emotional, it won't feel logical. You can't isolate with this, put it in neat little boxes," says Anna. "There aren't going to be any little boxes."

Jan now admits his fear. "Especially dealing with Lindsay is something that I know I can't do by myself because of where she is in terms of growing up. She's going to have to have some surrogate women around." Both say that Roseann—childless, immersed in her full-time career and life with her husband, could not handle this task.

Dottie starts to ask, "What about—" Jan breaks in. "There are some of our Richmond friends, Lockie and Tina and people like that." Anna says, "But they're not here, that's the problem. Those kids have known Lockie and Tina for years and feel pretty comfortable with them." Anna cannot bring herself to think of someone taking her place. "Again, the one-on-one isn't there. I can't think of who that could be."

The dog, Peaches, snuffles into the room, plaintively whimpering. Jan gets up to take him out. Dottie suggests that someone outside the family might help. "Sometimes what's helpful, while Mom is still alive and here, is to introduce them into a counseling situation. You set up some visits as an introduction because—and it's just that clear, honest, and simple—'what's happening in our lives is tough.' You can tell them, 'It's not usual, it's not what all your friends are going through. We deserve to have as much support as we can and there are wonderful people who do that.' I'm not saying it has to be me."

Anna interjects firmly, "No, I want it to be you." "There are lots of wonderful, good people out there," continues Dottie. "It's not uncommon to do this. The kids come in and you meet with them three, four times, whatever. And then periodically. So if and when you die, your kids don't need to find a stranger. There's this support network. And when there is a miracle and your bone marrow comes through—they've met somebody nice and there's somebody who can celebrate with them and say good-bye to. It has not been a negative experience. That's one thing that we can do, even when there are lots of people in the family."

"Would you want to work with them together or separately or both?"

"It depends. When you're working with children, you follow them. Initially I generally spend a bit of time with the kids together and then have some private time. Family situations are all different. There have been times when I've worked with whole families. But when there are brothers and sisters, there usually needs to be some private time because the guy things are separate. And sometimes the guy wants a guy counselor. It has to be individual and respectful of who the kids are and what's right for them. We all need to do this."

Dottie points out a fact that families often neglect to their detriment, that bereavement begins at the time of diagnosis. "This kind of stuff is wonderful even for people who are probably going to get better, absolutely. We all need support in our lives sometimes." Often a neutral, non–emotionally charged outsider is best at supplying that support, she explains. Anna tells her that they have always encouraged the children to talk to their school guidance counselor. "They've both been very good at doing that. We're happy they have other ways to express themselves besides just trying to talk with us. I'm all for it."

While Jan is out, Anna uses the opportunity to shift to the hardest subject. "What about dying at home? Does it affect . . . I mean, this is something . . . it's a real plummet for me," she begins haltingly. "On the one hand, I think, for a patient who's dying, to be at home is neat. But in my case, I'm looking at this and thinking, 'No way!' I don't want this house associated with that kind of trauma for Nils—that's his middle name—or the kids. I don't want them to walk back in that bedroom and have a vision of their mother, lying probably bloated and looking really . . ." She cannot finish the sentence. "If they're going to have that vision, let it be in some antiseptic place where they can disassociate themselves.

Is that a smart thing to do? This has been a real head twister for me and I don't know. My instinct is 'Don't die at home.' "

"Where do you want to be?" asks Dottie.

"I don't care. They haven't built a hospice place in Montgomery County yet. I don't like hospitals—but I'd go there. Once I'm in morphine land, I'll be pretty whacked out. I just don't want to traumatize them. I think it's going to be bad enough."

Dottie takes a breath and then quietly and calmly goes about trying to give Anna guidance concerning her jumbled feelings. "Kids are traumatized by things that they don't understand, by things that they can't participate in—that they have to stand there and watch and can't do anything about. And by things that they don't have a place to process afterwards and it's an open wound and it never has a chance to heal. Children are not necessarily traumatized [by experiencing dying]. I've worked with literally hundreds of families that have made these kinds of choices and when the decision is one that's made by all of you together, it's perfectly appropriate. Difficult, excruciatingly difficult, but very appropriate when the time is right for you guys to be talking about this and to ask, 'What's right for Mommy?'

"Because one of the things that's going to comfort them afterwards is knowing that they did everything they could, that they did the best they could for Mom. 'Mom said she wanted to die at home. Well, by God, we're going to do our best to make sure that happens.' Or 'Mom said she wants to die in the hospital, not at home. Well, by God, then we did our best to make that happen.' "

"So communicating it is—"

"Absolutely," jumps in Dottie. "It's not really *where* [one dies], it's how we deal with it. And in terms of a memory of you being bloated or not—again, those kinds of stark pictures that you view are sudden drastic shocks. Like when the last time they saw you, you were fine and healthy in tennis shorts and you had hair down to your shoulders and now they come in and see you, that's when it makes that kind of imprint.

"But they're looking at you every day. They're not looking at you physically. They're looking in your eyes. They're cuddling up to you. They don't know whether they're laying on a boob or a rib. They're laying on Mommy. There needs to be a connection. And the business of Lindsay being more cuddling now, that's fine. This isn't all conscious kinds of stuff. Some of it is generated by a scaredness. And some of it is generated by an awesome appreciation of 'she's here now, I'm going to love her while I can.' Your husband said it to you. 'If you don't spend time with the kids, I'm never going to forgive you.' If you didn't spend time with the kids, you wouldn't forgive yourself. They gravitate to you—some of it from this kind of scary, sad place and some of it is from 'This is wonderful,' a sense of appreciation that it's not all bad."

"I never even thought about that," says Anna. "They have been wonderful, like when I can't get out of bed, they love to feed me dinner. They call me 'baby bird.' 'Feed the baby bird.' Ellery, I've used that boy to walk. He's said, 'Here, Mom, lean on me.' And I've been able to support myself with my son, my eleven-year-old kid, holding me up."

Dottie nods. "That's good for them; allowing them to help is very important. It's a terrible feeling to be shut out. It's much better for you, too, to be around them even if being around them is hard, because it allows you to be included and not isolated and it allows you to be able to participate and to give something. And you will all have that later—'I gave, I tried. We did everything we could do.' And that's an enormous comfort."

Anna seems in awe. "I never thought . . . all I kept thinking about was all they'll see and how they won't be able to go in the room and they'll start to hate the house because I'd died here."

"Talk to them about it," suggests Dottie. "Again, you're a creative family—are you kidding? You'll do it in the garage if that's what's right." Anna laughs. "Some people say, 'I want to be at home, but I don't want to *die* in the house, so when I'm just about ready to die, put me in the ambulance and take me to the hospital.' Whatever," continues Dottie. " 'Put me in the car and let me ride around the block.' That may sound nuts—but this is *your life, this is your time, their life and times.* There is nothing that you can decide to do with that time that's wrong."

"But I want it to be as right as it can be for everybody," protests Anna, "not just me. What makes me the happiest is what's right for the unit." "How many times have you been through this before? I don't think too many," says Dottie archly as Anna smiles. "So you don't know until you're in the middle of it. With the children, you'll make some decisions together. You'll write them in pencil. So if you're in the bedroom and all of a sudden Dad, one of the kids, or you say, 'This is too hard, it's not what I bargained for, take me to the hospital,' that's okay, because you've written it in pencil. Nobody's making promises. The only promise is that you will do this together in the best way that you can and your promise is that you will tell each other what you need as you go through it because you can't plan it in advance."

"That's so wonderful," says Anna, sobbing. "That's a great way. I didn't think like that. I was stupid not to. We've done that all the way, but for some reason, suddenly I'm thinking, 'No, no, I've got to protect them.' And the word 'protection' is equated as shutting them out and that's wrong." She wipes her eyes. "That's really cool. I like that. Yeah."

"You let them self-protect," says Dottie. "They will do that."

"Now, when is the time to talk about this?" asks Anna. "At this point, they know that I'm fighting. I haven't decided yet I'm definitely going to die," says Anna, firmly. "I know the score and it may happen, but I keep going, 'Hey, I can do this for another year, come on liver, keep functioning.' So there's the 'what if' game. What if you sit 'em down and say, 'Guys, you know there is a chance that I can die'—and then you hang around!" Anna laughs. "And so you've put them on pins and needles—and I don't want to make the situation scary. Yet, I don't know. That's why I was asking—"

Jan has returned and he nods in agreement with Anna. "The problem is striking a balance between being up-front and dwelling on it. They know all about the cancer, but you don't want to sit around talking about it all day. That just doesn't make sense. You've got to go on with things."

Dottie smiles. "As much as I'd like you to need me and my advice, it sounds like you people have a wonderful knack for striking balances already." She reiterates what she told Anna about counseling for the children and stresses, "If the kids say, 'Everything's okay, I don't need this anymore,' fine. You all keep the phone numbers. From time to time, they'll come or they won't. Sometimes they don't come at all, which is fine, but because they know it's there, they don't have to. There's that little cushion."

They talk about how will they know if something drastic happens emotionally for the children, what are the warning signs. "One key word is 'changes,' " says Dottie. "Just be aware if the child has a real big change that persists. There's a difference between Lindsay becoming cuddly, which is fine, and this normally independent kid not wanting to go to dance class, Girl Scouts, whatever, because she needs to be near you all the time. That's off balance. Look for a big change. A child who is normally a crappy student suddenly starts getting straight A's?—you worry a bit. What's he bargaining out here in order to try and keep things safe? And you just look at them in the four regular areas: Are they eating fine? Sleeping fine? Playing fine? How is their schoolwork? The area of big changes."

Anna mentions outside forces that could be compounded by her illness, such as Lindsay's departure from a one-on-one nurturing teacher to several different teachers. "I've noticed a real change; she doesn't like this new situation. Is that normal or is this part of her worries about me?" "It makes sense," remarks Dottie. "She had one nice teacher and now she has three that she's not connected with." Anna says, "Fifth grade is more adult, there's more responsibility placed on her. I just worry between that and what's happening with me is that she's not going to do as well. She got straight A's last year, but grades are slipping some. I harp on it a little bit."

Dottie makes the situation less drastic. "So she doesn't like it, plus she's distracted," she says with a shrug. Anna interrupts. "She's distracted by what's happening here." "You can't ignore that," agrees Dottie, "it plays into it. But it's not just you that's causing what's happening at school." "I know," replies Anna, "but it's all happening at the same time and it's a lot." She talks about how Lindsay is spreading herself too thin with ballet and chorus and how she and Jan drew the line and would not let her be in the variety show. "I said, 'You've got to have time for you.' "

"You said something very important—for the kids, for Jan, and for you—and that is 'You've got to have time for you.' Meaning you've got to take care of you." Dottie starts in on her last project of the day, to make Anna and Jan realize that they too need help. "He's going to throw something at me," she says, smiling as she points to Jan. "It might be useful for you, too, to be introduced perhaps to a counselor, just to meet once or twice. I'm not saying this lightly: *the most important thing that a parent does for his child is to take care of himself.* If you want statistics, I can pull out a Boston study. Kids who get grief support and their parent who gets none do not do as well as the kid who gets grief support and the parent does too. This has been my big concern with those who say, 'I don't have to worry, I'm going to be the one that's simply fine—' "

"I know!" exclaims Anna. "That's what worries me about Jan." She champions Dottie's suggestion of counseling—but only for Jan. "So I agree a hundred billion percent. I think that's going to be critical and he will try and be Superdad and he will get stressed out." Anna, who generally feels that her open personality conquers all problems, ignores a salient point. Dottie is suggesting counseling for them both. "Get recommendations from people that you trust. Talk to 'em, meet a person once. If you don't connect, I don't give a shit if they're Einstein and Sigmund Freud rolled into one. This work is done from here," she says, pointing to her heart, "it's not done from here," pointing to her head. "I can give you some names."

Anna sails right on, back to Jan. "I've already bugged him because I got the book *How We Die,* given to me by a friend. I read it, felt wonderful and uplifted, and thought it was great. He wouldn't read it. I was like, 'Come on! Read this book!' "

Dottie stops her firmly. "Let's understand, we are talking here about a process—we are *not* talking about rules and milestones. It's like you two are out in a canoe and neither one of you knows how to swim and the canoe tips over. Sometimes the worst thing you can do is try to hold on to each other, because you'll both drown. You each have to reach for your life preservers. You can swim side by side, sometimes you'll be paddling here and he'll be paddling there. You can keep calling to each other, but you're going to be doing this not always at the same rate."

"Well, I'm so straight, up-front, in your face. It's the way I am," says Anna. Jan adds, "She's not going to quit until everything on the list is done. With me, it's 'Aw, do it tomorrow.' I don't take well to regimented situations."

"May I ask a tough question?" asks Dottie, looking at Anna and placing her hand on her arm. "Is there one thing in particular that really scares you, maybe terrifies you, about this?"

"Well," says Anna, quickly turning to tears. "Hurting my kids. Hurting my kids. I know—I think—Jan'll get through it. Our friends are the most wonderful people in the world and will be there for him forever. I worry that he'll hide, or whatever, but hurting my kids, I just can't stand hurting them." Her words come out strangled as she sobs heavily. "And this hurts them and I hate it, I hate it, just knowing it hurts everybody and there's nothing I can do about it. I'm not scared for me," she goes on. '"Hey, I'm doing the best I can do and I feel really good about my life, I feel very good about me. I look back and I have nothing to complain about, so I'm happy about that. And if I do die early, that's the way it goes. But the thought of causing or being the cause of so much pain to my kids, it tears my heart out. They're at such a young age too." The sobs come harder. All the while, Dottie has quietly and lightly patted Anna's arm, not interrupting or attempting to stop her tears.

"When my mom died, she was seventy-nine, we got to say good-bye. I'd been able to grow up with her and I feel like there's going to be so much I could have done with them that they're not going to get. It's going to hurt them. It's not going to give them quite the edge. It's not going to give them the advantage, and I hate that. I really hate that."

As Anna grows quiet, Dottie asks, "Do you know it's not your fault?"

"Yes, I know there's nothing I can do about it, but it's frustrating. I'm a person who likes to control that. See, that's the problem. I know it's not my fault and I know there's nothing I can do about that and *dammit* I want to do something about that and I can't. I can't. I know that."

"But there are ways to be there for them," suggests Dottie. "There are ways to kind of direct them as they grow and it might be as simple as having a videotape."

Anna nods. "I'm going to do that. And letters, yes."

"Write not just about them. Tell them your story. Write them what you remember about being sixteen for Lindsay to open on her sixteenth birthday. Write about what it was like for you to go on a date for your son to read when he thinks about dating. 'What's it like on the other side, to be a girl?' Tell them your story. Give them you. You might not be here physically, but your story can be. Your story can be a part of their lives. And that's important. Write down all of your memories."

"I had planned to do things for odd moments. 'Watch this when you are so mad at Dad that you want to take a brick and whack him'—you know. I could spend time and do this for the kids." "Write all the instructions in pencil," cautions Dottie, "so that you are saying, 'If you don't want to watch these ever, you never have to. They're just here.' Because sometimes the thought of having to look at Mom and having to remember hurts. So write it in pencil. Then it's a gift with absolutely no strings. And they will open it and they might show them to their grandchildren. There are so many ways."

Anna returns to her thoughts of dying. "Oh, I hate it—" Dottie insists, "You're not hurting them." Anna says, "Yes, but they *will* hurt." Dottie says, "They will hurt in life a thousand times," then lets Anna know that she understands—"As a mom, your job is to keep them from hurting and this flies in the face of that." Then she turns the conversation around. "You've thought obviously a lot about this. What do you want from them? All things being equal, say, you don't need to protect them. They're fine. Is there anything that you need that you would want?"

"I don't know what it is." "While you're dying?" "Oh, I don't know, just their love and support." "Do you want to be alone, do you want somebody with you?"

"To be honest with you, it changes," says Anna. "I think I would like them all to be with me but not necessarily in the house—but now I'm ready to say to them, 'Do you want me in the house?' I want to be with them, I really don't care where we are. But I care if they care. I guess that's what's important to me. If they don't want me in the house because that is a hurtful memory and they see this house then as a sad place, I don't want to be here. Because I've never been a sad person. There have always been jokes, fun, that's what I want them to remember. But I want to be with them, yes. In that book *How We Die,* he says that about ninety percent of people die alone. My dad and my sister were in the house, but Mom died alone in that bedroom, nobody was with her."

As Anna winds down, exhausted, Jan looks at her with empathy in his eyes. Dottie gets up to leave. Anna says she will be calling her to set up an appointment for the children. Dottie gives her a long embrace, then turns to include Jan in the circle. For several seconds, the three of them hold on to one another. Tears course down Jan's face as he too sobs.

Later that week, Anna reflects on their meeting. "Dottie is so wonderful, she reminds me of my mother, sitting there, listening, patting one softly on the hand. What was fascinating was what Dottie said to me—about them participating so much and how I should not take that away from them. She really opened my eyes. My whole thought about dying at home and all. And she is so right, how they are helped by helping me. So when I thought about that, I went, 'Wow, this is going to be a group decision.' And I never saw that as how it would be."

Anna sighs and says, "I can't let my preconceptions get in the way of reality."

A few weeks later, in January of 1996, Anna and Jan sit down with the children and tell them about Dottie. "The timing couldn't be better," says Anna. Marcia, the school counselor who had helped Ellery and Lindsay in the past, was in a car accident and on leave indefinitely. "I used this situation as the doorway. I said, 'Guys, Dad and I met a person named Dottie and she counsels all kinds of kids. Kids who have AIDS, kids who have this, kids with that. Kids who have sick parents. You guys have extenuating circumstances, I can't quite do what I always did and you guys have to pick up the burden of that. You don't have Marcia any more and I know there's a lot on your mind and sometimes you can't tell us or don't want to tell us everything because we're the problem.'

"I said, 'You have nobody really as an adult who can understand, and I think Dottie would be perfect. She's going to be your person. I am very excited about it because we had an immediate warm feeling about Dottie and we just connected and I think this will happen to you. She is a professional and understands children and she's going to know how you feel. She's going to keep whatever you say or do private. You guys need one person like that who's continuous in your life. It's really nice to have that one person you can talk with.' And I told them about the clay wall. 'She's got this wall where if you get mad about something you go pick up clay and whack it at the wall.'

"Well, they thought it was a great idea! They never balked at it."

Their first Sunday afternoon together, Dottie explains to Ellery and Lindsay that they will meet a few times and then go from there. Purposely in front of their mother, she stresses that "this is your time to talk about whatever you want. Or not to talk. Just play for an hour." Ellery and Lindsay smile. "Nothing you say or do will be repeated by me to anyone. The only time I would ever say anything to your mother is if there was something that would possibly physically harm you. She needs to know about that. Other than that, you can tell your mom and dad what you want—or you don't have to."

During their first session, Anna stays downstairs while her children walk up to the third floor with its huge, floppy beanbag chairs and toys and stuffed animals.

Although the children seldom tell their parents what transpires during these monthly sessions, Anna and Jan have learned to listen in other ways. The first time, as Anna hears the slamming of clay against a wall, over and over, and then sees the flushed and relieved faces of her children, she knows that she has made the right choice.

CHAPTER NINE

All in the Family: Masculine and Feminine Grieving

On a balmy Florida morning in January 1996, Anna is as happy as a released prisoner, having left behind a D.C. blizzard and freezing winds. Her clownishness abounds. This time, Anna's chemo treatment is not drastically damaging her hair follicles. Anna's dark eyebrows have returned and she is growing a head of dark hair, the fledgling outlines of an attractive short cut. The texture is as silky soft as puppy fur. "I tell you, it's animal hair!

"Look," she says, jumping up in her father's den in his Cocoa Beach home and rubbing her hand across her face. "I've never had so much hair on my face ever!" There is dark fuzz down her cheeks and the back of her neck. Looking at her children, sprawled in pajamas on the floor in front of the TV, Anna contorts her face, makes monkey sounds, dangles one arm low, and scratches herself under the armpit with the other. The family howls and Ellery says, "Mom makes the best monkey faces." Her father's eyes shine with happiness as he watches Anna. "Friends tell me I can wax it off, but I'm going to wait and see the upcoming MRI, which will tell whether the medicine is shrinking the tumors. If it isn't working, I'll be on another chemo set and it will all probably fall out again."

Anna is genuinely able to joke about her plight at this moment, but she is also performing a valuable service for her family, helping them adjust to changes and stages of her illness in a nonthreatening way—casually introducing the thought, for example, that she might have to turn to another set of chemotherapy treatments. Anna is following her instincts, without any guidance, yet she would make an enviable text case as the near-perfect way to achieve what the experts call redefining. This step of redefining—being able to look at oneself honestly and adapt to the changes in one's condition—is critical, in order for the patient and the entire family and circle of friends to accommodate to adaptations dictated by illness.[1]

When patients succeed in redefining, as Anna does, they ease the process for the rest of the family. The family can enjoy one another and get on with what has to be done, adjusting behavior and patterns of living, rather than struggling to "maintain a false sense of normalcy."[2] Anna's family show signs of successfully redefining Anna and understanding her current goals. "I think Anna has made the decision that she's going to try to raise the kids as much as she can in the time that she has," says her brother Steve. Her mother-in-law, Phoebe, shared that thought at Thanksgiving. "I think she's trying to stay around as long as possible. She knows there's very little chance [of a cure], but if anybody has a chance, she'll have it."

When patients cannot redefine themselves, they are filled with a sense of rage, worthlessness, and curdled frustration that permeate the entire household. If any family member remains unwilling to redefine the patient, this too affects everyone; tension results "as family members try to evade the effects of the illness. . . ." The pattern in such families is not to acknowledge feelings or uncertainties. "There is no resolution because they ignore problems, assign blame, refuse help. Instead of coming together, they focus on their own emotional needs with little regard for others." The resulting pain, resentment, and anger can rule their emotions for years.[3]

A classic example of how damaging this can be lies close to home, in Anna's extended family. "My brother, a heavy smoker, died of lung cancer when his twins were fifteen," recalls Phoebe. "It was treated like this terrible secret. His children were told nothing. His wife couldn't talk about it at all. That was in 1984, and she still hasn't gotten over it. The twins have a lot of anger still because they weren't told enough and weren't able to talk to their father or mother about his illness."

One troubling common factor among men is that even in long-term illness there are often no good-byes. The story of one adult son illustrates how one can suffer when a father refuses to talk about his illness. His father's daily jokes placed few burdens on friends or family. As admirable as this was, the son wanted deeper moments. His father's approach left no opening for sentiment, discussions, or, importantly, farewells. If the dying person or the survivor cannot express his or her feelings, creating closure is always difficult. His doctor joined forces with the patient, telling the family nothing and giving false hope.

Redefining, of course, does not come easily for Anna or anyone. Realistically, altering one's sense of self is a wrenching passage, achieved only over time; it is marked by anguish in letting go and in such grieving as Anna's loss for her full-time career and concern for her children's future.

Yet, when the patient can redefine himself or herself as Anna does—viewing herself as someone who still has accomplishments, still sees the "essence" of self and life—he or she is showing those around him or her that redefining does not mean giving up. Because Anna has hope, others can hope as well. Her attitude—"I'm not dying *now.* I'm living"—makes it easier for her to adapt to everything from new ways to utilize her mind and talents to coping with the medical roller coaster: "It's a new chapter, much more geared to my physical capability." So if one chemo doesn't work, we'll try another. So if I can't work full-time, I will work full speed on the ballet and help to edit a friend's attempt at a first novel. If Lindsay and Ellery need to be prodded about homework, by God, I'm there instead of at the store. If I have to lie down, I'll lie down. The specter of dying is offset by heightened appreciation of life and an urge to live it to its fullest.

And Jan is the near-perfect husband for Anna. Although she is disturbed by his inability to express feelings, he is firmly by her side, redefining their life together, step by step, with a near-intuitive ability to understand and adapt. He may not be able to speak of it, but he shows his love and concern daily in countless ways. Like other spouses who successfully redefine the patient, Jan acknowledges physical changes but takes them in stride. He patiently recognizes that Anna's changes in moods or abilities stem from her medical treatments or cancer, listening quietly and reassuringly as Anna obsesses at times about the children or what will happen to him, taking over chores while not interfering with Anna's fierce desire for independence. He knows that her dignity demands this, even if she sometimes stubbornly overdoes it.

Before they left for Florida, for example, there was Anna, shoveling snow while loaded with chemotherapy. On the day they were supposed to leave for the South, her doctors wanted to hospitalize her for a transfusion. Anna knew as well as the doctors that her white and red cells were dangerously low. "I just told them, 'No way!' My body and soul needed care and contentment, something that I knew no hospital could offer." For all her directness, Anna compassionately shields those she loves. Unbeknownst to her father, Anna and Jan go into the bathroom and shut the door. Jan fills a vial with liquid as clear as water and shoots it just under the skin of her stomach. These series of shots will help the bone marrow to resupply the body with red and white cells. "I'm taking a slower route to recovery," says Anna, "but it is right for me, nonetheless."

On Thursday night, the family celebrates a trio of January birthdays—Jan, forty-three; Anna's father, Stephen, eighty-one; and Anna's brother Marty, forty-five. Husbands and wives and nephews and nieces and cousins filled a U-shaped table at the nearby Country Club of Rockledge as twenty-two Megregians share dinner. As the dinner ends, the Megregians mill around. Anna listens to a seventeen-year-old niece who is crying, telling Anna about the cyst on her ovary. Anna holds her hands, hugs her, listens with a total concentration reminiscent of her mother. At the far end of the table, brother Steve, the university comptroller and master punster, tops himself with each play on the word "lapsadaisical," stemming from a sentence in which someone used the word "lapse." "Hey," he says, waiting for the groans, "I never promised you a prose garden."

That weekend, Anna and her father are determined to play golf, no matter that both of them have been battered by illnesses that make walking and swinging difficult. This was always their special time together, kibitzing and laughing as they circled eighteen holes. And so early on Sunday morning, after a bulging breakfast at the country club, they move toward the first tee, along with Jan and Anna's brother Steve.

Although the upper body of Anna's father is strong and muscular, he is stooped from the waist with pain from a back operation that did not properly heal. His bedroom nightstand is cluttered with medication for diabetes and high blood pressure and with painkillers, yet, although he never complains, the pain is seldom dulled. His craggy face is creased with the grimaces of agony, and his deep brown eyes speak eloquently of his sorrows for the loss of his wife and for his daughter's illness, but Stephen Megregian's smile is as buoyant as his jokes. "I've had so many illnesses, I figure I should have died years ago. Nowadays I'm just happy I'm on the right side of the grass—looking down instead of up."

More than a half century of golfing are in Stephen's arms and so his sureness of form overrides crippling pain as he swings and hits the ball a respectable distance. Anna, rusty and clumsy on feet and legs filled with the pain of neuropathy, hits the ball a shorter distance. She shakes her head in disgust as they move on down the hill and out of sight. (Afterward she beams, once again able to redefine her definition of success. "I thought I'd only do half, but out of eighteen holes, I sat out only three.")

Meanwhile, Ellery and Lindsay eagerly race off with a friend to an amusement park where go-carts and video games gulp quarters like a weary runner gulps air. Ellery is all over the place, trying machine after machine, expertly wasting enemy aliens and bad cowboys who fall down to his touch at the lever. Both are so mesmerized that the friend has to call a halt in order to get them back to the country club in time for lunch.

The day before, Anna's dad sits in his favorite worn leather chair and talks, taking time out from his *New York Times* puzzle books that Anna buys him by the handfuls. He is expressive, volatile, and intense as he brags about Anna. "She has friends coming out her ears—keeps 'em forever and really cares." He cannot, however, talk about how he feels about her cancer or a fear of losing her. Instead, he speaks of illnesses in general and runs through his own medical saga, including his own operation horror stories. The loquacious Stephen, however, cannot express his emotional suffering regarding his wife's searing death and his continued loneliness, or his current pain about Anna. Neither can his son or Jan. Men often seem relieved when women take on the process of open grieving, coping, and adjusting for the entire family.

The multigenerational ripple effect of prolonged illness, grieving, and accommodating overlap in the Megregian-Johannessen homes, as they do in so many families. The death of Anna's mother continues to spawn disparate emotions; Ro's resentment at her brothers for "having to do it all" when she was dying, Anna's reliving her days with her mother now that she is seriously ill, her father reeling from one severe loss only to be hit by the potential horror of losing his daughter, disagreement among the siblings as to what should be done to help their father.

As for Jan's parents, there is increased concern for their son as well as their daughter-in-law. "In some ways, it's probably more difficult for Nils to watch this than to have it happen to you," says his mother, "particularly when he knows so much about it." Many family members experience guilt, resentment, anger, and helplessness when they are torn between caring for someone who is ill and their own responsibilities and lives. Often it is the adult child, facing the disruption of caring for elderly parents. Other times, as with Anna, it is a parent who experiences such feelings. Phoebe says, "The cancer recurred just after we moved to Seattle. Had we known, we probably would have stayed nearby, to help with the children and at home. We moved not knowing she would need us. We felt a number of guilt pangs about it." She adds, with finality, "But it was done." An unspoken guilt seems to linger, but she is adamant. "I can't come here again. I am very fond of the children and I can have them for visits and I can visit them, but I can't do much." Phoebe cannot describe how this makes her feel. As she states often, "We do not talk about our personal feelings. We never did it."

That stiff-upper-lip upbringing feeds Jan's general male inability to discuss feelings. Like so many women who live with men who cannot speak about their emotions, Anna not only is frustrated, she is convinced it would be cathartic for him. "When we were young, I used to pick a fight just to get his reaction," says Anna. "I wasn't very successful. No reaction! Once when we were driving, he just turned around and started screaming at me—over things I had done six months to a year prior! I looked at him and burst out laughing and said, 'If you've got a problem with what I'm doing, you'd better tell me at the time. I can't do anything about what I did six months ago. From now on, you've got to communicate with me right here and now.' I realized, 'You poor guy, you've held all this in, and we could have had a good fight!' He's gotten a lot better but often remains this big giant clam." "Nils learned a lot from Anna about talking more," says Phoebe, "but it doesn't come naturally."

Nor does it come naturally to the males in Anna's own family when it involves serious emotions, no matter how close they feel to one another. Listen to Stephen, the father, and Steve, the brother, dance around their emotions.

What about when Ro got cancer?

"That was very upsetting," recalls brother Steve. "As a matter of fact, when they did the mastectomy, she didn't know I was coming. I walked into her hospital room and shocked her. I told my wife, 'I've got to go.' And she said, 'Okay, go, I understand.' So I went."

How did you handle your emotions then? Did you talk to your wife, Bonnie, or anybody, about it? "No, I don't talk much about how I feel. But I figured that, well, there's not a whole lot I can do. That's the way it is. They gave Ro six months to live and it was very upsetting to everybody. Dad wore it more on his sleeve than I did. But he didn't feel any more or less upset about it than I; he was just a little more open. I figured, 'Hell, she's my sister and I love her, but what can I do? She's got it.' "

His father continues, "All of a sudden out of the clear blue, Ro's got this cancer thing. I don't, what should I say, jump at the first bump. It has to sink into me for a while." The clichés flow. "Like Steve says, we have to take the things that we can't control and just roll with the punches." His son nods and says, "If you can't do something about it, you can't." "If there's something to be said, we say it," says Anna's father, "but if there is a problem that we can't do anything about, we don't go into any histrionics. I expected Audrie to outlive me. I figure I should have died long ago. But I survived and she didn't."

How did you cope with that?

"What can you do? Religion? No." He shakes his head firmly. "It doesn't belong in my life at all." Did you ever go to a survivor group and talk? "Naah, I didn't do that stuff," says Stephen. "I've got a strong head. Maybe too strong." He pauses. "You may have a picture of our family as having an intense nature, yet we live every day without any thinking back."

Stephen does not seem to fathom that, despite his words, he goes through a cathartic grieving ritual every time he sees Audrie's face and medals on the den wall, talks about her, relives their life together, and cries. "When we start talking about the old days, tears will come to his eyes—but he *loves* to talk about it," says his son Steve. "I think that's one of the reasons why he'll never leave this house." Both Anna and Ro feel it would be best for their father to move, but he had made a deathbed promise to Audrie to stay. They feel their brothers don't do enough to help with the upkeep. "Look," says Anna, pointing to the screen affixed to a part of the roof that has collapsed. "It goes to the roof! The whole damn thing is going to fall." "So what if the roof leaks?" says Steve. "We'll fix it. I don't get mad, I just ignore it."

Their father resists pleas to move. "I don't need this big house," he admits, "but it has Audrie all through it." He is comfortable having her in the house. "He's not a bit spooked about it," says his son. "In order to try to ease their minds a little bit about me being alone," says Stephen, who is adapting to getting on with life, "I got a girlfriend. It's nothing special. I have fun. I play duplicate bridge three times a week. I took a cruise. And I have my crossword puzzles and golf three days a week."

How do you cope with a mother dying? Steve is asked. He does not talk about what he did to handle her death but concentrates on the positives. "She was almost eighty, she lived a good, full life. I would have felt differently if she would have died at a young age. Quite frankly, it was a blessing when she died because she needed to be out of her misery." And then another platitude, "When your time has come, it's come."

Even Wayne, Anna's dearest male friend from Richmond, who feels "closer to Anna and Jan than my family," admits that he and Jan do not discuss feelings. "My job is to make people comfortable. I'm the approachable icebreaker. I empower them." Wayne thinks of active ways to help Jan. "I want to make sure we get him out on the water with us. I crew for Chuck, another friend. We need to get Jan in with us, a break from all of this." Anna loves talking with Wayne, who concentrates on the good times and encourages her with "Let's just live another day." Yet there is far less an attempt to hear her out than her female friends. "When she does break down at times and worries about the kids," says Wayne, "I try to defuse the emotion, talking matter-of-factly." Wayne stops and acknowledges what he has just revealed—how he closes down any opening for more expression by endeavoring to "defuse the emotion." "I'm probably like Jan," he says ruefully. "I'm taking it like a man."

"Taking it like a man," "Only sissies cry," "You have to be the big man in the family and take care of your momma." Any number of clichés of past culturation come quickly to mind that explain to some degree why men are trained by society to show less emotion. The men in Anna's life are the norm. Many women consider that men are emotional cripples in all walks of life, but particularly as grievers, because of societal emphasis on so-called masculine attributes of self-reliance. A more realistic question for women should be not whether men grieve—because they do—but why they grieve the *way* they do. Silent or private mourning and immersing oneself in activity are both patterns of male grieving. Taking action is not ducking the emotional but rather a form of coping and healing, and can be very effective. Bottling up one's feelings without any accompanying positive action, however, can lead to major blocks in family relations and often dysfunctional ways of handling grief—denial, closing off from spouse and children, misdirected anger, heavy drinking.

"Men and women tend to be suspicious about the others' mode of grief," writes Thomas R. Golden, a psychotherapist who specializes in masculine grieving. "He may think she is 'overdoing it' as she emotes. . . . She may feel that the man is not actually grieving because he grieves in private or through action."[4] Women generally seek more help than men, either through friends or professionally, while many males believe, as one man put it, "I don't think a stranger can say anything that would help me." Men often attend counseling sessions as protectors, patting the wife's hand, sitting stolidly next to her, not as seekers of help.

"Many men find some of the current counseling approaches very intrusive," says Kenneth Doka, internationally known death educator and minister. "The 'how are you handling it?' directness often interferes with that self-reliance sense." The trick is to find new ways of dealing with masculine grieving, says Doka, who finds that counselors are often unprepared to deal with grieving men.[5]

Often these silent grievers find some oblique way to work out their feelings. For example, one son who resented his father's constant and critical interference with his hobbies refused to finish a model boat. When his father died, the man went back and finished the boat, coming to some resolution regarding their relationship. No longer are male relatives able to take charge in such a hands-on way as making the simple pine coffin, but many find comfort in such activity as making funeral arrangements, planning and building some memorial, as do some women.

Of course, there is no absolute gender pattern to mourning. Don't tell the Mothers Against Drunk Driving (MADD), for example, that action is solely a masculine trait. Nor Anna, the fiercely proactive cancer patient. What is termed "masculine grieving" is not determined by gender, emphasizes Doka. Today, women incorporate much of the male passion for activity, exercise, and immersion in work as a valuable healing process. One widow searches for meaning by writing a book about her husband. Another, who says, "You can never heal the hole in your heart," has found some surcease from the death of her young daughter, an author, by championing her causes. Women, however, have the added bonus of being able to relate their feelings with others, to endlessly replay their grief with compassionate, listening friends. During prolonged grief, their actions, more often than men's, are directed in a caregiving manner toward the sick person. Women find catharsis for their grief in helping.

During a prolonged life-threatening illness, men as well as women often find some active form of showing their connection and love for the person. Jan does it with furious exploration of new scientific routes to prolong or enhance Anna's life. Lockie does it with weekly hilarious greeting cards, Wayne with crazy phone conversations.

When men like the Megregians say, "There is nothing we can do," they are not recognizing the many ways they can help the patient and themselves, even if they cannot do anything about the illness. While the person is alive, it is healthy and comforting to honor and acknowledge the attachment that exists. "When you sit with that person and reminisce about old times and what you have done together, that is the work of grief," writes Golden. "When you tell that person how they have affected your life, how they are important to you, that is the work of grief." Prolonged illness affords a chance for closure that sudden death can never provide. "Anticipatory grief is a process that means completing your business," says Golden. "Heart-to-heart talks are for the living and the dying, a time even to settle grievances." Concluding one's business with another is the cornerstone of grief work whether through action or talking.[6]

Anna's brother is asked if he would suggest to males that they heighten the relationship with the sick person during the time that is available—make every moment count. "Why would you heighten a relationship if you didn't have it in the first place? It's not like Ro and Anna, who talk to each other all the time, about everything," says Steve. Jan says, "Steve shows his affection by action, like surprising Anna with a visit. He's really a big teddy bear and Anna knows it."

Steve expresses one form of anticipatory grief, the "what ifs" that go through his head about the future. "Anna married perfectly. The thing that worries me the most, if it turns out the way we don't want it to, is those two kids. They are spectacular—and have no idea how much talent they have. You never know, if Jan has to finish raising the kids, whether he can substitute for her personality and all that. Lindsay has got a hell of a lot of learning yet to do and values to get set in place. And same with Ellery. Ellery's a mega-sensitive kid." He sounds not unlike Jan's mother, Phoebe, who expresses concerns. "I just think Nils would be so frightfully overworked with the kids. And emotionally, I have no idea; I mean, that frightens me to death, I hate to think about it."

Steve sees his major role as helping his dad. "I worry about Dad being able to handle anything that happens, more than anything else. I believe the rest of the family is strong enough. But Dad will take it so hard. He doesn't say much, but he is very upset about it. He has said, 'I don't want to live if it is to live through this.' He calls Anna the spark plug of the family because she's got this wild personality—happy, funny, have a good time."

Do you feel you can do anything to help?

"Yeah, and I'm doing it. Well, just a little. For one thing, I'm there, okay? Marty's a little too removed and a little too busy, so I don't think he's in the position to do what I can. If he was, he'd do it." Steve takes the view that his father should be occupied, not left alone to reflect. "I keep him busy and talking about other things. If something did happen to Anna, I think my presence would help a lot. I would get him on the golf course, get him to the card table, be the force around him that says life goes on. To try to get him stable and back to normal."

Although distraction can be helpful, rushing someone to "get back to normal" is perilous; grieving can take years, subsiding into different forms as time goes on. No one ever "gets over" a loss, but there can be healing, which takes time. Many people need to know that there are people who can help explain ways to work through grief. Among men, conversations about grieving rituals being "normal" are rare, even though they provide a comforting structure for healing.

In today's frenetic society, there are few socially sanctioned rituals for grieving, for males or females. We are expected back at the job and to work as efficiently as ever, no matter how distracted and confused we are—a normal component to early grief. We are expected to get the kids dressed and off to school rather than stay in bed and succumb to grieving moments. We are expected to get back to the golf clubs and the card table. We are expected to find new companions, the sooner the better. Friends look with impatience at unhappy reminders of grief extended, thinking, "Aren't you 'over that' yet?" With increasing technology, we have moved farther away from contact with ritual, writes Golden. "It is almost as if we assume that we can think our way out of everything, that logic and technology can supply an answer to every problem."[7] Ritual is regarded as superstitious, foreign, not something to submit to.

Obviously there is nothing as striking in our modern culture as ancient mourning customs passed down in different societies. An Ethiopian couple, living a modern life in Washington, D.C., nonetheless adhere to Coptic customs of deep mourning—twelve straight days of wrenching and wailing mourning for both genders, a year in black for the women, a ritual celebration at the end of the year as the clothing is changed to lighter garb. "By the end of those twelve days," says the husband, Kyros Hagos, "you've earned a right to lessen your mourning; it is very hard to hear those wailing chants, 'Why have you left me?' and so forth, but it is very cleansing."

One African tribe recognizes that men have much to learn from women about grieving. The men stand and view the women who are crying and keening over a death. They do not taunt the women; rather the females are viewed as healthier specimens. They closely watch the women in order to bring forth their own sense of loss and to feel their own emotions. The Bara people of southern Madagascar, on the other hand, see differences between male and female grieving and provide support for both. They build two different huts when a member of the tribe dies, one designated the "male house" and the other the "house of tears." Activity is constant in the "male house" as the men organize rituals, receive condolences from other men, and take responsibility for burying the body. The "house of tears" is a private place for women mourners; there they weep and wail and receive condolences from other females.[8] In some parts of China, mourners wear armbands of different colors to designate whether the relative who died was a mother, father, sibling, or child. These armbands register, even to a stranger, the specifics of their deep mourning and serve as a guide for offering gentle sympathy.[9]

Saying no to grief, ironically, can prolong grief. If there are few honored rituals, the answer is to make up one's own. For the religious, rituals ordained by churches or synagogues or temples concentrate on mourning. But rituals can be simple and private. Taking a specific time each day to think about, honor, and mourn the person in the quiet of one's home can become a ritual of comfort. Looking at pictures in an album is another way of entering into grief. Such action has a beginning and an end, thus comforting the griever who desires to put those emotions away after he or she has experienced them. The son whose father dies and builds a memorial bench in the woods where he walked, the mother whose son is killed in an automobile accident and devotes the rest of her life to highway safety programs are working through their grief. The act of solitary jogging, accompanied by tears, is a manner of individual, contained grieving, as is rolling up the windows of the car and sobbing where no one can hear.

Although there is no one correct way to grieve, some theorists and therapists cling to the idea that the only way to get through grieving is to live through the core of grief, letting out all the stops and experiencing the necessary emotional effects. Only then, they assert, can one eventually resolve the loss. Such "letting go," however, can be elusive—to men, in particular. "Many of us don't know what it is we need to let go of," says Golden.

Acculturation plays a major role. "Rugged individualism" epitomized the male mystique, from the days of the earliest settler to today's Jockocracy. Frightening displays of machismo and honor, such as duels or settling injustices with a gun, were prevalent in earlier centuries, but there were also shared intimate relationships forced upon men and women in the preindustrial lifestyle of codependent community living. Depending on each other to bring in the crops or raise the barn or tend to livestock necessitated common caring. Death came often and with it neighborly coping with the common grief of infants and wives dying in childbirth.[10] With industrialization, work became more central to male identity. Long hours in a steel mill or moving to a new job left little time for neighborly bonding. Gone was the small community, where everyone was directly involved in the marriages and birthing and deaths of neighbors.

A key developmental issue was the manner in which men were taught to master emotions. Men had to be models of self-restraint for boys, who could not "control their enthusiasms." Long before John Wayne loped into view, ruggedness was prized, embodied in Rough Rider Theodore Roosevelt. It was not known for years that Roosevelt, with his ever-robust public persona, sank into profound, debilitating depression following the death of his first wife. His public would have frowned on such a display of grief. (In modern times, a picture of Israeli soldiers weeping on one another's shoulders emphasized that manliness can include showing one's emotions.)

Homophobia often played a role in fostering the tough-guy image. Homosexuals were hardly viewed as models for "red-blooded American boys"—therefore, it became more difficult to acknowledge feelings for other men. Thus came the "strong silent type" matinee-idol actor—no matter that their own sexual preferences were sometimes questionable. Homophobia, unfortunately, remains prevalent and surfaces in torturous cruelty when AIDS patients, for example, are shunned by male family members, particularly fathers. Males today carry on the tradition of minimal emotional expenditure, watching sports together, drinking in bars. The closest expression of affection is the high five or a hearty slap on the shoulder. That is why one man, responding to the loss of his stillborn son, could extol his behavior: "I knew I could hide my feelings very well. I had learned that and counted it as a strength." It was unthinkable to him that anyone would "try to draw out someone's feelings *unless they wanted to humiliate him or her.*" (Italics added.) He remained thankful for those discreet souls, "for there were times when I was very close to that *fearful state of being out of control of my emotions.*" (Italics added.)[11]

On the other hand, emotional expressiveness is rewarded, not repressed, among women, although women, who increasingly enter into careers governed by male-dominated hierarchies, often feel that they must keep emotions in check as well. Still, nothing in the female role denies them the support of others. In fact, the ability to give and accept nurturing is considered a critical mark of the woman's role.

"When Anna's mastectomy happened, my impression is that everyone has so much fear of the unknown," recalls Lockie. "We all think, 'What should I say, how should I react, am I saying the right thing, how do I talk to her?' My advice for anyone is 'Don't act any other way than you would. Just be there and don't be afraid of it.' " Anna cherishes Lockie for her reaction to her illness. "You crave that! We have normal conversations, but if I want to talk about the disease and what it is doing to me, I can. Some people aren't accepting of that and shy away. It's not easy to listen to someone deal with it and talk about it. Lockie's always been able to listen to this straight on. And I know she's always paying attention. It is not someone going on 'Yeah, yeah, blah de blah' She remembers things that even I don't."

Lockie says, "It's one thing to talk about illness—I've had enough problems to know I can do that—but when someone starts talking about 'How are my kids going to grow up without me?' and 'What my funeral plans are . . .' " Lockie's eyes tear and she can't finish the sentence. She starts again. "I remember the first time Anna started saying those things, I thought, 'Well, isn't this a little weird?' But if she wants to talk about it, that's fine. I don't exactly know what to say because no one's shared these thoughts with me before and isn't it terrific that she can? And I learned from that."

Anna touches Lockie's arm. "With people who aren't as comfortable with letting me deal with this illness on that personal a level, I could say the same thing and they just don't hear it. They shut down. They want to know that everything's 'okay.' " Anna's laugh is hollow. Her thoughts echo those of bereavement counselors; listening—really listening—to a sick or dying friend is key. One doesn't have to act as if one has all the answers. Nor does it help to compare illnesses or spin off to other topics.

If a friend acts as if he or she doesn't want company, it is better to err on the side of persistence. Communicate by E-mail or letters or phone, but keep communicating. With prolonged illness, despair comes when patients think they are forgotten. "I called a close friend I hadn't heard from in six months," says Anna. "She was in my wedding." Anna's openness has its hazards. When her cancer became worse, Anna remarked to her, "I don't know that I'm going to be here in a year." Recalls Anna, "After that, she was scared to call. So I said, 'Don't ever feel afraid to pick up the phone.' "

Denial and avoidance remain strong but injurious forms of dealing with illness. "I know a lot of people who've dealt with me that way," continues Anna. "I have to call them. Sometimes they just don't want to invade, don't want to catch me on a day if I don't feel good. At times you think, 'Well, that's a real cop-out,' but if you have a different personality than mine, you may not think that. I try not to get upset by it. When someone has lost somebody, look at how people duck them! They just don't know what to do or say. And they don't know that *that's* okay. They don't know that they can walk up and say, 'I don't even know what to say,' and the person will be grateful."

Unlike many who find comfort in the ubiquitous support groups now available—for widows or AIDS or cancer or many other illnesses or the grieving—Anna balks at them. "It would be a real search to find a group that's compatible for me. I rely on my friends when I need to vent; I can't see sitting around nit-picking every detail. If it's a cancer support group, I don't know if I would have anything in common except that—and to me it's got to be more. Having breast cancer and going through all of this is an aspect of my life—a damn big one. But to make it all-consuming is a waste of my time. Some of these groups just live and breathe each other's misery.

"This one group was in Ken's office—and I just wanted to smack 'em! I told Suzanne, 'Don't you ever schedule me when these people are in again.' They dwell on it. They're living for their [tumor marker] numbers. Normally, when your numbers go up that's a bad sign. But if a big tumor dies, say, and all these proteins are released at the same time, your numbers can go up too. I want to say, 'Calm down.' One friend in that group is terrified of having a bone marrow transplant; she's got stats on which hospitals have the highest mortality rate. Hey, I don't blame her—but you get ten people in a room all doing that, it would make me crazy. Everybody's going to get different facts. I'd be asking, 'How did you get your facts?' I'd rather find my own."

Anna says her major role is teaching others to know their cases. "The more people can understand it, the more they can make their days better. Those who sit around saying [she whines], 'What can you do?' drive me crazy. Recently I sat next to two ladies in the waiting room both in their early seventies, and they were so sweet. I asked one, 'What are you taking?' and she said, 'I don't know,' and I asked, 'You don't know what chemo you're on?!' and she said, 'Oh, no, I just do what the doctor tells me.' I thought, 'These "gods" don't have the time.' You catch errors if you're familiar with your case. I'm never just going to do what I'm told." Not once in this continuing conversation does Anna use the word "cancer" or the term "terminal illness," referring only to "it." "I know there are a lot of people who are afraid of it—and yet, if they try to hide in a box, they don't know what that's doing to them and everybody around them. To me, the scariest thing in the world is fear. That drives people in such negative ways. The more we can learn and take the fear away, the better off we are."

Do you find that people who are ill take their cue from you, because you make it easy for them to talk, or for healthy friends to gripe about something as trivial as a head cold? "Oh, yes. I've had friends actually apologize because they forget that I can't quite keep up. I'm glad they don't need to think about it and can regard me as one of them." Other patients seek Anna out because of her attitude. "One woman and I had chemo at the same time and I went bopping in with a movie. She was very depressed because her cancer recurred after thirteen years. And I had her in hysterics by the time we were out. And I know people who have felt *guilty;* one friend felt she needed to have as bad a breast cancer as I did because 'what happens if Anna goes and I don't?' "

Anna pauses and then shifts into a quieter tone. "It's very hard to go on living. I felt that way when Mom died. I felt terrible that I was going on and she wasn't. That I would see the sunrise and she wouldn't. And it was all about the things that I felt bad about—for *me.* But I think that's what this grief business is about—feeling *loss* and missing someone in *your* life. The person who is dead doesn't have a clue. Grieving is a very selfish act—but it has to be. You're feeling bad for the person who is dying, but you're feeling sad for yourself. They are going to be in your life as memory or inspiration or whatever—but the future with the person has been severed.

"I've always said that being the patient in a weird way is the 'escapist route.' " She exhales a shaky you-won't-understand-that laugh. "It sounds stupid, but it is." Anna's thoughts echo Thomas Mann, who wrote, "A man's dying is more the survivor's affair than his own." Says Anna, "I-don't-have-to-continue-this. When I've been sick in the hospital, I think, 'What do I have to do?' " Anna does her slightly dopey dog voice. " 'I'll just wait for the nurse. I don't have to do *anything.*' Jan has to do it all. Sure, you're suffering in a different way, in terms of removal from life. But it's very different than the people who are facing the loss of this person being out of their lives. I think it's harder."

Now Anna says fiercely, "In order to help each other, people need to read and learn about death and dying and long-term illness." Many people looking at this subject from the outside feel humbled, that they could never behave the way Anna and others have. Anna is told about one man who was praised for the brave way he handled his cancer; he stopped the compliments with a rhetorical question, "What choice do I have?" Anna nods her head. "We're very adaptable creatures. The kids and I and Jan have learned to take a day at a time. When I wake up it's a brand-new day. I don't know if I can get up. I don't know if I can walk to the end of the room. I don't know if my muscles will work. I don't know if I've got red cells that day. I don't know what this disease has in store. It's a little different every day. They have to pretty much take their cue from me as to what I can accomplish that day. If I say to Lindsay, 'I can't drive' and it's a ballet day, we have to work out other transportation. I can't push myself."

It is Sunday, before dawn; the illuminated hands on the clock say five in the morning. Anna wakes Jan and her children in the darkness. In silent stupor, they drive through quiet streets to the nearby beach. All is still and dark in the houses that nestle on the beach. They stumble down the driftwood-colored steps and hear hard slapping waves. One huge house, shuttered and surrounded by palm trees, is barely lit by the moon; the scene evokes the setting of a tropics novel by Graham Greene. In the far distance at Cape Canaveral, a vertical light glows. "That has to be the space rocket," says Jan. An unmanned satellite will soon be launched. To many, the marvel of space has become routine; no one else watches from the beach, this launch will not make the papers, but to Anna and her family, it remains a marvel not to be missed.

The children shiver, stamp their feet, race around to get warm. Lindsay is learning the lyrics to the musical *Oklahoma* and she starts with "OOOOOOOklahoma," which trails off into giggles. "I'm just a girl who cain't say no" has better success and the family sings together. The wait is longer than scheduled. Just as Lindsay races back to the car to see if there is a launch announcement on the radio, the rocket glows. "Lindsay, it's taking off!" shouts Anna. They all yell, "Come back!"

She makes it back to the beach just as a strong glow of fuel seems to suspend the rocket off the ground for seconds and then it mounts up and up, arcing into the air, and looks as if it is coming straight toward the Johannessens. "It's higher up than it looks," says Jan, the scientist. Ellery asks, "Is it into space yet?" "Not quite." The first separation leaves a small trail of vapors. Then comes the second. A golden ball unfurls, splashing across the darkened sky; colors begin to spread, gold, blue, and at the top left, brilliant red. Behind, the trail is a distinct white arc. Everyone oohs and aahs, especially Anna. "It's magical!" she shouts, using her favorite word for things or people she feels are extraordinary. Everyone talks at once about what they can see in the unusual remains of the second separation—a duck, some strange animal with a tutu, a racing dog—the magic of it spreading and changing minute by minute. As it opens further, the center takes the shape of a billowing skirt, then drifts outward with a hole in the center. Scientific explanations are forgotten, even by Jan, in the glory of a unique moment and a cloud unlike any they have seen.

As it fades and the sun begins its competing glow, Ellery and Lindsay play tag, racing and giggling, coming too close to Anna. "This is an out-of-bounds zone," she warns. The next time, she says forcefully, "Don't play that close! I don't want you bumping into me so that I take a tumble." They calm down and soon the four of them walk arm in arm down the beach. Ellery is especially protective and solicitous, giving her hugs. The horizon glows in the dawning of a new morning. As they walk back up to the car, Anna and Jan give each other a special hug.

"Just think, Nils!" says Anna, as he touches her face with a kiss and she tucks this cherished morning away in her memory. "That rocket's probably halfway round the world by now."

CHAPTER TEN

Riding the Roller Coaster

Anna returns from Florida rested and a bit energized by the shots that had boosted her red and white cells. Now she and Jan are experiencing anxiety again; it is time to get the results of her chemo treatments. Conquering fear through knowledge, an Anna axiom, is not always possible. "When I have to wait for results, I go crazy. I hear what Ken says, but I can't make a decision quick enough, I can't help participate in the next step. I need to think about it by myself, absorb it, before I can do anything."

A few days later, Anna has an MRI to determine whether the tumors have responded, standard practice after two cycles. She wonders and worries for a week, until the reports are back. Anna sits down as Miller reads her results from the report issued to him by the radiologist. Based on their comparison to Anna's "most recent MRI in July," he says, Miller recommends that Anna stay on the treatment. Anna sits there thinking, This has to be a slip of the tongue. This can't be happening to me! Her last MRI had *not* been in July of 1995, but *October*—just before Anna started her two-month chemo treatment in November. Anna looks at the report. "They *did* screw up!" She exclaims later, "The radiologist, who gets around fifteen hundred dollars for this procedure and analysis, compared my current MRI to the *wrong* set of films. And Ken made a decision to continue his treatment from the wrong files!" Anna angrily alerted Miller's office of the misreading. "The upshot of this reevaluation," says Anna, "is that Ken reassessed my treatment and completely changed his mind, halting the Mitomycin. So I am *now* on this brand-new drug that Ken found—it's called Arimidex—which shuts off the production of estrogen right at the adrenal gland faucet!"

Despite the error, Anna empathizes with Miller, "who is so overloaded." Does that bother you? "He's no different than anyone else. That's the scary part. There's been such an explosion of cancer. It's the same, I'm sure, for doctors who treat AIDS patients—they barely have time." Jan thinks that the genesis of the mixed-up report was probably a clerical error, a clerk for the radiologist pulling the wrong file. It took Anna, the vigilant patient, to notice. For the next thirty days, Anna will be free of chemo, taking only the Arimidex pill. "From what I've read—Jan pulled three abstracts from the science Internet—it seems like this is going to be a cakewalk. A good thirty percent of the women in one large study had absolute stability for twelve months." After one month of treatment, Anna will be checked and possibly go back on chemo. "So isn't that nuts? Had I not said, 'Hello-oh,' they would have not taken this adventurous treatment, which I'm all for."

Miller understands his patients' emotional need for quick results. "It's hard to live waiting for results. *Very* hard. It's possible that I may have spoken with Anna about the written report without having looked at the films myself because I was trying to answer her needs." Anna holds no grudge; Ken had in fact previously mentioned that Arimidex would probably be the next course of action. It would just have taken a little longer. "Human error is acceptable and undeniable. But when I found the error, that's what makes Ken such a good doctor. I am so happy that he is not one of the many arrogant M.D.'s who does not listen to his patients and does not allow himself to change his mind because he thinks he is never wrong in the first place. He was right on with Arimidex. It couldn't have been on the market for more than two weeks. My pharmacy had never heard of it and had to call the manufacturer. So I'm very, very happy that Ken stays on top of it pretty well. Plus his connections with Johns Hopkins and NIH [National Institutes of Health] help."

Now Anna is concentrating on another chemo holiday. "I think I'm going to have the best thirty days of my life. I get to grow more hair. And it's just going to be a fun time." She does not look ahead to the possibility of more debilitating chemo treatments. Her current half-joking comment is "As long as I can have hair in the winter and go bald later, I'll be fine. It's great to have hair around your neck when it's freezing outside."

* * *

As each February day dawns colder and grayer than the last, Anna sinks into worries and depression, exhausted from neuropathy pain and hot flashes that remain months after stopping Taxol and tamoxifen. Now Anna takes a white pill each night at dinner—Arimidex, the hormone blocker—and has had no side affects. It is too soon for an MRI to see if the tumors have decreased. The pain from nerve damage seems unending. "God, when is it ever going to stop? This is enough! Going down steps is really scary, because I don't feel my feet landing, all I know about having hit the stair is that my knees jerk. And my back is spasmed lately. Jan massages me at night."

One night, Anna tells Jan that she is "so depressed by all of this. In one sense I am grateful for these drugs, which are fighting a disease to keep me alive, but it's taking my life in a different way. One day, you stop and look in the mirror and say, 'Who in the hell are you?' I feel sorry for Jan and I told him, 'It's not fair. You're now married to a different person. The person you married is stuck in a body that doesn't work the way it used to.' And then I said, 'Maybe I'm addicted to the Percocet, maybe I'm actually fine.' Jan looked at me like I had three eyes. He said that it was stupid to think that was the problem. Still, I said, 'I'm not taking any painkillers today because I don't want to be addicted to Percocet.' So I don't take it until I'm in so much pain that I'm curled up in a ball. It's totally stupid, I know. What it's come down to is a battle for control—'Dammit, I'm going to make that decision.' Really pathetic, but that's what I do."

Still, nothing is so bad as Anna's lowest ebb in May and June of 1995, when the double dose of Taxol caused searing pain. "I thought, 'Dying has to be easier than this. If you die, you're not going to feel this bad anymore. You will feel nothing.' One night I woke up screaming, thinking I was being burned alive! It takes a lot to have pain interfere with my life, but I was suffering more from the treatment than the cancer.

"No, I never considered suicide. I just felt dying would be easier. I've actually thought, 'Wouldn't it be chic to think of suicide?' You meet a lot of intense people who've thought about it, so I said maybe I should be thinking about suicide, but it's just not my personality. The only time I can think of it is in terms of the Kevorkian effect. If I get to the point where

I am so sick, I hope the old morphine comes out and I'm overdosed. I don't want to lay around and be a vegetable and just drag on and on. I would much prefer 'Give that girl the overdose' and let me go on my way."

It has been coldly cruel, the winter of discontent for everybody who lives in or around the nation's capital. Anna notices that Jan is also depressed and frustrated at work. Talk switches to the natural depression that cold weather and sunlight deprivation can cause. "I have a friend who does not acknowledge the month of February at all," says Anna, laughing. "He goes into January thirty-second, January forty-seventh and forty-eighth, to the first of March. There just is no February."

Have you thought about light treatment? "I had a girlfriend who had the bulbs replaced in her office with that kind of lighting, but, no. Actually," she says, "I've thought of just taking a vacation by myself, to get somewhere warm and sunny. But I figure we need to keep each other bolstered up; Jan needs me now." Anna sighs. Her losses are so abiding. "I get up, help clean around the house a little, dust furniture, the easiest job I could find so I wouldn't get tired. I went out Saturday afternoon with two girlfriends to have lunch. That's all I did. I was so exhausted from pain, I had to take a two-hour nap to be able to go to the Ice Capades with Lindsay. Walking up and down those arena steps just about killed me. Thank God I had handicapped parking."

Do you need a Dottie person for yourself? Brushing off the question, Anna says, "I really don't think I need to yet." She is eking out the days until a Mexico vacation with Jan, planned for April. "We can talk then. I tell him everything, so it's not as though it's all bottled up inside. I think that what I'm going through is real normal and when the weather gets nice again and I'm out there planting bulbs and growing my vegetables and all that, it'll go away." It doesn't occur to her that Jan might need a rest from her problems, nor has Jan made a move to find counseling. "I know I agreed with Dottie when she suggested it for us . . . but I'm not there yet."

Toward the end of February, Anna sits down to write about "Who I am, how I feel, and why." Putting one's feelings on paper is a commonly recommended therapy, but Anna does it with extraordinarily reflective wisdom. "Often I am so busy doing and forging along, that I recognize the need to stop and reflect on my feelings, and it helps to write them down. Managing my cancer is quite time-consuming, so there has not been much time to articulate how I feel. I am usually too busy fighting this report or questioning that doctor or reading about treatment options, or dealing with family and the kids. I am not good at reading self-help books nor, as you know, do I feel compelled to join a support group and spend endless hours talking about the disease. It's a waste of my time.

"First the negative, what I call 'let's be gloomy and feel sorry for ourselves.' So, how do I feel about cancer? I was quite shocked when it returned in '94." Anna returns to her basic theme—the more she knows about her disease, the less her panic. The more control she has over treatment, "the easier I can cope with knowing I will die of this disease. Fighting my cancer daily on a physical and mental level helps to keep me alive. Yet I know that this disease is taking me away piece by piece, and I am filled with hatred over the vile, contemptible way that this cancer has opted to claim my life.

"I had always wished that when I died, it would be sudden and painless because I dreaded losing myself, my dignity, my very essence, to something so slowly consuming. Imagine being strapped down and eaten alive by some small tiny bugs that crawl all over you. In a way, that's cancer. Something is eating me up inside and I cannot stop it, I cannot kill it, and it is maniacally consuming me one piece at a time. And I do feel it! Not only do I feel the pain from the nerve damage left by the Taxol, but I feel the pain from the liver tumors, from the rib, from the small bump on my chest. I feel it every day and it is a constant reminder that cancer is so fucking cruel that it tears at my soul. We are a civilized society and I hate to see that anyone should have to suffer chronically, much less me! I search for the reason why, intellectually. What is the purpose to all of this?

"My girlfriend Nancy Bauer sent me Viktor Frankl's *Man's Search for Meaning.* He articulates certain things that I have accidentally encountered and realized about suffering, pain, and death; how we suffer is one way we give meaning to our lives." Anna adds wryly, "I find this true but quite bothersome—I would rather find other ways to obtain meaning that aren't so morosely productive. I am a happy soul by nature and dwelling simply on suffering gets on my nerves! So hence my search continues."

Two months later, Anna's search for meaning takes on a more sanguine note. "Sorrows, death, and dying are necessary dimensions to living. Grief and loss are such critical dimensions that require more individual, private, personal attention than we've given it, but look how it has been sensationalized out of all meaning in America! Here's today, the anniversary of the Oklahoma bombing, and they're beating us over the head with it all day on television. It takes away the personalness of the incident—they've taken a human tragedy and made it a circus." With feigned pathos, TV commentators position themselves among the genuinely tearful survivors for their broadcasts. "Out of that tragedy there may be some act that will profoundly affect people's lives in a meaningful way. But it's not going to come from those tacky newscasters."

Anna says she can't imagine a life without turmoil or sorrow or tragedy.

"What would people know about really appreciating what they have without it?" She speaks of her friend Jane Bittner, whose son was killed four years ago in a motorcycle accident. Sometimes when Bittner talks about the accident, raw tears still come, but Anna feels her friend has grown through her tragedy. "She now sees the world very differently and appreciates so much more what she sees. This is the first brand-new ballet she's choreographed in years and I'm feeling like she's a new bird spreading her wings and part of what's happening is that Carl's right there with her in her head. I don't know that she thought of him every single day when he was alive, because, with all of us, the kids are just there. You take your life so for granted before something bad happens. Jane puts a smile on her face and she's amazing. I'm not saying there's a good side, but she's found strength and beauty from her loss and made wonderful things from it. I think everybody's capable of that in time, if they can get out of themselves a bit.

"Anyway, Jane and I were sitting together the other day and we talked about how we were not afraid to die. She's had to live with one of the worst things in life, her child dying. I think there's a natural order to life, but I don't believe that there's a 'religious rule book.' Everybody says, 'Well, do you believe in this and do you believe in that?' And I just say, 'Well, I don't have a rule book.' Somehow there's just a natural order to the universe and I'm just a piece of that order and that's fine. As I die, something else will be born and on goes creation. I feel worse for the people left who have to grieve for me."

When Anna was writing in February of 1996, her anger was not about dying, but about the form it was taking. "As happy as I am to be alive and set an example to my children and friends about boldly facing this disease and continuing on with my life, I hate the fact that I will have to die a slow death. I hate it for my family, who will have to endure such long-term suffering. I, at least, will see an end to it, but they will suffer even longer. The sense of responsibility that I am the cause of this pain is depressing." She repeats her helpless anger about treatment for cancer being such a crapshoot.

"So, there is my anger. Anger at the disease, at the medical community, anger that I probably won't see and participate in important moments of my kids' lives, anger that my entire family will have to suffer and probably suffers each day right now as they gaze at me. Suffering and joy are intermingled. We're happy I am here, but we suffer the terrors of the unknown of how much time we have together. At this point, my kids do not know for sure that my disease is terminal. They keep thinking that I can be cured. I have had to make a solid choice about when will be the right time for them to know the entire truth. I refuse to tell them something like this when, in fact, I could still live on for years. Why make them more sad and more miserable?"

Anna leaps to another thought. "Then too, there is plain old embarrassment. Did you ever feel like you overstayed your welcome? This is another reason for wishing for a fast death. I guess I'll just call myself a clinging vine. One feels like an albatross. Everyone could get on with their lives and not worry about me if I just died out now. Having cancer is as much about the people around you, those you love, as it is about you, the patient, dealing with it. On an optimistic note, if you asked my family which they would prefer, keeping me around would be their choice. The patient feels he or she is causing a burden, but the love my family feels makes caring for me a joy as much as it is a task. How does one separate the two? Can't be done."

Anna fears for something she could never become. "Another odd feeling that my change has brought is that I am becoming a boring person. When I was working and interacting more with others, I felt useful, knowledgeable, and a part of life. Self-doubt was nonexistent when it came to feeling whether I had anything worthwhile to contribute to a conversation. That has changed since this recurrence—because I am not working now and my exposure to adults is limited because I physically do not have the stamina. I now feel stupid—yep, that's it, plain and simple—I feel stupid. I fear going to dinner parties because I am quite convinced that I will have nothing of interest to add to the conversation, unless it is to talk about the latest events regarding my disease. I even believe that I am deadly dull to my husband. I know that this is untrue on an intellectual plane. I had a girlfriend who went through exactly the same situation. As a homemaker, she became convinced that she was a noncontributing member of society, could not socially carry on, and finally went back to work. However, I never viewed her in that negative fashion. It is this remembrance of her feelings versus reality that keeps me from going off the deep end."

Her writing sounds so much like Anna talks that one can almost hear Anna taking a breath, and then going on, as she writes, "So, are we depressed yet? That is a very quirky aspect to me." Anna repeats her inability to remain depressed—"regardless of how much I hurt—the latest bad cancer news, the weather, a friend dying. I have my odd day of sobbing, curled up in bed feeling sorry for myself, but then something just happens. I make plans for something fun to occur. I create more goals and volunteer for something that will be a challenge and VOILÀ, depression is gone. I don't get caught up in the quagmire of my own martyrdom.

"Now on the positive side. If anyone can lick this disease by sheer willpower, I can. I love my life. I have too much to do yet, although I am in a holding pattern while focusing my energies on staying healthy and fighting this bloody disease. I want to grow old with Nils and retire on a perfect sunny island. I want to see my grandchildren and laugh at my kids when they start dealing with the issues that are forever circular. I want to help my children through the trials of teenage life and have long conversations with them over the merest trivia or world issues. I want to write again, and maybe direct a show again, and maybe work again! There are too many places I have yet to explore, so damn it, cancer, just go somewhere else!

"I have had a very meaningful and wonderful life, providing joy and laughter to my family and friends. Although I am not religious at all, I have treated others with respect and care. I feel very much loved by a large number of friends whose lives I have touched. My greatest joys come from hard work and having fun with other people—doing things for people that make them smile and ease their burdens."

Anna changes gears and turns to decision making during prolonged illness. "When I realized the cancer was back, I made the decision to get my personal affairs organized. I do not believe that it would be considerate to leave all my final wishes and arrangements to Nils. The poor man will have enough on his plate. So, I called the funeral home and got a price list so that Jan can follow my wishes and I will have it all written out. I wrote up a telephone tree for him too. This will eliminate his need to be on the phone to pass on the news because others can take that list and do the phoning. I will write my own obituary too—this way the facts will be right. My will and his are sort of up to date and as written are okay. I am having the car transferred into his name once I really get sick. These little things will make life easier on him. [Wrestling with the bureaucracy over changing credit cards, titles to cars or property, is not only overwhelming at the time of the death of a loved one, but a constant jarring reminder every time one has to write "deceased" on a piece of paper or supply a death certificate.]

"It is unconscionable for a perfectly capable person who endures a long-term illness to leave these chores undone," explodes Anna. "It is selfish and truly cruel to leave it all to the relatives, who must cope with the pain, the loss and grieving. And again it allows me a sense of control which provides me that feeling of mental peace."

A month later, in March, although Anna's physical strength has improved and she is continuing with Arimidex, death is on her mind. "It has been a week of funerals," she explains. The Sunday before, March 10, Anna and Jan were waiting at the St. Francis Bereavement Center while Lindsay and Ellery had their session with Dottie Ward-Wimmer. Anna checked their home phone answering service for messages and heard a friend's voice telling them that Lockie's father had died. "He was getting to the stage where he was going to have to go to a nursing home. It was a blessing for them all, including his wife, Alice, who is very religious," says Anna. She is so close to Anna that Anna is the second listing in her prayer book, after Lockie and her now deceased husband. Lockie drove from her parents' home in Danville, Virginia, to Charlottesville to tell her brother in person; his wife, a heavy smoker, was dying of throat cancer and Lockie didn't want to break it to him on the phone. That same week, Lockie's brother watched his wife, Nan, die.

Lockie told Anna and other friends not to come for her father's funeral. "I'll just be so busy and I won't have time to spend with you." Anna replied, "I'm coming. And you'll be glad I did." Anna refused to take Lockie's request seriously because Anna had her own memories. "When Mom died, I had no friends there, it was all family, and sometimes friends are as close, if not closer, than family." Anna reiterates to others what counselors feel; good friends should err on the side of persistent caring, rather than take grieving friends at their word.

The "Richmond contingent" went to the funeral. When Wayne saw them, he said, "What is it about you women? Is this *The Big Chill* [referring to the 1980s movie about boomers bonding at a funeral]?" "Yes," Anna replied. "Hey, she needs us and we're here."

And Anna was correct. "When she saw us, Lockie, who just doesn't cry around others, burst into tears. Just the hug around the shoulder was important. Lockie was able to laugh and reminisce. Her family is very formal southern, an old Virginia blood family. Lockie never felt that unconditional love outwardly and her friends gave it to her. She was very touched." Once again, Anna uses the funeral to offer a lesson on life to her children. "Lindsay was there when I walked in crying. They knew I was going to Danville for Lockie's dad's funeral. I told them how important it was for Lockie and that this is what friendship is all about."

Anna's caring is deepened by her own feelings of loss, a sensitivity that the seriously ill often develop. She also purposefully spent time with Lockie's mother and the brother who had lost his wife. "He had had the time and had reached a sense of acceptance. He was very pleased with the hospice people who cared for his wife and told me that he would never have traded these times with Nan, that the illness had made them closer. I was able to tell him about Frankl's book. He hadn't read it in twenty years and was going to reread it. I also could help Lockie about the legal aspects—multiple copies of the death certificate and so forth. And I sang all five choruses of 'Amazing Grace.' First time I've ever done *that* for anybody."

Back home, exhausted both mentally and physically, Anna falls into bed but can't sleep. It is another evening of conversation in bed with Jan. Anna wonders how many more deaths she will witness now that she is getting to an age when friends have parents who are dying. For those living with life-threatening illness, funerals are always reminders of their own sickness. She tells Jan about how she and Nan had sat together a year ago, "talking about how we were both going to lick this thing. We were both so positive. I am sad she's not here—but I'm feeling so damn good right now. I feel like I've cured this thing." She laughs. "Then I start to think, 'If I'm feeling this great, is the cancer feeling this good too?' I used to tell myself when I was feeling so rotten that somehow my system was working away at those damn tumors."

So Anna, six weeks off chemo, is now worried about feeling good. "I just don't trust Arimidex. It's treating only a *part* of the cancer. With chemo, you know something is dying." Anna wants something to kill the cancer tumors, period, not just halt them at the current stage. "I don't want to waste time by not taking chemo." Once again, Anna rides the roller coaster; panic takes over as she waits for her checkup next week to see what's happened with Arimidex.

On a positive note, Anna says that Lindsay and Ellery can't wait for their sessions with Dottie. "I don't hear the clay wall being slammed on so much. It's a great release for anger, but now she has gone on to other activities. I think they need that. But last night, Ellery was upstairs and I heard that clay wall thump-thump, so he must have been really working stuff out. I'm reading and laughing to myself—'Wow! I've got to throw a couple.' The stairs are a hard climb for me, but I went up and threw a couple of times for fun. I was amazed I still could throw and I could actually hit what I targeted. It's a neat wall. The whole place is. I said to the kids, 'Think of all these children who are coming here—instead of throwing toys away, you can donate things for all these little kids."

Ellery and Lindsay see their counselor separately—"They have different issues that have come up over the school year," says their mom. Anna likes that because one of them stays downstairs to keep her company. "We have a good time goofing around, sampling the various hot chocolates and other goodies that are in the front hall." Neither Jan nor Anna has ever probed what the children do or discuss with Dottie and there are few gleanings from their conversations.

On the way into the center from Olney that day, Ellery asks his mother incessant, curious questions. "Do you believe in heaven?" "What happens when you die?" "Are you afraid to die?" "How long will my grandfathers live?" and finally, "Mom, how long do you think you will live?" Anna answers, "I don't know." Ellery says, "I talked to Missy [a friend who is Jewish] and she said that in her religion they believe that when you die, the soul gets released and then it gets to go somewhere. So what does that really mean, Mom?" Answer: "Hey, I don't know. Where does it get released to? Good question."

From Ellery's conversation with Anna after his session, she knows that a relaxed Ellery has asked Dottie similar questions. "She didn't try to answer the unknowable and took an ambivalent course so that he could help make up his own mind," says Anna. "I think that's neat. And she told him she hoped I would be around a long time. So it's really interesting and they have someplace to talk and think."

That night as the children get ready for bed, Anna turns to Jan and says, " 'You're going next time. You cannot *not* be a part of this—too much is going on. Too many interesting things, too many questions are coming out of Ellery's mouth, and I don't want this experience just to be associated with me. That's not right. You have to be there because this is going to eventually be a family thing.' " Anna speaks so fervently to him that Jan agrees quickly. Anna recalls, "When I told him all these things that came out of Ellery's mouth, he realized he was missing the boat."

Anna treasures the conversation she overheard that afternoon, driving Lindsay and Ellery home. They were talking about playing with the sandbox. Lindsay had drawn a big heart in the center. "Where are you?" Dottie had asked. "In the center of the heart," Lindsay replied. Dottie asked, "Where's your mom?"

"My mom *is* the heart."

Anna finds solace in such moments. Little does she know that in a few weeks, she will be savoring many more.

CHAPTER ELEVEN

Reprieve

Anna sits in the doctor's office with her mouth agape. She has trouble absorbing the news on this April day. Then, with mouth still wide open, a grin starts to spread. Her tumors have shrunk dramatically—eight, many of them large, have vanished and only two remain. As she walks out, a numbed Anna says, "I guess I'm in remission!" A few weeks later, Anna bubbles away. "I feel like a whole different person. Now I can deal with the pain to a degree because I stay busy and divert myself. I didn't have the energy to do that before. So far, Arimidex has no side effects. If there were, it's worth it for the benefit I'm getting from the drug. For me, the benefits are tremendous."

For the first time in weeks, Anna shows up for ballet, cuing recorded music as Lindsay and four others swoop out as fireflies, then laughing as they leap and wings pop and molt onto the floor. Anna jokes, "Got to fix those firefly butts." She plants bulbs and seeds and tomatoes, even plays softball with the community team, hitting solidly while someone runs for her. She delights in walking the dogs, no task for sissies. "Being able to walk the dogs for an hour this morning and feel good about it!" she marvels, as if she has just won the lottery. "I won't poop out till eight or nine tonight."

Despite her joy, Anna is bombarded by yet another emotion. She is plagued by feeling like "the guest who won't go away." During this "stay of execution," Anna jokes, "What did the dying person say to the doctor when she learned she was getting better? 'Oh, hell. I've just ruined the makings of a really good funeral party!' Well, that is my condition now. I was prepared to die and no one knows what's happening now.

The price for remission is uncertainty every day. When I knew I was fighting death, I was able to make the most of each day because in the back of my mind, this was it. But now I am lazy and actually more depressed at times because what I am fighting is not clear anymore. How do I keep fighting when I am winning?! What horrible thing could I do to accidentally change it? I so desperately want to be normal again!

"*I don't have any answers!* Jan tries to reassure me to just enjoy myself, be a mom to the kids and hang loose. He is right—but it doesn't stop me from wondering and fearing." Anna is told that there is even a name for what she is going through—*Lazarus syndrome,* as in rising from the dead. "Well, it's nice to know you're not original," she says dryly, "but it's interesting to find out there is a pattern." As described by Dr. Stephen P. Hersh, when a person has a life-threatening illness, the patient and family accommodate to the decline. "Then, unexpectedly, the ill person's heath improves. . . . Experiences like these are emotionally wrenching, especially for family members. All are challenged by the sudden need to shift expectations." Patients have guilt for the burden they perceive they have become and families have guilt because they have indulged in secret thoughts that it is, indeed, time to go.[1]

"There's a tension, an anxiety, that being ill puts on everyone around you," says Anna. "No matter what I say or do, I can't stop my friends from worrying or wanting to do things for me. At times, I say, 'Stop, it's enough.' Now I worry that they're going to want to do more to keep me better. I'm constantly on the receiving end and can't give back.

"I know it's all in my mind, but you feel like you're letting people down in a different way," says Anna. "When you're told that someone is very ill, you think about your life without that person and the difficulties ahead. Everybody's doing that with me and all of a sudden it seems like I'm better. And they're thinking, 'Is this some kind of a bad joke? Are you going to get better and then, boom, get worse?' It's almost even a bigger piece of gloom hanging over them.

"This respite is very, very nice but can be confusing. I'm sure the shoe is out there. How big it is, when it'll drop, I don't know." Anna's optimism returns. "I'm going to get some very good months out of this. A year ago, Arimidex wasn't available. That's what's so neat. Maybe something else new will come along that even will be better."

Anna faces a new challenge. "It's odd, but I don't think I am any good at prioritizing all of this 'free time.' There's a part of me, the person I was before I got sick, that's resurfacing—'You should get a job again, you should contribute, this is *living*!' The other part of me says, 'No, no, no! Even more than when you were sick, enjoy this day, because it may be taken away from you tomorrow.' And Jan helps me to stop and say, 'Don't go get a job. Keep doing all the special things you wanted to do when you thought that was the last you'd ever see of that.' "

Jan's hopes soar. "He's doing a lot of 'Oh, boy, she's in good shape; let's take advantage of it.' We're trying to get to Canada and the Outer Banks this summer, and Jan's considering a science meeting in San Francisco in the fall." Anna adds, "I look at all the slack Jan took up and I feel terrible. More than ever, the kitchen is a foreign place." She laughs. "I don't speak the language—I can't communicate with that room."

This new lease on life, has it made you able to say, *"Que será, será"*?

"Oh, absolutely! If I got hit by a truck today, hey, I wasn't supposed to be here, this has all been a gift. Plus, if I get hit, there's a folder and Jan can say, 'Okay, here's the funeral, here's why I need this many death certificates, here's her insurance policy.' He will be able to sort through things in a heartbeat." At her most optimistic, Anna reveals why she can so breezily make end-of-life plans. "This can all be real—but part of me thinks it never will happen, the part that says, 'Hey, I'm gonna lick this sucker.' "

On May 3, Anna and Jan drive to Johns Hopkins in Baltimore to see Nancy Davidson, the oncologist who had shown them the disastrous "sausages in my liver" X rays seventeen months ago. Anna seeks a magic bullet as she asks Davidson if there is anything else she can do. Davidson greets Jan and Anna pleasantly but is not effusive. Slim and tall, Davidson wears minimal makeup, a white T-shirt, red jacket, navy skirt and tights, and blue flats. They sit in a small room, knees almost touching.

Anna's X rays are slapped up on the light box on the wall. "See all of these guys have disappeared," says Anna, glowing. "Since Arimidex, I have just two little guys." Davidson and Anna discuss medications. Anna tells Davidson that she takes sleeping pills nightly. Never an insomniac before her cancer recurred, Anna thinks that one of the reasons is "I feel I have to be awake—I don't want to miss a minute of my life." Such a reaction depends on the individual; for some, tension, exhaustion, pain, and depression causes sluggishness and withdrawal.

Anna asks the doctor, "The big question is, What do I do now?"

"Okay," she replies. Behind a curtain, Davidson palpates Anna's stomach, pushing down around the liver. Then they are back sitting with Jan. "Well, I wouldn't change a thing," Davidson says. "You look very good, you're feeling well, you're not having any side effects."

Anna asks why hormone-blocking medication—without chemotherapy—is working. "All of a sudden, we've gone whomp with hormones only, and even the bones have cleaned up, so we're definitely somewhat confused."

"Hormone-dependent or -independent cancers, both are going to respond to chemotherapy," explains Davidson. "But hormone-dependent cancers are more likely to respond to hormones. I'd stay with the Arimidex."

Davidson quietly inserts a reality check; they will dot her conversation. "In all the times we've talked, we've talked about the fact that we're not going to cure this illness, right? And that the goal of our therapy just is to let you and the breast cancer live in harmony with each other—and at this point, you seem to be very harmonious." Anna voices concerns about Arimidex not lasting longer than nine to twelve months in clinical trials. Davidson says, "The natural history of metastatic breast cancer is that it's intrinsically resistant; it may get better for a while, but cancer cells are smart and they've learned how to get around it. So they start growing again. Arimidex is very useful and has a niche, but it's not going to be any more or less effective than other kinds of hormones that are available."

Anna twice returns to her sister's theme, voicing doubts about not having had an adrenalectomy. Davidson demurs, reiterating Dr. Miller's argument that chemicals are just as effective. "What about the bone marrow transplant?" ask Anna and Jan. "No," Davidson responds flatly, noting that Anna's cancer has not been adequately responsive to chemotherapy, a major component of bone marrow transplants. "With a transplant, anything could happen. I was never really enthusiastic about that for you.

"When Arimidex stops working," Davidson says, "there are other hormone blockers and chemotherapies to try. That's the time to go into your information-gathering mode again—call me or yack with those guys at the NCI and Georgetown and see if there's anything that interests you that's available then. One thing about investigational therapy, as you know well, is that they come and go and only a few pan out." Davidson cautions Anna to stay with these three "really good breast institutions" at hand rather than seek distant cancer centers. "There isn't one area so incredibly promising that you would want to do that. We would all know about it immediately. It's an information society and we would all be doing it because we're not anxious to mess around with ideas if somebody else has a better mousetrap."

"Well, I'm definitely on my information-seeking track," says Anna, "but I agree with staying on the Arimidex and riding it out. At least I will have gotten extra months."

Anna leaves, fiercely punching an elevator button. "Well, it's nice to know I'm still gonna die." Still, Davidson's negative assessments do not bother her. "She has a very logical, earnest manner. I get irritated with people who've seen her and come out devastated because they think she was cold. That woman is not cold. But she's very scientific, which is good because I don't need to be patted on the back. I want to hear the truth." Anna is a doctor's dream in that regard, no matter how emotionally difficult her questions may be to answer. Many patients avoid the truth as long as possible.

On the drive home, Anna still obsesses about the adrenalectomy. "I'm a victim of time. Seven years ago, tamoxifen had just come out; it was working but wasn't time tested. None of this stuff has been out long enough to know its long-term efficiency versus the adrenalectomy. Had we done that maybe seven years ago, who knows? God, I hope Ro doesn't beat herself silly someday going, 'Dammit, she should have done this,' because it may not have made a difference, you know?" Jan lets Anna ruminate on an issue so hard to put to rest. Many months later, Jan admits that for both of them, "the doubt always remained. I can tell you it was never resolved."

Anna digs for reassuring nuggets. "Nancy kinda said, 'Keep on going until they come up with something new.' Who knows, I might hit the jackpot. But again it's very patient proactive! I'll have to circle like the hawk to find something we think is right and then ask about it." Jan tries to reassure her, repeating Davidson's comment that any extremely effective treatment would be picked up instantly everywhere."You still have to monitor the situation," says Anna, adding lightly, "They're not going to keep a little note that says 'Call Anna.' " Jan smiles. Anna shrugs. "So, what the hell. This is just a reprieve—but we'll take it. That's fine with me."

On June 1, 1996, Anna trots off to the wedding of her former Happy Feet partner, Connie Giordano. A year earlier, while Anna was still on the debilitating Taxol, Giordano told her, "I have a big favor to ask—I want you to be my matron of honor." Anna started crying. "To see Anna cry is very unusual," recalls Giordano. Anna said to her, "You've given me another goal to shoot for." It cannot be stressed too much that the best friends are those who treat the sick naturally, to "give them another goal to shoot for," even the simplest venture or moment that can be shared. At the time, Jan felt it was problematic that Anna would make it, but said nothing.

Shortly before the ceremony, Anna excitedly called Giordano. "I've found a pair of shoes!" she fairly shouted. "I'm getting feeling back in my feet and I'm gonna *dance* at your wedding." Says Giordano later, "And I mean she danced. She had a great time."

In mid-June, Anna meets a friend for lunch at The Cheesecake Factory. She looks fresh in a white T-shirt under a long, sleeveless denim summer dress. She wears earrings and, for the first time in months, a trace of lipstick. Her thick hair needs shaping, but Anna cannot bear to cut an inch. Anna sips a concoction of Chambord and juices and explodes with her latest project, producing pictures of her Richmond house surrounded by greenery. To the uninitiated, it looks like bushes, huge, yes, but benign. "That's *weeds*! Those people let the whole yard go to pot." Anna and Jan are suing the tenants they evicted for nonpayment of rent and for damages to their home. (When the trial date is postponed until October, Anna says, "Great. I want her to have to take off from work, not now when she has time off." Revenge, a seemingly unknown quantity in Anna, sounds justifiable as she ticks off their weeks of consuming work. Eventually the Johannessens were successful in receiving back rent and collecting on some of the damage and sold the house within days.)

"I've been down there cleaning up the place to get it ready to sell. There's crayon all over the walls, floors are a mess, we're going to have to paint, inside and out. It's so bad that it looks like most of the summer I'll be commuting to Richmond." Anna is not complaining; rather, she seems ecstatic that she is well enough to participate in such a taxing assignment.

Now that she is feeling well, talk of cancer fades. Anna's present priorities remind one of the old saying that when sex is bad in a relationship, it consumes 90 percent of one's thoughts, but when it is good, it consumes 10 percent. Anna's cancer was now consuming only 10 percent of her thoughts.

As for sex, often it is a searing problem, as illness takes away not only one's desire but a vital sense of one's sensuality. Experts recognize that this loss can create serious depression and anxiety regarding one's partner as well as oneself. Now Anna giggles and says that she even felt good enough for sex for the first time in ages. "But it was crazy! I was trying to get comfortable, moving my leg this way, my arm that way, and Jan was trying to make it easy on me." She and her friend joke that they had invented the *Kama-Sutra* for the physically challenged.

Anna slurps the bottom of her drink. "Isn't it neat that I never said anything to the kids? I don't know why, but I just knew that the time was not right. I'm so glad, however, that I got things started with Dottie; I don't know what ups and downs we're going to have with this ride."

Anna announces, "I may become a guinea pig—which is kind of exciting." She and Jan are exploring experimental clinical trials, even as she counts her blessings. "I thought I would be dead by now. It's been two years since my recurrence and I didn't think I'd see two years. I don't think Jan did either. I know I will definitely be here by the end of 1996. Now I can see lasting until Lindsay's middle school graduation in another three years. We've made such progress. With Taxol and Arimidex I got more than a free year! Maybe I'm getting cocky, but I'm starting to say, 'Weelll, maybe a little more, depending on what drugs come out.' " Anna is taking a mental holiday from the incessant drumbeat of cancer—her blood work, the checkups. "Ken and I agreed to just back off over the summer."

The long, glorious summer spins on. Jan and Anna exult in the joys of a near-normal life. "It gave us a window of hope," says Jan. There are many weekend trips to Richmond for them and the children. Anna relives memories as she scours and paints walls, scrubs and sands floors. Friends drop by. They had a wonderful evening at a Japanese steak house, celebrating Wayne's birthday.

One fine day in late summer, Jan and Anna go sailing with friends in waters so calm that they drift more than sail. Anna sits in the back of the boat, alone. She is memorizing everything about nature, burning memories into her brain, looking at the greater beauty of the whole world.

Twelve-year-old Ellery has shot up more than two inches and slimmed down over the summer, and is virtually unrecognizable. "Nils went on a trip and came back four days later and said, 'You've grown.' He's really become a handsome guy." But Ellery does not sound himself when he answers the phone on August 20. Friendly questions about his summer are greeted with monosyllables, then the phone is quickly turned over to his mother. "Hi there," says Anna, but the bounce is not in her voice. Asked if she had been awakened, Anna says no, in a flat voice. Something is very wrong. The easy flow is missing. The caller mentions not being able to reach her doctor for an interview. "Well, he's there now. I saw him yesterday."

"You went in for your blood work?" "Yeah." Pause. "My markers are going way up." "Oh, no!" "Well, we always knew Arimidex gave us just a little skating time." Her laugh is without mirth. Even though the tumors had disappeared on X rays, the cancer cells remained in her system and, as Davidson predicted, were surfacing again. The caller feels as if a knife is twisting in her stomach. Fear grips her chest and a tingling chill settles in her arms. She doesn't know what to say. A deep breath from Anna courses through the phone. "Anyway, Ken tells me there is another new chemo drug, the name sounds like a Hawaiian dessert—cookoo coca, pooko poka, something like that. [A month later, she says, "I can't spell it, but it sounds like top-o-teek-an."] That may be premature, but anyway, we'll see, we'll see."

Her friend grasps for anything positive. "Didn't you tell me that rising markers are not necessarily a negative sign?"

"When you're killing off a lot of tumors with chemo, they can rise," says Anna. "But that isn't the case now, I'm not on chemo. In three months, they've gone from seventy to one hundred sixteen to one hundred seventy-eight." After seven months of extraordinary health, she is trying to absorb this blow. "No matter what we do, I think I should stay on the Arimidex. It's really fighting the estrogen; it's really low and that's good." After a few minutes of small talk, Anna gets off the phone; she cannot bear to talk about the end of her golden summer any longer.

Six days later, Jan is chipper. "Weellll, things go up and down," he says. "Remember when NIH said Anna could be a candidate for some new trials, except that she was doing too well? I thought, 'What the hell,' and called them back. They're interested. Maybe while the tumors are still small, something different will give it the old knockout punch." The head of the clinical trial will meet with them in two days. To be eligible for the trials, Anna must be off Arimidex, so she stopped this week, just in case.

Once again, they are cliff-hanging. Jan remembers their frantic struggle for a bone marrow transplant two years before. "In hindsight, it was a lot of work for nothing. You're in the hospital for a month and whacked out for six, with all that poison dumped into you. Anna has a friend who went through it and in ten months, it's all back. Evidence shows that it has not panned out so well for breast cancer."

Miller is asked if he thinks the NIH study would be beneficial. "I don't think it's harmful and I don't think we're going to lose anything if we need to go back to the Arimidex. Anna is exploring a totally different avenue of cancer therapy, which is immune therapy. One of the very basic, interesting, and difficult issues of breast cancer is how is it that it can remain quiescent for five, six, seven, ten, even fifteen years and then show up again? What happened in that period of time? What were those cells doing? There is an implication that maybe the immune system was keeping them dormant. Anna had a long time in remission and so maybe there is something we can do to help her body get back into remission."

By September 5, Anna's mood was skyrocketing. "Lots of excitement here. Lindsay broke her clavicle on August 31. She was racing on her bike and hit the steel pole of the basketball hoop. Brakes didn't work. She was in a lot of pain and slept with me; I had her packed so she wouldn't roll off the bed." Lindsay wears a clavicle brace that pins her shoulders back so that the clean break will come together. "One doctor said, 'Put two pieces of a clavicle bone in the same room and they'll find each other.'

"Now for some more news. I'm in the program! I've started prednisone; I'll be the size of a house. The prednisone is to lower my immune system, to suppress the antibodies so they don't see these foreign antibodies—which come from mice spleen!—that will be pumped into my system and go charging off, yelling, 'Kill, kill!' " Miller comments, "God willing, the mouse antibodies that NIH is trying will kill cancer cells. There's rationale to it. There was a real interest in vaccines a number of years ago and it didn't seem to be panning out, so it was dropped. But this is a whole new generation of vaccine trials. She'll be in a wonderful place, getting good care."

"Ken has sent a lot of people to NIH and they've all been rejected," says Anna. "I'm a fluke. I'm *perfect* for this study. Physically and agewise, I'm in good shape. Basically I'm a 'clean' subject, even after having had so many medicines." Grateful for Arimidex—"I was able to do so much and it gave me seven very good months"—Anna now dismisses it as the hope of the past. "Been there, done that. Now it's on to the next, whatever." She says, cheerfully, "We'll see!"

Monday, September 9 Anna has taken so much prednisone that she seems on speed—flying high, talking nonstop, engorged with energy. "Hiiii!" she fairly shouts, sitting cross-legged on her hospital bed at NIH this first day of her experimental treatment. She looks great, her eyes wide and bright, lips brushed with gloss. Hair floats around her ears and down her neck. She wears two gold chains, gray Donna Karan sweatpants (discounted), a low-necked loose-fitting purple tank top that reveals her life port, unencumbered and ready for action. "Imagine what my arms would be like if they had to shoot up my veins! I'd have more tracks than a heroin addict.

"Boy, they spare no expense around here. I wonder what all this is costing? Everything is paid by the government. As long as I'm in the study, it's all free to me." The room's decor is an attempt at restful serenity. Walls are covered in a combination of textured lavender-and-gray wallpaper and matching gray-lavender paint. A discreet lavender-and-gray pattern marches across the curtains. Even the leather chairs are lavender, a departure, to say the least, for hospital furniture.

Anna explains her treatment. "I take massive amounts of prednisone—so high that the steroid suppresses my immune response, but it also gives me all this energy and I am *starving all the time.*" She imitates marking her menu. "Chocolate cake? Yeah! . . . Ice cream? Oh, yeah!" At 2:00 P.M., Anna had had her first shot of the "mouse-spleen protein," or LMB1—a liquid administered through her port every other day that hopefully kills cancer cells. Although some studies have been conducted, Anna is the first to try such high doses of prednisone along with the LMB1. The National Institutes of Health is trying to find a dosage tolerance that would keep the body from making antibodies that would fight off LMB1, the foreign mouse-spleen-protein derivative, as it enters her system. "Now I don't want to sound too altruistic," says Anna, "but I am part of a study that may turn up a wonderful drug for a bunch of other people down the road." Several more phases must be conducted before that could be achieved.

The esteem surrounding the National Institutes of Health filled Anna with awe at first. "You think, 'Jeez, I'm at NIH! Then you go through the halls to get a chest X ray and there are dust bunnies and paper and boxes of chemicals and all right in the halls, and you think, '*This* is NIH?' " But she quickly switches, raving about the efficiency. She checks her watch. "It's six twenty-eight and they're supposed to take my blood by six-thirty exactly and she hasn't shown." Two minutes later, on the dot of 6:30, the nurse appears. "See?" says Anna, beaming. Dr. Lee Pai, who is conducting the trial, "is very scientific and straightforward. They are incredibly thorough and explain everything. I love it here."

Anna is out of bed, padding down the hall in her tennis shoes, not giving a fig about the absent boob/bra. More than once, she will refer to this week as her "NIH holiday." She could be selling a tentative spa customer on memberships: "They've got Ping-Pong tables, unlimited free phone calls so patients can call back to wherever they're from, a refrigerator down the hall here." She waves at the nurses' station, passes through a door, and opens the refrigerator. "Here's the stash"—pointing to RC Cola, Sprite, milk, chocolate and white, juices.

Back in the room, Anna introduces her roommate, who has returned from her walk in time for their early dinner. In April of 1995, Janet (not her real name) had a sudden seizure and collapsed. Doctors found an inoperable brain tumor. Although her mental capacity is fine, the tumor has affected her motor skills; she walks with a limp and one arm is quite useless. Janet is another young mother, with an eight-year-old son. For forty-two weeks, she has been flying in from the West Coast every other week for treatment with experimental drugs. Janet is almost anorexic thin, wears glasses, and seems very private. Unlike Anna, she is reluctant to discuss her treatment or even to reveal her name, but she is equally as fierce a fighter. Despite the painful disruption of her family life, Janet clings to this exhaustive regimen. At one point when she is out of the room, Anna explains, "It's all that has kept her alive and stable. Unfortunately, one of the long-term effects of these drugs is that it causes depression."

Anna speaks protectively of her roommate. They have entered into one of those instant friendships, a bonding that can occur when people endure trauma together—whether it be soldiers in battle, families in war-torn communities or those ravaged by disasters such as floods or hurricanes, or two women lying side by side in a cancer ward. At night, they talk about their children, sobbing at times. Janet searches in agony to find meaning to their cruel fate, and has come to a small glimmer of acceptance that it is God's will. Anna thinks that it may be just the unhappy roll of the dice. She has also discovered and encouraged a vein of humor in Janet. Anna recounts the gag she had devised that morning with her roommate. Expecting "grand rounds," the two women and a doctor decided to pull a gag on the collection of doctors who stand around their beds—to stare at them and ask endless questions. "Janet would be covered in Post-it notes and she would just point to them when they asked questions. I thought, 'Why not do it in languages, since there are doctors from so many countries?' We had *nein* and *sí* and *oui* and so on plastered all over her—and they didn't show up! Isn't that disgusting?"

Talk turns to the children. Not only is Lindsay facing the discomfort of her body brace, she is disoriented by a sudden switch in math classes. "It's a big trauma for this kid. She doesn't like to have attention called to herself. She says, 'Mom, can I wear the brace under my clothes?' '*No,*' I say. 'I want it to be a warning sign so that someone won't accidentally hit you.' "

The phone rings, a crazy high sound that sends Anna into laughter. "Can you believe it? The 'chirping cricket.' " It's Ellery. Anna peppers him with questions: "Hey, how ya doin'? Aced your math quiz? That's great. . . . Tons of homework? . . . Really? . . . You'll love *Tom Sawyer*. . . . You sound like you're getting a cold and I think you should not come tonight. . . ." Lindsay gets on the phone. "Now tell me, who's in your new accelerated math? . . . Oh, good, you'll have someone to help you. Is it as hard as seventh? Harder? Great! . . . How's your shoulder? Don't pick up anything now!" Jan is now on the phone. "I know," she says, her face showing that they are not coming that night. "It sounds like they both have masses of homework plus he's got a cold. . . . I don't know if they'll let me out tomorrow. I feel great. I'm oinky pig and always hungry." Off the phone, Anna says, "I feel so sorry for that little boy. Now that Jan has to drive Lindsay to school, Ellery has to leave on the bus at six and doesn't get home until after four."

Wednesday, September 11 Anna awakens to the taking of blood and urine, the administering of potassium pills. "I got a pass yesterday—you have to be back by dark—from Dr. Rivera. He jokes about this being 'Hospitality Central.' I went home and cleaned the bathrooms. Coming back here is my *vacation*."

Anna is sweating. Looking at her prednisone-swollen face, she jokes, "Cheeks, cheeks, where are you?" She jumps out of bed. "Let's say we go up to the recreation area." As she gets off the elevator, a chapel is directly to Anna's left. She clownishly makes an exaggerated detour, charging forward to the huge gym with its full-sized basketball court, used by NIH employees, visitors, and patients who are well enough.

The next day, Anna is home on a pass and drastically different. Her friend Lockie answers the phone, her voice low because Anna is resting on the couch. "She's very tired and doesn't want to see anyone." Anna asks to get on the portable phone. "I took a shower and was so short of breath—*panting* from just drying myself—and I got terribly dizzy. I tried to walk down the hall and had to keep stopping. I didn't know if I had the muscle strength to keep myself up." Anna has a sore throat and, although fully dressed, is freezing. She crawls into bed until it is time to return.

*　　*　　*

Friday, September 13 Anna explains that her reaction was "totally normal. The drug causes capillary leak. You're not able to make the fluids go into the kidneys. The capillaries will get repaired when I'm off the drugs." It is Anna's last day at NIH and the end of the LMB1 drug. Anna's arms and legs are so swollen that she has to sleep on her back with her legs up. "My cheeks are disappearing into my eyeballs. Dr. Pai said that I would feel tired, but I couldn't imagine *this* tired; she's very pleased with the results." Anna looks over a questionnaire she has to fill out, evaluating her NIH stay. Anna laughs at the wording. "They ask if the food 'exceeded expectations.' Well, when you think of hospital food, *anything* would exceed expectations."

The family arrives for their last afternoon at NIH. Lindsay's eyes widen when she sees her mother's face; she stiffly embraces her, because of her brace. Ellery, stuck with homework all week, curiously examines the room for the first time. "Mom, you're a happy lab rat!" Anna shows him how the bed works and her tiny television that zooms in and out at the merest touch. She pulls it up close and makes a face in it. Ellery turns it every which way. Lindsay says little and sits close to her mom. Ellery begs for a turn on the video games in the recreation room. Anna asks about homework and Ellery relates that he has to write a journal for science and English. Immediately, Anna turns her experience into a learning venture. "You gotta check out this hospital, how this stuff works." Grateful for the suggestion, Ellery inspects everything even closer. After they leave, Anna comments on Lindsay's quietness. "She's been very low-keyed. She seems very mature at times. I don't know if it has to do with me or that it's just her age—she'll be eleven in a few weeks—or embarrassment or what."

A social worker walks in to chat and soon they are talking about how people don't want to face living wills and other matters of death. "My mother is so stubborn, she wouldn't do it," says the social worker. "I *made* my parents do it," says Anna. "I said, 'If you want us to do it the way you want, you have to have it in writing.' They asked me about mine here and I said I had it at home and they said bring it in. I'm for that."

Anna's room is besieged by staff. A research nurse says, "I've come to touch base with you concerning your questions on cancer research," but immediately makes it clear that Dr. Pai is in control and should be consulted. "I'm hoping this is going to work," says Anna, "but I'm also concerned about what happens if . . . Once I am in the system, I would love to stay. . . ." Anna describes Ro's cancer, her concerns for Lindsay, and asks if she could be a candidate for gene research. The nurse says gently but firmly that she should talk to Dr. Pai for any information on breast cancer trials. "Thank you," says Anna, adding with a rueful smile, "Insert foot in mouth." Anna wants the nurse to understand her emphasis on "staying in the system." She recounts her disastrous attempt at the bone marrow clinical trial. "Since then, I'm really not confident in those 1-800 government [phone] numbers." The nurse says, "PDQ gets updated monthly."

Then she softens and explains her frustration in getting data in order to make precise criteria for eligibility. "I am trying to get Mass. General involved in helping us for a lymphoma study. They have used this study three times—but we haven't a shred of their evidence. We can't get them to collect this information. Satellite research centers just don't care about eligibility criteria as much. It's a disservice. We have to start over and it adds up to government waste." Anna nods sympathetically. The nurse sighs. "Research nursing used to be outstanding—annual bonuses and so forth. Now it's a pass-fail system—and no monetary incentive. And the government wonders why they can't keep talented people." She continues with her frustration regarding NIH satellite research centers, how she's "written memo after memo" to no avail. "They all blow it off, even if the NIH is trying to do good." She mentions in particular the site at nearby Frederick, Maryland. "That's where Mr. Science came from!" says Anna.

Anna relates one of the few support group meetings she attended. It was last November, a bitter, freezing night, and about twenty-five male and female cancer survivors had turned out for a lecture on the prospect of new treatments. Many wore ill-fitting wigs. "These were desperate people seeking information about cancer—and this major science nerd was talking about T cells," she recounts. Anna questioned him as to why protocols were changed without proper notification. "He couldn't say anything except 'All I do is this. I don't know anything about anything else.' " The reasons protocols were changed were, in part, he said, because "in clinical trials we kill people." When the scientist spoke in mystifying jargon, one person in the audience asked caustically, "Is it too much trouble to speak English? These people want answers that will help." The scientist smiled and said, not without pride, "Some of my colleagues say I'm too technical." Anna says, "See what us average patients are up against?"

After the nurse leaves, Anna says, "Everybody around me is a whole lot sicker than I seem to be, so I kind of have a good time. It's friendly here. The patients get out in the halls and yack." Anna fervently hopes that she is a successful guinea pig and can return. "I really like this place," she reiterates softly. "They care on a personal basis. They had an eighty-year-old in here and you could tell by the way they treated him." At the end of three weeks, she will know the results. "Oh," she says, "let's hope!"

CHAPTER TWELVE

In Limbo

For the rest of September, Anna tries not to think about the impending results of the NIH trials. On glorious Indian summer days, she eats lunch with friends on her back deck, gazing at golden floating leaves, brushing away hovering bees, closing her eyes and turning her face toward the fading sun. Anna is not prepared for the extent of her fatigue. Ellery helps his mother down the deck steps to the garden. "I shouldn't have done it, but I wanted to just stand there and pick the last tomato of the season." She drives to the ballet studio to work on *The Nutcracker.* She becomes the tough Warden of Homework Detail, prodding, insisting. "You are not by the computer—you are not even *close* to the computer!" Anna shouts down the steps to the den; even though she cannot see him, her mother's instinct has caught Ellery playing hooky.

In October, Anna and Jan return to NIH for results of the clinical trial. Anna stumbles out, crying. Her "happy lab rat" days are over. "The good news is that my immune system was so low that it didn't fight the mouse stuff. The bad news is that it didn't matter; LMB1 didn't do a thing to shrink my tumors." A sadness creeps into Anna's voice as she remembers how cosseting life had been as a favored NIH human guinea pig. Although she has always known the rules, Anna can't help characterizing her termination in tough terms—"They kicked me out"—because she feels so abandoned. She had kept in the back of her mind that if this trial didn't work, something else would come up for which she would be eligible. "I stopped by to see my roommate—they're kicking her out too. After all this time, she's going home; it's not working for her anymore." Unlike others who bond in fleeting moments of togetherness, their connection is not broken, and they talk to each other long distance for months. One day in January 1997, Anna calls Janet and gets her husband instead. Janet had died two weeks before. Her frail and wracked body could not survive pneumonia. Anna sinks into deep depression, not only for the loss of Janet but for her own uncertain future.

On October 22, 1996, D day for another new chemotherapy treatment, Anna walks into Miller's office. She is sweating from a hot-flash attack, in pain, tired, and angrily obsessed by a misreading once again of her MRI by the radiology center. She fired off a critical letter, demanding to "see and discuss every film of every future scan with both doctors [Miller and the radiologist]." She radiates a new sense of purpose, steely urgency, determination, and anxious concern. Dedicated to monitoring everything, she is armed with her NIH X-ray folder and studies on various chemotherapy treatments gleaned from the Internet.

"This stuff is growing," she says in quiet fury to the nurse, pointing to her neck and throat. "NIH found these when your guys didn't in August. That's the *second* time in eight months that they've given me bad readings!" "Are you in pain?" asks the nurse. "*Yes,* I am in pain!" Anna has another gripe, the latest insurance wrinkle—her tumor marker tests will no longer be paid by them. "That's eighty-five dollars a pop at least once a month."

The door opens and Anna surveys a tall, lean man who looks like a *GQ* ad—gleaming polished tassel loafers, tan slacks, tan patterned socks, blue jacket, blue, tan, and maroon tie, well-trimmed beard, brushed-back dark hair, mustache, glasses. The opposite of rumpled Miller. "Well, here is the wonderful Dr. Kaplan, who looks like James Taylor," Anna banters. "If he could sing and play, he wouldn't be here."

"So," says Kaplan, "are you starting something new and exciting?" "Navelbine, yes—but I have some questions first." Anna bombards him and he explains that this chemotherapy stops the cells from dividing. Uncharacteristically, Anna stops him in midexplanation, so urgent is she to get to the tumors in and around her neck. "I want to know if we can start radiation. It's killing me now." Kaplan probes around her neck with his fingers, then as Anna starts her chemo drip, he holds her neck X rays up to the light. "See this mongo round guy on the soft tissue?" says Anna.

"They're on this [NIH] X ray, but they *missed* it here! And now the clavicle really hurts and the neck and I have tumor fever and this sucks.

"Another question I have, and this might sound bizarre—tell me what you know about hydrazine sulphate." Kaplan says, "It's mostly to improve nutritional status, gives you a sense of well-being, energy—" "There was a story in *Mediaweek,*" interjects Anna, "about what's-her-face, Bob Guccione's wife, who had this amazing reaction—boom—remission. But you read other articles and it's all so convoluted." Kaplan nods. "I've got some articles that would make you swear by it." "If it is primarily for nutrition," Anna asks, "how can it cure breast cancer?" She shakes her head at the claims of Mrs. Guccione. Kaplan replies, "You don't know, she could have had some sort of spontaneous remission." (Guccione's wife died in 1997.) Kaplan opens the door for trying experimental methods: "If we run out of options, I'm all for that. We know that a lot of what we do in traditional medicines doesn't work on some people. But we're not there yet." "I don't want to be there," says Anna. She lowers her voice and says in robot fashion, "I-do-not-want-to-go-there."

A week later, Anna is at the Shady Grove Radiology Center, a half hour from home. She lies on the radiology table; areas where radiation will hit are finitely calibrated, then indelible black lines, like crosshairs on a gun, are drawn on her skin to mark these points. Three days later, on November 2, an early Saturday morning, Anna casually shows the marks on her neck to her ballet friends. They are busily cleaning out a barn in the rolling hills of Maryland near Anna's home. Anna hoists boxes and shifts garden tools and sweeps the floor. Jan and some other fathers are in a van, on their way to unload Jane Bittner's basement of scenery so that the ballet group will have space to build additional *Nutcracker* sets. It is one of those glorious cold-apple-cider days, with piled leaves drifting in gusts. The van lumbers into the yard and there is much tugging and pulling as fake trees and lumber, a large papier-mâché wishing well, human-sized gingerbread men, and other items that turn a bare stage into magic are stacked in the barn. Now Bittner's basement is empty and ready. The mood is jocular and Jan seems especially happy in the company of friends. One of the male parents who will dance in the ballet's opening party scenes, he attacks the task with relish.

The following Monday, Anna plunges into three weeks of radiation, which turn out to be far more terrifying than she ever imagined. In her usual jaunty manner, Anna greets the receptionist, a pleasant blond who goes out of her way to show kindness to patients. Later she confides that her empathy was ingrained when her mother died of cancer. The waiting room is small, decorated in rose and green, and on one wall are pamphlets reminding people of why they are here: "When Mommy Has Cancer" is one. A counter is stacked with nutrition-building milk shake drinks, tea, and hot chocolate.

Anna enters the radiation room. The metal door is two feet thick. The chilly room looks like a stage for some minimalist play. The centerpiece is the table on which Anna will lie, strapped in place, that can be mechanically tipped to whatever angle is necessary. Overhead a lumbering piece of equipment hovers, looking something like the cab of a semitrailer. It will turn by remote control to move over and around Anna. From this, a red laser line marks the center of the beam of radiation to be zapped directly at the crosshairs on her neck and chest and upper stomach and will reach into her back and spine. The ceiling and walls are plastered with scenes of flowers, waterfalls, trees, mountains, seasides, placed for patient viewing no matter how they are turned. Technicians leave the room for their safe operating spot in the room next door. Anna is alone as the two-foot-thick door thumps shut.

After a few treatments, Anna almost trembles when she has to walk through that door. "It's the most horrible experience ever," she says. "Worse than chemotherapy. Part of it must be psychological. I don't like the smell of burning, and I could smell and feel my neck burn! Dr. Stinson says I smell the ozone, that I'm not burning, but ozone is produced from burn, so there's no difference to me. I had been told, 'Oh, its not painful, it doesn't hurt at all. You'll have very few side effects—a little trouble swallowing and the area will get sore and swollen.' I was not prepared for this horrible feeling."

Anna describes the sensation. "Think of when you're in the tropics and take a deep breath and feel that wonderful moisture go way into your lungs and back out. Then picture yourself in the desert; you take a deep breath and feel a dry, hot, parched burn in your lungs. When I breathe while being radiated, I feel as if I've gone into a hot desert wasteland and am burning up inside. Ellery asks, 'Why didn't you try and hold your breath?' I try but can't always manage. Radiation zaps are like twenty to twenty-five seconds long and I'm in such tension that I have to breathe." When Anna comes out, she rushes to the cool milky drinks to sooth her fiery insides.

Even knowing that she has only one last session to endure doesn't quell Anna's anxiety. As she is driven to the radiology center, Anna sits with arms folded, bending over as if she has stomach pain. "I hate this, I hate this!" she says in a tortured, keening tone. "I know many others who don't think radiation is so bad. I must have some phobic sensitivity. I just can't stand it!"

But stand it she does, and when it is over, one of the technicians, Tom Krupa, shakes her hand admiringly and wishes her luck. "I wish more patients were like you, looking at the disease and what's out there for you, knocking on doors, asking questions, really good questions. Not like 'Do you validate tickets or is there free parking or when are my treatments?' but questions like 'There's nothing in my C2, my spine, is there?' 'In my bone scan, I can see there was something there, but how come they're saying such and so?' You're terrific. Your husband was real good support too, coming here and asking questions. Some of these people are all alone."

Anna smiles wanly before guzzling another mouthful of chocolate drink, then carries on a discussion about getting patients to "pay attention to their own diseases." Krupa nods. "It's fear. Fear of the unknown. And, hey, what about just trying to get your own medical history from your family? I asked my mother, 'What did Grandma die from?' 'She died of something, something down below.' I said, 'What do you mean, down below?' And she says, 'I think it was the coln.' [Krupa pronounces it without the second *o*.] I said, 'You mean "colon"?' 'No, well, it was something. I don't know.' And I said, 'Mom, I want to know what my grandma and granddad died from!' "

While Anna is undergoing her treatment, Dr. Susan Stinson discusses Anna and radiation. She is tall and willowy with curls artfully streaked, wearing a plum pantsuit with matching plum velvet cuffs and collar. A small silver pin and a gold wedding band are her only jewelry. She quickly gets to the point; Anna is in for palliative treatment, not cure—and they can relieve pain only in the areas they treat, not the liver and other areas of spread. The optimum goal for Anna? "That the areas we're treating will stay pain free." Like Miller, Stinson mentions that Anna seems to be among a growing cohort of young breast cancer patients. "I really love older people, they have such a wealth of experience, and I thought that's what I was going to be dealing with, hoping to provide pain relief in their waning years." The doctor sighs. "It's hard for me to deal with people my own age or younger."

Anna then enters the room and fires off questions. "So do you expect more tumors or will this be it for the neck area?" Anna wants radiation to be over for good; she is also concerned that she can't take chemotherapy for liver tumors while doing radiation. Anna tells her that she is in deep pain, taking Percocet, antinausea drugs, and "good old Mary's Magic Mouthwash"—a liquid medication which numbs the mouth.

Dr. Stinson repeats that "our best result would be that your pain will go away in the radiated areas and will stay away. Eighty percent of breast cancer patients do respond to palliative radiation very well." Anna pushes again. "We think the test at NIH lowered my immune system drastically with whomping doses of prednisone. Could that have made the body more susceptible? Why did it grow so fast?" Stinson has no answer. Anna insists that she could feel herself burning. Stinson says she wasn't. "When we treat the brain, head, and neck area, some people really complain about how bad it smells, so you may just have a good strong sense of smell." Stinson explains how radiology works—it makes a break in the DNA of all cells. Overnight, repair takes place in both normal and cancer tissues, but the cancerous ones are less good at repairing themselves. "There's the differential that we're working toward."

It is six days before Thanksgiving when Anna closes the door to the Shady Grove Radiology Center for the last time. In the car going home, Anna shouts, "YEAHHHH!" It's over and I'm so glad! I want to go and see the new *Star Trek* movie, my hope is that I could talk everybody into going. It opens tonight." (They did.) She mulls over her conversation about stress and cancer with Dr. Stinson. "The ballet is happy stress, the medical crap is exasperating stress."

Anna turns into the driveway and sees Ellery, returning from school. Her son chose a particularly rough time to take a nosedive in school, while Anna was at NIH. Although her illness may have been part of the cause, she brooks no excuses. Rolling down the window, Anna says, "Is there a report card in your backpack?" Ellery nods. He pulls it out for her. Anna smiles and says, "You are awesome," as she runs her eyes down the card. "You're on the honor roll, dude!" Ellery smiles and continues into the house. "He went from three D's at the interims to B's in his magnet courses. See?" she says with satisfaction. "That's why we have to push on the homework."

For Thanksgiving, Anna nests calmly with Jan and the children, quiet time needed by everyone. In the first days following radiation, Anna's throat is so swollen and raw that it pains her to eat. She winces as she forces herself to swallow fluids. By Thanksgiving, her throat is better, but, ever since the radiation, Anna has developed severe headaches. Although in pain, Anna dresses up in gold lamé and feathers while Linda Suarez, her photographer "cancer buddy," also a Ken Miller patient, snaps photos that reveal an altogether different vision, a stunning, smiling Anna.

After Thanksgiving, Anna skips a chemotherapy treatment. "I just have too much to do with the ballet and I can't be that drained of energy." In addition to creating the *Nutcracker* program, supervising the printing, writing stories and news releases for the local papers, pitching in with costumes, managing the volunteer parents, Anna is much in demand as the only one with professional training in stage lighting. She works the lights for all performances. Lindsay, now on pointe, is luminous. Ellery works on stage props, Jan struts smartly on stage in Victorian costume, dancing a reel. The high school's impressive auditorium is filled—2,000 attendance over four performances. For an amateur group, the production is surprisingly professional. Afterward, Anna comes down from her exacting task in the lighting booth for the postperformance party.

The Friday before Christmas, Anna finds out that the chemotherapy poison has done its damage. "My white blood count is really low again." They plan to give Anna shots at the office, but Anna is in a hurry and says, "Just give me the prescription for Neupogen and I'll do it at home." That way, Anna can shoot up whenever she needs to during the holidays. Since she is not able to travel, Anna has talked her father into coming north, and Ro and Cliff and her father are all arriving that afternoon. The pharmacist cannot fill Anna's prescription until the day after

Christmas. "There wasn't a white cell left in my body. On Christmas day, I couldn't do anything."

Anna's "Christmas from hell" has its good moments with Jan and the children and Cliff and Ro and her father. "I wish my dad would move right in. He's so easy to deal with. We all had a grand time. They love to eat and cook and drink beer, but I was sick as a dog. On Christmas night, we had this lovely standing rib roast. I forced myself to do the dishes because I wanted to do something—they had lived in the kitchen—and then I lay down, taking Compazine [an antinausea drug] so the food will stay down."

Anna had been concerned about this holiday for several days. Because both brothers and their families had planned to be away from Cocoa Beach, Anna had invited her father. Now, it turns out that one set has decided to descend on Anna and Jan, and the others are visiting relatives nearby. As Anna rests after the Christmas Eve meal, Marty, Anita, and their two children arrive. Her headaches persist, along with blurred vision, and all she wants to do is sleep. "We fed everybody. It was only four new people, but it seemed like ten," Anna recalls. "It was their kids—and mine too. When kids get together, everything gets louder. But their kids are screamers. They're shouting at you and jumping about. It drives me crazy!"

She is angry that her brother, Marty, and his wife have brought a television set for Ellery. "Would you give a twelve-year-old a television set without asking the parents? You'd think they would ask, 'Is this appropriate?' They didn't give it a thought. I told him we could keep it somewhere, but that he was not going to have a TV in his room."

Anna struggles through Christmas day, and on the twenty-sixth they serve nineteen for dinner, including her two brothers and their families, and assorted extended relatives. "That was chaos, just too many people. Ro said I passed out on the sofa. I don't remember a thing, I was so sick. By eight, they put me to bed. But I had had my first Neupogen shot, so that I knew I would get better every day."

But the news is not good when she returns to the doctor's after Christmas. Anna looks good, having lost 14 pounds from her bloated prednisone days of 170 pounds. But blood tests show that Navelbine is definitely not working. "One test checks your carcinogen level. A regular person is zero to four, a smoker is between four and twelve. I was one hundred eighty-something! That was *bingggg*—off the charts. The tumor marker was so bad that they had to dilute the blood to measure it because it was so thick—that's bad." Anna is put on Taxotere, the chemo that Anna had heard about last spring, now on the market.

A few days after Anna starts Taxotere, she is stricken by a malady so terrifying that she gasps for air, as if she had been socked in the stomach. While performing one of those mundane necessities of life, writing out a check for groceries at the supermarket, Anna is suddenly seized with a massive headache and her vision blurs drastically. "It came on out of nowhere," she recalls afterward. "I couldn't focus on anything—the check or the person in front of me—I couldn't read the register. No matter how hard I blinked and tried to organize my eyeballs, they wouldn't focus."

The checkout clerk helps fill out the check and Anna manages to stumble to the car, cautiously backs out of the parking lot, and drives the few minutes to her house, where she lies down, petrified and exhausted. "I didn't know how long this was going to last. Had I ruined something permanently? Or has this [Anna cannot bring herself to say "cancer"] gone up into my head? Everything just starts to go very dim and I can still see, but it fades and gets really dark, like it's night. And white becomes this weird yellow. It's got to be associated with these headaches." Her vision is too weak for her to walk. She mostly sleeps because keeping her eyes open is too painful.

No one in the family mentions what everyone is thinking. Brain scans are immediately taken. Nerve-racking days ensue until the results are available. Relief enters the Johannessen household. Says Anna, "I didn't have even the *beginnings* of a brain tumor." But the baffling headaches and vision attacks continue. One afternoon, Anna sits in her living room, concern clouding her eyes. "The CAT scan doesn't see anything in my brain, and they've done one spinal-fluid tap and that's negative, but you're supposed to have three before you can tell for sure. Nobody can tell what's going on in my head and it's driving me crazy."

In the first weeks of January 1997, as her problems continue, Anna confronts issues that are "all of a sudden real life changes, like what if I'll never drive again? What am I going to do? A *shut-in*!? For five days, I couldn't go out of this house. To have to ask yourself, 'What are you going to do if you find out you can't drive anymore? If you find out you can't read and you can't see the television set? What are you going to do with yourself?' I feel so much fear," she says, curling in her corner, while a friend sits nearby, touching her arm. "I can't function and the days just drag and drag. I'll be up at six and sitting here thinking, 'What the hell am I doing with myself?' And I can't do anything. I can't read. Can't pay the bills, watch television. I have to lie absolutely flat, because of my head. And so I go to bed by six o'clock."

Fearing the reason, the usually direct Anna doesn't tell anybody that her vision problems are continuing. "I should have gone right to Ken and had him have a neurologist see me," she reflects later. Anna is terrified, a fairly rare emotion for Anna but not uncommon for those whose options are dwindling. "The scariest thing for anybody is losing sensory faculties," Jan says later. "Anna could take pain but not this fear that she was getting to the point where she was losing control. Losing your mind is like losing yourself." Anna says, "I didn't say anything to the kids about my own fears, I just withdrew, even though I was happy when they came home. They let me know they would do anything for me. They've been very nurturing."

Anna had continued to take Compazine for nausea throughout radiation and chemotherapy. Compazine can cause severe reactions in some people, but Anna never had any problems taking it. When she told Miller that she was still having vision problems, he said, 'Get off of the Compazine. It may be the problem in combination with Taxotere.' " A happy Anna reports by mid-January that her vision has cleared. "That did it!"

Despite her relief, those fearful days had jarred her like no other since that day two and a half years ago when she learned her cancer had metastasized. In addition, her body was under assault from Taxotere. "Every time I go in, they tell me another piece of lovely information, another little piece isn't quite working the way it used to work. The side effects of Taxotere seem to be lasting longer than Taxol. Maybe my system has had so many drugs—they've just been pumping me so full of so much stuff—that it can't jump back anymore. I feel like my insides are being burned out and I feel really, really draggy. Of course my hair is going, going, gone."

* * *

No matter how sick she gets, Anna pushes for special moments with the family. "We need to do something theatrical, cultural, with the kids once a month because otherwise you get into a daily grind and it's terrible. We took them to see *Cinderella* at the Olney Theater in December and now this in January." For Jan's birthday, the family went to hear the Baltimore Symphony. "That is the most wonderful concert hall. It is so designed for acoustics. It was Barry Tuckwell's last performance. He stands up to play, which most French horn players don't. He did a Mozart piece and then a modern one by a composer who musically illustrates Maurice Sendak's art, those really neat creatures. You can close your eyes and see them come to life. This music was amazing! One of those pieces where you have to watch the conductor put the baton down to realize it's over. And Tuckwell's last note is ringing quietly and then you hear *ring, ring, ring,* and somebody's goddamn cell phone went off!"

Anna now sees heightened fear in her children's eyes. "Ellery's definitely scared, seeing me get so sick, so strange. He is all over me, pats me, like a pet, saying, 'Mommy, oh, I love you, Mom. I love you, Mom.' He will not leave me alone." He and Lindsay stay close to home, play together instead of seeking friends or wanting to go places. "They're hovering. If I get into a coughing spasm, Lindsay's right there—'Oh, my God, Mommy, are you okay? Are you okay? Can I do something? What can I do?' I'm trying to say, 'I'm fine, I'm just coughing.' Sometimes I just have to say, 'Guys, give me some time and give me some space!' I tell everybody to back off. I have to. I can't take the hovering. If I'm lying there feeling awful, I have to just push them away. That makes me feel terrible. It's so selfish, I just want to kick myself.

"Ellery can't visualize something as huge as my death, but I know he's thought about it," says Anna. "One day, he told me he was convinced that the universe was going to die, not just me. And one night we watched the TV show *The Single Guy,* and the lead's father was remarrying. Ellery flat-out said, 'Well, I'm not going to let Dad get married again.' And I stopped him in a joking way. 'Excuse me? *I'm* still here. What am I, chopped liver? You're getting rid of me? Where did you send *me,* Ellery?' We all had a laugh, but I know he's thinking that there's going to come a time when Mom's not here. So I said to him, 'Wouldn't you want your dad to have female companionship? It wouldn't interfere with your relationship with him, and that person would never be Mom. I'm your mom. That person would be someone who could maybe be a new friend for you. Wouldn't it be nice not for Dad to be lonely? He doesn't deserve that.' " Anna laughs. "Ellery thought about it and said, 'Yeah, okay, he can get married.'

"I worry that Jan doesn't fill that emotional void for the kids when I can't. I keep saying, 'Talk to them, you've got to talk to these kids.' He doesn't take as much cuddle time with the kids. He's more"—she imitates a gruff he-man voice—" 'Okay, guys, let's sit down, let's do your math, let's go out and chop down the tree, tote that barge. . . .' Jan's just living day to day, not looking down the road. He gets upset when he hears bad news—especially big changes. Then he goes off and madly does research. That's his way of coping, trying to come up with new approaches. And I'm grateful for that, but he doesn't say to me, 'Oh, honey, I'm so scared that you're going to die'—talk to me as I would like. He'll tell me how much he loves me and plan the next thing to do. He sees this as a more positive attitude. He won't verbalize his introspection."

Anna's bout with her vision left her vulnerable and introspective. "The blurriness scared all of us. I flat-out said to Jan, 'If it goes to my brain, you will do something about that, thank you, if I go into a coma. Do *not* let me live under those circumstances. I don't want to be a vegetable.' It could happen and that thought's terrifying. I have moments of 'What am I heading into?' I'm not looking for a cure, I just want as much time as I can get. Yet this disease is one of the nastiest because it takes you piece by piece. I'm realizing it's happening; there's blood in my stool, blood in the urine. Now the cancer's going to grab something else. And I just absolutely hate it, hate it, hate it. I'm seeing a distinction between my quality of life six months ago and my quality of life now. I get tired so much faster. I feel lazier. I look at the kids and wonder, 'Will I get to see this or that?' I can send myself into a real tailspin with that if I'm not careful, send myself, like now, into moments of hysteria, thinking like that. So I take a breath and say, 'Okay, you're not there yet. You're not there yet. Take the next drug.' But I'm experiencing this slow decline. It's real. I know Ken knows it's real. And yet I should be lucky because there are four women I know of who had breast cancer who are already dead and I'm not. And a lot of people actually can live like this. It's just amazing how long you can keep going. I'm starting to really resent being sick now because it's invading my life."

Anna says one survival skill is making plans. "I'm still doing my ballet stuff, which I love. I've broached Jan with places I want to go, things to do. That does keep you going." Then Anna admits something she would never have thought possible. As her body slows down, she has moments of being "almost secure and happy just staying in the house and crawling under a blanket. I know I'm entitled to that, but is that a good thing? Or a bad thing? It'll be seven o'clock and I can't wait to get my pajamas on sometimes. I hurt everywhere and I know if I can just lay down, I'll be better. But what a damn shitty quality of life that I am relegated to, compared to six months ago. Radiation has deprived me of sunshine. Can't sit out, they say, for a year. And it's my favorite thing to do in the whole world. Screw it, I'm going out, I don't care, let me burn."

Anna is scrupulous about distinguishing between what she can't do because of her illness and what she simply does not want to do. "I don't want the kids to think that every disappointment they're going to have is related to my illness—that's a lie. So when I don't want to do something, I tell them, and they can be mad at me instead of blaming this illness." Everyone in the household is now getting testy. "Anna was a lot more short-tempered than I have ever seen her. We all were," recalls Jan. "There was just so much stress with Anna's frightening condition."

The endless battle with homework feeds into Anna's fears for the future. "Jan's going to butt heads with them and not take the time to emotionally work this out. That's why he's going to need a Dottie. Not yet, but he's going to need somebody to help him understand how to talk to his own kids, because Ellery was all flattened out after Jan yelled at him. I quietly said, 'Ellery, you had an A in the magnet science program, and that's something to really crow about, but you're now settling for a B. Dad wants to see you feel so proud of yourself, he can't stand it. You're not letting yourself experience that yet and Dad wants you to have that experience.' Jan was the same way in college; the fights we had when we were first married were because of my getting on him to finish his Ph.D.—he'd do everything for everybody else and wouldn't do his own work. I think he sees a lot of himself in Ellery and doesn't want him to repeat his ways."

*   *   *

January drags to an end. As Jan and Anna search for new ways to attack her cancer, a desperate urgency creeps in. Jan is now prodding Anna to go for an adrenalectomy. In his constant search, he has found a doctor in Portland, Oregon, who has done a fair number. Letters are quickly dispatched. The doctor replies that he is no longer surgically removing adrenals and suggests Anna continue on the Arimidex—now his drug of choice, not surgery. Another last shot to end any possible estrogen is to have Anna's ovaries removed. "The operation is called oophorectomy," says Anna. "Sounds weird!" She and Jan decide to go ahead.

The day after her oophorectomy, performed in an outpatient procedure, Anna gallops through her latest adventure on the phone with friends. "It was a bilateral-something oophorectomy, laparoscopy, blah-blah oophorectomy. It was a breeze. The doctor took pictures inside, a little camera zooming in there! 'Here's your ovaries; now you see 'em, now you don't.' The color pictures, man, I couldn't believe it. The ovaries were bright orange and the tumors on my liver looked like pink Pepto-Bismol tablets. . . ."

Meanwhile, Anna has been listening sympathetically to a male friend's eight-month dilemma regarding serious surgery for his young daughter. From June to January, her friend was highly distracted as he continued his demanding career. His eight-year-old daughter, Julie, had developed puberty early and there was concern about her pituitary gland. "God forbid there is a tumor," her father prayed as he waited for the MRI scan. "I got a message to call radiology. It was like the experience when Kennedy was shot. I remember exactly where I was, what I was doing. The radiologist said, 'Oh, by the way'—those were her words—'her pituitary's fine, but there's an abnormality. "And that 'oh, by the way' turned out to be a big *big* deal."

The man's ordeal had just begun. First he and his daughter saw a neurologist who said to "keep an eye on her" but added that they should "see a neurosurgeon to get his opinion." "So we saw a neurosurgeon," the man continued. "Again, I remember this like the day Kennedy was shot—the neurosurgeon looked at the films, didn't look at Julie at all, never met her, and proceeded to tell me about this huge operation she needed, a six-hour procedure with opening the skull and putting a shunt in. I thought I was going to fall down from shock." Seeking another opinion, the man saw "another excellent neurosurgeon who said, 'Keep an eye on it.' So we had one saying, 'Do a big operation,' and the other saying, 'Do no operation, just watch her.' So I said, 'We'll see a third neurosurgeon.' He said, 'No, no, you have to operate, but don't do what the first one said, do a less-extensive operation.' And that's when it became really awful, because what was the right answer?"

Different opinions, different thoughts, accumulated as the frantic father consulted more medical experts. "We finally found a very good neurosurgeon in Chicago who had a less-invasive surgical approach; they simply take the bone off and leave the brain alone. I felt comfortable with that. My wife and Julie and I went out there, after months of tremendous strife, debating, 'What's the right thing to do? What's the right thing to do for your child?'

"Most parents would have gone to the first doctor; he would have said, 'Operate,' and the parents would have said, 'Fine, let's do it.' I had totally educated myself about it, and I was getting different opinions and that's when it got to be crazy. What was the right answer? No matter what I did, someone was going to disagree with it—which is a very tough feeling. Especially when it involves your child. If we did nothing and she gets worse, which had been threatened to us as a possibility, then that's awful. If she had a surgical complication or wasn't the same afterward, that's awful too. A child depends upon you to make the decision! It was an awful period, not knowing what the right answer was. There's a sense that there's supposed to be a 'right' answer.

"We finally chose the surgeon in Chicago." In icy January chill, the family flew to Chicago. Julie had an MRI that night and the next morning was prepped and in the operating room. "We were in the holding area—and the doctor rushed in and said, 'You know, I looked at the studies from last night and I don't think we need to do it!' The relief was enormous." On the way home, the man formed a thank-you letter to the surgeon—adding a comment on his experience with the medical profession. "What does a patient do? I've learned that eventually, as a patient or a parent of a patient, one has to have a certain leap of faith and say, 'I'm making the best decision I can.' I wrote to the other doctors, telling them that we decided to do a watch-and-wait approach and why. And I got a letter back from one of the doctors, who basically said, 'That is the wrong decision and you are doing absolutely the wrong thing.' And I was thinking, 'I didn't need this letter! I'd finally reached a point of comfort and he does this.'"

When Anna's friend recounted his eight-month odyssey of strife and despair, she empathized but couldn't resist a rather triumphant comment, "Welcome to my world. Now you know what it's like." The man was her longtime oncologist, Ken Miller.

Miller has to concede that Anna's point was apt; he now better understands his patients. "We all read about serious illness and you see television programs that dramatize it, and it's almost like a love story. But most of living with serious illness is just that—living and the day-to-day stuff, the dog to walk, the kids' report cards.

"Anna's life is a profile in courage of a meaningful person and points up all of the handicaps that people live with that don't go away," Miller concludes. He is one of millions who witness firsthand chronic diseases or disabilities. "My oldest daughter is deaf. It's not life and death, it's not cancer, but it's a day-to-day issue that doesn't go away.

"All of us would like the happy ending, and it doesn't always happen." Miller pauses. "Thankfully, Anna's been able to live with this disease a long time."

PART III

A New Level of Existence

There's a natural order to the universe and I'm just a piece of that order. . . . As I die, something else will be born and on goes creation. . . . I feel like I'm one of the flowers that popped out of the ground and bloomed and everything around me for a while enjoyed the bloom and whoops winter came and the bloom fell over. . . . It saddens me that I'm going to miss out in some fun, but I don't have terrifying feelings about it at all.

ANNA JOHANNESSEN

Anna's mother, Audrie (1985)

Anna—and siblings—
Steve, Marty, Ro,
and (seated) Steve (1995)

Anna and her father

CHAPTER THIRTEEN

Anna's Choice

On Friday, February 14, Valentine's Day, 1997, Anna tells a friend that she has decided to quit chemotherapy. Her friend catches her breath. This is a monumental decision and so she struggles for the right thing to say. Finally she elects to do what they have done so often, keep the tone light. "Are you being naughty?" Anna laughs and says, "Weellll, I won't call it naughty. Let's say I've taken my brain to a new level of existence. And that plain says, 'This is bull! You've gotta stop doing this!' "

A few days before, Anna's checkup showed that her tumor markers were alarmingly elevated, now at a thousand. Again pain and anger heighten the expletives. "I thought to myself, 'How long should I stay on this drug, which is so damn effing debilitating?' If it were two years ago and I was taking Taxotere for the first time, I don't think it would be so bad. But as the result of having had so much chemo, my system just isn't able to bounce back. This Taxotere experience is just miserable. I'm puking my guts out. I want a drug holiday. I want to go back to last summer when I stayed on that one pill, Arimidex. The cancer grew to some degree, but I felt good. I felt like I could *live.* I feel that while I'm alive, I'm alive, dammit. I'm not a piece of chemical crap running around. I started thinking, 'Why am I poisoning myself to the point where I can't function anymore? I can't go from the bedroom to the living room.' That's when I said, 'I'm not doing this anymore, unless there's a hell of a good reason. I've had my ovaries out, I've done surgery, I've done years of chemotherapy, I've been fighting, but I can't put up a fight if I'm so devastated physically from chemotherapy.' I'm going to have a heart attack; just carrying laundry up the steps, I get so out of breath. That cancer's never going to get a chance to kill me because the damn chemo's going to do it first."

Anna cries. She tells Jan, "I want to be strong enough to take walks again. I want my immune system to strike back." Jan puts his arms around Anna on the sofa and says, "Life to you is not laying in a bed like that." He sees Anna's deep depression as she fears being a nonfunctioning shut-in. Her words slow. "I think this is the last year I've got and I don't want to spend it three-quarters of the time in bed."

On Monday, her blood count is so low, the doctors try to put Anna in the hospital for a transfusion, saying it is a matter of life or death. Anna explodes. "Give me my little shots, let me stay around my little germs at home—we're all friends—and I'll be fine." Anna recalls, "They were ready to slam me into the hospital, the worst place I could possibly be. I realized then that I had to stop the madness. I want my body to be able to still help command this fight somewhat. Once you get to the transfusion stage, you don't have the tools."

On Tuesday, Jan and Anna face Joe Kaplan in a tiny examining room. Anna smiles brightly. He says, "Okay, you can't fool me. Suzanne told me." Anna had discussed her pain with the nurse. "With these tumor markers going through the roof, where is my cancer going?" responds Anna. "*Where is it going?* I know where it's going." Anna points to her right side. "I've got rib pain. It started two weeks ago and I waited to see if it would go away." Kaplan asks, "Does it hurt when you breathe?" "Oh, yeah. Big time." Anna continues, "I take my Percocet and I go merrily about my way. But I'm curious, if this is getting in my ribs and lots of places, what can I look forward to?" Kaplan tells her that while those ribs are not weight bearing, Anna could end up with several fractures. He wants her to take radiation in any weight-bearing areas. Anna tells him, "There's no way in hell I will have radiation again."

Now, this Valentine's Day, 1997, Anna ponders her choices as she gets a bone scan. "I have to ask, 'Gee, what healthy tissue is going to get zapped in the process? What good stuff are we going to kill?' From now on," says Anna, with a grim laugh, "I'm looking at these trade-offs. There's no odds in it the other way." She is dubious that Taxotere has been effective, but the MRI, scheduled for next month, is needed for proof. Anna balks, refusing to take the third cycle. "This sure makes me feel real crappy. What idiot would want to do this?! It is a very logical decision. I think I'd be much more happy with that. Happy in one way, scared in another, cuz you don't know what's coming up. Somehow, I will find a way to manage pain."

Anna says she wants definite answers on how long she has to live. A major obstacle for dying patients is doctors, trained not to let go but to try just one more treatment. Many cannot conceive of giving a terminal patient—even one who prefers the truth—an educated guess as to how long he or she has left. "But such information gives you some way to chart the rest of your life. It gives you some road map markers," argues Anna. "There is no way you have to buy it. You could say, 'I'm going to show you, I'm going to live three or four more years,' but at least you have a way station."

For all her insistence on knowing, however, Anna admits she is as hesitant as any patient to confront a time frame. "I'm not good at pushing that, but I'm going to try. I think I can push it with Joe. Ken would be Mr. Butterball." Later, Miller points out that in the past, Anna has evaded definitive discussions. He had mentioned the option of stopping therapy more than once after her cancer had metastasized, says Miller, but Anna was not ready to hear it. "I first started bringing it up to Anna when two, three therapies didn't work. Each time I said to her, 'Anna, we've got a couple of choices. One is that people always have the right to say, "I don't want to do this anymore. I'm more interested in quality of life and I don't want aggressive therapy." Or we could try a different type of chemotherapy or experimental therapy.' Most people aren't ready the first time they hear that. Now Anna says she is at that point."

She thinks it is the chemo that makes her feel bad, Miller is told. "That's a part of it, yes. It's very, very hard when people are on therapy and they don't feel well. You say to yourself, 'Is it the disease? Is it the treatment? Or is it unrelated? Is it a virus or some other process? Or is it aging, or what?' And the only way to find out sometimes is to give people a break and if they start feeling better, then it was the therapy that was doing it." When a cancer metastasizes, Miller is never free from scrutinizing his treatment. "You can't help agonizing, and retrace your steps to see if there was anything different you could have done." Anna's anger at the X-ray snafus is mentioned. "She was right! I don't blame her. I was pissed off too, because we're depending upon our consultants, our radiologists, and the lab to have things just right. But thankfully I don't look back at anything with Anna and say, 'Oh, my God, this was a major screwup. This poor woman, her life would be different.' Thankfully I don't feel that way."

Miller talks of the struggle and anguish doctors face at this stage in an illness. "Over the years in my practice, I have noticed something. What Anna or some other patient might discuss with friends and family may be different than what they would ask me. It's a different experience thinking about wanting to know when you may die and actually asking the doctor. It's very difficult for the doctor also because when cancer returns, when someone has advanced cancer, on one hand, you have to share information about the seriousness of the disease, but on the other hand, I would want to leave a ray of hope. I think it's fair to say to people, 'This is a very serious disease and many people die of this disease.' But my belief is that we have treatments that will hopefully help. I don't remember ever saying to someone, 'You're incurable.'

"When people do ask, 'How long?' I'll start off by saying, 'I'm not God and I don't know.' " Ken then will add, if he believes so, "However, I don't think it's going to be days or weeks, but it's probably not going to be a year either. It's probably life measured in months. In terms of how many months, I don't know for sure." This kind of answer provides a comfort zone for those who, as Miller says, are "sick enough that they know that things are not going well. Sometimes people will take it further, they'll ask, 'Well, how many months?' And then I might say, 'I think it may be less than six.' Sometimes I turn the question around: 'I know this is a hard question, but what do you think?' " Ken does this with family members who pull him aside outside the patient's hearing or who call on the phone. "Usually the family knows or has a feel for this and they'll say, 'I don't think she's going to be alive by Christmas.' Or 'I don't think she's going to be alive for the wedding.' Or 'I do think she'll make the wedding.' And so on."

Miller remembers an unsettling experience early in his career. "A patient forced me to give him an exact time; he said, 'You've got to tell me, I'm not getting up from this chair until you do.' And I said six months. Well, he lived for eight months and he was mad at me for those entire two months! That taught me a lesson."

Speaking of lessons, Miller is asked if doctors are given any preparation for the difficult, awkward, and emotionally painful task of dealing with dying patients. "Very little," he says, "very little." Oncologists choose a field that involves long-term interaction with patients that may end with death. In recent months, medical training has been excoriated for its neglect in teaching caring skills. "In medicine in general, no one teaches you how to prepare people for this," says Miller. "We don't take medical exams that go over how well you do the counseling part, which is a big part of our job. There's no peer review for that. Nor does a doctor really get feedback. The only feedback you get is from your day-to-day work, your patients and families, and hopefully it's favorable."

Another problem is that often doctors have to be mind readers with patients who tend to minimize their problems when they go for office visits. "Actually, I have had to say to Anna, 'You know, you present yourself so positively that you've got to remind me that you've got problems. You need to be specific and tell me.'

"With every patient, your relationship's a little different, the illness is different, their perspective on their illness is different, their life story is different." He pauses. "Anna's life means a great deal to me," he says as pain shows in his eyes. "I've known her a long time now. She's about my age and her kids are about the same age as mine. Anna was one of the first people I saw when I started my practice in a tiny little office. I remember very well seeing Anna and Jan that first day."

On February 18, "blood-work day," as Anna terms it, she forcefully tells Ken that she wants to quit chemotherapy. "It's ruining the quality of my life and it's not making me any better. I'm very serious about wanting to have really a good quality life and I don't want to spend days lying in a bed in so much pain from the chemo. I'm not saying I don't want to take chemo ever again. But right now, there's nothing that we know of, let's face it, that's out there that's really going to set off any bells and whistles.

"Why am I having all this pain?"

"We could take millions of tests," says Miller, then gently, "but,

Anna, we know. It's probably in your ribs and just not showing yet. Let me take a look." Anna climbs up on the table; Miller lifts up her sweatshirt and gently pushes on her ribs on the right side. Anna winces and says "Aarrrgghh!" at the sharp pain. Ken tells her that the cancer may be in new areas. Both of them feel that an MRI at this point won't tell them anything they don't already suspect.

Ken looks at Anna. "I know you have an agenda and part of my job as your doctor is to help you fulfill that agenda."

"Yes," says Anna, "and my agenda is that I want to enjoy myself. I'm going to Florida in early April and I want to be strong enough to have a good time. I don't want to be so drugged out that I take three steps and I fall over. Ever since the NIH thing—I think it really whacked my immune system—and if I just build my own body strength up, I'm going to feel a whole lot better."

"Okay," says Miller. "Let's take a drug holiday; I want you to go and have ten days to just play. Then come back in and we're going to take your blood counts." Miller assures her that "we can go back and revisit any of this at that point."

Anna says, "So if we find out in ten days that nothing's working, then what do we do? What's out there? Not a whole hell of a lot. I'm not totally averse to trying the 5-FU [an abbreviation for a chemo regimen, 5-fluorouracil], but I want to get stronger before I jump into it." On the way out, Anna says, "But I'm sitting there saying to myself, 'If I have to wear the 5-FU bag and it's not going to work, what the hell for?' " Anna is happy that she doesn't have to make that decision right now and is pleased that Miller agreed to stop chemotherapy. "What I need to do is just get back to trying to be me. I'm trying to eat sensibly. I'm taking two Percocets at night for the pain and I'm still doing the Arimidex." Hope, so important for survival, remains, and it is not unrealistic. "They come out with an alternative to Arimidex, I'll be first in line! The next pill that comes along may be able to fool the cancer for a while and I may get a respite again. Who knows? After these ten days, if the tumor markers are still going up, I'm just going to say, 'Okay, that's it. I'll call you if I'm in major pain, now leave me the hell alone."

In her weekly conversation with her father, Anna expresses her determination to rebuild her strength while off chemo. "He's still on this 'you've got to get rid of this disease' kick. I tell him, 'I'm *trying.*' I'm trying to make him understand that I'm not at all giving up, that as a matter of fact, I can get stronger and feel better, that there's no reason to be so sick from treatments. I think he does kind of get it.

"I told him we were coming down and he was so funny. He said, 'Well, do you think you can play golf?' And I said, 'Dad, I don't know that I can necessarily lift a golf club, much less twist my torso with the side being so sore. But I might try. . . .' I can still putt. I can go along with him and he can hit all the long stuff and I'll be his putter."

Ten days later, there is no improvement in the tumor markers. Anna makes the decision to stay off chemotherapy. Instead of being depressed, her mood is high. "Free at last!" she says a few days later. "Since this decision, I have taken walks every day, I'm out there enjoying the day and it's been so beautiful and wonderful. I'm tired, but I'm happy tired. I'm liberated from taking the stuff that was killing me. I'm stronger now."

Anna begins her next visit with Miller by saying, "Listen, I have to bring up a subject I know you hate. I think it's getting to be the right time to tell the kids. They're eleven and thirteen," she reminds him. "They are beginning to ask questions—and they are going to ask in one way or the other 'When is it going to happen?' " Anna fights back tears. "And I need to give them some answer." She takes a deep breath. "I don't see me going through '97. What do you think?" Ken replies, "Oh, I see you getting through '97. But '98?" He finishes the thought with a palms-up "Who knows?" gesture. Anna smiles broadly. "Great! I'll take your odds."

The conversation leads to a much broader discussion. "I think she had a lot of relief and so did I," Miller recalls. "It opened up conversations that actually were very comfortable—but then Anna's a unique person. She's so easy to get close to, so great to be with. I'm not sure that she shares everything with me as much as she does with friends, and I have to give her the right to do that. But I asked her something I've really never asked anyone, well, maybe I have once or twice. She talked about the end of life and I said, 'Where will you go?' She said, 'I'll be on the Hale-Bopp comet. Look for me.' I've just been thinking and laughing about it. And believing it too."

Ken reflects on his years of experience with the dying. "Most people,

I don't think, go through those stages that Elizabeth Kübler-Ross wrote about—they don't reach that point of acceptance and almost spiritualism. Most people are probably getting chemotherapy until they die. Or some type of therapy, because it's too profound to picture the end of one's life."

As a result, people often view hospice as death's doorway instead of seeing the positive quality of life one can achieve with its palliative care. Pain-free is their goal. Unlike patients who opt for continuing futile treatments, Anna says it's how you live your life that counts, not how many days you have. Anna raves about a book she is reading, *Dying Well*, written by a hospice physician, Ira Byock, whom Miller knows from his days on the Academy of Hospice Physicians board. "I love Ira and his work. He and I—we all know people like Anna, but it's a minority. It's a very unusual person who can talk about all this." For Anna, Byock's book provides comfort and she is mystified by those who cannot respond with her sense of practicality. "I couldn't put it down. The guy is a real humanitarian and gives me information that's usable. It's not pie in the sky. I've been trying to find out what's going to happen to me, what happens to the inside of my body. And I've seen this only in hospice books."

At this point, Anna seems far from end-of-life decisions. "Anna comes across as very, very functioning at a much higher level than she feels," says Miller. "So it is very easy to be fooled, including for me. But she is active and is nowhere near that." During such a period, well-meaning friends and family members often cannot gauge a patient's needs. Some, for example, have urged Anna to get help in the home, instead of, for example, lugging laundry from the basement. "You know what? She *wants* to," says Miller. "And that's important. This is the living part, helping your kids do their homework, that kind of stuff. If nothing else, it's a respite from your illness when you get involved with someone or something else.

"Generically speaking, there's a couple of things I advise my patients. One is that they need to tell their family and friends what they need. For example, if someone is getting adjutant therapy for breast cancer, I think it's fair to tell their family and friends, 'I don't *have* breast cancer. I *had* breast cancer. I've had surgery and this is preventative therapy.' That's not ignoring the fact that it might come back, but at that point, she's not a cancer patient. For someone with more advanced cancer, they also need to tell their family what they need."

For Anna, it is difficult to ask for any help. Miller smiles. "That's probably how she's been all her life and probably how she will be. So you know what? Let's celebrate that."

For months, Anna has played out in her mind how and what she will tell her children if and when her disease progressed. As she contemplated her drug holiday in February, she wrestled with uncertainty. "Just last week," she recalls, "Ellery said, 'Mom, when you kick this thing and you get better, are you going to go back to work?' And I said, 'Weellll, I don't know.' I focused on the work aspect rather than 'when you kick this thing.' It's not too far around the corner when we're going to have to have that conversation. Again, I don't want to have it too soon. One of the things I'm going to do is ask Dottie about that."

In a household so open, her children witness their mother's ups and downs daily, overhear her blunt phone conversations, develop deep concerns and equally deep denial systems. About the time his mother is worrying about when to talk to them, Ellery is having his own conversations. He volunteers in a long-distance phone call that he is taking a stress course at school. "No one in there is really talkative. We sit around and try to talk about what is causing the stress. One kid got kicked out on Thursday. We were talking about things that made us stressed and one girl said that two years ago her dad died. When we were talking about her dad's dying, he said, 'Well, think about it this way, it's just one less human being screwing up the world'—and me and a girl and another friend, we *made* him go over to her and apologize." How did you do that? "Well, he had some"—Ellery pauses for effect—" 'help.' She told him off right then and there. She said, 'You're lying and you're a stupid, short idiot.' And he is short." What did the teacher do? "I know she's going to be talking to the counselor." How did he make you feel? "It pissed me off. When we took him over to apologize, he said, 'That was a perfectly valid statement' and so I said, 'Then *you're* screwing up the world.' He just, like, stood there."

The group was asked to write down their areas of stress. Ellery wrote "math" and "science" and then "My mom has cancer." On the phone,

Ellery says, "Mom is in bad shape, you know." How does that make you feel? "I just keep reassuring myself that they will solve the problem. Just keep reassuring myself that nothing's going to happen." It must be very hard for you. There is no response. Does Dottie relieve the stress? "Oh, definitely. She makes me forget about everything. She's very helpful." Is the clay wall helpful? "Oh, *yeah.*" What is important about those times with Dottie? "Just being with her, talking to her. The last time we were there, we played the game called the Ungame. It's a talking game. You go around the board, like Monopoly, and we discuss things. Like if you're having a bad day, you go there, stuff like that." What is Dottie's ability to make you forget the bad things? "She calms me down. A lot of times I get panicky. She makes me not care about that stuff for the moment." Panicky about your mother? "That's mostly what she talks about. She always assures me that everything is just going to be fine."

Later his mother says, "Dottie never says something that is not true, that's just what Ellery wants to take from the meeting." Dottie adds, "You never, ever lie. You never say, 'Don't worry about it, things are going to get better.' But kids, like grown-ups, hear selectively. I can try to let a kid down gently until I was purple. And if they don't want to hear it, they're going to hear the *tone* of my voice as hopeful. If I use the word 'hope' in any way, that's what they latch on to. If you say, 'I understand how you really want Mom to get better,' that can be interpreted as 'Mom's going to get better.' You don't ever contradict and you never, ever take away that hope." She points out, "Very few illnesses are absolutely straight declines, so these kids have lots of reasons to believe in miracles. You have a woman who had lots of metastases and the liver cured up for a good length of time. That's unheard of! So there's lots of medical reasons. Let them hang on to that. What would it accomplish for a kid to have to say, 'I know my mother's going to die.' So *what*?! If it clouds and messes up that day, that's one less good day that they have. Everybody knows it! We ain't kidding. 'I know that she or he is going to die and I know after he or she is dead, I'm going to have to deal with it. But let me now have this time to enjoy you. So it makes sense to allow me to say, "Okay, put this little 'know' in a bucket and leave it over there." So you and I have this moment. And be fully in this moment.'

"Kids are extraordinarily bright, extraordinarily intuitive. That's how they operate. That's what they bring into this world, before we beat it out of them and teach them not to trust it anymore. They know. They also know that this moment is precious."

Ellery is now extremely protective of both his sister and his mother. "Mom can never do anything she wants to do now. But we understand that and help her out." Do you have some idea how or if your life is different from other children's? "Yeah. It's really quite simple. We have a lot more to do around the house." Has her illness made you grow up more? "I understand more. And I have a better comprehension about all this stuff." He doesn't verbalize how it has clearly sensitized him and made him more compassionate, as demonstrated in his angry response to the cruel comments of the hostile boy in his stress class to the girl who was grieving over the death of her father. "I almost hit him," recalls Ellery. He and his father are spending more time together, not talking about problems but working actively on a science project. "I went to Dad's office. It was great. Dad has a gram scale that can measure one-tenth of a milligram. We got that scale and measured out fifteen amounts of yeast, one gram or really close. . . ."

Ellery still stalls on projects and needs pushing from his parents, but there has been no startling decline, although stress about his mother has increased and his hormones are hard at work. Now twelve, Ellery is over five feet seven inches, taller than his father, his body has slimmed, his voice has lowered, a faint brush of mustache is visible, and, much to his disgust, phone calls from girls have increased. In no way does he resemble the short, pudgy boy of two years ago. Now in the seventh grade, Ellery is doing pre-algebra on an eighth-grade level. "I have to go at this pace. Otherwise I'll get bored." Computer games—"They're more powerful than video games"—are Ellery's latest passion, as well as his old standby, TV. "And, I watch," he says slowly, knowing it will get a rise out of his listener, "violent movies." With that dumbfounding ability of adolescents to do several things at once, like studying intricate homework and listening to booming music, Ellery says, "I'm watching one as we speak. *Showdown in Little Tokyo.*" With the exasperation of a parent who has experienced the same with her son, his listener asks, "What is so wonderful about violent movies?" "I don't know." Then Ellery laughs, teasingly. "Hey, it's a guy thing."

CHAPTER FOURTEEN

Telling the Children

Dottie Ward-Wimmer comes to Anna's house on the afternoon of February 21, while the children are at school. The women hug each other and Anna bubbles on about feeling much better. It is still a few days before Anna returns to the doctors to find that she is getting no better and decides to go off chemo permanently. Even without that knowledge, Anna desperately knows she needs this meeting.

"I think I have to tell the kids. I think it's time from signs I'm just getting inside." Her run-on sentences and disparate feelings collide into one another. "I'm not sure if it's time, oh, it's so scary to know when the right time is! But there are a couple of indicators. Ellery has said things to me like, 'Mom, when you're cured, are you going back to work?' It really worries me that he's now in delusion land. A neighbor and I were walking the other day and she asked how I felt and I said I was better. She said, 'I knew you hadn't been well.' And I said, 'How did you know?' And she said that she asked Lindsay how I was doing and that Lindsay replied, 'Oh, she's okay. She just lays around the house.' And I said to myself, 'Man, I can't let this be the picture that Lindsay will remember.' " Anna starts to weep. "It just . . . It can't be the picture."

Dottie pats Anna's arm until Anna gains control. "I can't let them see that. I mean, they're going to see that, but let them see that for the right reason—that it's not the damn chemotherapy that's causing Mom to lie around the house. Let 'em understand what it is for what it is. And I was reading in this book—and they made an interesting point—that if I tell the kids now, they'll have me to share their sadness with. I told Jan last night, 'It's not fair *not* to do that. What happens if this thing takes me out quick, because the liver can just go, and I'll be jaundiced and three weeks later I'll be dead?' The liver's already pushing around in places, they think it may be in my lungs, and I said to Jan, 'If this happens quickly, they're going to be cheated out of knowing I was sick and dying, and thinking instead that they could have done something, maybe.' I don't know what they would think—levelwise, where would they be? But do you think that's a good idea to tell 'em? I was thinking of telling them Sunday, March ninth."

Tears spring to Anna's eyes again and she laughs a hollow laugh. "I thought, 'We'll sit down Sunday and have a nice breakfast. We'll tell 'em not that 'oh, gee, Mom's dying,' but that this disease, that we can't stop it and that it might kill me and I'm fighting all the time and I've taken all these drugs and I'm very weak and I need to get my strength back, and, I mean, I'll walk 'em through what's going on. But the bottom line is I know Lindsay's going to flip out and think she's going to die of cancer. I can see the scenarios of fear that are going to come up in their heads—and I can do so much to calm them down and I think we'll have some amazing dialogues from that point on, especially with Ellery."

Anna races on, almost as if afraid to stop and think about what she is saying. "I think he's going to ask a lot of questions and he's going to want to know things and he's going to feel a lot and I think he'll communicate that. I think he'll be okay overall in the process because we already talk about our feelings. Lindsay doesn't, you know, but I thought, 'What better time than us to sit down on a Sunday morning,' and then we would be prepared for . . . And I don't know if I should call the schools even and say, 'Listen, if you see a behavioral change, let us know. We've had some changes in terms of this stuff and the kids may be distracted, they may be not all there for a while.' " Anna gulps for breath. "But we don't know how to tell them. I don't have a clue. Oh, my God!"

Dottie steps in, reassuringly. "Nobody ever does. It's so much of a process, it really is. And to say that you're going to do it on March ninth, at seven-thirty in the morning . . . ?" She shrugs. "I can tell you how some other families have done this and generally what seems to 'work,' and I use that word in quotes because there's no easy way. But it is imperative to have a real good sense of the core of what you want them to know. You need to be able to say it in two sentences essentially. You can use more words, if you like, but you need to be very clear with yourself what it is that you want to say. Are you trying to say that 'I need a break from chemotherapy because I need a rest?' Are you trying to say that 'Maybe this isn't going to work?' Or are you in fact trying to say, 'I'm probably going to die from this disease?' It's real important that you're clear inside yourself about the message that you want to give them. Otherwise you'll be all over the place, because you'll start to say something, you'll watch them get sad, and the mother in you will just automatically back up and say, 'But'—and you'll somehow make it nicer or different. You have to know what it is you're trying to say to them."

Anna replies, "It's going to be 'I'm probably going to die from this disease.' " "Then you and Jan decide, Are you going to tell them separately or tell them together?" "I want them to be together." "Okay, then you're just real clear with them. You and Jan might even practice saying your words back and forth to each other because those words will choke in your throat."

"I know. And I have to be able to say it, I have to be able to tell them."

"When the moment is right, it will happen. Just let it come to you. And the time will come. Who knows, the sun will be shining, your kids will be sitting there. They'll say something that is the perfect cue—and to let that moment go by because it's not March the ninth!" Dottie rolls her eyes. Anna laughs weakly and nods. Dottie continues. "Generally speaking, if you can be open to those moments, you might find that, say, on a Friday afternoon—where you have a weekend to process it and they have time to do what they need to do and they don't have to take an algebra test the next day—that's the right time. But if it happens on a Monday and they need to take Tuesday off from school, that's fine. It's different in each family, but it opens up those possibilities for a kid to say, 'God, I just want to be with Mom today.' So you'll write him a note, so maybe he'll be absent a few times, maybe his grades will take a nosedive. What he will have—as difficult as it is to say to you now—are far fewer regrets."

Anna jumps in. "They're trying to be caregivers right now as it is. 'Mom, can I get you this? Do you need help?' And they don't know why. They know I'm sick, of course, but they keep grasping on to this 'when she gets better.' We could be building a really big block of anger here in that they're going to say, 'You lied to us or didn't level with us.' " Anna remembers Phoebe's brother and the anger that his children still feel for being told nothing about his illness. "I don't want to see that happen. And I've got all these indicators that things are breaking down, which is not a good sign. I've got blood in my stool, in my urine. I have to be able to be ready, knowing how fast this can come. I want to be able to tell my kids that this is the way it really is and we're all together and we're all okay with it and we can work through some of the pain together."

Anna's urgency to tell her children is driven, in part, by her need to control and affect situations while she is alive. "Jan and I talked about it last night and he kind of went, 'Ugh!' He hedged—" Dottie interrupts, "And you will from time to time too." Anna rushes on. "I know, I know. But then I explained to him that it wasn't fair. I said, 'What if this goes quickly and all of a sudden they're looking at me and they've got so much pain and I could have shared it? If they wanted to cry? I could have been the person holding them. We can't take that away from them.' And he said, 'Wow, you're right!' " "Then *don't* take it away from them," says Dottie. Anna nods. "If we go to Florida in the spring, we'll have a much more meaningful vacation if those kids can think, 'I may never do this again with my mother; let's have a good time, make the most of it.' And they won't have regrets later, thinking, 'Why didn't she tell us.' "

Dottie says softly, "Once the word 'die' gets said, it's amazing how you can then focus on living." "Exactly," murmurs Anna. "You're so right." "This isn't about tolerating chemotherapy and how we're going to get through it until Mommy gets cured," continues Dottie. "This is about 'Probably, at least that's what my body's telling me, I'm going to die from this disease. It may be months. I may have another year or so. Nobody knows for sure. I just want to be honest and real. And I want this time to be spent with us being able to live in the best way that we can. And I can't do that when I'm taking all these drugs that now we know aren't helping, so I'm going to stop taking those drugs because I want to be able to live out my time with you.' And you'll cry and it'll be sad because the thought of living only this much time will be sad. But you put it out there." Anna sobs. "I know. I know. And I have to."

"And in time, knowing your family, you will wind up in all places—perhaps they will plan your funeral." Anna tries to interrupt, to tell Dottie how much she will mean to the children during this time. Dottie puts her hand up. "Don't talk about me, I'm going to be there, I'm going to be a part of the mix, but it will not be the awfulness there is when you first face it, because your life becomes the joy. And you are a life-filled family."

As tears stream down Anna's face, she says, "I'm so glad to hear that, that's wonderful. That helps a lot. We'll practice. That's a good idea. So I don't choke on the words and I don't beat around the bush, that's a great idea, because I will otherwise."

"You need to just put it out there. And shut up and just wait and see what happens. And it will be a process—they may decide the next time they see me that they don't want to talk about it and that's okay because there has to be places where they *cannot* deal with it. School might be the safe place for them to not have to face it. There are things to be said about telling the counselors or the teachers, but we also need to honor Ellery and Lindsay's need for what they can control. That's part of what's so awful for you right now is this lack of control. The only thing perhaps you can control is whether or not you're going to take the damned chemo."

"That's right," says Anna. "That's *my* decision."

"Build in some choices for them," recommends Dottie. "And you might have to make decisions for them. If they're having a hard time at school and the teachers are coming down on them, there's nothing wrong with taking over your parental rights and saying, 'I know you don't like this, but I need to tell the counselor because we need to get something moving here.' "

"Well, Ellery's taking this stress class. He came home with a paper showing areas or things that cause him stress. One was "My Mom has cancer." Next to that was a plus and I said, 'What's that for?' And he says, 'That means we can do something about it mentally. I can think positively about this.' All I could think of was guilt, *my* guilt. It was good that he could think positively, but I've contributed to that because I haven't told him what's happening now."

Dottie protests, "But that feeling doesn't have to change when it moves to dying rather than chemo. You can think positively about how you're going to choose to live your time. You can think positively about what this time is going to be. They can do something about it because now they can decide, given this new information, if they want to spend an extra hour with you. If they're going to give up a baseball game, I don't know what, in order to take a day with Mom and Dad on a picnic, where ordinarily kids this age would say, 'Heck, no.' It gives them a chance to do something positive about how they're going to live this time out. I'm not saying this is easy, I'm saying you don't have to give up all the control pieces. It gives you different kinds of options and controls." Anna repeats out loud, "Different kinds of controls—and you're right, they have to have them too. Okay, we'll see how they do and see if they can assimilate school. Maybe you're right. Maybe it's a safe place and they'd do fine and it goes on."

Again Dottie repeats her theme, knowing that in such a high-stress situation people need the repetition and the time to reflect, in order for it all to penetrate. Always she stresses asking the children their permission before doing anything when it comes to their roles. "You'll talk to them and you'll tell them. They'll get over the shock of hearing it and one of the next things you'll talk about fairly soon is 'How do you want us to handle this with school? Do you want to tell your counselor at school? Do you want us to tell the counselor at school?' And they'll say, 'No, don't tell anybody,' or they'll say, 'Talk to them,' or 'I'll tell them,' or whatever. You're not alone in this. Nobody's going to be alone in this anymore. Not that you have been, you've been very good, your kids really know so much. This is a new phase of it, a new part, and you've made a very important decision that you're not going to leave them alone in this part."

Anna nods. "Yes, and I don't want their fears to take over where reality can be so much nicer and better. And I don't want to give them false hopes and have them later say, 'Why did you do that to me?' " Dottie smiles and touches Anna. "Do you know how courageous this is on your part?" Anna laughs, embarrassed. "Sometimes I think it's selfish too. I want my kids with me, I don't want them not knowing. I want them with me. . . ." Anna begins to weep again. Struggling through her tears, she says, "I don't want them not thinking the truth. I just think that we'll be stronger and we'll be closer and I can help more. I can help Lindsay and say, 'Just because I have this, you don't have to get this; let's make a list of things. Here's how women prevent that breast cancer, Lindsay, here's what they do. Talk to your Auntie Roseann; look, she's okay. Talk to this person; she's okay. This is what women are doing, these are the good things you can do.' My telling her may open a door she can't open now—for her to finally express the fear that she thinks that it's going to kill her. She's just terrified about it."

"She may not be willing to open that right now," Dottie cautions, "but you can give her all the information." Anna says, "I know." Dottie continues, "When it's time. You can plant all the right seeds." Anna races on. "Up to now, she's been thinking, 'It's not really in my world because Mom will be fine.' And I'm going to get worse, I can't keep saying, 'Oh, I'm getting better.' " Anna playacts an imaginary conversation, imitating Lindsay in a "Mr. Bill" (from *Saturday Night Live*) voice: " 'Gee, Mom, you don't look like you're getting better, *you're* turning *yellow*!' " Anna flutters her voice like a twittery old woman. " 'Oh, it's just the jaundice, my dear, nothing to worry about.' " Dottie can't help but laugh. Anna continues, "That's just terrible, not to be real with them."

Dottie says reaffirmingly, "Yes, this family has too much style and too much history with putting it out there to isolate you now. They wouldn't even know how to deal with that. It's not what they're used to." Anna shudders. "It's scary, scary, scary, but we have to do it. And I was so glad Jan agreed. He's been a real surprise to me. I thought, for sure, he was going to scientifically argue. Actually, he did say, in this quiet little voice, 'Well, why don't we find out about the 5-FU being placed directly into the liver?' I looked at him and said, 'No!' He said, 'How do you know you won't have side effects?' I said, 'Honey, they can put it in my liver, they can give it to me through my life port, it still circulates through my system, it's going to get to my mouth and my vascular areas. Just because they shoot it directly into the liver doesn't mean I'm not going to get any side effects from it. Come on, you're the scientist!' He feels getting off chemo was a very liberating thing. But he's still holding hard to 'Try this, try this,' and I tell him I can't do it. I'm just tired of being brought to the brink of death by chemotherapy."

"It's interesting," comments Dottie about Anna's decision. "It's not at all about giving up, it's about giving life a chance." She lets that sink in and then suggests, "In deciding what to say to the kids—and of course nobody knows; you could go on like this for years, you could go on for three months—but if you can get some time frame from Ken, that can be helpful for the kids. Knowing that it's not an absolute commitment, the kids will need something. And then you can go on to say, 'We're shifting our focus to accommodate that time frame.' "

"I've said to friends that the doctors didn't think I'd live this long," recalls Anna. "I don't know if the kids ever heard that, but that's one thing I can tell them. As you know, I haven't sat down and said to myself or anyone, 'Oh, gee, I'm dying.' I'm just not like that." "Exactly! What you're doing now is *staying* in their life. It's not saying, 'I'm dying,' and go off in a closet. You're saying, 'I still want to be a part of their lives.' " Dottie gives voice to an exuberant thought. "You know what else we can do? Instead of coming down to the center the next time, let me come here. Ellery's been wanting to do that for a while. Let's do that, make it a bit easier for you. You can come down the next time, if you feel like it, but let's do this in a way that honors your time.

"I just realized something else. If and when it comes up with Lindsay, this fear of cancer, a counselor at the center has beaten breast cancer twice. Twice. Chemo. Radiation. The whole nine yards. Second clean bill of health. I was thinking maybe I'd introduce Lindsay to her."

Worries about Jan are discussed. "I said, 'Be there for Lindsay, talk to her, don't let this child go in a hole,' " Anna says. "She'll probably work out a lot through dance, but Jan's going to have a really hard time. I said, 'Whatever you do, don't withdraw from those kids. You might have to withdraw from everything else for a while to regroup. That's fine. But don't withdraw from the kids, because they'll take it so personally. They'll think, 'What have I done wrong?' " Anna says to Dottie, "I hope he will talk to you. His nature is to not verbalize. He was very quiet last night after we talked about this, and a few tears came. And then he couldn't sleep. He got up and got on the Internet. And I went right to sleep. I feel so much better. We've got this plan. I am thrilled. He is so glad that you and I are talking. If we do this now, I can help deal with the children. It may be a saving grace for all three of them."

Dottie reassures Anna that she will always be there, either on the phone or in person, and offers to come to the house anytime. "It's easy for me to stop here on my way to work in the morning. And that's what this is about. It's not about making schedules, it's not about regular therapy time, it is about honoring your life and us just being there as you need it, as you want it, as you deserve it to be. You have so much natural wisdom and experience and it's so helpful. And your example will be taken to the next family," says Dottie, just as she has incorporated previous stories to share with and comfort Anna and others in grief.

Anna races on, avoiding the compliment. "I'm so glad you do what you do and you're there. The kids just love you to death." "Oh, I just love *them,* they are so precious. They are good kids." "They're very unique people. I don't think it's just me, Mom, talking," she says with a laugh. "They are unique in their own right—and they've got a unique dad."

Faking an admonishing tone, Dottie says, "And *you* just can't take a compliment. God forbid!" Anna echoes, "Yeah. God forbid!" They laugh and hug. As Dottie gets ready to leave, Anna, almost lost in thought, mumbles, "It's going to be tough, Lindsay's got a party Saturday night. . . ." Dottie edges in. "There's not going to be any right time." Anna says vehemently, "No, but she's got outdoor ed [education]. She goes away Monday, Tuesday, and Wednesday next week; they sleep over. I can't do it before she goes away and have this fear or sadness come up out there." Her voice drifts off.

Anna is so cheerful the following week that it staggers a visitor. "I feel like a different person. Mentally. And physically; I have much more energy. It's been three weeks without chemo, I would have had it today. Thursday I go in for blood tests, but this is the best decision I ever made. I feel wonderful." There is a settled calm about her decision to go off chemo. She had lunch the day before with a friend and drove in the country. "We went to this *great* potter, Tatiana, who has fabulous glazed stuff. Then on the way home, we drove along a little teeny diddly winding country road and when I got home, I was green. I was *so* car sick. But it was so great to be out." Anna is now about to pick up a prescription and go to the grocery store. Chores that most people would find mundane irritants Anna now looks on as miracle moments.

Once again, she is back helping others. Anna is organizing and editing material for a friend's disjointed thesis. And once again, she is getting out of her own sorrows through curiosity; she enthuses about the theme of the thesis as if it were her own—looking at children's understanding of their own day care experience.

Anna and her sister talk often now. At one point before Anna's meeting with Dottie, recalls Roseann, "Anna was not going to tell the kids at that time. I said, 'Anna, they *have* to know. You've got to tell them and Dad. They've got to know it's not playing out the way we thought it would.' She wasn't sure." Roseann worked on her some more. "There's a lot they're going to have to learn. Each child handles it differently. It gives them time to start working through this. They know I'm a survivor. Lindsay needs to see that."

By the end of February, Anna still has not found an appropriate time to tell them. Meanwhile, Dottie's advice remains uppermost in her mind: "Practice what you will say. Jan can be the kids for you and you can be the kids for him. He has to say it too. Maybe not at the exact same moment, but the time will come when he will need to say those words with them." At night, the two of them sit in the bedroom and practice. Anna even laughs now and then as she gets into it, distancing herself from the reality by pretending it's role playing. "Hey, Jan, okay, what do you think of this?" she says, lying on the green coverlet as he stands by the bed. " 'Listen, you guys, there is something I need to tell you. I think I'm going to die of cancer.' " A wincing Jan protests, "No, no, no! That's way too severe. That's too hard." Anna is now working on "something more like . . ." She laughs. "I haven't gotten it all down. 'Kids, for eight years, you know I have fought breast cancer. I've taken every chemotherapy I can. I've tried everything I can and I think the breast cancer is going to win the battle and I think it's going to kill me.' It's a little bit longer, which scares me because I've got to be able to not crack up and cry. I've got to be able to get this statement out of my mouth.

"Dottie had a helluva point. 'Make sure you know what you want to say to them.' I can't throw too many ideas out because that's going to confuse them. So I've narrowed it down to 'I've been fighting this fight, I will keep fighting this fight, but I suspect the cancer is going to win.' "

In early March, there are two reasons—one frightening, the other joyous—why Anna and Jan have not yet told the children.

Anna's blood work reveals that she is severely anemic. She repeatedly throws up and develops shortness of breath. Stumbling into the bathroom, Anna sees herself in the mirror and screeches, "Oh, my God!" Jan comes running. Anna hysterically asks, "What's wrong with my lips? Look at my lips!" To Anna, they look blood purple, even though Jan tells her "they're completely normal." Anna insists that they must be infected. She has lost so much color that her lips stand out in vivid contrast to her chalk white face. Anna is inconsolable. "I'm finally starting to look like a cancer patient," she sobs to Jan. "This really sucks. Obviously my bone marrow can't produce enough red blood cells." Joe Kaplan, on duty that day, looks at Anna and immediately schedules an all-day transfusion for the next morning. Jan spends the day with her. Anna looks over at Jan and jokes, "I vant to dreeenk your blood." Pinkness returns to her cheeks. Anna is relieved that she hadn't given the children her speech before her collapse. "Otherwise, they might have thought that I was dying."

The second reason for holding off is Ellery's sudden comic fame. A few weeks before, Ellery had an assignment that gave him three options—to write and memorize an original piece, to memorize a dramatic piece, or to memorize a comedic piece—and that had to be presented in front of the class. Ellery's love of comedy inspired him to re-create an old Bill Cosby skit on Noah's ark. In an at-home rehearsal, his mother saw no inspiration as her son just spilled it out in a monotone, without inflection. The project had become big competition, with every English class participating in the three categories, challenging one another for the title of "Best of Seventh Grade." The winner would compete with those in the sixth and eighth grades.

"Ellery won the first round!" says Anna, bubbling over. "Ellery is now the funniest boy in seventh grade! They had to do this in assembly, in front of huge masses of rowdy, wild kids. I'm just extremely amazed. There's this whole other person. He's very self-assured." Anna has begun to realize that her children have unknown lives. "I'm just totally amazed, because he didn't do it at home. It's the same as when Lindsay played flute solos in the fifth-grade band concert. I had no idea she could play all these pieces. These are those moments when you realize your children are becoming really independent beings. It smacks you in the face."

It is March 7. "Tonight we're going to see Ellery perform for the overall win. I can hardly wait," says Anna. "Tonight we were going to tell the kids. That's not going to happen. This boy may come home with a trophy and I'm not going to say, 'Well, now that we've had our fun for the day, let me pop your bubble.' "

The Johannessens scurry in out of a chill, driving wind to sit in the audience, fidgeting while they wait for their son. Ellery again is hysterically funny and beams as he listens to a new sensation—laughter and applause rolling toward him. He places second, following an eighth-grade girl who gave a polished dramatic reading. Ellery basks in new-found popularity. "Everyone knows who I am," he says in wonderment.

The big moment comes the following morning, a crystal-clear sunny Saturday. Ellery gets up first and snuggles up to his mother on the sofa in his "jammies," as Anna calls them, consisting of boxers and a T-shirt. Anna has taken her usual position in the corner bend of the L-shaped sectional. She wears an old robe over her pajamas and a green hat "to cover my bald little head." She continues to praise Ellery for his performance. Jan nervously sits, then leaves to take a shower. Lindsay protests loudly at being awakened and grouchily moves over to the blue chair in front of the bay window, wearing white pajama shorts and T-shirt. Jan has again disappeared, to start a load of laundry. Anna decides she can't wait, sensing that the kids will soon start to pick on one another.

She clears her throat and begins her rehearsed, rethought, and revised speech. "You guys know that I have been fighting breast cancer for eight years now. Well, you need to know that I may be slowly losing this battle and that I may die from this disease." She did not cry. "*Whew!*" she thought. "I got it out!" As Jan moves in and sits at the end of the couch, Anna continues to tell them how long she has fought, how her body is tired out, that there are no new drugs for her, that the cancer is slowly spreading. She says, "I know you kids aren't stupid and have been afraid of this for a long time." No one says anything. Then Ellery says, "Get a liver transplant!" Anna and Jan have to explain twice that she has too much cancer to be eligible for a liver transplant, because he refuses to hear it. "Why can't they do the transplant?" he keeps saying. Lindsay is slowly curling up behind a favorite old stuffed toy, Forest the Bear, hiding, as if shielding herself from the words. Anna looks at her. "Hey, this doesn't mean you will get this disease, Lindsay. But you, like *all* women, will have to check and watch that you don't—just like men have to check for prostate cancer. Just look at Aunt Ro, who has beaten it!"

Anna starts to tell them, "Now we can share this pain and deal with our fears together." She barely gets the sentence out as her tears begin to flow. She asks Lindsay to come over by her. Lindsay curls up on the left side; Ellery is on her right. All three are sobbing now and Anna constantly kisses their heads and tells them, "I love you. I love you. I'm sorry to cause this pain, but we have no choice and we will all have to face this. This is all new to me too, and we will muddle through together. I'm going to keep on fighting as long as I can." As they sob and hug her, Jan, with tears in his eyes, moves over next to Lindsay. Through her sobs, Anna tells them, "I am a lucky person because I have had such a wonderful life with you and Daddy. Hey, you guys," she says, snuffling, "what about Dad?" They turn to hug and cuddle with him as he sobs. Anna urges them to say anything. "You can ask me absolutely anything about my disease." But no questions come.

Tears begin to subside and silence fills the room. Anna knows they are finished, for now. "Okay," she says, "let's get on with it—we have a house to clean!" Jan quickly repeats the call to action. Anna puts on a Candy Duffler saxophone CD—"Great kick-ass music"—and the Johannessens start to clean the cluttered, dusty house.

CHAPTER FIFTEEN

"I Want Wonder"

Anna and Jan now go about the task of redefining their lives, once again. Aims and achievements are more limited, but Anna remains positive. More than ever, she embraces each day, clinging to the comforting thought that she may get through the year remaining relatively active. Her pains continue, but her days are filled with long-distance phone calls with friends, lunches with those nearby, nights with Jan and the children, various projects, including the final ballet performance of the season in May.

"I walk around the block and it hurts to breathe," she says, the week after she tells the children. In addition to leftover nerve damage from Taxol, the pain comes from her now-weakening bones. She pops Percocets, but there is an incredible amount of energy and relief in Anna's voice. "It's all on the table and I think that's a healthier perspective." Anna walks a tightrope with her silent daughter, broaching the subject at times but not overwhelming her. "Last night, I hugged her, saying I was sorry I had to give her such bad news. She faded off into another world, but that's very normal. It's her way of handling it. But she heard. I saw this incredible sadness in her eyes. Ellery's finding his own ways to help himself. I wouldn't be surprised if his grades go down."

On occasion, Anna sees snapping tempers in her children, a consequence of the tremendous anger they feel at her illness. "I make it very clear that they can never blame themselves, which I understand children can do for no reason, but I think I have to reinforce this." She is grateful that "it is their nature to be self-centered at this age. If we can help them stay in that world, that's fine with me. And I am so glad we found Dottie. When they're mad, they can now whomp on that wall."

Anna continues to draw sustenance from facing situations head-on; knowing all she can about her cancer, planning the next move, finding humor in the situation when she can, help her fend off fear and panic. Practical planning is part of her nature and the fact that at times she can also distance herself by pretending it's about someone else remains a defense. Still, she goes forth ducking nothing.

One day, before deciding to go off chemo, Anna asks to take the exercise on facing one's death—called Death Personalization—given by the St. Francis Bereavement Center to prospective volunteers. Then she carefully writes out her answers on the computer. The instructor begins by telling everyone to sit comfortably, loosen any tight clothing, let go of tension by repeating the word "relax" with eyes shut, then follows with general relaxation techniques: "Feel the tension leave your forehead . . . your jaw. . . ." Anna skips the initial exercise, in which she is to imagine a doctor is telling her that she has one year at best to live. Unfortunately, this is no fantasy for Anna.

She proceeds to questions contemplating the final year: "How do your friends and family respond to your illness?" Her answers reveal an undercurrent of emotional pain—her melancholy at being the cause of sorrow. "This disease is causing my family to fight their own set of demons and it makes me so sad. I try to give them a sense that I have some control over this disease. My husband just looks at me and quietly cries. His face gets bright red and tears stream from his eyes. He vocalizes nothing. He cannot talk about it, still. My brothers both express sorrow, but they live in Florida and are removed from the day-to-day living with the disease. They check up on me . . . but they seem to be able to live with this because they don't have to see me all the time. . . . My dad talks about it but gets all choked up because he is fighting the demons of my mom's death too. He refuses to believe that this will kill me." When her father gets in the "battle the disease mental state," Anna can tell over the phone that he is crying. "It makes me so sad to see him hurt so very much. . . . My sister is fighting her old battle again. She just cannot admit that my case is different and I may not be as lucky as she is. She wants to blame someone for our situations not being the same. She is driven by frustration and anger and the pain I see in her face just tears me up. Sometimes I fear that she thinks I am giving up. I just know the situation is different. . . . So she, like my dad, is in the fight mode—fight with everything I've got. And I do." Anna feels that when she does tell everyone, " 'I am dying of cancer,' they will believe me and probably be relieved that a long, fierce battle that has drained us all will be drawing to a close."

She mentions friends. "Most have remained true, close, loyal, helpful, allowing me to vent my frustrations and allowing me to become a bit less exciting. . . . It can overwhelm some people, but none of my friends who are close has abandoned me. . . . They seem to be a tough lot and willing to give of themselves to support me." The calls from Richmond and visits from those nearby are daily. "My ballet friends and my few lady Jiffy Lube friends have been marvels of support, letting me go on about illness, taking me out to lunch so I still think I am a part of the human race. We talk about our kids, husbands, the usual stuff. They all treat me normally and we carry on about day-to-day things as though the cancer is not the center of attention. It is wonderful! They still call to ask my advice on issues. It is nice to know that friends don't associate my cancer with any mental inability to function as I have in the past."

The exercise asks, "If you had to choose only one person, whom would you choose to be with you now? What do you want him or her to do? Does that person know your wishes?" "As I die, it would be Jan. In his silence, I find love, strength, compassion, and I know that he will put me first. If I am decrepit, he will help me end all this with the least amount of pain to my family. He is gentle, kind, and always giving. He would have made a fabulous doctor. . . . It will be the hardest thing for him, but he will know how much I appreciate his nearness. As we have so often, we will lie in bed and he will just hold my hand and stroke it. He demands so little of me and I am so lucky that he has plain-out not rejected or gotten angry with me due to the situation. It would be reasonable for a man, while going through watching his wife ebb away, to be hostile and angry with her for making his life so difficult and making his pain so hurtful. If Jan has ever felt those things, I know they have never been channeled toward me.

"I want Jan to try to help me die peacefully, without a lot of fuss, with my mental faculties still intact, I hope. He cannot control that, I know. He knows not to let me linger in a coma, brain-dead. He is aware of my wishes for dying and funeral stuff. I want to be cremated and have a celebration party of my life. I sure love life and enjoy all my time here."

The exercise moves on: "Now that you are dying, what emotions arise in trying to live your remaining time?" Anna writes about her "quite varied" emotions. "I am jealous that I won't be able to be a continuing part of my children's lives—only a 'past tense' reference. I hate that! So I am living my remaining time trying to impress some guidelines, values, etc., on the kids so they will know right from wrong and remember what 'Mom' said." She comments on the question, "How do you want to live your remaining time?" "My career interests are sort of dead. I want to travel and see the world. I want to see the constellations on the other side of the world and I want to do these things with Jan." Anna wants out of life something that she has been able to produce in the past by virtue of her personality and will. "I want wonder."

Anna tackles such questions as "What has been the purpose of my life?" "What is the meaning of it now?" "Am I satisfied with that meaning?" "I feel that dying is part of the ever-moving life cycle—as one thing dies, another is being born. Whether there is any 'justice' to who dies and why, I don't know—but I am happy with life. I believe my life's purpose was to make people laugh and make them feel special." The knowledge that she has done that for numerous people "has made me feel as though I have lived a very full life; although the years will have been short, the life experiences and personal rewards were quite ample. The meaning of my life now? Part of me feels my job now is to go through this slow-death process while filling my family with life! I want my kids to love life and see all the wonder around them and appreciate what they have and who they are. . . . How I deal with this cancer day to day I hope will help them to see what a huge sea of choices and positive choices they have! It sounds so Pollyannaish, but I have learned that my approach and attitude generally dictated how things went. We make our lives what they are. . . . I really am a 'glass half full' person. As I consider these questions, I feel quite at peace with myself. This sure is not the mission that I had set for myself—thinking I would become some hotshot corporate ad executive (well, I was a few times)—but I can still gain rewards."

The questions get grimmer; the person is asked to visualize being bed bound. "Who would be the main caretakers?" "Imagine loved ones as they visit your bedside." Anna writes that Jan and the children will be the main caretakers. "They will not be afraid to see me in this condition. . . . I can picture them coming in to talk to me, read to me, feed me ice chips, stroke my arm, adjust my blanket, and caress my face. I can also see them hold each other outside of my view, crying." When she summons them, what does she want? "I would hope for a touch, which will be real and enduring—and remind me that they are there as I drift off into morphine land."

A question about dying is placed in the context of being very tired and letting go: ". . . Just moving seems to take monumental effort—and suddenly you begin to feel that it is time. Imagine you are standing at the opening of a tunnel." The person is instructed to enter the tunnel and "proceed at your pace. . . . There will be a warm, bright light through which images are visible. What do you see?" The person is asked to make a choice, to go forward or return to life. "The tunnel spells relief!" writes Anna. "It signifies joy and rebirth for me and everyone I leave behind, who can now get on with their lives. . . . I think I will see the essence of my mother within the light at the tunnel's end. I have asked not to be resuscitated, so hopefully, people won't be frantically working over my body, so that it can be let go."

Asked to imagine services, Anna writes, "I envision a memorial party where people better be laughing about some of the antics I have experienced with them. . . ." For all of Anna's inner spirituality, she eschews religion to the last. "I hope there is no religious person there who talks about me—because I did not go to church. The Quakers have a nice thing where people stand up and tell stories about the deceased. That would be nice . . . something everyone could share without some blowhole giving a speech about me when he or she did not even know me. I find that revolting." Her great concern is that all of their friends will work hard at being with Jan.

Anna's resistance to pain management unnerves those who want to provide more relief, including Dr. Miller. During her discussions with Dottie, the counselor manages to plant the seed for pain-free palliative care. "Pain experts are really good at pain control nowadays." Anna sighs. "I have to do something because I don't think my oncologist is really tuned in to that. [In reality, Miller has suggested stronger pain control, but Anna has resisted, fearful of being a drugged-out zombie.] I know that's going to be my own stupidity—I let pain go way too long without doing anything about it—and I will also think I'm doing something about it and not have scratched the surface. 'Well, I took two Percocets and it still hurts, but it's a little better.' "

"The idea is to *stop* the pain, to find the rhythm of the pain, what works for you, and to take it all the time," urges Dottie. "I'm not saying you're dying tomorrow. I'm saying you have pain now. Start learning about it. There's this myth that 'If I take it now, it won't help me when I need it.' Not true. We can max out on aspirin, on nonnarcotic pain controls, there's a limit to their efficacy. But there's not to narcotics. You just keep increasing the dose. There is this myth; people say, 'I don't want to be a drug addict.' That's crap. You're not an addict, you are physically dependent. All that means is that your body gets used to having it in its system and if you need to stop it, you have to wean yourself off it. But you can. I've seen it many, many times because I did hospice for years and people would have these remissions and they'd be on high doses and in three weeks they're weaned off it. You're a drug addict if you take it because you need to feel an emotional high. Taking it so that you feel no pain, so that you can just live in this world, that's not a craving. That's very, very different."

Anna admits, "I have a stigma about going to morphine. It's my little indicator that says, 'Uh-oh, you're really sick now.' It's a complete psychological game that I play—'Anna, once you go to morphine, that's it. You're in big trouble now.' Dottie says soothingly, "Of course that's a big step. It can say to people, 'Uh-oh'—and that's what the movies do to us—" Anna interrupts. "Well, I read that it takes about ten days for your body to acclimate to it, and you have all these crazy effects and have nausea and all—" "You may," interjects Dottie, "and you'll be constipated and all of that. . . ."

Anna asks, "And then your body adjusts?" "Yes, then you get acclimated. I work with hundreds and hundreds of kids, and I see them on morphine and morphine derivatives literally for years. If you knew what these kids were taking, you'd drop your teeth. As you learn more, you'll chart the rhythm of your pain and discover where the triggers are and you'll know, for example, 'usually my hardest time is in the afternoon,' so you don't *wait* until you're miserable. You'll develop a pattern of popping these pills in a way that gets the pain before it even starts." Anna finally admits, "I don't do that—and it's terrible. I get to the point where I can't move. I'm my own worst enemy."

"After you start on a regular pattern, you actually wind up taking less over the long run, because you're mitigating it," advises Dottie. "You're getting it before it breaks through. Pain has a threshold. What they look for in hospice is this place around the threshold, where a drug works, doesn't give you all the sleepy crappy side effects and is also effective. And that's what you're looking for."

Anna startles her with a sudden query. "How do you know when to call hospice?" "That's a good question. If you've made a decision not to take chemo, then you might want to just call them and meet them and get some information. I was doing hospice work before the feds were involved, we were part of the team that people were introduced to when they were diagnosed with the disease. Period. We were called hospice/special services. We were just part of the support team. So when it got to the point where they weren't going to be taking chemo or whatever anymore, and they were kind of looking at issues of dying, they didn't have to be introduced to strangers. They just saw more of us than they did of the oncologist. Whether or not you were on chemo, our job, our responsibility to you, never changed, to help support your living. But there are federal regulations now, so I'm not exactly sure what the particular guidelines are."

Many in the hospice field decry the limit of six months in hospice care—set not by them but by Medicare—which implies a death sentence from the start. Studies show that some people thrive on the nurturing concept of hospice and survive longer. (A larger picture of hospice, its pros and cons, will be discussed later.) Anna asks, "How do you *know*? I don't know if I've got six months to live or a year or what." "It's such crap," fumes Dottie. "I can't believe what the feds have done to this. There is a program out at Gaithersburg called Hospice Caring [which takes no federal funding and therefore is not limited to six months]. They are simply volunteers; they don't do direct nursing care—they pull in those services somehow. You might want to investigate it."

Anna wants more actual details about "what's going to happen—how my body's going to behave." Dottie suggests a hospice expert might provide that information or put Anna in touch with doctors "who are used to talking about end-of-life issues and are used to being honest. Now is the time to learn—and to consider getting yourself out of pain. If you want to live your life, then do it as pain free as you can." Dottie smiles.

Anna says slowly, "It makes a whole lot of sense. A friend of mine gets on the phone and just cries and cries over this and I'm saying, 'Pat, it is what it is. I can't sit and cry about it.' I think I'm really lucky—I know myself and I've liked and been happy with who I was. I feel sorry for people who get diagnosed with cancer and their entire lives have been about what their accomplishments are, the money they made. You lose all of that and if you have no other way to define yourself, you have nothing. I didn't define myself that way. I was a pay-and-play person—if I couldn't have a good time, I didn't care what I was making financially, I'd quit and do something fun. And I am still doing it, not on as grand a scale, but I can have a good time and share it with others. So the pressure's off," Anna explains to Dottie, "I don't have all those angry coulda, woulda, shoulda things hanging over me. Anything I wanted to do I did."

Dottie says, "You're still going to make jokes from your bed." That pleases Anna.

Anna's typical need for preparedness and consideration for others prompts her to give advice about this topic to the readers of this book. She titles it "All Sorts of Things You Should Do Before You Die":

- Don't wait, get your will done today and get it finalized! I may outlive many readers, but my affairs are in order so that I don't screw my family with having to deal with these issues as well. This is also a major control issue. If you get your affairs in order, things are done your way. If not, hey, don't bitch about it in your afterlife when cousin Gomer gets your favorite leather coat that you wanted your nephew to have.
- Make sure the title to the car is out of your name before you die. It is easier than making your spouse prove you are dead so that he or

she can get the title changed. [There are many horror stories about the trauma of spouses having to reiterate the cold word "deceased" every time they try to get a name changed on property or a bank account or to close a credit account. For example, one top executive, shattered by the murder of his sister by her estranged husband, found this exercise one of the most invidious of his many duties as her executor.]

- Call and ask your banker what your spouse needs to convert the checking and savings and all other accounts to his name.
- Find out what it takes for your spouse to get your life insurance money and make sure your spouse has the information at the ready. I did learn that you need to get death certificates from the state government and, based on holdings and assets, your spouse may need an original death certificate for every asset you have. The funeral home can arrange for these to be procured quickly for a meager cost. *Do it!* Sometimes a Xerox copy will not suffice and it can take up to six weeks to get death certificates from the state, whereas the funeral home can do it within days. There will be enough unforeseen burdensome things for your spouse, so get that taken care of.
- If you don't want to be hooked up to machines, then get your living will done, witnessed, and keep it in a prominent place with you, your doctor, and your mate. The scary part is that once the hospital guys hook you up to life support, they cannot unhook you easily—*even with the documentation.* You need to be sure they see the documentation *before* they attach you to life-support stuff. Make sure everyone has the paperwork on your living will wishes.
- If you are on disability and did not provide for your kids, do so immediately. Take some of your disability money and put it into their bank accounts. After you die, your spouse will have a much easier time having the rest of your disability money switched over to them.
- Be nice and while you are mobile (or someone in the family can), clean out your junk. Don't let your family have to deal with all of this as well. This is not the nice things that you want them to have—this is the real junk!
- Make your own funeral arrangements. You can do this by discussing the arrangements and writing down the instructions so that

your spouse does not have to do anything but follow them. You can even go so far as to write down the deal with the funeral home and put funds in a joint savings account for you and the funeral home. I am not going that far. Jan can write the check because he may want to do stuff that I don't care one way or the other about.

- Write all this down so that your spouse has a list of what needs to be done and how to do it. Write out a telephone-tree list so that your spouse knows whom to call when you die. Each person he calls can be given a list of others to call.
- If you have children, hopefully you have begun some sort of counseling process before you die. If not, try to do so—so that the process is under way and your children already trust another person and can continue talking with him or her. You may suggest this to your spouse as well, with or without kids. Each family must decide this, but from my experience, having a bereavement counselor in place is wonderful—someone to whom my kids can display their fears about losing me. They try to be brave with me, but they need someone who can allow them to be vulnerable. I had no idea that they would act like this, hence the relief to have a counselor!
- Make sure that you and your spouse have decided what would happen if he or she were to die suddenly, leaving the kids without parents. What relative would take them? Have you asked that relative, in case? Have you and your spouse figured all of this out? In our case, this is a weird one because it will depend on the age of our kids at the time as to what relative we would have them be with. [It is comforting to the disorganized to know that Anna is not perfect.] We have to get this done in writing yet—but we will!

Anna drives down to visit Lockie in Richmond, in mid-March, soon after she tells the children about the extent of her cancer. After the two-and-a-half-hour ride, she walks with difficulty as she approaches Lockie's house. Lockie lives alone in a charming cottage-style house—Anna says that it looks like a gingerbread house. It reflects Lockie's artistic talents as well as her immaculate order—bibelots on desktops and end tables, a rich apricot Oriental rug, an interesting stained-glass windowpane, artfully draped airy cream-colored swags over bay windows. In Lockie's beautiful backyard, yellow and violet flashes of spring flowers glint in the pale sun of early spring. "You're at least three weeks earlier than we are," remarks Anna. Her enthusiasm revives and she raves about Lockie's recently completed guest bedroom, especially the handsome maroon-and-gold draperies and bedspread, mixing plaid and print in perfect harmony.

Over a gourmet dinner, excellently prepared by Lockie—a roast, fresh vegetables, salad with fabulous homemade dressing, a decadent dessert—the two of them reminisce about good times, but Anna eats little. Although she carries on, her face is pale and she becomes quiet, about the only sign to indicate that she is in pain. Anna rallies in Lockie's bedroom as they hoot about an old dress that Lockie drags from the closet, but this weekend is a strain. Lockie looks sad as Anna—the one who kept parties alive for hours—goes to bed early. Anna, nonetheless, is content to be with Lockie, knowing that her longtime pal is so in tune with her that she will empathize, without being maudlin. As Lockie putters in the kitchen the next morning, making coffee, heating homemade bread, Anna leans against a wall. "Wow, I'm really hurting." Lockie says, "I'm glad you can be here with me while your hurting," patting her arm as she passes by. Later Anna remarks that "Lockie had a hard time learning how to open up. There's a night-and-day difference from when we met."

Lockie knows every detail about Anna's condition and is aware that Anna has told the children. Lockie's eyes swim with tears and, as she blinks, they fall on her cheeks. "That's probably touched me more than anything else." There is a long pause as she struggles to control tears. "I pray a whole lot. And I cry a whole lot with my mother. And try not to be selfish about myself." Anna says softly, touching her, "That's what grieving is for, feeling sorry for ourselves and healing."

Wayne joins them that noon for brunch. He hugs Anna, standing in line, and cheerfully says, "How ya doin'!?" Anna leans against him and says in a whimper, "I'm hurtin'." He holds on to her as she says, "I've been better." Wayne looks at Anna's black turban with a white sash tied to one side, one of those numbers created for cancer patients that passes for feminine headgear. He seeks to deflect: "You look like a nun." Anna flaps her arms. "Just call me Sally Field."

As they sit in a booth, talk turns to a favorite song Wayne had written, "Life Goes On and I'm Okay." The week before, Anna had cried when she hummed it in the shower. The trio mumble over the words, not certain of them anymore. Anna looks at Wayne, laughing. "You're the music maestro for my funeral, so you have to get it right!" Wayne picks up her mood and intones, Martin Luther King–preacher style, "And in death, she reaches out and says, 'Play the damn song!' "

After lunch, Wayne drives over to their impressive studio compound and sits in his white Mustang Cobra in the parking lot, talking about Anna while she goes into the studio with Lockie. "Lockie's been much better at staying in touch. Anna is just incredible. Anna is engulfed with this, and at the same time, she is taking classes in film editing! Just like when I was up there earlier this month, she waited until the kids were gone and took me aside. She and Jan were crying and Jan said, 'Anna's talking to the kids.' I remembered back—my mom died of cancer when I was young and it was all 'trusting the Lord' and I was never given an option to deal with it while she was alive. Anna decided to allow her kids to have the option to grieve, be angry, whatever, while she is here." Wayne sighs, then says positively, "Today will leave its mark. I see the way the two of them are dealing with this and it helps me put perspective in my life. Like 'big deal' about work—'God, *that's* a problem!' " he says derisively. "When she first said for me to get the songs that 'I want played at the funeral,' I didn't know what to say. Jan said, 'Yeah, we can do that.' The longer I'm around them, the more I realize it's not macabre. It's logical. Why not? I hope that's the way I'd be. You have an option to wallow in it or do what you can to realistically face the future."

Nonetheless, Wayne was terribly upset when Anna told him she was going off chemotherapy. "If you go cold turkey, what can you be doing to put this thing in check?" he had asked her. He listened to her explanations about how it was a positive move. Now Wayne says, "Just look at her a year ago. She was so beautiful, her hair grown back. I never told her, 'You look good,' or 'Look at all that beautiful hair.' I was afraid she was going to lose it again and I didn't see any reason to equate her esteem with a physical thing. It's Anna that matters, not her hair."

Wayne gets out of his sporty car and enters Mainstreet Productions, their successful visual production company. It now takes up 10,000 square feet spread over three buildings. In one exquisitely decorated office, Wayne leads Anna over to a coffee table. "Now time to give you a present." An intricately carved crushed-marble elephant about a foot and a half high sits there. Anna's eyes fill with tears as she hugs Wayne, who wraps it and lugs it to her car. It remains prominent in her living room.

As Anna leaves that afternoon, Lockie hugs her hard, worry clouding her eyes—but only when she holds Anna so close that she is sure Anna cannot see her face.

Four days later, Anna visits Dr. Miller. She remains jaunty and bantering with the nurses and aides. Miller walks in with her bound records, the size of a Manhattan phone directory, and lugs it to a counter as Anna's barrage hits him: "Hey, things are looking good. I just want you to order me some more Lortab [a liquid painkiller Anna uses to augment Percocet]. I'm finally doing pain management. Instead of taking two Percocets every four hours, I take less, every two hours, and that keeps things pretty pain free." Anna's tendency to paint the brighter picture is an edited version of reality. At times, she doubles over with pain from the liver tumors.

But Miller is not fooled. He suspects that Anna is popping Percocets like M&M's. "I've got another plan," he says pleasantly. Anna protests, "Oh, no . . ." He puts his hand up in a "now listen" gesture. "You're not getting enough relief. How about a long-acting medicine?" Anna looks at him dubiously. "What's happening with your pain now is that it is up and down, up and down, all day long. You can have choices, a patch or MS Contin in pill form." MS Contin stands for "morphine sulfate continuous." When said fast, it sounds like MS Cotton. Ken makes Anna smile, telling her that that was what he thought his instructor said "in my green first year in med school. These medicines can give you relief all the time by taking one pill only twice a day."

"Can I drive?" asks Anna. "Will I be completely here—not out of it?" (Anna's onetime experience with a large dose of morphine made her throw up and feel woozy.) Ken carries on. "Over the weekend, why don't we start with the lowest dose? I can promise you that you will need more. It's not going to help that much, but I want to start at this dose so that hopefully you will feel comfortable taking it." Anna swallows. "I have this mental block on morphine." "Percocet is in the same class," emphasizes Miller, "but this is a better drug. It's very good!" Recognizing that he sounds like a spielmeister, he jokes, "I have stock in the company." This brings a small smile from Anna. "Seriously, wouldn't it be great if you only had to take two pills a day? We'll start with this really low, baby dose," he keeps emphasizing. "If it is not benefiting, call me on Monday." [This is Thursday.] Anna resignedly agrees. Ken offers, "You can still take Percocet for breakthrough pain, but with the right dose, ideally we can handle the pain."

Anna says, "I can't take a breath without pain." She wants a direct answer. "Is the liver functioning?" Miller looks at her recent blood tests. "Your liver is functioning slightly above normal—but not that bad." He motions to the examining table. Anna says, "My whole right side feels pooched out." Ken raises her sweatshirt and lowers her sweatpants at the waist and gently presses on her liver, a procedure he has performed countless times on Anna. "I think it's enlarged, all the way to the center," says Anna. "You're right," says Miller. Nothing more is said—there is nothing more to say. Anna's thoughts have been confirmed. Anna and Miller hug good-bye, she takes the prescriptions and heads for the drugstore.

Anna's spirits are high as she marks the days off until they leave for Florida at the Easter holidays. She looks and feels better than she did in Richmond. She jokes that life is now measured around her constipation—the latrine humor is another way of coping. As she and a friend stock up on laxatives at her drugstore, they are hysterical over the array of bottles and pills.

One afternoon, Anna stretches out on her bed to talk. Lindsay gets testy and stomps out of the house with two tugging dogs when Anna asks her to walk them. No matter the level of her worry, Anna fights for normalcy. Later, she comes up to Lindsay and makes a whimpering puppy noise. Lindsay's mouth curls up. "I'm sorry, Mommy, but I was right in the middle of my homework. Sorry I was grouchy." Anna deadpans, "I hadn't noticed." They laugh together.

The afternoon of her visit to Dr. Miller, Anna feels energetic enough to make dinner. She prepares a new recipe for chicken breasts with *herbes de Provence,* potatoes, asparagus. "I'm just so glad there are nights when I can fix dinner and Jan doesn't have to." Lindsay enters wearing pale pink lipstick, and light eye makeup, with glitter on her lids. Anna admires the look, realizing Lindsay is into preteen glamour by now. "Mom, do we have any nail polish besides light pink?" she says, making a face. "What color did you have in mind?" "Blue!" Anna gives her a look. "Honey, those colors look so tacky." Lindsay returns with pink fingernails with sparkles on them.

Jan comes in late, tired. He had been working hard on a cohesive study covering needed changes at FDA and had presented it that afternoon at a conference. The children talk about school, then grab dessert and race to the rec room. Jan listens as Anna tells him the details of Miller's new treatment for pain. Jan has agonized over Anna's refusal to better medicate and encourages her to use the morphine.

After dinner, Jan plugs in the computer at the dining room table to do even more work. Queen bellows up the stairs on a 1975 record that Lindsay plays on an old phonograph. "Can you believe my daughter likes Queen?" says Anna. Lindsay shouts that she has found an ancient Beatles record of "Hard Day's Night"—"not even opened!" Her father raises his voice so she can hear, "Put it back." "Why?" "Because I said so." Jan is stressed, tired, and so worried about Anna that he is in no mood to jolly anyone.

Anna moves off to the bedroom. Jan leaves his computer and goes in to help with her pain medicine, to hug her, and to give her a kiss good night, again, as always, wondering what Anna's next day will bring.

CHAPTER SIXTEEN

April

It is April 1 and Anna and the family are relaxing in Cocoa Beach, after the long drive. Sitting by the pool, Jan escapes into a Patricia Cornwell thriller while restless Anna, dissatisfied with the neglected poolside Japanese garden her mother had planted, pulls weeds. She has lost twenty-seven pounds recently, but her sculptured face and visible cheekbones provide a new form of beauty. She leans back and seeks the sun. This time her hair has grown back sparsely so that it resembles the fine fuzz of a gosling. Ellery and Lindsay are out back, on the wooden dock by the canal. Both are anxious to "*do* something." Lindsay's buddy, who lives across the canal, is away, much to her disappointment. After some nudging, the family go to the beach.

Anna and Jan walk very slowly, arm in arm. Lindsay and Ellery dart in and out of the water like human sandpipers, racing on the hard sand, but keep running back to their mother to walk the slow walk with her. Although they now know their mom may not beat cancer, they choose to avoid it. Only Ellery alludes to the possibility of life without her, being sure to use the qualifier "if." Staring at his feet, which are sucking up sandy water with each step, he comments, "Mom says that if anything happens to her, she wants us to get Dad down here to live. Grandpa really loves him and Dad loves this. So do I. I would come in a minute. It's paradise, plus the cousins are here."

Young Ellery is not alone in the use of softening euphemisms; countless numbers of grievers do so. Last year, his uncle Steve avoided directness in his conversations about Anna. "If it turns out the way we don't want it to . . . if something did happen to Anna . . ." Euphemisms for death are legion—people don't die, they "expire" or "pass away" or are "called home" or are "with the angels" or, in a vague imprecise status, are "no longer with us." Death is called the Big Chill. There are euphemisms with shock value—"kicked the bucket," "bought the farm." A man used to rolling with the punches, Richard Rymland, nonetheless gasps years later, remembering: "When my mother died, the nurse called me. 'I hate to tell you this, Richard,' she said, 'but your mother just conked.' She was a Caribbean woman. To her, that was how they talked about it."

Explaining why such evasions survive, J. S. Neaman and C. G. Silver write, "The motives for euphemizing death are in many ways similar to those for disguising references to pregnancy and birth. Great superstition surrounded these events, as did great distaste and a sense of social impropriety. Propelled by these feelings, we have attempted to strip death of both its sting and its pride—in fact to kill death by robbing it of its direct and threatening name."[1]

Later that afternoon, Anna's father is happier reminiscing than he is dealing with the present. Stephen laughs. "I guess Anna was on the edge of being a bad girl. That's secondhand knowledge from Audrie—and by that time, it was usually a call for enforcement. Seems it was mostly staying out late, smoking, drinking some. We didn't like it, but it was never to the point where we had any great concern. Audrie knew more—she had eyes in the back of her head." Did you feel like you were the absent father? "With the first two, yes. The other two, Audrie *made* me be involved, read to them and play games with them. And I did. Bored as I might be." He laughs. "Well, they all turned out okay. I just love 'em all. Every chance I get. Like most ethnic people, we would have liked very much if our kids were even interested—but our kids never once wanted anything to do with the word 'Armenian.' It didn't bother me, but we thought that if they met nice Armenians, it might make a very stable relationship." Anna's marriage is a "great match," he adds beaming. "Jan's such a beautiful kid."

The Armenian religion was not followed, however. "Audrie used to take the kids to an *Episcopal* church Sunday school. Armenian? No! You could fall asleep just staring out into the blue. The constant 'yuda, yuda da da.' [His voice goes singsong.] Constant intonation for *hours.*" Do you think religion is a comfort for people going through horrible times? "I think so. A lot of people go into religion because it's another means of coping. To me, religion is a sop. You can just kind of forget about the problems."

Anna's disillusionment with religion came not so much from parental attitudes as through experience. As she walks through the room, she interrupts. "I was thirteen years old, a confused kid about protocol, and I called this young Episcopalian priest Gary—instead of Father Gary. *His* father was also a priest and I just got mixed up. He actually *swore* at me, he got so mad! It all seemed so wrong and unfair."

The Megregians are like many who practice no form of religion and rely on an inner spirituality of caring and giving, yet vast legions of people derive consolation in prayer and religious beliefs. After Anna leaves the room, Stephen is asked how he personally handles Anna's impending death—what comforts him instead of religion? "I just cry. She told me the first night down here. The only thing I can do is just sit here and wait. I realize what the inevitable will be, but I hope she can beat it somehow. I feel so bad that she's gonna go. When she told me she was on morphine, I thought, 'Oh, God, they haven't been able to stop the damn thing.' "

Stephen fights to control his voice as tears spring to his eyes. "Those kids are so young—they *need* her so." He remains grateful that Anna has been able to guide her children during the past crucial years. "At their age, I think now they're going to have enough sense to know what to do, and I think their father will keep them on the straight and narrow too." He takes a deep breath, eyes brimming again. "She's been such a wonderful mother, unbelievable. She looks stronger today than when she first came down." Yet Anna's father takes little comfort in this. His voice is barely above a whisper as he sinks into sadness. "I expect this will be her last trip down here."

That night, Stephen takes them out to dinner, a form of pleasure he has enjoyed for years. But now Anna is having real difficulty eating. She picks at her food and can only ingest small amounts. Even so, she sometimes throws up spontaneously. By seven o'clock the next morning, eighty-one-year-old Stephen has already left for the golf course. The children sprawl on the den floor, watching television as Jan fixes breakfast. Anna keeps up banter as she glances at the TV. "Would you look at those clones?" she says, watching what passes for daytime news. "They all look alike, cloned from Ken dolls." The movie *Tammy and the Bachelor* is on one station and Anna warbles the theme song. As channels are flipped, the fare goes from bad to worse. Anna cracks, "We're experiencing technical and mental difficulties."

Lindsay has been working on her mother for several minutes about having some candy. An angry Anna says with finality, "This is getting old!" Lindsay protests that Anna said she could have some if she asked. "I never give an open-ended answer like that," Anna says, firmly. In another room, Jan and Anna exchange one of those parental pacts that take seconds. "I'm not going to put up with this," she says. Jan is in total agreement. The next time Lindsay asks, Anna says, truthfully, "I threw it out." Over the noise of the TV, Jan commands, "Turn it off." In the silence, Lindsay sighs and says, "Anybody for cards?" Ellery says, "I will," and a halfhearted game of Go Fish starts while breakfast dishes are washed. Energies are released with a walk on the beach. In the afternoon, Ellery and Lindsay beg for a trip to Jungle Village, the land of go-carts, putt-putt golf, and, of course, money-gulping video games.

Anna quietly leaves and curls into a fetal position on a bed. Jan brings her a morphine pill and also drops into her mouth a small amount of liquid Lortab, which cuts the pain fast. Jan strokes her on the head and arm and gently takes off her glasses. "Is it okay if I nap for about twenty minutes? I just want the pain pill to kick in." "Sure, honey," says Jan, turning off the light and closing the door. Lindsay hovers. "Should I take Mom some Jell-O?" "No, honey, she's sleeping." Barely twenty minutes pass before Anna walks out of the bedroom. "Okay, guys. I'm ready to go."

Thirteen days later, Anna is back in Olney, getting ready for a fancy dinner at Nora's, a chic restaurant in the District. She has lost another seven pounds, and is almost ethereal in her beauty as she walks into a small banquet room to join sixteen people. She and Jan are guests of the Hospice Foundation of America, which is sponsoring a teleconference on prolonged illness the next day. Anna is a stranger to most, yet her incandescent smile and effervescence quickly charm everyone. She wears an avocado-colored silk pantsuit and a cream-colored silk blouse. A crimson silk scarf shot with gold flecks catches the light, as do her gold dangling earrings. There is a trace of pink lip gloss. Her hair is still thin but confidently uncovered. She looks terrific and several women tell her they admire her not wearing a hat or wig.

Over dinner, she talks animatedly with Dr. Ken Doka. Knowing about her cancer, he had resigned himself to an evening of hard work, wanting nothing more than to relax. Afterward, he burbles like a lovestruck teenager. "She's extraordinary! She talked about her illness a bit—she is so unusual to be so frank and open—but soon she was talking about other things, and drew me out about my work and so forth." Other guests marvel as, even at this stage, her luminous spirit eclipses others. Says Doka, "It took me a few days to think, 'Oh, my God, this wonderful woman who lights up everything is dying."

An equally easy conversationalist, Jan talks to the others with quiet assurance. He is now facing the depth of Anna's illness and for a moment lets it show. He talks to a friend about the fun he had performing in the *Nutcracker* ballet last Christmas. "But then I go backstage and I see Lindsay—" Jan cannot finish the sentence. His head goes down, elbows on the table, chin resting in his hands. He blows his nose and wipes at tears. Anna notices, and later surmises that "Jan's terrified about how he is going to handle Lindsay, how he is going to get her through this." In fact, she is wrong, as Jan explains later in detail. "*The Nutcracker* was a very difficult time for me. Learning the parent's role was fun, but during the second act, I spent a lot of time in the wings, helping and watching. When I first saw Lindsay onstage, with her full costume and makeup, being such a lovely young lady, I became very angry and upset that her grandmother couldn't be there. I remember Audrie telling me that her greatest regret was that she was not going to live to see Ellery and Lindsay grow up. She would have given all she had, all her professional accomplishments, all her awards, to be able to see that. It was such an injustice that she missed out on that wondrous scene. I had a very hard time watching Lindsay; I suppose it was compounded by knowing that Anna probably wouldn't be seeing next year's performance. I cried every night as I watched."

As April rolls on, Anna continues to worry about Lindsay—"so quiet, so into denial. And yet just a few days ago, she asked me, 'Mom, how do you get cancer?' It was out of the blue, and direct, but with a little trepidation. She wouldn't look at me when she formed the question, but she would when I talked to her. I told her that all cells reproduce and as cells reproduce, all they have to do is reproduce a little bit wrong and these are called mutations and they can become cancer cells. I told her what kinds there were—breast, liver, prostate, stomach, and so on. I said we don't know if it is because of the environment or that people are living longer and getting more cancer, but everyone has to be careful and keep on top of it, with exams and so forth." Anna ponders the sudden interest. "When I told her about how bad things were with me, she never even acknowledged it. Never asked one question. Maybe now a couple of her friends are saying something or their mothers have asked, 'How is your mom feeling?' Maybe this has caused this search for knowledge."

Lindsay can pout, and, as a preteen, there are natural changes, rebellion. Anna notices she is "getting snappier quicker." Jan is quick to anger if he thinks Lindsay is stressing out Anna, but no one has ever said for her to be better because her mom is sick. It would never occur to Anna or Jan to lay that guilt trip on either Lindsay or Ellery. "I am glad that she is acting like a normal adolescent," says Anna. Do you think this is anger about your cancer? "No. All the mothers of her friends say they are the same way. I'm sure it feeds on itself. They get together and start to complain, 'Oh, my *mother* won't let me—and blah blah.' " Anna's elephantine memory saves the day. "I was the same *way.* My God, the histrionics, the high drama." Once, her father reached to restrain a raging Anna, she moved, and by mistake, he caught her neck. One can picture teenage Anna, palm to forehead, striking a pose, as she responded, "If you're going to *kill* me—go ahead!" She shakes her head and laughs. "What a jerk I was."

The day of the hospice teleconference, Anna waits until the last minute, hoping she will feel better, then calls to regret that she can't make it. "I don't know what hit me, I am just so tired. I think it must be allergies."

On Friday, April 18, Anna and Jan meet with Dr. Miller for the hardest session that the three of them will ever have. Both she and Jan fight to hold themselves together, Anna by joking with the nurse and Jan by trying for scientific distance. Anna is now doctorlike in her ability to read her MRIs. "The tumors are just *all* over the liver," she says, "and the liver is so enlarged, it's pushing on the ribs. My bones feel like knuckles cracking." While she waits in Miller's office, an ashen-faced Jan is in another room, discussing Anna's MRI, illuminated by a light box. He strives for the impersonal, as if this MRI is not his wife's. "See all those white things? They're all tumors. All over the place." The liver, a not quite round mass, blots out the lung on the right side. Tumors dot the liver like snow in a crystal ball. Following their path is almost like viewing a galaxy of stars, some bigger and brighter, some smaller and cloudy. Jan points to a small sphere, scrunched by the liver. "That's her poor stomach. That's why she's having so much trouble eating." Jan still grasps for something to work. "There's a technique—they put the catheter right into an artery that takes drugs to the liver; it delivers a real high dose." (Miller later tells him 5-FU is as effective.) Jan returns to Anna, sitting in Miller's office. He pulls his chair close, holds her hand with one of his, and puts the other arm around her shoulder, stroking her softly. "So did you see?" she asks. "Yeah. They're all over the place." He holds up the X ray to the light from the window. "See why you're having pain on the right side?" Anna knows this before Jan shows her anything; her body has told her. "Your poor little stomach is getting smushed." Anna nods.

In walks Miller. Jan points to the X ray, saying, "These are some pretty ugly pictures." Miller sits across from the couple, looking at them steadily as he takes a deep breath. "It's been a great change." Anna says, "Yeah. Major." He says, "There has been a dramatic increase in liver metastases." Anna asks, "Any one really big?" as she holds her hands under her ribs. Miller nods. "What your feeling, it's exactly right there." The doctor reinforces Anna's thought. "Good," she says in a flat voice, "I'm not crazy."

As Anna listens, her face is shiny with sweat that drops down her chin. She sits stock-still. Miller hands her a Kleenex. "You're really having a hot flash." Tumor fevers had raised her temperature to 102.8 and she has just taken medication, she explains. "The temperature's gone and it's just me, cooling off."

Miller keeps the concern out of his voice but not his eyes. "I think the cancer has got a lot worse." He now draws back from his earlier optimistic time frame. "The time is more limited." Anna asks about the liver shutting down. "You can have a small part of the liver doing a lot of the normal duties of a bigger liver. But you'll be more tired and will spend more time in bed," says Miller, quietly. "It will be gradual, but then you will spend all the time in bed."

Jan swallows and puts both of his arms around Anna. She continues to ask questions, trying not to cry. "Is 5-FU worth exploring?" Answers the doctor, "That's where you guys can steer the ship." Anna picks up on Miller's tone. "I don't know, should we? You're kind of hedging." He responds, "The decision has to be yours. It's not my body." Before, when Miller saw more hope, he had urged Anna to try new treatments. Now he leaves the impression that he might like her to try, but since the situation is so drastic now, it may not be helpful. Miller gently says, "Don't do it for me." "Will it stop the tumors where they are?" asks Jan. "Hopefully it will shrink them," says Miller. Anna ponders. "It could possibly relieve pain for a while. . . ." Miller says, "Hopefully. It's not a home run drug . . . but it may slow the cancer or push it back some."

"I'll do it," says Anna, despite her earlier decision to stop chemotherapy. Miller asks, "What do you think, Jan?" "With any drug, you can't guarantee it'll work," says Jan. "If the side effects are not bad . . ." His unfinished sentence implies that he thinks it is worth a try. "What effect does it have on energy level and tiredness?" Miller responds, "The difficulty is in figuring out what is caused from the cancer and what is caused by the drugs." They sit there saying little; all three recognize that the choices are minimal. "This is a big change and I'm concerned about it," Ken reiterates. "I think the time is getting shorter."

Anna nods. "I can feel it." She starts to cry. Her voice is a strangled, high pitch as she talks over her tears. "If we start this thing, can I wait until after Wednesday?" She looks at Jan and almost whimpers, "I don't want to go to that lunch with a fanny pack." Miller's office had recommended Anna to appear at a luncheon to publicize the Race for the Cure breast cancer event to take place in June. Her face reddens as she holds back more tears. Miller almost tears up. "You're making me cry too." "No, no," Anna says, brushing at her cheek. Miller says softly, "I go with hope. It's a different pharmacology than you've ever had. So I'm hoping it is going to work for you."

Sherwin B. Nuland, in his book *How We Die,* chastises doctors in general and himself specifically, recalling the painful treatment to which he subjected his brother, Harvey, because "I could not deny him a form of hope that he seemed to need. I would marshal the forces of cutting-edge medicine and rescue him from the brink of death. . . . Had I been wiser . . . I might have understood that my way of giving Harvey the hope he asked for was not only a deception but, given what we knew about the toxicity of the experimental drugs, an almost certain source of added anguish for all of us."[2] Like Anna, Nuland's brother was given 5-FU with other chemotherapies at the end. Had his brother developed cancer thirty years ago, before chemotherapy, Nuland believes he would have lived as long and possibly less painfully. Despite our common fascination with the latest biotech discovery, one study in fact showed that people who opted for palliative care instead during their last days lived longer than those who stayed with aggressive treatment.[3]

"Doctors rarely *want* to give up," states Nuland.[4] Frequently it is up to the patient and family to stop exercises in costly and painful futility. Then, they face another cruel jolt when they are beyond recovery—abandonment by doctors who cannot face what they subconsciously deem a failure of science and their expertise.

There is another reason why doctors often run away from death. "Of all the professions, medicine is the one most likely to attract people with high personal anxieties about dying," writes Nuland. "We become doctors because our ability to cure gives us power over the death of which we are so afraid. . . ."[5] Loss of that power heightens their own anxiety. Oncologist E. Roy Berger recounts how it was getting harder each year to help patients face death because he had not resolved his own fears. "I realized that if I could somehow feel less anxious about my own demise and separation from life, I might be able to impart more comfort and peace to my patients. After years of denying any thoughts of an unscientific nature about the afterlife or the soul, my life's work was forcing me to confront that very issue."[6]

For doctors who care, end-of-life treatment is an agonizing call. Miller says later that he felt Anna needed to cling to hope at that time and that he felt 5-FU would not be painful and would do no harm. Jan says, "The 5-FU was palliative; we were not trying for a dramatic reversal but perhaps a stabilization to relieve the pain and allow her to eat. The main reason to go ahead was that it was supposed to have almost no side effects."

With yet another attempt to possibly shrink her tumors, the close bond between Anna and her doctor remains. Even the clear-eyed Anna demonstrates the depth of one's hope to borrow time, the desire to live overpowering reason. "Well, we'll try," says Anna as Jan hugs her, his eyes never leaving her face. Miller gives voice to a concern. "I don't want to be a drug pusher and I don't want you to feel that I'm serving my own purpose." Anna waves that off and says she's willing to try now, firmly explaining that her drug holiday in January was her own good decision. "I got a lot of my own energy back." She offers a wry smile. "Now, all I have is the cancer."

Miller urges Anna to eat. "Don't worry about cholesterol." "Hey," says Anna, "this [cancer] is the only thing that ever brought my cholesterol down." Miller shifts topics. "I'm so happy you're going on Wednesday." He hugs her close. "Good luck and enjoy your luncheon." Anna says, "I'm excited about it."

Anna reels from this crushing blow, the suddenness with which death is intruding. Still she manages to joke to the staff as she leaves about how she will be sitting with "the drug people—my pushers" at the luncheon. "And I'm supposed to have my little photo opportunity with Betty Ford!"

Anna embodies the theory that people die like they live. With grace and courage, she cheers up Miller's staff, rather than it being the other way around. Despite her limited horizon, Anna is concentrating on day-by-day rewards. On the drive home, however, Anna and Jan are quiet. "That's the first time Ken ever said anything about the dying process," she reflects, "how you get more and more tired and then you stay in bed all the time. He's always refused to look down that road before." Jan tries to switch moods. "Honey, how about watching *Help!*, that old Beatles movie? We haven't seen it in ages. I thought you might be starting the 5-FU drip tonight and got it for you." "I'll see how I feel," Anna replies, distractedly. Jan prompts her to take her double dose of morphine. He joins those in the medical and scientific field who abhor doctors who resist giving narcotics to dying patients and those who claim they can be addictive. Hospital stories abound of relatives pleading to give painkillers to dying loved ones. "They use it for what they need, to stop the pain, and it is *not* a craving," Jan says. In the final stages, in any event, one has to ask, Would it matter?

They walk into the house and, as if changing clothes, shift to daily duties, after having just been told that Anna is going to die sooner than expected. Before she left for the doctor's, Anna had said firmly to Lindsay, without raising her voice, "These clothes have been in the living room for two days to be folded. I don't want to see them when I get back." Lindsay complained, "Ellery's supposed to do it." Anna interrupted Lindsay's litany regarding the division of chores. "I don't care who does what," said her mother. "I don't want to see them." On her return, Anna notes that they are still in the living room but neatly folded and en route to being put away.

Dinner has been brought in—matzo ball soup, roast chicken, potato latkes with applesauce, green beans, and a special treat, chocolate mud pie. Anna eats a small amount of the soup and a healthier amount of fresh green beans. Her stomach can't hold more. The woman who once ate chocolate by the pound can no longer tolerate it. She drinks Ensure and Gatorade for the electrolytes. Walking around, Anna gets hiccups and the pain is sharp. "Oh, that hurts." She winces but shows little expression. There have never been melodramatics about her illness. Jan leads her to the couch and her special L-shaped pillow, which helps cradle her right side. "Honey, just lay down, try to relax." He sits on the couch, stroking her head and her arms, shushing with soothing sounds. Ellery has disappeared into computer games. Lindsay sits at the bottom of the couch, stroking her mother's legs.

It is a cold night and Jan, in sweats, walks their friend to the car, barefoot. He jokes, "I'm a Wiking"—for Viking. "First thing I'm going to do is make Anna as comfortable as I can." They hug good-bye. "And then we will talk about all of this tomorrow."

A few days later, on Wednesday, April 23, the vast ballroom in the downtown Marriott Hotel reverberates with the sound of 500 chatting women. At a reception, Anna sits as crowds surround the former first lady Betty Ford, who will be praised often for speaking out about her breast cancer in 1974. At a press conference, Ford is asked whether she would endorse today's procedures of lumpectomies or less radical mastectomies. She sidesteps suggesting procedures for other women but says, "I'm awfully glad I had the radical twenty-three years ago. I'm still here!" At seventy-nine, she remains youthful—model slim and erect in a lime green dress and coat.

Anna, in emerald green silk long skirt and jacket, is starkly changed from a week ago, when she sparkled at the hospice dinner. Her responses are slower; she seems a bit dazed. As she passes by, Betty Ford reaches over and holds Anna's hand in hers. She makes the stock phrase "It's so wonderful to meet you" sound genuine. Anna mentions that the effects of chemotherapy and cancer "force you to rethink what is normal." Ford listens, nods, and says, "Good luck."

Now, in the ballroom, Anna is in the Land of the One-Breasted Women. Judy Mann, a columnist for the *Washington Post,* herself a breast cancer survivor, gets strong applause when she cracks, "We may be missing a few breasts in this room, but there's no shortage of guts." The lunch, sponsored by the Susan G. Komen Breast Cancer Foundation, emphasizes the vastness of breast cancer, which touches millions of women and their families in all walks of life. Bright-colored turbans, elaborately wrapped bandanas, cloche hats, and chic-looking short cuts reveal that chemotherapy has visited a large number in the audience. At Anna's table, Bristol-Myers-Squibb is not dancing in attendance. No representative is present at the unfilled table. Anna sits with two older African American patients of Miller's. Speakers stress that more must be done to provide insurance and to urge African American women, who die in disproportionate numbers, to seek early detection. This month's big news is that the National Cancer Institute has finally switched its recommendations to include mammograms starting at age forty, rather than the previous fifty. Maryland senator Barbara Mikulski congratulates woman Congress members who, like herself, led the fight on the Hill for earlier mammograms. Anna harrumphs, "A little too late," noting that it took years to reverse the decision, remembering her bone-marrow-transplant letters that went unheeded on the Hill. "They are all great at writing form letters," she mutters.

Air-conditioning frosts the room. Anna crosses her arms, repressing shivers, as she first sweats from hot flashes, then freezes in damp clothes. Dark patches appear on her silk jacket. Anna piles on a warmer jacket offered by a tablemate. Tipper Gore arrives with fanfare. Anna is interviewed by a well-known local reporter for WTOP radio, Bob Madigan. A few weeks later, he would find the place and time to run snippets of Anna's conversation. Although Anna's spirit returns for this interview, her enthusiasms throughout the luncheon are muted. For the first time, one gets the feeling that Anna is thinking that hoped-for miracles have passed her by.

The next day, Anna is startlingly, staggeringly worse. Her face is shrinking into her cheekbones, she is dazed, not talkative, remembering little. Anna is in now-baggy sweats and a green turban. The fanny pack of 5-FU is attached. Her friend, Patty Williams, supports her on a slow walk. Jan confides to another friend as they walk behind, "It's more than the morphine. Suzanne [Miller's nurse] thinks it could be the liver." The day is mockingly beautiful; red-pink dogwoods, white dogwoods, cherry blossoms, yellow forsythia, vibrant flames of red and yellow tulips—all are bathed in warm spring sunlight. On the way back, more awake after the airy walk, Anna points to a neighbor watering his tulips. "There's our tiny patch of tulips and there's Bob's all in a neat and orderly same-colored red row." She raises her voice. "What are you doing again this year, Bob, trying to embarrass the neighborhood with your neat, orderly, straight row of tulips?" Her friends laugh as they help her into the house.

As the sun goes down, a chill invades the house. Anna sits in her favorite sofa corner. Friends call constantly. Jan lines up a relay of friends, spacing the time so that one person will be with her throughout the day. He is worried about her disorientation and sleepiness. He has left work early—his boss and colleagues urge him to take all the time he needs. Jan fixes a casserole, as airy as a soufflé, of baked sole with a light covering of mashed potatoes. He is pleased that Anna can eat a serving along with green beans. Ellery is staying more and more in the basement. He is slim, eating less, looks grim-faced and distracted. Lindsay is also downstairs, cleaning up the rec room for Lockie, who is coming on Friday and will sleep on the pull-out sofa. When Lindsay protests that some of the mess is Ellery's, Jan, shattered by Anna's rapid decline, snaps, "No nonsense. Just get it done." Anna softens the moment, appealing to Ellery to help, which he does. It is six-thirty and Anna can hardly keep her head up.

After Jan walks her to the bedroom, puts on her long red T-shirt jams, and gets her to bed, he looks at his watch. He is reinventing their days to accommodate Anna. "We'll just have earlier dinners." He makes a list of foods she manages to eat—custards, Ensure, ice cream, mashed potatoes, green beans, Gatorade, water. In a few minutes, Jan will drive Lindsay to ballet class. Both children suddenly seem years beyond their age.

A far happier Jan reports that Anna rallied over the weekend. "But she could not remember anything that she had done on Thursday. She signed papers to turn the cars over to me, but she did not remember that."

Jan later recalls how that day was a panicky turning point. "The gut realization that she had missed a whole day scared the heck out of me." He was crying before he took her for the walk, terrifyingly aware that life was slipping out of control and might end immediately. On Monday, April 28, they are back in Miller's office. Anna says she is "feeling a little better" since the 5-FU, "but I can't tell if it's working. I'm getting the side effects—my tongue definitely is starting to feel it. I'm doing Mary's Magic Mouthwash." "At this dose," says Miller, "we hope we can keep it going for a while." He feels that the 5-FU is psychologically important to Anna at this stage and may be relieving pain.

Anna's strange reaction last week troubles her. "Thursday, I went crazy." Jan interjects, "But Friday you were great. Very much better." He tells Miller, "Thursday I thought she was not going to make it." Miller says that high protein in the liver sometimes causes the reaction she experienced. "Her liver enzymes are high but the liver is still working well. She is not jaundiced."

Anna abruptly switches the subject to a television taping set for May 14, a little over two weeks from now. Anna admits that "talking about it [end-of-life issues] makes it too real for some." To the end, she wants to help others by relaying her experience. "It's going to be on family issues and counseling and how you go through the dying process."

CHAPTER SEVENTEEN

Caregivers

With shocking speed, cancer consumes Anna. The ravages of malignancy, the fluids in the liver, have so swollen her stomach that Anna looks five months' pregnant. Roseann cuts out shorts and sweatpants at the waist for comfort. A battalion of buddies appear. Anna is deeply moved by ballet friends Patty Williams and Jane Bittner, who have taken a hospice volunteer course in order to be better caregivers.

No matter how prepared Anna is to die, neither she nor anyone close to her is ready for such shattering quickness. She never got the chance to write letters to her children to be read at various milestones in their lives. Anna's planned video never happened; so swift was her progression that Anna did not want to be immortalized as she now looks.

But she has made a vital decision. Anna's memory of her mother dying, wasted and in pain, initially guided her decision to spare her children from seeing her die. "I've changed my mind," said Anna in March. "Dottie helped me rethink that. I have to ponder what role they have played and would I be taking that away." She will stay at home, "but only up to the point when one person in the family says no. Everybody has to be sensitive to how people are able to *cope* with it." The dying process is never so tidy, however, and Anna is losing much of her ability to make decisions as cancer consumes her. Jan is so in tune with her, however, that he would know if she wanted to leave home. His own resolve remains firm. "I felt very adamant from the beginning that Anna would stay at home," Jan says later. "This is one thing I *could* do for Anna. I would never forgive myself if I sent her to a facility, no matter how nice it was."

During the first week in May, Anna still walks around the block, wearing her 5-FU fanny pack, with the designated pal caregiver-of-the-moment. She naps longer and longer. Jan deems Friday the second a "great day" because Anna is able to sit up for two hours at a time and eat a fair portion of the dinner Jan makes—soft, creamy mashed potatoes and chicken potpie. Anna talks often about the impending panel discussion. She tries to eat in order to have strength for it, but her system is rejecting food.

What is happening to Anna is not so simple as the fact that insatiable, gobbling tumors are robbing her of essential nutrients. There are many ways for a malignancy to starve its host, the patient, into malnutrition. Changes in taste perception make it difficult for Anna to eat, as do the side effects of chemotherapy. Moreover, certain malignancies release a substance called cachetin—which decreases appetite by acting directly on the brain's feeding center. The malevolence of cancer inspires even doctors to personify this disease as "the enemy."[1] By May 8, Anna's 5-FU treatment is junked. Chemotherapy has come to an end.

A ballet-teacher friend, Nancy Wiltz, arrives one day with a maddeningly complex three-dimensional puzzle of the Taj Mahal. Hundreds of squiggly pieces of pasteboard, replicating stone and marble, sprawl across the coffee table. Anna, sitting on the sofa, and her parade of friends laboriously match up pieces. A few days before Mother's Day, Anna talks long distance with a friend who is crying because she cannot be there. She is dealing with family illness of her own. "Hey, these things happen," says Anna, who knows better than most. Anna then goes on in a manner that makes her friend wonder if she is hallucinating. "I took a walk with Ann Wylie, looking for the bald eagle, and couldn't find him. I haven't seen a bald eagle forever." It turned out, however, that Anna was clear as a bell. That week, Wylie had provided Anna with moments of inexplicable happiness—her last outdoor adventure. They drove to nearby Great Falls, where Anna had found the eagle's nest, if not the eagle.

Anna has talked to the hospice people but has not yet engaged them. As for medication, Anna says, "I need the Lortab, which is a quick hit, as much as the morphine. I need the two." Anna switches from herself and continues on with some of her old enthusiasm. "We're doing great strides on this puzzle. Lindsay did some and Nancy went crazy and did all the doorways." Anna talks about how slow-going everything is for her—walking, thinking, getting to the bathroom. "Everybody says, 'Everything takes time,' " she says, with weariness. "That line is getting old."

Ever since May 9, Anna has been hooked up by her life port at night to a bag filled with clear liquid that contains glucose, vitamins, and other nutrients. The bag is attached to an intravenous pole that has a beeper and flashing green light to alert caregivers it is empty. Because IV feeding is considered life sustaining, hospice cannot care for Anna yet. (Various hospices differ on this crucial end-of-life decision, which will be discussed later.) Home health care is begun in this intermediate period. Jan administers the feeding, making precise notes. Says Jan, "The reason I went with the TPN [total parenternal nutrition] is because she *really* wants to see Ellery's birthday." (He will be thirteen on May 15, the day after Anna's panel taping.) The refrigerator crisper drawer holds vials upon vials of clear fluid now, not lettuce and carrots. Jan's handwritten notes indicate amounts and the time he administers the IV.

Every night, Jan lies beside Anna in their king-sized bed. He gets little sleep. One night, at 3:00 A.M., he notes that Anna has shortness of breath and that her temperature spiked at 103.2. Jan gets up, groggily, and gives Anna a pill to lessen her tumor fever and laboriously changes her sweat-soaked pajamas. One day, Anna is left for only minutes by Jan and three friends. When one returns, Anna is on the floor, trying to reach the bathroom. It takes Jan and two friends to lift her, get her to the bathroom, and sit her back on the bed, while another rescues a pair of shorts from the clean laundry basket. Although Anna's legs will not hold her, she is determined, shaking her head no, when asked, "Do you want to lie down?" She sits straight up, braced by Jan, as Bittner gives water and ice cream. Anna takes it obligingly, like a baby bird opening its mouth, then very slowly swallows. Everyone hovers, anxious to get more food in her, asking questions. One says, "We're rushing her, asking too many questions."

While on IV at night, Anna's thought processes fluctuate and friends and family witness widely varying reactions. With so much fluid coursing inside her, Anna wakes up at least twice a night to go to the bathroom. She adamantly refuses bedpans or a commode at her bedside, shaking her head and saying, "No, no!" To her, they are a devastating sign of retreat, of giving up her dignity, a feeling shared by many who are dying. So Jan is up with her, turning on a dim light, guiding her through the obstacle of a cluttered bedroom, past a trunk piled high on top with blankets, sheets, and pillows, to the adjoining bathroom. However, there are three of them now—Jan, Anna, and her IV pole, which creaks along on wheels, dragging behind her as if it is some robot, its green light blinking. Anna feels as if it's pulling somebody else hooked to it. She tells Jan, "Something's coming to get you! To kill you." Jan says later, "She was absolutely convinced of it."

As it was happening, "Anna's nighttime experiences seemed like waking dreams," says Jan. "I had to gently calm her down. She couldn't explain them at the time." Ann Wylie caught a different mood when Anna related her remembrances of the IV pole. "For three nights in a row, she had had the same experience. She was very interested and wanted to understand the significance of these dreams. All three had the same basic theme; there were things on the pole and it was her duty to give them to someone else. One was a piece of jewelry that she had found that belonged to a mother of a friend—something that the mother had lost many years before. Anna had to give it to her. The second time it was money. It was meant for someone; she had to give it to him. The third was not specific. It had to do with the pole belonging to someone else. She was frustrated because she couldn't make Jan understand. 'He just wanted me to get on the potty and go back to bed,' " Anna told Wylie. " 'I started sobbing, because he didn't understand what I was saying about these three consecutive dreams.' She was fascinated, not scared, when she told me," says Wylie. "I thought maybe it was the morphine, but then she recollected it so clearly."

Symbolic dreams of the dying take on special significance and caregivers should pay close attention to them, especially if they are vivid and recur, no matter how murky or confusing they sound. When a patient is puzzled, as was Anna, a good listener might be able to help him or her find the information he or she needs not by trying to interpret the dreams but by drawing the patient out with careful questions. Some scary dreams connote a fear of death.[2] Anna never evinced such fears, either in conversations or in her dreams. Dream interpretations are tricky, at best, but here is a pleasant suggestion for Anna's. It could be that, to the end, she was thinking of others and her obligation to complete unfinished business. Her generous spirit needed to find the owners of the baubles and money on the pole and, even, to give the pole—whatever that represents—to its rightful owner.

A trail of friends from Anna's past and present meet for the first time in the Johannessen home. The range is from age twenty to late forties, for the most part. There are Christopher and Peggy, a charming young couple who are professional clowns; he was boss clown for one of the Ringling units. Other longtime theater pals, Terry and Linda, mingle with Anna's steady troop of caregivers—Nancy Wiltz, Jane Bittner, Patty Williams, Marcia DuVal, Ann Wylie, Linda Suarez, Jeanette Golden, Pat Wirth, Andrea Roberson. Dottie Ward-Wimmer visits the children, who gratefully hug her; the three of them have private time together.

On May 10, the day after Anna starts IV feeding, Lockie gives a party, but sadness intrudes on levity; the absent Anna is harsh reality for Lockie that her days with Anna are numbered. The night before Mother's Day, Jan buys flowers and keeps them in the carport. The next morning, he brings them in; lilacs and other spring flowers top the TV set at the foot of Anna's bed, flanked by two handwritten cards. "Dear Mom, we hope you like the flowers. Happy Mother's Day. [A happy face consisting of a curve for a smile and two short lines for eyes is drawn.] Today is for you. We are your slaves today. Anything you want or need will be done. Love, Ellery." "Dear Mom, happy Mother's Day! We hope you enjoy your day today. Tara and Missy send you flowers on the Internet, and well, so do Ellery and me. Love, Lindsay." Anna smiles, takes a deep smell of the flowers, closes her eyes.

Anna's room is filling up with the paraphernalia of the afflicted. The end table holds baby wipes and a bottle of water. On the dresser, pale latex gloves curl in a box. An ointment tube ("for diaper rash, chafed skin, abrasions and minor burns") is at hand to rub on Anna's bottom. Aloe Vesta Perineal Solution II, a cool aqua liquid skin cleanser ("Apply to wet skin, rinse thoroughly"), is next to dry-hair shampoo. There is a jar of Vaseline for dry lips and bottles of Naproxen (similar to Aleve) for fever and Ambien for sleep. Bright red Mary's Magic Mouthwash

("Swish and swallow 1 tablespoon 15 minutes before meals") sits next to various strengths of morphine, in liquid and pill form. Jan's handwritten notes on IV feeding lay nearby. Amidst all of this is an old-fashioned silver hairbrush with brushed roses and filigreed top, dusty from disuse. Next to it is a jar of hand cream, Forever Spring.

By the morning of Wednesday, May 14, all of Anna's friends and family worry about Anna's ability to make that night's panel discussion. For the last few days, Anna has slept most of the time, but she is unpredictable. One night, Anna suddenly sits up and dresses in clothes placed on a nearby chair, determined to go to Lindsay's ballet rehearsal. Jan talks her back down. Alertness seems erratic at best to those who cannot understand her talk, but surfaces in noticeable ways. One day while she can still walk by herself, Anna stares into the den at a brown-and-orange Afghan, walks ploddingly to the Afghan, and straightens it, without saying a word. She is living more inside her own world, a typical response of the dying.

Now, on this Wednesday, she sleeps all day, waking only for morphine. Jan calls Linda Suarez, Anna's friend and Miller patient, telling her, "Be prepared to get someone at the last minute." Anna's mind is easily sidetracked. She is pale, not jaundiced. She has a very hard time walking on swollen feet and Jan worries about whether she can endure sitting up for two hours of taping and whether she will be able to articulate her thoughts. But Anna miraculously rises to the occasion, just as her mother had four years ago to attend her farewell party three weeks before her death. "That's Anna," Jan says. "When push comes to shove, you produce."

That night, Anna gives the best performance of her life. She sits at a table as the videotape rolls, wearing a black-and-white print sleeveless dress over a white T-shirt, and, although quite thin, carries on clearly, with dignity and humor, inspiring others about how to live until the moment you die. Only occasionally does she grope for a word. She weaves new and lively twists into her general themes of learning all you can, telling your children the truth, the need to educate everyone about death and dying and how to face it. Anna does not feel that there is enough known about hospice: "I don't see that much in the media at all."

The moderator asks the panel to consider seriously ill people or their families who are "worrying about dying and are not as comfortable as the three of you are in talking about this—they're afraid of it, see no hope, are living in darkness. What would be the things you could say to them that might help them take a step toward some light?" "I know one thing," says Anna. "When I started learning about hospice, I was amazed to find out that it wasn't a place to go and die. It didn't mean the end of the road. It meant, 'We're going to make you not hurt. Period. For as long as you want to be around, you don't have to hurt.' I felt a lot more comfortable after that. I didn't feel like the Grim Reaper was waiting here." She dangles her hand over her head " 'Okay! *anytime,*' I thought. 'No pain? *This* could be a first!' " The audience laughs. *"I can guarantee you people don't know what the concept is,"* she says forcefully. "Just to keep you pain free and as comfortable as you want to be." Afterward, Jan helps an exhausted Anna into the car. This is the last time Anna will ever leave her home.

The next day, Anna fades heavily, although she manages to sign a birthday card. On Friday, she revives a bit for Ellery's party. She lies propped up in her corner on the sofa, smiling wanly at the balloons, ice cream, and cake. Ellery's major present is tickets to the Bill Cosby show next week. Shortly after Ellery's Cosby impersonation in March, Anna had reserved four tickets.

After the panel discussion, Patty Williams writes down her thoughts about how much Anna means to her. Williams waits for some time alone with Anna, then reads it to her. Anna's eyes are closed and Williams isn't sure she hears her, but then tears roll down Anna's cheeks. Williams bends close. "I love you, Anna," she says as she kisses and hugs her, knowing now that Anna has heard her. Aside from the satisfaction they receive in being able to help dying friends, caregivers must struggle with their own ways of saying good-bye. Like Williams, they savor their time alone with the dying, vital private moments of closure.

The puzzle sprawl of the Taj Mahal has metamorphosed into a nearly completed edifice, rising from the glass coffee table in pasteboard splendor. On May 17, two days after Ellery's birthday party, the Sunday avalanche of newspapers surrounds the Taj Mahal and flows onto the sofa. Jan's crossword, worked on while Anna dozes, is almost finished. A friend who has not seen Anna in two and a half weeks is stricken by the decline of her bouncy, talkative pal. Anna sits straight up on the living room sofa, eyes open. Her silence is eerily out of character. Other voices fill the air, but they cannot make up for her vigorous amusement at life. Wayne has returned again from Richmond and sits on the far side of the sofa; Jan is next to Anna.

She is scrubbed to a shine, smells sweetly of talcum powder, and wears a pink-and-white-checked pajama top and plaid shorts. In cruel mockery, her hair is growing back beautifully, fitting her head like a cap. She has full eyelashes and eyebrows. Her eyes express some recognition of her latest visitor's kiss. Her mouth opens but nothing is uttered. She does not seem to be in much pain. Always attentive, Jan asks if she wants another pillow. Anna shakes her head no. With great effort, she says what sounds like "It's just the way it is." The phrase becomes a one-liner for Wayne. Whenever Anna is asked something and there is no answer, he gently glides into "It's just the way it is." Anna smiles when she hears him. Her dark eyes fade behind fluttering lids, then open wide, then close again. "Do you want more water? Want to sit back?" Jan asks, although she seldom responds. "Let's get your legs back up." He lifts her legs onto the sofa, then fifteen minutes later asks, "Do you want to lie down on the chaise on the sundeck? It's beautiful out." He and Wayne lift her up. Anna mumbles, "You just got me down." Jan laughs, "I know, honey, but it will be good to get outside." Wayne says, "Let's catch some rays. They'll feel good."

In order to get Anna in the right direction, Jan moves her around, in that slow dance caregivers learn—Anna's hands on Jan's shoulders, his securing her at the waist, then turning, slow step by slow step. As Wayne holds her on the other side, Anna shuffles slowly between them, certain to fall without their support, and settles into a chair. Afternoon sun slants across the deck and onto the yard. Jan leaves Anna with Wayne, knowing his time with her is precious. Light beads of sweat appear. Anna smiles as Wayne spreads a cool cloth on her face and then gently dries it. Anna sips water from a cup with a picture of a woman in a large hat and the words "Of course women don't look as busy as men. We do it right the first time." Anna tries to form a sentence: "See the woman with the hat . . ." She stops. Wayne prods, pointing to the cup. Anna stares. The thought is gone. She dozes, then nods when Wayne asks if she wants to go in. Anna leans her head on his shoulder and smiles, back on the sofa. Simon and Garfunkel waft from the stereo—"Hello, darkness, my old friend . . ."

This horrible irony, the loss of Anna's talent for expressive verbalization, is not caused by medication, experts feel. "Morphine just doesn't do that," says William Lamers, a physician and psychiatrist and premier hospice consultant who, in forty years, has witnessed close to 3,000 dying patients and families go through the death process. "I've seen people on massive doses of morphine whose speech remains lucid. It is more likely lesions in the brain. Almost all kinds of tumors are little cellular factories that can produce complicated chemicals. We know for instance that lung tumors can produce neurotransmitters that influence brain activity. Breast tumors can do the same. There's a state of confusion, agitation, delirium, that results purely from the products of the cancer cells themselves. It's not terribly well examined because it is usually seen in the extreme circumstance when the patient is nearing death and the focus of those treating them is 'God, keep them comfortable.' I've seen this so many times."

Somehow life must go on, small pleasures must be found. As Wayne stays with Anna, Ellery and Jan pile into Wayne's white Cobra Mustang. "Dad, can we hit some of those detours on the way home?" Ellery eagerly asks. He is referring to the sharp turns and high speeds on the side roads where Jan lets out the Cobra full throttle. Jan answers, "We'll see what time we have."

Parents sit on bleachers in the studio filled with dancers staring at themselves in mirrors. It is hard to imagine that the graceful and authoritative Lindsay is only eleven. Willowy in soft peach, she twirls to Enya's "China Rose," a favorite of Anna's. Patty Williams and other friends struggle with tears as they watch Lindsay, who looks more like her mother each day. On the way home, Lindsay pulls her hair out of its bun and reveals a transition. Her hair is cut to shoulder length. She fans it out. "I love it." Her long hair now hangs, like a pony's tail, on her bedroom wall. Both children plead for a quick spin. Jan, anxious to see Anna, says, "Let's go home first."

At home, Jan helps Wayne get Anna up to go to the bathroom. Shakily, Anna stands uncertainly by the bathroom door, hesitating to go over the doorsill. Jan puts Anna to bed. For many nights now, Jan has tried to stay awake or respond when Anna needs to get up, but one night Anna does not want to disturb him. A snoring Jan cannot rouse himself. He finds Anna on the floor, halfway to the bathroom, with the drip still attached. That moment convinces Jan that the IV feeding is an impediment and no longer helping. "The purpose was to try to give Anna more strength in her final days," he says. "I thought it would make her more comfortable and she did feel better for a short time." He now makes the decision to stop, knowing that the feeding can be a load on Anna's failing system. "The hospice nurse says the IV feeding—putting a high-protein load into a liver that is working less and less—could even make it worse."

Ken Miller calls one evening. He tells Jan that he considers Anna a friend and asks Jan to call him any time of the day or night if he needed him and he would be right over. He agrees with Jan about stopping the feeding. Unlike some who decide to cut off feeding, there are no grinding conflicting emotions for Jan. He and Anna had talked endlessly about doing so when this time came. He is without hesitation, feeling that it would be cruel to prolong this stage. For those who adhere to such wishes of the dying or their own instincts, the knowledge that it will end a painful process provides steely courage. Others are torn by conflicting wishes of family members or a sense of guilt and often wish for a helpful doctor to encourage their decision. But as has been noted, doctors are loath to participate in such a dire acknowledgment of death. Death educators stress that learning about the dying process makes it easier.

By Monday, May 19, the Johannessen house has taken on the appearance of a command post, with Jan, unfailingly polite as always, scheduling shifts of Anna's volunteer friends. Ro has gone home but will return the following weekend. Jan has not shaved and a dazed look occasionally overtakes him, but he experiences an amazing adrenaline high, juggling detail after detail—up with Anna in the middle of the night, up at five-thirty to get the children off to school, racing to the office if he feels Anna is well covered, hugging everyone who comes into the house, spending time with Anna and the children after everyone leaves, then on the phone with Ro. The kitchen is filled with comfort food: donuts and carrot cake, spaghetti and pizza, deli sandwiches, soups and salads, brought by the crew. His uniform is shorts, flip-flops, and a T-shirt. He has taken to putting the ever-ringing cellular phone in his shorts pocket as he moves energetically around the house. His customary "hi there" greets everyone. "Not much, hanging out, got a couple of calls to make. . . ." "I'm trying to transfer the videotape of Lindsay's ballet so we can play it in Anna's room. . . ." "The kids can go to the farm if they get their homework done. Remind me later, cuz I'll forget. . . ."

Hospice is alerted on Sunday night, May 17. Monday is an exercise in futility as attempts to coordinate with hospice fizzle. In recent years, hospice patient loads have changed dramatically; it is no longer just a vestibule for the elderly. Younger cancer and other terminally ill patients, AIDS, and a growing desire to die at home have swelled the numbers of pre-Medicare patients under age sixty-five. "There is some mix-up about officially transferring from home health care," explains Jan. "My Blue Cross policy will cover it, but hospice wants to make sure they will pay."

The nurse assigned to Anna that first day is out sick. No one calls the Johannessens and no one comes. Anna's friends work so efficiently that the absence does not affect them for one day. A friend and nurse, Belinda, shows them how to wash Anna, carefully and lovingly. On Tuesday, a hospice nurse, not the permanent nurse who is still out sick, shows up. She is efficient and warm and apologizes for yesterday. She checks Anna's vital signs, while Jan puts Vaseline on Anna's lips. "Her mouth gets dry, sometimes she breathes with her mouth open." The nurse suggests a hospital bed; "raising her head up will help with her breathing." The nurse is quietly insistent. "The hospice likes twin beds, that you can raise and lower. If there is only one aide or caregiver, you can turn her much easier. It's more comfortable."

But Jan will not hear of it. He and Anna had made a pact; for the children's sake, Anna desperately wanted the bedroom to look as natural as possible, not like a hospital cubicle. And they wished to be able to sleep together to the end. Inconvenience aside, the king-sized bed becomes a magic carpet for friends and family. Anna is not in pain as they sprawl around her, hugging, stroking her arm, leaning close to have intimate conversations. When she grimaces slightly or moans, they are ready with morphine. Unencumbered by visiting hours, they come and go at will; Anna is seldom alone. Without rails, they can hold her hand with ease, sitting on a chair next to the bed. When Anna awakes, her gibberish is often indecipherable, but her calm face, the upraised-eyebrows greeting, reassure everyone that Anna knows she is surrounded by friends, not alone and fumbling for a call button to summon a fleeting hospital nurse.

"Pain control is a must," says the nurse. If Anna cannot communicate, they must watch for signs—groans, winces, discomfort when moved. Outside of Anna's hearing, talk turns to durable power of attorney and DNR (do not resuscitate) papers. "We have them," says Jan. But bureaucracy is no stranger to hospice; the nurse says this must be noted in a hospice book, which Jan has yet to receive, "in the event she stops breathing and doesn't want to be resuscitated."

Jane Bittner expresses anger about yesterday's inefficiency, stressing that speed is essential. "Anna's gone down so fast, she may not be here tomorrow." The nurse assures her that it will not be that fast. Like many, Bittner is disturbed that hospice rules make it difficult to take patients as long as they are receiving treatment—based on the regulation that hospice patients must relinquish attempts at curative care. Indeed, hospice members sometimes make independent decisions. Some hospice doctors and directors, for example, admit patients while they are receiving some treatment or IV feeding, reasoning that this is "palliative"—rather than "life sustaining"—since such procedures may ease pain for those who are clearly dying.

Bittner also feels that Anna and Jan postponed setting up hospice too long. This is a nationwide failing. Instead of viewing hospice as quality-time pain-free treatment, as Anna stresses in her videotape, many patients and their families suffer needlessly while waiting far too long to turn to hospice. Although attitudes are changing greatly, some are still held hostage to the corrosive myth that hospice connotes giving up. Relatives who ease their own burdens by removing loved ones to hospitals can also do a major disservice—often dying patients are all but abandoned and in pain because hospital staffs resist following hospice's pioneering steps in pain management and maintain aggressive treatment to keep them alive, even if they are comatose. The nurse urges Bittner to call hospice and stress that Anna needs them right away. "I'm only a field nurse, not a supervisor." By midweek, hospice is functioning; insurance will pay, the aide is set to come four days a week to bathe Anna and change sheets, the nurse twice a week. Jan and Ro will be the main caregivers.

At Anna's request, Jan refuses the services of a chaplain or social worker, and Anna's friends provide far more hours of tender care than would a hospice volunteer, in addition to washing endless mounds of laundry and cleaning the house. Dottie will provide counseling for the children and Jan reasons he does not need social worker assistance, although they provide help in everything from educating caregivers (which was not properly addressed with Jan and the other helpers) to making funeral arrangements. In addition, they are a neutral force that can further harmony among family and friends in a highly emotionally charged atmosphere. As for religion, hospice adheres to strictly nondenominational spiritual guidance, and their chaplains assiduously make no effort to alter or disapprove of a family's beliefs or, as is frequently the case, nonbeliefs. For countless other families without a support system as strong as Anna's, the unique hospice team concept is invaluable in making an ordeal bearable and provides lasting memories of comforting support.

Friday, May 23, is the big night—the Bill Cosby show in downtown D.C. No one mentions how sad they feel that Anna will not be there. Ellery takes a friend instead. Jan hesitated until friends urged him to go. Four of them will stay with Anna until they return following the early show and dinner. A new sign is up in the dining room, made by Anna's friends. "CONGRATS to LINDSAY! Good for You!!" Lindsay had earned a World Studies Achievement and Honor Roll Award. Friends can envision Anna, the vigilant mom, saying, "See? I told you, you need to push!"

As time goes on, Ellery and Lindsay choose to withdraw more and more from the hubbub around them. Lindsay's method of control is to avoid any conversations about her mother, however well meaning, for fear that she will "lose it." The house is constantly full and Lindsay appears more startled than annoyed at the takeover. She retreats to her bedroom to do homework while Ellery communes more and more with his computer games. Says Dottie Ward-Wimmer, "Remember there's a control piece here. 'I'm already out of control, don't you dare make me talk about it, don't you dare make me think about it, don't you dare make me cry. Don't put your arm around me.' "

Despite Jan's all-consuming devotion to Anna, he becomes aware of how much the activity is disrupting his children. After Ro returns, Jan asks caregivers and friends to come earlier so that the house will be quieter when the children return from school. "These friends who love Anna are there with all good intentions, but there's a real balance that needs to be maintained," explains Ward-Wimmer. "The very turf that the kids need in order to feel settled to do this processing is now being overtaken. And how can you get mad? They're taking care of your mother! It's not that they're unsociable, or don't understand. It's that they have no place to go, to feel it all out."

As Jan and the children leave for the Cosby show, the women tend to Anna. She sits up and seems to understand them. Scrubbed, hair brushed smooth, wearing Walt Disney pajamas, Anna looks like a docile child. At soft commands, she opens her mouth to drink water, one sip at a time, take drops of morphine, swallow tiny spoonfuls of sherbet (hospice nurses have informed them that ice cream can create mucus, which makes breathing more difficult). With Williams bracing her from behind on the bed, Anna sucks on a mix of crushed ice cubes and Gatorade. When asked if she wants Jell-O, Anna's eyebrows go up. At times, Anna seems agitated, moving her head with slight grimaces, spreading a curled hand over her face. Morphine drops are given. When she sits up, friends take advantage to push pads under her and change her diapers. Anna does not protest what she would have considered an indignity a month ago. All the while, *Breakfast at Tiffany's* is playing on the VCR; friends too young to have seen the movie are transfixed. Outside Anna's bedroom world is another time and place of routine living; birds sing, a hammer pounds, a lawn mower buzzes.

Tina, in blue jeans, lies across the bed, talking to Anna. Everyone is convinced that Anna can hear them. This view is bolstered by caregiving professionals who warn family caregivers never to talk about anything dire or upsetting and never to presume the patient cannot hear, even in a coma. Hearing is the last sense to go. One hospice caregiver tells the story of a man in a coma who had expressly told his mother he wanted no priest. As he lay motionless and comatose, the mother sneaked in a priest to give him last rites. Her son thrashed in horrible anger, his body telling his mother what his voice could not—that she had betrayed him.

In the kitchen, Anna's friends take breaks and pick at a mishmash of food—homemade tomato and basil sauce with pasta, leftover Greek salad. The women become confidantes, exchanging their stories and times with Anna. Jane Bittner's sorrowful remembrances include deep mourning for her twenty-six-year-old son who died in a motorcycle accident. "One never 'gets over it.' It just changes, but you will always remember."

Bittner's tears flow. For her, every mother's worst nightmare came true—the call in the middle of the night. Bittner leans heavily against the sink counter. Her friendship with Anna is immensely helpful. "When I met Anna, I felt instantly that this is someone I have to know." Bittner is one of many, as Marcia DuVal points out: "Her personality is intoxicating—you can't be around her without feeling uplifted." DuVal says that Anna changed her life. "I had a difficult family life. Here was this abandoned puppy on the side of the road, and she took me home. I had a chance to see what really loving people could be like with their children." Because Anna makes them feel special, each friend carries around this warmth, this certitude, that he or she is the one really special friend to Anna. In reality, they all are.

Tina McCarthy met Anna in Richmond. Anna has told Tina, as well as Jan and just about everyone, that she hopes Jan and Tina get together after she is gone. Jan and Tina shake their heads, letting Anna live her fantasy. After all these years, they are more like brother and sister. In March, Anna had had a long discussion at Lockie's house regarding a rift that had grown between Lockie and Tina. It disturbed Anna greatly. Now, during these fading days, Tina and Lockie lie on the bed with Anna and tell her that they have made up. Anna's contented grin tells them that she has heard them—and that they have made her dying days happier.

Reconciliation—either the patient dealing with discord in his or her life or a reuniting of others within the close circle, like Lockie and Tina—can be paramount for the dying. Often they will hang on until this is achieved. One of the cruelest cases of reconciliation thwarted is that of an AIDS victim whose father refused to speak to him after finding out his son was gay. Other family members' frantic attempts to intercede came to naught. The son died a sad, lingering death after being "held back" from his desired destination while waiting for the father who never came.[3]

Breakfast at Tiffany's has ended. The ubiquitous fare of hospitals—loud, intrusive TV shows complete with cackling laugh tracks—is absent in Anna's room; classical music flows soothingly on tape. It is a night of many phone calls. The bubbly voice of Christina, who sells TV airtime, asks if it is okay if she brings her newborn baby to see Anna. (When the message is relayed later that night, Jan says, "That might be a good idea. Anna's been waiting for that baby to come.")

The phone is held to Anna's ear when Lockie calls and later, Wayne. He carries on in an effortless manner that some people find so easy, and others envy, when dealing with the dying. Everyone is convinced that Anna understands as Wayne does his monologue, his laughter coursing through the phone. "Remember when we did this?"; he sings snatches of favorite songs. "I know you can't talk, so I'll just talk, and I know you can hear me. Love you, Anna." Anna's eyes open at times, then close.

The dogs bark frantically to announce the return of Jan and the children. Although Ellery is exhausted and stuffed with pizza, he raves, "Cosby was great! He did a lot of new material." Both children come to Anna's bedside and tell her good night, kissing her on the forehead. Lindsay is elegant, taller than ever in slight platform shoes, wearing glistening plum-colored silk pants that belonged to her mother. In the kitchen, Lindsay gives her dad a hug good night, then moves to the piano and starts to play a lyrical piece. Anna hears the sound in her bedroom and moves in an effort to sit up. The tape is turned down. Anna, leaning on friends, rocks slowly. As she listens to her daughter playing, tears run down her cheeks.

At eight-thirty the next morning, Ro and Cliff arrive, having driven all night from New York. It is clear that Anna's sister has come to take charge. Jan's mother, Phoebe, had offered to come, but says Jan, "I was in complete agreement that this was Ro's place and I really was grateful she could come. I really needed her." That weekend, Ro and Jan made the decision to tell Anna's father not to come from Florida. Stephen agrees. "The trip, alone, will be rough," Jan says. Unmentioned, but certainly respected, is the trauma of such a final visit to this loving and emotional father, who cannot face the thought of the natural order being reversed, his daughter dying before him, and cannot talk to her on the phone after he is told that she probably would not respond.

Even in the best of families, duties and desires of relatives during the dying process can create unsettling disharmony—but this can be diffused through discussions on what each one should do. In the dysfunctional, discord can devastate. Occasionally very bad families can find closure. "Caregiving out of a sense of obligation rather than love might not be a negative," says Ken Doka. "It might be positive. A sense of saying, 'I'm a good person because I've done what I was supposed to do. It can validate me.' In one case, a father had a severe drinking problem and was very physically abusive to his children, who held him responsible for their mother's early death, of cancer, because her life was so stressful with him. But they were very good caregivers, though probably a part of them just wanted to walk away." A lifetime of abuse and loss flooded back and the daughter acknowledged that "my father was not the best father." Then she added, "He had better children than he deserved." Says Doka, "That's a nice thought. Her way of closing down on it."

For any family, seldom will emotions be so heightened, so convoluted, so fierce, as at this time. They can battle over decision making. The mother of a son dying of Hodgkin's fights with the sister who is trying to enforce her brother's decision to stay at home instead of going to the hospital, for example. Some members can bear lasting grudges against siblings or other relatives who shirk their duties or shun the death process. Husbands who were not so faithful can be subsumed by guilt. The weary wife of an Alzheimer's patient can feel guilty at the relief she feels as the end nears.

Among the Johannessens and their friends, another common emotion surfaces, the desire to be the one most helpful source of comfort. It was natural that those who had cared so diligently for Anna would have to take a back seat when Ro arrived. There are some awkward moments and ruffled feathers, but they quickly pass. Ro observes the necessity for friends to have private time with Anna, and backs out of the room accordingly. But the main reason that the system continues to work is that Roseann recognizes and respects their help during her absence and knows it will continue. She later relates, "The unconditional love and caring they gave is something in today's day and age that you don't see and people don't know about. I commend every one of them. It overwhelms me when I think about it."

One should not romanticize caregiving, which can be trying under the best of circumstances and brutal at worst, depending on the patient or the situation. Yet for many who care for loved ones at home, the benefits are enormous—as it is with the Johannessen clan. Despite sadness, at times accompanied by searing emotional and physical exhaustion and disagreeable chores, the gratification, even joy, of helping relieve pain and suffering can be manifold. Caregiving camaraderie—a raw closeness seldom found in day-to-day living—can be a blessed memory for the rest of one's life.

With Anna's group, there is time for sweet remembrance but not, as yet, for mourning. Being busy, doing for a loved one, supersedes fatigue. Jan finds a deep reward in being able to care for Anna, make her comfortable, talk to her, hold her, lie next to her at night, and seems almost incapable of stopping. Ro runs a close second—even though friends repeatedly tell the two that they will spell them. Jan and Ro feel that it will take two to handle Anna—and they want to be the two. When Cliff is present, he provides his own gift, gourmet meals, which are often eaten on the run.

Ro is not pleased with the reports on hospice. "It's one thing to train the volunteers, but they should train the family better." When Jan comes into the room, she asks, '"Did the nurse tell you what to do?" "Very little," responds Jan, who learned more about shifting Anna in bed and changing diapers through watching the hospice-trained volunteer friends. This is a crucial factor; often families are not given explicit information on the dying process and its progression. Luckily, Jan's science background makes him an assured administer of morphine, waiting until it takes effect, a matter of minutes, before attempts are made to move or change her.

Memorial Day, May 26, provides a lesson in how no one can predict the time of death. After somnolent days when it seemed the end was near, Anna is suddenly alert. She sits in bed with her eyes open and, although she doesn't smile, says very clearly, "How ya doin'?" as a friend kisses her on the cheek, before tumbling into a world of words unknown to her listeners. Seeing her Richmond friend J.P., John Pishko, walk into the bedroom with Wayne, her eyes open wide and she utters a very distinct "Holy shit!" Pishko laughs heartily as he sprawls on the bed and Anna smiles a bit. Downstairs, Wayne puts on a tape of Anna and the old crowd singing a song he wrote, "Give Me a Life Full of Love (and Make It a Life Full of Love for Yourself"). When they finish, Anna's youthful voice bursts forth on tape, "Wow! That's the best we ever did that!" As they move into "Will the Circle Be Unbroken?" Lockie and Anna provide strong, tight harmony. After, Wayne says wistfully, "We were good."

Wayne has brought the tape for Anna, but Jan cautions him not to play it for her. The night before, Jan had put on some old ballet tapes and Anna seemed fine with them. Then he showed a family video. "Anna started crying, sobbing. I didn't know if she didn't want to see herself or whether she didn't want to be reminded of the good times, but she was really upset." Jan feels Wayne's tape might have the same effect.

Anna is unusually restless and Ro predicts, having seen Anna's mom, that she is going into "the next phase." At one point, Anna opens one eye, then the other, then very deliberately starts to move herself up and out of bed. In her confusing speech, the words "the kids!" are very clear. She moves with astounding force as a friend attempts to restrain her. "Lindsay's right here," her friend says calmly. "Ellery's at the movies. No!" she says more sharply, struggling with Anna. "You don't have to get up. I'll get Lindsay." Instantly Ro and Jan are in the room. "Hi there!" says Ro in a cheerful voice, positioning herself in front of Anna like a blocking guard. Jan sits on Anna's left side, holding her, saying soothingly, "Everything's okay, hon." Lindsay comes in. "Hi, Mom, I'm here." Anna looks at Lindsay sitting by her side, but there is no sign of recognition. Jan drips morphine into Anna's mouth. With some urging, she lies back down.

CHAPTER EIGHTEEN

Letting Go

A long nightmare for Jan and Ro begins Anna's descent to yet another level during the early hours before dawn. The agitation that Anna experienced throughout Memorial Day blows into gale force as the rest of the house sleeps. All is calm when Anna goes to sleep around 10:00 P.M., but then she wakes up at 2:00 A.M. on Tuesday morning and never stops talking for eleven hours. Jan is awakened first by thrashing and loud talking. Ro and Cliff hear her from the basement and Ro bounds out of the sleep sofa and rushes up to help. Lindsay and Ellery are awakened by the noise. Ro and Jan sit on either side of Anna on the king-sized bed, trying to restrain her. So weak and docile in the hours before, Anna suddenly summons amazing strength. Her ability to move is astounding. "It took the two of us to hold her," Ro recalls.

Even so, she breaks away, moving all over on the bed on her knees, refusing to be calmed. It is as if she has no pain. "Her adrenaline was such that any pain she had was superseded by the fact that she wouldn't give in to sleep," comments Ro. "And the reason she wouldn't give in to sleep—she kept saying over and over again, in so many words—was that she didn't want to die. She was associating sleep with death and this is a stage they go through."

Yet something else is taking place. Anna may be experiencing her last rebellion, but there are other forces at play. Unfortunately, these all-too-common moments of the dying are viewed by observers as morphine-induced hallucinations or visions caused by oxygen deprivation. However, they are too frequent to be discounted on such terms alone. The most prevalent theme in nearing-death awareness seems to be being in the presence of someone not alive. The dying person often stares past those in the room, fixated on one spot. "Timing varies; the experience can happen hours or days or sometimes weeks before the actual death," write Maggie Callanan and Patricia Kelley, two hospice nurses. "Dying people often interact with someone invisible to others—talking to them, smiling or nodding at them. . . . Generally they recognize someone significant from their lives who is already dead."[1]

During this phase, Ro watches Anna "communicating with something she sees when she looks at the fan. No, I don't think it's the morphine." Anna talks to her mother, calling her by name, then to Rufus, one of her favorite dogs of the past, and to the grandfather who used to buy her ice cream and died when she was about five. "I could hear the names, and she would go in and out," recalls Ro.

Sometimes this other life is so vivid that it stuns observers. One man, Ralph, whose swimmer friend became a paraplegic after an accident and died before Ralph, is seen by Ralph in a final vision, whole and healthy, ready to help him cross over into death: " 'Oh, look!' he said excitedly. 'Here comes Steve! He's come to take me swimming.' "[2] In Florida, Millie Cowan cared for her elderly brother at her apartment. He steadfastly denied his dying but performed symbolic rituals. He insisted on keeping a suitcase packed and a fanny pack with money nearby and talked about "going home." Said his sister, "I knew he wasn't talking about Maryland."

Rather than dismissing such messages as the result of medicine, hallucination, or loss of intellectual function, observers can better respond to such symbolic communing by expecting it to happen. It may even be possible to talk to the patient to find out what he or she is experiencing. "The most important thing to remember when a dying person sees someone invisible to you is that death is not lonely. . . . These people tell us . . . that they didn't die alone, and neither will we."[3] Anna has Rufus, her mother, and her grandfather, and perhaps others, as companions on her journey.

Yet Anna has other indecipherable fears about unfinished business that take the form of anger, so inexplicable and out of character. Sometimes she shouts, "Where are the kids? Lindsay! Ellery!" Lindsay gets up and goes into the room. Anna stares at her and speaks in a sharp tone, then says, "That Lindsay—you've gotta watch out for her." Jan and Ro never understand the reference. It could be that she is talking about her concerns for Lindsay, and that they had to literally watch out—to care—for her. But Jan cannot fathom her lashing out. "Poor Lindsay didn't need that." He soothes and holds his daughter in the hallway outside the bedroom, telling Lindsay that her mother is talking that way to others and not to take it personally, that she is awakening from bad dreams. They cry together. Later, Lindsay and Anna have their tender moments as Anna holds her daughter's hand, which makes up for this wild night.

At dawn on Tuesday, Anna's need to control, to rebel, resurfaces dramatically. "The aide came in," relates Ro. "I needed to have Anna sponge-bathed. She would not let it happen. She was up all over the bed, buck naked, and would not let anybody touch her. She was adamant. Moving all over. I'm not sure, but I think she associated the aide with death—not being able to do things for herself." Anna's anger turns to Ro and even Jan. Anna scowls and shouts at the sister and husband she so loves. "She didn't want us to touch her!" says Ro. Anna broke the skin on her sister's arm as she struggled. "She wouldn't let us put anything on her or put the diaper on. Fortunately, I had those chucks down when she finally let go."

The aide suggests that they give Anna a Valium derivative, Lorazepam, to calm her down and leaves. It takes Jan, Ro, and two caregiver friends to get Anna clothed and diapered. Jan races to Miller's office five minutes away for the antianxiety prescription and then to the pharmacy. While Jan is away, Miller comes to visit, having called to say he was going to stop by. It is rare for doctors to visit dying patients, although Miller does it on occasion.

Unfortunately for Miller, this is the worst possible time for a visit. "I'm not talking to you," Anna says with a clarity that came with this agitated state. Angrily she turns on Ro. "I *told* you not to let him in my room!" Miller sits down and Anna says through clenched teeth, "*I have something to tell you.* It's your fault that I am this way. You misread things, you weren't quick enough with new things," she says loudly, gathering steam. Miller sits there and takes this barrage and then quietly says, "Can we change the subject?" Anna is not about to let this happen.

Peaches and Cream bark loudly, signaling that Jan has returned. Ro slips out and tells him to hurry. "Ken is here and she is *mad*!" When the two of them walk into the bedroom, Anna is pointing to the wedding picture of Jan and her on the wall and shouts at Jan to bring it to her. "You ruined this family! This was a beautiful family," she says, shaking her finger at Miller. She doesn't stop, even when he tries to change the subject again by asking Anna how she feels physically. As Miller leaves the bedroom, Jan gives her the Valium derivative.

Later Jan says, "I've gotta call Miller. I feel terrible about this because that is not how Anna sees him." Ro feels otherwise and responds angrily to the suggestion that Anna may have been rambling and confused. "No! You could understand every word she said, blaming him for the reason she is where she is now. And I don't disagree."

As Ken leaves Anna and walks into the living room where Ro is sitting he is saddened, but feels that Anna did not mean her attack except in a general, final frustration. "I'm really happy to have the opportunity to meet you," he says to Ro. She responds, "I need to say a couple of things to you. I'm really not happy about a lot of things." Later Ro relates, "And *he* tried to pass off to me the kind of thing that 'life doesn't pick who gets this.' I know that! And how what is happening to his daughter is an example of how you can't control it—and how fond he is of my sister.

"I believe that, but I addressed the fact that there needs to be more flexibility in the medical profession [concerning protocols, providing a central data base of information regarding new treatments that doctors and patients could quickly tap into]. He passed that off. He would not listen or take that seriously." Ro's voice rises in indignation. "That's when he said that life chooses and you can't do anything about it and one thing and another. I found this very inadequate, but I was not going to take the time to challenge him right then. However, if the man feels that way, to me, it is a great injustice to his patients. Because if what you are prescribing does *not* work, then where are the avenues to go? And he said, 'Jan was a great help.' I looked at him and said, 'This is *your* job! It wasn't Nils's!' He didn't answer. And then he left."

Miller recalls his sadness, his own grieving, and why he had no desire to debate his treatment or discuss the merits of a centralized medical-information data base for patients. Indifference played no part. "This woman I care for deeply is *dying* in the other room! It was not the time for that. I just let it go."

Jan is too wired to nap. He can't stop talking about how Anna could not stop talking. Anna finally sleeps, but she wakes up two hours later. Ro finally dozes but soon wakes up. Her head pounds and the circles under her eyes are deep. All seems serene in Anna's room. Classical music plays softly; friends climb up and down the basement stairs, doing laundry, load after load. They are comforted by the knowledge that Anna is getting the best care imaginable—theirs.

Friends compare stories about this agitated state, which seems to be common. One remembers a distinguished former White House cabinet member reduced to the indignity of a supposedly superior hospital where indifferent nurses and aides barely looked in on him. He had huge bed sores and was often left in dirty diapers. Agitated, his bony fingers picking at his covers, although he seemed in a coma, he would shout, "Help me, please. Somebody, help me! I'm dying, help me!" Another mentions a gay friend recounting that, as frail as his dying lover was, he "had the strength of ten men" when he became agitated. For Anna's mother, this period lasted for about twenty-four hours, not as violently as Anna's, before she fell into a coma and died. The hospice nurse has seen patients rant. So much for the concept of going quietly into the night. Loved ones find relief in knowing that patients in this state are often not in pain.

Jane Bittner suggests that Anna needs to know that all is fine, particularly with the children. Jan had already begun reassuring her, giving Anna permission—a common need among the dying—that it is all right to go. There are numerous accounts of dying patients staying on in order to reach a certain goal—the patient who lingers until a relative or close friend flies in, or revives enough to attend a wedding or birthday, or waits until family and friends provide ease and closure by saying that it is all right to go. Jan feels certain that Anna, such a stickler for getting everything completed, is agitated and fighting because life is slipping too fast. He remembers Anna's instructions: "If any one of the four of us does not want me at home, I'm outta here." Leaning on a kitchen counter, he says softly, "Can you imagine how scared she'd be waking up in a hospital room with no one she knows around her? If she can get this agitated even with us? Last night was very difficult for Lindsay, but I still don't think she'd want her mother"—he gulps and tears come—"to go anywhere."

Jan brightens when he says, "Ken said she was looking good, she isn't jaundiced." Anna indeed remains astonishingly pretty. Her arms are thin, and her cheeks are gaunt, but an alabaster beauty remains. "She laps up the Gatorade," says Jan. "You can go a long time without food if you drink." Her liver and kidneys continue to function. Miller tells Jan that it could be another two weeks.

On Wednesday, Anna is calm again. Jan does not want to dull her with antianxiety medication and stops the Lorazepam—but not before he gives her some in the morning to make sure she will not fight her bath. Annie, the tall and pretty nurse's aide, is an invaluable source of help. She warms the water, the soft rag, and the washing liquid she will spray on Anna as she works gently, limb by limb. Ro talks baby talk to Anna, a steady stream in a high voice, as a child talks to a doll, reverting to the past, when she was Anna's minimother. "We're going to have Anna's *spa* day. A spa day for my sisser. A sponge all over and then a massage. . . ."

Although Anna sleeps the deep sleep of the dying now, she is never left alone. A friend spells Ro, who sits in the living room, pausing from a chore begun when Anna began to need less care, cleaning out closets. Some coats, including a chubby fur coat Ro loaned Anna years ago, are slung over the sofa back. Ro cannot let rest her disquiet at the medical profession in general and Miller in particular and insists on making her point for the record. She is adamant about the medical profession providing a central clearinghouse for disseminating news to patients through their doctors. She returns to her long-standing complaint. "Ken didn't encourage adrenalectomy, didn't try to get my sister to have a hysterectomy, which *might* have helped early on. I had one immediately. . . . There were just too many things that were kept in Miller's realm and even though they went to Hopkins, it was Anna pushing—it wasn't his suggestion." (That is not so; Miller recommended it.)

Although perhaps more vehement than most, Ro's anger is not

uncharacteristic of family members who blame doctors and treatments as their loved ones die. Anyone who listens to survivors hears far more displeasure at doctors than praise. Miller says that his patients often complain to him, blaming their primary doctors for not detecting the cancer—just as Anna's father did regarding her mother's initial incorrect evaluation—but has seldom had it directed with such belligerence at him. Oncologist E. Roy Berger describes how he has been the "butt of anger and abuse" from relatives. "The woman on the phone was obnoxious, but her reaction wasn't rare. Accusations rising from the misdirected anger of family members is one of the major heartaches in dealing with people and their diseases. These frustrated relatives are not just venting their hostilities toward doctors, they are actually blaming the doctors for the diseases of their loved ones. Even though the irrational wrath can be understood intellectually," Berger states, such abusive antagonism has a negative result, with doctors appearing "more and more aloof in order to mask the aggravation they are feeling."[4]

Linda Suarez, Anna's cancer buddy and photographer, arrives. She has heard Ro's comments and says, "I'm going to have to stick up for Ken. First of all, he saved my life. I should not be alive. And Anna had complete faith in him." An exhausted Ro, like a bulldog with a bone, does not give up, arguing her central complaints as Suarez counters in vain. "Patients shouldn't have to read up on everything on the Internet," as Suarez does, says Ro. "What if you don't have the Internet? Or a scientific background like Jan? The patient is *not* medically trained." Doctors like Miller should provide vital new information. Linda protests, "It did happen at times like that! Ken made lots of suggestions that she either took or did not."

Suarez, knowing Anna's decisive manner, adds, "If she really was unhappy with Ken, why didn't she leave?" "She actually did talk about that with me," says Ro. "I don't know, there is a loyalty in her. I can't explain it." Linda says firmly, "I tell you, Ken adored Anna. He would do anything in the world for her, and he would do the same for me." Ro gives no quarter. "I think he put forth what he could—to the best of his abilities." The argument continues and finally Ro says, "Well, I've said my piece."

The two women try to end the discussion on a grace note. They talk about life after death. Ro says, "Anna and I aren't religious at all, but I also believe that we have been here in some form before and come back again in some form." "When I first started my chemo and was drifting off," recalls Linda, "all of a sudden it was like my two aunts, who had died, were there, trying to put this white plastic sheet over me. I kept thinking, 'You've gotta scream, you've got to wake up, do something!' and finally I just shouted, 'No!' and it all went away. I found that very comforting because I felt like, 'Okay, if you can fight with that magnitude on a subconscious level, then you have a real fighting chance.' I also felt that to me that was a sign that there was something out there and people who loved me."

Linda was fine until this spring. "After seven years, I had it again. It was like, 'Whupp!'—snapped with the choke chain. I was right back in the cancer mainstream. After seven years, you kind of go, 'La-di-da di-da.' It wasn't recurrence. It was a totally different cancer. It was very small and the surgery got it. There is no cancer anymore."

Linda says, more softly now, "Maybe it's a simplistic view. I think everyone has a time to die. It's Anna's time." Yesterday Linda and Anna had a private moment when Anna was talking clearly. "She told me, 'It could have been you.' And I said, 'It *should* have been me, based on the severity of my cancer.' " (Ro says, "It should have been me, more than twenty years ago.") "Then I said to Anna," continues Linda, " 'God's still working on me. You are absolutely perfect.' And I think that's true. A person reaches a state of grace and then they are perfect. To me, yesterday with Ken was frustration and panic. I think she would be surprised at herself." Ro lets that go.

"She resigned herself that there was no place else to fight," Ro says. "But she's been very happy with her life. There is nothing that she would probably do over again. But she wanted to do things she hadn't done, like go to Australia and watch the water go down the drain the reverse way. She was fascinated with the fact that that happens when you go to the other side of the equator." Linda says, "I lived in Uruguay—believe me, it's no big deal." Says Ro, "But it was something she wanted to see." "I remember the first time Anna saw Hale-Bopp," recalls Linda. "It was aglow. She said, 'I knew in that instant that I was going to be riding comets.' "

In those hours when Anna talked to her dead mother, Ro says, "I told Anna, and I wasn't joking, 'Mom is pulling you, she's pulling you too hard, she wants you back.' " Her words cascade in anguish as tears come. She is stung by a memory. "When my mother died, it wasn't me she wanted—it was Anna—to take care of her." Linda says, "That hurts." Ro blows her nose. "I understood why, it was okay—my mother loved having Anna with her. And ever since my mother died, I have felt this tug. She pulled—and we couldn't pull anymore."

"People have the right to let go," says Linda, "and we should help them." Roseann nods.

Later that afternoon, four old Richmond friends arrive at the same time by happenstance. Tina and Lockie drive up together and whoop when they see the two others, whom they have not seen in ages. Red wine is uncorked as they sit on the bed, talking to Anna constantly, singing, joking. When Tina and Lockie say, "Anna, let's party," Anna smiles with her eyes closed. She also cries with happiness when Tina and Lockie tell her they drove up together, reinforcing once more that they have made up. Anna gives every indication that she, like many patients who are semicomatose, can hear and that it is important for those around her to provide pleasurable moments. Thursday morning, Anna wakes with a smile on her face and says to her friends, "Let's party!" The nurse checking her vital signs says, "She's very happy this morning." Tina says, "She partied last night." Lockie laughs. "It's happiness hangover."

By noon on Thursday, May 29, an assembly line of friends are with Anna. She complies when they gently roll her to change diapers but it elicits a slight moan. Morphine is dripped into her mouth. Tina warms the washcloth, sprays it with washing solution. Anna does not protest as her old friend bathes her bottom. Others reach for ointment and efficiently diaper Anna. All the while, they speak endearingly to Anna. "It's okay, babe," says Lockie, leaning close to her. "You're worn out from partying." Lockie and Tina hug and kiss her. Speaking into Anna's ear, Lockie says, "We love you. We're going back to Richmond now. See ya soon."

Anna's last weekend on earth is peaceful. The weather is unseasonably cold and gray, the temperature dipping down to record-breaking numbers. It seems like an omen, as if the sun would never shine again. By Monday, June 2, Anna lies still, drifting into a coma. A friend looks at her, shrunken in size, devoid of her spectacular energy and warmth, and hopes, as she kisses her on the cheek, that the end will come soon. The hospice nurse, Margaret, indicates to Jan and Ro that based on low blood pressure, low pulse rate, and other signs, she didn't think Anna would last the week. Jan calls Dottie, who has been on vacation, to alert her to prepare the children. They know that their mother is going to die, but they view it as something in the future, not imminent. Jan makes plans for Dottie to come tomorrow night for dinner.

By Tuesday, June 3, Anna has visibly deteriorated. "When Annie came to wash and give her a lotion rub," recalls Jan, "I helped turn Anna. I noticed several small places on her back where blood was pooling—a sign that her blood pressure was so low that there was very poor circulation. Anna's temperature was up to one hundred and four, but her pulse and blood pressure were actually better than the day before. At Margaret's suggestion, I zoomed up to Safeway and got some Acetaminophen suppositories, to lower the temperature. We continued with the morphine solution, and gave her more Acetaminophen at bedtime."

Everyone senses that the end is near. "Nancy wanted to take down the 3-D Taj Mahal puzzle, but I wanted to give Lindsay the opportunity to help, since she worked on it quite a bit. I took some pictures of it and if they come out okay, I might give them to everyone who helped so much. It was a strong symbol of group effort."

Jan and Ro are jumpy. "Being restless, playing the waiting game, we both found it very therapeutic to clean, and the kids' rooms were in dire need," says Jan. "We rearranged some things (so that clean clothes actually had a drawer to go in, imagine that!)." Winter clothes are moved into another closet that Ro had cleaned out. When the children return from school, Jan and Ro show them their spotless rooms. Dottie comes that evening and they all eat Roseann's lasagna. Then Dottie disappears with the children to the downstairs rec room. "She worked her magic as I guess she always has," says Ro, "making them able to open up and express their feelings. It was very helpful for them and came just in time." After the session, Dottie tells Ro and Jan that they should not have cleaned the children's rooms. "The one thing Ro and I were clued in to was to leave the kids' rooms alone! In retrospect, I am in complete agreement with Dottie. The kids have been subjected to so much coming and going that they needed to have a space all their own, and though well meaning, we violated that space. They are at the age where those types of issues are very important."

That night, Dottie says her farewell to Anna. Leaning close, she reassures Anna about her children. " 'I will keep my promise, I didn't forget it. I will be there.' I have no doubt that she heard me and knew exactly what I was saying."

Later, as Jan snuggles up to Anna, holding her close, he whispers, "I love you."

The next evening, June 4, at six forty-five, Jan writes, "This morning I awoke about 4:10 A.M. to Anna's labored breathing. Her breathing rate was slow, but each breath was more as if she was gasping for air, making a determined effort to hang on. She was also making some noise, which I would describe as a soft groan as she exhaled. I got up and gave her a good slug of morphine, stroked her, and talked to her a bit, then went back to sleep. I got up at six and gave Anna another cc of morphine. Her breathing was still very labored (it was almost as if she was gasping). Ro came up and we noticed that there was blood pooling in her toes and heels. I couldn't feel a pulse at the ankles or wrist and her hands and feet were very cold, despite the fact that her underarm temperature was 102+. Ro and I agreed that Margaret should be called, because we wanted to know what to do to make Anna as comfortable as possible. We called hospice to page Margaret and ask her to come right over. We kept up with the morphine, and I gave her a little Acetaminophen to ease her temperature.

"In the meantime, I had gotten the kids up, fed the dogs, made lunches. Jane Bittner had been scheduled for 7:00 A.M., and when she arrived, I asked her to take Ellery to school, as I wanted to stay close by. After Lindsay got off to school, Ro and I just sat with Anna, each of us holding a hand and whispering to her that she could relax, that she could go, that everything was taken care of thanks to all her work. I put on a CD of Rubinstein playing Chopin and turned it up so Anna could hear it in the bedroom. She was somewhat responsive, managing little groans when we talked to her and stroked her. The breathing continued to be labored, and her fingertips and toes got very blue. Ro and I continued to hold her hand and talk to her."

Roseann says later, "When I looked at the catheter bag, I noticed that there had been a very, very small amount of urine since the night before. I knew her kidneys were in a major shutdown. At that point, she was very hot, then cold, then hot."

The house was very still, except for the voices of Jan and Roseann and Anna's groans and breathing. They kept soothing Anna, telling her that everything was just as she wanted it and that it was time to stop fighting and let go so that she would stop suffering, and giving her morphine now and then. "She was groaning a lot, but we weren't sure if she was uncomfortable or what," says Roseann. "It was very hard to know. I think it was probably just a moan and she was not in pain. Her breathing was very short and shallow. Margaret had explained to me that when her body shut down, there would be less and less oxygen to the brain and—although she was breathing a lot—the breathing was so shallow that the body would not be getting enough oxygen."

Meanwhile, the normally frisky Cream became very quiet. She lay outside the room, looking in. "She looked depressed, and stayed that way the whole day, and a good part of the next day," recalls Roseann. "It seemed as if she knew her friend was gone, you could really see it.

"We continued to talk to Anna and talk and talk and talk over a period of forty-five minutes. About eight thirty-five, Nils got up and went to the bathroom and at that point I believe the first of what I call cardiac arrest started. All of a sudden, she gasped—you could see her chest expanding, as if she were taking a deep breath—then stopped. She was breathing again, then it happened again. Jan came out of the bathroom. 'I think she's going,' I called. We were both with her. This happened four times in the space of five minutes."

"She finally died about eight-forty," recalls Jan. "She stopped breathing, but she still had a faint pulse visible on her chest. She took a couple of last-minute gulps of air and then was still. During these few minutes between life and death, I found that Ro and I were concentrated on Anna's comfort; grief was not yet part of the emotional milieu. After Anna had been still for a few minutes, the grief washed over us. We cried separately, each one taking some private time with Anna, then we hugged and cried some more. I think we both felt relief for Anna; it must have been very hard for her to give up, and I think she was conscious at some level almost to the end."

Margaret arrived quickly. By now, any disputes with hospice are history. Jan cannot praise them enough. "Margaret was an absolute gem. She bathed Anna, cleaned up everything, and got her into a nice pink nightgown" Jane Bittner also helped with this ritual, deriving comfort in preparing her friend properly. "I have to say that it worked out for the best," comments Roseann. "The kids had gone. Nobody else was in the house. It was as if Anna had organized it." Ro and Jan had their private good-bye. It is not inconceivable that Anna indeed had waited until the children were gone to die.

Jan and Roseann felt that perhaps Anna's body should be removed before the children came home. Margaret and Jane weren't so sure. "I got on the phone with Dottie," says Ro, "who said that it was best that the kids had a chance to say good-bye." As always, Dottie stressed that the children needed to make their own choices. "If they didn't want to see her, they didn't have to, but they *had* to be given the option."

While Jan left to get the children, Dottie arrived. "Because Margaret needed someone to be a witness," says Roseann, "I watched as she dumped medication; we flushed thousands of dollars down that toilet." This included unopened medications, an incredible waste, considering worldwide shortages, but it is the law. "You can't even give it away legally," Jan explains. The funeral home is advised that they would be called for removal of the body shortly and reminded that Anna had requested immediate cremation. Says Ro, "We were just waiting for Jan to come back with the kids."

"So," writes Jan, "I left to get first Ellery, then Lindsay. I had asked Ro to call the school counselors and tell them I was on my way, but not to say anything to the kids. I cried most of the way to Ellery's school, which is about thirty minutes away, hoping I could cry myself out enough to hold things together when I got there. I managed to get into the office okay, sign him out, and meet with the counselor in one piece. We walked to Ellery's third-period class and I asked the counselor to go in and get him, as I wanted to create as little disturbance as possible. Ellery came out and asked what the deal was and I told him I was taking him home. He asked me why and I held off until we were out of the building, then I managed to tell him between sobs that Anna had died this morning. I think he knew right away, but was holding on, hoping it was something else. When I managed to get that out, we both cried, and I just kept us walking arm in arm. I didn't think he wanted his friends to see him like that. In the car, we had a good hug and more crying.

"On the way, we were both fairly quiet, me staring ahead and Ellery with his head down. I did rub his back at every stop sign and manage to say that this really sucked. Ellery stayed in the car when we got to Lindsay's school. We arrived just at lunchtime. After signing Lindsay out, I was just going to the lunchroom to get her, when she and a friend appeared. She had her lunch bag and a soda in hand, and I put my arm around her and said she needed to come home. She asked about getting her book bag and I said she should leave it in her locker."

Once again, Jan's tears course down his face as he holds his daughter and tells her that Anna has died. Jan comments, "The crying is extremely therapeutic. I am blubbering right now as I write this. I have been keeping my crying time to myself. While time to get with the kids and talk and cry about things has come up, I feel you need to balance the grief with the getting on with things. As such, I find that driving in the car by myself has been a good time to let it all out. It allows one to recharge the batteries to face the next day, hour, minute. . . ."

It takes Jan four and a half months before he can bring himself to finish his thoughts. In October he writes, "This has been a long break, but I will finish my recollections of the day, as they are very much in my mind, still. We got home to find Ro and Margaret and Dottie there." Roseann looks at the children anxiously as they walk in. "Ellery was just unbelievably shaken, he was crying from the depth of his soul," she recalls. "The first person he walked to was me and he gave me a big hug and I hugged him back, crying too. Lindsay was very quiet. She went over to Dottie."

Jan and the children have their own group hug and more tears in the kitchen by themselves. "Then I asked the kids if they wanted to say good-bye to Anna, which they both did. The three of us went in together. Margaret had cleared away all the medical paraphernalia and Anna looked as if she was sleeping. All morning had been very gray and gloomy, but when I was picking up the kids, it turned into a brilliant, clear day. It was bright in the room. Each of the kids stood and stared for a short time and said good-bye. We left the room and had some good hugging and crying all round. I had decided to take the kids out, now that they had some closure, so I said we would climb up Sugerloaf Mountain, since that has been a favorite spot of Anna's.

"Ro, Margaret, Jane, and Dottie would stay and take care of all the unpleasant details. I have never asked Ro about the things she had to do that day. I know it must have been wrenching for her to see Anna carried away. I am having a very hard time just thinking about it. The kids changed and we went off, trying to be a little upbeat, deciding that Anna had given us the beautiful weather. Clear, dry, and in the seventies.

"We got to Sugarloaf in midmorning and had the place all to ourselves, since it was a weekday. We hiked up the mountain, exploring as we went all the little overlooks and big rocks and half-fallen trees we had explored many times before with Anna. The view from the top is spectacular in good weather. The breeze was so gentle that everything was absolutely still. I tried to get the kids to use their imagination and try and see Anna in the clouds; they thought that was pretty corny.

"While we were all sad, we were all very aware of a strong sense of love and unity—perhaps we felt some collective relief that Anna's suffering had ended. We didn't talk too much on our hike. We decided to stop for lunch at the Comus Inn, which is nearby and has a wonderful view of Sugarloaf. The patio was empty, so we got some sandwiches and sat there, soaking up the warm sun and lovely view. We made several toasts to Anna, and kept thoughts of her in our conversation. I wanted to emphasize to them that this was it—it was just the three of us now, and we had to stick together. We talked about what we thought Anna would want for us and what we would do over the summer. We also talked about school, and I let them know it was their decision as to when they would go back. I also emphasized that we had to talk a lot and tell each other things, that we would have to try hard to do things together and have dinners together as much as possible.

"We touched on various vacation wishes for the summer and Lindsay's ballet plans for the fall. While we came to the brink of tears a few times (me mainly), it was generally a happy time. We even had a couple of laughs over some fond memories. I think we were all focusing hard on the immediate future, bucking ourselves up by immersing ourselves in plan making while savoring the warmth and feeling of togetherness of the moment.

"I think subconsciously we were also dreading going home, wanting the loveliness of the outing never to end. After lunch, we decided to go to a driving range and hit a few balls, which was a lot of fun, since none of us is particularly good at it. We talked of Anna and her brother Steve; they both loved to golf. Golf is a good connection for Steve, as he loves to teach the kids and will have lots of opportunities when we go to Florida.

"The afternoon stretched on, and we had to go. We rented a silly movie for the evening (I can't remember what, I didn't watch it) and may have picked up some takeout, I don't remember. I don't remember much more about the evening. There were some papers I had to sign and phone calls to make, though Ro and company had done everything—made phone calls to get the phone tree going, dealt with the funeral home, called the schools to let them know we didn't want the kids getting undue attention when they came back. I can't tell you what a comfort it was to have Ro here, and how indebted I am to her for that day I was able to spend alone with the kids."

Jan is a young man of forty-four, but he has lived almost forever with Anna. For the first time in nearly three decades, since he was sixteen, Jan is without Anna. For twenty-three years, they had slept together as man and wife. On the night of June 4, Jan sleeps in the big king-sized bed, without Anna by his side, knowing that never will she be there again. For Anna, there had been only one man in her entire life, Jan. He cries himself to sleep.

PART IV

Grieving: Our Common Bond

When we are dead, and people weep for us and grieve, let it be because we touched their lives with beauty and simplicity. Let it not be said that life was good to us, but rather that we were good to life.

JACOB P. RUBIN

The friend who can be silent with us in a moment of despair or confusion, who can stay with us in an hour of grief and bereavement, who can tolerate not-knowing, not-curing, not-healing, and face with us the reality of our powerlessness—that is a friend who cares.

HENRY NOUWEN, *Out of Solitude*

Anna and Wayne Westbrook (1995)

Jan, Lindsay, Anna, and Ellery (summer 1996)

Jan Johannessen

Photo by Linda Suarez

November 1996 (seven months before Anna died)

CHAPTER NINETEEN

Love Beyond Death

No matter how prepared a family is, no matter how thorough a patient is in prearranging the "unpleasant details," survivors can be overwhelmed by cold technicalities that intrude on grief at its rawest. Arranging for the body to be taken away; choosing caskets or urns; signing paperwork with funeral homes, hospitals, or hospice; writing and notifying newspapers of obituaries; alerting friends; planning funerals or memorial services—all are emotion-fraught decisions.

While Jan waits, the hospice nurse calls the funeral home and they indicate that Roseann can sign the papers for Jan. As Jan leaves with the children for Sugarloaf Mountain, the duties for Ro and Anna's friends are just beginning. Margaret and Jane deal with the removal of the body. At times, Roseann dissolves in tears and is comforted by Patty and Jane. "I truly appreciate them because periodically I became a basket case, not being able to mentally function," she recalls. Funeral home attendants arrive and take Anna's body, wheeling her down the hall on a gurney and out the front door that Anna never used while alive. Jane and Dottie strip and change the bed and straighten up. Roseann and Margaret take care of hospice papers and then Margaret hugs everyone as she leaves. Dottie also leaves. Jane and Patty stay with Roseann, comforting her. Ann Wylie house-sits until equipment is picked up, such as the hulking green oxygen tank that has sat all this time in the dining room, unused. Jane drives Roseann to the funeral home.

Roseann is anxious to complete business at the funeral home. "The last thing I wanted to do was stress Jan when he got back." But Roseann cannot legally sign the document regarding cremation, after all. She is told that Anna's husband could sue the funeral director, saying that he had not agreed to it. "It's Maryland law," says Roseann. Jan signs the paper when he returns from Sugarloaf.

Roseann has nothing but praise for the small Barber Funeral Home, in Laytonsville, Maryland, and understands why Anna chose it. Mrs. Barber encourages Ro to buy their own memorial guest book. "It will save you money rather than buying it from me." Her attitude is foreign to most funeral homes now owned by conglomerates, where no expense is spared, so long as it comes from the pockets of bereaved families. In those cool and darkened rooms, assistants are instructed to lead families across soft plush carpets, moving inexorably from the least-expensive to the most-expensive caskets—those burnished wood-and-brass silk-lined enclosures that can cost up to $20,000 or more. Like car salesmen writ large, they pause at the Cadillacs of caskets, trying to make families ashamed if they opt for anything less. Cremation has become a growing alternative, but those expenses can run as high as funerals.

Because children are involved, Mrs. Barber suggests that the memorial should not be at the funeral home. "This can leave a negative, lasting effect on the children," she says. Ro adds, "She was very gracious and helpful. She stressed some place that the kids could accept, saying that children seldom get the opportunity to hear how people feel about their parents and it would be a lasting, positive memory."

Jan settles on a Quaker-style memorial service and sets it for Sunday, June 14, because Lindsay has a ballet recital on June 7, and it will give out-of-towners more time to make arrangements to attend. An anguished Roseann again urges her father not to come, fearful that the travel and the emotional pain would be too much for him. They will videotape the memorial and show it to him when they all meet in Florida in July. She and Jan are in daily communication with him. "He has been very depressed since all of this," Ro recounts the day before the memorial service. "I have grave concerns about him, because of what's happened, even though he was prepared for it."

On Friday, June 6, two days after Anna died, an eerie moment occurs. Jan and friends hear Anna's clear, cheerful voice coming over the radio. Thousands of listeners who have never met Anna hear her say of cancer,

"So I am fighting it again right now." Bob Madigan, the interviewer, says, "Through the chemotherapy, you've lost your hair, but you haven't lost your will." "Oh, no!" Anna's emphatic voice booms. "Haven't lost your good sense of humor," says Madigan. "Oh, no! I haven't lost much of anything. . . . I was in the media biz, the marketing and advertising business, and I had to walk away and say, 'It's time to be with your family'—smell the flowers finally and enjoy myself—and that's what I've done. And it's really been the best thing." "And the best thing she did for her two children, eleven-year-old Lindsay and thirteen-year-old Ellery," says Madigan, over the recording of Anna, taped just six weeks before at the Race for the Cure luncheon. "You see, Anna Johannessen of Olney died this past Wednesday, at home with her husband, Jan, by her side. Anna is proof the Race for the Cure [to be run the next day] is not just an event. It's real people facing a very real and deadly disease."

Roseann repeats often her urgency to "get everything back to normal," how the house was "as normal as possible" when Jan and the children returned from Sugarloaf on Wednesday. This quest for normalcy is a common reminder of how little time we allow for grieving—yet being disoriented, numb, distracted, relieved, anguished is normal at this stage. Lindsay chooses to return to school the next day; it seems to be her haven. Ellery stays home, keeps to himself. On Friday, Lindsay performs in a band recital that the whole family attends. Jan and Ro busily make and field phone calls, distribute Anna's phone tree to friends to call. When Cliff comes on Friday, Ro tells Jan, "I really need to get home."

Roseann feels that they "need to have the opportunity to get started on their own life together without a fourth party. It's going to be a bonding and evolution of coming together in a different way. And also, quite frankly, I felt very surrounded. I went through this with my mother and now I had gone through it with Anna and it left me with the feeling of"—her voice becomes strained—"being left to bury everybody and this is very hard on me." Roseann, emotionally and physically drained, starts to sob. "It's very hard for me to talk about." Some of Roseann's tears are for herself, feeling that a heavy burden has been placed on her due to life's circumstance. She doesn't mention that she may feel, as some designated family caregivers do, that no one really understands what a task this is. She is grateful for every Anna friend who appreciated her.

* * *

Anna's preparations make this time so much easier for her family and friends. They zip through the telephone tree, contacting people in no time. The two cars in Anna's name had been transferred to Jan and their other possessions were jointly held, thus saving Jan from the emotional blow experienced by many survivors—having to, in effect, cancel a loved one out of their lives. Still, there is much to do in the days preceding the memorial service, says Jan. "Making arrangements, talking with friends and relatives, getting to ballet rehearsals and recitals, going to the schools to talk with the teachers and counselors, getting to work as I could, cleaning the house, fetching relatives, visiting folks, writing notes. Dottie came, and reinforced my sense that Ellery should go back and face school, for emotional reasons, and he did that week. I didn't want him to go through the summer wondering and worrying whether he would cry when he saw his friends and teachers in the fall and I didn't want him to feel badly about not having had the courage to do it (especially in light of Lindsay's decision). He had a couple of tough days, but the stress of worry about Anna was relieved."

There is one task Anna never finished, and that is her obituary. She had planned to write it—"That way, it will be right"—but she left nothing in writing or in her computer. A friend uses Anna's résumé to help compose the piece. Unless one is famous or prominent, obituaries are about as personal as tax return forms. A reader learns where the deceased went to school, worked, what he or she died of, the names of survivors—but these bloodless accounts reveal nothing about how the person lived or the impact he or she made on others. Within those confines, Anna Johannessen was duly observed in the *Washington Post* and the *Richmond Times-Dispatch.*

One final act, however, is pure Anna. Anyone who knew her even slightly smiles when they learn of it. One day, when she and Roseann were discussing cremation, Anna said, "I don't want you to buy any urn, we have plenty of things around here to use. How about the cookie jar that you gave me?" Roseann stared at her. Years ago, when Jan and Anna were first married, Roseann bought them a Cheshire cat cookie jar. Roseann recalls, "I thought it looked like Anna. It had that funny grin and was humorous." The Cheshire cat cookie jar is tucked under Ro's arm as she goes to the funeral home. It is white ceramic, with a black bow of a grin, whiskers, and mischievous shiny eyes. No one who knew Anna can think of a better final resting place.

A memorial service, often termed a "celebration of life," has increasingly become a substitute for the traditional funeral. Some in the death education field warn that such celebrations should include recognition of major loss; such finality allows the bereaved to give vent to full mourning. For many who are less steeped in tradition or eschew somberness, an occasion that combines love and laughter, taking on the aspects of roasts as well as toasts, is an appropriate ritual. Certainly Anna felt that way. How could anyone forget her written request not to have "some blowhole giving a speech about me when he or she didn't even know me."

On the other hand, there are those who find great comfort in and would feel deeply incomplete without a church or synagogue or other religious service. There are as many variables as there are individuals. Ken Doka, a minister who trains funeral directors, says, "With Anna, some of the things that funerals can do to help tell you about the reality of death were unnecessary; her survivors had been actively involved and had witnessed it. And Anna's wishes didn't contradict the rest of the family. In a situation where that was not the case, I would go with the survivors. The one problem I have with the celebration of life is that it should acknowledge the many ambivalent feelings that people have—'We're glad her suffering is over, glad it's over for us, *but* we still miss her.' That has to be validated. And that's a funeral—no matter what you call it. A funeral is a ritual that surrounds death." William Lamers, physician and psychiatrist and one of the founders of the American modern hospice movement, invented a definition of the word "funeral." "It's been published all over the world," says Lamers. It's as inclusive as it can be, yet succinct: "An organized, purposeful, flexible, time-limited, group-centered response to a loss."

"When I train funeral directors, I tell them to ask families to talk about rituals and funerals that meant something to them. 'What are the things you liked? What are the things you hated? What do you want to see avoided?' " says Doka. "I don't teach directors to tell families what they should do. The art is not giving advice; the art is asking the right questions, and you can only do that by listening—to the verbal and nonverbal—and recognizing that communication is very complex."

Anna's celebration of life is a special page out of Americana, as more than 300 friends and family gather in the Olney Lutheran Church of the Good Shepherd social hall, not the church itself. It is June 14, 1997—ten days after Anna died. The service starts late, as they wait in a long line to reach the front, where a casket or urn might have been. Instead there are two large display boards, filled with snapshots and enlarged pictures of Anna in wide-mouthed smile and laughter, the glamorous mixed with the clowning. More are placed on a table that holds the guest book. In one, Anna is clumping on the sand in a black bikini, wearing flippers and mask, arms outstretched like some crazed bird, her long hair trailing, looking like the Creature from the Black Lagoon. In their wedding picture, Jan and Anna look like kids, mouths wide, ready to burst out of the frame. Friends have come prepared, some with brand-new Kleenex boxes placed by their chairs, but the many grinning faces of Anna produce smiles.

In this Family Life Building, children's rainbow pictures decorate, rather than stained glass. Folding chairs, instead of pews, line the room and face the "altar" of Anna pictures—a comforting, encircling U-shaped configuration of friends. Some friends wear black, but several know that Anna would want brightness. Patty Williams, who held Anna against her chest so many times in those days when she was fed water or morphine, is in red-and-white polka dots. "I picked out the brightest dress I could find for Anna." Jane Bittner wears a bright peach top and white slacks. Anna had requested intimate informality and, although there is the scattered tie and sports coat, the mood is more of a summer's picnic moved inside—children in shorts and sandals, women in flowing skirts and blouses, men in shirts, infants cradled in arms. A cross section of ages, races, and creeds comingle. Roseann wears a cream jacket and black slacks, Cliff is in a brightly patterned shirt, Anna's trim mother-in-law, Phoebe, wears slacks and a white shirt. Jan is in a bright blue golf shirt, Ellery in a white one, Lindsay in a midcalf blue skirt and white blouse. She and Ellery, both so tall, slim, and attractive, stand frequently as friends and family hug them continuously.

Although Anna had instructed Wayne to be her music director, Jan bypassed music, opting for uninterrupted expressions of bearing witness. It seems perfect. There are no prayers, no dignitaries, no official speakers, no clergy, no flowers. Anna had requested that donations be sent to the Olney Ballet and the St. Francis Bereavement Center instead. Jan begins with a casual greeting, explaining that Wayne will be moving throughout, making a video, especially for Anna's father and for posterity. "So if any of you are on the lam from the CIA . . ." Jan's sentence is interrupted by welcoming laughter. Although it is sad without Anna, says Jan, that is not the thrust of the day. "Anna would like to see lots of smiles. It's important to note that today would have been her mom's eighty-third birthday." Jan's voice rings out clearly, trembling only occasionally. "I'm going to get started and if anyone wants to get up, just go ahead.

"Three words describe Anna," he begins, " 'courage,' 'compassion,' and 'justice.' When I think about courage, I've never known Anna to back down from anybody or anything. When she ran into something or some kind of a problem, she'd take it on straight on. I'm kind of reminded of that little cartoon you sometimes see around offices, of the frog who is about to be swallowed by this large bird. And the frog's lying down, he's got his hands around the bird's neck [he demonstrates, to much laughter], and the caption says, 'Never give up.' That frog took lessons from Anna. And in terms of compassion, although Anna was a fierce competitor, if there was a friend in need, she was always willing to lend her time or money or help out or offer a place to stay, anything like that. And as for her incredible sense of justice, Anna had a real thing for things being right. In this day and age of finger-pointing and assigning blame to this, that, and the other, Anna was probably one of the most honest people that I ever met." Jan chokes, tears descend. "And I think that everyone would agree to that. That was one of her really special traits. Many people have those traits, but Anna had an absolute commitment to hold on to them. Just uncompromising.

"Anna had a great sense of fun and adventure and was always willing to try something new. I remember one of the things that Anna was never able to master, although she always tried, was waterskiing. [Laughter ensues.] Starting back when we were in college, Patty and Jimmy, who are here, went out with Patty's folks on their boat on the Severn River. Anna just couldn't quite get up. She'd be going along halfway out of the water, but she wouldn't let go. And she'd try again and again. You would see this huge wall of water [there is huge laughter]—and she just wouldn't let go.

"The final thing I want to say is about Anna's sense of friendship. Many people in this room I would not have met had it not been for Anna. She had a real ability to be friends with everybody and pick up on everybody. Lots of people who had just met her have this sense of wanting to sit down and tell her their whole life story. That quality had led me to the conviction that women really are the glue that holds together families and communities and societies."

Voices chant, "Hear! Hear!" Immediately friends bear witness one after another—from high school and college, colleagues in Anna's various careers, the Richmond pals, relatives. Comedians would be lucky to have such willing audiences as friends and family provide on such occasions. Jimmy has them howling with his reminiscences of college life in the form of a letter to Anna. "Remember Lloyd—the only person to be listed in the phone book as an alias? . . . Remember when we measured everybody's mouth? [Laughter.] And yours was the largest? [Guffaws.]"

Lockie picks up the postgraduate days—how they met, a gardening truckload of chicken manure fiasco, the time Lockie's dog got drunk on paint stripper and Jan raced out with his medical book and a solution of hydrogen peroxide and water. "Anna gets this big turkey baster and pumps this solution down. . . ." Lockie blows her nose. "She saved my dog's life. . . . And Anna could never let an injustice stand. I had a bad relationship with my mom. Oil and water. After Anna became sick, she just couldn't see that rift remain. So she writes a four-page letter to my mother and says everything I'm sure I never would have said. Mom called Anna and said, 'Lockie's so lucky to have a friend like you.' Now Mom and I are best friends." Lockie chokes back tears. "When Anna's cancer got worse, I told her, 'Anna, if I'm going to lose you, you're going to have to be my guardian angel. . . . I will carry you with me.' "

Terry Snyder, a tall man with dramatic flair, relates a pathetic Shakespeare players performance. "Anna was stage manager for *Two Noble Kinsman,* a strange story—and a much stranger director. I was one of the two noble kinsmen"—he pauses—"and I wore a *dress.* . . . Through it all, Anna made it a good time and made us understand that being together was more important than whatever we were producing on the stage. She's been my friend ever since. I miss her."

Connie Giordano, her Happy Feet Shoe Store partner, addresses Anna's oft-mentioned genius for making instant friends. "She could reach right inside you and she always had faith in the people that she loved." Jan's older sister, Lisbeth, stands, addressing "Nils—we never call him Jan." She reads two poems, one written at the wedding, August 17, 1974; the other dated yesterday. "It came to me last night." Jan is moved to sobbing. His sister comes over to hug him. His mother races over from her chair on the opposite side of the room to hold him.

Jane Bittner says, "Anna made OCBT [Olney Children's Ballet Theater] what it is," and speaks of her courage. "When there would be a technical rehearsal at five-thirty, Anna would only say, 'I might be a little late. I don't get out of chemo until five-fifteen.' I'd say, 'You don't have to come, it may be too hard,' and Anna would reply, 'Just get a mat out in case I need to lie down.' "

Several women testify to Anna's giving them the confidence to try new careers. One adds, "The thing I remember most about Anna is her inner beauty." There are nods of awareness around the room. "I always felt like Anna was an angel here on earth. . . . I know she is happy." She cries. "She's not hurting anymore and that's a comfort to me. The last time I saw her was on Mother's Day and I told her how much I admired her—she was a wonderful mother. She said, 'Finally I've played all my cards.' I told her, 'They were really damn good cards!' "

Tributes continue, poetic and funny, halting and assured, sad and uplifting: "Anna was a six-speed convertible Corvette—red, of course—and God left out speeds one through five." "Sadness and Anna are an oxymoron, like military and intelligence." "I can't think of Anna without smiling." "Everything I ever learned about life I learned from Anna." "She got involved with the Race for the Cure so others would not have to go through what she did." "I want to be just like Anna, she is my hero."

Roseann winds up. "She was my baby doll. My live baby doll." She pauses. "She was my best friend . . . and everything everyone said here is true. She emulated our mother in many ways—but Anna also came from another place. A very special sister. How much it means to hear how all of you loved her! It helps me get through this. Thank you personally for the unbelievable love expressed to my sister. You don't see that in today's world. I think it helped my father, who is having a hard time with this; understanding that she was not alone."

If one has to lose the battle with cancer or any other disease, Roseann's final comment proves that love does last. "The love poured out was love poured back."

Kleenex tissues have piled up, along with the laughter, and Jan says, "I just want to say, 'Let's blow our noses—and let's *party*!' "

Much later, Jan recalls, "I had a difficult time getting though the memorial, but was helped by looking at the sea of friends and relatives. Many of the kids' teachers and friends came as well." Being surrounded by their own friends helped Ellery and Lindsay immensely; they smiled more than they cried.

Guests plow through a sudden summer thunderstorm, soaking shoes in puddles, and the house soon explodes with people, laughter, and noise; many of Anna's friends are as gregarious as she was. Throughout the house are displays of even more pictures of Anna and friends and family. Miraculously the rain ends so that the crush spreads onto the deck, where buckets of white and red wine, champagne, and beer will soon need replenishment. Every conceivable horizontal surface in the dining room is loaded with food, and one guest, carrying hot pizza, lifting the tray high over the heads of guests, barely finds room.

An unbelievable mix—from scientists to clowns, from dancers to baseball players—shmooze together. "Look at the people she's touched," says Christopher Hudert, the young, attractive boss clown at Ringling Brothers. "For one person to do all of this in such a short life. Nothing was impossible for Anna; it was not 'No' but 'How can we?' She was always one step ahead, in the jungle cutting the growth down. She wasn't a team player, she was our team *leader*." No one can think of negatives—Anna could be stubborn, not graceful at accepting compliments or help, but what was that compared to her magnanimity? She was never yucky or saccharine, never bragged about what she did for friends. Peggy, Hudert's wife and also a clown, says, "The only negative is a positive. Everyone she moved on from could have still used her."

The community baseball crowd gathers: "Over the years, she got really good—a good hitter, fielded balls. She came last year, half her hair sticking out of baseball cap, but she was still hopping around. She played left field," says a women named Lorie. A man interjects, "When she'd catch one, she'd raise her hands," imitating the jock *Yesssss!* moves. "Everything she did was contagious," says Lorie, who works for a plastic surgeon. She remembers Anna's disinterest in breast reconstruction—" 'I don't need that'—and that was very inspiring. She was very comfortable with herself. She taught me—and this will stay with me forever—that she lived to live. She didn't live to die, even though she was dying; she'd take it as long as she could handle it."

Male teammates talk about why they liked Anna. "She was a great character. . . . She'd jump in the pool and play with the kids." "She didn't give a damn—she went out to have fun." "She was one of the guys. She got the beer—or the scotch." Janet Carbone recalls, "I had only heard of Anna through Bill." She lowers her voice in tough-guy imitation of her husband. " 'She's the broad plays baseball and she's got cancer and she hits the ball. . . .' It didn't affect me. *I* didn't have cancer. Then I got ovarian cancer. People didn't want to talk about it, but Anna was right there. She was an inspiration. If she could kick it, I could kick it." Janet pauses. "She's not kicking it anymore—but she went down like a trooper."

In another corner of the deck, a sailing friend, Chuck Shasky, recounts an insane sailing adventure with novices Jan and Anna and the nephew of a Saudi sheikh in 1982. Jan and Anna thought they were going on a pleasure ride; they hit thunder, lightning, and violent rain—then found out they were actually in a race on the Chesapeake Bay. As fog rolled in, they crossed the finish line. "We had won! With three rookies onboard!" recalls Shasky. "The sheikh guy said, 'Let's go to the Chart House to celebrate! This is on me!' We were just soaked slimy. Needless to say, Anna enjoyed the largesse of her newfound friend and led the partying."

Roars of laughter come from the far corner of the deck. Christopher Hudert is showing how to cure neck pain. He takes one arm and turns his neck—creating the most godawful cracking sound. Hidden in his armpit is a plastic cup; unnoticed by his audience, he presses that arm to his side, creating the intense cracking sound precisely as he turns his neck with the other arm. It seems more hilarious each time. Children start imitating him, and as the evening wears on, so do adults.

Down in the rec room, sprawled every which way, are Lindsay and Ellery and a band of adolescents, watching a Schwarzenegger movie.

As darkness begins to fall and the plastic cup supply is being noisily depleted behind him, Wayne stands in a corner, looking forlorn for a minute. "Don't kid yourself," he says. "Anna could be as depressed and lonely and negative as everybody else. But she chose to look beyond that." When she met an unlikable person, "she could cut to the chase pretty quick—but at the same time, she believed you had your universe and she had hers. Her perspectives were just incredible."

Wayne makes the most important point of the day. "Anna wasn't 'trying' to be good. She wasn't 'trying' to be all these things that people loved in her. She didn't work at it. It was just there."

CHAPTER TWENTY

How to Go On Living

For Jan, the long, slow process of grieving and learning to live without Anna brought vast sweeps in emotions. At the memorial service, a friend had warned Jan that after everyone is gone and ordinary life resumes, "things can get real quiet." Jan frenetically avoided such solitude. He took the path journeyed by many in grief, the fastest highway he could find. He and the children whirled from one activity and location to another—Florida, North Carolina, Seattle.

Although the Fourth of July trip to Florida was bittersweet—"We all had our sad hugs at various points"—Jan took pleasure in how elated Anna's father was to see them. "His subliminal fear that we wouldn't visit now that Anna was gone evaporated immediately." Jan's experience reminds one of the saying, "Grief shared, is grief diminished." Roseann was there also and many of the family gathered with them to see the videotape of the memorial. Anna's father was very impressed with the outpouring of love for his daughter. Says Jan, "I think it helped him with closure." It was hard on Jan. "I started to watch, but had to leave and take a walk after a couple of minutes."

Later that month, the trip to a beach in North Carolina with Jan's siblings took on all the aspects of a troop movement. The clan flew into Washington's National Airport from Seattle, Minneapolis, and St. Louis. "Full carloads to the beach, then masses of people sleeping all about the house on returning to Olney," recalls Jan. "We all had a really marvelous time—some twelve of us." It was wonderfully therapeutic for Lindsay and Ellery, who raced with the other children on the beach, swam, flew kites. "The first night, we had a full moon," recalls Jan. Several of the grown-ups and Lindsay and Ellery walked along the beach in the moonlight. "I had brought some of Anna's ashes. In the last-minute chaos which always precedes trips, I looked around for something to put some of Anna's ashes into, and not finding anything obvious, grabbed a jar of instant coffee, dumped out the coffee, rinsed and dried it, and put some ashes in. You remember Anna and coffee—she would have approved.

"We stood calf-deep in the surf, looking directly into the rising moon, each savoring a few memories of Anna, as we tossed her ashes to the wind and surf. We all surrendered to the emotion and gathered to hug and cry." Like many who have recently experienced the death of someone they love, Jan saw Anna's hand in everything that was pleasurable. "We were all struck by how marvelous it was for Anna to arrange for such a perfect confluence of natural phenomena."

Then came the inevitable crash. "The week after the beach was our hardest up to that point," recalls Jan. "We were all very depressed by the sudden transition from hubbub to lonely quiet. This was the first week since Anna died that we didn't have plans to make, so the weight of losing Anna really hit us with full force. We three had been on our own plenty of times before, while Anna was traveling, but that she would not be back became real. I would have this odd expectation that she would call any second or think there would be a letter from her as I walked down to fetch the mail. None of us could really muster enthusiasm for doing anything, and we all withdrew.

"Lindsay, who had been very strong, had a very hard week and cried a lot, as we all did. She watched all the *Star Wars* movies every day—at first for diversion, perhaps, but I think she was drawn to the strong symbolism of Princess Leia, identifying with her as a brave girl with no mother. Not a bad role model, and not all that inaccurate."

Jan rouses himself to get the children off to Seattle, a week before he will join them. Jan plans to use this time to catch up on the residue of those busy months—thank-you notes, sorting pictures and medical files—but he lacks enthusiasm for such tasks, a common lethargy that often accompanies grief. A friend talks to him on the phone and thinks Jan has a cold, but he has been crying. "I have definitely found the therapeutic effects of crying," Jan says poignantly, months after Anna's death. "Afterward you feel like you've run ten miles. It's a release."

In the roller coaster of grief, Jan can be laughing one moment, then crying the next, can go from having a good day to one of shattering depression. Moods can shift over the smallest happenstance. The day after the children leave for Seattle, Jan reaches for pages on a cluttered desk and finds Anna's glasses. He crumples on the sofa, clutching them and crying.

Self-pity would be understandable, but Jan does not indulge in "why me?" pursuits. "Sure, you get angry and envious at times when you see happy couples and families that are whole, but I never felt it was an isolated instance that was set upon me. Somebody at work whose brother died suddenly a year ago said he felt like the only person that such a bad thing ever happened to. I always felt that if you woke up to food in your mouth and a roof over your head, you were probably better off than ninety-nine percent of the population. In this case, I *do* have something to bitch about, but it is not unique. It happens every day to lots of people. Certainly single parents can relate and I know there are lots and lots of widows and widowers. In fact, this is a source of strength; I look at how many fairly ordinary people have done this and I think, 'If they can do it, I can do it too.' People say that support groups help you realize you are not alone. But I already know that." Jan knows that he is among millions who lose loved ones each year. Anna, in fact, was one of 47,000 women who died of breast cancer in 1997.

While such facts can give one perspective, it should not be expected to lessen grief. "We ask people to have a perspective that is really unfair," says bereavement counselor Ken Doka. "I remember I got very angry at a fifty-five-year-old woman who had lost a breast to cancer. I was very new at this and very young, and that view probably reflected a little gerontological insensitivity, but part of it reflected anger. Here was this woman who had a very, very good prognosis who was complaining about the loss of her breast, while I was upstairs dealing with eight- and four-year-olds who were dying. But *now* I would think differently. It's the old saying that the worst loss is the one that happens to you. For her, that was devastating. I hate that old proverb 'I cried because I had no shoes until I saw someone who had no feet.' It's still kind of hard being without shoes."

"No one gets over a meaningful loss," reminds psychiatrist Stephen P. Hersh. "We just place losses in our personal kaleidoscope. We try to live without constant pain."[1] Grieving over the loss of a child may last a lifetime; for a spouse, it may take years.

A common grieving pattern is loss of sleep, although Jan has not experienced this often, even as he sleeps in the bed he shared with Anna for so long. "Except," he says, "for the night of the memorial." The clowning wedding picture on the bedroom wall had been taken down for display at the service. As Jan went to bed, he noticed the empty spot on the wall. After tossing and turning, he went out to the living room, found the picture, and placed it back where it had been for years. Only then could he sleep.

Casting one's mind back to the final days of dying is a common grief reaction, searing at first, then lessening with time. Jan's reverberating memories fit this pattern of intense preoccupation with the past and a need to relive events over and over again. "What haunts me is the private mental anguish she suffered when she realized she was going so rapidly. For a short time after our trip to Florida, in April, I would say her quality of life was still good. She was still able to have fun with family, walk on the beach, go to the planetarium and see Hale-Bopp. But when she started to have difficulties remembering or losing part of a day altogether, she was deeply distressed. The realization that she had deteriorated to the point that she wouldn't be able to finish such things as leaving last messages for the kids frustrated her terribly."

Sheer determination propelled her to the panel discussion three weeks before she died, but that resolve "couldn't reverse the disease and her unstoppable mental deterioration," says Jan. "That must be one of the most terrifying experiences imaginable. Had Anna felt that everything had been completed, I think she would have fought her death less. Jane was wise, realizing the source of Anna's frustration and cluing the caregivers that we needed to continuously reassure Anna that everything was taken care of, that the kids and I would be okay, that she had done a wonderful job of organizing everything, and that she could let go with a clear conscience."

Giving the dying person permission to die is, in fact, one of the cornerstones of hospice teaching. Robert Abbo, a Washington restaurant owner who shared the business with his mother, recalls how she simply refused to die. Finally a hospice nurse soothed her, recognizing the one concern that his mother could not assuage. She told her that the restaurant was going along fine without her and that, in fact, there was a full house! That was all Mama Abbo needed to know. She died soon thereafter.

Although Anna had no fear of death, for someone so used to being in control, giving up was excruciating. As Anna said in the panel discussion just twenty-one days before she died, "Until this, I was never, ever high maintenance at all. I was always, 'Leave me alone. I can do it myself.' " Assuaging her concerns "helped Anna and gave her some comfort," says Jan. "But I know she was still fighting at the very end."

Those who have been able to care for the dying may have an easier time in their grieving. It is a comfort to Jan. "I feel good about the fact that I was able to keep Anna at home in her own bed. Though Anna couldn't always speak or respond, I know she was aware of her surroundings until the very end. I was able to do this only because of the outpouring of help from Ro and many close friends who organized themselves into shifts to come and help. I will be forever grateful for their unselfish generosity. I could not have done it by myself."

In keeping with Anna's reputation as the Queen of the Thank-You Notes, who never let the smallest present or the smallest gesture go by without a rapid thank you, Jan early on set about the task of answering hundreds of condolence letters. One of the first was to Ken Miller. The doctor had written a long letter to Jan and the family that was an outpouring of love, reminiscence, assurance, and mourning. "I know that I lost a friend this week. . . . There was, for me, tremendous joy in getting to know Anna, who was one of the most outstanding individuals that I have ever met. Anna's unique gift of oneness, honesty, warmth, spontaneity, humor, and goodness were all rolled up in one person. . . . Her openness and her willingness to talk about her own illness and about dying have helped me as a doctor, but even more as a person." Miller praised Jan—"Each step of the way you were there for Anna to provide your love and support." He lauds Jan's ability to keep her at home with the family. "I know that is where her heart is. I will be thinking of you and I will remember Anna in my heart."

Jan thanked Miller for coming to see Anna, then added, "and [to] apologize for what I later learned was not entirely a pleasant interaction. I want to reinforce what you already know, that Anna does, and has always, thought the world of you. During the couple of days she was in her excited state, she also let me, Ro, and anyone else who was around have it about one thing or another." He reiterated the reasons why Anna had fought her death. Then Jan enclosed a letter that he had found on Anna's computer, written two years before when her treatment did not seem to be working. It was intended to be read at the end of her life or after her death.

"By now I am either in a comatose-type state or I have boldly gone where I have not gone before," wrote Anna. She thanked Miller for giving her "a very special gift—time. I know it is so hard to put on a 'happy' face every day when you see your patients and suspect the worst for us. Well, my *Star Trek* pal, just remember, focus on the joy of the life that each person in your office is getting for whatever time they have! . . . The choices and decisions are ours, the recommendations are yours; you cannot make the decisions for us, so don't be so hard on yourself. Read that again—don't be so hard on yourself! And don't be afraid to get close to some of us. Sometimes it is the people who have to confront death a bit abruptly who are filled with the most life and they can remind you how to live it. . . . I am so glad that I was given the time to bring just that bit more of joy and tomfoolery into the world. I owe much of that to you," she writes, then includes his partner and staff. ". . . Coming into that office was like visiting a second home. . . . You guys make your patients feel so comfortable, wanted, and welcome. . . ."

Anniversaries, birthdays, holidays such as Christmas and Hanukkah and Thanksgiving, New Year's Eve, Mother's Day and Father's Day, Passover, Easter, Bar and Bas Mitzvahs, weddings, confirmations—all of these special events that celebrate the togetherness of family and friends—can be especially traumatic, so much so that grief counselors offer special advice on how to get through them. "How Can I Handle That Empty Chair?" is the headline in one bereavement newsletter at Christmastime. A group of widows' responses to that question were varied. Some changed traditions, moving to a buffet instead of a sit-down dinner. Some asked the eldest child to take the place of the father, reaffirming the family of its own continuity even in death. Yet another left the chair empty to remind everyone of their loss, which for them was therapeutic. And a take-charge survivor said, "*I* sat there!"[2]

While a real trauma, the empty chair is also a metaphor for the especially difficult significant events. As time goes by, sometimes the dreaded anticipation of an upcoming anniversary, a summer's vacation spot, or activity shared in the past with the deceased is worse than the actual reality. Facing it sometimes brings closure. Grieving survivors are given some helpful hints: Acknowledge grief work is real work that can leave one unable to deal with extra demands of the holiday season. Exercise and relaxation techniques are priority measures to deal with stress and depression. Plan ahead—perhaps do things differently, take a trip; a change can be helpful if one recognizes that it cannot bring an end to grieving. Others, conversely, need to settle in with loving friends or family members as in the past. Follow your own dictates. Don't fight with your emotions. Whatever they are, they're normal, including getting angry or resentful of others' happiness, and sudden bouts of sobbing. It is, in fact, helpful to build in time and places where you can withdraw from festivities for private time as the mood strikes.

Communing with the departed loved one about what you are experiencing, or recalling fond shared remembrances of holidays past, is not a sign of disorientation. Rather, it can be an aid in absorbing the reality of your loss. Many survivors, unfortunately, feel guilty if they experience moments of joy and laughter, as if that somehow cheapens their grief. For Jan and Anna's friends, this guilt was nonexistent; Anna would have approved, they all knew. Remembering the dead in a way meaningful to you provides valuable connection—whether it be lighting a candle, viewing home videos, writing a letter to the loved one, looking at old photos. And don't forget interludes of emotional and spiritual respite—a quiet walk, meditation, prayer.[3]

In August, Jan had joined his children in Seattle and had a wonderful day of hiking with them on Mount Rainier. Then he was socked in the stomach the next day, August 17, 1997. This would have been his and Anna's twenty-third wedding anniversary. "I had a hard evening, staying awake 'til about three A.M. two nights in a row, alternately crying and trying to occupy my mind with a who-dun-it." Yet, as in many steps along the way, Jan was helped by friends and family and coworkers. He remains appreciative of the thoughtfulness of his brother, Erik, and his wife, Lisa, who had spent the day before with them, without mentioning or celebrating their own anniversary. "I feel sure they decided to keep quiet about it because ours would have been the next day."

A friend visits one hot Saturday afternoon in September when the family returns. Anna's absence sits heavily in the house; a strange, empty silence permeates the rooms. Jan is digging up the garden with a friend, sweating as he turns the soil. A handful of Anna's ashes are mixed in, to commemorate her favorite tomato patch. On Anna's birthday, October 2, Jan climbs up Sugarloaf Mountain once more and scatters some of Anna's ashes. "Strangely, Anna's ashes have no strong meaning for me. I had no problem picking them up at the funeral home. I do find it meaningful to take some of the ashes with me when I go places that were special to her and scatter them. But when I am thinking of her, I do not feel drawn to her ashes, which are stored out of sight; I'm not sure how the kids would feel about the cookie jar. Nor do I avoid them. They are simply there, remnants of her body, but not of Anna."

The need to have a connection with the deceased is common and can take many forms. In the fall of 1997, Jan throws himself into every single task Anna had executed for the ballet's *Nutcracker* performance. He seems driven to be her stand-in, bringing her presence close to him and everyone involved. He distracts himself from grief to the point of exhaustion—personally posting thousands of announcements, taking all the pictures, writing and producing the program, handling the ads. He and Jane Bittner wisely provide a role for Ellery, who dances onstage with grown-up élan as one of the parents. Jan has graduated to the role of the tipsy grandfather celebrating Christmas Eve. During dress rehearsal, Jan sits part of the time with a friend, enthusiastically explaining how they made the layer of fog that was rolling across the stage during a dream scene. He smiles at Lindsay, the youngest of the troupe to perform a multitude of roles. It seems in that moment as if Jan has completely integrated Anna's death into his active life. It is cathartic that they are all so involved and have a common project to occupy their time, he says.

"Given the hard time I had during last year's performances, I was dreading them this year, assuming I would be a basket case after every show. To my surprise, as I watched from the wings, I found myself happy and smiling," he recalls. "Not that I didn't get misty-eyed on occasion, but overall, the experience was a happy one. It seems that doing the show was helping me make a transition. Happy, fond memories of Anna were taking the place of anguished recollections of her suffering and death. I would sense she was smiling with me as I watched all the elements everyone had worked on for months all come together to create a magical effect. The entire show was a worthy reflection of the enthusiasm and positive energy Anna's presence would have brought." Unperturbed throughout the shows, Lindsay had her moments of lonely sorrow afterward. She sobbed in the dressing room when she saw other mothers coming back to hug their children. Soon she was laughing at the cast party.

Jan's rosy recollections are balanced by a later reality of "*Nutcracker* madness," as he terms those driven days. "It really was too much." Frantic activities that helped to occupy them ultimately would have become stressful under normal circumstances. "But the magnitude of my emotional swings was magnified," he recalls. Jan's duties running the household were already stressful. "Many days went smoothly, but there were several when I felt I was drowning in a confusing sea of grief, anger, guilt, loneliness, frustration, and hopelessness. (I still have those days, and I'm sure will continue to have them). On bad days, I would feel pressured to finish things, then more duties would pile up. On top of supreme frustration, I'd be feeling guilty that I couldn't juggle all the responsibilities with the same cool matter-of-factness that Anna had in spades. Layer on this a sudden pang of loss and sadness and abject loneliness and lack of direction. Despite the bad days (maybe one a week), things got done."

Despite, or perhaps because of, the children, who are countless reminders of Anna, Jan experiences the special loneliness of a widow or widower. "Until now, I have never really known the meaning of loneliness," Jan says in the early days of 1998. "I've always enjoyed solitude, and have cherished occasional quiet afternoons sans family. When I was in graduate school, I remember thinking it odd when one of my single fellow students said how she hated living alone—but I was confusing solitude with loneliness. When you are by yourself, you are not lonely when the connections to significant others are possible, but when they are simply gone, what is left is a gaping hole. While that is a cliché, it is the most accurate description and can't be fully appreciated until it is experienced.

"The consequences of loneliness shadow many aspects of life—motivation, for example. Many of the things I enjoyed doing was because I was doing them for or with Anna. It is no fun to fix a gourmet dinner if no one is there to appreciate it, for example. For now, I don't take pleasure in too many activities, though I know that will gradually change." When something exciting or fun does happen, says Jan, the luster is lost "when you realize the person you most want to share it with is gone. The kids and I do share things, but it is on a different level." He still struggles with profound lethargy at times. "It must be what it is like to be clinically depressed (maybe we are, I understand a temporary depression is not uncommon after the death of a loved one)."

It is, indeed, common enough to be addressed in all books and articles regarding grieving. "Sadness and depression . . . certainly are understandable—someone you love has died. The death has changed your life. Old activities are different now. You may grieve not only the death . . . but all the other losses of routine, companionship and activity," writes Ken Doka.[4] It is important to acknowledge that the coldness and grayness of winter, which hamper activity, can compound depression, especially if someone suffers from seasonal affective disorder (SAD). In the winter of 1998, Jan is doing everything the experts suggest—expecting and not fighting periods of sadness, planning respite and diversion, finding support through friends.

The death of a loved one tops the stress scale. Now Jan is coping not only with grief but with the travails of becoming a single parent for two adolescents. On Halloween night, 1997, around 7:00 P.M., Jan relates some frantic moments. "I am finally home. After rushing from work, getting Lindsay to ballet, going back home, getting Ellery and taking him to a distant friend to spend the night, stopping at the grocery to get last-minute candy and the liquor store to treat myself to a bottle of an Islay single malt, ordering gyros, getting Lindsay, picking up gyros, rushing home, feeding the dogs while Lindsay got her costume on (a real, genuine, hippie, complete with head scarf, tie-dye shirt, and about a thousand necklaces, rings, and bracelets), taking Lindsay to her party (and sleep-over), then back home just in time to dump the candy in a big bowl, shut the dogs in Ellery's room, turn on the front-hall light, put on a CD with cheesy Halloween sounds, and greet the first customer. In short, a rather typical day. So I decided to sit and type a bit while I listen to a plethora of creaks, groans, screams, and organ music oozing from the stereo, occasionally jumping up for the door or fortifying myself with a sip of scotch, as the moment dictates."

Soon comes another crush of holidays, Thanksgiving and Christmas. A half year after Anna died, Jan observes a low-key Christmas, in the past a time of much decorating and feasting. "Ro came and I think that helped with the kids, but it would have been okay with just us three." They are helped by the knowledge that they would leave the next day for Florida and its magic diversions.

The first days of 1998 are spent with Anna's father, who displays but a glimmer of zestier days. When he takes the family and a friend to dinner, he refuses offers to pay, insisting on picking up the check. "I'm spending my children's inheritance," he jokes. Now close to eighty-three, Stephen Megregian remains sharply attuned, but his body is no match for his brain. He make jokes about his "pharmacy"—the card table in his bedroom—but the stories of his aches and pains now overshadow the jokes. He is pale and quieter; Anna's father has been dealt a hard blow by Anna's death, but he rejects the idea that this sorrow contributes to his excruciating, intractable pain, although grief experts note that existing illnesses can be heightened and that there is a real chance of contracting a serious illness within the first year after a significant loss. Stephen rails at the crippling pain that halts his busy activities, always a source of strength in the past that kept him from sinking into depressing reflection. He cries the instant he starts talking about Anna. "I try to keep my daily thoughts away from past events like that. My wife passed away five years ago, Anna passed away six months ago, and just last week, my best golf buddy passed away. They're gone, I can't do anything about it."

Fearful worries do intrude, however, regarding a possible secondary loss. "What am I going to do with these kids? Now that Anna's gone, are they going to come down and see me as much as they did? How long? They're growing up fast." He is assured that Jan and the children love him. "I would just love to have them come down and take the place over and do anything they want," he says wistfully. "It's so much fun to watch them." The father is so much like the daughter—Stephen is determined to keep the conversation light. "I keep reminding them that they've got to come down here and check up on their inheritance."

His sense of humor is vital. "I'm hanging on to that as long as I can because if you start getting grumpy, it would be easier to go out and buy a gun and shoot yourself." Still, the fanciful suggestion that his wife and daughter may be having fun together somewhere right now elicits a sad response. "Well, I hope they're not watching me, because I'm not having any fun. Not anymore."

The next morning, however, Stephen is up at dawn, before his grandchildren, prepared to take them to his country-club golf pro for lessons. Lindsay and Ellery attack golf with enthusiasm, especially Ellery, who hits the ball 200 yards. "He smacked the heck out of it," says Jan. "He loves it." Lindsay has ballet for physical release of her emotions, now Ellery has found the same satisfaction in golf. In addition, says his now more sensitive father, "it's another good thing he can do."

The children have great fun in Florida. They joke and laugh in their grandfather's bedroom, watching *Beavis and Butt-Head,* not an acquired taste for the adults who watch football in the den. Two gold chains, one delicate and the other masculine, always worn by Anna, now encircle her children's necks. After their father gave them to Lindsay and Ellery, they have never removed the chains. On Lindsay's is a miniature figurine of mother and child, given to her by Jane Bittner, Ann Wylie, Patty Williams, and Nancy Wiltz on Lindsay's twelfth birthday in October. She seems to be emerging with new self-confidence, talking easily and warmly, with facial expressions and movements uncannily like her mother's. Like so many adolescents, she now wears dramatic nail polish—today it is dark blue, the color her mother had despised. Ellery has a girlfriend, "well, sort of." They convey no deep thoughts, but at times they can easily mention fun moments they had with their mother.

Back in Olney, however, the three hit bottom once again. "We were all miserable," says Jan, as he tries to "wipe the slate clean" with New Year's action—making some order out of Anna's medical files and getting the children to discard old clothes and toys. Plummeting grades inspire Jan to contact Dottie Ward-Wimmer, whose helpful insights had been missing during the past overloaded months. She suggests that Ellery and Lindsay might benefit from a teenage support group at St. Francis but gave them the choice to do that, see her separately, or to do nothing.

A month later, after a few phone calls with Ward-Wimmer, no decision is made to see her, but the children visit her a couple of times in the spring. Jan wisely lightens up on bad grades, an absolutely expected form of grief; children often do not express grief in traditional ways but in such indirect ways of acting out. "I tried to emphasize that I am not going to talk about what happened before Christmas in terms of grades. I know some are going to be crappy. I keep telling myself I have to look at the big picture. Some bad grades don't make a lifetime. Ellery's too bright to mess up his life; he feels bad about it himself. I know lots of parents with kids who are grown. They've gone to the best private schools, the best universities, gotten great grades all along, and now have very ordinary jobs. It doesn't always compute."

By February's end, a small corner seems to have been turned. Ellery comes back ecstatic from a week's school trip in Florida—he had even finished most of his math work before he left. Jan watches as Lindsay and Ellery happily reunite; he is able to feel elation, a numbed emotion these past months, at such a happy family moment.

As the months go by in 1998, Jan feels his way along the uneven path of single parent child rearing, dealing always with the overlay of his grief and his children's, which are mostly unspoken. "Sometimes I feel that I'm never going to catch up with anything," says the harried father, "never get a breather." Although Anna so often had voiced concern that Jan might not be up to the task, Jan says, rightfully, "I think she would be proud of me." The man who had difficulty expressing emotions and lacked the patience to understand the nuances of his children's actions, now expresses his feelings with his children, cries openly as Lindsay hugs him and pats him reassuringly, and encourages them to talk to him about anything. Still, his worries are numerous.

"I worry about a lack of insight when it comes to making decisions concerning Ellery and Lindsay. Anna just seemed to know the right thing to do—what parties were okay to go to, what friends were okay, what clothes or jewelry were age appropriate. We didn't always agree, but her choices always had a certain logic. She had a sixth sense about interpersonal relationships. The kids are plunging headlong into adolescence, and I have been taken by surprise with this rapid transition. I worry about striking the right balance between too little freedom and too little supervision. I worry that I'll be restrictive in an arbitrary way and that I'm too negative with them; too many no's and don't's. Anna and her mother, especially, had a great knack of making a criticism without ever using a negative word. It's something I have to work on."

Jan remarks about the manner in which roles get played out when there are two parents. The task of listening nurturer naturally fell to Anna, the mother. Now he takes a page from her book and is able to show his own imperfections. One night he sat down for an open discussion with his children as to how they could all do better. Taking the initiative, Jan allowed as how he was at times "more critical than I should be." As they grinned and nodded, he noted that his plan had worked. "I offered that first, so they could agree." It sounds as if Jan is setting impossibly high standards for himself during a time when testiness and anger on his part is to be expected. One axiom while experiencing grief is to be kind to yourself. Yet Jan admonishes himself when he behaves in a manner that seems reasonable, given the pressures and his own grieving. "The kids, true to their ages, had made a huge mess and just left it, assuming some benevolent genie would clean up. I remember on one occasion pleading with them through tears, 'You guys just can't *do* this to *me* right now!' "

He notes that their adjustments are compounded by witnessing years of illness. The last three of Anna's life, filled with cataclysmic ups and downs, "were more than a quarter of Lindsay's lifetime." Does he think there is a sense of relief, which sometimes can turn to guilt among survivors? "It's hard to know. It seems to come out more in depression with Ellery. Lindsay seems pretty normal, then lets it out when she has to."

Jan does worry about the long-term effects of Anna's illness and death on the children. "I got a Christmas card from a very old friend of the family whose husband was killed in a car accident about thirty years ago, when her four children were from six to twelve years old. She enclosed a note saying the one serious mistake she made was not talking about her husband's death with her kids, trying to be strong for them. Consequently, there was some delayed grieving and depression with difficulties later in life. I will have to depend on instinct and Dottie's advice and ongoing evaluations of the kids for help. I know we all will be affected by Anna's death always, but I hope the effects do not impair our ability to enjoy life in the future."

Dottie Ward-Wimmer has comforting words for Jan. Although generations ago, dying used to be a normal part of family life, the prospect now raises questions among concerned parents, like Jan, as to whether witnessing death can scar their children later. "The answer depends on the attitude of the adults in the home. If the caregivers are uncomfortable with it, if all the children see is the wasting and can't get past that, that's different. If a person chooses to die at home and has to do it without support and adequate pain control, it would be *very* traumatic for children. But in a home where there is love and acceptance—'sure this is difficult, but I also have all of my hours with you now. This is part of our life together'—and children are allowed to come and go as they wish, it doesn't hurt them at all.

"Yes, it's hard to go through, but in the years down the road, think of the comfort that kids exposed to this can have. There was not a thing that could have been done for their mother that was left undone. Anna was never left alone, never with strangers. They didn't have to worry if a nurse would give her medicine on time. They never had to be in some strange place."

The extraordinary care that Anna's children witnessed "is a beautiful lesson—'look at how wasted, look how difficult, and yet Daddy didn't turn his back. *He'll never turn his back on me either.* Boy, this is what love is about, this is what commitment is about.' It's a very, very tough time, but it's a part of life."

During Anna's remission in 1996, at a remove from the immediacy of her own death, Anna elaborated on her thoughts about the unavoidable in anyone's life—funerals, death, mourning, deep grieving. "Let's face it, we cannot escape death. Many of my friends are now suffering family loss, and I am seeing in them a new awakening," said Anna, "a new realization that money, power, fame can't make death go away, can't take away hurt, can't help." She wrote, "Time, one's own attitude about living and loved ones, will make the harsh reality of grief and anger soften slowly into fond remembrance and learned truths about oneself, I think. It has for me." Anna learned that not facing life's realities "will prevent your life from being fruitful. I have a relative who is still fighting the battles of her long-dead spouse; she dwells on bad memories and they eat her alive. I wish she could get help because she is living in the past and the past is over! It will be up to Jan whether or not he chooses to be lonely. As I constantly tell him, I hope that he finds a woman to provide love and companionship for the rest of his life. I don't want him to pine away. What we had can never be replaced; I know that and am comforted by it."

Jan considers her point. Nine months after her death, he says, "While I worry about being alone, I also worry about not being alone—that is, considering the possibility of dating and remarrying. The whole idea scares the hell out of me right now. I can understand, being so vulnerable, how one could reach out for adult companionship and it could be a terrible mistake. One cannot predict when new connections will be made, but I'm steering clear of that now.

"When you have been with someone constantly since the age of sixteen, all your major decisions about lifestyle, philosophy, child rearing, and so forth evolve in tandem. When we married, we had very few preconceived notions about married life, so we didn't have a lot of disagreements. I have heard horror stories about couples meeting later in life, when they are very set in their ways. Huge fights ensue over something as trivial as which shelf the dishes get stored on. After being with Anna for almost two-thirds of my life, we knew each other completely and decisions were made often through wordless communication. I don't know how accommodating I'm willing to be."

For now, Jan cherishes his time with his children. "I worry about being alone as I see that Ellery and Lindsay will be off to college in four and five years, respectively. I miss them terribly when they are away. I wonder whether they will live nearby, whether they will visit often. They are already following their natural instincts as they get older and preferring to spend time with friends."

And says Jan, "I worry about going through life but not *living* life. Anna was often the prime mover when major changes in direction needed to be made. I have to make sure that we move ahead when the time comes. If there is one lesson Anna taught everyone, it's that life is to be lived."

Above all, Jan is sustained and guided by what he prefers to call symbolic rather than religious expressions of Anna's spirit. "Clearly, her spirit lives on in many of us. For me, symbolism took on much more importance during her illness and after her death. I found myself putting extra effort into keeping all the plants alive that Anna received during her first bout with cancer in 1989. I felt subconsciously that keeping them alive was helping Anna stay alive.

"We saw a lot of unusual natural phenomena during this past year, both before and after Anna's death. In the spring, it was Hale-Bopp, which we watched whenever possible. I remember waking Anna up before five A.M. one morning, so she could see it in the east before sunrise. She was thrilled by her first view in a completely childlike way. I remember the beautiful day that emerged from gray dreariness just after Anna died. I remember walking in shallow ocean water with the kids in July and finding ourselves surrounded by scores of rays, gracefully floating by. I remember the kids and I playing in the canal behind Steve's house for two hours with a pair of manatees. I remember arriving for our first evening at the beach in late July and being greeted by a full moon. I remember hearing about a meteor shower on the late news in August, when the kids were in Seattle, and going out and lying on the deck at midnight, watching the meteors streak by, just as Anna and I had done years before."

Jan, the scientist, suspends his insistence on relying on that which can be proved. "It is," he writes, "a harmless comfort to think that we were seeing Anna's influence in all of these wondrous moments."

Indeed, Anna's perceptive thoughts continue to echo. Her certainty that someday there would be a cure for cancer, as she sought to relieve Lindsay's fears, became partially true a year after her death. It involved the very drug that stopped working for Anna after nearly five years. For the first time in history, there is now a chance that cancer can be *pre-*

vented in healthy but high-risk women. A 1998 landmark study found that the use of tamoxifen in such women, who have no cancer but a family history of cancer or precancerous lesions, reduces the rate of expected breast cancers by 45 percent.[5] At the time of publication, more hope for preventing cancer had surfaced. By the time Lindsay becomes a young adult, hopefully major advances will have been discovered.

As the first year since Anna's death nears its close, Jan indicates that the old cliché, time heals, was true for him. "The days of overwhelming despondence are fewer and farther apart. I am beginning to heal a little and am realizing how much of a toll Anna's illness and death have taken. After Anna died, I felt in poor health for the first time in my life. I see the physical healing (losing some weight, getting exercise) as an essential parallel to the emotional healing. Spring has certainly provided an emotional and symbolic lift." Jan now shares his garden with a couple, and he basks in the "wonderful afternoons, digging in the earth, enjoying the sun on our backs."

Some joys of life are returning. "I am noticing the world around me more and paying attention to it, feeling more like entertaining and mingling with friends. I find myself thinking more about what meaning I choose to attach to life and what I want for my future. The happy visions of Anna jumping up and down with enthusiasm while saying 'Yea, man, lets *do* it!' in response to some new plan or idea—and then actually just doing it—give me confidence while reminding me that life is short. Gee, so what wild things have I done yet? Not much. I did agree to let Ellery have a co-ed party. Oh, well, you have to start somewhere."

Jan has not sorted his life out enough to make "any big lifestyle changes." His single parent duties make it difficult to "find large chunks of time to sit and think. I need to figure out how to spend more time on fun things and less on work." An unresolved situation is "how to keep the kids on the right track. Because they are getting older, the idea of them being after school alone is more worrisome." He resolves to plan for some after-school supervision. "I see so many kids drifting into trouble, not consciously, but by slipping into bad habits in imperceptibly small increments. I don't worry about them drifting away, however. We are still very close and will always be."

In April, Jan attended a birthday party for Anna's buddy, Linda Suarez, herself a study in courage. So certain that her cancer was gone at the time of Anna's death, Suarez was hit with uterine cancer a few months later. Now she was preparing to enter Johns Hopkins for a bone marrow transplant. Jan brought her a picture of Anna to take with her. Suarez said, "Anna always goes everywhere with me."

Then she turned to another matter. "I'm going to fix you up with a date, Jan. I'm giving you a year, and then I'm going to get your butt in gear!" In the hospital, following the success of the major stage of her transplant, Suarez was as cheerful as ever. "It hasn't been bad at all." She has a woman all picked out, she told Jan. "You *know* Anna wouldn't want you to drop out of life." With a laugh Jan recalled, "I just let that one slide by. Things are not settled enough to think about it." He feels that way about all major decisions—contemplating a new job, a new home, a new car, possibly relocating.

Says Jan, "While the coming of spring has been uplifting, it is also a reminder that this time last year Anna was going downhill rapidly. I'll be admiring a daffodil or the flowering crab-apple tree and suddenly be reminded of Anna's suffering, so incongruous amidst such a riotous flourish of new life.

"Well, that's the news from Lake Woebegon."

June 4, 1998, the first anniversary of Anna's death, was not especially observed by Jan. It was too rainy for a trip to Sugarloaf Mountain, the children were busy with end-of-school functions, and Jan was inundated by a work project that he was racing to finish. Still, the day did not go unnoticed. "We're conditioned to pay attention to anniversaries of all kinds. I think there was a symbolic shift. Not that all of a sudden you change the way you feel. But you do stop and look back a year and say, 'I managed to get through this.' Now it's time to move ahead."

Jan realizes that many of the goals he had set up "were goals to fill up the time and now I can see that the fact I didn't get them done doesn't really matter." Now his time is genuinely swallowed by the "condition of my *life.* You talk to any single parent with two teenage kids and they'll tell you they haven't time for themselves. Even a *couple* with teenage kids!" Hiring a person to clean house once a week has lessened the stress.

The children seem happy with their friends and their lives. (Dotty Ward-Wimmer commented recently that the children's adjustment demonstrated that they were "a great example of having done much of their grief work" during Anna's illness.) Lindsay is off to summer ballet schools; Ellery is now fourteen years old and five foot ten, has just graduated from the eighth grade, and is already planning parties for the summer. As the trio leave for a one-week vacation at some North Carolina beaches, Jan enthuses about much—"a fabulous African wedding I went to and that fabulous movie I saw, *The Truman Show.* It said so much on so many levels."

He is not dating anyone and contemplates staying in Olney for now. The one family member facing the biggest change is Anna's father. His son, Steve, took a job with a college in Houston, thus forcing the reality that the father must move into a condo. "He actually seems quite chipper about it," says Jan. "It's closer to the country club and Marty's home." Marty is the last of the siblings in Florida.

Anna is not forgotten by anyone. A few days after the anniversary of her death, a dedication of commemorative plaques took place at St. Francis. Thanks to friends and family, a plaque in memory to Anna Johannessen is now placed outside Anna's favorite door, the office of Dottie Ward-Wimmer.

Jan finds moments when he communes with Anna. "When things get difficult, I sometimes say, 'Anna, you gotta help me out.' I draw strength thinking about what she would have done—or would have told me to do."

And Anna's is the first face he sees in the morning and the last he sees at night. He always takes a look at that happy, clowning picture on the bedroom wall of two happy people in their early twenties—Jan and Anna on their wedding day.

CHAPTER TWENTY-ONE

Lessons and Reflections

It is more than one year since Anna died and yet she remains vividly in the present tense for me. I miss her terribly. I still expect an enthusiastic E-mail filled with exclamation points or a letter with her silly version of a happy face beside her signature or an upbeat message on my phone. I replay our hours of tapes, watch the video of her distinctive, gutsy last appearance, three weeks before her death, when she talked about living, really *living* until the very end. I reread her letters and know that, in some way, she is with me. I feel right now that she is looking over my shoulder and giving me guidance and enthusiastic encouragement but also teasingly saying, "Now be sure to get this right!!"

I have felt heavy sadness because I will never physically see her again; this overlaps with smiling moments as I think about all that she was, what she would be saying about today's events. Remembering Anna is an enforced constancy as I write in a rush to deadline. Friends have said, "This must be very difficult for you." At times, yes; however, I am sustained by the knowledge that I am doing what Anna so wanted.

Any chronicler lives in a voyeur's world; there seems to be an affliction of the brain, if not the soul. We live outside as well as inside the moment. Even the deepest events in one's life are transposed into mental, if not physical, notes in order to remember every detail. One protective flak jacket is to detach oneself from one's subjects. After a few weeks of knowing Anna, this was impossible. She became a beloved friend. I became much too involved for the distancing that journalists prize—not unlike the medical profession. Certain, for example, that I had taken precise notes, I would find vague scribblings. When she was in remission, I was joyous; to hell with the book. When the cancer resurfaced, I worried and prayed as her vision blurred.

She wrote me after that Christmas: "It is over and it was too much for me, really. . . . Many thanks for Christmas goodies. . . . We are on the red ball hunt. I still can't believe they were sold out. We are seeing Dottie this weekend, since I have gotten so much worse with this head business. It will be good for the kids. Aha, we are now on the Internet—way cool! Much love and we can get together soon to chill out! That is my prescription for after holidays!"

At our next meeting, I dissolved in tears, then wrote: "That was selfish of me, because it certainly does you no good to have me sobbing all over the place. Your fabulous ebullience in the face of this crap is part of what makes you so wonderful to all who know you. It is so touching that, in the midst of all this, you were trying to find a red ball for me! . . ." I feel a lump in my throat now, remembering how she had searched for a giant exercise ball to help my painful muscle condition. My awe was compounded, knowing that I was but a small part of her universe treated so lovingly despite her pain.

Denying the depth of her illness, as a friend, was in contrast to what I saw, as a reporter. When Anna mentioned having had radiation for cancer in her spine, for example, I was shocked. I had completely forgotten it and had sloughed off "cancer in the vertebrae" as if it had nothing to do with her spine. Then one precious moment just hours before Anna died, I stood alone by her bed and could deny no longer. She looked peaceful, as if she was between worlds. I did not cry, this time. I was glad for her and, for the first time, became convinced that the Anna I knew was no longer in that frail, inanimate body. I knew in that instant if anyone I loved came to such a point in life, and I had some choice in the matter, I would not hesitate to help end that suffering.

One day, I confided to a wonderful former hospice nurse, now a bereavement therapist in private practice, Pat Murphy, how involved I had become with Anna. She looked at me as if to say, "So what else is new?" Then she said, "I would worry about you if you *didn't.*" And therein is the nutshell of the caregiving hospice and counseling movement. Unlike other medical professionals, they assume that one's feelings will and must come into play. The best give of themselves, over and over. At that moment, Pat was grieving herself, for a client, a young mother who had just died. In grief, "everyone is struggling to get back to 'normal,' and that's impossible, because 'normal' includes that person," she says. "You have to redefine normal and that takes a long time."

I have been asked what it felt like to enter such an intimate world of dying and grief and how I handled the relationship with Anna and her family. At times, the paradoxes were painful. During her illness, I was comforted that Anna was a willing partner; she so wanted to leave something of herself, to last after she had died. The book was a catharsis. Once, we talked late into the night in a shared hotel room. Her curiosity about dying was vivid. She wanted me to be with her, listening to her describe her final moments. "Wouldn't that be exciting? To learn about it, up to the last, and have it all written down?"

As it so sadly happened, Anna lost her capacity to express. In those final weeks, it was vital for me to take a backseat in order that Anna's legion of friends and family could have their private and caregiving time with her. Despite their all-consuming devotion to Anna, Jan and Roseann nevertheless graciously recognized the need for my fly-on-the-wall presence, in order to vividly retell Anna's story. But I, too, was grieving. Anna and I had had an intense relationship of twenty months—a speck in time compared to others—yet we deeply shared daily confidences and caring. As Anna once wrote in a letter, "Just writing a book is not the impetus for a person to drive forty miles plus round-trip [repeatedly] to take a person to a fifteen-minute doctor's appointment. Actually, when you really stop and think about it, it's downright insane! Myra, thanks for being nuts!" Nearing the end, I wanted to stop being the reporter and, as much as everyone in the room, bathe her forehead, spoon her morphine, tell her I love her by being helpful in the here and now. And so I felt helpless as I struggled with the conflicts.

As I later wrote to Jan, "When I started this project, I had hoped I would find someone with whom I would have a close rapport. Never did I think I would fall in love—with Anna, you, Lindsay, Ellery, and your friends and family. I know at times it has been difficult; times when I wanted to put away the tape recorder and just embrace the warmth and love that I witnessed, times when you all wanted me to just disappear, yet I have always known that we are united in trying to produce the best possible remembrance of Anna and the things she wanted to tell those who were never fortunate enough to know her. I thank all of you for letting me into your life so generously."

As I gaze back, I feel there are important issues upon which to reflect—religion and spirituality, hospice and dying at home, caregiving and an afterlife, mourning and the lessons we have learned from Anna.

I will tackle first that which is hardest for me. Religion. So much of what we believe is set in childhood. As in Anna's and Jan's home, religion was not followed or taught in mine. While I envy the serenity my husband and other family members and friends obtain through the Bible and other religious reading, attending synagogues or churches, I have yet to find such solace. According to polls, there are many who feel as I do. I have a sense of spirituality—more so since I have witnessed Anna's dying—but I have not found an organized religion I can embrace.

For those who do, the comfort provided during times of sorrow is immeasurable. My Catholic son-in-law, Joe Drape, says, "It's never too late to try." A writer, Joe can be sardonic and cynical about much in life, but his religious faith is rock solid. He suffered a grievous loss when his parents died, but, he says, "My thirty-six years of my faith prepared me for those moments. A lot of it is thoroughly irrational if you break it down—Christ rose from the dead, we eat his body and drink his blood—but there is a deep sense that someone who dies is gone but not out of your life and that you're going to be unified again. To me it would be unfathomable to think that this is all there is. There is a celebratory feeling in my faith, that someone has gone to a better world. Believing means accepting that some matters are out of your control."

And perhaps that is what it is all about. The journey of discovery, finally, comes down to this: knowing that there are no easy answers—and often no answers—to much that is mysterious and mesmerizing about our living, our dying, and a possible afterlife.

Organized religion, as we have seen, was not for Anna or Jan. Both derided what they viewed as hollow sentiments. "We had no time for the hypocritical self-righteousness and xenophobia of fundamentalists of any ilk," remarks Jan. The couple had a "healthy disregard for traditional rituals." They wrote their own wedding vows and discarded a traditional funeral.

Yet Anna was not troubled, as I and, I suspect, many others are, by doubt or a longing for religious sustenance. She was among the most spiritual, living her life with a caring honesty and personal values that many a churchgoer could emulate. Her acts of generosity were unknown to many who call themselves religious. Anna did not pray, but she was a walking answer to many people's prayers. Which begs one of those monumental questions, What is religion, anyway?

"We are certainly not antireligious," says Jan. "We count among our closest friends people who have deep religious convictions, and we respect each other's freedom to choose what is right for them." Indeed, most of Anna's caregivers are religious and prayed openly for Anna. "Anna and I were very comfortable finding ourselves in the miracle of life, accepting that as a gift," says Jane Bittner.

One study indicates that a vast majority in the United States, 96 percent, believe in God. More than half were concerned that they would not be forgiven, either by others or by God (56 percent), and 42 percent worried "a great deal" that God would not forgive them. Such a punitive God would never occur to Anna, who neither believed in hellfire and brimstone tirades, nor the stringent ethos of not sinning in order to make it to heaven. George Gallup, Jr.'s, critical conclusion was that "a lot of spiritual needs are not being answered" and that clergy must be better trained to help people deal with end-of-life matters.[1]

The perception that a religious malaise exists today—polls show that 60 percent of respondents feel it is a waning force in this country—is not borne out by facts. The same numbers of Americans pray today, 90 percent, as did in 1947. (In this poll, 5 percent prayed for something bad to happen to someone else. Tsk, tsk.) As the millennium approaches, there seems to be a resurgence in religion and a search for meaningful answers—both on how to live well and how to die well. The difference is the form that this may take. "A new breed of worshiper is looking beyond the religious institution for a do-it-yourself solution," write the editors of the *New York Times Magazine.*[2] Young Americans in this spirituality-seeking era of mobile living, interfaith marriages, and lifestyle freedoms are finding paths never imagined by parents. Baptists become

Catholics, Pentecostal storefronts host Catholics, Jews practice Buddhism, former Baptists worship in Muslim mosques.[3] Prayer has entered the once strictly clinical world of medicine. Some mainstream doctors, humbled by fruitless decades of trying to cure the most intractable diseases, now resort to prayer, hypnosis, and stress management to help patients as surely as any New Age or alternative medicine guru.

No matter the modern permutations that religion may take, one strong and true law remains the backbone of otherwise dissimilar religions. Remarkably similar wording admonishes that one is not a true believer unless one follows the Golden Rule to do unto others as you would have them do unto you. It is the credo of Christianity, Judaism, Brahmanism, Buddhism, Confucianism, Taoism, Zoroastrianism, and Islam.[4] Anna epitomized the Golden Rule.

One widely held belief is in a life hereafter, another cornerstone of cultural and religious thinking throughout the world, throughout the ages. Making meaning out of death, believing that there is more to come, is a galvanizing hope for most, whether or not they follow organized religions. Since no living being will ever know, accepting that there are unexplained mysteries in one's passage from this world allows for full mental exploration and, for many, ease of mind.

"Anna believed there was something after life, but was not sure what," recalls Jan. "Perhaps pure energy." Anna's insistence that she would be riding the comet Hale-Bopp was like a mantra. Just days before her death, she had perfected that image in the videotaped panel discussion—"Hey, and I'll be up front, I thought of it *first,*" she said to audience laughter, referring to the members of the California cult who had killed themselves en masse, believing that was the way to reach the comet.

"I have a deep faith," says Linda Suarez, Anna's cancer buddy. "We talked about what would happen after we die; I know Anna thought that there was more to life than just this." Suarez feels that "although Anna was very accepting of death, she might have had it just a tad easier" if she could have been sustained by prayer.

But Anna found her own resources. She delved into philosophy and was sustained by the words of others, such as Viktor Frankl, and quieting thoughts compiled by Dame Cecily Saunders, the kindly British pioneer of the modern hospice movement and its emphasis on pain-free care. In one book, Anna underlined paragraphs that dealt with what the authors called stillpoints. "Stillpoints are a technique that allows you to stay calm and feel safe in the midst of threat. . . . A stillpoint is not a sense of being in control of everything. It is a sense of confidence that things are as predictable as possible and that they will work out as best they can. . . . A stillpoint is like an emotional companion. It is the oasis in a desert. A stillpoint strengthens the spirit to deal with that which may be beyond one's control."[5] Suggestions for reaching this stage included self-hypnosis techniques of relaxation and positive imagery. Anna was finding, through spiritual awareness, an acceptance of what she could not control and a point of serenity others gain through prayer.

The Gallup poll indicated a deep desire for loving companionship at the end, one of the hallmarks of hospice. There was a need to have someone with whom they could share their fears and concerns, to have someone pray for them, not to be alone. Dr. William Lamers is an assured candidate for the *Guinness Book of World Records* for having witnessed more deaths and surviving grievers—"in the thousands"—than any other doctor in the United States. He founded the first hospices in the western states, taught those who developed the first 250 hospices in the United States, and, "at a time when no one told me that doctors don't make house calls, saw patients every day for six months until they died. I remember hearing the past president of the American Medical Association say that, 'in looking over fifty-five years as a physician, I've never actually seen a patient die.' And I thought, 'Where in hell were you?' "

"Religion," says Lamers, "cuts both ways. I remember an old priest, age ninety-eight. After years of preaching that there was a heaven, as he was dying he winked his eye and said, 'Now, we'll see!' But I've seen the old Catholics, screaming as they're dying because they think they're going to go to hell. I've seen Mormons who are beautifully relaxed, saying, 'This day I will be in paradise; I'm going to be reunited with my family.' And I've seen Native Americans say, 'I'm going south for the winter,' like the geese—such a beautiful thought. We've had people who are lifetime Protestants saying, 'I want to see a rabbi.' They want to see if they're missing something. We've had people who are total agnostics and their husbands or wives write us later, 'Thank you for not pushing religion down my throat.' One guy sent something into the *Congressional Record* about the wonderful care we gave to agnostics. We've seen them all. The gypsies, the whole bit. It's a wonderful education.

"There is no such thing as a norm. Everyone is unique. The circumstances in life, spirituality, psychology, family makeup—everybody's different. But there are some commonalities in dying. Facing death prods people to come to some sort of terms with what existence is and with what death might imply for them and their survivors."

Most people can recite the so-called five stages of dying—denial, anger, bargaining, depression, acceptance. As easy as reciting the names of the Seven Dwarfs, these stages are not that helpful as guidelines. Thirty years ago, the pioneering work *On Death and Dying,* by Swiss-American psychiatrist Dr. Elizabeth Kübler-Ross, formulated these stages that quickly became international gospel. While most death educators recognize that her unresearched observations stimulated a lot of discussion and "brought dying into the popular, public focus," as Dr. Lamers states, there is broad agreement that dying people do not necessarily progress through the five-stage dying sequence Kübler-Ross proposed. "There is no single right, proper, or correct way," says Lamers. In fact, some critics argue that her stages are misleading. No evidence indicates patients respond in such a manner and that the totality of one's life is neglected in favor of these supposed stages, they say, which ignore the complexities of human behavior and thinking. This point is illustrated by a cartoon showing five disconcerted doctors surrounding a man in bed. "*Dead?* Impossible!" says one doctor. "First there should be acceptance."[6]

"To speak about 'denial,' for example, makes it so hard and fast, when in reality it is a much more complex phenomenon," says Ken Doka.

Avery Weisman, in his classic refutation *On Dying and Denying,* argues that such broadly formulated stages are meaningless; he illustrates by dissecting "denial," which could mean: (1) I am not ill; (2) I am ill, but it is not serious; (3) I am seriously ill, but not dying; (4) I am dying, but death will not come for a long time . . . and so forth.[7] "Acceptance" could mean anything from quiet serenity to surly resignation.

Weisman also coined the term "middle knowledge"—which helped build away from the concept that denial and acceptance are two separate things. Middle knowledge recognizes that people drift in and out of attitudes concerning their mortality. This explains why Anna could talk about living forever and could also see the end of her life simultaneously. "The real question is not that one knows—but when, where, or with whom he chooses to acknowledge it," says Doka. Rather than Kübler-Ross stages, a more accepted approach today is that there are a swirling range of experiences to dying—feelings, attitudes, and emotions—that are ongoing, ever changing, and revisited again and again and can be experienced simultaneously. Ambivalence is among the most common. That is why Anna could genuinely accept death but at the same time fight against its untimeliness. As Jan remembers so well, there were thunderbolt moments of terror during Anna's illness—the day they learned her cancer had returned, the day they realized the terrible truth when they saw the large tumors and were flatly told that metastasized breast cancer was incurable, the day they knew that Anna was going to die much faster than thought. But those moments were interspersed by months of numbed reality during which they could face the cancer easier, if not accept it, and could discuss it almost abstractly.

"There is quite a difference between acceptance and resignation," says Lamers. "I *have* seen, most beautifully, a kind of spirituality that arises at the end, as people go through what I sense is a paradoxical shift," he says. "They go from being anxious to suddenly having an overwhelming sense of calm that comes from their recognizing that 'this is the way it happens.' "

The guiding message is to remember that this stage does not come to everyone.

So what is hospice, asked a seventy-five-year-old cancer survivor who was on the panel with Anna in May of 1997. "Is it a place or what?" Hospice is not a place but a philosophy, based on a humanism that requires hospice workers to accept patients unconditionally. Sometimes, say, a lifelong history of family dysfunction is difficult to tolerate. "Hospice caregivers learn not only to tolerate but to respect individual differences in the family. . . . It is a core part of hospice philosophy that to approach the human encounter with death is to face what is noblest in humanity. Even the poorest in spirit can be transformed by the experience," writes Stephen R. Connor, clinical psychologist and former executive director of the Hospice of Central Kentucky.[8] He is now vice president of the National Hospice Organization.

Some hospices have facilities and they do attend patients in nursing homes, but the basic thrust is to teach the families how to care for the dying in their homes. The best in the movement are unrelentingly nonjudgmental givers and teachers, both for patients and families, with an emphasis on pain management and psychological preparation for death. A little-known but major component is that hospice offers at least twelve months of bereavement counseling for families following a death.

Hospice, which began as hostels for the weary traveler, the poor, the sick, and the dying in the Middle Ages, has become an astounding modern movement in the United States in less than thirty years, growing from just 1 in 1971 to nearly 3,000 in 1998; hospices now serve almost half a million dying patients annually. The hospice concept has grown worldwide. When Jack Gordon, president of the Hospice Foundation of America, was interviewed on Voice of America television in 1996, calls came in from Malawi and Argentina and Romania, asking how to start hospices. In the United States, a negative reaction to depersonalized high-tech care—no matter how futile—spurred the movement. Hospice, of course, is not perfect and has its pitfalls, but, despite complaints, I have yet to hear a family say they would have preferred a hospital.

As Anna said, knowledge is the greatest antidote to fear. Doubtful before I experienced Anna's at-home dying and listened to countless personal stories, I am now positive that hospice is what I would chose for myself or loved ones. But this includes my strong warning to thoroughly check out those available to you. Statistics on their efficacy are rare because hospices functioned for years as ad hoc entities. Sometimes there are administrative and coordinating snags, such as we saw in Anna's case. As the patient load grows, hospice leaders acknowledge that some recruits need better training on the hospice philosophy. "Effective hospice takes time and requires the work of an experienced, supervised, and carefully trained interdisciplinary team," says Lamers. "I will say, 'I'll do a physical exam. You sit in the kitchen with the wife and find out what's going on here. Where are the kids, the parents, brothers, sisters, what needs to be done, what are your plans and priorities?' "

Although many families reject nonnursing aspects, such as chaplains, social workers, or volunteers, I would strongly suggest trying the full hospice team initially and then discarding that which seems unnecessary. A volunteer may be indispensable running errands, buying groceries, listening to the patient while you take a breather. The social worker's role is far different from the usual connotation of working with the poor or dysfunctional. In hospice, they are there to expedite details on many fronts—funeral homes, financial planning—and, above all, to help educate families on what to expect as one goes through dying. Hospice team members who ignore this crucial aspect should be reported immediately to the supervisor. Doka stresses that sometimes "not nearly enough is done to teach family members." As for chaplains—who are strictly discretionary—their presence could be beneficial even for those with no expressed faith. "It's got to be a really grounded person who has been through a lot of deaths, a lot of experiences. It is *nondenominational* help," Lamers stresses. "One wonderful hospice chaplain said that the 'chaplain's major role is that of spiritual broker.' It's saying, 'Do you want to make contact with your church? If so, I'll arrange it.' Or, 'If you want to talk about it, what can we do to foster that?' " Sometimes this means just listening to underlying spiritual doubts, needs, desires, or, conversely, negative questions.

Tales of hospice care can run the gamut. Some survivors say that hospice nurses and aides came only a few hours a week. Others say that the nurses and aides stressed that they could be called at any hour and duly showed up when summoned. Reports vary even within the same hospice, depending on the individual caregiver. One woman received no follow-up bereavement calls from a Northern Virginia hospice center. She opened her mail six months after her husband died to find herself on the hospice mailing asking for donations—which should go out only after one year of grieving. A gay couple intensely disliked a coordinator from the same hospice. "She was about as comfortable as going to Bloomie's customer service," says Don Wilder Plett. "She treated Alan like a tomato—'If he won't be able to understand me, you'll have to fill this out . . .' and spoke to me as if I was a nanny from another country. I told her, 'He's in pain. I want to have him hooked up tomorrow [for a morphine drip].' We got rid of hospice and called home care service.

Their nurse was kind and loving and treated Alan like a recovering person, not a terminal victim. It was psychological therapy for him. She came to the memorial."

There are others, like the much younger sister of an eighty-four-year-old brother, Millie Cowan, who says, "We could not have done it without hospice. He had an unbelievable bond with the nurse's aide, who bathed him for six months. She could get him to do anything." And a forty-year-old daughter, Tammy Haddad, who quit her high-powered job to help her father for five months, says, "The hospice team treated the whole family. The social worker still calls my mother to ask how she is doing. We kept saying, 'Who *are* these people? They must be angels.' They come into your house, they don't know you at all. They're able to perceive your essence and help you to appreciate it and help you move to another life in the most comforting way possible. Fear is the worst feeling imaginable. There's no book, no doctor, no nurse; there's no one out there that can make this situation better. They helped me realize that there was no answer and that that wasn't necessarily a bad thing. This is just what it is and what you need to accept."

One major block to the hospice goal of making death a process of growth and completion of life is psychological—the denial of death and the unwillingness to stop aggressive care. Hence half of all patients are in hospice care for no more than a month. Government regulations feed such attitudes. When Medicare began reimbursing hospice in 1983, this was considered a great boon and it did indeed help hospice expand and reach larger numbers of patients. (Since then, for-profit hospices have burgeoned and have been criticized for such practices as providing commissions to staff members for signing up doctors who refer patients.)[9] A pitfall is the arbitrary six-month limitation set by Congress on Medicare funding. "Hospice people at the time thought that a year was more reasonable, but that was the legislative compromise," says Gordon. "When people have an incurable disease and you're trying to keep them alive and functioning as long as possible, that's the wrong kind of limit." Sometimes families resort to subterfuge. Cowan's brother was never told he was in hospice care. Haddad's hospice nurse was also a chemotherapy expert and home health care nurse; she treated him at home while he was on chemo and later as a hospice nurse. Others find religious caregiving organizations that act as hospices, without the restraint of "palliative care only" rules.

In this cost-cutting medical era, hospices additionally find themselves embroiled in catch-22 bureaucracy. "Government auditors have questioned hospices about a small percentage [one half of 1 percent] of their patients who live longer than six months," says Gordon. "Doesn't it seem crazy that the government is telling us that we're helping people live too long? The kind of care that they get probably extends their life, so hospices are being penalized for success. It also points up that an arbitrary six months is difficult to predict." Instead of cutting back, says Gordon, "the kind of holistic care given to the terminally ill ought to go to everybody."

Health care in this country is organized to provide primarily acute-care services, although the greatest need is for chronic care. Many in the field seek to educate the public, legislators, and the medical profession to recognize the value of hospice for more than the immediately terminal. "Hospice could be extended to chronic diseases and severe disabilities," says Gordon, "and could be extended to conditions that we know are terminal but take a lot longer, like emphysema or Parkinson's or Alzheimer's or Lou Gehrig's disease. The government and/or insurance companies would have to make the benefit available on a diagnosis/prognosis basis, with different levels of care at different times." (Since 80 percent of all hospital days are for chronic care, an expanded hospice system—proven less costly than hospitals—could cut health costs.)

The best proselytizers for hospice are surviving family members and friends. Tammy Haddad's story embodies the experience of countless survivors. "We were really skeptical early on because, first of all, when you face hospice, you're facing death and there is the element of not knowing what is going to happen that is so painful. It was hospice nurses, not the hospital or doctor's nurses, who helped prepare my parents for each step along the way. They alleviated much of the fear by saying, 'In the next week, you're going to be noticing this or feeling this,' and so on. Just reading this may sound like cold comfort, but it was the most wonderful thing that you could give someone."

The raw wounds of losing her father six months ago bring tears. A successful businessman who had run lives, companies, and families, Haddad's father, like many people, felt angrily out of control. "The nurses, aides, and social workers helped him regain control of even the small things and helped him realize that letting go is part of it." After his death, the social workers talked to Haddad and her mother about "how at first he was such an angry man and then how he grew and how he accepted it. They kept telling him something which is so true, and that is 'You could have had a heart attack and died; instead you have this whole period to say good-bye to your family and reflect about all that you've accomplished—not in *work* but with your family and all the loved ones now around you.' " Because of them, her father positively reordered his waning days. "He was so sweet, a pussycat," says Haddad, sobbing again.

They emphasized that Haddad and her mother should take breaks. "Someone telling you that it's okay to go, that you just can't go flat out the whole time, made me realize that it was important to walk away and fall apart so that you don't fall apart in front of the person dying.

"I guess death is the ultimate equalizer," says Haddad. She has worked among the powerful and famous as the executive producer and creator of both the Larry King radio show and *Larry King Live* television show, a vice president of CNN, and senior broadcast producer for the *Today* show. "Sure these people can have big egos, can be arrogant—but some can be absolutely terrific." Since her father's death, "my appreciation has grown for those who care about their families, who care about you—it sounds so trite, but it's true." There were surprises. Comedian Don Rickles, who was not close, became kindly solicitous and shared his own experiences when he found out Haddad's father was dying. A noted female columnist whose dying father was in a coma for months became a new best friend, although Haddad had known her only slightly before. "She was there for me every step of the way." Haddad reflects that until one experiences it, "we just *don't* know how to die, or to help those who die. Hospice helps. This has totally changed my life. Part of that was the hospice people. They were there, helping us to take stock and figure out our priorities. Their beliefs were so strong that you just absorbed it in their presence. It made all the difference."

When Haddad quit her job, she says, "I was frankly embarrassed to publicly say, 'I'm leaving. I'm going to spend time with my father.' You're competing in a man's business and it felt like it was a wussy girlie thing to say.

But as it turns out, I've gotten more calls and notes from people who said, 'Good for you, I didn't spend time with my dying parents. I didn't do this or that.' Or people who said, 'You know what, this is the best thing you've ever done. Call me if I can do anything to help.' I have acquired four or five really good friends because of this experience."

Haddad now belongs to what can be the most caring group, those who have been there. Her experience has sensitized her to give back—as others did for her. "I'm more sensitive to other people's problems and am more helpful to friends and family by talking about them. A lot of people go through life not having that opportunity. You have to feel like you've gained something from this and that maybe you can help others who are in this situation." Haddad expresses a common sentiment of the newly bereaved. "I'm much more conscious of the shortness of life—to appreciate what I have and really how fragile it is."

Although some people apply the Kübler-Ross five-stage theory of dying to grief, this is, again, not sufficient. Ambivalent, conflicting, and simultaneous emotions are also part of grieving. Today there is growing acceptance that some survivors never do end their grieving. If mourning persisted after two years, it used to be considered unacceptable complicated grief with other underlying causes. More compassion for long-term grief exists today. Denise Scali, one widowed friend, more than two years after the death of her husband, describes her grief as coming in waves. So does Jan. It is a good metaphor; one goes along, safely treading water, and then is flattened by an unexpected wave that swells suddenly and slaps one in the face.

One aspect of this book was to examine how all of us can help console friends or loved ones. Ideas thread throughout this book, but they bear reviewing, along with more suggestions. They can sound simple and obvious, but putting them into practice takes thoughtful and conscious effort. St. Francis Bereavement Center includes the following: Be there. "Grieving people need support and presence much more than advice." Initiate and anticipate. "Intensely grieving people often don't know or can't ask for what they need. Suggest specific tasks and times you would like to help." Anna's friend Jane Bittner, who has survived the death of her son, both parents, and a brother, adds, "Do not wait to be asked. Just show up. I remember people saying to me, 'If there is anything I can do, please call.' They meant it, but I think grieving people don't call."

Every manual on grief emphasizes listening—that silence is golden—and advise not to push or force conversation. Expect to listen to the same details repeatedly; grieving people often need to tell their stories over and over. One of the most important gifts you can give is not to interrupt or relay your own stories.

During my volunteer bereavement course at St. Francis Center, I promptly flunked Not Talking 101. We have all heard ourselves flailing on, so discomfited by silences, particularly in emotional moments, offering anecdotes or rolling out platitudes. To really listen and absorb what others are telling us, either verbally or through body language, is an extraordinary gift. Some seem born with what a friend of mine, Pat Altobello, calls the "nursing gene." I call it the "caregiving gene." And then there are the rest of us. The excuses come. "Can't visit now," "I hate hospitals," "I don't know what to do or say," "I'll wait until later. . . ." Does this tell us that we are more concerned about our own awkward helplessness and unpleasant feelings? Perhaps. "But," says Grace Metz, director of volunteer services at St. Francis, "sometimes we're so concerned about causing pain or that we won't say it right that we don't say anything. And that contributes to the sense of being invisible or disenfranchised."

Listening is a delicate balancing act. "Some people want to be asked how they feel, and some people say 'That's the last damn question I want,' " Metz says. An old man in a video said that asking him how he felt put the burden on him. "Ask me something that involves *you, that doesn't objectify me,*" he said vehemently. He also wanted to be treated normally. "I really appreciated someone . . . saying 'Oh dude, you got a nuclear haircut (chemo-zapped baldness).' " For some very private people, who have their own way of navigating, any conversation can be a definite invasion. Yet, as caring strangers, volunteers can often free up the patient or mourner. A gift for them can be telling their story to someone brand new, who has no emotional frame of context.

Caregiving may not seem natural, but one can learn. It is exhilarating to know that we can help friends and family in many ways—from wiping a warm forehead to sending notes to running errands to letting a dying or grieving friend talk if so desired. In the beginning, I couldn't believe professional caregivers who told me how blessed and rewarded they felt, how their own lives were so enriched by the humbling experience of helping others in their most intimate moments. Now I know.

Another gift we can provide is a safe haven, so that the bereaved can open up if they feel like it. Opening a door can be a delicate, sometimes thankless effort. Don't have expectations; they may chose not to walk through it, now or ever. "I have said a number of times to Lindsay, 'How are you doing?' " says Bittner. "And she will say"—imitating a chipper response—" 'Oh! I'm fine!' So that was it. The door was opened, but she didn't have to walk through." Comments about missing her mother are met with one word, "yep," which brooks no discussion.

If a friend chooses not to open up, it is important not only to accept that, but to keep showing support on whatever level you can. Grieving people need listening, but they also need friends who treat them as they always have—inviting them to movies or parties or lunch, even if they decline. Providing moments of laughter and diversion are wonderful ways to help a bereaved friend regain energy and some perspective.

Condolence letters can be of great help if they include the positive way in which the deceased touched your life; many survivors savor such remembrances and reread them over the years. One son who lost his father says that such letters "remind me of all the things he had given me over the years." And, remember, "consoling" clichés should be curbed. Rabbi Earl A. Grollman writes an imaginary inner dialogue to accompany some: " 'I know just how you feel.' ('No, you don't! How can you possibly know what I'm going through?') 'You are doing so well.' ('How do you know how I feel when you leave?') 'Your loved one lived to a ripe old age.' ('At any age death is a robber.') 'Others have lived through it.' ('At this moment I'm concerned about myself.') 'It's God's will.' ('Then this vindictive and vengeful God must be my enemy.') 'You're so young. You have the rest of your life ahead of you.' ('Don't you know I'm hurting and I feel like I'll hurt forever?')"[10]

Finally, be kind to yourself. If what you do comes from the heart, any mistake along the way will be forgiven by grieving friends, who realize the depth of your caring.

There are many books, articles, and organizations that the bereaved can turn to for help. (Some are listed at the back.) Perhaps your community will be fortunate to have as caring a place as Washington's St. Francis Center. Sometimes the most succinct guides offer practical help on a variety of matters: what to expect upon returning to work, what to do when friends withdraw, finding spiritual strength when you are not religious, how numbness can be a temporary gift from the torrent of emotions, dealing with the anniversary of the death. ("The issue after the first year is not *if* we're feeling better, but if we're feeling better *more* of the time. . . . Recognize that this is a difficult time. Often when we accept that fact, we do not feel as bad about feeling bad.")[11] I have included information on how some excellent journals can be purchased inexpensively.

At the end of this long journey, I have learned to be more tolerant of the beliefs and attitudes of others regarding dying, death, and grieving; to recognize that some mysteries are not only unsolvable but exciting to contemplate. I am willing to believe in the mystic moments of others; it is the truth for them and therefore enough for me. I believe that Anna conversed with her mother in her nearing-death awareness stage. And when Jane Bittner tells me that her dead son came to her one day in radiant light, I believe her. When Don Wilder Plett says that his greatest healing occurred "when Alan came down to me; I could feel his presence," I do not scoff. He was scattering Alan's ashes on Mount Rainier. Plett pulls out snapshots. "See the sky change from clear to that wide swatch of cloud? That could be in the shape of an angel wing if you use your imagination." Jan, the scientist, was himself contemplating a mystic end. "I wondered whether at the time of Anna's death there would be some indication of some nonphysical part of Anna leaving her body. One reads numerous accounts of people seeing what could be termed a soul leaving the body at the time of death. I saw nothing and felt nothing other than Anna's life ending." He adds that this has nothing to do with "Anna's spirit living on in many of us. It clearly does."

On a practical note, Anna's messages about constant vigilance regarding doctors, tests, X rays, diagnoses, and so forth should be a strong lesson to us all. Second and third opinions should be sought. Roseann's suggestion that doctor's offices should provide up-to-the-minute information regarding clinical trials or new drugs is a sound idea. It would be a boon to patients if doctors were to hire case workers of sorts who would not only handle such information but would be able to explain in laymen's terms, step by step, in detail, what the doctor usually does not have time, or the ability, to outline. Given today's cost-cutting medical situation, such a person might have to be hired by a patient, but it would be worth it; also there are some people who will, for a small fee, search the Internet for detailed information on what one needs to know about illnesses and diagnoses.

I cannot imagine why people are unwilling to provide every available piece of information for those who will survive them—up-to-date wills, living wills, do-not-resucitate papers, and the like should be done while one is healthy, so as not to be a burden in case of sudden death. Anna's All Sorts of Things You Should Do Before You Die list (on pages 244 to 246) is invaluable.

As for humane end-of-life measures, it would be a boon if hospital bed manufacturers were to make twin beds that can be attached together, so that a loved one could stay in the same bed if so desired. After all, one can purchase a motorized regular king-sized bed with individual mattresses and up and down controls for either side. Anna's caregivers were told by the hospice that guard rails were not available for the Johannessen's king-sized bed. That also seems a simple enough product to design.

It is absurd to think that Anna's wisdom and selflessness and undaunted optimism would wash over me—but I was able to retain the spirit, if not the totality, of her mind-set. Her gift of giving was so strong that I never left Anna without being uplifted. I felt when my son, Michael, and daughter, Leah, were born, creations of such magnitude, I would never sweat the small stuff again. It didn't happen that way, then or now; deadlines still stress me out, the driver who cuts me off still gets cursed, the pace of life remains frenetic. But my journey has found me pondering more and more what I can do to give back for the richness of my life.

When I started this book, I thought that finding Anna was pure luck. Now I think there is a much more profound reason, a higher power that brought us together. For all the pain of loss, the joy of knowing Anna has enriched my life far more. I am better able to accept death and dying and feel more sensitized to helping others. I think more generously about people I meet, for one never knows what sorrows they are carrying quietly inside them as they laugh and talk at work or at a social gathering.

The finest tribute to Anna, or to anyone you know like Anna who came to live out loud, would be to try to live as she did. This saying is a reminder: "Alas for those who cannot sing, but die with all their music in them. Let us treasure the time we have and resolve to use it well, counting each moment precious—a chance to apprehend some truth, to experience some beauty, to conquer some evil, to relieve some suffering, to love and be loved, to achieve something of lasting worth."

Resources

Candlelighters Childhood Cancer Foundation
1901 Pennsylvania Avenue, NW
Suite 1001
Washington, DC 20006
(202) 659-5136

Headquarters for local groups that provide education and support for parents.

Centers for Disease Control AIDS Information Hotline
1-800-342-2437

General Information about AIDS, directory of AIDS treatment and support organizations, advice and support for people with AIDS or HIV.

Compassionate Friends
P.O. Box 3696
Oak Brook, IL 60522-3696
(708) 990-0010

Headquarters for local chapters that provide support and education for parents and siblings on childhood loss.

Concern for Dying
250 West 57th Street
New York, NY 10107
(212) 246-6962

A clearinghouse for death-related information. They also provide copies of model durable power of attorney and living will forms.

The Dougy Center
P.O. Box 66461
Portland, OR 97286
(503) 775-5683

Provides support for bereaved children.

Foundation for Thanatology
630 West 168th Street
New York, NY 10032

An educational organization providing workshops and materials for professionals working with the dying and bereaved.

Hospice Foundation of America
2001 S Street, NW
Suite 300
Washington, DC 20009
(202) 638-5419

Promotes education on death, dying, and bereavement through newsletters, audio and video resources, and an annual teleconference on "living with grief." Books that supplement the teleconference, edited by Kenneth J. Doka, include Living with Grief: Who We Are, How We Grieve *(1998);* Living with Grief: When Illness Is Prolonged *(1997);* Living with Grief: After Sudden Loss *(1996); and* Children Mourning, Mourning Children *(1995), published by Hospice Foundation of America, Taylor and Francis.*

Journeys Bereavement Newsletter

A monthly newsletter featuring well-known grief specialists who offer advice and insight to aid in bereavement. Available in both bulk and individual subscriptions. Contact Hospice Foundation of America for ordering information. (202) 638-5419.

Make Today Count
P.O. Box 222
Osage Beach, MI 65065
(314) 346-6644

A national program providing model educational programs for people coping with cancer and other life-threatening illnesses.

National AIDS Hotline
American Social Health Association
P.O. Box 13827
Research Triangle Park, NC 27709
1-800-342-AIDS

A twenty-four-hour-a-day hotline with recorded information on AIDS and referral capability for medical care and testing.

National Association for Widowed People
P.O. Box 3564
Springfield, IL 62708

Promotes support groups and resources for widowed people.

National Cancer Institute, Cancer Information Service
1-800-422-6237

Offers information about conventional and experimental cancer treatment, trials, and protocols and referral to specialized cancer centers.

National Hospice Organization
1901 N Moore Street
Suite 901
Arlington, VA 22209

A major organization for hospices in the United States.

National Organization for Victim Assistance
717 D Street, NW
Washington, DC 20004
(202) 232-8560

An organization that advocates for the rights of victims of crime and disaster and provides services to local programs.

Parents of Murdered Children
100 East Eighth Street
Room B41
Cincinnati, OH 45202
1-800-327-2499

A national organization that provides support and educational information for parents of murdered children.

St. Francis Center
4880 MacArthur Boulevard NW
Washington, DC 20016
(202) 333-4880

Provides support during illness, dying, and bereavement.

Survivors of Suicide
Suicide Prevention Center, Inc.
184 Salem Avenue
Dayton, OH 45406

A national organization providing services to suicidal people and their families.

Widowed Persons Service
American Association of Retired Persons
601 E Street, NW
Washington, DC 20049
(202) 434-2260

Provides support groups and resources for the newly widowed.

Notes

Prologue: Learning

1. *New York Times,* Sunday, 12 April 1998. Sports section, p. 21.
2. *The Facts About Breast Cancer*, (Dallas: The Susan G. Komen Breast Cancer Foundation, 1998).

1. Meeting Anna

1. Ibid.
2. *Washington Post,* 1 December 1995, p. A28. Tamoxifen remains the best-selling cancer drug in the world, but it is not the panacea to match its hype. It reduces the risk of recurrence by about 40 percent. One can argue that this is a major improvement—but it still leaves a 60 percent chance that cancer can recur. Studies from 1998 have paved the way for use as a preventative in women with high risk of breast cancer.

3. A New Stage

1. *Florida Today,* 27 February 1989, People section, p. 1.
2. Ibid. Also *Florida Today,* 7 August 1996, p. A7.
3. *Florida Today,* 27 February 1989, People section, p. 1.
4. Ibid.

4. "The Return of the Big C," Insurance Companies, and Other Snafus

1. In one study, the National Cancer Institute tracked breast cancer survivors for eighteen years. Ruling out all causes of death other than breast cancer, NCI found that 97 percent of the women were alive after one year, 80 percent after five years (another study found that there was a 97 percent five-year survival rate for early-stage breast cancer), 63 percent after ten years, and only 50 percent after eighteen years. As reported by Michael Castleman in "The Real Truth about Breast Cancer," 1996. NABCO. Ubs.com/focus/archives/features/Breast Cancer.html.

5. Resilience, Anger, and Humor

1. Charles A. and Donna M. Corr and Clyde M. Nabe, *Death and Dying, Life and Living,* 2d ed. (Pacific Grove, Calif.: Brooks/Cole Publishing Company, a division of International Thompson Publishing Company, 1997), p. 177.

2. Ronna Fay Jevne, Ph.D., and Alexander Levitan, M.D., *No Time for Nonsense: Getting Well Against the Odds* (San Diego, Calif.: LuraMedia, 1989), pp. 136 and 137.
3. Ibid., p. 56.
4. Ashleigh Brilliant, *Appreciate Me Now and Avoid the Rush* (Santa Barbara, Calif.: Woodbridge Press, 1981). As quoted by Jevne and Levitan in *No Time for Nonsense,* p. 140.
5. Myra MacPherson, *Long Time Passing: Vietnam and the Haunted Generation* (Garden City, N.Y.: Doubleday and Company, 1984), p. 368.
6. Jevne and Levitan, *No Time for Nonsense,* p. 62.
7. As quoted by Dr. Sheldon Blau from a study by the Harvard School of Public Health, in *How to Get Out of the Hospital Alive* (New York: Macmillan, 1997), p. 57.
8. Ibid.
9. E. Roy Berger, M.D., with Linda A. Mitiga, *Common Bonds: Reflections of a Cancer Doctor* (Westbury, N.Y.: Health Education Literary Publisher, 1995), p 198.

7. The Clay Wall

1. Kenneth J. Doka, Ph.D., with Joyce Davidson, eds., *Living with Grief: When Illness Is Prolonged,* (Washington, D.C.: Hospice Foundation of America, 1997), chapter by Betty Davies, R.N., Ph.D., pp. 23–24.
2. Ibid.

8. Paving the Way

1. Study conducted by Dr. Bruce E. Compas and colleagues, University of Vermont, *New York Times,* 12 February 1997, p. B12.

9. All in the Family: Masculine and Feminine Grieving

1. Information for the section on redefining came from Betty Davies, RN, Ph.D., University of British Columbia and British Columbia's Children's Hospital; Joanne Chekryn Reimer, RN, MSN, Canuck Place, a Hospice for Children, Vancouver, British Columbia; Pamela Brown, RN, MSN, Calgary, Alberta; Nola Martens, RN, MSN, Families in Supportive Care Project, Sherwood Park, Alberta; *Fading Away: The Experience of Transition in Families with Terminal Illness* (Amityville, N.Y.: Baywood Publishing Company 1997). Also Kenneth J. Doka, Ph.D., with Joyce Davidson, eds., *Living with Grief: When Illness Is Prolonged* (Washington, D.C.: Hospice Foundation of America, 1997), chapter by Betty Davies, R.N. Ph.D.
2. Ibid., p. 25. Chapter 2.
3. Ibid., p. 20. Chapter 2. Also, see *Fading Away* for more detail.
4. Thomas R. Golden, LCSW, *Swallowed by a Snake: The Gift of the Masculine Side of Healing* (Kensington, Md.: Golden Healing Publishing, L.L.C., 1996), p. 83.
5. Unless otherwise indicated, research for this section came from conversations with Doka as well as an unpublished paper by Kenneth J. Doka, Ph.D., and Terry Martin, Ph.D., "Taking It Like a Man: Masculine Responses to Loss," November 1994.
6. Golden, *Swallowed by a Snake,* p. 21.
7. Ibid., p. 35.
8. From a study by Tom Golden, grievance counselor, reported in "Grieving Men," *Washington Post,* 7 November 1994.

9. Author's conversation with Paul Tschudi, then director of the St. Francis Bereavement Center.
10. Doka and Martin, "Taking It Like a Man."
11. Cynthia Bach Hughes and Judith Page-Lieberman, "Fathers Experiencing Perinatal Loss," *Death Studies* 13 (1989): 537–56. As quoted by Doka and Martin in "Taking It Like a Man."

11. Reprieve

1. Stephen P. Hersh, M.D., "Death from the Cancers," in *Living with Grief: When Illness Is Prolonged,* edited by Kenneth J. Doka, Ph.D., with Joyce Davidson (Washington, D.C.: Hospice Foundation of America, 1997), p. 101.

16. April

1. J. S. Neaman and C. G. Silver, *Kind Words: A Thesaurus of Euphamisms* (New York: Facts on File Publications, 1983), pp. 144–45. As quoted in Charles A. Corr, Donna M. Corr, and Clyde M. Nabe, *Death and Dying, Life and Living* (Pacific Grove, Calif.: Brooks/Cole Pubishing Company, 1997), p. 88.
2. Sherwin B. Nuland, *How We Die: Reflections on Life's Final Chapter* (New York: Alfred A. Knopf, 1994), p. 229.
3. "The Survival and Expense of Traditional Care and Hospice Care," *Oncology Reports* 1(1994):993–96.
4. Nuland, *How We Die,* p. 257.
5. Ibid.
6. E. Roy Berger, M.D., with Linda A. Mittiga, *Common Bonds: Reflections of a Cancer Doctor* (Westbury, N.Y.: Health Education Literary Publisher, 1995), p. 197.

17. Caregivers

1. All information and quoted material in this paragraph are from Sherwin B. Nuland, *How We Die: Reflections on Life's Final Chapter* (New York: Alfred A. Knopf, 1994), p. 218.
2. Maggie Callanan and Patricia Kelley, *Final Gifts: Understanding the Special Awareness, Needs, and Communications of the Dying* (New York: Poseidon Press, 1992), pp. 163–64.
3. Ibid. Reconciliation and "held back" are discussed in Chapters 11 and 12.

18. Letting Go

1. Maggie Callanan and Patricia Kelley, *Final Gifts: Understanding the Special Awareness, Needs, and Communications of the Dying* (New York: Poseidon Press, 1992), p. 85.
2. Ibid., p. 87.
3. Ibid., p. 97.
4. E. Roy Berger with Linda A. Mittiga, *Common Bonds: Reflections of a Cancer Doctor* (Westbury, N.Y.: Health Education Literary Publisher, 1995), p. 197.

20. *How to Go On Living*

1. Dr. Stephen P. Hersh, *Journeys: A Newsletter to Help in Bereavement,* December 1994, p. 3. Published by Hospice Foundation of America, Washington, D.C.
2. Information for this section came from *Journeys,* December 1994. Articles were written by Hersh; Kenneth J. Doka, Ph.D.; Ellen Zinner; and Rabbi Earl A. Grollman.
3. Ibid.
4. Kenneth J. Doka, Ph.D., "Sadness and Depression," *Journeys,* December 1996, p. 1.
5. *Miami Herald,* Monday, 6 April 1998, p. 1; *New York Times,* Tuesday, 7 April 1998, p 1. A concern that tamoxifen can cause an increase in uterine cancer—which is much easier to detect early and cure than breast cancer—was outweighed by the benefits in the study.

21. *Lessons and Reflections*

1. *New York Times,* 6 December 1997, Religion page, "Journal" column.
2. "God Decentralized," *New York Times Magazine,* 7 December 1997. Comments on page 55, statistics on page 60, with source notes on page 114.
3. April Witt, "Seeking Spiritual Renewal," *Miami Herald,* Sunday, 12 April 1998, p. 1.
4. As quoted in *The Great Quotations,* compiled by George Seldes (New York: Lyle Stuart Publishers, 1960), p. 283.
5. Ronna Fay Jevne, Ph.D., and Alexander Levitan, M.D., *No Time for Nonsense: Getting Well Against the Odds* (San Diego, Calif.: LuraMedia, 1989), p. 174.
6. Charles A. Corr, Donna M. Corr and Clyde M. Nabe, *Death and Dying, Life and Living,* 2d ed. (Pacific Grove, Calif.: Brooks/Cole Publishing Company, a division of International Thompson Publishing Company, 1997), p. 154.
7. Ibid., p. 153. As described from Weisman's work: *On Dying and Denying: A Psychiatric Study of Terminality* (New York: Behavioral Publications, 1972).
8. Stephen R. Connor, *Hospice: Practice, Pitfalls, and Promise* (Washington, D.C.: Taylor and Francis Publishers, 1998), p. 9.
9. Charles Babcock, *The Washington Post,* 14 June 1998, p. 1. This look at hospice practices noted that a federal audit review of more than two thousand hospice patients who lived longer than the arbitrary six months concluded that nearly two-thirds were not terminally ill when they were enrolled. However, hospice organizations argue that the article failed to point out that, if this were true, it is a miniscule number of hospice patients—less than one half of 1 percent of the four hundred fifty thousand annual patients, the majority of whom receive humane, quality treatment that family survivors endorse. In fact, the sad statistic is that the majority of doctors and families resist hospice until the very last, hence half of hospice patients receive but one month care, far less than the six months set by the government. Vitas Healthcare Corp. of Miami, the largest chain of for-profit hospices, was questioned by the auditors. (No report was issued by the publication date.) It is a major supporter of the nonprofit Hospice Foundation of America, an educational organization that I mention often and favorably in this book; it is a separate entity, not connected to any hospice facility or organization. As I have mentioned in the body of the book, my husband, Jack D. Gordon, is the president of the Hospice Foundation of America.
10. *Journeys: A Newsletter to Help in Bereavement,* December 1996, p. 2. Published by Hospice Foundation of America, Washington, D.C.
11. Ibid.

Suggested Bibliography

Attig, Thomas. *How We Grieve: Relearning the World.* New York: Oxford University Press, 1996.

Berger, E. Roy, with Linda A. Mittiga. *Common Bonds: Reflections of a Cancer Doctor.* Westbury, N.Y.: Health Education Literary Publisher, 1995.

Blau, Sheldon P., and Elaine Fantle Shimberg. *How to Get Out of the Hospital Alive.* New York: Macmillan, 1997.

Byock, Ira. *Dying Well: The Prospect for Growth at the End of Life.* New York: Riverhead Books, 1997.

Callahan, Daniel. *What Kind of Life: The Limits of Medical Progress.* New York: Touchstone Books, 1990.

Callanan, Maggie, and Patricia Kelley. *Final Gifts: Understanding the Special Awareness, Needs, and Communications of the Dying.* New York: Poseidon Press, 1992.

Carter, Rosalynn, with Susan K. Golant. *Helping Yourself Help Others: A Book for Caregivers.* New York: Times Books, 1994.

Connor, Stephen R. *Hospice: Practice, Pitfalls, and Promise.* Washington, D.C.: Taylor and Francis, 1998.

Corr, Charles A., Donna M. Corr, and Clyde M. Nabe. *Death and Dying, Life and Living,* 2d ed. Pacific Grove, Calif.: Brooks/Cole Publishing Company, 1997.

Davies, B., J. C. Reimer, P. Brown, and N. Martens. *Fading Away: The Experience of Families with Terminal Illness.* Amityville, N.Y.: Baywood, 1995.

DeSpelder, Lynne Ann, and Albert Lee Strickland. *The Last Dance: Encountering Death and Dying,* 4th ed. Mountain View, Calif.: Mayfield Publishing Company, 1996.

Diamond, Nina L. *Purify Your Body: Natural Remedies for Detoxing from Fifty Everyday Situations.* New York: Random House, 1996.

Doka, Kenneth J., ed. *Children Mourning, Mourning Children.* Washington, D.C.: Hospice Foundation of America/Taylor and Francis Publishers, 1995.

———. *Disenfranchised Grief: Recognizing Hidden Sorrow.* Lexington, Mass.: Lexington Books, 1989.

———, ed. *Living with Grief: When Illness Is Prolonged.* Washington, D.C.: Hospice Foundation of America/Taylor and Francis Publishers, 1997.

Field, Marilyn J., and Christine K. Cassel, eds. *Approaching Death: Improving Care at the End of Life.* Washington, D.C.: National Academy Press, 1997.

Frankl, Viktor E. *Man's Search for Meaning.* New York: Pocket Books, 1984.

Golden, Thomas R. *Swallowed by a Snake: The Gift of the Masculine Side of Healing.* Kensington, Md.: Golden Healing Publishing, L.L.C., 1996.

Grollman, Earl A. *Living When a Loved One Has Died.* Boston: Beacon Press, 1995.

———. *Concerning Death: A Practical Guide for the Living.* Boston: Beacon Press, 1974.

———. *Straight Talk about Death for Teenagers: How to Cope with Losing Someone You Love.* Boston: Beacon Press, 1993

Haller, James. *What to Eat When You Don't Feel Like Eating.* Hantsport, Nova Scotia: Robert Pope Foundation, 1994.

Hennezel, Marie De. *Intimate Death: How the Dying Teach Us How to Live.* New York: Alfred A. Knopf, 1997.

Infeld, Donna Lind. *The Hospice Journal: Physical, Psychosocial, and Pastoral Care of the Dying,* vol. 12, no. 3. Washington, D.C.: National Hospice Organization/Haworth Press, Inc., 1997.

Jennings, Bruce, ed., *Ethics in Hospice Care: Challenges to Hospice Values in a Changing Health Care Environment.* Binghampton, N.Y.: Haworth Press, Inc., 1997.

Jevne, Ronna Fay, and Alexander Levitan. *No Time for Nonsense: Getting Well Against the Odds.* San Diego, Calif.: LuraMedia, 1989.

Kessler, David. *The Rights of the Dying: A Companion for Life's Final Moments.* New York: HarperCollins, 1997.

Lang, Susan S., and Richard B. Patt. *You Don't Have to Suffer: A Complete Guide to Relieving Cancer Pain for Patients and Their Families.* New York: Oxford University Press, 1994.

Levine, Stephen. *Who Dies? An Investigation of Conscious Living and Conscious Dying.* New York: Doubleday, 1982 (1996).

MacPherson, Myra. *Long Time Passing: Vietnam and the Haunted Generation.* New York: Doubleday, 1984.

McCue, Kathleen, with Ron Bonn. *How to Help Children Through a Parent's Serious Illness.* New York: St. Martin's Press, 1996.

Mendelsohn, Robert S. *Male Practice: How Doctors Manipulate Women.* Chicago: Contemporary Books, Inc., 1981.

Neaman, J. S., and C. G. Silver. *Kind Words: A Thesaurus of Euphemisms.* New York: Facts on File Publications, 1983.

Nuland, Sherwin B. *How We Die: Reflections on Life's Final Chapter.* New York: Alfred A. Knopf, 1994.

Parachin, Victor M. *Grief Relief.* St. Louis: CBP Press, 1991.

Quinlan, John. *Loved and Lost: The Journey Through Dying, Death, and Bereavement.* Collegeville, Minn.: Liturgical Press, 1997.

Rando, Therese. *Grieving: How to Go on Living When Someone You Love Dies.* New York: Bantam, 1991.

Reoch, Richard. *Dying Well: A Holistic Guide for the Dying and Their Carers.* London: Gaia Books Limited, 1997.

Saunders, Cicely. *Beyond the Horizon: A Search for Meaning in Suffering.* London: Darton, Longman and Todd, 1990.

Spufford, Margaret. *Celebration.* London: Fount Paperbacks, 1989.

Viorst, Judith. *Necessary Losses.* New York: Simon & Schuster Inc., 1986.

Waugh, Evelyn. *The Loved One.* Boston: Little, Brown and Company, 1977.

Webb, Marilyn. *The Good Death: The New American Search to Reshape the End of Life.* New York: Bantam Books, 1997.

Weintraub, Simkha Y. *Healing of Soul, Healing of Body: Spiritual Leaders Unfold the Strength and Solace in Psalms.* Woodstock, Vt.: Jewish Lights Publishing, 1994.

Weisman, Avery D. *On Dying and Denying: A Psychiatric Study of Terminality.* New York: Behavioral Publications, 1972.

Acknowledgments

I cannot thank Anna and her friends and family enough for their gracious and valuable contribution; this book would have been impossible without them: Jan, Lindsay, and Ellery Johannessen; Anna's sister Roseann and her husband, Clifford Beutell; Anna's father, Stephen Megregian, and her brother Steve Megregian; Jan's parents, Phoebe and Jo Johannessen; Lockard "Lockie" Fuller; Wayne Westbrook; Tina McCarthy; Patty Williams; Jane Bittner; Ann Wylie; Nancy DuVal; Linda Suarez. A special thanks to Suarez for her grand cover-photo of Anna.

Nor can I express adequately my appreciation to the experts who taught me as much about life as they did death, dying, and bereavement: Kenneth J. Doka, Dr. William Lamers, Dr. Ira Byock, and many of the other members of the Association for Death Education and Counseling and the International Work Group on Dying, Death, and Bereavement. St. Francis Bereavement Center tops my list for caring counseling; included are past president Paul Tschudi, current president Robert Washington, Grace Metz, and, notably, child counselor Dottie Ward-Wimmer. Without the gracious input of Dr. Kenneth Miller, Dr. Joe Kaplan, and the cooperation of the staff, Anna's story would be most incomplete. Among them are Suzanne Krikawa, Darlene Gebicke, Anneka Wheaton, Vivien Steinberg, and Rhonda Schoem.

Although our friendship was far too fleeting, I remember and thank my fellow trainees for the richness of our time together in the St. Francis Center volunteer course: Nancy Muller, Delia Cordero, Mary Jo Devine, Candice Evans, Amy Gates, Lisa Harris Kelly, Lisa Michelle Lewis, Janie Miller, and LaShaun Williams. Also Pat Gouldner, who helped enormously through a hospice volunteer course at Hospice Care of D.C.

The Hospice Foundation of America was a major support in providing advice and materials and in expediting the completion of this manuscript: Lisa Veglahn, Sophie V. Berman, David Abrams, Jon Radulovic, Chris Procunier, and Michon Lartique. Also Hugh Westbrook, president of Vitas Health Care Corp. The dedicated former first lady Rosalynn Carter taught me much in her books and lectures on caregiving. Other fine teachers were Kathleen Foley, M.D., director of Project on Death in America and chief of Pain and Palliative Services at Sloan Kettering Memorial Cancer Center; Joanne Lynn, M.D., director of Americans for Better Care of the Dying, Washington, D.C. My thanks to Olwen Price, of the *Washington Post,* who deciphered and transcribed many long and rambling tapes.

A secondary reward of writing this book is that I came to meet new friends and to know many friends and family even better as we explored a more serious side of our lives than the usual bonhomie of friendship; I cherish the many discussions about life and death, religion and bereavement, as well as the kindness of those who shared their own experiences with death, dying, and grieving. (And, of course, I remain grateful for those who put up with my trials and tribulations and encouraged me to keep going.) Among them are my father,

Douglas MacPherson, and my children, Michael Siegel and Leah Siegel and her husband, Joe Drape (a special thanks goes to Leah, for her superb editing suggestions). Also children-by-marriage, Andy Gordon and Vicki Simons, Deborah Gordon and Ben Crow, Melanie Somers and Jonathan Gordon. And, of course, grandchildren, who made me laugh, no matter how sad I sometimes felt about Anna: Jessica, Hannah, James, Eleanor, and Sam. Other helpful friends include my sister-in-law Ann and her husband, Harvey Kramer; Bob Sherrill; Marthena and Joe Cowart; Gar and Sharon Alperovitz; Janet Donovan; Barbara Raskin; Faith Jackson; Jeff Frank; Molly Ivins; Betty Friedan; Jack Skuce; Richard Rymland and Cathy Wyler; Robert and Prudy Squier; Molly and Jim Dickenson; Linda Burgess and Bill Dunlap; Hodding Carter and Patt Derian; Ruth Noble Groom; Tom Bryant; Len and Zelda Glazer; Marilyn Bloom; Ruth Greenfield; Millie and Harold Cowan; Bob and Alice Yoakum; Laura Cosgrove and her son, Kevin.

Lisa Drew has managed an amazing feat—being a tough but enthusiastic editor and a close friend through two books. Joy Harris is also a writer's dream, a hands-on agent with savvy, who cares.

Last—but forever in the forefront of my life—I give enormous thanks and love to my husband, Jack Gordon. His expertise in this field is matched only by his loving patience.

Index

lonely planet

Portu

D0971943

Regis S
Robert La

RETIRÉ DE LA COLLECTION UNIVERSELLE
Bibliothèque et Archives nationales du Québec

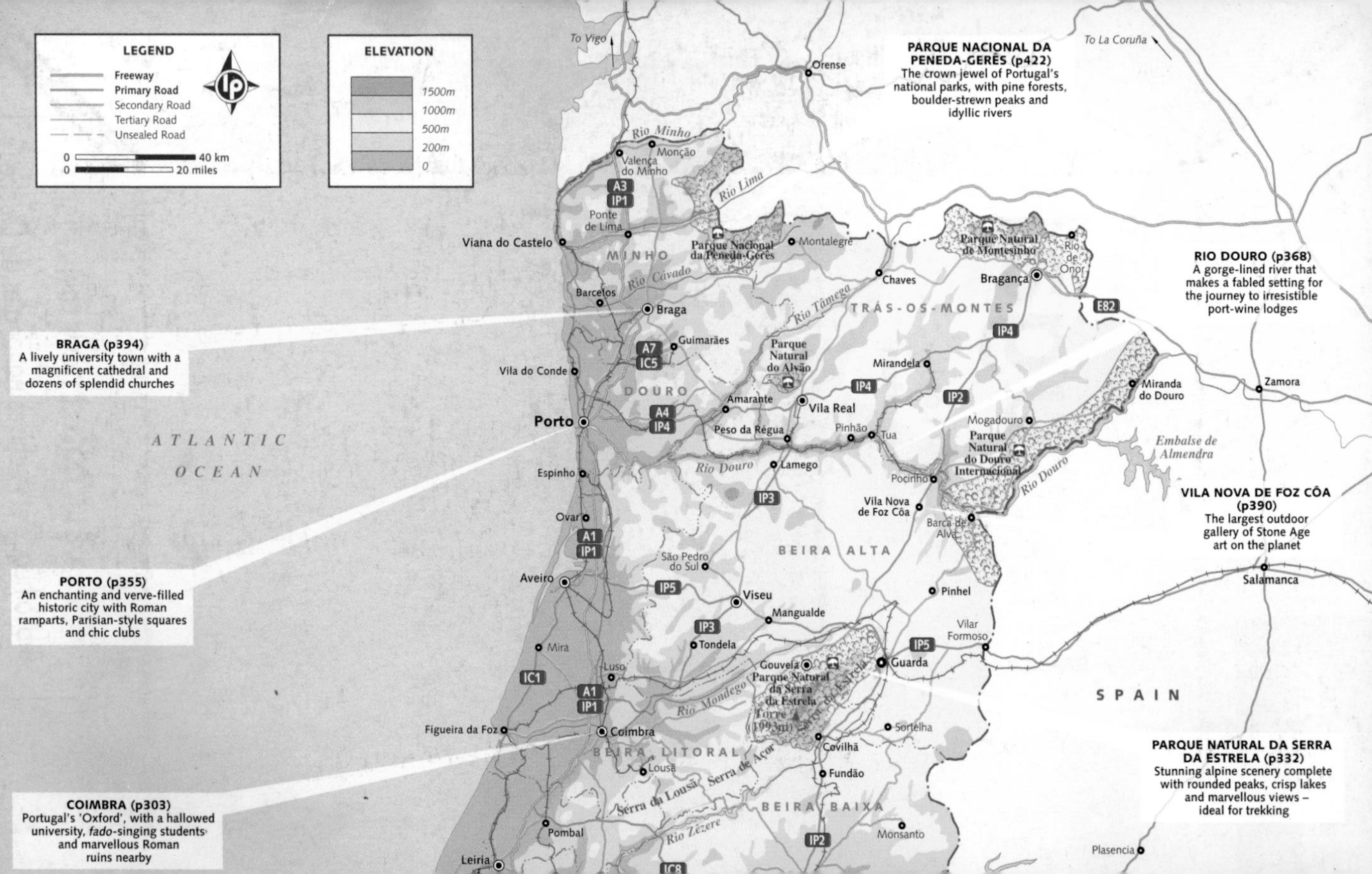
LEGEND
Freeway
Primary Road
Secondary Road
Tertiary Road
Unsealed Road
0 40 km
0 20 miles
ELEVATION
1500m
1000m
500m
200m
0
PARQUE NACIONAL DA PENEDA-GERÊS (p422)
The crown jewel of Portugal's national parks, with pine forests, boulder-strewn peaks and idyllic rivers
RIO DOURO (p368)
A gorge-lined river that makes a fabled setting for the journey to irresistible port-wine lodges
BRAGA (p394)
A lively university town with a magnificent cathedral and dozens of splendid churches
PORTO (p355)
An enchanting and verve-filled historic city with Roman ramparts, Parisian-style squares and chic clubs
VILA NOVA DE FOZ CÔA (p390)
The largest outdoor gallery of Stone Age art on the planet
COIMBRA (p303)
Portugal's 'Oxford', with a hallowed university, fado-singing students and marvellous Roman ruins nearby
PARQUE NATURAL DA SERRA DA ESTRELA (p332)
Stunning alpine scenery complete with rounded peaks, crisp lakes and marvellous views – ideal for trekking
ATLANTIC OCEAN
SPAIN
MINHO
DOURO
TRÁS-OS-MONTES
BEIRA ALTA
BEIRA LITORAL
BEIRA BAIXA
To Vigo
To La Coruña
Orense
Zamora
Salamanca
Plasencia
Valença do Minho
Monção
Ponte de Lima
Viana do Castelo
Barcelos
Braga
Guimarães
Vila do Conde
Porto
Espinho
Ovar
Aveiro
Mira
Figueira da Foz
Coimbra
Luso
Lousã
Pombal
Leiria
Parque Nacional da Peneda-Gerês
Montalegre
Chaves
Parque Natural de Montesinho
Rio de Onor
Bragança
Parque Natural do Alvão
Amarante
Vila Real
Peso da Régua
Lamego
Pinhão
Tua
Mirandela
Mogadouro
Miranda do Douro
Parque Natural do Douro Internacional
Embalse de Almendra
Pocinho
Vila Nova de Foz Côa
Barca de Alva
Pinhel
São Pedro do Sul
Viseu
Mangualde
Tondela
Vilar Formoso
Guarda
Gouveia
Parque Natural da Serra da Estrela
Torre (1993m)
Sortelha
Covilhã
Fundão
Monsanto
Rio Minho
Rio Lima
Rio Cávado
Rio Tâmega
Rio Douro
Rio Mondego
Rio Zêzere
Serra da Lousã
Serra de Açor
Serra da Estrela
A3
IP1
A7
IC5
A4
IP4
A1
IP5
IP3
IP2
E82
IC1
IC8

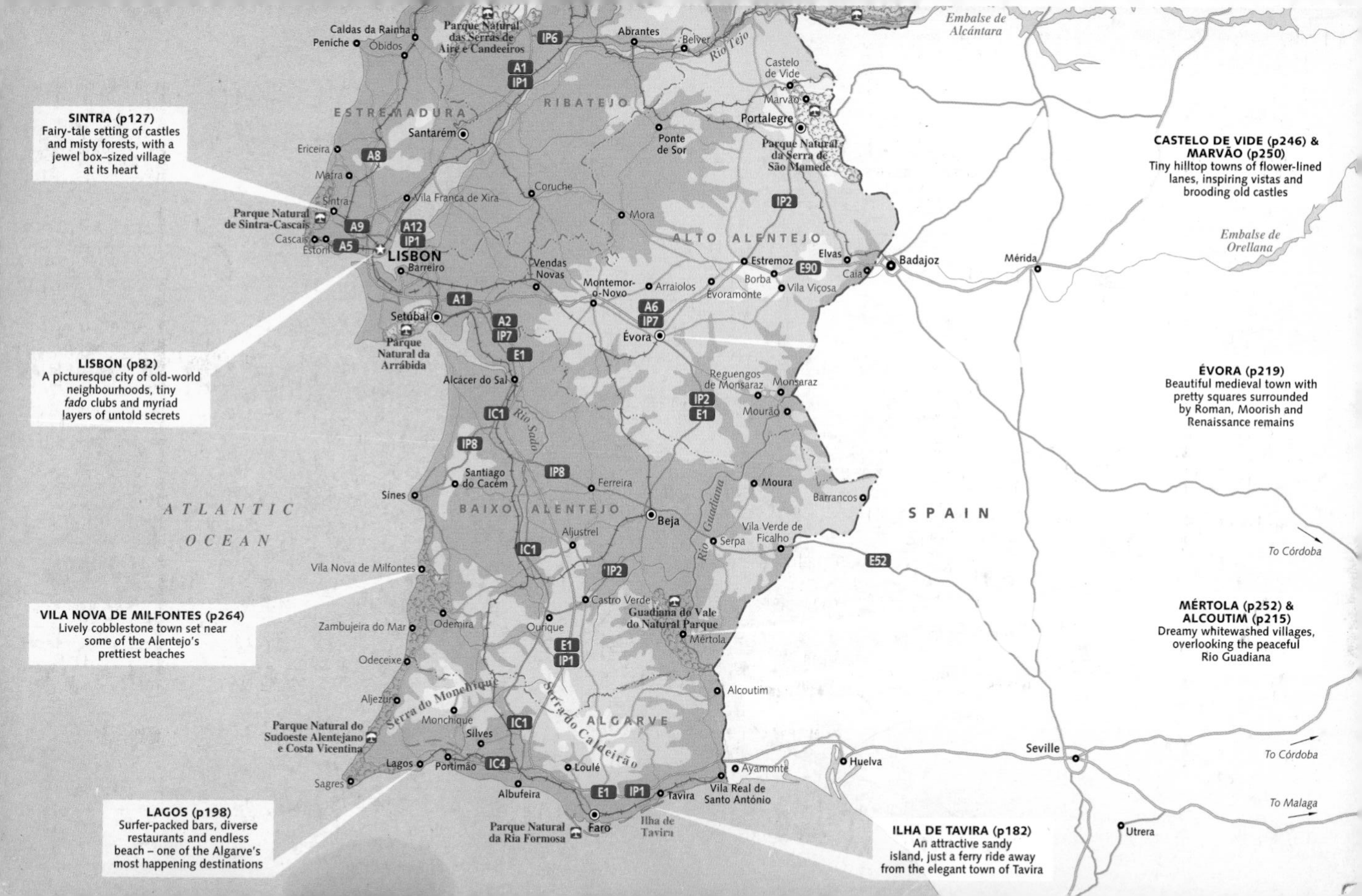

SINTRA (p127)
Fairy-tale setting of castles and misty forests, with a jewel box–sized village at its heart
LISBON (p82)
A picturesque city of old-world neighbourhoods, tiny *fado* clubs and myriad layers of untold secrets
VILA NOVA DE MILFONTES (p264)
Lively cobblestone town set near some of the Alentejo's prettiest beaches
LAGOS (p198)
Surfer-packed bars, diverse restaurants and endless beach – one of the Algarve's most happening destinations
ILHA DE TAVIRA (p182)
An attractive sandy island, just a ferry ride away from the elegant town of Tavira
MÉRTOLA (p252) & ALCOUTIM (p215)
Dreamy whitewashed villages, overlooking the peaceful Rio Guadiana
ÉVORA (p219)
Beautiful medieval town with pretty squares surrounded by Roman, Moorish and Renaissance remains
CASTELO DE VIDE (p246) & MARVÃO (p250)
Tiny hilltop towns of flower-lined lanes, inspiring vistas and brooding old castles
ATLANTIC OCEAN
SPAIN
ESTREMADURA
RIBATEJO
ALTO ALENTEJO
BAIXO ALENTEJO
ALGARVE
Caldas da Rainha
Peniche
Óbidos
Parque Natural das Serras de Aire e Candeeiros
Abrantes
Belver
Rio Tejo
Castelo de Vide
Marvão
Portalegre
Parque Natural da Serra de São Mamede
Santarém
Ponte de Sor
Ericeira
Mafra
Sintra
Parque Natural de Sintra-Cascais
Cascais
Estoril
LISBON
Barreiro
Vila Franca de Xira
Coruche
Mora
Vendas Novas
Montemor-o-Novo
Arraiolos
Évoramonte
Estremoz
Borba
Vila Viçosa
Elvas
Caia
Badajoz
Mérida
Embalse de Alcántara
Embalse de Orellana
Setúbal
Parque Natural da Arrábida
Évora
Alcácer do Sal
Reguengos de Monsaraz
Monsaraz
Mourão
Rio Sado
Santiago do Cacém
Ferreira
Moura
Barrancos
Sines
Beja
Aljustrel
Serpa
Vila Verde de Ficalho
Rio Guadiana
Vila Nova de Milfontes
Castro Verde
Guadiana do Vale do Natural Parque
Odemira
Ourique
Mértola
Zambujeira do Mar
Odeceixe
Alcoutim
Aljezur
Serra do Monchique
Monchique
Serra do Caldeirão
Parque Natural do Sudoeste Alentejano e Costa Vicentina
Silves
Lagos
Portimão
Loulé
Ayamonte
Huelva
Seville
Sagres
Albufeira
Vila Real de Santo António
Tavira
Faro
Ilha de Tavira
Parque Natural da Ria Formosa
Utrera
To Córdoba
To Córdoba
To Malaga
A1
A2
A5
A6
A8
A9
A12
IP1
IP2
IP6
IP7
IP8
IC1
IC4
E1
E52
E90

Destination Portugal

Tucked away in one of Europe's oft-overlooked corners, Portugal is a land of old-fashioned charm, where medieval castles and picture-perfect villages lie scattered over meandering coastlines and flower-covered hillsides. This nation of great explorers still clings to ancient traditions, from its deep connection to the sea, to its Roman-era vineyards. Meanwhile, laid-back cities and sun-kissed beaches offer enticements of a more modern sort.

Portugal's capital, Lisbon, and its northern rival, Porto, are gems among the urban streetscapes of Western Europe. Both are magical places for the wanderer, with riverside views, cobblestone streets and rattling trams framed by looming cathedrals. Narrow lanes hide old book and record stores, tiny boutiques and an eclectic mix of restaurants, bars and nightclubs, giving new life to the time-worn setting.

Outside the cities, rambling vineyards and groves of cork and olive roll off into the distance, towards jagged peaks in the north and gentler slopes in the south. Among such rural scenery, picturesque whitewashed villages slumber beneath the shadows of ancient fortresses, each providing a glimpse of the Portugal of centuries past.

Portugal's breathtaking shoreline has long enchanted visitors and locals alike. Stretching along the Atlantic are dramatic, end-of-the-world cliffs, wild dune-covered beaches, protected coves and long, sandy islands fronting calm blue seas.

While it's true that Portugal is no longer the Iberian Peninsula's best-kept secret, it's fairly easy to escape the crowds. Even at the busiest resorts in the Algarve, it only takes a short bus ride or a walk across countryside to reveal rarely visited places that still offer the feeling of discovery – a sentiment close to the Portuguese soul.

DAMIEN SIMON

Lisbon

GREG ELMS

Spoilt for choice: bar crawling in the Bairro Alto (p117)

GREG ELMS

Lose yourself in the medina-like maze of streets in the Alfama (p97); looming in the background is the Igreja de São Vicente de Fora, and on the right is the Panteão Nacional (National Pantheon)

Built to last: Lisbon's Romanesque *sé* (cathedral; p97), dating back to 1150

GREG ELMS

GREG ELMS

Feel the passion at the Alfama's Clube de Fado (p121)

Around Lisbon

A surfer sets up his next move at Praia do Guincho (p138), a prime surfing spot near Cascais

ANDERS BLOMQVIST

BETHUNE CARMICHAEL

Tormented by turrets: Sintra's highly romantic Palácio Nacional da Pena (p130)

The wildly extravagant Palácio Nacional de Mafra (p143) – the last word in decadence

ANDERS BLOMQVIS

The Algarve

PAUL BERNHARDT

Get an historical slant on Lagos (p198) as you walk through Moorish arches

JULIA WILKINSON

Enjoy a taste of local life at the *mercado municipal* in Tavira (p181)

Look out from stunning Praia de Beliche (p208) at the sheer cliffs of distant Cabo de São Vicente

ANDERS BLOMQVIST

Alentejo

ANDERS BLOMQVIST

Megaliths mingle at the Cromeleque dos Almendres (p230), west of Évora

ANDERS BLOMQVIST

Cork oak trees (p63) – keeping the Portuguese economy afloat

Flower-filled and castle-topped Marvão (p250) offers staggering views

ANDERS BLOMQVIST

ANDERS BLOMQVIST

Roman know-how lives on at the Templo Romano (p223), Évora

9

Estremadura & Ribatejo

The lean Gothic Mosteiro de Santa Maria de Alcobaça (p281), once known for its not-so-lean monks

ANDERS BLOMQVIST

ANDERS BLOMQVIST

Angels, saints, apostles and kings congregate in the western doorway of the Mosteiro de Santa Maria da Vitória (p283)

A pilgrim juggles candles in the basilica at Fátima (p289)

PAUL BERNHARDT

The Beiras

Make like a native at the outdoor cafés of Coimbra (p303)

ANDERS BLOMQVIST

MARTIN MOO

Study in style in the Biblioteca Joanina (João V Library; p307) of Coimbra's Velha Universidade (Old University)

Prepare to be floored by the elaborate mosaics in Conimbriga (p315)

JULIA WILKINSON

The Douro

BRENT WINEBRENNER

Medieval alleys with river views await in Porto's Ribeira district (p360), the city's historic heart

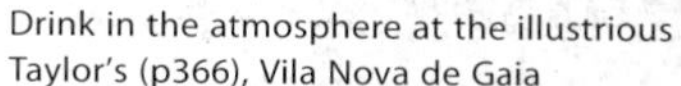

Drink in the atmosphere at the illustrious Taylor's (p366), Vila Nova de Gaia

ANDERS BLOMQVIST

MICHAEL GEBICKI

Tiled with style: Pinhão train station (p389) boasts impressive *azulejos* depicting wine harvesters at work

Far North

Only unmarried boys need apply: Festa dos Rapazes (p452), Trás-os-Montes

PAUL BERNHARDT

ANDERS BLOMQVIST

Decked out in Semana Santa (Holy Week) finery: Braga cathedral (p395), the country's oldest

ANDERS BLOMQVIST

Espigueiros (p424) in Parque Nacional da Peneda-Gerês: quirky corn-storage units

Contents

Regional Map Contents

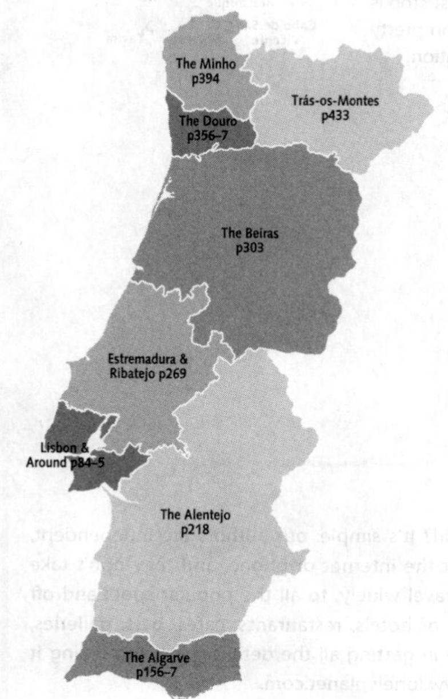

The Authors

REGIS ST LOUIS

Coordinating Author, Lisbon & Around, The Algarve, The Alentejo

A lover of wine, rugged coastlines and a bit of *bacalhau* (dried salt-cod), Regis was destined for a romance with small, irresistible Portugal when he first began exploring the country some years back. Favourite memories of his most recent trip include watching Portugal win surprise World Cup victories from village squares in the Alentejo, walking the empty country roads in the Serra de Monchique and discovering hidden beaches in the south. Regis has written many guidebooks, and his travel essays have appeared in the *Los Angeles Times* and the *San Francisco Chronicle*, among other publications. He lives in New York City.

My Favourite Trip

The journey begins in the Alfama (p97), where I soak up the sights and sounds of village life. Next is a meandering drive down the Alentejo coast, stopping at Vila Nova de Milfontes (p264) and taking dirt roads to some of Portugal's undiscovered shores. I make my way to easy-going Sagres (p206), a good base for seeing Cabo de São Vicente's end-of-the-world cliffs. Then I head to the hilly forests and sweeping views near Monchique (p213), and east to Tavira (p169) to dine at one of its excellent riverside restaurants. I follow Rio Guadiana north to Mértola (p252) for a swim in the river and a stroll through the enchanting fortress town. The last stop is Évora (p219), for good Alentejan cuisine, sunset drinks on pretty squares and plenty of historical lore to fuel my imagination.

LONELY PLANET AUTHORS

Why is our travel information the best in the world? It's simple: our authors are independent, dedicated travellers. They don't research using just the internet or phone, and they don't take freebies in exchange for positive coverage. They travel widely, to all the popular spots and off the beaten track. They personally visit thousands of hotels, restaurants, cafés, bars, galleries, palaces, museums and more – and they take pride in getting all the details right, and telling it how it is. For more, see the authors section on www.lonelyplanet.com.

ROBERT LANDON

Estramadura & Ribatejo, The Beiras, The Douro, The Minho, Trás-os-Montes

At 19, Robert spent a memorable week in Lisbon and the Algarve – his first, intoxicating experience as a solo traveller. Since then he has returned regularly to Portugal and has travelled (with and without company) throughout Portugal's far-flung former empire, including stays in Macau, Guinea-Bissau and Cape Verde as well as a year living in Rio de Janeiro and São Paulo. Writing has paid for most of his travels, with work appearing in the *San Jose Mercury-News*; Bloomberg.com; an early iteration of Travelocity; Paris' *Boulevard Magazine*; and countless other websites (most now defunct). He is the author of the Lonely Planet *Portuguese Phrasebook*. He currently lives in Berkeley, California.

CONTRIBUTING AUTHOR

Dr Caroline Evans wrote the Health chapter. Having studied medicine at the University of London, Caroline completed general practice training in Cambridge. She is the medical adviser to Nomad Travel Clinic, a private travel-health clinic in London, and is also a GP specialising in travel medicine. Caroline has acted as expedition doctor for Raleigh International and Coral Cay expeditions.

Getting Started

As prices rise all over Western Europe, Portugal takes your euro further, with lodging and dining to accommodate every budget. When planning a trip, keep in mind that from June to September, the holiday crowds arrive, and you'll need to book accommodation well in advance. Portugal has a good bus system and decent train system connecting major towns, but if you're heading to out-of-the-way places, renting a car will save you a lot of time; bus services die out on weekends in rural areas.

Other things to keep in mind: most museums close on Monday, and restaurants often close on Sunday.

WHEN TO GO

See Climate Charts (p457) for more information.

Portugal's high season runs from mid-June to mid-September, when temperatures across the country average around 27°C. In July and August it gets hot, particularly in the Algarve, the Alentejo and the upper Douro valley, where the mercury can climb to over 45°C.

If you'd rather skip the crowds (and the heat), consider a trip in spring, when the countryside is at its most verdant, or in autumn, when it's still warm but the summer crowds have dispersed. During winter (November to March) the rains arrive, falling most heavily in the north and most lightly in the south (the Algarve gets near year-round sunshine), with a handful of places closing down. Travelling then, however, will net you substantial savings at many hotels, and you'll see the country's most traditional side.

It's worth making a beeline for a Portuguese festival, particularly Carnaval in February or March, and Holy Week (the week before Easter) in March or April. Dates vary annually, so check with a turismo (tourist information office; p464).

COSTS & MONEY

HOW MUCH?

Meia de leite (coffee with milk) €0.80-1.20

Pastel de nata (custard tart) €0.80

Ceramic tile €2.50-100 or more

Lulas assadas (grilled squid) €7-10

Ticket to football €20-50

See also the Lonely Planet Index, inside front cover.

Portugal remains excellent value for money, whether you're travelling on the cheap or trying to spend your inheritance. If you're on a shoestring budget, you could get by on around €30 per day, as long as you camp (around €4 per person, plus a charge for your tent and car) or stay in youth hostels (€11 to €16 for a dorm bed), buy your own food and do free stuff such as lying on the beach. Travelling in the low season will help, too.

Many museums are free on certain days (often Sunday). Purchasing family tickets to attractions usually saves a few euros, and student or senior cards often get you discounts. In restaurants you can sometimes share a main course or order a *meia dose* (half serving). Drink promotions are prevalent in the Algarve, particularly during happy hour, making for a cheap night out. See p74 for more on food and drink.

Midrange travellers can expect to pay around €40 to €50 per person per day, while a cushier holiday with more-stylish digs and fancier meals and cocktails starts at around €90 per person per day.

TRAVEL LITERATURE

The Portuguese: The Land and Its People (2006), by Marion Kaplan, is an excellent one-volume introduction to the country, covering history, culture and other facets of Portuguese identity.

Lisbon: A Cultural and Literary Companion (2002), by Paul Buck, takes readers on a journey through some of Lisbon's well-known neighbourhoods, sharing curious anecdotes spanning the past 500 years or so.

TOP TENS

Books

Get under the Portuguese skin with these great reads (see p44 for more on these titles, authors and Portuguese literature in general):

- *Balada da Praia dos Cães* (Ballad of Dog's Beach) by José Cardoso Pires
- *Memorial do Convento* (Baltasar and Blimunda) by José Saramago
- *Deus Passeando Pela Brisa da Tarde* (A God Strolling in the Cool of an Evening) by Mario de Carvalho
- *A Ordem Natural das Coisas* (The Natural Order of Things) by António Lobo Antunes
- *Over the Edge of the World* by Laurence Bergreen
- *O Vale da Paixao* (The Painter of Birds) by Lídia Jorge
- *A Ilustre Casa de Ramires* (The Illustrious House of Ramires) by Eça de Queirós
- *A Small Death in Lisbon* by Robert Wilson
- *Contos da Montanha* (Tales from the Mountain) by Miguel Torga
- *O livro do Desasossego* (The Book of Disquiet) by Fernando Pessoa

Films

Go on a trip without leaving the sofa (these films and Portuguese cinema in general are covered on p46, unless otherwise noted):

- *Capitães de Abril* (April Captains)
- *The Convent*
- *Terra Estrangeira* (A Foreign Land)
- *Ganhar a Vida* (Get a Life)
- *A Lisbon Story* (p98)
- *Noite Escura* (In the Darkness of the Night)
- *O Delfim* (The Dauphin)
- *Ossos* (Bones)
- *Um Filme Falado* (A Talking Picture)
- *Porto da Minha Infância* (Porto of my Childhood)

Festivals & Events

There are plenty of ways to celebrate *a maneira Portuguesa* (Portuguese style).

- Carnaval, February or March, nationwide, but try Loulé (p186) or Nazaré (p280)
- Procissão do Senhor Ecce Homo, Holy Thursday (usually March or April), Braga (p398)
- Festa das Cruzes, May, Barcelos (p402)
- Festa de Santo António, June, Lisbon (p107)
- Festa de São João, June, Porto (p368) and Braga (p397)
- Super Bock Super Rock, July, Lisbon (p107)
- Évora Classical Music Festival, summer (p226)
- Festival do Sudoeste, summer, Zambujeira do Mar (p266)
- Sagres Surf Festival, August (p208)
- Feiras Novas, September, Ponte de Lima (p419)

DON'T LEAVE HOME WITHOUT...

You'll be able to find most essentials in Portugal, but it's worth packing certain things, to avoid hassle rather than anything else.

- A phrasebook will help both practically and socially.
- Sunscreen is widely available, but you can avoid paying high prices or trying to find some in a remote village on a Sunday if you take it with you. If you wear contacts, take enough lens-care solution.
- Sunglasses – again, you can buy them in many places (Lisbon has a sector of touts specialising in overpriced shades and fake hash) – but you may want some that suit you.
- Even if you're not dreaming of trekking, a compass can be useful for getting your bearings.
- Finally, you may want an umbrella if you're heading to the showery north.

Journey to Portugal: A Pursuit of Portugal's History and Culture (1981) is José Saramago's account of his travels in 1979. Unfortunately, the richly imaginative style found in the Nobel Prize winner's novels is surprisingly absent in these rather dull travel essays.

Stepping back in time, Fernando Pessoa's *Lisbon: What the Tourist Should See* (1925) portrays the many faces of the poet's home town, though it too can be a bit of a plod. A more successful work by a great writer is Almeida Garrett's *Travels in my Homeland* (1846), which is full of wry observations about Portugal but also touches on philosophy, poetry, nature and other Romantic-era topics.

Representing one of the country's many expat admirers is the work by 19th-century Gothic novelist William Beckford. He wrote a rollicking tale of his stay in Sintra and travels around Estremadura in *Journals and Recollections of an Excursion to the Monasteries of Alcobaça and Batalha* (1835).

INTERNET RESOURCES

Lifecooler (www.lifecooler.pt in Portuguese) Excellent for insider up-to-the-minute reviews, including restaurant, bar, club and hotel listings.

Lonely Planet (www.lonelyplanet.com) Where else would you go for damn fine travel information, links and advice from other travellers?

Plateia (www.plateia.iol.pt in Portuguese) Good for booking tickets (shows, sports) and for seeing what's on.

Portugal Tourism (www.visitportugal.pt) Portugal's official tourism site; includes tips on itineraries and upcoming events.

Portugal Virtual (www.portugalvirtual.pt) General information, and good hotel, restaurant and practical listings.

Itineraries
CLASSIC ROUTES

ALONG THE ATLANTIC COAST
One Week / Lisbon to Porto

Start in **Lisbon** (p82), making sure not to neglect café culture, *fado* (traditional, melancholic Portuguese singing) in the Alfama, or Bairro Alto's street parties. After this urban revelry, head north for a relaxing stay in the hillsides of **Sintra** (p127), then make your way to the hilltop village of **Óbidos** (p274). Next, drink in the heady architecture of **Alcobaça** (p281) and **Batalha** (p283). After all that culture, take a stroll along the coastal pinewood of **Pinhal de Leiria** (p288) before dropping in at the colourful university town of **Coimbra** (p303). From here, it's a day trip to Portugal's best-preserved Roman ruins – the mosaics at **Conimbriga** (p316). More sylvan scenery awaits on a walk to the go-for-baroque palace at **Buçaco** (p316), a prelude to the imposing sight of the castle **Montemor-o-Velho** (p322). Then, go north to **Porto** (p355), Lisbon's rival in beauty. Enjoy a night out on the town, then head across the river to **Vila Nova de Gaia** (p364), a dreamy spot for the port-wine lover. End with a boat trip along the **Rio Douro** (p368), taking in the dramatic gorge scenery.

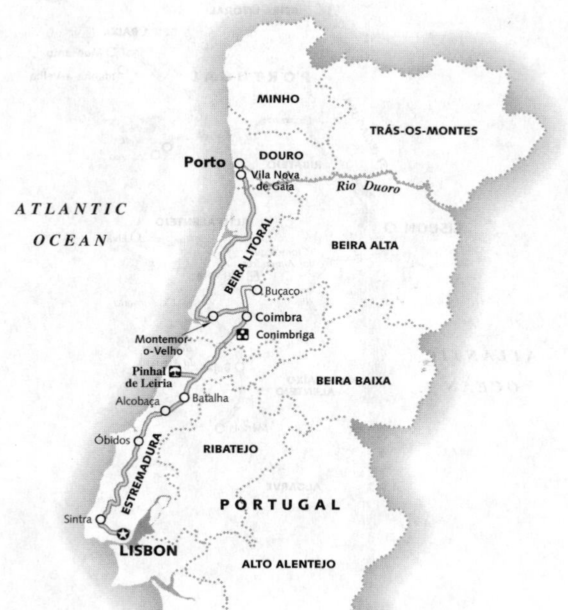

With detours along the way, it's around 355km from Lisbon to Porto. Frequent and inexpensive train connections link the towns, and there is also a decent bus service, which will be your main transport to the suggested stop-offs on the way.

VIEW FROM THE CASTLE

Two Weeks / Lisbon to Lisbon

The wondrous old Moorish castle atop **Lisbon** (p82) is an excellent starting point for this journey into Portugal's medieval history. After taking in the capital's fine panoramas, head northeast to **Monsanto** (p329), a fairy-tale village dating back to Visigoth times. From there stop off in neighbouring **Idanha-a-Velha** (p330), an extraordinary town with Roman and Visigoth roots and, like Monsanto, a fine castle. Head south to the Alto Alentejo's twin fortress hilltop towns of **Castelo de Vide** (p246) and **Marvão** (p250), the latter rising from a craggy peak.

The next stop is **Elvas** (p240), with its extraordinary zigzagging fortifications protecting narrow streets, only 14km from Spain. Its tiny size contrasts nicely with the pristine, walled town of Unesco-listed **Évora** (p219). Linger here for high culture, cathedral-gazing and Alentejan haute cuisine, and take a day trip out to see the striking Neolithic ruins – particularly the **Cromeleque dos Almendres** (p230), one of the most important megalithic sites on the Iberian Peninsula. After a bit of Stone Age musing, head to the magical hilltop village of **Monsaraz** (p232), overlooking ancient olive groves and land littered with yet more Neolithic sites. From there dip down to **Beja** (p256), the sedate, pretty capital of Baixo Alentejo, to access **Mértola** (p252), one of the Alentejo's most dramatic hilltop villages. An open-air museum with a Moorish legacy, it's set high above the meandering Rio Guadiana.

This route is around 850km. It's possible to cover it by public transport, though you'd spend a lot of time on buses, and transport to some of these remote towns is infrequent.

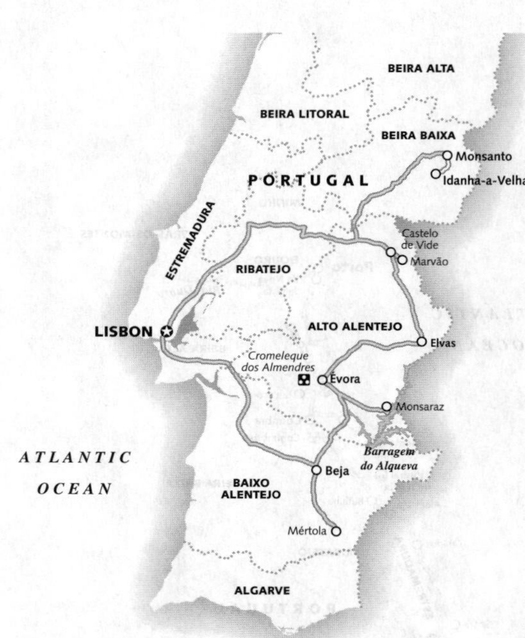

SOUTHERN BEAUTY

Two Weeks / Lisbon to Serpa

This trip will give you a chance to see spectacular contrasts in scenery by following Portugal's southern rivers, beaches and ridges. From **Lisbon** (p82) head to the **Costa da Caparica** (p145), going far south of the tourist hordes to wild, sparsely visited beaches. Next, stop in **Setúbal** (p147) for a seafood feast and a visit to the beautiful protected area of the **Parque Natural da Arrábida** (p152).

From here, it's up to the mountains of **Monchique** (p213), where you'll find densely wooded hills and the Algarve's highest point at 902m. Take advantage of the picturesque walking, biking and pony-trekking opportunities, followed by a spa visit in refreshing **Caldas de Monchique** (p214).

From here you can dive back down to the coast, heading west to the surreal cliffs of **Cabo de São Vicente** (p207), with an overnight in the laid-back beach town of **Sagres** (p206).

Go straight east along the coast to **Faro** (p158), where you can take in its fine medieval centre before journeying out to the lush **Parque Natural da Ria Formosa** (p167), a lagoon system full of marsh, creeks, dune islands and the wetland birds that live there. From there, head to **Tavira** (p169), set with genteel 18th-century buildings straddling the Rio Gilão. This picturesque river town is a fine base for a boat trip across to the peaceful, sandy **Ilha de Tavira** (p182).

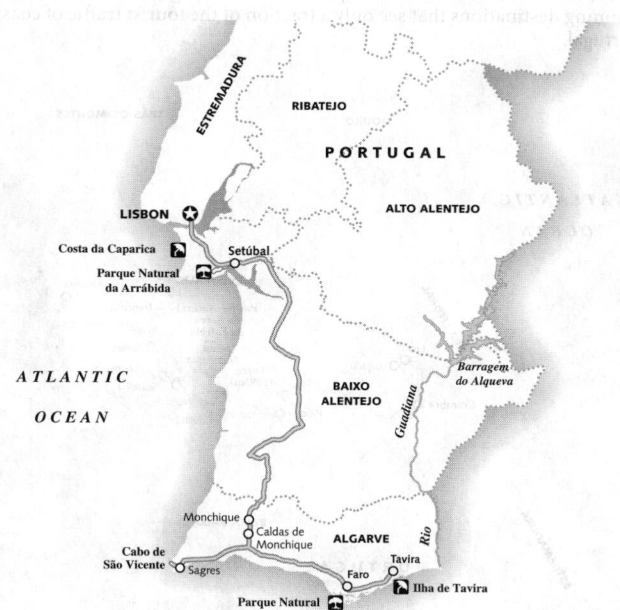

This route is around 340km, and can be done largely on public transport, though you'll be able to explore more-remote regions and less-travelled coastline if you hire a car.

ROADS LESS TRAVELLED

BLAZING THE BEIRA BAIXA Two to Three Weeks / Coimbra to Sortelha

This highly rewarding trip through the Beira Baixa takes you past striking scenery with plenty of opportunity for outdoor adventure and leaves the crowds far behind – the deeper you delve, the fewer travellers you'll see. Start your foray from **Coimbra** (p303), soaking up the sights before hitting the photographer's paradise and royal retreat and spa of **Luso** and **Buçaco** (both p316).

From here you'll lose the crowds by breaking west to pristine rural idylls such as **Piódão** (p318), or any of the traditional hamlets and villages in the beautiful **Parque Natural da Serra da Estrela** (p332), packed with exquisite scenery, outdoor pursuits and Portugal's highest point – **Torre** (p339), also home to the country's only ski resort. Base yourself bang in the middle at **Manteigas** (p337) to give you the run of the whole mountain range; afterwards, visit beautiful **Belmonte** (p349), a hill town that overlooks the Serra da Estrela and has a fascinating secret history.

You could start the descent from these heady heights via the chilly highland towns of **Covilhã** (p340) or **Guarda** (p347), and then head up north to **Trancoso** (p350), a perfectly preserved medieval walled town.

Other fabulous castles and fortified towns you can visit in the lowland Beiras include northern **Almeida** (p352) and far-flung **Sortelha** (p331), both stunning destinations that see only a fraction of the tourist traffic of coastal Portugal.

This trip has some of Portugal's most spectacular scenery and sights, but a severe dearth of public transport. With your own wheels you could whiz around this 410km path in two weeks, but relying on buses, you'd have to skip the more remote villages.

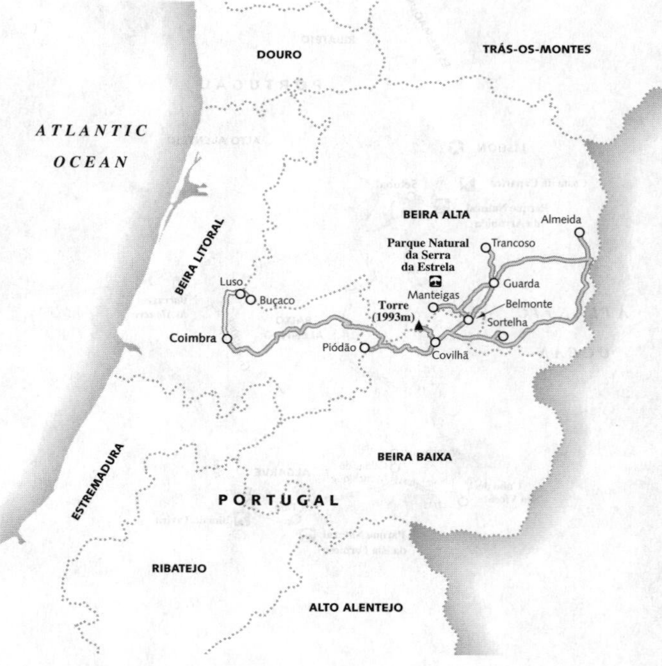

MEANDERINGS IN THE MINHO

Two to Three Weeks / Porto to Porto

Portugal's oft-ignored northern region makes a great destination for outdoor adventures, as well as exploring colourful markets or catching a lively festival. From **Porto** (p355), head up the coast to the north's festival capital – folklore-rich **Viana do Castelo** (p409), which is also just a short ferry ride from the north's best beaches. Continue north to the border fortresses of **Valença do Minho** (p413), taking a good long gaze at the Spaniards on the other side of the river.

From here, travel south to charming backwater **Ponte de Lima** (p416), and its picture-book Roman bridge. Nearby **Ponte da Barca** (p420) is a springboard to the remote villages of **Soajo** (p425) and **Lindoso** (p426), little changed for centuries.

From **Braga** (p394), the spiritual epicentre of Portugal, you could head back up north, into eastern **Parque Nacional da Peneda-Gerês** (p422), to spa town **Vila do Gerês** (p427) and nearby spots for canoeing, mountain biking and fantastic hiking. Alternatively, if you're passing on a Thursday – head the short distance west to **Barcelos** (p401) to catch its famous midweek market.

Back in Braga, head down south via the pilgrimage site of **Bom Jesus do Monte** (p400) and Celtic ruins at **Citânia de Briteiros** (p408) to the cradle of the nation in history-rich **Guimarães** (p404).

For a refreshing dose of greenery, stop in the small but enchanting **Parque Natural do Alvão** (p436), which has spectacular waterfalls and 800-year-old traditional villages. Nearby stands picturesque **Amarante** (p379), famous for its monastery and phallic cakes. Check out Vila Real's must-see **Palácio de Mateus** (p434), then it's back to Porto, squeezing in a river cruise from **Peso da Régua** (p387) and a quick trip down to **Lamego** (p383).

Apart from remote corners of the national parks, this route isn't difficult to traverse by public transport. Completing the whole 550km loop will take a long two weeks, or a leisurely three if you want to linger in Peneda-Gerês.

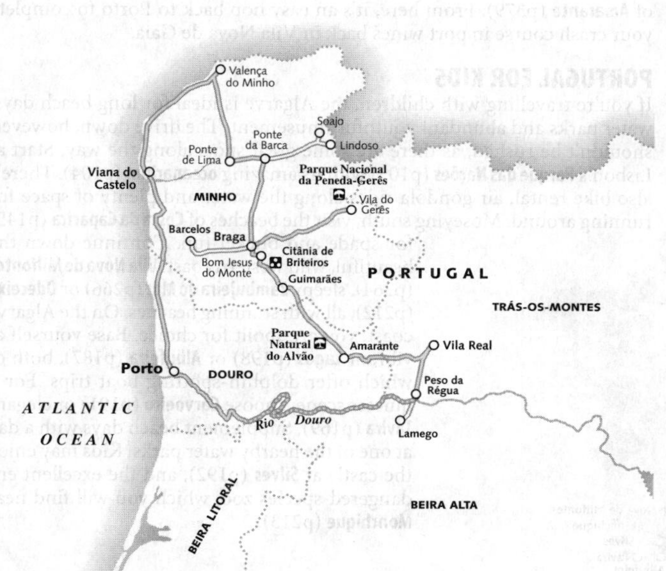

TAILORED TRIPS

A VITICULTURAL VOYAGE

Oenophiles have much to look forward to on a leisurely journey through the north, Portugal's premier wine-growing region. How quickly you cover this 360km route depends on how much imbibing you plan to do along the way. You can cover the distance in just over a week, but you may want to linger at some of the delightful guesthouses and rural manors along the way.

Any self-respecting port-wine tour will probably begin and end in **Porto** (p355) at the mouth of the Rio Douro, the heart of the world's best port-wine region. Across the river from the city is **Vila Nova de Gaia** (p364). Packed with port-wine lodges, this is an excellent place to sample the goods and has fine views to the city.

After preliminary tastes, it's time to journey up the wine's ancient highway, on a river cruise up the Douro valley to **Peso da Régua** (p387) and beyond to the very heart of vineyard country, the tiny village of **Pinhão** (p389). Asking locally will give you any number of different vineyards and *adegas* (wine cellars) to visit.

While in the vicinity, don't miss **Lamego** (p383), which is surrounded by beautiful architecture and is home to one of Portugal's few sparkling wines. You could also stop in **Vila Real** (p433), erstwhile home of its eponymous rosé wine.

Returning along the Douro, catch the train back as far as Livração and change to the Linha da Tâmega narrow-gauge train up to the historic town of **Amarante** (p379). From here, it's an easy hop back to Porto to complete your crash course in port wines back in Vila Nova de Gaia.

PORTUGAL FOR KIDS

If you're travelling with children, the Algarve is ideal for long beach days, water parks and abundant youthful amusement. The drive down, however, shouldn't be rushed, as there are some great spots along the way. Start at Lisbon's **Parque das Nações** (p103) with its amazing **oceanarium** (p104). There's also bike rental, air gondola rides along the water and plenty of space for running around. Moseying south, visit the beaches of **Costa da Caparica** (p145) for spade and bucket fun. Continue down the beautiful, wild western coast: **Vila Nova de Milfontes** (p264), sleepy **Zambujeira do Mar** (p266) or **Odeceixe** (p212), all with stunning beaches. On the Algarve coast, you are spoilt for choice. Base yourself at vibrant **Lagos** (p198) or **Albufeira** (p187), both of which offer dolphin-spotting boat trips. For a quieter scene, choose **Carvoeiro** (p191) or elegant **Tavira** (p169). Supplement beach days with a day at one of the nearby water parks. Kids may enjoy the castle at **Silves** (p192), and the excellent endangered-species zoo, which you will find near **Monchique** (p213).

Snapshot

Portugal has come a long way in the last three decades. It's hard to believe that in 1974 this small, peaceful country had tanks rolling through the streets and a people on the edge of revolution, having just waved goodbye to Western Europe's last dictatorship.

How far Portugal has come economically is even more startling given the shambles the economy was in when António de Oliveira Salazar's regime was toppled (as a marker, Portugal's GDP currently stands at 70% of the EU average, compared to 53% in 1986 when it joined the European Community). The end of Salazar was the dawn of a boom time for the country not only economically, but also socially and politically.

However, the days of abundance ended in 2000, and by 2006 Portugal was still in the grip of a five-year-long economic slump. The dispiriting statistics show six straight years of rising unemployment, with very little (or sometimes negative) annual growth, and a ballooning budget deficit, signalling alarm bells elsewhere in the EU.

FAST FACTS

Population: 10.6 million

GDP: US$19,300

Inflation: 2.6%

Unemployment rate: 7.6%

Bottles of wine produced per annum: 750 million

Per capita olive-oil consumption per annum: 7.1kg

Global events, particularly the disastrous war in Iraq, no doubt affected the economy. In a 12-month period from 2005 to 2006, prices rose considerably. Petrol shot up 37% and mortgage rates skyrocketed, in some cases rising by 28%. The costs of public transport and natural gas were both on the rise.

For much of the population, the government has seemed obsessively focused on addressing budget deficits rather than social concerns. The Portuguese president of the Anti-Poverty League, Father Jardim Moreira, has spoken out against the seeming indifference to Portugal's most disadvantaged (20% live below the poverty line), describing the distribution of wealth as 'scandalous'. 'While Ireland invests in education, Portugal invests in concrete,' he says.

The effects of poverty, inflation and rising costs have certainly taken their toll on the country's outlook. In a 2006 poll, 44% of respondents said the family budget was getting tighter, 57% said that the education system was deteriorating, and 34% said that the health system was inadequate. In another recent poll – this one done throughout the EU and in the US – only 3% of Portuguese surveyed said they were very satisfied with their lives, compared with 44% in Sweden and 58% in the US. Only 28% of Portuguese surveyed felt their life had improved in the last five years, compared with Spain's 46% and Ireland's whopping 63%. Yet in the final question of the survey – do you feel optimistic about life improving in the future? – half of Portuguese respondents answered yes, placing them among the top five countries (but still below the US, Ireland and the UK).

Optimism indeed hasn't been crushed despite the damning figures. Portugal and Spain, once former enemies, have grown closer in their old age, and in 2006 were entering new phases of trade and cooperation (Spain is Portugal's biggest trading partner, and has fared far better economically than its neighbour during the last five years). Public environmental awareness is growing. In 2006 recycling was up by 18% from the year before. Even bigger news was the start of construction of the new €58 million solar-power station in the Alentejo. When completed in 2007, the station will be the world's largest, bringing electricity to 8000 homes, and saving an estimated 30 tonnes of carbon dioxide emissions (around 1% of the country's current emissions).

On other fronts, Portugal surprised millions with its unprecedented appearance in the quarterfinals of the 2006 World Cup. Whether the country can approach its social and economic woes with the same verve will be a defining issue in years to come.

History

PRE-ROMAN & ROMAN ERAS

The Iberian Peninsula has been inhabited for at least 30,000 years. If you want to see the earliest evidence of human habitation in Portugal, check out the ancient Palaeolithic inscriptions near Vila Nova de Foz Côa in the Alto Douro (p390). For Neolithic ghosts, head for the atmospheric fortified hilltop settlements, dating from 5500 BC, in the lower Tejo (Tagus) valley.

Portugal: A Traveller's History (2004), by Harold Livermore, is an entertaining but scholarly history that explores some of the richer episodes from the past – taking in cave paintings, vineyards and music, among other topics.

In the first millennium BC Celtic people started trickling into the Iberian Peninsula, settling northern and western Portugal around 700 BC. Dozens of *citânias* (fortified villages) popped up, such as the formidable Citânia de Briteiros (p408). Further south, Phoenician traders, followed by Greeks and Carthaginians, founded coastal stations and mined metals inland.

When the Romans swept into southern Portugal in 210 BC, they expected an easy victory. But they hadn't reckoned on the Lusitani, a Celtic warrior tribe based between the Rio Tejo and Rio Douro that resisted ferociously for half a century. Unable to subjugate the Lusitani, the Romans offered peace instead and began negotiations with Viriato, the Lusitanian leader. Unfortunately for Viriato and his underlings, the peace offer was a ruse, and Roman agents, posing as intermediaries, poisoned him. Resistance collapsed following Viriato's death in 139 BC.

By 19 BC the Romans had eliminated all traces of Lusitanian independence. A capital was established at Olisipo (Lisbon) in 60 BC, and Christianity became firmly rooted in Portugal during the 3rd century AD. For a vivid glimpse into Roman Portugal, you won't see a better site than Conimbriga (p315), near Coimbra, or the monumental remains of the so-called Temple of Diana (p223), in Évora.

By the 5th century, when the Roman Empire had all but collapsed, Portugal's inhabitants had been under Roman rule for 600 years. So what did the Romans ever do for them? Most usefully, they built roads and bridges. But they also brought wheat, barley, olives and vines; large farming estates called *latifúndios* (still found in the Alentejo); a legal system; and, above all, a Latin-derived language. In fact, no other invader proved so useful.

The First Global Village (2002), by Martin Page, is a compact and fascinating survey of Portuguese history from the Romans up to the Revolution of the Carnations.

MOORS & CHRISTIANS

The gap left by the Romans was filled by barbarian invaders from beyond the Pyrenees: Vandals, Alans, Visigoths and Suevi, with Arian Christian Visigoths gaining the upper hand in 469.

Internal Visigothic disputes paved the way for Portugal's next great wave of invaders, the Moors – North African Muslims invited in 711 to help a Visigothic faction. They quickly occupied large chunks of Portugal's southern coast.

Southerners enjoyed peace and productivity under the Moors, who established a capital at Shelb (Silves). The new rulers were tolerant of Jews and Christians. Christian smallholding farmers, called Mozarabs, could keep their land and were encouraged to try new methods and crops, especially citrus and rice. Arabic words filtered into the Portuguese language, such as *alface* (lettuce), *arroz* (rice) and dozens of place names (including Fatima,

TIMELINE

22,000 BC
A gallery of Palaeolithic art is carved on rocks in the Alto Douro

5500 BC
Neolithic fortified hilltop settlements appear in the lower Tejo (Tagus) valley

Silves and Algarve – the latter stemming from the Arabic El-Gharb ('the west') – and locals became addicted to Moorish sweets.

Meanwhile in the north, Christian forces were gaining strength and reached as far as Porto in 868. But it was in the 11th century that the Reconquista (Christian reconquest) hotted up. In 1064 Coimbra was taken and, in 1085, Alfonso VI thrashed the Moors in their Spanish heartland of Toledo; he is said to have secured Seville by winning a game of chess with its emir. But in the following year, Alfonso's men were driven out by ruthless Moroccan Almoravids who answered the emir's distress call.

Alfonso cried for help and European crusaders came running – rallying against the 'infidels'. With the help of Henri of Burgundy, among others, Alfonso made decisive moves towards victory. The struggle continued in successive generations, and by 1139 Afonso Henriques (grandson of Alfonso VI) won such a dramatic victory against the Moors at Ourique (Alentejo) that he named himself Dom – King of Portugal – a title confirmed in 1179 by the pope (after extra tribute was paid, naturally). He also retook Santarém and Lisbon from the Moors.

By the time he died in 1185, the Portuguese frontier was secure to the Rio Tejo, though it would take another century before the south was torn from the Moors.

In 1297 the boundaries of the Portuguese kingdom – much the same then as they are today – were formalised with neighbouring Castile. The kingdom of Portugal had arrived.

The Contemporary Portuguese Political History Research Centre's website (www.cphrc.org.uk) is a great resource – if a tad dense for bedtime reading.

THE BURGUNDIAN ERA

During the Reconquista, people faced more than just war and turmoil: in the wake of Christian victories came new rulers and settlers.

The Church and its wealthy clergy were the greediest landowners, followed by aristocratic fat cats. Though theoretically free, most common people remained subjects of the landowning class, with few rights. The first hint of democratic rule came with the establishment of the *cortes* (parliament). This assembly of nobles and clergy first met in 1211 at Coimbra, the then capital. Six years later, the capital moved to Lisbon.

Afonso III (r 1248–79) deserves credit for standing up to the Church, but it was his son the 'Poet King' Dinis (r 1279–1325) who really shook Portugal into shape. A far-sighted, cultured man, he took control of the judicial system, started progressive afforestation programmes and encouraged internal trade. He suppressed the dangerously powerful military order of the Knights Templar, refounding them as the Order of Christ (p298). He cultivated music, the arts and education, and founded a university in Lisbon in 1290, which was later transferred to Coimbra (p307).

Dom Dinis' foresight was spot-on when it came to defence: he built or rebuilt some 50 fortresses along the eastern frontier with Castile, and signed a pact of friendship with England in 1308, the basis for a future long-lasting alliance.

It was none too soon. Within 60 years of Dinis' death, Portugal was at war with Castile. Fernando I helped provoke the clash by playing a game of alliances with both Castile and the English. He dangled promises of marriage to his daughter Beatriz in front of both nations, eventually marrying her off to Juan I of Castile, and thus throwing Portugal's future into Castilian hands.

210–139 BC

Invading Romans face fierce resistance by Lusitani, but eventually win through treachery

AD 400–500

The Roman Empire crumbles, making way for the Vandals, Alans, Visigoths and Suevi

On Fernando's death in 1383, his wife, Leonor Teles, ruled as regent. But she too was entangled with the Spanish, having long had a Galician lover. The merchant classes preferred unsullied Portuguese candidate João, son (albeit illegitimate) of Fernando's father. João assassinated Leonor's lover, Leonor fled to Castile and the Castilians duly invaded.

The showdown came in 1385 when João faced a mighty force of Castilians at Aljubarrota. Even with Nuno Álvares Pereira (the Holy Constable) as his military right-hand man and English archers at the ready, the odds were stacked against him. João vowed to build a monastery if he won – and he did. Nuno Álvares, the brilliant commander-in-chief of the Portuguese troops, deserves much of the credit for the victory. He lured Spanish cavalry into a trap and, with an uphill advantage, his troops decimated the invaders. Within a few hours the Spanish were retreating in disarray and the battle was won.

An ambitious and beautiful romance novel, *Distant Music* (2003), by Lee Langley, spans no less than six centuries of Portugal's history since 1429, not to mention different classes and diverse regions.

The victory clinched independence and João made good his vow with Batalha's stunning Mosteiro de Santa Maria da Vitória (aka the Mosteiro da Batalha or Battle Abbey; p283). It also sealed Portugal's alliance with England, and João wed John of Gaunt's daughter. Peace was finally concluded in 1411.

THE AGE OF DISCOVERIES

João's success had whetted his appetite and, spurred on by his sons, he soon turned his military energies abroad. Morocco was the obvious target, and in 1415 Ceuta fell easily to his forces. It was a turning point in Portuguese history, a first step into its golden age.

It was João's third son, Henry, who focused the spirit of the age – a combination of crusading zeal, love of martial glory and lust for gold – into extraordinary explorations across the seas. These explorations were to transform the small kingdom into a great imperial power

The biggest breakthrough came in 1497 during the reign of Manuel I, when Vasco da Gama reached southern India. With gold and slaves from Africa and spices from the East, Portugal was soon rolling in riches. Manuel I was so thrilled by the discoveries (and resultant cash injection) that he ordered a frenzied building spree in celebration. Top of his list was the extravagant Mosteiro dos Jerónimos in Belém (p102), later to become his pantheon. Another brief boost to the Portuguese economy at this time came courtesy of an influx of around 150,000 financially savvy Jews expelled from Spain in 1492.

Spain, however, had also jumped on the exploration bandwagon and was soon disputing Portuguese claims. Christopher Columbus' 1492 'discovery' of America for Spain led to a fresh outburst of jealous conflict. It was resolved by the pope in the bizarre 1494 Treaty of Tordesillas, by which the world was divided between the two great powers along a line 370 leagues west of the Cape Verde islands. Portugal won the lands to the east of the line, including Brazil, officially claimed in 1500.

The rivalry spurred the first circumnavigation of the world. In 1519 the Portuguese navigator Fernão Magalhães (Ferdinand Magellan), his allegiance transferred to Spain after a tiff with Manuel I, set off in an effort to prove that the Spice Islands (today's Moluccas) lay in Spanish 'territory'. He reached the Philippines in 1521 but was killed in a skirmish there. One of his five ships, under the Basque navigator Juan Sebastián Elcano, reached the Spice Islands and then sailed home via the Cape of Good Hope, proving the earth was round.

711 The Moors arrive and camp out on the southern coast, remaining for another 500 years

1139 Afonso Henriques declares himself first king of Portugal

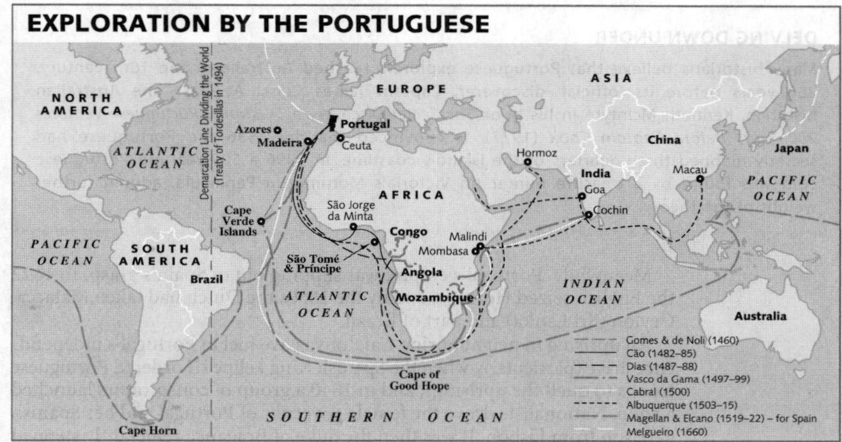

As its explorers reached Timor, China and eventually Japan, Portugal cemented its power with garrison ports and trading posts. The monarchy, taking its 'royal fifth' of profits, became stinking rich – indeed the wealthiest monarchy in Europe, and the lavish Manueline architectural style symbolised the exuberance of the age.

It couldn't last, of course. By the 1570s the huge cost of expeditions and maintaining an empire was taking its toll. The expulsion of commercially minded refugee Spanish Jews in 1496 and the subsequent persecution of converted Jews (*marranos*, or New Christians) during the Inquisition, which began in the 16th century under João III, only worsened the financial situation.

The Portuguese were the first Westerners to reach Japan in 1543. They founded Nagasaki, introduced the mosquito net and brought new words to the language, including *pan* (bread) and *arrigato* (thank you).

The final straw came in 1557, when young idealistic Prince Sebastião took the throne, determined to take Christianity to Morocco. He rallied an 18,000-strong force and set sail from Lagos only to be disastrously defeated at the Battle of Alcácer-Quibir. Sebastião and 8000 others were killed, including much of the Portuguese nobility. His aged successor, Cardinal Henrique, drained the royal coffers ransoming those captured.

On Henrique's death in 1580, Sebastião's uncle, Felipe II of Spain (Felipe I of Portugal), fought for and won the throne. This marked the end of centuries of independence, Portugal's golden age and its glorious moment on the world stage.

SPAIN'S RULE & PORTUGAL'S REVIVAL

Spanish rule began promisingly, with Felipe vowing to preserve Portugal's autonomy and attend the long-ignored parliament. But commoners resented Spanish rule and held on to the dream that Sebastião was still alive (as he was killed abroad in battle in Morocco, some citizens were in denial); pretenders continued to pop up until 1600. Though Felipe was honourable, his successors proved to be considerably less so, using Portugal to raise money and soldiers for Spain's wars overseas, and appointing Spaniards to govern Portugal.

1297
The Moors are driven from Portugal, and the kingdom of Portugal is complete

1385
João defeats the Castilians at Aljubarrota, sealing Portugal's independence and alliance with England

DELVING DOWN UNDER

Many historians believe that Portuguese explorers reached Australia in the 16th century, 250 years before its 'official' discoverer, Captain James Cook. At least one Australian historian, Kenneth McIntyre in his book *The Secret Discovery of Australia: Portuguese Ventures 200 Years Before Captain Cook* (1977), is convinced that by 1536 the Portuguese had secretly mapped three-quarters of the island's coastline. In 1996 a 500-year-old Portuguese coin was found by a treasure hunter on Victoria's Mornington Peninsula, adding further weight to the theory.

Meanwhile, Portugal's empire was slipping out of Spain's grasp. In 1622 the English seized Hormoz, and by the 1650s the Dutch had taken Malacca, Ceylon (Sri Lanka) and part of Brazil.

An uprising in neighbouring Catalunya gave fuel to Portugal's independence drive (particularly when the Spanish King Felipe III ordered Portuguese troops to quell the uprising), and in 1640 a group of conspirators launched a coup. Nationalists drove the female governor of Portugal and her Spanish garrison from Lisbon. It was then the duke of Bragança reluctantly stepped forward and was crowned João IV.

With a hostile Spain breathing down its neck, Portugal searched for allies. Two swift treaties with England led to Charles II's marriage to João's daughter, Catherine of Bragança, and the ceding of Tangier and Bombay to England.

In return the English promised arms and soldiers: however, a preoccupied Spain made only half-hearted attempts to recapture Portugal, and recognised Portuguese independence in 1668.

The Portuguese were the first Westerners to reach Japan in 1543. They founded Nagasaki, introduced the mosquito net and brought new words to the language, including pan (bread) and arigato (thank you).

Moves towards democracy now stalled under João's successors. The Crown hardly bothered with parliament, and another era of profligate expenditure followed, giving birth to projects like the wildly extravagant monastery-palace in Mafra (see p143).

Into the ensuing economic chaos of the 18th century stepped a man for the moment – the Marquês de Pombal, chief minister to the epicurean Dom José I (the latter more interested in opera than affairs of state). Described as an enlightened despot, Pombal dragged Portugal into the modern era, crushing opposition with brutal efficiency.

Pombal set up state monopolies, curbed the power of British merchants and boosted agriculture and industry. He abolished slavery and distinctions between traditional and New Christians, and overhauled education.

When Lisbon suffered a devastating earthquake in 1755 (see p83), Pombal swiftly rebuilt the city. He was by then at the height of his power, and succeeded in dispensing with his main enemies by implicating them in an attempt on the king's life.

He might have continued had it not been for the accession of the devout Dona Maria I in 1777. The anticlerical Pombal was promptly sacked, tried and charged with various offences, though never imprisoned. While his religious legislation was repealed, his economic, agricultural and educational policies were largely maintained, helping the country back towards prosperity.

But turmoil was once again on the horizon, as Napoleon swept through Europe.

1415
Prince Henry the Navigator kicks off the seaborne Portuguese Age of Discoveries

1487
Pêro da Covilhã, master spy, heads off to discover India, paving the way for Vasco da Gama's epic voyage

THE DAWN OF A REPUBLIC

In 1793 Portugal found itself at war again when it joined England in sending naval forces against revolutionary France. Before long, Napoleon threw Portugal an ultimatum: close your ports to British shipping or be invaded.

There was no way Portugal could turn its back on Britain, upon which it depended for half of its trade and protection of its sea routes. In 1807 Portugal's royal family fled to Brazil (where it stayed for 14 years), and Napoleon's forces marched into Lisbon, sweeping Portugal into the Peninsular War (France's invasion of Spain and Portugal, which lasted until 1814).

To the rescue came Sir Arthur Wellesley (later Duke of Wellington), Viscount Beresford and their seasoned British troops, who eventually drove the French back across the Spanish border in 1811.

Free but weakened, Portugal was administered by Beresford while the royals dallied in Brazil. In 1810 Portugal lost a profitable intermediary role by giving Britain the right to trade directly with Brazil. The next humiliation was João's 1815 proclamation of Brazil as a kingdom united with Portugal – he did this to bring more wealth and prestige to Brazil (which he was growing to love) and in turn to him and the rest of the royal family residing there. With soaring debts and dismal trade, Portugal was at one of the lowest points in its history, reduced to a de facto colony of Brazil and a protectorate of Britain.

The Last Kabbalist of Lisbon (2000), by Richard Zimler, is a thriller cast as a long-lost manuscript about the murder of a 16th-century Jewish mystic. It reveals the harrowing life of secret Jews during Portugal's Inquisition.

Meanwhile, resentment simmered in the army. Rebel officers quietly convened parliament and drew up a new liberal constitution. Based on Enlightenment ideals, it abolished many rights of the nobility and clergy, and instituted a single-chamber parliament.

Faced with this *fait accompli*, João returned and accepted its terms – though his wife and son Miguel were bitterly opposed to it. João's elder son, Pedro, had other ideas: left behind to govern Brazil, he snubbed the constitutionalists by declaring Brazil independent in 1822 and himself its emperor. When João died in 1826, the stage was set for civil war.

Offered the crown, Pedro dashed out a new, less liberal charter and then abdicated in favour of his seven-year-old daughter Maria, provided she marry uncle Miguel and provided uncle Miguel accept the new constitution. Sure enough, Miguel took the oath, but promptly abolished Pedro's charter and proclaimed himself king. A livid Pedro rallied the equally furious Liberals and forced Miguel to surrender at Évoramonte in 1834.

After Pedro's death, his daughter Maria, now Queen of Portugal at just 15, kept his flame alive with fanatical support of his 1826 charter. The radical supporters of the liberal 1822 constitution grew vociferous over the next two decades, bringing the country to the brink of civil war. The Duke of Saldanha, however, saved the day, negotiating a peace that toned down Pedro's charter, while still radically modernising Portugal's infrastructure.

The latter half of the 19th century was a remarkable period for Portugal, and it became known as one of the most advanced societies in southern Europe. Casual visitors to Lisbon like Hans Christian Andersen were surprised to find tree-lined boulevards lined with gas-lit street lamps, efficient trams and well-dressed residents. Social advances were even less anecdotal. The educational reformer João Arroio dramatically increased the number of schools, doubling the number of boys' schools and quadrupling the number of girls' schools. Women gained the right to own property; slavery was abolished throughout the Portuguese empire, as was the death penalty; and

1580–1640
The Spanish seize the throne, ending the Portuguese golden age

1755
Lisbon is levelled: three major earthquakes, followed by fire and a tsunami, kill thousands

even the prison system received an overhaul – prisoners were taught useful trades while in jail so they could integrate into society upon their release.

Professional organizations, such as the Literary Guild, emerged and became a major impetus to the advancement of ideas in public discourse, inspiring debate in politics, religious life and the art world.

As elsewhere in Europe, this was also a time of great industrial growth, with a dramatic increase in textile production, much of it to be exported. Other major works included the building of bridges and a nationwide network of roads, as well as a flourish of major architectural works like the Pena Palace (p130) above Sintra.

A Small Death in Lisbon (1999), by Robert Wilson, is a vivid award-winning thriller that cuts between 1941 and a post-1974 murder investigation, showing the impacts of WWII and the Revolution of the Carnations on the Portuguese psyche.

However, by 1900 the tides of discontent among workers began to grow. With increased mechanisation, workers began losing jobs (some factory owners began hiring children to operate the machines), and their demand for fair working conditions went unanswered. Those who went on strike were simply fired and replaced. At the same time, Portugal experienced a dramatic demographic shift: rural areas were increasingly depopulated in favour of cities, and emigration (especially to Brazil) snowballed.

Much was changing, and more and more people began to look towards socialism as a cure for the country's inequalities. Nationalist republicanism swept through the lower-middle classes, spurring an attempted coup in 1908. It failed, but the following month King Carlos and Crown Prince Luis Filipe were brutally assassinated in Lisbon.

Carlos' younger son, Manuel II, tried feebly to appease republicans, but it was too little, too late. On 5 October 1910, after an uprising by military officers, a republic was declared. Manuel, dubbed 'the Unfortunate', sailed into exile in Britain where he died in 1932.

THE RISE & FALL OF SALAZAR

After a landslide victory in the 1911 elections, hopes were high among republicans for dramatic changes ahead, but the tides were against them. The economy was in tatters, strained by an economically disastrous decision to join the Allies in WWI. In postwar years the chaos deepened: republican factions squabbled, unions led strikes and were repressed, and the military grew powerful.

One of Portugal's best period dramas to date, *O Milagre Segundo Salomé* (2004), directed by Mário Barroso, is a tear-jerking romance film about a prostitute in early-20th-century Portugal.

The new republic soon had a reputation as Europe's most unstable regime. Between 1910 and 1926 there were an astonishing 45 changes of government, often resulting from military intervention. Another coup in 1926 brought forth new names and faces, most significantly António de Oliveira Salazar, a finance minister who would rise up through the ranks to become prime minister – a post he would hold for the next 36 years.

Salazar hastily enforced his 'New State' – a corporatist republic that was nationalistic, Catholic, authoritarian and essentially repressive. All political parties were banned except for the loyalist National Union, which ran the show, and the National Assembly. Strikes were banned, and propaganda, censorship and brute force kept society in order. The sinister new secret police, Polícia Internacional e de Defesa do Estado (PIDE), inspired terror and suppressed opposition by imprisonment and torture. Various attempted coups during Salazar's rule came to nothing. For a chilling taste of life as a political prisoner under Salazar, you could visit the 16th-century Fortaleza at Peniche (p272) – used as a jail by the dictator.

1793–1811
French troops invade Portugal, but are fought off with help from the British

1908
Portuguese King Carlos and his son are assassinated: Portugal is declared a republic within two years

THE FAMILY MAN

When General António Carmona was named Portugal's new president in 1926, he inherited a country in serious debt. Doing what most rulers do when faced with a problem that they are unable to solve, Carmona called in an expert, a man by the name of Oliveira Salazar. At the time, Salazar was a 37-year-old bachelor, sharing spartan quarters with a priest (who would later become Cardinal of Lisbon). Salazar himself was no stranger to religious life. He spent eight years studying to become a priest, and some residents from his small native village even called him 'father' on his visits. Only a last-minute decision led him to veer into law instead.

Upon graduating, he went into the then fledgling field of economics, becoming one of the country's first economics lecturers, and soon garnered wide respect for his articles on public finance. When General Carmona approached him with the job of finance minister, Salazar accepted on one condition: that the spending of all government ministries fall under his discretion. The general agreed.

Salazar achieved enormous success at firing up the national economy. He severely curtailed government spending, raising taxes and balancing the budget during his first year. Unemployment decreased significantly. Salazar quickly became one of Carmona's star ministers. He also took on adjoining posts as other ministers resigned. In this way he consolidated power until Carmona eventually named him prime minister.

This is when Salazar set the tone for civilian life that would last for many decades to come. He drafted a new constitution around his New State ideals, which were partly modelled on the family as a political idea. Families had no organised internal strife so there was no need for unions or for political parties; a family had a head of household, who would determine where to spend the money. Naturally, Salazar saw himself as the father figure who would be running the family ship; he also saw the church as the 'mother', which would continue to fulfil society's thirst for spiritual values.

Under his authoritarian rule, he did bring stability and prosperity to the country, though at enormous cost: censorship, imprisonment and, in some cases, torture of political opponents. Among his most damning attributes was his attitude towards the working class. He believed in giving them a diet of '*fado*, Fátima and football,' to keep them happily compliant, but had no intention of bettering their lot; at the end of his rule, Portugal had the highest rate of illiteracy and tuberculosis in Western Europe, and women were still not allowed to vote. Given the socially backward condition of the nation when Salazar relinquished power, the advancements of the last 30 years seem all the more startling.

The only good news was a dramatic economic turnaround. Through the 1950s and 1960s Portugal experienced an annual industrial growth rate of 7% to 9%.

Internationally, the wily Salazar played two hands, unofficially supporting Franco's nationalists in the Spanish Civil War, and allowing British use of Azores airfields during WWII despite official neutrality (and illegal sales of tungsten to Germany). It was later discovered that Salazar had also authorised transfer of Nazi-looted gold to Portugal – 44 tonnes according to Allied records.

But it was something else that finally brought bought the Salazarist era to a close – decolonisation. Refusing to relinquish the colonies, he was faced with ever more costly and unpopular military expeditions. In 1961 Goa was occupied by India, and nationalists rose up in Angola. Guerrilla movements also appeared in Portuguese Guinea and Mozambique.

1910–26
An astounding 45 governments are sifted through power in 16 years

1932
António de Oliveira Salazar ushers in an era of repression that was to last 36 years

Salazar, however, didn't have to face the consequences. In 1968 he had a stroke, and died two years later.

His successor, Marcelo Caetano, failed to ease unrest. Military officers sympathetic to African freedom fighters - the officers had seen the horrible living conditions in which the colony lived beneath the Portuguese authorities – grew reluctant to fight colonial wars. Several hundred officers formed the Movimento das Forças Armadas (MFA), which on 25 April 1974 carried out a nearly bloodless coup, later nicknamed the Revolution of the Carnations (after victorious soldiers stuck carnations in their rifle barrels). Carnations are still a national symbol of freedom.

The big-budget Portuguese film *Capitães de Abril* (April Captains; 2000), directed by Maria de Medeiros, is a must-see for those interested in the events of 1974's Revolution of the Carnations.

FROM REVOLUTION TO DEMOCRACY

Despite the coup's popularity, the following year saw unprecedented chaos. It began where the revolution had begun – in the African colonies. Independence was granted immediately to Guinea-Bissau, followed by speedy decolonisation of the Cape Verde islands, São Tomé e Príncipe, Mozambique and Angola.

The transition wasn't smooth: civil war racked Angola, and East Timor, freshly liberated in 1975, was promptly invaded by Indonesia. Within Portugal, too, times were turbulent, with almost a million refugees from African colonies flooding into Portugal.

The country was an economic mess, with widespread strikes and a tangle of political ideas and parties. The communists and a radical wing of the MFA launched a revolutionary movement, nationalising firms and services. Peasant farmers seized land to establish communal farms that failed because of in-fighting and poor management. While revolutionaries held sway in the south, the conservative north was led by Mário Soares and his Partido Socialista (PS; Socialist Party).

It took a more moderate government, formed in 1975, to unite the country after a coup by radical leftists was crushed. At last, the revolution had ended.

THE ROCKY ROAD TO STABILITY

Portugal was soon committed to a blend of socialism and democracy, with a powerful president, an elected assembly and a Council of the Revolution to control the armed forces.

The law allowing all Portuguese women to vote was only established as late as 1975.

Soares' minority government soon faltered, prompting a series of attempts at government by coalitions and nonparty candidates, including Portugal's first female prime minister, Maria de Lourdes Pintassilgo. In the 1980 parliamentary elections a new political force took the reins – the conservative Aliança Democrática (AD; Democratic Alliance), led by Francisco Sá Carneiro.

After Carneiro's almost immediate death in a plane crash (of which evidence of foul play later surfaced), Francisco Pinto Balsemão stepped into his shoes. He implemented plans to join the European Community (EC).

It was partly to keep the EC and the International Monetary Fund (IMF) happy that a new coalition government under Soares and Balsemão implemented a strict programme of economic modernisation. Not surprisingly, the belt-tightening wasn't popular. The loudest critics were Soares' right-wing partners in the Partido Social Democrata (PSD; Social Democrat Party), led

1974
Army officers overthrow Marcelo Caetano, Salazar's successor, in the Revolution of the Carnations

1974–75
Most Portuguese colonies gain independence, and refugees flood the country

by the dynamic Aníbal Cavaco Silva. Communist trade unions also organised strikes, and the appearance of urban terrorism by the radical left-wing Forças Populares de 25 Abril (FP-25) deepened unrest.

By mid-1985 the government collapsed over labour-reform disagreements, and the PSD emerged a narrow winner in subsequent elections. But this wasn't the end of Soares. In the February 1986 presidential elections the veteran socialist became the country's first civilian head of state in 60 years.

In 1986, after nine years of negotiations, Portugal joined the EC. Flush with new funds, it raced ahead of its neighbours with unprecedented economic growth. The new cash flow also gave Prime Minister Cavaco Silva the power to push ahead with radical economic reforms. These included labour law reforms that left many disenchanted workers; the 1980s were crippled by strikes – including one involving 1.5 million workers – though all to no avail. The controversial legislation was eventually passed.

The PSD, now also stricken by corruption scandals, suffered massive losses in municipal elections but still managed to hold onto power. The electorate may have been disgusted by scandals, unemployment, inflation and public-sector shortcomings, but they were wooed nonetheless by the PSD's promises of growth.

Portugal only narrowly missed claiming Europe's first woman PM: in 1979 Margaret Thatcher snatched the honour just three months before Maria de Lourdes Pintassilgo (1930–2004).

It was soon obvious that these promises would be hard to fulfil. In 1992 EC trade barriers fell and Portugal suddenly faced new competition. Fortunes dwindled as recession set in, and disillusionment grew as Europe's single market revealed the backwardness of Portugal's agricultural sector.

Strikes, crippling corruption charges and student demonstrations over rising fees only undermined the PSD further, leading to Cavaco Silva's resignation in 1995.

PORTUGAL TODAY

The general elections in 1995 brought new faces to power, with the socialist António Guterres running the show. Despite hopes for a different and less conservative administration, it was business as usual, with Guterres maintaining budgetary rigour that qualified Portugal for the European & Monetary Union (EMU) in 1998. Indeed, for a while Portugal was a star EMU performer with steady economic growth that helped Guterres win a second term. But it couldn't last. Corruption scandals, rising inflation and a faltering economy soon spelt disaster. Portugal slipped into economic stagnation. The result saw a political swing to the centre-right, with Guterres resigning just before his party was squashed in the 2002 general elections by the PSD.

The Political Science Resources website (www.psr.keele.ac.uk/area/portugal.htm) has good links for politics and current events as well as history.

Things were far from rosy for the new prime minister, José Manuel Durão Barroso, who had to form a coalition government with his former foe, the radically right-wing Centro Democrático Social-Partido Popular (CDS-PP; Popular Party). Like his predecessors, Durão had the unenviable job of tackling Portugal's financial and budgetary crisis, in hopes of promoting growth and productivity. Under his watch, he faced rising unemployment and stiff rigours for meeting EU fiscal requirements.

Perhaps, given the obstacles, it's not surprising that he would resign – taking over, instead, as head of the EC – Portugal's first appointee to that post. This caused a flurry of political shuffling that brought Lisbon mayor Pedro Santana Lopes to Portugal's top post.

1975
Portuguese women are finally granted full voting rights

1986
Portugal joins the EC along with Spain on 1 January

On the international stage, Portugal received some worldwide criticism for hosting the Iraq War Conference in the Azores in 2003 (attended by George Bush, Tony Blair and Spain's José María Aznar). Initially, Portugal contributed a small force to Iraq (later withdrawn in 2005), which made then prime minister Lopes extremely unpopular at home and ultimately contributed to his political downfall.

With more than 210 million speakers worldwide, Portuguese is among the top 10 of the world's most widely spoken languages – a considerable achievement given the tiny size of Portugal.

Meanwhile, 2004 was a time for Portugal's success as host nation in the European Football Championships, and the refocus on sport did wonders for the country's morale, despite its 1–0 loss in the final to Greece.

Unfortunately, Lopes proved unprepared for the transition to national politics and, by the end of 2004, President Sampaia lost confidence in Lopes' government, dissolved parliament and called for new elections.

Parliamentary elections in 2005 brought to power socialist José Socrates, who models himself on Blair and Spain's José Luís Zapatero. Still early in his tenure, he's sought to reposition the PS as part of the modern left – one that is more fiscally prudent and committed to IMF reforms (including pension reform and privatisation of public services – contentious topics among many citizens). At the same time, Socrates has tried to stay true to his supporters – vowing to slash unemployment and create jobs.

In 2006 another old face returned to the stage, with the unprecedented election of Cavaco Silva, a former PSD prime minister, who won with just a hair over 50% of the vote. The new government has the same problems to face: ballooning budget deficits, rising unemployment and stagnant growth. The 2004 enlargement of the EU hasn't helped, as countries with much lower labour costs have overturned Portugal's former competitive advantage.

Despite its attention to domestic problems, Portugal continues to play an active role in the EU. When it takes over the rotating EU presidency in 2007, it plans to focus on deepening relations between Europe and Africa, fully taking on political responsibilities among its former colonies. Along those lines, Portugal is proving to be a driving force in the Community of Portuguese Speaking Countries, and has announced proposals to achieve a drastic reduction of poverty among member countries by 2015.

1998	2007
José Saramago wins Portugal's first Nobel Prize in literature	Portugal takes over the rotating EU presidency

The Culture

THE NATIONAL PSYCHE

People tend to come to Portugal without a preconceived notion of its people. However, if any international image sticks, it is one from the Salazar years: that of a quietly resigned people drowning their sorrows in smoky bars, with plenty of wine and nostalgic music. While this image is far behind the times, its legacy lingers.

In particular, the Portuguese like to indulge in a little *saudade,* the nostalgic, often deeply melancholic longing for better times. The idea is most eloquently expressed in bittersweet *fado* music, traditional, melancholic Portuguese singing with yearning laments that express fatalism and exquisite frustration about matters that cannot be changed. It's also partly thanks to repression under Salazar that Portugal – especially in the north – remains very traditional and conservative. Extremism is definitely not encouraged. While people are friendly, honest, unhurried and gracious, they can also be extremely formal and polite, and religious festivals and pilgrimages are taken very seriously.

The Portuguese are the world's biggest drinkers, according to a survey by – we are assured unbiased – French researchers. Apparently the home of port imbibes 11.2L of pure alcohol per person every year.

The Salazar years did nothing to wipe out Portugal's fierce sense of national identity, which was forged through a plucky history of expelling numerous invaders and a seafaring tradition in which Portugal once led the world. These days the national pride also finds expression through football – less a pastime than a countrywide narcotic.

But the nation's huge outflow of emigrants and influx of immigrants has inevitably given the national character a certain fluidity, as has its geographic diversity; the colder northern reaches seem to breed a tougher, more reserved character, while the scorching plains in the south encourage an open, sunny outlook. The Portuguese are not averse to mocking their compatriots with blunt stereotypes. For example, the sleeves-up people of Porto recite an old saying about the country's biggest cities: 'Coimbra sings, Braga prays, Lisbon shows off and Porto works', and they call their southern counterparts Moors.

However, it is the urban–rural divide that is most dramatic. It's easy to see Portugal as a dynamic, forward-looking nation when you're in one of its cities, but the contrast in the countryside could not be bigger. As their young desert them, many tiny rural communities almost seem to intensify their adherence to the old ways.

The Portuguese were recently declared the laziest nation in the EU by a study on sedentary lifestyles carried out by scientists at the University of Navarra in Spain.

LIFESTYLE

Portugal has undergone rapid transition. Held back for decades under Salazar, it has since been sprinting to catch up with the rest of Western Europe. Few other countries could claim to have urbanised so quickly, let alone set up a welfare state, reduced family sizes, improved employment for women, developed a middle class, changed consumer lifestyles and set an empire free – all in a blink of the political eye.

Like any society changing at a frantic pace, it's inevitable that yawning chasms have opened up between the lifestyles of city-dwellers and rural folk, young and old. In urban centres you'll see many old houses that are shabby on the outside, but step inside and you'll find them packed with mod cons – shiny computers, modern kitchenware and a widescreen TV.

The number of cars has almost tripled in the last decade, mostly in city and coastal areas. Even in the smaller settlements you can see grandmas whizzing by on mopeds, a handbag swinging from one arm. But on their journeys, these vehicles will flash past any number of donkey-drawn carts on country roads.

A BAD CASE OF THE BLUES

It's been described as nostalgia for a glorious past, a fathomless yearning and longing for home, but unless you're Portuguese you'll probably never really grasp the uniquely Portuguese passion for *saudade*. Its musical form is the aching sorrow of *fado*, a melancholic submission to the twists and turns of fate. In Portuguese and Brazilian poetry, *saudade* is a mystical reverence for nature coupled with a brooding sense of loneliness, especially popular among certain 19th- and early-20th-century poets who fostered a cult of *saudosismo*. In tangible form, *saudade* is the return of thousands of émigrés to their home villages every August, drawn not just by family ties but by something deeper, a longing for all that home and Portugal represents – the heroism of the past, the sorrows of the present and wistful hopes for the future.

Also, while the urban Portuguese are worrying increasingly about crime, their country compatriots frequently leave their doors unlocked and windows open. In smaller country towns it's also common for two-thirds of the population to be aged 65 years or over. Partly as a result of this, Portugal's interior remains staunchly traditional, and pious *romarias* (religious festivals in honour of a patron saint), fairs and markets are a big part of life.

In terms of personal liberty, it's hard to imagine now that only decades ago the Portuguese could not vote freely, or dress or write uninhibitedly, or even own a cigarette lighter without first having a state licence. In light of this, it's extraordinary to consider the government's recent softer drug laws (aimed at rehabilitating rather than criminalising), its pioneering schemes for public access to the internet, and the widespread tolerance shown towards the southern coast's hedonistic resorts.

Attitudes towards women are changing, albeit at a snail's pace (see p44), and acceptance of gay and lesbian lifestyles largely depends on your location (see p460).

ECONOMY

While economic growth in Portugal remained above the EU average for much of the 1990s, it hit a speed bump in 2000, and has been in a serious slump ever since. Its GDP shrank in 2003, and recovered slightly in subsequent years, but still only grew by 1% in 2006, making it one of the lowest in the EU. At present, Portugal's per capita GDP lags behind that of Slovenia, Malta, Cyprus and, since 2002, Greece.

Portugal was one of seven countries in the EU to reduce its energy consumption (by 5%) in 2005. Elsewhere in the world consumption increased by an average of 2.7%.

Unemployment has also slowly risen over the last five years, peaking at 7.6% in 2005, although in some areas it was more than twice that. To add to the country's financial woes, the budget deficit and consumer prices have continued to rise, while wages increased only slightly. All this has made for a rather unhappy population.

The government has certainly had its work cut out for it, trying to walk a fine line between keeping the EU happy (ultimatum from Brussels: 'reign in your budget deficit!') and helping its own citizens. As is often the case, economic priorities trumped social concerns, and the government has adopted austere measures to bring the country economic equanimity. Measures it undertook included raising the value-added tax (VAT) from 19% to 21%, initiating a hiring and promotion freeze on various parts of the public sector and reforming pensions – never a pretty topic in a country with 17% of its population over the age of 65.

In other economic areas Portugal still lumbers beneath a significant trade deficit; it spent €20 billion more than it exported in 2005. Incidentally, Portugal's leading market for both imports and exports is Spain, though Germany, France, Italy and the UK are also players. The Portuguese economy is still based on traditional industries such as textiles, clothing, footwear, cork, paper products, wine and glassware.

Agriculture, once a mainstay of the economy, now only accounts for 3% of GDP, though it employs 12% of Portugal's workforce. This statistic is a small indication of the country's old-fashioned tendency towards manpower over machinery – and a reason why it has difficulty competing with cheaper, better located Eastern European countries that are the new kids on the EU block.

The service industry, particularly tourism, is playing an increasingly important role, and certainly more changes are underfoot as Portugal stumbles its way towards the light of economic stability. On the horizon, the country will lose its training wheels as the EU cuts its funding from 2007 to 2013 by 10%, a whack of more than €2 billion.

You won't get a better insider glimpse of the harsh life of 20th-century rural Portugal than in *The Creation of the World* and *Tales from the Mountain* by Miguel Torga, a renowned writer from Trás-os-Montes.

POPULATION

Portugal's population breakdown has seen dramatic changes in the last few decades. The country's emigration rate has long been among Europe's highest, but its immigration rate shot up during the mid-1970s when around 500,000 to 800,000 African *retornados* (refugees) immigrated from former Portuguese colonies.

They later came from war-torn Angola and Mozambique, followed by others from Guinea-Bissau and São Tomé e Príncipe. Officially, in 2006, there were just over 400,000 legal immigrants in Portugal – the majority from Africa – plus many illegal immigrants. Africans compose Portugal's largest ethnic group (including 68,000 Cape Verdeans), with especially big communities in Lisbon.

Another influx resulting from Portugal's empire building is of Brazilians, and some have now put down roots here. There's a small resident Roma population and increasing numbers of immigrant workers from Central and Eastern Europe – particularly from Ukraine, with 43,000 Ukrainians living in Portugal. One of the biggest inflows in recent years has been sun-seekers from Western Europe buying properties and settling in southern regions.

Most native Portuguese share typically Mediterranean features, such as brown eyes and dark hair. The majority still live in rural areas, such as in the Minho, one of Portugal's poorest and most densely populated regions, and the ever more crowded Algarve coast. But the urban population has increased dramatically since the 1960s, from 22% of the total to around 42%; smaller villages are fast disappearing as their youth move away and ageing populations fizzle out.

RESPONSIBLE TRAVEL

In many popular destinations the summer tourist influx puts a real strain on local infrastructure. It's not uncommon for as many as 40,000 annual visitors to squeeze into villages with usual populations of less than 2000 – stretching local services to the limit.

One way to minimise your impact is to visit outside the high season. Spending your money in less-visited areas also helps to even out tourism's financial impact, while simultaneously broadening your view of the country.

In traditionally minded rural areas, extreme dress can cause offence. While beachwear (and even nudity on some beaches) is fine in coastal tourist resorts, shorts and skimpy tops on a visit to a church are a definite no-no (as is intruding during church services).

Speaking Portuguese – however clumsily – will earn you lots of brownie points. Politeness is highly valued, so be sure to address people correctly (*senhor* for men, *senhora* for women, *senhora dona* followed by the Christian name for an elderly or respected woman).

SPORT

Football

Football (soccer) is not a game here: it's a national obsession. Life – male life, at any rate – and often the national economy come to a near standstill during any big match, with bar and restaurant TVs showing nothing else.

Boozy postmatch celebrations are a tradition in themselves, with fans taking to the streets, honking car horns, setting off fireworks and gridlocking entire town centres until the wee hours.

Football hysteria consumed the country in 2006 when it made it to the quarterfinals of the 2006 World Cup, beating the Netherlands and England en route. Madness also took hold in 2004 when Portugal hosted the UEFA European Football Championships, the biggest sporting event ever staged there. Sports authorities were counting on the tournament to provide a big shot in the arm for Portuguese football, and they got it. Local clubs, with mounting debts and ageing stadiums, watched the country's star players earn a fortune abroad (for example, Luís Figo at Real Madrid and Cristiano Ronaldo at Manchester United). But sure enough, the authorities set about building and sprucing up stadiums and building vital new transport links to the venues.

On a national level, the story of Portuguese football is mainly about Lisbon and Porto. The big three teams – Lisbon's Sporting Clube de Portugal and Sport Lisboa e Benfica and Porto's Futebol Clube do Porto – have among them won every national championship but two since the 1920s (Porto's upstart Boavista Futebol Club briefly broke the spell in 2001). Regional titles haven't been lacking either for the country's top teams, with the Futebol Clube do Porto picking up the 2004 European Champions League title.

The season lasts from September to May, and almost every village and town finds enough players to make up a team. Major teams and their stadiums are noted under bigger towns in this book.

Since traditional bullfighting is outlawed in the US, Portuguese emigrants in central California invented a bloodless bullfight using Velcro-tipped spears. Read more on this bizarre sport at www.ranchcardoso.biz.

Bullfighting

Love it or loathe it, bullfighting is a national institution. First recorded in Portugal a staggering 2000 years ago by a Roman historian, it was honed in the 12th century, when the *tourada* became a way to maintain military fitness and prepare nobles for battle on horseback. But the gory death of a nobleman in 1799 resulted in a less bloodthirsty version, in which the bull's horns are covered in leather or capped with metal balls and the animal is not killed publicly.

A typical *tourada* starts with an enraged bull charging into the ring towards a *cavaleiro*, a dashing horseman dressed in 18th-century finery and plumed tricorn hat. The *cavaleiro* sizes up the animal as his team of *peões de brega* (footmen) distract and provoke the bull with capes. Then, with superb horsemanship, he gallops within inches of the bull's horns and plants several barbed *bandarilha* (spears) in the angry creature's neck.

The next phase, the *pega*, features eight brave (read: foolhardy) young *forcados* dressed in breeches, white stockings and short jackets, who face the weakened bull barehanded. The leader swaggers towards the bull, provoking it to charge. Bearing the brunt of the attack, he throws himself onto the animal's head and grabs the horns while his mates rush in to grab the beast, often being tossed in all directions. Their success wraps up the contest and the bull is led out. Though Portuguese bullfighting rules prohibit a public kill, the animals are killed after the show – you just don't witness the final blow.

Bullfighting remains popular here despite opposition from international animal-welfare organisations. Portugal's own anti-bullfighting lobby is vocal but small. If you feel strongly, contact the **Liga Portuguesa dos Direitos dos Animais** (LPDA; Portuguese League for Animal Rights; ☎ 214 578 413; www.lpda.pt in Portuguese) for more information and suggestions of action.

The season runs from March or late April to October. The most traditional contests take place in bull-breeding Ribatejo province, especially in Santarém (p294) during the June fair, and in the otherwise unexceptional Vila Franca de Xira during the town's July and October festivals. Frequent *touradas* in the Algarve and Lisbon are more tourist-oriented.

MULTICULTURALISM

Portugal's emigration rate has long been one of Europe's highest, but in the 1970s the tables were turned and the country was flooded with *retornados*. They generally integrated exceptionally well into Portuguese society, with many picking up work in the booming construction industry. Their culture and music has also helped to shape that of the Portuguese, most notably in the kicking African beats so popular in Lisbon clubs. Similarly, the big Brazilian population in Portugal has helped promote its mellow musical tastes here.

However, it's not all jazz and funk in Lisbon's multicultural society. While Portugal has one of the lowest percentages of avowed racists in the EU, at times racism does rear its ugly head in the capital. Gang-related tensions between Angolans and Cape Verdeans have exploded there. The slum living conditions of many immigrants are a depressing indication of the lack of government and national attention to the Afro-Portuguese community.

A lower-profile prejudice is sometimes present in rural Portugal and rails against outsiders, especially the Roma population, although some people from small towns can also be wary of tourists. The latest stream of immigrants, mainly expats from Britain and Germany, has been to the southern Algarve; locals often regard them simply as long-stay tourists.

But it's comforting to note that by international standards none of the teething troubles associated with Portuguese immigrant populations are serious. The country seems to take each new wave in its stride.

The nation of explorers is still on the move. An estimated five million Portuguese live abroad; some 100,000 emigrate each year – though many return.

RELIGION

Christianity has been a pivotal force in shaping Portugal's history, and religion still plays a big part in the lives of its people. The country is famous for its impressive pilgrimages and *romarias*, which continue unabated and are celebrated with a special fervour in the north. One of Europe's most important centres of pilgrimage is in Portugal at Fátima (p289), where up to 300,000 pilgrims congregate every May and October. See p459 for a list of Portugal's myriad *romarias*.

However, it's not just through rousing events and festivals that the Portuguese demonstrate their faith. Around half of northern Portugal's population still attends Sunday Mass, as do more than a quarter in Lisbon – though there are noticeably fewer churchgoers on the southern coast.

In the more traditional north, Catholic traditions often mingle with curious folk practices. For example, Trás-os-Montes is renowned for its wild and untamed dancing (p452), while Amarante's patron saint is associated with the swapping of phallic cakes (p379). In Tomar, the singular Festa dos Tabuleiros (p299) also has colourful pagan roots. And on a hill above Ponte de Lima (p418) is a chapel dedicated to Santo Ovídio, patron saint of ears, with walls covered in votive offerings of wax ears. Similar chapels, adorned with wax limbs of all kinds, can be found even inside churches, revealing a pragmatic tolerance by the Catholic Church.

According to statistics, around 94% of the population is Roman Catholic, although the number of practising Catholics is steadily dropping. Other Christian denominations make up much of the remaining population, along with many Muslims and a small number of Jews.

The Portuguese are getting cold feet in record numbers. In 2005 weddings had fallen for the seventh consecutive year (down to 48,700 weddings, compared with 103,000 in 1975).

WOMEN IN PORTUGAL

Women didn't earn full voting rights until 1975, making Portugal one of the last pockets in the northern hemisphere to grant universal suffrage (women in Afghanistan, by comparison, gained the right to vote in 1963). This was one of the many sad legacies of Salazar. In addition to lacking voting rights, women did not have the authority to administer their own property or to leave the country without a father's or husband's permission, and if a woman married a foreigner she automatically forfeited her citizenship along with her inheritance. It wasn't until 1969 that a married woman was allowed to have a passport or leave the country without her husband's consent.

Maria Velho da Costa is one of the three authors of *Novas Cartas Portuguesas* (The Three Marias: New Portuguese Letters; 1972), whose modern feminist interpretation of the 17th-century *Letters of a Portuguese Nun* so shocked the Salazar regime that its authors were put on trial. The story was made into a film by Jesus Franco in 1977.

Portugal has come a long ways since the dark days of the dictatorship. Equality is now enshrined in the civil code. Of students enrolled in higher education in 2005, 56% were women, and women make up about 47% of the working population. Although women haven't achieved equality in professional occupations, the gap is narrowing. At last count, 40% of physicians were female, with a similar figure for lawyers.

Women enjoy just protection under the legal system, with cases of rape, domestic violence and sexual harassment punishable by imprisonment. Traditional attitudes, however, still discourage abused women from using the legal system, and domestic abuse remains prevalent. Of the more than 13,000 crimes reported annually to the Association for Victim Support, roughly 80% involve domestic violence.

But in aspects of women's rights, Portugal still has some way to go. Despite legal equality, gender stereotypes continue to persist, keeping women from playing a more central role in society. Abortions are still illegal in the country. And despite being among the first countries in Europe to elect a female prime minister in 1979, women are grossly underrepresented in senior-management positions in both public and private sectors. Women earn about 30% less than men in both professional and working-class jobs, and comprise only 10% of Portugal's parliament; the government has toyed with the idea of enforcing minimum quotas of women candidates in elections.

One of the finest all-round books about the Portuguese is Marion Kaplan's perceptive *The Portuguese: The Land & Its People* (2006). Ranging from literature to emigrants, its female perspective seems appropriate for a country whose men so often seem to be abroad.

ARTS

Literature

Portuguese literature has long been moulded by foreign influences – notably that of Spain – but has retained its individuality throughout. Two major styles dominate: lyric poetry and realistic fiction. The country's most outstanding literary figure is Luís Vaz de Camões (1524–80), a poet who enjoyed little fame or fortune in his lifetime. Only after his death was his genius recognised, thanks largely to an epic poem, *Os Lusiados* (The Lusiads; 1572). It tells of Vasco da Gama's 1497 sea voyage to India, but it's also a superbly lyrical paean to the Portuguese spirit, written when Portugal was still one of the most powerful countries in the Western world. Four centuries after its humble publication, it's considered the national epic and its poet a national hero.

In the 19th century a tide of romanticism flooded Portuguese literature. A prominent figure in this movement was poet, playwright and romantic novelist Almeida Garrett (1799–1854), who devoted his life to stimulating political awareness through his writings. Among his works is the novel *Viagens na Minha Terra* (Travels in My Homeland; 1846), an allegory of contemporary political events, presented as a home-grown travelogue. Despite being Portugal's most talented playwright since 16th-century court dramatist Gil Vicente, Garrett was exiled for his political liberalism.

Garrett's contemporary Alexandre Herculano (also exiled) was meanwhile continuing the long Portuguese tradition of historical literature, which flourished most strongly during the Age of Discoveries. Herculano produced a vast body of work, most notably his magnum opus, *História de Portugal* (1846). Towards the end of the 19th century several important writers emerged, among them the ever-popular José Maria Eça de Queirós, who introduced a stark realism to Portuguese literature with his powerful novels and more-entertaining narratives, such as *Os Maias* (The Maya; 1888).

Fernando Pessoa (1888–1935), author of the 1934 *Mensagem* (Message), is posthumously regarded as the most extraordinary poet of his generation. His four different poet-personalities, which he referred to as heteronyms, created four distinct strains of poetry and prose. *A Centenary Pessoa* (1995), published in English, provides a fascinating insight into his work.

The Anarchist Banker (1997), edited by Eugénio Lisboa, is a collection of late-19th- and 20th-century fiction from Portugal. Big names include Eça de Queirós, Antonio Patricio, Irene Lisboa, Fernando Pessoa and José Rodrigues Migueis.

However, Portugal's creative juices were soon to be stoppered. The Salazar dictatorship, spanning much of the early modern era, effectively buried freedom of expression. Several writers suffered during this period, including the poet and storyteller Miguel Torga (1907–95), whose background in Trás-os-Montes brought a radical individualism to his writings, so much so that several of his writings were banned.

One of the most notable writers who survived and often documented this repressive era was José Cardoso Pires (1925–98), a popular novelist and playwright whose finest work, *Balada da Praia dos Cães* (Ballad of Dog's Beach; 1982), is a gripping thriller based on a real political assassination in the Salazar era. Prominent poets of the time were Jorge de Sena (1919–78), a humanist thinker who also wrote much fiction and criticism; and David Mourão-Ferreira (1927–97), whose works include the novel *Un Amor Feliz* (Lucky in Love; 1986). In Portugal's former colonies (particularly Brazil), writers such as Nobel Prize winner Jorge Amado (1912–2001) have also made their mark on modern Portuguese-language literature.

One of José Cardoso Pires' novels, *O Delfim* (The Dauphin), set at the end of Salazar's reign, has been made into a great melodramatic film (2002); Fernando Lopez directed.

Today's literary scene is largely dominated by two names: José Saramago (1922–) and António Lobo Antunes (1942–). Saramago, who won the Nobel Prize in 1998, is king of the discursive, brilliantly funny and politically astute novel. Some of his best works are *O Evangelho Segundo Jesus Cristo* (The Gospel According to Jesus Christ; 1991), in which Saramago retells the famous story, written from a much more humanistic point of view. *Cegueira* (Blindness; 1995), a modern-day fable in which everyone in the world goes blind, is a much darker work revealing the human condition in a most wretched and horrific state – themes that recur in his many novels, along with a mild touch of redemption.

Antunes produces magical, fast-paced prose, often with dark undertones and vast historical sweeps. His novel *O Regresso das Caravelas* (The Return of the Caravels; 2002) features a surreal time warp where 15th-century navigators meet 1970s soldiers and contemporary Lisboêtas. His *Manual dos Inquisidores* (The Inquisitors' Manual; 1996) is a dark look at the run-up to and aftermath of the 1974 revolution.

The Sin of Father Amaro is a powerful 19th-century novel by Eça de Queirós. The book is set in Portugal, though it was relocated for a popular Mexican film, *El Crimen del padre Amaro* (2002).

Hot names on the late-20th-century poetry front included Pedro Tamen and Sophia de Mello Breyner (awarded the Portuguese Camões Prize in 1999), the latter finding fame both as a poet and as a writer of children's stories, using the sea as her central theme. Up-and-coming novelists include Ana Gusmão, whose stories are set in urban landscapes and reflect conflicts in relationships, cultures and traditions; and José Riço Direitinho, whose haunting novel *Breviário das Más Inclinações* (The Book of Bad Habits; 1994) is peopled by folk memories, superstitious peasants and rural traditions. Also consider the work of Mario de Carvalho, who won the Pegasus Prize for Literature with his gripping novel *Deus Passeando Pela Brisa da Tarde* (A God Strolling in the Cool of an Evening; 1996), which is set in Roman Portugal.

Look out for the beautiful novels of Lídia Jorge, whose book *O Vale da Paixao* (The Painter of Birds; 1995), a tale about an Algarve family split by emigration, won her several Portuguese and international awards.

Cinema

Portugal has a distinguished history of film making, though poor foreign distribution has left the world largely ignorant of it. The only internationally famous director is Manoel de Oliveira, described by the British *Guardian* newspaper as 'the most eccentric and the most inspired of cinema's world masters'. The ex-racing driver has made more than 20 films, with all except three made after he turned 60. His 1995 film, *The Convent,* starring Catherine Deneuve and John Malkovich and set in a Portuguese convent, follows Malkovich and Deneuve as they travel to Portugal to research the theory that Shakespeare is Spanish-Jewish. Also of gossipy interest, this Portugal connection has led to Malkovich being a player in several Lisbon businesses – Lux nightclub and Bica do Sapato restaurant. Malkovich and Deneuve also appear in the director's French-language *Je Rentre à la Maison* (I'm Going Home; 2002), set in Paris. Oliveira's *Viagem ao Princípio do Mundo* (Voyage to the Beginning of the World; 1997) is a deceptively simple road movie that explores Portugal's rural past. It's a melancholy meditation on ageing and also tells us a great deal about its director. *Um Filme Falado* (A Talking Picture; 2003) is a thought-provoking film exploring how Europe has been moulded by the past. It examines countries through a series of characters on a cruise from the Mediterranean to India. Slow, but well worth sticking with. In 2004 Oliveira directed the period film *O Quinto Império* (The Fifth Empire; 2004), which follows the disastrous story of Sebastião. Oliveira's rather theatrical, fastidious films often feature long, silent takes and can be an acquired taste.

Terra Estrangeira (A Foreign Land; 1995), directed by Walter Salles and Daniela Thomas, is a modern film-noir thriller that jumps between São Paolo and Lisbon at a time when Brazilians were leaving the country in droves.

Ossos (Bones; 1998), directed by Pedro Costa, is a dark and disturbing film about life in a creole Lisbon slum. Not for the faint-hearted.

Other well-established Portuguese film makers include João Botelho, Paulo Rocha and the maverick sexagenarian João César Monteiro. Monteiro's last film, *Vai e Vem* (Come and Go; 2002), raised the usual international eyebrows because of its forthright sexual content.

Alongside the older film makers, a new generation of directors has now emerged, producing works that are often provocative and harrowing, exposing the darker side of Portugal. Ground-breaking films include those by Pedro Costa and Teresa Villaverde, whose 1999 film, *Os Mutantes* (The Mutants), is a disturbing work about unwanted youngsters.

The country's best-known actress is Maria de Medeiros who turned director with her *Capitães de Abril* (April Captains; 2000), based on the 1974 Revolution of the Carnations. Significantly, this was funded by the Instituto de Cinema Audiovisual e Multimédia (ICAM; Institute for Cinema Audiovisuals & Multimedia), which has grown more daring in its approach. Other up-and-coming female directors include Catarina Ruivo.

You can find a wealth of information on Portuguese films, companies, directors and upcoming events on the multilingual website of the Instituto de Cinema Audiovisual e Multimédia: www.icam.pt.

Portugal's talent for dark social commentaries has continued past the millennium. Another directorial name to emerge in this genre is João Canijo, whose films *Ganhar a Vida* (Get a Life; 2001), about a Portuguese émigré in France, and *Noite Escura* (In the Darkness of the Night; 2003), set around Portugal's seedy rural nightlife, have caused waves internationally. If you can track it down, the hard-hitting film *A Passagem da Noite* (Night Passage; 2003) by Luís Filipe Rocha, about a raped girl who discovers she is pregnant, is also good, if harrowing.

However, despite the growing confidence of the Portuguese film industry, cinemas still tend to favour subtitled European and American films. Cinema buffs will find international festivals in Porto in February, the Algarve and Viana do Castelo in May, Tróia in June and Figueira da Foz in September.

Music

Fundamental to Portugal's history of musical expression is its foot-tapping folk music, which you can hear at almost every festival. It traces its roots to the medieval troubadour, and is traditionally accompanied by a band of guitars, violins, clarinets, harmonicas and various wooden percussion instruments. In fact, the instruments are often more attractive than the singing, which could be generously described as a high-pitched, repetitive wail.

Far more enigmatic is Portugal's most famous style of music, *fado* (Portuguese for 'fate'). These melancholic chants – performed as a set of three songs, each one lasting three minutes – are also said to have their roots in troubadour songs, although African slave songs have had an influence, too. They're traditionally sung by one performer accompanied by a 12-string Portuguese *guitarra* (a pear-shaped guitar). *Fado* emerged in the 18th century in Lisbon's working-class districts of Alfama and Mouraria and gradually moved upmarket.

There are two styles of *fado* music, one from Lisbon (still considered the most genuine) and the other from the university town of Coimbra. The latter is traditionally sung by men as it praises the beauty of women. In 1996 *fadista* (*fado* performer) Manuela Bravo caused an outcry when she recorded a CD of Coimbra *fados* – the entire issue of CDs mysteriously disappeared almost as soon as it had appeared.

The greatest modern *fadista* was Amália Rodrigues, who brought *fado* international recognition. She died in 1999 aged 79, after more than 60 years of extraordinary *fado* performances ('I don't sing *fado,*' she once said, 'it sings me'). Pick up a copy of her greatest hits to hear what *fado* should really sound like.

However, while *fado* brings to mind dark bars of the Salazar years, this is not a musical form stuck in time. Top-notch contemporary performers

MUSICAL TOP 10

- *Transparente* (2005) One of the best albums by Mariza, whose enchanting voice is the success story of modern *fado*.
- *Amália Rodrigues: The Essential Collection* (2005) A collection of classics from Portugal's *grand dame* of *fado* music.
- *Ainda* (2001) Folk-group Madredeus is known for mesmerising music accompanied by guitar, accordion and cello. This was the soundtrack for Wim Wenders' film *A Lisbon Story*.
- *Afro-Portuguese Odyssey* (2002) Wide-ranging look at how the African colonies have musically influenced Portugal, and vice versa.
- *Music from the Edge of Europe* (1998) A good one-disc introduction to some of Portugal's leading contemporary vocalists.
- *Changing with the Times* (1999) Sonic Fiction, a talented fusion band, mix jazz and rock on this bright, well-played album.
- *Re-Definições* (2006) The latest album from the musical gurus of Da Weasel, one of Portugal's most popular hip-hop bands.
- *Undercovers* (2003) Portuguese jazz at its best, performed by Maria João and Mario Laginha.
- *Garras dos Sentidos* (1998) The best album by Mísia, another of Portugal's contemporary and very enchanting *fadistas*.
- *Underground Sound of Lisbon* (2004) For a housey take on the roots of Lisbon's evolving club scene, check out this fine album by DJ Vibe.

and exponents of a new *fado* style include the dynamic young *fadista* Mísia, who broke new ground by experimenting with instrumentation and commissioning lyrics by contemporary poets. She has since been followed by several excellent performers.

The current darling of the *fado* industry is Mariza, whose extraordinary voice and fresh contemporary image has struck a chord both at home and internationally. But the men aren't outdone: one of the great young male voices in traditional *fado* these days is Camané.

Venues for live *fado* include Lisbon (p120), Coimbra (p313), Porto (p374) and elsewhere. See p107 for details on an annual *fado* festival, and p98 for a museum dedicated to its history.

Both *fado* and traditional folk songs – and, increasingly, strains from Europe and Africa – have shaped Portugal's *música popular* (modern folk-music scene). Often censored during the Salazar years, its lyrics became overtly political after 1974, with singers using performances to support various revolutionary factions.

The Portuguese guitar, too, took on a new range of expression under masters such as Carlos Paredes and António Chaínho. Well-known folk groups include the venerable Madredeus. At the grass-roots level are student song groups, called *tunas académicas,* who give performances all over the country during March.

Jazz is also hugely popular in Portugal, which hosts several jazz festivals. One of the leading lights of Lisbon's lively African jazz scene is diva Maria João. If you spend time in Lisbon and want a taste of Portuguese jazz, make a beeline for the Hot Clube (p119).

On the rock scene, don't miss the old masters Xutos & Pontapés, the quirky Gift and the popular Blind Zero. Or if fresh-faced pop is more your scene, you'll soon discover chart sensation David Fonseca, who sings in English.

African-influenced urban music is now all the rage. Dozens of Lisbon nightclubs resonate to the rhythms of the former colonies. African jazz was at the forefront of this trend, and big names include Cesaria Évora from Cape Verde and drum-maestro Guem from Angola.

THE LYRICAL LUSOSPHERE

Large numbers of immigrants filling the streets of Portugal over the last three decades may have added stress to the infrastructure, but it's left the country much richer musically. As one of the core founders of the Community of Portuguese Language Countries, Portugal is now awash in the rhythms and sounds of its former colonies – particularly Cape Verde, Angola and Mozambique.

Among the most popular singer to appear now and again on Lisbon's stages is Cesaria Évora, a singer from Cape Verde who's enjoyed worldwide popularity for her melancholic *mornas* – a haunting and melodic style with roots in *fado.* Other great singers from the African island include Tito Paris, Herminia and Maria Alice; the latter also performs from time to time in the capital.

Angola's musical contributions are also evident in the Portuguese music scene. Lisbon dance clubs feature music such as the Angolan *merengue* (a relative of the Dominican dance style), *semba,* which has roots in Brazilian samba, and *kizomba,* a native style based around the marimba. Be on the lookout for performers such as singer-guitarist Waldemar Bastos, or pick up a CD by musical legend Bonga, an Angolan expat who was a soccer star in Portugal before turning to songwriting.

Though often overlooked, Mozambique has a wide range of musical styles, owing to influences from other African nations. *Marrabenta* is among the best known of Mozambique music. The word derives from *rebentar* (to break), in reference to the guitar strings that break while playing this fast-paced music. Wazimbo and Orchestra Marrabenta are among the classic names associated with *marrabenta.*

However, the hottest urban clubs around the country are now dominated by DJ culture. You'll hear lots of hip-hop and funk, made popular by the likes of Hip-Hop Tuga and the hugely popular Da Weasel, and a new wave of Portuguese dance-floor music, increasingly being exported around Europe. Look out for names like Micro Audio Waves, Mike Stellar, and the Space Cowboys. Plus the biggest names at the time of writing were house DJs Rui da Silva and Rui Vargas, who regularly play in Lisbon's hottest club venue, Lux (p119).

Visual Arts

The earliest visual arts to be found in Portugal were several treasure-troves of 20,000-year-old Palaeolithic carvings (see the boxed text, p391).

The cave-dwellers' modern successors were heavily influenced by French, Italian and Flemish styles. The first major exception was the 15th-century primitive painter Nuno Gonçalves, whose polyptych of the *Panels of São Vicente* is a unique tapestry-style revelation of contemporary Portuguese society.

Instituto Camões' website (www.instituto-camoes.pt/cvc) presents background information on Portuguese language, literature and theatre, plus potted biographies of the country's most important authors and poets.

The 16th-century Manueline school produced some uniquely Portuguese works, remarkable for their incredible delicacy, realism and luminous colours. The big names of this school are Vasco Fernandes (known as Grão Vasco) and Gaspar Vaz, who both worked from Viseu; their best works are in Viseu's first-rate Museu de Grão Vasco (p343). In Lisbon, other outstanding Manueline artists were Jorge Afonso, court painter to Dom Manuel I, and Cristóvão de Figueiredo and Gregório Lopes.

Hot on the heels of the Renaissance, in the 17th century artist Josefa de Óbidos made waves with her rich still lifes. However, the fine arts waned somewhat until the 19th century, when there was an artistic echo of both the naturalist and romantic movements, expressed strongly in the works of Silva Porto and Marquês de Oliveira. Sousa Pinto excelled as a pastel artist in the early 20th century.

Naturalism remained the dominant trend into the 20th century, although Amadeo de Souza-Cardoso struck out on his own path of cubism and expressionism, and Maria Helena Vieria da Silva came to be considered the country's finest abstract painter (although she lived in Paris for most of her life).

Other eminent figures in contemporary art include Almada Negreiros, often called the father of Portugal's modern art movement, and Guilherme Santa-Rita, who had a short career in abstract art. Their works and others can be seen in Lisbon's Centro de Arte Moderna (p101) and Porto's Museu Nacional Soares dos Reis (p363).

The conservative Salazar years that followed didn't create the ideal environment to nurture contemporary creativity, and many artists left the country. These include Portugal's best-known modern artist, Paula Rego, who was born in Lisbon in 1935 but has been a resident of the UK since 1951.

Rego's contemporary Helena Almeida has had a particularly strong influence on Portugal's younger artists. Her large-scale often self-reflective photographic portraits combine drawing, photography and painting, challenging the relationship between illusion and reality.

Among the younger generation, born around the time of the 1974 revolution – an event that inspired a surge of artistic development – Miguel Branco is the link between the new and old eras. His small, evocative paintings bring to mind the Renaissance masters, despite being contemporary in presentation. Eduardo Batarda produces influential works in acrylic, often adapting paintings in comic-strip style. Other 20th-century stars to keep an eye out for are António Areal, Angelo de Sousa and Nadir Afonso.

THE MAGICAL WORLD OF PAULA REGO

One of Portugal's best-known painters, Paula Rego is a major presence in the art world. Born in 1935 in Lisbon, Rego grew up in a wealthy family during the early days of the repressive Salazar regime, in an atmosphere that would one day set the mood for her darkest works. Rego's artistic talents were recognised at a young age, and she went to England – studying at the Slade School of Art – where she would eventually emigrate.

Her first solo show was held in Lisbon in 1965, and it was highly praised for its jarringly expressive images, though it was years before the rest of the world would acclaim her work. Rego's signature style developed around fairy-tale paintings given a nightmarish twist. Her works deal in ambiguity and psychological and sexual tension, such as *The Family* (1988) where a seated business man is either being tortured or smothered with affection by his wife and daughter. Domination, fear, sexuality and grief are all recurring themes in Rego's paintings, and the mysterious and sinister atmosphere, heavy use of chiaroscuro (stark contrasting of light and shade) and strange distortion of scale are reminiscent of surrealists Max Ernst and Giorgio de Chirico.

Rego, now in her 70s, is considered one of the great early champions for painting from a female perspective, and she continues to contribute to a sizable volume of work. She has also painted portraits, including one of Germaine Greer, which hangs in London's National Portrait Gallery, and the official presidential portrait of Jorge Sampaio. In Portugal you can see some of her work at Lisbon's Centro de Arte Moderna (p101).

Graça Morais, a figurative artist from Trás-os-Montes, paints moving scenes from her village life.

However, the biggest trend in Portuguese contemporary art is in innovative video and multimedia projects. Most notably, João Onofre's primitive grainy creations take a humorous look at social dynamics; Miguel Soares' futuristic, slightly unsettling works reflect Portugal's rapidly changing times; and João Penalva's music and video installations are well worth looking out for. Minimalist painter Julião Sarmento has also dabbled in video and photographic works to explore different ways of seeing.

Other exciting breaks with tradition include the work of young collectives such as the Tone Scientists (Carlos Roque, Rui Valério and Rui Toscano), which blends visual art with classical music, and offbeat events such as the Festival Internacional de Banda Desenhada da Amadora (www.amadorabd.com in Portuguese), held every November near Lisbon, showcasing the talents of Portugal's comic-strip artists.

SCULPTURE

Sculptors have excelled throughout Portugal's history. Among the first masterpieces are the carved tombs of the 12th to 14th centuries, including those of Inês de Castro and Dom Pedro in the Mosteiro de Santa Maria de Alcobaça (p281).

In the Manueline era sculptors including Diogo de Boitaca went wild with Portuguese seafaring fantasies and exuberant decoration. At the same time, foreign influences were seeping in, including Flemish, followed in the 16th century by the flamboyant Gothic and plateresque styles of Spanish Galicia and Biscay. During the Renaissance, several French artists settled in Portugal and excelled in architectural sculpting. The ornate pulpit in Coimbra's Igreja de Santa Cruz (p307) is regarded as Nicolas Chanterène's masterpiece.

Foreign schools continued to influence Portuguese sculptors in the 18th-century baroque era, when Dom João V took advantage of the assembly of foreign artists working on the Convento do Mafra to found an influential school of sculpture. Its most famous Portuguese teacher was Joaquim Machado de Castro.

A century later the work of António Soares dos Reis reflected similar influences. However, Soares also tied himself in knots by attempting to capture in sculpture the melancholic feeling of *saudade* (p40), a uniquely Portuguese and impossibly intangible concept. You can see one of his most famous works, *O Desterrado,* at the museum dedicated to the great sculptor – and other 19th-century artists – in Porto's Museu Nacional Soares dos Reis (p363).

At the turn of the 20th century two names were prominent: Francisco Franco and the prolific sculptor António Teixeira Lopes, whose most famous work is his series of children's heads. These, along with work by Soares, are on display in the Museu Nacional Soares dos Reis in Porto (p363).

Leading lights on the contemporary scene include Noé Sendas, who creates life-size figures in thought-provoking poses and dress; Leonor Antunes, whose sculptural installations invite viewers to explore how they relate to their surroundings; and Lisbon's Pedro-Cabrita Reis, who also creates impressive architectural installations designed to stimulate memories. Also keep an eye out for the dramatic modern sculptures by Rui Chafes, influenced heavily by the romantic period.

HANDICRAFTS & INDIGENOUS ARTS

You only have to visit the big weekly markets in Portugal to see the astounding range of traditional handicrafts available – from myriad forms of ceramics to baskets of rush, willow, cane or rye straw, and from the fabulously painted wooden furniture of the Alentejo to the carved ox yokes of the Minho.

Long traditions of hand-embroidery and weaving are also found throughout Portugal, as is lace-making, which is mainly found along the coast ('where there are nets, there is lace,' goes the saying).

For details of where to buy these crafts, see p462.

Apart from Lisbon, the biggest single community of Portuguese is found in Paris.

Theatre & Dance

The theatre scene has finally cast out the demons of the Salazar years. The venerable Teatro Nacional Dona Maria II of Lisbon and Teatro Nacional de São João of Porto have now been joined by numerous private companies, boosted by increased funding from the Ministry of Culture. Portugal's biggest recent theatre success has been the musical *Amália* (about *fado*'s greatest diva), seen by more than a million people. Also keep an eye out for Tomar's innovative theatre company, Fatias de Cá, which tends to perform in amazing venues, such as castles and palaces.

The Gulbenkian Foundation, one of Portugal's most generous and wide-ranging private arts sponsors, also continues to support new theatre companies and dance. Indeed, Portuguese modern dance is capturing increased international acclaim, and every November contemporary dance fans flock to Lisbon's Festival Internacional de Dança Contemporânea. One of the country's leading choreographers is Vera Mantero, previously a ballerina, now an exponent of cutting-edge experimental dance styles. Prestigious ballet performances also take place in palatial settings in Sintra during August.

The in-depth Portuguese Culture Web (www.portcult.com) is an amusing personal look at Portuguese culture from an immigrant's perspective.

However, it's good old folk dancing that you'll most frequently see in the north. Almost every village has its own dancers, all in flamboyant costumes, with the women draped in jewellery. Their whirling, foot-stomping and finger-waggling routines make great watching. Some, such as the flowery *pauliteiros* (stick dancers) of Miranda do Douro (see the boxed text, p452), have gone professional, touring the country and abroad.

Architecture

Portugal's varied assortment of cathedrals, castles and *cromeleques* (circle of prehistoric standing stones) are just a few small pieces of the country's great architectural jigsaw puzzle. Travellers with an interest in the past and an eye for the aesthetic have hundreds of sights to satisfy them.

Among the many famous icons here are wildly baroque monasteries, complete with masterfully carved façades, blinding interiors of gold-and-stone towers stretching to the sky. Medieval, Renaissance and Gothic churches are other top destinations for experiencing Portugal's architectural masterpieces, many of them dating from the Age of Discoveries.

Vestiges of the Roman Empire live on in well-preserved temples and in ruins of former villas scattered about the countryside. There are also low-rising stone cathedrals left by the Romans' Visigothic successors, and neighbourhoods first laid out during Moorish times – narrow, winding lanes crisscrossing past whitewashed houses whose façades haven't changed much in the last 1000 years.

Medieval castles and walled fortress towns offer a glimpse into Portugal's early nationhood. Visitors to remote outposts are often rewarded with sublime castle-top views over the countryside.

Works from the 19th and 20th centuries show Portugal at its most eclectic, from playful, wrought-iron elevator towers (diminutive cousins of Monsieur Eiffel) to sweeping plazas framed with beaux-arts backdrops, with a handful of modernist architects adding new touches to Portugal's handsomely set stage.

PALAEOLITHIC PALETTE

A most mysterious group of 95 huge monoliths form a strange circle in an isolated clearing among Alentejan olive groves near Évora. It's one of Europe's most impressive prehistoric sites: the Cromeleque dos Almendres.

All over Portugal, but especially in the Alentejo, you can visit such ancient funerary and religious structures, built during the Neolithic and Megalithic eras, about 6000 years ago. Most impressive are the dolmens: funerary chambers – rectangular, polygonal or round – reached by a corridor of stone slabs and covered with earth to create an artificial mound. King of these is

ARCHITECTURAL TOP 10

- Cromeleque dos Almendres (p230) – a mystical setting of 95 prehistoric big stones.
- Templo Romano (p223) – straight from Rome in the heart of Évora.
- Mosteiro de Santa Maria de Alcobaça (p281) – lean Gothic at its best.
- Palácio Nacional de Mafra (p143) – vast, vast, vast extravagance.
- Convento de Cristo (p297) – mysterious Manueline, Gothic and Renaissance styles.
- Mosteiro de Santa Maria da Vitória (p283) – Gothic grandeur.
- Mosteiro dos Jerónimos (p102) – Manueline masterpiece.
- Gare do Oriente (p104) – hyper-modern breeziness.
- Torre de Belém (p102) – one of Lisbon's iconic landmarks.
- Boa Nova Casa-Chá (p372) – Alvaro Siza Vieira's modernist-magic ocean-fronting teahouse. It's in Leça da Palmeira, 20 minutes north of Porto.

the Anta Grande do Zambujeiro, also near Évora, and Europe's largest dolmen, with six 6m-high stones forming a huge chamber. Single monoliths, or menhirs, often carved with phallic or religious symbols, also dot the countryside like an army of stone sentinels. Their relationship to promoting fertility seems obvious.

With the arrival of the Celts (800–200 BC) came the first established hilltop settlements, called *castros*. The best-preserved example is the Citânia de Briteiros, where you can literally step into Portugal's past. Stone dwellings were built on a circular or elliptical plan, and the complex was surrounded with a dry-stone defensive wall. In the *citânias* (fortified villages) further south, dwellings tended to be rectangular.

ROMANS & RUINS

The Romans left their typical architectural and engineering feats – roads, bridges, towns complete with forums (marketplaces), villas, public baths and aqueducts. These have now largely disappeared from the surface, though the majority of Portugal's cities are built on Roman foundations and you can descend into dank foundations under new buildings in Lisbon and Évora. At Conimbriga, the country's largest Roman site, an entire Roman town is under excavation. Revealed so far are some spectacular mosaics, along with structural or decorative columns, carved entablatures and classical ornamentation, which give a sense of the Roman high life.

Portugal's most famous and complete Roman ruin is the Templo Romano, the so-called Temple of Diana in Évora, with its flouncy-topped Corinthian columns, nowadays echoed by the complementary towers of Évora cathedral. This is the finest temple of its kind on the Iberian Peninsula, its preservation the result of having been walled up in the Middle Ages, and later used as a slaughterhouse.

At the well-produced panoramic creation 360°Portugal (www.360portugal.com) you can peer around castles, megaliths, churches, archaeological sites and more.

The various Teutonic tribes who invaded after the fall of Rome in the early 5th century left little trace other than a few churches built by the Visigoths, a fierce bunch of Arian Christians. Though heavily restored over the centuries, these ancient churches still reveal a Roman basilica outline, rectangular and divided by columns into a nave and two aisles. Two fine examples are the Capela de São Pedro de Balsemão and the Igreja de Santo Amaro. Most unusual is the Capela de São Frutuoso (near Braga) – Byzantine (Graeco-Asiatic) in character and laid out in the shape of a Greek cross.

The Visigoths also rebuilt the Roman town of Idanha-a-Velha, now a quiet hamlet near Castelo Branco; you can see their influence in parts of the cathedral here. Many other Visigothic churches were destroyed by the Moors after they kicked out the Visigoths in AD 711.

MOOR STYLE

Unlike Spain, Portugal has no complete buildings left from the Moorish period. You will find the odd Moorish arch or wall, bits of fortresses, and the atmospheric remains of several *mourarias* (Moorish quarters), notably in Moura, which retains a well and a Moorish tower as part of its castle. Nearby Mértola retained much of its Islamic characteristics (nothing like a bit of economic torpor to halt development) and includes a distinctive former mosque converted into a church. Silves was the Moorish capital of the Algarve, and retains an enormous well, now on display as part of the archaeological museum.

The Moors did, however, powerfully influence Portuguese architecture, no matter how hard the Christians tried to stamp out their mark. This is particularly noticeable in private homes, and especially in the south: terraces and horseshoe arches, wrought-iron work and whitewash, flat roofs and geometric ornamentation, and the use of water in decoration.

FORTRESS-CHURCHES

During the Christian recapture of Portugal from the Moors, completed by 1297, most mosques were torn down and replaced by a church or cathedral, often on the same site. These were in the simple, robust Romanesque style – with rounded arches, thick walls and heavy vaulting – originally introduced to Portugal by Burgundian monks. As in Lisbon and Coimbra, they often resembled fortifications – demonstrating concerns about the Moors wreaking revenge, and anticipating the Castilian threat.

Fires of Excellence: Spanish and Portuguese Oriental Architecture, by Miles Danby & Matthew Weinreb (1998), is a stunningly photographed exploration of Portugal's Arabian history and aesthetics.

More delicate Romanesque touches can be found in several small, lovely churches, notably the Igreja de São Salvador in Bravães, where portals often display fine animal or plant motifs in their archivolts. Only one complete example of a secular building remains from this time – Bragança's endearing five-sided Domus Municipalis, Portugal's oldest town hall.

GREAT GOTHIC

Cistercians introduced the Gothic trend, and this reached its pinnacle in Alcobaça, in one of Portugal's most ethereally beautiful buildings. The austere abbey church and cloister of the Mosteiro de Santa Maria de Alcobaça, begun in 1178, has a lightness and simplicity strongly influenced by Clairvaux Abbey in France. Its hauntingly simple Cloisters of Silence were a model for later cathedral cloisters at Coimbra, Lisbon, Évora, and many others. This was the birth of Portuguese Gothic, which flowered and transmuted over the coming years as the country gained more and more experience of the outside world. For centuries Portugal had been culturally dominated and restricted by Spain and the Moors.

By the 14th century, when the Mosteiro de Santa Maria da Vitória (commonly known as Mosteiro da Batalha or Battle Abbey) was constructed, simplicity was a distant, vague memory. Portuguese, Irish and French architects worked on this breathtaking monument for more than two centuries. The combination of their skills and the changing architectural fashions of the times, from Flamboyant (late) Gothic to Gothic Renaissance and then Manueline, turned the abbey into a seething mass of carving, organic decorations, lofty space, and slanting stained-glass light. It's a showcase of High Gothic art. It exults in the decorative (especially in its Gothic Royal Cloisters and Chapter House), while the flying buttresses tip their hat to English Perpendicular Gothic.

Portuguese Decorative Tiles, by Rioletta Sabo (1998), is an all-out wallow in the dazzling colours and diversity of Portugal's favourite wall-covering.

Secular architecture also enjoyed a Gothic boom, thanks to the need for fortifications against the Moors and to the castle-building fervour of the 13th-century ruler, Dom Dinis. Some of Portugal's most spectacular, huddled, thick-walled castles – for example, Estremoz, Óbidos and Bragança – date from this time, many featuring massive double-perimeter walls and an inner square tower.

AMAZING MANUELINE

Manueline is a uniquely Portuguese style, a specific, crazed flavour of late-Gothic architecture. Ferociously decorative, it coincided roughly with the reign of Dom Manuel I (1495–1521) and is interesting not just because of its extraordinarily imaginative designs, burbling with life, but also because this dizzyingly creative architecture skipped hand in hand with the era's booming confidence.

During Dom Manuel's reign, Vasco da Gama and fellow explorers claimed new overseas lands and new wealth for Portugal. The Age of Discoveries was expressed in sculptural creations of eccentric inventiveness, drawing heavily on nautical themes: twisted ropes, coral and anchors in stone, topped by the ubiquitous armillary sphere (a navigational device that became Dom

AZULEJOS

Portugal's favourite decorative art is easy to spot – polished painted tiles called *azulejos* (after the Arabic *al zulaycha,* meaning polished stone). These tiles cover everything from churches to houses to train stations with the best examples being at Aveiro, Pinhão and Porto's São Bento. The Moors introduced the art, having picked it up from the Persians, but the Portuguese liked it so much they tiled anything that stayed still long enough.

Portugal's earliest 16th-century tiles are Moorish, from Seville. These were decorated with interlocking geometric or floral patterns (figurative representations aren't an option for Muslim artists for religious reasons). After the Portuguese captured Ceuta in Morocco in 1415, they began exploring the art themselves. The 16th-century Italian invention of majolica, in which colours are painted directly onto wet clay over a layer of white enamel, gave works a fresco-like brightness and kicked off the Portuguese *azulejo* love affair.

You can easily spot the earliest tiles, polychrome and geometric, either imported by the Moors or produced by the Portuguese. The earliest home-grown examples date from the 1580s, and may be seen in churches such as Lisbon's Igreja de São Roque, providing an ideal counterbalance to fussy, gold-heavy baroque. Some of Portugal's earliest tiles adorn the Palácio Nacional da Sintra.

The late 17th century saw a fashion for huge panels, depicting everything from cherubs to commerce, saints to seascapes. As demand grew, mass production became necessary and the Netherlands' blue-and-white Delft tiles started to appear all over the walls.

Portuguese tile makers rose to the challenge of this influx, and the splendid work of virtuoso Portuguese masters António de Oliveira Bernardes and his son Policarpo in the 18th century springs from this competitive creativity. You can see their work in Évora, in the breathtaking Igreja de São João.

Fantastic 17th- and 18th-century tiling also covers the Igreja de São Vicente de Fora in Lisbon. Rococo themes appeared at this time, as can be seen in Lamego's Igreja de Nossa Senhora dos Remédios, or Lisbon's Palácio Nacional de Queluz and Quinta dos Marquêses da Fronteira, offering lots of buxom mythological ladies, and providing religious scenes with a chintzy garden-party look.

By the end of the century, industrial-scale manufacture began to affect quality, coupled with the massive demand for tiles after the 1755 Lisbon earthquake. Tiling answered the need for decoration, but was cheap and practical – a solution for a population that had felt the ground move beneath its feet.

From the late 19th century, the Art Nouveau and Art Deco movements took *azulejos* by storm, providing fantastic façades and interiors for shops, restaurants and residential buildings – notably by Rafael Bordalo Pinheiro (visit Caldas de Rainha, where there is a museum devoted to his work), Jorge Colaço and Jorge Barradas, whose work you can see at the Museu da Cidade in Lisbon.

Azulejos still coat contemporary life, and you can explore the latest in *azulejos* while going places on the Lisbon metro. Maria Keil designed 19 of the stations, from the 1950s onwards – look out for stunning block-type prints at Intendente (considered her masterpiece) and Anjos. Oriente also showcases extraordinary contemporary work. Artists from five continents were invited to contribute, including Austria's Hundertwasser. Look out also for public works by Júlio de Resende, responsible for Ribeira Negra, Porto (1987).

For more information on this beautiful art, and a visual feast, visit Lisbon's Museu Nacional do Azulejo. There are also many impressive pieces in Lisbon's Museu de Cidade. Lisbon and Porto have the best on-the-street examples.

Manuel's personal symbol) and the Cross of the Order of Christ (symbol of the religious military order that largely financed and inspired Portugal's explorations).

Manueline first emerged in Setúbal's Igreja de Jesus, designed in the 1490s by French expatriate Diogo de Boitaca, who gave it columns like trees growing into the ceiling, and ribbed vaulting like twisted ropes. The style quickly caught on, and soon decorative carving was creeping, twisting and crawling over everything (aptly described by 19th-century English novelist William Beckford as 'scollops and twistifications').

Outstanding Manueline masterpieces are the Mosteiro dos Jerónimos, masterminded largely by Diogo de Boitaca and João de Castilho and the Mosteiro de Santa Maria da Vitória's otherworldly Capelas Imperfeitas (Unfinished Chapels).

Other famous creations include Belém's Torre de Belém, a Manueline-Moorish cake crossed with a chesspiece by Diogo de Boitaca and his brother Francisco, and Diogo de Arruda's fantastical organic, seemingly barnacle-encrusted window in the Chapter House of Tomar's Convento de Cristo, as well as its fanciful 16-sided charola – the Templar church, resembling an eerie *Star Wars* set. Many other churches sport a Manueline flourish against a plain façade.

The style was enormously resonant in Portugal, and reappeared in the early 20th century in exercises in mystical Romanticism, such as Sintra's Quinta da Regaleira and Palácio Nacional da Pena, and Luso's over-the-top and extraordinary neo-Manueline Palace Hotel do Buçaco.

Memorial do Convento (Baltazar and Blimunda; 1982) is José Saramago's Nobel prize–winning novel about the Mafra extravaganza – a convent-palace dreamed up by size-junkies and compulsive builders.

RENAISSANCE TOUCHES

After all that froth and fuss, the Portuguese were somewhat slow to take up the Renaissance style, which signalled a return to Roman classical design and proportion. One of its protagonists, the Italian Andrea Sansovino, is thought to have spent some time in Portugal, though he seems to have made little impression. The Quinta da Bacalhoa, a 15th-century house at Vila Nogueira de Azeitão (near Setúbal) is his only notable contribution. The French sculptor Nicolas Chanterène was the main pioneer of Renaissance ideas here, and from around 1517 onwards, his influence abounds in both sculpture and architectural decoration.

Portugal has few Renaissance buildings, but some examples of the style are the Great Cloisters in Tomar's Convento de Cristo, designed by Spanish Diogo de Torralva in the late 16th century; the nearby Igreja de Nossa Senhora da Conceição; and the Convento de Bom Jesus at Valverde, outside Évora.

Work on the Palácio Nacional de Mafra was so lavish and expensive it nearly bankrupted the country.

MOODY & MANNERIST

Sober and severe, the Mannerist style reflects the spirit of its time, coinciding with the years of Spanish rule (1580–1640) and the heavy influence of the Inquisition and the Jesuits.

This style persisted throughout much of the 17th century. Lisbon's marvellous Igreja de São Vicente de Fora, built between 1582 and 1627 by Felipe Terzi, is a typical example of balanced Mannerist classicism. It served as a model for many other churches.

BRAZIL, BAROQUE & BUCKETS OF GOLD

With independence from Spain re-established and the influence of the Inquisition on the wane, Portugal burst out in baroque fever – an architectural style that was exuberant, theatrical and fired straight at the senses. Nothing could rival the Manueline flourish, but the baroque style – named after the

MATERIAL MATTERS

Local architecture varies according to climate and building materials to hand. Northern Portugal is packed with granite, a hard material perfect for constructing thick-walled, two-storey houses with slate roofs that keep out winter weather. In the coastal Beiras, local limestone is used for houses that are faced with painted stucco or, occasionally, *azulejos*.

On the coast near Aveiro, several villages are famous for their candy-striped houses built of wood from nearby pine forests. Brick houses in the Ribatejo and the Alentejo are long, single-storey structures, stuccoed and whitewashed, with a single colour (usually blue) outlining their architectural features. To keep out the summer heat these houses have few doors and windows; their huge fireplaces and chimneys provide both warmth and a place to smoke the meat and sausages typical of the region.

Perhaps most extraordinary are the marble towns in the Alentejo – Estremoz, Vila Viçosa and Borba – where there is such a surfeit of fine marble that it is casually used everywhere, from kerbs to cobblestones, giving the towns a luminescent pinky-golden glow.

By contrast, the Algarve's clay or stone houses appear modest. Those with flat terraces (used for drying produce, catching rainwater and generally hanging out), instead of the usual red-tile roofs, are a Moorish legacy. Such characteristics are a combination of Arabic tradition and architectural influences absorbed on long-distance travels abroad. In Tavira, for example, pagoda-like red-tiled roofs are a souvenir of visits east. Typical, too, of Mediterranean houses are the Algarve's shaded porches and arcaded verandas at ground level.

Portuguese word for a rough pearl, *barroco* – cornered the market in flamboyance. At its height in the 18th century (almost a century later than in Italy), it was characterised by curvaceous forms, huge monuments, spatially complex schemes and lots and lots and lots of gold.

Financed by the 17th-century gold and diamond discoveries in Brazil, and encouraged by the extravagant Dom João V, local and foreign (particularly Italian) artists created mind-bogglingly opulent masterpieces. You'll see prodigious *talha dourada* (gilded woodwork) in church interiors all over the place, but it reached its most extreme in Aveiro's Convento de Jesus, Lisbon's Igreja de São Roque and Porto's Igreja de São Francisco.

The baroque of central and southern Portugal was more restrained. Examples include the chancel of Évora's cathedral, and the massive Palácio Nacional de Mafra. Designed by the German architect João Frederico Ludovice to rival the similar palace-monastery of San Lorenzo de El Escorial (near Madrid), the Mafra version is relatively sober, apart from its size – which is such that at one point it had a workforce of 45,000 working on it, looked after by a police force of 7000.

Earth Architecture in Portugal, edited by Felipe Jorge (2005), contains more than 50 essays dealing with the technique, history and anthropology of building with natural materials, aka dirt.

Meanwhile, the Tuscan painter and architect Nicolau Nasoni (who settled in Porto around 1725) introduced a more ornamental baroque style to the north. Nasoni is responsible for Porto's Torre dos Clérigos and Igreja da Misericórdia, and the whimsical Palácio de Mateus near Vila Real (internationally famous as the image on Mateus rosé wine bottles).

In the mid-18th century a school of architecture evolved in Braga. Local artists such as André Soares built churches and palaces in a very decorative style, heavily influenced by Augsburg engravings from southern Germany. Soares' Casa do Raio, in Braga, and much of the monumental staircase of the nearby Bom Jesus do Monte, are typical examples of this period's ornamentation.

Only when the gold ran out did the baroque fad fade. At the end of the 18th century, architects flirted briefly with rococo (best exemplified by Mateus Vicente's Palácio de Queluz), begun in 1747, or the palace at Estói before embracing neoclassicism.

POST-EARTHQUAKE SOBRIETY

After Lisbon's devastating 1755 earthquake, the autocratic Marquês de Pombal invited architect Eugenio dos Santos to rebuild the Baixa area in a plain style, using classical elements that could be easily built and repeated. This new 'Pombaline' style featured a grid pattern marked by unadorned houses and wide avenues. It had a knock-on effect and led to a reaction against the excesses of the baroque period in other parts of the country. In Porto, for instance, the Hospital de Santo António and the Feitoria Inglesa (Factory House), both designed by Englishmen, show a noticeable return to sober Palladian and classical designs. Lisbon's early-19th-century Palácio Nacional da Ajuda was also designed on neoclassical lines and served as the inspiration for the elegantly restrained Palácio de Brejoeira (near Monção, in the Minho).

Houses were tiled on the outside after the 1755 earthquake as a cheap and more expendable means of decoration.

NEO-EVERYTHING, ART NOUVEAU & THE NEW

In the early 19th century most new building of major monuments came to a halt. This was partly due to the aftereffects of the Peninsular War (1807–14) and partly because a liberal decree in 1834 dissolved the religious orders, allowing their many buildings to be appropriated by the state. Some former monasteries are still used by the government today – notably Lisbon's Benedictine Mosteiro de São Bento, now the seat of parliament.

Alvaro Siza, by Brigitte Fleck (2001), is a handy monograph on the great contemporary architect, whose nationwide projects include the clean cubism of Porto's Museu de Arte Contemporânea.

When new buildings did emerge they tended to draw on all the architectural styles of the past, from Moorish (as in Lisbon's Rossio station) to neoclassical (Porto's stock exchange, the Palácio da Bolsa). A distinctly French influence can be seen in many grand apartment blocks and office buildings built at this time.

Towards the end of the 19th century the increased use of iron and steel reflected Portugal's emergence as an industrial nation. Train stations (eg Lisbon's Alcântara station) and other grand buildings were covered in iron and glass. Gustave Eiffel built iron bridges across the rivers Minho, Lima and Douro, and his followers were responsible for several Gustav Eiffel design-aesthetic (exposed ironwork) lookalikes, including Lisbon's wonderfully eccentric Elevador de Santa Justa (kind of like the Eiffel Tower crossed with a doily).

One of the most delightful movements during this period was Art Nouveau, a burst of carefree, decorative fancy that produced many beautifully decorated cafés and shops – check out Lisbon's Versailles and Pastelaria São Roque, or Braga's Café Astória.

HAIL, SIZA

One of Portugal's great contemporary architects, Álvaro Siza Vieira (born 1933) remains fairly unknown outside his home country. In fact, even outside of Porto, many Portuguese can't quite place his name. This is surprising given his loyal following in the architecture world, his long and distinguished career and his award-winning designs (which garnered him the coveted Pritzker Prize in 1992). Part of the reason for this is perhaps his deceptively minimalist creations.

On the surface, his work may seem less than dazzling. Stucco, stone, tile and glass are his building materials of choice, and his designs might seem to the casual observer like low-rising boxlike structures. Yet, once inside, it's a different story: the whole trumps the parts, and everything – inside and out – morphs into a smoothly integrated work. Place means everything in Siza Vieira's work, with geography and climate carefully considered before any plans are laid.

In recent years, Siza Vieira has begun designing household objects in collaboration with New York–based Ohm Design. This includes a curiously reimagined port glass. You can see images of his work on www.pritzkerprize.com/siza.htm.

The Salazar years favoured decidedly severe, Soviet-style, state commissions (eg Coimbra University's dull faculty buildings, which replaced elegant 18th-century neoclassical ones). Ugly buildings and apartment blocks rose on city outskirts. Notable exceptions dating from the 1960s are Lisbon's Palácio da Justiça in the Campolide district, and the gloriously sleek Museu Calouste Gulbenkian. The beautiful wood-panelled Galeto café-restaurant is a time capsule from this era.

The tendency towards urban mediocrity continued after the 1974 revolution, although architects such as Fernando Távora and Eduardo Souto Moura have produced impressive schemes. Lisbon's postmodern Amoreiras shopping complex, by Tomás Taveira, is another striking contribution.

Portugal's greatest contemporary architect is Álvaro Siza Vieira. A believer in clarity and simplicity, his expressionist approach is reflected in projects such as the Pavilhão de Portugal for Expo 98, Porto's splendid Museu de Arte Contemporânea and the Igreja de Santa Maria at Marco de Canavezes, south of Amarante. He has also restored central Lisbon's historic Chiado shopping district with notable sensitivity, following a major fire in 1988.

Spanish architect Santiago Calatrava designed the lean organic monster Gare do Oriente for the Expo 98, architecture that is complemented by the work of many renowned contemporary artists. The interior is more state-of-the-art spaceship than station. The longest bridge in Europe, the Ponte de Vasco da Gama built in 1998, stalks out across the river from nearby.

The Lisbon metro is not just about transport – it's an art gallery, showcasing the best of Portuguese contemporary art and architecture, with especially wonderful *azulejos*. Check out Metro Lisboa's website at www.metrolisboa.pt.

Environment

THE LAND

Portugal is one of Europe's smallest countries, covering an area of just 92,389 sq km and measuring only 560km north to south and 220km east to west. But despite its pipsqueak size, its land is impressively diverse. A single day's travel could see you pass from dramatic mountain ranges in the north to undulating meadows in the south; meanwhile the coast switches its mood from wicked surf-crashing Atlantic waves to balmy Mediterranean beaches, perfect for paddlers.

Landscapes of Portugal, by Brian and Eileen Anderson (1993) and the more up-to-date *Landscapes of the Algarve* (2000) are great sources for country walks and car journeys in Portugal.

Together with Ireland and Spain, Portugal dips its toes into the Atlantic at the westernmost extreme of Europe; and it's no accident that, with 830km of Atlantic coastline, Portugal is one of the greatest nations of seafarers and explorers in history. In many ways though, Portugal is at the mercy of its rivers, which bring precious water to its parched southern lands due to its lack of rainfall.

One of Portugal's most important waterways, the Rio Tejo, slices the country almost perfectly in half, flowing northeast to southwest and spilling its contents into the Atlantic at Lisbon, one of Portugal's few natural harbours. The mountains loom mostly north of the Tejo, while vast plains spread to the south.

Topping the country, the heavily populated northwestern Minho is blessed with fertile rolling plateaus and rivers flowing through deep gorges. Step down and neighbouring Beira Alta, Douro and Trás-os-Montes are all carved from high granite, schist and slate plateaus. This region, rising to 800m, is nicknamed the *terra fria* (cold country) for its winter chill.

Portugal is home to the most endangered big cat in the world.

Meanwhile the southern and eastern Alto Douro (in southern Trás-os-Montes) rightly scores the name *terra quente* (hot country), a scorched landscape of sheltered valleys with dark schists that trap the heat and create the perfect microclimate – described by locals as 'nine months of winter and three months of hell' – for pumping out Portugal's famous port wine.

However, for real mountains you need only look to the Serra da Estrela, which tops out at the 1993m Torre, the highest peak in mainland Portugal and home to a winter ski resort. Rolling down further south, you'll reach the low-lying, often marshy Atlantic coastline of Beira Litoral and Estremadura, sprinkled with river-mouth lagoons and salt marshes.

Inland, between the Rio Tejo and the Rio Guadiana, the Alto Alentejo joins the Spanish tablelands in wide flat plateaus. Further south still, in northern Baixo Alentejo, are ridges of quartz and marble, and a vast undulating landscape of wheat, cork trees and olive trees – a large swath of which is now submerged by the vast Barragem do Alqueva (Alqueva Dam).

RESPONSIBLE TOURISM

Every year around six million sun-seeking visitors cram into the overdeveloped beaches of the Algarve, permanently transforming the coastline and once-remote habitats. You can't halt the inexorable rise of hotel, villa and apartment-block complexes, but if you want to minimise your impact on the south's delicate landscapes, do beware of supposedly 'ecofriendly' tours such as jeep safaris that, though great fun, damage and disrupt natural habitats.

Instead you could choose organised walks, which are far less destructive plus you learn first-hand knowledge of environmental issues. Walks organised by the Associação Nacional de Conservação da Natureza (Quercus; p66), the country's leading environmental organisation, are recommended, but we also note other organisations that offer guided walks in local listings in the regional chapters throughout this guide.

THE LYNX EFFECT

No endangered animal in Portugal plucks at the heartstrings quite like the tufty-eared Iberian lynx. Though not much bigger than the common house cat, this is the only big cat endemic to Europe and is easily the world's most endangered feline. There are thought to be just 120 Iberian lynx are now left in Spain and Portugal, its numbers decimated by disease, poachers, wildfires, dam- and road-building and the scarcity of wild rabbits (its favourite food).

The last remaining hide-outs of the animals in Portugal are mostly in scattered, remote regions of the Algarve – though some conservationists wonder if any lynx remain in Portugal. A network of protected areas, habitat corridors and captive breeding programmes are now being thrown together to save the species. For details of how to help, check the website of **SOS Lynx** (www.soslynx.org). It's alarming to think that if the species dies out, it may well be the first feline extinction since prehistoric times.

Only the eastern Serra do Caldeirão and western Serra de Monchique break the flatness of the south, and are a natural border between the Alentejo and the Algarve. They also act as a climatic buffer for the Algarve, which basks in a Mediterranean glow.

The islands of Madeira and the Azores, originally colonised in the 15th century, are also part of Portugal: Madeira lies 900km to the southwest, off Africa's west coast; the nine-island Azores archipelago sprawls 1440km west of Lisbon.

WILDLIFE

While few visitors come to Portugal specifically to track down its wildlife, the country is nonetheless home to some of the rarest and most interesting creatures in Europe. Northern Portugal has forests and hills rich in animal and bird life, while the south's parched plains and coastline also shelter their fair share of fauna.

Birdwatching Guide to the Algarve, by Kevin and Christine Carlson (1995), has all the information you'll need on south-coast birds.

Animals

Several of Portugal's rarest creatures are the shaggy-bearded Iberian lynx (see above), now teetering on the brink of extinction, and the much-maligned wolf. However, the fauna you're most likely to stumble across are hares and bats. With luck, in more remote areas you might be able to spot foxes, deer, otters or even foraging wild boars.

A few North African species have also sneaked into the picture. The most delightful settler is the Mediterranean chameleon, which was introduced to the eastern coastal Algarve about 70 years ago. Two more such species are the spotted, weasel-like genet, which hides during the day, and the Egyptian mongoose, which you may stumble upon as it trots across quieter Algarve roads.

To read reports and view photos of bird watchers who have travelled in Portugal, visit www.travellingbirder.com.

Bird fanciers will also be kept busy. Portugal has a mixed bag of bird life – from temperate to Mediterranean species, plus migrants too. You've an excellent chance of admiring wetland species – including flamingos, egrets, herons, spoonbills and many species of shore birds – in reserves, such as the Reserva Natural do Sapal de Castro Marim e Vila Real de Santo António and the Parque Natural da Ria Formosa.

You may even score a glimpse of more unusual birds: nimble lesser kestrels and the shy black stork near Mértola and around Castro Verde, vividly coloured purple gallinules in the Parque Natural da Ria Formosa, hefty bustards and sandgrouse on the Alentejo plains, and Iberian species such as the great spotted cuckoo, red-winged nightjar, rufous bushchat and azure-winged magpie.

However, if it's birds of prey that ruffle your feathers, your best bet is in the Parque Natural do Douro Internacional, over which soar various species of eagles, kestrels and vultures.

Portugal's leading ornithological society is the **Sociedade Portuguesa para o Estudo de Aves** (SPEA; ☎ 213 220 430; www.spea.pt in Portuguese; Rua da Vitória 53, 1100-618 Lisbon), which runs government-funded projects to map the distribution of Portugal's breeding birds. **Naturetrek** (☎ 01962 733051 in the UK; www.naturetrek.co.uk) runs an eight-day bird-watching excursion around southern Portugal.

Grupo Lobo is a wolf-conservation organisation and runs volunteer programmes. For more information on the disappearing Iberian wolf, see their website (http://lobo.fc.ul.pt).

ENDANGERED SPECIES

The most high profile of Portugal's endangered animals is the fast-dwindling Iberian lynx (p61). But this iconic species is not the only one set to disappear.

Moving from cats to dogs – the rusty-coloured Iberian wolf is also in serious decline. Shockingly, there are only around 200 left in Portugal (out of an estimated 1500 on the Iberian Peninsula). Most live in the Parque Natural de Montesinho in Trás-os-Montes and adjacent areas of Spain. But despite being protected by law, the wolf is still illegally shot, trapped or poisoned on a regular basis as it is blamed (often mistakenly) for attacking cattle and domestic animals.

The Mediterranean chameleon, resident of the south coast, has a tongue longer than its body.

Dog-lovers will be fascinated by the web-footed wonder, the Algarve water-dog. This little creature's unique webbed feet once made it the fisherman's best friend, able to dive down to depths of 6m to retrieve broken nets. Now practically extinct (dog fanciers in the USA have snapped up many in recent years) it's the subject of a special breeding programme at the Parque Natural da Ria Formosa's Quinta de Marim headquarters. The park is also home to the strictly protected Mediterranean chameleon, though its shifting colours can make it hard to spot!

Portugal's protected areas also harbour several endangered birds, including the majestic Spanish imperial eagle, the tawny owl in the Parque Nacional da Peneda-Gerês, and the purple gallinule in the Parque Natural da Ria Formosa.

Outside the parks you can see endangered species in Mértola, which hosts the country's largest nesting colony of lesser kestrels between March and September, or in the Castro Verde region, a haunt of the great bustard, Europe's heaviest bird, weighing in at a whopping 17kg! (This is one of the heaviest birds capable of flight.)

The Algarve Tiger, by Eduardo Goncalves et al (2002), is a passionate book about the world's most endangered feline, the Iberian lynx.

Plants

Like its climate, Portugal's flora is a potent cocktail of Mediterranean and Atlantic elements. In spring, Mediterranean flowers set the countryside ablaze in the Algarve and Alentejo; especially enchanting are the white and purple rockroses. The pretty Bermuda buttercup, a South African invader, also paints Algarve fields a brilliant yellow in the winter. Orchid lovers will also have a wild time. They thrive in the Algarve, especially around Faro. Meanwhile, in the rainier northern climes, gorse, heather and broom cloak the hillsides.

Early settlers in the south cultivated vines and citrus trees, while the Moors introduced almonds, carobs, figs, palms and the gorgeous white irises that decorate roadsides. Portuguese explorers and colonists also got in on the act, bringing back various exotics, including South African figs and American prickly-pear cacti.

In Sintra you'll see dozens of exotic species, planted as fashionable novelties in the 18th and 19th centuries. More recently, profitable plantations of Australian eucalyptus have engulfed vast areas with their thirsty monoculture. Eucalyptus trees grow faster than cork (cork takes about 40 years of growing before the tree is commercially viable versus 12 years for the eucalyptus), and they earn farmers more money – eucalyptus nets about €150 per hectare versus €45 for the cork. Eucalyptus is used in Portugal to make paper and pulp.

PUT A CORK IN IT

Doggedly battling it out with commercial giants like the eucalyptus are two home-grown trees that have long crafted Portugal's landscape and lifestyle: the olive and the cork oak, the latter now a threatened species. Since Roman times both have been grown and harvested in harmony with the environment, providing not only income but protection for many other species.

The olive tree, in fact, is one of the oldest known cultivated trees in the world, and the Romans considered those who used animal fats instead of olive oil in their diets to be barbarians. Olives have long had a prominent place on the Portuguese table, and the country produces 50,000 tons of olive oil annually. Different regions produce different types of olives, and there's much local lore tied up in the rich, oily fruit.

Travel across the vast Alentejo plains and you'll see wild twisted groves of olive trees. Even more predominant however, are the thousands of cork oak trees: they're the tall, round-topped evergreens with glossy, holly-like leaves and wrinkled bark that's often stripped away, leaving a strangely naked, ochre trunk.

Indeed the cork oak has long been one of the country's prize agricultural performers and Portugal is the biggest cork producer in the world. Treasured for its lightness, admired for its insulating and sealing qualities, and more versatile than any synthetic alternative, cork is used for everything from footwear to floors, gaskets to girders. And – of course – for bottle stoppers. The absence of smell and taste make it the essential 'bung' for quality wines.

Cork is cultivated as carefully as port wine. Trees mature for at least 25 years before their first stripping; indeed, there are laws against de-barking too early. After that they may only be shorn every ninth year. Cork cutters slice and snip by hand, as skilfully as barbers. Treated with such respect, a tree can produce cork for up to 200 years: moreover, the largest cork tree in Portugal produced over a tonne of raw cork last time it was harvested. Now that's a lot of bottles bunged!

Every year around 15 billion natural cork bottle-stoppers are produced in Portugal.

But this exceptionally sustainable industry is now under threat. There have long been critics of cork stoppers – some 300 million bottles of wine a year do indeed end up 'corked', contaminated by an organic compound in the cork. Now there's growing worldwide use of a synthetic alternative: plastic.

And much is at stake if cork forests decline. These are areas of exceptional biological diversity on which various threatened species depend, including the Iberian lynx and Bonelli's eagle. An international campaign has been launched to promote 'real cork' and urge producers and retailers to publicise its importance. Check out the website www.corkqc.com for more on the natural cork campaign and the multimillion euro battle to improve the quality of organic bottle stoppers in the face of their synthetic competition.

NATURAL PARKS & RESERVES

Portugal's myriad natural parks offer vast areas of unspoilt mountains, forests and coastal lagoons. And the reluctance of most Portuguese to go walking anywhere, let alone venture into remote areas, can be a huge bonus for travellers. Step even a short distance off the beaten track and you'll find that you have extraordinary landscapes all to yourself.

The Parque Nacional da Peneda-Gerês is the only bona-fide *parque nacional* (national park) in Portugal, but there are also 24 other *parques naturais* (natural parks), *reservas naturais* (nature reserves) and *paisagens protegidas* (protected landscape areas). These areas total some 6500 sq km – just over 7% of Portugal's land area.

The Instituto da Conservação da Natureza (ICN; Map p90) is the government agency responsible for the parks. Its **Divisão de Informática** (Information Division; ☎ 213 507 900; www.icn.pt in Portuguese; Rua de Santa Marta 55, Lisbon) has general information, but detailed maps and English-language materials are sur-

TOP NATURAL PARKS & RESERVES

Parks & Reserves	Features	Page
Parque Nacional da Peneda-Gerês	lushly forested mountains, rock-strewn plateaus; deer, birds of prey, hot springs, wolves, long-horned cattle	p422
Parque Natural da Arrábida	coastal mountain range, damaged by wildfire; birds of prey, diverse flora	p152
Parque Natural da Ria Formosa	salty coastal lagoons, lakes, marshes & dunes; rich bird life, beaches, Mediterranean chameleon	p167
Parque Natural da Serra da Estrela	pristine mountains – Portugal's highest; rich bird life, rare herbs	p332
Parque Natural da Serra de São Mamede	forest- & brush-covered mountains; vultures, eagles, kites, rare plants, black storks	p244
Parque Natural das Serras de Aire e Candeeiros	limestone mountains, cave systems; covered in gorse & olive trees	p291
Parque Natural de Montesinho	remote oasis of peaceful grassland & forest; last wild refuge for Iberian wolf	p446
Parque Natural de Sintra-Cascais	rugged coastline & mountains; diverse flora	p128
Parque Natural do Alvão	granite basin, pine forest, waterfalls; rich bird life, deer, boar	p436
Parque Natural do Douro Internacional	canyon country with high cliffs & lakes; home to many endangered birds of prey	p453
Parque Natural do Vale do Guadiana	gentle hills & plains, rivers; rare birds of prey, snakes, toads, prehistoric sites	p254
Parque Natural do Sudoeste Alentejano e Costa Vicentina	coastal cliffs & remote beaches; unique plants, otters, foxes, 200 bird types	p210
Reserva Natural da Berlenga	remote islands in clear seas, rock formations, caves; sea birds	p274
Reserva Natural das Dunas de São Jacinto	thickly wooded coastal park; rich in bird life	p325
Reserva Natural do Estuário do Sado	estuary of mud, marshes, lagoons & dunes; bird life incl flamingos, molluscs, bottlenose dolphins	p104
Reserva Natural do Sapal de Castro Marim e Vila Real de Santo António	marshland & salt pans; flamingos, spoonbills, avocet, caspian terns, white storks	p184

prisingly scant. Standards of maintenance and facilities vary wildly, and hopeful hikers may be disappointed by resources: 'trails' often turn out to be roads or nothing at all; the park 'map' may simply be a glossy leaflet for motorists; and 'park accommodation' a couple of huts, which are geared towards school groups.

Nevertheless, exploring Portugal's mixed bag of natural parks is worth the effort. Browse the table that shows Portugal's parks and nature reserves (opposite) to get a picture of all the rich wildlife and diverse landscapes on offer.

ENVIRONMENTAL ISSUES

Portugal has been slow to wake up to its environmental problems, notably soil erosion, pollution, rubbish disposal and the effects of mass tourism on fragile coastal areas. Of growing concern, too, is the spread of huge, water-thirsty eucalyptus plantations that effectively destroy regional wildlife habitat and aggravate an already serious drought problem brought on by climatic change. They're also a highly flammable species, making for some destructive fires (see p66). While such intensively cultivated plantations continue to proliferate (now accounting for over one-fifth of the country's forest area), Portugal's traditional, sustainable cork plantations are under serious threat.

Litter is a growing problem, but industrial development is to blame for Portugal's most polluted seasides – you'd be wise to avoid beaches near the industrial centre of Sines. Having said that, around 160 Portuguese beaches claim an international Blue Flag for cleanliness and some areas have undergone radical clean-ups in recent years.

More than 400 bird species have been spotted in Portugal.

However, disaster was narrowly averted along Portugal's northwestern coast in November 2002 when the oil tanker *Prestige* spilled 6000 tonnes of oil off the Spanish Galician coast, causing one of the world's worst environmental catastrophes. The ship emptied its oily slick over much of the western Spanish and part of the French coastline. To keep up to date with water quality, get hold of the free, regularly updated map of coastal water, *Qualidade da Água em Zonas Balneares* from **Instituto da Água** (☎ 218 430 022; inforag@inag.pt).

Fire & Drought

It's water – or rather the lack of it – that is fast becoming Portugal's worst environmental nightmare. Years of terrible drought in the mid-1990s heralded an alarming trend that continues to grow. Every year around 3% of Portugal's forest goes up in flames, worsening soil erosion and devastating farmland. And matters have only worsened in recent years.

Brush and forest fires in northern and central Portugal on average wipe out 1900 sq km per year, though fires in 2003 and 2005 were particularly bad. Adding to the devastation was the horrendous drought of 2005 – the country's worst since 1931 – completely wiping out its wheat crop.

An excellent general website on Portuguese environmental and nature-related topics is www.naturlink.pt.

Portugal is not alone in its thirst. Squabbles with Spain continue over shared water sources. Unfortunately for Portugal, three of its major rivers – the Douro, the Tejo and the Guadiana – originate in Spain. And both countries desperately need this water for agriculture (which accounts for three-quarters of water use in Portugal), hydroelectricity and to counter their dire drought situation in the south. Despite water-sharing agreements with Portugal, Spain is increasing its withdrawals from the Guadiana in order to divert the water to its dry southern lands.

Environmentalists point out the stress that the holiday-making economy places on local infrastructure. One 18-hole golf course, for instance, can use as much water in a year as 10,000 homes, and plans to build some 100,000 holiday homes in the Algarve over the next 10 years are likely to create problems of much greater magnitude.

PORTUGAL IN FLAMES

In the crackling summer heat, Portugal suffers annual fires that dart through the forests, attack houses and singe or kill wildlife. In 2003 massive infernos burned 5% of land and 13% of forests, and killed 18 people; damages were estimated at €1 billion. In 2005 fires were even more numerous, devastating some 3380 sq km of Portuguese land. The government has been criticised for its slow approach and for failing to prevent these serious fires. It's not out of the question that some were started by arsonists. Make sure you extinguish that cigarette butt.

Meanwhile, Portugal's own answer to this water problem has been to erect large dams – some 100 at last count – to control its precious water supply. Its most recent dam, the Barragem do Alqueva near Beja (p223), is a behemoth, which caused enormous environmental damage during its construction. The huge reservoir (Europe's largest manmade lake) now submerges around 260 sq km of the arid Alentejo. Among its casualties are over a million oak and olive trees and the habitats of several endangered species, including Bonelli's eagle, the otter, black storks, bats and the Iberian lynx. And that's not even mentioning the Stone Age art and Roman fortress now under water. Even the supposed beneficiaries – the farmers themselves – may increasingly find irrigation costs too high.

More than 400 bird species have been spotted in Portugal.

Environmental Organisations

Almargem (☎ 289 412 959; Alto de São Domingos 14, 8100-536 Loulé) Active in the Algarve.

Associação Nacional de Conservação da Natureza (Quercus; National Association for the Conservation of Nature; ☎ 217 788 474; www.quercus.pt in Portuguese; Apartado 4333, 1503-003 Lisbon) Portugal's best and busiest environmental group has branch offices and education centres scattered around Portugal. In addition to churning out studies and publishing environmental guides, Quercus members are Portugal's most active campaigners for environmental causes. Some Quercus branches arrange field trips.

Grupo de Estudos de Ordenomento do Território e Ambiente (Geota; ☎ 213 956 120; www.geota.pt; Travessa do Moinho de Vento 17, 1200-727 Lisbon) This environment study group is also an activist organisation that arranges weekend trips.

Liga para a Proteção da Natureza (LPN; League for the Protection of Nature; ☎ 217 780 097; www.lpn.pt; Estrela do Calhariz de Benfica 187, 1500-124 Lisbon) This is Portugal's oldest conservation group and often publicises environmental issues.

An excellent general website on Portuguese environmental and nature-related topics is www.naturlink.pt.

Portugal Outdoors

Blessed with some of Europe's loveliest Atlantic coastline, Portugal has some spectacular settings for outdoor adventure. Water sports are perhaps the top draw to the country, with dozens of excellent surfing and windsurfing beaches. Those who'd rather gaze at the waves than ride them can enjoy great views from some of the best golf courses on the continent. Taking a boat trip is another way to enjoy the dramatic coastline, whether heading off on leisurely dolphin-watching outings or sailing en route to good scuba-diving sites.

Popular inland activities include hiking, horse riding, mountain biking and canoeing. Adrenaline-fuelled sports like rappelling (abseiling) and paragliding are also growing in popularity, with some enticing options in the north.

No matter what you decide to do, you'll generally enjoy lower prices than elsewhere in Europe and, owing to Portugal's small size, you can take advantage of a range of diverse activities (and settings) on even a short holiday to the country.

CYCLING

If you want to take it faster, Portugal has many exhilarating mountain-biking (*bicyclete tudo terrano;* BTT) opportunities too. Monchique and Tavira in the Algarve, Sintra and Setúbal are all popular starting points for guided rural tours.

The country's most important cycling race is *Volta á Portugal,* a 10-stage, two-week race that follows immediately after the Tour de France.

For practical information on cycling in Portugal, see p472.

In the north try **PlanAlto** (☎ 253 311 807; Parque de Campismo de Cerdeira, Campo do Gerês, 4840-030 Terras de Bouro), with BTT trips around the Minho and Trás-os-Montes. Parque Nacional da Peneda-Gerês is also a great area for mountain biking.

For cycling tours, try the following UK- and US-based companies:

Easy Rider Tours (☎ 978-463 6955, 800 488 8332; www.easyridertours.com) Based in the US, and with a long menu of guided cycling and walking itineraries.

Rough Tracks (☎ 0870-066 0396; www.roughtracks.com) Offers one-week mountain-biking and road tours.

Saddle skedaddle (☎ 0191-265 1110; www.skedaddle.co.uk) Offers eight-day tours through isolated countryside.

DIVING

There are a handful of good dive sites in the country, most located in the Algarve. The water temperature is a bit crisp (around 14°C to 16°C, though it doesn't vary much between summer and winter); most divers prefer a 5mm suit.

Visibility is usually between 4m and 6m, though on the best days, it can range from 15m to 20m.

One of the best places for beginners to learn is off Praia do Carvoeiro, with several operators offering PADI-accredited courses in English. **Tivoli Diving** (☎ 282 351 194; www.tivoli-diving.com) offers a range of courses, including a five-dive open-water course (€395). **Divers Cove** (p191; www.diverscove.de) is a reputable, German-run outfit offering a similar range of courses.

More experienced divers can visit a wreck dive – that of a German U1277 submarine – off Matosinhos. **Mergulho Mania** (☎ 934 837 434; www.mergulhomania.com in Portuguese) offers dives there as well as PADI-certified courses.

There are also diving outfits at Costa da Caparica and Reserva Natural da Berlenga (p272).

GOLF

A golf mecca, Portugal is famous for its rolling greens, and is full of championship courses. The Algarve has the lion's share of courses – 29 at last count – but the Estoril coast (read on) is big business too, and there are also courses in Beira Alta and the Minho and one in the Alentejo near Marvão. Although many courses are the domain of club members and local property owners, anyone with a handicap certificate can play here. Greens fees usually run from €70 to €100 per round.

Get the complete rundown on the golfing scene by visiting www.portugalgolf.pt and www.algarvegolf.net.

Estoril has nearly a dozen spectacular golf courses. **Golf do Estoril**, one of Portugal's best-known courses, has hosted the Portuguese Open Championship 20 times. It's 5262m long and set among eucalyptus, pine and mimosa. **Quinta da Marinha**, 9km to the west, was designed to give both high handicappers and scratch golfers a challenge, with the course rolling over windblown dunes and rocky outcrops, with fantastic views.

Some 10km to the northwest is the **Penha Longa Club** with superb views of the Serra de Sintra. It's ranked one of the best courses in Europe, and has also hosted the Portuguese Open. Nearby are **Estoril-Sol**, with one of the country's best practice areas; and **Quinta da Beloura**, designed by Rocky Roquemore, also responsible for beautiful **Belas Clube de Campo**, 22km northeast of Estoril in the Carregueira hills.

Estoril and Cascais turismos (www.estorilsintragolf.net) have full details of all courses. For golfing packages in the Algarve, try UK-based **3D Golf** (☎ 0870-122 5050; www.3dgolf.com).

HORSE RIDING

Lusitano thoroughbreds hail from Portugal, and experienced riders can take dressage lessons in Estremadura (see below). Apart from such exclusive equitation, there are dozens of horse-riding centres – especially in the Algarve and Alentejo – and some gorgeous settings for rides, particularly in the Parque Natural de Montesinho (p446). This is a fantastic way to experience Portugal's beautiful countryside. Rates are usually around €25 per hour.

The origins of the Lusitano horse date back at least 25,000 years, with Neolithic cave paintings showing the horse in action.

Escola de Equitaçã o de Alcainça (☎ 219 662 122; Rua de São Miguel, Alcainça) There are many places to pony trek and horse ride, but this school near Mafra offers dressage lessons on Lusitano horses, and is world renowned.

Equitour (☎ 61 303 31 08; www.equitour.com) For riding holidays, this Swiss-based organisation offers several rewarding treks, including an eight-day journey along the Costa Azul (the Alentejo coast), starting at €1200, including accommodation and some meals.

Equitours (☎ 307-455 3363 in the US; www.ridingtours.com) This US-based outfit offers several week-long, intermediate-level rides across some of Portugal's most stunning scenery. Prices range from US$1500 to US$1800, and includes accommodation and some meals.

JEEP TOURS

Many companies in the south offer jeep tours. These can be particularly useful for exploring national parks, such as Parque Natural da Arrábida (p152), if you don't have your own transport. Be aware that some operators are more environmentally aware than others (see p60 for further information on being environmentally aware).

Also mistrust tours that promise you explorations of the 'real Algarve' – you're more likely to find this hopping on a bus than in a convoy with 30 other people.

Although there's generally a good safety record for these jeep trips, in 2006 one trip from Albufeira ended tragically when the jeep went off the road, killing the driver and injuring eight passengers.

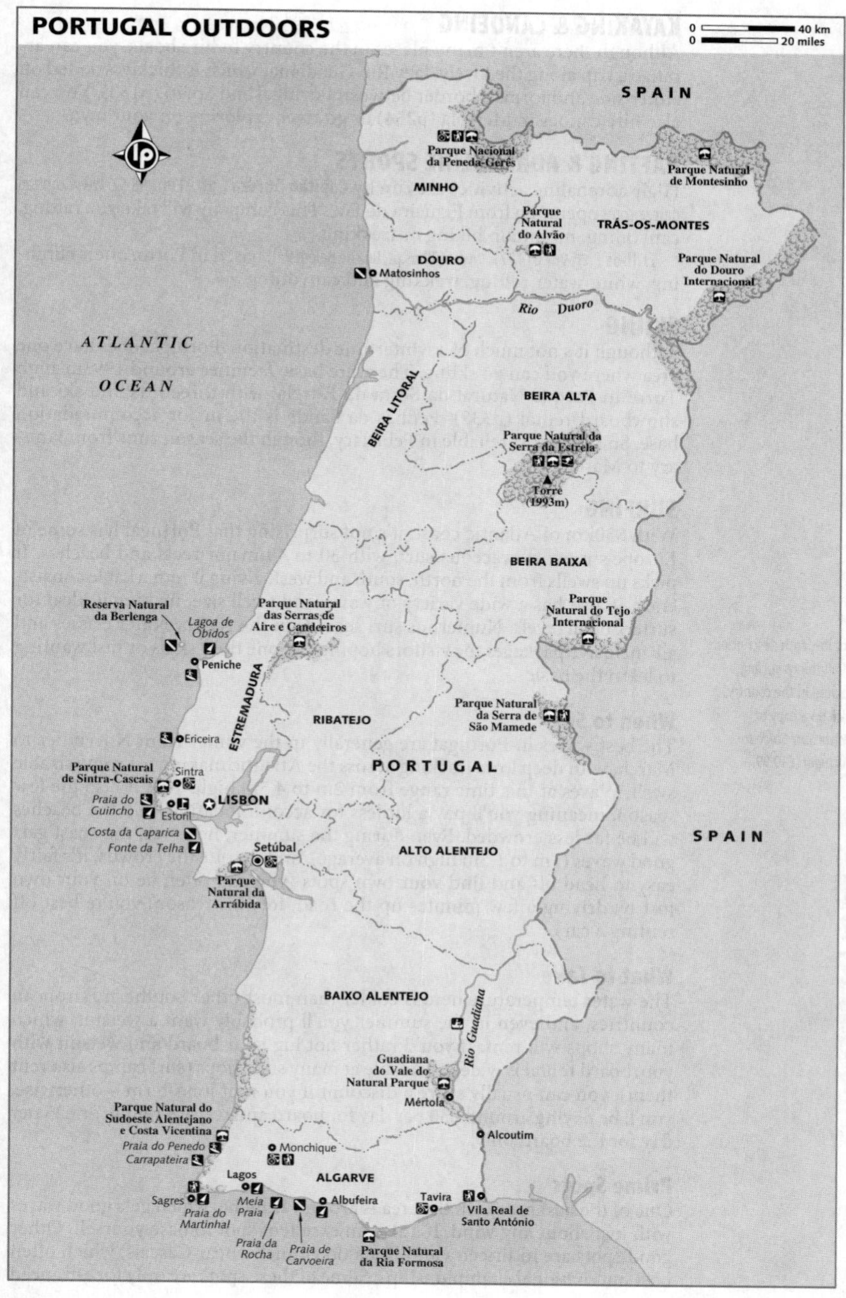
PORTUGAL OUTDOORS
0 40 km
0 20 miles
SPAIN
Parque Nacional da Peneda-Gerês
Parque Natural de Montesinho
MINHO
Parque Natural do Alvão
TRÁS-OS-MONTES
DOURO
Matosinhos
Parque Natural do Douro Internacional
Rio Duoro
ATLANTIC OCEAN
BEIRA LITORAL
BEIRA ALTA
Parque Natural da Serra da Estrela
Torre (1993m)
BEIRA BAIXA
Reserva Natural da Berlenga
Lagoa de Óbidos
Parque Natural das Serras de Aire e Candeeiros
Parque Natural do Tejo Internacional
Peniche
ESTREMADURA
RIBATEJO
Parque Natural da Serra de São Mamede
Ericeira
Parque Natural de Sintra-Cascais
Sintra
PORTUGAL
Praia do Guincho
Estoril
LISBON
Costa da Caparica
Fonte da Telha
Setúbal
ALTO ALENTEJO
SPAIN
Parque Natural da Arrábida
BAIXO ALENTEJO
Rio Guadiana
Guadiana do Vale do Natural Parque
Mértola
Parque Natural do Sudoeste Alentejano e Costa Vicentina
Alcoutim
Praia do Penedo
Monchique
Carrapateira
Lagos
ALGARVE
Sagres
Praia do Martinhal
Meia Praia
Albufeira
Tavira
Vila Real de Santo António
Praia da Rocha
Praia de Carvoeira
Parque Natural da Ria Formosa

KAYAKING & CANOEING

Although there aren't many places in the country to hire boats, you can arrange a trip along the lovely, lazy Rio Guadiana, which is thickly wooded on either side and forms a border between Portugal and Spain (p183). You can also hire canoes in Mértola (p254) or go river exploring on your own.

RAFTING & ADRENALINE SPORTS

High-adrenaline activities are run by **Capitão Dureza** (☎ 91 907 98 52; www.capitaodureza.com) operating from Figueira do Foz. This company will take you rafting, canyoning, mountain biking or trekking.

Trilhos (☎ 967 014 277; www.trilhos.pt; Rua de Belém 94), based in Porto, offers climbing, white-water rafting, trekking and canyoning.

SKIING

Although it's not much of a wintertime destination, Portugal does have one area where you can go skiing. There are basic facilities around 1993m-high Torre in Parque Natural da Serra da Estrela, with three lifts and ski and snowboard rental (p338). Penhas da Saúde is the major accommodation base. Snow is most reliable in February, though the season runs from January to March.

SURFING

With 830km of Atlantic coast, it's not surprising that Portugal has some of Europe's most curvaceous surf, with 30 to 40 major reefs and beaches. It picks up swells from the north, south and west, giving it remarkable consistency. It also has a wide variety of waves and swell size, making it ideal for surfers of all levels. Numerous surf schools in the Algarve offer classes and all-inclusive packages for visitors hoping to hone their skills or just wanting to learn the basics.

For in-depth descriptions of all things surfing related in the country, pick up a copy of *Ocean Surf Guide to Portugal* (£10.99).

When to Surf

The best waves in Portugal are generally in the winter from November to March, with deep lows tracking across the Atlantic making for some sizable swell. Waves at this time range from 2m to 4.5m high. This is also the low season, meaning you'll pay a lot less for accommodation, and the beaches will be far less crowded. Even during the summer, however, the coast gets good waves (1m to 1.5m high on average), and despite the crowds, it's fairly easy to head off and find your own spots (you can often be on your own just by driving a few minutes up the road; for this reason, you're best off renting a car).

What to Take

The water temperature here is colder than most other Southern European countries, and even in the summer you'll probably want a wetsuit, which many shops will rent. If you'd rather not lug your board and wetsuit with you, board rental is widely available at many surf shops (surf camps also rent them); you can usually score a discount if you rent long-term – otherwise, you'll be paying around €30 per day for board and wetsuit rental, or €25 per day for the board only.

Prime Spots

One of the best breaks in the area is around Peniche, which gets good waves with just about any wind. It's also an excellent spot to base yourself. Other good spots are in Ericeira and Praia do Guincho near Cascais, which often host international championships. Some of these spots are only for advanced surfers, however. Another break that's famous among the global surfing community is on the west coast of the Algarve around Carrapateira. Schools and clubs head over this way from Lagos and further afield to take advantage of the crashing waves. Nearby, the area around Praia do Penedo is a good choice for beginners.

Information

There are dozens of schools that can help you improve your surfing game. One thing to consider when choosing an operator is location – whether you want to be in a lively town (like Lagos, where several outfits are based) or enjoying the quiet out on the beach (either camping or in bungalows).

Recommended surf camps in Peniche include two German-run schools: **Maximum Surfcamp** (www.maximumsurfcamp.com in German) and **Baleal Surfcamp** (www.balealsurfcamp.com), as well as the Portuguese-run **Peniche Surfcamp** (www.penichesurfcamp.com). Read more about these schools on p272.

In the Algarve, there are many operators, including the popular **Algarve Surf Camp** (www.algarvesurfcamp.com), which has camps in Sagres and in Carrapateira. There's also the smaller, local outfit **Surfcamp Carrapateira** (www.surfcamp-algarve.com). See page 000 for details.

Surf Experience (☎ 282 961 743; www.surf-experience.com) Based in Lagos, this English-Aussie outfit offers one- to four-week surf packages that include accommodation, breakfast and lunch and transport to the beach. Sample high-season/low-season rate including board hire are £329/299 per week.

You can read the latest surf report on www.magicseaweed.com.

WALKING

Portugal's wonderful walking potential is all the better because few people know about it. Most organised walking clubs are in the Algarve, with marked trails and regular meetings. Those interested in walking the breadth of the country should consider trekking along the Via Algarviana, a 250km route following paved and unpaved roads between Alcoutim and Sagres that takes from two to three weeks. Visit www.algarveway.com for more info.

When to Walk

Summer temperatures can get stiflingly hot in some regions (particularly the Alentejo and the Algarve). To beat the heat, consider travelling in Spring (April to May) or Autumn (late September and October).

What to Take

If you're headed to the showery north, be sure to bring reliable rain gear. Otherwise, bring a good compass, maps, a hat and strong sun protection and some type of palliative for aching feet. Be mindful that in some rural areas, you may encounter dogs wandering the road; they bark but generally pose no harm.

Prime Spots

There is a cluster of organisations around Monchique (p213) but other good bases are Vila Real de Santo António, Sagres and Parque Natural Serra de São Mamede. Some good companions include *Algarve: Let's Walk* by Julie Statham (1999), describing 20 easy walks, and two *Discovery Walking Guides* to areas around Loulé (1999) and Silves (2000), featuring 1:25,000 map sections. *Walking in Portugal* by Bethan Davies and Ben Cole (2002) covers walks in the north and as far down as Setúbal.

There's fantastic walking in the north, where the Parque Natural da Serra da Estrela (p337) has a fine network of marked trails you are likely to have to yourself. Most demanding is Serra da Estrela with 1993m Torre, Portugal's

RESPONSIBLE WALKING

To help preserve the ecology and beauty of Portugal, consider the following tips when walking.

Rubbish

- Carry out *all* your rubbish. Don't overlook easily forgotten items, such as silver paper, orange peel, cigarette butts and plastic wrappers. Empty packaging should be stored in a dedicated rubbish bag. Make an effort to carry out rubbish left by others.
- Never bury your rubbish: Digging disturbs soil and ground cover and encourages erosion. Buried rubbish will likely be dug up by animals, who may be injured or poisoned by it. It may also take years to decompose.
- Minimise waste by taking minimal packaging and no more food than you will need. Take reusable containers or stuff sacks.
- Sanitary napkins, tampons, condoms and toilet paper should be carried out despite the inconvenience. They burn and decompose poorly.

Human Waste Disposal

- Contamination of water sources by human faeces can lead to the transmission of all sorts of nasties. Where there is a toilet, please use it. Where there is none, bury your waste. Dig a small hole 15cm (6in) deep and at least 100m (320ft) from any watercourse. Cover the waste with soil and a rock. In snow, dig down to the soil.

Washing

- Don't use detergents or toothpaste in or near watercourses, even if they are biodegradable.
- For personal washing, use biodegradable soap and a water container (or even a lightweight, portable basin) at least 50m (160ft) away from the watercourse. Disperse the waste water widely to allow the soil to filter it fully.
- Wash cooking utensils 50m (160ft) from watercourses using a scourer, sand or snow instead of detergent.

Erosion

- Hillsides and mountain slopes, especially at high altitudes, are prone to erosion. Stick to existing trails and avoid short cuts.
- If a well-used trail passes through a mud patch, walk through the mud so as not to increase the size of the patch.
- Avoid removing the plant life that keeps topsoils in place.

Fires & Low-Impact Cooking

- Portugal has hundreds of devastating fires every year, the majority of them caused by humans. Don't depend on open fires for cooking: open fires are prohibited in Portugal. Cook on a lightweight kerosene, alcohol or Shellite (white gas) stove and avoid those powered by disposable butane gas canisters.

Camping & Walking on Private Property

- Always seek permission to camp from landowners.
- Public access to private property without permission is acceptable where public land is otherwise inaccessible, so long as safety and conservation regulations are observed.

highest peak. Or head to Parque Nacional da Peneda-Gerês (p424) for more glorious, empty hill trails. Parque Natural do Alvão in Trás-os-Montes also has some splendid hiking spots.

Information

Based in Lisbon, **Rotas do Vento** (☎ 213 950 035; www.rotasdovento.pt) offers country-wide walks. **Quercus** (p66) offers environmental trips.

Approximately 10km north of Sagres Julie Statham, author of *Portugal Walks*, runs **Portugal Walks** (☎ 282 697 298; 0871 711 3315 in the UK; www.portugalwalks.com; 37 Quinta do Montinho, Budens, Vila do Bispo), which offers all-inclusive week-long packages (from €425/655) for unguided or guided walks.

Try the following UK-based companies for organised walking tours:

ATG Oxford (☎ 0186-531 5678; www.atg-oxford.co.uk) Guided walking holidays.

Headwater (☎ 0160-672 0099; www.headwater.com) Weeklong jaunts and self-guided tours.

Ramblers Holidays (☎ 0170-733 1133; www.ramblersholidays.co.uk) Guided walking holidays.

Sherpa Expeditions (☎ 0208 577 2717; www.sherpa-walking-holidays.co.uk) Good self-guided walks in the north.

Winetrails (☎ 0130-671 2111; www.winetrails.co.uk) Gentle rambles with fine wining and dining.

Jogo do pau is the country's ancient martial art, whereby two combatants engage in stick fighting. It was a common form of duelling in medieval times.

WINDSURFING

Praia do Guincho, west of Sintra, is one of the most popular beaches for windsurfers. Another good spot is Lagoa de Óbidos, which is a pretty lagoon that draws both sailers and windsurfers. Closer to Lisbon, the Costa da Caparica's Fonte da Telha is also a prime windsurfing spot. In the Algarve, Sagres attracts pros (its strong winds and fairly flat seas are ideal for free-riding, with a rental outfit on Praia do Martinhal), while Lagos, Albufeira and Praia da Rocha cater to all.

Escola de Vela da Lagoa (p277) rents sailboards and Hobie sailing boats out at Lagoa de Óbidos; it also offers courses in windsurfing and sailing.

Windsurf Point (☎ 282 792 315; www.windsurfpoint.com) Based at Meia Praia near Lagos, this Portuguese-run outfit offers classes in windsurfing for both beginners and the advanced. The price for a six-/10-hour course is €140/180. They also offer kite-surfing classes (€250 for eight hours). You can rent equipment here for a variety of water sports – including sea kayaks – and you can also arrange to go parasailing here (€35 for 10 minutes).

Food & Drink

Portugal's abundant coastline and fertile fields are the key ingredients to its long culinary traditions. All along the coast, you'll find a wide variety of fresh fish, seafood stews and shellfish. Further inland, pork, steak and chicken are the staples, with fresh olives, warm loaves of bread and very drinkable wines rounding out the meal. No matter where you are, you won't be far from the exalted *bacalhau* (dried salt-cod), which is served many ways, but appears most often in casseroles.

In *Portuguese Homestyle Cooking,* by Ana Patuleia Ortins (2002), 'frugal cuisine' is made rich and satisfying with an ample collection of authentic recipes.

While Portuguese cuisine doesn't hold the same lofty status as French cuisine or offer the diversity of Chinese cooking, its simple ingredients are blended nicely, offering aromatic and delightful dishes full of tradition and prepared with familial care. In addition, Portugal's large immigrant population has contributed to an eclectic dining scene in Lisbon and a handful of other cities. Here, the spices and flavours of North Africa, Brazil and the Far East add to an increasingly diverse restaurant scene.

Dining in Portugal offers excellent value for money. You can eat better here for less than probably anywhere else is Western Europe, and the fact that Portuguese cooking is so little known outside its borders means that there's much to discover.

STAPLES & SPECIALITIES

Portugal's centuries-old love affair with the sea means that there's no shortage of cooks who know how to handle their *espadarte* (swordfish). Nearly anything that swims in the ocean is fair game when it comes to seafood. In towns all along the Atlantic, there are prawns, squid, clams, crayfish, cuttlefish, octopus and magnificent large barnacles (sounds strange, but try them and you'll know why they're such a treasured delicacy here). You'll also find dozens of fish, including sea bass, salmon, red snapper, scabbard fish, sea bream, tuna, swordfish and monkfish. These are usually served grilled, sometimes prepared atop sizzling hot coals, just outside the restaurant's entrance, which might be on a sandy beach or a cobblestone square. In any event, follow the smoke and the enticing fresh-roasted scent.

Portuguese wild boar are fattened on an exclusive diet of acorns – makes them yummy!

In coastal Portugal, the seafood stews are well worth seeking out. *Arroz de tamboril* (monkfish rice) and *arroz de marisco* (rice and seafood stew) are savoury, nicely spiced dishes where all the juices blend delightfully together. *Cataplana,* named after the copper pot in which the seafood stew is cooked, is another exquisite speciality, made of seafood and rice (there are many varieties); this is similar to *caldeirada,* a kind of Portuguese bouillabaisse, made of fish or shellfish along with peppers, potatoes, tomatoes and onions. It's highly recommended.

THE COST OF COUVERT

There's one essential commandment regarding Portuguese dining etiquette: whatever you eat you must pay for, whether or not you ordered it. Throughout the country, in both dives and flash bistros, waiters bring bread, olives and other goodies (sometimes cheese and fish paste) to your table the moment you sit down. This unordered appetiser is called 'couvert' and can cost anywhere from €1 per person to over €12 at the priciest places. If you don't want it, you can send it away, no offence taken. There's also no shame in asking the price – *'quanto e isso?'* You may also receive extras throughout your meal or a shot of something at dessert. Unless told otherwise, you will have to pay for these.

NO FISH MONDAYS

Because fish markets are closed on Mondays (the fishing fleet takes a rest on Sundays), it's better to start your week off with something nonfishy. Otherwise, you'll be eating leftovers that certainly won't be very fresh.

Probably the most common fish you'll encounter (on grills and menus alike) is the *sardinha* (sardine). These are also usually grilled, and are served uncleaned, with guts and all. Another common foodstuff is *bacalhau*. Pieces of *bacalhau* look like bits of wizened shoe leather in the grocery store, and must be soaked in water before they regain their fishy consistency. *Bacalhau*, because it's rather, ahem, bland, is usually cooked with other rich ingredients. *Bacalhau com natas* (shredded cod with cream and potatoes) and *bacalhau a brás* (shredded fried cod with potato and scrambled egg) are two of many popular cod dishes.

Meat dishes are generally less imaginative than seafood dishes here, though you will find a few intriguing combinations. *Cabrito assado* (roast kid) is a major crowd pleaser in the north. Another northern favourite is *posta de barrosã,* an amazing beef from one of a rare breed of cattle in Minho and Trás-os-Montes. Pork is more common than beef in many places, and among the better variants is *porco preto* (black pork) a tender, free-range meat; you'll also find grilled *costoletos* (chops) and *lombo* (loin). *Borrego* (lamb) and *coelho* (rabbit) also appear on menus and can be excellent depending on who's in the kitchen.

Cod: A Biography of the Fish That Changed the World (1998) by Mark Kurlansky is a fascinating account of how this simple yet crucial food affected the peoples whose lives it touched and the historic events that ensued.

Another popular dish is *feijoada* (a hearty stew of beans, sausage and pork), which is not quite as heavy as the Brazilian version. *Leitão* (roast suckling pig) is a Portuguese speciality though rare to find on menus (it's more common at festivals and such). Grilled and roasted chicken are both quite good in Portugal; nearly every town has one restaurant (often with names like *Rei dos Frangos,* King of Chickens) that's *the* place to go for grilled chicken. It's cheap, tasty, and there's usually a takeaway counter where you can get your bird to go. *Piri piri* (chilli sauce) adds a bit of fire to the meat.

Travellers on a budget, or those getting sick of the same old-same old, can usually rely on a good, inexpensive bowl of soup. You can try *caldo verde* (cabbage or other green vegetable, potatoes and possibly sausage), *sopa de legumes* (mixed vegetables) or in the north *nabos* (turnips).

For snacks, try the markets, which offer a delectable range of seasonal fruits: cherries in spring; peaches, melons and apricots in summer, with guavas, mangoes and figs widely available in the Algarve; there are excellent late summer grapes (including black muscatel); and chestnuts and pomegranates in the winter. The markets also stock a range of good goat and sheep cheeses (with some of the best hailing from Serra da Estrela), as well as fresh breads, plump olives and sausages (including *morcela* – blood sausage).

The Portuguese don't drink much port. It's more an English drop.

A few things to keep in mind: Sometimes a main dish (or *dose,* portion) is big enough for two (when in doubt, ask the waiter). If you're alone, you can often order a *meia dose* (or half-portion), which will usually be around half price. Also, when you order fish it comes with peeled, boiled potatoes; meat dishes come with chips (French fries). Both dishes also come with rice and salad (some lettuce and tomato). Although eating the same side dishes gets old very quickly, tradition is tradition, and in Portugal this is simply the way it has been and always will be. Amen.

Cafés and patisseries are a big part of Portuguese life, as they provide not only delectable desserts and strong coffee, they're also important meeting places to catch up on the latest village or neighbourhood gossip. There are

TOP FIVE RESTAURANTS

There are many atmospheric places to experience Portugal's best dishes. The following are a few of our highly subjective picks.

- Mariazinha (p371) – a rustically elegant spot, where you can enjoy creative *haute cuisine* made with the freshest ingredients. Each of the five courses comes with a surprise, along with a different Portuguese wine.
- Palace Hotel do Buçaco (p318) – this ex-royal retreat hidden in the forest is as much about devouring your fairy-tale surroundings as the excellent food.
- Adega Faustino (p441) – on a more earthy footing, this cavernous old wine warehouse offers a taste of Northern specialities passed down through generation after generation.
- A Ver Tavira (p181) – overlooking the medieval quarters of Tavira, this charming new restaurant has already earned many fans for its exquisitely prepared dishes.
- Restô (p115) – more about the views than the food (though it's Portuguese with an exotic twist), this restaurant seems to float above the twinkling city.

dozens of local specialities, some so artfully prepared, it seems sinful to eat them. This is also where most Portuguese head in the morning, having a small cup of coffee, a pastry, or *torrado* (toast).

Pastéis de nata (custard tarts) may be the national dessert of Portugal. These are small and round, easily held in one hand and highly addictive. You'll also be tempted by *queijadas* (cheesecakes), *palhas de ovos* (egg pastries), *suspiros* (meringues) and *bolinhos de maçapão* (marzipan), which is most common in the Algarve.

DRINKS

Wine

Portuguese wines may not be very well known abroad, but the country certainly produces some excellent drops. Although ports are the best known viticultural produce from the country, Portugal also produces a wide-ranging assortment of reds (*tinto*), whites (*branco*), rosés and *vinhos verdes* (literally, green wines), with a further classification of *maduro* (mature). For the complete details on port, see the boxed text on p365.

A good website for information on Portuguese wines, especially port, is www.vino.com. It also includes some recipes and words on cuisine.

Most restaurants stock a decent selection of wines, though at smaller rural outposts, you're only options may be regional varieties (which may not be such a bad thing). There's almost always a house wine, sometimes served in small jugs (*jarros*), and which often goes down remarkably well.

Some of the best wine-growing regions are the Douro, Bairrada, Alentejo, Dão, Estremadura and Ribatejo. According to tradition, wines become more user-friendly as you travel from north to south, with the Douro producing some of the most unique and complex reds.

Portugal has its own indigenous grapes – over 100 varieties – making for some distinctive imbibing. When buying a quality wine look for the label 'Denominação de Origem Controlada', often abbreviated DOC.

The next tier down is Indicação de Provenência Regulamentada (IPR). Both levels of grape varieties are controlled but an IPR wine is allowed a greater yield per acre than a DOC so it could be more tannic. It also means the grapes are pressed a second time to extract more juice.

The next tier down is Vinho Regional (VR), which covers larger regions, allowing more grape varieties and greater yields. These are often good value for the money. The last tier is Vinho da Mesa (table wine), which is often quite decent.

Most labels show the name of the grapes (*castas*) on the back label, with the first one listed being the predominant one. Full berry fruit flavours include Castelão Frances (nicknamed Periquita), Trincadiera Preta, Moreto, Aragones, among others. Full-bodied dry reds come from grapes like Touriga Nacional, Jaen, Tinta Roriz, Bastardo, Alfrocheiro. Bairrada wines from the Beiras are dominated by the Baga grape, making for an elegant and full flavoured wine.

Whites are dry and crisp. Grapes to look out for include Fernão Pires, Malvasia Vina Rabigato Loureiro and Gouveio.

Estremadura and Ribatejo are still coming into their own as far as reputable wine producers (they've long been relegated to making cheap mass-market froth). However, you can generally find some nice drinkable wines here, a bit fruitier than in northern regions, but fairly good value for the money. Another good region for reds is in Colares (near Sintra).

The world's only source of cork for closing wine bottles is Portugal.

Perhaps the best known table wine of Portugal is the innocuous Mateus Rosé. It can be refreshing on a hot day, but it's a bit too sweet to be taken seriously. Better than its rosé, however, is *vinho verde* (semisparkling young wine), perhaps Portugal's signature wine. Available throughout the country, *vinho verde* takes its name from its youth rather than its colour, as it's intended to be quaffed when young – less than a year old. These wines are characteristically light, crisp and dry.

Although there are red *vinhos verdes,* most are white and the best are made from the Alvarinho grape (with the best of the best found in Monção and Melgaço, along the Rio Minho).

Other Drinks

Beer (*cerveja*) is almost as popular as wine and comes in a few different varieties. Sagres and Super Bock are among the best sellers with Cristal and Cintra coming in third and fourth. All of these are fairly standard European-style lagers. To order a draught, you may order *um imperial* (300mL) or *uma caneca* (500mL). If you prefer a bottle, request *uma garrafa.*

Aguardente is the generic term for distilled spirits and can be made from whatever is on hand. When it's good it's pretty smooth, and when it's bad it's horrid. Good or horrid, this is what the Portuguese like to end a meal with.

As for nonalcoholic drinks, coffee is good in Portugal, and you can have it espresso-style (*uma bica*), coffee with milk (*um meia de leite*) or tall and weak, with milk (*um galão*). Tea is fairly lacklustre – surprising given the Portuguese were the first to India and even introduced England to tea. Expect a generic tea bag of black tea, though some places have a few herbal-tea choices.

The Portuguese still season fish with *garum,* a fermented fish sauce (like the Thai version) used by the ancient Romans.

Water (*água*) is almost as important as wine, and you can order it *com gas* (sparkling) or *sem gas* (still). Your waiter might ask if you'd like it *fresca* (cold) or *natural* (room temperature). For the simple stuff, order *água da torneira,* (tap water). If you're feeling fancy, go for *água com gelo e limão* (water with ice and lemon).

CELEBRATIONS

Throughout the year, the Portuguese have some lively festivals, which are an excuse for a city or neighbourhood to let its hair down, and dance, drink, eat and be merry. Many celebrations have religious roots, such as the lively saints' days celebrations in Lisbon and Porto.

On the religious calendar Pascoa (Easter) is by far the most important date. Just as in the Anglophone world, eggs play a part in the festivities, though the Portuguese prefer to make omelettes rather than hide eggs. Also on the Easter table are roast lamb, piglet or kid, again symbols of new life.

Carnaval, which is the Latin for 'farewell to meat', marks the beginning of Lent, the 40 days before Easter during which the pious take no meat and vow to give up other goodies or vices. The Portuguese have goodies and vices in abundance, so they pull out all the stops the day before Lent. The signature dish of Carnaval is *cozida à portuguesa,* a soupy stew of sausages, meats and vegetables.

Sometimes the Portuguese don't need any excuse to celebrate. Witness Domingos Gastronomicos (Gastronomic Sundays). Every Sunday from February to May in many parts of Portugal selected restaurants will prepare local regional dishes and publish their historical or social significance. Even schools take part, with children doing the cooking or learning from their parents.

Portugal also has some festivals, which revolve exclusively around food. In the Algarve, for instance, there are festivals celebrating stuffed sausages, seafood, sardines and even desserts. It's well worth attending one of these if you're in the area. See p194 for details.

WHERE TO EAT & DRINK

Portugal has a variety of places where you can stop in for a meal besides the unambiguous *restaurante*. If you're looking for a small, casual neighbourhood tavern, you might end up at a *tasca* or a *casa de pasto*. These often walk a fine line between charming and tiled and dingy and smoky. There's usually a daily special or two on offer, and meals are fairly straightforward affairs (the menu will likely be some variant of sardines and pork).

Meat lovers should seek out local *churrasqueiras*. These are places where you'll find good chargrilled chicken, sausages, pork chops, steak and the like. Its distant relative is the *marisqueira* (seafood house), where you'll find a wide variety of fish and crustaceans, and quite often 20,000-leagues-under-the-sea type décor (fish tanks, shiny blue tiles, fishing nets hung from the rafters). These places can be pricey, as you often pay by the kilo (a nicely turned out fish for instance might run €45 per kg).

TRAVEL YOUR TASTE BUDS

While Portuguese cooks tend to keep things pretty straightforward when it comes to meal preparation, there are occasions when invention gets the better of them. To experience the racier side of Portuguese dining try one of these curious dishes:

- *açorda* – a kind of bread-based stew with olive oil, garlic, herbs and sometimes an egg. If you like olive oil, this one may be for you.
- *carne de porco à alentejana* – a popular dish of braised pork with baby clams, a sort of Portuguese surf and turf.
- *lapas* (limpets) – tiny little conical molluscs with garlic and butter.
- *migas* – if you like *açorda*, try its kindred spirit: a dish of fried breadcrumbs flavoured with sausage.
- *pastéis de toucihno* – sweet bacon tartlets, a treat in the south.

We Dare You

When the Portuguese slaughter a pig for food then food it shall be – all of it. Not just hams and trotters and shoulders, but brains, organs, guts and all. They will eat everything but the oink. The blood will be made into sausage, rather like an English black pudding. The entrails will be fried or tossed into a stew. The stomach lining will be removed and consigned to soup. Bits of brain and hunks of heart and kilos of kidneys will find their way to market, and to the menu you'll soon be holding in your hand.

GETTING TIPSY

Service is usually not added to the bill, and it's fairly customary to leave 5% or even 10% if the service was exceptional. Many places still do not accept credit cards. Always ask if you're planning to use plastic.

For snacking and socialising over a cold beer, the *cervejaria* (beer hall) is a good option. These popular local places are usually colourfully decorated in tiles and rustic décor and they stay open all day and well into the night. Besides cold brew, *cervejarias* serve hearty plates of the usual favourites (seafood, meat), along with a respectable assortment of snacks.

Another atmospheric option is the *adega,* which literally means wine cellar. As per the name, these are indeed often lined with large wine casks and have cellar-like ambience. You often find communal wooden tables and a good mix of people there to eat simple, hearty meals (similar menus to restaurants) and drink a fair house wine.

Customary meal times (and opening hours for the above establishments are) noon to 3pm and 7pm to 10pm. Cafés that dole out coffee, pastries and sandwiches open by about 8am.

VEGETARIANS & VEGANS

Vegetarianism is slowly gaining attention in Portugal, though outside of urban areas and popular tourist destinations like the Algarve, options are scarce for strict vegetarians and vegans. Soups, omelettes and salad – along with bread, olives and cheese – may be your best bet at many restaurants. You can always ask *'tem alguma hortaliça?'* (do you have a plate of vegetables?), and you might get it.

Luckily, most towns have excellent local markets, where you can load up on fresh fruits and veggies and with a little imagination put together a good meal. Health-food stores are also becoming more common, and you'll be able to gather cereal bars, organic dried fruits and the like before heading off into more remote parts.

Lisbon, Porto and a handful of towns in the Algarve have the best assortment of vegetarian and ethnic (Italian, Indian, Asian) restaurants.

Check out www.palcus.org/network/food.html. It is a page of links to recipes, Portuguese restaurants worldwide and online suppliers of Portuguese foods and wines.

EATING WITH KIDS

The Portuguese are a very family-oriented people and welcome children to all but the fussiest of restaurants. At particularly busy places, you might consider trying to miss the lunch or evening rush, by going early. Children's menus are not common, but they are usually able to take a *meia dose* (half-portion) at about half-price. (Adults have the same option in traditional places.)

For between-meal snacks you can take the kids to the *minimercado* (a kind of convenience store, though with fruit on hand) or the *hipermercado* (like an inexpensive supermarket). Keep in mind that Portuguese pastries can be very heavy, and can spoil an appetite easily if eaten before meal time. For more on travelling with children see p456.

HABITS & CUSTOMS

Welcome to the most user-friendly tables of Europe. You'll usually get a plate, a knife, a fork, a wine glass and a paper serviette. None of these will be changed in the course of the meal unless you break one. If you ask for it you'll get a water glass. If you order a shot of spirits afterwards, as the locals will probably do, you'll receive another glass for that.

Table manners are couth but casual, and the Portuguese eat most things – including pizza – with a knife and fork. If you see a wash basin in a *tasca* (a working-class restaurant or tavern), avail yourself of it before eating. It's the custom.

Smoking is still quite common in most restaurants; there are very rarely nonsmoking sections.

EAT YOUR WORDS

Want to know *piri piri* from *pimenta*? Get behind the cuisine scene by getting to know the language. For pronunciation guidelines see p481.

Useful Phrases

Table for ..., please.
Uma mesa para ..., se faz favor. — oo·ma *me*·za *pa*·ra ..., se faz fa·*vorr*

Can I see the menu, please?
Posso ver o menu, por favor? — *po*·so verr o me·*noo*, porr fa·*vorr*

Can I see the wine list, please?
Posso ver a carta de vinhos, por favor? — *po*·so verr a *kar*·ta de *vee*·nyozh, porr fa·*vorr*?

Can you recommend a good local wine?
Pode recomendar-me um bom vinho da regiao? — *po*·de rre·ko·*meng*·darr·me oong bong *vee*·nyo da rre·*zheeow*?

Do you have a high chair for the baby?
Tem uma cadeira de bebe? — teng *oo*·ma ka·*day*·ra de be·*be*?

I'll have a beer, please.
Vou tomar uma cervejar, se faz favor. — vo to·*mar oo*·ma ser·ve·*zhar* se faz fa·*vorr*

Can I have the bill/check, please.
A conta, se faz favor. — a *kong*·ta se faz fa·*vorr*

I'm vegetarian.
Sou vegetariano/a. (m/f) — so ve·zhe·ta·ree·*a*·no/a

Check out www.paleys.org/nataverk/food.html; it has a page of links to recipes, Portuguese restaurants worldwide and online suppliers of Portuguese foods and wines.

Food & Drink Glossary

adega	a·*de*·ga	cellar, usually wine cellar; may also denote a winery; also a traditional bar or bar-restaurant serving wine from the barrel
aguardente	a·gwar·*deng*·te	strongly alcoholic 'firewater'
almôndegas	ow·*mong*·de·gazh	meatball served in tomato gravy
camarão	ka·*ma*·rown	a tinned sausage usually served on a roll
cachucho	ka·*shoo*·sho	sea bream
casa de pasto	*ka*·za de *pash*·to	casual eatery
cervejaria	ser·ve·zha·*ree*·a	beerhouse
chanfana	shang·*fa*·na	mutton or goat stew cooked with red wine
choco	*sho*·ko	cuttlefish
churrasqueira	shoo·rrash·*kay*·ra	grilled-chicken restaurant
confeitaria	kon·fay·ta·*ree*·a	cake and pastry shop
dose	*do*·ze	serving or portion
empada	eng·pa·*da*	a little pot pie
escabeche	esh·ka·*besh*	raw meat or fish marinated in vinegar and oil
espetada	esh·pe·*ta*·da	kebab
favas	fa·*vazh*	a dish of broad beans
gamba	gang·*ba*	prawn
gelado	zhe·*la*·doo	ice cream
marisqueira	ma·reesh·*kay*·ra	seafood house
meia dose	*may*·a *do*·ze	half-portion
merenda	me·*reng*·da	light snack
paio	pay·*oo*	smoked pork sausage

pastéis de nata *pash*·taysh de *na*·ta custard tarts
pastelaria pash·te·la·*ree*·a pastry and cake shop
pernil no forno *per*·neel no *forr*·no roast leg of pork
pequeno almoço pe·*ke*·no ow·*mo*·so breakfast, traditionally just coffee and a bread roll
pimenta pee·*meng*·ta pepper
piri piri *pee*·ree *pee*·ree fiery chilli sauce; it is the signature condiment of Portugal
pudim poo·*deeng* pudding
queijada kay·*zha*·da a cheesecake pastry
rota dos vinhos *ro*·ta dozh *vee*·nyosh wine route
salmão sal·*mown* salmon
sardinhas assadas sar·*dee*·nyazh a·*sa*·dash grilled sardines
simples seeng·*plezh* plain, no filling or icing
tasca *tash*·ka tavern
uma bica *oo*·ma *bee*·ka short black
vindima veeng·*dee*·ma grape harvest
vinho da casa *vee*·nyo da *ka*·za house wine
vinho maduro *vee*·nyo ma·*doo*·ro *wine matured for more than a year*
vinho verde *vee*·nyo *ver*·de emisparkling young wine

Lisbon & Around

Spread across steep hillsides that overlook the Rio Tejo, Lisbon offers all the delights you'd expect of Portugal's star attraction, yet with half the fuss of other European capitals. Gothic cathedrals, majestic monasteries and quaint museums are all part of the colourful cityscape, but the real delights of discovery lie in wandering the narrow lanes of Lisbon's lovely backstreets.

As bright yellow trams wind their way through curvy tree-lined streets, Lisboêtas stroll through the old quarters, much as they've done for centuries. Village-life gossip in old Alfama is exchanged at the public baths or over fresh bread and wine at tiny patio restaurants as *fadistas* (proponents of *fado,* Portugal's traditional melancholic singing) perform in the background.

Meanwhile, in other parts of town, visitors and locals chase the ghosts of Pessoa in warmly lit 1930s-era cafés or walk along the seaside that once saw the celebrated return of Vasco da Gama. Yet, while history is very much alive in centuries-old Lisbon, its spirit is undeniably youthful.

In the hilltop district of Bairro Alto, dozens of restaurants and bars line the narrow streets, with jazz, reggae, electronica and *fado* filling the air and revellers partying until dawn. Nightclubs scattered all over town make fine use of old spaces, whether on riverside docks or tucked away in 18th-century mansions.

The Lisbon experience encompasses so many things, from enjoying a fresh pastry and *bica* (espresso) on a petite leafy plaza to window-shopping in elegant Chiado. It's mingling with Lisboêtas at a neighbourhood festival or watching the sunset from the old Moorish castle.

Just outside Lisbon, there's more to explore: the magical setting of Sintra, glorious beaches and traditional fishing villages.

HIGHLIGHTS

- Strolling the narrow streets of Alfama, searching for the soul of **fado** (p120)
- Joining the street party in **Bairro Alto** (p117), Lisbon's nightlife centre
- Indulging in heavenly *pastéis de Belém* (custard tarts) at one of many atmospheric **cafés** (p116)
- Hopping aboard **tram 28** (p105) for a rattling, roller-coaster ride through the city
- Experiencing the royal decadence at the **Mosteiro dos Jerónimos** (p102)
- Visiting the fairy-tale castles and rolling woodlands of **Sintra** (p127)

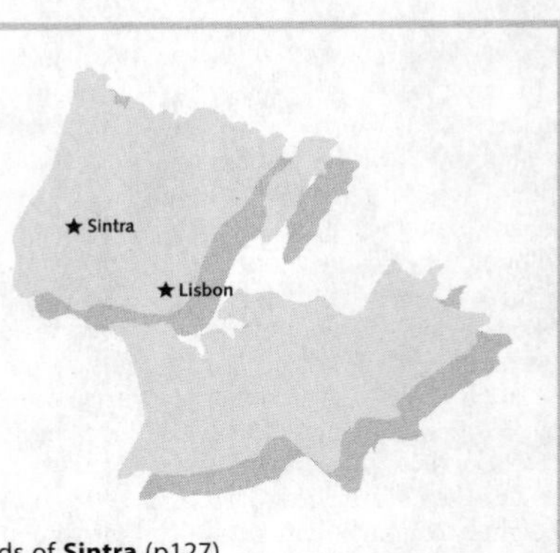

- POPULATION: 580,000
- AREA: 86.5 SQ KM

HISTORY

Immense riches, fires, plague, Europe's worst recorded earthquake, revolutions, coups and a dictatorship – Lisbon has certainly had its ups and downs.

It's said that Ulysses was here first, but the Phoenicians definitely settled here 3000 years ago, calling the city Alis Ubbo (Delightful Shore). Others soon recognised its delightful qualities: the Greeks, the Carthaginians and then, in 205 BC, the Romans, who stayed until the 5th century AD. After some tribal chaos, the city was taken over by North African Moors in 714. They fortified the city they called Lissabona and fended off the Christians for 400 years.

But in 1147, after a four-month siege, Christian fighters (mainly British crusader hooligan-pillagers) under Dom Afonso Henriques captured the city. In 1260, Afonso III moved his capital here from Coimbra, which proved far more strategic given the city's excellent port and central position.

In the 15th and 16th centuries Lisbon boomed as the opulent centre of a vast empire after Vasco da Gama found a sea route to India. The party raged on into the 1800s, when gold was discovered in Brazil. Merchants flocked to the city, trading in gold, spices, silks and jewels. Frenziedly extravagant architecture held up a mirror to the era, with Manueline works such as Belém's Mosteiro dos Jerónimos.

But at 9.30am on All Saints' Day, 1 November 1755, everything changed. Three major earthquakes hit, as residents celebrated Mass. The tremors brought an even more devastating fire and tsunami. Some estimate that as many as 90,000 of Lisbon's 270,000 inhabitants died. Much of the city was ruined, never to regain its former status. Dom João I's chief minister, the redoubtable Marquês de Pombal, immediately began rebuilding, in a simple, cheap, easily managed style that created today's formal grid. (Though the famous quote 'We must bury the dead, and feed the living' was uttered by the Marquês de Alorna and not the Marquês de Pombal, to whom it is often attributed.)

In November 1807, Napoleon's forces occupied the city, where they would remain for the next four years, and Lisbon slid with the rest of the country into chaos. In 1908, at the height of the turbulent republican movement, Dom Carlos and his eldest son were assassinated in Praça do Comércio. The next 16 years saw 45 changes of government, and another high-profile assassination (President Sidónio Pais, at Rossio station in 1918). During WWII Lisbon, although officially neutral, harboured numerous spies.

Two bloodless coups (in 1926 and 1974) rocked the city. In 1974 and 1975 there was a massive influx of refugees from the former African colonies, changing the demographic of the city and adding to its richness culturally, if not financially.

After Portugal joined the European Community (EC) in 1986, massive EC funding started to boost redevelopment, which was a welcome boost after a 1988 fire in Chiado. Streets became cleaner and investment improved facilities. Lisbon has spent recent years dashing in and out of the limelight as 1994 European City of Culture, and host of Expo 98 and the 2004 European Football Championships. Meanwhile, 2006 saw the continuation of major development projects throughout the city, from the reopening of the restored Praça de Touros (Lisbon's bullring) to ongoing work on the metro system and, most importantly, much needed building rehab in the Alfama.

ORIENTATION

Lisbon's seven hills – Estrela, Santa Catarina, São Pedro de Alcântara, São Jorge, Graça, Senhora do Monte and Penha de França – sit on the northern side of Portugal's finest natural harbour, the wide mouth of the Rio Tejo. São Jorge is topped by the *castelo* (castle), and each of the others by a church or a stunning *miradouro* (viewpoint).

At the river's edge is the grand Praça do Comércio. Behind it march the streets of the Baixa (lower) district, up to Praça da Figueira and Praça Dom Pedro IV (aka the Rossio).

Here the city forks along two arteries. Lisbon's splendid main street, Avenida da Liberdade, stretches 1.5km northwest from the Rossio and the adjacent Praça dos Restauradores to Praça Marquês de Pombal and the large Parque Eduardo VII. The other fork is the commercial strip of Avenida Almirante Reis, running north for almost 6km from Praça da Figueira (where it's called Rua da Palma) to the airport.

From the Baixa it's a steep climb west, through swanky shopping district Chiado, into the narrow streets of nightlife-haven Bairro Alto. Eastwards from the Baixa it's

(Continued on page 92)

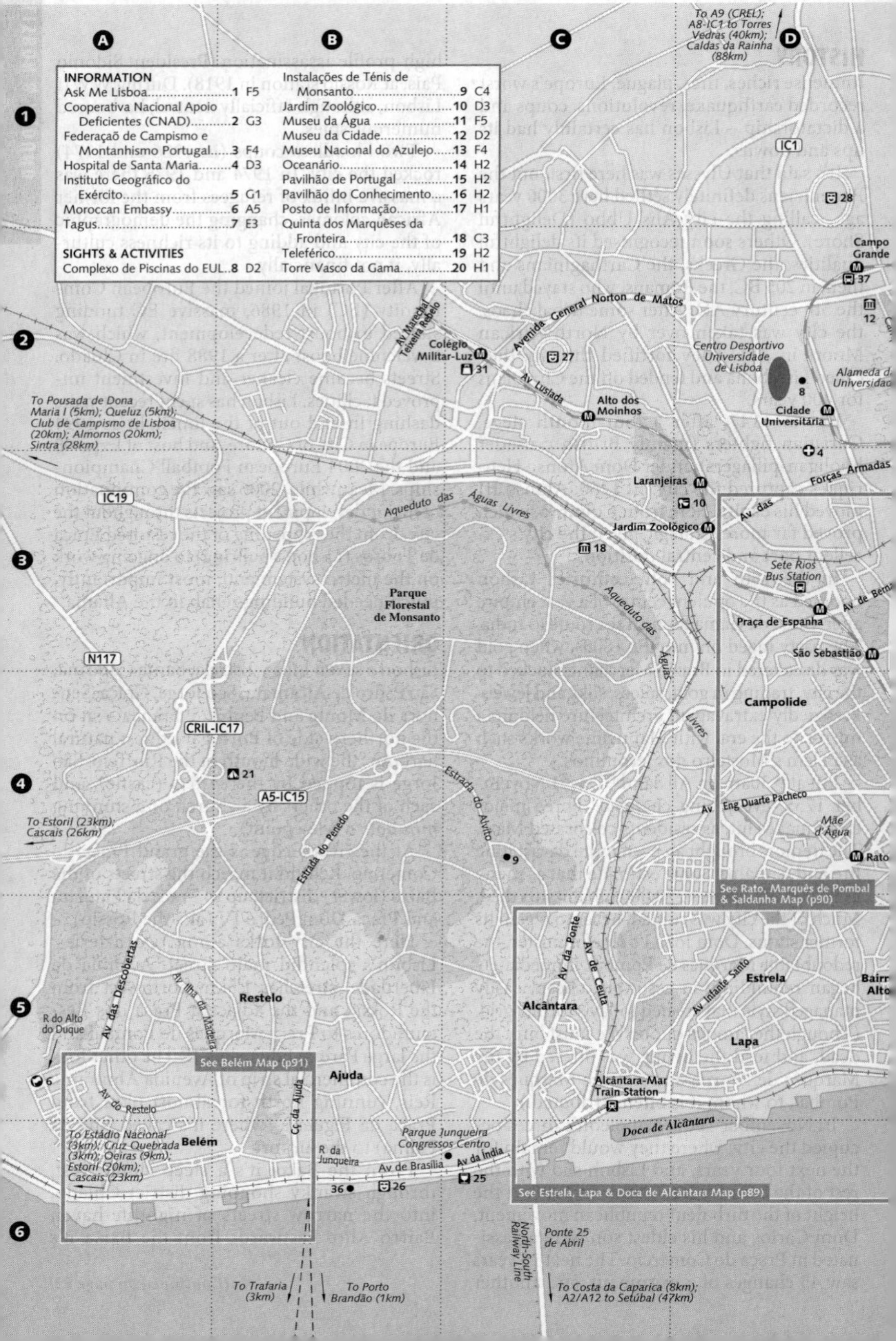

A B C D

1 2 3 4 5 6

INFORMATION

Ask Me Lisboa........................1 F5
Cooperativa Nacional Apoio Deficientes (CNAD)...........2 G3
Federaçaõ de Campismo e Montanhismo Portugal......3 F4
Hospital de Santa Maria.........4 D3
Instituto Geográfico do Exército.....................5 G1
Moroccan Embassy..................6 A5
Tagus...........................7 E3

SIGHTS & ACTIVITIES

Complexo de Piscinas do EUL..8 D2
Instalações de Ténis de Monsanto..............................9 C4
Jardim Zoológico.......................10 D3
Museu da Água 11 F5
Museu da Cidade.......................12 D2
Museu Nacional do Azulejo.....13 F4
Oceanário................................14 H2
Pavilhão de Portugal 15 H2
Pavilhão do Conhecimento......16 H2
Posto de Informação...............17 H1
Quinta dos Marquêses da Fronteira..............................18 C3
Teleférico.................................19 H2
Torre Vasco da Gama..............20 H1

To A9 (CREL); A8-IC1 to Torres Vedras (40km); Caldas da Rainha (88km)

IC1

28

Campo Grande

37

12

Avenida General Norton de Matos

Av Marechal Teixeira Rebelo

Colégio Militar-Luz

31

27

Av Lusíada

Alto dos Moinhos

Centro Desportivo Universidade de Lisboa

8

Alameda da Universidade

Cidade Universitária

4

To Pousada de Dona Maria I (5km); Queluz (5km); Club de Campismo de Lisboa (20km); Almornos (10km); Sintra (28km)

Laranjeiras

Forças Armadas

IC19

10

Aqueduto das Águas Livres

Av das

Jardim Zoológico

18

Sete Rios Bus Station

Av de Berna

Praça de Espanha

Parque Florestal de Monsanto

Aqueduto das Águas Livres

São Sebastião

N117

Campolide

CRIL-IC17

21

A5-IC15

Estrada do Alvito

Av Eng Duarte Pacheco

To Estoril (23km); Cascais (26km)

Mãe d'Água

Estrada do Penedo

9

Rato

See Rato, Marquês de Pombal & Saldanha Map (p90)

Av da Ponte

Av de Ceuta

Av das Descobertas

Av Ilha da Madeira

Restelo

Av Infante Santo

Estrela

Bairro Alto

Alcântara

R do Alto do Duque

See Belém Map (p91)

Lapa

6

Ajuda

Alcântara-Mar Train Station

Av do Restelo

Cç da Ajuda

Doca de Alcântara

To Estádio Nacional (3km); Cruz Quebrada (3km); Oeiras (9km); Estoril (20km); Cascais (23km)

Belém

Parque Junqueira Congressos Centro

R da Junqueira

Av de Brasília

Av da Índia

36

26

25

See Estrela, Lapa & Doca de Alcântara Map (p89)

North-South Railway Line

Ponte 25 de Abril

To Trafaria (3km)

To Porto Brandão (1km)

To Costa da Caparica (8km); A2/A12 to Setúbal (47km)

0 1 km
0 0.5 miles
E
F
G
H
1
2
3
4
5
6
To A1-IP1 to Santarém (60km); Porto (305km)
To Ponte Vasco da Gama (1.5km); A12 to Setúbal (45km); A2-IP1 to the Algarve (240km)
Aeroporto de Lisboa
Av Dr Alfredo Bensaúde
Av Dom João II
Av de Boa Esperança
Parque das Nações
Fil; Lisbon Exhibition Centre
Oceanos
R da Pimenta
Av Cidade do Porto
Av de Berlim
Olivais Norte
Gare do Oriente
Doca dos Olivais
Alameda dos Oceanos
Teatro Camões
R D Fuas Roupinho
Avenida Marechal Craveiro Lopes
Av Marechal Gomes da Costa
Cabo Ruivo
Olivais
Chelas
Av Infante Dom Henrique
Avenida Almirante Gago Coutinho
Av do Santo Condestável
Alvalade
Biblioteca Nacional
Av dos Estados Unidos da América
Roma
Entrecampos
Entrecampos Poente Train Station
Entrecampos Train Station
Bela Vista
Areeiro
Campo Pequeno
Av da República
Av 5 de Outubro
Olaias
Alameda
Estrada de Chelas
Saldanha
Arroios
Av Almirante Reis
Picoas
Igreja de Penha de França
Av Dom Afonso III
Av Mouzinho de Albuquerque
Parque
Anjos
Xabregas
Marquês de Pombal
Intendente
Avenida
Martim Moniz
Rossio Train Station
Restauradores
Graça
Rossio
Castelo
Baixa-Chiado
Alfama
Baixa
Cais do Sodré Train & Metro Station
Praça do Comércio
Santa Apolónia Train Station
See Baixa, Alfama & Castelo Map (pp86–7)
RIO TEJO
To Cacilhas (2km); Almada (3km)
To Barreiro (9km)
To Montijo; Seixal; Reserva Natural do Estuário do Sado
SLEEPING
Lisboa Camping – Parque Municipal 21 B4
Pousada da Juventude da Lisboa Parque Nações 22 G1
EATING
Bica do Sapato 23 F5
Casanova 24 F5
Deli Delux (see 23)
DRINKING
Café In 25 C6
ENTERTAINMENT
Belém Bar Café 26 B6
Estádio da Luz 27 C2
Estádio José de Alvalade 28 D1
Fnac (see 31)
Lux 29 F5
Pavilhão Atlântico 30 H1
SHOPPING
Centro Comercial Colombo 31 C2
Centro Vasco da Gama 32 G1
Cerâmica Viúva Lamego 33 E4
Livraria Bertrand (see 31)
Olaria do Desterros 34 E4
TRANSPORT
Eurolines Ticket Office (see 35)
Gare do Oriente 35 G1
Tejo Bike 36 B6
Tejo Bike (see 17)
Terminal Campo Grande 37 D2

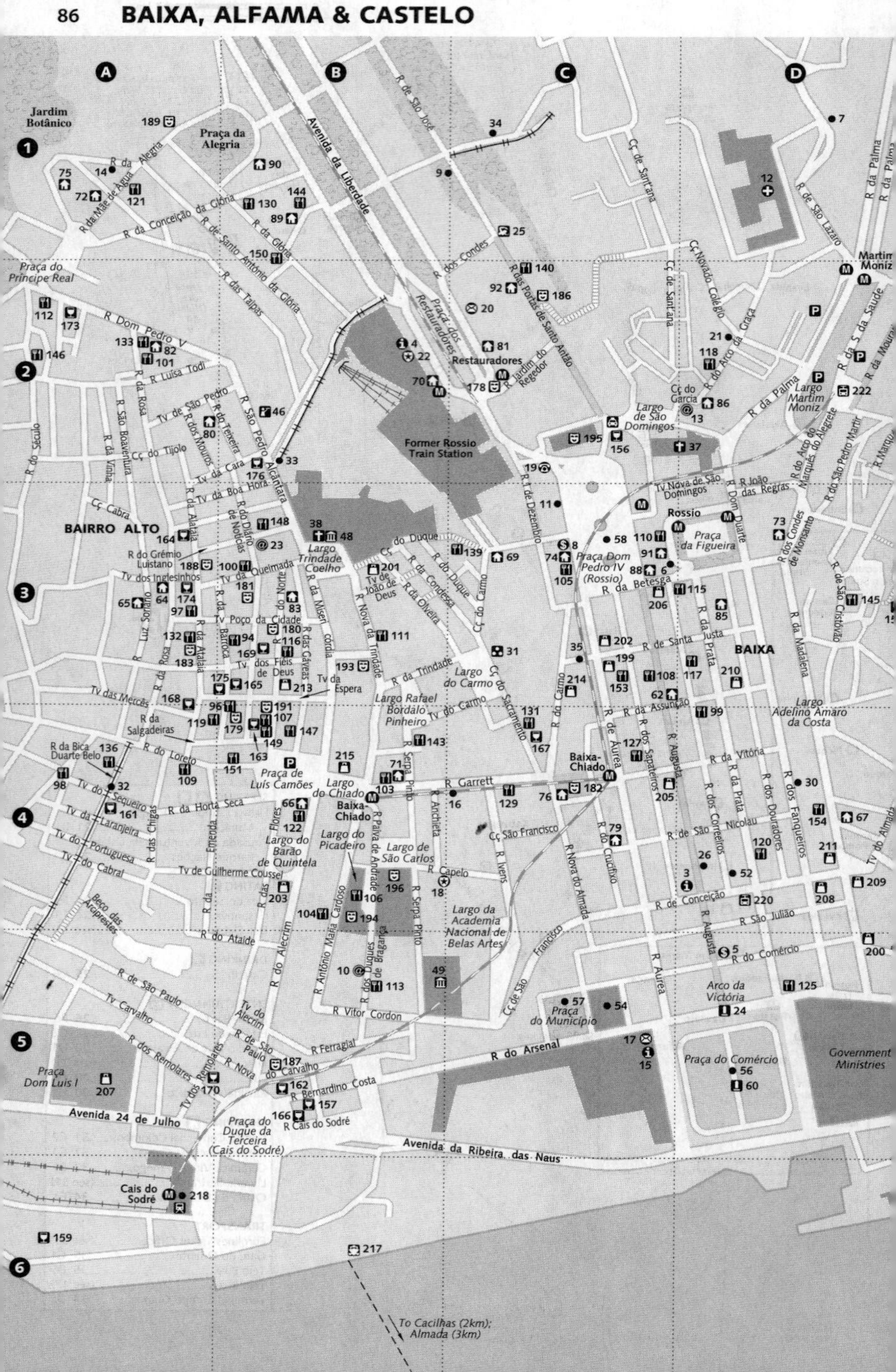
Jardim Botânico
Praça da Alegria
Avenida da Liberdade
Former Rossio Train Station
Restauradores
Praça do Príncipe Real
BAIRRO ALTO
Largo Trindade Coelho
Largo do Carmo
Largo Rafael Bordalo Pinheiro
Praça de Luís Camões
Largo do Chiado
Baixa-Chiado
Largo do Picadeiro
Largo de São Carlos
Largo do Barão de Quintela
Largo da Academia Nacional de Belas Artes
Praça Dom Pedro IV (Rossio)
Praça da Figueira
Rossio
BAIXA
Largo de São Domingos
Largo Martim Moniz
Martim Moniz
Largo Adelino Amaro da Costa
Praça do Município
Arco da Victória
Praça do Comércio
Government Ministries
Praça Dom Luís I
Praça do Duque da Terceira (Cais do Sodré)
Cais do Sodré
R do Arsenal
Avenida 24 de Julho
Avenida da Ribeira das Naus
R Garrett
R Augusta
R da Prata
R do Ouro
R Áurea
R dos Fanqueiros
R Nova do Almada
R Dom Pedro V
R da Misericórdia
R do Alecrim
R de São Paulo
R dos Remolares
R Ferragial
R Vítor Cordon
R Serpa Pinto
To Cacilhas (2km); Almada (3km)

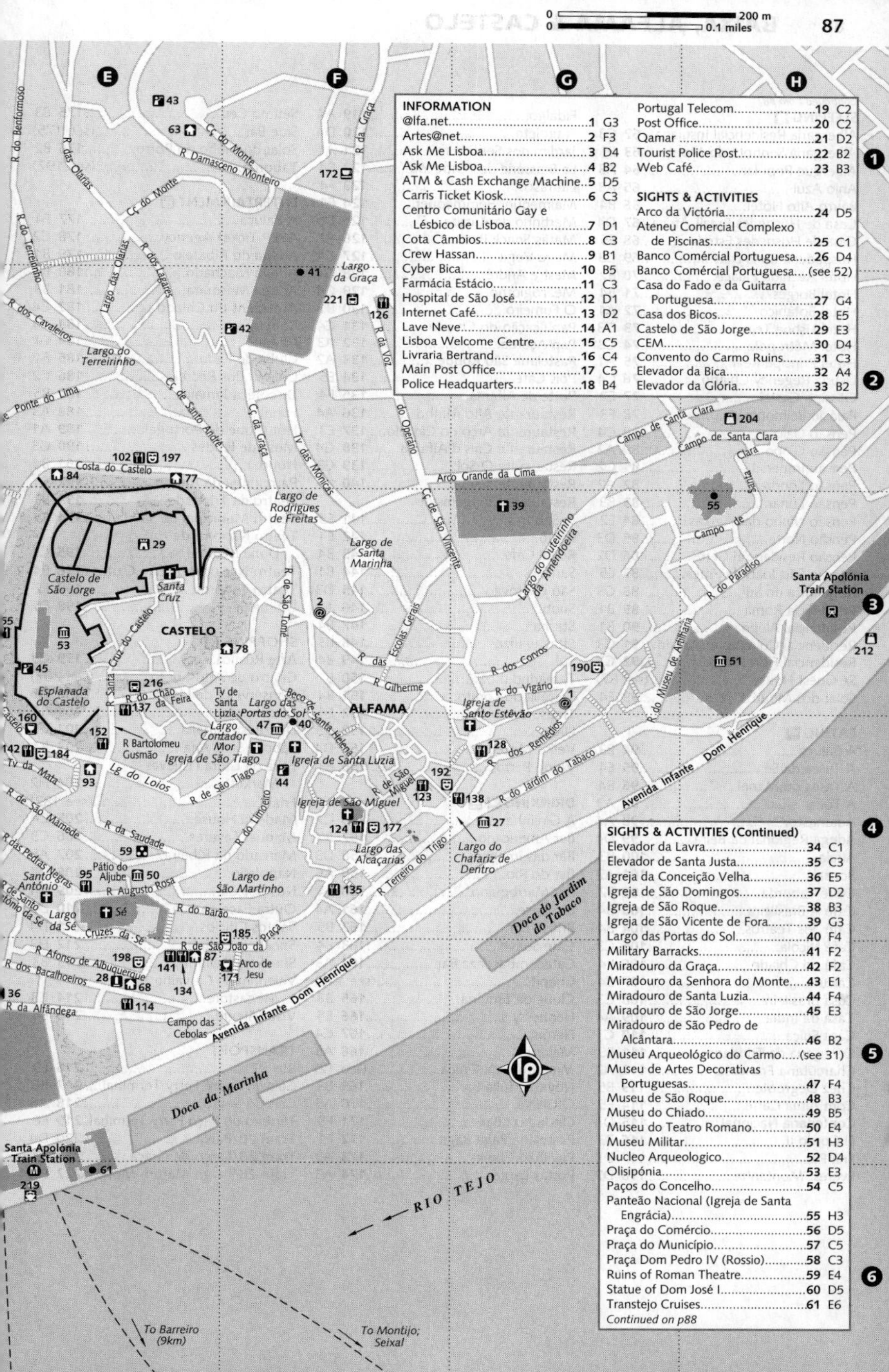
0 200 m
0 0.1 miles
INFORMATION
@lfa.net 1 G3
Artes@net 2 F3
Ask Me Lisboa 3 D4
Ask Me Lisboa 4 B2
ATM & Cash Exchange Machine 5 D5
Carris Ticket Kiosk 6 C3
Centro Comunitário Gay e Lésbico de Lisboa 7 D1
Cota Câmbios 8 C3
Crew Hassan 9 B1
Cyber Bica 10 B5
Farmácia Estácio 11 C3
Hospital de São José 12 D1
Internet Café 13 D2
Lave Neve 14 A1
Lisboa Welcome Centre 15 C5
Livraria Bertrand 16 C4
Main Post Office 17 C5
Police Headquarters 18 B4
Portugal Telecom 19 C2
Post Office 20 C2
Qamar 21 D2
Tourist Police Post 22 B2
Web Café 23 B3
SIGHTS & ACTIVITIES
Arco da Victória 24 D5
Ateneu Comercial Complexo de Piscinas 25 C1
Banco Comércial Portuguesa 26 D4
Banco Comércial Portuguesa (see 52)
Casa do Fado e da Guitarra Portuguesa 27 G4
Casa dos Bicos 28 E5
Castelo de São Jorge 29 E3
CEM 30 D4
Convento do Carmo Ruins 31 C3
Elevador da Bica 32 A4
Elevador da Glória 33 B2
SIGHTS & ACTIVITIES (Continued)
Elevador da Lavra 34 C1
Elevador de Santa Justa 35 C3
Igreja da Conceição Velha 36 E5
Igreja de São Domingos 37 D2
Igreja de São Roque 38 B3
Igreja de São Vicente de Fora 39 G3
Largo das Portas do Sol 40 F4
Military Barracks 41 F2
Miradouro da Graça 42 F2
Miradouro da Senhora do Monte 43 E1
Miradouro de Santa Luzia 44 F4
Miradouro de São Jorge 45 E3
Miradouro de São Pedro de Alcântara 46 B2
Museu Arqueológico do Carmo (see 31)
Museu de Artes Decorativas Portuguesas 47 F4
Museu de São Roque 48 B3
Museu do Chiado 49 B5
Museu do Teatro Romano 50 E4
Museu Militar 51 H3
Nucleo Arqueologico 52 D4
Olisipónia 53 E3
Paços do Concelho 54 C5
Panteão Nacional (Igreja de Santa Engrácia) 55 H3
Praça do Comércio 56 D5
Praça do Município 57 C5
Praça Dom Pedro IV (Rossio) 58 C3
Ruins of Roman Theatre 59 E4
Statue of Dom José I 60 D5
Transtejo Cruises 61 E6
Continued on p88
CASTELO
ALFAMA
Castelo de São Jorge
Santa Apolónia Train Station
RIO TEJO
Doca da Marinha
Doca do Jardim do Tabaco
Avenida Infante Dom Henrique
To Barreiro (9km)
To Montijo; Seixal

Continued from p87

SLEEPING

Albergaria Residencial Insulana....62 C3
Albergaria Senhora do Monte....63 E1
Albergue Popular....64 A3
Anjo Azul....65 A3
Bairro Alto Hotel....66 B4
Casa de Hóspedes Brazil-África....67 D4
Casa de Hóspedes Estrela....68 E5
Hospedaria Bons Dias....69 C3
Hotel Avenida Palace....70 B2
Hotel Borges....71 B4
Hotel Botânico....72 A1
Hotel Lisboa Tejo....73 D3
Hotel Métropole....74 C3
Hotel Príncipe Real....75 A1
Lisboa Regency Chiado....76 C4
Olissipo Castelo....77 E2
Palácio Belmonte....78 F3
Pensão Galizia....79 C4
Pensão Globo....80 A2
Pensão Imperial....81 C2
Pensão Londres....82 A2
Pensão Lunar....83 B3
Pensão Ninho das Águias....84 E2
Pensão Norte....85 D3
Pensão Residencial Gerês....86 D2
Pensão São João da Praça....87 E5
Residência do Sul....88 C3
Residência Roma....89 B1
Residencial Alegria....90 B1
Residencial Coimbra e Madrid....91 C3
Residencial Florescente....92 C2
Sé Guest House....(see 87)
Solar dos Mouros....93 E4

EATING

A Baîuca....94 B3
A Tasca da Sé....95 E4
A Tasca do Manel....96 B4
A Toca....97 A3
Adamastor....98 A4
Adega Regional da Beira....99 D4
Alfaia....100 B3
Bonsai....101 A2
C@fé Taborda....102 E2
Café A Brasileira....103 B4
Café dos Teatros....104 B4
Café Nicola....105 C3
Café no Chiado....106 B4
Calcuta....107 B4
Casa Brasileira....108 C3
Casa da India....109 A4
Casa Suiça....110 C3
Cervejaria da Trindade....111 B3
Charcutaria Francesa....112 A2
Chez Degroote....113 B5
Com Alma Caffé....114 E5
Confeitaria Nacional....115 D3
El Gordo II....116 B3
Ena Pai....117 D3
Everest Montanha....118 D2
Fidalgo....119 A4
Fragoleto....120 D4
Jardim dos Sentidos....121 A1
La Brasserie de l'Entrecôte....122 B4
Lautasco....123 F4
Malmequer Bemmequer....124 F4
Martinho da Arcada....125 D5
Matas Snack Bar....126 F2
Mega Vega....127 C4
Mestre André....128 G4
Mezzogiórno....129 C4
O Fumeiro....130 B1
Panificação do Chiado....131 C4
Pap'Açorda....132 A3
Pastelaria São Roque....133 A2
Pois Café....134 E5
Porte de Alfama....135 F4
Restaurante Alto Minho....136 A4
Restaurante Arço do Castelo....137 E3
Restaurante Cais d'Alfama....138 G4
Restaurante O Sol....139 C3
Restaurante Solmar....140 C2
Restaurante Viagems de Sabores....141 E5
Restô....142 E4
Royal Café....143 B4
Sancho....144 B1
São Cristóvão....145 D3
Snob....146 A2
Stasha....147 B4
Stravaganza....148 B3
Sul....149 B4
Tamarind....150 B1
Tertúlia do Loreto....151 B4
Treasure Island....152 E4
UMA....153 C3
Velho Macedo....154 D4
Verde Perto....155 E3

DRINKING

A Ginjinha....156 C2
Bar Americano....157 B5
Bar das Imagens....158 D3
Bar do Rio....159 A6
Bar Marroquino....160 E4
Bicaense....161 A4
British Bar....162 B5
Café Suave....163 B4
Catacombas Jazz Bar....164 A3
Chapitô....(see 142)
Clube da Esquina....165 B3
Hennessy's....166 B5
Heróis....167 C4
Majong....168 A3
Miradouro da Graça....(see 42)
Nova Tertúlia Bar....169 B3
O'Gilín's....170 A5
Onda Jazz Bar....171 F5
Pastelaria Baga Baga....172 F1
Pavilhão Chines....173 A2
Portas Largas....174 A3
Sétimo Ceu....175 B3
Side Bar....(see 175)
Solar do Vinho do Porto....176 B2
Taborda....(see 197)

ENTERTAINMENT

A Baîuca....177 F4
ABEP Ticket Agency....178 C2
Adega do Ribatejo....179 B4
Adega Machado....180 B3
Adega Mesquita....181 B3
Armazéns do Chiado....182 C4
Capela....183 A3
Chapitô....184 E4
Clube de Fado....185 F4
Coliseu dos Recreios....186 C2
Discoteca Jamaica....187 B5
Frágil....188 A3
Hot Clube de Portugal....189 A1
Mesa de Frades....190 G3
Nono....191 B4
Parreirinha de Alfama....192 F4
Teatro da Trindade....193 B3
Teatro Municipal de São Luís....194 B4
Teatro Nacional de Dona Maria II....195 C2
Teatro Nacional de São Carlos....196 B4
Teatro Taborda....197 E2
Última Sé....198 E5

SHOPPING

Arte Rustica....199 C3
Centro de Artesanato....(see 207)
Conserveira de Lisboa....200 D5
Discolecção....201 B3
Discoteca Amália....202 C3
Fábrica Sant'Ana....203 B4
Feira da Ladra (Thieves Market)....204 H2
Fnac....(see 182)
Madeira House....205 C4
Manuel Tavares....206 C3
Mercado da Ribeira....207 A5
Napoleão....208 D4
Nós por Cá....209 D4
Outra Face da Lua....210 D3
Santos Ofícios....211 D4
Sneakers Delight....212 H3
Sneakers Delight....213 B3
Valentim de Carvalho Megastore....214 C3
Vista Alegre....215 B4

TRANSPORT

Bus 37....216 E3
Cais do Sodré Ferry Terminal....217 B6
Cais do Sodré....218 A6
Terreiro do Paço Ferry Terminal....219 E6
Tram 28/Baixa....220 D4
Tram 28/Largo da Graça....221 F2
Tram 28/Largo Martim Moniz....222 D2

0 — 300 m
0 — 0.2 miles
INFORMATION
British Council 1 F1
Espaço Ágora 2 E3
French Embassy 3 E3
Hospital Britânico 4 D1
Irish Embassy 5 E2
Netherlands Embassy 6 C2
UK Embassy 7 E1
SIGHTS & ACTIVITIES
Basílica da Estrela 8 D2
Casa Museu de Amália Rodrigues 9 E1
Cemitério dos Ingleses 10 D1
Jardim Botânico 11 F1
Jardim da Estrela 12 E1
Miradouro de Santa Catarina 13 F3
Museu da Carris 14 A4
Museu da Marioneta 15 E3
Museu Nacional de Arte Antiga 16 D3
Palácio da Assembleia da República 17 E2
Praça do Príncipe Real 18 F1
SLEEPING
As Janelas Verdes 19 D3
Casa de São Mamede 20 F1
Lapa Palace 21 D3
Maná Guesthouse 22 E3
Residencial Beira Tejo 23 E3
York House 24 D3
EATING
A Confraria (see 24)
Café Apolo XI 25 E3
Cha da Lapa 26 D3
Espalha Brasas 27 B4
Esplanada 28 F1
Lusitália 29 F1
Picanha Janelas Verdes 30 D3
Sitio do Pica Pau 31 D2
DRINKING
Bar 106 32 F1
Bar Água no Bico 33 F1
Bric-a-Bar 34 F1
Doca de Santo 35 B4
Foxtrot 36 F1
Max 37 F1
Op Art Café 38 B4
Tuareg 39 E3
ENTERTAINMENT
A Lontra 40 E1
Blues Café 41 C4
Buddha Bar 42 B4
Dock's Club 43 C4
Finalmente 44 F1
Incógnito 45 F2
Kapital 46 E3
Kremlin 47 E3
Luanda 48 B3
Memorial 49 F1
Paradise Garage 50 B3
Senhor Vinho 51 E2
Trumps 52 F1
SHOPPING
Carla Amaro 53 F1
ESTRELA
LAPA
MADRAGOA
BAIRRO ALTO
ALCÂNTARA
Jardim Botânico
Jardim da Estrela
Cemitério dos Ingleses
Tapada das Necessidades
Tapada da Ajuda
Doca de Alcântara
Doca de Santo Amaro
Gare Maritima de Alcântara
Gare Maritima Rocha do Conde de Óbidos
Santos Train Station
Alcântara-Mar
Casa da América Latina
RIO TEJO
To Belém (1km)
Avenida 24 de Julho
Avenida da India
Avenida de Brasília
Avenida da Ponte
Avenida Infante Santo
Avenida Dom Carlos 1

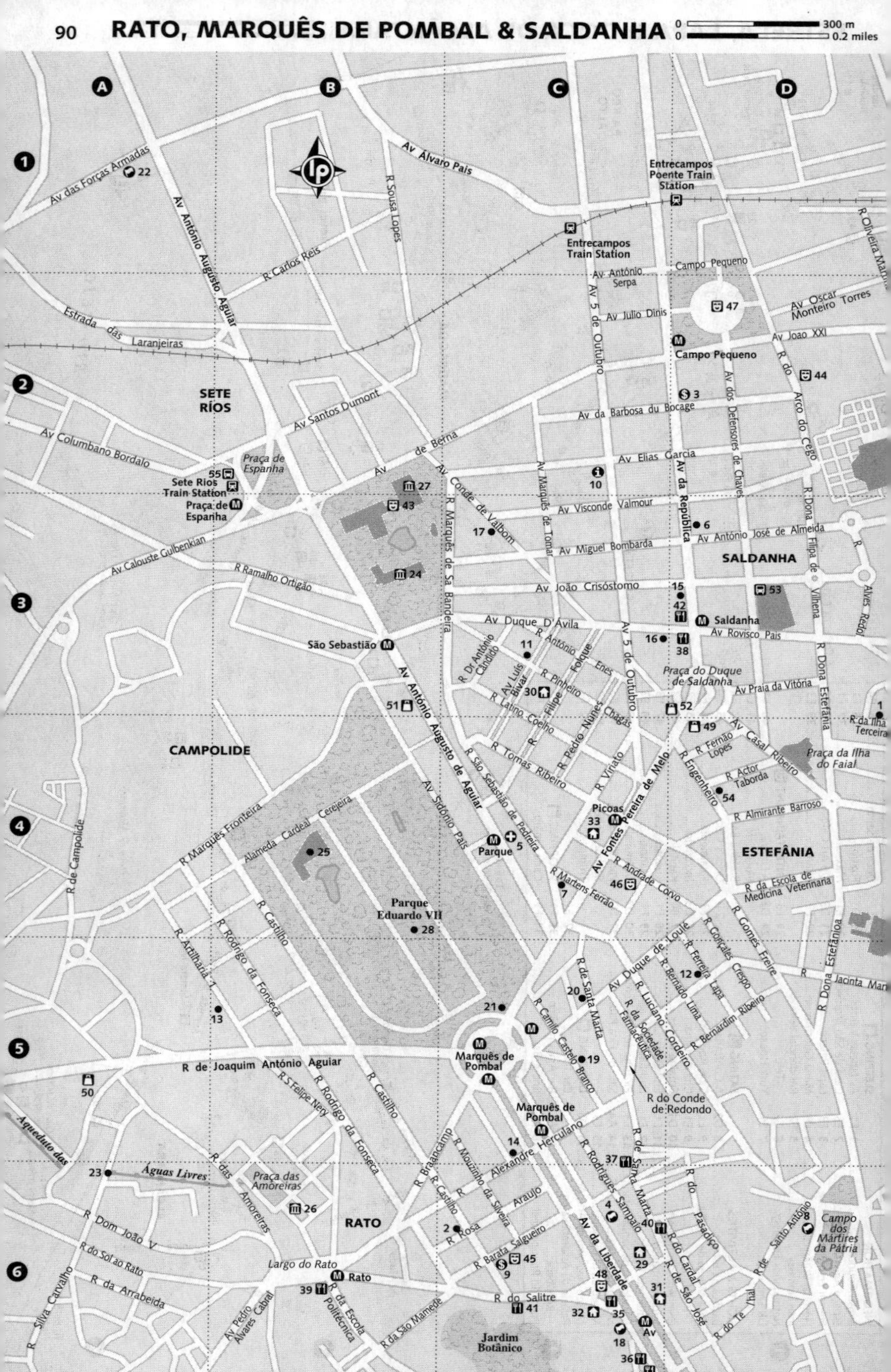
0 300 m
0 0.2 miles
SETE RÍOS
CAMPOLIDE
SALDANHA
ESTEFÂNIA
RATO
Entrecampos Poente Train Station
Entrecampos Train Station
Sete Rios Train Station
Praça de Espanha
Campo Pequeno
São Sebastião
Saldanha
Picoas
Parque
Marquês de Pombal
Rato
Av
Parque Eduardo VII
Jardim Botânico
Praça do Duque de Saldanha
Praça da Ilha do Faial
Praça das Amoreiras
Campo dos Mártires da Pátria
Largo do Rato
Aqueduto das Águas Livres
Av das Forças Armadas
Av António Augusto Aguiar
Av Álvaro Pais
R Sousa Lopes
R Carlos Reis
Estrada das Laranjeiras
Av Santos Dumont
Av Columbano Bordalo
Av de Berna
Av Calouste Gulbenkian
R Ramalho Ortigão
Av Conde de Valbom
R Marquês de Sa Bandeira
Av Marquês de Tomar
Av 5 de Outubro
Av da República
Av dos Defensores de Chaves
R do Arco do Cego
R Dona Filipa de Vilhena
R Dona Estefânia
R Oliveira Martins
Av Oscar Monteiro Torres
Av Joao XXI
Campo Pequeno
Av António Serpa
Av Julio Dinis
Av da Barbosa du Bocage
Av Elias Garcia
Av Visconde Valmour
Av Miguel Bombarda
Av António José de Almeida
Av João Crisóstomo
Av Duque D'Ávila
Av Rovisco Pais
R António Enes
R Pinheiro Chagas
R Dr António Cândido
Av Luís Bivar
R Filipe Folque
R Latino Coelho
R Pedro Nunes
R Tomas Ribeiro
R Viriato
Av Fontes Pereira de Melo
Av Praia da Vitória
Av Casal Ribeiro
R Fernão Lopes
R Actor Taborda
R Engenheiro
R Almirante Barroso
R da Ilha Terceira
R Alves Redol
R São Sebastião da Pedreira
Av Sidónio Pais
R Martens Ferrão
R Andrade Corvo
R da Escola de Medicina Veterinaria
R Gomes Freire
R Gonçalves Crespo
R Ferreira Lapa
R Bernado Lima
R Luciano Cordeiro
R da Sociedade Farmacêutica
R Bernardim Ribeiro
R Jacinta Marto
Av Duque de Loulé
R de Santa Marta
R Camilo Castelo Branco
R do Conde de Redondo
R Marquês Fronteira
Alameda Cardeal Cerejeira
R de Campolide
R Artilharia 1
R Rodrigo da Fonseca
R Castilho
R de Joaquim António Aguiar
R S Felipe Nery
R Braancamp
R Mouzinho da Silveira
R Alexandre Herculano
R Rodrigues Sampaio
R Rosa Araujo
R Barata Salgueiro
Av da Liberdade
R do Pasadiço
R do Cardal
R de São José
R de Santo António
R do Telhal
R das Amoreiras
R Dom João V
R do Sol ao Rato
R da Arrabeida
R Silva Carvalho
Av Pedro Álvares Cabral
R da Escola Politécnica
R da São Mamede
R do Salitre

INFORMATION
Associação Opus Gay........1 D3
Australian Embassy........(see 4)
Automóvel Club de Portugal (ACP)........2 C6
Barclays Bank........3 D2
Canadian Embassy........4 C6
Clínica Médica Internacional........5 C4
Comissão para a Igualdade e para os Direitos das Mulheres.6 D3
Foreigners' Registration Service..7 C4
German Embassy........8 D6
Grupo Deutsche Bank........9 C6
ICEP Turismo........10 C2
Institut Franco-Portugais de Lisbonne........11 C3
Instituto da Conservação da Natureza (ICN)........12 D5
Instituto Geográfico Português..13 B5
Instituto Português da Juventude (IPJ)........(see 33)
Livraria Buchholz........14 C5
Livraria Municipal........15 D3
Movijovem........16 C3
Secretariado Nacional de Reabilitação........17 C3
Spanish Embassy & Consulate...18 C6
Tagus........19 C5
Top Atlântica........20 C5
Tour Bus Terminal........21 C5
US Embassy & Consulate........22 A1

SIGHTS & ACTIVITIES
Aqueduto das Águas Livres........23 A6
Centro de Arte Moderna........24 B3
Estufas........25 B4
Mãe d'Água Reservoir........26 B6
Museu Calouste Gulbenkian........27 B2
Parque Eduardo VII........28 B4

SLEEPING
Hotel Britannia........29 C6
Hotel Impala........30 C3
NH Liberdade........31 C6
Pensão Residencial 13 da Sorte..32 C6
Pousada da Juventude de Lisboa........33 C4

EATING
Ad Lib........34 C6
Cervejaria Ribadouro........35 C6
La Caffé........36 C6
Luca........37 C5
Pastelaria Sequeira........38 D3
Real Fábrica........39 B6
Restaurante Estrela de Santa Marta........40 C6
Restaurante Os Tibetanos........41 C6
Versailles........42 D3

ENTERTAINMENT
Concert Halls (Fundação Calouste Gulbenkian)........43 B3
Culturgest........44 D2
Instituto do Cinemateca Portuguesa........45 C6
Mussulo........46 C4
Praça de Touros........47 D2
São Jorge Cinema........48 C6

SHOPPING
Atrium Saldanha........49 D4
Complexo das Amoreiras........50 A5
El Corte Inglés........51 B3
Galerias Monumental........52 D3

TRANSPORT
Arco do Cego Bus Station........53 D3
Eurolines (Intercentro) Ticket Office........54 D4
Sete Rios Bus Station........55 B2

BELÉM

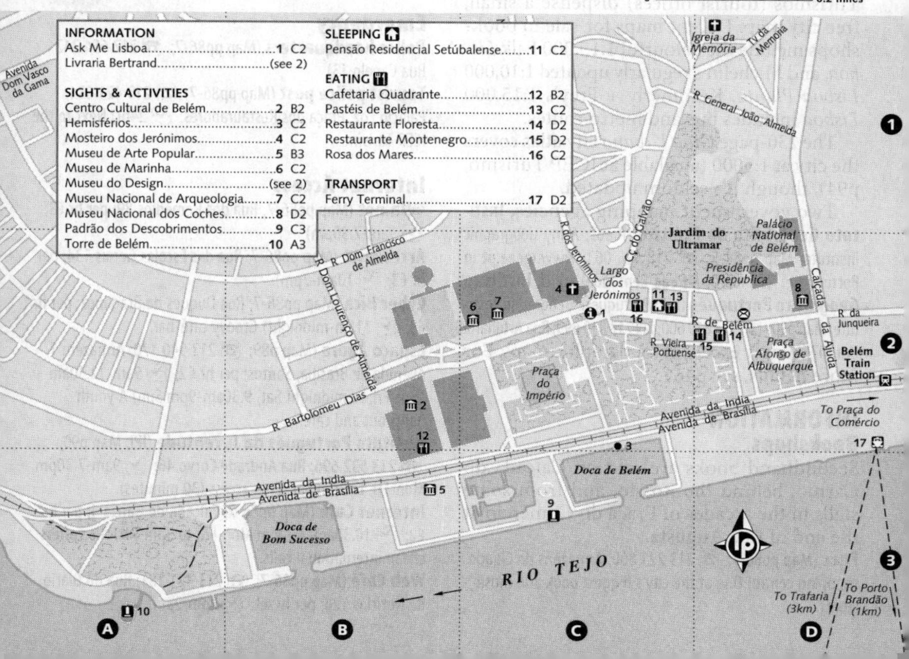

(Continued from page 83)

another climb to Castelo de São Jorge and the ancient, mazelike Alfama district around it.

River ferries depart from a pier near Praça do Comércio and from Cais do Sodré to the west. Lisbon's long-haul train stations are Santa Apolónia, Sete Rios, Cais do Sodré and Barreiro (across the Tejo). Gare do Oriente is the newest station, combining bus, train and metro stations on the northeastern outskirts of town.

Aside from Gare do Oriente, the main long-distance bus terminal is Sete Rios, near Praça da Espanha metro station. Besides metro and buses, there are old-fashioned trams, with smart new ones running 6km west from Praça da Figueira to the waterfront suburb of Belém.

Lisbon is connected south across the Tejo to the Costa da Caparica and Setúbal Peninsula by the immense, 70m-high Ponte 25 de Abril, Europe's longest suspension bridge, which also carries trains to the south. Vasco da Gama bridge – 17.2km long – reaches across the Tejo further north, from Sacavem (near Parque das Nações) to Montijo, speeding up north–south traffic.

Maps

Turismos (tourist offices) dispense a small, free city map. Decent maps for sale in bookshops include the colourful 1:15,000 Falk *Lisboa*, and Michelin's regularly updated 1:10,000 *Lisboa Planta*. Kümmerly + Frey's 1:15,000 *Lisboa* includes bus and metro routes.

The 230-page *Guia Urbano* city atlas covers the city at 1:5000 (available at ICEP Turismo, p94), though it's seldom updated.

Two government mapping agencies, **Instituto Geográfico do Exército** (IGeoE; Army Geographic Institute; Map pp84-5; ☎ 218 520 063; www.igeoe.pt in Portuguese; Avenida Dr Alfredo Bensaúde) and **Instituto Geográfico Português** (IGP; Portuguese Geographic Institute; Map p90; ☎ 213 819 600; fax 213 819 699; Rua Artilharia Um 107) supply excellent topographic maps. For more details, see p461.

INFORMATION

Bookshops

Secondhand books are sold on Calçada do Carmo, behind the Rossio, and from some stalls in the arcades of Praça do Comércio at the end of Rua Augusta.

Fnac (Map pp86-7; ☎ 213 221 800; Armazéns do Chiado shopping centre) One of the city's biggest book and music stores.

Livraria Bertrand Chiado (Map pp86-7; ☎ 213 421 941; Rua Garrett 73); Greater Lisbon (Map pp84-5; Centro Comercial Colombo shopping centre); Belém (Map p91; Centro Cultural de Belém) Dating from the 18th century, Bertrand has excellent selections amid old-world charm.

Livraria Buchholz (Map p90; ☎ 213 170 580; Rua Duque de Palmela 4) Huge collection of literature in Portuguese, English, French and German.

Livraria Municipal (Map p90; ☎ 213 530 522; Avenida da República 21a) A spacious, tiled bookshop devoted entirely to Lisbon, with some titles in English.

Cultural Centres

British Council (Map p89; ☎ 213 214 500; www.britishcouncil.org/portugal; Rua Luís Fernandes 1-3) In a palatial building; has a huge library (open from 2pm to 6pm, Monday to Friday), with current English newspapers.

Crew Hassan (Map pp86-7; ☎ 213 466 119; www.crewhassan.org; 1st fl, Rua das Portas de Santo Antão 159; 🕑 2pm-midnight) Manifesting the more creative side of the Lisboêta spirit, this place hosts a wide range of events: readings, film screenings, art openings. It's a comfy place of armchairs, high ceilings and balconies if you want to stop in for a beer or *bica* (espresso).

Institut Franco-Portugais de Lisbonne (Map p90; ☎ library 213 111 421; www.ifp-lisboa.com; Avenida Luís Bívar 91) Has regular cultural (including film) events, and a library called Mediateca.

Emergency

Police headquarters (Map pp86-7; ☎ 217 654 242; Rua Capelo 13)

Tourist police post (Map pp86-7; ☎ 213 421 634; Palácio Foz, Praça dos Restauradores; 🕑 24hr) Next to the ICEP Turismo.

Internet Access

@lfa.net (Map pp86-7; Rua dos Remédios 89; per hr €3; 🕑 9am-7.30pm)

Artes@net (Map pp86-7; Rua das Escolas Gerais 134; per hr €3; 🕑 10am-7pm)

Cyber Bica (Map pp86-7; Rua Duques de Bragança; per hr €3; 🕑 11am-midnight) Groovy café-bar.

Espaço Ágora (Map p89; ☎ 213 940 170; Armazém 1, Avenida de Brasilia, Santos; per hr €2; 🕑 9am-12.30am Mon-Fri, to midnight Sat, 9.30am-9pm Sun) A youth hang-out and café.

Instituto Português da Juventude (IPJ; Map p90; ☎ 213 532 696; Rua Andrade Corvo 46; 🕑 9am-7.30pm Mon-Fri, to 3pm Sat) Free access (30 minutes).

Internet Café (Map pp86-7; Calçada do Garcia 4; per hr €2; 🕑 10.30am-7.30pm Mon-Fri, to 3pm Sat) Also offers cheap international calls.

Web Café (Map pp86-7; ☎ 213 421 181; Rua do Diário de Notícias 126; per hr €3; 🕑 2pm-2am)

Internet Resources

www.luso.u-net.com/lisbon.htm John Laidlar's labour of love is train-and-tram-spotting heaven.
www.askmelisboa.com Turismo de Lisboa's multilingual website.
www.ccb.pt Centro Cultural de Belém's site; lists current and forthcoming events.
www.musica.gulbenkian.pt The Gulbenkian Foundation's bilingual site, with what's on.
www.parquedasnacoes.pt Parque das Nações' site, with current and forthcoming events.
www.cm-lisboa.pt The groovy municipal site – in Portuguese but self-explanatory.

Laundry

Lave Neve (Map pp86-7; Rua da Alegria 37; per 5kg €8.70; 9am-1pm & 3-7pm Mon, 10am-1pm & 3-7pm Tue-Fri, 9am-1pm Sat) The only self-service laundrette in Lisbon.

Medical Services

ICEP Turismo keeps a list of private doctors and dentists who speak English or other languages.

Clínica Medica Internacional (Map p90; ☎ 213 513 310; Ave Antonio Augusto de Aguiar 40) A quick, pricey, private clinic with English-speaking doctors.
Farmácia Estácio (Map pp86-7; ☎ 213 211 390; Rossio 62) A central pharmacy.
Hospital Britânico (British Hospital, Hospital Inglês; Map p89; ☎ 217 213 400, 217 276 353; Rua Saraiva de Carvalho 49) English-speaking staff and doctors.
Hospital de Santa Maria (Map pp84-5; ☎ 217 805 000; Avenida Professor Egas Moniz)

Money

Multibanco ATMs are widespread throughout the city.

Barclays Bank (Map p90; ☎ 217 911 100; Avenida da República 50)
Cota Câmbios (Map pp86-7; ☎ 213 220 480; Rossio 41; 8.30am-10pm) The best bet for changing cash or travellers cheques is a private-exchange bureau such as this one.
Grupo Deutsche Bank (Map p90; ☎ 210 001 200; Rua Castilho 20)
Top Atlântica (Map p90; ☎ 213 108 800; Avenida Duque de Loulé 108) Lisbon's American Express representative.

Post

Airport (24hr) Post office.
Main post office (Map pp86-7; Praça do Comércio) Has poste restante.
Post office (Map pp86-7; Praça dos Restauradores) Another central post office.

Telephone & Fax

Equipped with a phonecard, including the Portugal Telecom card, you can make international direct-dial (IDD) phone calls from most payphones. At Portugal Telecom booths in post offices you can pay after you've made the call.

Portugal Telecom (Map pp86-7; Rossio 68; 8am-11pm) Has rows of booths.
Qamar (Map pp86-7; Rua do Arço da Graça 35; 10am-10pm) Offers bargain-basement international calls (€0.10/0.35 per minute to USA/Europe).

LISBON IN...

Two Days

Start your day with a *bica* (espresso) and pastry in **Chiado**, followed by some first-rate window-shopping and museum-hopping in the neighbourhood. Have lunch at one of the many outdoor cafés secreted about the area. Afterwards, take a roller-coaster ride through the city aboard **tram 28** as it heads up to **Alfama**. Hop off near the **Castelo de São Jorge** (p98) for impressive views over the city. After a few hours exploring Alfama's narrow lanes, book a table at a *fado* (traditional melancholic Portuguese style of singing) restaurant for dinner and song (p120).

On day two, catch a tram to **Belém** for heavenly custard tarts and a packed day of cultural attractions – starting with the marvellous **Mosteiro dos Jerónimos** (p102). In the evening eat in **Bairro Alto**, followed by drinks and late-night pub-crawling in the area. End the night at **Lux** (p119), **Buddha** (p120) or one of Lisbon's other favourite nightspots.

Four Days

On your third day in town, catch a train to **Sintra** (p127) for surreal castles and idyllic scenery. On day four, rise early for a visit to the **Museu Calouste Gulbenkian** (p100); in the afternoon, head to **Cascais** (p136) or **Caparica** (p145) for a drink or sunny stroll along the beach. End the day back in Lisbon with a seafood finale.

Tourist Information

Ask Me Lisboa Rua Augusta (Map pp86-7; near Rua Conceição; ⌚ 10am-1pm & 2-6pm); Santa Apolónia (Map pp84-5; door 47, inside train station; 8am-4pm Tue-Sat); Belém (Map p91; Largo dos Jernónimos; ⌚ 10am-1pm & 2-6pm Tue-Sat); Palácio Foz (Map pp86-7; near Praça dos Restauradores; ⌚ 9am-8pm) Turismo de Lisboa runs several information kiosks; these are the most useful.

ICEP Turismo (Map p90; ☎ 217 909 500; Avenida 5 de Outubro 101) For national inquiries try here, efficiently run by the state's tourism organisation.

Lisboa Welcome Centre (Map pp86-7; ☎ 210 312 810; Praça do Comércio; ⌚ 9am-8pm)

Turismo de Lisboa Airport (☎ 218 450 660; ⌚ 8am-midnight) Doles out maps, advises on transport and makes hotel reservations. Also runs Ask Me Lisboa kiosks.

Excellent free publications available at hotels and tourist offices include the following:

Follow Me Lisboa A fortnightly Portuguese/English leisure guide.

Guia Convida (www.guiasconvida.com) Among the best-designed guides to Lisbon, these are semi-annual publications, one for each major neighbourhood: Bairro Alto, Chiado, Baixa, Liberdade and Príncipe Real.

Guia Gay e Lésbico Gay and lesbian leaflet guide.

Lisboa Step by Step A quarterly tourist guide, produced by Turismo de Lisboa, featuring what's on in the city.

Best Guide: Lisboa (www.myguide.pt) Lists museums, restaurants and nightlife.

Travel Agencies

Tagus Rato (Map p90; ☎ 213 525 986; www.viagenstagus.pt in Portuguese; Rua Camilo Castelo Branco 20); Arreiro (Map pp84-5; ☎ 218 491 531; Praça de Londres 9c; ⌚ 9.30am-7pm Mon-Fri, 10am-1.30pm Sat) Leading youth-oriented travel agency, offering budget hotel, bus, train and air bookings (plus ISIC and ITIC cards).

Top Atlântica (Map p90; ☎ 213 108 800; Avenida Duque de Loulé 108)

DANGERS & ANNOYANCES

Lisbon has a low crime rate, but take care, as you would in any large city. Most crime against foreigners involves car break-ins, pick-pocketing or bag-snatching. Use a money-belt and keep valuables hidden. Be especially mindful when in crowded trams and buses. If you do get challenged, it's far better to hand stuff over than take a risk. Park cars in guarded or locked garages.

Late at night (especially on weekends), avoid walking alone through the Bairro Alto, Alfama and Cais do Sodré districts; take a taxi. Parks and gardens are best avoided after sunset.

SIGHTS

Aside from blockbuster attractions like Belém's majestic Mosteiro dos Jerónimos, Lisbon boasts an assortment of refreshingly compact sights that reveal fascinating aspects of the country's past.

Highlights here include a Moorish castle, a convent from the middle ages and museums devoted to *azulejos* (hand-painted tiles), *fado* performers, gilded coaches and Portuguese decorative arts. Those who prefer nature may enjoy a day at the city's excellent aquarium, the zoo, or an afternoon in one of many green spaces. Among the best ways to approach the city is simply to wander through its quaint neighbourhoods (Alfama should be high on your list), stopping at lovely viewpoints and atmospheric cafés along the way.

Baixa & the Riverfront

Following the destructive 1755 earthquake, the Baixa was reborn along the grid that had been envisioned by the autocratic Marquês de Pombal, Dom José I's chief minister. From the riverside to the Rossio, wide, commercial streets with footpaths were laid, each named after the trade that flourished there – Áurea (formerly Ouro, gold), Sapateiros (shoemakers), Correeiros (saddlers), Prata (silver), Douradores (gilders) and Fanqueiros (cutlers).

While touristy, this *baixa* (lower town) today is still an attractive place to wander, with pedestrianised streets lined with cafés and boutiques, and hustlers selling everything from hash and sunglasses to dicey portraits and jewellery.

The sights in the following section are all on Map pp86–7, unless otherwise noted.

PRAÇA DO COMÉRCIO & AROUND

The city's grandest square is **Praça do Comércio**, an architectural fanfare of Portugal's wealth and might. All visitors arriving by river or sea used to disembark here, and the huge square still feels like the city's portal, with Joaquim Machado de Castro's bronze **equestrian statue** of Dom José I; the 18th-century, arcaded **government ministries** along three sides; and Verissimo da Costa's **Arco da Victória**, the arch opening onto Rua Augusta. The stock exchange was once on the southeastern corner. Before the earthquake, the *praça* (town square) was called Terreiro do Paço (Palace Sq), after the royal Palácio da Ribeira that overlooked it until the morning of 1 November 1755. In 1908 the square witnessed the death of the monarchy, when anarchists assassinated Dom Carlos I and his son.

Just off the square's northwestern corner, the smaller **Praça do Município** is dominated on the eastern side by the 1874 **Paços do Concelho** (town hall), where the republic was proclaimed from its balcony on 5 October 1910; on the southern side by the former marine arsenal; and centrally by a finely carved, 18th-century *pelourinho* (stone pillory).

To the west is the spike-domed **Mercado da Ribeira**, housing the city's former main food market, with an arts and crafts centre (p124).

CENTRAL BAIXA

Under the *baixa* is the **Núcleo Arqueológico** (☎ 213 211 700; admission free), a web of tunnels believed to be the remnants of a Roman spa (or a temple) and probably dating from the 1st century AD. You can descend into the depths via the **Banco Comercial Portuguesa** (Rua dos Correeiros 9) on a guided tour run by the Museu da Cidade. Tours take place on Wednesday (🕓 3-5pm) and Saturday (☎ 10am-noon & 3-5pm), though you'll need to phone ahead to book.

From Largo Martim Moniz, tram 28 twists up into Alfama and Graça. At the Baixa's other end sits the **Elevador de Santa Justa**, a charming, eccentric wrought-iron lift designed by Raul Mésnier du Ponsard (a follower of Gustave Eiffel) and completed in 1902.

ROSSIO & PRAÇA DA FIGUEIRA

The northernmost boundary of the Baixa is this pair of squares, a meeting place for Lisbon's multicultural population, filled with hustle, bustle, cafés and fountains. You are bound to cross these squares repeatedly during your visit – all roads seem to lead here.

In the middle of the Rossio is a **statue**, allegedly of Dom Pedro IV, after whom the square is named (but everyone calls it the Rossio). On the northern side of the square is the restored 1846 **Teatro Nacional de Dona Maria II**, topped by a statue of 16th-century playwright Gil Vicente.

The Rossio was once the scene of animal markets, fairs and bullfights. The theatre was built on the site of a palace in which the unholiest excesses of the Portuguese Inquisition took place from the 16th to the 19th centuries. In the nearby **Igreja de São Domingos** (admission free; 🕓 7.30am-7pm Mon-Fri, noon-6pm Sat) the Inquisition's judgments, or autos-da-fé, were pronounced. Inside it's imposing, with gashed pillars like a damaged rock face. The much-battered church (just about) survived earthquakes in 1531 and 1755, and fire in 1959. The high altar, designed by the Mafra architect Friedrich Ludwig, dates from 1748.

Chiado & Bairro Alto

The Chiado, a wedge of wide streets between Rua do Crucifixo and Rua da Misericórdia, is elegantly 18th century, with upmarket shops and cafés. It leads up to the contrastingly weblike Bairro Alto (upper district), a fashionable 17th-century residential quarter, now the Lisbon Soho with one-off designers, vintage boutiques, record shops, restaurants and boho bars and cafés. The following are on Map pp86–7 unless otherwise noted.

In the Chiado the graceful ruins of the **Convento do Carmo**, uphill from Rua Garrett along Calçada do Sacramento, are Lisbon's only remaining example of Gothic architecture, mostly devoured by the 1755 earthquake. Just the tall slender pillars, arches, walls and flying buttresses remain of one of Lisbon's largest churches, built in 1423; it's now regularly used as an open-air theatre. The **Museu Arqueológico do Carmo** (☎ 213 478 629; adult/child under 14 €2.50/free, 10am-2pm Sun free; 🕓 10am-6pm Apr-Sep, to 5pm Oct-Mar) was set up to safeguard religious treasures after the abolition of religious orders in 1834. It has an outstanding collection of 14th-century carved tombs, some prehistoric implements and a dishevelled trio of mummies – one battered Egyptian and two gruesome 16th-century Peruvians.

LISBOA CARD

With this discount card you get free travel on the metro, buses, trams and lifts, plus the train to Belém; free admission to 27 museums and monuments including some in Sintra; and discounts of up to 50% on sights, tours, cruises and other admission charges. The 24-/48-/72-hour versions cost €13.50/23/28 (children from five to 11 €6/9.50/11.50) – reasonable value if you are a tenacious tourist. You validate the card when you want to start it.

The card is sold at all Turismos de Lisboa and Carris ticket kiosks.

INHARMONIOUS HETERONYMS: A PEOPLE'S POET

'There's no such man known as Fernando Pessoa,' swore Alberto Caeiro, who, truth be told, didn't really exist himself. He was one of more than a dozen 'heteronyms' (identities) adopted by Fernando Pessoa, Portugal's greatest 20th-century poet.

Heralded by literary critics as one of the icons of modernism, Pessoa was also among the stranger characters to wander the streets of Lisbon. He worked as a translator by day (having learned English while living in South Africa as a young boy), and wrote poetry by night – but not just Pessoa's poetry. He took on numerous personas, writing in entirely different styles, representing different philosophies, backgrounds and levels of mastery. Of Pessoa's four primary heteronyms, for instance, Alberto Caeiro was regarded as the great master by other heteronyms Alvaro de Campos and Ricardo Reis (Fernando Pessoa was the fourth heteronym, but his existence, as alluded to earlier, was denied by the other three). Any one style would have qualified Pessoa as a major poet of his time, but considered together, the variety of his styles places him among the greats of Western literature.

Pessoa for many is inextricably linked to Lisbon. He spent his nights in cafés, writing, drinking and talking until late into the evening, and many of his works are set very precisely in Lisbon's old neighbourhoods. Among Pessoa's phobias were lightning and having his photograph taken. You can see a few of the existing photos of him at the Café Martinho da Arcada (p112), one of his regular haunts.

Despite his quirks and brilliance, Pessoa published very little in his lifetime, with his great work *Livro do Desassossego* (The Book of Disquiet) only appearing in 1982, 50 years after it was written. In fact, the great bulk of Pessoa's work was discovered after his death: thousands of manuscript pages hidden away inside a wooden trunk.

By contrast, the gutted buildings that pockmarked the Chiado after a massive fire in 1988 have been magnificently restored by architect Álvaro Siza Vieira (p58), most now housing elegant shopping malls. One survivor of the fire is **Teatro Nacional de São Carlos** (p122), Lisbon's opera house and well worth a visit. It's a delirious gold-and-red, cherub-and-garland extravaganza built in the 1790s.

Nearby, in the strikingly converted Convento de São Francisco, is the **Museu do Chiado** (☎ 213 432 148; www.museudochiado-ipmuseus.pt; Rua Serpa Pinto 4; adult/under 26/senior €3/1.50/1.50, 10am-2pm Sun free; ⏲ 2-6pm Tue, 10am-6pm Wed-Sun), beautifully lit and laid out with contemporary art exhibitions plus a permanent display of 19th- and 20th-century Portuguese and foreign art, including works by Rodin and Maillol. Highlights are the marvellous panels (1927–32) by José de Almada Negreiros from San Carlos Cinema.

From Praça dos Restauradores, the **Elevador da Glória** climbs up to a superb viewpoint atop one of Lisbon's seven hills, **Miradouro de São Pedro de Alcântara**, and is a less tiring way of getting to Bairro Alto. Across the road is the inviting **Solar do Vinho do Porto** (p118), where you can sample some of the country's best ports.

A short walk southeast of the viewpoint is 16th-century Jesuit **Igreja de São Roque** (☎ 213 235 381; Largo Trindade Coelho; admission free; ⏲ 8.30am-5pm), whose plain façade, designed by the architect of São Vicente, hides a dazzling interior of gold, marble and Florentine *azulejos* – an elaborate canvas bankrolled by Brazilian riches.

Most spectacular is the **Capela de São João Baptista**, to the left of the altar, a stylistic tussle between classical austerity and decorative hysteria. Commissioned in 1742 by Portugal's most extravagant king, Dom João V, this chapel was designed and built in Rome over eight years, using the most expensive materials possible including amethyst, alabaster, agate, jade, lapis lazuli and Carrara marble. The four mosaics representing events from the saint's life are as elaborate as oil paintings. After its consecration by Pope Benedict XIV, the chapel was dismantled and shipped across to Lisbon for the staggering sum of UK£225,000.

The adjacent **Museu de São Roque** (☎ 213 235 381; adult/child €1/free, Sun free; ⏲ 10am-5pm Tue-Sun) contains more evidence of flash ecclesiastical cash, with lavish devotional items, weird reliquaries, and 16th- and 17th-century paintings.

If you carry on northwest of the viewpoint, you'll hit **Praça do Príncipe Real**, a relaxing shady square around which is Lisbon's principal gay district.

Near Príncipe Real is the venerable, 19th-century **Jardim Botânico** (Map p89; ☎ 213 921 802; www.jb.ul.pt; Rua da Escola Politécnica 58; adult/child €1.50/0.60; 9am-6pm Mon-Fri, 10am-6pm Sat & Sun Oct-Apr, 9am-8pm Mon-Fri, 10am-8pm Sat & Sun May-Sep). Its diversity of international flora is a tribute to Portugal's worldwide tendrils at the time. It is a marvellous, exotic escape, shaded by magnificent old trees.

From the southern end of the Bairro Alto (walking distance from Cais do Sodré) the **Elevador da Bica** creeps up to Rua do Loreto, a few blocks west of Praça de Luís Camões. At the end of Rua Marechal Saldanha, on another of Lisbon's seven hills, is the **Miradouro de Santa Catarina** (Map p89) with a popular outdoor café, offering exhilarating views across the river and the Ponte 25 de Abril.

Alfama, Castelo & Graça

This area east and northeast of the Baixa is Lisbon's oldest district. Unlike anywhere else in the city, its tangled web of semimedieval, quasi-Arabic steeply slanted streets leads up to outstanding views from three of Lisbon's seven hills – São Jorge, Graça and Senhora do Monte. The following are on Map pp86–7 unless otherwise noted.

ALFAMA

The haphazard, medina-like Alfama has a distinctively Arabic legacy, like its name. The Arabic *al-hama* means 'springs' or 'bath', a name perhaps inspired by hot springs found near Largo das Alcaçarias. Once an upper-class Moorish residential area, after earthquake damage it reverted to a working-class and fisherfolk quarter. The sharply stepped, rock-built hills meant it was one of the few districts to survive the big one in 1755.

Diving down from the castle to the river, the district's *becos* and *travessas* (alleys) and steep stairways are a world away from the Baixa's tidy European grid. By day, with its lively enclave of restaurants and thimble-sized grocery stores, the area retains a strong sense of community. For a real rough-and-tumble atmosphere, visit during the Festas dos Santos Populares in June (p107).

East from the Praça do Comércio is Campo das Cebolas (Field of the Onions), with the bizarre 16th-century **Casa dos Bicos** (House of Points) – a pincushion façade built by Afonso de Albuquerque, a former viceroy in India. It now houses a private organisation; if the lobby is open you can see bits of the old Moorish city wall and brick streets.

Directly north is the **sé** (cathedral; admission free; 9am-7pm Tue-Sat, to 5pm Mon & Sun). This Romanesque cathedral was built in 1150, on the site of a Moorish building (possibly a mosque), soon after the city was recaptured from the Moors by Afonso Henriques. The fortresslike appearance of the building shows that the Christians may have been victorious, but they weren't taking any chances. It was damaged in the 1755 earthquake, and extensively restored in the 1930s. The interior is largely baroque, with religious riches on display in the **treasury** (admission €2.50; 10am-5pm Mon-Sat). The Gothic **cloister** (admission €2.50; 10am-5pm Mon, to 6.30pm Tue-Sat May-Sep, to 5pm Mon-Sat Oct-Apr) dates from the 13th century, and holds intriguing archaeological excavations, with stonework from the 6th century BC, a medieval cistern and the Islamic foundations.

Nearby is the **Museu do Teatro Romano** (☎ 217 513 200; Pátio do Aljube 5; admission free; 10am-1pm &

HILLTOP EXPRESS

For a quick ride up some of the city's steepest hills, Lisbon operates three bee-yellow *elevadores* or *ascensores* (funiculars), which were originally water-powered, and a wonderful bit of 19th-century elegance, the **Elevador de Santa Justa**. It's a frilly, wrought-iron lift in the Baixa, which elevates you around 45m to a café with a superb view across the rooftops, the ruins of Carmo and the river. Perhaps the most charming ride is on the **Elevador da Bica** through the Santa Catarina district, at the southwestern corner of Bairro Alto. The other two funiculars are the **Elevador da Glória**, from Praça dos Restauradores up to the São Pedro de Alcântara viewpoint; and the **Elevador do Lavra**, the first street funicular in the world, opened in 1884 and running from Largo de Anunciada, on the eastern side of Restauradores. All funiculars cost €1.20 one way, operating from 7am to 9pm Monday to Saturday and 9am to 9pm Sunday.

2-6pm Tue-Sun), displaying the city's ruined Roman theatre. Built during Emperor Augustus' time, it was extended in AD 57 to seat up to 5000. The theatre was abandoned in the 4th century, and its stones were appropriated to build the city. Not much is left but the museum cleverly re-creates the scene.

Just off the tram line, the **Museu de Artes Decorativas Portuguesas** (☎ 218 814 651; Largo das Portas do Sol 2; adult/child/senior €5/free/2.50; ⌚ 10am-5pm Tue-Sun) is set in a petite, beautifully restored palace, complete with 16th- to 19th-century furniture, textiles and baroque tiles.

Facing the museum is the stunning viewpoint **Largo das Portas do Sol** (the 'sun gateway'), originally one of the seven Moorish gateways. Nearby **Miradouro de Santa Luzia** is another fine overlook. Both have well-placed cafés for purposeful lingering.

Fado was born in Alfama. To learn more, visit the **Casa do Fado e da Guitarra Portuguesa** (☎ 218 823 470; Largo do Chafariz de Dentro; adult/student €2.50/1.25; ⌚ 10am-12.30pm & 2-5.30pm), a vibrant museum that traces *fado*'s history from its working-class roots to international fame, and finishing at a re-created *fado* house.

CASTELO DE SÃO JORGE

The **castle** (☎ 218 800 620; adult/child/student €3/free/1.50; ⌚ 9am-9pm Mar-Oct, to 6pm Nov-Feb) has stupendous views across the city. From its Visigothic beginnings in the 5th century, it was later fortified by the Moors in the 9th century, sacked by Christians in the 12th century and used as a royal residence from the 14th to 16th centuries – and as a prison in every century.

A LISBON STORY

You can take a crash course in Lisbon's allure by watching Wim Wenders' sweet, meandering film *A Lisbon Story* (1994), in which a sound engineer goes in search of a missing director, discovering the city through footage he has left behind. Some of the most memorable scenes take place in Alfama, making good use of the villagelike ambience and the neighbourhood's fine views over the river.

Musical greats Madredeus play a supporting role, and add a lush soundtrack to the film. Venerable Portuguese director Manoel de Oliveira, who's been making movies since they were silent, also makes a cameo.

The building itself is a series of open courtyards, filled with trees and birdsong, and you can climb and walk around the battlements. Inside one of the towers, a **camera obscura** offers fascinating 360-degree views of the city, with demonstrations every half-hour. Near the castle entrance is **Olisipónia** (☎ 218 877 244; adult/under 26 €1.50/0.75; ⌚ 10am-1pm & 2-5.30pm), an exhibition with multilingual commentary about Lisbon's history. It uses a video wall to jazz up the already exciting history, but glosses over anything unpalatable (did anyone say slave trade?).

Northwest of the castle is the former **Mouraria Quarter**, the Moorish district after the Reconquista (Christian reconquest).

To get to the castle from the Rossio, take bus 37.

GRAÇA

Northeast of the castle lies Graça. Following Rua de São Tomé up from Largo das Portas do Sol, you pass Largo de Rodrigues de Freitas and reach Calçada da Graça, which leads to the splendid **Miradouro da Graça** (with a café). To the east is a former Augustinian convent, now a military barracks, and about 700m beyond the convent is the area's third major viewpoint, on another of Lisbon's hills, the **Miradouro da Senhora do Monte**, the best in town for views of the castle, Mouraria and the centre.

Two cultural sites lie just to the east (tram 28 also passes close by). Dominating the scene is the huge dome of the Igreja de Santa Engrácia. When work began in 1682, it was planned as one of Lisbon's grandest churches. After centuries of dithering and neglect, the sombre, marble edifice was finally inaugurated in 1966 (after work on the dome was completed) as the **Panteão Nacional** (National Pantheon; ☎ 218 854 820; Campo de Santa Clara; adult/child €2/1, 10am-2pm Sun free; ⌚ 10am-5pm Tue-Sun; ♿). It contains chilly marble cenotaphs to historic and literary figures. Vasco da Gama and Henry the Navigator are in their usual pride of place, with new-kids-in-town tucked away in side chapels; look for General Humberto Delgado, the opposition leader assassinated by the secret police in 1965, and Amália, the famous *fado* singer.

Walk up to the rooftop (there is a lift for the disabled) for a sunbake and great views of Alfama, the river and a vast stretch of the Vasco da Gama bridge.

Nearby is wonderful **Igreja de São Vicente de Fora** (☎ 218 824 400; adult/child €4/2; 🕒 10am-6pm Tue-Sun). Founded in 1147, this monastery – 'St Vincent of Outside', as it was outside the city walls – was built on the burial sites of foreign crusaders and later, between 1582 and 1627, reconstructed by the master of the Italian Renaissance, Felipe Terzi. In 1755's earthquake, the roof and dome collapsed on worshippers. Building works continued until the early 18th century, when finally the canons got to live here in peace – that is, until 1834, when religious orders were banished. Today it has a wide, strikingly stark nave and coffered vault.

Remarkable blue-and-white *azulejos* date from the 18th century. They dance across almost every wall, echoing the curves of the architecture, across the serene, white cloisters and up to the 1st floor. Here there is a unique collection of panels depicting La Fontaine's fables (entertaining 17th-century moral tales), accompanied by excellent English and French background text.

Under the sacristy, decorated in eye-tiring polychrome marble, lie the crusaders' tombs. The former refectory holds a mausoleum containing the sombre marble tombs of most of the Braganças. A lone, weeping, cloaked woman holds stony vigil, to great dramatic impact.

The monastery rooftop has more fantastic views.

SANTA APOLÓNIA

About 1km northeast of Santa Apolónia train station is Lisbon's most beautiful museum, the **Museu Nacional do Azulejo** (National Tile Museum; Map pp84-5; ☎ 218 100 340; Rua Madre de Deus 4; adult/under 26/senior €3/1.50/1.50, 10am-2pm Sun free; 🕒 2-6pm Tue, 10am-6pm Wed-Sun; ♿). It's housed in the 16th-century convent of Igreja de Nossa Senhora da Madre de Deus, with lovely small tiled courtyards, Manueline cloister and gold-smothered baroque chapel, set off with more blue-and-white tiles. Illustrating the history and development of the tile, the museum has many exquisite pieces, from early Ottoman geometry to zinging blue-and-yellow altars, and from chintzy religious scenes to Goan intricacies. Among the exhibits is a fascinating 36m-long panel with a rare depiction of pre-earthquake Lisbon. (For more on *azulejos*, see p55.). There's also a lovely restaurant in the museum, and disabled access. Buses 104 and 105 stop nearby.

West of Santa Apolónia station, in a suitably florid building, is the **Museu Militar** (☎ 218 842 300; Largo do Museu de Artilharia; adult/child under 10/under 18 €2.50/free/1.80; 🕒 10am-5pm Tue-Sun), with the biggest collection of artillery in the world. It's a mind-blowing, if fusty, display of ways to do damage. One for Charlton Heston types.

The **Aqueduto das Águas Livres** (p101) and **Mãe d'Água** reservoir (p101) are part of the **Museu da Água** (Map pp84-5; ☎ 218 135 522; Rua do Alviela 12; admission €3; 🕒 10am-6pm Mon-Sat), in a restored 19th-century pump station. The museum explains the complex watering system and is run by Empresa Portuguesa das Águas Livres (EPAL), the municipal water company.

Estrela, Lapa & Doca de Alcântara

The sights in the following section are on Map p89, unless otherwise noted.

Estrela and Lapa, west of Bairro Alto, are wealthy districts with a discreet, moneyed look. Getting here on a westbound tram 28 is fun (you can also take bus 13 from Praça do Comércio).

In Largo de São Bento is one of the area's most imposing sights, the **Palácio da Assembleia da República**, Portugal's parliament, once the enormous 17th-century Benedictine Mosteiro de São Bento. The national assembly has convened here since 1833.

Nearby is **Casa Museu de Amália Rodrigues** (☎ 213 971 896; Rua de São Bento 193; admission €5; 🕒 10am-1pm & 2-6pm Tue-Sun). More pilgrimage site than museum, this ochre house is where *fado* diva Amália lived; along the street you'll notice graffiti announcing it Rua Amália. The short tours include recordings of performances.

At the top of Calçada da Estrela bulge the dome and belfries of the **Basílica da Estrela** (☎ 213 960 915; admission free; 🕒 8am-1pm & 3-8pm). Completed in 1790 by order of Dona Maria I (whose tomb is here) in gratitude for a male heir, the church is all elegant neoclassicism outside and chilly, echoing baroque inside, with fabulous views from the dome.

Across the road is an attractive public park, the **Jardim da Estrela**, with a children's playground. Beyond this lies the unkempt Protestant **Cemitério dos Ingleses** (English Cemetery), founded in 1717. Expats at rest here include Henry Fielding (author of *Tom Jones*), who died during an unsuccessful visit to Lisbon to improve his health in 1754. At the far corner are the remains of Lisbon's old Jewish cemetery.

To the south of Estrela is **Lapa**, Lisbon's diplomatic quarter. Here is the fine **Museu Nacional de Arte Antiga** (National Museum of Ancient Art; ☎ 213 912 800; www.mnarteantiga-ipmuseus.pt; Rua das Janelas Verdes 9; adult/under 26/senior €3/1.50/1.50, 10am-2pm Sun free; ⏲ 2-6pm Tue, 10am-6pm Wed-Sun). Housed in a grand 17th-century palace (take bus 60 from Praça da Figueira or tram 15 west from Praça do Comércio), this has an amazing European art collection, bursting with Portuguese works, including painting, sculpture, ceramics, textiles and furniture. There is also a superb collection of decorative art from Africa, India, China and Japan. You can buy a guide (€1) in Portuguese or English.

Masterpiece of the collection is the *Panels of São Vicente* by Nuno Gonçalves, most brilliant of the Flemish-influenced 15th-century Portuguese painters. His genius was to depict contemporary society with extraordinarily naturalistic portraits, so the centuries-old faces look like ones you might meet today. The six fabulously detailed panels show a social lucky dip (from fishermen, sailors and priests, to the Duke of Bragança and his family) paying homage to São Vicente, Portugal's patron saint. The frequently reproduced central panels include Henry the Navigator.

Foreign highlights include Bosch's hallucinatory *Temptation of St Anthony,* populated by strange creatures and flying fish; a haunting, glowing *Salomé* by Lucas Cranach; *St Jerome* by Dürer; *Works of Mercy* by Brueghel; Poussin's *Philistines Attacked by the Plague;* Courbet's bleak *Snow;* and *Danaide* by Rodin.

Artefacts from India, China and Japan include Japanese *namban* screens. *Namban* ('southern barbarians'), the Japanese name for the Portuguese who landed on Tanegaxima island in 1543, now refers to all Japanese art inspired by this encounter. The 16th-century screens show the arrival of the huge-nosed Portuguese in absorbing detail. Vastly rich inlaid Goan furniture is another treat.

Gem-smothered religious treasures include the *Monstrance of Belém* (1506), a reliquary made with gold brought back by Vasco da Gama on his second voyage. There's also some amazing jewellery, mostly from convent collections. A gleaming silverware display features dozens of masterpieces by the French silversmith Thomas Germain and his son François-Thomas, which were made in the late 18th century for the Portuguese court and royal family.

The building's wing integrates the beautiful baroque chapel, the sole remnant of a Carmelite convent that adjoined the palace.

For something entirely different, head to charming **Museu da Carris** (☎ 213 613 087; Rua Primeiro de Maio; adult/child €2.50/1.25; ⏲ 10am-1pm & 2-5pm Mon-Sat), which is housed in the Carris headquarters and tells the history of Lisbon's most endearing means of transport using the models-in-glass-cases method. Tram 15 passes right by so you can have a holistic experience.

Museu da Marioneta (Puppet Museum; ☎ 213 942 810; Rua da Esperança 146; adult/under 26/senior €2.50/1.30/1.30; ⏲ 10am-12.30pm & 2-5.30pm Tue-Sun), in the eastern part of the district, houses a bewitching collection of puppets in the splendid Convento das Bernardas. A surprisingly grand restaurant (dishes €16.50 to €32), open for lunch Tuesday to Sunday, adjoins the space.

Rato, Marquês de Pombal & Saldanha

Head north for hothouses and high culture. The sights in this section are on Map p90 unless otherwise noted.

Chief must-see is the eclectic, brilliant collection of the **Museu Calouste Gulbenkian** (☎ 217 823 461; www.museu.gulbenkian.pt; Avenida de Berna 45a; adult/child €3/free, Sun free; combined ticket with Centro de Arte Moderna €5; ⏲ 10am-6pm Tue-Sun; metro São Sebastião). One of Europe's unsung treasures, this museum, set in a sleek 1960s building, houses more than 6000 pieces (with 1500 on permanent display) spanning major epochs of Western and Eastern art. Idyllic gardens surround the space, and there are bilingual touch screens with information on some of the museum's most exceptional works.

Within the classical and Oriental collections, the **Egyptian Room** houses an exquisite 2700-year-old alabaster bowl, a gilded silver mummy mask, small female statuettes (each differently coiffed), and some naturalistic bronze cats. In the adjoining **Greek & Roman** section are a 2400-year-old Attic vase, luminescent Roman glassware and Hellenic coins with finely carved heads.

Oriental Islamic treasures include some 16th- and 17th-century Turkish faïence glowing with brilliant greens and blues, Persian carpets and 14th-century mosque lamps from Syria, with strikingly sensuous shapes. The **Armenian** collection features illuminated manuscripts from the 16th to 18th centuries.

In the **Chinese & Japanese** section, huge pieces of 18th-century Chinese porcelain contrast with small neat Japanese writing boxes and lacquered picnic sets of the same era.

Going west, **European Art** sweeps from medieval ivories and jewel-like manuscripts to 15th- to 19th-century masterpieces. All the big names are here, including Rembrandt *(Portrait of an Old Man)*, Van Dyck and Rubens (including the frantic *Loves of the Centaurs*). Particularly lovely is the 15th-century *Portrait of a Girl* by Ghirlandaio and a white marble *Diana* by Houdon.

Eighteenth- and 19th-century European art doesn't get skimped, with Aubusson tapestries, wonderfully fussy furniture (including items from Versailles), Sèvres porcelain and intricate clocks. Outstanding works include Gainsborough's *Mrs Lowndes*, two atmospheric La Tour portraits, turbulent Turners, a passionate *Spring Kiss* by Rodin, several Manets *(Boy Blowing Bubbles)* and Monets *(Still Life with Melon)*, and a pretty Renoir.

The grand finale is the incredible collection of **René Lalique** glass and jewellery. Here are fabulous, unique fantasies, such as the outrageous, otherworldly *Dragonfly*, glittering with gold, enamel, moonstones and diamonds.

Nearby is the Fundação Calouste Gulbenkian's other major museum, the **Centro de Arte Moderna** (Modern Art Centre; ☎ 217 823 474; admission €3, combined ticket with Museu Calouste Gulbenkian €5, free Sun; 2-6pm Tue-Sun), a white, warehouselike space with an unparalleled collection of modern Portuguese art. These include influential Amadeo de Souza Cardoso, who caused a scandal with his experiments in cubism, expressionism and futurism; abstract works by iconic modernist José de Almada Negreiros; the haunting grotesque fairy tales of Paula Rego, Portugal's best-known contemporary artist; and the geometric brilliance of Angelo de Souza. Works by modern British artists such as David Hockney, Bridget Riley, Anthony Gormley and Julien Opie serve as points of reference. The café is a Lisbon institution, and good for vegetarians.

Parque Eduardo VII (Avenida da Liberdade) is down the road. The huge park (named after England's Edward VII, who visited Lisbon in 1903) provides a fine escape, especially in its gorgeous **estufas** (greenhouses; adult/child under 12 €1.20/free), filled with brilliant exotic flowers. The **estufa fria** (cool greenhouse; 9am-5pm Oct-Apr, to 6pm May-Sep) and **estufa quente** (hot greenhouse; 9am-4.30pm Oct-Apr, to 5.30pm May-Sep) were built on an old quarry site; planting began in 1910. There's also an **outdoor area** (9am-4.30pm Oct-Apr, to 5.30pm May-Sep), with a large pond. Access is from Rua Castilho on the park's western side. There's a great playground nearby.

The 109 arches of the **Aqueduto das Águas Livres** lope across the hills into Lisbon from Caneças, more than 18km away; they are most spectacular at **Campolide**, where the tallest arch is an incredible 65m high. Built between 1728 and 1835, by order of Dom João V, the aqueduct brought Lisbon its first clean drinking water.

The king laid the aqueduct's final stone at **Mãe d'Água** (Mother of Water; Praça das Amoreiras; adult €3; 10am-6pm Mon-Sat), the city's massive, 5500-cu-metre main reservoir. The reservoir's cool, echoing chamber (check out the start of the narrow aqueduct passage), completed in 1834, now hosts art exhibitions. See p99 for details of the related museum in Santa Apolónia.

Belém

The sights in this section are on Map p91 unless otherwise noted.

Stately Belém, 6km west of the Rossio, has immense historical importance and architectural riches, and makes a great day trip. (Note: everything's closed Monday.) Most famously, this was the place from which the great explorer Vasco da Gama set sail on 8 July 1497 for the two-year voyage on which he discovered a sea route to India, shifting the world's balance of power and showering riches on the Portuguese.

FREE LISBOA

Many museums are free on Sunday morning. The **Centro Cultural de Belém** (p103) presents regular free music and dance performances. Everything during its day-long Festa da Primavera (Spring Festival) in March is also free. The **Museu Calouste Gulbenkian** (opposite) gives free musical recitals at noon some Sundays in the library foyer.

In shopping venues, **Fnac** (p119) has a regular programme of free exhibitions, concerts and films. The **Mercado da Ribeira** (p124) also has free concerts and exhibitions.

The **BaixAnima Festival** puts the bizarre into Baixa on weekends from mid-July to the end of September with flamboyant street performers, centred on Rua Augusta.

When Vasco da Gama returned safely, Dom Manuel I ordered the construction of a monastery on the site of the riverside chapel (founded by Henry the Navigator) where da Gama and his officers had kept an all-night vigil before departing.

The Jerónimos, like its predecessor, was dedicated to the Virgin Mary, St Mary of Bethlehem (Belém) – hence the district's name.

The fantastical monastery and an offshore watchtower (both Unesco World Heritage sites) are prime examples of splendidly over-excited Manueline architecture (p54).

The best way to get here is on the modern tram 15 from Praça da Figueira or Praça do Comércio; alternatively take bus 14 from the Rossio or Praça da Figueira. Frequent trains from Cais do Sodré to Oeiras stop at Belém.

A miniature **tourist train** (☎ 213 582 334; ticket €3; 🕑 10am-7pm Apr-Aug) makes a regular tour of the slightly spread-out sights.

MOSTEIRO DOS JERÓNIMOS

Vasco da Gama's discovery of a sea route to India inspired the glorious **Mosteiro dos Jerónimos** (www.mosteirojeronimos.pt), a Unesco World Heritage site with an architectural exuberance that trumpets 'navigational triumph'. It later became a pantheon for Manuel I and his royal descendants (many now entombed in its chancel and side chapels). Huge sums were funnelled into the project, including pepper money, a 5% tax on income from the spice trade with African and Far Eastern colonies.

Work began around 1501, following a Gothic design by architect Diogo de Boitaca, considered a Manueline originator. After his death in 1517, building resumed with a Renaissance flavour under Spaniard João de Castilho and, later, with classical overtones under Diogo de Torralva and Jérome de Rouen (Jerónimo de Ruão). The monastery was completed in 1541, a riverside masterpiece – the waters have since receded. The huge neo-Manueline western wing and domed bell tower were added in the 19th century.

The monastery was populated with monks of the Order of St Jerome, whose spiritual job for about four centuries was to give comfort and guidance to sailors – and to pray for the king's soul. When the order was dissolved in 1833 the monastery was used as a school and orphanage until about 1940.

The façade has a horizontal structure, to encourage a feeling of repose. It looks like no-one told João about the repose idea – his fantastic southern portal is a filigree frenzy, dense with religious and secular significance.

You enter the **church** (☎ 213 620 034; Praça do Império; admission free; 🕑 10am-6.30pm Tue-Sun May-Sep, to 5.30pm Tue-Sun Oct-Apr) through the western portal. The first thing you notice about the interior is its height, reaching up to an unsupported baroque transept vault 25m high. Tall, tree-trunk-like columns seem to grow into the ceiling, which is itself a spiderweb of stone. Windows cast golden light over the church. Superstar Vasco da Gama is interred in the lower chancel, just to the left of the entrance, in a place of honour opposite Luís Vaz de Camões, the venerated 16th-century poet.

From the upper choir you get a superb view of the church; the rows of seats are Portugal's first Renaissance woodcarvings.

Peaceful even when crowded, the monastery's golden-stone **cloisters** (adult/child under 15/under 26 €4.50/free/2.25, 10am-2pm Sun free; 🕑 same as church) dance with Manueline organic detail and exotic influences from overseas. The simple tomb of renowned poet and writer Fernando Pessoa is here. One wall is lined with 12 confessionals so monks could hear penitents who came to the church. The sarcophagus in the echoing chapterhouse on the northeastern corner belongs to the 19th-century Portuguese historian Alexandre Herculano (he of many street names).

TORRE DE BELÉM

Another World Heritage site, the **Torre de Belém** (Tower of Belém; ☎ 213 620 034; Avenida da Índia; admission €4; 🕑 10am-6.30pm Tue-Sun May-Sep, to 5pm Oct-Apr) has come to symbolise the Age of Discoveries. The brilliant Arruda brothers, Diogo and Francisco, designed the pearly grey chesspiece in a shaken-not-stirred mix of early Gothic, Byzantine and Manueline styles. It's just offshore, about 1km from the monastery; before the shoreline shifted south, the tower sat right out in midstream. Manuel I built it around 1515 to guard the entrance to Lisbon's harbour, perhaps to catch invaders off guard.

PADRÃO DOS DESCOBRIMENTOS

The huge limestone **Padrão dos Descobrimentos** (Discoveries Monument; adult/child under 7/under 18 €2/free/1.50; 🕑 9am-5pm Tue-Sun), inaugurated in 1960 on the 500th anniversary of Henry the Navigator's death, is shaped like a stylised caravel, chock-full of Portuguese bigwigs. At the prow is Henry; behind him are explorers

Vasco da Gama, Diogo Cão and Fernão de Magalhães, poet Luís Vaz de Camões, painter Nuno Gonçalves and 27 other greats. Inside are exhibition rooms, an audiovisual show introducing the city, and a lift and stairs to the top, with impressive monastery and river views.

CENTRO CULTURAL DE BELÉM & MUSEU DO DESIGN

One of Lisbon's most important cultural venues, **Centro Cultural de Belém** (CCB; ☎ 213 612 400; www.ccb.pt; Praça do Império) is a mottled grey-peach modern building hosting music, dance and exhibitions. Inside is the world-class **Museu do Design** (☎ 213 612 934; adult/child under 12/under 15 €3.50/0.50/2; 11am-8pm, last admission 7.15pm; ♿).

Financier Francisco Capelo began his collection in 1937. The wonderful array includes the lean lines of Charles and Ray Eames, the 1960s bright excesses of Vernon Panton, late-'60s beanbags, Frank Gehry's '70s *Wiggle Side* chair, and Michael Graves' scary 1981 *Plaza* dressing table (an overgrown Barbie set). Not only are these beautiful, humorous pieces of design, but the museum also puts their development in a social context. The contest for the most uncomfortable-looking chair is impressive, but Philippe Starck's *WW* stool has the edge.

Other halls feature changing modern-art exhibitions. There's an excellent bookshop, and disabled access.

OTHER MUSEUMS

The **Museu Nacional dos Coches** (National Coach Museum; ☎ 213 610 850; Praça Afonso de Albuquerque; adult/student €3/1.50; 10am-5.30pm Tue-Sun), in the former royal riding school, has a fairy-tale collection of 17th- to 19th-century coaches. The oldest belonged to Philip II, who toured Portugal in it in 1619. Cunningly plain on the outside, inside it has a suitably regal golden globular ceiling. Most spectacular are three triumphal vehicles sent to Pope Clement by spendthrift Dom João V. Festooned with symbols of triumphant Portuguese navigation, these coaches are so gold and heavy it's surprising they could move at all.

The **Museu de Arte Popular** (Folk Art Museum; ☎ 213 011 282; Avenida de Brasília; adult/child under 12 €2/free; 10am-12.30pm & 2-5pm Tue-Sun) should house a regional folk-art collection. As of 2006, the main museum was still closed for long-term renovations.

Opened in 1893, the **Museu Nacional de Arqueologia** (National Museum of Archaeology; ☎ 213 620 000; Praça do Império; adult/child under 15/under 25 €3/free/1.50, 10am-2pm Sun free; 2-6pm Tue, 10am-6pm Wed-Sun), in the Mosteiro dos Jerónimos' western wing, has exhibits from prehistory to Moorish times, including reverentially lit Graeco-Roman antiquities such as funerary masks, mummies, tiny mummified crocodiles, sandals and combs. The other highlight is the Treasures Room, with a great haul of gleaming, burnished antique gold jewellery, from massive Bronze Age torques to a delicate Roman snake bracelet.

Next door is the **Museu de Marinha** (Naval Museum; ☎ 213 620 019; adult/child under 6/under 17 €3/free/1.50; 10am-5pm Tue-Sun Oct-Mar, to 6pm Tue-Sun Apr-Sep). Among the armadas of model boats, this museum has gems such as Vasco da Gama's portable wooden altar and the rich, polished private quarters of the 1900 UK-built royal yacht *Amélia*. There are also ornate royal barges, the biggest a 1780 neo-Viking number. A **children's museum** (weekends) offers brightly coloured creative activities.

Greater Lisbon

One of Lisbon's newest areas offers waterfront eye-candy for adults and kids alike. Greater Lisbon also has the zoo and several historically edifying sights. All sights in this section are on Map pp84–5 unless otherwise noted.

Quinta dos Marquêses da Fronteira (☎ 217 782 023; Largo de São Domingos de Benfica 1; admission €5; tours at 10.30am, 11am, 11.30am & noon Mon-Sat) is a charming, run-down 17th-century mansion, with tiles covering any space that's not formal Renaissance garden. Reserve ahead for a tour.

Two metro stops north of Parque Eduardo VII is the kid-pleasing but somewhat cooped-up **Jardim Zoológico** (Zoological Garden; ☎ 217 232 910; www.zoolisboa.pt; Praça Marechal Delgado Humberto; adult/child €12.50/9.50; 10am-6pm Oct-Apr, to 8pm May-Sep), in attractive gardens with more than 2000 animals. There's also a dolphin show and rowing boats.

Further north, the **Museu da Cidade** (City Museum; ☎ 217 591 617; Campo Grande 245; admission €2, 10am-1pm Sun free; 10am-1pm & 2-6pm Tue-Sun), in the Palácio Pimenta, careers through Lisbon's amazing roller-coaster history with an enormous model of the pre-earthquake city and an excellent collection of tiles. The nearest metro station is Campo Grande.

PARQUE DAS NAÇÕES

On the northeastern riverfront, the **Parque das Nações** (nas-*oish;* Nations Park; Map pp84–5) was built for Expo 98. The development includes a huge world-of-its-own aquarium, the Oceanário, plus the Pavilhão do Conhecimento, a cable car and a landscaped riverside park with restaurants and bars. There's some stunning modern architecture here: the ribbed Death Star structure of **Gare do Oriente** and the **Pavilhão de Portugal** by Portugal's leading architect, Álvaro Siza Vieira.

Designed by acclaimed Spanish architect Santiago Calatrava, Gare do Oriente is an extraordinary vaulted, vented structure that creates spectacular, haunting, organic and skeletal shapes. The metro station below features *azulejo* works by international artists from Hundertwasser to Zao Wo Ki.

The other spectacular development born of Expo 98 was the Ponte de Vasco da Gama. This 30m-wide bridge is unbelievably long (17.2km), and vanishes into the distance. The curvature of the earth had to be taken into account when building, so as to place the piers evenly. The foundations go down to 85m below sea level and it's been built to withstand a major earthquake and winds of up to 250km/h.

The 2km-long park site sometimes feels as if you have wandered into an architectural model, but it's an entertaining place to visit, especially for families. The Atlantic Pavilion hosts major concerts, such as Depeche Mode in 2006.

Take the metro to Gare do Oriente and walk through the Centro Vasco da Gama to the park's main **Posto de Informação** (Map pp84-5; ☎ 218 919 333; www.parquedasnacoes.pt; ⌚ 10am-8pm Apr-Oct, to 6pm Nov-Mar), with free maps and information. The Cartão do Parque (adult/child €15.50/8.50) gives admission to the Oceanário, Pavilhão do Conhecimento, cable car and Vasco da Gama tower, as well as some restaurant discounts.

Europe's largest aquarium, the superb **Oceanário** (Oceanarium; ☎ 218 917 002; www.oceanario.pt; adult/child under 4/under 12 €10.50/free/5.25; ⌚ 10am-7pm Apr-Oct, to 6pm Nov-Mar; ♿) has 450 different species from the world's seas, accompanied by loads of fascinating facts to wow your inner anorak (did you know the Pacific covers a third of the world?). Splendid sea creatures include the 2.5m-wide giant manta (seemingly flying through the water), sea otters, penguins, 3m-long sharks, plantlike seadragons, and Nemo from *Finding Nemo,* aka the clown fish.

Lie on a bed of nails or play an invisible harp at the **Pavilhão do Conhecimento** (Knowledge Pavilion; ☎ 218 917 100; www.pavconhecimento.pt; adult/child €6/3; ⌚ 10am-6pm Tue-Fri, 11am-7pm Sat & Sun; 💻 ♿), with lots of fun exhibits explaining scientific phenomena and pointing out how reality and perception often contradict. There's an indoor playground for three- to six-year-olds, a free cybercafé and disabled access.

The 140m-high **Torre Vasco da Gama** (☎ 218 918 000; adult/child 5-14 €2.50/1.50; ⌚ 10am-8pm Apr-Oct, to 6pm Nov-Mar) has panoramic views of the park, river and city, and an upmarket restaurant.

A riverside **teleférico** (cable car; return ticket adult/child 5-14 €5.50/3; ⌚ 11am-7pm), more than 1km long and 20m high, gives stunning views of the river and the Vasco da Gama bridge.

Tejo Bike (bike per hour adult/child/tandem €4/3/7; ⌚ 10am-8pm Apr-Oct, noon-6pm Nov-Mar), next to the information post rents out bikes.

A **minitrain** (adult/child €2.50/1.50; ⌚ 10am-7pm Apr-Sep, to 5pm Nov-Mar) trundles around hourly, too.

ACTIVITIES

Bird-Watching

The **Reserva Natural do Estuário do Tejo** (☎ headquarters 212 341 742; Avenida dos Combatentes da Grande Guerra 1, Alcochete) is upriver from Lisbon. A vitally important wetland area, it hosts around 40,000 migrant wading birds during the winter, including avocets and teals. It's accessible from Montijo, a ferry ride from Lisbon's Terreiro do Paço (p124).

Golf

There are six major courses (p68), plus the **Lisbon Sports Club** (☎ 214 321 474; Casal da Carregueira, Belas), which is just north of Queluz.

Swimming

The handiest swimming pool to the centre of the city is the small, rooftop, indoor **Ateneu Comercial Complexo de Piscinas** (Map pp86-7; ☎ 213 430 947; Rua das Portas de Santo Antão 102; admission €4; ⌚ 9am-noon, 1.30-4.30pm & 9-10pm Mon, Wed & Fri, 7.30am-10am, 1.30-4pm & 9-10pm Tue & Thu, 3.30-7pm Sat). Professional-standard **Complexo de Piscinas do EUL** (Map pp84-5; ☎ 217 994 970; Avenida Professor Gama Pinto; admission €8; ⌚ 6.45am-10pm Mon-Fri, to 7pm Sat) is part of the university's sports complex; head north 400m from Cidade-Universitária metro.

Tennis

Also at the university sports complex are the university's **tennis courts** (☎ 217 932 895). More courts are at the **Instalações de Ténis de Monsanto** (Map pp84-5; ☎ 213 648 741; Parque Florestal de Monsanto); to get there take bus 24 from Alcântara or bus 29 from Belém. You'll need to reserve at both places.

WALKING TOUR
Tram 28 & Alfama

This viewpoint-to-viewpoint route starts on tram 28 from Largo Martim Moniz or the Baixa, thus taking in the city's best tram route *and* avoiding uphill slogs. Take the tram up to Largo da Graça – just to the east of the huge barracks. From here you can walk northwards and turn left behind the barracks to pay a visit to the **Miradouro da Senhora do Monte** (**1**; p98). Or, walk south and turn right in front of the barracks to **Miradouro da Graça** (**2**; p98). Retrace your steps and walk eastwards to visit the tiled glories of **Igreja de São Vicente de Fora** (**3**; p99), and the cool, echoing **Panteão Nacional** (**4**; p98). If it's Saturday, make a detour to the **Feira da Ladra** (Thieves Market; **5**; p123). Otherwise, walk directly west along Arco Grande da Cima until you reach Largo de Rodrigues de Freitas. Take the Costa do Castelo fork, continuing west. This way you can walk right around the outskirts of the castle, along narrow cobbled streets, with some stunning views. Pass in front of **Hotel Solar dos Mouros** (**6**; p110), then turn left up to the **Castelo** (**7**; p98) and a **viewpoint** (**8**). Next head down the steep lanes to Largo

WALK FACTS
Start Largo Martim Moniz or Baixa
Finish Near Praça do Comércio
Distance 2km
Duration Two to three hours

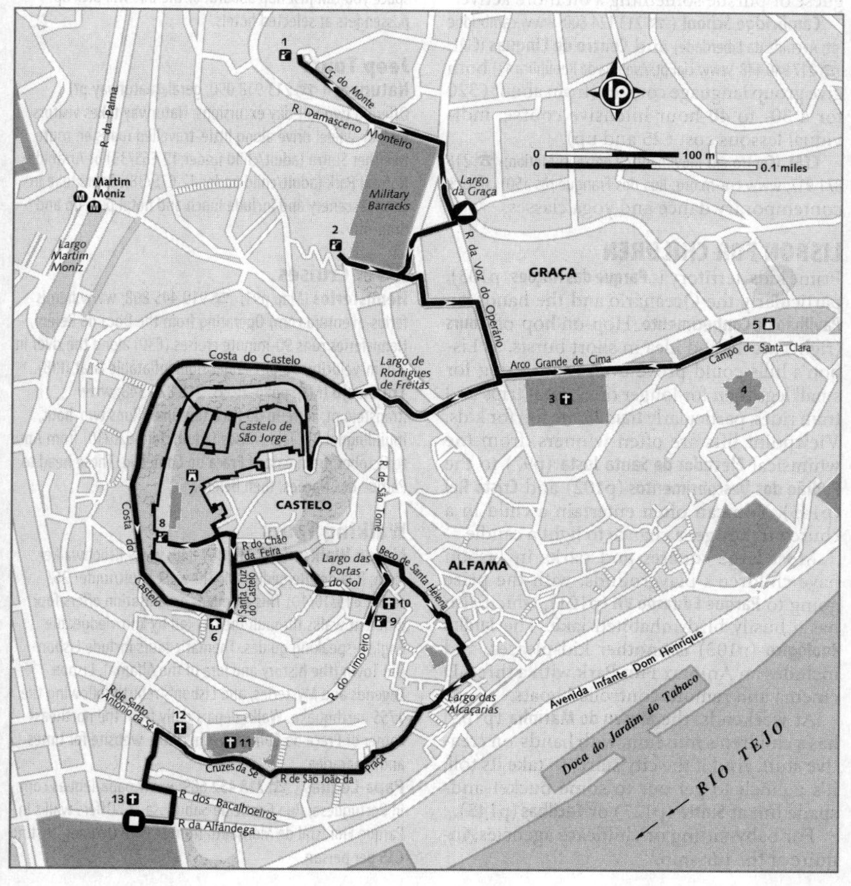

das Portas do Sol, and another fine view from **Miradouro de Santa Luzia** (**9**; p98). From here walk northward, past **Igreja de Santa Luzia (10)** on your right, and turn right in the atmospheric lane of Beco de Santa Helena. This will take you through one of Alfama's most colourful neighbourhoods, to Largo das Alcaçarias, from where you can take Rua de São João de Praça westwards to the **sé** (**11**; p97) and the **Igreja de Santo António (12)**. Downhill from here, your final stop is gazing at the amazing Manueline façade of **Igreja da Conceiça o Velha (13)**, just east of Praça do Comércio.

COURSES

There are a handful of places in the capital where you can take a crash course in Portuguese or pursue something a bit more active.

Cambridge School (☎ 213 124 600; www.cambridge.pt; Avenida da Liberdade) and **Centro de Linguas** (CIAL; ☎ 217 940 448; www.cial.pt; Avenida da República 41) both give group language courses (from about €320 for a 30- to 40-hour intensive course; individual lessons cost €25 and up).

CEM (Centro em Movimento; Centre in Motion; ☎ 218 871 917; www.c-e-m.org; Rua dos Frangueiros 150) offers contemporary dance and yoga classes.

LISBON FOR CHILDREN

Prime kids' territory is **Parque das Nações** (p103), particularly the Oceanário and the hands-on **Pavilhão de Conhecimento**. Hop-on hop-off **tours** (right) are a good idea in short bursts, as Lisbon's hills could prove even more tiring for small legs than for longer ones. Boat trips and tram rides, particularly **tram 28**, are fun for kids. Viewpoint lifts are often winners, from the whimsical **Elevador de Santa Justa** (p97) to the **Padrão dos Descobrimentos** (p102) and **Cristo Rei** (p145). You can often entertain a child in a church if they get a chance to light a candle.

Most large squares and parks in Lisbon have children's playgrounds, with the prize going to **Parque Eduardo VII** (p101), which also has a busily bird-inhabited lake. The **Jardim Zoológico** (p103) is another kid-pleaser, and includes an Animax Fun Park with a three-D cinema and remote-controlled boats.

At weekends, the **Museu do Marinha** (p103) has a children's museum, with hands-on creative stuff. And if the city starts to take its toll, it's a cinch to get out to some bucket-and-spade fun at **Sintra** (p127) or **Cacilhas** (p145).

For baby-sitting or childcare agencies, inquire at the turismo.

TOURS

Bus & Tram Tours

Carris (☎ 213 582 334, 966 298 558; carristur@carris.pt) The municipal transport company runs 1½-hour tram tours (adult/child €17/8.50): one around the Baixa and Alfama (13 to 18 daily); and one that continues to Belém (three daily). Carris also runs frequent hop-on, hop-off open-top bus tours (€14/7) from Praça do Comércio such as the Tagus Tour of the city and Belém; and the Orient Tour of northeast Lisbon, including Parque das Nações and Museu Nacional do Azulejo.

Cityrama (☎ 213 191 090; www.cityrama.pt) This outfit runs sightseeing bus tours of Lisbon and the surrounding region, including a 5½-hour city tour (€31); Lisbon by Night (€61 including two drinks, four hours); and Lisbon plus Sintra and the Estoril coast (€76, full day with lunch). All depart from Marquês de Pombal (Map p90). If there's space you can just hop aboard, or the bus will pick up passengers at selected hotels.

Jeep Tours

Naturway (☎ 213 918 090; geral@naturway.pt) Offering two full-day excursions, Naturway takes visitors by four-wheel drive along little-travelled roads en route to either Sintra (adult/child under 12 €65/33) or Arrábida Natural Park (adult/child under 12 €75/38). Tours take in coastal scenery and include lunch and hotel pick-up and drop-off.

River Cruises

Hemisférios (Map p91; ☎ 919 445 868; www.hemisferios-aventura.com) Operating from the Doca de Belém, Hemisférios runs 90-minute cruises (€30) along the river in a high-velocity, 12-passenger rigid inflatable boat (RIB).

Transtejo (Map pp86-7; ☎ 218 820 348; www.transtejo.pt; Terreiro do Paço terminal) Runs two-hour, multilingual Rio Tejo cruises (adult/child €20/10) from April to October, from east of Praça do Comércio. These head to Parque das Nações, then Belém.

Walking Tours

Lisbon Walker (☎ 218 861 840; www.lisbonwalker.com; Rua dos Remédios 84; 3hr walk adult/under 26/senior €15/10/10) This excellent organisation offers four different walks through the city led by knowledgeable English-speaking guides. Thematic tours include Lisbon Old Town (the history and lore of the Alfama), Lisbon Legends and Mysteries, and Lisbon's rebirth following the 1755 earthquake. Walks depart daily from the northeast corner of Praça do Comércio. Check the website for times and itineraries.

Papa-Léguas (☎ 218 452 689; www.papa-leguas.com in Portuguese; Rua Conde de Sabugosa 3f) Offers walks in Parque Florestal de Monsanto from May to October, costing €15 per person.

LISBON'S FAVOURITE EXPAT

Calouste Sarkis Gulbenkian was born to Armenian parents in Istanbul in 1869 and educated in Marseilles and London. He became one of the 20th century's wealthiest philanthropists, an astute and generous patron of the arts even before he struck it rich in Iraqi oil. His guiding tenet for this collection was 'only the best is good enough for me' and he was advised by experts such as art historian Sir Kenneth Clark. His great artistic coup was buying works from Leningrad's Hermitage between 1928 and 1930, when the young Soviet Union desperately needed hard currency. He fell out with the British in 1942, who declared him a 'technical enemy' and waved his collection goodbye. Washington had beady eyes on his loot, but during the war years Gulbenkian chose Portugal as his safe haven. He lived in Lisbon's Hotel Aviz for 13 years until his death in 1955, when he bequeathed the nation the stupendous lot (some pieces had already gone to the Museu Nacional de Arte Antiga in Estrela) along with establishing a charitable foundation, the Fundação Calouste Gulbenkian – Portugal's main cultural life force.

FESTIVALS & EVENTS

Like most people, Lisboêtas love an excuse for a party, and the city hosts a wide mix of festivals, many in summer (especially June). Apart from those listed here, there is a much broader array of one-time festivals and concerts. Stop at the tourist office to see what's on.

March

Moda Lisboa (www.assoc-modalisboa.pt) One of two fashion weeks in Lisbon (the other is held in October), Moda Lisboa showcases the work of more than a dozen established and up-and-coming Portuguese designers.

April

Festa da Música Classical-music lovers shouldn't miss this event, with more than 100 concerts held at Centro Cultural de Belém (p103) in mid- to late April. Visit www.ccb.pt (in Portuguese) for details.

Indie Lisboa (☎ 213 158 399; www.indielisboa.com) This small but worthwhile independent film fest usually takes places in the last 10 days of April.

May

Super Bock Super Rock (www.superbock.pt) Lisbon's biggest rock event is held in Parque das Nações on two weekends in May and June: it features 18 concerts and some fairly big names.

June

Festa do Fado (Fado Festival) Lisbon's celebration of its long song tradition is held at various venues throughout the city, including the Centro Cultural de Belém and the Castelo de São Jorge. Most of the action takes place in early to mid-June.

Festival Internacional de Cinema de Tróia (☎ 265 525 908; www.festroia.pt) Held in Setúbal, this long-established film festival screens more than 100 films from dozens of countries.

Festas dos Santos Populares (Festivals of the Popular Saints) The city goes crazy in June with Christianised versions of the summer solstice, featuring Festa de São João, Festa de São Pedro and Festa de Santo António.

Festa de Santo António (Festival of St Anthony) The climax of three weeks of partying known as the Festas de Lisboa, this lively fest is celebrated with particular fervour in Alfama and Madragoa from 12 to 13 June, with some 50 *arraiais* (street parties). The highlight is the Marchas Populares on the evening of 12 June when dozens of communities march along Avenida da Liberdade, with the ultimate *arraial* in the Alfama on the same night.

Festa de São João (Festival of St John) Held from 23 to 24 June.

Festa de São Pedro (Festival of St Peter) Held from 28 to 29 June.

August

Jazz em Agosto (Jazz in August) Early August sees another music festival at the Fundação Calouste Gulbenkian (p100).

September

Festival de Cinema Gay e Lésbico (Gay & Lesbian Film Festival; www.lisonfilmfest.org) One of Europe's largest gay and lesbian film fests, this one takes place over 10 days in late September.

Festa Avante (www.pcp.pt) Brought to you by Portugal's communist party, this three-day fest is held in Seixal and features an excellent combo of music, food and drink.

SLEEPING

It's wise to reserve ahead during the high season (July to mid-September), but if you do arrive without a reservation you can head to a turismo, where staff can call around for you.

 Book accommodation online at lonelyplanet.com

Rossio, Praça dos Restauradores & Baixa

In the valley between Alfama and Bairro Alto, this centrally located area attracts a wide mix of budget travellers to its basic *pensões* (guesthouses), with a handful of polished options as well. Unlike Bairro Alto, it's fairly quiet at night, making the area a good choice if you still want to be near the action.

BUDGET

Many cheap places in the Baixa are on the upper floors of old residential flats.

Residencial Coimbra e Madrid (Map pp86-7; ☎ 213 421 760; fax 213 423 264; 3rd fl, Praça da Figueira 3; s/d with shared bathroom €25/30, s/d €30/35) This good-value place has spacious rooms with polished cork floors and nice views (some face the castle, others the plaza), though sometimes the corridors are a little musty.

Casa de Hóspedes Brazil-África (Map pp86-7; ☎ 218 869 266; www.pensaobrasilafrica.com; 2nd fl, Travessa das Pedras Negras 8; s/d with shower €25/35) This friendly travellers' favourite has a mix of rooms, all with balconies, and some with wood floors. The inviting lounge is a nice feature.

Hospedaria Bons Dias (Map pp86-7; ☎ 213 471 918; 5th fl, Calçada do Carmo 25; s/d with shared bathroom €15/35) Secreted among several other guesthouses on this street, this is a popular budget option with bright, carpeted rooms; some (like room 502) have a small balcony.

Pensão Norte (Map pp86-7; ☎ 218 878 941; fax 218 868 462; 2nd-4th fl, Rua dos Douradores 161; d with shower €35) Hides a warren of small, nice functional rooms with telephone. Some rooms have balconies over the street.

Residência do Sul (Map pp86-7; ☎ 213 422 511; 2nd fl, Rossio 59; s/d/tr with shower €30/40/60) Overlooking the *praça*, this no-nonsense place has six bright, breezy rooms with tile floors and high ceilings; there are also darker quarters out the back.

Pensão Galizia (Map pp86-7; ☎ 213 428 430; 4th fl, Rua do Crucifixo 50; s/d with shared bathroom from €15/40) In a good Baixa location, this small top-floor guesthouse has 11 small but cosy rooms, the best with balconies and antique furnishings.

Pensão Imperial (Map pp86-7; ☎ 213 420 166; 4th fl, Praça dos Restauradores 78; s/d with shower €25/40) This clean, cheery place has an irresistible location (but no lift) and mix of rooms with either tile floors or carpeting. The best quarters have flower-draped balconies overlooking the *praça*.

MIDRANGE

Pensão Residencial Gerês (Map pp86-7; ☎ 218 810 497; www.pensaogeres.web.pt; Calçada do Garcia 6; d with/without bathroom €45/55;) A small, clean, efficient guesthouse, with attractive, carpeted rooms overlooking the narrow street down to the hustle of the Largo.

Residencial Florescente (Map pp86-7; ☎ 213 425 062; www.residencialflorescente.com; Rua das Portas de Santo Antão 99; s/d/tw/tr €45/55/70/80) On a pedestrianised street lined with tourist restaurants, Florescente has comfortable, snug, mundanely decorated rooms with telephone.

Albergaria Residencial Insulana (Map pp86-7; ☎ 213 423 131; www.insulana.cjb.net; Rua da Assunção 52; s/d €45/55) Although it's not the most elegant option in town, this guesthouse is fair value for its rooms with big windows and decorative balconies. You'll also find floral-patterned duvets, silvery wallpaper and worn carpeting.

Residência Roma (Map pp86-7; ☎ /fax 213 460 557; Travessa da Glória 22a; s/d/apt €50/60/70;) Rooms at Roma are spacious, with wood floors and trim and modern bathrooms with tubs, but dated furnishings. The 20 apartments here are good value with separate bedroom, living room and small but serviceable kitchens.

Hotel Borges (Map pp86-7; ☎ 213 461 951; fax 213 426 617; Rua Garrett 108; s/d/tr/q €65/75/85/95;) Housed in a classic, 19th-century building along Chiado's main drag, this simple but comfortable hotel offers good value for the money. The best rooms have French windows with small verandas and views onto the Chiado's elegant 19th-century façades. Service can be brusque at times.

TOP END

Hotel Lisboa Tejo (Map pp86-7; ☎ 218 866 182; www.evidenciahoteis.com; Rua dos Condes de Monsanto 2; s/d €105/120) In a fine old building, this hotel has adventurously decorated doubles in dashing colours. The ancient *poço* (well) near the entrance was probably used from Roman times, and survived the 1755 earthquake.

Hotel Métropole (Map pp86-7; ☎ 213 219 030; www.almeidahotels.com; Rossio 30; s/d €160/170) Built in the 1920s, small, low-key Métropole has spacious, renovated but endearingly old-fashioned rooms with antique furnishings. There are views over the Baixa, Alfama and to the castle.

Lisboa Regency Chiado (Map pp86-7; ☎ 213 256 100; www.regency-hotels-resorts.com; Rua Nova do Almada 114; s/d from €182/194) In an elegant building, this has sleek, plush rooms, neutrally decorated but with flashes of colour. Go for a top-floor one with terrace, taking in the castle, cathedral and river. The 7th-floor bar and outdoor terrace, open from noon to midnight, offers lovely views for all.

Hotel Avenida Palace (Map pp86-7; ☎ 213 218 100; www.hotel-avenida-palace.pt; Rua 1 de Dezembro 123; s/d €180/205) This gorgeous *belle époque* jewel has spacious, handsomely furnished rooms (though the carpeting doesn't match the antique design) and lavish common areas, such as the beautiful marble-floored atrium lobby.

Bairro Alto

Even closer to the heart of the action, Bairro Alto is perfect for stepping out your door and into the nightlife.

BUDGET

Albergue Popular (Map pp86-7; ☎ 213 478 047; Rua da Rosa 121; s/d with shared bathroom €15/25) Despite the decorative balconies overlooking the (often noisy) street and the *azulejos* in one room, this place has simple, well-worn rooms, and it's cheap.

Pensão Globo (Map pp86-7; ☎/fax 213 462 279; Rua do Teixeira 37; s/d €35/45) In a blue building with white trim, this popular, 17-room guesthouse offers simple, tidy rooms of varying sizes. It's just steps from the nightlife district but on a quietish, narrow street. Laundry service available.

Pensão Luar (Map pp86-7; ☎ 213 460 949; www.pensaoluar.com; Rua das Gáveas 101; s/d with shared bathroom €20/35, s/d €40/45) A lacklustre budget option, Luar has tiny but clean rooms with pressed wood floors and decent natural light. This low-key guesthouse can be noisy at night as it's in central Bairro Alto.

MIDRANGE

Residencial Alegria (Map pp86-7; ☎ 213 220 670; www.alegrianet.com; Praça da Alegria 12; d €48; ❄) Overlooking a small lush plaza, this charming guesthouse offers spacious rooms with polished wood floors, and big windows (or French doors) opening onto the peaceful street. Flower boxes adorn the decorative balconies.

Anjo Azul (Map pp86-7; ☎ 213 478 069; http://anjoazul.cb2web.com; Rua da Luz Soriano 75; d from €50) This handsomely restored place has trim, modern rooms done in splashy colours with a bit of homoerotic artwork adorning the walls. The Anjo Azul is a gay-friendly hotel that attracts a wide mix of travellers.

Pensão Londres (Map pp86-7; ☎ 213 462 203; www.pensaolondres.com.pt; Rua Dom Pedro V 53; d with/without bathroom from €68/46) This lovely atmospheric place has a range of comfy rooms: the best have high ceilings, decorative balconies and handsome furnishings. The 4th floor has great views over the city. Book well ahead in summer.

TOP END

Hotel Botânico (Map pp86-7; ☎ 213 420 392; www.hotelbotanico.net; Rua Mãe d'Água 16; s/d from €80/85; ❄) Inside an ugly grey building is this recently renovated old gem with wild red carpeting and attractive rooms done in masculine tones. Some rooms boast excellent views, and all have CD players.

our pick **Casa de São Mamede** (Map p89; ☎ 213 963 166; Rua da Escola Politécnica 159; s/d incl breakfast €80/90) In a former magistrate's 1758 town house, this elegant guesthouse has beautifully set rooms amid period furnishings and exquisitely tiled walls. It has a good location near Bairro Alto nightlife, but be steeled for a staid reception if you stumble back in the early hours.

Hotel Príncipe Real (Map pp86-7; ☎ 213 407 350; www.hotelprincipereal.com; Rua da Alegria 53; s/d/ste from €97/115/149; ❄) This charming boutique hotel has stylish rooms, with handsome furnishings, flat-screen TVs and marble bathrooms; most also have balconies.

Bairro Alto Hotel (Map pp86-7; ☎ 213 408 288; www.bairroaltohotel.com; Praça Luís de Camões 8; s/d from €290/310; ❄) The neighbourhood's loveliest boutique hotel has a lobby full of artwork, an inviting café-bar and elegant designer rooms – decorated with richly hued fabrics, dark woods and artful furnishings.

Alfama & Graça

Alfama has some of Lisbon's most charismatic hotels; it's a steep walk or short tram ride from the centre.

BUDGET

Casa de Hóspedes Estrela (Map pp86-7; ☎ 218 869 506; 1st fl, Rua dos Bacalhoeiros 8; s/d with shower €25/35) Among several waterfront cheapies, this is our favourite, with simple, tile-floored rooms and sweet and cheerful staff. The best rooms have tiny balconies overlooking a small plaza.

Pensão Ninho das Águias (Map pp86-7; ☎ 218 854 070; Costa do Castelo 74; s/d/tr with shared bathroom €30/40/60) Despite the grumpy staff, it's hard to knock this amazing bargain house-on-a-hill. Located just below the castle, 'the eagle's nest' has stunning city views, decent rooms and a garden terrace. Reserve well ahead.

Pensão São João da Praça (Map pp86-7; ☎ 218 862 591; 218862591@sapo.pt; 2nd fl, Rua São João da Praça 97; d with/without bathroom from €50/35) Next to the cathedral, this characterful 19th-century house has a range of rooms from small quarters with high ceilings to more-spacious wood-floored rooms with big windows and river-facing verandas.

MIDRANGE

Sé Guest House (Map pp86-7; ☎ /fax 218 864 400; 1st fl, Rua São João da Praça 97; d with shared bathroom €70) On the 1st floor of a 19th-century house is this charming guesthouse, filled with unusual knick-knacks. The doubles are romantic, some facing onto the cathedral. Bathrooms are gleamingly clean.

TOP END

our pick Solar dos Mouros (Map pp86-7; ☎ 218 854 940; www.solardosmouros.pt; Rua do Milagre de Santo António 4; d €80-200; ❄) This stylish guesthouse features eight uniquely designed rooms, each bearing the imprint of artist Luís Lemos. Nicely lit rooms are hung with contemporary art and decorated with handsome furniture; some quarters feature river or castle views.

Albergaria Senhora do Monte (Map pp86-7; ☎ 218 866 002; senhoradomonte@hotmail.com; Calçada do Monte 39; s/d €95/120, d with terrace €145; P) Near the Miradouro da Senhora do Monte, with pale, comfortable rooms, this hotel has top-of-the-world views. The terrace rooms are worth the extra. Tram 28 runs close by.

Olissipo Castelo (Map pp86-7; ☎ 218 820 190; www.olissipohotels.com; Rua Costa do Castelo 112-126; d from €165; ❄) Some of the city's best views arrive courtesy of this well-appointed option in Castelo. Rooms are spacious with huge windows but fairly traditional furnishings. Third-floor rooms have sizable verandas.

Palácio Belmonte (Map pp86-7; ☎ 218 816 600; www.palaciobelmonte.com; Páteo Dom Fradique 14; d from €320; ❄ 🏊) Set in a gorgeously restored palace (parts of which date from the 15th century), this is Lisbon's most atmospheric hotel. Luxurious rooms, gorgeous views and excellent but unobtrusive service are just a few of the palace charms. There's also the lush garden, the pool, the gorgeous 18th-century tile work.

Lapa

Lisbon's sleek and leafy diplomatic district has some beautiful top-notch places.

Residencial Beira Tejo (Map p89; ☎ 213 975 106; residencial-beira-tejo@clix.pt; 2nd fl, Calçada do Marquês de Abrantes 43; d with/without shower €40/30) This pleasant guesthouse has just seven cosily furnished rooms, each with wood floors, high ceilings and balconies.

Maná Guesthouse (Map p89; ☎ 213 973 196; pensaomana@sapo.pt; Calçada do Marquês de Abrantes 97; d €50-70) This small, welcoming guesthouse has attractive rooms with polished wood floors, high ceilings and elegant furnishings. Breakfast is served in the small back garden.

York House (Map p89; ☎ 213 962 435; www.yorkhouselisboa.com; Rua das Janelas Verdes 32; s/d from €195/220) Hidden among greenery, this former 17th-century convent with 34 antique-furnished rooms is beautiful and knows it. The restaurant spills into a sun-dappled courtyard.

As Janelas Verdes (Map p89; ☎ 213 968 143; www.heritage.pt; Rua das Janelas Verdes 47; s/d/tr €215/235/295) In an 18th-century palace that novelist Eça de Queirós used as a model in his novel *Os Maias*, this hotel has fine rooms (some with balcony) and a courtyard, as well as a library with a terrace. Welcoming and lovely.

Lapa Palace (Map p89; ☎ 213 949 494; www.lapapalace.com; Rua do Pau de Bandeira 4; d from €325; ❄ 🏊 ♿) A 19th-century country mansion, Lapa Palace has glorious river views and rooms of sumptuous old-world decadence. There is also disabled access.

Rato, Marquês de Pombal & Saldanha

Pousada da Juventude de Lisboa (Map p90; ☎ 213 532 696; lisboa@movijovem.pt; Rua Andrade Corvo 46; dm/d €16/43; 🕑 24hr) Well located and well run, this youth hostel is in a fine old building, near Parque Eduardo VII. The nearest metro station is Picoas, or take buses 46 or 90 from Santa Apolónia or Rossio, or AeroBus from the airport; buses stop at the end of the road.

Pensão Residencial 13 da Sorte (Map p90; ☎ 213 539 746; www.trezedasorte.no.sapo.pt; Rua do Salitre 13; s/d/tr €40/50/60; ❄) This pleasant place has smart rooms with tile floors, cheery curtains (and bedspreads) and sizable windows, as well as telephones and fridges.

Hotel Impala (Map p90; ☎ 213 148 914; fax 213 575 362; Rua Filipe Folque 49; 2-/4-person apt €75/90) Impala offers bargain modern apartments with tiny kitchens in a peaceful area. Sixth-floor apartments have terraces.

NH Liberdade (Map p90; ☎ 213 514 060; www.nh-hoteles.es; Avenida da Liberdade 180b; s/d €102/114; P ✖ ≋) This sleek high-rise hotel has comfortable ultramodern rooms (chrome lamps, black wood desk and headboard) that attract largely business travellers. Other features include a top-floor pool, a good restaurant and an attractive lounge bar.

Hotel Britannia (Map p90; ☎ 213 155 016; www.heritage.pt; Rua Rodrigues Sampaio 17; s/d €154/164; ✖) In a beautifully restored Art Deco building, Hotel Britannia has large plush rooms with eclectic furnishings and marble bathrooms. The inviting bar with two-toned wood floors warrants a visit.

Belém

Pensão Residencial Setúbalense (Map p91; ☎ 213 636 639; Rua de Belém 28; s/d from €30/40) A short walk east of the monastery, this guesthouse has rooms of varying size, though all have tile floors (faux-wood finish), large windows and modern bathrooms. Ask for a room with a bridge view.

Greater Lisbon

As well as the camp sites and a hostel, Lisbon's outskirts harbour a palatial *pousada* (guesthouse).

Lisboa Camping – Parque Municipal (Map pp84-5; ☎ 217 623 100; fax 217 623 106; adult/tent/car €5.60/5.80/3.50; ≋ ♿) In the huge, green, forested Parque Florestal de Monsanto, 6km west of the Rossio, this big and well-equipped camping ground has tennis courts, playground, restaurant, bar and disabled access. Bungalows for two to six are also available. To get there, take bus 43 from Cais do Sodré or bus 50 from Gare do Oriente.

Clube de Campismo de Lisboa (☎ 219 623 960; fax 219 623 144; adult/tent/car €1/4.40/1; ≋ ♿) Open to Camping Card International (CCI) cardholders only, and 20km northwest of Lisbon at Almornos, this is a shady, large site, with restaurant, bar, disabled access, playground and pool (admission fee).

There are other camp sites at Costa de Caparica (p146) and Praia do Guincho (p139).

Pousada da Juventude de Lisboa Parque Nações (Map pp84-5; ☎ 218 920 890; lisboaparque@movijovem.pt; Via de Moscavide 47; dm/d €13/37; ⏲ reception 8am-midnight) This is near Parque das Nações, 1km north of Gare do Oriente (take a metro to the centre). It has a restaurant, plus cooking and laundry facilities.

There are other *pousadas da juventude* (youth hostels) across the Tejo at **Almada** (☎ 212 943 491; almada@movijovem.pt; Quinta do Bucelinho, Pragal; dm/d €16/36), and near the beach at **Catalazete** (☎ 214 430 638; catalazete@movijovem.pt; Estrada Marginal, Oeiras; dm/d €13/36), 12km west of Lisbon, accessible by frequent trains from Cais do Sodré. Both these have bargain four-person apartments (€70) and dorms. Reservations are essential – at least a month ahead in summer.

EATING

Lisbon boasts an excellent range of restaurants, catering to all budgets.

Turismo de Lisboa's Restaurant Card (person/couple/family €6.15/8.10/10.75) offers discounts of 10% to 15% in more than 35 restaurants. It's valid for 72 hours and available at turismos and some hotels.

Dining in Lisbon can be a great value, especially at lunch, when daily specials can cost as little as €5.

Many places close on Sunday night or Monday.

Rossio, Praça dos Restauradores & Baixa

The traditional dining rooms and outdoor cafés along the pedestrian streets of the Baixa cater largely to tourists, though there are some gems here – and unbeatable ambience at outdoor spots on the plazas and in the backstreets of Chiado.

BUDGET

our pick **Fragoleto** (Map pp86-7; Rua da Prata 74; one-scoop €1.80; ⏲ 9am-8pm Mon-Sat, 10am-7pm Mon-Sat-winter) Serving the tastiest gelato this side of Genoa, pint-sized Fragoleto should not be missed. The ice cream here is divine, featuring a changing selection of seasonal fruits and even vegan options. Our current favourites: pistachio, green tea and wild berries.

Restaurant O Sol (Map pp86-7; Calçada do Duque 21; dishes €2-5; ⏲ lunch & dinner; V) This small veggie café with healthy food has outdoor tables on the stepped, cobbled lane.

Casa Brasileira (Map pp86-7; Rua Augusta 267; pastries €1.50; ⏲ 7am-1am Mon-Sat, 8am-1am Sun) Take your place around the stand-up counter at this popular local café for tasty pastries, fresh juices and sandwiches. There are also outdoor tables at the front.

Confeitaria Nacional (Map pp86-7; ☎ 213 461 720; Praça da Figueira 18; lunch from €5.50; ⏲ 8am-8pm Mon-Sat)

This 170-year-old café has a dizzying array of pastries and sweets. Upstairs, you'll find an inviting restaurant serving heartier cuisine, including good quiches and soups.

Velho Macedo (Map pp86-7; Rua da Madalena; dishes €6; lunch & dinner) An excellent, untouristy backstreet restaurant, with simple food cooked to perfection. Try the delicious squid.

Com Alma Caffé (Map pp86-7; ☎ 218 870 246; Rua da Alfândega 114; dishes €4-6; lunch Mon-Fri, dinner Mon-Sat) Indeed, this newcomer to the dining scene has a lot of *alma* (soul). Modern moulded furniture contrasts with the exposed stone walls. On offer is good Mediterranean fare, and on weekends DJs or world music groups add to the scene.

Royal Café (Map pp86-7; ☎ 213 469 125; Largo Raphael Bordallo Pinheiro 29; dishes €4-6; 10am-8pm Sun-Tue, 10am-midnight Wed-Sat) This stylish café has moulded plastic furniture, tasty create-your-own sandwiches and a small backyard patio, with hipster kids sprinkled about. Laptop not included.

Rua dos Correeiros has lots of good-value places, catering to Portuguese at lunchtime and tourists at night, with set menus and mains at around €6. Try **Ena Pai** (Map pp86-7; ☎ 213 421 759; Rua dos Correeiros 182) and **Adega Regional da Beira** (Map pp86-7; ☎ 213 467 014; Rua dos Correeiros 132).

There are supermarkets and *minimercados* (grocery shops) everywhere. The Baixa also has a small but well-stocked health food store, **Celeiro** (Map pp86-7; Rua 1 de Dezembro 65; 8.30am-8pm Mon-Fri, 8.30am-7pm Sat; V).

MIDRANGE

Café no Chiado (Map pp86-7; ☎ 213 460 501; Largo do Picadeiro 10; dishes €4-8; noon-2am Tue-Sun) Tree-shaded outdoor tables make a fine setting at this peaceful café in Chiado. There are quiches and salads, as well as daily specials.

Mega Vega (Map pp86-7; Rua dos Sapateiros 113; lunch €6-10; 8.30am-11pm Mon-Fri, 10am-11pm Sat; V) This small cheerful vegetarian restaurant serves fresh salads, tasty homemade tortes and juices, and spreads a fine lunch buffet.

Mezzogiórno (Map pp86-7; ☎ 213 421 500; Rua Garrett 19; dishes €6-11; lunch Tue-Sat, dinner Mon-Sat) The scent of piping-hot pizzas lures many would-be passers-by to this well-located Chiado pizzeria. Many varieties of tasty thin-crust pizzas are on offer, baked in a wood-burning oven. Our only gripe: plant some trees in that blindingly barren courtyard!

Everest Montanha (Map pp86-7; ☎ 218 876 428; Calçada do Garcia 15; dishes €7-9.50; lunch & dinner Mon-Sat; V) Tucked away just north of Praça da Figueira, this small, simple restaurant serves decent Nepalese and Indian dishes, with many vegetarian options.

UMA (Map pp86-7; ☎ 213 427 425; Rua dos Sapateiros 177; dishes €7-10; lunch Mon-Fri) With a delicious, award-winning *arroz de marisco* (rice and seafood stew), and other great dishes, this backstreet place earns good reviews.

Sancho (Map pp86-7; ☎ 213 469 780; Travessa da Glória 14; dishes €7.50-17.50; lunch & dinner Sun-Fri, dinner Sat) Amid dark wood furnishings and a beamed ceiling, this place serves excellent fish and seafood. Look for the wooden Sancho (Quixote's sidekick) out the front.

Jardim do Sentidos (Map pp86-7; ☎ 213 423 670; Rua da Mãe d'Água 3; dishes €8-10; lunch Mon-Fri, dinner Mon-Sat; V) This attractive vegetarian restaurant serves a changing menu of nicely prepared dishes such as lasagne, chilli and vegetable kofta. Lunchtime crowds come for the good-value buffet and the pleasant garden dining.

Chez Degroote (Map pp86-7; ☎ 213 472 839; Rua dos Duques de Bragança 4; dishes €9; lunch Mon-Fri, dinner Mon-Sat) Away from the tourist crowds, this good-value restaurant has colourful walls, wrought-iron chandeliers and nicely prepared dishes. Straightforward specialities feature roasted meats or fish (sea bass, salmon).

Martinho da Arcada (Map pp86-7; ☎ 218 879 259; Praça do Comércio 3; dishes €11-18; breakfast, lunch & dinner) In business since 1782, this tiled, yellow-and-white-tablecloth place was once a haunt of Pessoa. Although the literary lions have since moved on, Martinho's outdoor tables beneath a colonnade make a fine spot for a traditional meal.

TOP END

Tamarind (Map pp86-7; ☎ 213 466 080; Rua da Glória 43; dishes €12-18; lunch Mon-Fri, dinner daily) You'll find exquisite Indian cuisine at this attractive Zenlike space near the Elevador da Glória. Popular dishes such as the succulent prawn curry have earned fans all over the world. Reservations advised.

O Fumeiro (Map pp86-7; ☎ 213 474 203; Rua da Conceição da Glória 25; dishes €12-20; lunch & dinner) This cosy blue-and-white-tiled restaurant specialises in the earthy, aromatic cuisine of the mountainous Beira Alta and Serra da Estrela regions. Rich meat dishes pair nicely with the wines.

Restaurante Solmar (Map pp86-7; ☎ 213 423 371; Rua das Portas de Santo Antão 106; dishes €12-24; ⏲ lunch & dinner Mon-Sat) This enormous columned place has underwater sea murals and fusty waiters labouring beneath large seafood platters.

Bairro Alto

Lisbon's most extensive restaurant district has charming Portuguese options along with international spots.

BUDGET

Restaurante Alto Minho (Map pp86-7; ☎ 213 468 183; Rua da Bica Duarte Belo 61; dishes €2.50-5.50; ⏲ lunch Sun-Fri) Next to the Elevador da Bica, this traditional tiled place does cheap, filling Portuguese staples with plenty of *bacalhau* (dried salt cod) options. It's a popular local spot.

Adamastor (Map pp86-7; ☎ 213 471 726; Rua Marechal Saldanha 24; dishes €4.50-9; ⏲ lunch & dinner Mon-Sat) This tiny wedge-shaped café serves inexpensive meals (chicken or sardines, anyone?) amid first-rate people-watching. Get there early to snag an outdoor table.

Casa da India (Map pp86-7; ☎ 213 423 661; Rua do Loreto 49; dishes €5-8; ⏲ 9am-2am Mon-Sat) Despite the name, this is a traditional joint with a Portuguese menu. It's popular and lively, always busy, and the *gambas á guilho* (garlic prawns) are divine.

Esplanada (Map p89; ☎ 962 311 669; Praça do Príncipe Real; mains €4-6; ⏲ 9am-9pm) This pleasant indoor-outdoor café is a good spot for a coffee break among trees and twittering birds.

A Toca (Map pp86-7; ☎ 213 467 160; Rua da Atalaia 85; dishes €5-8.50; ⏲ lunch & dinner Mon-Sat) Basic, small and cheerful with mainstream Portuguese fare.

MIDRANGE

Bonsai (Map pp86-7; ☎ 213 462 515; Rua da Rosa 248; dishes €2.50-16.50; ⏲ lunch & dinner Mon-Sat, lunch Tue-Fri only Nov-Mar) Surprisingly spacious, Bonsai features rush walls, black tables, tinkling music and good authentic Japanese food, with a regularly changing menu.

Alfaia (Map pp86-7; ☎ 213 461 232; Travessa da Queimada 18; dishes €4-12; ⏲ noon-2am Mon-Sat, 7pm-2am Sun) This cosy spot serves tapas, sandwiches and hearty Portuguese fare, though port is the main event here. Grab a seat at one of the peaceful outdoor tables for premium imbibing.

Fidalgo (Map pp86-7; ☎ 213 422 900; Rua da Barroca 27; dishes €6.50-10; ⏲ dinner Mon-Sat) An award-winning sitting-room with bottle-lined walls, Fidalgo is a lively, sophisticated, gay-friendly, buzzing choice. It offers interesting, well-executed fish and meat dishes and delicious desserts.

A Tasca do Manel (Map pp86-7; ☎ 213 463 813; Rua da Barroca 24; dishes €7-12; ⏲ lunch & dinner) Tiled and wooden, this is a hip *tasca* (tavern), always packed and lively, with tasty traditional fish and meat dishes.

Tertúlia do Loreto (Map pp86-7; ☎ 213 426 731; Rua do Loreto 12; dishes €8-12; ⏲ lunch & dinner) In a former bakery with stone walls and a wood-beamed ceiling, this friendly spot dishes up creative Portuguese cuisine. Try the Brazilian-influenced cod with coconut milk and palm oil.

Stasha (Map pp86-7; ☎ 213 431 131; Rua das Gáveas 29; dishes €8-12; ⏲ lunch Mon-Fri, dinner Tue-Sun; Ⓥ) A funky, lively restaurant-bar, Stasha has adventurous dishes with international flavours and good veggie choices. Inside is peachy and dim, brightened with paintings.

Cervejaria da Trindade (Map pp86-7; ☎ 213 423 506; Rua Nova da Trindade 20c; dishes €8-13; ⏲ lunch & dinner) In a former convent building, this has a fine, tiled and bustling dining room. Beef and seafood dishes are particularly popular but you can also pop in for a sandwich.

Snob (Map pp86-7; ☎ 213 463 723; Rua do Século 178; dishes €8-13.25; ⏲ 9pm-3.30am) This is where journalists come to huddle in brown-leather booths against walls comfortingly lined with whisky bottles. It has a gentlemanly, wide-ranging menu with renowned steaks. Food served until late.

Stravaganza (Map pp86-7; ☎ 213 468 868; Rua do Grémio Lusitano 18; dishes €8-15; ⏲ noon-1am Mon-Sat) This popular Italian spot serves decent pizzas and pastas in a buzzing late-night atmosphere. Check out the red, spray-painted sunflowers mounted on the wall.

Charcutaria Francesa (Map pp86-7; ☎ 213 432 389; Rua Dom Pedro V 52; mains €10-14; ⏲ lunch & dinner Mon-Sat) For a date-pleasing picnic, stop in at this attractive food market and grab cheeses, wines, smoked meats, chocolates and other tasty bites. There's also a good French restaurant at the back, serving a noteworthy Saturday brunch.

Other atmospheric options:

A Baîuca (Map pp86-7; ☎ 213 423 813; Rua da Barroca 24; dishes €8-9; ⏲ dinner) Small, cosy and garlicky; trad Portuguese grub.

Calcuta (Map pp86-7; ☎ 213 428 295; Rua do Norte 17; dishes €6-9; ⏲ lunch & dinner Mon-Sat; Ⓥ) Colourful North Indian, nice, and good for vegies.

Baralto (Map pp86-7; ☎ 213 426 739; Rua do Diário de Notícias 32; dishes €9-12; ⌚ lunch & dinner Mon-Sat) Traditional Portuguese cuisine with a few unique options (vegetarian lasagne, paella) in a cosy setting.

Café dos Teatros (Map pp86-7; ☎ 213 257 640; Rua António Maria Cardoso 38; dishes €4-10; ⌚ noon-1am Mon-Sat) A theatrically lit setting with excellent soups, salads and sandwiches and ample dessert choices.

TOP END

El Gordo II (Map pp86-7; ☎ 213 426 372; Travessa dos Freis de Deus 28; dishes €3.25-28; ⌚ dinner Tue-Sun) Lit with a rosy glow from cloth lanterns, and decorated with mirrors and carved wooden screens, this has excellent, though not cheap, Spanish tapas such as octopus in smoked paprika, or pimento peppers. There are outdoor tables on the cobbled steps.

Sul (Map pp86-7; ☎ 213 462 449; Rua do Norte 13; dishes €12-16; ⌚ dinner) Romantic, candlelit and exotic, with mainly Italian dishes.

Pap'Açorda (Map pp86-7; ☎ 213 464 811; Rua da Atalaia 57; dishes €13-19; ⌚ lunch & dinner) The beauty crowd gathers at this elegant spot, set with cascading glass chandeliers and exposed brick walls. The speciality is the old working-class Alentejan staple *açorda* (bread and shellfish soup served in a clay pot). Save room for the legendary chocolate mousse.

La Brasserie de l'Entrecôte (Map pp86-7; ☎ 213 428 344; Rua do Alecrim 117; steak €15; ⌚ lunch & dinner) Here candlelight flickers across the high ceiling, and a refined crowd tucks into the only choice on the menu: entrecôte steak with herb and nut sauces.

Alfama & Graça

Alfama is the place to head for small, traditional, family-run eateries.

BUDGET

Restaurante Cais d'Alfama (Map pp86-7; ☎ 218 873 274; Largo do Chafariz de Dentro 24; dishes €4-12; ⌚ lunch Mon-Sat & dinner Thu-Sat) Attracts locals with its cheerful atmosphere and extensive tasty choices, including fresh barbecued sardines. There are a few outside tables on the square.

A Tasca da Sé (Map pp86-7; ☎ 218 875 551; Rua Augusto Rosa 62; dishes €5.50-11.50; ⌚ lunch & dinner) Near the cathedral, this terracotta- and brown-tiled small and welcoming family restaurant offers delicious home-cooked dishes.

São Cristóvão (Map pp86-7; ☎ 218 885 578; Rua de São Cristóvão 30; mains around €6; ⌚ lunch & dinner) A cheerful, tiny, family-run restaurant famous for its Cape Verdean dishes and other African fare, such as a punchy *moamba de galinha* (Angolan chicken stew).

Matas Snack Bar (Map pp86-7; Largo da Graça 8; dishes €4-8; ⌚ 8am-midnight) Fronting a tree-shaded courtyard in a quiet stretch of Graça, this colourful café serves simple lunch plates, though most come here for coffee, pastries and the pleasant open-air setting.

Porte de Alfama (Map pp86-7; ☎ 218 864 536; Rua de São João da Praça 17; dishes €6-7; ⌚ lunch & dinner) A tiny place with outdoor tables serving simple dishes such as barbecued fish. Free *fado* on Saturday.

Frescos & Co (Map pp86-7; Rua da Graça 115; ⌚ 8am-8pm) One of several good fruit and grocery shops in Graça.

MIDRANGE

Restaurante Viagems de Sabores (Map pp86-7; ☎ 218 870 189; Rua São João da Praça 103; dishes €8.50-12.50; ⌚ dinner Mon-Sat) This superb, amazing-value international restaurant is small, with warm décor. It offers a journey for your taste buds from Thai to Indian. Grilled tuna and eggplant lasagne are good picks. Book ahead.

Treasure Island (Map pp86-7; ☎ 918 902 778; Rua Bartolomeu Gusmão 11; dishes €4-12; ⌚ lunch & dinner) Set with antiques and colourful artwork, this eclectic restaurant serves sandwiches (including a vegetarian option) and tapas as well as heartier fare.

our pick **Pois Café** (Map pp86-7; ☎ 218 862 497; Rua São João da Praça 93; dishes €4-12; ⌚ 11am-8pm Tue-Sun) This large, airy café has big tables, comfy armchairs and plenty of books and newspapers on hand for whiling away a lazy afternoon. The fresh salads, hearty sandwiches and desserts are delicious (and nice accompaniments to tangy juices).

Verde Perto (Map pp86-7; ☎ 218 870 488; Costa do Castelo 20; dishes €7-9; ⌚ noon-midnight Tue-Sat) Shiny pink placemats and black wooden lightboxes along the wall lend a minimalist chic to this friendly restaurant. Huge, creative salads are tops here, though you can also opt for crepes, open-faced sandwiches or other light fare.

Mestre André (Map pp86-7; ☎ 218 871 487; Calçadinha de Santo Estevão; dishes €6.50-12.50; ⌚ lunch Mon-Fri, dinner Mon-Sat) A charming neighbourhood restaurant with small tables under a star-spangled ceiling, André has tasty *bacalhau con nata* (dried salt-cod with cream), and cheesecake made with Portuguese cheese.

Casanova (Map pp84-5; ☎ 218 877 532; Cais da Pedra á Bica do Sapato; dishes €7-13; 🕑 lunch Wed-Sun, dinner Tue-Sun) Close to Bica do Sapato and under its wing, this is *the* place for authentic Italian pizza in an airy modern space, as swinging as its light bulbs. There is some riverside seating. No reservations – just turn up and wait.

Deli Delux (Map pp84-5; ☎ 218 862 070; Armazem B, Avenida Dom Henrique; dishes €7-13; 🕑 noon-10pm Wed-Sat, 10am-8pm Sun) Next door to Casanova, this enticing grocery shop has a casual restaurant at the back where you can enjoy good salads, gourmet sandwiches and tasty desserts. There's riverside seating, too.

C@fé Taborda (Map pp86-7; ☎ 218 879 484; Costa do Castelo 75; mains from €7; 🕑 lunch & dinner; Ⓥ) Up near Castelo de São Jorge is this high-up vegetarian and fish restaurant with marvellous views through its large windows.

Restaurante Arço do Castelo (Map pp86-7; ☎ 218 876 598; Rua do Chão da Feira 25; dishes €7-11; 🕑 lunch & dinner Mon-Sat) A small, relaxed Indian restaurant lined with bottles, this place has good Goan dishes. Try the coconut tiger-prawn curry and *piri piri* (red hot chilli pepper) chicken.

Malmequer Bemmequer (Map pp86-7; ☎ 218 876 535; Rua de São Miguel 23; dishes €6-12.50; 🕑 lunch & dinner Wed-Sun) Located on a small square, this bright restaurant is adorned with murals, with an extensive menu of excellent charcoal-grilled dishes and blue-and-white cheery check tablecloths.

Lautasco (Map pp86-7; ☎ 218 860 173; Beco do Azinhal 7; dishes €9-12; 🕑 lunch & dinner Mon-Sat) Lautasco has a wonderfully romantic location, tucked in a leafy, decorated courtyard. Grilled salmon is among the favourites.

our pick **Restô** (Map pp86-7; ☎ 218 867 334; Costa do Castelo 7; tapas €4-5, restaurant dishes €10-16; 🕑 7.30pm-2am Mon-Fri, noon-2am Sat & Sun) Part of the Chapitô arts cooperative, Restô has a tree-filled open-air terrace, an arty tapas bar (open till 2am) and an enchanting top-floor restaurant with magical views over Lisbon. Tasty unusual dishes feature a range of international flavours.

Bica do Sapato (Map pp84-5; ☎ 218 810 320; Cais da Pedra, Avenida Infante Dom Henrique; sushi €2-7, café €14-22, restaurant €18-32; 🕑 lunch Tue-Sat, dinner Mon-Sat) An über-hip minimalist dockside venue part-owned by actor John Malkovich, this comprises restaurant, café and sushi bar.

Alcântara, Lapa & Docas

Sitio do Pica Pau (Map p89; ☎ 213 978 267; Rua Remédios; 🕑 8am-5.30pm Mon-Fri) This sweet café has a small, shrub-surrounded terrace looking down a steep, cobbled, pastel-painted street to the river.

Café Apolo XI (Map p89; Rua de Santos-o-Velho 92; dishes from €5; 🕑 closed Sun) A small charming café far from the tourist trail, Apolo XI attracts a low-key workaday crowd who come for meatballs, stuffed cuttlefish, grilled pork ribs and other daily specials.

Cha da Lapa (Map p89; ☎ 213 957 029; Fritz ldr do Olival 6; 🕑 9am-7pm) A smart, English-feeling tearoom, refined and well mannered, with flock wallpaper, tea and scones.

Lusitália (Map p89; ☎ 916 169 736; Praça das Flores 40; dishes €6-8; 🕑 noon-10pm Tue-Sun) One of several outdoor cafés facing the leafy *praça,* Lusitália serves toasted sandwiches, salads and a daily pasta, as well as decadent desserts.

Picanha Janelas Verdes (Map p89; ☎ 213 975 401; Rua das Janelas Verdes 96; set-price lunch/dinner €7/13.50; 🕑 lunch daily, dinner Mon-Sat) This cosy spot has tiles on the wall and chequered tablecloths. The main event here is *picanha* (steak seasoned with garlic and olive oil), an enormously popular Brazilian dish.

A Confraria (Map p89; ☎ 213 962 435; Rua das Janelas Verdes 32; dishes €12-24; 🕑 lunch & dinner) This upmarket restaurant at York House (p110) is renowned for its esoteric French delicacies (mainly more than €20). Sit outside in the sun-dappled courtyard.

There's a string of waterfront restaurants and bars around the Docas area, under the thundering Ponte 24 de Abril, which gives the area some *On the Waterfront* cachet. See Drinking (p119) for more details.

It's worth wandering along the strip to see what takes your fancy, but one of the nicest places, with delicious food and especially good salads is **Espalha Brasas** (Map p89; ☎ 213 962 059; Avenida de Brasilia; dishes €9-15; 🕑 lunch & dinner Mon-Sat).

Rato, Marquês de Pombal & Saldanha

Real Fábrica (Map p90; ☎ 213 852 090; Rua da Escola Politécnica 275; dishes €7.25-14.50; 🕑 lunch & dinner) A trendy converted 19th-century silk factory, Real Fábrica throngs with people tucking into fine meat and fish. There's a long bottle-lined bar, and big plate-glass windows onto the street.

Restaurante Os Tibetanos (Map p90; ☎ 213 142 038; Rua do Salitre 117; dishes €4-7; 🕑 lunch & dinner Mon-Fri; Ⓥ) Part of a school of Tibetan Buddhism in an old house topped with prayer flags, this

TOP 10 CAFÉS & PASTELARIAS

The Portuguese know a thing or two about cakes. Here is a tenaciously researched survey.

- **Pastéis de Belém** (Map p91; Rua de Belém 84; tart €0.80; 🕑 8am-midnight) Sublime, divine traditional *pastéis de Belém* (custard tarts) – the eggiest, lightest, crispiest tarts, served warm with a sprinkling of cinnamon and sugar. The recipe is secret, but these tarts taste like they've been made by angels. Founded in 1837, the traditional tiled tearoom is pretty.
- **Café A Brasileira** (Map pp86-7; ☎ 213 469 547; Rua Garrett 120; mains €6-12) This wonderful original Art Deco café has literary credentials – the seated bronze statue outside is writer Fernando Pessoa, a former habitué. It's touristy but still a local favourite with lots of atmosphere.
- **Versailles** (Map p90; ☎ 213 546 340; Avenida da República 15a; dishes €11-18) One of Lisbon's grandest *pastelarias* (pastry and cake shops), this is a splendid marble, column, chandelier and icing-sugar stucco confection, matched by delicious cakes and desserts, and frequented by battalions of well-coiffed elderly ladies. It also serves good savoury food.
- **Café Nicola** (Map pp86-7; ☎ 213 460 579; Rossio 24; dishes €1.35-10; 🕑 8am-10pm Mon-Fri, 9am-10pm Sat, 10am-7pm Sun) The grande dame of Lisbon's cafés, Nicola has shiny 1930s Art Deco features and outside tables. The white-tablecloth restaurant at the back is a good place for lunch.
- **Pastelaria São Roque** (Map pp86-7; Rua Dom Pedro V; dishes €1-5; 🕑 daily) A mirrored, templelike café, with gold-topped columns and alcove tables for window-watching. It justifiably declares itself a *catedral do pão* (cathedral of bread) in tiles behind the counter. The homemade soup is delicious.
- **Panificação do Chiado** (Map pp86-7; Calçada do Sacramento; pastries €1-2; 🕑 7am-7pm Mon-Fri, 7am-1pm Sat) This elegant, refreshingly smoke-free pastry shop serves delicious chocolate croissants, fresh-baked breads, homemade jams and plenty of other temptations.
- **Pastelaria Baga Baga** (Map pp86-7; Largo da Graça 108; pastries €1-2; 🕑 6am-midnight) A charming option off the well-trodden tourist path, this tiny Graça café serves tasty bites at diminutive prices.
- **Pastelaria Sequeira** (Map p90; ☎ 213 140 749; Avenida da República 11c; 🕑 7am-8pm Mon-Sat) Way out in Saldanha, this delightful pastry shop has enormous glass windows, through which one can glimpse flaky pastries, creamy tarts and the neighbourhood regulars that love them.
- **Casa Suiça** (Map pp86-7; ☎ 213 214 090; entrances at Rossio 96-101 & Praça da Figueira; pastries €1-2; 🕑 8am-8pm Mon-Sat) A long-established favourite doing a brisk trade with tourists outside and sedate elderly locals inside.
- **Cafeteria Quadrante** (Map p91; ☎ 213 622 722; Centro Cultural de Belém; dishes €5-8; 🕑 12.30-9.30pm Mon-Fri, 12.30-7pm Sat & Sun) On the 3rd floor, this is a calm, spacious, modern café with a lovely terrace overlooking the river.

ever-popular vegetarian eatery will fill you up with daily specials such as quiche or rice with vegetables. Desserts are delicious – try rose-petal ice cream with yogurt.

Restaurante Estrela de Santa Marta (Map p90; ☎ 213 548 400; Rua de Santa Marta 14a; dishes €6.50-13.50; 🕑 lunch & dinner) This smart, low-key, classy restaurant serves typical Portuguese dishes, such as fresh grilled fish and seafood rice. It gets busy with a Portuguese crowd at lunchtime.

Luca (Map p90; ☎ 213 150 212; Rua Santa Marta 35; dishes €9-16; 🕑 lunch Mon-Fri, dinner Mon-Sat) Known for its contemporary Italian cuisine, Luca is a favourite among Lisboêtas. Here you'll find a large, open dining room, a well-dressed but laid-back crowd and inventive risotto and pasta dishes (try the ravioli with tiger prawns), and grilled meats. Upstairs is an enticing tapas bar, where you can snack (and drink) while you wait for a table. Reservations are recommended.

Ad Lib (Map p90; ☎ 213 228 350; Avenida da Liberdade 127; dishes €18-25; 🕑 lunch & dinner Mon-Fri, dinner Sat & Sun) This modern, artfully decorated restaurant serves up imaginative (and delicious) plates of Franco-Portuguese cuisine. A blend of seafood, pastas and roasted meats round out the menu.

La Caffé (Map p90; ☎ 213 256 736; Avenida da Liberdade 129; dishes €18-25; ⏲ lunch Mon-Sat, dinner Tue-Sat; 🖳) Above the Lanidor fashion store, this stylish restaurant serves good but pricey international fare (risottos, pesto dishes, grilled meats). ...ere's also an attractive bar-lounge, with ac-...hion mags and free internet.

...empting restaurants are on Rua Vieira ...ense, with outdoor seating overlooking ...ark.

...staurante Floresta (Map p91; ☎ 213 636 307; ...ieira Portuense 2; dishes €5-8; ⏲ lunch & dinner Tue-... The best value along this strip, popular ...oresta is cheerful and reliable, with outside ...bles.

Restaurante Montenegro (Map p91; ☎ 213 638 279; Rua Vieira Portuense 44; dishes €6-11; ⏲ lunch Tue-Sun, dinner Tue-Sat) This is a lovely, friendly place to sit outside and linger over lunch. Has good shellfish-rice.

Rosa dos Mares (Map p91; ☎ 213 637 277; Rua de Belém 110; dishes €9-18; ⏲ lunch & dinner) This smart, bright 1st-floor restaurant is intimate, with craggy white walls and excellent seafood.

Greater Lisbon

Museu Nacional do Azulejo (National Tile Museum; Map pp84-5; ☎ 218 100 340; Rua Madre de Deus 4; dishes around €7; ⏲ lunch Tue-Sun) This is a bright courtyard-facing restaurant, lovely for a long lunch, with tiled walls and white tablecloths.

Complexo das Amoreiras and Centro Comercial Colombo (both p123) are very big malls with useful supermarkets for self-caterers.

DRINKING

Lisbon offers up some pretty enticing settings when it comes to raising a glass. Breezy riverside terraces, leafy hilltop manors and atmospheric wine cellars are just a few of the places that you're liable to stumble across while you're out drinking up the town. You'll also find slinky lounges, smoky jazz bars and wildly eclectic old gems tucked away in the old city streets.

Most bars have free admission, are open from around 10pm until 3am, and have a relaxed dress code. For information on nightclubs, see p119.

In addition to the areas listed here, Parque das Nações offers riverside views, with dozens of interchangeable restaurant-bars along Rua da Pimenta.

Rossio

A Ginjinha (Map pp86-7; Largo de São Domingos 8; ⏲ 7am-midnight) Inebriating locals and visitors since the 1840s, this hole-in-the-wall bar serves up shots of *ginjinha* (a cherry liqueur), which tastes like cough syrup but sure puts a zing in your step. You can take your medicine *com* (with) or *sem* (without) whole cherries. Espinheiro, the drink's inventor, keeps a beady watch over the door.

Bairro Alto

This web of narrow lanes is Lisbon's liveliest bar district, with revellers spilling out onto the streets most nights. The best approach is to wander, and halt when something takes your fancy.

Clube da Esquina (Map pp86-7; Rua da Barroca 30) Current favourite among young partiers, this place has smart design – old radios decorate the wood-floored space – though on weekends you'll have to squeeze past caipirinha-swilling crowds. DJs spin hip-hop, electronica and house.

Catacombas Jazz Bar (Map pp86-7; Rua da Rosa 154) This bar hosts live jazz on Thursday night, and on other nights its small rooms, tables and chairs are packed. It's a relaxed place to be, and not as self-consciously trendy as some other bars.

Nova Tertúlia Bar (Map pp86-7; www.novatertulia.com; Rua do Diário de Notícias 60) This Bairro Alto newcomer hosts live jazz most weekends amid plenty of smoky atmosphere.

Café Suave (Map pp86-7; Rua Diário de Notícias 6) This unpretentious place attracts a hip, laid-back crowd more interested in conversation than getting blitzed. Minimalist artwork and friendly staff.

Portas Largas (Map pp86-7; Rua da Atalaia 105) A well-worn, well-loved linchpin of Bairro Alto, this was once a *tasca* (tavern) and retains its original fittings – the long bar, black-and-white tiled floor and a smattering of columns and porticos. People-wise it's a mishmash – gays, straights and not-sures linger around the bar and spindly marble tables.

Majong (Map pp86-7; Rua da Atalaia) Scruffy, with school chairs, deep-red walls and drowsy cabbage-leaf lamps, this is a choice hang-out that gathers a somewhat boho crowd. It gets superpacked on weekends.

Bicaense (Map pp86-7; Rua da Bica Duarte Beló 42a) Out of the main action, this place has so-hip-it-hurts clientele. It's dimly lit and decked out with old radios and projectors; the back room is used to stage the occasional live-music act.

Heróis (Map pp86-7; Calçada do Sacramento) A Chiado bar, Heróis is packed with white Panton chairs (plastic retro classics). It hosts a cool, largely gay crowd listening to laid-back house.

our pick **Solar do Vinho do Porto** (Map pp86-7; ☎ 213 475 707; Rua de São Pedro de Alcântara 45; glass €1-24.50; 11am-midnight Mon-Sat) In a suitably awed atmosphere, here is an excellent opportunity to taste over 200 varieties of port – dark and red or light and tangy – either upstairs, which does a genteel-tearoom impression, or downstairs in a cosy cavern. Bottles cost €7 to €1200. Top tip: taste here and buy at the supermarket later.

Alfama

Alfama is perfect for a drink with a view.

Bar das Imagens (Map pp86-7; Calçada Marquês de Tancos 1; 11am-2am Tue-Sat, 3-11pm Sun) Set with outdoor tables overlooking a lovely stretch of the city, this friendly bar serves potent caipirinhas and other nicely prepared cocktails. Jazz plays in the background.

Bar Marroquino (Map pp86-7; Costa do Castelo 22; 9pm-2am Tue-Sat) The Arabian Nights–inspired 'Moroccan Bar' provides a cosy setting for smoking banana- or cherry-flavoured tobacco out of large waterpipes. Look for the blue lantern out the front.

Onda Jazz Bar (Map pp86-7; www.ondajazz.com; Arco de Jesus 7; 9pm-2am Wed-Sat) This narrow, underground space features an eclectic menu of mainstream jazz as well as more eclectic beats of bands hailing from Brazil, Angola and Cape Verde.

Miradouro da Graça (Map pp86-7; 10.30am-3am) There are brilliant views from this terrace, with soothing music during the day that gets heavier as the night wears on.

Two alternative theatres affording fantastic views from their bars are **Chapitô** (Costa do Castelo 7; noon-midnight) and **Taborda** (Costa do Castelo 75; noon-2am) – both excellent choices for a sundowner or a late-night drink overlooking the city.

Príncipe Real & São Bento

Centre of the Lisbon gay scene, this area also houses some unique drinking dens.

Pavilhão Chines (Map pp86-7; Rua Dom Pedro V 89-91) Probably the most fabulous bar in Lisbon, or perhaps anywhere, this Luís Pinto Coelho creation features walls lined with polished cabinets, full of carefully arranged kitsch, such as outfitted Action Men. A well-executed cocktail, a deep sit in a comfy armchair and a game of pool beneath squadrons of suspended model aircraft: what more could you want?

Foxtrot (Map p89; Travessa de Santa Teresa 28) By the same designer as Pavilhão Chines, this splendidly stately place feels like it has been here since the 1940s (actually only since the '80s), with low lighting, staid sofas, Oriental silks and rambling rooms.

Cais do Sodré & Avenida 24 de Julho

Old favourites and large clubs cluster around this trendy nightlife area, where people come for a change from Bairro Alto. During the Salazar years, this area was the only place for a bit of night-time seed, and some areas retain this seedy feel – particularly tacky Rua Nova do Carvalho.

Bar do Rio (Map pp86-7; Cais do Sodré Armazém A Porta 7) Intimate, funky and on its lonesome at Cais do Sodré, Bar do Rio is worth hitting for a drink before heading to Lux (opposite). Get there too late and it might seem like too much of an effort if it's crowded, but the staff are friendly and relaxed. They play good soul, funk and house.

O'Gilíns (Map pp86-7; Rua dos Remolares 8-10) Lisbon's oldest Irish pub gathers homesick expats who come for the frothy heads of Guinness and live music in the evening from Thursday to Saturday.

Hennessy's (Map pp86-7; Rua Cais do Sodré 32-38) Offers a similar pubby atmosphere to O'Gilíns.

Tuareg (Map p89; Calçada Marquês de Abrantes 72) Throw pillows, flickering candles and Arabian music set the mood at this atmospheric drinking den. In addition to cocktails and ambience, Tuareg serves up several dozen teas, waterpipes and Saturday-night belly dancers.

British Bar (Map pp86-7; Rua Bernardino Costa 52; Mon-Sat) Resembling an early-20th-century railway bar, this bottle-lined bar has an old-fashioned clientele and a backwards clock. There's even a resident shoe shiner.

Bar Americano (Map pp86-7; Rua Bernardino Costa 35) Across the road from the British Bar, this place is similarly classic. It dates back to the 1920s.

Docas & Alcântara

More modern (and somewhat tackier) than Bairro Alto, the Docas nightlife district comprises two separate areas: Doca de Alcântara and, to the west, Doca de Santo Amaro, which has a breezy setting under the lit-up, rumbling 25 de Abril bridge. Most people taxi here, but you can also take the train from Cais do Sodré to Alcântara Mar, then follow *maritima* signs, turning right to Doca de Santo Amaro; or catch tram 15 from Praça da Figueira.

Doca de Santo (Map p89; ☎ 213 963 535; Doca de Santo Amaro) This is clatteringly large, but with style and lots of open-air, leafy seating – a glamorous yet relaxed place to settle with a cocktail. Serves good salads (among other things).

Op Art Café (Map p89; Doca de Santo Amaro) On the water's edge, this slightly hidden spot attracts a better crowd than other Docas joints. On Saturday nights you'll also find some decent music with DJs spinning until dawn.

Café In (Map pp84-5; Avenida de Brasilia, Pavilhão Nascente 311) About 1km west of Doca de Santo Amaro, Café In offers good views of the bridge from either the riverside terrace or the all-glass bar inside. DJs spin ambient tunes for a fairly well-dressed crowd.

ENTERTAINMENT

Despite its diminutive size, Lisbon has a lot going on: dance parties, classical concerts, ballet, theatre, opera, live bands and, of course, *fado*, the Portuguese blues.

For details of events during your stay, grab a copy of the monthly *Follow Me Lisboa* (free) from a turismo. In Portuguese, the free monthly **Agenda Cultural Lisboa** (www.lisboacultural.pt) includes details of performances and screenings; cinema listings can also be found in the daily *Diário de Notícias*. Tickets are available from the following outlets:

ABEP Ticket Agency (Map pp86-7; ☎ 213 475 824; Praça dos Restauradores)

Fnac Greater Lisbon (Map pp84-5; ☎ 217 114 237; Centro Comercial Colombo); Baixa Chiado (Map pp86-7; ☎ 213 221 800; Armazéns do Chiado, Rua do Carmo 3)

Ticket Line (☎ 210 036 300; www.ticketline.pt)

Nightclubs

Lisbon's wide-ranging club scene offers a little something for everyone – from smoky, hole-in-the-wall dance bars to brash-and-sexy discos as well as some of Europe's most exciting African clubs.

Most venues charge admission (particularly on weekends – around €5 to €20, which includes a drink or two), and some operate a card-stamping system to ensure you spend a minimum amount.

Opening hours vary but most places won't get going before 2am or 3am. The music dies when people leave – any time between 4am and 10am.

BAIRRO ALTO

Capela (Map pp86-7; Rua da Atalaia 45) This atmospheric former chapel hosts experimental electronica and occasional house. Get there early (before midnight) to appreciate the DJs before the crowds descend.

Frágil (Map pp86-7; Rua da Atalaia 126) Granddaddy to the Lisbon nightclub scene, this is not the happening place it once was, but Frágil can be fun, with a small dance floor and a relaxed, mixed gay-straight crowd. At weekends it's mainly house; weekdays, you're at the DJ's mercy.

A Lontra (Map p89; Rua de São Bento 155) Near Bairro Alto, A Lontra hosts an eclectic, mainly African-Portuguese clientele bumping and grinding to African sounds, R&B, hip-hop and house. It fills up about 3am and stays open late.

ALFAMA

Última Sé (Map pp86-7; www.ultima-se.com; Travessa da Almargem 1) Hidden behind the Casa dos Bicos, Última Sé is an atmospheric place with old arched stone walls and a fun crowd. It features nights of world beats and reggae.

PRÍNCIPE REAL & SÃO BENTO

Hot Clube de Portugal (Map pp86-7; www.hcp.pt; Praça da Algeria 39; 🕙 10pm-2am Tue-Sat) Here the masters play you jazz in a small, smoky setting, just the way it should be. Shows are at 11pm and 12.30am.

our pick **Lux** (Map pp84-5; ☎ 218 820 890; Avenida Infante Dom Henrique) Near Santa Apolónia train station is Lisbon's ice-cool, must-see club. Run by ex-Frágil maestro Marcel Reis and part-owned by John Malkovich, it's lots of fun, with an oversized shoe, a mirrored tunnel and violet light setting the scene. It's huge and airy, special but not snooty, and hosts the best big-name house DJs and live acts. Weekends are less hip but the music is still tip-top. Lux-style policing is heartwarmingly lax but get here after 4am on a Friday or Saturday and you might have trouble getting in because of the crowds.

DOCAS & ALCÂNTARA

Buddha Bar (Map p89; www.buddha.com.pt; Gare Maritima de Alcântara, Doca de Santo Amaro) This big multilevel club is the best of the bunch out in Docas. Buddha statues and other Near Eastern props (red lanterns, gauzy curtains, fountains) decorate the space. Good DJs, a fun dance-happy crowd and that breezy outdoor terrace with bridge views makes it rather worthwhile.

Luanda (Map p89; Travessa Teixeira Júnior 6) This is a big, African club and Lisbon's favourite booty shaker, with a fantastically steamy, glitzy atmosphere. Things get hot and sweaty around 3am, when everyone hits the floor for Luandan *kuduro*, Brazilian or R&B music.

Mussulo (Map p89; Rua Sousa Martins 5d, Estefânia) If you like Luanda, try this place as well.

Dock's Club (Map p89; Rua Cintura do Porto) This is another people-packed place, with mirrors and glitterballs, pop hits and dudes looking to score.

Belém Bar Café (Map pp84-5; www.belembarcafé.com; Avenida Brasília, Pavilhão Poente) About 1.5km west of the Docas mayhem, this slinky riverside spot brings a well-dressed and strait-laced crowd, with DJs spinning a mix of house, hip-hop and R&B.

Blues Café (Map p89; Rua Cintura do Porto) One of the most popular on the strip, this is a happening place, playing mainstream pop, R&B and hip-hop.

Incógnito (Map p89; Rua Poiais de São Bento 37) At this small, attractive dance-bar you'll find a good mixed crowd and a broad spectrum of music – electropop, rock and a little something for those stuck in the '80s. It's a nice alternative to the big club scene.

CAIS DO SODRÉ & AVENIDA 24 DE JULHO

Kapital (Map p89; Avenida 24 de Julho 68) For young, wealthy Lisboêtas (blazers, V-necks, big hair on the men; oh-so-casual glam on the women), this is nightclub nirvana. Expect a door policy, chrome, people so cool they're almost frozen and matching music. If it feels too much like a 1980s teen movie, there's an adjoining tunnel to next-door Kremlin.

Kremlin (Map p89; Escadinhas da Praia 5) Lisbon's home of house doesn't really heat up until around 3am. These days it's generally only packed on weekends with upwardly mobile Lisboêtas keen to dance at this legendary club. While it's a far cry from the heady days of the Summer of Love in '88, it can still transcend.

Discoteca Jamaica (Map pp86-7; Rua Nova do Carvalho 8; 11pm-4am or 6am) At most of the clubs on this seedy street, dancing involves laps, but this is a gem. Everyone in the know (gay/straight, black/white, old/young) has a great affection for offbeat Jamaica, where weekends get busy with a mixture of mostly retro and reggae.

Fado

Bairro Alto and Alfama are where the dark melancholy of *fado* was born, and there are many places where you can indulge in a bit of dignified solemnity. Backed by the bright-toned 12-string Portuguese guitar, with Arabic influences that make it resemble flamenco, *fado*'s fun-packed themes are love, *saudade* (p40), destiny, death, bullfighting, social injustice and *fado* itself. If it's *fado vadio* (open *fado*), anyone can get up and sing. Most places cater heavily to tourists, but this means they often host the finest singers – although counterbalanced by the often overpriced, mediocre food and phoney feel. However, a *fado* concert depends entirely on the night in question – one night a singer might create an electric, tangible atmosphere, the next night, with the same ingredients, it can feel entirely different.

Following is a smattering of *fado* venues in the city. It's a good idea to make a reservation, especially at weekends. Most places require you to spend a minimum amount, which will include the cost of the *fado*, and many empty out by midnight. For more on *fado*, see p47.

BAIRRO ALTO

Adega Machado (Map pp86-7; 213 224 640; Rua do Norte 91; minimum €16; 8.30pm-3am Tue-Sun) Filipe de Arajo Machado runs this place, started by his *fadista* mother and father. Clientele is largely groups, but there is a good and lively atmosphere.

Adega do Ribatejo (Map pp86-7; 213 468 343; Rua Diário de Notícias 23; minimum €15; 8.30pm-12.30am Mon-Sat) This small place has some professionals and some amateurs, who can be very good.

Adega Mesquita (Map pp86-7; 213 219 280, Rua Diário de Notícias 107; minimum €15; 9pm-1am) A long-established *fado* house, Mesquita hosts singers and folk dancers.

Nono (Map pp86-7; 213 429 989; Rua do Norte 47; minimum €10, tourist menu & cover €27.50, dishes €9-16; 9pm-2.30am Mon-Sat) Smaller and less formal, Nono has more of a local atmosphere.

GAY & LESBIAN LISBON

Take a look at www.portugalgay.pt for more pink listings.

Bars

While no longer in the closet, gay and lesbian venues remain discreet; ring the bell.

Bar 106 (Map p89; www.bar106.com; Rua de São Marçal 106) Stylish and popular, Bar 106 packs crowds on weekends.

Bar Água No Bico (Map p89; Rua de São Marçal 170) A cheerful place with rotating art exhibitions.

Bric-a-Bar (Map p89; Rua Cecilio de Sousa 82-84) Cruisy, with a dark room, but often empty.

Max (Map p89; Rua da São Marçal 15) Attracting a somewhat older crowd, Max hosts strip shows, a leather night and other weekly fests.

Sétimo Ceu (Map pp86-7; Travessa da Espera 54) An old-school bar that's still one of the most popular gay drinking spots in town.

Side Bar (Map pp86-7; Rua da Barroca 33) Next door to Sétimo Ceu, this fun, tiny place is also worth checking out. It's a mixed bar run by the same owner.

Clubs

Finalmente (Map p89; Rua da Palmeira 38) This fun, absurdly popular place has a tiny dance floor, nightly drag shows and wall-to-wall crowds.

Memorial (Map p89; Rua Gustavo de Matos Sequeira 42a) Mainly lesbian, this laid-back place attracts a mixed crowd, often men looking for women.

Trumps (Map p89; www.trumps.pt; Rua da Imprensa Nacional 104b) Lisbon's premier gay club boasts two bars and a sizable dance floor. This is the place to dance.

Organisations & Events

Gay Pride Festival is in June, and the Festival de Cinema Gay e Lésbico is in late September.

Associação Opus Gay (Map p90; ☎ 213 151 396, after hours 962 400 017; opus@opusgayassociation.com; 2nd fl, Rua da Ilha Terceira 34; 5-8pm Wed-Sat;) Also has a visitors centre, including internet café.

Centro Comunitário Gay e Lésbico de Lisboa (Lisbon Gay & Lesbian Community Centre; Map pp86-7; ☎ 218 873 918; ilga-portugal@ilga.org; Rua de São Lazaro 88; 4-8pm Mon-Sat Sep-Jul;) Has a café, library, internet and counselling facilities.

Grupo de Mulheres (Women's Group; ☎ /fax 218 873 918; gmulheres@yahoo.com) Part of ILGA-Portugal, it organises regular social gatherings and lesbian film screenings.

ALFAMA

A Baîuca (Map pp86-7; ☎ 218 867 284; Rua de São Miguel 20; dishes €10-13) This is a special place with *fado vadio,* when anyone can take a turn. On a good night A Baîuca is packed with locals, with spectators hissing if anyone dares make a noise during the singing. The food is simple and tasty; the *fado* performance goes on until midnight, and the food stops around 10pm. Reserve ahead.

Clube de Fado (Map pp86-7; ☎ 218 852 704; Rua de São João da Praça; dishes €12-18, minimum €10; 9pm-2.30am Mon-Sat) Overpriced, with mediocre food and a touristy feel, Clube de Fado hosts some fine artists in an arched, colonnaded hall. It's popular with groups.

Mesa de Frades (Map pp86-7; ☎ 218 871 452; Rua dos Remédios 139a; dishes €13-16; dinner Tue-Sun) One of the Alfama district's magical settings for hearing *fado,* this tiny old-fashioned spot is decorated with lovely tiled murals and has just a handful of tables. Hearty traditional meals are made with care. Reservations are recommended.

Parreirinha de Alfama (Map pp86-7; ☎ 218 868 209; Beco do Espírito Santo 1; minimum €15; 8pm-3am) Another local favourite, this place offers good food and ambience; it seems to attract an audience that often falls hard for the top-quality *fadistas.*

LAPA

Senhor Vinho (Map p89; ☎ 213 972 681; www.restsrvinho.com; Rua do Meio á Lapa; minimum €15; 8pm-2am) Small, with good singers, this place has a dramatic atmosphere.

Cinema

For blockbusters try the multiplexes in **Complexo das Amoreiras** (Map p90; ☎ 213 810 200; opposite), **Centro Comercial Colombo** (Map pp84-5; ☎ 217 113 222; opposite) and **Centro Vasco da Gama** (Map pp84-5; ☎ 218 922 280) malls. More-traditional cinemas are the grand **São Jorge** (Map p90; ☎ 213 579 144; Avenida da Liberdade 175) and, just around the corner, **Instituto do Cinemateca Portuguesa** (Museu do Cinema; Map p90; ☎ 213 596 200; www.cinemateca.pt; Rua Barata Salgueiro 39), which shows offbeat, art-house, world and old films. French films are screened at the **Institut Franco-Portuguais** (Map p90; ☎ 213 111 427; Avenida Luís Bívar 91).

For details of screen times and venues, visit www.7arte.net.

Theatre

Teatro Nacional de Dona Maria II (Map pp86-7; ☎ 213 250 827; Rossio) Underfunding means the impressive national theatre has a somewhat hit-and-miss schedule. There's a charming café on site.

Teatro Nacional de São Carlos (Map pp86-7; ☎ 213 253 045; www.saocarlos.pt; Rua Serpa Pinto 9) Worth visiting just to see the wonderful gold-and-red interior, this theatre has opera, ballet and theatre seasons. There's an excellent terrace restaurant attached.

Teatro Municipal de São Luís (Map pp86-7; ☎ 213 257 640; Rua António Maria Cardosa 38) This venue stages opera, ballet and theatre.

Teatro Taborda (Map pp86-7; ☎ 218 854 190; Costa do Castelo 75; 💻) This cultural centre shows contemporary dance, theatre and world music. It also has spectacular views and an excellent restaurant.

Teatro da Trindade (Map pp86-7; ☎ 213 420 000; Rua Nova da Trindade 9) Bairro Alto's early-20th-century gem stages an assortment of national and foreign productions.

Chapitô (Map pp86-7; ☎ 218 855 550; www.chapito.org; Costa do Castelo 1-7; 💻) Chapitô offers original physical theatre performances, with a theatre school attached. There's a jazz café downstairs with dentist-chair décor, with live music Thursday to Saturday. Like Teatro Taborda, come here for spectacular views and an excellent restaurant.

Music & Dance

Pavilhão Atlântico (Map pp84-5; ☎ 218 918 409; www.atlantico-multiusos.pt; Parque das Nações) International acts, from Moby to Madonna, play here, Portugal's largest indoor arena.

Paradise Garage (Map p89; ☎ 213 243 400; www.paradisegarage.com; Rua João Oliveira Miguens 38-48) This is one of Lisbon's chief small venues for bands, festivals and club nights.

Excellent classical concerts and ballets are held at Fundação Calouste Gulbenkian's three **concert halls** (Map p90; ☎ 217 935 131; www.musica.gulbenkian.pt; Avenida de Berna) or the **Centro Cultural de Belém** (CCB; Map p91; ☎ 213 612 444; www.ccb.pt; Praça do Império, Belém) and the **Coliseu dos Recreios** (Map pp86-7; ☎ 213 240 580; Rua das Portas de Santo Antão 92). The CCB and the Coliseu dos Recreios also host bands and dance events.

A versatile exhibition venue is **Culturgest** (Map p90; ☎ 217 905 155; Rua do Arco do Cego).

Sport

FOOTBALL

Of Portugal's 'big three' clubs, two – SL Benfica (Sport Lisboa e Benfica) and Sporting (Sporting Club de Portugal) – are based in Lisbon. They've been rivals ever since Sporting beat Benfica 2–1 in 1907.

The season runs from September to mid-June, with most league matches on Sunday; check the papers (especially *Bola,* the daily football paper) or ask at the turismo. Tickets cost €20 to €55 and are sold at the stadium on match day or, for higher prices, at the **ABEP ticket agency** (Map pp86-7; ☎ 213 475 824; Praça dos Restauradores).

Estádio da Luz (Map pp84-5; ☎ 217 219 555; www.slbenfica.pt) SL Benfica plays at this 65,000-seat stadium in the northwestern Benfica district. Euro 2004's big games were played here. The nearest metro station is Colégio Militar-Luz.

Estádio Nacional (☎ 214 197 212; Cruz Quebrada) Hosts the national Taça de Portugal (Portugal Cup) each May. Take the train from Cais do Sodré.

Pavilhão Atlântico (Map pp84-5; ☎ 218 918 409; www.atlantico-multiusos.pt; Parque das Nações) Major sporting events are held at this park.

Estádio José de Alvalade (Map pp84-5; ☎ 217 514 069; metro Campo Grande) Sporting's attractive new stadium (which hosted Euro 2004 matches) seats 54,000 and is just north of the university. Take the metro or bus 1 or 36 from Rossio.

BULLFIGHTING

Lisbon's grand **Praça de Touros** (bullring; Map p90; ☎ 217 932 442; Avenida da República; tickets €15-60), near Campo Pequeno metro, reopened in 2006 following six years of restoration. The red-brick Moorish-style arena sees action from

May to October, with fights usually held on Thursday or Sunday. Tickets are sold outside the bullring, or at higher prices from the **ABEP ticket agency** (Map pp86-7; ☎ 213 475 824; Praça dos Restauradores).

MARATHON RUNNING

Lisbon hosts an international **marathon** (☎ 213 616 160; www.lisbon-marathon.com) in December, with a half-marathon as well, starting and finishing at Praça do Comércio. Around March another half-marathon, the **Meia Maratona Cidade de Lisboa**, starts from Almada with around 35,000 runners crossing the Ponte 25 de Abril, finishing in Belém; contact the **Federação Portuguese de Atletismo** (☎ 214 146 020; www.fpatletismo.pt) for details.

SHOPPING

Shopping in Lisbon is wildly diverse, with charming stuck-in-time shops dealing exclusively in hats, buttons or canned fish, but also the brilliant, funky boutiques of Bairro Alto – which often open around 4pm and stay open until midnight, with DJs to blur the nightlife/shopping distinction further.

Shopaholics may like to take advantage of the Lisboa Shopping Card, which offers discounts of 5% to 20% in more than 200 selected stores. It costs €3.70/5.80 for 24-/72-hour versions, and is available at Turismos de Lisboa.

If you're after a huge shopping mall, try the following:

Atrium Saldanha (Map p90; Praça Duque de Saldanha) Swanky.

Centro Comercial Colombo (Map pp84-5; Avenida Colégio Militar) Colossal.

Centro Vasco da Gama (Map pp84-5) Near Gare do Oriente, at Parque das Nações.

Complexo das Amoreiras (Map p90; Avenida Engenheiro Duarte Pacheco) Modernist. To get here, take bus 11 from Praça do Comércio.

El Corte Inglês (Map p90; Avenida António Augusto de Aguiar 31) Massive and Spanish.

Galerias Monumental (Map p90; Praça Duque de Saldanha)

Colourful street markets are among the best places to browse for buried treasure. One of the city's biggest weekly markets is the **Feira da Ladra** (Thieves Market; Map pp86-7; 🕑 8am-5pm Sat & 8am-noon Tue), which spreads riotously across Campo de Santa Clara, and has antiques, clothes, shoes, records and indecipherable junk.

Azulejos & Ceramics

Fábrica Sant'Ana (Map pp86-7; ☎ 213 638 292; Rua do Alecrim 95) One of Lisbon's finest *azulejo* factories and showrooms, this place sells wonderful elaborate tiles, as well as cherubs and candlesticks.

Cerâmica Viúva Lamego (Map pp84-5; ☎ 218 852 408; www.viuvalamego.com; Largo do Intendente Pina Manique 25) Another good showroom for *azulejos* (including made-to-order items) and other ceramic ware.

Olaria do Desterros (Map pp84-5; ☎ 218 850 329; Rua Nova do Desterro 14) This family-run pottery factory is a few blocks west of Cerâmica Viúva Lamego. The factory (there's no obvious showroom) is at entry F in an alley, seemingly within the grounds of the Hospital do Desterro.

Museu Nacional do Azulejo (National Tile Museum; Map pp84-5; ☎ 218 100 340; Rua Madre de Deus 4) *Azulejos* central also sells a few *azulejo* souvenirs.

Vista Alegre (Map pp86-7; ☎ 213 461 401; Largo do Chiado 20) The most famous name in ceramics. Their finely crafted products can be found at a number of Lisbon stores.

Arte Rústica (Map pp86-7; ☎ 213 421 127; Rua d'Áurea 246) This place has an excellent range of more-rustic ceramics.

Clothes & Jewellery

Bairro Alto is home to a concentration of über-cool boutiques selling retro-inspired clothes, unusual local design and Brazilian imports. Good places to start are the Rua do Norte and Rua da Rosa. Many of the shops here open around 4pm and stay open until midnight.

Sneakers Delight (Map pp86-7; ☎ 213 479 976; Rua do Norte 30) Here trainers are treated with the reverence they nearly deserve. DJs spin on weekends.

Outra Face da Lua (Map pp86-7; ☎ 218 863 430; Rua da Assunção 22) This former Bairro Alto outpost is blazing new trails in Baixa, hoping to entice hipsters down the hill with its rambling collection of vintage clothes and wallpapers, kitschy old toys and fashion pieces from young designers. There's also an in-store coffee shop and jazz or electronica playing overhead.

Carla Amaro (Map p89; ☎ 213 474 043; Rua Cecílio de Sousa 72; 🕑 11am-7pm Tue-Fri, 3-7pm Sat) This tiny jewellery shop sells a colourful mix of whimsy and elegance, all handcrafted by Portuguese designer Amaro.

Handicrafts, Textiles & Canned Goods

Santos Ofícios (Map pp86-7; ☎ 218 872 031; Rua da Madalena 87) A fascinating, chichi *artesanato* (handicrafts shop), stocking an eclectic range of folk art from all around Portugal. This street is a good one for browsing for knick-knacks.

Nós por Cá (Map pp86-7; Rua da Madelan 76) Near Santos Ofícios, this spot sells vintage post-cards, old-fashioned toys and aromatic soaps.

Madeira House (Map pp86-7; ☎ 213 426 813; Rua Augusta 131) At this shop you'll find hand-embroidered linen from its most famous source, Madeira.

Mercado da Ribeira (Map pp86-7; ☎ 210 312 600; Ave 24 de Julho; 🕒 10am-11pm Mon-Sat, 7.30am-2pm Sun) On the 1st floor of the central food market, the Centro de Artesanato sells high-quality handicrafts and has demonstrations about artisanal products and regional cuisine. The ground floor retains the flower and food market, and on Sundays there's a collectors' market (9am to 1pm).

Conserveira de Lisboa (Map pp86-7; ☎ 218 871 058; Rua dos Bacalhoeiros 34) Canned fish may not be the first souvenir you were thinking of taking home, but this is a brilliant place to shop, with piles of cans in retro wrappings, a monstrous old till and elderly ladies wrapping up your purchases in brown paper.

Music

Valentim de Carvalho Megastore (Map pp86-7; ☎ 213 241 570; Rua do Carmo) Lisbon's longest-established music store.

Fnac (Map pp86-7; ☎ 213 221 800; Rua Nova do Almada 110) Fnac also sells a vast array of music and audiovisual gear.

Discoteca Amália (Map pp86-7; ☎ 213 421 485; Rua de Áurea 272) Specialises in *fado* and cheap classical CDs.

Enticing vinyl and CD shops lie in and around Bairro Alto, like **Discolecção** (Map pp86-7; Calçada do Duque 53).

Wine

Portuguese wine is excellent value. In most supermarkets you can buy something decent for as little as €4 a bottle.

If you prefer port, there are dozens of wine shops, including **Napoleão** (Map pp86-7; ☎ 218 861 108; Rua dos Fanqueiros 70) or **Manuel Tavares** (Map pp86-7; ☎ 213 424 209; Rua da Betesga 1a). Staff here can also offer recommendations.

GETTING THERE & AWAY

Air

Aeroporto de Lisboa (Aeroporto da Portela; ☎ flight information 218 413 700) is about 4km northeast of the centre.

Portugália and TAP both have multiple daily flights to Lisbon from Porto and Faro, and more than 20 carriers operate scheduled international services (p467).

Boat

The **Transtejo ferry line** (www.transtejo.pt) has several riverfront terminals. From the eastern end of the Terreiro do Paço terminal (Map pp86–7), swanky catamarans zip across the Tejo to Montijo (€1.90, 30 minutes) and Seixal (€1.55, 30 minutes, half-hourly weekdays, every hour or so weekends). From the main part of the terminal, called Estação do Sul e Sueste, Soflusa ferries run very frequently to Barreiro (€0.75, 30 minutes), for rail connections to the Alentejo and Algarve. From Cais do Sodré, passenger ferries go to Cacilhas (€0.70, 10 minutes, every 10 minutes all day). Car (and bicycle) ferries also go from Cais do Sodré to Cacilhas.

From Belém, ferries depart for Trafaria and Porto Brandão (€0.75, every 30 to 60 minutes), about 3.5km and 5km respectively from Costa da Caparica town.

Bus

Lisbon's new long-distance bus terminal is **Sete Rios** (Map p90; Rua das Laranjeiras), conveniently linked to both Jardim Zoológico metro station and Sete Rios train station. From here the big carriers, **Rede Expressos** (☎ 24hr 707 223 344; www.rede-expressos.pt) and **Eva/Mundial Turismo** (☎ 213 147 710; www.eva-bus.com), run frequent services to almost every major town. Destinations with 10 or more services a day include Coimbra (€10.80, 2½ hours), Évora (€9.80, 1¾ hours), Porto (€13.50, 3½ to four hours) and Faro (€15, 4½ to five hours). You can buy your ticket up to seven days in advance.

The other major terminal is **Gare do Oriente** (Map pp84–5), concentrating on services to the north and to Spain. On the 1st floor of this architectural stunner are bus company booths (mostly open 9am to 5.30pm Monday to Saturday, to 7pm Friday, closed lunch; smaller operators only open just before arrival or departure). At weekends you may have to buy your ticket on the bus, though it's wise to phone ahead. The biggest companies operating from here are **Renex** (☎ 218 956 836) and the Spanish operator **Auto-Res** (☎ 218 940 250; www.auto-res.net).

Many Renex buses take passengers 20 minutes early at Campo das Cebolas in Alfama, before Gare do Oriente.

Several regional companies with destinations in the north include **Mafrense** (www.mafrense.pt; for Ericeira & Mafra), **Barraqueiro Oeste** (www.barraqueiro-oeste.pt; for Malveira & Torres Vedras) and **Rodoviária do Tejo** (www.rodotejo.pt; for Peniche). These companies operate from **Terminal Campo Grande** (☎ 217 582 212) outside Campo Grande metro station.

Buses to Sesimbra and Costa da Caparica go from a terminal (Map p90) at Sete Rios bus station.

Eurolines (Map pp84-5; ☎ 218 957 398; www.eurolinesportugal.com; Loja 203, Gare do Oriente; 9.30am-1pm & 2-6.30pm Mon-Fri, 9am-1pm & 2-4pm Sat) runs coaches to destinations all over Europe, with all coaches serving both Sete Rios and Gare do Oriente. You can also go to many European cities from Sete Rios with Eurolines affiliate **Intercentro** (Map p90; ☎ 213 571 745; Rua Engenheiro Vieira Silva 55).

Information and tickets for international departures are scarce at weekends, so try to avoid that last-minute Sunday dash out of Portugal.

Car & Motorcycle

The nearest place to rent a motorbike is Cascais (see p141). The big-name car-hire companies are all on hand, though you can often save substantially by booking local agencies. Most agencies offer pick-up and delivery service to your hotel.

Autojardim (☎ 800 200 613; www.auto-jardim.com; from €26 per day)
Avis (☎ 800 201 002; www.avis.com.pt)
Europcar (☎ 219 407 790; www.europcar.pt)
Hertz (☎ 219 426 300; www.hertz.com)
Holidays Car (☎ 217 150 610; www.holidayscar.com; from €22 per day)
Sixt (☎ 218 407 927; www.e-sixt.com)

Train

Lisbon is linked by train to other major cities. See p477 for domestic services and p470 for international services. Check www.cp.pt for schedules. Some sample 2nd-class direct journeys to/from Lisbon are below. The abbreviations relate to international train services (IN) and express services (*intercidade*; IC).

Destination	Service	Price (€)	Duration (hr)	Frequency (per day)
Coimbra	Alfa	20.50	2	8
	IC/IN	15	2¼	6
Faro	Alfa	19.50	3	1
	IC	18	3¾	3
Porto C	Alfa	24	3	8
	IC	19.50	3½	4

Lisbon has several major train stations, plus some smaller ones. **Santa Apolónia** (Map pp84–5) is the terminal for trains from northern and central Portugal. It has a helpful **information desk** (☎ 808 208 208; 7.30am-9pm) at door 8. The international section at door 47 includes an international ticket desk, bank, ATM and cash-exchange machine, snack bar, car-rental agencies and a **Turismo de Lisboa desk** (10am-6pm). Left-luggage lockers are nearby.

All of Santa Apolónia's services also stop at the **Gare do Oriente** (Map pp84–5). All trains to the Algarve and to international destinations depart from here. Ticket booths are on the 1st floor (platforms are on the 2nd) and car-rental offices, banks and shops are at street level. Left-luggage lockers are on the basement metro level.

The other major terminal is at **Sete Rios** (Map pp84–5), which is connected to the Jardim Zoológico metro station; it serves the northern suburbs, including Sintra and Queluz.

Most services (including that from Sintra) continue on to **Entrecampos** (Avenida 5 de Outubro). Either of these stations provide services (on Fertagus trains; www.fertagus.pt) across the Ponte 25 de Abril to Setúbal, among other destinations.

Cais do Sodré (Map pp84–5) is the terminal for train service to Cascais and Estoril.

GETTING AROUND

To/From the Airport

The AeroBus (bus 91) departs from outside Arrivals (€3, 30 to 45 minutes, roughly every 20 minutes from 7.45am to 9pm). It goes via Marquês Pombal, Avenida Liberdade, Restauradores, Rossio and Praça do Comércio to Cais do Sodré. You get a Bilhete Turístico, which gives free passage on all city buses, trams and funiculars for the rest of the day. Passengers with a TAP boarding pass get a free ticket.

Local buses 44 and 45 also run from the centre but they're bad news in rush hour if you have baggage.

If you're arriving by train just to get to the airport, the quickest option is bus 44 from Gare do Oriente (with Vasco da Gama shopping centre behind you, the stop is under the station's arches to the left).

Taxi rip-offs can occur on the airport-to-city route. You can buy a prepaid Táxi Voucher from the Turismo de Lisboa desk in Arrivals at set prices for specific destinations (eg most of central Lisbon costs about €15/18 per day/night and weekends). Only taxis involved in the scheme – marked with a coloured sticker – will accept the vouchers.

With nonvoucher taxis, expect to pay about €10 to the city centre, plus €1.60 if your luggage needs to be placed in the boot. Avoid long queues by flagging down a taxi at Departures.

Car & Motorcycle

Lisbon can be quite stressful to drive around, thanks to heavy traffic, maverick drivers, narrow one-way streets and tram lines, but the city is at least small. If you're used to driving in other European capitals you probably won't find it too problematic. There are two ring roads, both useful for staying out of the centre: the inner Cintura Regional Interna de Lisboa (CRIL); and the outer Cintura Regional Externa de Lisboa (CREL).

Once in the centre, parking is the main issue. Spaces are scarce, parking regulations complex, pay-and-display machines often broken and car-park rates expensive (about €10 to €12 per day). On Saturday afternoon and Sunday parking is normally free.

Upmarket hotels usually have their own garages. If you need to park for more than a few days, there are cheaper car parks near Parque das Nações (metro Gare do Oriente – the multistorey here costs around €5 per day) or Belém (free car parks), then catch a bus or tram to the centre. Always lock up and don't leave any valuables inside or anything visible, even if it's worthless, as theft is a risk.

Bicycle

Traffic, trams, hills, cobbles and disgruntled drivers equal a cycling nightmare. You're better off stashing your bike with the left-luggage office at the bus station or airport and seeing the city by public transport. Better hotels and *pensões* may have a storage room. On the Lisbon–Sintra train you can take your bike for free on weekends or for €2.50 return on weekdays (only outside the rush hour).

There are two pleasant places to ride a bike in Lisbon: Parque das Nações, where you can rent from **Tejo Bike** (Map pp84–5); and a 5km stretch on the Rio Tejo promenade, from 1km west of Doca de Santo Amaro to Belém and Praia d'Algés. Here you will find a bike stall run by **Tejo Bike** (Map pp84-5; 10am-8pm Jun-Sep, 10am-7pm Sat & Sun Oct-May).

Public Transport

BUS, TRAM & FUNICULAR

Companhia Carris de Ferro de Lisboa (Carris; ☎ 213 613 054; www.carris.pt) operates all transport except the metro. Its buses and trams run from about 5am or 6am to 1am; there are some night bus and tram services.

You can get a transport map, *Planta dos Transportes Públicas da Carris* (including a map of night-time services) from turismos or from Carris kiosks, which are dotted around the city. The Carris website has timetables and route details.

Individual tickets cost €1.20 on board or €0.75 if you buy a Bilhete Único de Coroa (BUC; a one-zone city-centre ticket) beforehand. These prepaid tickets are sold at Carris kiosks – most conveniently at Praça da Figueira, at the foot of the Elevador de Santa Justa, and at Santa Apolónia and Cais do Sodré train stations.

The Carris kiosks also sell a one-/five-day (€3.30/13.20) Bilhete Carris/Metro valid for buses, trams, funiculars *and* the metro.

These passes aren't great bargains unless you're planning a lot of travel outside the centre. A better deal is the Lisboa Card (p95), good for most tourist sights as well as bus, tram, funicular and metro travel.

Don't leave the city without riding tram 28 from Largo Martim Moniz or tram 12 from Praça da Figueira through the narrow streets of the Alfama.

Two other useful lines are tram 15 from Praça da Figueira and Praça do Comércio via Alcântara to Belém, and tram 18 from Praça do Comércio via Alcântara to Ajuda. Tram 15 features space-age articulated trams with on-board machines for buying tickets and passes. Tram stops are marked by a small yellow *paragem* (stop) sign hanging from a lamppost or the overhead wires.

METRO

The expanding **metropolitano** (underground; www.metrolisboa.pt; 1-zone single/return €0.70/1.30, 2-zone single €1, 1-/2-zone caderneta €6.65/9.85; 6.30-1am) system is useful for short hops and to reach the Gare do Oriente and nearby Parque das Nações.

Buy tickets from metro ticket offices or machines. Lisboa Cards (p95) are also valid. Buy a *caderneta* (10-ticket booklet) if you'll be using the metro often.

Entrances are marked by a big red 'M'. Useful signs include *correspondência* (transfer between lines) and *saída* (exit to the street). There is an impressive array of contemporary art at various stations, for example, Angelo de Sousa at Baixa-Chiado, and various artists including Hundertwasser at Oriente.

Watch out for pickpockets in rush-hour crowds.

Taxi

Lisbon's *táxis* are reasonable and plentiful. If you have trouble hailing one, try the ranks at Rossio, Praça dos Restauradores, near all stations and ferry terminals, and at top-end hotels. To call one, try **Rádio Táxis de Lisboa** (☎ 218 119 000) or **Autocoope** (☎ 217 932 756).

All taxis have meters, but rip-offs occasionally occur (the airport route is the main culprit). If you think you've been cheated, get a receipt from the driver (and note the car's registration number and your time of departure and arrival) and talk to the tourist police.

For more information about taxis and taxi fares, see p475.

AROUND LISBON

Just outside of Lisbon, the city unfolds into rolling hillsides, untainted beaches and quaint villages that seem several centuries removed from the urban hustle of the capital. The star attraction here is Sintra, with its enchanting castles set against a lush, mountainous backdrop. Northwest of there, the 18th-century palace of Mafra, handcrafted by thousands of artisans, provides an even more extreme version of royal decadence.

During the summer, Lisboêtas head south to the lovely sands lining the Costa da Caparica. Further south, seafood-lovers can get their fix at active fishing towns like Setúbal or sleepy Sesimbra. Natural parks near Setúbal offer a glimpse of coastal beauty, as do rugged capes near the city, such as Cabo Espichel and Cabo da Roca.

Even closer to Lisbon is the western stretch of coast leading out to Cascais, with attractive beaches, and ample guesthouses and dining options.

SINTRA

pop 26,400 / elevation 280m

With richly hued palaces, mist-covered forests and the ruins of a craggy Moorish castle overlooking a sleepy village, Sintra is like a page torn from a fairy tale. Not surprisingly, it's long been a favourite with out-of-towners. The Portuguese royals summered here, as did the Moors before them, and it was one of the few places in Portugal that Lord Byron liked, inspiring his travel epic *Childe Harold's Pilgrimage* ('Lo! Cintra's glorious Eden intervenes, in variegated maze of mount and glen').

Sintra makes a marvellous getaway. Its exceptional microclimate encourages exotic vegetation, and you can undertake some pleasant walks through the countryside, either clambering beneath turrets guarded by gargoyles or investigating a cork-lined monastery deep in the woods.

In addition to its bizarre and beautiful palaces, mansions and finely manicured gardens, Sintra boasts a historic centre that's listed as a Unesco World Heritage site. The early Iberians made it a site of cult worship; the Moors built the castle; the Middle Ages brought monasteries; the nobility bolted here after the 1755 earthquake; then, in the 19th century, it became one of the first centres of European romantic architecture.

Even if you're only in Lisbon for the weekend, it's worth making the short journey up to Sintra, if not for an overnight, at least for the day.

Orientation

There are four parts to Sintra: the historic centre (Centro Histórico) is called **Sintra-Vila** or Vila Velha ('old town'); the new-town district of **Estefânia**, where the railway terminates, lies 1.5km northeast; modern **Portela de Sintra**, 1km east of Estefânia is where you'll find Sintra's bus station, Portela Interface (beside the Portela de Sintra train station); and tiny **São Pedro de Penaferrim** slumbers 2km southeast of Sintra-Vila.

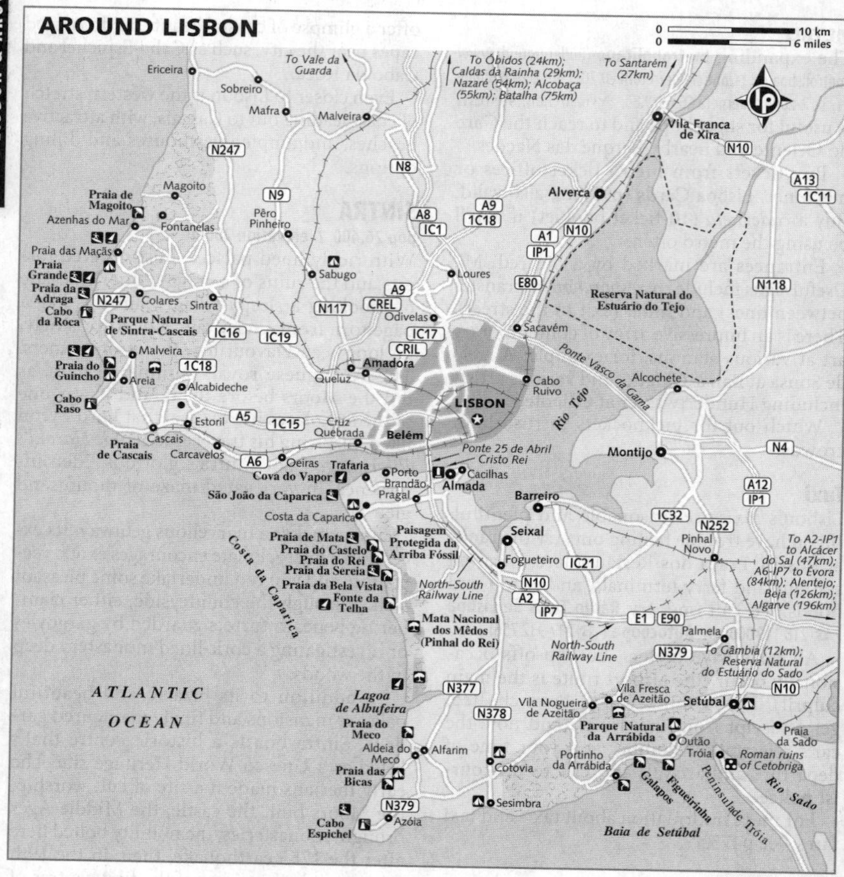

The Parque Natural de Sintra-Cascais encompasses both the Serra de Sintra and nearby coastal attractions, including Cabo da Roca, Europe's most westerly point.

Information

EMERGENCY

Police station (Map p132; ☎ 219 230 761; Rua João de Deus 6)

MEDICAL SERVICES

Centro de saúde (medical centre; Map p132; ☎ 219 106 680; Rua Dr Alfredo Costa 34)

MONEY

There's an ATM in the turismo building, or try the following banks (with ATMs):

Montepio Geral (Map p130; ☎ 214 248 000; Avenida Heliodoro Salgado 42)

Totta (Map p132; Rua das Padarias 2)

INTERNET ACCESS

Loja do Arco (Map p132; Rua Arco do Teixeira 2; per hr €3.50; ⌚ 11am-7.30pm) Internet access, and also stocks a wide range of Portuguese literature, music and crafts.

Sabot (Map p132; ☎ 219 230 802; Rua Dr Alfredo Costa 74; per hr €3; ⌚ noon-midnight Mon-Sat) Internet access near the station.

POST

Post office Sintra-Vila (Map p132; Rua Gil Vicente); Estefânia (Map p130; Avenida Movimento das Forças Armadas) Has NetPost.

TOURIST INFORMATION

Parques de Sintra – Monte da Lua (☎ 219 237 300; www.parquesdesintra.pt) Runs the gardens and parks, most of which have visitors centres.

Parque Natural de Sintra-Cascais Headquarters (Map p130; ☎ 219 247 200; Rua Gago Coutinho 1) Opens usual business hours.

Turismo (🕑 9am-7pm Oct-May, 9am-8pm Jun-Sep); Main office (Map p132; ☎ 219 231 157; www.cm-sintra.pt; Museu Regional, Praça da República 23); Train station (Map p132; ☎ 219 241 623) These turismos provide a free, information-packed map, and will also help with accommodation.

Sights

PALÁCIO NACIONAL DE SINTRA

Dominating the town is the **palace** (Sintra National Palace; Map p132; Paço Real or Palácio da Vila; ☎ 219 106 840; adult/under 14/15-25 €4/free/2, free 10am-2pm Sun; 🕑 10am-5.30pm Thu-Tue), with its two huge white conical chimneys and vast plaza. Of Moorish origins, the palace was first expanded by Dom Dinis (1261–1325), greatly enlarged by João I in the early 15th century (when the kitchens were built), adorned with Manueline additions by Manuel I in the following century, and repeatedly restored and redecorated right up to the present day. It was often occupied when royalty went hunting in the region or took refuge from Lisbon's heat or outbreaks of plague.

Passing through these three different royal residences, you'll notice a brilliant collection of 15th- and 16th-century *azulejos*, which are among the oldest in Portugal. Highlights include the delightful Sala dos Cisnes (Swan Room), with a polychrome ceiling adorned with 27 gold-collared swans. Used for plays and dance recitals, it was damaged in the 1755 earthquake but rebuilt to its original design.

Another notable hall is the Sala das Pêgas (Magpie Room), its ceiling thick with painted magpies, each holding in its beak a scroll with the words *por bem* (all to the good). The alleged story goes that the queen walked in on João I making advances to one of her ladies-in-waiting. Caught red-handed, the king claimed the kisses were harmless, that it was all '*por bem*' ('for good'). Naturally, much court gossip followed, and the king responded by commissioning the cheeky decoration – one bird for every lady-in-waiting.

The Sala dos Brasões (Coat of Arms Room) carries the heraldic shields of 74 leading 16th-century families on its wooden coffered ceiling.

The Sala dos Árabes (Arab Room) was João I's bedroom, and features amazing Manueline tiles from the early 16th century – some of the oldest tiles in Portugal.

Busily patterned, the Palatine chapel dates from the 14th century, but was altered in the 15th, and then restored in the 1930s. Islamic influences remain in the decorated ceiling and ceramic tile carpet; in fact, the Christian chapel may even have been a mosque in an earlier incarnation.

The room alongside the gallery located above the chapel served as Afonso VI's cell during his imprisonment by his brother Pedro II for nine years. He died of apoplexy in 1683 while listening to Mass through a grid in the wall.

Finally, the kitchen, of twin-chimney fame, is suitably huge and was once a separate building, to lessen the risk of fire.

CASTELO DOS MOUROS

Snaking over the mountain above Sintra-Vila, the ruined **castle** (Map p130; ☎ 219 107 970; adult/child under 6/under 17 €3.50/free/2; 🕑 9am-8pm mid-Jun–mid-Sep, 9am-7pm May–mid-Jun & mid-Sep–Oct, 9.30am-6pm Nov-May, last admission 1hr before closing) is set in enchanted woodlands. First built by the Moors, the castle was captured by Christian forces under Afonso Henriques in 1147. By the 15th century it was no longer used, and in the 19th century was converted to a 'romantic ruin' at Don Fernando's instigation. Its battlements offer sublime views over the twisting greenery of the woods and their huge Gothic mansions. The best walking route here from Sintra-Vila is not along the main road (a steep and car-busy 3km) but the quicker, partly off-road route via Rua Marechal Saldanha. The steep route is around 2km, but rewarding and quiet.

PARQUE DA PENA

A further 200m up the road from Castelo dos Mouros is **Parque da Pena** (Map p130; ☎ 219 079 955; adult/child €3.50/2, combination ticket with Palácio Nacional da Pena €6/4; 🕑 9am-8pm mid-Jun–mid-Sep, 9am-7pm May–mid-Jun & mid-Sep–Oct, 9.30am-6pm Nov-Apr, last admission 1hr before closing), filled with lakes and exotic plants, huge redwoods and fern trees, camellias and rhododendrons. It's cheaper to buy the combination ticket if you want to visit the Palácio Nacional da Pena too, as the only entrance to the palace is via Parque da Pena.

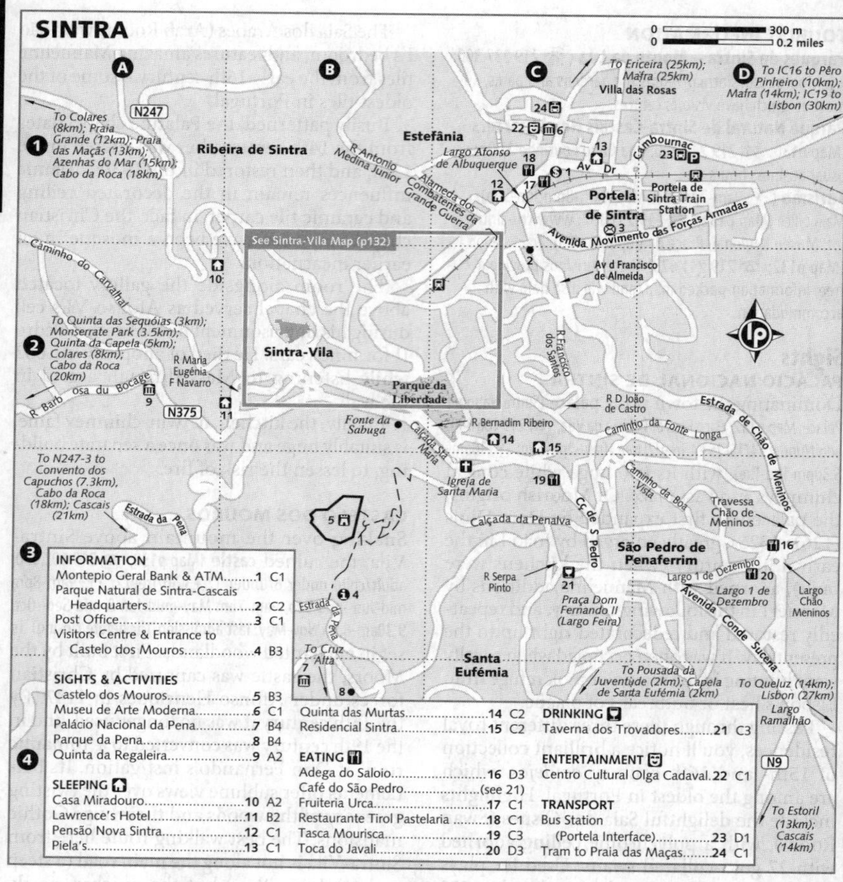

PALÁCIO NACIONAL DA PENA

The lavender-, lemon- and rose-tinted turrets and battlements of the ludicrous, magical **Palácio Nacional da Pena** (Pena National Palace; Map p130; ☎ 219 105 340; adult/child under 6/under 17 €6/free/4; ⏲ 10am-6.30pm Tue-Sun, 10am-5pm Nov-May, last admission 1hr before closing) rise up from a thickly wooded Sintra peak.

There had long been a convent here, reduced to 16th-century ruins when Ferdinand of Saxe Coburg-Gotha (artist-husband of Queen Maria II) became enchanted with the site, bought it, and began restoration of the convent. He then commissioned Prussian architect Ludwig von Eschwege in 1840 who, egged on by the king, delivered this Bavarian-Manueline epic (and as a final flourish added a statue of himself in armour, overlooking the palace from a nearby peak).

The kitsch, extravagant interior is equally extraordinary. The rooms, which have been left much as they were when Queen Amélia left after the 1910 declaration of the republic, are a curious mix of grandeur and kitsch. There's Eiffel-designed furniture, Ferdinand-designed china and a wall of unfinished nudes painted by Dom Carlos I. Every room is crammed with fascinating treasures. One room is filled with chintzy pastel Meissen porcelain furniture; in the Arab room, walls are painted to look like stucco. The ballroom has a chandelier holding 72 candles, and just in case those didn't do it, there are four statues of Turks bearing electric candles. Queen Amélia's teak-furnished tearoom is dominated by a bas-relief showing a terrible cholera outbreak.

A ghostly 16th-century carved white and blue-black alabaster altarpiece by Nicolas Chanterène and the Manueline cloister remain from the convent. The dining room was once the monks' refectory.

If you can't face the steep 10-minute climb, there's a shuttle bus from the park entrance to the palace for €2 return.

Inside the palace, an elegant **restaurant** (mains €9-18.50; lunch & dinner) serves up risottos, lamb and a stately cod amid vaulted ceilings and starched white tablecloths. There's also a cheaper terrace **café** (snacks €2-8; 10am-6pm Tue-Sun) with snacks and good pastries, before entering the grounds.

Buses to the park entrance leave from Sintra train station and near the turismo. A taxi will cost around €8 one way. The charming but steep woodland walk from Sintra-Vila is around 3km.

QUINTA DA REGALEIRA

This magical **villa and gardens** (Map p130; ☎ 219 106 650; Rua Barbosa du Bocage; adult guided/unguided visit €10/5; 10am-6pm Jun-Sep, to 4pm Mar-May, Oct & Nov, 11am-3.30pm Dec-Feb) is one of Sintra's striking architectural gems. Mythological symbols and elements from the Knights Templar, freemasonry and alchemy cover this early-20th-century, neo-Manueline extravaganza. It was dreamed up by an opera-set designer, Italian Luigi Manini (who also designed the stunning Palace Hotel do Buçaco in the Beiras), under the orders of António Carvalho Monteiro, a Brazilian-born mining and coffee tycoon known as Monteiro dos Milhões (Moneybags Monteiro).

The villa is surprisingly small and homely inside, despite its ferociously carved fireplaces and floors of Venetian glass. By the main house is a beautiful small chapel, **Capela da Santíssima Trindade**, with more Venetian glass mosaics. The playful gardens are brilliant to explore, with winding paths leading through exotic foliage to follies, fountains, grottoes, lakes and underground caverns. All paths seem to eventually end at the revolving stone door, which leads to the initiation well, **Poço Iniciáto**, plunging down some 30m. You walk down the nine-tiered spiral (3 x 3; three being the magic number) to thrillingly mysterious hollowed-out underground galleries, lit by fairy lights.

CONVENTO DOS CAPUCHOS

Hidden in the woods is another magical sight, the hobbit-hole-like **Convento dos Capuchos** (Capuchin Monastery; ☎ 219 237 300; adult/child under 6/under 17 €3.50/free/2; 9am-8pm Jun-Oct, to 6pm Nov-May, last admission 1hr before closing), which is a far remove from lavish palaces. Built in 1560 to house 12 monks, the monastery's builders took Matthew's gospel literally when it said 'the way to heaven is sinuous and its doors low and narrow'. The monks lived in incredibly cramped conditions, their tiny cells having low and narrow doors in preparation for the trip to heaven. Byron mocked the monastery in his poem *Childe Harold*, referring to one recluse, Honorius, who spent an astonishing 36 years here (dying at age 95 in 1596).

It's often known as the Cork Convent, because the diminutive cells are lined with cork. Visiting here is an *Alice in Wonderland* experience as you squeeze through to explore the warren of cells, chapels, kitchen and cavern. The monks lived a simple, touchingly well-ordered life in this idyllic yet spartan place, hiding away here up until 1834 when it was abandoned.

You can walk here – the monastery is 7.3km from Sintra-Vila (5.1km from the turn-off to Parque da Pena) along a remote, wooded road. There's no bus connection (taxis charge around €16 return; arrange for a pick-up about an hour later). Admission is by guided visit only (lasting 45 minutes), usually every 15 to 30 minutes, and it's preferable to book in advance. Visits are run in English or Portuguese, depending on who was first to book a tour.

MONSERRATE PARK

Marvellous, rambling, partly wild, **Monserrate Park** (☎ 219 107 806; www.parquesdesintra.pt; adult/child under 6/under 17 €3.50/free/2; 9am-8pm mid-Jun–mid-Sep, to 7pm May–mid-Jun & mid-Sep–Oct, 9.30am-6pm Nov-May, last admission 1hr before closing) is a romantic 30-hectare garden. The wooded hillsides feature a vast range of exotic flora, from roses and conifers to Chinese weeping cypress, dragon trees, eucalyptus, Himalayan rhododendrons and more than 24 species of palm. The park is over 3.5km west of Sintra-Vila; take care of traffic on the narrow road if you're walking.

The gardens were created in the 18th century by wealthy English merchant Gerard de Visme. In the 1850s, they were enlarged

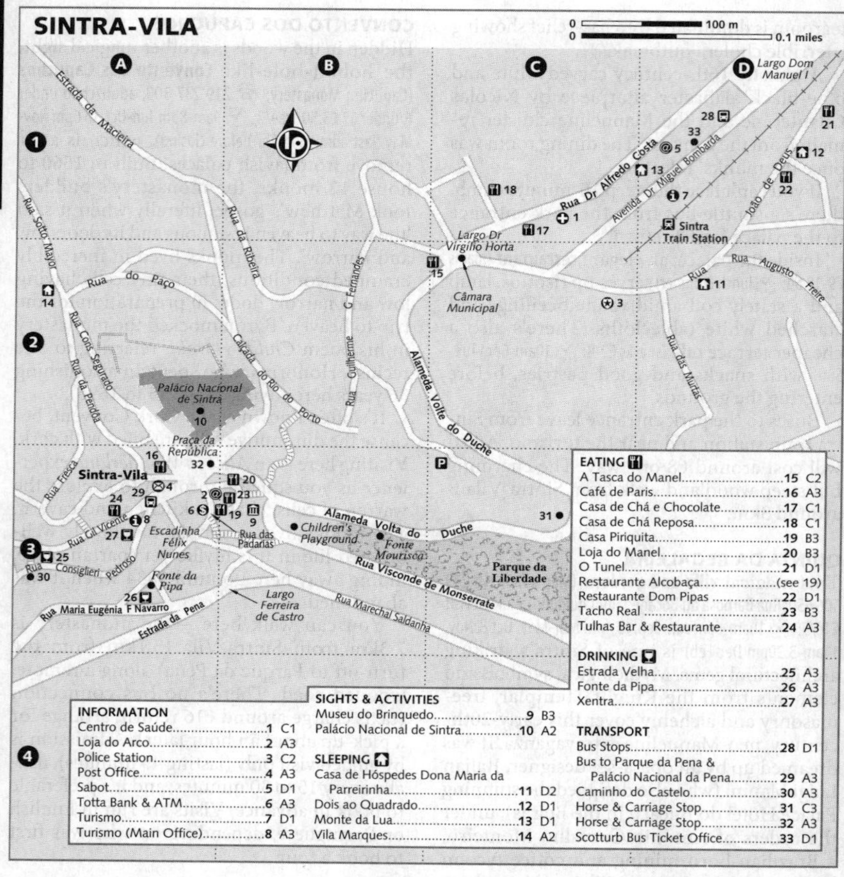

by the painter William Stockdale (with help from London's Kew Gardens), who imported many plants from Australasia and Mexico. Neglected for years (the site was sold to the government in 1949 and forgotten), it's now maintained by Parques de Sintra but still retains an aura of wild abandon.

At the heart of the gardens is a Moorish-inspired **palácio** (☎ 219 237 300; adult/child under 6/under 17 €7/free/5.50; ⏲ guided visits 10am & 3pm) constructed in the late 1850s by James Knowles for another wealthy Englishman, Sir Francis Cook. A Gothic-style villa previously stood on the site, rented by the rich, infamous British Gothic writer, William Beckford, in 1794 after he fled Britain in the wake of a homosexual scandal. Visits to the recently restored Monserrate Palace are by 90-minute guided tour (including the grounds); reservations are essential.

MUSEU DO BRINQUEDO

In the former fire station, the **Museu do Brinquedo** (Toy Museum; Map p132; ☎ 219 242 171; www.museu-do-brinquedo.pt; Rua Visconde de Monserrate; adult/child/student €3/1.50/1.50; ⏲ 10am-6pm Tue-Sun; ♿) has a delightful international collection, from 3000-year-old Egyptian stone counters to Christian Dior Barbies, via tin cars, lead soldiers, Dinky toys and spooky porcelain dolls. João Arbués Moreira, an engineer by profession, began this collection (now more than 20,000 pieces) more than 50 years ago when he was 14. On the 3rd floor is a toy-repair workshop, where a man sits studiously working in a glass case, beside a bizarre tray of disembodied heads.

The museum also has a café, a small shop and disabled access.

MUSEU DE ARTE MODERNA

The world-class **Museu de Arte Moderna** (Modern Art Museum; Map p130; ☎ 219 248 170; Avenida Heliodoro Salgado; adult/under 18 €3/free, 10am-2pm Sun free; 🕑 10am-6pm Tue-Sun; ♿), set in Estefânia's splendid former casino, has a spectacular collection of postwar art (especially good pop art) including works by Warhol, Lichtenstein, Pollock, Kossoff, Klein and Nauman. There are also excellent temporary exhibitions and disabled access.

Activities

Walking through pretty countryside is a much-loved activity in the Sintra region, and **mountain biking** is increasingly popular. A pleasant walking trail is from Sintra-Vila to Castelo dos Mouros, a relatively easy 50-minute hike. You can continue to Palácio Nacional da Pena (another five minutes). From here you can ascend the Serra de Sintra's highest point, the 529m Cruz Alta (High Cross) named after its 16th-century cross, with amazing views all over Sintra. You can continue on foot to São Pedro de Penaferrim and loop back to Sintra-Vila.

Ozono Mais (☎ 219 619 927; www.ozonomais.com; Rua General Alves Roçades 10) offers a variety of excursions, including canoeing, mountain-biking and jeep tours (the jeep tours are around €55 per person).

Cabra Montez (☎ 917 446 668; www.cabramontez.com), or 'mountain goat', runs trekking/canoeing/mountain-biking trips for €25/30/40 per person.

Centro Hípico O Paddock (☎ 219 283 308; Rua do Alecrim, Janas; per hr €20; 🕑 10am-1pm & 3-6pm Tue-Sun Oct-May, 10am-1pm & 4-7pm Jun-Sep) offers horse rides around Sintra.

Festivals & Events

Sintra's major cultural venue is the **Centro Cultural Olga Cadaval** (☎ 219 107 110; www.ccolgacadaval.pt; Praça Francisco Sá Carneiro), beautifully converted from an old cinema.

Festival de Música This classical music festival is Sintra's big cultural event, and runs from mid-June to mid-July.

Noites de Bailado From mid-July to the end of August, the equally international classical and contemporary dance festival follows, held in the lovely gardens of hotel Palácio de Seteais. Contact the turismo for details.

Sleeping

It's worth staying overnight, as Sintra has some attractive options, from quaint village guesthouses to lavish manors. The turismo can advise on private apartments (€50 to €70).

BUDGET

Dois ao Quadrado (Map p132; ☎ 219 246 160; www.doisaoquadrado.web.pt; Rua João de Deus 68; dm/d with shared bathroom from €15/40; 💻) New in 2006, this cosy hostel has bright, airy rooms with simple but attractive furnishings and an on-site bar.

Casa de Hóspedes Dona Maria da Parreirinha (Map p132; ☎ 219 232 490; Rua João de Deus 12-14; d €40; 🅿) This small, friendly guesthouse is a welcome addition to Sintra-Vila, with attractive, nicely kept rooms and big windows.

MIDRANGE

Monte da Lua (Map p132; ☎/fax 219 241 029; Avenida Miguel Bombarda 51; d €30-50) This quaint guesthouse has lovely tidy rooms (with telephone), the best overlooking the wooded valley at the back.

Piela's (Map p130; ☎ 219 241 691; Avenida Dr Cambournac 1-3; s/d €35/50) Piela, who used to run a popular Sintra-Vila guesthouse, has opened a slightly more upscale one in nearby Estefânia. The new locale has attractive wood-floored rooms and a pleasant terrace.

Vila Marques (Map p132; ☎ 219 230 027; www.vilamarques.net; Rua Sotto Mayor 1; s/d with shared bathroom from €35/50) Rooms at this attractive place in Sintra-Vila range from small to spacious, but most have good views and high ceilings if somewhat frilly décor. There's also a terrace.

Pensão Nova Sintra (Map p130; ☎ 219 230 220; www.novasintra.com; Largo Afonso de Albuquerque 25; d €75; ❄ 💻) A renovated mansion above the main road offering small doubles with views and a big outdoor terrace. Rooms on upper floors are better.

Quinta das Murtas (Map p132; ☎ 219 240 246; www.quinta-das-murtas.com; Rua Eduardo Van Zeller 4; d €75; 🏊) A grand salmon-pink manor house with charmingly pale rooms overlooking the wooded exterior. Don't miss the handsome sitting room with peacock mural.

Residencial Sintra (Map p132; ☎ 219 230 738; www.residencialsintra.blogspot.com; Travessa dos Avelares 12; d from €75; 🏊) In a picturesque position between Sintra-Vila and São Pedro, this is a stately, faded 1850s mansion with 10 spacious high-ceilinged rooms and wooded views. It's perfect for families, with a large terrace, beautiful pool and rambling garden.

TOP END

Casa Miradouro (Map p130; ☎ 219 107 100; www.casa-miradouro.com; Rua Sotto Mayor 55; s/d €112/125) An imposing Battenberg cake of a house, built in 1890, with six elegant rooms and excellent views.

our pick **Quinta da Capela** (☎ 219 290 170; s/d incl breakfast €130/140; mid-Mar–mid-Oct;) Dating back to the 16th century and rebuilt in the 18th, this grand manor house is an exquisite setting for an overnight stay. Amid a secluded valley just beyond Monserrate Park, the manor has nine bright, beautiful rooms each filled with antiques, and blessed with great views. The manicured gardens are populated by peacocks and gliding swans.

Quinta das Sequóias (☎ 219 243 821; www.quintadasequoias.com; d €160;) This superb five-bedroom manor house adorned with art and flowers is en route to Monserrate Park. Rooms are charming, homely and gloriously comfortable, and the views are fantastic. No children under 12.

Lawrence's Hotel (Map p130; ☎ 219 105 500; www.lawrenceshotel.com; Rua Consiglieri Pedroso 38; s/d €188/245;) This charming 18th-century hotel, where Lord Byron stayed in 1809, has beautifully restored rooms (some with tiles, antique furnishings or views over the wooded valley), and no two are alike. There's also an excellent restaurant and disabled access.

Eating

BUDGET

Restaurante Tirol Pastelaria (Map p130; Largo Afonso de Albuquerque 9; mains €1-4.50; daily) This big, busy café has decadent desserts and outside tables.

Casa Piriquita (Map p132; Rua das Padarias 1-5; sandwiches from €2.50; Thu-Mon) This busy café is a popular destination for inexpensive bites as well as Sintra's famous *queijadas* (sweet cheese cakes) and *travesseiros* (almond pastries).

Café do São Pedro (Map p130; Rua Serpa Pinta 5; mains €4-8; 9am-7pm Tue-Sun) Gold-framed prints and an old Victrola lend an old-fashioned elegance to this inviting café. You'll find coffees, teas, desserts and *queijadas*.

O Tunel (Map p132; ☎ 219 231 286; 29 Rua Conde Fereira, Estefânia; mains €6-8) Brightly lit, popular with locals, simple and large, this place serves tasty traditional dishes in a cheery atmosphere.

Tasca Mourisca (Map p130; Calçada de San Pedro 28; mains from €6.50; lunch & dinner Mon-Sat) This small local gem serves up tasty traditional dishes.

A Tasca do Manel (Map p132; ☎ 219 230 215; Largo Dr Virgílio Horta 5; mains €5-6.50; breakfast & lunch Mon-Sat) Small, good-value, TV-and-tiles place.

Fruiteria Urca (Map p130; Largo Afonso de Albuquerque 34) Tiny grocery, good for picnics.

Loja do Manel (Map p132; Rua do Arco do Teixeira) Grocery store.

MIDRANGE

Tulhas Bar & Restaurante (Map p132; ☎ 219 232 378; Rua Gil Vicente 4; mains €9-14; lunch & dinner Thu-Tue) A converted grain warehouse; dark, tiled and quaint, with twisted chandeliers and a relaxing, cosy atmosphere. Try the *bacalhau com natas* (shredded cod with cream and potato).

Casa de Chá e Chocolate (Map p132; ☎ 219 234 825; Rua Dr Alfredo Costa 8; mains around €11; V) This cheerfully painted café serves decent vegetarian plates, Portuguese standards and a tempting assortment of desserts.

Tacho Real (Map p132; ☎ 219 235 277; Rua da Ferraria 4; mains from €12; closed Wed) Nicely prepared lunch specials such as grilled salmon are good value (€6 to €10) here. There's a handsome dark wood interior, and a sunny front terrace.

Café de Paris (Map p132; ☎ 219 232 375; Praça da República 32; mains €6-14; 10am-8pm) Facing the palace, this handsome but somewhat snooty terrace café serves baguettes, savoury crepes and other international fare, though the setting is more impressive than the cuisine.

Adega do Saloio (Map p130; ☎ 219 231 422; Travessa Chão de Meninos; mains €10-18, half-portions €6.50; Wed-Mon) Popular with locals, Adega do Saloio has two outlets across the road from each other, both specialising in grills, but one is more formal than the other. Both have bustling atmospheres and are decorated with strings of garlic.

Restaurante Alcobaça (Map p132; ☎ 219 231 651; Rua das Padarias 7; mains €7.50-13; lunch & dinner) This is the best-value and most traditional restaurant in the old town; it's a simple place that's busy and bright.

Casa de Chá Reposa (Map p132; Rua Conde Fereira 29; Tue-Sun) An amazing tearoom with a view, crammed with interesting things for sale. A chandelier hung with tissue-paper-covered teapots dangles from the high stuccoed ceiling. Good cakes.

Restaurante Dom Pipas (Map p132; ☎ 219 234 278; Rua João de Deus 60, Estefânia; mains €8-10; Tue-Sun) Near the train station, popular Dom Pipas attracts a mix of locals and out-of-towners who enjoy good traditional dishes at fair prices.

Toca do Javali (Map p130; ☎ 219 233 503; Rua 1 de Dezembro 12; mains €7-15; ⏰ lunch & dinner) Boasting a delightful tree-shaded courtyard, Toca do Javali serves delicious barbecued mains, including wild boar.

Drinking

Fonte da Pipa (Map p132; ☎ 219 234 437; Rua Fonte da Pipa 11-13; ⏰ from around 9pm) A hip tiled bar, this has craggy, cavelike rooms and comfy seats.

Estrada Velha (Map p132; ☎ 219 234 355; Rua Consiglieri Pedroso 16) Another popular bar, this place is vaguely publike, laid-back though busy, with jazzy music in the background.

Xentra (Map p132; ☎ 219 240 759; Rua Consiglieri Pedroso 2a) This cellar bar has a vaguely medieval feel with stone walls and an arched ceiling.

Taverna dos Trovadores (Map p130; ☎ 219 233 548; Praça Dom Fernando II 18) In São Pedro, this atmospheric, upmarket tavern has live Portuguese music Friday and Saturday nights.

Getting There & Away

Buses run by **Scotturb** (Map p132; ☎ 214 699 100; www.scotturb.com; Avenida Dr Miguel Bombarda) or **Mafrense** (☎ 219 230 971; www.mafrense.pt) leave regularly for Cascais (€3.10, 60 minutes), sometimes via Cabo da Roca (€3.10). Buses also head to Estoril (€3.10, 40 minutes), Mafra (45 minutes) and Ericeira (45 minutes). Most services leave from Sintra train station (which is *estação* on timetables) via the Portela Interface terminal, in Portela de Sintra. For a handy bus service to the airport, see p125. Scotturb's useful information office, open 9am to 1pm and 2pm to 8pm, is opposite the station.

Train services (€1.50, 45 minutes) run every 15 minutes between Sintra and Lisbon (Sete Rios or Entrecampos train stations). Bikes travel free on weekends and holidays (€2.50 return weekdays, not permitted from 7am to 10am Sintra to Lisbon, 4pm to 8pm Lisbon to Sintra).

Getting Around

BUS

From the station, it's a 1.5km scenic walk into Sintra Vila – a good way to get your bearings – or you can hop on a bus. Bus 433 runs regularly from Portela Interface to São Pedro (*Largo 1 Dez* on timetables; €0.80, 15 minutes, at least half-hourly 7am to 8pm) via Estefânia and Sintra-Vila. To get to Palácio Nacional da Pena (€3.85, 15 minutes), catch bus 434, which starts from Sintra train station and goes via Sintra-Vila (every 20 to 40 minutes, from 9.35am to 6.05pm). The last one from Pena returns at 6.20pm.

For €8.50 you can buy a Day Rover, valid on all Scotturb bus routes, including the Pena service.

A one-day Train & Bus Travelcard (€12) is valid on Lisbon–Cascais and Lisbon–Sintra trains and all Scotturb buses. Ticket kiosks are at Portela Interface (near the car park) and opposite Sintra train station.

You can hire bikes at **Caminho do Castelo** (Map p132; Rua Consiglieri Pedroso 15; ⏰ 10am-7pm).

HORSE & CARRIAGE

These clip-clop all over the place, even as far as Monserrate (€60 return). The turismo has a full list of prices (€15 to €100). The carriages wait by the entrance to the Parque da Liberdade (on Alameda Volta do Duche) or by the *pelourinho* (pillory) below Palácio Nacional de Sintra.

TAXI & CAR

Taxis are available at the train station or opposite the Sintra-Vila post office. They aren't metered, so check fares with the turismo. Count on about €8 one way to Palácio Nacional da Pena, or €16 return to Convento dos Capuchos. There's a 20% supplement at weekends and on holidays.

There's a free car park below Sintra-Vila; follow the signs by the *câmara municipal* (town hall), in Estefânia. Alternatively, park at Portela Interface and take the bus.

WEST OF SINTRA

Spectacular beaches lie just 12km west of Sintra. Here **Praia Grande** and **Praia das Maçãs** draw local crowds on summer days. Praia Grande lives up to its name, a big sandy beach with ripping breakers, which hosts heats of the European Surfing Championships. It also has a 102m-long oceanwater **swimming pool** (adult/child Mon-Fri €6/3, Sat & Sun €7/4; ⏰ Jun-Oct). **Praia das Maçãs** has a smaller beach, backed by a lively little resort. **Azenhas do Mar**, 2km further, is spectacularly set on a clifftop, with a small beach below.

En route to the beaches, the ancient ridge-top village of **Colares** makes a pleasant pit stop. In addition to panoramas and slow-paced village life, Colares is famous for its wines, which have been around since the 13th century. In fact, vines grown today are the only ones in Europe to have survived the 19th-century phylloxera plague, saved by their deep roots and sandy soil. Call in advance to arrange a visit to **Adega Regional de Colares** (☎ 219 291 210; Alameda Coronel, Linhares de Lima 32), where you can taste some of its velvety reds.

Cabo da Roca (Rock Cape) is a sheer cliff of around 150m, facing the roaring sea, about 18km west of Sintra. It's Europe's westernmost point and a highly recommended setting around sunset. Wild and wind-lashed, it's very uncommercialised, perhaps because it feels so remote; there are a couple of stalls, a café and a turismo where you can buy a certificate to show you've been here.

Sleeping

BUDGET

Senhora Maria Pereira (☎ 219 290 319; tucha38@hotmail.com; Avenida Maestro Frederico de Freitas 19; s/d/tr incl breakfast €40/45/50, 3-person apt €60) A kilometre before Praia Grande beach, here delightful *quartos* (private rooms) overlook a large rambling garden with barbecue facilities. Three self-catering apartments are also available.

Residencial Real (☎ 219 292 002; Rua Fernão Magalhães, Praia das Maçãs; d incl breakfast around €45) A faded, spacious place, Real is at the northern end of the Praia Grande village, with expansive ocean views.

Village Praia Grande (☎ 219 290 581; www.villagepraiagrande.com; Avenida Atlântico; studio/1-/2-bedroom/3-bedroom apt €56/73/95/124) Just 500m from the beach, these rustic but serviceable bungalows come equipped with kitchens, TV and telephone. You can also arrange surf classes here (€13 for 90 minutes).

MIDRANGE & TOP END

Hotel Miramonte (☎ 219 288 200; www.viphotels.com; Avenida do Atlântico 155, Pinhal da Nazaré; s/tw/tr €50/60//70;) A large endearingly old-fashioned 1970s place on the Sintra–Praia das Maçãs road, 400m before the turn-off to Praia Grande; an odd location but the hotel has appealing countryside views.

Hotel Arribas (☎ 219 292 145; www.hotelarribas.com; Avenida Alfredo Coelho, Praia Grande; s/d/tr/q €68/80/111/137;) While this 39-room, scallop-shaped hotel isn't the prettiest sight, its sea views over Praia Grande are magnificent, and guests have access to its 100m-long oceanwater pool. The rooms themselves are trim and neat, if slightly underwhelming. There's disabled access.

Casal St Virginia (☎ 219 283 198; www.casalstvirginia.com; Avenida Luis Augusto Colares 19; d from €105) On a cliff overlooking the sea, this lovely manor house is full of character, with a central wooden staircase, artwork and antiques decorating the common areas and a marvellous terrace. It sits near the small village of Azenhas do Mar.

Eating

Restaurante Pôr do Sol (☎ 219 291 740; Rua António Brandão de Vasconcelos 25; mains €8-12; daily Jul & Aug, Wed-Mon Sep-Jun) Fantastically located at the top of the village, this small place in Azenhas do Mar, has good *pratos do dia* (daily specials) and great views. Staff can recommend *quartos*.

D'Adraga (☎ 219 280 028; Praia da Adraga; mains €7-14; lunch & dinner) This lone restaurant has big windows over the wild, rocky little beach. Decorated with lanterns and anchors, it gets packed due to a great location and fabulous seafood. It's a good lively place for families. Buses run here from Sintra and Praia Grande; the beach and restaurant are 2km from the bus stop.

Many cafés and restaurants are scattered along Praia Grande and Praia das Maçãs.

Getting There & Away

Bus 441 from Portela Interface goes frequently via Colares to Praia das Maçãs (€2.40, 25 minutes) and on to Azenhas do Mar (€2.25, 30 minutes), stopping at Praia Grande (€2.40, 25 minutes) three times daily (more in summer). Bus 440 also runs from Sintra to Azenhas do Mar (€2.40, 35 minutes).

A brilliant way to reach the beach is aboard the century-old tram service (€2), which connects Sintra with Praia das Maçãs. In summer it runs hourly from Friday to Sunday, starting at 10.05am; the last tram from Praia das Maçãs returns at 6pm. Catch the tram on Rua J Almeida in Estefânia (Map p130). Schedules often change, so check at the turismo.

Bus 403 to Cascais runs regularly via Cabo da Roca (€3.10, 45 minutes) from Sintra station.

CASCAIS

pop 33,255

The attractive seaside town of Cascais, with its lovely beaches and youthful air, is a favourite among weekending Lisboêtas and travellers. While its resort status is undisputed – many shops and cafés cater largely to summertime crowds – it remains an active fishing port, with an appealing old town full of narrow, winding lanes.

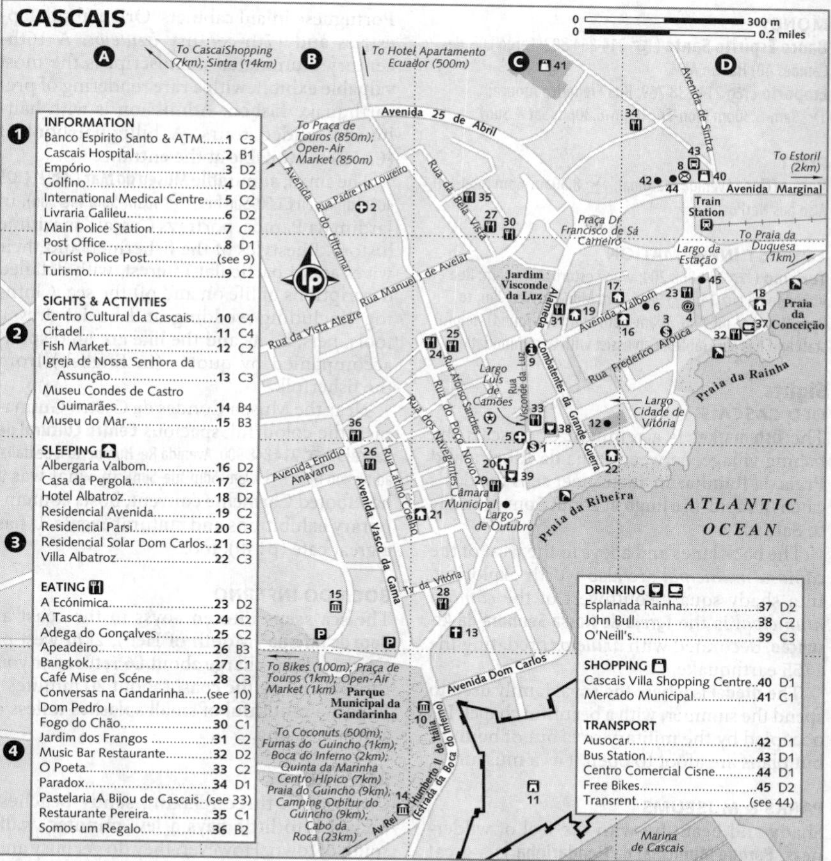

Cascais was once a fishing village, but in 1870 the royal court came here for the summer, with a trail of nobility in its wake. Such patronage has left it with some grand pastel-coloured buildings and a striking citadel. Apart from beaches, Cascais has a few quirky museums, some wild gardens and a lively fish market.

Orientation & Information

The train station and nearby bus station are about 250m north of the main pedestrianised Rua Frederico Arouca.

BOOKSHOPS

Livraria Galileu (☎ 214 866 014; Avenida Valbom 24a) Good source of secondhand English, Spanish, Italian, French and German books.

EMERGENCY

Main police station (☎ 214 861 127; Rua Afonso Sanches)

Tourist police post (☎ 214 863 929; Rua Visconde da Luz) Next to the turismo.

INTERNET ACCESS

Golfino (Rua Sebastião J Carvalho e Melo 17; per hr €6; 🕑 9.30am-8pm Mon-Sat)

MEDICAL SERVICES

Cascais Hospital (☎ 214 827 700; Rua Padre JM Loureiro)

International Medical Centre (☎ 214 845 317/8; Largo Luis de Camões) Staffed by English-speaking personnel; offers fast but pricey treatment and has 24-hour service available.

MONEY

Banco Espírito Santo (☎ 214 864 302; Largo Luís de Camões 40) Has an ATM.

Empório (☎ 214 838 769; Rua Frederico Arouca; ⌚ 9am-6.30pm Mon-Fri, 10am-6.30pm Sat & Sun)

POST

Post office (Avenida Marginal; ⌚ 8.30am-6pm Mon-Fri) Also has NetPost.

TOURIST INFORMATION

Turismo (☎ 214 868 204; www.estorilsintra.com; Rua Visconde da Luz 14; ⌚ 9am-7pm Mon-Sat Sep-Jun, to 8pm Mon-Sat Jul-Aug, 10am-6pm Sun year-round) Helpful staff and has surf tables. Can assist with accommodation.

Sights

OLD CASCAIS

The **fish market** is a remnant of Cascais the fishing village, between Praia da Ribeira and Praia da Rainha; an auctioneer sells the day's catch in rapid-fire lingo at about 5pm Monday to Saturday.

The back lanes and alleys to the west of the *câmara municipal* are also worth exploring. In a shady square southwest of the *câmara municipal* is the **Igreja de Nossa Senhora da Assunção**, decorated with *azulejos* predating the 1755 earthquake.

The **citadel** is where the royal family used to spend the summer, with a beautiful chapel. It's occupied by the military so is out of bounds, but plans are afoot to open it as a museum.

PARKS & MUSEUMS

Shady and beautiful with the feel of wilderness, **Parque Municipal da Gandarinha** is a great place to explore. It's dotted with birch and pine trees, palms and eucalyptus, rose gardens and flowering shrubs, and there are peacocks, aviaries, duck ponds and a playground scattered among the flora.

The grounds also contain the delightful **Museu Condes de Castro Guimarães** (☎ 214 825 407; admission €1.60; ⌚ 11am-4pm Tue-Sun), the late-19th-century mansion of Jorge O'Neill. Designed by a painter (apparently inspired by Luigi Manini's opera-set designs), it's a dreamlike mix of styles, with castle turrets and an Arabic cloister. O'Neill was Irish, hence the clover leaves inside. But they didn't bring him luck – he went bankrupt and had to sell up.

The interior displays the lavish furnishings installed by his successor, Count of Castro Guimarães, including 17th-century Indo-Portuguese inlaid cabinets, Oriental silk tapestries and 17th-century *azulejos*. A 16th-century illuminated manuscript is the most valuable exhibit, with a rare rendering of pre-earthquake Lisbon. Admission is with half-hourly guided tours. A bilingual booklet (€2.50) is available at the entrance.

The small, admirable **Museu do Mar** (☎ 214 825 400; admission €1.50, Sun free; ⌚ 10am-5pm Tue-Sun), in Jardim da Parada, portrays Cascais' maritime history. Lifestyles of the fishermen and their wives are of particular interest, with detailed descriptions of life on and off the sea. Clothing (including wedding and burial dress), tools, nets, boats and the like are on display, accompanied by quotes (in English) from the fisherfolk.

Near the Museu Condes de Castro Guimarães, the colourful, spacious **Centro Cultural de Cascais** (☎ 214 848 900; Avenida Rei Humberto II de Itália; admission free; ⌚ 10am-6pm Tue-Sun), in what was a barefooted Carmelite convent, hosts contemporary exhibitions and cultural events. It has a great café (p140), too.

BOCA DO INFERNO

The sea seeps into an abyss in the coast at **Boca do Inferno** (Mouth of Hell), 2km west of Cascais. Taxis charge about €6 return, or you can walk along the coast (about 20 minutes). Expect a mouthful of small splashes unless a storm is raging.

Activities

Cascais has three relaxing sandy beaches, tucked into little bays a few minutes' walk south of town. However, they do get busy and the water quality is not great.

Largest and closest is **Praia da Ribeira**, but the best beach is **Praia do Guincho**, 9km northwest. This long, wild beach is a surfer's and windsurfer's paradise (the site of previous World Surfing Championships) with massive crashing rollers. The strong undertow can be dangerous for swimmers and novice surfers.

John David's Watersports Centre (☎ 214 868 099; www.exclusive-divers.net) at Praia da Duquesa, midway between Cascais and Estoril, rents out sailboards (€25 per hour) and organises water-skiing jaunts (€25 per 15 minutes) and banana-boat rides (€24 per five people). It can also take you scuba-diving around the Cascais coastline and beyond.

Moana Surf School (☎ 964 449 436; www.moanasurfschool.com; Praia do Guincho; introductory 75min lesson €20,

4 x 75min classes €75) and **Guincho Surf School** (☎ 965 059 421; Praia do Guincho) run surfing courses. You can ring Pedro Barbudo, who runs the Guincho school, for a surf report.

Surfboards can be rented from **Aerial Wind e Surf** (☎ 214 836 745; Loja 129, Cascais Marina); there's also a branch at **Praia do Guincho** (☎ 917 890 036).

You can charter a yacht for six people from **Tuttamania** (☎ 934 843 636; Cascais Marina; half-/full day incl skipper & insurance €750/1200).

The **Guia Climbing School** (☎ 214 847 084; www.adesnivel.pt; 3-6pm Mar-Oct) is west of the Boca do Inferno, with sea-cliff climbs of around 10m to 20m, suitable for beginners or experienced climbers. It also has a climbing wall (€3) open from 8pm to 11pm Monday to Friday, and 4pm to 8pm Saturday.

Quinta da Marinha Centro Hípico (☎ 214 869 084; www.quintadamarinha-centrohipico.pt; per hr around €22; 9am-noon & 3-7pm Tue-Sun, 9am-noon & 4-8pm Apr-Sep), 2km inland from Praia do Guincho, offers horse rides to the sand dunes and through forest as well as around Sintra.

Festivals & Events

Events for children are laid on every month, such as games, concerts and theatre. These are mainly in Portuguese, but some are suitable for foreigners too; inquire at the turismo.

Festas do Mar Held at the end of June, this festival celebrates Cascais' marine ties and honours the patron saint of fishers, the Senhora dos Navegantes, with a procession and a parade of fishing boats.

Estoril Festival de Jazz Held in both Cascais and Estoril in July.

Festival de Música da Costa do Estoril Also held in both towns, also in July.

Free outdoor entertainment A programme runs from July to mid-September with live bands at around 10.30pm nightly, usually at Estoril's Praia de Tamariz and/or Cascais' Praia de Moitas (en route to Estoril).

Fireworks displays From July to mid-September there are fireworks on Saturdays around midnight, usually over Praia de Tamariz.

Sleeping

Advance reservations are essential if you're visting in summer.

Camping Orbitur do Guincho (☎ 214 870 450; www.orbitur.pt; adult/tent/car €4.65/5.05/4.55) In Areia, about 1km inland from Praia do Guincho and 9km from Cascais, this is a large, shaded site, with restaurant, playground and disabled facilities. It gets busy in July and August. Buses run regularly to Guincho from Cascais.

Residencial Avenida (☎ 214 864 417; Rua da Palmeira 14; d with shared bathroom €40) So long established that its sign is practically invisible, Avenida is a quiet spot; it's like staying in someone's flat. There are just four plainly decorated but comfortable doubles.

Residencial Parsi (☎ 214 845 744; fax 214 837 150; Rua Afonso Sanches 8; d with/without bathroom €35/60) In a crumbling, characterful old building near the waterfront, Parsi has a range of carpeted rooms, some with tall ceilings and gorgeous views, but it's a bit run down.

Albergaria Valbom (☎ 214 865 801; albergariavalbom@mail.telepac.pt; Avenida Valbom 14; s €53-58, d €68-73) You'll find dated design and uninspiring pale-green walls at this fairly bland but centrally located option. In its defence, the rooms are clean and comfortable, and the staff efficient.

Residencial Solar Dom Carlos (☎ 214 828 115; www.solardomcarlos.com; Rua Latino Coelho 8; s/d from €50/65; P) A 16th-century former royal residence with a chapel where Dom Carlos used to pray, this charming guesthouse has spacious, old-fashioned rooms on a quiet leafy street. Breakfast is in a lavishly muralled room. Laundry and bike hire.

Hotel Apartamento Ecuador (☎ 214 826 500; hotelequador@mail.telepac.pt; Alto da Pampilheira 396; 2-person apt with breakfast & kitchen €95; ♿) This high-rise on the northern outskirts of town offers some of Cascais' most reasonably priced apartments. There's disabled access.

our pick **Casa da Pergola** (☎ 214 840 040; www.pergolahouse.com; Avenida Valbom 13; d incl breakfast with/without balcony €129/119) In the same family for more than a century, Casa da Pergola as been maintained with obvious affection, from the lush flower garden to its beautifully intricate façade. Inside, guests can enjoy more of the same: an antique-filled sitting room, marble staircase and six rooms, each classically furnished, with artwork on the walls. Several rooms have balconies overlooking the garden.

Villa Albatroz (☎ 214 863 410; www.albatrozhotels.com; Rua Fernandes Tomás 1; s/d incl breakfast from €175/215, breakfast €12.50; ♿) This boutique hotel (smaller sibling of Hotel Albatroz) has just 11 rooms, each handsomely furnished in a contemporary design. The best rooms have terraces, Jacuzzi tubs and ocean views. There's disabled access.

Hotel Albatroz (☎ 214 847 380; www.albatrozhotels.com; Rua Frederica Arouca 100; s/d from €200/240; P) Set in a beautiful 19th-century building, this magnificent hotel has lavish interiors – imagine gilded mirrors and orchids – plus huge, classically decorated rooms. The saltwater pool overlooks the bay of Cascais. Excellent service and a great restaurant; breakfast is €15.

Eating

You'll find the widest selection of outdoor restaurants along the pedestrian Rua Frederico Arouca and in the cobbled Largo Cidade de Vitória. Behind the nearby fish market is a string of upmarket fish restaurants.

BUDGET

A Económica (☎ 214 833 524; Rua Sebastião J C Melo 11; mains €5.50-8; lunch & dinner Fri-Wed) This popular low-key spot serves large, cheap plates of Portuguese standards. Outdoor tables.

Dom Pedro I (☎ 214 833 734; Beco dos Invalides 5; mains €6.50-9; lunch & dinner Mon-Sat) A marvellous small restaurant unexpectedly tucked away in a small courtyard, serving great-value grilled fish.

Jardim dos Frangos (☎ 214 835 695; Avenida Marginal; mains €5-10; lunch & dinner Mon-Sat) Grilled chicken is the featured attraction at this no-nonsense local favourite.

Somos um Regalo (☎ 214 865 487; Avenida Vasco da Gama 36; mains €1.50-9; Thu-Tue) Another top grilled-chicken option; you can either eat in or you can take away.

Pastelaria A Bijou de Cascais (☎ 214 830 283; Largo Luis de Camões 55; mains €6; 8am-7pm) Locals and visitors alike flock to this attractive, jewel box–sized pastry shop. Inexpensive lunch specials are also available.

Paradox (☎ 214 843 004; Avenida Costa Pinto 91; mains €5-7; lunch Mon-Sat; V) This good-value vegetarian restaurant serves simple but filling plates of freshly prepared cuisine in a vaguely institutional setting.

MIDRANGE

Apeadeiro (☎ 214 832 731; Avenida Vasco da Gama 252; mains €6.50-11; lunch Tue-Sun, dinner Tue-Sat) This is an airy, cut-above yet relaxed restaurant, renowned for its excellent, beautifully cooked grilled fish, with chequered tablecloths, big windows and walls hung with fishing nets.

Conversas na Gandarinha (☎ 214 866 402; Avenida Rei Humberto II de Itália; mains €7.50-11) The Centro Cultural de Cascais (p138) has this fantastic airy, pastel courtyard, where you can nibble cakes or enjoy a delightful lunch. The deserts are good.

Fogo de Chão (☎ 214 820 196; Rua Carlos Ribeiro 50; meals €7-14) A traditional Brazilian *rodízio* (all-you-can-eat meat restaurant), Fogo de Chão serves up heaps of juicy barbecued meat, accompanied by an extensive salad buffet. There's not much ambience but there is high-powered air-conditioning.

Music Bar Restaurante (☎ 214 820 848; Largo Praia da Rainha 121; mains €9-14) For unusually good sea views (and fair cuisine), the Music Bar is hard to top. Grab a seat on the spacious terrace for premium wave-watching.

Restaurante Pereira (☎ 214 831 215; Rua de Bela Vista 92; mains €7-10) Simple, good value and off the beaten track, this is a good, unassuming restaurant with chequered tablecloths and TV, serving up lots of seafood.

Café Mise en Scène (☎ 214 842 313; Rua Luís Palmieiri 14; mains €9-14; noon-midnight Tue-Sun) This colourful French café has artwork on the walls, eclectic furnishings and a few outdoor tables. Delightful choices include *coq au vin*, fish soup and chocolate fondue, though it's also a nice destination for afternoon *café au lait*.

O Poeta (☎ 214 832 242; Largo Luis de Camões 55-61; mains €6-9) Serving pizzas, baguette sandwiches and speciality salads, O Poeta has a nice location on the square. Upstairs is a more upmarket restaurant and wine bar (mains from €10 to €16) of the same name.

Other local favourites:

A Tasca (☎ 214 820 726; Rua Afonso Sanches 61; mains €6-9; lunch & dinner Mon-Sat)

Adega do Gonçalves (☎ 214 830 287; Rua Afonso Sanches 54; mains €7-9; lunch & dinner Thu-Tue)

TOP END

Furnas do Guincho (☎ 214 869 243; Estrada da Guincho; mains €10-16) Stunningly situated upmarket seafood restaurant about 1km along the road to Guincho, with views over the sea as you tuck into its bounty.

Bangkok (☎ 214 847 600; Rua da Bela Vista 6; mains €12-18) The smiliest restaurant in town, this Thai place with patio seating is exquisitely decorated with green tiles, wood and scented candles. The chef is no less imaginative, turning out excellent, aromatic and authentic dishes.

Drinking

Bars cluster around Largo Luís de Camões, and tend to be publike, loud and lively and stuffed with a good-time crowd that gets crazy after a round of golf.

John Bull (☎ 214 483 319; Largo Luís de Camões 4) Lined with comfy chairs and authentic English pub ambience, this spot is usually busy.

O'Neill's (☎ 214 868 230; Largo 5 de Outubro) One of Cascais' cheeriest pubs (Irish, draught Guinness, lots of wood), O'Neill's has live music on Thursday to Saturday evening around 11pm.

Coconuts (☎ 214 844 109; Avenida Rei Humberto II de Itália 7; 11pm-4am) Cascais' most popular nightclub, Coconuts is most impressive, boasting seven bars, two dance floors and an esplanade by the sea. It's packed with cool dressed-up locals as well as tourists. Coming here feels like an event.

For a sea view with your drinks, head for outdoor **Esplanada Rainha** (Largo da Rainha; 10am-10pm), which overlooks Praia da Rainha.

Shopping

Serious shoppers should head for CascaiShopping, a vast mall to get lost in, which also has a cinema (some films in English), en route to Sintra. Bus 417 passes by regularly. Cascais also has the **Cascais Villa shopping centre** (Avenida Marginal) by the bus station.

The *mercado municipal* (municipal market), on the northern outskirts of town, is best on Wednesday and Saturday morning, while an open-air market – a mix of clothes, bags, antiques, junk and so on – fills the area next to the former bullring, 1km west of town, on the first and third Sunday of the month.

Getting There & Away

Buses go frequently to Sintra from both Estoril and Cascais (€3.10, 40 minutes) and to Cabo da Roca (€2.40, 30 minutes). You pay more aboard the bus than at the kiosk.

Bus 498 goes to Lisbon's airport (Day Rover €7.50, 30 minutes, hourly) via Estoril train station. At the weekend, services between 8am and 6pm continue to Lisbon's Parque das Nações (last bus back at 6.55pm).

Trains from Lisbon's Cais do Sodré run to Cascais via Estoril (€1.30, 30 minutes, every 20 minutes daily). Bikes travel free on this line on weekends.

It's only 2km to Estoril, so it doesn't take long to walk the seafront route.

Getting Around

Since car parking is tricky (try near Museu do Mar), a good option is to park on the outskirts (eg at Praça de Touros) and take the **BusCas minibus** (☎ 214 699 100; per day/ticket €1.20/0.90) into town. It does a circular route via the centre every seven minutes from 7.30am to 9.20pm (to 10.20pm July to September) Monday to Thursday and Sunday, and to 12.20am on Friday and Saturday.

Free bikes are available from 8am to 7pm daily at various points around town, including Largo da Estação near the train station – you just have to show ID. Or you can rent them from **Transrent** (☎ 214 864 566; www.transrent.pt; basement level, Centro Comercial Cisne, Avenida Marginal), for €8.50 per day. Transrent also rents scooters/cars/motorbikes for €20/30/33 a day. There's a bicycle path that runs the entire 8km length from Cascais to Guincho. Buses 405 and 415 go to Guincho (€2.40, 20 minutes, seven daily).

Often waiting at Jardim Visconde da Luz are horse carriages, which do half-hour trips to Boca do Inferno.

Near the bus station are numerous car-rental agencies including **Ausocar** (☎ 214 822 472; www.ausocar-rentacar.pt; loja D, Edifício Sol de Cascais, Avenida 25 de Abril 16). For a taxi, call ☎ 214 660 101.

ESTORIL

pop 23,770

Packed with upmarket hotels, seaside villas and a swish casino, the palm-fringed resort of Estoril (shtoe-*reel*) once fancied itself as the Portuguese Riviera.

Now, its days of grandeur have passed, and the nouveau riche have been replaced by a more sedate and elderly clientele, preferring golf clubs and comfortable shoes to high-stakes gambling. Praia de Tamariz, the town beach, remains Estoril's loveliest feature, with a seaside promenade lined with restaurants and bars.

Estoril was where Ian Fleming hit on the idea for *Casino Royale*, as he stalked Yugoslav double agent Dusko Popov at its casino. During WWII, the town heaved with exiles and spies (including Graham Greene, another intelligence man turned author).

Orientation & Information

The bus and train stations are a stone's throw from the beach on Avenida Marginal, opposite shady Parque do Estoril. The casino is at the north end of the park, while the **turismo** (☎ 214 663 813; 9am-7pm Mon-Sat Sep-Jun, to 8pm Mon-Sat Jul & Aug, 10am-6pm Sun year-round) faces the train station, near the southwest corner of the park.

Sights & Activities

The glitzy **casino** (☎ 214 667 700; www.casino-estoril.pt; Avenida Marginal; gaming room/slot machine room €5/free; 3pm-3am) has everything from roulette to poker, French bank and blackjack to the ubiquitous slot machines. Its vast main restaurant, **Preto e Prata** (☎ 214 684 521; floor show with/without dinner €55/15), stages an international floor show nightly at 11pm. There is disabled access for both the casino and the restaurant.

Estoril's small but pleasant Praia de Tamariz has showers, cafés and beach-side bars and an ocean **swimming pool**, east of the train station.

For details on Estoril's renowned golf scene, see p68.

Festivals & Events

Feira do Artesanato (Handicrafts Fair) From mid-June to August, from 6pm to midnight, this fair takes place beside the casino to catch big winners.

International Naïve Painting Salon In October, the 1st-floor casino art gallery hosts what is acknowledged as the biggest and best such exhibition in Iberia.

Sleeping

Casa Londres (☎ 214 682 383; www.casalondres.com; Avenida Fausto Figueiredo 7; s/d from €35/50) This pleasant guesthouse has attractive rooms with white-washed walls, wood floors and a trim design. Some rooms have large terraces.

Pensão Pica Pau (☎ 214 667 140; www.picapauestoril.com; Rua do Afonso Henriques 48; s/d €40/65) A charming, modern option 400m west of the casino, Pica Pau has fine rooms, friendly service and an inviting pool. Some rooms have a balcony.

Pensão Residencial Smart (☎ 214 682 164; www.residencialsmart.com; Rua José Viana 3; s/d €60/70) About 700m northeast of station, this tidy, wood-floored classic has spotless rooms and friendly service.

Comfort Hotel São Mamede (☎ 214 659 110; www.hotelsmamede.com; Avenida Marginal 7105; s/d €66/80) With some rooms offering sea views, this is a good-value if uninspiring option. It's along a busy road, 200m uphill from the station.

Hôtel Inglaterra (☎ 214 684 461; www.hotelinglaterra.com; Rua do Porto 1; s/d €192/200) Recently renovated, this lavish, early-20th-century mansion houses a top-notch hotel, with stylish rooms and abundant amenities.

Eating

Garrett do Estoril (☎ 214 680 365; Avenida de Nice 34; snacks €1-4) An upstanding old-fashioned *pastelaria* (pastry and cake shop) and tea salon on the eastern side of the park, this has lots of pastries, sandwiches and so on, wowing the formidable, small-dog–toting clientele.

Praia de Tamariz (☎ 214 681 010; Praia de Tamariz; mains €10-14; lunch & dinner) A beachfront venue serving fresh fish and a tasty Spanish paella, this is a tempting and relaxing dining choice.

La Villa (☎ 214 680 033; Praia do Estoril; mains €14-18; Tue-Sat; V) Estoril's best restaurant lies in a classically decorated seafront villa, and specialises in delectable seafood dishes with a twist. Try the risotto with sea scallops. Vegetarian options are available.

Getting There & Away

Bus 412 goes frequently to Cascais, or it's a pleasant 2km walk or cycle along the seafront. For other train and bus services, see p141.

QUELUZ

Versailles' whimsical cousin-once-removed, the powderpuff **Palácio de Queluz** (☎ 214 343 860; admission €4; 9.30am-5pm Wed-Mon) was once a hunting lodge, converted in the late 1700s to a royal summer residence. It's surrounded by queen-of-hearts formal gardens, with tree-lined walkways, fountains (including the Fonte de Neptuno, ascribed to Italian master Bernini), statues and an *azulejo*-lined canal where the royals went boating. One wing of the palace is still used to accommodate state guests.

The palace was designed by Portuguese architect Mateus Vicente de Oliveira and French artist Jean-Baptiste Robillon for Prince Dom Pedro in the 1750s. Pedro's niece and wife, Queen Maria I, inspired the best gossip about the place; she lived here for most of her reign, going increasingly mad. Her scheming Spanish daughter-in-law, Carlota Joaquina, was just as bizarre, a match for eccentric British visitor William Beckford. On one occasion she insisted that Beckford run a race with her maid in the garden and then dance a bolero (which he did, he related, 'in a delirium of romantic delight').

Inside is like living in a chocolate box, with a mirror-lined Throne Room, marble-floored Ambassador's Room with a painted ceiling, and Pedro IV's bedroom where he slept surrounded by *Don Quixote* murals, under a circular ceiling. The palace's vast kitchens now house a palatial, fine-dining restaurant, **Cozinha Velha** (☎ 214 356 158; lunch & dinner Wed-Mon).

You've seen the palace, now live the life. Part of the palace is a dazzling *pousada*, so you can stay here. The Royal Guard of the Court quarters in this ice-cream-pink rococo palace have been converted to the beautiful **Pousada de Dona Maria I** (☎ 214 356 158; recepcao.dmaria@pousadas.pt; s/d incl breakfast €173/185; ❄), with high-ceilinged, at-home-with-the-royals rooms.

Getting There & Away

Queluz (keh-*loozh*) is 5km northwest of Lisbon. Frequent trains from Sete Rios station in Lisbon stop at Queluz-Belas (€1.05; 20 minutes).

MAFRA

pop 11,276 / elevation 250m

Mafra, 39km northwest of Lisbon, makes an excellent day trip from Lisbon, Sintra or Ericeira. It's home to the Palácio e Convento de Mafra, Portugal's most extravagant building, a hulking, ludicrous monastery-palace hybrid with 1200 rooms. Nearby is the beautiful former royal park, Tapada de Mafra, once a hunting ground and now a fascinating place to explore, still full of wild animals and plants.

Orientation

The huge palace façade dominates the town. Opposite is a pleasant little square, Praça da República, where you can find cafés and restaurants. Mafra's **bus terminal** (☎ 261 816 152) is 1.5km northwest but buses also stop in front of the palace (called 'convent' on timetables). A Mafrense bus **ticket office** (Avenida Movimento Forças Armadas 22) is near the square.

Information

The **turismo** (☎ 261 817 170; Terreiro Dom João V; 🕒 9.30am-1pm & 2.30-6pm) is in part of the palace. It has a picturesque (though outdated) map of the Mafra area and a bilingual *Mafra Real* booklet describing the palace and park.

Sights

PALÁCIO NACIONAL DE MAFRA

Constructed during the 18th-century reign of wild-spending Dom João V, the mammoth baroque **palace** (Mafra National Palace; ☎ 261 817 550; adult/child under 14/under 25/senior €4/free/2/free, 10am-2pm Sun free, 🕒 10am-5pm Wed-Mon) is a combination of palace, monastery and basilica, covering almost 4 sq km. Built from mock marble, the symmetrical structure centres on the basilica. The German architect Friedrich Ludwig had trained in Italy and the structure shows the influence of the Vatican palaces.

However, it is the extravagance that stuns, rather than the architecture. The building was begun in 1717, six years after Dom João V promised to build a monastery if he received an heir: a daughter, Dona Maria, was fortuitously born the same year. As gold from Brazil flowed into the king's coffers, he found ways to make it flow out again: the initial design for 13 monks was expanded to house 280 monks and 140 novices and include two royal wings. No expense was spared to build its 1200 halls and rooms, over 4700 doorways, 2500 windows and two bell towers with the world's biggest collection of bells (92 in total). When the Flemish bell-founders queried the extravagant order for a carillon of bells, Dom João is said to have doubled the order and paid in advance.

Up to 20,000 artisans (including Italian carpenters and masons) worked on the monument – a mind-boggling 45,000 in the last two years of construction, all of them kept in order by 7000 soldiers. The presence of so many outstanding artists spurred João V to establish a school of sculpture here from 1753 to 1770, which employed Portugal's most important sculptors. Though the building may have been an artistic coup, the expense of its construction and the use of such a large workforce helped destroy the country's economy.

After all this, it was only briefly used as a palace; the royal family visited for short periods, the longest being for a year in 1807. But when the French invaded Portugal, Dom João VI and the royal family fled to Brazil, taking most of Mafra's furniture with them. When the French arrived here in 1807, they found only 20 elderly Franciscan friars. General Junot billeted his troops in the monastery, followed by Wellington and his men. From then on the palace became a favourite military haven. Even today, most of it is used as a military academy.

A ROYAL EXTRAVAGANCE

For a fascinating glimpse at the building of Dom João V's megalith, read *Memorial do Convento,* the magical novel by Nobel Laureate José Saramago (translated into English as *Baltasar and Blimunda*). It's set in the 18th century, with Mafra's creation at the centre of this quasi-love story, though Saramago casts a wide net in capturing the era: the Inquisition, Brazilian gold, corrupt clergymen and the toils of peasant life are all part of the backdrop of this richly layered tale.

CODENAME TRICYCLE

During WWII, Portugal's neutrality, coupled with its strategic position on the Atlantic, made the country a hotbed of intelligence activity. Among the most famous spies operating within Portugal was the Yugoslav agent Dusko Popov, a young wealthy businessman, recruited early in the war by Nazi Germany. He later became a double agent, working for British intelligence, as he gave the dirt on the Nazis, whom he despised. Unlike other spies at the time, Popov lived a life of luxury, winning large sums of money at baccarat in the Estoril Casino, and seducing scores of women. Rumour had it that his codename, Tricycle, came from his penchant for *ménages à trois*. Yet, in spite of his playboy reputation, Popov's intelligence work was among the most valuable to the British effort, as he both misled the German military on British military plans, and gathered valuable data on Nazi capacities.

Popov died in 1981 at the age of 69 in Cannes. For more on the danger and debauchery courted by the real-life James Bond, check out Popov's memoir *Spy, Counterspy* (1974).

On the one-hour visit, escorted by a guard, the long corridors (one measuring 230m!) and countless salons and apartments are overwhelming. It's no surprise the royal family spent so little time here; its scale and chill are hardly cosy and even huge furniture looks lost, though the 19th-century quarters are more homely. There are some memorable sights: a room full of grotesque hunting décor (with furniture made from antlers, including a scary sofa with a boar's head); 18th-century wooden pinball machines; the monastery's infirmary beds on wheels so ailing monks could be trundled out for Mass; and a walled bed for mad monks (maybe sent over the edge by all those corridors).

Most impressive is the 83.6m-long barrel-vaulted baroque library, an unreal expanse, housing nearly 40,000 books from the 15th to 18th centuries. Many bound by the monks themselves, the books look like the sort painted on disguised doorways to secret passages. It seems an appropriate fairy-tale coda to all this extravagance that they're gradually being gnawed away by rats.

When the royals returned to Portugal, Mafra was mainly used during the hunting season. Manuel II spent his last night here before his exile following the Republic's establishment.

The central basilica, with its two bell towers, is wonderfully restrained by comparison, featuring multihued marble floors and panelling and Carrara marble statues.

Guided English-language tours usually set off at 11am and 2.30pm. A leaflet (€1) helps a bit if you catch a non-English tour. If it's a Sunday, stay till 4pm to hear a **Concerto de Carrilhão**, a concert of the basilica's infamous bells (preceded by a free guided bell-tower tour at 3.15pm). The palace's **Jardim do Cerco** (Enclosed Garden; admission free; ⌚ 10am-5pm) at the northern end of the palace, where the queen once picked her flowers, is a charming place to wait.

TAPADA NACIONAL DE MAFRA

The palace's 819-hectare park and hunting ground, **Tapada Nacional de Mafra** (☎ Mon-Fri 261 817 050, Sat & Sun 261 814 240; www.tapadademafra.pt; walker €4.50-6, cyclist €10) was created in 1747 and is still partly enclosed by its original 21km perimeter wall; the king enclosed the land and stocked it with game after nabbing it from locals. It's a rolling, beautiful, varied park, full of wild boar and deer. People still hunt here.

In 2003 there was a devastating fire, but a remarkable planting project has helped alleviate the loss. The beautiful trails around Tapada allow you to interpret the landscape; they pass a 350-year-old cork oak saved from the fire by a ring of people with buckets of water.

There are 2½-hour tours by **tourist train** (adult/child under 10/senior €10/6/8; ⌚ 10.45am & 3pm), which go via the park's carriage and wildlife museums. Weekday visits are for schools, but you may be able to join in if there's room: call to check.

There are several different walking trails, one of 4km (€4.50) and two of 7.5km (€6). There's also a 15km **mountain-bike trail** (ride with/without own bike €10/20; ⌚ 10am-4pm), with bikes available. For walking trails, gates open between 9.30am and 10am as well as between 2pm and 2.30pm daily; you can stay until 6pm. In recent years the Tapada has begun opening the gates at night during full moons. Ask at the information desk for details.

The Tapada is about 7km north of Mafra, along the road to Gradil. It's best reached by private transport, as buses are erratic; from Mafra, taxis charge around €8 one way.

SOBREIRO

At the village of Sobreiro, 4km northwest of Mafra (take any Ericeira-bound bus), sculptor José Franco has created an enchanting miniature, faintly surreal **craft village** (admission free; 9.30am-around 7.30pm;) of windmills, watermills and traditional shops. José Franco himself can often be seen crafting clay figures at the entrance. Kids love it here; so do adults, especially when they discover the rustic *adega* (winery) serving good red wine, snacks and meals. Ramped walkways make it accessible for wheelchair users.

Sleeping & Eating

Hotel Castelão (261 816 050; fax 261 816 059; Avenida 25 de Abril; s/d incl breakfast €55/75) If you get stuck here, this hotel offers comfortable, bland rooms, north of the turismo.

Café-Restaurante Paris (261 815 797; Praça da República 14; mains €6-9; lunch & dinner Mon-Sat) This smartish, genteel pink place is among several café-restaurants around Praça da República and offers decent Portuguese dishes.

If you want something lighter, there are lots of nice *pastelarias* around the square selling local crusty Mafra bread and good traditional cakes, such as *bizarros* or *pastéis de feijão,* a concoction of eggs, sugar and almonds.

Getting There & Around

There are regular **Mafrense** (261 816 159; Avenida Dr Francisco Sá Carneiro) buses to/from Ericeira (€1.70, 20 minutes, at least hourly), Sintra (€2.80, 45 minutes) and Lisbon's Campo Grande terminal (€3.10, 75 minutes, at least hourly). Mafra's train station is 6km away from the town centre with infrequent buses (taxis charge around €9 between the train station and the town centre); go to Malveira station instead for easier connections (20 minutes) to Mafra.

Taxis (261 815 512) are available in Praça da República.

SETÚBAL PENINSULA

When Lisboêtas head to the beach, that usually means going south, to the idyllic seascape of the Costa da Caparica. Here, vast stretches of sandy shore draw sunseekers of every shape and fashion. You'll find good surf here as well as lovely scenery, generally wilder the further south you go. Also in this region are favourite former fishing-village Sesimbra and seafood-central Setúbal. Two fine nature reserves, Reserva Natural do Estuário do Sado and Parque Natural da Arrábida, provide great settings for outdoor adventure such as surfing, dolphin-watching, mountain biking and walking.

CACILHAS

This sleepy seaside suburb lies just across the Rio Tejo from the capital. Its principal attraction, visible from almost everywhere in Lisbon, is the **Cristo Rei** (212 751 000), a 28m-high statue of Christ with outstretched hands, on a pedestal, doing a European impression of Rio de Janeiro's *Christ the Redeemer*. Built in 1959, it was partly paid for by Portuguese women grateful for the country having been spared the horrors of WWII. A **lift** (€3.50; 10am-6pm Apr-Sep, to 5pm Oct-Mar) zooms you up to a platform, from where Lisbon is spread out like a patchwork before you. It's a fantastic place for photos.

Cacilhas is also famous for its many seafood restaurants.

Near the ferry terminal, **Marisqueria Cabrinha** (212 764 732; mains €7-12; daily) is a cheery, friendly place that buzzes with locals. On offer are especially tasty shrimps, garlicky clams, and crab.

A 15-minute walk towards the bridge along the waterfront you'll find more excellent seafood and elegant views at Brazilian eatery **Atira-te ao Rio** (212 751 380; Cais do Ginjal 69; 1-4pm & 8pm-midnight Tue-Sun). The Saturday *feijoada* (black-bean stew) buffet is recommended.

Getting There & Away

Ferries to Cacilhas (€0.70, 10 minutes) run frequently from Lisbon's Cais do Sodré. A car-ferry service runs (every 40 minutes between 4.30am and 2.30am) from Cais do Sodré and back, or you can take bus 101 from the bus station beside the Cacilhas terminal.

COSTA DA CAPARICA

This extraordinary 8km beach disappearing into the horizon on the western coast of the peninsula is, unsurprisingly, Lisbon's favourite weekend escape. Restaurants and high-rises line the beginning of the beach, but as you head south, the land takes over, in a line of long, low-rising sandstone cliffs and pine forests. Sun-worshippers pack the beaches in July and August, but out of the high season you can easily find a tranquil space; the water is clean, but beware of the currents. Overall, the crowd is local rather than foreign, and the look smart rather than trashy. The town confusingly has the same name as the coastline, and is a cheery but tatty seaside place with lots of essential beach-side tack and shops.

During the summer a narrow-gauge railway runs most of the length of the beach from Costa da Caparica town, and you can jump off at any one of 20 stops. Each stop marks a distinctive neighbourhood: the nearer beaches, including **Praia do Norte** and **Praia do São Sebastião**, tend to attract families, while the further ones are younger and trendier. **Praia do Castelo** (stop 11 on the train) and **Praia da Bela Vista** (stop 17) are gay and nudist havens.

Continuing along the coast all the way to Lagoa de Albufeira is the Paisagem Protegida da Arriba Fóssil, a protected fossilised cliff of geological importance backed by the Mata Nacional dos Mêdos (aka Pinhal do Rei), a 600-hectare pine forest originally planted by Dom João V to stop the encroaching sand dunes.

Surfing and windsurfing are big here, especially along the northern part of the coastline.

Orientation & Information

Costa da Caparica town focuses on Praça da Liberdade. West of the *praça*, pedestrianised Rua dos Pescadores, with hotels and restaurants, leads to the seaside. The main beach (called Praia do CDS, or Centro Desportivo de Surf), with cafés, bars and surfing clubs along its promenade, is a short walk north. The **bus terminal** (Avenida General Humberto Delgado) is 400m northwest of the Praça da Liberdade; additional stops are by the *praça*.

The **turismo** (☎ 212 900 071; Avenida da República 18; ⏲ 9.30am-6pm Mon-Sat Jul–mid-Sep, 9.30am-1pm & 2-5.30pm Mon-Fri, 9.30am-1pm Sat mid-Sep–Jun) is just off the *praça*.

Policlínica São Filinto (☎ 212 954 064; Avenida da República 21) is a medical centre just nearby.

Activities

Among the hottest **surfing** spots are São João da Caparica, Praia da Mata and Praia da Sereia. **Fonte da Telha** (where the train terminates) is the best spot for **windsurfing**. Check the handy *Tabela de Marés* booklet (available at the turismo), which lists tide times, surf shops and clubs. There are plenty of water sports facilities to be found at Fonte de Telha.

Caparica Surfing School (☎ 212 919 078; www.capa ricasurfing.com; Praia do CDS; ⏲ 10am-6pm Sat & Sun) is the main surfing school. **Caparica Surf Center** (☎ 212 913 338; Avenida General Humberto Delgado 49a; ⏲ 10am-8pm) facing the beach, just south of Rua dos Pescadores, offers private lessons as well as board rentals.

Centro de Mergulho (☎ 212 977 711, 919 390 278; www.cabanadivers.com; Fonte da Telha), with a nicely set-up bar featuring wicker and basket chairs by the endless beach, provides diving lessons and equipment.

Sleeping

Costa da Caparica (☎ 212 903 894; adult/tent/car €4.65/5.05/4.55) There are masses of camp sites along the coast (most requiring camping-club membership), but Orbitur's site, 1km north of town, is closest and best. It has excellent facilities and a pine wood, and it's only 200m from the beach.

Residencial Copacabana (☎ 212 900 103; fax 212 910 462; Rua dos Pescadores 34; s/d €30/35) Among several cheap *pensões* along this street, Copacabana is a good pick offering spacious rooms with satellite TV. It's above a popular restaurant – noisy until midnight, but well placed for breakfast.

Residencial Real (☎ 212 918 870; www.hotel-real.com; Rua Mestre Manuel 18; s/d/ste €45/60/70) This has a range of trim, tidy rooms, the best of which have balconies with sea views. It's one street north of Rua dos Pescadores, 50m from the beach.

Eating & Drinking

In Costa da Caparica town, a touristy mix of seafood restaurants line Rua dos Pescadores. Along the beaches are bars and restaurants galore.

Merendeira (Rua dos Pescadores 20; mains €1.50) Fresh sandwiches (chorizo or cod) are on offer at this popular and attractive spot on the main street. It also has good daily soups and desserts.

Carolina do Aires (☎ 212 900 124; Avenida General Humberto Delgado; mains €7-12; ⏲ lunch & dinner) A big shady greenhouse of a restaurant, this pleasant indoor-outdoor spot serves up tasty seafood dishes. It's along the walking path to the beach.

Tarquino Bar (☎ 212 900 053; Avenida 1 de Maio; mains €6-10) Along Praia do Costa de Caparica, this rustic wooden restaurant serves heaps of prawns, grilled sardines and other pulls from the sea, with nice beach views.

Manuel dos Frangos (☎ 212 961 819; mains €5.25-12.50; ⌚ lunch & dinner) In Fonte da Telha, set a little back from the beach, this is a welcoming venue with a relaxed atmosphere serving grilled fish as well as roast chicken.

Bar Waikiki (☎ 212 962 129; Praia da Sereia; snacks €2.50-7; ⌚ 10.30am-7.30pm May-Sep) Nicely on its own, this is popular with surfers, on a great stretch of beach that's a surfing and parasurfing watering hole. You'll find it at stop 15 on the train.

Another beach-side haunt is **Kontiki** (☎ 212 914 391; Praia de Sao Joao).

Getting There & Away

Transportes Sul do Tejo (TST; ☎ 217 262 740; www.tsuldotejo.pt) runs regular buses to Costa da Caparica from Lisbon's Praça de Espanha (€2.30, 20 to 60 minutes). Carris bus 75 does a Costa da Caparica run (€3, every 15 minutes Saturday and Sunday from June to September) from Campo Grande metro station; the ticket gives you one-day use of all Carris transport.

The best way to get here is by ferry to Cacilhas (every 15 minutes) from Lisbon's Cais do Sodré (or to Trafaria, half-hourly, from Belém), where bus 135 runs to Costa da Caparica town (€2.20, 30 to 45 minutes, every 30 to 60 minutes); buses 124 and 194 also run here but are slower, also stopping at the train station. Bus 127 runs from Cacilhas to Fonte da Telha (50 minutes, at least hourly). Bus 130 runs from Trafaria to Fonte da Telha (45 minutes, at least hourly) via Costa da Caparica and Pinhal do Rei (near Praia do Rei).

Another option to avoid the worst of the traffic is the Fertagus air-conditioned train across the Ponte 25 de Abril, from Entrecampos in Lisbon to Fogueteiro via Sete Rios and Campolide. From Campolide you can take a train direct to Sintra (€1.50).

At Pragal (14 minutes from Entrecampos), the stop nearest Costa da Caparica, five daily buses run to town (€2.40, 25 minutes, half-hourly).

Getting Around

The train along the beach operates daily to Fonte da Telha (€4 return, every 15 minutes June to September, weekends from Easter to May, depending on the weather), about 1km before the end of the county beach. Although this is the end of the line, the beaches continue along the coast.

SETÚBAL

pop 114,000

Despite being a sizable port town with no beaches, Setúbal (*shtoo*-bahl) still draws its fair share of visitors. Among its attractions are Portugal's first-ever Manueline church; a castle with sweeping views; and a compact pedestrian centre with a jumble of clothing shops, outdoor cafés and simple guesthouses. Still, it's the seafood that draws most people here, particularly regional specialities like *caldeirada* (fish stew). Setúbal is also the closest town to the lovely beach-edged Parque Natural da Arrábida, and the Reserva Natural do Estuário do Sado, which is home to around 30 bottlenose dolphins and the winter abode of more than 1000 flamingos. The estuary's mud banks, marshes, lagoons, dunes and former salt pans house white storks (spring and summer) and resident marsh harriers and little egrets.

The Romans did a lot of fish-salting here, then came the Barbarians, then the Moors. The town developed after the 13th-century Reconquista, but it only boomed after 19th-century industrialisation.

Orientation

The mostly pedestrianised centre focuses on Praça de Bocage and Largo da Misericórdia, with most sights within easy walking distance. The bus station is about 150m northwest of the municipal turismo. The main train station is 700m north of the centre, and there's a local station (serving only Praia da Sado, by the Rio Sado) at the eastern end of Avenida 5 de Outubro. Frequent ferries shuttle across the Rio Sado to the Tróia peninsula from terminals around Doca do Comércio.

Information

EMERGENCY & MEDICAL SERVICES

Hospital (☎ 265 549 000) Near the Praça de Touros (bullring), off Avenida Dom João II.

Police station (☎ 265 522 022; Avenida 22 de Dezembro)

INTERNET ACCESS

Cyber Tody (Avenida Rua de São Cristóvão 7; per hr €2; ⌚ 10am-midnight Mon-Fri, 2.30pm-midnight Sat & Sun) Good central location.

Instituto Português da Juventude (IPJ; ☎ 265 532 707; Largo José Afonso; free internet access; ⌚ 9am-5pm Mon-Fri) Maximum 30 minutes.

Sobicome Cybercafé (1st fl, Avenida Luísa Todi 333; per hr €3; ⌚ 3pm-4am) About 500m west of the centre.

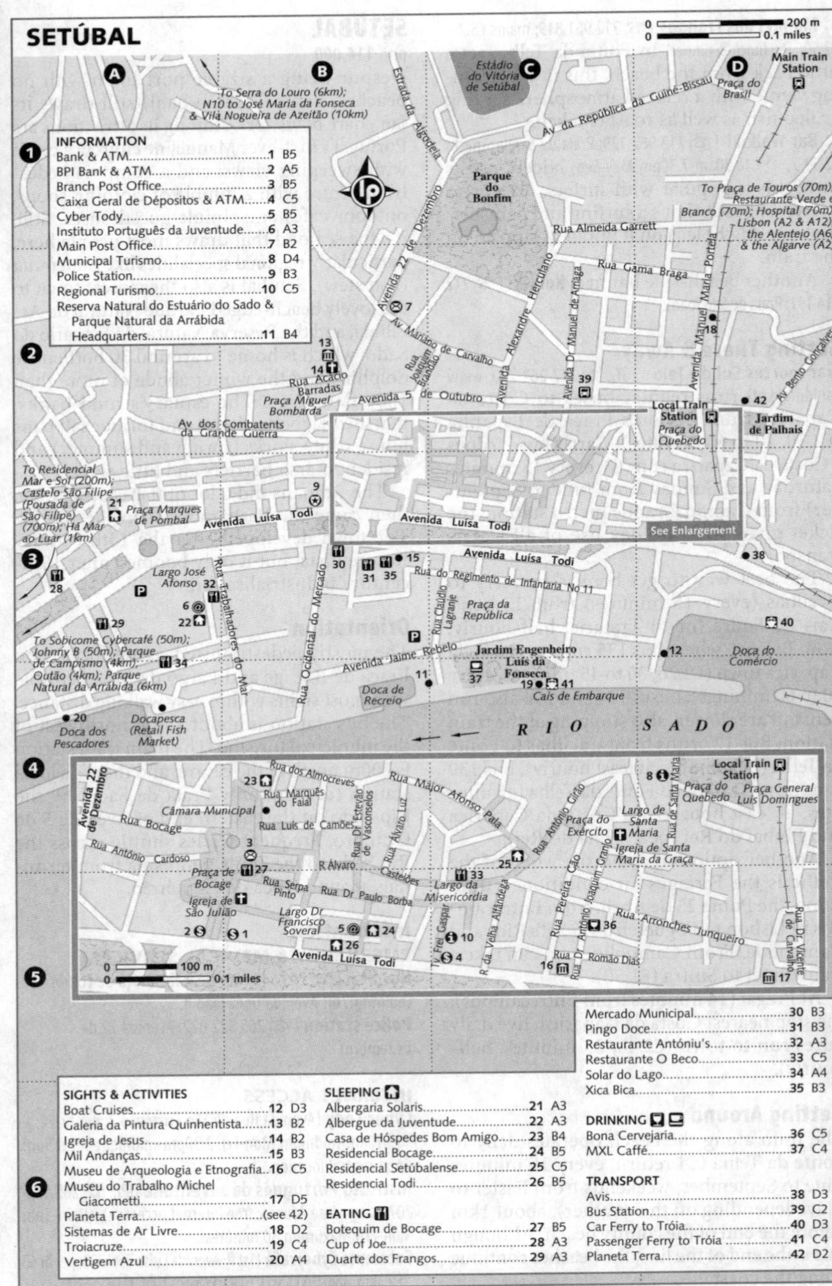
SETÚBAL
0 200 m
0 0.1 miles
A
B
C
D
1
2
3
4
5
6
INFORMATION
Bank & ATM....1 B5
BPI Bank & ATM....2 A5
Branch Post Office....3 B5
Caixa Geral de Dépositos & ATM....4 C5
Cyber Tody....5 B5
Instituto Português da Juventude....6 A3
Main Post Office....7 B2
Municipal Turismo....8 D4
Police Station....9 B3
Regional Turismo....10 C5
Reserva Natural do Estuário do Sado & Parque Natural da Arrábida Headquarters....11 B4
To Serra do Louro (6km); N10 to José Maria da Fonseca & Vila Nogueira de Azeitão (10km)
Estrada da Algodeia
Estádio do Vitória de Setúbal
Av da República da Guiné-Bissau
Praça do Brasil
Main Train Station
Parque do Bonfim
To Praça de Touros (70m); Restaurante Verde e Branco (70m); Hospital (70m); Lisbon (A2 & A12), the Alentejo (A6) & the Algarve (A2)
Rua Almeida Garrett
Rua Gama Braga
Avenida 22 de Dezembro
Avenida Alexandre Herculano
Avenida Dr Manuel de Arriaga
Avenida Manuel Maria Portela
Av Bento Gonçalves
Av Mariano de Carvalho
Rua Joaquim Brandão
Rua Acácio Barradas
Praça Miguel Bombarda
Avenida 5 de Outubro
Av dos Combatentes da Grande Guerra
Local Train Station
Praça do Quebedo
Jardim de Palhais
To Residencial Mar e Sol (200m); Castelo São Filipe (Pousada de São Filipe) (700m); Há Mar ao Luar (1km)
Praça Marques de Pombal
Avenida Luísa Todi
See Enlargement
Largo José Afonso
Rua Trabalhadores do Mar
Rua Ocidental do Mercado
Rua do Regimento de Infantaria No 11
Rua Cláudio Lagranje
Praça da República
To Sobicome Cybercafé (50m); Johnny B (50m); Parque de Campismo (4km); Outão (4km); Parque Natural da Arrábida (6km)
Avenida Jaime Rebelo
Jardim Engenheiro Luís da Fonseca
Doca do Comércio
Doca de Recreio
Cais de Embarque
Doca dos Pescadores
Docapesca (Retail Fish Market)
RIO SADO
Rua dos Almocreves
Rua Major Afonso Pala
Rua Marquês do Faial
Câmara Municipal
Rua Bocage
Rua Luís de Camões
Rua António Cardoso
Rua Dr Estevão de Vasconcelos
Rua Álvaro Luz
R Álvaro Castelões
Praça de Bocage
Rua Serpa Pinto
Rua Dr Paulo Borba
Largo da Misericórdia
Igreja de São Julião
Largo Dr Francisco Soveral
Tv Frei Gaspar
R da Velha Alfândega
Rua Pereira Cão
Rua Dr António Joaquim Granjo
Rua António Girão
Praça do Exército
Largo de Santa Maria
Rua de Santa Maria
Igreja de Santa Maria da Graça
Praça General Luís Domingues
Rua Arronches Junqueiro
Rua Romão Dias
Rua Dr Vicente J de Carvalho
0 100 m
0 0.1 miles
SIGHTS & ACTIVITIES
Boat Cruises....12 D3
Galeria da Pintura Quinhentista....13 B2
Igreja de Jesus....14 B2
Mil Andanças....15 B3
Museu de Arqueologia e Etnografia....16 C5
Museu do Trabalho Michel Giacometti....17 D5
Planeta Terra....(see 42)
Sistemas de Ar Livre....18 D2
Troiacruze....19 C4
Vertigem Azul....20 A4
SLEEPING
Albergaria Solaris....21 A3
Albergue da Juventude....22 A3
Casa de Hóspedes Bom Amigo....23 B4
Residencial Bocage....24 B5
Residencial Setúbalense....25 C5
Residencial Todi....26 B5
EATING
Botequim de Bocage....27 B5
Cup of Joe....28 A3
Duarte dos Frangos....29 A3
Mercado Municipal....30 B3
Pingo Doce....31 B3
Restaurante Antóniu's....32 A3
Restaurante O Beco....33 C5
Solar do Lago....34 A4
Xica Bica....35 B3
DRINKING
Bona Cervejaria....36 C5
MXL Caffé....37 C4
TRANSPORT
Avis....38 D3
Bus Station....39 C2
Car Ferry to Tróia....40 D3
Passenger Ferry to Tróia....41 C4
Planeta Terra....42 D2

MONEY

Caixa Geral de Depósitos (☎ 265 530 500; Avenida Luísa Todi 190) Has an ATM.

POST

Branch post office (Praça de Bocage)
Main post office (Avenida Mariano de Carvalho; ⌚ 8.30am-6.30pm Mon-Fri, 9am-12.30pm Sat) Has NetPost.

TOURIST INFORMATION

Municipal turismo (☎/fax 265 534 402; Praça do Quebedo; ⌚ 9am-12.30pm & 2-5.30pm Mon-Fri, 9am-7pm Sat & Sun Jun-Aug) Located in an 18th-century house.
Regional turismo (☎ 265 539 120; www.costa-azul.rts.pt; Travessa Frei Gaspar 10; ⌚ 9.30am-7pm Tue-Fri, 9.30am-12.30pm Sun May-Sep, to 6pm Mon-Fri, closed Sun Oct-Apr) Has a glass floor revealing the remains of a Roman *garum* (fish condiment) factory. The office sells a multilingual *Artesãos e Artesanato* (Craftsmen & Handicrafts) booklet (€1.50), the booklet *Parques e Reservas Naturais* (Parks & Natural Reserves; €1.50), with an English translation, and many more.

Sights

IGREJA DE JESUS

Setúbal has an architectural treasure, the early-Gothic **Igreja de Jesus** (Praça Miguel Bombarda; admission free; ⌚ 9am-1pm & 2-5pm Tue-Sat), containing the earliest known examples of Manueline decoration such as extraordinary twisted pillars, like writhing snakes, that spiral upwards to the ceiling. Nebulous-seeming and organic, they are made from delicately coloured Arrábida marble. Around the altar, 18th-century dark-blue and white geometric tiles form a stunning contrast with the curling arches of the roof.

Constructed in 1491, the church was designed by Diogo de Boitaca, better known for his later work on Belém's fantastical Mosteiro dos Jerónimos (p102).

GALERIA DA PINTURA QUINHENTISTA

This **gallery** (Gallery of 16th-Century Painting; Rua do Balneário Paula Borba; admission free; ⌚ 9am-noon & 1.30-5.30pm Tue-Sat) displays the marvellous panels that were once contained in the Igreja de Jesus, just around the corner. The set of 14 panels from the Lisbon school of Jorge Afonso (sometimes attributed to the anonymous 'Master of Setúbal') and four other later panels attributed to Gregório Lopes show extraordinarily rich colours and detail. Also on display is the stained glass of the church's main window. The gallery has a fine collection of Renaissance paintings, too.

MUSEU DO TRABALHO MICHEL GIACOMETTI

This **museum** (Largo Defensores da República; admission free; ⌚ 9.30am-6pm Tue-Sat) is set in a cavernous former sardine-canning factory. In pride of place is an entire 1920s grocery, transported from Lisbon wholesale. Portuguese rural life is the main subject, with implements collected in northern and central Portugal in 1975 by the famous Corsican ethnographer Michel Giacometti.

MUSEU DE ARQUEOLOGIA E ETNOGRAFIA

This small, rambling **museum** (Museum of Archaeology & Ethnography; ☎ 265 239 365; Avenida Luísa Todi 162; admission free; ⌚ 9am-12.30pm & 2-5.30pm Tue-Sat) has a wildly divergent collection. Some of its more curious pieces are Roman mosaics found nearby. Setúbal was founded by the Romans after their fishing port of Cetobriga (now Tróia), on the opposite side of the river mouth, was destroyed by an earthquake in AD 412. You'll also find endearing 19th-century religious devotional paintings on wood, showing invalids having holy visions.

CASTELO SÃO FILIPE

Worth the 500m schlep west uphill, the **castle** (⌚ 10am-9pm) was built by Filipe I in 1590 to fend off an English attack on the invincible Armada. Converted into a *pousada* in the 1960s, its ramparts are huge and impressive with wonderful views, and its chapel is fetchingly smothered in blue-and-white 18th-century *azulejos* depicting the life of São Filipe – you can view them through a glass wall if the door is locked. The restaurant is open to the public.

Activities

BEACHES

Head west to the Parque Natural da Arrábida for long, white-sanded **Figueirinha**, **Galapos** or, best of all, **Portinho da Arrábida** overlooked by a small 17th-century fort built to protect the monks from Barbary pirates. Here there are some *quartos* right on the beach. Buses from Setúbal run in the summer to Figueirinha.

WALKING

The company **Sistemas de Ar Livre** (SAL; ☎ 265 227 685; www.sal.pt; Avenida Manuel Maria Portela 40; per person Sat/Sun €5/6; 10am Sat & Sun Sep-Jun) organises three-hour guided walks in or around Setúbal.

Tours

JEEP TOURS

Mil Andanças (265 532 996; www.mil-andancas.pt; Avenida Luísa Todi 121; half-day €30) offers jeep tours in Arrábida.

Planeta Terra (265 080 176; www.planetaterra.pt; Praça General Luís Domingues 9) organises jeep safaris in Arrábida. A half-day tour encompasses a nature tour and a wine cellar (€35). The Storks Route concentrates on bird-watching, history and culture (€35).

CRUISES, CANOEING & DOLPHIN-WATCHING

Plenty of companies run trips around the estuary (leaving from Doca do Comércio) and to Arrábida, mostly with the intention of spotting the local dolphins and porpoises.

Nautur (265 532 914; www.nautur.com; Rua António Feliciano Castilho 9) Offers cruises with lunch, starting on the estuary, then visiting Arrábida beach, returning to the river for dolphin-spotting (€44).

Mil Andanças (265 532 996; www.mil-andancas.pt; Avenida Luísa Todi 121) Runs dolphin-spotting river tours (€35 per person).

Troiacruze (265 228 482; www.troiacruze.com; Rua das Barroças 34) Offers dolphin-spotting (five-hour trip per person €25 to €35) and other cruises, such as a sailing galleon along the Sado estuary (€65 including meals).

Vertigem Azul (265 238 000; www.vertigemazul.com; Rua Praia da Saúde 11d) Offers three-hour dolphin-watching tours in the Sado estuary (with a stop for snorkelling; €28); five-hour canoeing trips in the estuary (€35); or a day's dolphin-watching and jeep tour (€65). It's located 500m west of the centre.

WINE TOURS

There are recommended free wine-cellar tours of **José Maria da Fonseca** (212 198 940; www.jmf.pt; Rua José Augusto Coelho 11; 10am-1pm & 2-5pm), the oldest Portuguese producer of table wine and Moscatel de Setúbal, in nearby Vila Nogueira de Azeitão. The company is now run by the sixth generation of the family. Ring ahead to arrange a visit to the house and museum. From Setúbal, buses leave frequently to Vila Nogueira de Azeitão (20 minutes).

The tourist office has a free useful leaflet, *Rota de Vinos da Costa Azul*, detailing all the wine producers in the area you can visit.

Sleeping

BUDGET

Parque de campismo (265 238 318; Outão; adult/tent/car €3.50/4.10/2.50) A fairly shady site, right on the coast 4km west of Setúbal, accessible by regular bus (25 minutes).

Albergue de juventude (265 534 431; setubal@movijovem.pt; dm €9, d with/without bathroom €19/16; curfew 11pm-7am) Attached to the IPJ, this curved building is close to the busy fishing harbour. It's the usual bargain, with adequate facilities and a small adjoining café.

Residencial Todi (265 220 592; Avenida Luísa Todi 244; s/d with shared bathroom €20/30, with bathroom €25/35) This friendly and recently renovated guesthouse has simple, tidy rooms with good natural lighting, and it's right on the main drag.

Casa de Hóspedes Bom Amigo (265 526 290; 2nd fl, Rua do Concelho 7; d with/without shower €35/30) A welcoming choice, this place is homely and traditional, with clean, neat rooms and lots of doilies and old-fashioned furnishings.

MIDRANGE

Residencial Setúbalense (265 525 790; Rua Major Afonso Pala 17; s/d incl breakfast €30/40;) Another nice value in town, Setúbalense has clean, carpeted rooms and decent bathrooms, all with bathtubs.

Residencial Bocage (265 543 080; www.residencialbocage.pt; Rua de São Cristóvão 14; s/tw €36/46;) In the old-town centre, this small *residencial* (guesthouse) has pleasant, but small, carpeted rooms with dark wood trim.

Residencial Mar e Sol (265 534 603; www.resmaresol.com; Avenida Luís Todi 606; s/d/tr €36/47/54; P) About 1km west of the *praça*, this clean, modern hotel has comfortable carpeted rooms with marble verandas and big bathrooms. Book a top-floor room for a view.

Albergaria Solaris (265 541 770; albergaria.solaris@netc.pt; Praça Marquês de Pombal 12; s/d €45/55;) Efficient and smart, this building has a tiled façade and overlooks a square. Some of the comfortable, plain, businesslike rooms have small balconies.

TOP END

Há Mar ao Luar (265 534 901; www.hamaraoluar.com; Alto San Filipe; apt/windmill €90/110) Near the castle, this is a rural tourism place, a gorgeous house that has spacious, strikingly decorated apartments with big beds, tranquil shaded terrace, sea views and even a windmill.

Pousada de São Filipe (☎ 265 550 070; recepcao.sfilipe@pousada.pt; d €200;) Entertain royal notions at Setúbal's most luxurious option, hidden inside the town's hilltop castle.

Eating

Setúbal is packed with good fish restaurants (most with outdoor seating), especially along the western end of Avenida Luísa Todi.

BUDGET

If you're only in town for one meal, treat yourself to the seafood feast of *caldeirado*, a hearty fish stew prepared in a covered brass pot. There are many outdoor seafood restaurants along Avenida Luísa Todi, but some are rather touristy and none too unimpressive.

Cup of Joe (Avenida Luísa Todi 558; 10am-midnight) A youthful crowd gathers at this attractive coffee shop with outdoor seating. In addition to potent cappuccinos, you'll find toasted sandwiches, crepes and other light bites.

Duarte dos Frangos (☎ 265 522 603; Avenida Luísa Todi 285; roast chicken for 1/2 people €5.50/8.50; lunch Fri-Wed, dinner Fri-Tue) Roast chicken is the dish at this cosy local favourite just south of the old town. Takeaway service is next door.

MIDRANGE

Solar do Lago (☎ 265 238 847; Parque das Escolas 40; mains €7.50-16) This airy restaurant has high ceilings, big wooden tables, wrought-iron decorations and plenty of country charm. Excellent seafood dishes include *caldeirado* and grilled squid. A few outdoor tables overlook a quiet plaza.

Restaurante Antóniu's (☎ 265 523 706; Rua Trabalhadores do Mar 31; mains €7-11; Thu-Tue) This long-popular, old-fashioned venue serves a good *açorda de marisco* (seafood stew with eggs, bread and herbs) and a top-notch *arroz de marisco* (rice and seafood stew).

Restaurante O Beco (☎ 265 524 617; Rua da Misericórdia 24; mains €9-12; lunch Wed-Mon, dinner Mon & Wed-Sat) Since opening in 1966, this friendly family-run place has charmed locals. Try tasty traditional plates like *arroz de pato* (duck with rice), stone bass fillets and other seafood dishes.

Botequim de Bocage (Praça de Bocage 128; desserts €2-3) One of several attractive outdoor cafés on the main square, this is a good pitstop for coffee and desserts.

TOP END

Restaurante Verde e Branco (☎ 265 526 546; Rua Maria Batista 33; mains around €9; lunch Tue-Sun Oct-Aug) Beside the Praça de Touros and famous for miles around, this traditional hot spot serves only grilled fish: simple and superb.

Pousada de São Filipe (☎ 218 442 001; mains €17-23; lunch & dinner) This restaurant has a top-of-the-world sea-view terrace, and is the town's most spectacular place to eat, with impressive traditional food, too.

Xica Bia (☎ 265 522 559; Avenida Luísa Todi 131; mains €9-12; breakfast, lunch & dinner Mon-Sat) An upmarket, charming option near the market, this fancy place has delicious traditional food in a big arched room with exposed brickwork and wrought-iron chandeliers.

For self-catering, try the supermarket **Pingo Doce** (Avenida Luísa Todi 149; 8am-9pm) or the large market next door.

Drinking

Café-bars staying open until around 4am are plentiful along the western end of Avenida Luísa Todi, and you'll find a young local crowd out for a good time.

Johnny B (1st fl, Avenida Luísa Todi 333; 11pm-4am Tue, Fri & Sat Oct-Apr, daily May-Sep) With its dance and karaoke nights, this is a good starting point to check out the scene.

MXL Caffé (Jardim Engenheiro Luís da Fonseca; 10am-2am) Near the ferry terminal, this stylish waterfront café is a good spot for coffee or a drink. All glass walls inside and terrace seating at the front.

Bona Cervejaria (☎ 967 717 505; Rua Dr Antóniu Joaquim Granjo 32; noon-2am) A German-run option, this bar has a range of entertainments, from Friday and Saturday transvestite shows (2am) to live *fado* on Tuesday evening and a stripper on Sunday at midnight.

Getting There & Away

BOAT

Car and passenger ferries to Tróia depart half-hourly to hourly every day (car and driver €5.50, passenger €1.10). Note that car ferries, cruises and passenger ferries all have different departure points.

BUS

Buses run between Setúbal and Lisbon's Praça de Espanha (€3.40, 45 to 60 minutes, at least hourly) – or from Cacilhas (€3.10, 50 minutes, every 15 minutes Monday to Friday, at least every two hours Saturday and Sunday), a quick ferry-hop from Cais de Alfândega. Services also run to Évora (€5.75, 1¾ hours) and Faro (€13.90, four hours, two daily), and to Santarém (€9.40, three hours 20 minutes, six daily Monday to Friday, three daily Saturday and Sunday).

TRAIN

From Lisbon's Terreiro do Paço terminal you can take the ferry to Barreiro station, from where there are hourly *suburbano* (suburban) trains to Setúbal (€1.75, 45 minutes, at least hourly).

Getting Around

You can rent bikes for €10/15/20 per one/two/three days from **Planeta Terra** (☎ 919 471 871; Praça General Luís Domingues 9).

Car-rental agencies include **Avis** (☎ 265 538 710; Avenida Luísa Todi 96).

PARQUE NATURAL DA ARRÁBIDA

Stunning, thickly green and hilly, edged by gleamingly clean, golden beaches, the Arrábida Natural Park stretches along the southeastern coast of the Setúbal Peninsula from Setúbal to Sesimbra. Covering the 35km-long Serra da Arrábida mountain ridge, this is an area rich in Mediterranean plants, from olive, pistachio and strawberry to lavender, thyme and camomile, with attendant butterflies, beetles and birds (especially birds of prey) and even 70 types of seaweed.

In 2004 it suffered huge fire damage, when 700 hectares were scorched and Portugal had to appeal to the EU for assistance to put out blazes across the country, but there is still much to visit.

Local honey is delicious, especially that produced in the gardens of the whitewashed, red-roofed **Convento da Arrábida** (☎ 212 180 520), a 16th-century former monastery overlooking the sea just north of Portinho (best days to visit are Tuesday or Thursday, but call ahead). Another famous product is Azeitão ewe's cheese, with a characteristic flavour that owes much to lush Arrábida pastures and a variety of thistle used in the curdling process.

Public transport through the middle of the park is nonexistent; some buses serve the beach from July to September (around four daily to Figueirinha). Your best option is to rent a car or motorcycle, or take an organised trip by jeep and/or boat (p150). Be warned: parking is tricky near the beaches, even in the low season.

Headquarters for both this park and the **Reserva Natural do Estuário do Sado** (☎ 265 541 140; fax 265 541 155) are on Praça da República, Setúbal. They're not much use if you don't speak Portuguese – guided walks can be arranged here, but only in Portuguese. However, you can buy a useful map of the park (€4).

SESIMBRA

pop 37,570

A tiny picturesque castle perched on a steep hillside forms the backdrop to this attractive former fishing village. While traces of Sesimbra's seafaring days can still be spotted, today it's better known as a popular resort for day-tripping Lisboêtas.

Summertime crowds arrive here en masse (particularly on weekends), but Sesimbra remains a surprisingly low-key place. Narrow cobbled streets lead down to a picturesque waterfront, where bustling fish restaurants and outdoor cafés are just a stone's throw from the town's long, pretty beach. It's 30km southwest of Setúbal, sheltering under the Serra da Arrábida at the western edge of the beautiful Parque Natural da Arrábida.

Cruises, guided walks and scuba-diving activities are on offer here, including trips to Cabo Espichel, where dinosaurs once roamed.

Orientation & Information

The **bus station** (Avenida da Liberdade) is about 250m north of the seafront. Turn right when you reach the bottom of the *avenida* (avenue) and pass the small 17th-century Forte de Santiago to the helpful **turismo** (☎ 212 288 540; www.mun-sesimbra.pt; Largo da Marinha 26; 🕑 9am-8pm Jun-Sep, 9am-12.30pm & 2-5.30pm Oct-May), set back slightly from the seafront.

Sights

CASTELO

Big coastal panoramas sit below the imposing Moorish **castle** (admission free; 🕑 7am-8pm Mon-Wed, Fri & Sat, to 7pm Sun & Thu), 200m above Sesimbra. It was taken by Dom Afonso Henriques in the 12th century, retaken by the Moors, and snatched back by Christians under Dom Sancho I the following century.

The empty ruins contain the pretty 18th-century **Igreja Santa Maria do Castelo**, with heavy gold altar and blue-and-white tiles, and its cemetery. The small **Centro de Documentação** (admission free; 🕑 9am-12.30pm & 2-5.30pm Mon & Tue,

9am-12.30pm & 1-7pm Wed & Fri, 10am-1pm & 2-6pm Sat & Sun) details the castle's history. The shady castle grounds are great for picnics.

Fortaleza de Santiago (admission free; 8am-8pm), a 17th-century fort that was once part of Portugal's coastal defences, is now open to the public, and offers fine views over the sea.

PORTO DE ABRIGO

About 1km west of town is **Porto de Abrigo**, a busy fishing centre. Early morning and late afternoon, when fishermen auction their catch, is still a good time to catch a more traditional atmosphere.

Activities

Aquarama (☎ 965 263 157; Avenida dos Náufragos; adult/child €15/9; 10am-6pm) runs one to four trips per day to Cabo Espichel on a glass-bottomed partially submerged boat. Buy tickets at the office or on the boat.

Nautilus (☎ 212 281 769; www.nautilus-sub.com; Porto de Abrigo) is an IDC PADI Dive Centre offering courses (including some for kids) and dives in the Sesimbra area. **Sersub** (☎ 962 608 026; Porto de Abrigo) also runs diving courses and offers fishing trips. **Tridacna** (☎ 936 233 313; Rua da Casa Nova 2) is another diving school.

Surf Clube de Sesimbra (☎ 210 875 139, 933 845 595; www.scs.pt; Edifício Mar de Sesimbra, Rua Navegador Rodrigues Soromenho, Lote 1a, Loja 5) offers lessons and board hire. Or you can windsurf with **O Lagoa** (☎ 212 683 109; Lagoa de Albufeira).

You can go pony trekking with **Granja Paraíso** (☎ 212 680 171; Fonte de Sesimbra), a local horse-riding school.

Vertente Natural (☎ 210 848 919; www.vertentenatural.com; Zambujal de Baixo; hiking/canoeing/climbing from €12/20/25) offers a wide range of excursions, from trekking and canyoning to canoeing, hiking and rappelling. It's headquartered a few kilometres northwest of town. Visit the website for upcoming outings.

Festivals & Events

Senhor Jesus das Chagas In early May, a procession stops twice to bless the land and four times to bless the sea, carrying an image of Christ that is said to have appeared on the beach in the 16th century (usually kept in Misericórdia Church).

Cabo Espichel festival Most spectacularly set, this festival celebrates an apparition of the Virgin during the 15th century; an image of the Virgin is carried through the parishes, ending at the Cape. It takes places on the last Sunday in September.

Sleeping

Forte do Cavalo (☎ 212 288 559; www.mun-sesimbra.pt; adult/tent/car €1.80/2.65/0.85) This basic tree-shaded municipal camp site, 1km west of town, sits up on a hill with views over the sea. Restaurant on site.

Parque de Campismo de Valbom (☎ 212 687 545; adult/tent/car €3.35/2.90/2.90) In Cotovia, this is a smaller, well-equipped facility 5km north of Sesimbra, with restaurant, disabled access and some shade. To get here from Sesimbra, take any Lisbon-bound bus.

Senhora Garcia (☎ 212 233 227; Travessa Xavier da Silva 1; s/d with shared bathroom €30/40) This place has well-advertised *quartos* that are plain, dark and functional, but right in the centre.

Residencial Chic (☎ 212 233 110; Travessa Xavier da Silva; s/d €30/40) More cheap than chic. Rooms are run down and above a bar, but they are bright and central and in some you can glimpse the sea from the window.

Residencial Náutico Club (☎ 212 233 233; info@nautico.com; Avenida dos Combatentes 19; d incl breakfast from €60) About 500m uphill from the waterfront, this friendly, attractive choice has comfortable doubles, some with terrace.

Quinta do Rio (☎ 212 189 343; www.azenhadaordem.pt; s/d €40/70) Around 7km towards Setúbal is this attractive converted *quinta* (estate) set among orange groves – a really lovely, relaxing place to stay. Also available are horse rides, a swimming pool and a tennis court.

Sesimbra Hotel & Spa (☎ 212 289 000; www.sesimbrahotelspa.com; Praça da Califórnia; s/d from €120/150) One of Sesimbra's top new addresses, this seaside hotel has modern, nicely designed rooms, each with balcony and ocean views. There's also a workout room and full spa services.

Eating & Drinking

Fish restaurants abound on the waterfront just east of the fort.

Rodízio (☎ 212 231 009; Largo da Marinha 13; mains €7-12; lunch & dinner Tue-Sun) Just behind the turismo, Rodízio is one of several indoor-outdoor spots, specialising in fresh grilled seafood. This one has daily specials, including all-you-can-eat feasts.

Tony Bar (☎ 212 233 199; Largo de Bombaldes 19; mains €8-16) A classy restaurant with excellent fish mains in huge portions, and good service. The swordfish with tomatoes is delicious. Inside it's cosy or there are seats on the square.

Ribamar (☎ 212 234 853; Avenida dos Náufragos 29; mains €15-20) One of Sesimbra's best restaurants is this attractive, airy spot facing the beach. Beautifully prepared seafood and outdoor seating.

Restaurante A Sesimbrense (☎ 212 230 148; Rua Jorge Nunes 19; mains around €7; ⏰ lunch & dinner Thu-Tue) One of the cheaper places along Rua da Liberdade or Largo do Município (near the market). A short walk up from Largo de Bombaldes, this is a nice, cosy local restaurant, with more fresh fish and a local clientele.

For evening snacks and late-night drinks, stroll Avenida dos Náufragos.

Getting There & Away

Buses leave from Lisbon's Praça de Espanha (€3.40, 60 to 90 minutes, at least four to five daily); from Setúbal (€2.80, 45 minutes, at least nine daily Monday to Saturday, six Sunday); and from Cacilhas (€2.90, around one hour, at least hourly). There are runs to Cabo Espichel (€2, 20 minutes, two daily) and more frequent runs to the village of Azóia (€2, 10 daily Monday to Saturday, six Sunday), about 3km before the cape.

AROUND SESIMBRA

Aldeia do Meco

Like nearby Alfarim, this tiny village 12km northwest of Sesimbra is famous for its clustered seafood restaurants.

SLEEPING & EATING

Country House (☎ 212 685 001; www.countryhouse-meco.com; Rua Alto da Carona, Alfarim; d €50, 2-/4-person apt €65/80) A big, fairly modern whitewashed house with sloping red roofs, 1.4km north of the village in a wooded setting, with four spacious rooms (with coffeemakers and fridge) and three apartments, most with balconies. It's 2km from the beach, and well signposted.

Campimeco (☎ 212 683 394; adult/tent/car €3.35/2.90/2.90; 🏊 ♿) This large camp site is 3km from the village, above Praia das Bicas and close to several beaches. It has a great situation, right up on the clifftop, with lots of shady trees, good facilities and disabled access.

Bar do Peixe (☎ 212 684 732; Praia do Meco; mains €7-11; ⏰ lunch & dinner Wed-Mon, daily Jul & Aug) North of Praia das Bicas, right on the beach, this is a big wooden building with a sea-facing terrace and a wonderful position overlooking the long sands. It's 500m from the bus stop.

Other top local seafood spots are found throughout the village, particularly on Rua Central do Meco, the town's main street.

GETTING THERE & AWAY

Buses run from Sesimbra (€2, 30 minutes, three to five daily).

Cabo Espichel

At strange, bleak Cabo Espichel, frighteningly tall greenery-topped cliffs drop down into the piercing blue sea, some met by swaths of beach. The only building on the cape is a huge church, the 18th-century Nossa Senhora do Cabo, flanked by two arms of desolately empty pilgrims' lodges.

It's easy to see why Wim Wenders used this spot as a location when filming *A Lisbon Story*, with its lonely, brooding, outback atmosphere. Rocks around the cape resemble prehistoric hides – an appropriate setting for dinosaurs, whose footprints have even been discovered imprinted in rock to the north, near Praia dos Lagosteiros.

It's worth your while trying to catch the Cabo Espichel festival if you are visiting in September (p153).

Buses run direct from Sesimbra (€2, 20 minutes, two daily), more frequently terminating at the village of Azóia (€2, 10 daily Monday to Saturday, six Sunday), about 3km before the cape.

The Algarve

Love it or hate it, the Algarve is Portugal's premier holiday destination, with pretty beaches, brash resorts and picturesque whitewashed towns that flood with foreigners when summer arrives. While the party atmosphere isn't for everyone, the setting is undeniably beautiful. Outside the touristy enclaves, there are quiet castle towns, flower-covered hillsides and enchanting stretches of shoreline still untouched by development.

The Algarve's long-time popularity is due to its dramatic scenery: breathtaking cliffs, wide golden sands, natural bays, scalloped beaches and long sandy islands with waves lapping at the shore.

The towns themselves aren't as varied as the coastline, but still offer a wide range of personalities. Lagos, with its cobbled streets, young crowd and abundant nightlife, is the carnival queen of the Algarve. Tavira, set along a peaceful river, remains elegant and laid-back, with a history dating back to the Romans. The hypermodern town of Praia da Rocha is a bit trashier, though its high-rise hotels overlook one of the region's best beaches. Out on the rugged west coast, small, charming towns like Sagres and Carrapateira attract a surf-loving crowd, while cliffside Albufeira sees a wider mix of travellers.

The quiet interior contrasts considerably with the coast. Here you'll find sleepy towns like Alcoutim, set overlooking the picture-perfect Rio Guadiana on the edge of Spain, and Monchique, a quaint town with fine views over the steep wooded countryside.

If you're not keen on crowds and high-season prices, avoid coming from July to mid-September. This is when most Portuguese and other Europeans take their holidays: spring and autumn are lovely alternatives (though the water will be a bit nippy).

HIGHLIGHTS

- Dining and bar-hopping in happening **Lagos** (p198).
- Taking in the stunning beauty of the cliffs of **Cabo de São Vicente** (p207).
- Frolicking in the waves off untouched islands in the **Parque Natural da Ria Formosa** (p167).
- Strolling the old, historic streets of riverside **Tavira** (p182).
- Enjoying country walks, followed by spa pampering in **Monchique** (p213).

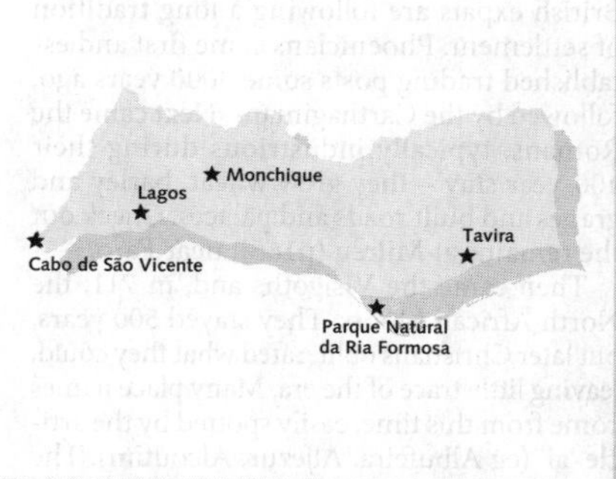

POPULATION: 396,000	AREA: 4995 SQ KM

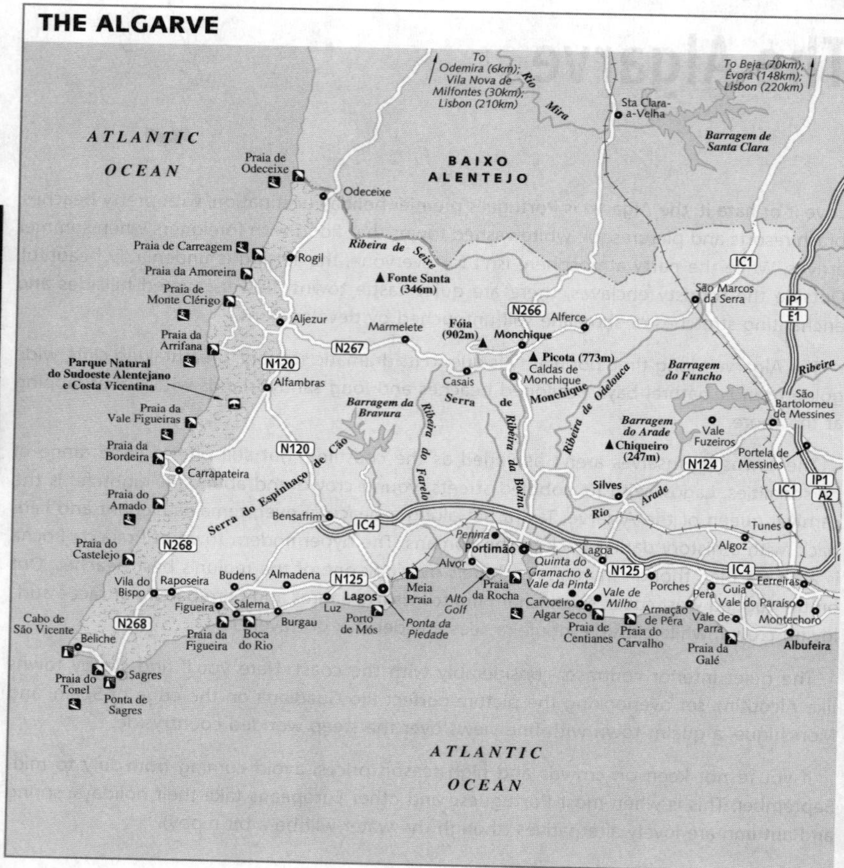

History

British expats are following a long tradition of settlement. Phoenicians came first and established trading posts some 3000 years ago, followed by the Carthaginians. Next came the Romans, typically industrious during their 400-year stay – they grew wheat, barley and grapes and built roads and palaces. Check out the remains at Milreu (p166), near Faro.

Then came the Visigoths and, in 711, the North African Moors. They stayed 500 years, but later Christians obliterated what they could, leaving little trace of the era. Many place names come from this time, easily spotted by the article 'al' (eg Albufeira, Aljezur, Alcoutim). The Syrian Moors called the region in which they settled (east of Faro to Seville, Spain) al-Gharb al-Andalus (western Andalucía), later known as 'Algarve'. Another Arabic legacy is the flat-roofed house, originally used to dry almonds, figs and corn, and to escape the night heat.

Trade boomed, particularly in nuts and dried fruit, and Silves was the mighty Moorish capital, quite independent of the large Muslim emirate to the east.

The Reconquista (Christian reconquest) began in the early 12th century, with the wealthy Algarve as the ultimate goal. Though Dom Sancho I captured Silves and territories to the west in 1189, the Moors returned. Only in the first half of the 13th century did the Portuguese claw their way back for good.

Two centuries later the Algarve had its heyday. Prince Henry the Navigator chose the

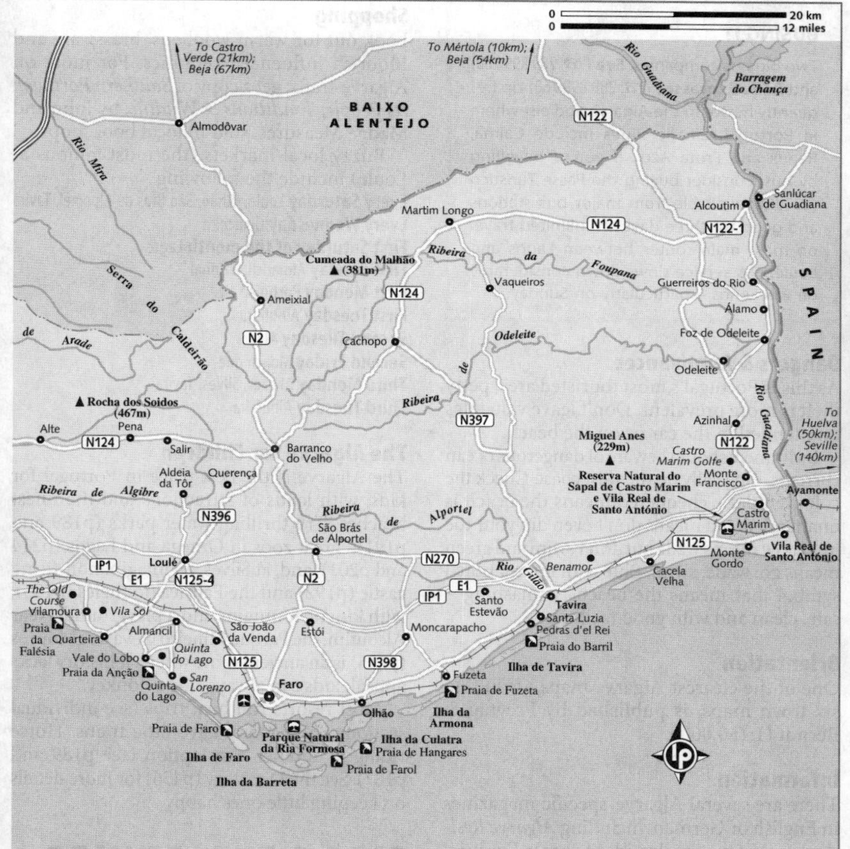

appropriately end-of-the-earth Sagres as the base for his school navigation, and had ships built and staffed in Lagos for the 15th-century exploration of Africa and Asia – seafaring triumphs that turned Portugal into a major imperial power.

The Algarve coastline is 155km long, with five regions: the leeward coast (Sotavento), from Vila Real de Santo António to Faro, largely fronted by a chain of sandy offshore *ilhas* (islands); the central coast, from Faro to Portimão, featuring the heaviest resort development; the increasingly rocky windward coast (or Barlavento), from Lagos to Sagres, culminating in the wind-scoured grandeur of the Cabo de São Vicente, Europe's southwesternmost corner; and the hilly, thickly green interior, which rises to two high mountain ranges the Serra de Monchique and the less-visited Serra do Caldeirão. The Costa do Ouro (Golden Coast) borders the Costa de Sagres (Bay of Sagres), while the Costa Vicentina stretches north of here, the windy, wild rim of a national park.

Climate

Blessed with good weather, the Algarve has a mild winter and sunshine almost year-round with 12/six hours' sunshine on a typical summer/winter day. Summertime temperatures average 25°C to 30°C, sometimes reaching as high as 40°C. In January and February, almond blossoms cover the countryside, while in March it's orange blossom; April is the best time for wildflowers.

BUSING IT

Two big bus companies, **Eva** (☎ 289 899 760) and **Rede Expressos** (☎ 289 899 760) zip frequently between the Algarve and elsewhere in Portugal. Smaller lines include Caima, Renex and Frota Azul. If you're travelling by bus, consider buying the Passe Turístico (€22.80), available from major bus stations and good for three days of unlimited travel on most main routes between Lagos and Loulé. Bus service slows down considerably on weekends – particularly on Sunday.

Dangers & Annoyances

As this is Portugal's most touristed area, petty theft is more prevalent. Don't leave valuables unattended in the car or on the beach.

Swimmers should beware of dangerous ocean currents, especially on the west coast. Check the coloured flags: chequered means the beach is unattended, red means don't even dip your toe in, yellow means wade but don't swim and green means go: wade, swim. Blue is an international symbol that means the beach is smashing – safe, clean and with good facilities.

Orientation

One of the clearest Algarve maps, including six town maps, is published by Freytag & Berndt (1:150,000).

Information

There are several Algarve-specific magazines in English or German, including *Algarve Resident* (www.portugalresident.com). *Essential Algarve* (www.essential-algarve.com) is a leisure and lifestyle mag.

Turismos (tourist offices) dole out information, maps and free leaflets, including the monthly *Algarve Guide*, which covers what's on, the quarterly *Welcome to the Algarve*, and *Algarve Tips*. Major towns have a monthly *Agenda Cultural* magazine. The *Best Guide Algarve* covers sights and activities, and has a basic road map. *Algarve Tourist Yellow Pages* is another freebie, with town maps and local information. There are also privately produced *Free Maps* in resorts (often available at bars and shops), good for up-to-date tips on local spots.

Far and away the best of many websites is www.visitalgarve.pt, with information on hidden beaches, upcoming events and festivals, activities and more.

Shopping

Look out for warm woollens, brassware and Moorish-influenced ceramics. For more on Algarve crafts, get a copy of *Southern Portugal: Its People, Traditions & Wildlife*, by John and Madge Measures, sold in local bookshops.

Buzzy local markets (the most famous at Loulé) include the following:

Every Saturday Loulé, Olhão, São Brás de Alportel, Tavira
Every Wednesday Quarteira
First Saturday of the month Lagos
First Sunday Almancil, Azinhal
First Monday Portimão
First Tuesday Albufeira
Second Tuesday Alvor
Second Friday Monchique
Third Monday Aljezur, Silves, Tavira
Third Tuesday Albufeira

The Algarve for Children

The Algarve is the best place in Portugal for kids, with loads of attractions and the finest beaches. Try thrilling water parks (p189 and p191); great zoos in Omega and Lagos (p214 and p201); and, at Silves, an imagination-firing castle (p192) and the Fábrica do Inglês (p195), with kinetic fountains and a playground. Near Alcoutim, the Parque Mineiro Cova dos Mouros (p215) is an ancient mine where, if history lacks appeal, kids can always ride a donkey.

Most resorts run boat trips (see individual sections), and many have little trains. Horse riding is another easy option (see p189 and p187). See the Directory (p456) for more details on keeping little ones happy.

FARO & THE LEEWARD COAST

FARO

pop 52,000

Algarve's capital has a more distinctly Portuguese feel than many other resort towns. While most people only pass through, laid-back Faro (*fah*-roo) makes a fine overnight stop. It has an attractive marina, well-maintained parks and plazas and an old town full of outdoor cafés and pedestrian lanes. Marvellously preserved medieval quarters harbour curious museums and churches (along with a bone chapel), and a vibrant nightlife – more local than expat. Nearby beaches, including island sands of Ilha de Barreta, add to Faro's allure.

History

After the Phoenicians and Carthaginians, Faro boomed as the Roman port Ossonoba. During the Moorish occupation, it became the cultured capital of an 11th-century principality.

Afonso III took the town in 1249 (the last major Portuguese town to be recaptured from the Moors), and walled it.

Portugal's first printed works – books in Hebrew made by a Jewish printer – came from Faro in 1487.

A city from 1540, Faro's brief golden age slunk to a halt in 1596, during Spanish rule. Troops under the Earl of Essex, en route to England from Spain in 1597, plundered the city, burned it and carried off hundreds of priceless theological works from the bishop's palace, now part of the Bodleian Library in Oxford.

Battered Faro was rebuilt, poking its head over the parapet only to be shattered by an earthquake in 1722 and then almost flattened in the 1755 big one. Most of what you see today is postquake, though the historic centre largely survived. In 1834 it became the Algarve's capital.

Orientation

The town hub, Praça Dr Francisco Gomes, adjoins the marina and small garden called Jardim Manuel Bívar. The Eva bus station and the train station, both on Avenida da República, are a short walk away. The airport is about 6km west, off the N125.

Offshore is the widest stretch of the Parque Natural da Ria Formosa. While many of the near-shore sand bars along here disappear at high tide, two of the bigger sea-facing islands – Ilha de Faro to the southwest and Ilha da Culatra to the southeast – have good beaches.

Information

BOOKSHOPS

Faro's main bookshop is **Livraria Bertrand** (☎ 289 828 147; Rua Dr Francisco Gomes 27), although souvenir shops and newsagents stock more local maps and guides.

EMERGENCY & MEDICAL SERVICES

Faro district hospital (☎ 289 891 100; Rua Leão Penedo) Over 2km northeast of the centre.

Police station (☎ 289 822 022; Rua da Polícia de Segurança Pública 32)

INTERNET ACCESS

Café Aliança (Rua Dr Francisco Gomes; per hr €2.50; 🕑 9am-11.45pm Mon-Sat, 10am-11.45pm Sun)

Instituto Português da Juventude (IPJ; Rua da Polícia de Segurança Pública 1; 🕑 9am-8pm Mon-Fri, 10am-1pm Sat) Free internet access next to the Pousada da Juventude (p162).

Planet (Rua Ferreiro Neto 5; per hr €2.50; 🕑 10am-11pm Mon-Fri, 10am-7pm Sat)

LAUNDRY

Lavandaria Sólimpa (☎ 289 822 891; Rua Batista Lopes 30; 1-day wash-&-dry service per kg €1.75, min 4kg; 🕑 9am-1pm & 3-7pm Mon-Fri, 9am-1pm Sat)

MONEY

Cota Câmbios (Rua Dr Francisco Gomes 26; 🕑 8.30am-6.30pm Mon-Fri, 10am-2pm Sat) A private exchange bureau.

POST

Main post office (Largo do Carmo)

TOURIST INFORMATION

ICEP turismo (☎ 289 818 582; 🕑 8am-11.30pm) At the airport.

Municipal turismo (☎ 289 803 604; Rua da Misericórdia 8; 🕑 9.30am-1pm & 2.30-5.30pm Mon-Fri) The chief information office: efficient, busy and helpful.

Regional turismo administrative office (☎ 289 800 400; rtalgarve@rtalgarve.pt; Avenida 5 de Outubro 18; 🕑 8.30am-8pm Mon-Fri) Provides a map and leaflets.

TRAVEL AGENCIES

Abreu Tours (☎ 707 201 840; www.abreu.pt; Avenida da República 124; 🕑 9am-12.30pm & 2-6pm Mon-Fri)

Tagus (☎ 289 805 483; www.viagenstagus.pt; Avenida 5 de Outubro 24c; 🕑 9.30am-7pm Mon-Fri, 10am-1pm Sat) The best student-oriented agency.

Sights & Activities

CIDADE VELHA

Within medieval walls, the picturesque Cidade Velha (Old Town) consists of winding, peaceful cobbled streets and squares, reconstructed in a mélange of styles following successive batterings – first by marauding British and then two big earthquakes.

Enter through the neoclassical **Arco da Vila**, built by order of Bishop Francisco Gomes, Faro's answer to the Marquês de Pombal (p31), who oversaw Faro's reconstruction after the 1755 earthquake. The top of the street opens into the orange tree–lined Largo da Sé, with the *câmara municipal* (town hall) on the left, the Paço Episcopal (Bishop's Palace) on the right and the ancient *sé* (cathedral) in front of you.

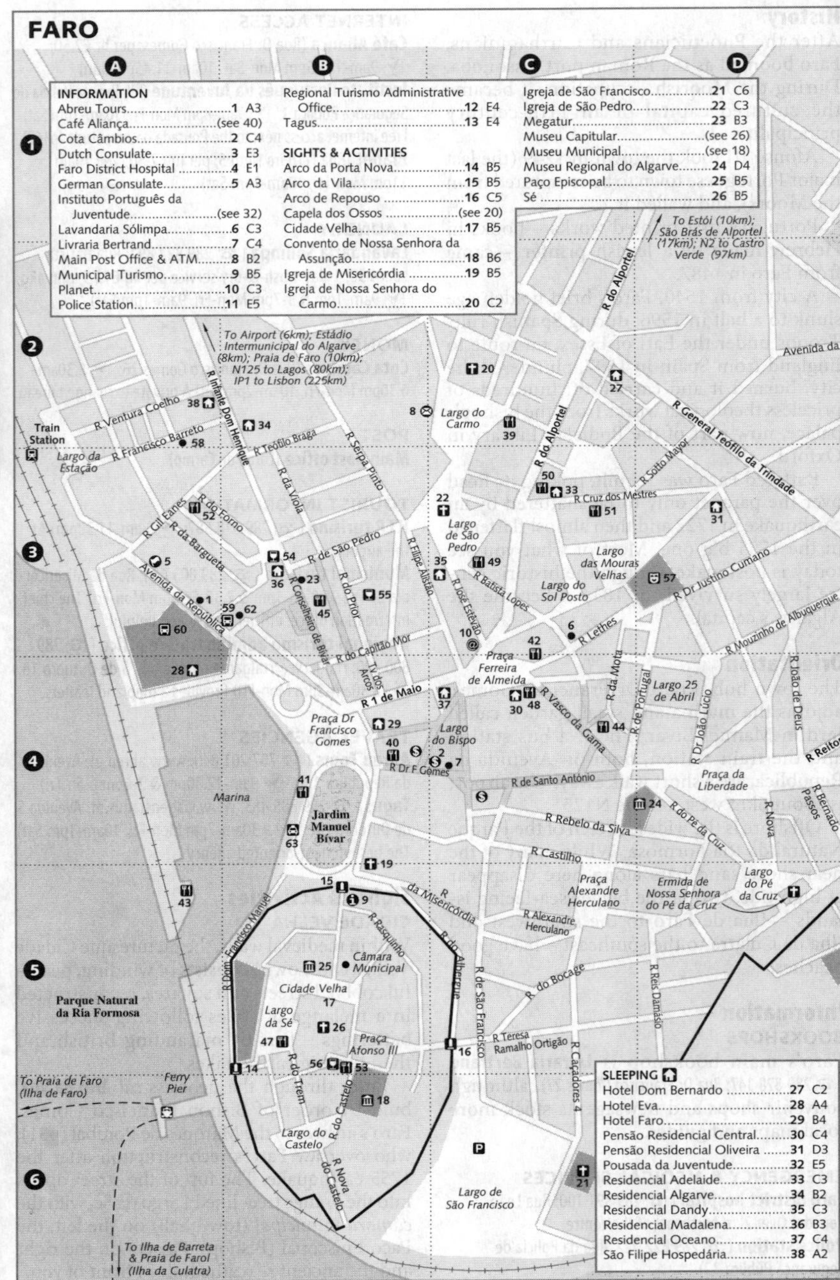
FARO
A
B
C
D
1
2
3
4
5
6
INFORMATION
Abreu Tours....1 A3
Café Aliança....(see 40)
Cota Câmbios....2 C4
Dutch Consulate....3 E3
Faro District Hospital....4 E1
German Consulate....5 A3
Instituto Português da Juventude....(see 32)
Lavandaria Sólimpa....6 C3
Livraria Bertrand....7 C4
Main Post Office & ATM....8 B2
Municipal Turismo....9 B5
Planet....10 C3
Police Station....11 E5
Regional Turismo Administrative Office....12 E4
Tagus....13 E4
SIGHTS & ACTIVITIES
Arco da Porta Nova....14 B5
Arco da Vila....15 B5
Arco de Repouso....16 C5
Capela dos Ossos....(see 20)
Cidade Velha....17 B5
Convento de Nossa Senhora da Assunção....18 B6
Igreja de Misericórdia....19 B5
Igreja de Nossa Senhora do Carmo....20 C2
Igreja de São Francisco....21 C6
Igreja de São Pedro....22 C3
Megatur....23 B3
Museu Capitular....(see 26)
Museu Municipal....(see 18)
Museu Regional do Algarve....24 D4
Paço Episcopal....25 B5
Sé....26 B5
SLEEPING
Hotel Dom Bernardo....27 C2
Hotel Eva....28 A4
Hotel Faro....29 B4
Pensão Residencial Central....30 C4
Pensão Residencial Oliveira....31 D3
Pousada da Juventude....32 E5
Residencial Adelaide....33 C3
Residencial Algarve....34 B2
Residencial Dandy....35 C3
Residencial Madalena....36 B3
Residencial Oceano....37 C4
São Filipe Hospedária....38 A2
To Estói (10km); São Brás de Alportel (17km); N2 to Castro Verde (97km)
To Airport (6km); Estádio Intermunicipal do Algarve (8km); Praia de Faro (10km); N125 to Lagos (80km); IP1 to Lisbon (225km)
Train Station
Largo da Estação
R Ventura Coelho
R Francisco Barreto
R Infante Dom Henrique
R Teófilo Braga
R Serpa Pinto
R da Viola
R Gil Eanes
R do Forno
R da Barqueta
Avenida da República
R de São Pedro
R Conselheiro de Bivar
R do Prior
R do Capitão Mor
Tv dos Arcos
R Filipe Alistão
R José Estêvão
R Batista Lopes
Largo do Carmo
Largo de São Pedro
Largo do Sol Posto
Largo das Mouras Velhas
R do Alportel
Avenida da
R General Teófilo da Trindade
R Sotto Mayor
R Cruz dos Mestres
R Dr Justino Cumano
R Lethes
R Mouzinho de Albuquerque
R João de Deus
R Reitor
Praça Ferreira de Almeida
R 1 de Maio
R Vasco da Gama
R da Mota
R de Portugal
Largo 25 de Abril
R Dr João Lúcio
Praça da Liberdade
Praça Dr Francisco Gomes
Largo do Bispo
R Dr F Gomes
R de Santo António
R Rebelo da Silva
R do Pé da Cruz
R Nova
R Bernardo Passos
Marina
Jardim Manuel Bívar
R Castilho
Praça Alexandre Herculano
Ermida de Nossa Senhora do Pé da Cruz
Largo do Pé da Cruz
R da Misericórdia
R Alexandre Herculano
R do Albergue
R de São Francisco
R do Bocage
R Reis Damásio
R Rasquinho
Câmara Municipal
R Dom Francisco Manuel
Cidade Velha
Largo da Sé
Praça Afonso III
R do Trem
R do Castelo
R Nova do Castelo
Largo do Castelo
R Teresa Ramalho Ortigão
R Caçadores 4
Largo de São Francisco
Parque Natural da Ria Formosa
To Praia de Faro (Ilha de Faro)
Ferry Pier
To Ilha de Barreta & Praia de Farol (Ilha da Culatra)

The **sé** (admission €2.50; 10am-6pm Tue-Fri, 10am-1pm Sat) was completed in 1251, on what was probably the site of a Roman temple, then a Visigoth cathedral and then a Moorish mosque. Only the tower gate and two chapels remain of the original Romanesque-Gothic exterior – the rest was devoured in 1755. It was rebuilt in a polygamy of Gothic, Renaissance and baroque styles, with intense gilded carving alongside elaborate tilework inside. Climb up to the rooftop *miradouro* (lookout) for views across the pretty walled town to the sea, as well as the storks nesting in the bell towers. The cathedral buildings also house the **Museu Capitular**, with an assortment of sacred artwork (vestments, chalices, saint statues in glass boxes), and a small shrine built of bones to remind you of your mortality.

Facing the cathedral is the 18th-century **Paço Episcopal** (admission €1.50; 10am-1pm & 2.30-6pm Tue-Sun), with a pointy red roof and finished in multicoloured *azulejos* (hand-painted tiles), successor to the previous Episcopal dwelling trashed by British troops in 1596. It houses changing exhibitions of sacred art, and is worth stopping in to glimpse the finely crafted interior. At the southern end of the square is a small 15th-century town gate, the **Arco da Porta Nova**, leading to the ferry pier.

Next to the cathedral is the stately 16th-century **Convento de Nossa Senhora da Assunção**, now housing the Museu Municipal (p162).

From here you can leave the old town through the medieval **Arco de Repouso**, or Gate of Rest (apparently Afonso III, after taking Faro from the Moors, put his feet up and heard Mass nearby). Around the gateway are some of the town walls' oldest sections – Afonso III's improvements on the Moorish defences.

IGREJA DE NOSSA SENHORA DO CARMO & CAPELA DOS OSSOS

The twin-towered, baroque **Igreja de Nossa Senhora do Carmo** (Our Lady of Carmel; Largo do Carmo; 10am-1pm & 3-5pm Mon-Fri Oct-Apr, to 6pm Mon-Fri May-Sep, 10am-1pm Sat & Sun year-round) was completed in 1719 under João V and paid for (and gilded to death inside) with Brazilian gold. The almost-edible butterscotch façade was completed after the 1755 earthquake.

A more ghoulish attraction lies behind the church. The 19th-century **Capela dos Ossos** (admission €1) was built from the bones and skulls of over 1000 monks as a blackly reverent reminder of earthly impermanence, and the ultimate in recycling. There's a similar chapel at Évora (p225).

OTHER CHURCHES

For more dazzling woodwork, head to the frenzied 18th-century baroque interior of the **Igreja de São Francisco** (Largo de São Francisco; Mass 6.30pm) with tiles depicting the life of St Francis.

The 16th-century **Igreja de Misericórdia** (Mass 9am), opposite the Arco da Vila, has a remarkable Manueline portico, the only remnant of an earlier chapel to withstand the 1755 earthquake.

At the southern end of Largo do Carmo is the 16th-century **Igreja de São Pedro** (9am-1pm & 3-7pm Mon-Fri), filled with 18th-century *azulejos* and fine-carved woodwork.

MUSEU MUNICIPAL

The splendid, domed 16th-century Renaissance Convento de Nossa Senhora da Assunção, in what was once the Jewish quarter, houses the **Museu Municipal** (289 897 400; Largo Dom Afonso III; adult/student €2/1; 10am-6pm Tue-Fri, noon-6pm Sat & Sun Mar-Oct; 9.30-5.30pm Tue-Fri, 11.30am-5.30pm Sat & Sun Oct-May). Highlights are the 3rd-century *Mosaic of the Ocean*, found in 1976 on a building site; 9th- to 13th-century domestic Islamic artefacts; and works by a notable Faro painter, Carlos Filipe Porfírio, depicting local legends.

MUSEU REGIONAL DO ALGARVE

The **Museu Regional do Algarve** (Algarve Regional Museum; 289 827 610; Praça da Liberdade; admission €1.50; 9am-12.30pm & 2-5.30pm Mon-Fri) Elements of old peasant life are on display here – like a small fishing boat and a wooden water cart (used until the owner's death in 1974). There are also enigmatically labelled displays of ceramics, fabrics and dioramas of typical interiors.

BEACHES

The town's beach, **Praia de Faro**, with miles of sweeping sand, windsurfing operators and some cafés, is on the Ilha de Faro, 10km away. It's crammed in July and August. Take bus 14 or 16 from opposite the bus station (€1.40, half-hourly in summer, via the airport). Ferries go out to **Praia de Farol** (Ilha da Culatra) and **Ilha da Barreta** (aka Ilha Deserta, p165), a long narrow-strip of sand just off the mainland.

Courses

You can have group and private lessons in Portuguese at **Centro de Linguas** (CIAL; 289 807 611; www.cial.pt; Rua Almeida Garrett 44). Prices are around €320 for a 30-hour intensive course.

Tours

Megatur (289 807 485; www.megatur.pt; Rua Conselheiro de Bívar, 80; half-day €15-25, full day €30-65) offers a wide range of excursions, from speedboat and jeep tours to trips to the Loulé market.

Festivals & Events

FolkFaro The city's big folk festival features lots of dance (with local and international folk groups), live music and street fests. It's held in late August over five days at various venues around town.

Feira de Santa Iria Held in mid-October, Faro's biggest traditional event honours St Irene with fairground rides and entertainment. It takes place in a temporary fairground to the northeast, by the municipal fire station.

Sleeping

BUDGET

Pousada da Juventude (289 826 521; faro@movijovem.pt; Rua da Polícia de Segurança Pública 1; dm €13, d with/without bathroom €36/28; reception 8am-noon & 6pm-midnight) At the Instituto Português da Juventude (IPJ), this hostel offers basic facilities and adjoins a park. The IPJ is buzzy, with a small café.

Pensão Residencial Oliveira (289 812 154; Rua Horta Machado 28; s/d with shared bathroom from €15/30) One of Faro's cheapest options, this well-worn place has nine rooms with frilly bedspreads and peeling wallpaper amid a cluttered old house. Some rooms have balconies.

Residencial Oceano (289 823 349; Rua Ivens 21; s/d/tr €25/35/45) Up the tile-lined stairs you'll find a simple, friendly option with tidy rooms and tile floors. Good value.

Residencial Adelaide (289 802 383; Rua Cruz dos Mestres 7; s/d €35/50;) Recently renovated, this small, pleasant guesthouse has trim and tidy rooms, some with terraces. Laundry service is available.

Pensão Residencial Central (289 807 291; Largo do Bispo 12; s/d €35/50) This popular place has cool, tiled and spacious rooms with balconies overlooking the pretty square, though the rooms at the back are quieter.

São Filipe Hospedária (/fax 289 824 182; www.guesthouse-saofilipe.com; Rua Infante Dom Henrique €35/45;) Renovated in 2006, this guesthouse has small colourful rooms with new mattresses, flower prints on the walls and spotless tile floors.

MIDRANGE & TOP END

Residencial Dandy (☎ 289 824 791; Rua Filipe Alistão 62; d with/without bathroom from €45/35) Looking as smart as its name, this good-value place has a range of rooms. The best are attractively furnished with wood floors, high ceilings and small wrought-iron balconies. More compact, tile-floored rooms are in back.

Residencial Madalena (☎ 289 805 806; Rua Conselheiro de Bívar 109; s/d €40/50) This place has simply furnished rooms, some with small balconies and excellent natural light. Others are small and a little cramped.

Residencial Algarve (☎ 289 895 700; www.residencialalgarve.com; Rua Infante Dom Henrique 52; s/d/tr €50/65/80; P) This friendly, small-scale place has bright, cheerful rooms, some with balconies.

Hotel Dom Bernardo (☎ 289 889 800; www.hoteldombernardo.com; Rua General Teófilo da Trindade 20; d from €83;) Rooms at modern Dom Bernardo are comfortable, if daring in their colour combinations. Striped bedspreads, floral curtains and chocolatey brown tile floors are set with big windows overlooking a busy street. A few extra euros buys you a sea view.

Hotel Faro (☎ 289 830 830; www.hotelfaro.pt; Praça Dr Francisco Gomes 2; s/d €123/143;) Newly opened in 2006, this square cube of a hotel hides plush rooms with huge beds and marble-filled bathrooms. The top-floor bar-restaurant with terrace is great for a sunset cocktail.

Hotel Eva (☎ 289 001 000; www.tdhotels.pt; Avenida da República 1; s/d €123/144;) This huge 150-room hotel has spacious, attractive rooms, most with balconies and views. There's a rooftop swimming pool for more marina-gazing.

Eating

BUDGET

Café Aliança (Rua Dr Francisco Gomes; snacks €0.60-8; breakfast, lunch & dinner) Head for this dog-eared, old-fashioned place for coffee, snacks and people-watching from the tables spilling into the square.

Café do Coreto (Jardim Manuel Bívar; mains €4-8; 10am-11pm) Overlooking the marina, this casual café has well-placed outdoor seating and many lighter bites and drinks.

Adega Nova (☎ 289 813 433; Rua Francisco Barreto 24; mains €6-10; lunch & dinner) Serving nicely prepared meat and fish dishes, this long, narrow restaurant has country charm: a lofty beamed ceiling overhead and rustic cooking implements along the walls.

Faro's big, daily *mercado municipal* (municipal market) is in Largo Mercado. Two supermarkets are **Alisuper** (Largo do Carmo) and small **Minipreço** (Praça Ferreira de Almeida 8).

MIDRANGE

Restaurante A Taska (☎ 289 824 739; Rua do Alportel 38; mains €6-13; lunch & dinner Mon-Sat) Popular with locals, this trattoria-style, high-ceilinged place serves delicious regional food, with an impressive wine list.

Faro e Benfica Restaurante Marisqueira (☎ 289 821 422; Marina; mains €7.50-16; lunch & dinner) Candle-lit at night, with a marina-side setting, big open windows and a plant-filled terrace, this is a classy seafood choice.

Gengibre e Canela (☎ 289 882 424; Rua da Mota; mains €8; lunch & dinner Tue-Sat; V) Tucked away on a pedestrian lane, this Zenlike vegetarian restaurant has a small menu of daily specials (tofu with vegetables etc), plus organic wine and fresh juices.

La Pizza (☎ 289 806 023; Travessa José Coelho 13; mains €6-10; lunch & dinner) On a quiet pedestrian lane near the bars, this pizzeria serves up tasty thin-crust pizzas. There's outdoor seating, too.

Tasca Rasca (☎ 289 825 996; Rua do Forno 21; mains €8-12; lunch & dinner Mon-Sat) In a charming old-fashioned setting (woodwork, curious murals), Tasca Rasca serves rich plates of seafood. Try the *cataplana a tasca* (seafood stew cooked in a copper pot).

Centenário (☎ 289 823 343; Largo do Bispo 4; mains €8-13; lunch & dinner) A smartly decorated restaurant, specialising in grilled fish and seafood stews, Centenário serves delectable *arroz marisco* (rice and seafood stew). Outdoor seating on the tree-shaded square in front.

Mesa dos Mouros (☎ 289 878 873; Largo da Sé 10; mains around €13; Tue-Sun) With splendid outdoor, cathedral-shaded seating, this place offers a large choice of seafood or unusual, hearty mains such as rabbit with chestnuts.

O Aldeão (☎ 289 823 339; Largo de São Pedro 54-57; mains €11.50-14) This fetching, upmarket place has outdoor seating in the square, and inventive Algarvian and Alentejan dishes, including steak with clams and fragrant black pork.

Vilaadentro Restaurante (☎ 919 191 021; Largo Afonso III 17; mains €11.70-16.50; lunch & dinner) This cathedral-side, tiled restaurant sets the scene for upmarket traditional Algarvian cuisine. There are outdoor tables, but for once inside could be even nicer.

THE ALGARVE

Sushi Ya (☎ 289 821 196; Rua Cruz das Mestras 36; platter for two €40; lunch & dinner Tue-Sun) Faro's sushi restaurant has an attractive dining room and an airy back courtyard, decorated with paper lanterns, bamboo and flickering candles. The sushi and sashimi is decent.

Drinking

Faro's student-driven nightlife clusters around Rua do Prior and surrounding alleys, with bars and clubs open most days till late, though things pick up considerably on weekends.

A Capelinha (Largo da Madalena 8; 8pm-2am Tue-Sat;) An attractive low-key bar, with outdoor tables scattered around the square's gurgling fountain. You'll also find good sangria, a small fish tank and computer for web-browsing.

Taverna da Sé (Praça Afonso III 26; 10am-midnight Mon-Sat) Hung with bohemian paintings, this cool, small in-crowd *taverna* is in the old town. There are some outdoor tables in the square.

Aktual Club (☎ 289 812 310; Rua do Prior 38) This warehouse club is one of the town's better dance venues, featuring housey sounds.

Entertainment

The 30,000-seat **Estádio Intermunicipal do Algarve** is a state-of-the-art stadium built for Euro2004, at São João da Venda, 8km northwest of Faro. Here you can watch Faro's own team, SC Farense, and Loulé's Louletano. Contact the turismo for transport information.

Small Italianate theatre **Teatro Lethes** (☎ 289 820 300; Rua Lethes) hosts drama, music and dance. Built in 1874, it was once the Jesuit Colégio de Santiago Maior and is now owned by the Portuguese Cruz Vermelha (Red Cross).

Getting There & Around

AIR

Portugália and TAP (Air Portugal) provide multiple daily Lisbon–Faro flights (40 minutes) as well as Lisbon–Porto connections (45 minutes). For international services, see p468.

For flight inquiries call the **airport** (☎ 289 800 800). **TAP** has a central booking office (☎ 707 205 700; www.tap.pt; Rua Dr Francisco Gomes; 9am-5.30pm Mon-Fri).

BUS

From the **Eva bus station** (☎ 289 899 760; Avenida da República 5) express coaches run to Lisbon (€17, five hours, at least hourly, one night service); some services involve changing at Vale do Paraíso, north of Albufeira. Opposite the bus station, **Renex** (☎ 289 589 602; 9-11.15am & 1.30-8pm Mon-Fri, to 9-11.15am & 30min before bus leaves Sat, noon-8pm Sun) sells tickets for the Renex Lisbon express bus (€15.50, four to six daily).

Buses run to Vila Real de Santo António (€4.20, 1¾ hours, six to nine daily), via Tavira (€3, one hour, seven to 10 daily); and to Albufeira (€3.60, 1¼ hours, at least hourly), with some going on to Portimão (€4.50, 1½ hours,

TOP 10 BEACHES OF THE ALGARVE

From small, secluded coves to wide stretches of rugged, dune-backed shores, the Algarve has enticing choices when it comes to sunbaking and wave frolicking. Our highly subjective picks include the following:

- Praia de Dona Ana (p201) Enchanting, golden rock formations that make this cove beach a photographer's favourite.
- Odeceixe (p212) Small and pretty, with decent swimming and good surfing.
- Meia Praia (p201) Popular and sceney, with options for water sports.
- Ilha de Tavira (p182) Crown jewel of the east-coast beaches, with a nudist area.
- Praia Verde – About 11km west of Vila Real de Santo António; the calm seas backed by cool pine trees are ideal for families.
- Vale Figueiras (p211) Long stretch of wild coast that's little frequented.
- Praia da Galé (p189) Attractive cove beach with striking rock formations.
- Praia da Bordeira (p210) Wild untamed beauty (and surfing).
- Praia do Ançâo – Sunbathe with the A-list crowd at this sandy stretch near the Quinta do Lago estate.
- Praia da Arrifana (p211) Lovely, pristine natural setting along a bay framed by black cliffs.

seven daily weekdays, two daily weekends) and Lagos (€4.50, 1¾ hours). For Sagres, change at Lagos. There are regular buses to Olhão (€1.50, 20 minutes, every 15 minutes weekdays) and buses to São Bras de Alportel (€3.20, 35 minutes, four to 10 daily) via Estói (15 minutes).

Eva services run to Seville in Spain (€13, five hours, two daily) via Huelva (€7.50, 3½ hours). For further details, see p469.

CAR

The most direct route from Lisbon to Faro takes about five hours. A nonmotorway alternative is the often traffic-clogged N125.

Major car-rental agencies are at the airport. Local heroes include **Auto Jardim** (☎ 289 800 881) and **Rentauto** (☎ 289 818 718). In town try **Megatur** (☎ 289 807 485; www.megatur.pt; Rua Conselheiro de Bívar 80).

Portugal's national auto club, **Automóvel Club de Portugal** (ACP; ☎ 289 898 950; www.acp.pt; Rua Francisco Barreto 26a; 9am-1pm & 2-4.30pm Mon-Fri) has an office here.

Faro's easiest parking is in Largo de São Francisco (free).

TRAIN

There are trains from Lisbon (€18 to €19.50, 3 to 3¾ hours, four daily). You can also get to Porto (€38 to €54, 6½ to 7½ hours, three daily) usually changing at Lisbon; there is also one train per week going via Coimbra (5½ hours to Coimbra, seven to 7½ hours to Porto).

Trains also run daily to Albufeira (€2.50, 30 minutes, eight to 12 daily); Vila Real de Santo António (€5, 1¼ hours, 10 daily) via Olhão (20 minutes); Lagos (€6.20, 1¾ hours, eight daily); and Loulé (€1.25, 20 minutes, 10 daily).

Getting Around

TO/FROM THE AIRPORT

Eva (☎ 289 899 740) buses 14 and 16 run into town via the bus station, Jardim Manuel Bívar and Hotel Dom Bernardo (€1.40, 20 minutes, half-hourly in summer, every hour or two in winter.

A taxi into town costs about €10 (€11.50 after 10pm and weekends).

BICYCLE

You can rent bikes (including kids' bikes) from **Megasport** (☎ /fax 289 393 044; www.megasport.pt; Rua Ataíde de Oliveira 39c; per day from €9; 10am-1pm & 3-7.30pm Mon-Sat). They offer free delivery between Faro and Albufeira. Bikes can be taken on the Algarve train line (if there's space in the goods van) for €2.

BOAT

May to September, **Animaris** (☎ 917 811 856; www.ilha-deserta.com) operates four ferries a day to/from Ilha da Barreta (return trip €7). The same company also runs 2½-hour year-round boat trips (€20) through Parque Natural da Ria Formosa (p167). Boats leave from the pier next to Arco da Porta Nova.

TAXI

Ring for a **taxi** (☎ 289 895 790) or find one at the taxi rank on Jardim Manuel Bívar.

SÃO BRÁS DE ALPORTEL

pop 10,030 / elevation 210m

Just 17km north of Faro, this quiet country town feels a world away from the coast. Although São Brás has few attractions, it's a pleasant place to stroll and see an authentic slice of Algarvian life. The town was a hot spot in the 19th-century heyday of cork and has stayed true to its agricultural roots. It lies in a valley in the olive-, carob-, fig- and almond-wooded Barrocal region, a lush limestone area sandwiched between the mountains and the sea.

Orientation & Information

Buses stop in the central Largo de São Sebastião.

The **turismo** (Largo de São Sebastião; 9.30am-1pm & 2-5.30pm Mon-Fri) distributes maps, including self-guided walking tours in the surrounding countryside.

Sights & Activities

MUSEU ETNOGRÁFICO DO TRAJO ALGARVIO

A small, eccentric **museum** (☎ 289 842 618; Rua Dr José Dias Sancho 61; admission €1; 10am-noon & 2-5pm Mon-Fri, 2-5pm Sat, Sun & holidays) 200m east of the Largo (along the Tavira road), this has a rambling collection of local costumes, handicrafts and agricultural implements. It's housed in a former cork magnate's mansion, and there are displays in the stables of the town's once buoyant cork industry.

OLD TOWN

For a fine stroll, follow Rua Gago Coutinho south from the Largo to the 16th-century **igreja matriz** (parish church), which has breezy views of orange groves and surrounding valleys. Nearby, below what was once a bishop's palace (now a nursery school), is a landscaped **municipal swimming pool** (☎ 289 841 243; ⏲ 10am-7pm Jun-Sep) and children's playground.

Sleeping

Estalagem Sequeira (☎ 289 843 444; fax 289 841 457; Rua Dr Evaristo Gago 9; s/d €28/50) Although the façade is uninspiring, rooms here are decent, with a trim modern design and polished cork floors.

Residencial São Brás (☎ /fax 289 842 213; Rua Luís Bívar 27; s/d €35/50) Round the corner from Sequeira (along the Loulé road), this delightful guesthouse has halls decked with plants, antiques and *azulejos*. Rooms are old-fashioned but big (more modern ones are in a back annexe).

Pousada de São Brás (☎ 289 842 305; d from €150) On a panoramic hilltop, this renovated 1950s low-riser offers cheerful, handsomely decorated rooms, most with terraces. You'll also find a pool with a view and a good restaurant here.

Eating

Pastelaria Ervilha (Largo de São Sebastião 7; pastries from €1; ⏲ breakfast, lunch & dinner) In the centre of town, this São Bras institution (around since 1952) sells tasty homemade cakes and pastries, as well as ice cream and fresh juice. Outdoor tables overlook the square.

Luís dos Frangos (☎ 289 842 635; Estrada de Tavira 8150; mains from €4.50-7; ⏲ lunch & dinner Tue-Sun) Five hundred metres east of the Largo (beyond the museum), this friendly, casual place is famous for its grilled mains – particularly its chicken. There's a good dessert selection, too.

Fonte da Pedra (☎ 289 841 413; Avenida da Liberdade; mains €9-14; ⏲ lunch Thu-Mon, dinner Wed-Mon) In a peaceful spot 700m north of the Largo, this attractive place serves a tasty mix of grilled meats and seafood. The wraparound porch has fine views.

Getting There & Around

Buses run from Faro (€3.10 via Estói, 35 minutes, four to 10 daily) and Loulé (€2.50, 25 minutes, two to four daily except Sunday).

MILREU & ESTÓI

The Roman ruins at Milreu and the nearby charming derelict rococo Estói palace and gardens make an ideal day trip from Faro, 10km to the south.

There are several simple local cafés fronting the main square in Estói.

Next to the old Roman bridge in Milreu, **V Terra** (☎ 289 997 198; Sítio do Guelhim; mains €5-8; ⏲ lunch & dinner Tue-Sun), a cheery spot, serves delicious international dishes, from Chinese chicken salad to vegetable lasagne. There's a sunny terrace on the top floor.

Buses run from Faro to Estói (€2.10, 20 minutes, 11 weekdays) continuing on to São Brás de Alportel.

Milreu

The ruins of a grand Roman villa are set in beautiful countryside at **Milreu** (adult/under 25 €2/1; ⏲ 9.30am-12.30pm & 2-6pm Tue-Sun Apr-Sep, 2-5pm Oct-Mar), providing a rare opportunity to get something of an insight into Roman life. The lst-century AD ruins reveal the characteristic form of a peristyle villa, with a gallery of columns around a courtyard. In the surrounding rooms geometric motifs and friezes of fish were found, but these have now been removed for restoration.

Tantalising glimpses of the villa's former glory include the **fish mosaics** in the bathing chambers, which are located to the west of the villa's courtyard.

The remains of the bathing rooms include the **apodyterium**, or changing-room (note the arched niches and benches for clothes and postbath massage), and the **frigidarium**, which had a marble basin to hold cold water for cooling off postbath.

Other luxuries were underground heating and marble sculptures (now in Faro and Lagos museums).

To the right of the entrance is the site's **nymphaerium**, or water sanctuary, a temple devoted to the cult of water. The interior was once decorated with polychrome marble slabs and its exterior with fish mosaics. In the 3rd century the Visigoths converted it into a church, adding a baptismal font and a small mausoleum.

Information sheets (€1) in various languages are available. The bus from Faro to Estói stops outside.

Palácio do Visconde de Estói

About 800m north of Milreu, this enchanting, dishevelled palace is the 18th-century version of Milreu. It's a short walk from Estói's sleepy main square (which was under construction when we passed through). Down a palm-shaded avenue, past abandoned stables and outhouses, are the palace's delightfully overgrown, wild **gardens** (admission free; 9am-12.30pm & 2-5.30pm Tue-Sat). To add to the romance are busts of poets, rococo sculpture, and gleaming 19th-century *azulejos* featuring naked mythological ladies prancing – their voluptuous stone cousins bask by an ornamental pool. The palace (closed to the public) is all rosy rococo overexcitement, reminiscent of Queluz Palace near Lisbon (p142).

OLHÃO

pop 40,800

A short hop east of Faro, Olhão (ol-*yowng*) is the Algarve's biggest fishing port with an active waterfront and narrow bustling lanes in its old quarters. Although there aren't many sights, Olhão is a pretty place, with crisp Moorish-designed neighbourhoods that lend the place a North African feel. It's long been known for its excellent fish restaurants.

The town is also a springboard for the sandy islands of the Parque Natural da Ria Formosa, with fine beach options on Ilha da Culatra and Ilha da Armona.

Saturday is the best day for the morning **market** (Avenida 5 de Outubro), which sells fish and vegetables.

Orientation

From the small **Eva bus terminal** (Rua General Humberto Delgado), turn right (west) or, from the train station, left (east) and it's a block to the town's main avenue, Avenida da República. Turn right and 300m down the Avenida you'll reach the parish church, at the edge of the central, pedestrianised shopping zone.

At the far side of this zone is waterfront Avenida 5 de Outubro. Here is the twin-domed market and to the left (east) is the town park, Jardim Patrão Joaquim Lopes.

Information

Centro de saúde (medical centre; ☎ 289 722 153; Rua Associação Chasfa)

Espaço Internet (Rua Teófilo Braga; 10am-9pm Mon, to 10pm Tue-Fri, to 8pm Sat) Free internet access.

Police (☎ 289 710 770; Avenida 5 Outubro 176)

Post office (☎ 289 700 600 Avenida da República) A block north of the parish church, opposite a bank with an ATM.

Turismo (☎ 289 713 936; Largo Sebastião Martins Mestre; 9.30am-7pm May-Sep, 9.30am-noon & 1-5.30pm Mon-Fri Oct-Apr) In the centre of the pedestrian zone; from the bus station bear right at the fork beside the parish church.

Sights & Activities

BAIRRO DOS PESCADORES

Just back from the market and park is the Bairro dos Pescadores (Fishermen's Quarter), a knot of whitewashed, cubical houses, often with tiled fronts and flat roofs. Narrow lanes thread through the *bairro* (neighbourhood), and there's a definite Moorish influence, probably a legacy of longstanding trade links with North Africa. Similar houses are found in Fuzeta (10km east).

BEACHES

Fine beaches nearby, sparsely sprinkled with holiday chalets, include **Praia de Farol** (the best); **Praia de Hangares** on Ilha da Culatra; and **Praia de Armona** and **Praia de Fuzeta** on Ilha da Armona. There are ferries to both islands from the pier just east of Jardim Patrão Joaquim Lopes (p169). You can also reach Armona from Fuzeta, and it is less busy, but narrower.

PARQUE NATURAL DA RIA FORMOSA

The Ria Formosa Natural Park is mostly a lagoon system stretching for 60km along the Algarve coastline from just west of Faro to Cacela Velha. It encloses a vast area of *sapal* (marsh), *salinas* (salt pans), creeks and dune islands. To the west there are also two freshwater lakes, at Ludo and Quinta do Lago, a vital habitat for migrating and nesting birds. You can see a huge variety of wetland birds here, along with ducks, shorebirds, gulls and terns. This is the favoured nesting place of the little tern and rare purple gallinule (see the boxed text p168).

You'll find some of the Algarve's quietest, biggest beaches on the sandbank *ilhas* of Faro, Culatra, Armona and Tavira. For transport there, see p169.

The **park headquarters** (☎ 289 704 134; pnrf@icn.pt; Quinta de Marim; 9am-5.30pm) is 3km east of Olhão and has an excellent visitors centre. Try the 2.4km nature trail across the dunes.

To get to Quinta de Marim, take a Tavira bus from Olhão, get off at the Cepsa petrol station, and walk seaward for 1km or take a bus to the camp site (200m before the visitor centre).

Festivals & Events

The **Festival do Marisco**, a seafood festival with food and folk music, fills the Jardim Patrão Joaquim Lopes during the second week of August.

WILDLIFE OF THE ALGARVE

Although not the most fauna-rich region of the country, the Algarve is home to some fascinating wildlife. The purple gallinule (aka the purple swamp-hen or sultan chicken) is one of Europe's rarest and most nattily turned-out birds, a large violet-blue water creature with red bill and legs. In Portugal it only nests in a patch of wetland spilling into the exclusive Quinta do Lago estate, at the western end of the Parque Natural da Ria Formosa, 12km west of Faro. Look for it near the lake at the estate's São Lourenço Nature Trail.

Another bizarre Algarve resident is the Mediterranean chameleon *(Chamaeleo chamaeleon)*, a 25cm-long reptile with independently moving eyes, a tongue longer than its body and skin that mimics its environment. It only started creeping around southern Portugal about 75 years ago, and is the only chameleon found in Europe, its habitat limited to Crete and the Iberian Peninsula. Your best chance of seeing this shy creature is on spring mornings in the Quinta de Marim area of the Parque Natural da Ria Formosa or in Monte Gordo's conifer woods, now a protected habitat for the species.

Bird lovers should consider a trip to the Serra do Caldeirão foothills. Approximately 21km northwest of Loulé, the dramatic Rocha da Pena, a 479m-high limestone outcrop, is a classified site because of its rich flora and fauna. Orchids, narcissi and native cistus cover the slopes, where red foxes and Egyptian mongooses are common. Among many bird species seen here are the huge eagle owl, Bonelli's eagle and the buzzard.

There's a *centro ambiental* (environmental centre) in Pena village, and a 4.7km circular walking trail starts from Rocha, 1km from Pena.

Sleeping

There are few places to stay and they fill up quickly in summer.

Camping Olhão (☎ 289 700 300; www.sbsi.pt; adult/tent/car €4/3/3.30, caravan/family bungalow €7.50/45; ♿) This large, well-equipped, shady camping ground is 2km east of Olhão and 800m off the N125. The downside: daily trains run past, starting from about 6.45am. In summer a bus runs here from Jardim Patrão Joaquim Lopes.

Parque de Campismo de Fuzeta (☎ 289 793 459; fax 289 793 285; adult/tent/car €3/2.30/3.20; 🕑 year-round) This small, shady municipal site is on the waterfront in peaceful Fuzeta, about 10km east of Olhão. You can go canoeing from the beach, and there are ferries to the offshore islands.

Pensão Bela Vista (☎ 289 702 538; Rua Teófilo Braga 65; s/d €30/45) A short walk west of the turismo, this is a friendly and efficient place with clean, brightly tiled rooms and a flower-filled courtyard.

Pensão Bicuar (☎ 289 714 816; www.pension-bicuar.net; Rua Vasco da Gama 5; dm/s/d/ste with shower €15/25/35/45) Run by a welcoming expat couple, this newly renovated guesthouse offers superb value for its rooms, which feature lovely old-fashioned details. There's also a kitchen for guests and a book exchange. Rua Vasco da Gama is to the left (east) of the parish church.

Pensão Boémia (☎/fax 289 714 513; Rua da Cerca 20; s/d €40/50; ❄) This quaint spot has clean, colourful rooms with tile floors and small fridges. Several rooms have a terrace with views over the old town.

Eating

Avenida 5 de Outubro is lined with excellent seafood restaurants; this is also where you'll find the **market** (🕑 7am-2pm Mon-Sat).

Padaria Café (Rua Vasco da Gama 24; 🕑 7am-8pm) On a pedestrian street, this small but enticing café serves rich chocolate croissants and other pastries. Outdoor seating.

Restaurante Ria Formosa (☎ 289 714 215; Avenida 5 de Outubro 14; mains €5-9) On the river side of Avenida 5 de Outubro, next to a small park, this popular restaurant has awning-shaded outdoor tables and tasty seafood and rice dishes.

Horta Restaurante (☎ 289 714 215; Avenida 5 de Outubro 146; mains €7-11) A mix of locals and travellers crowd the outdoor tables at this popular seafood restaurant. Grilled fish and seafood stews (try the rice with monkfish) are tops here.

Getting There & Away

BUS

Eva express buses run to Lisbon (€17, four to five hours, four to five daily), as do **Renex** (Avenida da República 101).

Buses run frequently from Faro (€1.50, 20 minutes), some continuing to the waterfront at Bairro dos Pescadores, and from Tavira (€1.85, 40 minutes, hourly).

TRAIN

Regular trains connect to Faro (10 minutes, every two hours) or east to Fuzeta (10 minutes) and Tavira (30 minutes).

Getting Around

Ferries run out to the *ilhas* from the pier at the eastern end of Jardim Patrão Joaquim Lopes. Boats run to Ilha da Armona (€2.60 return, 30 minutes, at least nine daily June to mid-September, hourly July and August, four daily mid-September to May); the last trip back from Armona in July and August leaves at 8.30pm.

Boats also go to Ilha da Culatra (€2.60, 30 minutes) and Praia de Farol (€3.20, one hour), with six daily from June to September and four daily mid-September to May.

Ferries also run from Fuzeta to the offshore islands.

TAVIRA

pop 12,600

Set on either side of the meandering Rio Gilão, Tavira is a charming town that makes good use of its pretty river setting. The ruins of a hilltop castle, an old Roman bridge and a smattering of Gothic and Renaissance churches are among the attractions, and its enticing assortment of restaurants and guesthouses can make it difficult to leave.

As elsewhere in the old Algarvian towns, Tavira is ideal for strolling: its warren of cobblestone streets hide shady plazas and patisseries, and despite the growing number of tourists, there's still a small, active fishing port. The town lies 3km from the coast, near the beautiful and unspoilt beaches of Ilha de Tavira.

History

The Roman settlement of Balsa was just down the road, near Santa Luzia (3km west). The seven-arched bridge the Romans built at Tavira (then called Tabira) was an important link in the route between Baesuris (Castro Marim) and Ossonoba (Faro).

In the 8th century, the Moors occupied Tavira. They built the castle, probably on the site of a Roman fortress, and two mosques. In 1242 Dom Paio Peres Correia reconquered the town. Those Moors who remained were segregated into the *mouraria* (Moorish quarter) outside the town walls.

As the port closest to the Moroccan coast, Tavira became important during the Age of Discoveries (p30), serving as a base for Portuguese expeditions to North Africa, supplying provisions (especially salt, wine and dried fish) and a hospital. Its maritime trade also expanded, with exports of salted fish, almonds, figs and wine to northern Europe. By 1520 it had become the Algarve's most populated settlement and was raised to the rank of city.

Decline began in the early 17th century when the North African campaign was abandoned and the Rio Gilão became so silted up that large boats couldn't enter the port. Things got worse when the plague struck in 1645, followed by the 1755 earthquake.

After briefly producing carpets in the late 18th century, Tavira found a more stable income in its tuna fishing and canning industry, although this too declined in the 1950s when the tuna shoals sensibly moved elsewhere. Today, tourists have taken the place of fish as the biggest money-earners.

Orientation

The train station is on the southern edge of town, 1km from the centre. The bus station is a 200m walk west of central Praça da República.

Most of the town's shops and facilities are on the southern side of the river.

Information

EMERGENCY & MEDICAL SERVICES

Police station (☎ 281 322 022; Campo dos Mártires da Pátria)

Riverside International Medical Centre Clinic (☎ 289 997 742; 24 hr); Hotel Vila Galé Albacora (☎ 919 657 860; 9am-noon & 4-6pm Mon-Fri) A private clinic.

INTERNET ACCESS

Espaço Internet (Câmara municipal, Praça da República; 9am-9pm Mon-Fri, to 2pm Sat) Free access.

Cyber-Café Tavira (Rua Jacques Pessoa 4; per hr €3; 10.30am-4pm & 6pm-10.30pm Mon-Sat)

LAUNDRY

Lavandaria Lavitt (☎ 281 326 776; Rua das Salinas 6; 9am-1pm & 3-7pm Mon-Sat, 9am-1pm Sun) Charges around €7 for 6kg wash and dry.

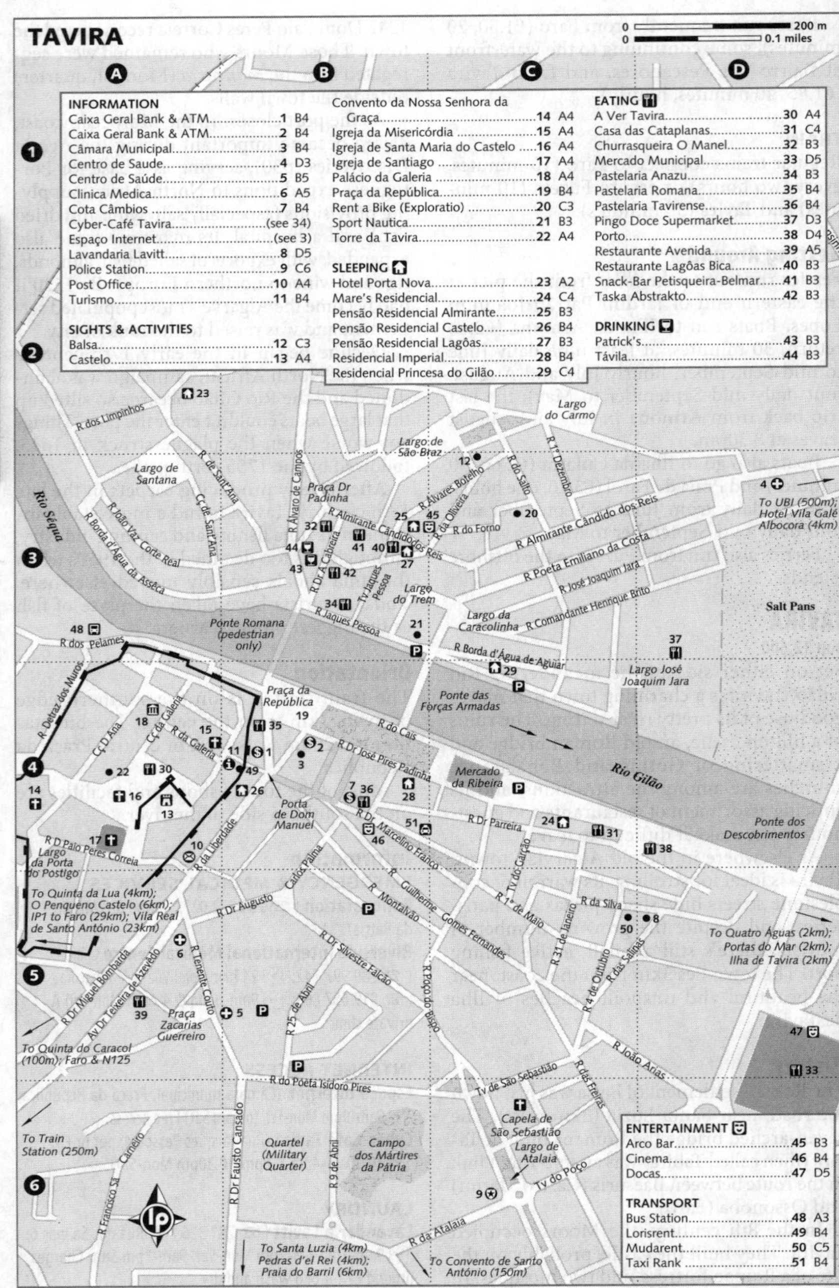
TAVIRA
0 200 m
0 0.1 miles
A
B
C
D
1
2
3
4
5
6
INFORMATION
Caixa Geral Bank & ATM....1 B4
Caixa Geral Bank & ATM....2 B4
Câmara Municipal....3 B4
Centro de Saude....4 D3
Centro de Saúde....5 B5
Clinica Medica....6 A5
Cota Câmbios....7 B4
Cyber-Café Tavira....(see 34)
Espaço Internet....(see 3)
Lavandaria Lavitt....8 D5
Police Station....9 C6
Post Office....10 A4
Turismo....11 B4
SIGHTS & ACTIVITIES
Balsa....12 C3
Castelo....13 A4
Convento da Nossa Senhora da Graça....14 A4
Igreja da Misericórdia....15 A4
Igreja de Santa Maria do Castelo....16 A4
Igreja de Santiago....17 A4
Palácio da Galeria....18 A4
Praça da República....19 B4
Rent a Bike (Exploratio)....20 C3
Sport Nautica....21 B3
Torre da Tavira....22 A4
SLEEPING
Hotel Porta Nova....23 A2
Mare's Residencial....24 C4
Pensão Residencial Almirante....25 B3
Pensão Residencial Castelo....26 B4
Pensão Residencial Lagôas....27 B3
Residencial Imperial....28 B4
Residencial Princesa do Gilão....29 C4
EATING
A Ver Tavira....30 A4
Casa das Cataplanas....31 C4
Churrasqueira O Manel....32 B3
Mercado Municipal....33 D5
Pastelaria Anazu....34 B3
Pastelaria Romana....35 B4
Pastelaria Tavirense....36 B4
Pingo Doce Supermarket....37 D3
Porto....38 D4
Restaurante Avenida....39 A5
Restaurante Lagôas Bica....40 B3
Snack-Bar Petisqueira-Belmar....41 B3
Taska Abstrakto....42 B3
DRINKING
Patrick's....43 B3
Távila....44 B3
ENTERTAINMENT
Arco Bar....45 B3
Cinema....46 B4
Docas....47 D5
TRANSPORT
Bus Station....48 A3
Lorisrent....49 B4
Mudarent....50 C5
Taxi Rank....51 B4
R dos Limpinhos
Largo do Carmo
Largo de São Braz
Largo de Santana
R de Sant'Ana
Cç de Sant'Ana
R 1º Dezembro
R do Salto
R Álvaro de Campos
Praça Dr Padinha
R Alvares Botelho
R da Oliveira
R do Forno
R Almirante Cândido dos Reis
R Poeta Emiliano da Costa
R José Joaquim Jara
R Comandante Henrique Brito
To UBI (500m); Hotel Vila Galé Albocora (4km)
Rio Séqua
R João Vaz Corte Real
R Borda d'Água da Asseca
R Dr A Cabreira
Tv Jaques Pessoa
Largo do Trem
Largo da Caracolinha
Salt Pans
R Jaques Pessoa
Ponte Romana (pedestrian only)
R dos Pelames
R Borda d'Água de Aguiar
Largo José Joaquim Jara
R Detraz dos Muros
Praça da República
Ponte das Forças Armadas
Cç D Ana
Cç da Galeria
R da Galeria
R do Cais
R Dr José Pires Padinha
Rio Gilão
Mercado da Ribeira
Porta de Dom Manuel
R Dr Parreira
Ponte dos Descobrimentos
R D Paio Peres Correia
Largo da Porta do Postigo
R da Liberdade
R Dr Marcelino Franco
Tv do Carção
R Carlos Palma
R Montalvão
R Guilherme Gomes Fernandes
R 1º de Maio
R da Silva
To Quinta da Lua (4km); O Penqueno Castelo (6km); IP1 to Faro (29km); Vila Real de Santo António (23km)
R Dr Augusto
R Dr Silvestre Falcão
R 31 de Janeiro
R 4 de Outubro
R das Salinas
To Quatro Águas (2km); Portas do Mar (2km); Ilha de Tavira (2km)
R Dr Miguel Bombarda
Av Dr Teixeira de Azevedo
R Tenente Couto
Praça Zacarias Guerreiro
R 25 de Abril
R Poço do Bispo
R João Arias
To Quinta do Caracol (100m); Faro & N125
R do Poeta Isidoro Pires
Tv de São Sebastião
R das Freiras
Capela de São Sebastião
To Train Station (250m)
R Francisco Sá Carneiro
R Dr Fausto Cansado
Quartel (Military Quarter)
R 9 de Abril
Campo dos Mártires da Pátria
Largo de Atalaia
Tv do Poço
R da Atalaia
To Santa Luzia (4km) Pedras d'el Rei (4km); Praia do Barril (6km)
To Convento de Santo António (150m)

MONEY

Banks with ATMs lie around Praça da República and Rua da Liberdade.

Cota Câmbios (Rua Estácio da Veiga 21; 8.30am-1.30pm & 2.30-7.30pm Mon-Fri, 9am-1.30pm & 2.30-6pm Sat) Private exchange bureau.

POST

Post office (Rua da Liberdade)

TOURIST INFORMATION

Turismo (☎ 281 322 511; Rua da Galeria 9; 9.30am-1pm & 2.30-5.30pm Mon-Fri Sep-Jun; 9am-7pm Mon-Fri Jul & Aug) Provides local and regional information, and helps with accommodation.

Sights

IGREJA DA MISERICÓRDIA

Built in the 1540s, this **church** (Rua da Galeria; admission free; 10am-1pm Mon, Wed & Fri) is the Algarve's most important Renaissance monument, with a magnificent carved, arched doorway topped by statues of Nossa Senhora da Misericórdia, São Pedro and São Paulo. The church's stone mason, André Pilarte, also worked on Mosteiro dos Jerónimos (p102).

IGREJA DE SANTA MARIA DO CASTELO

This 13th-century **Gothic church** (admission free; 9.30am-noon & 2.30-5pm), beside the castle, was built on the site of a Moorish mosque but rebuilt by an Italian neoclassicist following earthquake damage 500 years later. However, the architect retained traces of the former church – namely the main doorway, two side chapels and Arabic-style windows in the clock tower.

Inside is a plaque marking the tomb of Dom Paio Peres Correia, who won the town back from the Moors, as well as those of the seven Christian knights whose murder by the Moors precipitated the final attack on Tavira.

CASTELO

What's left of the **castle** (admission free; 8am-5pm Mon-Fri, 9am-5.30pm Sat & Sun) is surrounded by a decidedly unwar-like, small and appealing garden.

The defence might date back to Neolithic times; it was rebuilt by Phoenicians in the 8th century and later taken over by the Moors. What stands today dates mostly from 17th-century reconstruction. The restored octagonal tower offers fine views over Tavira.

OTHER OLD TOWN ATTRACTIONS

Enter the old town through the Porta de Dom Manuel (by the turismo), built in 1520 when Dom Manuel I made Tavira a city. Around the back, along Calçada da Galeria, the elegant **Palácio da Galeria** (gallery; admission free; 10am-12.30pm & 2-6pm Tue-Fri, 2-6pm Sat) holds occasional exhibitions.

Nearby, the **Torre da Tavira** (admission €3.50; 9.30am-5pm Mon-Sat) is the town's former water tower, now housing a camera obscura, with 360-degree views. Demonstrations point out the important monuments and buildings during a fascinating but stationary tour.

Just south of the castle is the whitewashed 17th-century **Igreja de Santiago** (Mass 8.30am Mon-Fri, 6pm Sun), built where a small mosque probably once stood. The area beside it was formerly the Praça da Vila, the old town square.

Downhill from here is the **Largo da Porta do Postigo**, at the site of another old town gate and the town's Moorish quarter.

PONTE ROMANA

This seven-arched **bridge** that loops away from Praça da República may predate the Romans but is so named because it linked the Roman road from Castro Marim to Tavira. The structure you see dates from a 17th-century reconstruction. The latest touch-up job was in 1989, after floods knocked down one of its pillars.

PRAÇA DA REPÚBLICA

For centuries, this sociable town **square** on the riverfront served as promenade and marketplace, where slaves were traded along with less ignominious commodities such as fish and fruit. The market moved to Jardim do Coreto in 1887 to improve hygiene, only moving again in 2000 to a new riverside location. A colourful affair, the *mercado municipal* is held on Monday to Saturday mornings.

SALT PANS & QUATRO ÁGUAS

You can walk 2km east along the river, past the fascinating, snowlike salt pans to Quatro Águas. The salt pans produce tiptop table salt and in summer attract feeding birds, including flamingos. Besides being the jumping-off point for Ilha de Tavira, the seaside hub of Quatro Águas has a couple of seafood restaurants and a former tuna-canning factory – now a luxury hotel, across the river.

For information on buses to Quatro Águas, see p182.

THE ALGARVE

Activities

You can rent kayaks for a paddle along the river at **Sport Nautica** (☎ 281 324 943; Rua Jacques Pessoa 26; kayak per hr/day €5/20; 🕑 9am-1pm & 3-7pm Mon-Fri, to 6pm Sat).

Tours

Balsa (☎ 281 322 882; Rua Álvares Botelho 51; 🕑 daily) This ceramics shop offers bike rental and four-hour guided trips around Tavira or Parque Natural da Ria Formosa for €10.

Rent a Bike (Exploratio; ☎ /fax 281 321 973; exploratio@netc.pt; Rua do Forno 33) Offers four-hour trips for €25 per person, including mountain-bike hire, in and around Tavira and the Parque Natural da Ria Formosa. They can also arrange half-day walking tours.

Riosul (☎ 281 510 200; www.riosultravel.com; Monte Gordo) Has a pick-up point in Tavira for its jeep tours and Rio Guadiana cruises.

Festivals & Events

You can't go wrong with free sardines, and that's what you'll get at Tavira's biggest festival, the **Festa de Cidade**, held on 23 to 24 June. Myrtle and paper flowers decorate the streets, and the dancing and festivities carry on till late.

Sleeping

BUDGET

Ilha de Tavira (☎ 281 321 709; www.campingtavira.com; camp site per 1/2 people plus tent €9/14; 🕑 Apr-Sep) Tavira's nearest campsite has a great location on the island (see p182). It gets crowded and noisy in the high season (mid-June to mid-September). There's no car access.

Pensão Residencial Lagôas (☎ 281 322 252; Rua Almirante Cândido dos Reis 24; s/d with shared bathroom €20/30, d €40-50) A long-standing favourite, Lagôas has small, clean rooms around a little courtyard decorated with plants. Some rooms feel cramped. There are good views from a roof terrace.

Pensão Residencial Almirante (☎ 281 322 163; Rua Almirante Cândido dos Reis 51; d with shared bathroom from €25) One block from the river, this cosy family house is full of clutter, but its six rooms are spacious and charmingly old-fashioned.

Residencial Imperial (☎ /fax 281 322 234; Rua Dr José Pires Padinha 24; s/d €35/50) This cosy, efficient *residencial* (guesthouse) has a family atmosphere and well-kept smallish rooms with cheery yellow curtains. Two classically decorated river-facing rooms are excellent value.

Residencial Princesa do Gilão (☎ /fax 281 325 171; Rua Borda d'Água de Aguiar 10; s/d €40/50; ❄) This eye-catching, modern, riverside place is laid-back and friendly. Go for a room with a small balcony overlooking the river.

MIDRANGE & TOP END

Mare's Residencial (☎ 281 325 815; maresresidencial@mail.telepac.pt; Rua Dr José Pires Padinha 134; d €40-60) Decorated with seafaring themes, this attractive 24-room riverside place has dapper, snug rooms with phone, satellite TV, tiled bathrooms and small balconies overlooking the river.

Pensão Residencial Castelo (☎ 281 320 790; fax 281 320 799; Rua da Liberdade 22; s/d/apt €30/50/65; ❄ ♿) Castelo offers nicely furnished rooms with spotless tile floors. Some also have balconies and castle views. It has wheelchair access.

Tavira Inn (Casa do Rio; ☎ 917 356 623; www.tavira-inn.com; Rua Chefe António Afonso 39; d €75, min 2 nights; ❄ 🏊) In a charming riverside spot, this place has original décor created by the owner's artist daughter, a small saltwater swimming pool and a zinging-yellow jazz bar. Children are not accepted.

Hotel Vila Galé Albacora (☎ 281 380 800; www.vilagale.pt; Quatro Águas; s/tw from €92/115; ❄ 🏊 ♿) Four kilometres east, overlooking Ilha de Tavira, this mustard-coloured, four-star 162-room hotel was converted from a tuna-canning factory. It has cheerful modern rooms with terraces set in attractive low-rise buildings. There's also a health club (with spa services), expansive pool and restaurant, and disabled access. The hotel runs a private boat service to Ilha da Tavira.

our pick Quinta do Caracol (☎ 281 322 475; www.quintadocaracol.pa-net.pt; São Pedro; s/d €98/120; 🏊 P) Overlooking a large exotic garden, this 17th-century farmhouse has nine separate apartments, each handsomely designed with traditional Algarve furnishings and rustic artwork; all have kitchenettes. Reserve well in advance.

Hotel Porta Nova (☎ 281 329 700; www.hotelportanova.com; Rua António Pinheiro; s/d/ste from €89/123/157; ❄ 💻 🏊) On a hill above town, this new whitewashed hotel offers trim and modern rooms with handsome wooden elements and splashes of colour. The rooms have balconies with fine views, and there's an attractive top floor bar.

Quinta da Lua (☎ 281 961 070; www.quintadalua.com.pt; Bernardinheiro, Santo Estevão; d/ste €130/150) Set among orange groves 4km northwest of Tavira, this peaceful place has eight bright, airy,

(Continued on page 181)

PAUL BERNHARDT

Romaria de Nossa Senhora d'Agonia (p411), Viana do Castelo, the Minho

PAUL BERNHARDT

Semana Santa (Holy Week) procession, Tavira (p169), the Algarve

Festa de Santo António (p107), Lisbon

ALA

Previous page:
Padrão dos Descobrimentos monument (p102), Belém district, Lisbon

GREG ELMS

PAUL BERNHARDT

Festival-goer, the Douro (p354)

Festa dos Rapazes (Festival of the Lads; p452), Trás-os-Montes

PAUL BERNHARDT

Festas dos Santos Populares (p107), Lisbon

ALAIN EVRARD

OLIVE

Mercado do Bolhão (p363), Porto, the Douro

Country fair, the Algarve (p155)

PAUL BERNHARDT

PAUL BERNHARDT

Fresh-produce market, the Alentejo (p217)

GREG ELMS

Pastéis de nata (custard tarts; p76)

Port barrels, the Douro (p354)

OLIVER STREWE

ANDERS BLOMQVIST

Outdoor café, Chiado district (p95), Lisbon

Conserveira de Lisboa (p124), Baixa district, Lisbon

GREG ELMS

Reconstruction of a hut in the Celtic hill settlement of Citânia de Briteiros (p408), the Minho

ANDERS BLOMQVIST

PAUL BERN

Fortified 13th-century castle (p254), Mértola, the Alentejo

Mosteiro dos Jerónimos (p102), Belém district, Lisbon

DAMIEN SIMONIS

ANDERS BLOMQVIST

Torre de Belém (p102), Belém district, Lisbon

Capela de São João Baptista in the Igreja de São Roque (p96), Lisbon

MARTIN MOOS

JULIA WILKINSON

Azulejo-adorned staircase of the Palácio do Visconde de Estói (p166), Estói, the Algarve

PAUL BERNHARDT

Praia dos Pescadores (p188), Albufeira, the Algarve

Coastline near Lagos (p198), the Algarve

ANDERS BLC

Sardines drying on the beach at Nazaré (p278), Estremadura

PAUL BERNHARDT

(Continued from page 172)

serene rooms set around a saltwater swimming pool. Hammocks and deck chairs are scattered about the extensive gardens, with birdsong part of the ambience.

Convento de Santo António (☎ 281 321 573; Rua de Santo António; r/ste from €150/240;) This former convent has lots of ambience, with antique-filled corridors and attractive grounds. Rooms themselves are furnished in a classic style, though some are too small to warrant the price.

Eating

BUDGET

Restaurante Avenida (☎ 281 321 113; Avenida Dr Teixeira de Azevêdo; mains €4-10; lunch & dinner Wed-Mon) A local favourite that has a long menu of fish and meat dishes.

Restaurante Lagôas Bica (☎ 281 323 843; Rua Almirante Cândido dos Reis 24; mains €5-11; lunch & dinner) Deservedly popular, here you can eat splendid food, such as fresh grilled fish (sole with orange is recommended), and down cheap bottles of decent Borba wine.

Churrasqueira O Manel (☎ 281 323 343; Rua Dr António Cabreira 39; mains €5-8) Great *frango no churrasco* (grilled chicken) and takeaway are on offer.

Cafés in town include the cheerful **Pastelaria Romana** (Praça da República 1; 8am-midnight), near the Ponte Romana, which has delicious ice cream and pastries, and outdoor tables facing the plaza. **Pastelaria Anazu** (Rua Jacques Pessoa; 8am-11pm Mon-Sat, 8am-8pm Sun) is another riverside spot with outdoor tables. **Pastelaria Tavirense** (☎ 281 323 451; Rua Dr Marcelino Franco 17; 8am-midnight), serves the town's best pastries.

There's also a huge modern **mercado municipal** (most stalls morning only) on the eastern edge of town and a **Pingo Doce Supermarket**.

MIDRANGE & TOP END

Portas do Mar (☎ 281 321 255; Quatro Águas; mains €6-14) Next to Quatro Águas, this place is also good and has a river-view terrace; try tasty shrimp curry or their speciality, spaghetti with shrimp.

Alquimia (☎ 281 323 298; Rua João Vaz Corte Real 80; meals around €15; dinner Mon-Sat) Serving a good mix of tapas, Alquimia is a stylish setting for a glass of wine and a light meal. Outdoor seating, expertly marinated seafood and a location just off the beaten path.

Quatro Águas (☎ 281 325 329; Quatro Águas; mains €8-15; lunch & dinner Tue-Thu Feb-Dec) For a splurge, head to this renowned restaurant, which serves delicious seafood, fish and meat dishes. You can eat inside or out.

Porto (Rua Dr José Pires Padinha 180; mains €10-13; lunch & dinner Tue-Sat) Imaginative dishes and a pleasant riverside setting make for a winning combination at Porto. Try the goat's-cheese samosas and octopus in red-wine sauce.

Taska Abstrakto (☎ 917 043 274; Avenida Dr Antônio Cabreira 34; mains €9-15) Decorated with eclectic artwork on the walls, this colourful place serves creative and nicely prepared dishes like coconut prawns in curry sauce and vegetarian couscous.

our pick **A Ver Tavira** (☎ 281 381 363; Calçada da Galeria 13; tapas/prix-fixe dinner €3-5/25; lunch Tue-Sun, dinner Tue-Sat) A handsome new addition to Tavira, this place has an airy interior and outdoor tables with lovely views over town. Lunchtime bites include great salads, quiche and sandwiches. For dinner, a delectable multicourse meal is served.

Casa das Cataplanas (☎ 281 326 278; Rua Dr José Pires Padinha 162; mains €6-11) Also with an excellent riverside situation, this place serves excellent *cataplanas*.

Drinking & Entertainment

The main bar area in town is along Rua Almirante Cândido dos Reis and Rua Poeta Emiliano da Costa, which have relaxing, welcoming places.

Arco Bar (Rua Almirante Cândido dos Reis 67; Tue-Sun) Run by a Portuguese-German couple, this small place attracts a mix of Portuguese and expats with its laid-back atmosphere and multicultural music.

Patrick's (Rua Dr António Cabreira 25; from 6pm Mon-Sat) This is a cosy expat-run bar with a few outside tables on the narrow cobbled street. It serves hearty British pub grub.

Távila (Praça Dr António Padinha 50) Overlooking a small tree-filled plaza, this low-key spot has outdoor tables, ideal for an afternoon or evening drink. Other similar café-bars are nearby.

For a higher-velocity night, the **Docas**, an extension of the *mercado municipal*, hosts a row of dancier, preclub bars that play music from hands-in-the-air house to African. The area buzzes in July and August.

After that, head to **UBI** (Rua Almirante Cândido dos Reis; midnight-6am Tue-Sun May-Sep, Sat & Sun Nov-Apr), still the only nightclub, in a former factory, with an open-air bar and music until 5am.

Getting There & Around

Frequent buses (☎ 281 322 546) go to Faro (€3, one hour, 12/seven daily weekdays/weekends), via Olhão, and Vila Real (€2.85, 40 minutes). Buses also go to Lisbon (€17, five hours) and Huelva (Spain; €6.50, two hours, twice daily), with connections to Seville (€12, three hours).

Trains run daily to Faro (€2.25, 40 minutes, 12 daily) and Vila Real (€1.60, 35 minutes). A tourist train starts from Praça da Republica and visits the main sights (€3, 40 minutes, hourly 10am to 7pm September to May, to 8pm in June and to midnight in July and August).

Cheap local car-rental agencies include **Mudarent** (☎ 281 326 815; Rua da Silva 18d). **Lorisrent** (☎ 281 325 203, 964 079 233; Rua da Galeria 9a; 9.30am-1.30pm & 3-6.30pm Mon-Sat) charges €4/15 per day for a mountain bike/scooter. There's also **Rent a Bike** (bikes €6 per day) and **Sport Nautica** (☎ 281 324 943; Rua Jacques Pessoa 26; bikes per day €5).

Taxis (☎ 281 321 544, 281 325 746) gather near the cinema on Rua Dr Marcelino Franco.

AROUND TAVIRA

Ilha de Tavira

Sandy islands (all part of the Parque Natural da Ria Formosa) stretch along the coast from Cacela Velha to just west of Faro, and this is one of the finest. The huge beach at the island's eastern end, opposite Tavira, has water sports, a camp site (p172) and café-restaurants, including the world music–playing **Sunshine Bar** (☎ 281 325 518; Tue-Sun). Off-season, the island feels wonderfully remote and empty, but during July and August it's busy.

Heading west from the jetty, in 1km you'll reach the nudist area of the island. A few kilometres further west along the island is **Praia do Barril**, accessible by a miniature train that trundles over the mud flats from **Pedras d'el Rei**, a resort 4km southwest of Tavira. There are some eateries where the shuttle train stops, then sand, sand, sand as far as the eye can see.

GETTING THERE & AWAY

Ferries make the five-minute hop to the *ilha* (€1.50 return, from 9am to 7pm) from Quatro Águas, 2km southeast of Tavira. Times are subject to change – ask the crew when the last one runs! In July and August they usually run till midnight. From July to mid-September a boat normally runs direct from Tavira – ask at the turismo for details.

In addition, **Áqua-Taxis** (☎ 964 515 073, 917 035 207) operates 24 hours a day from July to mid-September, and until midnight May to June. The fare from Quatro Águas/Tavira to the island is €18 for six people.

A bus goes to Quatro Águas from the Tavira bus station July to mid-September (€0.70, eight daily).

A taxi to Quatro Águas costs about €5. For Praia do Barril, take a bus from Tavira to Pedras d'el Rei (€1.70, 10 minutes, eight daily weekdays), from where the little train runs regularly to the beach March to September. Off-season the timetable depends on the operating company's mood.

Cacela Velha

Enchanting, small and cobbled, Cacela Velha is a huddle of whitewashed cottages edged with bright borders, and has a pocket-sized fort, orange and olive groves, and gardens blazing with colour. It's 12km east of Tavira, above a gorgeous stretch of sea, with one café-restaurant, splendid views and a meandering path down to the long, white beach.

GETTING THERE & AWAY

There's no direct bus from Tavira, but Cacela Velha is only 1km south of the N125 (2km before Vila Nova de Cacela; €1.65), which is on the Faro–Vila Real de Santo António bus route. Coming from Faro, there are two signposted turn-offs to Cacela Velha; the second is more direct.

VILA REAL DE SANTO ANTÓNIO

pop 11,000

Perched on the edge of the wide Rio Guadiana, Vila Real de Santo António is a thriving, commercial town staring across at Spanish eyes. Its small pedestrian centre is architecturally impressive; in five months in 1774, the Marquês de Pombal stamped the town with his hallmark gleaming grid-pattern of streets (like Lisbon's Baixa district) after the town was destroyed by floods. From here you can head off on boat or biking trips along the Rio Guadiana (opposite).

Orientation & Information

The seafront Avenida da República is one of the town's two main thoroughfares; the other is the pedestrianised Rua Teófilo Braga, which leads straight from the seafront and past the main square, Praça Marquês de Pombal. The train station lies 350m north of the riverfront. Buses stop beyond the ferry terminal, 100m east of Rua Teófilo Braga.

Espaço Internet Free internet access, opposite the turismo.

Turismo (☎ 281 542 100; Rua Teófilo Braga; 🕑 10am-1.30pm & 2.30-6pm Mon-Fri Apr-Oct, 9.30am-1pm & 2-5.30pm Mon-Fri Nov-Mar) Housed in the Centro Cultural António Aleixo, a former market hall.

Sleeping

Parque de campismo (☎ 281 510 970; adult/tent/car €5/2/3.15; ♿) Frequent buses go to this mammoth municipal camping ground outside the built-up Monte Gordo, 3km west of town. It has shade and beach access but gets jampacked in July and August. There are disabled facilities, a restaurant and bar.

Residência Matos Pereira (☎ 281 543 325; Rua Dr Sousa Martins 57; s/d €30/40) This friendly place near the turismo has frilly, small rooms and a family feel. There's a sunny terrace.

Residência Baixa Mar (☎ 281 543 511; Rua Teófilo Braga 3; s/d €30/40) This decent guesthouse has small, tidy rooms, some of which have river views (although these also face onto a busy road) and some of which open onto a tiny, viewless terrace.

Villa Marquês (☎ 281 530 420; Rua Dr José Barão 61; s/d €30/45) A few streets back from the waterfront, near the bus station, this place has bright, spotless rooms and a rooftop terrace with views over town.

Hotel Guadiana (☎ 281 511 482; www.hotelguadiana.com.pt; Avenida da República 94; s/d/tr/ste €45/55/65/80) Vila Real's fanciest lodging is housed inside a grand old mansion that overlooks the Rio Guadiana. You'll find a mix of colourful and classically furnished rooms with old-fashioned details.

Eating

Snack-Bar Mira (☎ 281 544 773; Rua da Princesa 59; mains €4-7; 🕑 lunch & dinner) This cheery, pocket-size place with blue-chequered tablecloths serves good-value daily dishes and is a winner with the locals.

Snack-Bar Cuca (☎ 281 513 625; Rua Dr Sousa Martins 64; mains €5-10; 🕑 lunch & dinner) Small, friendly and popular with the locals for its fresh fish, this snack bar has outdoor tables on the pedestrianised street.

Associação Naval do Guadiana (☎ 281 513 085; Avenida da República; mains €5-10; 🕑 lunch & dinner Wed-Mon) A big blue waterfront building, this place has a terrace with views over the river and good seafood.

Caves do Guadiana (☎ 281 544 498; Avenida da República 90; mains €8-10) With outdoor seats and a tiled interior, this long-standing waterfront favourite serves some of the city's best seafood.

GLIDING ALONG THE GUADIANA

One of the major rivers of Portugal, the slow-flowing Rio Guadiana makes an idyllic setting for a bit of adventure. Several outfits offer excursions along the river, which forms the border with Spain for some 50km.

Riosul (☎ 281 510 200; www.riosultravel.com; Monte Gordo) This company runs small-scale trips from Vila Real de Santo António to Foz de Odeleite at least four times weekly in summer and twice-weekly the rest of the year. The trips cost €41, including lunch and a stop for a swim. Periodically, they also offer night-time cruises, which cost €40, including dinner.

Conrad Turismo (☎ 916 823 565, 917 694 129; one-day/two-day trip adult €85/120, child €40/60) This outfit offers one- and two-day trips along the Guadiana aboard its 14m sailboat. It also offers sunset cruises and one-day trips along the coast, though you can arrange just about anything. Ask for Conrad Turismo at the entrance to the marina.

Lands – Turismo na Natureza (☎ 289 817 466; www.lands.pt; Rua Bento de Jesus Caraça 22) Based in Montenegro, about 2km from Faro, this outfit runs kayak tours from Foz de Odeleite; they cost €40 for a day including lunch, for groups with a maximum of 10 people. They also arrange walks around the Rio Guadiana, or bird-spotting in the Parque Natural da Ria Formosa (adult/child €20/10).

The quiet back road along the river from Foz de Odeleite to Alcoutim (14km) is also popular with bikers. Along this scenic route are several villages worth visiting, including Álamo, with its Roman dam, and Guerreiros do Rio, with its small **Museu do Rio** (River Museum; ☎ 281 547 380; admission €1; 🕑 9am-12.30pm & 2-5.30pm Tue-Sat) about traditional river life.

Getting There & Away

BUS

Buses (☎ 281 511 807) run daily to Tavira (€2.85, 30 to 45 minutes, six to nine daily) via Faro (€4.50, 1½ hours), some going on to Lisbon (€17, 4¾ hours, four to five daily). Regular buses go to Monte Gordo (€1.65, 10 minutes, eight to nine daily) and Huelva (Spain; €5.40, 2½ hours, two daily), with connections on to Seville (€10 total from Vila Real de Santo António, 3½ hours).

BOAT

Ferries cross the river border every 40 minutes to whitewashed Ayamonte; buy tickets from the waterfront office (€1.30/4.40/0.65 per person/car/bike), open from 8.20am to 7pm Monday to Saturday, 9.15am to 5.40pm Sunday.

TRAIN

Trains to Lagos (€9.50, 3½ hours, eight daily) require changes at Faro and/or Tunes. There are regular train services to Faro (€4.80, 1¼ hours, 11 daily).

Getting Around

The nearest place to rent bikes is in Monte Gordo, from **Riosul** (☎ 281 510 200). Bikes can be delivered if you call in advance.

CASTRO MARIM

pop 3100

Slumbering in the shadows of a 14th-century castle, Castro Marim is a picturesque village that sees only a handful of foreign visitors. It has a quaint, tree-shaded centre, but not much going on aside from a few restaurants and the fortifications, which afford views across salt pans, the bridge to Spain, and the fens and marshes of the **Reserva Natural do Sapal de Castro Marim**, which is famous for its flamingos. It's 5km north of Vila Real de Santo António.

Information

Odiana (☎ /fax 281 531 171; www.odiana.pt; Rua Dr José Alves Moreira 3; 9.30am-1pm & 2.30-6pm) An organisation promoting the Baixo (lower) Guadiana region, it distributes an excellent guide covering regional culture with suggestions for day trips.

Turismo (☎ 281 531 232; Praça 1 de Maio 2-4; 9.30am-12.30pm & 2-5.30pm Mon-Fri) Below the castle in the village centre, the turismo also provides decent guides.

Sights

CASTELO & AROUND

In the 13th century, Dom Afonso III built Castro Marim's **castle** (admission free; 8am-7pm Apr-Oct, 9am-5pm Nov-Mar) on the site of Roman and Moorish fortifications in a dramatic and strategic position for spying on the Spanish frontier. In 1319 it became the first headquarters of the religious military order known as the Order of Christ, the new version of the Knights Templar (p298). Until they moved to Tomar in 1334, the soldiers of the Order of Christ used this castle to keep watch over the estuary of the Rio Guadiana and the border with Spain, where the Moors were still in power.

The grand stretch of ruins today, however, date from the 17th century, when Dom João IV ordered the addition of vast ramparts. At the same time a smaller fort, the **Castelo de São Sebastião**, was built on a nearby hilltop (still closed to the public). Much of the area was destroyed in the 1755 earthquake, but the ruins of the main fort are still pretty awesome.

Inside the wonderfully derelict castle walls is a 14th-century church, the **Igreja de Santiago**, where Henry the Navigator, also Grand Master of the Order of Christ, is said to have prayed. The best time to see the castle is during the **Feira Mediéval**, which takes place for three days in late August or early September. There's a parade on the first day from the castle to the village, food stalls selling local products, music, and a medieval banquet.

RESERVA NATURAL DO SAPAL DE CASTRO MARIM E VILA REAL DE SANTO ANTÓNIO

Established in 1975, this nature reserve is Portugal's oldest, covering 20 sq km of marshland and salt pans bordering the Rio Guadiana north of Vila Real. Important winter visitors are greater flamingos, spoonbills and Caspian terns. In spring it's busy with white storks.

The park's **administrative office** (☎ 281 510 680; Sapal de Venta Moínhos; 9am-12.30pm & 2-5.30pm Mon-Fri) is 2km from Monte Francisco, a five-minute bus ride north of Castro Marim; get directions from the turismo at Castro Marim as there are no signs.

There are two accommodation centres in the park but they are popular with groups, so you need to book ahead. Another rewarding area for spotting the park's birdlife is around Cerro do Bufo, 2km southwest of Castro Marim. Ask staff at the park office or at Castro Marim's turismo for details.

Getting There & Around

Buses from Vila Real run to Castro Marim (eight minutes, €1.70) and go on to Monte Francisco, a short distance north.

THE CENTRAL COAST

LOULÉ

pop 21,700 / elevation 160m

One of Algarve's largest inland towns, Loulé (lo-*lay*) is a peaceful place with an attractive old quarter and Moorish castle ruins. Its history spans back to the Romans. Loulé's artisan traditions are still evident today, with crafty folk hard at work on cane furniture, wicker baskets and embroidery at tiny workshops scattered about town. For the casual visitor, Loulé, lying some 16km northwest of Faro, makes a popular day trip, particularly on Saturday when it hosts a weekly open-air market. Loulé's small university lends it some verve, but apart from its wild Carnaval (Carnival, the festival that takes place just before Lent), the town remains pretty snoozy.

Orientation

The bus station is about 250m north of the centre. The train station is 5km southwest (take any Quarteira-bound bus).

Information

Bookshop (Praça da República; 9.30am-1pm & 3-6pm Mon-Fri, 9am-1pm Sat) Has an excellent range of guidebooks and maps.

Espaço Internet (289 417 348; Largo de São Francisco; per hr €2; 9am-noon Mon-Sat, 4-11pm Sun) Provides internet access.

Turismo (289 463 900; Avenida 25 de Abril; 9.30am-5.30pm Mon-Fri Oct-May, 9.30am-7pm Mon-Sat Jun-Sep) Get maps and the lowdown on Loulé at this friendly, efficient office.

Sights & Activities

The restored castle ruins house the **Museu Municipal de Arqueologia** (289 400 642; Largo Dom Pedro I; admission €1.05; 9am-5.30pm Mon-Fri, 10am-2pm Sat), containing well-presented fine fragments of Bronze Age and Roman ceramics. A glass floor exposes excavated Moorish ruins. The admission fee includes entry to a stretch of the castle walls and the **Cozinha Tradicional Algarvia**

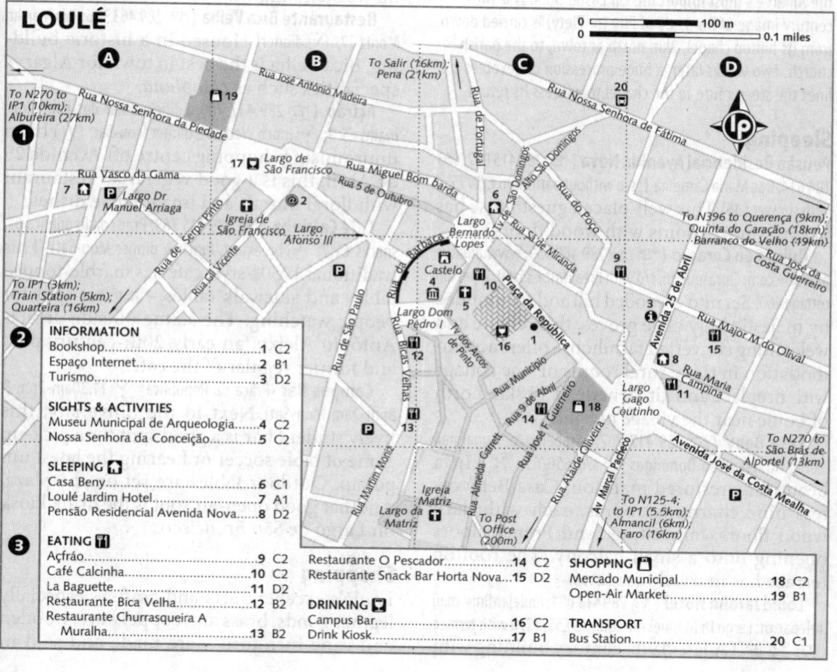

(9am-5.30pm Mon-Fri, 10am-2pm Sat), a recreation of a traditional Algarve kitchen, featuring a cosy hearth, archaic implements and burnished copper.

Opposite the castle, **Nossa Senhora da Conceição** (admission free; 9.30-1pm Tue, Thu & Sat) dates from the mid-17th century. It's a small chapel with a plain façade nonchalantly hiding a heavily decorated mid-18th-century interior with a magnificent gold altarpiece.

An environmental group, **Almargem** (289 412 959; www.almargem.org; per walk €3), welcomes visitors on its 10km Saturday walks. Each year they try to cover every area of the Algarve.

Festivals & Events

Carnaval (late February or early March) Just before Lent, Loulé shimmies into something sexy and sequinned, with parades, tractor-drawn floats and lots of musical high jinks. Friday is the children's parade, and Sunday the big one.

Loulé International Jazz Festival (July; www.ccloule.com) The town dons jazz boots on selected evenings; international and Portuguese musicians jam in the convent and castle.

Nossa Senhora da Piedade (Easter Sunday) Linked to ancient maternity rites, this *romaria* (religious festival) is the Algarve's most important. On Easter Sunday a 16th-century image of Our Lady of Pity (or Piety) is carried down from its hilltop chapel, 2km north of town, to the parish church. Two weeks later, a huge procession of devotees lines the steep route to the chapel to witness its return.

Sleeping

Pensão Residencial Avenida Nova (289 415 097, 963 104 614; Rua Maria Campina 1; s/d without bathroom €20/25, d with shower €35) This well-placed guesthouse has bright, sunny rooms with wood floors.

Quinta do Coração (/fax 289 489 959; www.algarveparadise.com; Carrasqueiro; s/d with breakfast €35/50, 2-person cottage €60) Set into a wooded hill and surrounded by majestic hilly olive groves, this remote and welcoming converted farmhouse offers accommodation in three rural rooms or one cottage with fireplace and kitchenette. It's 18km north of Loulé near the village of Salir.

Casa Beny (289 417 702; casabeny@portugalmail.com; Travessa São Domingos 13; s/d €50/65;) In a beautifully restored mansion, Casa Beny offers nine charming rooms, each with dark wood floors, tall ceilings and French doors opening onto a small balcony. The rooftop terrace has marvellous views.

Loulé Jardim Hotel (289 413 094; loulejardim@mail.telepac.pt; Largo Dr Manuel Arriaga; s/d €55/72, d with terrace €77;) A late-19th-century building with smart, large rooms, this efficient, popular place overlooks a pretty square. Book ahead for a terrace.

Eating & Drinking

Restaurante O Pescador (289 462 821; Rua José F Guerreiro; mains €7-9) Right by the market, this is the place for a good family hubbub (especially on market days), big helpings and reasonable prices.

La Baguette (Avenida 25 de Abril 2; mains €2-4; 10am-7pm) This low-key café serves a range of tasty baguette sandwiches as well as big cups of coffee and croissants.

Restaurante Snack Bar Horta Nova (289 462 429; Rua Major Manuel do Olival; mains €6-10; breakfast, lunch & dinner Mon-Sat) Offers open-air, cheap-and-cheerful dining in a large, walled garden under shady trees. They specialise in home-made pizzas and charcoal-grilled meat and fish.

Restaurante Churrasqueira A Muralha (289 412 629; Rua Martim Moniz 41; mains €7-13; lunch Tue-Sat, dinner Mon-Sat) Set in a former bakery, A Muralha has tasty regional favourites, and you can eat in the walled garden under a banana tree, surrounded by the old ovens. There's live music on weekend nights.

Restaurante Bica Velha (289 463 376; Rua Martim Moniz 17; dinner) Housed in a historic building, Bica Velha is the best in town for Algarve specialities such as *cataplana*.

Açfrão (289 417 700; Edifício Solar das Palmeiras; mains €5-9; lunch Wed-Sat, dinner Mon-Sat; V) In an unpromising shopping centre off Avenida 25 de Abril, this is a good vegetarian restaurant with floral murals and imaginative dishes.

Café Calcinha (289 415 763; Praça da República 67; snacks €1-7; breakfast, lunch & dinner Mon-Sat) This traditional 1950s-style café has marble-topped tables and sidewalk tables – a great spot for people watching. The statue outside depicts António Aleixo, an early-20th-century poet and former regular of the café.

Campus Bar (Praça da República; 11.30am-2pm & 8pm-2am Mon-Sat) Next to the university, this lively student bar is a good spot for a pick-up game of table soccer or hearing the latest uni gossip. Outdoor tables are set on the plaza. Another good open-air spot is the drink kiosk on Largo de São Francisco.

Shopping

Loulé's excellent arts and crafts – especially leather goods, brass and copperware, wooden and cane furniture – are made and sold in craft shops along Rua da Barbaca (behind the castle). The *mercado municipal* also has traditional craft stalls.

On Saturday morning head for the open-air **market** (9am-1pm) northwest of the centre, with masses of everything from clothes, shoes, toys and souvenirs.

Getting There & Around

Trains to Faro (€1.25, 15 minutes, eight daily) and Lagos (€4.80, 1½ hours, eight daily) stop at Loulé station (5km south of town). More conveniently, there are regular **bus** (289 416 655) connections from Faro (€2.45, 40 minutes, at least every two hours), Albufeira (€3.40, 55 minutes, four to seven daily) and Portimão (€4.85, 1¾ hours, four daily). For Lisbon (€17, 3¾ hours, four daily), change at Albufeira.

If you're coming by car on market day (Saturday), get here early or park outside town.

ALMANCIL

It's worth making a detour here, 13km northwest of Faro and about 6km south of Loulé, to visit the marvellous **Igreja de São Lourenço de Matos** (Church of St Lourenço; admission free). The church was built on the site of a ruined chapel after local people, while digging a well, had implored the saint for help and then struck water.

The resulting baroque masterpiece, which was built by fraternal master-team Antão and Manuel Borges, is smothered in *azulejos* – even the ceiling is covered in them. The walls depict scenes from the life of the saint. In the earthquake of 1755, only five tiles fell from the roof.

One of the Algarve's longest-established horse-riding centres is here too: **Paraíso dos Cavalos** (289 394 189; Almancil; per hr around €20).

Buses between Albufeira (40 minutes) and Loulé (15 minutes) stop here.

ALBUFEIRA

pop 20,200

Once a scenic fishing village, Albufeira (from the Arabic *al-buhera*, meaning 'castle on the sea') sold its soul to mass-market tourism in the 1960s. Development is rampant throughout the area, but the town still boasts picturesque beaches backed by cliffs, with a scenic old centre spreading up the hillside. It has loads of tourist facilities, accommodating a mix of families, couples and young travellers – most from the UK.

Although much of the town was damaged in the 1755 earthquake, the Moorish feel still lingers, and its quiet cobbled streets west of the centre make for some quiet wandering if you need to escape the carnival atmosphere. If you're looking for a lively, but not terribly authentic place, Albufeira may be the ticket, with artisan stalls, buskers and live music spilling out of bars at night.

The town's modern extension is Montechoro, apartment-block heaven, 3km to the east where 'the Strip' leads up from crowded Praia da Oura. Quieter beaches like Praia da Galé lie to the west.

Orientation

Albufeira's old town lies below the busy N526 (Avenida dos Descobrimentos). Its focal point is Largo Engenheiro Duarte Pacheco, where most of the cafés, bars and restaurants are clustered.

Sprawled to the north and east is modern-day Albufeira: the market, the bus station and main police station are almost 2km north. The train station is 6km north at Ferreiras, connected to the bus station by shuttle bus.

Information

BOOKSHOPS

Julies (289 513 773; Rua da Igreja Nova 6; 10am-4pm Mon-Fri, to 1pm Sat, to 3pm Sun) This is packed with second-hand books in English and other languages.

EMERGENCY & MEDICAL SERVICES

Centro de saúde (medical centre; 289 585 899; 24hr) Two kilometres north of the old town.

Clioura Clinic (289 587 000; 24hr) A private clinic in Montechoro.

GNR police post (289 583 210; Avenida 25 de Abril 22) More central than the police station. Next to Hotel Baltum.

GNR police station (289 590 790; Estrada Vale de Pedras) North of town, near the *mercado municipal*.

INTERNET ACCESS

Windcafé.com (289 513 786; 2nd fl, Centro Comercial California, Rua Cândido dos Reis 1; per hr €3.50, per 10min €1; 11am-9pm) Also has second-hand books on sale.

MONEY

Banco Português do Atlântico (Largo Engenheiro Duarte Pacheco 23) Along and near Avenida 25 de Abril are several banks with ATMs, including this one.

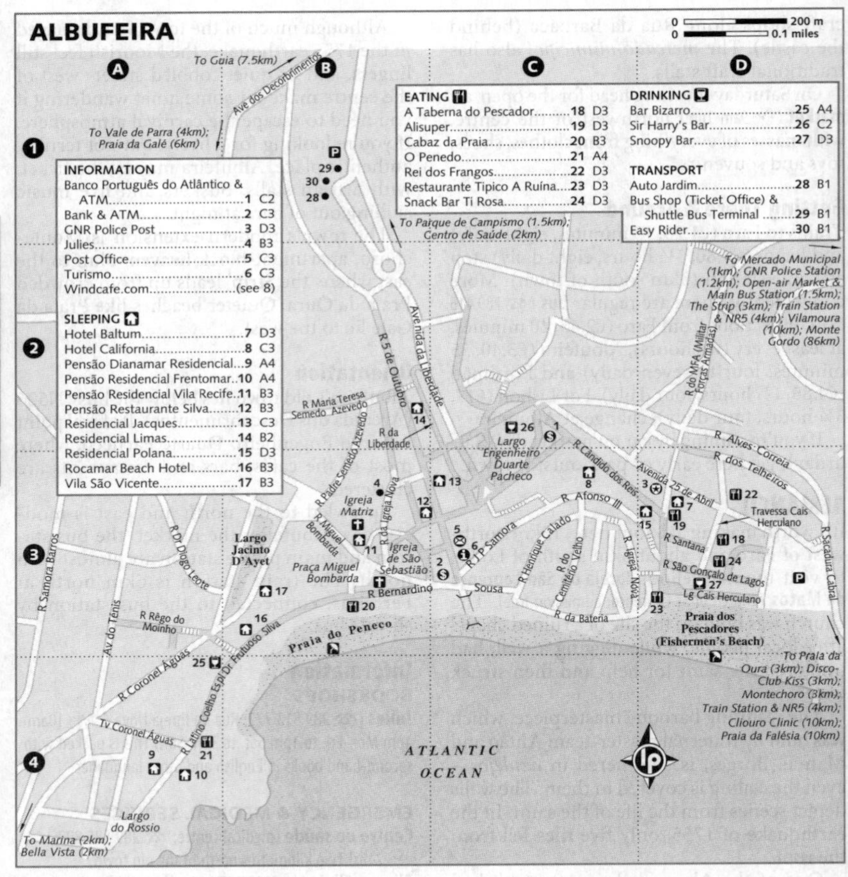

POST

Post office (Rua 5 de Outubro)

TOURIST INFORMATION

Turismo (☎ 289 585 279; Rua 5 de Outubro 8; ⏲ 9.30am-1pm & 2-5.30pm Mon-Sat) By a tunnel that leads to the beach.

Sights

Albufeira's pedestrianised seafront is made for seaside strolls. The town's beach, **Praia do Peneco**, through the tunnel near the turismo, is clean and scenic, but often head-to-toe with sun loungers.

For a hint of local flavour, head 400m east to **Praia dos Pescadores** (Fishermen's Beach, also called Praia dos Barcos), where you might find a remnant of Albufeira's fishing past, with fishermen mending their nets beside their high-prowed, brightly painted boats.

Further afield – both east and west of town – are numerous beautifully rugged coves and bays, though the nearest are heavily developed and often crowded. The easiest to reach is **Praia da Oura**, at the bottom of 'The Strip' 3km to the east (roughly 30 minutes on foot; follow Avenida 25 de Abril and climb the steps at the end to reach the road to the beach). It's wide and sandy, though backed by buildings.

Between Praia da Oura and **Praia da Falésia**, a wonderfully long and remote-feeling beach 10km to the east, is a string of less crowded beaches, including **Balaia** and **Olhos de Água**, whose western end is best for swimming and sunbathing. Buses run to Olhos de Água (€1.60, 10 minutes, half-hourly), mostly continuing to Praia da Falésia (20 minutes).

One of the best beaches to the west, **Praia da Galé**, about 6km away, is long and sandy, not so crowded and a centre for jet-skiing and water-skiing. It's easily accessible by car, but there's no direct bus service to this beach or the others en route, though local buses to Portimão do run along the main road about 2km above the beaches (get off at Vale de Parra).

Activities

Amorita Cruises (☎ 289 302 984; www.algarve-cruises.com; Marina Vilamoura; 3/6hr cruise €40/20) offers two different sailing cruises aboard a 17m yacht; the itinerary takes in caves and coastal rock formations, untravelled bays and pristine beaches, with a stop for swimming. Cruises leave from both Marina Vilamora and Praia dos Pescadores in Albufeira.

Riosul (☎ 281 510 200; www.riosultravel.com; Monte Gordo) offers jeep safaris (€25/65 half-/full day) and cruises up the Rio Guadiana (€38 to €49). They can pick you up at your hotel for a bit extra.

South Adventures (☎ 916 126 305; www.southadventures.com.pt) offers fast-sailing watery adventure in the form of kite surfing. Prices start at €100 for a three-hour lesson.

At Guia, 8km northwest, **Zoomarine** (☎ 289 560 300; www.zoomarine.com; adult/child €19/11.30; 10am-7.30pm Jul–mid-Sep, to 6pm mid-May–Jun & mid-Sep–Oct, to 5pm Tue-Sun Jan–mid-May & Nov, closed Dec) will satisfy all desires for aqua-entertainment, with huge swimming pools and slides, as well as lakes, an aquarium and dolphin shows.

Other water parks near Albufeira include **Aqualand – The Big One** (☎ 282 320 230; www.aqualand.pt; Alcantarilha; adult/child €16.50/13.50; 10am-6pm Jun-Sep) with huge a loop-the-loop slide and rapids and **Aqua Show** (☎ 289 389 396; www.aquashowpark.com; adult/child €19.50/15; 10am-6.30pm Apr-Aug, to 5.30pm Sep-Mar) in Vilamoura, 10km east of Albufeira, with flamingos, parrots and Europe's biggest wave pool.

The English-run **Albufeira Riding Centre** (☎ 289 542 870; Vale Navio Complex; 1 hr €25) on the road to Vilamoura offers one- to three-hour horse rides for all ages and abilities.

You can play tennis at the professional-standard **Ténis da Quinta da Balaia** (☎ 289 586 575; www.quintadabalaia.pt), a resort located 1km east of Albufeira.

Festivals & Events

The major local shindig is **Festa da Ourada**, held on14 August. It honours the fishermen's patron saint, Nossa Senhora da Ourada (Our Lady of the Oracle), with a procession that goes from the parish church along the seaside promenade and culminates in a mighty midnight fireworks display over Praia dos Pescadores.

Sleeping

You'll need to book well ahead to bag accommodation in July and August. Off-season (November to March), many places close.

BUDGET

Parque de Campismo de Albufeira (☎ 289 587 629; www.campingalbufeira.net; adult/tent/car €5.20/5.60/5.20;) Near Alpouvar, 2km north of town, this well-equipped, shady camp site has eateries, facilities for the disabled, swimming pools, a children's playground and caravans for rent. Bus 20 stops nearby.

Pensão Restaurante Silva (☎ 289 512 669; Rua 5 de Outubro 23; d with shower €40) Rooms at this small-scale centrally located spot are clean, bright and nicely kept.

Pensão Residencial Frentomar (☎ /fax 289 512 005; Rua Latino Coelho 25; d €40) This simple guesthouse has basic but tidy quarters. It's a steal if you can snag a room with terrace – these overlook the crashing waves.

Residencial Limas (☎ 289 514 025; Rua da Liberdade 25; d €40) Limas offers a range of carpeted rooms, some in better shape than others. The best are bright and colourful; some have shared bathrooms.

MIDRANGE & TOP END

Pensão Dianamar Residencial (☎ 289 587 801; www.dianamar.com; Rua Latino Coelho 36; s/d/tr from €30/50/70) Scandinavian-run Dianamar has lovely details, with fresh flowers and attractive rooms, many with balconies and two with sea views. There's also an inviting roof terrace.

Residencial Jacques (☎ 969 584 933; Rua 5 de Outubro 36; d €55) In a lovely old-fashioned building, Jacques offers eight cheery, spacious rooms with tile floors, some with tiny balconies over the street. There's a terrace for guests.

Hotel Baltum (☎ 289 589 102; www.hotelbaltum.com; Avenida 25 de Abril 26; s/d from €50/70;) This modern, low-rise hotel has neat and trim rooms with a beach-holiday feel; some rooms have small balconies.

Pensão Residencial Vila Recife (☎ 289 586 747; fax 289 587 182; Rua Miguel Bombarda 12; s/d/tr incl breakfast €45/55/75;) With a pleasant front garden, Recife has a range of rooms, from dated but spacious quarters with sea views to more modern, comfortable rooms with balconies.

Rocamar Beach Hotel (☎ 289 540 280; www.rocamarbeachhotel.com; Largo Jacinto D'Ayet; s/d €70/90, d with sea view €114;) Albufeira's newest hotel has sleek, stylish rooms with balconies. It's in a whitewashed building perched over the beach.

Residencial Polana (☎ 289 583 401; hotelcalifornia@mail.telepac.pt; Rua Cândido dos Reis 32; s/d €92/110;) Polana has nicely decorated rooms with Alentejan traditional painted furniture and attractive terraces. Guests check in and can use the pool at the nearby Hotel California.

Vila São Vicente (☎ 289 583 700; www.sao-vicente-hotel.com; Largo Jacinto D'Ayet; s/d from €85/110;) This peaceful, classically decorated guesthouse has handsome rooms with polished-wood floors. Some rooms have balconies with ocean views.

Hotel California (☎ 289 583 400; hotelcalifornia@mail.telepac.pt; Rua Cândido dos Reis 12; s/d incl breakfast from €97/140;) This hotel offers nice, simple, bright rooms with terracotta and patterned tiles, and terraces (without views).

Eating

Albufeira has a wide range of dining options, from traditional seafood feasts to Indian and Thai.

Snack Bar Ti Rosa (Rua Diogo Cão; mains €4-5; lunch & dinner) This tiny restaurant has many local admirers for its simple but tasty home-cooked meals (in the form of one or two daily specials).

Rei dos Frangos (☎ 289 512 981; Travessa dos Telheiros 4; mains €5-9; lunch & dinner) Good, inexpensive grilled chicken is the dish of choice at this tiled local favourite. *Cataplana* and grilled fish are also on offer.

Bella Vista (marina; mains €6-10) This marina-side restaurant serves hearty salads, pizza and pasta, and is a good spot to sit in the outdoor squashy chairs and watch the boats bobbing on the water.

A Taberna do Pescador (☎ 289 589 196; Travessa Cais Herculano; mains €5.50-12) This fun, cavernous place has a big fish mural and pavement tables and specialises in grilled fish.

O Penedo (☎ 289 515 072; Rua Latino Coelho 36; mains €6-12; V) This restaurant offers some unusual, tasty mains with vegetarian choices amid yellow walls hung with paintings; it overlooks the sea.

Restaurante Tipico A Ruína (☎ 289 512 094; Largo Cais Herculano; mains €7-15; lunch daily, dinner Mon-Sat) This restaurant covers all seating options, with superb sea views from the rooftop terrace, a pleasantly rustic setting and beach-side tables. It offers tiptop seafood and fish.

Cabaz da Praia (☎ 289 512 137; Praça Miguel Bombarda 7; mains €10-16) With its clifftop views over the crashing waves, this lovely French-influenced restaurant serves expertly prepared grills and seafood and decadent desserts. Book a table on the terrace for stellar views.

There is an **Alisuper supermarket** (8am-8.30pm) in the town centre, at the end of Rua Cândido dos Reis.

Drinking

Summertime events include live dance or music shows on various evenings in Largo Engenheiro Duarte Pacheco.

Bars throng the area around Largo Engenheiro Duarte Pacheco and nearby Rua Cândido dos Reis. Nearly all offer happy hours (at various times of the day) and open until at least 4am in summer.

Snoopy Bar (Rua S Gonçalo de Lagos) Overlooking the beach, this casual spot hosts live music most nights of the week.

Bar Bizarro (Esplanada Dr Frutuoso Silva 30; 9am-2am Mon-Sat) High above the beach, this colourful bar has cork-lined walls decorated with vintage bric-a-brac. There's lovely views from the front terrace.

Sir Harry's Bar (Largo Engenheiro Duarte Pacheco 37) One of the older (and pricier) British-style pubs, this is so authentic and cosy inside you can pretend you're in Britain with better weather. British brews on tap and live music daily.

Disco-Club Kiss This is the Algarve's most famous club, at Praia da Oura, with international poppy house DJs and usually with the addition of glitzy dancers.

Shopping

An open-air market, mostly selling clothes and shoes, is held on the first and third Tuesday of the month near the main bus station, 2km north of the old town.

Getting There & Away

The **main bus station** (☎ 289 580 611; Rua dos Caliços) is 2km north of town. Passengers travelling to

Lisbon can purchase tickets at a more conveniently located **bus shop** (☎ 289 588 122; Avenida da Liberdade); outside the bus shop, shuttle buses go to the main bus station (€1), every 15 minutes from 7am to 8pm.

Buses run to Lagos (€4.50, 65 to 75 minutes, 12 daily) via Portimão; Faro (€3.80, 40 minutes, hourly); Silves (€3.40, 40 minutes to one hour, seven daily); and Loulé (€3.40, 40 minutes, four to seven daily). There are two to Huelva in Spain (€10, 4¼ hours, via Faro), and on to Seville (€15, 5½ hours). Services shrink at weekends.

Trains run to Lagos (€4.80, 1¼ hours, nine daily) and Faro (€2.35, 35 minutes, nine daily) – but beware of slow local services. Go to Tunes (10 daily) to pick up trains to Lisbon.

Getting Around

To reach the train station, take the *estação* (station) shuttle bus (€2, 20 minutes, at least hourly 6.45am to 8pm) from the main bus station (opposite).

A major car-rental agency is **Auto Jardim** (☎ 289 580 500; www.auto-jardim.com; Edifício Brisa, Avenida da Liberdade). **Easy Rider** (☎ 289 501 102; www.go-easyrider.com; Avenida da Liberdade 115) rents mountain bikes/scooters for €10/20 per day.

CARVOEIRO

Carvoeiro is a cluster of whitewashed buildings rising up from tawny, gold and green cliffs and backed by hills. Shops, bars and restaurants rise steeply from the small arc of beach that is the focus of the town, and beyond lie hillsides full of sprawling holiday villas. This diminutive seaside resort 5km south of Lagoa is prettier and more laid-back than many of the bigger resorts, but its size means that it gets full to bursting in summer.

Orientation & Information

Buses from Lagoa stop right by the beach, beside the **turismo** (☎ 282 357 728; ⏲ 10am-1.30pm & 2-6pm Fri-Mon, 9.30am-6pm Tue-Thu). The post office and several banks are on Rua dos Pescadores (the one-way road in from Lagoa).

Sights & Activities

The town's little bite of sandy beach, **Praia do Carvoeiro** is surrounded by the steeply mounting town. About 1km east on the coastal road is the bay of **Algar Seco**, a favourite stop on the tour-bus itinerary thanks to its dramatic rock formations.

If you're looking for a stunning swimming spot, continue east along the main road, Estrada do Farol, to **Praia de Centianes**, where the secluded cliff-wrapped beach is almost as dramatic as Algar Seco. Buses heading for **Praia do Carvalho** (nine daily from Lagoa, via Carvoeiro) pass nearby – get off at Colina Sol Aparthotel, the Moorish-style clifftop hotel. The nearest water park is **Slide & Splash** (☎ 282 341 685, adult/child €16.50/13.50; www.slidesplash.com; Estrada Nacional 125), 2km west of Lagoa.

Golfers can be choosy: there's the nine-hole **Gramacho** and 18-hole **Pinta** (☎ 282 340 900; www.pestana.com; both at Pestana Golf Resort); and the challenging **Vale de Milho** (☎ 282 358 502; www.valedemilhogolf.com) near Praia de Centianes, good for all levels and with some of the Algarve's best-value play. The **David Leadbetter Golf Academy** (☎ 282 340 900; www.pestanagolf.com), at the Pinta course, can arrange golfing packages.

The (German) family-run **Divers Cove** (☎ 282 356 594; www.diverscove.de; Quinta do Paraíso; ⏲ 9am-7pm) diving centre provides equipment, dives and PADI certification (three-hour introduction €60, one-day discovery €120, two-day scuba diver/four-day open water €225/410).

Sleeping

In July and August, it may be impossible to find a room, so reserve well ahead. Some guesthouses may require a minimum three-night stay.

O Castelo (☎ 282 357 416; casteloguesthouse@netvisao.pt; Rua do Casino 59; d €40-60) Across the other side of the bay, this welcoming castle-shaped guesthouse gets the sunrise view, and offers spotless well-kept rooms, some with sea views.

Casa von Baselli (☎ 282 357 159; Rua da Escola; d with shared bathroom €45) Around the corner from Brigitte Lemieux, this is a cosy five-room, German-run place. There is a shared terrace, high above the bay, for breakfast and sunset.

Brigitte Lemieux (☎/fax 282 356 318; Rampa da Nossa Senhora da Encarnação 4; d/studio €50/62) Brigitte, an amiable Canadian woman, rents out two lovely rooms and one studio with kitchenette in this sea-facing little house on the cliff. Facing the sea take the steep road up to the left.

Vila Horizonte (☎ 282 356 047; http://vila-horizonte.com; Estrada do Farol 1260; d with/without balcony €70/56; 🅿) A 10-minute walk northeast of the beach, this white-washed place offers attractive, nicely furnished rooms overlooking a pool and gardens. Several rooms have sea-facing terraces.

THE ALGARVE

Eating

There are a handful of restaurants clustered near the beach and scattered along Estrada do Farol.

Rafaiol Restaurante & Bar (☎ 282 357 164; Rua do Barranco; mains around €12; ⌚ dinner Fri-Wed) About 1km north of the beach, Rafaiol is set in an atmospheric old mansion, with a wraparound porch and a small elegant dining room inside. Grilled seafood and meat dishes are the main attractions, followed by rich chocolate cake.

Restaurante Boneca Bar (☎ 282 358 391; mains €8-13; ⌚ 10am-midnight) Hidden in the rock formations out at Algar Seco, this place is a good spot for fresh grilled fish or a scenic cocktail. It has outdoor tables just a short hop from the foaming waves.

Getting There & Around

Buses run on weekdays from Portimão to Lagoa (€1.70, 20 minutes, half hourly) from where there are regular connections to Carvoeiro (10 minutes).

You can rent scooters from **Scooterent** (☎ 282 356 551; Rua do Barranco; 50/125cc per 3 days from €50/65) on the road back to Lagoa. Several car-rental agencies are also along this road. There's a taxi rank at the bottom of Estrada do Farol.

SILVES

pop 10,800

Boasting one of the best-preserved castles in the Algarve, Silves is a town of jumbling orange rooftops scattered above the banks of the silted up Rio Arade. Although it's an undeniably pretty setting, there isn't much to the town apart from Silves' red-stone walls and fortress, a handful of sleepy backstreets and one very lively restaurant. It's 15km northeast of Portimão.

History

The Rio Arade was long an important route into the interior for the Phoenicians, Greeks and Carthaginians, who wanted the copper and iron action in the southwest of the country. With the Moorish invasion from the 8th century, the town gained prominence due to its strategic hilltop, riverside site. From the mid-11th to the mid-13th centuries, Shelb (or Xelb), as it was then known, rivalled Lisbon in prosperity and influence: according to the 12th-century Arab geographer Idrisi, it had a population of 30,000, a port and shipyards, and 'attractive buildings and well-furnished bazaars'.

The town's downfall began in June 1189, when Dom Sancho I laid siege to it, supported by a horde of (mostly English) hooligan crusaders who had been persuaded (with the promise of loot) to pause in their journey to Jerusalem and give Sancho a hand. The Moors holed up inside their impregnable castle with their huge cisterns, but after three hot months of harassment they ran out of water and were forced to surrender. Sancho was all for mercy and honour, but the crusaders wanted the plunder they were promised, and stripped the Moors of their possessions (including the clothes on their backs) as they left, tortured those remaining and wrecked the town.

Two years later the Moors recaptured the town. It wasn't until 1249 that Christians gained control once and for all. But by then Silves was a shadow of its former self. The silting up of the river – which caused disease and stymied maritime trade – coupled with the growing importance of the Algarvian ports hastened the town's decline. Devastation in the 1755 earthquake seemed to seal its fate. But in the 19th-century local cork and dried-fruit industries revitalised Silves, hence the grand bourgeois architecture around town. Today tourism and agriculture are the town's lifeblood.

Orientation & Information

The centre of Silves is 2km north of the train station, a mostly downhill walk on a busy highway. Buses stop on the riverfront road at the bottom of town, crossing the Rio Arade on a modern bridge slightly upriver from a picturesque 13th-century version (for pedestrians only).

Espaço Internet (Rua João de Deus; ⌚ 11am-7pm Mon-Fri) Two blocks downhill from the turismo.

Post office (Rua Correira)

Turismo (☎ 282 442 255; Rua 25 de Abril; ⌚ 9.30am-1pm & 2-5.30pm Mon-Fri) It's a short climb from the bottom of town to the turismo.

Sights & Activities

CASTELO

The russet-coloured, Lego-like **castle** (☎ 282 445 624; adult/child under 12 €1.30/free; ⌚ 9am-7pm mid-Jul–mid-Sep, to 6pm mid-Sep–mid-Jul) has great views over the town and surrounding countryside. It was restored in 1835 and you can walk around its chunky red-sandstone walls, which today enclose unfinished archaeological digs that reveal the site's Roman and pre-Roman past. In the north wall you can see a treason gate (an escape route through which turncoats would sometimes let the enemy in), typical of castles at the time. The Moorish occupation is recalled by a deep well and a rosy-coloured water cistern, 5m deep. Inside, the cistern's four vaults are supported by 10 columns. Probably built in the 11th century, the castle was abandoned by the 16th century. It is to be restored and an interior walkway installed so that visitors can walk inside the structure. This development may mean admission increases once it's all finished.

SÉ & IGREJA MISERICÓRIDIA

Just below the castle is the **sé** (cathedral; admission free; 8.30am-6.30pm), built in 1189 on the site of an earlier mosque, then rebuilt after the 1249 Reconquista and subsequently restored several times following earthquake damage. The stark, fortresslike building has a multiarched Portuguese-Gothic doorway, and some original Gothic touches left, including the nave and aisles and a dramatically tall, strikingly simple interior. There are several fine tombs, one of which is purported to be of Joao do Rego, who helped to settle Madeira. Nearby is the 16th-century **Igreja Misericórdia** (9am-1pm & 2-7pm), plain apart from its distinctive, fanciful Manueline doorway decorated with curious heads, pine cones, foliage and aquatic emblems.

MUSEU DE ARQUEOLOGIA

Just below the cathedral, is the impressive, well laid-out **Museu de Arqueologia** (Archaeological Museum; 282 444 832, Rua das Portas de Loulé; adult/child under 14 €1.50/free; 9am-6pm Mon-Sat). In the centre is a well-preserved 4m-wide, 18m-deep Moorish well surrounded by a spiral staircase, which was discovered during building works. The find, together with other archaeological discoveries in the area, led to the establishment of the museum on this site; it shows prehistoric, Roman and Moorish antiquities. One wall is of glass, showing a section of the fort wall (also of Almohad origin) that is used to support the building.

MUSEU DA CORTIÇA

The award-winning **Museu da Cortiça** (Cork Museum; 282 440 480; www.fabrica-do-ingles.com; Rua Gregório Mascarenhas; adult/child 7-12 €1.50/1; 9.30am-12.45pm & 2-6.15pm) is housed in the Fábrica do Inglês (English Factory; p195). The museum, with the former workshops, machine room and press room, has excellent bilingual displays on the process and history of cork production. Cork was a major industry in Silves for 150 years, until the factory's closure in the mid-1990s, largely due to the silting-up of the Rio Arade.

HORSE RIDING & ANIMAL PARK

At **Quinta Penedo** (282 332 466; Vale Fuzeiros; one/two hr €20/35), 13km to the northeast, you can ride horses through lovely fruit farm countryside. Or there is the **Country Riding Centre** (917 976 992; www.countryridingcenter.com; daily), about 4km east of Silves, left off the road to Messines (it is signposted), who offer hour-long to half-day hacks at all levels, with swimming opportunities.

Near São Bartolomeu de Messines, about 17km northwest, there's **Krazy World** (282 574 134; www.krazyworld.com; adult/child €17/10; 10am-7.30pm Jun-Aug, 10am-6pm Mar-May & Sep, Wed-Sun only Oct-Feb), an animal and crocodile park with minigolf, quad-bikes and pony rides. Transport can be arranged.

Festivals & Events

For 10 days in late June the Fábrica do Inglês swills to the **Festival da Cerveja** (Beer Festival), accompanied by music, folk dance and other entertainment.

Sleeping

BUDGET

Residencial Restaurante Ponte Romana (282 443 275; Horta da Cruz; s/d €20/30) At the end of the old bridge on the other side of the river from town, this nicely kept guesthouse has clean rooms with tile floors and frilly bedspreads, and some of the rooms have idyllic views across the river onto the town and castle. There's a cheery restaurant, too (p194). To get here, drive over the larger bridge towards Portimão and take the first right (west) after the big bridge.

Residencial Sousa (282 442 502; Rua Samoura Barros 17; s/d with shared bathroom €25/40) This place offers pleasant, simply furnished rooms with wood floors, tall ceilings and big windows.

Vila Sodre (/fax 282 443 441; Estrada de Messines; d with breakfast €40;) This pretty, modern blue-and-white villa is 1.4km east of the newer bridge, set back from the busy road. It's good value, with smart rooms.

ALGARVE FOOD FESTIVALS

Epicureans shouldn't miss a chance to eat and drink their way into a tizzy – Algarve-style.

Festival Mediterrâneo (Loulé; www.festivalmed.com.pt) Although primarily focused on music (with excellent bands), this festival in late June also has a culinary component, featuring a wide variety of Mediterranean dishes as well as Portuguese fare.

Festival da Sardinha (Portimão) This 10-day event in early August brings together wine, music and the exalted sardine, served in evermore imaginative ways (try the *sardinha no pão,* aka sardine baked in bread).

Festival do Marisco (Olhão) Held in mid-August, this lively seafood festival features all the great Algarvian oceanic dishes, including *caldeirada* (fish stew) and *cataplana*. Bands add to the fun – the Village People played in 2006.

Feiras dos Enchidos Tradicionais (Monchique) Head for the hills in early March if you want to get a taste of Monchique's country cooking at this traditional sausage festival. You'll also catch performances by folklore troops and find handicrafts for sale.

Festival da Cerveja (Silves) Usually held in July, this spirited fest is dedicated to beer though you'll also find traditional cuisine and singing and dancing to accompany all that beer-guzzling.

Feira Concurso Arte Doce (Lagos) Dessert is elevated to high art at this three-day sweets fair, with marzipan, an Algarvian favourite, taking centre stage. The fair takes place in July.

Feira da Serra (São Brás de Alportel) This down-home country fair held in late July sells locally produced cheese and meats, cakes, wine and other belly-fillers; there are also games for the kiddies and plenty of folkloric song and dance performances.

MIDRANGE

Quinta do Rio (☎/fax 282 445 528; d incl breakfast €55) You'll find rural tranquillity at this charming restored farmhouse set among orange groves and rolling hills, in 5 hectares of countryside. To get here, head 5.5km northeast (en route to São Bartolomeu de Messines) to Sítio São Estevão.

our pick **Quinta da Figueirinha** (☎/fax 282 440 700; www.qdf.pt; 2-/4-/6-person apt €60/88/120;) This 36-hectare organic farm, run by the kindly Dr Gerhard Zabel, produces fruit, vegetables, marzipan, marmalades and chutneys, and offers simple apartments in wonderfully remote and peaceful surroundings. Leaving Silves and crossing the bridge, take the first left and keep to the left in the direction of Fragura. Follow the road for around 4km – the *quinta* is signposted. You can completely self-cater or arrange breakfast, with organic produce, costing €5.

Eating

There are plenty of café-restaurants in the pedestrianised streets leading up to the castle or down by the river, where you'll also find a reasonable market (just west of the old pedestrian bridge).

Restaurante Ponte Romana (☎ 282 443 275; Horta da Cruz; mains €4-7) Adjoining the *residencial* (p193), this large basement restaurant has novel décor – antiquated sewing-machine tables scattered about – and hearty country fare.

Ú Monchiqueiro (☎ 282 442 142; mercado municipal; mains €4-9; lunch & dinner Thu-Tue) By the river and near the market, this restaurant serves punchy *piri-piri* chicken and has covered outdoor tables.

Suzie's Bar (☎ 282 442 107; Rua Coronel Figueiredo; mains €5-9; breakfast, lunch & dinner Thu-Tue; V) This cosy English-run café-restaurant on the waterfront serves home-made burgers, pastas, breakfasts, vegetarian fare and cakes, and has an evening bistro menu. Outdoor seating.

Café Inglês (☎ 282 442 585; mains €6-12; 9.30am-10.30pm Tue-Thu & Sun, to 6pm Mon, to midnight Fri, 6pm-midnight Sat) Below the castle entrance, this café has a wonderful shady terrace and is everyone's favourite spot. The food is excellent (try a delicious vegetarian salad with fruit and nuts, or home-made pizza). One of the Algarve's liveliest restaurants north of the coast, it has an elegant interior and in summer has occasional live jazz, Latin and 1930s Brazilian music.

Bistro O Cais (☎ 282 448 098; Rua José Estevão 2; mains €9-12; 5pm-10pm) Near Suzie's, this handsomely restored waterfront town house makes a cosy setting for eclectic cuisine. Choices include pork satay with peanut sauce and vegetable- and camembert-filled crepes.

Pastelaria (Largo do Município; 8am-midnight Mon-Sat) On the ground floor of the town hall building, this is a lovely setting for coffee and pastries. You can sit outside next to a small tree-shaded plaza or inside for rustic charm.

Restaurante Rui (☎ 282 442 682; Rua Commendatory Villain 27; mains €7-15; ⏰ lunch & dinner Wed-Mon) Situated in the old town, this deceptively simple place is Sagres' finest seafood restaurant: savour everything here from cockles, clams and crabs to sea snails, stone bass and grouper.

Entertainment

Fábrica do Inglês (English Factory; ☎ 282 440 480; Rua Gregório Mascarenhas) In the impressive surroundings of the converted 19th-century English Museu da Cortiça (cork factory; p193), 300m northeast of the new bridge, this complex has restaurants and bars and, from July to mid-September, hosts a nightly multimedia show, featuring dancers, clowns and singers, lasers and cybernetic fountains. During the day you can press a button and walk through these; by night they are illuminated kaleidoscope-style. The ticket includes dinner and admission to the Museu da Cortiça. Reservations are advised. Off-season, there's usually a weekly theme evening; check at the museum's reception. There's a big children's playground too.

Getting There & Around

Buses shuttle daily between Silves and its train station (€1.70, three to four daily), timed to meet the trains from Lagos (€1.70, 35 minutes) and Faro (€3.10, one hour, with a change at Tunes). There are buses to Albufeira (€3.40, 40 minutes, seven daily), and to Portimão (€2.40, 20 minutes, two to five daily) and Lagos (40 minutes). All buses leave from the riverfront, with fewer running at weekends. The **bus ticket office** (☎ 282 442 338; ⏰ 8am-noon & 2-6pm Mon-Fri, 8-noon Sat & 11am-noon Sun) is on the western side of the market.

PORTIMÃO

pop 37,000

Bustling Portimão is a commercial hub for fishing, canning and shopping, with a flurry of activity around its sprawling port. Although most tourists are only passing through en route to Praia da Rocha, the friendly city does have some appeal. Manicured parks and plazas stretch along the waterfront, with an assortment of relaxing outdoor cafés and sizzling fish restaurants; other shops and restaurants are hidden in the old quarter nearby. You can also arrange a boat trip up the Rio Arade.

Portimão's strategic position has long been recognised. It was an important trading link for Phoenicians, Greeks and Carthaginians (Hannibal is said to have visited). It was called Portos Magnus by the Romans and fought over by Moors and Christians. In 1189 Dom Sancho I and a band of crusaders sailed up the Rio Arade from here to besiege Silves. Almost destroyed in the 1755 earthquake, it regained its maritime importance in the 19th century, and is still the Algarve's second most important port (after Olhão).

Orientation

The town's focal point is the Praça Manuel Teixeira Gomes, next to a smart riverside promenade. There's no bus station, but buses stop at various points along the riverside Avenida Guanaré (look for the Shell petrol station) and the parallel Avenida Afonso Henriques (look for the Agip station). The train station is a 15-minute walk (1.1km) north of the centre – follow the pedestrianised Rua do Comércio and its continuation, Rua Vasco da Gama.

Information

There are several banks with ATMs around the riverside Praça Manuel Teixeira Gomes. The **Municipal turismo** (☎ 282 470 732; www.cm-portimao.pt; Avenida Zeca Afonso; ⏰ 9am-6pm Mon-Fri, to 1pm Sat Jun-Aug, 9am-12.30pm & 2-5.30pm Mon-Fri Sep-May) is opposite the football stadium, about 600m west of the river.

Sights

The town's parish church, the **igreja matriz** (admission free), stands on high ground to the north of the town centre and features a 14th-century Gothic portal – all that remains of the original structure after the 1755 earthquake. Other echoes of the past can be found in the narrow streets of the **old fishing quarter**, around Largo da Barca, just before the old highway bridge.

Activities

Lots of operators along the riverside promenade offer boat trips. Most charge around €15 for a three-hour cruise along the coast, visiting caves along the way. **Arade Mar** (☎ 282 419 998; Rua Serpa Pinto 19) runs day trips in a restored fishing boat, with chances to swim, visit caves and have a barbecue on the beach. **Pirate Ship Santa Bernarda** (☎ 987 023 840; www.santa-bernarda.com; half-/full-day trips adult €25/50, child under 10 €15/25; ♿) runs cruises visiting the caves and coast on a 23m wooden sailing ship with wheelchair access. The full-day trip includes a beach barbecue and time to swim. Several operators also offer big-game fishing, such as **Cepemar** (☎ 282 425 866 or 917 348 414).

The nearest place to go for a gallop is at **Centro Hípico Vale de Ferro** (☎ 282 968 444; www.algarvehorseholidays.com; per hr €20), near Mexilhoeira Grande (4.2km west of Portimão), which also offers riding-holiday packages.

Liga para a Proteção da Natureza (League for the Protection of Nature; ☎ 282 968 380; donation; ⏲ Sep-Jul) arranges long, easy walks on the first Saturday of each month. Meet in the square in front of the train station at 9.30am and bring a picnic.

Courses

Interlingua Instituto de Linguas (☎ 282 427 690; Largo 1 de Dezembro 28) offers lessons in Portuguese. In addition to intensive courses, you can take a two-hour crash course for around €30 per person.

Sleeping

Residencial Arabi (☎ 282 460 250; Praça Teixeira Gomes 13; s/d €35/45) Overlooking the main square on the waterfront, this pleasant residencial has small neat rooms with wood floors. The best rooms face the square and have French doors opening onto decorative balconies.

Hotel Globo (☎ 282 416 350; Rua 5 de Outubro 26; d €65) A few blocks west of the water, this high-rise hotel has trim and tidy rooms and sizable windows letting in abundant natural light. Some rooms have fine harbour views.

Eating

The fountain-lined pedestrian street Rua Direita, about 300m west of the river, is a good destination for restaurant browsing. For open-air seafood grub, head for the strip of restaurants by the bridge, where charcoal-grilled sardines and barbecued fish are the specialties.

Casa Inglesa (Praça Manuel T Gomes; mains €2-6; ⏲ 8am-11pm) Central to Portimão life this large café on the main square has a charming 1950s feel, with lots of snacks on offer, as well as tasty marzipan. Outdoor tables are pleasant.

Dona Barca (☎ 282 484 189; Largo da Barca; mains from €4.50) This restaurant is off the main strip, with a cluster of other terrace restaurants in the pleasant cobbled surroundings of the old fishing quarter, under the arches of the bridge; it's famous for its Algarve seafood specialities.

O Mané (☎ 282 423 496; Largo Dr Bastos 1; mains from €10) Just off Rua Direita, this is one of Portimão's best seafood spots, with incredibly fresh cockles, grouper, bream and other fresh catch. There are a handful of outdoor tables on the old street, or you can dine inside, with lobsters peering over your shoulder.

Simsa (☎ 282 423 057; Rua S Gonçalo; mains €14.50-17.50; ⏲ dinner Tue-Sat) Cosy, deep-red and Dutch-run, the well-regarded Simsa is decorated with mirrors and birdcages, and has fittingly rich mains such as duck in strawberry and pepper sauce.

Shopping

Trawl Rua do Comércio, Rua Vasco da Gama and the adjacent Rua Direita for handicrafts (especially ceramics, crystal and copper goods), shoes and cotton items. A big open-air market is held behind the train station on the first Monday of each month. A flea market also takes place on the first and third Sunday of the month (mornings only) along Avenida São João de Deus (west of Rua do Comércio).

Getting There & Around

Six daily trains connect Portimão with Tunes (via Silves) and Lagos. Change at Tunes for Lisbon.

Portimão has excellent bus connections, including the following:

Destination	Price	Duration	Frequency (weekdays/weekends)
Albufeira	€3.60	45min	14/6
Cabo São Vicente	€4.70	2½hr	2/0
Faro	€4.50	1½ hr	7/2
Lagos	€2.40	40min	19 daily
Lisbon	€17	3¾hr	6/4
Loulé	€4.85	1¾hr	2/4
Monchique	€2.60	45min	9/5
Sagres	€4.60	1¼hr	2/0
Salema	€3.40	1hr	2/0
Silves	€2.40	35min	8/5

Buses shuttle between Praia da Rocha and Portimão (€1.70 on the bus €3.60/7.20 per five/10 prepurchased tickets, at least half-hourly).

You can get information and tickets for Eva and Intersul (Eurolines) services at the **Eva office** (☎ 282 418 120; Largo do Duque 3), located by the riverside. Buses either leave from outside the Restaurante Chinés Dinastia, to the right of the ticket office, or from the Shell station.

The easiest parking is a free riverside area by the Shell station.

PRAIA DA ROCHA

One of the Algarve's finest beaches, Praia da Rocha is a wide stretch of sand backed by ochre-red cliffs and a petite 16th-century fortress.

The town itself has long known the hand of development, with high-rise condos and luxury hotels sprouting like weeds along the cliffside, with a row of restaurants, bars and dance clubs packed along the one main thoroughfare. Despite the concrete façade, Praia da Rocha still has vestiges from its more elegant past, including some 19th-century mansions that have been converted into atmospheric guesthouses.

There's also a sleek marina painted weirdly autumnal colours (to match the cliffs) and a casino where you can double (or deplete) your savings.

Orientation

Set high above the beach, the esplanade, Avenida Tomás Cabreira, is the resort's main drag and is lined with shops, hotels and restaurants. At the eastern end is the shell of the **Fortaleza da Santa Catarina**, built in the 16th century to stop pirates and invaders from sailing up the Rio Arade to Portimão. Down below is the Marina de Portimão, with more restaurants and bars.

Information

The post office is near the turismo.

Phone One Internet & Call Center (Avenida Tomás Cabreira; per hr €2; 9am-10pm) Near the *miradouro* (lookout) at the west end of the main street.

Police (9am-12.30pm & 2-5pm Mon-Fri) Next door to the turismo.

Turismo (☎ 282 419 132; 9.30am-7pm Jul & Aug, 9.30am-1pm & 2-5.30pm Mon-Fri Sep-Jun) In the centre of the esplanade, opposite Hotel Júpiter.

Activities

Marina-based **Dolphin Seafaris** (☎ 282 799 209, 919 359 359; dolphinseafaris@mail.com; €30; Apr-Oct) offers dolphin-spotting trips.

Sleeping

Accommodation is almost impossible to find in the high season if you don't have a prior reservation.

Residencial Toca (☎ 282 418 904; residencialtoca@iol.pt; Rua Engenheiro Francisco Bívar; d €45; P) One of Praia's more affordable spots, this friendly guesthouse has tidy rooms with sizable windows, wood floors and frilly bedspreads. The best rooms have balconies, costing fractionally more.

Albergaria Vila Lido (☎ 282 241 127; fax 282 242 246; Avenida Tomás Cabreira; d from €105; P) Near the fort, this hotel was converted from a delightful 19th-century mansion and retains the feel of a gloriously elegant era, with great sea views and 10 bright rooms, eight of which have terraces.

Hotel Bela Vista (☎ 282 450 480; www.hotelbelavista.net; s/d €115/120; P) Living up to its name, Bela Vista bags the best beach view from the middle of the esplanade. Though the hotel is a bit tired-looking, it's a marvellous place – a whimsical late-19th-century, vaguely Oriental creation, with carved wooden ceilings and colourful *azulejos*. Only two of the 14 tile-decorated rooms lack a sea view.

Hotel Oriental (☎ 282 480 800; www.oriental@tdhotels.pt; s/d €160/190; P) One of many a growing number of immense hotels rising over the beach, the Oriental has a lavish foyer, inviting pools and comfortable spacious rooms with splashes of colour. Most rooms have sea views and some feature balconies, though all come with the Moorish theme-park touch.

Eating

Snack Bar Scorpíus (Rua Bartolomeu Dias; mains €6; 8am-2am) A bit off the beaten path, this popular local café is a good spot to enjoy simple but nicely prepared plates of seafood and desserts.

Safari Restaurante (☎ 282 423 540; mains €6.50-10; lunch & dinner) Tucked behind Discoteca Katedral, this attractive restaurant has fine views over the beach and dishes up decent grills (swordfish, chicken) as well as a hearty lamb stew.

Cabassa Coxinhas (☎ 282 483 235; Avenida Tomás Cabreira; mains €8-12.50; lunch & dinner) This friendly place on the town's east end has an extensive menu – pizzas, salads, appetizers, grilled fish – though the Brazilian-style *picanha* (rump steak) is a meat-lover's delight. Spacious outdoor terrace.

THE ALGARVE

Cervejaria e Marisqueira (☎ 282 416 541; mains €5.80-14.50, 3-course menu €10; ⏲ lunch & dinner) An unusually traditional restaurant for Praia da Rocha, this popular and low-key *cervejaria* on a road opposite the casino offers decent Portuguese fare, with a hearty array of daily specials.

The marina has a row of romantic, upmarket dining and drinking spots, including **Bella Italia** (☎ 282 411 737; Marina; mains €2.50-8; ⏲ lunch & dinner) with glass-covered, candlelit terraces overlooking the marina or the sea.

La Dolce Vita (☎ 282 424 175; Avenida Tomás Cabreira; mains €7-9; ⏲ lunch & dinner) Another good Italian restaurant, this place is full of old-world charm and serves filling pasta dishes and pizzas. There's also outdoor seating.

Titanic (☎ 282 422 371; Edifício Colúmbia, Rua Engenheiro Francisco Bívar; mains €10-14; ⏲ dinner) An old-fashioned classic, still a favourite with out-of-towners, Titanic cooks up some of Praia's best seafood and steak dishes.

Entertainment

Praia da Rocha bristles with bars, full of sunkissed faces, satellite TV, live music and karaoke, and often run by Irish or English expats. Dressed-up Portuguese also flock here for a big weekend splash.

Bustling, but not pretty, Brit favourites are the **Celt Bar** (Rua António Feu) and adjacent **Temple Bar** (Rua António Feu) for their Irish atmosphere, brews and regular live music. More scenic and sedate is **Kerri's Bar** (☎ 282 483 195; Rua Jerónimo Buisel), just before the fort, for Finnish liqueurs and fairy lights.

Well-situated bars string along the main strip, most with outdoor seating. Try **Pé de Vento** (⏲ 4pm-4am), a two-floor disco bar.

The newest nightclub in town is **Voxx** (Avenida Tomás Cabreira), a sleek, multistorey discotheque that makes good use of its waterside setting. Monster **Discoteca Katedral** (Rua António Feu), nearby, gets busy to pop house, until 6am nightly during summer. **Horaga Club**, nearby, is a bit cooler and gets down to funky house.

The glitzy **casino** (☎ 282 402 000; Avenida Tomás Cabreira), midway along the esplanade in Hotel Algarve, has slot machines (admission free, open 4pm to 3am), a gambling room (admission €4, plus passport and smart attire; open 7.30pm to 3am).

Getting There & Around

Buses shuttle to Portimão (€1.70 on the bus, €3.60/7.20 per five/10 prepurchased tickets, every 15 to 30 minutes). Buy tickets from **Hotel Júpiter** (☎ 282 415 041; Ave Tomas Cabreira). There are services to Albufeira (€3.70), Lagos (€3.40, four to six daily) and Lisbon (€17, four daily). The bus terminus in Praia da Rocha is by the fort, with another stop behind Hotel da Rocha (Rua Engenheiro José Bívar).

Mova (☎ 282 483 555; Casa dos Arcos, Avenida das Comunidades Lusiadas) offers good car-rental deals.

THE WINDWARD COAST & COSTA VICENTINA

LAGOS

pop 17,500

Although it's undeniably touristy, Lagos (*lah-goosh*) is an attractive town with many charms. It lies along the bank of the Rio Bensafrim, with 14th-century walls enclosing the pretty, cobbled streets of the old town. Tiny plazas and picturesque churches add to the allure, although most visitors are more interested in what lies outside the city walls, namely a good range of beaches, from long sweeping sands on the scenery side to secluded coastal coves. Nightlife here is among the best in the Algarve, with an eclectic mix of lounges, bars and restaurants catering to young backpackers, surfers, not-so-spendthrifty couples and various other sorts who pass through Lagos' gates.

Aside from its hedonistic appeal, Lagos has historical clout, having launched many naval excursions during Portugal's extraordinary Age of Discoveries (see p30).

History

Phoenicians and Greeks set up shop at this port (which later became Roman Lacobriga) at the mouth of the muddy Rio Bensafrim. Afonso III recaptured it from the Moors in 1241, and the Portuguese continued harassing the Muslims of North Africa from here. In 1415 a giant fleet set sail from Lagos under the command of the 21-year-old Prince Henry the Navigator to seize Ceuta in Morocco, thereby setting the stage for the Age of Discoveries.

Lagos' shipyards built and launched Prince Henry's caravels, and Henry split his time between his trading company here and his navigation school at Sagres. Local boy Gil Eanes left here in 1434 in command of the first ship to round West Africa's Cape Bojador. Others continued to bring back information

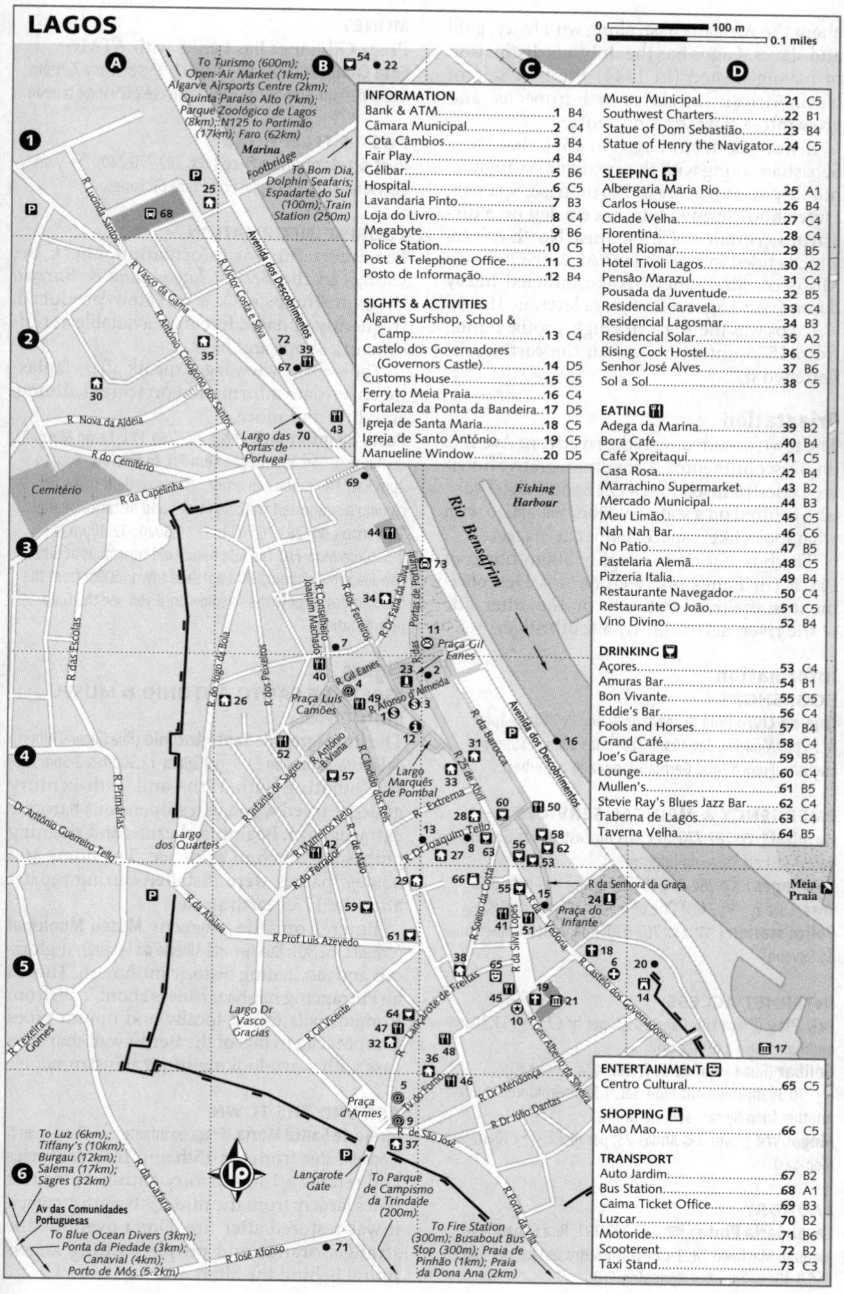
LAGOS
0 100 m
0 0.1 miles
A
B
C
D
1
2
3
4
5
6
INFORMATION
Bank & ATM........1 B4
Câmara Municipal........2 C4
Cota Câmbios........3 B4
Fair Play........4 B4
Gélibar........5 B6
Hospital........6 C5
Lavandaria Pinto........7 B3
Loja do Livro........8 C4
Megabyte........9 B6
Police Station........10 C5
Post & Telephone Office........11 C3
Posto de Informação........12 B4
SIGHTS & ACTIVITIES
Algarve Surfshop, School & Camp........13 C4
Castelo dos Governadores (Governors Castle)........14 D5
Customs House........15 C5
Ferry to Meia Praia........16 C4
Fortaleza da Ponta da Bandeira........17 D5
Igreja de Santa Maria........18 C5
Igreja de Santo António........19 C5
Manueline Window........20 D5
Museu Municipal........21 C5
Southwest Charters........22 B1
Statue of Dom Sebastião........23 B4
Statue of Henry the Navigator........24 C5
SLEEPING
Albergaria Maria Rio........25 A1
Carlos House........26 B4
Cidade Velha........27 C4
Florentina........28 C4
Hotel Riomar........29 B5
Hotel Tivoli Lagos........30 A2
Pensão Marazul........31 C4
Pousada da Juventude........32 B5
Residencial Caravela........33 C4
Residencial Lagosmar........34 B3
Residencial Solar........35 A2
Rising Cock Hostel........36 C5
Senhor José Alves........37 B6
Sol a Sol........38 C5
EATING
Adega da Marina........39 B2
Bora Café........40 B4
Café Xpreitaqui........41 C5
Casa Rosa........42 B4
Marrachino Supermarket........43 B2
Mercado Municipal........44 B3
Meu Limão........45 C5
Nah Nah Bar........46 C6
No Patio........47 B5
Pastelaria Alemã........48 C5
Pizzeria Italia........49 B4
Restaurante Navegador........50 C4
Restaurante O João........51 C5
Vino Divino........52 B4
DRINKING
Açores........53 C4
Amuras Bar........54 B1
Bon Vivante........55 C5
Eddie's Bar........56 C4
Fools and Horses........57 B4
Grand Café........58 C4
Joe's Garage........59 B5
Lounge........60 C4
Mullen's........61 B5
Stevie Ray's Blues Jazz Bar........62 C4
Taberna de Lagos........63 C4
Taverna Velha........64 B5
ENTERTAINMENT
Centro Cultural........65 C5
SHOPPING
Mao Mao........66 C5
TRANSPORT
Auto Jardim........67 B2
Bus Station........68 A1
Caima Ticket Office........69 B3
Luzcar........70 B2
Motoride........71 B6
Scooterent........72 B2
Taxi Stand........73 C3
To Turismo (600m); Open-Air Market (1km); Algarve Airsports Centre (2km); Quinta Paraíso Alto (7km); Parque Zoológico de Lagos (8km); N125 to Portimão (17km); Faro (62km)
Marina
Footbridge
To Bom Dia, Dolphin Seafaris; Espadarte do Sul (100m); Train Station (250m)
R Lucinda Santos
R Vasco da Gama
R Victor Costa e Silva
Avenida dos Descobrimentos
R António Crisógono dos Santos
R Nova da Aldeia
R do Cemitério
Largo das Portas de Portugal
Cemitério
R da Capelinha
Fishing Harbour
Rio Bensafrim
R das Escolas
R do Jogo da Bola
R dos Peixeiros
R Conselheiro Joaquim Machado
R dos Ferreiros
R Dr Faria da Silva
Portas de Portugal
R das
Praça Gil Eanes
R Gil Eanes
Praça Luís Camões
R Afonso d'Almeida
R da Barocca
R Primárias
Dr António Guerreiro Tello
R Infante de Sagres
R António B Viana
R Cândido dos Reis
Largo Marquês de Pombal
R 25 de Abril
R Extrema
R Dr Joaquim Tello
Largo dos Quartéis
R Marreiros Neto
R do Ferrador
R 1 de Maio
R Soeiro da Costa
R da Senhora da Graça
Meia Praia
Praça do Infante
R da Silva Lopes
R da Vedoria
R da Atalaia
R Prof Luís Azevedo
R Castelo dos Governadores
Largo Dr Vasco Gracias
R Gil Vicente
R Lançarote de Freitas
R Gen Alberto da Silveira
R Texeira Gomes
Tv do Forno
R Dr Mendonça
R Dr Júlio Dantas
Praça d'Armes
R de São José
To Luz (6km); Tiffany's (10km); Burgau (12km); Salema (17km); Sagres (32km)
R da Gafaria
Lançarote Gate
To Parque de Campismo da Trindade (200m)
R Porta da Vila
Av das Comunidades Portuguesas
To Blue Ocean Divers (3km); Ponta da Piedade (3km); Canavial (4km); Porto de Mós (5.2km)
R José Afonso
To Fire Station (300m); Busabout Bus Stop (300m); Praia de Pinhão (1km); Praia da Dona Ana (2km)

about the African coast, along with ivory, gold and slaves. Lagos has the dubious distinction of having hosted (in 1444) the first sale of black Africans as slaves to Europeans, and grew into a slave-trading centre.

It was also from Lagos in 1578 that Dom Sebastião, along with the cream of Portuguese nobility and an army of Portuguese, Spanish, Dutch and German buccaneers, left on a disastrous crusade to Christianise North Africa, which ended in a debacle at Alcácer-Quibir in Morocco. Sir Francis Drake inflicted heavy damage on Lagos a few years later, in 1587.

Lagos was the Algarve's high-profile capital from 1576 until 1755, when the earthquake flattened it.

Orientation

The town's main drag is the riverfront Avenida dos Descobrimentos. The administrative hub is the pedestrianised Praça Gil Eanes (zheel *yan*-ish), centred on a statue of Dom Sebastião with what looks like a space helmet at his feet.

The bus station is roughly 500m north of Praça Gil Eanes off Avenida dos Descobrimentos; the train station is on the other side of the river, accessible by a footbridge.

Information

BOOKSHOPS

Loja do Livro (Rua Dr Joaquim Tello; 10am-1pm & 3-7pm Mon-Fri, Sat 10am-1pm) Has a small supply of English-, French- and German-language paperbacks.

EMERGENCY & MEDICAL SERVICES

Hospital (282 770 100; Rua do Castelo dos Governadores) Just off Praça do Infante.

Medilagos (282 760 181; Amejeira de Cima, Bela Vista, Lote 2; 24hr) One of several private clinics.

Police station (282 762 930; Rua General Alberto da Silveira)

INTERNET ACCESS

Fair Play (Praça Luís Camões 23; per hr €2; 11.30am-midnight) Also a drinks café.

Gélibar (Rua Lançarote de Freitas 43a; per hr €3; 10.30am-midnight Mon-Sat, 1.30pm-midnight Sun) Another friendly café serving drinks.

Megabyte (Praça das Armas 23; per hr €2; 10am-9pm Mon-Sat)

LAUNDRY

Lavandaria Pinto (282 762 191; Rua Conselheiro Joaquim Machado 28; 1-day wash & dry service per 5kg €8; 9.30am-1pm & 3-7pm Mon-Fri)

MONEY

Praça Gil Eanes has banks with ATMs.

Cota Câmbios (Praça Gil Eanes 11; 8.30am-7.30pm Mon-Fri, 9am-6pm Sat & Sun) A private exchange bureau.

POST & TELEPHONE

Post & telephone office (282 770 240; 9am-6pm Mon-Fri) Central, just off Praça Gil Eanes.

TOURIST INFORMATION

For entertainment information, check the listings in the *Best of Lagos, Luz & Burgau* (www.freemaps.net), a privately produced, frequently updated free map available at *residenciais,* shops and bars.

The website www.lagos.me.uk offers fantastic up-to-date information on wining, dining, activities and more.

Posto de informação (282 764 111; Largo Marquês de Pombal; 10am-6pm Mon-Fri, to 8pm Jul-Aug, to 2pm Sat) The municipal office offers excellent maps (including a suggested walking route) and historical leaflets.

Turismo (282 763 031; 9.30am-12.30pm & 2-5.30pm Mon-Fri) The less handy old turismo is at Situo São João roundabout, 1km north of town (600m from the bus station). Follow the Avenida until you see the Galp petrol station.

Sights

IGREJA DE SANTO ANTÓNIO & MUSEU MUNICIPAL

The little **Igreja de Santo António** (Rua General Alberto da Silveira; admission €2; 9.30am-12.30pm & 2-5pm Tue-Sun), bursting with 18th- and 19th-century gilded, carved wood, is a stupendous baroque extravaganza. Beaming cherubs and ripening grapes are much in evidence. The dome and *azulejo* panels were installed during repairs after the 1755 earthquake.

Enter from the adjacent **Museu Municipal** (282 762 301; Rua General Alberto da Silveira), a glorious and fascinating historic mishmash. There's an entrancing haphazardness about it all, from Roman nails found locally and opium pipes from Macau to bits of the Berlin wall sharing a case with scary-looking surgical instruments.

AROUND THE TOWN

Igreja de Santa Maria (Praça do Infante; 9am-noon & 3-6pm) dates from the 15th and 16th centuries and retains a 16th-century entrance; the rest dates largely from the mid-19th century when it was restored after fire. Don't overlook the strange, orange and purple battling angels mural behind the altar.

Just south of Praça do Infante is a restored section of the stout **town walls**, built (atop earlier versions) during the reigns of both Manuel I and João III in the 16th century, when the walls were enlarged to the existing outline. They extend intermittently, with at least six bastions, for about 1.5km around the central town.

Rua da Barroca once formed the boundary between the town and the sea and retains some Arabic features.

Castelo dos Governadores (Governors Castle; in the southeast part of town at the back of the present-day hospital) was built by the Arabs. After the Reconquista in the 13th century, the Algarve's military government was established here in the 14th century. It's said that the ill-fated, evangelical Dom Sebastião attended an open-air Mass here and spoke to the assembled nobility from a small **Manueline window** in the castle, before leading them to a crushing defeat at Alcácer-Quibir (Morocco).

Near Praça do Infante is a less-than-glorious site – where slaves were auctioned off in Portugal in the 15th century. It now houses an art gallery.

FORTALEZA DA PONTA DA BANDEIRA

This little **fortress** (Avenida dos Descobrimentos; admission €2; 9.30am-12.30pm & 2-5pm Tue-Sun), at the southern end of the avenue, was built in the 17th century to protect the port. Restored, it now houses a museum on the Portuguese discoveries.

PONTA DA PIEDADE

Protruding south from Lagos, Ponta da Piedade (Point of Piety) is a stunning, dramatic wedge of headland. Three windswept kilometres out of town, the point is well worth a visit for its contorted, polychrome sandstone cliffs and towers, complete with lighthouse and, in spring, hundreds of nesting egrets. The surrounding area is brilliant with wild orchids in spring. On a clear day you can see east to Carvoeiro and west to Sagres.

PARQUE ZOOLÓGICO DE LAGOS

This **zoo** (282 680 100; www.zoolagos.com; Quinta Figueiras; adult/child €8/5; 10am-7pm Apr-Sep, to 5pm Oct-Mar) is a shady 3-hectare kid-pleaser, with small primates, a flight tunnel where you can observe exotic birds, lakes, and a children's farm housing domestic animals. It's near the village of Barão de São Miguel, 8km west of Lagos.

Activities

BEACHES & WATER SPORTS

Meia Praia, the vast expanse of sand to the east of town, has outlets offering sailboard rental and water-skiing lessons, plus several laid-back restaurants and beach bars. South of town the beaches – Batata, Pinhão, Dona Ana, Camilo among others – are smaller and more secluded, lapped by calm waters and punctuated with amazing grottoes, coves and towers of coloured sandstone. Avoid swimming at Batata and, to the east, at Ana. There's a ferry to Lagos beach.

Lagos is a popular surfing centre and has good facilities; surfing companies head to the west coast for the waves.

Algarve Surf Shop, School & Camp (282 767 853; www.algarvesurfcamp.com; Rua Dr Joaquim Tello 32; equipment hire & B&B €55/day, 1-/3-/5-day course or safari €35/90/140) will help you catch a wave.

If you want to go diving or snorkelling, contact **Blue Ocean Divers** (282 782 718; www.blue-ocean-divers.de; Motel Ancora, Ponta da Piedade), which offers a half-day 'Snorkelling Safari' (€30), a full-day diving experience (€85) and a three-day PADI scuba course (€280). It also offers kayak safaris (€28/45 half/full day, child under 12 €14/23).

BOAT TRIPS & DOLPHIN SAFARIS

Various operators have ticket stands at the marina or along the promenade opposite the marina.

The biggest operator is **Bom Dia** (282 764 670; www.bomdia.info), at the marina, which runs trips on traditional schooners, including a five-hour barbecue cruise (€44/22 adult/child), with a chance to swim; a two-hour grotto trip (€19/9.50, four daily); or a full-day sail to Sagres, including lunch (€75/44). They also organise big-game fishing and offer car rental.

Espadarte do Sul (282 767 252) offers 1½-hour trips to the grottoes beneath Ponta da Piedade, a three-hour coastal cruise and day-long big-game fishing.

Southwest Charters (282 792 681; www.southwestcharters.com; Marina de Lagos) provides power-boat or yacht charters carrying eight people for €160 to €265 per half-day, €295 to €460 per full day. Larger boats and week-long rentals are available. A skipper will cost you €55/110 per half-/full day.

Local fishermen offering jaunts to the grottoes by motorboat trawl for customers along

THE ALGARVE

the promenade and by the Fortaleza da Ponta da Bandeira.

The marina-based **Dolphin Seafaris** (☎ 282 799 209; dolphinseafaris@mail.com; €35; ⏲ Apr-Oct) offers dolphin-spotting trips.

OTHER ACTIVITIES

About 10km west of Lagos, **Tiffany's** (☎ 282 697 395; www.valegrifo.com/tiffanysriding; Vale Grifo, Almádena; ⏲ 9am-dusk) charges €25 an hour for horse riding and has other options, including a three-/five-hour trip (€65/100); the latter includes a champagne picnic. Another centre with similar activities is **Quinta Paraíso Alto** (☎ 282 687 596; Fronteira), 7km north of Lagos. Both also offer package horse-riding holidays.

Algarve Airsports Centre (☎ 914 903 384; www.gerrybreen.com; Aeródrome de Lagos, ⏲ Mon-Sat) offers courses, lessons and trial flights.

Courses

Centro de Linguas de Lagos (☎ 282 761 070; www.centrodelinguas.com; Rua Dr Joaquim Telo 32) offers classes in Portuguese. Students can choose from one of five levels, and can arrange private classes or intensive group lessons (four to eight students per class).

Sleeping

BUDGET

Accommodation options are extensive in Lagos, with more places out on Meia Praia and on Praia da Dona Ana. As elsewhere, rooms are pricier and scarcer from July to mid-September. Many agencies rent apartments (one-week minimum), including **Florentina** (☎ 282 761 001; Rua Joaquim Tello 8; apt per wk Jun/Aug €225/375).

Parque de Campismo da Trindade (☎ 282 763 893; cfelagos@clix.pt; adult/tent/car €3.10/3.60/4.10) A small site 200m south of the Lançarote gate in the town walls, this camping ground is a tent-peg's throw from the sea, has lots of shade, facilities for the disabled, a playground, a restaurant, bar and snack bar.

Pousada da juventude (☎ 282 761 970; lagos@movijovem.pt; Rua Lançarote de Freitas 50; dm/d €16/43, d with shared bathroom €35; ⏲ 24hr; 💻) One of Portugal's best, this hostel is often packed, and it's a great place to meet other travellers. There's a kitchen and pleasant courtyard, and the reception is helpful.

Carlos House (☎ 916 594 225; carloshousez@yahoo.com; Rua Jogo da Bola 8; dm/d from €16/36; 💻) Another popular hostel, this one's uphill from the centre and has a guest kitchen and a rooftop terrace.

Rising Cock Hostel (☎ 969 411 131; Travessa do Forno 14; dm €20; 💻) The double bunk beds and provocative décor are pretty yuck, but otherwise, this hostel is hard to fault. Rooms are colourful and nicely designed, and there's a comfy lounge, a terrace and free internet.

Senhor José Alves (☎ 282 762 864; Rua São José 22; d €30-35) Two small but cosy rooms available in this privately owned house. The upstairs room has a terrace.

Residencial Caravela (☎ 282 763 361; Rua 25 de Abril 16; s/d with shower €30/38, d without shower €35) In the central pedestrian zone, Caravela has nice breezy rooms, well kept but small, and most have wood floors.

Sol a Sol (☎ 282 761 290; Rua Lançarote de Freitas 22; s/d/tr from €35/45/50) This central, small hotel has rooms with tiny balconies and views over the town; it's a bit tired-looking but good value nonetheless.

MIDRANGE

Cidade Velha (☎ 282 762 041; residcidadevelha@netvisao.pt; Rua Dr Joaquim Tello 7; s/d/tr from €35/45/55; ❄ 💻) This friendly, welcoming guesthouse has trim and tidy rooms with tile floors and balconies. Top-floor rooms are best, with cosy touches and attractive wood furnishings.

Pensâo Marazul (☎ 282 770 230; www.pensaomarazul.com; Rua 25 de Abril 13; s/d incl breakfast €35/50; 💻) Also central, Marazul has comfortable, well-kept rooms with either sea views or inner balconies.

Hotel Riomar (☎ 282 763 091; Rua Cândido Reis 83; s/d €40/60; P ❄) Rooms here are small but comfortable, with wood floors and balconies (no view). Although the design is a bit dated, it's good value.

Residencial Solar (☎ 282 762 477; residencial-solar@netvisao.pt; Rua António Crisógono dos Santos 60; d €40-60; ❄) On a quiet street near the bus station and the waterfront, this modern, peaceful place has airy rooms with small balconies.

Residencial Lagosmar (☎ 282 763 722; Rua Dr Faria da Silva 13; s/d €65/75) A small whitewashed place on a narrow street, Lagosmar has comfortable but ageing rooms, each of which has a sizable terrace.

TOP END

Albergaria Marina Rio (☎ 282 769 859; www.marinario.com; Avenida dos Descobrimentos; d €102; P ❄ 🏊) Overlooking the harbour, this nautical-themed hotel has comfortable rooms with terracotta-tile floors and balconies. On the downside, it's on a fairly busy road, and most rooms are twins. There's a small pool and roof terrace.

Hotel Tivoli Lagos (☎ 282 790 079; www.tivolihotels.com; Rua Nova da Aldeia; d €170; P) This is Lagos' finest hotel, offering many creature comforts, including a health club and a lovely pool. It's popular with busloads of tour groups.

Eating

Lagos has some great dining spots, serving both Portuguese and international cuisine. Budget travellers should focus their attentions on lunchtime *pratos do dia* (daily specials), which often cost around €6.

BUDGET

Café Xpreitaqui (☎ 282 762 758; Rua da Silva Lopes 14; salads €2-5; 10am-2am Mon-Sat) A popular meeting point, this café serves up healthy juices, smoothies, salads, breakfasts and pizzas.

Bora Café (Rua Conselheiro Joaquim Machado 17; mains €3-5; 9am-7pm Mon-Sat, 10am-7pm Sun) Tiny Bora is a good spot for ice coffees, fresh juices and sandwiches, and there's outdoor seating on the pedestrian street.

Casa Rosa (☎ 966 884 317; Rua do Ferrador 22; dishes €2-6; 5pm-midnight) Backpacker-favourite Casa Rosa serves up simple, good-value mains such as veggie stir-fry, chilli con carne or fajitas.

Adega da Marina (☎ 282 764 284; Avenida dos Descobrimentos 35; mains €5-8; lunch & dinner) In a big barnlike building decorated with iron chandeliers and farming implements, this popular restaurant is well regarded for its tasty grilled chicken and fresh seafood dishes.

Pastelaria Alemã (Rua São Gonçalo 10; 8am-6pm Mon-Fri, 8am-1pm Sat) This delightful, German-run patisserie sells a variety of tempting fresh-baked goods, including flaky croissants, cherry tart and rhubarb cheesecake.

Nah Nah Bar (Travessa do Forno; mains from €6; lunch & dinner) A popular Aussie gathering spot for fat burgers, tuna melts, organic muesli and other fare. Grass-hut, Polynesian-type décor.

Marrachino (Avenida dos Descobrimentos 2; 8am-9pm) An accessible supermarket.

MIDRANGE & TOP END

Pizzeria Italia (☎ 282 760 030; Rua Garrett 26; mains €6-8; lunch & dinner) Enjoy good thin-crust pizzas cooked in a wood-burning oven on a pleasant terrace ringed with geraniums.

Meu Limão (☎ 282 767 946; Rua Silva Lopes 40; tapas/mains €4/9; lunch & dinner) This handsome tapas bar has a room hung with changing artwork, and a postcard view of Igreja Santo António from the outdoor tables. Tapas choices include shrimp with coconut, lemon chicken and mussels. They also have heartier plates and good wines.

Restaurante O João (☎ 282 761 067; Rua da Silva Lopes 15; mains €6-9; lunch & dinner Mon-Sat) An unpretentious, cosy nook, with arches and checked tablecloths, O João glimmers with candlelight at night. It attracts locals and tourists and serves up a pretty fine paella.

Vino Divino (☎ 917 009 238; Rua 1 de Maio 4; mains €8-13; dinner Tue-Sat) Rich and flavourful Italian dishes come beautifully prepared at this elegant restaurant. Appetisers like goat's cheese and roasted eggplant are fine preludes to homemade pastas and raviolis (try the tagliatelle with seafood). There are good wine selections and a rooftop terrace.

Restaurante Navegador (☎ 282 767 162; Rua da Barroca; mains €10-13; lunch & dinner Fri-Wed) With a sea view and pretty roof terrace, this smart restaurant rustles up some elaborately flambéed food, with lots of meat and fish dishes and port-based sauces.

No Patio (☎ 282 763 777; Rua Lançarote 46; mains around €14; dinner Tue-Sat, lunch Sun) Run by an English expat, No Patio (which means 'on the patio') is a charming and petite restaurant, with a sunny enclosed terrace, where fusion cuisine comes expertly prepared. Prawns and guacamole, asparagus risotto and tasty grilled fish go nicely with the sangria. Reservations advised.

Drinking

Dozens of bars litter the streets of Lagos, with some of the Algarve's most diverse drinking holes on hand.

Mullen's (Rua Cândido dos Reis 86; mains €6.50-13; dinner) A long-established *adega típica* (wine bar), this great arched tavern is filled with tiles, big barrels, unusual paintings and a lively crowd.

Taberna de Lagos (Rua Dr Joaquim Tello 1) Boasting a stylish space and brooding electronic music, this airy and atmospheric bar attracts a somewhat savvier bar-goer (higher cocktail prices also keep some punters away). It's set in a handsome town house, complete with high ceilings and old stone walls hung with vibrant paintings.

Taverna Velha (Rua Lançarote de Freitas 54) The snug Old Tavern is an old favourite and continues to haul in a lively crowd with its feel-good cocktail of where-it's-at popularity and sing-along pop.

Bon Vivante (Rua 25 de Abril 105) A multistorey place that attracts a sizable drinking crowd, this bar has an enticing roof terrace that's great for a sunset cocktail.

Eddie's Bar (Rua 25 de Abril 99) Another buzzing beer stop, this busy dark-wood bar gathers plenty of surfers and hangers-on – not surprising given its good-natured, down-to-earth atmosphere.

Stevie Ray's Blues Jazz Bar (Rua da Senhora da Graça 9; admission €5; 8pm-4am) This intimate two-level candlelit joint attracts a smart-casual older crowd, and has live music (blues, jazz, oldies) most weekends.

Fools and Horses (Rua António Barbosa Viana 7; mains €6-13.50, menu €13) This local boozer provides the English pub experience and all that it entails, and it's been around for over 30 years.

Joe's Garage (Rua 1 de Maio 78) With a dishevelled, bar-scene-from-*Star Wars* vibe (think Aussie backpackers, not aliens), this is the kind of place where you're not sure what might happen next, though shots and dancing on the tables are likely. Staff set fire to the bar to signal closing time and chase out stragglers with chainsaws.

Grand Café (Rua Senhora da Graça) This classy bar has lots of gold leaf, kitsch, red velvet and cherubs, over which are draped dressed-up local and foreign hipsters.

Lounge (Travessa Senhora da Graça 2) Small and sleek, Lounge plays a good range of music from drum 'n' bass and Brazilian to a spicy, want-to-dance-but-the-space-is-too-small crowd.

Açores (Rua Senhora da Graça 12) This Portuguese-run fun bar offers a lively atmosphere on two levels, with rock music and decent snack food.

Amuras Bar (Marina 10am-2am) One of half a dozen restaurant-bars overlooking the marina, this one attracts a slightly more staid crowd, who come for fruity cocktails and live music most nights.

Meia Praia has some beachfront gems just seconds from sun, swimming and sand, including Linda's Bar with fab food, good salads, cocktails and tunes, and Bahia Beach Bar, an essential hang-out with live music on Sundays and monthly beach parties.

Entertainment

Centro Cultural (☎ 282 770 450; Rua Lançarote de Freitas 7; 10am-8pm). Lagos' main venue for classical performances, including popular *fado* concerts, as well as contemporary art exhibitions.

Shopping

Lagos has some great little shops selling more style than you're likely to find in other Algarve towns.

Mao Mao (☎ 964 777 345; Rua Soeira da Costa 4; 10am-9pm Mon-Fri, to 1pm Sat) Fanciful T-shirts and lots of quirky designer bags, skirts and button-downs, this men's and women's store is a fun place to browse, if you're in need of a quick shopping fix.

Getting There & Away

BUS

From the **bus station** (☎ 282 762 944; Rua Vasco da Gama) buses travel to Portimão (€2.40, 20 minutes, four to eight daily) and Albufeira (around €4.50, one hour, four to five daily). Connections to Sagres run regularly (€3, 45 minutes to one hour, about hourly on weekdays, seven daily Saturday and Sunday), via Salema (20 minutes) and some go on to Cabo de São Vicente (€3.40, one hour, three daily on weekdays).

Eva express buses run to Lisbon (€17, 4¼ hours, five to six daily). To get to/from Carrapateira or Monchique, change at Aljezur (€3, 50 minutes, one to two daily) or Portimão. Buses to Aljezur also serve Odeceixe (1½ hours). There's a frequent express service to Lisbon (€17); tickets are available from the **Caima ticket office** (☎ 282 768 931; Rua das Portas de Portugal 101; 7am-1.30pm & 3-7.15pm daily, plus 10.30pm-12.30am Sun-Fri), which can also arrange minibus transfers to Faro airport.

Buses also go to Seville (via Huelva) in Spain (€17, 5½ hours, twice daily Monday to Saturday).

TRAIN

Lagos is at the western end of the Algarve line, with direct regional services to Faro daily (€6.20, 1¾ to two hours, eight daily), via Albufeira and Loulé (1½ hours), with onward connections from Faro to Vila Real de Santo António (€6.50, 3¼ hours) via Tavira (2¼ to 2¾ hours). Trains go daily to Lisbon (all requiring a change at Tunes; €21, 3½ hours, five daily).

Getting Around

CAR, MOTORCYCLE & BICYCLE

Auto Jardim and Luzcar are local agencies offering competitive car-rental rates.

Auto Jardim (☎ 282 769 486; Rua Victor Costa e Silva 18a; 8.30am-noon & 2.30-7pm)

Luzcar (☎ 282 761 016; www.luzcar.com; Largo das Portas de Portugal 10; 9am-1pm & 3-6pm)

Motoride (☎ 282 761 720; Rua José Afonso 23) Hires out bikes, scooters and motorcycles.

Scooterent (☎ 282 769 716; Rua Victor Costa e Silva) You can hire, you've guessed it, scooters (50/125cc per three days from €50/65).

Drivers are advised to leave their cars on the riverfront Avenida dos Descobrimentos, or head for a free car park on the outskirts. Close to the centre, parking spaces are metered.

BOAT

In summer, ferries run to and fro across the estuary to the Meia Praia side from a landing just north of Praça do Infante.

TAXI

You can call for **taxis** (☎ 282 763 587) or find them on Rua das Portas de Portugal.

LAGOS TO SAGRES

West of Lagos, the coast is sharp and ragged, and much less developed, though it's certainly not undiscovered. Once-sleepy fishing villages set above long beaches have now woken up to the benefits of tourism; they get busy in summer but are bewitchingly calm in the off-season.

Luz

Just 6km west of Lagos, Luz (meaning 'light') is a small resort, packed with Brits and fronted by a sandy beach that's ideal for families. Here **Azure Seas** (☎ 282 788 304; Avenida Pescadores 34) organises bike and car rental, jeep tours and just about everything else. Buses arrive at the central Praça da República.

SLEEPING & EATING

Camping de Espiche (☎ 282 789 265; adult/tent/car €5/4.80/4;) Turiscampo-run, this shady site – one of the two nearest camping grounds – is only 2km from Luz.

Valverde Camping (☎ 282 789 211; www.orbitur.pt; adult/tent/car €5.40/5.60/4.90;) Orbitur's typically slick camping ground is 3km from Luz and the beach, with shade. Both have wheelchair access, bars, restaurants, playgrounds, and caravans and chalets for hire.

Bella Vista (☎ 282 788 655; www.belavistadaluz.com; d €120;) This sizable place offers pleasant tiled rooms with verandas. There's also a large sunny terrace and pool. It lies 500m up from the beach, off a busy road.

Paraíso (☎ 282 788 246; mains €7-15; lunch & dinner) With a privileged location right on the beach, this attractive place serves up good grills as well as snacks, hamburgers, sandwiches and the like.

Fortaleza da Luz (☎ 282 789 926; Rua da Igreja 3; mains €10-14; lunch & dinner, barbecue closed Sun dinner) This dramatic 16th-century fort houses Luz's most spectacular restaurant, with a vaulted candlelit interior and covered sea-view terrace. Best of all is the garden overlooking the sea, with Brazilian barbecue on the menu. There's live music Sunday lunch time.

GETTING THERE & AWAY

Buses run frequently from Lagos (€1.80, 15 minutes).

Salema

This charmingly small coastal resort has an easy-going atmosphere; it's set on a wide bay 17km west of Lagos, surrounded by developments that manage not to overwhelm it. It's ideal for families, and there are several small, secluded beaches within a few kilometres – **Praia da Salema** by the village, **Praia da Figueira** to the west and **Boca do Rio** to the east.

Salema has a useful travel agency called **Horizonte** (☎/fax 282 695 920), opposite Hotel Residencial Salema. Horizonte can help with bookings for hotel and villa accommodation (often with discounts), car rental, boat or coach trips, and runs jeep trips within the Parque Natural do Sudoeste Alentejano e Costa Vicentina.

SLEEPING & EATING

Private rooms are plentiful along the seaside Rua dos Pescadores; expect to pay €35 or more for a double.

Quinta dos Carriços (☎ 282 695 201; www.quintadoscarricos.com; adult/tent/car €4.40/4.40/4.40, apt from €66;) Just 1.5km north of Salema, this camping ground is in an attractive and peaceful setting. It has studios and apartments and even its own naturist camping area.

Senhora Silvina Maria Pedro (☎ 282 695 473; Rua dos Pescadores 91; d/apt €35/60) These charming, tiny rooms with shared bathroom are in a former fisherfolk's house with a small terrace right on the beach.

Hospedaria Maré (☎ 282 695 165; www.algarve.co.uk; s/d €50/65) Just off the main road into town, this welcoming guesthouse has pretty rooms with terraces and sea views, a small garden for lounging and a kitchen for guest use. It's a short walk downhill to the beach.

Hotel Residencial Salema (☎ 282 695 328; www.hotel.salema.pt; s/d with breakfast €77/87) Fifty meters from the beach, Salema offers comfortable rooms with terraces (most with sea views) in a modern whitewashed building.

A row of restaurants along the beach includes **Restaurante Atlântico** (☎ 282 695 742; mains €10-13; lunch & dinner), which serves up an appealing selection of grilled fish on a large terrace. **Boia** (☎ 282 695 382; Rua dos Pescadores 101; mains from €9; lunch & dinner) is another attractive fish eatery with a covered sea-facing terrace.

GETTING THERE & AWAY

At least six buses daily connect Lagos and Salema (€2.20, 30 minutes).

SAGRES

pop 1940

Overlooking some of the Algarve's most dramatic scenery, the tiny village of Sagres has an end-of-the-world feel with its sea-carved cliffs and empty, windwhipped fortress high above the ocean. Despite its connection to Portugal's rich nautical past, there isn't much of historical interest in town. Its appeal lies mainly in its access to fine beaches and its laid-back vibe, with simple cheery, cafés and bars long popular with the surfing crowd. Outside of town, the striking cliffs of Cabo de São Vicente make for an enchanting visit.

Sagres is where dashing Prince Henry the Navigator built a new, fortified town and a semimonastic school of navigation that specialised in cartography, astronomy and ship design, steering Portugal on towards the Age of Discoveries.

At least, that's according to history and myth. Henry was, among other things, governor of the Algarve and had a residence in its primary port town, Lagos, from where most expeditions set sail. He certainly did put together a kind of nautical think-tank, though how much thinking went on out at Sagres is uncertain. He definitely had a house somewhere near Sagres, where he died in November 1460.

In May 1587 the English privateer Sir Francis Drake, in the course of attacking supply lines to the Spanish Armada, captured and wrecked the fortifications around Sagres. The Ponta de Sagres was refortified after the earthquake of 1755, which had left little of verifiable antiquity standing.

Sagres has milder temperatures than other parts of the Algarve, with Atlantic winds keeping the summers cool.

Orientation

From Vila do Bispo, the district's administrative centre at the western end of the N125, a 9km line of villas runs along the N268 to Sagres city centre.

From a roundabout at the end of the N268, roads go west for 6km to the Cabo de São Vicente, south for 1km to the Ponta de Sagres and east for 250m to little Praça da República at the head of unassuming Sagres town. One kilometre east of the square, past holiday villas and restaurants, is the port, still a centre for boat building and lobster fishing, and the marina.

Information

There's a bank and ATM just beyond the turismo, and a post office just east of there.

Turismo (☎ 282 624 873; Rua Comandante Matoso; 9.30am-12.30pm & 2-6pm Tue-Sat) Near a triangular monument, 100m east of Praça da República.

Turinfo (☎ 282 620 003; turinfo@iol.pt; Residência Dom Henrique; Praça da República; 10am-1pm & 2-7pm) A private tourist agency offering currency exchange, regional maps and books, excursions, bicycle hire (per 1/4/8 hr €2.50/6/9.50), car rental, bus tickets, and contacts for private rooms and flats. It also has an internet facility (€6 per hour).

Sights

FORTALEZA DE SAGRES

Blank, hulking and prisonlike, Sagres' **fortress** (☎ 282 620 140; adult/youth 15-25/child €3/1.50/free; 9.30am-8pm May-Sep, to 5.30pm Oct-Apr) has a forbidding front wall balanced by two mighty bastions. Inside, a few buildings dot the vast, open expanse, but otherwise a visit here is mostly about the striking views over the sheer cliffs, and all along the coast to Cabo de São Vicente.

Splash out on the guide (€1) that's sold at the entrance, or try to arrive in time for the free half-hour tour offered daily in English (at 3pm).

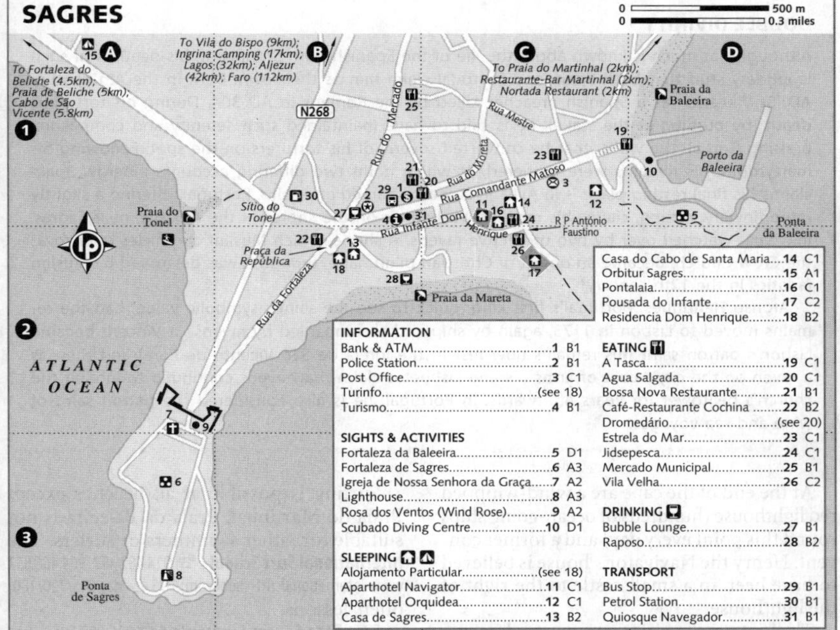

Inside the gate is a curious, huge stone called **rosa dos ventos** (wind rose, used to gauge the direction of the wind) that measures 43m in diameter. Excavated in the 18th century, it may date from Prince Henry's time – probably the only thing that does other than the foundations.

The village's oldest buildings, which include a cistern tower to the east; a house and the small, whitewashed, 16th-century **Igreja da Nossa Senhora da Graça**, with its worn golden altar, to the west; and the remnants of a wall, are possibly replacements for what was there before.

Many of the gaps you'll see between buildings are the result of a 1950s spring-clean of 17th- and 18th-century ruins, organised to make way for a reconstruction (later aborted) that was to coincide with the 500th anniversary of Henry's death.

Smack in the centre is a modern, rather unsightly exhibition hall, housing changing contemporary art installations. Near the southern end of the promontory is a **lighthouse**. Death-defying anglers balance on the cliffs below the walls, hoping to land bream or sea bass.

OTHER FORTS

Overlooking the harbour are the ruins of the small mid-16th-century **Fortaleza da Baleeira**.

The **Fortaleza do Beliche**, built in 1632 on the site of an older fortress, is 4.5km to the west of the Sagres roundabout on the way to Cabo de São Vicente. Inside is a small chapel on the site of the ruined Igreja de Santa Catarina (and possibly an old convent). It was once a hotel, but sadly it's crumbling, along with the cliff, and is now off-limits.

CABO DE SÃO VICENTE

A trip to Cabo de São Vicente (Cape St Vincent), Europe's southwesternmost point, is a must. This barren, thrusting headland is the bleak last piece of home that nervous Portuguese sailors would have seen as they launched into the unknown.

The cape – a revered place even in the time of the Phoenicians and known to the Romans as Promontorium Sacrum – takes its present name from a Spanish priest martyred by the Romans (see p208). The old fortifications, trashed by Sir Francis Drake in 1587, were later pulverised by the 1755 earthquake.

DOUBLE DIVINITY

Although not much is known about the life of the Spanish-born St Vincent, his death is of such legendary stuff that both Spain and Portugal claim him as their own. Born in the 4th century AD, St Vincent was a Spanish preacher killed by the Romans in AD 304. During his torturous death (by burning at the stake), he is said to have maintained such serenity and composure, praising God all the while, that he converted several of his torturers on the spot. Following his martyrdom, his remains were gathered, at which point two differing accounts emerge. Spain claims his final resting place is in Ávila in a church named after him. Portugal, offering a slightly more flowery version, claims his remains washed up on the shores of the Algarve, near Sagres, in a boat watched over by two protective ravens. A shrine, which Muslim chronicles refer to as the Crow Church, became an object of Christian pilgrimage, though it was destroyed by Muslim fanatics in the 12th century.

Afonso Henriques, Portugal's first king, quick to see the saint's symbolic value, had the remains moved to Lisbon in 1173, again by ship and accompanied by ravens. St Vincent became Lisbon's patron saint (his remains now rest in the Igreja de São Vicente de Fora) and there is a raven on the city's coat of arms – some Lisboêtas claim that ravens continued to inhabit the church's belltower for years afterwards. In Portugal, he is also considered the patron saint of wine and sea voyages.

At the end of the cape are a wind-whipped red lighthouse (hundreds of ocean-going ships round this point every day) and a former convent. Henry the Navigator's house is believed to have been in a small castle to the right of the lighthouse.

The best time to visit is at sunset, when you can almost hear the hissing as the sun hits the sea. It's a fantastic cycle along a quiet road, though 6km each way and windy.

There are cafés and restaurants along the way.

Activities

There are four good beaches a short drive or long walk from Sagres: **Praia da Mareta**, just below the town; lovely **Praia do Martinhal** to the east; **Praia do Tonel** on the other side of the Ponta de Sagres; and the isolated **Praia de Beliche**, on the way to Cabo de São Vicente. **Praia da Baleeira**, adjacent to the harbour, gets polluted from all the boat traffic. Praia do Tonel is especially good for surfing.

Turinfo (p206) can arrange **jeep tours** with Horizonte to the Costa Vicentina or into the Serra de Monchique (€46 per person) or weekend guided walks in southwest Alentejo or Costa Vicentina.

BOATING, SURFING & DIVING

Mar Ilimitado (☎ 282 215 814; www.marilimitado.com) offers a variety of boat trips from dolphin-spotting trips (€30) to excursions up to Cabo de São Vicente (€18).

Surfing is possible at all beaches except Praia do Martinhal. Praia da Baleeira is not suitable for either swimmers or surfers. The **International Surf School** (☎ 914 482 407, 964 466 851 www.internationalsurfschool.com; 1-/3-/5- day €45/120/180) offers lessons.

Free Ride Sagres Surfcamp (☎ 916 089 005; www.freeridesurfcamp.com; 1-/3-/5- day €45/100/150) gives lessons as well, and offers free transport from Sagres, Praia da Luz and Lagos.

The **Scubado Diving Centre** (☎ 282 624 594, 965 559 073; www.scubado-algarve.com; Porto da Baleeira; 🕑 dives at 10am & 3pm) organises diving trips (this is a great spot for shipwrecks between 12m and 30m). A dive and equipment costs €35/200/320 for one/six/10 days, while the four-day PADI open-water course goes for €290. Snorkel hire costs €10 per day.

Sleepy Sagres really comes to life during its annual **Surf Festival**, which is held during one weekend in mid-August and features music (with reggae bands taking centre stage) and surfy crowds.

Sleeping

Sagres fills up in summer, though it's marginally easier to find accommodation here than in the rest of the Algarve during the high season.

BUDGET

Many houses in Sagres advertise private rooms or apartments. Doubles generally cost €30 and flats cost €45 to €80.

Orbitur Sagres (☎ 282 624 371; www.orbitur.pt; adult/tent/car €4.40/4.60/4) Some 2km from town, just off the road to Cabo de São Vicente, this is a shady, well-maintained camping ground with lots of trees. You can hire bikes here.

Ingrina Camping (☎ 282 639 242; www.campingingrina.com; adult/tent/car €4.50/4.50/3.70) About 17km northeast of Sagres, this is a much smaller site, 600m from the beach south of Raposeira, with shade, a restaurant and bike hire.

Casa do Cabo de Santa Maria (☎/fax 282 624 722; Rua Patrão António Faústino; s/d/apt without breakfast from €25/35/60) Run by a former fisherman, this welcoming guesthouse is excellent value for its handsome, nicely furnished rooms and apartments.

MIDRANGE & TOP END

Alojamento Particular (☎ 282 624 096; alojamento.particular@netvisao.pt; Praça da República 1; d/apt €45-65/65-85) This beautifully located guesthouse has bright, cheery rooms and a lovely back garden overlooking the ocean. Half the rooms have terraces with sea views – well worth the extra cash.

Aparthotel Orquidea (☎ 282 624 257; aparthotelorquidea@sapo.pt; Rua das Naus; d/apt €50/55) This fairly worn place has large, simply furnished apartments, each painted in dull colours with carpeting. The price, however, is nice, as are the verandas – some with views over the marina.

Aparthotel Navigator (☎ 282 624 354; www.hotel-navigator.com; Rua Infante Dom Henrique; 1-/2-/3-person apt €50/55/60; ❄ 💻 🏊) This large, modern complex offers spacious, cheaply furnished apartments with sweeping views over the cliffs. Each has a balcony and satellite TV; a large pool in back.

Casa de Sagres (☎ 282 624 358; d €60) Efficient and pretty, Casa de Sagres has a great, almost beach-side, location, and the rooms are spacious with wood floors; the best have terraces with ocean views.

Residência Dom Henrique (☎ 282 620 003; fax 282 620 004; Praça da República; s/d €65/68, d with veranda €75; 💻) This friendly three-storey guesthouse has comfortable rooms with tile floors, big windows and beachcombers' décor. The best rooms have verandas with sea views.

Pontalaia (☎ 282 620 280; www.pontalaia.pt; Rua Infante Dom Henrique; apt from €90; ❄ 🏊) Next door to Navigator, this small, condo-like complex opened in 2005, and it offers attractive airy apartments set with blonde woods and stylish furnishings, each with a balcony.

Pousada do Infante (☎ 282 624 222; fax 282 624 225; d €170; ❄ 🏊) This modern *pousada* has large, luscious rooms in a great setting near the clifftop. Count on bright, cheerful colours, handsome furnishings and picture-perfect views from the terraces.

Eating

Many of the following places close or operate shorter hours during the low season (November to April). The *mercado municipal* provides great supplies for long beach days.

Estrela do Mar (Rua Comandante Matoso; mains €5-8; 🕑 lunch & dinner) This popular local restaurant offers good filling grilled dishes (such as chicken or swordfish) that won't break the bank.

Bossa Nova Restaurante (☎ 282 624 566; off Avenida Comandante Matasco; mains €5-10; 🕑 lunch & dinner) Behind Dromedário, this place is popular for its pizzas; there's an open-air dining area with wooden benches.

A Tasca (☎ 282 624 177; Porto da Baleeira; dishes €7-13; 🕑 lunch & dinner) Overlooking the marina and out to sea, this place specialises in seafood, has a sunny seaside terrace and a cosy interior with bottles embedded in the walls.

Agua Salgada (☎ 282 624 297; Rua Comandante Matoso; mains €10-17; 🕑 10am-2am; 💻 V) On the main drag, this stylish, two-storey restaurant and bar serves crepes, veggie burgers, sandwiches and plenty of cocktails when evening arrives. Good mix of music – soul, reggae and electronica. Free internet.

Dromedário (☎ 282 624 297; Rua Comandante Matoso; mains €10-17; 🕑 10.30am-2am; 💻) Right next door to Agua Salgada, this place offers similar food and ambience.

Vila Velha (☎ 282 624 788; Rua P António Faustino; mains €10-17; 🕑 dinner Tue-Sun; V) In a charming house with a lovely rose garden in front, Vila Velha offers rich seafood mains, a fine lamb and good vegetarian dishes.

Jidsepesca (☎ 282 620 280; Rua Infante Dom Henrique; mains €12-20; 🕑 dinner Fri-Tue) A stylish new restaurant serving top-quality seafood in an elegant dining room.

Praça da República has several eateries, including **Café-Restaurante Cochina** (mains €6-12.50; 🕑 breakfast, lunch & dinner), a casual snack spot with a large menu and seats on the square.

There are several inviting restaurants on the sands of Praia do Martinhal, including **Nortada** (☎ 282 624 147; mains €4-10; 🕑 10am-11pm Jun-Oct, 11am-6pm Nov-May), which serves grilled prawns and fish, as well as sandwiches, soups and oysters. Nearby is **Restaurante-Bar Martinhal** (☎ 282 624 032; Praia do Martinhal; dishes €1-10.50; 10am-9pm) offering similar bites.

Drinking

Raposo (10am-9pm) On the beach, laid-back Raposo enjoys an ideal setting, with lapping waves a few steps from the terrace.

Bubble Lounge (☎ 282 624 494; Rua Senhora da Graça; 6pm-2am Tue-Sun) Bright walls, beanbags, low seating, Indian lanterns and wall hangings: boho Bubble Lounge has an easy vibe and good beats. It's friendly and there's a small streetside terrace. Movies are screened here on some nights.

Getting There & Around

You can buy tickets from the newsagent kiosk on Praça da República. The bus stop is northeast of the turismo. For more information call ☎ 282 762 944.

Buses come from Lagos (€3, 50 minutes, 10 to 20 daily), via Salema, and Portimão (€4.60, 1¾ hours, three daily on weekdays). It's only 10 minutes to Cabo de São Vicente (three daily on weekdays).

Near the turismo, bike rental is available at **Quiosque Navegador** (€7.50 per day bike rental; 9am-9pm). Through Turinfo (p206) you can rent bikes, scooters or autos.

For a taxi, call ☎ 282 624 501.

NORTH OF SAGRES

Heading north along the Algarve's western coast you'll find some amazing beaches, backed by beautiful wild vegetation. It's so preserved because of building restrictions imposed to protect the Parque Natural do Sudoeste Alentejano e Costa Vicentina. This extraordinary area, protected since 1995, is rarely more than 6km wide, and runs for about 120km from Burgau to Cabo de São Vicente and up nearly the entire western Algarve and Alentejo shore. Here there are at least 48 plant species found only in Portugal, and around a dozen or so found only within the park.

It's home to otters, foxes and wild cats, and some 200 species of birds enjoy the coastal wetlands, salt marshes and cliffs, including Portugal's last remaining ospreys. Although the seas are sometimes dangerous, the area has a growing reputation for some of Europe's finest surf and attracts people from all over the world.

Carrapateira

Surf-central Carrapateira is a tranquil, pretty, spread-out village, with two exhilarating beaches nearby whose lack of development, fizzing surf and strong swells attract a hippy, surf-dude crowd. The coast along here is wild, with copper-coloured and ash-grey cliffs covered in speckled yellow and green scrub, backing creamy, wide sands.

Praia da Bordeira (aka Praia Carrapateira) is a mammoth swath merging into dunes, 2km off the road on the north side of the village, while the similarly stunning **Praia do Amado** (more famous for its surf) is at the southern end of the village and home to a controversial but low-key community of travellers.

For surfing courses contact **Algarve Surf** (p201). Or try the less official **Carrapateira Surf School & Camp** (☎ 964 432 324, 962 681 478; www.surfcamp-algarve.com; 1-week accommodation, equipment hire & lessons €295, €225 if camping; lessons per day €35; boards per hr/day €10/25), run by two local brothers who are passionate and experienced surfers. They built the camp (made up of basic but well-made three-bed wooden huts, with a communal kitchen) on family farmland, in a beautiful remote setting. They also hire out boards on both beaches from May to September.

SLEEPING & EATING

Pensão das Dunas (☎ /fax 282 973 118; Rua da Padaria 9; d with shared bathroom €28, 1-/2-room apts €39/58) This cosy French-run guesthouse has tidy, colourful rooms overlooking a flower-filled courtyard. It's 100m from the road at the southern end of the village.

Bamboo (☎ 282 973 323; d €40-50) About 500m from Praia da Bordeira, on the main road, this friendly, ecologically minded guesthouse has attractive, colourful rooms; the attached low-key bar is lined with aboriginal-inspired paintings.

Casa Fajara (☎ 282 973 123; www.casafajara.pt; d €50;) Some 500m from the village or 1.2km from Praia da Bordeira, this big modern house overlooks a valley and has rooms with shared kitchen, plus a swimming pool and tennis courts. Fajara doesn't accept children under the age of six and is closed from November to March.

Restaurante Torres (☎ 282 973 222; Rua da Padaria 7; mains €7-12.50; 8am-midnight Tue-Sun) Next door to Dunas, this simple place serves tasty grills (chicken and swordfish are favourites), and there are a couple of outdoor tables.

Restaurante do Cabrito (☎ 282 973 128; mains €8-13; ⏲ lunch & dinner) Near the main N268 and also specialising in grills, Cabrito is a big, friendly restaurant with lots of country charm and outdoor seating.

O Sítio do Rio (☎ 282 973 119; mains €9-16; ⏲ lunch & dinner Wed-Mon; V) Right on the dunes near Praia da Bordeira, this fine airy restaurant cooks up excellent grilled fish and meat mains with eclectic sauces; there are also vegetarian choices. It's hugely popular with Portuguese at weekends.

O Sítio do Forno (☎ 282 973 914; 2-person platters €22-28; ⏲ noon-9pm Tue-Sun) On the cliff overlooking Praia do Amado, this place serves excellent seafood to match those magnificent ocean views. A variety of grilled fish is on offer, but the speciality is the two-person *cataplana* or *arroz de marisco*.

Aljezur

Some 20km further north, Aljezur is a quiet village that straddles a river. One part, to the west, is Moorish – a collection of cottages below a ruined 10th-century hilltop castle; the other, called Igreja Nova (meaning 'new church'), is 600m up a steep hill to the east. Aljezur is close to some fantastic beaches, edged by black rocks that reach into the white-tipped, bracing sea – surfing hotspots. The countryside around, which is part of the natural park, is a tangle of yellow, mauve and green wiry gorse and heather.

ORIENTATION & INFORMATION

The high-up, pretty Largo Igreja Nova is the new town's focus, with some small cafés. Banks with ATMs, shops and restaurants can all be found on Rua 25 de Abril.

Espaço Internet (Largo Igreja Nova; ⏲ 3-8pm Thu-Tue).

Post office (Rua 25 de Abril; ⏲ 9am-12.30pm & 2-5pm Mon-Fri)

Turismo (☎ 282 998 229; ⏲ 9.30am-7pm Tue-Thu Jun-Sep, to 6pm Tue-Thu Oct-May, 7pm Tue-Thu Jun-Sep, 10am-1.30pm & 2.30-6pm Mon year-round) The turismo is next to a small covered market, just before the bridge leading to the Lagos N120 road (Rua 25 de Abril). Buses stop near here.

SIGHTS & ACTIVITIES

Nearby wonderful, unspoilt beaches include **Praia da Arrifana** (10km southwest, near a tourist development called Vale da Telha), a dramatic curved black-cliff-backed bay with one restaurant, balmy pale sands and some big northwest swells (a surfer's delight); and **Praia de Monte Clérigo**, about 8km northwest. **Praia de Amoreira**, 6km away, is a wonderful beach where the river meets the sea. More difficult to reach but worth the effort getting there is the fairly undiscovered **Praia de Vale Figueiras**, about 15km southwest of Aljezur on rugged dirt roads.

Beginners and more experienced riders can go **horse riding** (☎ 282 991 150; per 1/2hr €15/25, per half-/full day €45/70) in the natural park.

SLEEPING

Parque de Campismo Serrão (☎ 282 990 220; www.parque-campismos-serra.com; adult/tent/car €4.30/4.30/3; 💻 🏊 ♿) This calm, shady site is 4km north of Aljezur, then 800m down the road to Praia da Amoreira (the beach is 2.5km further). It has wheelchair access, tennis courts, a playground and apartments, plus bike rental.

Restaurante Oceano (☎ 282 997 300; d €35) The friendly owners here rent cosy rooms, with carved wooden beds and big windows overlooking palms and flowers. Brilliant seafood is just downstairs.

Residencial Dom Sancho II (☎ 282 998 119; turimol@iol.pt; Largo Igreja Nova; s/d €35/45) In Igreja Nova, just off the main square, this guesthouse has handsome rooms with homey touches (like the rocking chair). It's excellent value.

Hospedaria O Palazim (☎ 282 998 249; absent_zero@hotmail.com; N120; s/d €40/50) This modern, whitewashed two-storey place has pleasant rooms with verandas (and views over the hillsides and the town). It's 2km north of Aljezur on the busy Lisbon road.

Restaurante-Bar A La Reira (☎ 282 998 440; Rua 13 de Janeiro; d €45-60) Also in Igreja Nova, this place has clean and tidy rooms with wood details, and each opens onto a shared terrace with lovely views.

In Praia da Arrifana locals sometimes rent out private rooms (look for '*quartos*' signs). There are a few other options outside town.

EATING & DRINKING

Café Colmeia (Largo Igreja Nova; mains €3-8; ⏲ lunch & dinner) This casual spot in Igreja Nova has outdoor tables overlooking the main square and makes a good spot for coffee, sandwiches or other light fare.

Pontá Pé (☎ 282 998 104; Largo da Liberdade; mains €6-12; ⏲ lunch & dinner) Friendly, with wooden floors and a beamed ceiling, Pontá Pé does tasty fish dishes and good barbecue chicken. Adjoining it is a cheery bar with themed nights from Thursday to Sunday, from Brazilian live music to karaoke.

Two casual, popular places near Pontá Pé are the nautically themed **Restaurante Ruth o Ivo** (☎ 282 998 534; Rua 25 de Abril 14; mains €7.50-10; ⏰ lunch & dinner) and Palmeira, a friendly English-speaking café, that's right beside the bridge.

Facing Igreja Nova's main square, there's **Alisuper** (Largo Igreja Nova; ⏰ 9am-8pm Mon-Sat, 9.30am-1.30pm Sun), a small but adequate supermarket. Next to the turismo, the town **market** (⏰ 8am-2pm Tue-Sun) is a good place to buy fresh fruits and veggies.

Next to Hospedaria O Palazim, **O Chefe Dimas** (☎ 282 998 275; Aldeia Velha; mains €4-14; ⏰ lunch & dinner Thu-Tue) is one of Aljezur's top seafood restaurants, serving scrumptious fresh fish and shellfish or monkfish rice, with a breezy outdoor terrace.

In Praia da Arrifana there's a string of seafood restaurants (packed with Portuguese at weekends) on the road above the beach, where you can expect to pay around €8 for grilled fish.

At Praia da Amoreira try **Restaurante Paraíso do Mar** (☎ 282 991 088; mains from €6-13; ⏰ lunch & dinner), which offers fantastic panoramas overlooking the beach. The *caldeirada* is highly recommended.

GETTING AROUND

If you're driving, there's a free car park next to the turismo.

Odeceixe

Around here the countryside rucks up into rolling, large hills. As the Alentejo turns into the Algarve, the first coastal settlement is Odeceixe, an endearing small town clinging to the southern side of the Ribeira de Seixe valley, and so snoozy it's in danger of falling off, apart from the high season, when German, French and Portuguese visitors pack the place.

The sheltered **Praia de Odeceixe**, 3.5km down the valley is a wonderful bite of sand surrounded by gorse and tree-covered cliffs. There's a **turismo** (☎ 961 624 596; 10am-12.30pm & 2-6pm) near the car park before walking down to the beach. For surfboard rental, visit **Lokko** (Rua dos Correiros; surfboard/wetsuit per day €15/5), across from the Parque Hotel.

SLEEPING

There are a handful of well-advertised *quartos* (private rooms) in the village, especially along Rua Nova (en route to the beach). Expect to pay at least €35 for a double.

Parque de Campismo São Miguel (☎ 282 947 145; www.campingsaomiguel.com; adult/tent/car €5.50/5/4.50;) Facility-loaded and pine-shaded, this camping ground is 1.5km north of Odeceixe; wooden bungalows are also available.

Parque Hotel (☎ 282 947 117; Rua dos Correiros 15; d with breakfast €25; ⏰ Apr-Oct) Beside the post office, this quirky guesthouse has a wide range of clean, tile-floored rooms. The best are airy and bright, with balconies and views.

Pensão Luar (☎ 282 947 194; Rua da Várzea 28; d €45) At the western edge of the village, en route to the beach, this friendly *pensão* (guesthouse) is an excellent bargain, with modern, white spick-and-span rooms with balconies overlooking fields.

Restaurante Dorita (☎ 282 947 581; d with/without bathroom €50/35) Overlooking the beach (and near the turismo), this place has a gorgeous position overlooking the sea. Rooms are tidy and simple, and the best have terraces with views.

EATING

Restaurante Chaparro (☎ 282 947 304; Rua Estrada Nacional; mains €7-8.50; ⏰ lunch & dinner Mon-Sat) Opposite the post office, Chaparro has some good food and a cheery yellow interior.

Taberna do Gabão (☎ 282 947 549; Rua do Gabão 9; mains €8; ⏰ lunch & dinner Thu-Tue) Next to the fire station, this welcoming restaurant features good-value traditional dishes served in a charming old-fashioned wooden dining room. Outdoor seating.

You'll find several pleasant restaurants around Largo 1 Mai, a great spot to sit and watch the world amble by.

A Tasca da Saskia (Rua das Amoreiras; mains €2-7.60; ⏰ dinner Tue-Sun) With a small corner terrace laden with flowerpots, this arty little café off the main square has lots of veggie options as well as other mains, such as spaghetti with shrimp.

GETTING THERE & AWAY

Buses run from Lagos to Odeceixe (€3.60, 80 minutes, five daily) via Aljezur (€3, 50 minutes).

One daily bus connects Vila do Bispo with Carrapateira (€3.40, one hour). There's a twice-weekly service to Praia de Arrifana from Aljezur.

THE INTERIOR

MONCHIQUE

pop 5400 / elevation 410m

High up above the coast, the picturesque hamlet of Monchique makes a lovely base for exploring mountainous woodlands, with some excellent options for walking, biking or canoeing.

There's also an enticing spa town nearby and a marvellous private zoo for endangered species. It's set in the forested Serra de Monchique, the Algarve's mountain range, lying some 24km north of Portimão.

Fires regularly affect this area in the summertime, causing widespread damage and frustration at the lack of measures to prevent the annual devastation.

Orientation & Information

Buses will drop you off in the central Largo dos Chorões, with a café and clunking waterwheel sculpture.

Espaço Internet (☎ 282 910 235; Largo dos Chorões; 🕑 3-9pm Mon-Fri, 11am-9pm Sat & Sun)

Turismo (☎ 282 911 189; Largo da São Sebastião; 🕑 9.30am-5.30pm) A useful spot for picking up maps and getting recommendations for country walks. It's uphill from the bus stop (signposted to Portimão).

Sights

A series of brown pedestrian signs starting near the bus station directs visitors up into the town's narrow old streets and major places of interest.

The **igreja matriz** (parish church; admission free; 🕑 9am-5pm) has an extraordinary, star-shaped Manueline porch decorated with twisted columns that look like lengths of knotted rope, and a simple interior, with columns topped with more stony rope, and some fine chapels, including one whose vault contains beautiful 17th-century glazed tiles showing Sts Francis, and Michael killing the devil.

Keep climbing and you'll eventually reach the ruins of the 17th-century Franciscan monastery of **Nossa Senhora do Desterro**, which overlooks the town from its wooded hilltop.

Activities

All these require advance reservations.

The German-run **Nature Walk** (☎ 282 911 041, 964 308 767) organises one-day walking trips to nearby 773m Picota peak (€20 per person) and full-moon walks during summer.

Alternativ Tour (☎ 282 911 405, 965 004 337; www.alternativtour.com) offers many activities, including guided walks (€19), mountain-biking tours (€29); canoeing trips (€24) or combined mountain-biking and canoeing trips (€49).

Contact **Gunther** (☎ 282 913 657) for guided horse-riding (no beginners) trips.

Dutch-run **Outdoor Tours** (☎ 282 969 520, 916 736 226; www.outdoor-tours.net; based in Alvor) offers biking (€24 tp €35), canoing (€23) and walking trips (€19) both in and around the Serra Monchique.

Sleeping

BUDGET

Residencial Estrela de Monchique (☎ 282 913 111; Rua do Porto Fundo 46; s/d €25/35) Near the bus station, this is a cheery place in the centre, with good-value rooms above a café.

Residencial Miradouro (☎ 282 912 163; Rua dos Combatentes do Ultramar; s/d €30/40) Up steep Rua Engenheiro Duarte Pacheco (signposted to Portimão), near the turismo, this 1970s hilltop place, run with great seriousness, offers sweeping, breezy views and neat rooms, some with balcony.

> **MONCHIQUE'S MOONSHINE**
>
> You can find commercial brands of *medronho* (a locally made firewater) everywhere in Portugal, but according to those who have suffered enough hangovers to know, the best of all is the Monchique privately made brew.
>
> The Serra de Monchique is thick with *medronho*'s raw material – the arbutus, or strawberry tree. Its berries are collected in late autumn, fermented and then left for months before being distilled in large copper stills (for sale as souvenirs all over the Algarve).
>
> Home-made *medronho* is usually clear and drunk neat, like schnapps. It's strong, of course, but as long as you don't mix it with other drinks it doesn't give you a hangover (say the connoisseurs). Early spring, when distilling is under way, is the best time to track down some of this brew in Monchique: ask around.

THE ALGARVE

MIDRANGE

Albergaria Bica-Boa (☎ 282 912 271; enigma@mail.telepac.pt; d with breakfast €70;) One kilometre out of town on the Lisbon road, this gorgeous four-room place overlooks a wooded valley. There's a decent restaurant here, too (with vegetarian dishes).

Quinta de São Bento (☎ /fax 282 912 143; Rua do Fóia; s/d incl breakfast €70/85) A former holiday home of the Portuguese royal family, this is on the road to Fóia and has a balmy pool amid lush gardens.

Eating & Drinking

Restaurante Central (☎ 282 913 160; Rua da Igreja; mains €7-9; lunch & dinner) Without a doubt the winner of the eccentricity award, this pint-sized place is run by the characterful Nita Massano, who dishes out *piri-piri* chicken when the conditions are right. The walls are smothered in an array of mixed testimonies from previous diners.

A Charrete (☎ 282 912 142; Rua Dr Samora Gil 30-34; mains €7-12; lunch & dinner) Offering a wide range of regional specialities, this place serves reliably good cuisine amid country rustic charm. A few favourites include cabbage with spicy sausages, stuffed squid and honey flan for dessert.

Barlefante (Travessa das Guerreiras; mains €2.40-3.50; noon-2am Mon-Thu, to 4am Fri-Sun) Signposted off the town's main drag, this is a great find, decked out with golden-yellow walls, red-velvet alcoves, ornate mirrors, some outside tables in the narrow cobbled lane, and excellent tapas (aka sandwiches) with home-made bread. It's young Monchique's hippest haunt.

There are lots of restaurants on the way to Fóia offering *piri-piri* chicken. In a nice setting, about 2km from Monchique and off the main road is **Jardim das Oliveiras** (☎ 282 912 874; mains €4-18.50; lunch & dinner) Off Rua do Fóia, this place has regional dishes, shady trees and outside seating.

Shopping

Distinctive, locally made 'scissor chairs' – wooden folding stools – are a good buy here. Try shops along Rua Serpa Pinto, which runs from Largo dos Chorões.

Getting There & Away

Buses run from Portimão (€2.60, 45 minutes, six to eight daily).

AROUND MONCHIQUE

Fóia

The 902m Fóia peak is the Algarve's highest point, 8km west of Monchique. The road to the summit climbs through eucalyptus and pine trees and opens up vast views over the rolling hills. On the way are numerous *piri-piri* pit stops offering spicy chicken. Telecommunication towers spike the peak, but ignore them and look at the panoramic views. On clear days you can see out to the corners of the western Algarve – Cabo de São Vicente to the southwest and Odeceixe to the northwest.

Omega Parque

In a beautiful hilly setting, this marvellous, small-but-spacious **zoo** (☎ 282 913 149; www.omegaparque.com; adult/child €8/5; 10am-5.30pm, 10am-7pm) is dedicated to endangered animal species and is a family-run labour of love. You can decide whether the sweetest is the red panda, the pygmy hippo, the winsome ring-tailed lemur or Waldrapp ibis (cartoonlike birds resembling elderly men). Our favourite is the Ne Ne Hawaiian goose, so-called because of its despondent 'ne ne' cry (perhaps bemoaning its scarcity). It's humankind's fault – all the species have been threatened due to hunting and loss of habitat.

There's also a café with a view. The zoo is on the N266, just before Caldas de Monchique. Buses running between Portimão and Monchique stop here.

Caldas de Monchique

Caldas de Monchique is a faintly fantastical place, with a therapeutic calm, and pastel-painted buildings nestling above a delightful valley full of birdsong, eucalyptus, acacia and pine trees, 6km south of Monchique. It has been a popular spa for over two millennia – the Romans loved its 32°C, slightly sulphurous waters, which are said to be good for rheumatism and respiratory and digestive ailments. Dom João II came here for years in an unsuccessful attempt to cure his dropsy.

Floods in 1997 led to the closure of the spa hospital, after which it was redeveloped into a spa resort, and its picturesque buildings repainted pale pink, green and yellow.

ORIENTATION & INFORMATION

The hamlet is 500m below the main road. At reception (the first building on your left) you can book accommodation. Spa treatments and other luxuries are available at the spa.

SIGHTS

The most peaceful patch is a pretty, streamside garden above the hamlet's central square. Down the valley is the spa itself and below this is the huge bottling plant where the famous Caldas waters are bottled.

In the wooded valley below town, at the **Termas de Monchique Spa** (☎ 282 910 910; www.monchiquetermas.com; admission €25, hotel guests €11; 10.30am-1pm Tue, 9am-1pm Wed-Mon & 3-7pm daily), admission allows access to the sauna, steam bath, gym and swimming pool with hydromassage jets. You can then indulge in special treatments, from a Cleopatra bath to a Tired Legs treatment.

SLEEPING & EATING

There are two private places: **Restaurante & Residencial Granifóia** (☎ 282 910 500; fax 282 912 218; s/d/tw €30/35/40;), in a quiet location, has small basic rooms, some with balconies and views. Coming from Monchique, it's 400m past the turn-off to the hamlet, in a modern, unattractive building. In the village, **Albergaria Lageado** (☎ 282 912 616; fax 282 911 310; s/d €45/55;) is an attractive hotel with a red-sloped roof. It provides old fashioned, appealing rooms, a small camellia-surrounded pool and a restaurant.

The three other hotels all belong to Termas de Monchique. **Hotel Termal** (s/d €80/105), next to the spa, is the cheapest and biggest; **Hotel Central** (s/d €90/115), next to Termas' main reception, has 13 beautifully furnished rooms and **Estalagem Dom Lourenço** (s/d €90/115), opposite reception, is the most luxurious. The Termas also runs the self-catering **Apartamentos Turísticos D Francisco** (apt €83). You can book weekend or weeklong packages that include treatments.

The upmarket **Restaurante 1692** (mains €13-17; lunch & dinner) has tables in the tree-shaded central square and a smart interior.

About 200m uphill from the turn-off to Monchique, **Rouxinol** (282 913 975; mains €10-14; lunch & dinner) offers a range of unique dishes, including a Nordic-style *caldeirada*, vegetable curry and grilled fish and meat dishes. It has a lovely outdoor patio shaded by trees and a cosy dining room.

GETTING THERE & AWAY

The Monchique to Portimão bus service goes via Caldas de Monchique (€1.40); the bus stop is on the road above the hamlet. Alert the driver as to where you're going, because it's easy to miss.

ALCOUTIM

pop 1100 / elevation 334m

Strategically positioned along the idyllic Rio Guadiana, Alcoutim (ahl-ko-*teeng*) is a small village just across the river from the Spanish town of Sanlúcar de Guadiana. What-are-you-looking-at fortresses above both villages remind one of testier times. Phoenicians, Greeks, Romans and Arabs have barricaded themselves in the hills here, and centuries of tension have bubbled across the river, which forms the Algarve's entire eastern boundary. In the 14th century, Dom Fernando I of Portugal and Don Henrique II of Castile signed a tentative peace treaty in Alcoutim. Today the best activities are lazing along the riverside, strolling the cobbled streets or hopping a ferry to Spain.

Orientation & Information

Alcoutim has a new town development 500m north of the square across the Ribeira de Cadavais stream.

Café Vila Velha (Rua da Misericordia; per hr €2; 10am-2am Mon-Sat) Just off the central square; another internet facility (when the connection's working).

Casa dos Condes (☎ 281 546 104; 9am-1pm & 2-5pm) Opposite the turismo; has free internet access, a small display of local crafts and offers guided visits of Alcoutim.

Turismo (☎ 281 546 179; Rua 1 de Maio; 10am-1.30pm & 2.30-6pm Fri-Mon, 9.30am-6pm Tue-Thu) Behind the central square, just a few steps from the river, this office distributes maps and information on walks in the countryside.

Sights & Activities

The flower-ringed 14th-century **castelo** (admission €2.60; 9am-1pm & 2-5pm) has sweeping views. Inside the grounds is the small, excellent **Núcleo Museológico de Arqueologia** (archaeological museum), displaying ruined medieval castle walls and other artefacts.

You can cross the river on the small local **ferry** (€1.50, 9am-1pm & 2-7pm). Rent bikes or canoes from the **pousada da juventude** (see p216).

The prehistoric **Parque Mineiro Cova dos Mouros** (copper mine; ☎ 281 498 505; minacovamouros.sitepac.pt; adult/child €5/4.20; 10.30am-6pm Tue-Sun Mar-Oct, to 4.30pm Nov & Feb), 38km west of town near Vaqueiros, is over 4500 years old and includes Roman remains. You can follow a 1km walk, peer down the ancient old mine shafts and visit a reconstructed prehistoric

VIA ALGARVIANA

Covering some of the most beautiful scenery in the Algarve, this 250km walking trail crosses the breadth of Portugal from Alcoutim to Cabo de São Vicente, taking in the wooded hillsides of the Serra Monchique and the rugged coast near Carrapateira. The Via Algarviana has been tested by both walkers and horse riders and is largely marked; it takes two to three weeks to walk the trail. For more information, including directions and maps, check out www.algarveway.com.

house. For kids there are donkey rides and a nature trail, and you can also swim in the Ribeira da Foupana.

Sleeping & Eating

Ask at the turismo about the availability of private rooms (from €25 per night).

Pousada da juventude (☎ 281 546 004; alcoutim@movijovem.pt; dm/d €16/43; reception ⏰ 8am-noon & 6pm-midnight;) One kilometre north of the square, past the new town and fire station, is this fantastically situated, well-appointed hostel, with an excellent pool and kitchen facilities, plus bikes and canoes for rent.

Ildo Afonso (Rua Dr João Dias; s/d €25/35) This private house rents smartly decorated, bright rooms at good prices.

Estalagem do Guadiana (☎ 281 540 120; www.grupofbarata.com; s/d €65/80) Below the *pousada da juventude*, this place has trim and colourful rooms, with huge windows overlooking the river. The palm-surrounded pool in back is particularly refreshing.

Riverside Tavern (☎ 963 187 698; Avenida Duarte Pacheco 3) Just south of the boat dock and overlooking the river, this attractive café is a lovely spot for a drink or a light meal. Its sunny terrace is perfectly placed for gazing out across the water.

Snack Bar Restaurante O Soeiro (☎ 281 546 241; Rua do Município; daily special €6.50; ⏰ lunch & dinner Mon-Fri) A local favourite, this place serves hearty lunch plates, and also has outdoor tables overlooking the river.

Getting There & Around

Buses coming from Vila Real de Santo António (€3.40, 1¼ hours, two daily Monday to Friday) go on to Beja (two hours) via Mértola (50 minutes).

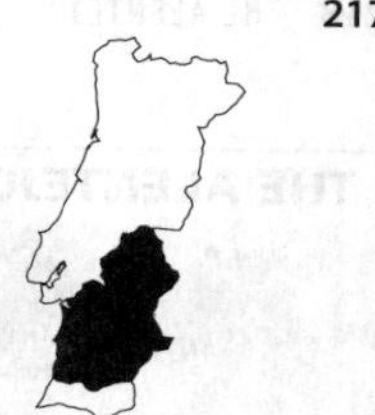

The Alentejo

Portugal's largest region, the Alentejo spreads across nearly one third of the country, encompassing vast stretches of rolling hillsides, with majestic medieval cities, whitewashed villages and picturesque mountaintop castles all woven into the landscape.

A journey into the heart of the Alentejo reveals a tradition of farming dating back many centuries: cork plantations, vineyards and olive groves are the unchanged markers of time's slow passage here. The scattered remains left by previous civilisations offer an even more illuminating vision of Alentejo's rich past. These include hillsides covered with the mystical stone carvings left by Palaeolithic tribes, fragments from various Roman conquerors (Roman baths and a beautifully preserved Roman temple notwithstanding), stolid Visigothic churches, Moorish-designed neighbourhoods and the awe-inspiring fortresses built at eagle's-nest heights, peering over the edge of Spanish-speaking Castile, Portugal's former nemesis.

Évora is the Alentejo's star attraction, with a walled, medieval centre that has changed little over the last 400 years. Cathedrals and cloisters, macabre bone chapels, attractive town squares and nearby Neolithic ruins are all part of the allure. Outside of Évora the crowds dwindle considerably, and you can witness traditional village life in the rarefied, flower-filled towns of Marvão and Castelo de Vide, take in the peaceful river views of Mértola or glimpse the fine craftsmanship in the marble towns of Estremoz, Vila Viçosa or Borba.

The Alentejo's long, unblemished coastline provides another reason to linger. Pretty towns like Vila Nova de Milfontes and Zambujeira do Mar overlook lovely stretches of beach and attract a mixed summertime crowd in search of sun, good waves and a lively but laid-back nightlife scene.

HIGHLIGHTS

- Following the trail of past civilisations in historically rich **Évora** (p219), a Unesco World Heritage–listed city
- Enjoying the sand, surf and sunset cocktails of **Vila Nova de Milfontes** (p264)
- Gazing out over the countryside from the castle perch of enchanting **Marvão** (p250)
- Canoeing along the Rio Guadiana beneath the shadow of tranquil **Mértola** (p252)
- Watching the shadows play on the megaliths at **Cromeleque dos Almendres** (p230) and **Monsaraz** (p232)

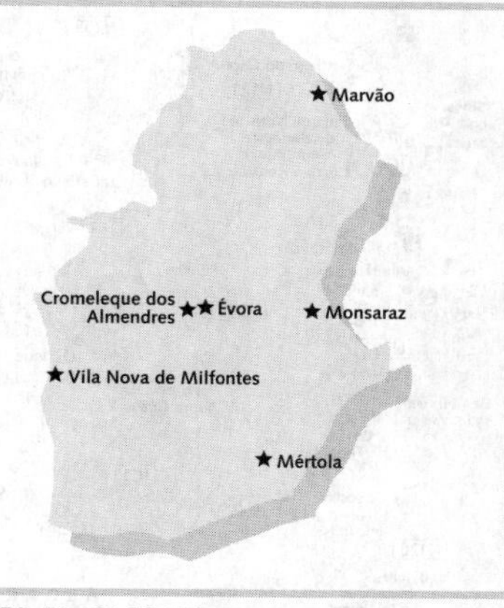

- POPULATION: 770,000
- AREA: 31,483 SQ KM

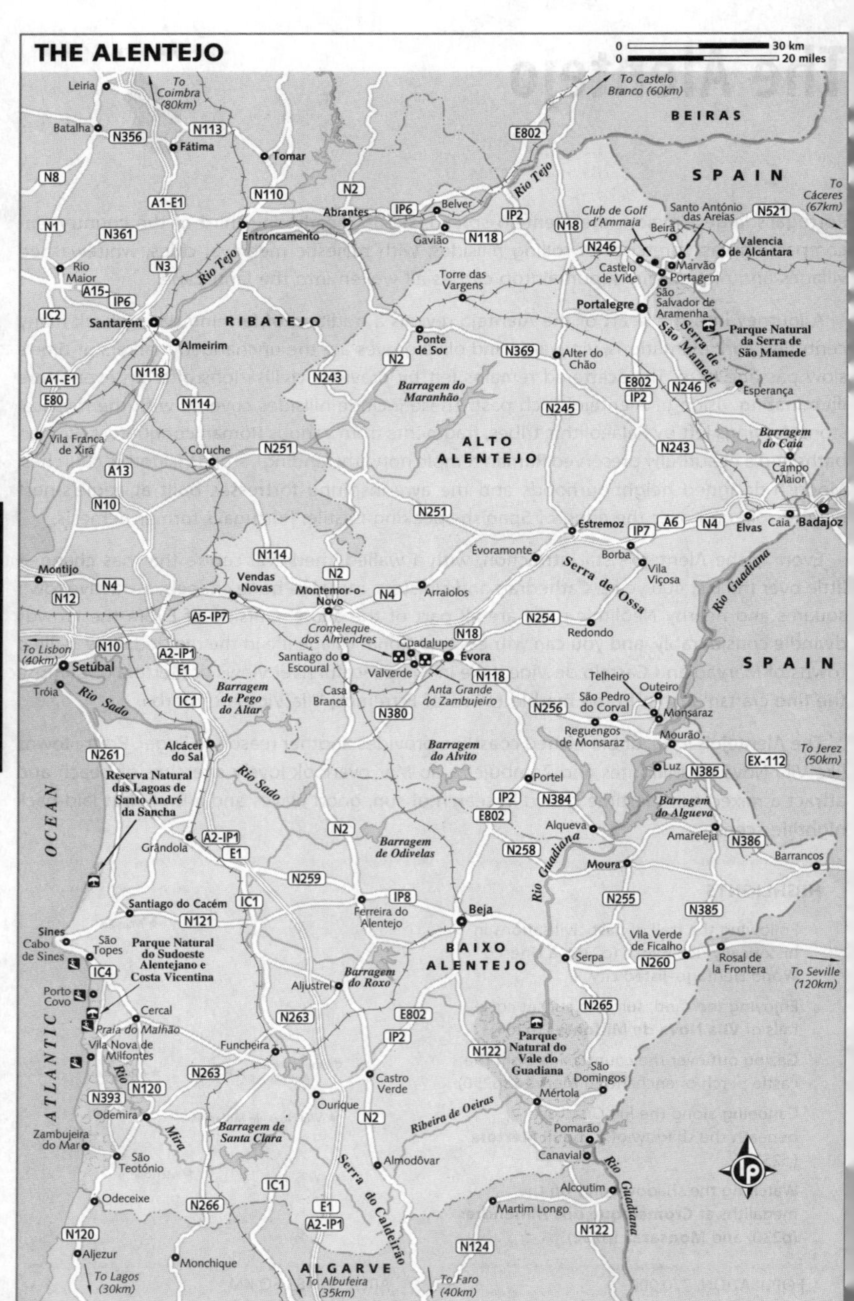

THE ALENTEJO

History

Prehistoric Alentejo was a busy place, and today's landscape is covered in megaliths. But it was the Romans who stamped and shaped the landscape, introducing vines, wheat and olives, building dams and irrigation schemes and founding huge estates called *latifúndios* (that still exist today) to make the most of the region's limited rivers and poor soil.

The Moors, arriving in the early 8th century, took Roman irrigation further and introduced new crops such as citrus and rice. By 1279 they were on the run to southern Spain or forced to live in *mouraria* (segregated Moorish quarters) outside town walls. Many of their hilltop citadels were later reinforced by Dom Dinis (p29), who threw a chain of spectacular fortresses along the Spanish border.

Despite Roman and Moorish development, the Alentejo remained agriculturally poor and backward, increasingly so as the Age of Discoveries (p30) led to an explosive growth in maritime trade and seaports became sexy. Only Évora flourished, under the royal patronage of the House of Avis, but it too declined once the Spanish seized the throne in 1580.

During the 1974 revolution (p34) the Alentejo suddenly stepped into the limelight; landless rural workers who had laboured on the *latifúndios* for generations rose up in support of the communist rebellion and seized the land from its owners. Nearly 1000 estates were collectivised, although few succeeded and all were gradually reprivatised in the 1980s. Most are now back in the hands of their original owners.

Today the Alentejo remains among Europe's poorest and emptiest regions. Portugal's entry into the EU, increasing mechanisation, successive droughts and greater opportunities elsewhere have all convinced young people to head for the cities, leaving villages to slowly die out. Although its cork, olives, marble and granite are still in great demand, and the deep-water port and industrial zone of Sines is of national importance, this vast region contributes only a small fraction to the gross national product. But the huge Barragem do Alqueva (Alqueva dam) and its reservoir have changed the region's prospects dramatically (p223). Supporters of the project cite the clean energy provided. Currently the hydroelectric dam meets the energy needs of more than 160,000 consumers in the Beja region.

ALTO ALENTEJO

The northern half of the Alentejo is a medieval gem, with a scattering of walled fortress towns (like Elvas and Estremoz) and remote clifftop castles (like Marvão and Castelo de Vide). Only a handful of visitors to Alto Alentejo travel beyond Évora, so once outside the city you'll see traditional life at its most authentic.

ÉVORA

pop 56,500 / elevation 250m

One of Portugal's most beautifully preserved medieval towns, Évora is an enchanting place to delve into the past. Inside the 14th-century walls, Évora's narrow, winding lanes lead to striking architectural works: an elaborate medieval cathedral and cloisters; the cinematic columns of the Templo Romano (near the intriguing Roman baths); and a picturesque town square, once the sight of some rather gruesome episodes courtesy of the Inquisition. Aside from its historic and aesthetic virtues, Évora is also a lively university town, whose students nicely dilute the tourist population, and there are a number of attractive restaurants serving up hearty Alentejan cuisine. Outside of town, Neolithic monuments and rustic wineries make for fine day trips.

History

The Celtic settlement of Ebora had been established here before the Romans arrived in 59 BC and made it a military outpost, and eventually an important centre of Roman Iberia, when it was known as 'Ebora Liberalistas Julia'.

After a depressing spell under the Visigoths, the town got its groove back as a centre of trade under the Moors. In AD 1165 Évora's Muslim rulers were hoodwinked by a rogue Portuguese Christian knight known as Giraldo Sem Pavor (Gerald the Fearless). The well-embellished story goes like this: Giraldo single-handedly stormed one of the town's watchtowers by climbing up a ladder of spears driven into the walls. From there he distracted municipal sentries while his companions took the town with hardly a fight. The Moors took it back in 1192, clinging on for another 20 years or so.

The 14th to 16th centuries were Évora's golden age, when it was favoured by the Alentejo's own House of Avis, as well as by scholars and artists. Declared an archbishopric in 1540, it got its own Jesuit university in 1559.

When cardinal-king Dom Henrique, last of the Avis line, died in 1580 and Spain seized the throne, the royal court left Évora and the town began wasting away. The Marquês de Pombal's closure of the university in 1759 was the last straw. French forces plundered the town and massacred its defenders in July 1808.

Ironically, as in many other well-preserved ancient cities, it was decline itself that protected Évora's very fine old centre – economic success would have led to far greater redevelopment. Today the population is smaller than it was in the Middle Ages.

Orientation

Évora climbs a gentle hill above the Alentejo plain. Around the walled centre runs a ring road from which you can enter the town on one of several 'spoke' roads.

The town's focal point is Praça do Giraldo, 700m from the bus station to the southwest. The train station is outside the walls, 1km south of the square.

If you're driving, it's best to park outside the walls at one of the many signposted car parks (eg at the southern end of Rua da República). Except on Sunday, spaces inside the walls are limited and usually metered; pricier hotels have parking.

Information

BOOKSHOPS

Livraria Nazareth (☎ 266 741 702; Praça do Giraldo 46) Opposite the turismo. Sells a few maps, including *Alentejo & Évora* (€4.95) and some books in English.

Livraria Som das Letras (1st fl, Rua João de Deus 21) Attractive bookshop with a handful of French- and English-language titles.

EMERGENCY & MEDICAL SERVICES

Évora district hospital (☎ 266 740 100; Rua do Valasco) East of the centre.

PSP police station (☎ 266 746 977; Rua Francisco Soares Lusitano) Near the Templo Romano.

INTERNET ACCESS

Câmara Municipal (town hall; Praça de Sertório; 🕑 9am-5.30pm Mon-Fri) Free internet access in the same building as the old Roman baths.

Cybercenter (Rua dos Mercadores 42; per hr €2; 🕑 9am-2am)

Instituto Português da Juventude (IPJ; ☎ 266 737 300; ipj.evora@mail.telepac.pt; Rua da República 119; 🕑 10am-6pm Mon-Fri, to 1pm Sat) Free access; 30-minute limit.

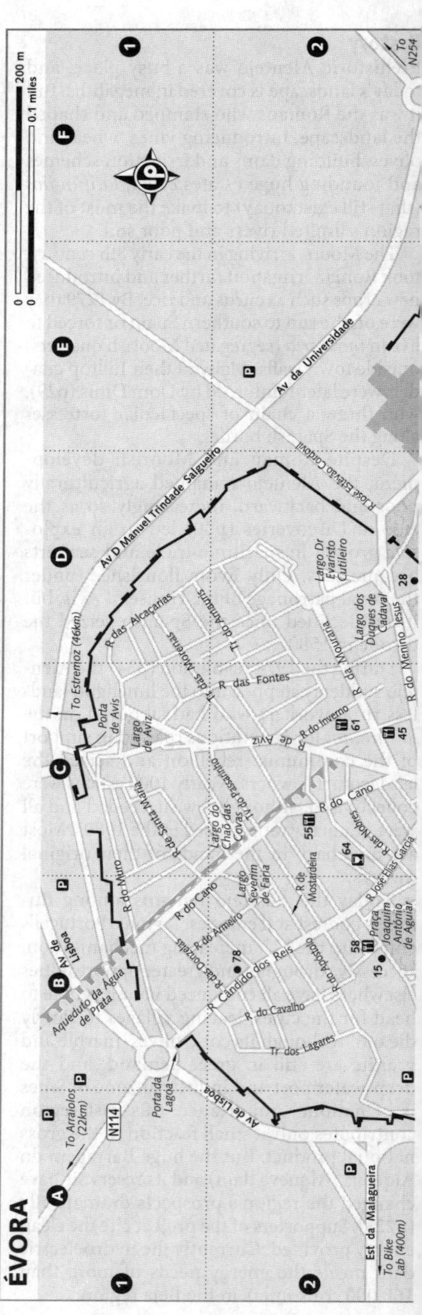

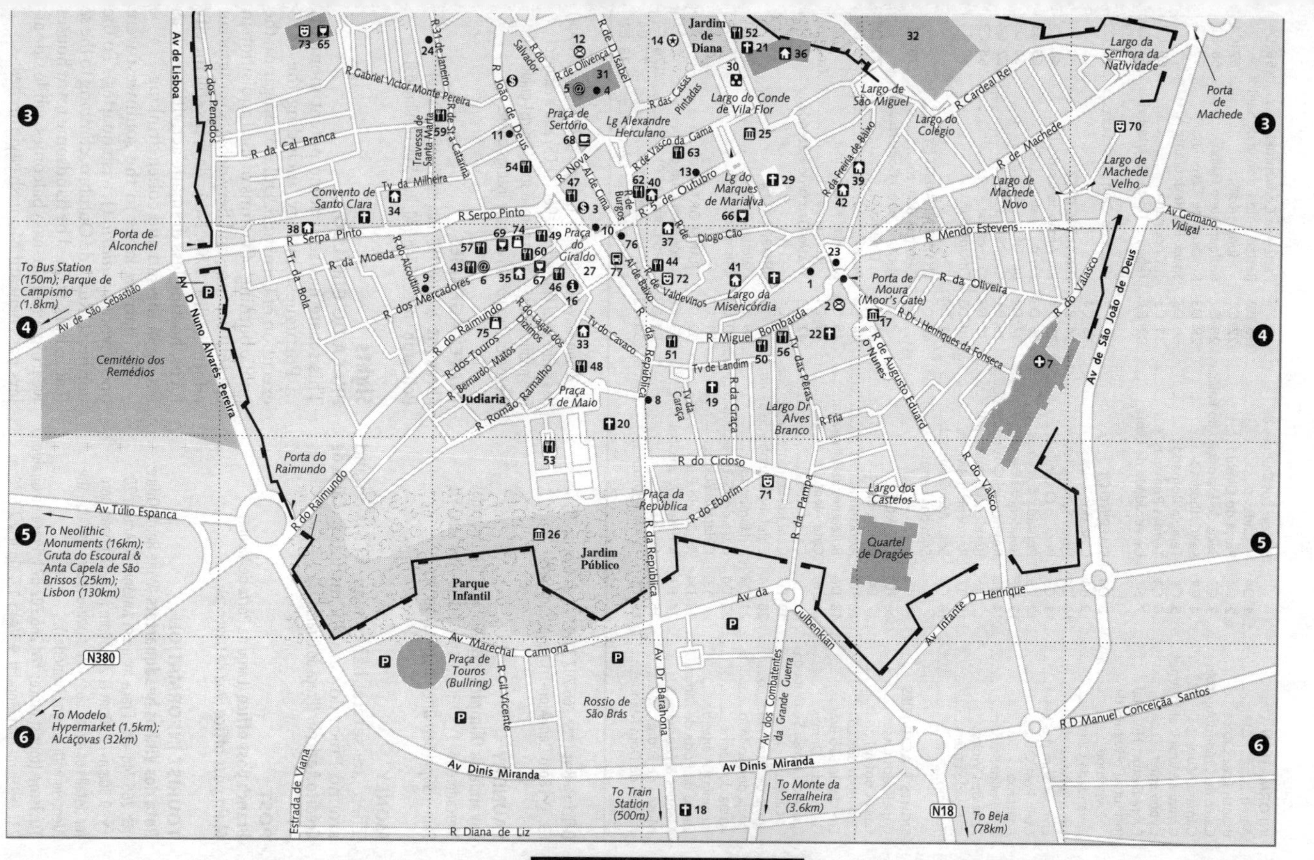
Porta de Machede
Largo da Senhora da Natividade
Largo de Machede Velho
Av Germano Vidigal
Av de São João de Deus
R do Valasco
R de Machede
Largo de Machede Novo
R Cardeal Rei
Largo do Colégio
Largo de São Miguel
R Mendo Estevens
R da Oliveira
R Dr J Henriques da Fonseca
Porta de Moura (Moor's Gate)
R de Augusto Eduard o Nunes
R do Valsco
Av Infante D Henrique
Quartel de Dragões
Largo dos Castelos
R da Pampa
Av da Gulbenkian
Av dos Combatentes da Grande Guerra
R D Manuel Conceição Santos
To Beja (78km)
N18
To Monte da Serralheira (3.6km)
Av Dinis Miranda
Jardim de Diana
Largo do Conde de Vila Flor
R da Freiria de Baixo
Lg do Marquês de Marialva
R Miguel Bombarda
Tv das Pêras
Largo da Misericórdia
Largo Dr Alves Branco
R Fria
R da Graça
Tv de Landim
Tv da Caraça
R do Cicioso
R do Eborim
Praça da República
R da República
Av Dr Barahona
Rossio de São Brás
To Train Station (500m)
Casas Pintadas
Lg Alexandre Herculano
R de Vasco da Gama
R 5 de Outubro
R de Diogo Cão
R de D Isabel
R de Olivença
Praça de Sertório
R Nova
Al de Cima
Al de Baixo
R de Burgos
R de Valdevinos
Praça do Giraldo
Tv do Cavaco
Praça 1 de Maio
Jardim Público
Parque Infantil
R do Salvador
R João de Deus
R Serpa Pinto
R do Lagar dos Dízimos
R Romão Ramalho
R Bernardo Matos
R dos Touros
Judiaria
R do Raimundo
R dos Mercadores
R do Alcoutim
R da Moeda
R 31 de Janeiro
R de Sta Catarina
Travessa de Santa Marta
R Gabriel Victor Monte Pereira
Tv da Milheira
Convento de Santo Clara
Tr da Bola
R da Cal Branca
R dos Penedos
Porta do Raimundo
Av Marechal Carmona
R Gil Vicente
Praça de Touros (Bullring)
R Diana de Liz
Estrada de Viana
Av D Nuno Álvares Pereira
Av de Lisboa
Porta de Alconchel
Av de São Sebastião
Cemitério dos Remédios
Av Túlio Espanca
N380
To Bus Station (150m); Parque de Campismo (1.8km)
To Neolithic Monuments (16km); Gruta do Escoural & Anta Capela de São Brissos (25km); Lisbon (130km)
To Modelo Hypermarket (1.5km); Alcáçovas (32km)

INFORMATION
Abreu ... 1 D4
Branch Post Office ... 2 D4
Caixa de Crédito Agrícola ... 3 C3
Câmara Municipal ... 4 C3
Câmara Municipal Internet ... 5 C3
Cybercenter ... 6 C4
Évora District Hospital ... 7 E4
Instituto Português da Juventude ... 8 D4
Lavandaria Olimpica ... 9 B4
Livraria Nazareth ... 10 C4
Livraria Som das Letras ... 11 C3
Main Post Office ... 12 C3
Policarpo ... 13 D3
PSP Police Station ... 14 D3
Rota dos Vinhos Headquarters ... 15 B2
Turismo ... 16 C4

SIGHTS & ACTIVITIES
Capela dos Ossos ... (see 20)
Casa Cordovil ... 17 E4
Convento dos Lóios ... (see 36)
Ermida de São Brás ... 18 D6
Galeria das Damas ... (see 26)
Igreja da Nossa Senhora da Graça ... 19 D4
Igreja de São Francisco ... 20 C4
Igreja de São João ... 21 D3
Igreja do Carmo ... 22 D4
Incoming Alentejo ... (see 13)
Largo da Porta de Moura ... 23 D4
Mendes & Murteira ... 24 B3
Museu de Évora ... 25 D3
Palácio de Dom Manuel ... 26 C5
Palácio dos Duques de Cadaval ... (see 28)
Praça do Giraldo ... 27 C4
Salas de Exposição do Palácio ... 28 D2
Sé (Cathedral) ... 29 D3
Templo Romano ... 30 D3
Termas Romanas ... 31 C3
Universidade de Évora ... 32 E3

SLEEPING
Casa dos Teles ... 33 C4
Hotel Santa Clara ... 34 B3
Pensão O Giraldo ... 35 C4
Pousada dos Lóios ... 36 D3
Residencial Diana ... 37 D4
Residencial O Alentejo ... 38 B4
Residencial Policarpo ... 39 D3
Residencial Riviera ... 40 D3
Solar Monfalim ... 41 D4
Som das Letras ... 42 D3

EATING
Adega do Neto ... 43 C4
Aquário ... 44 D4
Botequim da Mouraria ... 45 C2
Café Alentejo ... 46 C4
Café Arcada ... 47 C3
Café Restaurante Repas ... 48 C4
Cafetaria Cozinha de Santo Humberto ... 49 C4
Casa dos Sabores ... 50 D4
Gelataria Zoka ... 51 D4
Jardim do Paço ... 52 D3
Mercado Municipal ... 53 C5
O Antão ... 54 C3
O Aqueduto ... 55 C2
Pastelaria Conventual ... 56 D4
Restaurante Cozinha de Santo Humberto ... 57 C4
Restaurante o Fialho ... 58 B2
Restaurante Taverna ... 59 C3
Snack-Bar Restaurante A Choupana ... 60 C4
Taberna Tipica Quarta-Feira ... 61 C2
Time Out ... 62 C3
Vasco da Gama Cafetaria ... 63 D3

DRINKING
Bar Amas do Cardeal ... 64 C2
Bar do Teatro ... 65 B3
Bar UÉ ... 66 D3
Capítulo 8 ... 67 C4
Cup of Joe ... 68 C3
Oficin@Bar ... 69 C4

ENTERTAINMENT
Casa dos Bonecos ... 70 F3
Eborim Centro Comercial & Cinema ... 71 D5
Praxis ... 72 D4
Sociedade Harmonia Eborense ... (see 16)
Teatro Garcia de Rezende ... 73 B3

SHOPPING
Galeria Velharias ... 74 C4
Oficina da Terra ... 75 C4

TRANSPORT
Automóvel Club de Portugal (ACP) ... 76 C4
Bus to Camp Site ... 77 C4
Silvano Manuel Cégado ... 78 B2

Oficin@Bar (☎ 266 707 312; Rua da Moeda 27; per hr €3; 8pm-2am Mon-Fri, 9pm-2am Sat)

LAUNDRY
Lavandaria Olimpica (☎ 266 705 293; Largo dos Mercadores 6; 9.30am-1pm & 3.30-7pm Mon-Fri, 9am-1.30pm Sat) Offers next-day service.

MONEY
There are several banks with ATMs on and around Praça do Giraldo, including **Caixa de Crédito Agrícola** (Praça do Giraldo 13).

POST
Branch post office (Largo da Porta de Moura)
Main post office (Rua de Olivença)

TOURIST INFORMATION
Rota dos Vinhos headquarters (Wine Route Office; ☎ 266 746 498; Praça Joaquim António de Aguiar 20; 9.30am-12.30pm & 2-5.30pm Mon-Fri) Head here for details of a *rota dos vinhos* (wine route) through the Alentejo with *adegas* (wineries).
Turismo (tourist office; ☎ 266 702 671; Praça do Giraldo 73; 9am-7pm Mon-Fri, 9.30am-12.30pm & 2-5.30pm Sat & Sun May-Sep, 9.30am-12.30pm & 2-5.30pm Oct-Apr) Has a *Historical Itineraries* leaflet (€1.05) and a range of free publications – town map, a spiral tourist guide and the useful *Viva por Cá,* a glossy listings guide.

TRAVEL AGENCIES
Abreu (☎ 266 769 180; Rua da Misericórdia 16)
Policarpo (☎ 266 746 970; Rua 5 de Outubro 63)

Sights
PRAÇA DO GIRALDO
This **square** has seen some potent moments in Portuguese history, including the 1483 execution of Fernando, Duke of Bragança; the public burning of victims of the Inquisition in the 16th century; and fiery debates on agrarian reform in the 1970s. Nowadays it's still the city focus, hosting less dramatic activities such as sitting in the sun and coffee drinking.

The narrow lanes to the southwest were once Évora's *judiaria* (Jewish quarter). To the northeast, Rua 5 de Outubro, climbing to the *sé* (cathedral), is lined by handsome town houses wearing wrought-iron balconies, while side alleys pass beneath Moorish-style arches.

SÉ

Évora's **cathedral** (Largo do Marquês de Marialva; admission €1; ⌚ 9am-12.30pm & 2-5pm) looks like a fortress, with two stout granite towers. It was begun around 1186, during the reign of Sancho I, Afonso Henriques' son – there was probably a mosque here before. It was completed about 60 years later. The flags of Vasco da Gama's ships were blessed here in 1497.

You enter the cathedral through a portal flanked by 14th-century stone apostles, flanked in turn by asymmetrical towers and crowned by 16th-century roofs. Inside, the Gothic influence takes over. The chancel, remodelled when Évora became the seat of an archdiocese, represents the only significant stylistic change since the cathedral was completed. Golden light filters through the window across the space.

The cool **cloister** (admission with cathedral & museum €3; ⌚ 9am-noon & 2-4.30pm Tue-Sun) is an early-14th-century addition. Downstairs are the stone tombs of Évora's last four archbishops. At each corner of the cloister a dark, circular staircase (at least one will be open) climbs to the top of the walls, from where there are good views.

Climb the steps in the south tower to reach the choir stalls and up to the **museum**, which demonstrates again the enormous wealth poured into the church, with fabulous ecclesiastical riches, including a revolving jewelled reliquary (containing a fragment of the true cross); encrusted with emeralds, diamonds, sapphires and rubies, it rests on gold cherubs that would dazzle Liberace, is flanked by two Ming vases and topped by Indo-Persian textiles.

MUSEU DE ÉVORA

Adjacent to the cathedral, in what used to be the archbishop's palace (built in the 16th century), is this elegant **museum** (€2; ⌚ 9.30am-12.30pm & 2-6pm Tue-Sun). Fragments of old Roman and Manueline statuary and façades line the courtyard, which has been excavated to reveal Visigothic, Roman and medieval remains. In polished rooms upstairs are former Episcopal furnishings and a gallery of Flemish paintings. Most memorable is *Life of the Virgin*, a striking 13-panel series that was originally part of the cathedral's altarpiece, created by anonymous Flemish artists, most or all of them working in Portugal around 1500.

TEMPLO ROMANO

Opposite the museum is a complete Roman **temple** (Largo do Conde de Vila Flor) dating from the 2nd or early 3rd century. It's the best-preserved Roman monument in Portugal, and probably on the Iberian Peninsula. Though it's commonly referred to as the Temple of Diana, there's no

DAM STATISTICS

The 250-sq-km Alqueva reservoir, Europe's largest, created by an enormous dam (Barragem do Alqueva) near Moura, is undeniably beautiful. But there is something strange and otherworldly about it: it's not so much a lake as drowned land, with islands poking out of the water and roads disappearing off into nowhere.

It is hoped that this huge water mass will save the arid Alentejo. One of Portugal's major agricultural regions, and its poorest, it employs a host of irrigation schemes and reservoirs to keep its soil from cracking. The most important source of water is the Rio Guadiana, which rises in Spain and flows through the Alentejo. Various agreements with Spain were meant to ensure that its waters were fairly shared. But successive droughts strained the arrangement. Although the idea for the dam was first mooted in 1957, the Portuguese finally took matters into their own hands in 1998 and started work on the giant dam to guarantee both irrigation water and electricity for years to come, flooding 2000 properties and completely rehousing one village (the now strangely antiseptic Luz), all of which cost €1.7 billion.

Critics say that the dam may not even fulfil its remit, that irrigation schemes will be vastly expensive, that it is an ecological disaster, and that ancient rock art has been enveloped in the waters. A few outfits in Évora offer boat trips out on the reservoir (p225).

Completed in 2002, the dam creates an 83km-long reservoir, with a 1100km perimeter. This is big enough to affect the climate of the surrounding region, as it increases air humidity and reduces maximum temperatures during summer. It's well worth driving to the dam for a look if you have your own transport. There are no buses running here.

consensus about the deity to which it was dedicated, and some archaeologists believe it may have been dedicated to Julius Caesar. How did these 14 Corinthian columns, capped with Estremoz marble, manage to survive in such good shape for some 18 centuries? The temple was apparently walled up in the Middle Ages to form a small fortress, and then used as the town slaughterhouse. It was only rediscovered late in the 19th century. Obviously these unwitting preservation techniques worked, as the imposing colonnade is stunningly complete.

TERMAS ROMANAS

Inside the entrance hall of the *câmara municipal* on Praça de Sertório are more Roman vestiges, discovered only in 1987. These impressive **Roman baths** (admission free; 9am-5.30pm Mon-Fri), which include a *laconicum* (heated room for steam baths) with a superbly preserved 9m-diameter circular pool, would have been the largest public building in Roman Évora. The complex also includes an open-air swimming pool, discovered in 1994.

IGREJA DE SÃO JOÃO & CONVENTO DOS LÓIOS

The small, fabulous **Church of St John the Evangelist** (admission €3, plus Salas de Exposição do Palácio €5; 10am-12.30pm & 2-6pm Tue-Sun), which faces the Templo Romano, wasU founded in 1485 by one Rodrigo Afonso de Melo, count of Olivença and the first governor of Portuguese Tangier, to serve as his family's pantheon. It's still privately owned, by the Duques de Cadaval, and notably well kept.

Behind its elaborate Gothic portal is a nave lined with glorious floor-to-ceiling *azulejos* (hand-painted tiles) created in 1711 by one of Portugal's best-known tile-makers, António de Oliveira Bernardes. The grates in the floor reveal a surprising underworld: you'll see a deep Moorish cistern that predates the church and an ossuary full of monks' bones. In the sacristy beyond are fragments of even earlier *azulejos*.

The former **Convento dos Lóios**, to the right of the church, has elegant Gothic cloisters topped by a Renaissance gallery. A national monument, the convent was converted into a top-end *pousada* (upmarket inn; p226) in 1965. If you want to wander around, wear your wealthy-guest expression – or have dinner at its upmarket restaurant.

PALÁCIO DOS DUQUES DE CADAVAL & SALAS DE EXPOSIÇÃO DO PALÁCIO

Just northwest of the Igreja de São João is the 17th-century façade of a much older palace and castle, as revealed by the two powerful square towers that bracket it. The **Palácio dos Duques de Cadaval** (Palace of the Dukes of Cadaval) was given to Martim Afonso de Melo, the governor of Évora, by Dom João I, and it also served from time to time as a royal residence. A section of the palace still serves as the private quarters of the de Melo family; the other main occupant is the city's highway department.

The well-proportioned 1st-floor rooms are relaxing to amble around, and form the **Salas de Exposição do Palácio** (admission €3; 10am-12.30pm & 2-5pm Tue-Sun), a well laid-out, if enigmatically labelled, collection of family portraits, early illustrated manuscripts, royal documents and 16th-century religious art.

UNIVERSIDADE DE ÉVORA

Outside the walls to the northeast is the **university**, a descendent (reopened in 1973) of the original Jesuit institution founded in 1559 (which closed when the Jesuits got shooed out by Marquês de Pombal in 1759). Inside are arched, Italian Renaissance-style courtyards, a brazilwood ceiling and beautiful *azulejos*.

THE WINE ROUTE

Wines here, particularly the reds, are fat, rich and fruity. But tasting them is much more fun than reading about them, so drop in on some wineries. The Rota dos Vinhos do Alentejo (Alentejan Wine Route) splits the region into three separate areas – the Serra de São Mamede (dark reds, full bodied, red fruit hints), Historic (around Évora, Estremoz, Borba and Monsaraz; smooth reds, fruity whites), and the Rio Guadiana (scented whites, spicy reds).

You'll see the brown signs announcing that you are on the wine trail all over the place, and can pick up the booklet that lists wineries and their details at any local tourist office. Otherwise visit the helpful **Rota dos Vinhos headquarters** (☎ 266 746 498; Praça Joaquim António de Aguiar 20, Évora; 9.30am-12.30pm & 2-5.30pm Mon-Fri).

TOWN WALLS

About one-fifth of Évora's residents live within the town's old walls, some of which are built on top of 1st-century Roman fortifications. Over 3km of 14th-century walls enclose the northern part of the old town, while the bulwarks along the southern side, such as those running through the *jardim público* (public gardens), date from the 17th century.

LARGO DA PORTA DE MOURA

The so-called **Porta de Moura** (Moor's Gate) to the inner town stands beside busy **Largo da Porta de Moura**, just southeast of the cathedral. Among several elegant mansions around the square (and contemporary with the strange-looking, globular 16th-century Renaissance fountain in the middle of it) is **Casa Cordovil**, built in Manueline-Moorish style. Across the road to the west have a look at the extraordinary knotted Manueline stone doorway of the **Igreja do Carmo**.

IGREJA DE SÃO FRANCISCO & CAPELA DOS OSSOS

Évora's best-known **church** (Praça 1 de Maio) is a tall and huge Manueline-Gothic structure, completed around 1510 and dedicated to St Francis. Exuberant nautical motifs celebrating the Age of Discoveries deck the walls and reflect the confident, booming mood of the time. It's all topped by a cross of Christ's order and dome. Legend has it that the Portuguese navigator Gil Vicente is buried here.

What draws the crowds, though, is the **Capela dos Ossos** (Chapel of Bones; admission €1; 🕑 9am-1pm & 2.30-5.30pm Mon-Fri, from 10am Sat & Sun, to 6.30pm Jul-Aug), a mesmerising *memento mori* (reminder of death). A small room behind the altar has walls and columns lined with the bones and skulls of some 5000 people. This was the solution found by 17th-century Franciscan monks for the overflowing graveyards of several dozen churches and monasteries. There's a black humour to the way the bones and skulls have been carefully arranged in patterns, and the whole effect is strangely beautiful, if not one you would want to recreate at home. Adding a final ghoulish flourish are two hanging desiccated corpses, including one of a child. An inscription over the entrance translates as: 'We bones await yours'. A great (Addams) family day out.

The entrance is to the right of the main church entrance. It costs €0.25 extra to take photos.

JARDIM PÚBLICO

For a lovely tranquil stroll, head to the light-dappled **public gardens** (with a small outdoor café) south of the Igreja de São Francisco. Inside the walls of the 16th-century **Palácio de Dom Manuel** is the **Galeria das Damas** (Ladies' Gallery), an indecisive hybrid of Gothic, Manueline, neo-Moorish and Renaissance styles. There are also frequent temporary art exhibitions.

From the town walls you can see, a few blocks to the southeast, the crenellated, pointy-topped Arabian Gothic profile of the **Ermida de São Brás** (Chapel of St Blaise), dating from about 1490. It's possibly an early project of Diogo de Boitac, considered the originator of the Manueline style.

IGREJA DA NOSSA SENHORA DA GRAÇA

Down an alley off Rua da República is the curious baroque façade of the **Igreja da Nossa Senhora da Graça** (Church of Our Lady of Grace), topped by four ungainly stone giants – as if they've strayed from a mythological tale and landed up on a religious building. An early example of the Renaissance style in Portugal is found in the cloister of the 17th-century monastery next door.

AQUEDUTO DA ÁGUA DE PRATA

Jutting into the town from the northwest is the beguilingly named **Aqueduto da Água de Prata** (Aqueduct of Silver Water), designed by Francisco de Arruda (better known for Lisbon's Tower of Belém) to bring clean water to Évora and completed in the 1530s. At the end of the aqueduct, on Rua do Cano, the neighbourhood feels like a self-contained village, with houses, shops and cafés built right into its perfect arches, as if nestling against the base of a hill.

Tours

In addition to taking one of the tours listed here, you can hire multilingual audio guides (€2) at the turismo for use on a 2.5km self-guided walk (maps provided) that takes in the town's historic sights. The audio guides are available in English, French, Spanish and Portuguese.

Agia (☎ 963 702 392; agia@iol.pt; adult/child under 12 €12/free, minimum 2 people; 🕑 10am) Agia offers daily 90-minute guided tours of Évora from outside the turismo on Praça do Giraldo.

Incoming Alentejo (☎ 266 709 000; Rua 5 de Outubro 65) This outfit offers daily tours to the megaliths near

Évora (three hours, €20), the village of Monsaraz (3½ hours, €20), and less frequently to Alqueva (3½ hours, €25), which includes a 30-minute boat ride.

Mendes & Murteira (☎ 266 739 240; www.evora-mm.pt; Rua 31 de Janeiro 15a) Operating out of the Barafunda boutique, this company offers flexible three-to four-hour tours (price negotiable) of surrounding megaliths or around the city itself with knowledgeable guides.

Policarpo (☎ 266 746 970; www.policarpo-viagens.pt; Rua 5 de Outubro 63) Policarpo organises numerous trips, including daily 2½-hour city tours on foot (€20 per person), half-day minibus tours to nearby megaliths (€20) and five-hour trips to Alqueva (€25).

Festivals & Events

Évora Classical Music Festival This four-day event (sometimes held in early July) formerly featured a strictly classical programme, but today encompasses a wide range of contemporary and world musical styles. Concerts are held at various indoor and outdoor venues in Évora.

Feira de São João Évora's biggest, bounciest annual bash, and one of the Alentejo's best country fairs is held in late June or July.

Feira dos Ramos Palm Fair is celebrated with a large market on the Friday before Palm Sunday.

Rota de Sabores Tradicionais A gastronomic festival that lasts from February to April, celebrating pork in February, soups in March and lamb in April – traditional restaurants throughout the city serve specialities accordingly.

Sleeping

In high season it's essential to book ahead.

BUDGET

Parque de campismo (☎ 266 705 190; www.orbitur.pt; adult/tent/car €4.60/4.80/4.20) flat, grassy and tree-shaded, with disabled access, Orbitur's well-equipped camping ground is 2km southwest of town. Urban Sitee bus 5 or 8 (€1.20) from Praça do Giraldo, via Avenida de São Sebastião and the bus station, goes close by.

Casa dos Teles (☎ 266 702 453; casadosteles@yahoo.com; Rua Romão Ramalho 27; s/d/apt €25/35/45) These are the best of the *quartos* (rooms in private houses) run by a gentlemanly English speaker; attractive rooms at the back overlook a tiny courtyard.

Pensão O Giraldo (☎ 266 705 833; Rua dos Mercadores 27; s with shared bathroom €25, s/d €30/40) Offering a wide range of rooms, O Giraldo is a popular, well-run place with tile floors and floral-print bedspreads; the best rooms have small balconies overlooking the town. Cheaper, smaller digs are in a nearby building.

MIDRANGE

Residencial O Alentejo (☎ 266 702 903; Rua Serpa Pinto 74; s/d/tr from €35/45/55; ❄) A pleasant spot with an old-fashioned feel, O Alentejo has a range of rooms, each with colourfully painted wooden furnishings, high ceilings and handsomely polished floors. Doors are locked at 1am.

Residencial Policarpo (☎ 266 702 424; www.pensaopolicarpo.com; Rua da Freiria de Baixo 16; s/d with shared bathroom €30/35, s/d €50/55; P) Run by the Policarpos for three generations, this hotel is housed in the splendid holiday home of a 16th-century count – the family was purged by the Pombals in the 18th century. Your stay will be more peaceful, amid painted ceilings, 17th-century *azulejos* (in room 101), carved wooden and traditionally hand-painted Alentejan furniture.

Hotel Santa Clara (☎ 266 704 141; www.hotelsantaclara.pt; Travessa da Milheira 19; s/d €63/73; P ❄) A whitewashed building tucked away in a quiet, narrow back street, this Best Western hotel has unexciting but comfortable rooms.

Residencial Diana (☎ 266 702 008; residencialdiana@mail.telepac.pt; Rua de Diogo Cão 2; s/d with shared bathroom €40/45, s/d €60/65) Diana is a good central choice, with high-ceilinged, wood-floored rooms. Drawbacks are the slightly dour décor, and rooms facing the main street are noisy.

Residencial Riviera (☎ 266 737 210; www.residencialriviera.com; Rua 5 de Outubro 49; s/d €60/70; ❄) In a great location one block from the *praça* (town square), this charming, carefully renovated place has bright rooms with wood floors, brick arched ceilings and wooden carved beds. Bathrooms are gleamingly tiled.

There are 10 converted *quintas* (estates) around Évora, including **Monte da Serralheira** (☎ 266 741 286; monteserralheira@mail.telepac.pt; 2-/4-person apt €50/85;) a big, blue-bordered farm, 4km south, offering self-catering or B&B, with horses and bikes to ride. The Dutch owner is a qualified local guide.

TOP END

Solar Monfalim (☎ 266 750 000; www.monfalimtur.pt; Largo da Misericórdia 1; s/d/tr €70/85/112; P ❄) A delightful former 16th-century mansion with elegant rooms and a lovely colonnaded terrace overlooking the square, Monfalim is the place to head for cherub-decorated beds. It's been a hotel since 1892.

Pousada dos Lóios (☎ 266 730 070; Largo do Conde de Vila Flor; recepcao.loios@pousadas.pt; d €215; ❄) Occupying the former Convento dos Lóios opposite the Templo Romano, this is one of the country's most beautiful *pousadas,* with gorgeously furnished rooms set around the pretty cloister.

Eating

Scattered around Praça do Giraldo are a handful of attractive cafés with outdoor seating – a good spot for coffee or an early evening drink.

BUDGET

Casa dos Sabores (☎ 266 701 030; Rua Miguel Bombarda 50; snacks €2-4; 🕑 8am-7pm) A sleek café with solid small wood tables, marble floors and nice sandwiches, this place sells local wine, cheese and meats here, too.

Aquário (☎ 266 785 055; Rua de Valdevinos 7; mains €5; 🕑 lunch Mon-Fri; V) This small quaint vegetarian restaurant serves beautifully prepared dishes – but just one changing lunch special per day – along with freshly squeezed juices and vegan desserts. Checked tablecloths and old stone walls add to the ambience.

Snack-Bar Restaurante A Choupana (☎ 266 704 427; Rua dos Mercadores 16; mains €5-7; 🕑 lunch & dinner Mon-Sat) This is a tiled, busy place where you can sit at a long bar on tall stools. There's a TV, lots of knick-knacks and bargain mains of the day. The next-door restaurant could be a granny's kitchen – cosy, tiled and doilied.

Café Restaurante Repas (☎ 266 708 540; Praça 1 de Maio 19; mains €5-9; 🕑 breakfast, lunch & dinner) Repas may be nothing special cuisine-wise, but its location and outdoor seating are irresistible.

Pastelaria Conventual (Rua Miguel Bombarda 56; pastries from €1; 🕑 8am-8pm) This atmospheric pastry shop serves strong coffee and sweet desserts to a largely local crowd. Try regional specialities like *toucinho da abadessa,* a kind of almond fruitcake.

Gelataria Zoka (Largo de São Vicente 14, Rua Miguel Bombarda; ice creams from €1; 🕑 8am-midnight) Zoka is heaven for ice-cream lovers and you can sit at tables on the pedestrianised street.

You can pick up fruit and vegetables at the **mercado municipal** (municipal market; Praça 1 de Maio; 🕑 8am-5pm Tue-Sun) and eat them in the adjacent *jardim público*. Or try Modelo Hypermarket, a supermarket just beyond the town limits on the road to the camp site and Alcáçovas.

MIDRANGE

Adega do Neto (☎ 266 209 916; Rua dos Mercadores 46; mains €6-7; 🕑 lunch & dinner) Cheap daily specials, such as fried chicken, *feijoada* (pork and bean casserole), are the name of the game at this small, cheerful local eatery. There are a handful of tables and counter service (great for solo travellers).

Vasco da Gama Cafetaria (Rua de Vasco da Gama 10; mains €6.50-8; 🕑 breakfast, lunch & dinner Mon-Sat) This is a popular student eatery with outdoor seating.

Café Arcada (Praça do Giraldo 10; meals €6-10; 🕑 breakfast, lunch & dinner) Always busy, this barn-sized meeting place is great for coffee, crepes and cakes – and you can sit at an outdoor table on the lovely plaza.

Restaurante Taverna (☎ 266 700 747; Travessa de Santa Marta 5; mains €6-10; 🕑 lunch & dinner Tue-Sun) Set beneath a vaulted ceiling with drawings of Évora's plazas along the stone walls, Taverna serves good traditional food (codfish, lamb stew, pork ribs) at fair prices.

Taberna Típica Quarta-Feira (☎ 266 707 530; Rua do Inverno 16; mains €6-11; 🕑 lunch & dinner Mon-Sat) A jovial spot in the heart of the Moorish quarter, this place is decked with wine jars, and has robust cuisine, with hearty pork dishes and regional daily specials.

Café Alentejo (☎ 266 706 296; Rua do Raimundo 5; mains €10-13; 🕑 lunch & dinner Mon-Sat) With arched rooms painted in pale gold and red, and blues forming the soundtrack, this is an appealing, relaxed restaurant, with well-spaced tables and traditional Alentejan specialities, featuring lots of bread, coriander and garlic.

O Aqueduto (☎ 266 706 373; Rua do Cano 13a; mains €10-14; 🕑 lunch Tue-Sun, dinner Tue-Sat) A cut above the rest, this much-recommended restaurant offers inspiring food that has won prizes, and service to match.

TOP END

Time Out (☎ 266 107 242; Rua de Burgos 6; mains €8-13; 🕑 dinner) A tiny sushi restaurant with a trim and colourful look, Time Out serves a wide variety of Japanese bites. Reservations are recommended.

O Antão (☎ 266 706 459; Rua João de Deus 5; mains €10-14; 🕑 lunch & dinner Thu-Tue) With a white, arched, leafy interior, this restaurant offers beautifully cooked rural showpieces, such as rabbit Alentejana (cooked with clams) or duck rice, and has won prizes for its cuisine.

Restaurante Cozinha de Santo Humberto (☎ 266 704 251; Rua da Moeda 39; mains €9-15; 🕑 lunch Fri-Tue, dinner Fri-Wed) This is a traditional, long-established place, in a grand arched, whitewashed cellar hung with brass and ceramics. It offers a big menu of regional fare – try the hearty, inventive *carne de porco com amêijoas* (pork and clams). There is a nearby café serving similar (but lighter) bites with seats on the *praça*.

Restaurante O Fialho (☎ 266 703 079; Travessa dos Mascarenhas 16; mains €12-17; 🕒 lunch & dinner Mon-Sat) Smallish with wood panelling and white tablecloths, this restaurant manages to be both smart and relaxed, and is the kind of place people talk of in awed tones.

Botequim da Mouraria (☎ 266 746 775; Rua da Mouraria 16a; mains €14; 🕒 lunch Mon-Sat) Poke around the old Moorish quarter to find this small cosy spot that serves some of Évora's finest food. They don't take reservations, and there are no tables – just stools at the counter.

Jardim do Paço (☎ 266 744 300; Jardim de Diana; mains €11-16, dinner for two €40-65; 🕒 lunch Tue-Sun, dinner Tue-Sat) Beside Igreja de São João, in the former garden of the Palácio dos Duques de Cadaval, this is a lovely setting amid orange trees – or there is an indoor hall decorated with wedding-reception chic.

Drinking

Most bars open late and don't close until at least 2am (4am at weekends). There are no cover charges at these places.

Bar do Teatro (Praça Joaquim António de Aguiar; 🕒 8pm-2am) Next to the theatre, this small, inviting bar has high ceilings and old-world décor that sees a friendly mixed crowd pass through most nights. Music tends toward lounge and electronica.

Capítulo 8 (Rua do Raimundo 8; 🕒 10pm-2am) A stylish newcomer to the Évora scene, this bar has atmospheric lighting and walls lined with wooden masks. It attracts a slightly trendier crowd.

Oficin@Bar (☎ 266 707 312; Rua da Moeda 27; 🕒 8pm-2am Mon-Fri, 9pm-3am Sat) Attracting all ages, this is an appealing, relaxed bar with little wooden tables in a white-arched cave-like space. It's convivial, with jazz and blues playing gently in the background.

Bar UÉ (☎ 266 706 612; Rua de Diogo Cão 21; 🕒 Mon-Sat) At the Associação de Estudantes da Universidade de Évora, this is the main central student hang-out, with a nice owner and great outdoor drinking area – relaxing in the day, and like an outdoor party in the evening. They occasionally have karaoke.

Bar Amas do Cardeal (☎ 266 721 133; Rua Amas do Cardeal 4a; 🕒 10pm-3am) Popular, darkly lit and weirdly decorated, this bar attracts a chilled, eclectic crowd for post-1am drinking, and weekend dancing on the small dance floor. Regular DJs play cool and funky house.

Cup of Joe (Praça de Sertório 3; mains €3.50-5; 🕒 noon-2am) Part of a coffee chain, this attractive café has peaceful outdoor seating overlooking a plaza, and a good mix of lighter fare – crepes (savoury and sweet), salads, wraps and plenty of caffeine on hand. Electronic music and a friendly cocktail-sipping crowd arrives by night.

Entertainment

For theatre, film, concerts and art expositions, stop in at the imaginative cultural centre **Sociedade Harmonia Eborense** (☎ 266 746 874; Praça do Giraldo 72) to see what's on.

NIGHTCLUBS

Praxis (☎ 266 707 505; Rua de Valdevinos; 🕒 midnight-6am) Still the favoured destination for most students in town, Praxis has one big dance floor, one small dance floor and DJs spinning house, R&B and hip-hop. It's a lively, good-time crowd that doesn't get busy until around 2am.

CINEMA

Eborim Centro Comercial (☎ 266 703 068; Rua do Eborim) This is home to the town's cinema.

THEATRE & PUPPET THEATRE

Casa dos Bonecos (☎ 266 703 112; tickets €3, children's matinees €2) Five actors from the grand municipal Teatro Garcia de Resende studied for several years with the only surviving master of a traditional rural puppetry style called *bonecos de Santo Aleixo* (Santo Aleixo puppets). They perform this, other styles, and hand-puppet shows for children, at this little theatre off Largo de Machede Velho.

SPORT

Évora has a *praça de touros* (bullring) outside the southern walls, near the *jardim público*. Three to four bullfights take place between May and October.

Shopping

Rua 5 de Outubro has rows of *artesanatos* (handicrafts shops) selling pottery, knick-knacks and cork products of every kind – postcards, wine bottles, hats, shoes, even umbrellas made of cork. The shady side of the *mercado municipal* (municipal market)

THE ALENTEJO

is a good spot for finding cheaper pottery. There are more upmarket shops along Rua Cândido dos Reis, northwest of the centre. On the second Tuesday of each month a vast open-air market, with everything from shoes to sheep's cheese, sprawls across the big Rossio de São Brás, just outside the walls on the road to the train station.

Oficina da Terra (☎ 266 746 049; www.oficinadaterra.com; Rua do Raimundo 51a; 🕑 10am-7pm Mon-Fri, to 3pm Sat) If you're lucky you'll see the resident artist in action at this imaginative and award-winning handicraft and clay-figure workshop and gallery.

Galeria Velharias (Rua da Moeda 46) This small charming shop sells lace, bric-a-brac, old bullfighting photos and antiques.

Antique market (Largo do Chão das Covas; 🕑 8am-2pm) A wide assortment of trash and treasure can be found at this market held near the aqueduct on the second Sunday of each month.

Getting There & Away

BUS

The **bus station** (☎ 266 769 410) is off Avenida de São Sebastião. Note that there can be a real difference in the time you take to get to Lisbon, depending on which bus you board.

Destination	Price*	Duration*	Frequency (daily)
Beja	€7.80	1½hr	3-5
Coimbra (via Santarém)	€12.80	4½hr	2-6
Elvas	€5.50/9	2¼/1¼hr	2-4
Estremoz	€3.60/7	1½hr/30min	6-14
Faro (via Albufeira)	€12.70	5¼hr	2
Lisbon	€10.50/6.20	4/2hr	18-26
Portalegre	€6/8.90	2½/1½hr	3
Reguengos de Monsaraz	€3/6	1¼/¾hr	3-4
Vila Viçosa	€4.60/6.70	1½/1hr	3

* normal/express

TRAIN

The **Évora station** (☎ 266 742 336), 600m south of the Jardim Público, is on a branch of the Lisbon–Funcheira (via Beja) train line. There are daily trains to/from Lisbon (€10.20 2½ hours, five daily) with a change at Casa Branca. Trains also go to/from Setúbal (€8, 2¼ hours, five daily), Lagos (€20.66, five hours, two daily) and Faro (€19.80, 4½ hours, two daily).

Getting Around

CAR & BICYCLE

If you want to rent a car, get in touch with Abreu or Policarpo (p222).

Évora has a branch of the **Automóvel Club de Portugal** (ACP; ☎ 266 707 533; fax 266 709 696; Alcárcova de Baixo 7).

You can rent a bike from **Silvano Manuel Cégado** (☎ 266 703 434; Rua Cândido dos Reis 66; per day €10; 🕑 9am-7pm Mon-Fri, to 1pm Sat) or from **Bike Lab** (☎ 266 735 500; bikelab@mail.telepac.pt; Centro Comercial da Vista Alegre, Lote 14; per day €8-15), 800m northwest of the centre, which also offers guided bike tours.

TAXI

If you want a **taxi** (☎ 266 734 734) you'll find them waiting in Praça do Giraldo and Largo da Porta de Moura. On a weekday you can expect to pay about €3.50 (€5 with baggage) from the train station to Praça do Giraldo.

AROUND ÉVORA

Megaliths – derived from the Ancient Greek for 'big stones' – are found all over the ancient landscape that surrounds Évora. Such prehistoric structures, built around 5000 to 6000 years ago, dot the European Atlantic coast, but here in Alentejo there are an astounding amount of Neolithic remains. Dolmens (Neolithic stone tombs, or *antas* in Portuguese) were probably temples and/or tombs, covered with a large flat stone and usually built on hilltops or near water. Menhirs (individual standing stones) point to fertility rites – as phallic as skyscrapers, if on a smaller scale – while *cromeleques* (cromlechs, stone circles) were also places of worship.

Évora's turismo sells a *Historical Itineraries* leaflet (€1.05) that details many sites. Also on offer is the *Guide du Mégalithisme d'Évora*, in French, which contains maps, routes and background information. Dolmen devotees can buy the book *Paisagens Arqueologicas A Oeste de Évora*, which has English summaries. The turismo and the Museu de Évora also sell an English-language video, *Megalithic Enclosures*.

You can see more megaliths around Reguengos de Monsaraz, Elvas and Castelo de Vide.

ARRAIOLOS: THE GREAT CARPETS OF PORTUGAL

About 20km north of Évora, the small town of Arraiolos is famed for its exquisite *tapetes* (carpets). These hand-woven works show a marked influence from Persian rugs, and they have been in production here since the 12th century. It seems half the town is involved in this artistry, and on a casual stroll through town, you'll probably encounter half a dozen people stitching in front of their homes. Rug patterns are based on abstract motifs, *azulejo* designs or flower, bird or animal depictions. Shops are abundant, and you can pay anything from €50 for a tiny runner to €2000 for the most beautiful pieces, which feature more elaborate designs.

The village itself dates from the 2nd or 3rd century BC, and is laid out along traditional lines, with whitewashed blue-trimmed houses topped with terracotta roofs and the ruins of a castle overlooking town.

Take a peak at the centuries-old dye chambers in the main square, which is also where you'll find the **turismo** (☎ 266 490 254). There are cafés in town for lingering, and a flashy **pousada** (☎ 266 419 340; www.pousadas.pt; d €200) just outside Arraiolos.

CROMELEQUE DOS ALMENDRES

From Guadalupe a dirt track winds through a beautiful landscape of olive and cork trees to the Cromeleque dos Almendres (Almendres Cromlech). This huge, spectacular oval of standing stones, 15km west of Évora, is the Iberian Peninsula's most important megalithic group and an extraordinary place to visit.

The site consists of a huge oval of some 95 rounded granite monoliths – some of which are engraved with symbolic markings – spread down a rough slope. They were erected over different periods, it seems with geometric and astral consideration, probably for social gatherings or sacred rituals. The setting itself is magnificent.

Just off the dirt track en route to the *cromeleque* you can follow a short path to the solitary **Menir dos Almendres**, a single stone about 4m high, with some very faint carvings near the top.

ANTA GRANDE DO ZAMBUJEIRO

The Anta Grande do Zambujeiro (Great Dolmen of Zambujeiro), 13km soutwest of Évora, is a national monument and Europe's largest dolmen. Under a huge sheet-metal shelter in a field of wildflowers and yellow broom are seven stones, each 6m high, forming a huge chamber, more than 50m in diameter. Archaeologists removed the capstone in the 1960s. Most of the site's relics – potsherds, beads, flint tools and so on – are in the Museu de Évora.

ANTA CAPELA DE SÃO BRISSOS

Built in the 17th century from the surviving stones of an *anta*, this thick-walled whitewashed **chapel** is an unusual example of megalithic remains being recycled for Christian use, indicating acknowledgement of the stones' religious significance. It's an endearing sight, with tubby rounded walls and a curved tiled roof. It's beside the Valverde–N2 road (just beyond the turn-off to São Brissos).

GRUTA DO ESCOURAL

About 2km east of the village of Santiago do Escoural (25km west of Évora) is a bat-filled **cave** (☎ 266 857 000; admission €2.50; 9am-noon & 1.30-5.30pm Tue-Sun, 1.30-5.30pm Mon) with twisted rocks inside, adorned with Palaeolithic and Neolithic rock art, including a few faint ochre and black drawings of bison and engravings of horses, dating back 10,000 to 30,000 years.

Getting There & Away

There are no convenient buses to this area so your only option is to rent a car or bike (note that about 5km of the route is rough and remote). Alternatively, you can take a guided trip (p225) or you could hire a taxi for the day (€50).

With your own wheels, head west from Évora on the old Lisbon road (N114) for 10km, then turn south for 2.8km to Guadalupe. Follow the signs from here to the Cromeleque dos Almendres (4.3km).

Return to Guadalupe and head south for 5km to Valverde, home of the Universidade de Évora's school of agriculture and the 16th-century Convento de Bom Jesus. Following the signs to Anta Grande do Zambujeiro, turn into the school's farmyard and onto a badly potholed track. After 1km you'll see the Great Dolmen.

Continue west from Valverde for 12km. Before joining the N2, turn right for the cave at Santiago do Escoural.

ÉVORAMONTE

pop 700 / elevation 474m

Northeast of Évora, this sleepy hilltop village with its quaint 16th-century castle makes a fine detour on your way through the region. There are fine views all around across the low hills. A small turismo is just beyond the castle.

The **castle** (admission €1.50; 10am-1pm year-round, 2-5pm Oct-May & 2.30-6.30pm Jun-Sep) dates from 1306, but was rebuilt after the 1531 earthquake. Exterior stone carving shows unwarlike small bows, the symbol of the Bragança family – the knot symbolises fidelity. The interior is neatly restored, with impressively meaty columns topped by a sinuous arched ceiling on each cavernous floor. The roof provides sweeping panoramas.

You can stay at **A Convenção** (268 959 217; Rua de Santa Maria 26; d without/with terrace €35/45), where the two rooms – particularly the one with a terrace – have fantastic views from this peaceful spot.

It's also an unexpectedly smart **restaurant** (mains €8-12; Sun-Tue) with indoor-outdoor seating and views matched by good traditional specialities.

Nearby are also some attractive rural tourism options, including **Monte da Fazenda** (268 959 172) and **Quinta do Serafim** (268 959 360), both of which have doubles from around €75.

Two buses a day stop in Évoramonte from Évora (€1.20, 30 minutes), though it's a long uphill walk (1km) from the bus stop to the castle.

SÃO PEDRO DO CORVAL

Known for its fine pottery traditions, this tiny village, 5km east of Reguengos de Monsaraz, has dozens of workshops where you can see the artists in action and purchase a few fine pieces.

You'll have lots of choice – plain terracotta and bright rustic-patterned plates, pots, jugs, candlesticks and floor tiles. It's one of Portugal's largest pottery centres, and is cheap and cheerful rather than rare and refined. A good place to start is the reasonably priced **O Patalim** (266 549 117; 8.30am-noon & 1-7pm).

Buses between Reguengos and Monsaraz stop here.

REGUENGOS DE MONSARAZ

pop 11,300 / elevation 200m

This small working-class town once famous for its sheep and wool production is a stopping point and transport hub for Monsaraz. It's also close to the pottery centre of São Pedro do Corval as well as to an impressive half-dozen dolmens and menhirs (out of around 150 scattered across the surrounding plains). While you're here, try some of the great local red wine, Terras d'El Rei.

The rocket-like local church (built in 1887) was designed by José António Dias da Silva, who was also responsible for Praça de Touros, the Lisbon bullring.

Orientation

The town's focal point is Praça da Liberdade, 200m northeast of the bus station.

Information

Espaço Internet (266 519 424; Rua do Conde de Monsaraz 32; 10am-8pm Mon-Fri, 10am-1pm & 2-6pm Sat, 2-6pm Sun) About 100m northwest of the *praça*. Free internet access.

Turismo (266 503 315; Rua 1 de Maio; 9am-12.30pm & 2-5.30pm Mon-Fri, from 10am Sat & Sun) Just off the *praça*. On sale is *A Short Trip in the Alentejo* (€6.25) by locally based, award-winning novelist Robert Wilson. It's a useful detailed guide to parts of the eastern Alentejo.

Sights

There are several wineries around Reguengos, including the acclaimed **Herdade do Esporão** (266 509 280; esporao@mail.telepac.pt), 7km south of town. Operating as a winery for seven centuries, with some lovely old wine cellars, it produces mostly red wines for the domestic market. It has a wine bar, restaurant and wine shop.

Sleeping & Eating

Casa da Palmeira (266 502 362; fax 266 502 513; Praça de Santo António 1; s/d with shared bathroom €15/25) A fantastic old run-down mansion 200m northwest of the main square, this place has huge rooms with high ceilings and decorative wrought-iron balconies.

Pensão O Gato (/fax 266 502 353; Praça da Liberdade 11; s/d €25/30; lunch & dinner;) This friendly guesthouse has pleasant rooms that are nicely maintained. The best have small balconies (with flower boxes) overlooking the sleepy *praça*. It's above a charming restaurant (mains €6.50 to €9) that has red and white-checked tablecloths and reliably good Alentejan cuisine.

THE ALENTEJO

Restaurante Central (☎ 266 502 219; Praça da Liberdade; mains €8.50-12) Central offers tasty Portuguese mains and keeps up a busy trade. There is a small bar-café next door with high stools, where you can choose from an array of starters, such as tasty bean or tuna salads.

Shopping

The area is rich in handicrafts, the local speciality being *mantas alentejanas* (hand-woven woollen blankets).

Tear (Loom; ☎ 266 503 710; fax 266 501 104; 9.30am-1pm & 2.30-7pm) You can watch *mantas alentejanas* being made here, and they are available for sale, along with beautiful ceramics, wickerware and hand-painted Alentejan furniture, only at this award-winning shop near the Adega de Cooperativa de Reguengos, on the road towards Monsaraz. The workshop and showroom, which has been converted from an old slaughterhouse, belongs to an association of young artisans founded to preserve local skills, but who also sprinkle the traditional with contemporary and adventurous ideas. It's 1km from town, on the road to São Pedro.

Fabrica Alentejana de Lanificios (☎ 266 502 179; 9am-5pm Mon-Fri) Apart from Tear, this is the last remaining hand-loom producer of *mantas alentejanas*, but it only produces large commissions these days (which begs the question: where do all the small versions on sale come from?). If you're interested in seeing how they are made, check it out; it's on the Mourão road east of town.

Getting There & Away

Buses run daily to Évora (€2.90/6.40 normal/express, 1¼ hours/45 minutes, three to eight daily), with connections on to Lisbon. There are also direct Lisbon services (€11.20, 2½ hours).

MONSARAZ

pop 950 / elevation 190m

Perched high over the surrounding countryside, Monsaraz is a charmingly old-fashioned village with a looming castle at its edge, great views over the winding roads and olive groves sprinkling the landscape. The narrow streets here are lined with uneven-walled cottages and stoops dotted with flat-capped men watching the day unfold, while on the main square children chase soccer balls at dusk. Aside from the great views, it's a pleasant place to relax, walk the slumbering streets and sample Alentejan cuisine.

Settled long before the Moors arrived in the 8th century, Monsaraz was subsequently recaptured by the Christians under Giraldo Sem Pavor (Gerald the Fearless) in 1167, and then given to the Knights Templar as thanks for their help.

The castle was added in 1310. Now the village prospers on tourism, with a few restaurants, guesthouses and chichi foreign-run artisan shops, but it has not lost its magic or its community feel. It's at its best as it wakes up in the morning, in the quiet of the evening, or during a wintry dusk.

Orientation

Coaches or cars have to be parked outside the walled village, so your arrival at one of the four arched entrances will be as it should be – on foot. From the main car park, the Porta da Alcoba leads directly onto the central Praça Dom Nuno Álvares Pereira.

Porta da Vila, the main entrance to Monsaraz, is at the northern end of town (the castle is at the other end) and leads into Rua São Tiago and the parallel Rua Direita, Monsaraz' two main streets.

Information

Multibanco ATM (Travessa da Misericórdia 2) Off the main square.

Turismo (☎ 266 557 136; Praça Dom Nuno Álvares Pereira; 10am-6pm) Well stocked with regional information, including bus timetables.

Sights

IGREJA MATRIZ

The parish **church** (10am-1pm & 2-6pm), near the turismo, was rebuilt after the 1755 earthquake and again a century later. Inside is an impressive nave and a 14th-century marble tomb carved with 14 saints. An 18th-century *pelourinho* (stone pillory) topped by a Manueline globe stands outside. The 16th-century **Igreja da Misericórdia** (9am-1pm & 2-6pm) is opposite.

MUSEU DE ARTE SACRA

Housed in a fine Gothic building beside the parish church, the **Museum of Sacred Art** (admission €1; 10am-1pm & 2-7pm) houses a small collection of 14th-century wooden religious figures and 18th-century vestments and silverware. Its most famous exhibit is a rare example of a 14th-century secular fresco, a charming piece showing a good and a bad judge, the latter appropriately two-faced.

CASTELO

The **castle** at the southwestern end of the village was one in the chain of Dom Dinis' defensive fortresses along the Spanish border. It's now converted into a small bullring, and its ramparts offer a fine panoramic view over the Alentejan plains.

Festivals & Events

Accommodation must be booked far in advance at these times.

Bullfights If you want to see a bullfight, Easter Sunday is a good time to visit.

Music festival Monsaraz heaves with jollity during its week-long Museu Aberto (Open Museum) music festival, held in July on even-numbered years.

Festa de Nossa Senhora dos Passos Bullfights and processions feature in this festival on the second weekend of September.

Sleeping

Many villagers have converted their ancient cottages to guesthouses or self-catering apartments. Unless otherwise mentioned, all the following rates include breakfast. Each place also has cable TV. It's essential to book ahead in high season.

BUDGET

Casa Modesta (☎ 266 557 388; www.inoxnet.com; Rua Direita 5; s/d from €25/35) A charming option, this place has high ceilings, tile floors, traditional blue hand-painted furniture and flower boxes in the windows. It's run by a welcoming family who also have a café downstairs.

Casa Paroquial (☎ 266 557 101; Rua Direita; s/d €30/35) This is a welcoming place, with a friendly atmosphere in a family house, and the rooms and breakfasts are nice too.

MIDRANGE & TOP END

Casa Pinto (☎ 266 557 388; Praça Dom Nuno Álvares Pereira 10; d with/without view €50/40) Opposite the church, this pretty place has five comfortable rooms with nice wood furnishings and slate floors. There's also a breezy roof terrace with fine views.

Casa Dona Antónia (☎ 266 557 142; www.casadantonia-monsaraz.com; Rua Direita 15; d €40-50, ste €60) Accommodation in Dona Antónia's place means four neat, large, comfy rooms; the suite is huge and includes a terrace.

Casa Dom Nuno (☎ 266 557 146; fax 266 557 400; Rua José Fernandes Caeiro 6; d €55) One of several very fine Turihab properties (a government scheme for marketing private accommodation), this place has eight elegant doubles offering superb terrace views.

Estalagem de Monsaraz (☎ 266 557 112; www.estalagemdemonsaraz.com; Largo São Bartolomeu 5; s/d €63/84; ✖ 🏊) Outside the village walls, this atmospheric place has handsomely decorated rooms with dark-wood furniture and shuttered windows opening onto glorious views. There's a restaurant, a pool, a playground and open fires in winter.

Monte Alerta (☎ 266 550 150; fax 266 557 325; Telheiro; s/d €65/85; 🏊) This gorgeous example is one of several rural alternatives close by. It's a beautifully converted, blue-bordered *quinta* and though only 2.5km from Monsaraz at Telheiro it feels wonderfully remote. In spring it's surrounded by wildflowers. Inside are family antiques and eight spacious doubles; outside are wind chimes, gardens and horses.

Convento da Orada (☎ 266 557 414; convento@conventodaorada.com; s/d €70/90) Under the same management as the Estalagem, this beautiful, large remote convent with the atmosphere of a retreat (with satellite TV) is 2km from Monsaraz and only a couple of kilometres from a lake. It also houses the new museum in Telheiro and now neighbours the Cromeleque do Xerez (p234). There's a huge stork's nest on the roof, also inhabited by smaller birds – like a birds' block of flats.

Eating

Monsaraz has a handful of restaurants, all offering traditional Alentejan mains such as *borrego assado* (roast lamb). All close by 9pm.

Café Restaurante O Alcaide (☎ 266 557 168; Rua São Tiago 15; mains €7-10; 🕒 lunch & dinner Thu-Tue) This is Monsaraz' best restaurant. It is relatively smart, and you'll find good grilled fish here as well as lovely sunset views over the plains.

Café-Restaurante Lumumba (☎ 266 557 121; Rua Direita 12; mains €6.50-8.50; 🕒 lunch & dinner) A popular place, Lumumba has a great local atmosphere that's rare in the local restaurants. TV forms a backdrop – it's a good place to watch football.

A Casa do Forno (☎ 266 557 190; Travessa da Sanabrosa; mains €7-12; 🕒 lunch & dinner Tue-Sat) Food is fairly unexciting here, but the ambience is nice – an airy spot with a cool terrace.

Restaurante São Tiago (☎ 266 557 188; Rua São Tiago 3; mains €7-9; 🕒 lunch & dinner Thu-Tue) Close to O Alcaide, this is a lively venue with its own bar.

There are also a couple of cafés, including **Casa Modesta** (Rua Direita 11) with a patio and **Pastelaria Cisterna** (Rua Direita 25). Self-catering options are limited to bread and cheese from a **grocery shop** (Rua São Tiago 29) at the Porta da Vila end of the street and wines from **Castas & Castiços** (São Thiago 31; ⌚ 10am-6pm Tue-Sun), next door.

Getting There & Away

Buses run to/from Reguengos de Monsaraz (€2.30, 35 minutes, four daily on weekdays). The last bus back to Reguengos, where you can pick up connections to Évora, is around 5.15pm.

AROUND MONSARAZ

Neolithic megaliths are scattered throughout the landscape around Monsaraz – it is great to explore and discover these (they're signposted, but finding each one is an adventure) amid the tangles of olive groves and open fields of wildflowers. Most spectacular is **Cromeleque do Xerez**, which once stood 5km south of Monsaraz but was moved before flooding by the massive Barragem do Alqueva. The ensemble, including the triumphant seven-tonne menhir at its centre, forms part of the **Museu de Arqueologia** (☎ 266 557 414; admission free; ⌚ 9am-5pm Tue-Sat) in Telheiro (1.5km north of Monsaraz inside the Convento da Orada). A remaining highlight is the Menhir de Bulhoa, another phallic stone with intriguing carved circles and lines, 4km north of Monsaraz off the Telheiro–Outeiro road. A sketch map of several other accessible megaliths is available at the Reguengos **turismo** (☎ 266 557 136; Praça Dom Nuno Álvares Pereira; ⌚ 10am-6pm).

THE ALENTEJO

ESTREMOZ

pop 9000 / elevation 420m

Along with neighbouring Borba and Vila Viçosa, Estremoz is one of the region's well-known marble towns. Because there is so much fine marble in this region – rivalling that in Carrara, Italy – it's used all over the place: even the cobbles are rough chunks of marble.

Ringed by an old protective wall, Estremoz has an attractive centre set with peaceful plazas, orange tree–lined lanes and a hilltop castle and convent. It's a simple provincial town, with lots of elderly folk and shops selling farm tools, though visitors can also load up on earthenware pottery, preserved plums and goat's cheese – all of which are available at the great market that fills the huge central square on Saturday.

Orientation

The lower, newer part of town, enclosed by 17th-century ramparts, is arranged around a huge square, Rossio Marquês de Pombal (known simply as 'the Rossio'). Here you'll find most accommodation, restaurants and shops. A 10-minute climb west of the Rossio brings you to the old quarter, with its 13th-century castle (now a luxurious *pousada*) and keep.

The bus station is by the disused train station, 400m east of the Rossio.

Information

Caixa Geral de Depósitos Bank (☎ 268 339 710; Rossio Marquês de Pombal 43)
Centro de saúde (medical centre; ☎ 268 332 042; Avenida 9 de Abril) At the northeastern end of town.
Cybercafé (Rossio; ⌚ 2-8pm Tue-Sun) Free internet access inside the Centro Ciência Viva.
Police station (☎ 268 334 141) In the *câmara municipal*.
Post office (Rua 5 de Outubro; ⌚ 9am-6pm Mon-Fri) Has NetPost.
Turismo (☎ 268 333 541; fax 268 334 010; Largo da República; ⌚ 9.30am-12.30pm & 2-6pm)

Sights

LOWER TOWN

On the fringes of the Rossio are imposing old churches, former convents and, just north of the Rossio, monastic buildings converted into cavalry barracks. Opposite these, by Largo General Graça, is a marble-edged water tank, called the **Lago do Gadanha** (Lake of the Scythe) after its scythe-wielding statue of Neptune. Some of the prettiest marble streets in town are south of the Rossio, off Largo da República.

Museu de Arte Sacra

Overlooking the Rossio is the floridly bell-towered 17th-century **Convento dos Congregados**, which now leads a double life housing the police station, *câmara municipal* and the **Museu de Arte Sacra** (admission €1; ⌚ 9.30am-noon & 2.30-5.30pm), with stately 17th- to 18th-century ecclesiastical silverware and religious statues. You also get to see the restored marble church and, best of all, a rooftop view from the bell towers themselves. The stairway to the top is lined with *azulejos*.

UPPER TOWN

The upper town is surrounded by dramatic zigzagging ramparts and contains a gleaming white palace. The easiest way to reach it

on foot is to follow narrow Rua da Frandina from Praça Luís de Camões and pass the inner castle walls through the Arco da Frandina.

Royal Palace & Torre das Três Coroas

At the top of the upper town is the stark, glowing-white, fortress-like former royal palace, now the Pousada de Santa Rainha Isabel (p236).

Dom Dinis built the palace in the 13th century for his new wife, Isabel of Aragon. After her death in 1336 (Dinis had died 11 years earlier) it was used as an ammunition dump. An inevitable explosion, in 1698, destroyed most of the palace and the surrounding castle, though in the 18th century João V restored the palace for use as an armoury. The 27m-high keep, the Torre das Três Coroas (Tower of the Three Crowns), survived and is still the dominant feature. It's so-called because it was apparently built by three kings: Sancho II, Afonso III and Dinis.

Visitors are welcome to view the public areas of the *pousada* and climb the keep, which offers a superb panorama of the old town and surrounding plains. The holes at the keep's edges were channels for boiling oil – a good way of getting rid of uninvited guests.

Capela de Santa Isabel

This richly adorned **chapel** (admission free; 9am-11.30pm & 2-5pm Tue-Sun May-Sep) behind the keep was built in 1659. The narrow stairway up to the chapel, and the chapel itself, are lined with

USING YOUR MARBLES

The marble towns gleam with rosy-gold or white stone, but the effect is enhanced by the houses, which have a Hollywood-smile brightness. As if locals hadn't found enough uses for the stone stuff, with their marble doorsteps, pavements and shoes (OK, we made that last one up) a convoluted process has been cooked up to create marble paint: marble is recrystallised limestone, so if you heat marble chips in a clay oven for three days they turn into calcium oxide which is mixed with water to become whitewash. Cheaper than paint. People take pride in their houses' whiteness and retouch them annually.

While we're on the subject of colour, apparently the yellow borders keep away fever, while blue is the bane of flies (you can add these colours to the oxide). The blue theory may have some truth, or at least international adherents – in Rajasthan (India) local people also apply pale blue to their houses to ward off mosquitoes.

18th-century *azulejos*, most of them featuring scenes from the saintly queen's life.

Isabel was famously generous to the poor, despite her husband's disapproval. According to one legend the king once demanded to see what she was carrying in her skirt; she let go of her apron and the bread she had hidden to donate to the poor was miraculously transformed into roses.

To visit the chapel, ask for the custodian at the Museu Municipal.

Museu Municipal

This **museum** (☎ 268 339 200; adult/child €1.50/0.90; 🕓 9am-12.30pm & 2-5.30pm Tue-Sun) is housed in a beautiful 17th-century almshouse near the former palace. Pretty hand-painted furniture sits alongside endearing, locally carved wooden figures (charming rural scenes by Joaquim Velhinho) and a collection of typical 19th-century domestic Alentejan items. On the ground floor is an amazing display of the unique Estremoz pottery figurines – some 500 pieces covering 200 years, including lots of ladies with carnivalesque outfits, explosively floral headdresses and wind-rippled dresses. There's even an entire 19th-century Easter Parade.

Festivals & Events

The town's biggest event is the **Feira Internacional de Artesenato e Agro-Pecuária de Estremoz** (Fiape), a baskets, ceramics, vegetables and livestock bonanza, held for several days at the end of April in an open-air market area east of the bus station.

Sleeping

Residencial O Gadanha (☎ 268 339 110; Largo General Graça, 56; s/d €20/30) A splendid bargain, this sprightly little whitewashed house has bright, fresh, white and clean renovated rooms that overlook the square.

Residencial Carvalho (☎ 268 339 370; fax 268 322 370; Largo da República 27; s/d from €20/40) This simple place is decent value for its bright, spacious doubles (and smaller singles) with polished floors.

Pensão-Restaurante Mateus (☎ 268 322 226; Rua do Almeida 41; s €15-20, d €30-35) In an old house, Mateus is a cheerful spot offering a range of rooms: the best are spacious and tidy, the worst rather gloomy.

Café Alentejano (☎ 268 337 300; Rossio 14; s/d/tw €25/35/40) Facing the *praça*, this place has small attractive rooms with wooden floors and hand-painted Alentejan furniture; some rooms have views over the square. Bathrooms are elaborately marble-filled. It also has a café.

Hospedaria Dom Dinis (☎ 268 332 717; Rua 31 de Janeiro 46; s/d €25/35; ❄) This clean, friendly place has carpeted rooms in good shape. Some have big windows and others small verandas.

Monte dos Pensamentos (☎ 268 333 166; montedospensamentos@yahoo.com; Estrada da Estação do Ameixal; d from €60; 🏊) This lovely manor house offers pretty, traditionally furnished rooms in an idyllic setting 2km west of Estremoz. There's a pool surrounded by orange groves and mountain bikes for hire.

Pousada de Santa Rainha Isabel (☎ 268 332 075; recepcao.staisobel@pousadas.pt; d €250; ❄ 🏊) In the restored former palace, this lavish pousada offers spacious rooms with antique furnishings and views over the Alentejo plains. There are lovely palace gardens, a pool with views and common areas set with museum-quality tapestries.

Páteo dos Solares (☎ 268 338 400; www.pateosolares.com; Rua Brito Capelo; s/d from €140/150; ❄ 🏊) This converted bread factory – which is far more impressive than you might imagine – now houses a sumptuous guesthouse, partly situated on the old city walls. The rooms are quite comfortable and the attractive sitting room, spacious terrace and pool add to the appeal. There's also a smart restaurant here.

Eating

D Tea (Rua 31 de Janeiro 30; snacks from €3; 10am-midnight) This trim modern café is a popular student hangout; in addition to coffee and changing artwork, you'll find crepes, waffles and a tempting ice-cream display.

Café Alentejano (268 337 300; Rossio 14; mains €6.50-11; lunch & dinner) Packed with country folk throughout the week – particularly on market day – this is a pleasant café with outdoor tables facing the square. Upstairs a wood-floored, white-tablecloth restaurant offers heartier traditional fare. There are rooms upstairs.

Adega do Isaías (268 322 318; Rua do Almeida 21; mains €8-14; lunch & dinner Mon-Sat) To enter this award-winning, rustic *tasca* (tavern), you'll pass by a sizzling outdoor grill (cooking up tender fish, meat and Alentejan specialities), and enter into a cool cellar-like ambience – communal bench tables and huge bulbous wine jars, from which your wine is served.

Gastronomia do Monte (268 083 196; Rua Narciso Ribeiro 7; €7-8.50; lunch & dinner Mon-Fri) In a pleasant arched dining room decorated with rugs and black-and-white photos, this friendly spot serves up big portions of *bacalhau* (salt cod) and tasty regional fare.

São Rosas (268 333 345; Largo de Dom Dinis; mains €12-17; lunch & dinner Tue-Sun) White tablecloths under whitewashed arches equal rustic meets smart, and the food is great, featuring some unusual starters (such as smoked salmon and buttery, garlic-covered clams), pork and clams, and gaspacho in summer. It's just near the former palace.

O Figo (268 324 529; Rua Restauração; mains €4-11; lunch & dinner Tue-Sun) In the functional back room of a café, O Figo serves up Alentejan comfort food such as *bacalhau à brás* (salt-cod fried with onions and potatoes) among other specialities.

Drinking

Reguengo Bar (Rua Serpa Pinta 126; 8am-2am) This big barnlike space on the edge of the town walls is where Estremoz' youth kick their heels up. Live bands play most Friday nights.

Até Jazz Café (Rua Serpa Pinta 65) This cosy bar delivers a varied schedule of jazz or *fado* most weekends.

Shopping

The weekly Saturday market held along the southern fringe of the Rossio provides a great display of Alentejan goodies and Estremoz specialities, from goat's- and ewe's-milk cheeses, to a unique style of unglazed, ochre-red pots.

Casa Galileu (268 323 130; Rua Victor Cordon 16) If you miss the Saturday market, come to this great place, southeast of the Rossio. It has a fine collection of locally made ceramic figurines, as well as other essentials such as flat caps and cowbells.

Artesanato Santo André (268 333 360; Rua da Misericórdia 2) Hardly bigger than a breadbox, this charming shop is packed to the rafters with ceramic figurines and some pretty pieces of china.

Bonecos de Estremoz (268 339 200; Rua do Arco de Santarém 4) If you're after contemporary, Estremoz-style ceramic figurines, visit this workshop near the Museu Municipal.

Getting There & Around

Car rental is available at **Alenrent** (268 333 929; alenrent@iol.pt; Rua Capitão Mouzinho de Albuquerque 11). The **bus station** (268 322 282) is on the east side of town.

Destination	Price*	Duration*	Frequency (daily)
Borba	€1.85	15min	2
Elvas	€3.40/6.50	1½hr/45min	2-4
Évora	€3.60/7	1½/1hr	6-14
Évoramonte	€2	30min	2-4
Faro	€13.80	6hr	1
Lisbon	€10.50	2½hr	4-6
Portalegre	€3.60/7.10	1¼/1hr	3-4
Vila Viçosa	€2.60	45min	3 Mon-Fri

*normal/express

AROUND ESTREMOZ

Borba

pop 7800

The least visited of the marble towns, Borba glows with a peculiar rosy light. Its marble wealth hasn't brought it many obvious riches, so its marble-lined houses and public buildings have a remarkable simplicity.

This quiet small town is encircled by marble quarries (it's worth stopping en route to peer down a mine shaft) and is famous for its great red wines.

ORIENTATION & INFORMATION

Borba's main square, Praça da República, is the town focus, with its ornate 18th-century marble fountain, Fonte das Bicas, a rare sojourn into fanciness. The town comes to life once a year in early November, when it hosts a huge country fair. Access the Net for free at **Celeiro da Cultura** (Rua Fernão Penteado; 2-7pm Sun-Fri, 10am-1pm & 3-7pm Sat). There are a couple of tourist offices: one **turismo** (☎ 268 894 113; Rua do Convento das Servas; 11am-1pm & 2-5pm) is on the outskirts of town, just off the Estremoz–Elvas road (N4); the more central **turismo** (Rua 25 de Abril; 9.30am-12.30am & 2.30-5.30pm) is half a block from Praça da República.

SIGHTS

The **Adega Cooperativa de Borba** (☎ 268 894 264; Rua de San Bartolomeu; 9am-12.30pm & 2-5pm Mon-Fri) is the largest of three *adegas* in town, all producing the famous Borba full-bodied red and white *maduro* (mature) wines. The Adega operates a large **shop** (☎ 268 891 660; 9am-7pm Mon-Sat), 100m further up the road from the coop, where you can purchase some of their good-value wines.

SLEEPING & EATING

Residencial Inaramos (☎ 268 894 563; Avenida do Povo 22; s/d without breakfast €25/30) Up a marble staircase, this pleasant option offers bright, comfortable good-value rooms. It's nicely located on a street sprinkled with cafés, 1½ blocks east of the *praça*.

Casa de Borba (☎ 268 894 528; www.casadeborba.com; Rua da Cruz 5; s/d with breakfast €70/80;) An aristocratic 17th-century mansion, this place has high-ceilinged rooms filled with antiques – carved beds and canopies, rich rugs and marble-topped tables. There's also a peaceful garden and pool.

A Talha (☎ 268 894 473; Rua Mestre Diogo de Borba 12; mains €4-6.50; lunch & dinner Mon-Sat) Unsigned, splendid and in an arched cellar, A Talha has enormous urns indicating one of its specialities: punchy new wine. The other is home-cooked food, like *bacalhau com grau* (cod with chick-peas). To get here, walk down Rua Antonio Joaquim da Guerra (off Avenida do Povo, to the left of the large shrine). Take the first left (Rua Visconde Giâo), then the first right.

GETTING THERE & AWAY

Daily buses connect Borba with Estremoz (€1.85, 15 minutes, two daily) and Vila Viçosa (€1.25). Some buses drop you off on the edge of town (a 10-minute walk to the centre); others stop just east of the *praça*. For bus times, ask at **Café Briquete** (Avenida do Povo 31).

Vila Viçosa

pop 9100

If you visit just one marble town in the region, Vila Viçosa is the one to hit. It has a long attractive plaza, set with orange trees, a fountain and a few outdoor cafés, and a marvellous marble palace – one of the country's largest.

This was once home to the Bragança dynasty, whose kings ruled Portugal until it became a republic (Dom Carlos spent his last night here before his assassination). There is also a fine castle – one of the few nonmarble structures in town – some pretty churches and a friendly laid-back citizenry eager to show off their sparkling town.

ORIENTATION & INFORMATION

The huge, sloping Praça da República is the attractive heart of town, with the *mercado municipal* and gardens 200m to the southeast. At the top of the *praça* is the 17th-century Igreja de São Bartolomeu; at the bottom is Avenida Bento de Jesus, which lies at the foot of the castle.

The Paço Ducal (Ducal Palace) is 300m northwest of the *praça* (follow Rua Dr Couto Jardim). Pick up a town map and other info at the friendly **turismo** (☎ 268 881 101; www.cm-vilavicosa.pt; Praça da República 34; 9am-7pm). Free web access is available around the corner at **Espaço Internet** (Rua Padre Joaquim Espanca 19; 9am-7.30pm Mon-Sat).

SIGHTS

Terreiro do Paço & Paço Ducal

The **palace square** covers 16,000 sq metres, and it's ringed by the palace, the heavy-fronted Agostinhos Convent and graceful Chagas Nunnery. In the centre is a statue of Dom João IV.

The dukes of Bragança built their **palace** (☎ 268 980 659; adult/child under 10 €5/free; 10am-1pm Wed-Sun, 2.30-5.30pm Tue-Sun Apr-Sep, 2.30-5pm Oct-Mar) in the early 16th century when the fourth duke, Dom Jaime, decided he had had enough of his uncomfortable hilltop castle. The wealthy Bragança family, originally from Bragança in Trás-os-Montes, had settled in Vila Viçosa in the 15th century. After the eighth duke became king in 1640, it changed from a permanent residence to just another royal palace, but the family maintained a special fondness for it and Dom João IV and his successors continued to visit the palace.

The best furniture went to Lisbon after Dom João IV ascended the throne, and some went on to Brazil after the royal family fled there in 1807, but there are some stunning pieces, such as a huge 16th-century Persian rug in the Dukes Hall. Lots of royal portraits put into context the interesting background on the royal family.

The private apartments hold a ghostly fascination – toiletries, knick-knacks and clothes of Dom Carlos and his wife, Marie-Amélia, are laid out as if the royal couple were about to return (Dom Carlos left one morning in 1908 and was assassinated in Lisbon that afternoon).

A Portuguese-speaking guide leads the hour-long tours – some of the guides speak English well too, but if not you can buy a guidebook (€5).

Other parts of the Ducal Palace, including the 16th-century cloister, house more museums containing specific collections and with separate admission fees (armoury/coach collection/Chinese Porcelain/treasury €2.50/1.50/2.50/2.50).

Castelo

Dom Dinis' walled hilltop castle was where the Bragança family lived before the palace was built. It has been transformed into a **Museu de Caça e Arqueologia** (Game & Hunting Museum; admission €3; 10am-1pm Wed-Sun, 2.30-5.30pm Tue-Sun Apr-Sep, 2.30-5pm Oct-Mar), stuffed with endless unlucky animals – trophies that show how the dukes kept themselves busy on their 20-sq-km hunting ground north of Vila Viçosa.

Surrounding the castle is a cluster of village houses and peaceful overgrown gardens. There's a 16th-century Manueline *pelourinho* (the prison used to be nearby), with sculpted frogs. It's incongruously beautiful for a whipping post. Also near the castle is the brilliantly tiled 15th-century **Igreja de Nossa Senhora da Conceição**.

FESTIVALS & EVENTS

On the second weekend of September the **Fiesta dos Capuchos** takes place, with a bullfight and a *vacada* (a bull is released and locals try to jump over it to show how brave they are) in the main square.

SLEEPING

Casa da Mariquinhas (☎ 268 980 523; Avenida Duques de Bragança 56; s/d without breakfast €20/30) A few blocks north of the plaza on the road facing the castle, this welcoming spot offers three small, nicely furnished rooms with wood floors in a private house. Two rooms face the castle.

Hospedaria Dom Carlos (☎/fax 268 980 318; Praça da República 25; s/d without breakfast €30/35;) In an excellent location on the main square, this ageing place offers comfortable but bland rooms.

Casa de Peixinhos (☎ 268 980 472; fax 268 881 348; s/d incl breakfast €85/110) This turreted, classical 17th-century manor house, a few kilometres out on the Borba road, has rooms crammed with antiques and splendid tiling. Bathrooms are, of course, marble.

Hotel Convento de São Paulo (☎ 266 989 160; www.hotelconventospaulo.com; Aldeia da Serra; s/d from €105/120;) A marvellously romantic huge monastery on a 600-acre estate, this hotel has big, grand, striking rooms and a restaurant with a hugely lofty painted ceiling.

Pousada de Dom João IV (☎ 268 980 742; recepcao.djoao@pousadas.pt; d €215;) Next to the Ducal Palace, this former royal convent was once the 'House of the Ladies of the Court'. Today, this regal spot offers spacious rooms with wood floors, terraces and classic furnishings. Rooms open onto a striking inner courtyard. There's disabled access too.

EATING

Café Restauração (☎ 268 980 256; Praça da República; mains €6.50-10; lunch & dinner) This is the best and buzziest of several café-restaurants that sit on the square just below the turismo, and has pleasant outdoor seating.

O Forno (☎ 268 999 797; Rua Cristóvão Pereira; mains €5-12; lunch & dinner Mon-Sat) Signposted off Praça da República, this popular local place serves *bacalhau* (cod) and other favourites just like *vovó* (grandma) used to make.

Os Cucos (☎ 268 980 806; mains €5.90-8.30; lunch & dinner Mon-Sat) Hidden in the gardens near the *mercado municipal*, this peaceful spot has an airy interior and garden tables. Grilled fish and roasted pork are among the changing daily specials. To get here head uphill from the *praça*, then turn left after a block.

ENTERTAINMENT

Classical **concerts** (admission free) are held in the chapel of the Ducal Palace on the last Friday of the month at 9pm year-round.

THE ALENTEJO

GETTING THERE & AWAY

There are **buses** (☎ 268 989 787) to/from Évora (€4.60/7 normal/express, 1½/one hour, three daily), or Estremoz (€2.60, 35 minutes, three daily on weekdays).

ELVAS

pop 23,000 / elevation 280m

The impressive fortifications zigzagging around this pleasant little town reflect some of Europe's most sophisticated military technology of 17th-century Europe. Its moats, fort and heavy walls would indicate a certain paranoia if it weren't for Elvas' position, only 15km west of Spain's Badajoz. Inside the stout town walls, you'll find a lovely town plaza, some quaint museums and very few foreign visitors – aside from the occasional flood of Spanish day-trippers. Although there's not much to hold your attention beyond a day, Elvas is a fascinating place to visit, with its evocative frontier-post atmosphere, narrow medina-like streets and extraordinary, forbidding walls and buttresses.

History

In 1229 Elvas was recaptured from the Moors after 500 years of fairly peaceful occupation. The following centuries saw relentless attacks from Spain, interrupted by occasional peace treaties. Spain only succeeded in 1580, allowing Felipe II of Spain (the future Felipe I of Portugal) to set up court here for a few months. But the mighty fortifications were seldom breached: in 1644, during the Wars of Succession (1640–68), the garrison held out against a nine-day Spanish siege and, in 1659, just 1000 (an epidemic had wiped out the rest) withstood an attack by a 15,000-strong Spanish army.

The fortifications saw their last action in 1811, when the Duke of Wellington used the town as the base for an attack on Badajoz during the Peninsular War.

Orientation

Considering the extent of the walls, the centre feels small. Praça da República is at its heart, with all major sights a short walk away. Those arriving by train will find themselves disembarking at Fontaínhas, 4km north of town off the Campo Maior road.

It's possible to find central parking, but not always easy; if you don't like narrow one-way streets, park on the outskirts of town (or just inside Portas de Olivença).

Information

EMERGENCY & MEDICAL SERVICES

District hospital (☎ 268 622 225; Avenida de Badajoz) Opposite the Pousada de Santa Luzia.

Police station (☎ 268 622 613; Rua Isabel Maria Picão)

INTERNET ACCESS

Microluna (Avenida São Domingos 14; per hr €3; 9am-1pm & 3-7pm Mon-Fri, 9am-1pm Sat) Has three computers for internet access.

MONEY

Banco Espirito Santo (☎ 268 939 240; Praça da República) There are many banks with ATMs around town, including this one.

Cota Câmbios (Rua da Cadeia; 8.30am-1.30pm & 2.30-7.30pm Mon-Fri, 9am-1.30pm & 2.30-6pm Sat & Sun) A centrally located exchange bureau.

POST

Post office (Rua da Cadeia; 8.30am-6pm Mon-Fri, 9am-12.30pm Sat)

TOURIST INFORMATION

Turismo (☎ 268 622 236; Praça da República; 9am-6pm Mon-Fri, 10am-12.30pm & 2-5.30pm Sat & Sun May-Sep, 9am-5.30pm Oct-Apr) Near the police station, this small office distributes pamphlets and a rudimentary town map.

Sights

FORTIFICATIONS & MILITARY MUSEUM

Walls encircled Elvas as early as the 13th century, but it was in the 17th century that Flemish Jesuit engineer Cosmander designed the formidable defences that you now see, adding moats, ramparts, seven bastions, four semibastions and fortified gates in the style of the famous French military architect the Marquis de Vauban. To give you an idea of the level of security, you cross a door bridge to get to the main gate; inside is a 150-sq-metre square, surrounded by bastions, turrets and battlements, a covered road and three lines of trenches, some of which are carved out of rock.

Also added was the miniature zigzag-walled **Forte de Santa Luzia**, just 1.4km south of the *praça*. This now houses the **military museum** (☎ 268 628 357; 10am-1pm & 2-5pm Oct-Mar, 10am-1pm & 3-7pm Apr-Sep). The Forte de Nossa Senhora da Graça, 3km north of town, with a similar shape, was added in the following century; it's still in use as an army base and is closed to the public.

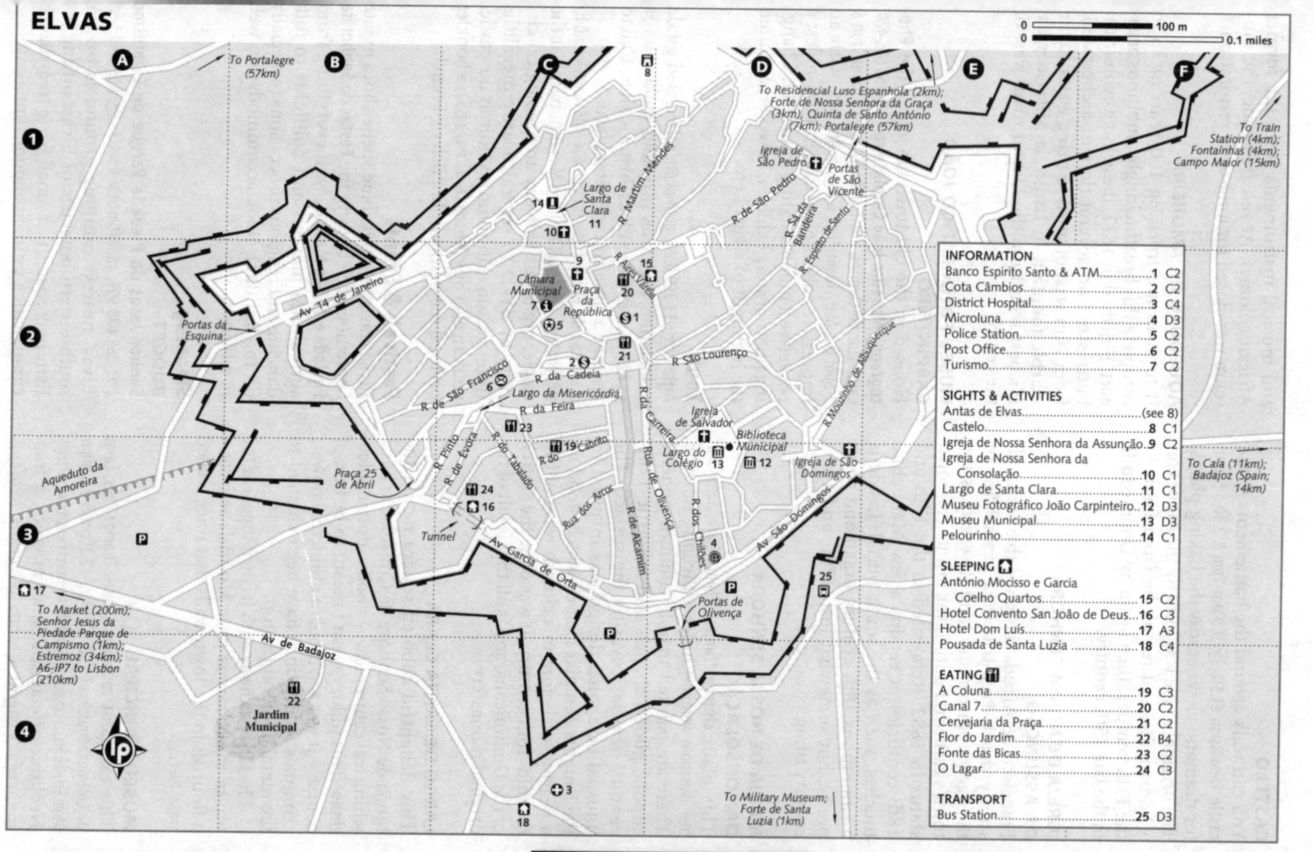

THE ALENTEJO

CASTELO

You can walk around the battlements at the **castle** (admission €1.50; 9.30am-1pm & 2.30-5.30pm) for dramatic views across the baking plains. The original castle was built by the Moors on a Roman site, and rebuilt by Dom Dinis in the 13th century, then again by Dom João II in the late 15th century.

IGREJA DE NOSSA SENHORA DA ASSUNÇÃO

Francisco de Arruda designed this fortified, sturdy **church** (Praça da República; admission free) in the early 16th century, and it served as the town's cathedral until Elvas lost its episcopal status in 1882. Renovated in the 17th and 18th centuries, it retains a few Manueline touches, such as the south portal. Inside is a sumptuous 18th-century organ and some pretty, but somewhat lost, 17th- and 18th-century tiling.

IGREJA DE NOSSA SENHORA DA CONSOLAÇÃO

This plain **church** (Largo de Santa Clara; admission free, donations welcome) hides a thrilling interior. There are painted marble columns under a cupola, gilded chapels and fantastic 17th-century *azulejos* covering the surface. The unusual octagonal design was inspired by the Knights Templar chapel, which stood on a nearby site before this church was built in the mid-16th century. It was once the church of the Dominicans, and is all that is left of the original monastery.

LARGO DE SANTA CLARA

This delightful cobbled square facing the Igreja de Nossa Senhora da Consolação has a whimsical centrepiece – a polka-dotted **pelourinho**. This pillory wasn't meant to be fun, of course – it was a symbol of municipal power: criminals would once have been chained to the metal hooks at the top.

The fancy **archway** with its own loggia at the top of the square is pure Moorish artistry – a flourish in the town walls that once trailed past here.

MUSEU MUNICIPAL

This excellent **museum** (Museu Thomaz Pires; Largo do Colégio; admission €0.50; 9am-12.30pm & 2-5.30pm Mon-Fri) is jam-packed with treasures, including Neolithic artefacts, Roman mosaics, a fragment of a Visigothic altar, folk crafts, *azulejos,* and musical instruments from the former African colonies. At research time, the museum was closed for long-term restoration.

AQUEDUTO DA AMOREIRA

It took an unsurprising 100 years or so to complete this breathtakingly ambitious **aqueduct**. Finished in 1622, these huge cylindrical buttresses and several tiers of arches stalk from 7km west of town to bring water to the marble fountain in Largo da Misericórdia. It's best seen from the Lisbon road, west of the centre.

MUSEU FOTOGRÁFICO JOÃO CARPINTEIRO

Housed in the old town cinema is the **Photography Museum João Carpinteiro** (☎ 268 636 470; Largo Luis de Camões; adult/child €2/1; 10am-1pm & 2-5pm Oct-Mar, 10am-1pm & 3-7pm Apr-Sep), with an impressive collection of cameras, the oldest a pocket-vest number dating from 1912. Changing photography exhibits, however, are often the highlight of a visit here.

Tours

Agia (☎ 933 259 036; agia@iol.pt), a licensed guide association, organises two-hour walking tours (€12) that explore Elvas' historic sites. Call to arrange a time and meeting place.

Antas de Elvas (☎/fax 268 626 403; Castelo; adult/student/senior €17.50/10/10; May-Oct), based at the castle, organises half-day archaeological circuits by 4WD to several nearby megaliths (four-person minimum). While at the castle, you can also buy *Antas de Elvas* (€5), a booklet on local megaliths in English or French.

Festivals & Events

Elvas starts to tap its blue suede shoes in late September, celebrating the **Festas do Senhor da Piedade e de São Mateus**, with everything from agricultural markets and bullfights to folk dancing and religious processions (especially on the last day). Book accommodation well in advance.

Sleeping

BUDGET

Senhor Jesus da Piedade Parque de Campismo (☎ 268 628 997; adult/tent/car €3/4/3; Apr–mid-Sep) Elvas' nearest camping ground is on the southwestern outskirts of Elvas, off the N4 Estremoz road. It's a small basic tree-shaded camp, with a municipal pool 1km away.

António Mocisso e Garcia Coelho Quartos (☎ 268 622 126; Rua Aires Varela 15; s/d €25/35;) The only budget place in the town centre has small, thin-walled but comfortable rooms with tile floors and a modern look.

MIDRANGE

Residencial Luso Espanhola (☎/fax 268 623 092; Rua Rui de Melo; s/d €30/45) A short way from town (2km north on the Portalegre road), this friendly 14-room hostelry has smallish, modern rooms with balconies overlooking a fine countryside view. There are two restaurants next door.

Hotel Dom Luís (☎ 268 622 756; fax 268 620 733; Avenida de Badajoz; s/d with breakfast €50/65;) A snappy, cheery little modern establishment, this hotel is 700m west of the centre, just outside the town walls and just across the road from the aqueduct. Rooms have small windows (but you can see the aqueduct) and satellite TV.

Quinta de Santo António (☎ 268 628 406; fax 268 625 050; Estrada de Barbacena; s/d with breakfast €75/80) This beautiful, stately old house sits in lush gardens 7km northwest of Elvas. There are tennis courts and horses to ride. You'll need your own transport to get to this place or the Residencial Luso Espanhola.

TOP END

Hotel Convento São João de Deus (☎ 268 639 220; www.hotelsaojoaodeus.com; Largo João de Deus 1; s/d Sun/Thu €64/70, Fri & Sat €74/80;) Spanish-owned, this is Elvas' finest hotel. It opened in 2004 and is a grand but not always sympathetic conversion of a 17th-century convent. Rooms here are cheerful and bright with handsome wood floors. There's also a small pool and a good restaurant.

Pousada de Santa Luzia (☎ 268 637 470; recepcao.staluzia@pousadas.pt; Avenida de Badajoz; d €140;) Dating from the 1940s, this is a comfortable, though relatively modern and characterless, *pousada* – the first in Portugal.

Eating

Cervejaria da Praça (☎ 268 628 270; Praça da República 26; mains €5-10; 10am-9pm) One of several indoor-outdoor cafés scattered around the plaza, this one serves soups, snacks and a range of Portuguese standards. It's a lovely setting for an evening drink.

Flor do Jardim (☎ 268 623 174; Avenida António Sardinho; mains €8-12; lunch & dinner) Set in the Jardim Municipal, this restaurant has a peaceful terrace where you can have drinks; the more traditional dining room inside is a good choice for nicely prepared meat and seafood dishes.

A Coluna (☎ 268 623 728; Rua do Cabrito 11; mains €5.50-8, tourist menu €9; lunch & dinner Wed-Mon) This whitewashed cavern is a cut above its competitors, with *azulejos* on the walls and lots of pork and *bacalhau* dishes on the menu.

O Lagar (☎ 268 624 793; Rua Nova da Vedoria 7; mains €5.50-12.50; lunch & dinner Fri-Wed) Smart and buzzing, O Lagar dishes up good regional cooking; it specialises in *bacalhau*, shellfish rice and *açorda* (bread soup) with prawns.

Canal 7 (☎ 268 623 593; Rua dos Sapateiros 16; mains €4-7) Serving inexpensive grills, Canal 7 is a simple eatery, long popular with locals.

Fonte das Bicas (Rua da Feira 15; 7.30am-8pm) A small accessible supermarket.

Shopping

On alternate Mondays there's a big lively **market** around the aqueduct, just off the Lisbon road west of town. The weeks it's not on, there's a **flea market** in Praça da República.

Getting There & Around

The new bus station is outside the city walls, on the road to Spain. It's an 800m walk mostly uphill (or a €4.50 taxi ride) to the main *praça*. There are buses to Estremoz (€3.40, 45 minutes, three daily on weekdays), Évora (€5.50, 1¼ to 1¾ hours, two daily), Portalegre (€4.50, 1¼ hours, two daily on weekdays) and Faro (€6.40, one daily on weekdays). Express coaches depart daily for Lisbon (€11.70, 3¼ to 3½ hours, nine daily).

There is daily train service to Lisbon (€22, 4¼ to 5¼ hours), with a transfer necessary at Entroncamento.

Taxis (☎ 268 623 526) charge around €4 from the train station at Fontaínhas into town.

PORTALEGRE

pop 26,800 / elevation 520m

Bunched up on a hilltop and at the foot of Serra de São Mamede – the mountain range that rears skywards from town – Portalegre is a pretty, whitewashed, ochre-edged city that's also Alto Alentejo's capital.

For a charming, low-key, off-the-beaten-track experience, it's a pleasant destination, and you'll find a lively student population and handy transport links to nearby mountaintop villages.

Inside the city walls, faded baroque mansions are all dressed up with no place to go – relics of the town's textile manufacturing heyday. In the 16th century, the town boomed through tapestry; in the 17th, silk. Bust followed boom after the 1703 Treaty of Methuen brought English competition. But, even today, Portalegre stays true to its legacy of natty threads – there is a factory here producing fine tapestries using a unique technique, and an impressive museum showcasing the work.

Orientation

Portalegre has an hourglass shape, with the new town to the northeast and the old town spread across a hilltop to the southwest. The waist is a traffic roundabout – the Rossio, which is close to the bus station, from where it's about 400m to the old town via the pedestrianised Rua 5 de Outubro.

Information

EMERGENCY

Hospital (☎ 245 301 000) About 400m north of town.

Police station (☎ 245 300 620; Praça da República) Just outside Porta de Alegrete.

INTERNET ACCESS

Espaço Internet (Praça da República; 10.30am-10pm Mon-Thu, 10am-10pm Fri & Sat) Free access, but often packed.

Instituto Português de Juventude (Estrada do Bonfim; 9am-12.30pm & 2-5.30pm Mon-Fri) Free access; 700m north of the Rossio.

Loja do Estudante (Praça da República; per hr €1.50; 9am-1pm & 2-6pm Mon-Sat)

MONEY

Caixa Geral de Depósitos (☎ 245 339 100; Rua de Elvas) Bank with ATM in the old town.

Sotto Mayor (Rossio) Another bank with ATM.

POST

Branch office (Rua Luís de Camões 39) In the old town.

Main post office (cnr Avenida da Liberdade & Rua Alexandre Herculano; 8.30am-6pm Mon-Fri, 9am-12.30pm Sat) About 250m north of the Rossio.

TOURIST INFORMATION

Parque Natural da Serra de São Mamede (☎ 245 203 631; pnssm@icn.pt; 2nd fl, Rua General Conde Jorge de Avilez 22; 9am-noon & 2-5.30pm Mon-Fri) The park's headquarters has a free map and leaflet in English,

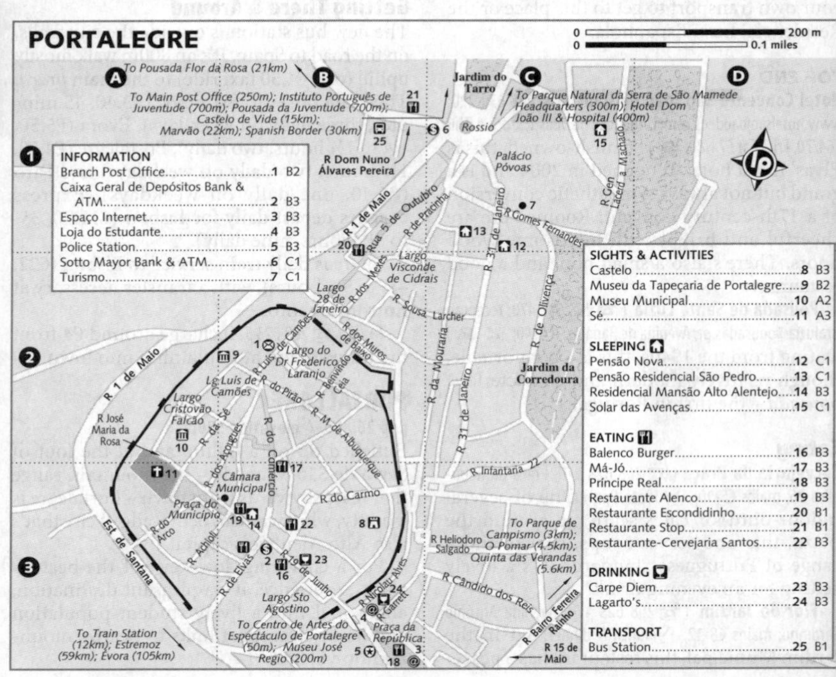

plus leaflets with suggested walks (€0.50), and several informative, well-produced publications (€5 to €10) about nature excursions, walking and biking in the Alto Alentejo, detailing trails.

Turismo (☎ 245 307 445; Rua Guilherme Gomes Fernandes 22; 10am-1pm & 2-6pm Mon-Fri, 10am-1pm & 3-6pm Sat & Sun) Has an excellent town map with suggested walking route, and four leaflets (€0. 50) detailing walks in the national park. Pick up the monthly *Agenda Cultural* – concerts are sometimes held in the Jardim do Tarro.

Sights

SÉ

In 1545 Portalegre became the seat of a new diocese and soon got its own **cathedral** (☎ 245 331 113). The pyramid-pointed, twin-towered 18th-century façade, with a broken clock, sombrely presides over the whitewashed Praça do Município. The sacristy contains an array of fine *azulejos*.

CASTELO

Portalegre's **castle** (admission €1; 10am-noon & 2-5pm Tue-Sat, morning Sun), off Rua do Carmo, dates from the time of Dom Dinis, with three restored towers that offer good views across the town. It was closed for long-term restoration during research.

MUSEU MUNICIPAL & MANSIONS

Beside the cathedral, in an 18th-century mansion and former seminary, is the charming but unlabelled town **museum** (☎ 245 330 616; Rua 19 de Junho; adult/child €2/1; 9.30am-12.30pm & 2-6pm Tue-Sun), with an attic-like collection of silver snuff boxes, porcelain, liturgical figures and a *Toad-of-Toad-Hall* two-seater car.

The town's former glory is recorded in stone: faded 17th-century baroque town houses and mansions dot Rua 19 de Junho to the southeast.

MUSEU DA TAPEÇARIA DE PORTALEGRE

Opened in 2001, this splendid **museum** (☎ 245 307 980; Rua da Figueira 9; admission €2; 9.30am-1pm & 2.30-6pm Tue-Sun) contains brilliant 20th-century creations from Portalegre's unique tapestry factory. It's named after the factory founder, who created an innovatory stitch. This reflects light in a certain way, enabling incredibly accurate copies of works of art. The museum shows a selection of the 6000 colours of thread used. French tapestry artist Jean Lurçat at first dismissed the technique, then the factory made a copy of one of his works – a cockerel – and asked him to identify the one made at Aubusson, in France. He chose the more perfect Portalegre copy – you can see them juxtaposed here. The huge tapestries are vastly expensive, and the museum includes copies of works by some of the most famous names in Portuguese 20th-century art, including Almada Negreiros and Vieira de Silva.

MUSEU JOSÉ REGIO

This small **museum** (9.30am-12.30pm Tue-Sun) is in poet José Regio's former house, and shows his magpie-like collection of popular religious art, with around 400 Christ figures. He was also particularly keen on Santo António. There are lots of rustic ceramics from Coimbra, which 18th-century migrant workers used to swap for clothes.

Sleeping

BUDGET

Parque de campismo (☎ 245 202 848; www.orbitur.pt; adult/tent/car €3.80/3.80/3.60; Apr-Sep) This lovely Orbitur camping ground at Quinta da Saúde is 3km northeast on the Estrada da Serra, high above town at 680m. It's shaded by pines, and there's a nearby swimming pool.

Pousada da juventude (☎ 245 330 971; portalegre@movijovem.pt; Estrada do Bonfim; dm/d with shared bathroom €9/24; 8am-10am & 7pm-midnight) A big white tower block labelled 'Centro de Juventude', 700m north of the Rossio, this youth hostel provides the usual not-fancy-but-fine bunks and bathrooms; the adjacent Instituto Português da Juventude (IPJ) is the town's main youth centre.

Pensão Nova (☎ 245 331 212; fax 245 330 493; Rua 31 de Janeiro 26; s/d €23/35;) A charming place in the old part of town, Pensão Nova has pretty rooms with wood floors and big, shuttered windows. Bathrooms are a bit cramped, but overall it's good value.

Pensão Residencial São Pedro (☎ 245 331 212; Rua da Mouraria 14; s/d €23/35), This is another snug place in a smart house, under the same management as Pensão Nova, which is where you'll find reception.

MIDRANGE & TOP END

Residencial Mansão Alto Alentejo (☎ 245 202 290; www.mansaoaltoalentejo.com.pt; Rua 19 de Junho 59; s/d €35/45;) This charming guesthouse offers small, bright rooms with tile floors, and traditional hand-painted furniture.

THE ALENTEJO

Hotel Dom João III (☎ 245 330 192; djoaoiii_portalegre@sapo.pt; Avenida da Liberdade; s/d €40/55) Near the garden, this modern, whitewashed hotel offers comfortable but somewhat bland rooms with carpeting and sizable verandas.

Solar das Avenças (☎ 245 201 028; www.rtsm.pt/solardasavencas; Jardim da Corredoura 11; s/d/ste €55/65/90) Overlooking the park, this 18th-century manor house has beautiful rooms with high ceilings, wood floors and antique furnishings. Some rooms have fireplaces.

Quinta das Varandas (☎ /fax 245 208 883; d with breakfast €75;) Rural options along the Estrada da Serra, on spectacularly high, vineyard-clad hillsides within the Parque Natural da Serra de São Mamede, include this fabulously remote and peaceful three-roomed *quinta,* about 2.6km beyond the camping ground.

Pousada Flor da Rosa (☎ 245 997 210; Crato; d €200;) In the middle of nowhere, 21km west of Portalegre, this strangely remote hotel is in a medieval castle, with arches and flagstone walls. Make sure you get a room in the old building. It's great for peace and quiet, and has a lovely pool.

Eating

Príncipe Real (Praça da República 2; mains from €2; 8am-2am) One of several attractive outdoor cafés on Praça da República, this place is a fine spot for baguette sandwiches, pastries and coffee. A garrulous young crowd arrives in the evenings.

Balenco Burger (Rua 19 de Junho 38; mains €3; lunch & dinner) This tiny snack spot serves cheap and tasty burgers made from scratch – though not much else.

Restaurante-Cervejaria Santos (☎ 245 203 066; Largo Serpa Pinto 4; mains €4-6.50; lunch & dinner Thu-Tue) On a pretty little square, this restaurant has a small outdoor wooden terrace under green umbrellas, and great grilled fish, as well as *migas* (pork and fried bread) and so on.

Restaurante Alenco (Rua 19 de Junho 62; mains €4-6; lunch & dinner) Attracting a mix of students and older folk, this friendly, low-key restaurant is a hit for its tasty inexpensive soups and daily Alentejan specials.

Restaurante Stop (Rua Dom Nuno Álvares Pereira 13; mains €5.50-7; lunch & dinner Sun-Fri) A decent budget choice near the bus station.

Má-Jó (Rua Dom Augusto Eduardo Nunes 1; 9am-1pm & 3-6pm Mon-Fri, 9am-1pm Sat) This tiny wine shop sells smoked meats, cheese and velvety rich reds.

Restaurante O Escondidinho (☎ 245 202 728; Travessa das Cruzes 1; mains €6-10; lunch & dinner Mon-Sat) A Portalegre charmer, this cosy spot has quaint country-style dining areas, a bar lined with tiles and a good selection of traditional mains.

Drinking

Portalegre's student population adds some life to the old streets, with outdoor drinking spots around Praça da República and to a lesser extent Largo do Dr Frederico Laranjo.

Carpe Diem (Rua 19 de Junho 33; noon-3pm & 7pm-2am) This nicely designed bar and bistro has exposed brick walls and a good mixed crowd. Plenty of cocktails and beer are served as are flavourful soups and sandwiches (the kitchen stays open late).

Lagarto's (Rua Garrett 16; 7pm-2am) This unpretentious student favourite has cheap drink specials, pinball and beer-drinking chit-chat.

Entertainment

Overlooking Praça da República, the **Centro de Artes do Espectáculo de Portalegre** (☎ 245 307 498; www.caeportalegre.blogspot.com in Portuguese; Praça da República 39), Portalegre's major new performance space, opened in 2006. Expect a regular line-up of *fado* singers, rock, jazz and acoustic groups, as well as dance and theatre. Ask at the tourist office or check the latest *Agenda Cultural* for current shows.

Getting There & Around

The **bus station** (☎ 245 330 723) has regular services to Lisbon (€11.70, 4½ hours), Estremoz (€3.60/7 normal/express, 80/50 minutes, three to five daily weekdays), Évora (€6 to €9, 1½ hours, one daily weekdays), Castelo Branco (€8.80, 1 hour 50 minutes, one daily) and Elvas (€4.50, 1½ hours, two daily weekdays).

Trains from Lisbon run daily (3½ hours, two to three daily); change at Abrantes. The station is 12km south of town but shuttle buses (€1.60, 15 minutes) meet all trains.

There are sometimes **taxis** (☎ 245 202 375, 966 772 947) outside the bus station. Car rental is available at the **Hotel Dom João III** (☎ 245 330 192) on Avenida da Liberdade.

CASTELO DE VIDE

pop 4100 / elevation 570m

High up above lush, rolling countryside, Castelo de Vide is one of Portugal's most attractive villages. It has a fine hilltop vantage point, dazzlingly white houses, flower-lined lanes and proud locals happy to share their well-kept village with visitors. Although there aren't many attractions in town, it's well worth spending the night, as you'll experience the town at its most disarming – at dusk and early morning. You'll see elderly ladies crocheting on doorsteps, children playing in the narrow streets, and neighbours chatting out of upper-storey windows. At night, the lanes are starlit.

By the castle is a small *judiaria* – the former Jewish district, strongest here in the early 15th century after their expulsion from Spain. A small synagogue is the main memento of this era. Castelo de Vide is famous for its crystal mineral water, which spouts out of various public fountains.

Orientation

At the heart of town are two parallel squares backed by the Igreja de Santa Maria da Devesa. The turismo is in a wide area in Rua Bartolomeu Álvares da Santa. Walk through the archway by the turismo to reach the southern square, Praça Dom Pedro V.

The castle, old quarter and *judiaria* lie to the northwest. Dive into the lanes behind the Igreja de Santa Maria da Devesa and follow the signs to Fonte da Vila (the old town fountain). From there it's a short, steep climb to the synagogue and castle.

Buses stop at the fountain near the post office; the train station is 4km northwest.

Information

Caixa Geral de Depósitos (☎ 245 339 100; Rua Elvas)
Centro de Interpretação (☎ 245 905 299; Rua de Santo Amaro 27; ⌚ 9.30am-12.45pm & 2-5.45pm Mon-Fri) Information centre for the Parque Natural da Serra de São Mamede.
Centro de saúde (medical centre; ☎ 245 901 105; Praça Dom Pedro V)
Open-air market Held every Friday (but the biggest is the last Friday of the month) in a car park just outside the old walls.
Police station (☎ 245 901 314; Avenida da Aramenha)
Post office (Rua de Olivença; ⌚ 9am-12.30 & 2-5.30pm Mon-Fri)
Turismo (☎ 245 901 361; cm.castvide@mail.telepac.pt; Rua Bartolomeu Álvares da Santa 81; ⌚ 9am-5.30pm Oct-Apr, to 7pm May-Sep) Friendly and helpful, with maps and leaflets.

Sights

OLD TOWN & JUDIARIA

A sizable community of Jews settled here in the 12th century, then larger waves came in the 15th. At first they didn't have an exclusive district, but Dom Pedro I restricted them to specific quarters. The tiny **synagogue** (Rua da Judiaria 16; admission free; ⌚ 9am-7pm May-Sep, to 5pm Oct-Apr), the oldest in Portugal, looks just like its neighbouring cottages, as it was adapted from an existing building. It's divided into two levels: one for women and one for men. In the bare interior is a wooden tabernacle and Holy Ark for Torah scrolls. Following Manuel I's convert-or-leave edict in 1496, many Jews returned to Spain, though some headed to Évora.

CASTELO

Originally Castelo de Vide's inhabitants lived within the castle's sturdy outer walls; even now there remains a small inner village with a church, the 17th-century **Igreja da Nossa Senhora da Alegria**.

There are brilliant views from here over the town's red roofs, surrounded by green and olive hills. The **castle** (admission free; ⌚ 9am-7pm May-Sep, to 5pm Oct-Apr), built by Dom Dinis and his brother Dom Afonso between 1280 and 1365, is topped by a 12m-high brick tower, thought to be the oldest part. There are great views from the roof of the fine vaulted hall.

FONTE DA VILA

In a pretty square just below and east of the *judiaria* is the worn-smooth 16th-century marble **Fonte da Vila**, with a washing area. This, along with several other fountains in the village, spouts out the delicious mineral water for which Castelo de Vide is known.

CENTRO MUNICIPAL DE CULTURA

This **cultural centre** (Rua 5 de Outubro 21; free admission; ⌚ 9am-5.30pm Mon-Fri) hosts a good range of temporary exhibitions – photographs of traditional and rural life in the Alentejo and the like. There's also a carving from a menhir on permanent display.

ANTA DOS COURELEIROS & MENHIR DA MEADA

In the wild, boulder-strewn landscape around Castelo de Vide are dozens of ancient megaliths. The two most impressive are the **Anta dos Coureleiros**, 8km north of town (with three other megaliths nearby making up what's called a Parque Megalítico), and the 7m-high **Menhir da Meada**, 8.5km further

on – supposedly the tallest menhir in the Iberian Peninsula – a large phallus for keeping the fields fertile.

Both megaliths are easily accessible by car or on foot. Turismos here and in Marvão should have *Paisagens Megalíticas Norte Alentejana* (Megalithic Landscapes North of Alentejo) a free, glossy photographic leaflet (English versions available) to help you track down these and other megaliths; follow the small wooden 'Antas' signs en route.

CIDADE DE AMMAIA

This excellent little **Roman museum** (admission €2.50; 9am-1pm & 2-5pm Mon-Fri, 10am-1pm & 2-5pm Sat & Sun) lies 7km east in São Salvador de Aramenha, en route to Marvão. From São Salvador head 700m south along the Portalegre road, then turn left, following the signs to Olhos d'Água restaurant.

In the 1st century AD this area was a huge Roman city called Ammaia, flourishing from the area's rich agricultural produce (especially oil, wine and cereals). Although evidence was found (and some destroyed) in the 19th century, it wasn't until 1994 that thorough digs began.

Here you can see some of the finds – engraved lintels and tablets, jewellery, coins and some incredibly well-preserved glassware – and also follow paths across the fields to where the forum and spa once stood and see several impressive columns and ongoing excavations.

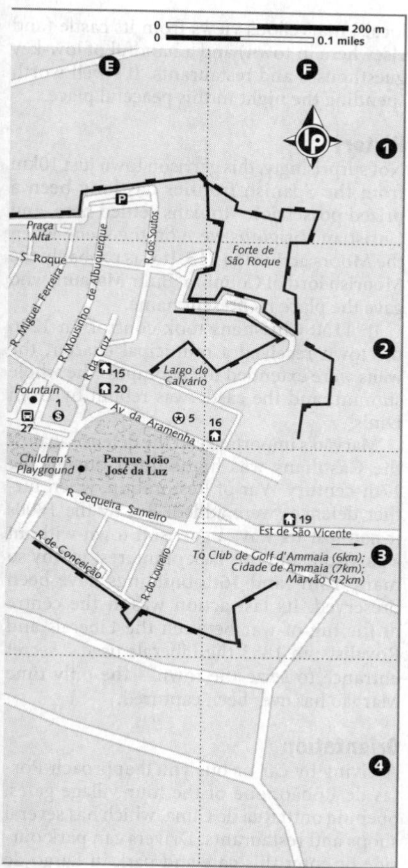

Activities

The **Club de Golf d'Ammaia** (☎ 245 993 755) golf course is 6km east towards Marvão.

Festivals & Events

Carnaval Held in February/March, this festival is great fun, too, with everyone out to watch processions of fantastically costumed folk, many in drag.

Easter festival Castelo de Vide's big bash is the four-day fair in March/April when hundreds of lambs go through the highs and lows of blessings and slaughter; processions, folk dances, band music and much revelry all take place.

Sleeping

BUDGET

Casa Janeco (☎ 245 901 211; Rua da Costa 56a; s/d with shared bathroom €15/25, apt €25) Run by the sweet Senhora Janeco, this private residence has two small rooms up for grabs and a bargain miniapartment in the narrow cobbled heart of town.

Casa Machado (☎ 245 901 515; Rua Luís de Camões 33; s/d €25/28) On the western edge of town, this friendly place has bright and airy modern rooms that are spotlessly maintained. There's a small, shared kitchen and outdoor patio. It's great for families.

Casa de Hóspedes Melanie (☎ 245 901 632; Largo do Paça Novo 3; s/d €25/35; ❄) This efficient place on a leafy square has five plain but spacious good-value rooms.

Quinta do Pomarinho (☎ 245 901 202; www.pomarinho.com; d with shared bathroom €25-35, adult/tent €4/4) A Dutch-owned old rural house 5km southwest of town, this *quinta* is a rural, ecologically friendly farm. It also has camping and a little roundhouse.

MIDRANGE & TOP END

Residencial Isabelinha (☎ 245 901 896; Largo do Paça Novo; d €40) Overlooking a leafy square, this *residencial* is beginning to show its age, though rooms are comfortable enough and some windows open onto the greenery.

Casa do Parque (☎ 245 901 250; casadoparque@mail.pt; Avenida da Aramenha 37; d €45-48) Overlooking the park, this lovely spot has inviting, well-maintained rooms with tile floors and big windows. It's worth the extra (currently 3€) euros for a balcony. A decent restaurant adjoins the space.

Albergaria El-Rei Dom Miguel (☎ 245 919 191; fax 245 901 592; Rua Bartolomeu Álvares da Santa 19; s €30, d €50-60) This seven-room place on the main street has charm and attention to detail – antique furniture, rooms with gleaming white linen, balconies and smart bathrooms.

Quinta da Bela Vista (☎ 245 968 125; Póvoa e Meadas; d €80) This is an old country house 13km north of Castelo de Vide. It's been in the same family since the 1920s and is a lovely choice.

Hotel Sol e Serra (☎ 245 900 000; www.grupofbarata.com; Estrada de São Vicente 73; s/d €62/82; ❄ 🏊) About 100m towards Marvão, this large, attractive hotel is a golfers' favourite with lots of amenities. Rooms are spacious and colourful, and each sports a veranda.

Casa Amarela (☎ 245 905 878; www.rtsm.pt/casaamarela; Praça Dom Pedro V; d/ste €100/125) On the main square with views over the *praça*, this beautifully restored guesthouse features stone staircases and antique-filled common areas; it has nine attractive rooms and two suites.

Eating & Drinking

Pastelaria-Restaurante Sol Nascente (☎ 245 901 789; Praça Dom Pedro V; mains €5-9; ⏲ breakfast, lunch & dinner Wed-Mon) This pleasant central café serves sandwiches, a decent vegetable soup, pastries and filling mains and has great outdoor seating.

ADCV (☎ 245 905 125; Rua Alexandre Herculano; mains €5-6) Known to locals as 'Johnny's' after its genial patron, ADCV (the initials stand for the local sports club) is packed with labourers at lunch and mainly men at night. Good-value seafood, pork and all the standards are here.

Restaurante Marino's (☎ 245 901 408; Praça Dom Pedro V, 6; mains €9-17; ⏲ dinner Mon-Sat) This smart-looking Italian restaurant offers good pasta dishes (like penne vodka) as well as lamb stew and Portuguese classics.

Brasil (☎ 245 901 407; Rua 5 de Outubro 13; ⏲ lunch & dinner) Bright and tiled, this enticing spot serves lots of traditional mains as well as a meat marathon on skewers – the Brazilian portion of the menu.

Bar da Vila (☎ 245 905 433; Rua de Olivença 11; ⏲ 11am-11pm) This bar has outdoor seating facing a garden square – perfectly placed for a relaxing drink.

Self-catering supplies are available at the minimarket **Meio Tostão** (Rua Bartolomeu Álvares de Santa 52).

Getting There & Away

BUS

Buses (☎ 245 901 510) run to/from Portalegre (€2.30/5 normal/express, 20 minutes, one to four daily) and Lisbon (€13, 4¼ hours, two daily). Regular buses stop just opposite the Pelourinho. Express buses stop five blocks east of there. Ask at the turismo for bus times.

TRAIN

You can get to/from Lisbon (€12.50, four hours, twice daily) – change at Abrantes and Torre das Vargens. The station is 4km northwest of town and there are no bus links. **Taxis** (☎ 245 901 271), available from outside the turismo, charge around €5 to the station.

MARVÃO

pop 800 / elevation 862m

On a jutting peak high above the surrounding countryside, the windswept lanes of Marvão feel like a retreat far removed from the proceedings of the world down below. The whitewashed village of picturesque tiled roofs and bright flowers has charmingly friendly locals, marvellous views from its castle (and elsewhere in town) and a handful of low-key guesthouses and restaurants. It's well worth spending the night in this peaceful place.

History

Not surprisingly, this garrison town just 10km from the Spanish frontier has long been a prized possession. Romans settled here, and Christian Visigoths were on the scene when the Moors arrived in 715. It was probably the Moorish lord of Coimbra, Emir Maraun, who gave the place its present name.

In 1160 Christians took control. In 1226 the town received a municipal charter, the walls were extended to encompass the whole summit, and the castle was rebuilt by Dom Dinis.

Marvão's importance in the defence against the Castilians was highlighted during the 17th-century War of Restoration, when further defences were added. But by the 1800s it had lost its way, a garrison town without a garrison, and this lack of interest is why so many 15th- and 16th-buildings have been preserved. Its last action was at the centre of the tug-of-war between the Liberals and Royalists; in 1833 the Liberals used a secret entrance to seize the town – the only time Marvão has ever been captured.

Orientation

Arriving by car or bus you'll approach Portas de Ródão, one of the four village gates, opening onto Rua de Cima, which has several shops and restaurants. Drivers can park outside or enter this gate and park in Largo de Olivença, just below Rua de Cima. The castle is up at the end of Rua do Espiríto Santo.

Information

There's a **Caixa Geral do Depósitos** bank (with ATM) on Rua do Espiríto Santo. Access the Net for free at the **Casa da Cultura** (Largo do Pauladino; ⏲ 9.30am-1pm & 2-5.30pm Mon-Fri). Near the castle and selling jam and local liquors is the **turismo** (☎ 245 993 886; Largo de Santa Maria; ⏲ 9am-noon & 2-5.30pm Sep-Jun, 9am-noon & 2-7pm Jul & Aug).

Sights

CASTELO

The formidable **castle** (admission free; ⏲ 24hr), built into the rock at the western end of the village, dates from the end of the 13th century, but most of what you see today was built in the

THE ALENTEJO

17th century. The views from the battlements are staggering. There's a huge vaulted cistern (still full of water) near the entrance, but it's swarming with little flies. At the far end, the **Núcleo Museológico Militar** (Military Museum; adult/student €1/0.80; 10am-1pm & 2-5pm Tue-Sun) offers a fine little display of Marvão and its castle's embattled history (in Portuguese only) with an accompanying flourish of 17th- to 18th-century muskets and bayonets.

MUSEU MUNICIPAL

Just east of the castle, the Igreja de Santa Maria provides graceful surroundings for the small **museum** (adult/child under 12 €1/free; 9am-12.30pm & 2-5.30pm). Here the scattershot approach to history reigns, with displays of medieval grave markers, carved stonework dating from the 3rd millennium BC, a near-complete skeleton and Roman pottery shards.

CASA DA CULTURA

In a restored building, this **cultural centre** (Largo do Pauladino; free admission; 9.30am-1pm & 2-5.30pm Mon-Fri), hosts changing exhibitions, and you can check out the rustic upstairs court room, dating from 1809. There's also a small handicrafts **shop** on site.

MEGALITHS

You can make a brilliant 30km round-trip via Santo António das Areias and Beirã, visiting nearby *antas* (dolmens). Pick up the free *Paisagens Megalíticas Norte Alentejana* leaflet from the turismo. Follow the wooden *'antas'* signs through a fabulously quiet landscape of cork trees and rummaging pigs. Some of the megaliths are right by the roadside, while others require a 300m to 500m walk. Be sure to bring refreshments: there's no village en route. You can continue north of Beirã to visit the megaliths in the Castelo de Vide area (p247). Ask at the turismo about bikes to rent.

Sleeping

Casa Rosada (☎ 245 993 491; Rua das Portas da Vila 14; d €25) This welcoming little house offers two clean and pleasantly furnished rooms with great views; one has a terrace.

Casa Dom Dinis (☎ 245 993 957; www.casaddinis.pa-net.pt; Rua Dr Matos Magalhães 7; s/d €45/55, d with terrace €60) Near the turismo, the friendly Dom Dinis has cool, colourful blocky murals and eight imaginatively decorated rooms of varying sizes, one of which has a terrace.

Albergaria El Rei Dom Manuel (☎ 245 909 150; alberg.d.manuel@mail.telepac.pt; Largo da Olivença; s/d €60/70) This friendly guesthouse has cosy rooms with tile floors and sizable windows. The best rooms have great views.

Casa da Árvore (☎/fax 245 993 854; Rua Dr Matos Magalhães 3; d with breakfast €70) This lovely guesthouse has five attractively furnished rooms incorporating some unusual elements, including original Roman funerary stones and a João Tavares tapestry from the famous Portalegre factory. The breakfast room has a stunning view.

Pousada de Santa Maria (☎ 245 993 201; www.pousadas.pt; Rua 24 de Janeiro; d €150;) Converted from two village houses, this is the most elegant and intimate option in town, with marvellous views from some rooms.

Casa das Portas de Ródão (☎ 245 992 160; Largo da Silveirinha 2; house from €100) This two-storey, three-bedroom house right by the entrance to town has a rustic, country feel, with curly iron bedsteads, wood or tiled floors and a terrace. It's a great family option. For info, ask at the handicraft shop Muralhas da Vila nearby.

Eating

Restaurante Casa do Povo (☎ 245 993 160; Rua de Cima; mains €7-10; 9am-midnight Fri-Wed) Boasting the town's loveliest terrace, Casa do Povo has wonderful views across the countryside, and the menu includes somewhat untraditional fare like grilled trout and shark with garlic and coriander, among other things.

Restaurante O Marcelino (☎ 245 903 138; Rua de Cima 3; mains around €8) This hidden gem has a grandmotherly cook dishing up home-style mains if you arrive at the right time.

Bar-Restaurante Varanda do Alentejo (☎ 245 993 272; Praça do Pelourinho 1; mains €5.50-8; lunch & dinner) This place serves up lots of hearty regional specialities, like *bacalhau dourada* (cod, onion and potatoes), which you can enjoy with a sangria on the terrace. They also have some *quartos* available.

Bar O Castelo (☎ 245 993 957; Rua Dr Matos Magalhães; snacks €2-3; 9am-10pm) This cosy, local eatery serves daily specials such as pork and clams, and other Alentejan hallmarks. Outdoor tables are around the side.

Getting There & Away

Two buses run daily on weekdays (one on weekends) between Portalegre and Marvão (€2.30, 45 minutes). There are two services from Castelo de Vide, but the first requires a change of buses at Portagem, a major road junction 7.5km northeast.

The nearest train station, Marvão-Beirã, is 9km north of Marvão, and has beautiful *azulejo* panels. Two trains run daily to/from Lisbon (€13.50, 4½ hours); change at Abrantes and Torre das Vargens. Taxis charge around €6 to the station. The daily Lisbon–Madrid *Talgo Lusitânia* train stops here just before 1am, en route to Valencia de Alcántara (Spain), and just before 5am on the journey to Lisbon (3¼ hours).

Taxis (☎ 245 993 272; Praça do Pelourinho) charge around €10 to Castelo de Vide.

BAIXO ALENTEJO

MÉRTOLA

pop 8700 / elevation 70m

Spectacularly set on rocky hills, high above the peaceful Rio Guadiana, the cobbled streets of medieval Mértola are a delightful place to roam. A small but imposing castle stands high over town, overlooking the jumble of dazzlingly white houses and a picturesque church that was once a mosque. A long bout of economic stagnation at this remote town has left many traces of Islamic occupation intact, so much so that Mértola is considered a *vila museu* (open-air museum). In the heat of the day – up to 47°C – the only sound is insects buzzing. Nearby are the beautiful, bleak disused copper mines of São Domingos.

History

Mértola follows the usual pattern of settlement in this area: Phoenician traders, who sailed up the Guadiana, then Carthaginians, then Romans. Its strategic position, as the northernmost port on the Guadiana, and the final destination for many Mediterranean routes, led the Romans to develop Mértola (naming it Myrtilis) as a major agricultural and mineral-exporting centre. Cereals and olive oil arrived from Beja, copper and other metals from Aljustrel and São Domingos. It was a rich merchant town.

Later the Moors, who called it Martulah and made it a regional capital, further fortified Mértola and built a mosque. Dom Sancho II and the Knights of the Order of Santiago captured the site in 1238. But then, as commercial routes shifted to the Tejo, Mértola declined. When the last steamboat service to Vila Real de Santo António ended and the copper mines of São Domingos (the area's main employer) closed in 1965, its port days were over.

Orientation

From the bus station in the new part of town, it's about 600m southwest to the historic old walled town. Old Mértola has few right angles or horizontal surfaces, and driving into it is asking for trouble – even a donkey would struggle.

Information

Biblioteca Municipal (town library; Rua 25 de Abril 16; ⌚ 10.30-noon Mon-Wed & Fri, 2.30-6pm Mon-Fri) Provides free internet access.

Caixa Geral Bank & ATM (Rua Dr Afonso Costa)

Centro de saúde (☎ 286 612 254; Cerca Carmo) Medical centre.

Espaço Jovem (Avenida Aureliano Mira Fernandes; per hr €0.50; ⌚ 9am-9pm) Disconsolate youth centre; offers internet access.

Millennium BCP Bank (Rua Dr Afonso Costa) Has an ATM.

Parque Natural do Vale do Guadiana headquarters (☎ 286 611 084; pnvg@icn.pt; Rua Dr Afonso Costa 40; ⌚ 9am-12.30pm & 2-5.30pm Mon-Fri Sep-Jun, 8am-2pm Jul & Aug) Administrative office but supplies information on the 600-sq-km park.

Police station (☎ 286 612 127; Rua Dr Afonso Costa)

Post office (Rua Alves Redol; ⌚ 9am-12.30pm & 2-5.30pm)

Turismo (☎ 286 610 109; Rua Alonso Gomes 18; ⌚ 9.30am-12.30pm & 2-5.30pm) Just inside the walled town; offers free internet access and can advise on *quartos*.

Sights

Stepping through the thick outer walls into the old town makes you feel as if you have stepped back in time. It's enchanting just to wander around the sleepy, sun-baked streets.

LARGO LUÍS DE CAMÕES

This is the administrative heart of the old town, a picturesque square lined with orange trees, with the *câmara municipal* at its western end. To reach the *largo* (small square), enter the old town and keep to the left at the fork in the road.

The **Torre do Relógio**, a little clock tower topped with a stork's nest and overlooking the Rio Guadiana, is northeast of the square. Alongside it is a municipal building with a rooftop worthy of Van Gogh.

IGREJA MATRIZ

Mértola's striking parish **church** (Rua da Igreja; admission free; Tue-Sun) – square, flat-faced and topped with whimsical little conical decorations – is most well known because in a former incarnation it was a mosque, one of the few in the country to have survived the Reconquista. It was reconsecrated as a church in the 13th century. Look out for an unwhitewashed cavity in the wall, on the right-hand side behind the altar; in former times this served as the mosque's mihrab (prayer niche). Note also the goats, lions and other figures carved around the peculiar Gothic portal and the typically Moorish horseshoe arch in the north door.

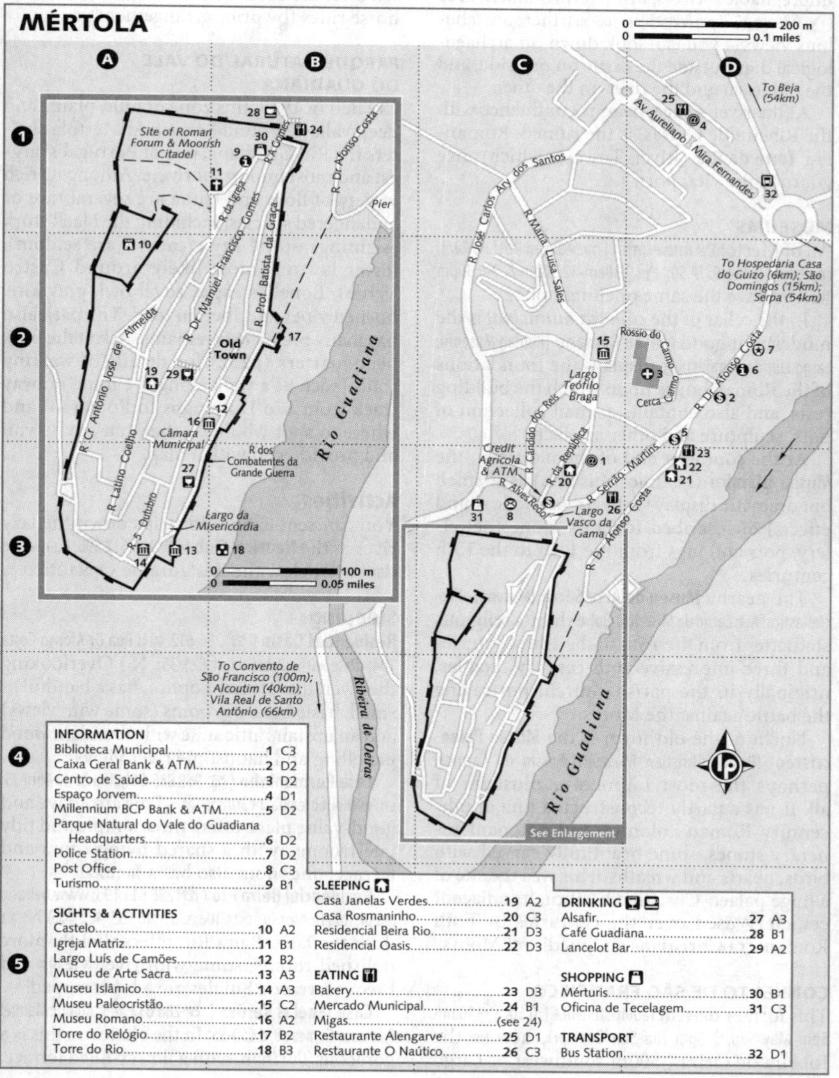

CASTELO & TORRE DO RIO

Above the parish church looms Mértola's fortified **castle** (admission free; 24hr), most of which dates from the 13th century. It was built upon Moorish foundations next to an Islamic residential complex and *alcáçova* (citadel), which itself overlaid the Roman forum. For centuries the castle was considered western Iberia's most impregnable fortress. From its prominent **keep** (9.30am-12.30pm & 2-5.30pm Tue-Sun) there are fabulous views – you can look down on archaeological digs outside the castle on one side, and the old town and the river on the other.

At the river's edge, near its confluence with the Ribeira de Oeiras, is the ruined, Roman-era **Torre do Rio** (River Tower), which once guarded the vital port.

MUSEUMS

All of Mértola's **museums** (1 museum adult/child €2/1, combined ticket €5/2.50; 9.30am-12.30pm & 2-5.30pm Tue-Sun) have the same opening hours.

In the cellar of the *câmara municipal* is the modest but good **Museu Romano** (Roman Museum; Largo Luís de Camões). It displays the foundations of the Roman house upon which the building rests, and also contains a small collection of pots, sculpture and other artefacts.

At the southern end of the old town, the **Museu Islâmico** (Islamic Museum) is a small but dramatic display (with atmospheric sound effects) of inscribed funerary stones, jewellery, pots and jugs from the 11th to the 13th centuries.

The nearby **Museu de Arte Sacra** (Museum of Ecclesiastical Art; Largo da Misericórdia) exhibits religious statuettes from the 16th to the 18th centuries and three impressive 16th-century retables, originally in the parish church, portraying the battle against the Moors.

North of the old town is the **Museu Paleocristão** (Palaeo-Christian Museum; Rossio do Carmo), perhaps the most impressive museum of all. It has a partly reconstructed line of 6th-century Roman columns and poignant funerary stones, some beautifully carved with birds, hearts and wreaths. This was the site of a huge palaeo-Christian basilica, its adjacent cemetery used over the centuries by both Roman-era Christians and medieval Moors.

CONVENTO DE SÃO FRANCISCO

This former **convent** (adult/student €1/0.50; 10am-5pm May-Sep, 2-6pm Tue-Sun Oct-Apr), across the Ribeira de Oeiras, 500m southwest of Largo Vasco da Gama along a track, has been owned since 1980 by Dutch artist Geraldine Zwanikken and her family. They have transformed it into a nature reserve and art gallery. The grounds are full of herbs, horses, rain temples and wildflowers; its former chapel exhibits Geraldine's extraordinary art; and its riverside is devoted to nesting storks and lesser kestrels. On offer are occasional workshops, as well as horse rides (by prior arrangement).

PARQUE NATURAL DO VALE DO GUADIANA

Created in 1995, this zone of hills, plains and deep valleys around Serpa and Mértola shelters the Rio Guadiana, one of Portugal's largest and most important rivers. Among its rich variety of flora and fauna are several rare or endangered species, including the black stork (sightings of the shy creatures are seldom), lesser kestrel (most likely around Castro Verde), Bonelli's eagle, royal owl, grey kite, horned viper and Iberian toad. The park also has many prehistoric remains. Ask at the park headquarters (p252) for details of walking trails (such as a walk along the mine railway track from São Domingos to Pomarão) and where to spot wildlife – they can advise you and provide you with a map.

Activities

You can rent canoes for trips down the lazy river at the **Nautical Club** (286 612 596; Rua Serrão Martins 16) below the Restaurante O Naútico.

Sleeping

Residencial Oasis (286 612 404; Rua Dr Afonso Costa 104; d/ste without breakfast €25/35;) Overlooking the river, this pleasant option has a handful of small, basic but tidy rooms (some with views) and an upstairs attic suite with abundant wood panelling and handsome river views.

Casa Rosmaninho (969 835 644; Rua 25 de Abril 23; s/d without breakfast €30/35;) This attractive and good-value place offers three simple and tidy guestrooms, with a shared living room and terrace; one room also has a Jacuzzi.

Residencial Beira Rio (286 611 190; www.beirario.co.pt; Rua Dr Afonso Costa 108; s/d from €35/40;) Next door to Oasis, Beira Rio offers slightly more polished rooms, some with river views and breezy terraces. Singles are a bit cramped.

Casa Janelas Verdes (286 612 145; Rua Dr Manuel Francisco Gomes 38; d €50-55) In the old town, this is a gorgeous Turihab, with a flower-filled terrace, lots of elderly ladies, old-fashioned rooms and a famously good breakfast.

There are also some appealing rural tourism options around: try **Hospedaria Casa do Guizo** (☎ 286 655171; Monte do Guizo, Moreaness; r €40;) or ask at the turismo for further options. Ask at the park headquarters (p252) about accommodation provided within the park near the border town of Canavial, 20km southeast of Mértola.

Eating

Mértola's specialities are *javali* (wild boar) and the regional pork dish *migas* – great labouring fuel, but perhaps heavier than necessary for sightseeing.

Restaurante Alengarve (☎ 286 612 210; Avenida Aureliano Mira Fernandes; mains €5-10; lunch & dinner Tue-Thu) The oldest restaurant in Mértola and run by the same family for years, this place serves up filling, traditional cuisine. A small terrace overlooks the street.

Migas (Municipal Market; mains €8) This is a superb little restaurant alongside the market, serving serious Alentejan specialities, such as aromatic, coriander-packed river-bass soup.

Restaurante O Naútico (☎ 286 612 596; Rua Serrão Martins 16; Mon-Sat; mains €6-8; lunch & dinner Mon-Sat) Above the riverside Nautical Club, this restaurant has a roof terrace and fabulous views, as well as light, nautical mains such as grilled squid or salmon.

Self-caterers and honey monsters should head to the **mercado municipal** (Praça Vasco de Gama; 8am-4pm Mon-Sat) with lovely fresh produce, including cheese, honey, nuts, fruit and vegetables. There's also an unsigned **bakery** (Rua Dr Afonso Costa 96) where you can buy fresh-baked bread (go in the evening for hot rolls).

Drinking

Lancelot Bar (Rua Nossa Senhora da Conceição) This vaguely medieval-feeling bar has friendly barkeeps and eclectic décor (colourful paintings and a wall of skeleton keys), with a shady wooden terrace attached.

Alsafir (☎ 286 618 049; Rua dos Combatentes da Grande Guerra 9; 9pm-4am) This bar hosts occasional dance-party nights in a simple tavern-like ambience.

Café Guadiana (☎ 286 612 186; Praça Vasco de Gama; snacks €1-4; lunch & dinner) With an excellent raised vantage point on the main square, this café has an outside terrace for watching comings and goings.

Shopping

Oficina de Tecelagem (Rua José Carlos Ary dos Santos; 9am-12.30pm & 2-5.30pm Tue-Sun Oct-May, 10am-1pm & 3-7pm Jun-Sep) A small wool-weaving workshop, this is a good place to see craftspeople at work in a wonderfully gossipy atmosphere. You can buy products here such as rugs and ponchos.

Mérturis (Rua da Igreja 35; 10am-1pm & 3-7pm) Next door to the turismo, this quaint shop sells regionally produced honey, teas, almonds and artwork.

Getting There & Away

There are **buses** (☎ 286 611 127) to Lisbon (€12.50, 4¼ hours, one or two daily) and Vila Real de Santo António (€8.10, 1½ hours); and a slower local Vila Real service (€5, two hours) via Alcoutim (50 minutes), which runs on Monday and Friday. Daily services (normal/express, €4.50/5.40, 75 minutes/one hour) run to/from Beja.

AROUND MÉRTOLA

The ghost town of **São Domingos** consists of desolate rows of small mining cottages. Once the mine closed in the 1960s, many miners emigrated or moved to Setúbal. But the village is amid beautiful countryside and next to a huge lake, where you can swim or rent a paddleboat or canoe.

The São Domingos mine itself is over 150 years old – though mining has been taking place here since Roman times – and is a deserted, fascinatingly eerie place to explore, with crumbling old offices and machinery. The rocks surrounding it are clouded with different colours, and the chief mine shaft is filled with deep, unnatural-seeming dark-blue water (no swimming), shot through with rust. The mines were established by a British firm, who apparently treated the workers badly, keeping them in line with a private police force.

Set in some of the mine's former administrative buildings, the grand new **Estalagem São Domingos** (☎ 286 640 000; www.hotelsaodomingos.com; s/d from €100/120;) features extensive facilities. The hotel's rooms are bright and spacious, with attractive furnishings. You'll also find a saltwater pool, a games room (with snooker) and elegant common areas, including a library.

Best visited with your own transport, São Domingos is 15km east of Mértola.

BEJA

pop 36,200 / elevation 240m

Baixo Alentejo's principal town, Beja is easy-going, welcoming and untouristed, with a walled centre and some beguiling sights. Pleasant, inexpensive guesthouses, quaint plazas and excellent transport links make it one of the best places to stop on your way through the Baixa.

Beja is at the heart of the regional tourist area called Planície Dourada (Golden Plain) – meaning it's surrounded by an endless sea of wheat fields. On Saturday there's the bonus of a traditional market, spread around the castle.

History

The Romans founded Beja on the pinnacle of the plains. They called it Pax Julia (shortened to Pax, which then became Paca, Baca, Baju and finally Beja), after Julius Caesar restored peace between the Romans and rebellious Lusitanians.

It became an important agricultural centre, booming on wheat and oil.

Little evidence remains of the 400 years of subsequent Moorish rule, except for some distinctive 16th-century *azulejos* in the Convento de Nossa Senhora da Conceição (now the Museu Regional). The town was recaptured from the Moors in 1162.

Orientation

Beja's historic core is circled by a ring road and surrounded by modern outskirts. The train station is about 500m northeast of the town centre, the bus station 400m southeast. The main sights are all within an easy walk of each other. Drivers are advised to park near the bus station.

Information

There are several banks with ATMs near the turismo.

Hospital (☎ 284 310 200; Rua Dr António Covas Lima)

Instituto Português da Juventude (IPJ; ☎ 284 325 458; Rua Acabado Janeiro; 9am-7pm Mon-Fri) Free internet access; 300m southeast of bus station.

Planície Dourada (☎ 284 310 150; Praça da República; www.rt-planiciedourada.pt; 9am-12.30pm & 2-5.30pm) The regional tourism office; will sell publications on the area if they are not available at the turismo.

Police station (☎ 284 322 022; Largo Dom Nuno Álvares Pereira)

Post office (Rua Luís de Camões; 8.30am-6.30pm Mon-Fri) Has NetPost.

Só Café (Loja 16, Centro Comercial Pax Julia, Avenida do Brasil; per hr €1.40; 9am-midnight) Provides internet access, but has just one machine.

Turismo (☎ /fax 284 311 913; Rua Capitão João Francisco de Sousa 25; 10am-1pm & 2-6pm Mon-Sat) Look out for the great multilingual *Tourist Guidebook to the Planície Dourada* (€2.50) and *Nature Trails* (€1), both with suggested itineraries and maps, on sale here or at the Planície Dourada office. There's one computer for free internet access.

Sights

PRAÇA DA REPÚBLICA

This renovated attractive **town square** with a *pelourinho* (stone pillory) is the historic heart of the old city. Dominating the square is the 16th-century **Igreja de Misericórdia**, a hefty church with an immense porch – its crude stonework betrays its origins as a meat market. The Planície Dourada building (above) features an elegant Manueline colonnade.

CASTELO

Dom Dinis built the **castle** (admission free; 10am-1pm & 2-6pm Tue-Sun May-Oct, 9am-noon & 1-4pm Nov-Apr)

BEJA'S LOVE LETTERS

A series of scandalous, passionate 17th-century love letters came from Beja, allegedly written by one of the convent's nuns, Mariana Alcoforado, to a French cavalry officer, Count Chamilly. The letters immortalised their love affair while the count was stationed here during the time of the Portuguese war with Spain.

The *Letters of a Portuguese Nun* first emerged in a French translation in 1669 and subsequently appeared in English and many other languages. Funnily enough, the originals were never found.

In 1972 three Portuguese writers, Maria Isabel Barreno, Maria Teresa Horta and Maria Velho da Costa published *The Three Marias: New Portuguese Letters,* a collection of stories, poems and letters that formed a feminist update of the letters – for which they were prosecuted under the Salazar regime.

THE ALENTEJO

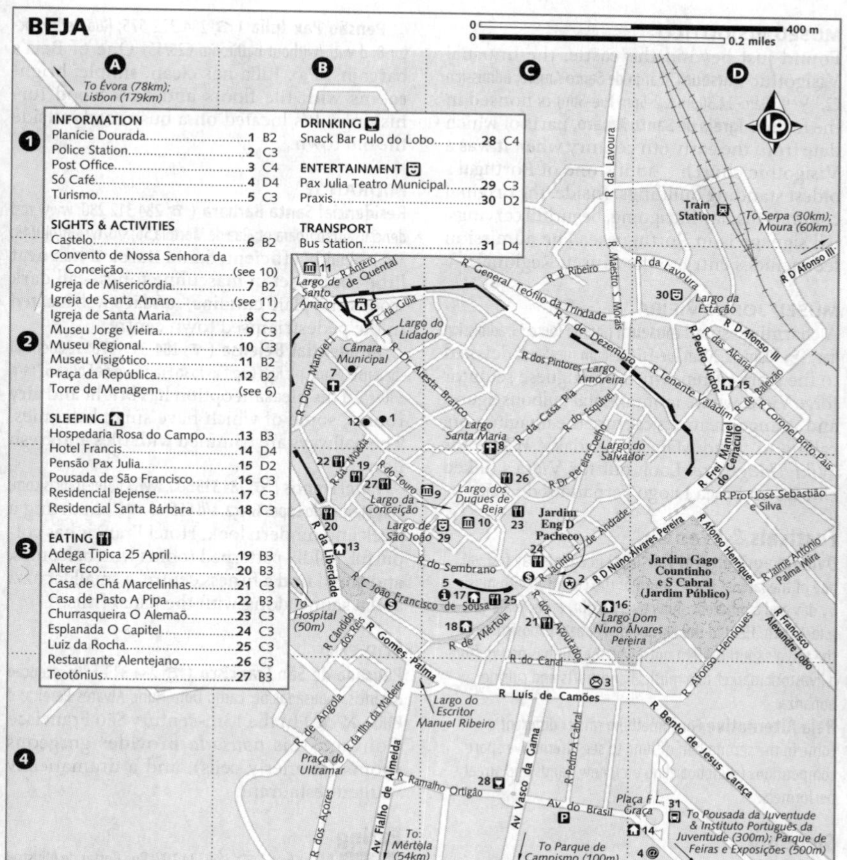

on Roman foundations in the late 13th century. There are grand views from the top of the impressive 42m-high **Torre de Menagem** (admission €1.35). The ticket office has free bilingual leaflets on Beja's culture, arts and heritage.

CONVENTO DE NOSSA SENHORA DA CONCEIÇÃO & MUSEU REGIONAL

Founded in 1459, this Franciscan **convent** (Largo da Conceição; adult/child €2/free, admission free 9.30am-12.30pm Sun; 9.30am-12.30pm & 2-5.15pm Tue-Sun) was the location for the romance between a nun and soldier that inspired *Letters of a Portuguese Nun*, which so caught the public imagination.

Indeed a romantic setting, it's a delicate balance between no-nonsense Gothic and Manueline flights of fancy. The interior is even more lavish than the exterior. Amazing highlights are the busily patterned rococo chapel with 17th- and 18th-century gloriously gilded woodwork, and a chapel seemingly effortlessly inlaid with intricate marble. The chapterhouse is also stunning if incongruously Arabian, with a beautiful ceiling painted with wild unfurling ferns, 16th-century tiles (the oldest in the building) and a carved doorway. The cloister has some splendid 16th- and 17th-century *azulejos*.

Tucked inside this splendid convent is the **Museu Regional**, displaying Roman lamps, glass bottles and stelae, and 16th-century paintings. The admission fee includes entry to the Museu Visigótico.

THE ALENTEJO

MUSEU VISIGÓTICO

Found just beyond the castle, the unusual Visigothic **museum** (Largo de Santo Amaro; admission €2; 9.30am-12.30pm & 2-5pm Tue-Sun) is housed in the former **Igreja de Santo Amaro**, parts of which date from the early 6th century when it was a Visigothic church – so it's one of Portugal's oldest standing buildings. Inside, the original columns display intriguing, beautiful carvings. All signage is in Portuguese. The admission fee includes entry to the Museu Regional.

MUSEU JORGE VIEIRA

A charming, small **museum** (Rua do Touro 33; admission free; 10am-12.30pm Tue-Fri & 2-6pm Tue-Sun), devoted to the work of renowned Portuguese sculptor Jorge Viera, whose monumental bulbous figures and strange creatures capture the imagination, calling to mind Maurice Sendak's *Where the Wild Things Are*. Look out for Viera's linked ellipses on Praça Diogo Fernandes de Beja.

Festivals & Events

Ovibeja agricultural fair This huge nine-day festival, one of the largest in the south of the country, with music by day and a different show every night, takes place in mid-March. Held in the Parque de Feiras e Exposições on the town's southeastern outskirts, the fair has grown from a livestock market to a music, handicrafts and cuisine bonanza.

Beja Alternative For something rather different, come in the second half of June to see alternative sport competitions (skateboarding etc), new bands and street performers.

Sleeping

BUDGET

Parque de campismo (☎ 284 311 911; Avenida Vasco da Gama; adult/tent/car €2.50/1.70/1.70) Beja's camp ing ground is part of a somewhat desolate municipal sports area on the outskirts of town, which also houses a swimming pool and tennis courts. There's disabled access, a restaurant and plenty of shade.

Pousada da juventude (☎ 284 325 458; Rua Professor Janeiro Acabado; beja@movijovem.pt; dm €11, d with/without bathroom €30/24) Next to the IPJ, 300m southeast of the bus station, the youth hostel is fairly new, fresh and spick-and-span. It has a laundry and kitchen facilities, plus bikes for rent.

Hospedaria Rosa do Campo (☎ 284 323 578; residencial.rosa.do.campo@netvisao.pt; Rua da Liberdade 12; s/d €28/40) This guesthouse has charming and polished rooms with wooden floors and small kitchen units, making for good value.

Pensão Pax Julia (☎ 284 322 575; Rua Pedro Victor 8; d with/without bathroom €25/15) One of Beja's bargains, Pax Julia has clean, simple, bright rooms with tile floors and dark-wood furnishings. It's located on a busy road outside the old town.

MIDRANGE

Residencial Santa Bárbara (☎ 284 312 280; www.residencialsantabarbara.pt; Rua de Mértola 56; s/d/tw €30/40/43;) Briskly efficient, Santa Barbara has neat little rooms set in masculine tones – all dark woods and plaid curtains – and it's well located in the pedestrianised town centre.

Residencial Bejense (☎ 284 311 570; residencial-bejense@sapo.pt; Rua Capitão João Francisco de Sousa 57; s/d €30/45) This pleasant option has bright and airy rooms, some of which have small balconies. The hallways are trimmed with tiles and fresh flowers.

Hotel Francis (☎ 284 315 500; www.hotel-francis.com; Praça Fernando Lopes Graça; s/d €55/65;) Sporting a sleek and modern look, Hotel Francis has colourful, boldly patterned rooms with balconies, and you'll find a fitness centre, a small Jacuzzi and a sauna along with the usual frills.

TOP END

Pousada de São Francisco (☎ 284 313 580; recepcao.sfrancis@pousadas.pt; Largo Dom Nuno Álvares Pereira; d €185;) In the 13th-century São Francisco Convent, this *pousada* provides gorgeous rooms (formerly cells), and a dramatically vaulted restaurant.

Eating

our pick **Alter Eco** (☎ 284 324 102; Rua Portas de Aljustrel 29; specials €4.50; 6pm-2am Mon-Sat; V) A favourite with Beja's alternative crowd, this attractive café-restaurant-bar is spread between two floors of an atmospheric old building, and has comfy chairs and sofas and cosy nooks beside the windows overlooking the street. Tasty vegetarian specials (like spinach lasagne) change daily and there's an enticing assortment of homemade desserts. Good music, art exhibitions, refreshing cocktails and a laid-back crowd are all part of the charm.

Churrasqueira O Alemão (☎ 284 311 490; Largo dos Duques de Beja 11; mains €5-7; lunch & dinner) Specializing in grilled chicken, steak and the like, this place has a popular takeaway counter and a cosy, sit-down restaurant next door. It's a local favourite for reliably good, reasonably priced dishes.

Restaurante Alentejano (☎ 284 323 849; Largo dos Duques de Beja 6; mains €4-7; ⌚ lunch & dinner Sat-Thu) This lively local eatery is a good bet for filling Alentejan plates of roasted pork or cod dishes. It has a relaxed but dapper atmosphere, with TV in the background.

Casa de Pasto a Pipa (☎ 284 327 043; Rua da Moeda 8; mains €6-9; ⌚ lunch & dinner Mon-Sat) A charmingly rustic eatery with a wood-beamed ceiling, blue-and-white checked tablecloths and farm implements on the walls, A Pipa dishes up good filling mains.

Casa de Chá Marcelinhas (☎ 284 321 500; Rua dos Açoutados 12; ⌚ 8.30am-8pm Mon-Sat) For delicious regional pastries head to this lovely, sedate tearoom, which serves typical *doces conventuais* (desserts traditionally made by nuns) and, particularly good, *pasteis de toucinho* (a delicious thin pastry and almond creation).

Luiz da Rocha (☎ 284 323 179; Rua Capitão João Francisco de Sousa 63; mains €5.50-10; ⌚ lunch & dinner) One of Beja's oldest cafés always gathers a chatty neighbourhood crowd, and it's justly famous for its cakes: *trouxas de ovos* (sweet egg yolks) and *porquinho doce* (a sweet little pig). It also serves up Alentejan staples.

Esplanada O Capitel (☎ 284 325 708; Jardim Engenheiro Duarte Pacheco; snacks €1-4; ⌚ breakfast, lunch & dinner) This is a relaxing, partly open-air café, in the centre of a quiet square – well-placed for fresh orange juice or an afternoon pick-me-up.

Adega Típica 25 Abril (Rua da Moeda; mains €6-9; ⌚ lunch & dinner Tue-Sun) Popular at lunch, this cavernous, rustic *adega* serves typical food, with good daily specials.

Teotónius (☎ 284 328 010; Rua do Touro; mains €6-10; ⌚ lunch & dinner Wed-Mon) A well-regarded whitewashed arched cellar, this places dishes up good traditional mains such as *carne de porco à alentejana* (pork with clams), and less-traditional ones, such as fondue and (so they claim) the best snails in the world.

Drinking

Snack-Bar Pulo do Lobo (Avenida Vasco da Gama; ⌚ noon-10pm) A café-restaurant with an outdoor terrace, Pulo do Lobo is a Beja favourite for an evening get-together over snails and cold beer.

Entertainment

Praxis (Rua General Teófilo da Trinidade; ⌚ midnight-6am) Near the train station, this big nightclub is the sister to the one in Évora, and equally popular for its good-time house sounds.

Pax Julia Teatro Municipal (☎ 284 315 090; www.paxjulia.org; Largo de São João 1) This cinema and theatre hosts regular concerts, dance performances and film screenings; pick up a bimonthly programme guide at the turismo or stop by their box office.

Getting There & Away

BUS

From the **bus station** (☎ 284 313 620) daily buses run to Évora (7.80, 1½ hours); Mértola (€4.50, 1¼ hours, two daily); and Serpa (€2.75, 45 minutes, seven daily), some continuing to Moura (€4.50, 65 minutes, five daily). Around half this number operates on weekends. Buses run to Faro daily (€10, 3¼ hours, three daily) via Albufeira (€9, 2¼ hours), and to Lisbon (€10.60, 3¼ hours, six daily).

Buses also run to the Spanish border town of Vila Verde de Ficalho (normal/express, €4.50/7.50), and on Tuesday, Thursday and Saturday to Seville (€17.50, 3½ hours).

TRAIN

Beja is on the Lisbon–Funcheira (near Ourique) railway line. There are three direct *intercidade* (IC) services from Lisbon (€15, 2½ hours) and three direct *regional* (R) trains (€9.50, 3¼ hours).

Getting Around

Bikes are available for free use within the city from the *câmara municipal* (near Praça da República) or the turismo. Some form of ID (eg a passport) must be left as a deposit.

SERPA

pop 18,200 / elevation 230m

Planted among the rolling hills of vineyards and dusty fields, Serpa is a sleepy town of bleached-white walls and narrow cobblestone streets, with cats stepping gingerly over hot roofs and children eyeing the town's famous creamy-cheese pastries in bakery windows. At its old medieval heart is a small pretty plaza carefully guarded by the elderly folk who have long called Serpa home.

Orientation

Those arriving by car must brave tight gateways into the old town and breathtakingly narrow streets (or park outside the walls).

The bus station, *mercado municipal* and *parque de campismo* are in the new town area, southwest of the old town. From the bus station,

turn left and then take the first right and keep walking till you see the walls.

Information

On the fourth Tuesday of the month a huge country market sprawls beside Rua de Santo António on the town's northeastern outskirts.

C@fe (Rua Dr Eduardo Fernando de Oliveira 18; per hr €1.20; ⌚ 9am-6.30pm) Provides internet access; 250m east of the *mercado municipal*.

Caixa Geral de Depósitos Bank & ATM (Largo Conde de Boavista) Around the corner from the turismo; also has an ATM.

Lavendaria Moderna (Rua das Portas de Beja; per kg €3.60; ⌚ 9am-12.30pm & 2.30-6pm Mon-Fri) Not self-service, but cheap.

Post office (Rua dos Lagares)

Turismo (☎ 284 544 727; Largo Dom Jorge de Melo 2; ⌚ 9am-12.30pm & 2-5.30pm) In the centre; has a map of the old town and sells local handicrafts.

Sights

CASTELO

You enter the small **castle** (admission free; ⌚ 9am-12.30pm & 2-5.30pm) through a dramatic entrance: a heavy cracked piece of wall. Inside it feels domestic in scale. You can walk around the battlements for long views over the flat plains, the aqueduct, town walls, rooftops and orange trees, and the slow life of Serpa residents. Also inside the walls is the small **Museu de Arqueologia** (admission free; ⌚ 9am-12.15pm & 2-5.15pm), housing a small collection of archaeological remnants that reveal bits of Serpa's history which reaches back to the arrival of the Celts over 2000 years ago.

TOWN WALLS & AQUEDUTO

Walls still stand around most of the inner town. Along the west side (follow Rua dos Arcos) run the impressive remains of an 11th-century **aqueduct**. At the southern end is a huge 17th-century wheel pump (aka noria), once used for pumping water along the aqueduct to the nearby **Palácio dos Condes de Ficalho** (still used by the de Ficalho family as a holiday home).

MUSEU ETNOGRÁFICO

No traditional rural trade is left unturned in the exquisite exploration of Alentejan life found at Serpa's **Ethnographic Museum** (Largo do Corro; admission free; 9am-12.30pm & 2-5.30pm Tue-Sun). Beautifully presented and polished tools, used by former wheelwrights, saddle makers, barrel makers and ironmongers are on display. The accompanying booklet is only in Portuguese, so nonlinguists get to play guess the use of the implement.

MUSEU DO RELÓGIO

This **museum** (284 543 194; www.museudorelogio.pa-net.pt; Rua do Assento 31; adult/child under 10 €2/free; 2-5pm Tue-Fri, 10am-noon & 2-5pm Sat & Sun) houses an amazing private collection of watches and clocks, from Napoleonic gilded timepieces to Swiss cuckoo clocks, in the cool vaulted surroundings of the former Convento do Mosteirinho. Also on display are two Roman urns used to keep food cool, found during excavations.

Festivals & Events

Festas de Senhora de Guadalupe Celebrations of Serpa's patron saint take place in March/April from Good Friday to the following Tuesday – there is a pilgrimage to bring the saint's image down to the parish church, and on the last day a procession takes it back to the chapel on horseback. On the Tuesday everyone eats roast lamb.

Noites na Noura Held in July and the first week of August, this festival features nightly local theatre and music shows on a terrace tucked behind the aqueduct.

Sleeping

Parque de campismo (284 544 290; Largo de São Pedro; adult/tent/car €2/1.80/1.50) The municipal camping ground is on scrubby land 400m northeast of the bus station on the southwestern edge of town. There's a restaurant and disabled access; rates include admission to the nearby pool.

Casa de Hóspedes Vírginia (284 549 145; Largo 25 de Abril; s/d with shared bathroom €15/25) A tiny guesthouse with basic but sizable rooms and somewhat thin walls, Vírginia is good value. It faces a square dotted with orange trees.

Residencial Beatriz (284 544 423; fax 284 543 100; Largo do Salvador 10; s/d €32/45, 2-/4-person apt €52/65;) A small modern building on a pleasant little square facing a church, this comfortable spot has smart rooms with big windows and minibalconies.

Casa de Serpa (284 549 238; www.casadeserpa.com; Largo do Salvador 28; s/d €40/56) This friendly guesthouse has a fine location in the centre of town, with bright, handsomely furnished rooms that open onto a courtyard. Home-made breakfasts include fresh orange juice and local produce.

Casa da Muralha (284 543 150; www.casadamuralha.com; Rua das Portas de Beja 43; s/d €60/75) Serpa's most atmospheric overnight is at this house nestled beside the town walls. Its spacious whitewashed rooms have arched or beamed ceilings, and are set with traditional, elegant wooden furniture. They open onto a courtyard shaded by lemon and orange trees, with the old walls looming overhead. You can rent canoes for river trips.

Eating & Drinking

All the local restaurants serve *tapas de queijadas de Serpa*, the salty and creamy local cheese, served as an appetiser.

Restaurante São Pedro (284 543 186; Avenida da Paz; mains €4.75-8; lunch & dinner Mon-Sat) Near the camping ground, São Pedro is a simple airy eatery, with outside tables – a good spot for grilled chicken or snails.

Restaurante Pizzeria A Adega (284 544 308, Rua do Rossio 76; mains €4-8; lunch & dinner Fri-Wed) With some outdoor tables on a sleepy square, this is a convivial pizzeria, good for families, that also serves Portuguese mains.

Restaurante O Casarão (284 549 295; Largo do Salvador 20; mains from €6-9; lunch & dinner) Not far from the town walls, this is a slightly more elegant option, with a small cosy interior and generous servings of traditional hearty mains.

Mohló Bico (284 549 264; Rua Quente 1; mains €5-9; lunch & dinner Thu-Tue) This great arched, rustic space, has exposed brickwork, long wooden tables and huge wine urns – a perfect setting for the good traditional cooking, particularly grilled plates of fish.

Café Alentejano (☎ 284 544 335; Praça da República; mains €7-12) Serpa's best-located café has outdoor tables on the main square and a vaguely Art Deco interior. Try a locally made *queijada de Serpa* (a cheesecake-like pastry). The upstairs restaurant has good food in an appealing, white-arched location.

Café Rotunda (Avenida da Paz; €6-10; ⌚ 9am-10pm) One of three cafés surrounding a small roundabout, this low-key spot is ideal for sitting outside and catching up on the local gossip. It's one block west of the bus station.

Cervejaria Lebrinha (☎ 284 549 311; Rua do Calvário 6; mains €6-9; ⌚ lunch & dinner Wed-Mon) Popular with the locals, Lebrinha is a no-nonsense restaurant that's touted as Serpa's choice spot to drink beer. You'll find plenty of cod, grilled shrimp and grilled pork loin to accompany those draughts.

Shopping

At the unsigned **Dom Luis** (Praça da República 15; ⌚ 10am-1pm & 3pm-6.30pm Wed-Sun) you can buy cheese (€14.50 per kg) in various varieties, as well as wine or smoked ham. Creamy rich *queijadas* are also available.

The **Casa de Artesanatos** (Rua dos Cavalos 31; ⌚ 10am-6pm) is a fun place to browse, with jams, olive oil, cheese, pottery, handicrafts and odd iron implements you might have seen at the Museu Etnográfico.

Getting There & Away

Buses (☎ 284 544 740) run to/from Lisbon (€10, four hours, two to four daily) via Beja (€2.75, 35 minutes, two to four daily). There are no direct buses to Évora. A daily service goes to the Spanish frontier east of Vila Verde de Ficalho (€11, 35 minutes, one daily).

MOURA

pop 17,600 / elevation 180m

This pleasant working-class city is flatter than most fortified towns in the Alentejo, and it's an intriguing place to wander, with some elegant buildings, an ageing castle and well-preserved neighbourhood with some remnants of its Moorish past. Well placed near water sources and rich in ores, Moura has been a farming and mining centre and a fashionable spa in previous incarnations, though nowadays it remains a backwater, with incongruously graceful buildings. It's also the nearest large town to the fairly new lake created by the Barragem do Alqueva, 15km to the north.

The Moors' 500-year occupation came to a end in 1232 after a Christian invasion. Despi the reconquest, Moorish presence in the cit remained strong – they only abandoned the quarter in 1496 (after Dom Manuel's convert or-leave edict).

The town's name comes from a legend re lated to the 13th-century takeover. Mooris resident Moura Salúquiyya opened the tow gates to Christians disguised as Muslims. The sacked the town, and poor Moura flung herse from a tower.

Orientation

The bus station is by the defunct train statio at the newer, southern end of town, aroun 500m from the old town and the main square Praça Sacardo Cabral (which has a Galp petro station on the corner). All the main places o interest are within easy walking distance.

Information

There are banks on the *praça* and along Ru Serpa Pinto, directly north of the turismo.

Espaço Internet (☎ Rua 5 de Outubro 18; ⌚ 8.30am midnight Mon-Fri, 12.30pm-midnight Sat) Free (and very swanky) Internet access.

Post office (Rua da República) East of Rua Serpa Pinto.

Turismo (☎ 285 251 375; Largo de Santa Clara; ⌚ 9am-1pm & 2-5pm Mon-Fri, 10am-1pm & 2.30-5.30pm Sat & Sun) Some 400m downhill from the bus station; turn left into the first main street, Rua das Forças Armadas, and right at the end.

Sights & Activities

MUSEU MUNICIPAL

In an appealing residential quarter off a lan about 200m east of the *praça*, this fine tiny **museum** (☎ 285 253 978; Rua da Romeira; admission free ⌚ 9.30am-12.30pm & 2.30-5.30pm Tue-Sun), contains local prehistoric and Roman remains, such as 1st- and 2nd-century needles, as well as Moorish funerary tablets.

LAGAR DE VARAS DO FOJO

With a system of production that would have been similar to that of Roman times, the **oil press** (Rua João de Deus 20; admission free; ⌚ 9.30am-12.30pm & 2.30-5.30pm Tue-Sun) re-creates the oil-pressing factory that functioned here until 1941, with giant wooden and stone-wheel presses.

IGREJA DE SÃO BAPTISTA

This 16th-century **church** (admission free) has a remarkable Manueline portal. Set against the plain façade, it is a twisting, flamboyant bit of decoration, with carvings of knotted ropes, crowns and armillary spheres. Inside, the church has some fine deep-blue and yellow 17th-century Sevillian *azulejos*. It's just outside Jardim Dr Santiago.

JARDIM DR SANTIAGO & SPA

The **thermal spa** was at the entrance to the lovely, shady Jardim Dr Santiago, at the eastern end of Praça Sacadura Cabral, but is pretty much defunct, though pitched for redevelopment into something a bit more 21st century. Bicarbonated calcium waters, said to be good for rheumatism, burble from the richly marbled **Fonte das Três Bicas** (Fountain with Three Spouts) by the entrance to the *jardim*. The garden itself has a good view, a bandstand, and is a favourite spot for elderly men to sit and chat.

MOURARIA

The old **Moorish quarter** (Poço Árabe) lies at the western end of Praça Sacadura Cabral. It's a well-preserved tight cluster of narrow, cobbled lanes and white terraced cottages with chunky or turreted chimneys.

The **Núcleo Árabe** (Travessa da Mouraria 11; admission free; 9.30am-12.30pm & 2.30-5.30pm Tue-Fri, 2.30-5.30pm Sat & Sun) just off Largo da Mouraria is a pocket collection of Moorish ceramics and other remains, such as carved stone inscriptions and a 14th-century Arabic well.

CASTELO

Offering fabulous views across the countryside, the **castle** (admission free) above the old town has been restored. One of the towers is the last remnant of a Moorish fortress. Rebuilt by Dom Dinis in the 13th century and again by Dom Manuel I in 1510, the castle itself was largely destroyed by the Spanish in the 18th century. There's a ruined convent inside the walls.

Sleeping

Residencial Santa Comba (☎/fax 285 251 255; Praça Sacadura Cabral 34; s/d from €23/35;) On the main square, this smart new place is in an old building, with clean rooms and balconies overlooking the square. There's disabled access.

Residencial Alentejana (☎ 285 250 080; www.residencialalentejana.com.pt; Largo José Maria dos Santos 40; s/d €25/35;) This green-shuttered house opposite the Galp petrol station near the bus station, has a gloomy foyer, but the rooms are comfortable and clean.

A Casa da Moura (☎/fax 285 251 264; Largo Dr Rodrigues Acabado 47; s/d €26/45;) Nicely located in the old Moorish part of town, this friendly spot has 10 clean, pleasant rooms and shared sunny terraces.

Hotel de Moura (☎ 285 251 090; www.hoteldemoura.com; Praça Gago Coutinho; s/d from €40/55) Moura's loveliest hotel is a grand place with sweeping staircases, polished floors and tall windows overlooking a pretty square. Rooms, however, vary considerably, from the classically furnished to the rather barren. It's worth paying extra for a superior room.

Eating & Drinking

There are several café-restaurants with outdoor seating around Praça Sacadura Cabral, where you'll also find the *mercado municipal* in a huge glass building.

O Ideal (☎ 285 251 182; Rua Serpa Pinto 12; mains €7-8.50; lunch & dinner Tue-Sun) A few blocks south of the *praça*, this is a good spot for traditional dishes. There's a casual café at the front and a tile-lined dining room at the back.

O Trilho (☎ 285 254 261; Rua 5 de Outubro 5; €6-10; lunch & dinner Tue-Sun) Three streets east of Rua Serpa Pinto, O Trilho is another local favourite, with excellent regional mains.

Bar do Castelo (2pm-4am Tue-Sun) In the castle complex, this small, smoky bar plays rock to a young friendly crowd. There's an open-air patio attached.

Getting There & Away

Buses run to/from Beja (€4.50, one hour, three to five daily) via Serpa (€2.60, 40 minutes). Rede Expressos run to Lisbon (€13, four hours, daily) via Évora (€8.20, 1½ hours).

COASTAL ALENTEJO

PORTO CÔVO

pop 1100

Perched on low cliffs with fine views over the sea, Porto Côvo is the first enticing coastal town you'll reach after heading south of the Setúbal Peninsula. Portuguese holidaymakers arrive en masse to this former fishing village during summer but somehow don't detract from Porto Côvo's sleepy charm. Its old town consists of just a handful of cobbled streets lined with sun-bleached houses and a pretty town square at its northern end. Modern villas and summer homes are spread outside the small centre.

THE ALENTEJO

Paths along the cliffs lead down to the harbour at the town's southern end and to the fantastic rock formations to the north, with access down to the fine Praia do Somouqueira, a beach that grows considerably during low tide.

The **turismo** (☎ 269 959 124; 🕑 9am-noon & 1-5pm Mon-Fri) is on the edge of the old town, just one block north of the main square and next to a free car park.

Sleeping & Eating

Parque do Campismo (☎ 269 905 136; campingportocovo@gmail.com; Estrada Municipal 554; adult/tent/car €3.20/4.50/4.90) This good, well-equipped camp site, with a restaurant, store and disabled access, is just outside of town on the road to Vila Nova de Milfontes.

Zé Inácio (☎ 269 959 124; Rua Vasco da Gama; d €40-70) Above a restaurant of the same name, this attractive spot has spacious rooms with tile floors, bamboo ceilings and white stucco walls.

Maresia (☎ 269 905 449; Rua Cândido da Silva 57; d/apt €50/60) Strategically placed above the narrow harbour, this place rents out comfortable rooms with ocean views, as well as a spacious apartment. Maresia, however, is better known for its excellent restaurant (mains €10 to €13), with the best views in town from its terrace. In addition to seafood, there are tasty desserts, including lemon meringue pie.

Restaurante Marquês (☎ 269 905 036; Largo Marquês de Pombal; mains €10-17; 🕑 lunch & dinner Wed-Mon) Porto Côvo's favourite dining spot is set on the town's main square, with inviting outdoor tables and scrumptious plates of grilled fish and seafood salads. There's also a low-key café-cum-ice-cream shop next door.

Getting There & Away

During summer at least five buses a day travel to/from Lisbon (€11.60, 2¾ hours). There are also regular connections to Vila Nova de Milfontes (€5, 25 minutes).

VILA NOVA DE MILFONTES

pop 3200

One of the loveliest towns along this stretch of the coast, Vila Nova de Milfontes has an attractive, whitewashed centre, sparkling beaches nearby and a laid-back population that couldn't imagine living anywhere else. It's set in the middle of the beautiful Parque Natural do Sudoeste Alentejano e Costa Vicentina and is still a port (Hannibal is said to have sheltered here) alongside a lovely, sand-edged limb of estuary.

No stranger to tourism, Vila Nova's narrow lanes and tiny plazas harbour some colourful eating and drinking options, with even more scenic restaurants out on the beach. Just the same, Vila Nova remains much more low-key than most resort towns in the Algarve, though all bets are off in August when surfers and sun-seekers pack the place.

Orientation & Information

The main road into town from Odemira and Lisbon, Rua Custódio Bras Pacheco, is lined with restaurants, banks, shops and the post office.

Police station (☎ 283 998 391; Rua António Mantas)

Turismo (☎ 283 996 599; Rua António Mantas; 🕑 10am-1pm & 2-6pm Tue-Sat) Off the main road, opposite the police station, en route to the centre of town if you're driving. Buses stop a bit further along the same road.

Beaches

Praia do Farol, the lighthouse beach just by the town, is sheltered but gets busy. Beaches on the other side of the estuary are less crowded. Be careful of the strong river currents running through the estuary. If you have your own transport, you could head out to the fantastic **Praia do Malhão**, backed by rocky dunes and covered in fragrant scrub, around 7km to the north (travel 2.5km to Bruinheras, turn left before the primary school, then travel another 3km until you see a sign to the beach where you turn left – the road is not paved all the way). The more remote parts of the beach harbour nudist and gay areas. The sea is quite wild here, but the coast is strikingly empty of development.

Activities

There are some gorgeous beaches around both near the town and extending out along the coast. Scuba diving is organised by **Alentejo Divers** (☎ 283 996 821, 939 145 368; gitte@netc.p Pousadas Velhas, Apt 129), who run PADI courses about 1km beyond the Parque de Campismo Milfontes (signposted).

You can rent surfboards at **Essential Surf Shop** (Rua Sarmento Beires 10; 🕑 10am-10pm), with discounts for longer rentals. Next door, **Sudaventura** (☎ 283 997 231; www.sudaventura.com; Rua Sarmento Beires 10; 🕑 10am-7pm) offers a range of excursions including canoe and jeep trips, river boat ou ings and the like. You can also rent bikes here. Surf lessons are available through **Surf Milfontes** (☎ 919 922 193; www.surfmilfontes.com).

Sleeping

Note that prices zoom upwards in August and you'll need to book in advance.

BUDGET

Sitava Turismo (☎ 283 890 100; www.sitava.pt; adult/tent/car €3.55/3.35/2.15;) Near Praia do Malhão (600m), this is a superb on-its-own camp site, with supermarket, pub and restaurant and disabled facilities. It's well situated on a tree-shaded 50-hectare site.

Campiférias (☎ 283 996 409; novaferias@oninet.pt; Rua da Praça; adult/tent/car €3.50/2.90/3.50;) A camp site 500m northwest of the turismo, this is only 800m from the beach, with disabled access and lots of shade.

Parque de Campismo Milfontes (☎ 283 996 140; parquemilfontes@netc.pt; adult/tent/car €3.80/3.20/4.20;) Near Campiférias, this is an even better-equipped site, in a pine forest close to the beach. It has a café and grocery, small bungalows (€54 to €75) and disabled access.

Casa Amarela (☎ 283 996 632; www.casaamarela milfontes.com; Rua Dom Luis Castro e Almeida; dm €12.50 d/tr/q €35/50/62.50;) A longtime backpacker favourite, this cheery yellow guesthouse is set with eclectic art and knick-knacks collected by the genial English-speaking owner, Rui, on his world travels. You'll find bright, tidy rooms, a cosy lounge space, shared kitchens and free internet. There's also a peaceful annexe nearby, with attractive dorm rooms, a courtyard and solar-heated showers.

MIDRANGE & TOP END

Residencial Mil-Réis (☎ 283 998 233; fax 283 998 328; Largo do Rossio 2; d/tr €40/50) Run by a friendly elderly couple, this modern place offers clean, well-kept rooms in a pretty house in the old town centre.

Pensão do Cais (☎ 283 996 268; Rua do Cais 9; d €45) The large flower-filled patio overlooking the river is the most charming feature in this modern three-storey building, while the rooms range from fair to charming, some with solid-wood furniture and brilliant views.

Casa dos Arcos (☎ 283 996 264; fax 283 997 156; Rua do Cais; d €50;) Jauntily painted in blue and white, this smart, airy guesthouse has comfortable beds, tiled floors and small balconies. There's disabled access.

Quinta das Varandas (☎ 283 996 155; fax 283 998 102; d €50, one-/two-bedroom apt €65/80) In a peaceful setting 700m west of the turismo (and 300m from the beach), this blue-and-white complex offers handsome rooms with cork floors and verandas. It also has simply furnished apartments. Many other similar apartment hotels are nearby.

our pick **Casa do Adro** (☎ 283 997 102; www.casa doadro.com; Rua Diário de Notícias 10; d €80;) Set in a house dating from the 17th century, this Turismo Rural option has antique- and artwork-filled common areas, with seven elegantly furnished bedrooms. Some rooms have private balconies, others have access to shared terraces, and each guest gets to request the hour of breakfast – a nice touch.

Castelo de Milfontes (☎ 283 998 231; s/d €110/145) Set in a small 16th-century castle, this is a marvellously atmospheric place to stay, with antique furniture, suits of armour, *azulejos* and superb views. Reservations are essential.

Eating

Paparoca (Largo Brito de Pais 11; mains €3-5; 7am-midnight) Paparoca is the sandwich king of Milfontes, with good, inexpensive sandwiches as well as soups, filling specials and rich desserts. It has a few outdoor tables.

Mabi (Largo de Santa Maria 25a; 8am-2am) Something of a Milfontes institution, this cheery and inviting café serves excellent pastries (€0.75 to €1.50), ice cream and coffee.

Patio das Pizzas (☎ 283 996 355; Rua do Pinhal 4; mains €6-8; lunch & dinner) This enticing Italian spot serves a good variety of pizzas and pasta dishes, and it has nice lighting, a bamboo ceiling and friendly staff.

Restaurante Portinho do Canal (☎ 283 996 255; mains €6.50-10; lunch & dinner Fri-Wed) Up from the fishing harbour, this is an old-school, family-run place that has superb views over the sea, and decent grilled fish.

A Telha (☎ 283 996 138; Rua do Pinhal 3; mains €7-10.50; lunch & dinner) This casual eatery is popular for simple but delicious dishes like grilled chicken, fried shrimp and the like.

Restaurante A Fateixa (☎ 283 996 415; mains €8-12; lunch & dinner Thu-Tue) With a perfect setting down by the river, A Fateixa delivers excellent seafood dishes (try the grilled squid or *tamboril* (monkfish) rice for two), and it has breezy outdoor tables.

Portal da Vila (☎ 283 996 823; Largo do Rossio; mains €8-12; lunch & dinner Tue-Sun) A cosy restaurant decorated in colourful tiles, this place serves up sizzling grilled fish (halibut, flounder, whatever's fresh) as well as *porco da pedra* (pork served on a hot stone) and other unusual plates.

Tasca do Celso (☎ 283 996 753; Rua dos Aviadores; mains €10-14; lunch & dinner Tue-Sun) Inside a charming blue-and-white building, you'll find neat, traditional décor and excellent cuisine, particularly the grilled seafood.

Restaurante Choupana (☎ 283 996 643; Praia do Farol; dinner for two €50; lunch & dinner) Set in a wooden structure right on the beach, this lovely but rustic spot is the best place in town for fresh grilled fish. Dishes here are pricey (you pay by the kilo), but the quality is top-notch. There's a pleasant little open-air terrace where you can just stop in for a drink and watch the grill master in action.

Drinking

Café Azul (Rossio 20) Always lively, whatever the time of year, even if the rest of the town is dead, this is a jovial bar with a pool table and lots of papier-mâché sharks, octopuses and squid hanging from the ceiling.

Green Island (Largo de Santa Maria 39) Run by a friendly couple, Green Island is an enticing garden bar that's open in the summer.

Discoteca SudWest (Estrada do Canal; midnight-6am) In season this is the big hip-and-happening house nightspot, with a packed dance floor and diverse crowds.

Café Turco (Rua Dom João II) With a touch of Moorish atmosphere, this café gathers a fun, slightly more bohemian crowd. It has a partly outdoor setting, but is only open in the high season.

Getting There & Away

Vila Nova has three bus connections daily on weekdays to/from Odemira (€2.70, 20 minutes). There are buses daily from Lisbon (€12, four hours, three daily) via Setúbal (€10.80, three hours) and one daily from Portimão (€8.90, two hours) and Lagos. The ticket office in Vila Nova is at Largo de Santa Maria, a few doors down from Mabi.

ZAMBUJEIRA DO MAR

pop 850

Enchantingly wild beaches backed by rugged cliffs form the setting to this sleepy seaside village. There are only a few quiet lanes in this tiny one-horse town, with the main street terminating at the cliff, down which paths lead to the attractive sands below. Quieter than Vila Nova, Zambujeira attracts a backpacker, surfy crowd, though in August the town throws some pretty big parties, including Festa do Sudoeste, one of Portugal's biggest music fests. The crowds give Zambujeira some uncharacteristic zip, but they obscure its out-of-season charms: fresh fish in mom-and-pop restaurants, blustering clifftop walks and a dramatic, empty coast.

There's a small **turismo** (☎ 283 961 14[illegible]; 9.30am-1pm & 2-5.30pm Tue-Sat) on the main street, which closes to traffic from July to mid September.

Festivals & Events

Held in early August, the **Festival do Sudoeste** is one of Portugal's best international contemporary music festivals. Recent years have seen PJ Harvey and Massive Attack.

Sleeping & Eating

Parque de Campismo Zambujeira (☎ 283 961 17[illegible]; www.campingzambujeira.com.sapo.pt; adult/tent/car €4/4.50/4) Just 800m east of the village, this is a wooded, well-appointed site with a playground. It's near the beach and also has bungalows for rent.

Residencial Mar-e-Sol (☎ 283 961 171, 283 961 19[illegible]; Rua Miramar 17a; d €40-50) In Zambujeira's main street, this is run by a charming landlady Dona Maria Fernanda. Rooms are spick-and-span and all have a private (though not always en suite) bathroom; there's also a shared kitchen.

Taverna Ti Vítoria (☎ 283 961 130; Rua da Fonte; mains €6-15; lunch & dinner Tue-Sun) Almost behind Residencial Mar-e-Sol, just off the main square, this is a traditional *churrasqueira* (grill restaurant), good for fish, and with a nice terrace.

Café-Restaurant Rita (Rua Miramar 1; mains €6-13.50; lunch & dinner Fri-Wed) has a fine vantage point with a raised terrace overlooking the sea; it gets mixed reviews on the grilled fish and seafood. **O Martinho** (Rua Miramar 2; mains €6-13.50; lunch & dinner), across the street, has similar views and seafood.

Getting There & Away

In summer, Zambujeira has one to three daily connections with Vila Nova (€7, 45 minutes) and Lisbon (€12.70, 3¾ hours) – buy tickets at the **bookshop** (Rua Miramar 9). Buses also run to Odemira (40 minutes) and Beja (three hours); for these you buy your ticket on the bus.

THE ALENTEJO

Estremadura & Ribatejo

Occupying the country's richest farmland yet within striking distance of the capital, the Estremadura and Ribatejo regions were a perfect choice for Portugal's great and good to build their most splendid monuments. The four grandest, each one equal parts political might and religious fervour, have earned World Heritage status: the massive palace-cum-monastery at Mafra; the masterly gothic Mosteiro de Santa Maria da Vitória (Battle Abbey); the distinctly epicurean Mosteiro de Santa Maria de Alcobaça (Alcobaça Monastery) and the Convento de Cristo, Portuguese headquarters of those mystical warriors, the Knights Templar.

And then there's Fátima. Similarly splendid in scale if aesthetically more dubious, it remains one of the Catholic world's most important pilgrimages, a scene of intense devotion since three children chatted with the Virgin Mary here in 1917. If you need a mass-produced bust of Pope John Paul II, Fátima's your place.

The region's coast is home to a series of fine, wide beaches and some of Europe's best surfing. Head for the Lisbon weekend getaways of Ericeira, Peniche and Nazaré, or wilder beaches backed by the Pinhal de Leiria – a 700-year-old forest of coastal pines. And don't miss Óbidos, a beguiling village of whitewashed houses girdled by bristling medieval walls.

Inland, Ribatejo ('Above the Tejo River') is, along with Lisbon, Portugal's industrial powerhouse. Santarém, Portugal's bullfighting centre and the region's scenic capital, overlooks rich, green plains that produce some very big, very bad bulls indeed.

HIGHLIGHTS

- Gaping at the Gothic heights and intricate Manueline tracery of **Batalha's abbey** (p283)
- Praying for victory at the Templar's 16-sided altar at Tomar's 12th-century **Convento de Cristo** (p297)
- Walking the medieval walls that girdle whitewashed, jewel-like **Óbidos** – the traditional wedding gift to future queens (p274)
- Catching whiff of the neat rows of coastal pines at **Pinhal de Leiria** (p288), planted some seven centuries ago by a forward-thinking king
- Conjuring the smells that once wafted from the kitchens at **Alcobaça's** distinctly epicurean abbey (p281)

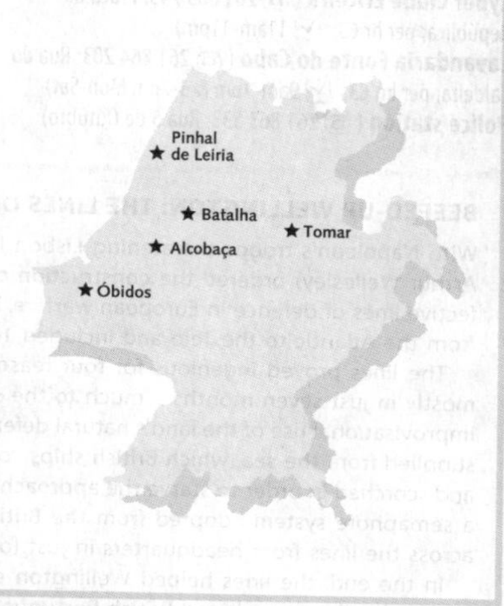

- POPULATION: 1,113,000
- AREA: 11,500 SQ KM

Book accommodation online at lonelyplanet.cc

ESTREMADURA

Running up the Atlantic coast from the mouth of the Rio Tejo almost to the Rio Mondego, Estremadura has long been a land of plenty, its rolling hills and valleys offering up some of Portugal's richest farmland. For proof, visit the elaborate kitchens that fattened up the monks at Alcobaça's extraordinary monastery. The coast, too, is blessed with miles-long strands, which also catch some of Europe's best surf. Estremadura earned its name the same way as Spain's Extremadura: for a time, it represented the farthest reaches of the Reconquista.

ERICEIRA

pop 6700

Sitting on bluffs above a series of sheltered coves, this fishing-village-turned-resort boasts grandstand views up and down the Atlantic coast. Long popular with weekending Lisboêtas, its outskirts have been overbuilt, but the narrow lanes of its whitewashed core remain remarkably preserved – though they're packed to the gills in August. If you're in search of succulent seafood or challenging surf, Ericeira also delivers.

The town's old centre is clustered around Praça da República, with a newer district to the south.

Information

Cyber Clube Ericeira (☎ 261 865 743; Praça da República; per hr €3; 🕑 11am-11pm)
Lavandaria Fonte do Cabo (☎ 261 864 203; Rua do Caldeira; per kg €3; 🕑 9am-1pm & 3-7pm Mon-Sat)
Police station (☎ 261 863 533; Rua 5 de Outubro)
Post office (☎ 261 860 501; Rua do Paço 2; 🕑 9am-12.30pm & 2.30-6pm Mon-Fri)
Turismo (tourist office; ☎ 261 863 122; www.ericeira.net; Rua Dr Eduardo Burnay 46; 🕑 10am-1pm & 2-6.30pm Mon-Fri, 10am-1pm & 3-7pm Sat & Sun)

Sights & Activities

There are three beaches within walking dis tance of the *praça* (town square): **Praia do S** (also called Praia da Baleia), **Praia do Nort** (also called Praia do Algodio) and **Praia d São Sebastião** to the north. Some 5km nort is unspoilt **Praia de São Lourenço**, while **Prai Foz do Lizandro**, a big bite of beach backed b a small car park and a couple of restaurant is 3km south.

Ericeira's big attraction is **surfing**. Prai da Ribeira de Ilhas, a World Championshi site, is just a few kilometres north, though th waves at the nearer Praia de São Sebastião ar challenging enough for most amateurs.

Recommended surfing outlets:

Ericeira Surf Clube (☎ 960 008 030; www.ericeirasur clube.cjb.net; Praia de Algodio) Hires out surfboards and gives lessons for €15 per hour.
Ultimar (☎ 261 862 371; Rua 5 de Outubro 37a; board/board & suit per day €17/25; 🕑 9.30am-1pm & 3-7.30pm) Hires out surfboards.

Sleeping

Book ahead in July and August. During th off-season, expect discounts of up to 30%.

BUDGET

Parque de Campismo Municipal de Mil Rego (☎ 261 862 706; www.ericeiracamping.com; adult/tent/ca €4.30/5.25/4) Just off the coastal highway 800m north of Praia de São Sebastião, this relatively

BEEFED-UP WELLINGTON: THE LINES OF TORRES VEDRAS

With Napoleon's troops threatening Lisbon from the north in 1809, Lord Wellington (then just Arthur Wellesley) ordered the construction of one of the cleverest, most efficient and most effective lines of defence in European warfare. Known as the Lines of Torres Vedras, they stretched from the Atlantic to the Tejo and included 108 forts and 151 redoubts.

The lines proved ingenious for four reasons. First, they were built with remarkable speed – mostly in just seven months – much to the surprise of the French. Second, they made brilliant, improvisational use of the land's natural defences, from rivers to cliff sides. Third, lines were easily supplied from the sea, which British ships controlled, while land north of the lines was stripped and scorched in order to starve the approaching French. Finally, battlements were equipped with a semaphore system adopted from the British navy that enabled orders to spread all the way across the lines from headquarters in just four minutes.

In the end, the lines helped Wellington eject some 300,000 French troops from the Iberian peninsula with a combined British-Portuguese force of fewer than 100,000.

expensive but high-quality site has lots of trees, a playground, disabled access and a municipal swimming pool next door. Also offers trim, two-bedroom cabins (€110).

Parque de Campismo Sobreiro (☎ 261 815 525; parque-campismo-sobriero@clix.pt; adult/tent/car €3.20/2.50/2.20) At Sobreiro, 6km east of Ericeira and 4km west of Mafra, this humbler site has limited shade, hot water, a restaurant and disabled access.

MIDRANGE

Pensão Gomes (☎/fax 261 863 619; Rua Mendes Leal 11; d with/without bathroon €50/40) With a pretty courtyard filled with bougainvillea, this old-fashioned boarding house has smallish rooms

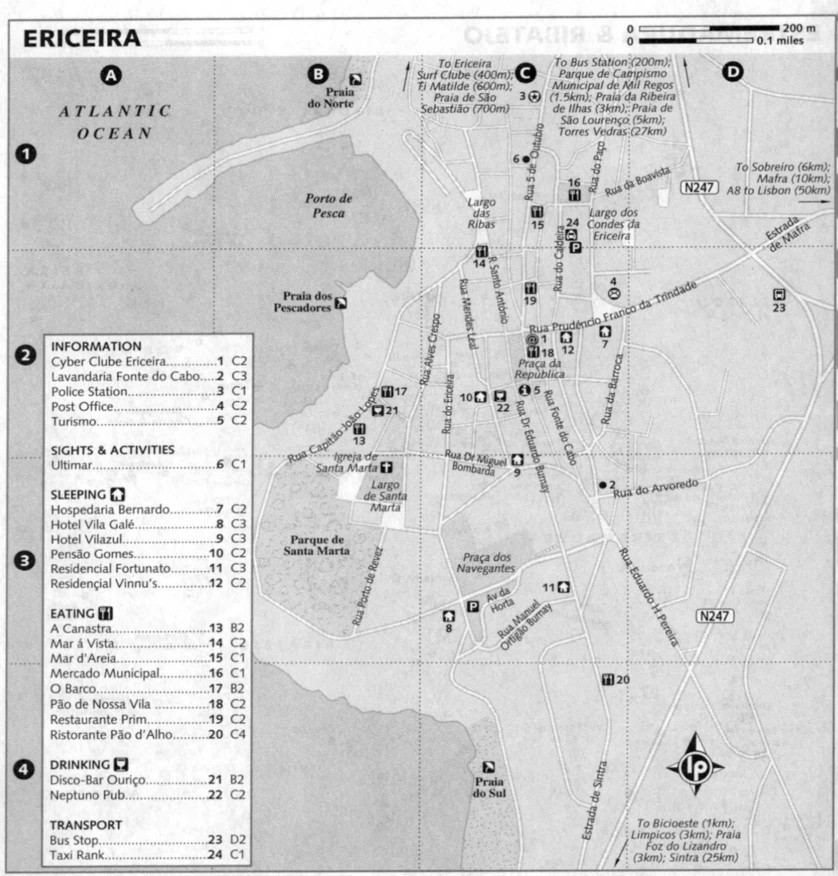

and floors that creak, but it still has more charm than most places in town. At the time of writing it featured prominently in a popular night-time soap opera.

Hospedaria Bernardo (☎ /fax 261 862 378; Rua Prudéncio Franco da Trindade 11; d from €50) This welcoming place has clean if slightly run-down rooms that vary in size and price. Ask to see your room before agreeing on a price. No breakfast.

Residencial Vinnu's (☎ /fax 261 863 830; Rua Prudéncio Franco da Trindade 19; d €50) Friendly, bright and modern, this place has simple and comfortable whitewashed rooms, some with pretty, blue-tiled bathrooms. Triples with kitchenette are a bargain at €60. No breakfast.

Residencial Fortunato (☎ 261 862 829; www.pensaofortunato.com; Rua Dr Eduardo Burnay 7; d €50; Ⓟ) A well-run, well-kept place with good-value rooms that are light, bright and all-white (including bedspreads and ceramic tile floors). The best digs are upstairs overlooking a small terrace with lovely sea views.

Hotel Vilazul (☎ 261 860 000; www.hotelvilazul.com; Calçada da Baleia 10; d €68; ❄) This place is bright and businesslike, although the carpeted rooms could use a bit of an update. A common terrace with sweeping views needs no improvement, however.

TOP END

Hotel Vila Galé (☎ /fax 261 869 900; www.vilagale.pt; Praça dos Navegantes; d from €100) A classic *fin de siècle* hotel with green mansard roof has been made over into Ericeira's top choice. It has panoramic vistas, a fine, cliff-side pool, and comfy, almost stylish rooms. An extra €20 buys you ocean views.

Eating

For true budget meals in this resort town, you'll have to self-cater. Self-caterers can find every kind of bread at **Pão de Nossa Vila** (Praça da República 12; 8am-8pm Wed-Mon), which is also excellent for a stand-up breakfast. For fresh produce and other foodstuffs, start at the **mercado municipal** (municipal market; Largo dos Condes da Ericeira).

Ristorante Pão d'Alho (☎ 261 863 762; Estrada de Sintra 2; individual pizzas from €5, mains €7-13.50; lunch & dinner Wed & Thu) Good value and the best pizza in town make this place worth seeking out. Also serves steaks, seafood and – a rarity in Portugal – imaginative salads.

Mar d'Areia (☎ 261 862 222; Rua Fonte do Cabo 49; mains €7-9; lunch & dinner Tue-Sun) Jauntily nautical, with antiseptic white tiling, Mar d'Areia is very friendly, popular with locals, and serves excellent fish. They'll show you the catch of the day and then barbecue your choice outside. Good value.

Mar á Vista (☎ 261 862 928; Rua Santo António 16; mains €5-11; lunch & dinner Thu-Tue) Another hearty local place in the same vein as Mar d'Areia, but known for its shellfish. Its cosy dining room looks out over the sea, while the bar pulls in the local tipplers.

Ti Matilde (☎ 261 862 734; Rua Dr Manuel Arraiga; mains €6-12; lunch & dinner Tue-Sun, daily Jul & Aug) At the north end of the old town, this unfussy place has windswept outdoor seating, fantastic views and a simple menu of grilled seafood and *caldeirada de peixe* (seafood stew).

Restaurante Prim (☎ 261 865 230; Rua 5 de Outubro 12; mains €7-12; lunch & dinner Thu-Tue) This bright, contemporary place dishes up high-quality, Brazilian-style grilled meats as well as several veggie mains, plus has outdoor seating on a pleasant little square.

O Barco (☎ 261 862 759; Rua Capitão João Lopes; mains around €15; lunch & dinner Fri-Wed) Just across from the sea, O Barco serves the highest-quality seafood, including grilled fish and *caldeiradas*, in its snug, nautical-rustic dining room as well as at some rather windswept outside tables.

A Canastra (☎ 261 865 367; Rua Capitão João Lopes; mains around €15; lunch & dinner Thu-Tue) O Barco's twin and near-neighbour delivers the other 'best' seafood in town. Trust yourself to either, if you have the funds.

Drinking

There are a couple of bars on Lizandro beach with outside tables overlooking the sandy expanse. In town, the terrace just above Praça dos Navegantes also has a clutch of bars and cafés.

Neptuno Pub (☎ 261 862 017; Rua Mendes Leal 12; 4pm-2am) As the name suggests, this place is decked out like an underwater cavern – one that hasn't been redecorated since the early '60s, we're guessing. It attracts fishermen and city-types in search of realness, and sometimes features *fado* (traditional, melancholic Portuguese singing) singers in summer.

Disco-Bar Ouriço (Rua Caminho Novo 9; 11pm-6am Fri & Sat, nightly Jul & Aug). One of Portugal's oldest discos caters to multigenerational hordes with a crowd-pleasing mix of pop dance, oldies, and disco standards. It's open every night in July and August.

Getting There & Away

The bus station is 800m north of the *praça*, off the N247 highway, but there is a bus stop at the top of town on the N247.

Regular **Mafrense** (☎ 261 816 152; www.rodeste.pt) buses travel roughly hourly from 6am to 8pm to/from Lisbon's Campo Grande station (€4.50, 80 minutes) via Mafra (€1.75, 20 minutes), and to/from Sintra (€2.35, 45 minutes). The turismo provides current timetables.

There is paid parking under Praça dos Navegantes and by the sea just north of the town centre near Praia de São Sebastião.

Getting Around

Regular local buses to Torres Vedras go past the Parque de Campismo and Praia da Ribeira de Ilhas (€1.20). For Praia Foz do Lizandro (€1.20), take any Sintra-bound bus to a stop on the N247 above the beach.

You can rent bicycles from **Bicioeste** (☎ 261 867 029; www.bicioeste.com), just south of Ericeira on the coastal road towards Sintra. There's a taxi stand in Largo Conde da Ericeira.

PENICHE

pop 26,100

The main access point to the beautiful rocky nature-reserve islands of Berlenga, the walled town of Peniche is equal parts tourist centre and busy fishing port. Once an island, it only joined the mainland in the 16th century, when silt created a narrow isthmus. Development around the outskirts is burgeoning, making the old town centre, with its excellent fish restaurants and looming, historically notorious fort, a pleasant surprise. Beaches to the north of town proffer some of Europe's best surfing.

Orientation

Driving into the old town walls, the main N114 turns left into Rua Alexandre Herculano, where you'll find the turismo, or continues straight on for 3km round the Peniche peninsula to Cabo Carvoeiro and its lighthouse. If you are arriving by bus, you will be dropped off at the market, about 20m northwest of the turismo. From the market it's a short walk south to the old town centre and fort, the harbour and Avenida do Mar, which is home to most of the seafood restaurants. Passenger boats for Ilha Berlenga leave from the harbour.

Information

Espaço Internet (☎ 969 195 895; Rua Dr João de Matos Bilhau; 10am-1pm & 3-10pm Mon-Sat, 10am-noon, 3-8pm Sun) Free internet access.
Hospital (☎ 262 781 900; Rua General Humberto Delgado) About 600m northwest of the market.
Police station (☎ 261 863 533; Rua Heróis Ultramar) About 400m west of the market.
Turismo (☎ /fax 262 789 555; 9am-8pm Jul & Aug, 10am-1pm & 2-5pm Sep-Jun) In a shady public garden alongside Rua Alexandre Herculano.

Sights

FORTALEZA

Dominating the southern end of the peninsula, Peniche's imposing 16th-century **fortress** (admission free; 2-5.30pm Tue, 9am-12.30pm & 2-5.30pm Wed-Fri, 10am-12.30pm & 2-5.30pm Sat & Sun) was in military use as late as the 1970s, when it was converted into a temporary home for refugees from the newly independent African colonies.

Twenty years earlier it served as one of dictator Salazar's infamous jails for political prisoners. By the entrance, where prisoners once received visitors – with the stark booths with their glass partitions all preserved – is the **Núcleo-Resistência**, a grim but fascinating display about those times, including the flimsy leaflets of the Resistance; educational materials for schools where pupils would learn phrases such as 'Viva Salazar!'; prisoners' poignant, beautifully illustrated letters to their children; and some secret letters, written in incredibly small handwriting.

Housed in another part of the fort is the **Museu Municipal** (☎ 262 780 116; admission €1.40; 2-5.30pm Tue, 9am-12.30pm & 2-5.30pm Wed-Fri, 10am-12.30pm & 2-5.30pm Sat & Sun). Outside is the desolate prison yard, and the top floor reveals the chilling, sinister interrogation chambers and cells, some used for solitary confinement. Floors below this contain a municipal mishmash, from Roman archaeological artefacts to shipwreck finds, and the grand, strangely out-of-place reconstruction of the bedroom of Peniche-born artist and politician Paulinho Montez.

LACE-MAKING SCHOOLS

Like Vila do Conde – another of Portugal's Atlantic fishing ports – Peniche is famous for lace. You can watch the nimble (and chatty) ladies in action at **Escola de Rendas** (9.30am-12.30pm & 2-5.30pm Mon-Fri) in the turismo building, as well as at **Rendibilrosa** (Rua Marechal Gomes Freire Andrade 57; 9am-12.30pm & 2-5.30pm Mon-Fri). The chaos of their bobbins produces some of the world's most exquisite lace.

BALEAL

About 4km to the northeast of Peniche is this scenic island-village, connected to the mainland village of Casais do Baleal by a causeway. The fantastic sweep of sandy beach here offers some fine surfing. Surf schools dot the sands, as do a couple of bar-restaurants.

Activities

Kite-surfing is taking off in Peniche. On the far side of high dunes about 500m before the entrance to the walled town you'll find **Peniche Kite Center** (☎ 919 424 951; www.penichekitecenter.com), which also gives lessons (three hours with equipment for €50).

For fishing trips, contact **Nautipesca** (☎ 917 588 358), which has a kiosk at the harbour.

DIVING

There are good diving opportunities around Peniche, and especially around Berlenga. Expect to pay about €35/50 for one/two dives (less around Peniche). Operators include **Berlenga Sub** (☎ 262 189 619; www.berlengasub.com; Largo da Ribeira Velha 4) and **Mergulhão** (☎ 262 785 795; www.mergulhao-dive.com).

SURFING

The beaches at Baleal, just north of Peniche, are a paradise of challenging but, above all, consistent waves, making it ideal for learners.

Camps charge around €250 to €400 for a week of classes plus equipment and shared, self-catering lodging. You can also take one half-day class (from €30) and rent boards (from €15). There are various surf schools:

Maximum Surfcamp (☎ 939 334 455; www.maximumsurfcamp.com; Rua do Gualdino 7)

Baleal Surfcamp (☎ 969 050 546; www.balealsurfcamp.com; Rua Amigos do Baleal 2)

Peniche Surfcamp (☎ 962 336 295; www.penichesurfcamp.com; Rua do Gualdino 4)

Sleeping

Prices are for high season; expect discounts of up to 30% outside July and August.

Parque de campismo (☎ 262 789 529; fax 262 780 111; adult/tent/car €2.30/1.90/1.90) The small municipal site is 2km east of Peniche (opposite the BP station) and 500m from the beach. It has disabled facilities and is near a swimming pool, though proffers little shade.

Parque de Campismo Peniche Praia (☎ 262 783 460; fax 262 789 447; adult/tent/car €3.30/3.30/3;) On the high, windy, north side of the peninsula, 1.7km from town and the beach, and 2km from Cabo Carvoeiro, this site has good facilities but no shade.

Residencial Popular (☎ 262 790 290; www.apopular.com; Largo da Ribeira 40; d €35) Simple but clean and recently refurbished rooms above the excellent restaurant of the same name deliver great value just a few steps from the ferry to Berlenga.

Residencial Rimavier (☎ 262 789 459; www.rimavier.com; Rua Castilho 6; d €40) This immaculate *pensão* (guesthouse) – run by the same lovely, helpful couple who run the downstairs souvenir shop – has small but spruce rooms with tile floors and nautically themed linens. No breakfast.

Residencial Maciel (☎ 262 784 685; www.residencial-maciel.com; Rua José Estevão 38; d from €50) Spotless, completely refurbished rooms are done up with gleaming antique-style furnishings at this pink-hued spot. Some are quite large, others just average-sized.

There are two great options in the more scenic Baleal:

Residencial Quelhas (☎ 262 185 794; Baleal Village; d with breakfast €60) This newly opened *residencial* (guesthouse) on the seaward side of Baleal has airy, pleasant, well-equipped rooms with tile floors with the blue sea visible from most rooms. There's also a shared rooftop terrace with fantastic views.

Casa das Marés (☎ 262 769 371/200/255; casamares1@hotmail.com; Praia do Baleal; d €75) At the picturesque, windswept tip of Baleal stands this imposing house – actually a row of three houses, owned by three sisters. The breezy, inviting rooms all have great sea views, especially out the back, which looks all the way to Berlenga.

Eating

Restaurante Popular (☎ 262 790 290; Largo da Ribeira; mains from €4.50) This breezy, harbour-side spot serves up delicious, freshly caught fish grilled before your eyes – and at terrific value.

Restaurante A Sardinha (☎ 262 781 820; Rua Vasco da Gama 81; mains €4.50-10; lunch & dinner) This simple place on a narrow street parallel to Largo da Ribeira does a roaring trade with locals and tourists alike. The house speciality is, as the name implies, grilled sardines.

our pick **La Rose de Picardie** (☎ 262 785 793; Rua Garrett 77; mains €7-12; lunch & dinner Mon-Sat) A French-Portuguese couple run this unassuming, classically provincial French restaurant. Between them they cook, serve, bake bread, make ice cream and even grow much of their own produce. A rare find. Recommended.

Oh Amaral (☎ 262 785 095; Rua Dr Francisco Seia 7; mains €10-13; lunch & dinner Fri-Thu;) It may be a little more expensive, but snug Oh Amaral reliably does the best seafood in Peniche. And, if you can believe this, smoking is strictly forbidden because it's an interference with the taste buds.

Drinking

The area around Igreja de São Pedro is the centre of the town's nightlife (think four walls, cold beer and a home stereo system). In Baleal you'll find several restaurants right on the beach, including the rather stylish wood-and-glass **Danau Bar** (☎ 262 709 818; lunch & dinner), a surfers' bar, open year-round and offering hot snacks and sometimes live music or karaoke on weekends. It's closed Monday in the low season.

Getting There & Away

Peniche's **bus station** (☎ 968 903 861) is located 400m northeast of the turismo (cross the Ponte Velha connecting the town to the isthmus). It's served by **Rodotejo** (www.rodotejo.pt) and **Rede Expressos** (www.rede-expressos.pt). Buses run to/from Lisbon (€7, 1¾ hours, hourly) via Torres Vedras, and to Coimbra (€10.80, 3½ hours, four daily) via Leiria (€9.60, 2½ hours), and every few hours to Óbidos (€2.40, 40 minutes). Service drops off at weekends.

Most days you can find ample free parking along Largo da Ribeira, the road that runs along the harbour.

Getting Around

Bikes can be rented from **Micro-Moto** (☎ 262 782 480; Rua António Conceição Bento 19a; per day €5), beside the market.

RESERVA NATURAL DA BERLENGA

Sitting about 10km offshore from Peniche, Berlenga Grande is a spectacular, rocky and remote island, with twisting shocked-rock formations and gaping caverns. It's the only island of the Berlenga archipelago you can visit – the group consists of three tiny islands surrounded by clear, calm, dark-blue waters full of shipwrecks that are great for snorkelling and diving (see p272).

In the 16th century Berlenga Grande was home to a monastery, but now the most famous inhabitants are thousands of nesting sea birds, especially guillemots. The birds take priority over human visitors: the only development that has been allowed includes housing for a small fishing community, a lighthouse, a shop and a restaurant-*pensão*. You can camp here – book at the turismo in Peniche. Paths are clearly marked to stop day-trippers trespassing on the birds' domain.

Linked to the island by a narrow causeway is the 17th-century **Forte de São João Baptista**, now one of the country's most dramatic but barren hostels (also reserve at the Peniche turismo). In 1666 a garrison of less than 20 men withstood attack by a Spanish fleet of 14 for two days, killing 500 men – only capitulating when they ran out of provisions.

The reserve's **headquarters** (☎ 262 787 910; fax 262 787 930; Porto da Areia Norte, Estrada Marginal) are in Peniche.

Tours

A number of companies offer day tours to Berlenga, plus other activities like fishing and diving. Tickets and information are available at Peniche's harbour, at the kiosks in Largo da Ribeira.

Barco-Noa (☎ 969 134 534; per person €18) Runs three boat trips a day, depending on demand and weather.

TurPesca (☎ 963 073 818; 4-5hr adult/child €18/12, minimum 6 people) Runs privately organised cruises on demand throughout the year. There's usually a 10am trip, plus at least two more daily during the summer, when you may have to book a few days ahead.

Sleeping & Eating

If you want to sleep on the island, you'll need to book well ahead. The two park facilities can only be reserved starting in May. Most places are already booked solid by the end of May.

Berlenga campsite (2-/3-/4-person tent €8/11.50/15; 🕒 May-Sep) There is a small rocky area for camping near the harbour; book in advance at the Peniche turismo.

Forte de São João Baptista hostel (☎ 262 750 244, 918 614 190; dm €9.50; 🕒 Jun-Sep) This was once a fine historic inn, but was abandoned for many years – and you can feel it. It's a dramatic but dead-basic hostel, with antiquated bathrooms: you need to bring your own sleeping bag and cooking equipment (though there is a small shop and a bar). To get a place in summer you'll have to make reservations in May. Bring a torch (the generator goes off at midnight).

Pavilhão Mar e Sol (☎ 262 750 331; d €77; 🕒 Jun-Sep) Rooms are decent but quite simple, considering the price. Downstairs is the island's only restaurant. Advanced reservations essential.

There's also a small grocery store on the island for self-catering.

Getting There & Away

Viamar (☎ 262 785 646; fax 262 783 847; adult/child €18/10; 15 May-15 Sep) does the 45-minute trip to the island once daily at 10am, returning at 4.30pm, between 15 May and 15 September (depending on the weather). During July and August there are three sailings, at 9.30am, 11.30am and 5.30pm, returning at 10.30am, 4.30pm and 6.30pm. Tickets tend to sell out quickly during this period as only 300 visitors are allowed each day.

If you're prone to seasickness, choose your day carefully – the crossing to Berlenga can be rough.

ÓBIDOS

pop 11,300 / elevation 80m

Encased in neatly elliptical medieval walls and set atop limestone heights, Óbidos looks forbidding from the plains it watches over. But enter its dreamy lanes and you'll instantly be disarmed. Chalk-white houses are bordered in zinging blue and yellow and, in summer, draped with roses and lilacs. Refined architectural elements, from the Renaissance church to the elaborate gates, add their own flourish. Portugal's prettiest town? It's definitely way up there. Its charms pull in an increasing number of day-trippers, and souvenir and 'aft shops await the waves. But backstreets main surprisingly serene. If you can, stay on absorb the quiet of the night.

istory

'hen Dom Dinis first showed Óbidos to his ife Dona Isabel in 1228, it must have already een a pretty sight, because she fell instantly love with the place. The king decided to ake the town a wedding gift to his queen, itiating a royal tradition that lasted until e 19th century.

Any grace it had in 1228 must be credited the Moors, who had laid out the streets and ad only recently abandoned the strategic eights. The Moors had chased out the Visioths, who in turn had evicted the Romans, ho also had a fortress here.

Until the 15th century Óbidos overlooked e sea; the bay gradually silted up, leaving e town landlocked.

formation

paço Internet (☎ 262 959 037; Câmara Municipal, a Direita; ⌚ 10am-9pm Mon-Fri, 11.30am-6.30pm Sat Sun Sep-Jun, 10am-10pm Jul & Aug) Free Net access.

ost office (Rua Direita; ⌚ 9am-12.30pm & 2.30-6pm on-Fri)

egião de Turismo do Oeste (☎ 262 955 060; www :-oeste.pt; Rua Direita 45; ⌚ 10am-1pm & 2-6pm Mon-i) Regional tourism headquarters.

urismo (☎ 262 959 231; ⌚ 9.30am-6pm Mon-Fri, 30am-12.30pm, 1.30-5.30pm Sat & Sun) Town tourist fice, just outside Porta da Vila near the bus stop.

Sights

CASTELO, WALLS & AQUEDUCT

You can walk around the unprotected **muro** (wall) for uplifting views over both the town and the surrounding countryside. The walls date from the time of the Moors (later restored), but the **castelo** itself is one of Dom Dinis' 13th-century creations. It's a stern edifice, as castles should be, with lots of towers, battlements and big gates. Converted into a palace in the 16th century, it's now a deluxe *pousada* (upmarket inn).

The **aqueduct**, west of the main gate, dates from the 16th century and is 3km long.

IGREJA DE SANTA MARIA

The town's elegant main **church** (Rua Direita; admission free; ⌚ 9.30am-12.30pm & 2.30-7pm May-Sep, to 5pm Oct-Apr), at the northern end of the street, stands on the foundations of a Visigothic temple that was later converted into a mosque. Begun in the 12th century but restored several times since, it dates mostly from the Renaissance. It had its 15 minutes of fame in 1444 when 10-year-old Afonso V married his eight-year-old cousin Isabel here.

Inside is a wonderful painted ceiling and walls done up in beautiful blue-and-white 17th-century *azulejos* (hand-painted tiles). Paintings by the renowned 17th-century painter Josefa de Óbidos (below) are to the right of the altar. There's a fine 16th-century Renaissance tomb on the left, probably carved by the French sculptor Nicolas Chanterène.

JOSEFA DE ÓBIDOS

In an age when the only acceptable vocations for a woman were as nun, or wife and mother, Josefa de Óbidos managed to establish herself not just as one of 17th-century Portugal's best but also one of its most respected artists. Daughter of minor Portuguese painter Baltazar Gomes Figueira, she was born in Seville but returned to Portugal as a child after the country regained its independence from Spain. She studied at the Augustine Convento de Santa Ana as a young girl, though later left the convent without taking vows, eventually settling in Óbidos, where she remained famously chaste and religious until her death in 1684.

A number of factors enabled her to carve out her unlikely public position. First, her father too was a painter, so that she was able to receive an education within her home – the only 'respectable' place a woman might have received training. Second, she allied herself closely with the church without ever taking vows. In this way, she never subjected her talents to the whims of a nay-saying mother superior, yet still could appear as a humble representative of the Mother Church rather than anything so brazen as an independent woman flogging her own works. By all accounts, she was a genuinely religious person, but this choice seems auspicious, too. Finally, and most important, there was the sheer appeal of her paintings. Often they ignore established iconography in favour of a certain domestic sweetness, but at the same time they combine a masterful use of colour and form.

MUSEU MUNICIPAL

The town's **museum** (☎ 262 955 557; Solar da Praça de Santa Maria: admission €1.50; ⏲ 10am-1pm & 2-6pm) is located in the Solar da Praça de Santa Maria, an 18th-century manor house just next to the church. It's now home to a haunting portrait by Josefa de Óbidos, *Faustino das Neves* (1670), remarkable for its dramatic use of light and shade. Among the other religious paintings and icons is a curious 18th-century roulette wheel made from wood and paper. The museum is next to the Igreja de Santa Maria.

Festivals & Events

Óbidos celebrates **Semana Santa** (Holy Week) with religious re-enactments and processions.

Sleeping

BUDGET

There are several unofficial private rooms available.

Casa dos Castros (☎ 262 959 328; Rua Direita 83; s/d with shared bathroom €25/35) Be short or at least prepared to stoop at this place near the church. The ceilings of its simple rooms are unbelievably low, but then again so are the prices. The old couple who run it are welcoming indeed, and make it all seem very normal. No breakfast.

Óbido Sol (☎ 262 959 188; Rua Direita 40; d €40) This old town house is kept neatly by its chatty proprietor, with cosy and comfortable rooms (with new bathrooms) around a snug living room. Two rooms have views across town to the adjacent hills. Very good value.

MIDRANGE

Casa do Relógio (☎ 262 959 282; casa.relogio@clix.pt; Rua da Graça 12; d €60) Just east of the town walls, this 18th-century house (named for a nearby sundial) has eight smallish but spotless, traditionally furnished rooms with handsome tile floors – plus a friendly welcome.

Hospedaria Louro (☎ 262 955 100; www.hospedarialouro.com; Casal da Canastra; d with breakfast €60; P ✱ 💻 🏊) Outside the walls 300m west of Porta da Vila, this modern hotel lacks the charm of other places, but a recent remodel has yielded simple but bright, comfortable, spotless rooms, some with nice rural vistas.

Casa d'Óbidos (☎ 262 950 924; www.casadobidos.com; Quinta de São José; d €80, 4-/6-person apt €120/160; P 🏊) In a whitewashed, 19th-century villa at the foot of the old town and affording sweeping views of its bristling walls and towers, t[his] place is worth the premium, with tenn[is,] swimming pool, lovely grounds and spacio[us] breezy rooms with good new baths and per[iod] furnishings.

Casa de São Thiago (☎/fax 262 959 587; Larg[o] São Thiago; d €80; P) Ridiculously charming la[b]yrinth of snug, 18th-century rooms and til[ed] flower-filled courtyards in the shadow of [the] castle. The rooms are a bit drearier but ha[ve] all the midrange comforts, plus some n[ice] antique touches.

TOP END

Pousada do Castelo (☎ 262 955 080; www.pousadas[...] d €220) One of Portugal's best *pousadas* o[c]cupies a gloriously bleached-white conve[nt] hidden within the town's forbidding, 13[th-]century castle. Rooms are also whitewash[ed] but done up mostly with sleek contempora[ry] furnishings. Book well in advance.

Eating & Drinking

There are no true budget options in touri[st] Óbidos, but what's available tends to be ve[ry] good. The larger inns, including the *pousa[da]*, have good if pricey dining rooms.

Bar Lagar da Mouraria (☎ 919 937 601; Rua da Mo[ur]aria; snacks €2-8; ⏲ noon-2am) North of Igreja [de] Santa Maria, behind the post office, is t[his] lovely traditional bar, with beamed ceili[ngs] and a flagstone floor. It's housed in a form[er] winery, with seats around a massive old wi[ne] press. You can snack on tapas, cheese, gril[led] *chouriço* (spicy sausage), *morcela assa[da]* (blood sausage), sandwiches or fish soup.

Café-Restaurante 1 de Dezembro (☎ 262 959 2[...] Largo de São Pedro; mains €7-12; ⏲ breakfast, lunch & d[in]ner) Set on a wonderful little square, this pla[ce] serves standard Portuguese fare that does[n't] quite measure up to the setting. Still, if y[ou] want to eat alfresco in the old town, this [is] the place.

Adega do Ramada (☎ 262 959 462; Travessa No[ssa] Senora do Rosário; mains €9-12; ⏲ lunch & dinner Tue-S[un]) Another great location with wooden tab[les] and benches in the cobbled lane next to 1 [de] Dezembro, Ramada specialises in grills cook[ed] on its outdoor barbecue.

Alcaide (☎ 262 959 220; Rua Direita 60; omelette €6.[..] mains €10-14; ⏲ lunch & dinner Thu-Tue) This upsta[irs] restaurant has wrought-iron chandeliers a[nd] windows overlooking town, while the me[nu] has creative dishes like *requinte de bacalh[au]* (salt cod with cheese, chestnuts and apples

Getting There & Away

The town's main gate, Porta da Vila, leads directly into the main street, Rua Direita. Buses stop on the main road just outside Porta da Vila. There is a paying car park just outside the gate, while the one just across the road is free.

Buses run frequently to Caldas da Rainha (€1.20, 15 minutes) and Peniche (€2.15, 45 minutes). There are seven weekday runs to Lisbon (€7.50, 70 minutes), with one on Saturday and none on Sunday. Otherwise change at Caldas da Rainha.

Óbidos' train station has at least six daily trains to Lisbon (€9.20, 2½ hours) via connections at Mira Sintra-Meclas station on the suburban Lisbon line. The station is located at the foot of the castle end of town. It's rather a hoof uphill.

CALDAS DA RAINHA

pop 43,600 / elevation 90m

Now that its sulphurous waters are restricted to hospital patients, dowdy Caldas da Rainha has limited interest to the traveller, though its old centre – particularly the leafy Parque Dom Carlos I – is pleasant enough.

If ceramics are your bag, the **Museu de Cerâmica** (☎ 262 840 280; Ilídio Amado; admission €2, 10am-12.30pm Sun free; 🕑 10am-12.30pm & 2-5pm Tue-Sun Oct-May, 10am-7pm Jun-Sep) makes an interesting stop. In a delightful, 19th-century holiday mansion, it features fantastic works by native son Rafael Bordalo Pinheiro, whose intricate works often involve effusions of flora and fauna. Most memorable are the fabulous jars and bowls (by both Pinheiro and Manuel Mafra), encrusted with animals, lobsters and snakes.

The **turismo** (☎ 262 839 700; fax 262 839 726; 🕑 9am-7pm Mon-Fri, 10am-1pm & 3-7pm Sat & Sun) is on Praça 25 de Abril, a block from the bus station and two blocks from the train station. They can offer information on opportunities to learn more about ceramics, including visits to local factories.

Sleeping & Eating

Residencial Dom Carlos (☎ 262 832 551; Rua de Camões 39a; d with/without bathroom €45/35) The English-speaking owner offers faded but clean, cheerful, carpeted rooms, a few with nice views across to leafy Parque Dom Carlos I.

Casa dos Plátanos (☎ 262 841 810; fax 262 843 417; Rua Rafael Bordalo Pinheiro 24; d €60) This white-washed, 18th-century manor house, located on a countrylike lane about 100m beyond the hospital and baths, has simple, mostly bright rooms with terracotta-tile floors and rustically elegant common areas. Ask to see the impressive library.

Supatra (☎ 262 842 920; Rua General Amílcar Mota; mains from €8; 🕑 lunch & dinner Tue-Sun) Do you believe that there is more to seasoning than salt and garlic? Thai diplomats drive all the way from Lisbon to dine at this fantastically fragrant Thai restaurant 700m south of the park.

Pastelaria Baía (Rua da Liberdade; 🕑 8am-8pm) This appealing little café has a small terrace overlooking the street alongside the park. The local speciality is the sweet *cavacas* (air-filled tarts covered with icing).

Getting There & Away

Buses run from Peniche (€2.75, 45 minutes, six daily) via Óbidos (€1.20, 15 minutes), and Leiria (€8, 50 minutes, about hourly). Service drops off on the weekend.

Four to six regional trains run to/from Lisbon (€7.40, 2½ hours) via connections at Mira Sintra-Meclas station on the suburban Lisbon line.

There is ample metered street parking around Parque Dom Carlos I.

FOZ DO ARELHO

pop 2500

With a vast, lovely beach backed by a lagoon ideal for windsurfing, Foz do Arelho remains remarkably undeveloped. It makes a fine place to laze in the sun, and outside July and August you'd hardly know it was a resort town. Still, development is starting to pick up the pace.

Escola de Vela da Lagoa (☎ 262 978 592; www.escoladeveladalagoa.com; Marginal da Lagoa) rents out sailboards (€14 per hour) and sailing boats (from €16 per hour) and also provides courses (windsurfing, 15 hours, €90; private sailing, two hours, €60; kitesurfing, three two-hour lessons with equipment, €130). Its base is 2.5km along the road that runs inland along the lagoon. From the village turn left when you approach the lagoon.

Sleeping

Parque de Campismo Foz do Arelho (☎ 262 978 683; www.orbitur.pt; adult/tent/car €4.60/4.80/4.20, 4-person cabins €81; ♿) This good, shady camp site, 2km from the beach, is run by Orbitur. It has a restaurant, bar, shade, and bikes for rent.

 Book accommodation online at lonelyplanet.com

Residencial Pendedo Furado (☎ 262 979 610; fax 262 979 832; Rua dos Camarções 3; d €70; P) Situated in the village, this smart, efficient and modern *residencial* offers simple, bright rooms with tiled floors, some with verandas and lagoon views.

O Facho (☎ 262 979 110; ofachoguesthouse@hotmail.com; Rua Francisco Almeida Grandela; d €82) Just above the beach past the cluster of cafés, this new pink confection has airy, bright rooms, many with terrific ocean views. There's also a cool bar and shady veranda on the ground floor.

Eating

Cabana do Pescador (☎ 262 979 451; Avenida do Mar; mains €4.50-18) Most renowned of the local fish restaurants, this place offers every manner of sea life as well as a sea-view terrace.

Restaurante-Bar Atlântica (☎ 262 979 213; Avenida do Mar; mains €4-10; lunch & dinner) The oldest and scruffiest of the restaurants along Avenida do Mar, Atlântica has a typically fish-heavy menu and more good views.

Getting There & Away

Buses connect Foz do Arelho with Caldas da Rainha (€1.20, 20 minutes, at least six daily on weekdays, fewer on weekends).

SÃO MARTINHO DO PORTO

pop 2700

Set on a moon-shaped bay ringed by sand beaches, São Martinho is an unassuming resort town whose warm, placid waters make it a big hit with families. Midrise development isn't making the place any more charming, but it still has a small centre of cobbled streets and open-air seafood restaurants to remind you of quieter days.

Orientation & Information

The **turismo** (☎ 262 989 110; Largo Vitorino Fróis; 10am-1pm & 3-7pm Tue-Sun May-Sep, 10am-1pm & 2-6pm Sat & Sun year-round, closed Mon Oct-Jun) is in the middle of the little town, a block back from the beach.

The train station is about 700m to the southeast. Buses stop on Rua Conde de Avelar, a block inland.

Sleeping

Colina do Sol (☎ 262 989 764; www.colinadosol.net; adult/car €4.30/3.85, tent €4.30-6;) This well-equipped and friendly camp site is 2km north of town, but only 1km from the beach, with disabled access, a children's playground, a pool and some sections shaded by pine trees.

Pensão Americana (☎ 262 989 170; fax 262 989 349; Rua Dom José Saldanha 2; d with breakfast €65) In a building that manages to be creaky without being terribly old, this is the closest this beach town comes to a budget *pensão*. Rooms received new bathrooms, beds and a fresh coat of paint in 2006 –all welcome.

Residencial Atlântica (☎ 262 980 151; fax 262 980 163; Rua Miguel Bombarda 6; d €80) In a modern building, Residencial Atlântica has bright, spotlessly white rooms with tiled floors to match. Friendly staff and large breakfasts are nice bonuses.

Palace do Capitão (☎ 262 985 150; www.palacecapitao.com; Rua Capitão Jaime Pinto 6; d around €100) This perfectly preserved, 19th-century sea captain's home is the town's only place of distinction, with much of its original Victoriana still intact. Some rooms are small but all are trimly appointed. Located right across from the beach.

Eating

O Largo (Largo Vitorino Fróis 27; mains €5-10) This good little cheapie near the turismo has outdoor seating, tasty grilled meat and fish, and daily specials for around €4.

Restaurante Carvalho (☎ 262 980 151; Rua Miguel Bombarda 6; mains €6-12) On the ground floor of the Residencial Atlântica, this place serves simple but good fish and meat dishes. The speciailty is *bife na pedra* (sizzling beefsteak).

Getting There & Away

Buses run from Alcobaça (€5.20, 40 minutes) six times a day on weekdays and at least twice daily on weekends to Lisbon (€7.30, 1½ hours). There are also trains about six times daily to Caldas da Rainha (€1.40, 15 minutes, seven daily), with connections to Lisbon.

Street parking is plentiful, though it can grow competitive on summer weekends.

NAZARÉ

pop 15,500

The most scenic of the region's coastal towns, Nazaré is an uncanny combination of fishing village and cheery, cheesy beach resort. Its grid of extra-narrow streets forces locals and tourists into remarkable intimacy.

In fact, the whole place is crammed to bursting in July and August – including the extra-wide sweep of beach. But even whe

ESTREMADURA & RIBATEJO

they're outnumbered by tourists, the town's womenfolk won't let you forget who's boss. Many still wear traditional costumes of short but voluminous skirts and brightly embroidered tops. They patrol the narrow streets with admirable swagger, touting *quartos* (private rooms) and selling dried fruits and nuts along the oceanfront promenade.

The old town is tucked up against honey-coloured cliffs at the north end of the beach. A funicular climbs to the cliff's edge, affording sweeping views as well as access to Promontório do Sítio, the town's original site.

Orientation

Until the 18th century the sea covered the present-day site of Nazaré; the locals lived inland at the hilltop Pederneira and the nearer Promontório do Sítio. Today, both places play second fiddle to Nazaré and its seafront Avenida da República. The former fisherfolk's quarter of narrow lanes now hosts restaurants and cafés.

Information

Centro de saúde (☎ 262 569 120; Urbanização Caixins) Medical centre on the eastern edge of town.
Hospital (☎ 262 569 120; Largo Nossa Senhora Nazaré) In Sítio.
Police station (☎ 262 550 100; Rua Sub-Vila)
Post office (Avenida da Independência Nacional; 9am-12.30pm & 2.30-6pm Mon-Fri)
Turismo (☎ 262 561 194; Avenida da República; 9.30am-1pm & 2-6pm Sep-Jun, 9am-9pm Jul & Aug)

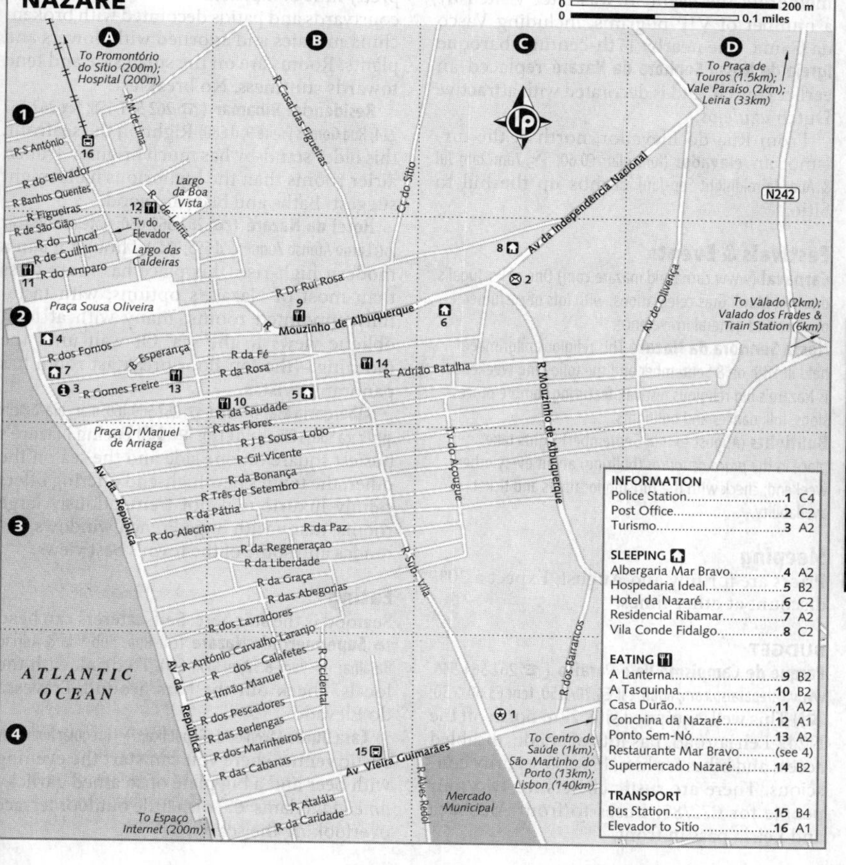

ESTREMADURA & RIBATEJO

Book accommodation online at lonelyplanet.com

Sights

The **Promontório do Sítio**, the clifftop area 110m above the beach, is popular for its tremendous views and, among Portuguese devotees, its mystical associations. According to legend it was here that a long-lost statue of the Virgin, brought back from Nazareth in the 4th century, was finally rediscovered in the 18th century.

Even more famously, it's said the Virgin appeared here on a foggy day in 1182. Local nobleman Dom Fuas Roupinho was in pursuit of a deer when the animal disappeared off the edge of the Sítio precipice. Dom Fuas cried out to the Virgin for help and his horse miraculously stopped right at cliff's edge.

Dom Fuas built the small **Hermida da Memória** chapel on the edge of the belvedere to commemorate the event. It was later visited by a number of VIP pilgrims, including Vasco da Gama. The nearby 17th-century, baroque **Igreja de Nossa Senhora da Nazaré** replaced an earlier church, and is decorated with attractive Dutch *azulejos*.

From Rua do Elevador, north of the turismo, an **elevador** (funicular; €0.60; 7am-2am Jul & Aug, to midnight Sep-Jun) climbs up the hill to Sítio.

Festivals & Events

Carnaval (www.carnavaldanazare.com) One of Portugal's brashest Mardi Gras celebrations, with lots of costumed parades and general irreverence.

Nossa Senhora da Nazaré This religious pilgrimage, held in Sítio on 8 September and the following weekend, is Nazaré's big religious festival, featuring sombre processions, folk dances and bullfights.

Bullfights (August to mid-September) Fights take place in the *praça de touros* (bullring) about every other weekend; check with the turismo for times and ticket availability.

Sleeping

Prices are for July and August. Expect a 30% discount at other times.

BUDGET

Parque de Campismo Vale Paraíso (☎ 262 561 546; www.valeparaiso.com; adult/car €4.20/3.50, tent €3.60-5.30;) This well-equipped site, 2km north off the N242 Leiria road, has lots of shade, disabled access and bikes for hire. It's also security conscious. There are rustic chalets for two/four people for €72/87. Buses to/from Alcobaça and Leiria pass in front.

Parque de Campismo Valado (☎ 262 561 111; www.orbitur.pt; adult/car €4.20/3.70, tent €4.10-5.70) This shady, well-equipped Orbitur site has a restaurant and bar. It's 2km east of town, off the Alcobaça road.

Hospedaria Ideal (☎ 262 551 379; Rua Adrião Batalha 98; d €35, full board €75) The gracious, French-speaking landlady has a little restaurant downstairs and six humbly old-fashioned rooms upstairs that are a little bigger than the beds. Books solid in August, when full board is sometimes mandatory.

MIDRANGE & TOP END

Vila Conde Fidalgo (☎ /fax 262 552 361; http://condefidalgo.planetaclix.pt; Avenida de Independência 21a; d €45, 2-/4-person apt €60/80) One of the only charming places in town and also a good value, this pretty little complex is built around a series of courtyards and patios decorated with broken-china mosaics and adorned with flowers and plants. Rooms are on the small side and tend towards stuffiness. No breakfast.

Residencial Ribamar (☎ 262 551 158; fax 262 562 224; Rua Gomes Freire 9; d €80) Right on the seafront this older stand-by has much brighter, frillier airier rooms than the lugubrious halls might suggest. Baths and beds are good.

Hotel da Nazaré (☎ 262 569 030; hotelnazare@cli.pt; Largo Afonso Zuquete; d €95;) Though it's in a modern high-rise, this place has more class than most of Nazaré's options, with tastefully appointed rooms, many with at least oblique views to the sea. Or wait until the morning – the top-floor breakfast room has panoramic vistas.

Albergaria Mar Bravo (☎ 262 569 160; mar_bravo@cl.pt; Praça Sousa Oliveira; d €120; P) Facing Nazaré's busiest square on one side and the sea on the other, the town's new high-end offering offers calmly luxurious if not tremendously large rooms, many with huge French windows, verandas and some of the town's best views.

Eating

Seafood is the star here. Self-caterers can head to **Supermercado Nazaré** (cnr Ruas Sub-Vila & Adrião Batalha; 9am-8.30pm Mon-Sat). To drink with the locals, check out the bars around Travessa do Elevador.

Casa Durão (Avenida da Republica; irregular hours) A rustic venue where you can start the evening with beer and a big plate of steamed garlicky *ameijoas* (clams; €5) on a little outdoor terrace overlooking the sea.

Conchina da Nazaré (☎ 262 186 156; Rua de Leiria 17d; mains €5.50-8; ⌚ lunch & dinner) This simple place with outdoor seating on a backstreet square serves good-value seafood, including wood-grilled fish and *açorda de marisco* (thick bread soup with seafood). Many nights there are more locals than tourists.

Ponto Sem-Nó (Rua Gomes Freire 54; snacks €4-8; ⌚ lunch & dinner Wed-Mon) An appealing local drinking hole in a back alley, serving *petiscos* (snacks) including tasty cheeses and octopus salads, as well as grilled sardines (€5).

A Tasquinha (☎ 262 551 945; Rua Adrião Batalha 54; mains €6-9; ⌚ lunch & dinner Tue-Sun) This snug family operation serves, you guessed it, seafood. High quality and reasonable prices make it hugely popular. Expect queues on summer nights.

A Lanterna (☎ 262 562 215; Rua Mouzinho de Albuquerque 59; mains €6-22; ⌚ lunch & dinner Wed-Mon) Specialising in the paella-like *cataplana* (seafood and sausage dish; mains for two €18 to €22), this cosy if touristy place delivers up good seafood in a low-ceilinged, pseudo-old-fashioned dining room.

Restaurante Mar Bravo (☎ 262 569 160; Praça Sousa Oliveira; mains €12-22; ⌚ lunch & dinner) On the ground floor of the town's top hotel you'll find its most upscale restaurant, with high-quality seafood simply prepared, plus ocean views.

Getting There & Away

There is a bus service to Lisbon (€7.90, 1¾ hours, about six daily) and Leiria (€6.70, 40 minutes, five daily). There are almost hourly runs to Caldas da Rainha (€5.20, 45 minutes, nine daily) and Alcobaça (€3.80, 20 minutes). The turismo has timetables.

Parking and, in summer, even driving, can be frustrating. But there is a large, free car park one block south of the municipal market.

ALCOBAÇA

pop 54,800

The town of Alcobaça is pleasant but unassuming, and when you first approach the Mosteiro de Santa Maria de Alcobaça (the one reason to come here), you may feel a little disappointed. Don't be. Hiding behind a handsome if uninspired baroque façade lies an extraordinary 12th-century Cistercian monastery whose stark grandeur easily deserves its Unesco World Heritage status. You too will marvel as you walk amid a bright forest of arches that are almost completely unadorned yet seem to reach ethereal heights.

Orientation

From the bus station in the new town turn right along Avenida dos Combatentes to cross the Rio Alcôa and reach the monastery, 500m downhill. The turismo, restaurants and hotels are all near the monastery.

Information

Valuables have been stolen from cars in the monastery car park; be sure to keep them with you.

Hospital (☎ 262 590 400; Rua Hospital) On the eastern edge of the new town, off Rua Afonso de Albuquerque.

Police station (☎ 262 595 400; Rua de Olivença)

Post office (☎ 262 590 351; Praça 25 de Abril; ⌚ 8.30am-6pm Mon-Fri) Almost next door to the turismo.

Turismo (☎ 262 582 377; Praça 25 de Abril; ⌚ 10am-1pm & 3-7pm Jun-Sep, 10am-1pm & 2-6pm Oct-May) Opposite the monastery's main entrance, providing useful bus timetables and free internet access for 15 minutes.

Sights

MOSTEIRO DE SANTA MARIA DE ALCOBAÇA

This **monastery** (☎ 262 505 126; adult/child/senior €4.50/2.25/2.25, church admission free; ⌚ 9am-7pm Apr-Sep, 9am-5pm Oct-Mar) was founded in 1153 by Dom Afonso Henriques, first king of Portugal, to honour a vow he'd made to St Bernard after the capture of Santarém from the Moors in 1147. The king entrusted the construction of the monastery to the monks of the Cistercian order, also giving them a huge area around Alcobaça to develop and cultivate.

Building started in 1178 and by the time the monks moved in, some 40 years later, the monastery estate had become one of the richest and most powerful in the country. In those early days the monastery is said to have housed 999 monks, who held Mass nonstop in shifts.

Switching from farming to teaching in the 13th century, the monks used the estate's abundant rents to carry out further enlargements and changes to the monastery to suit the fashions of the day. Towards the 17th century, the monks turned their talents to pottery and the sculpting of figures in stone, wood and clay.

Revived agricultural efforts in the 18th century made the Alcobaça area one of the most productive in the land. However, it was the monks' growing decadence that became famous, thanks to the writings of 18th-century travellers such as William Beckford who, despite his own tendency to overdo, was shocked at the 'perpetual gormandising…the fat waddling monks and sleek friars with wanton eyes…'. The party ended in 1834 with the dissolution of the religious orders.

Church

Much of the original façade was altered in the 17th and 18th centuries (including the addition of wings), leaving only the main doorway and rose window unchanged.

However, once you step inside, the combination of Gothic ambition and Cistercian austerity hits you immediately: the nave is a breathtaking 106m long but only 23m wide, with huge pillars and truncated columns. It is modelled on the French Cistercian abbey of Clairvaux.

Tombs of Dom Pedro & Dona Inês

Occupying the south and north transepts are two intricately carved 14th-century tombs, the church's greatest possessions, which commemorate the tragic love story of Dom Pedro and his mistress (see the boxed text, below).

Although the tombs themselves were badly damaged by rampaging French troops in search of treasure in 1811, they still show extraordinary narrative detail and are embellished with a host of figures and scenes from the life of Christ. The Wheel of Fortune at the foot of Dom Pedro's tomb and the gruesome Last Judgment scene at the head of Inês' tomb are especially amazing. The tombs are inscribed *Até ao Fím do Mundo* (Until the End of the World) and, on Pedro's orders, placed foot to foot so that, when the time comes, they can rise up and see each other straight away.

Kitchen & Refectory

The grand kitchen, described by Beckford as 'the most distinguished temple of gluttony in all Europe', owes its immense size to alterations carried out in the 18th century, including a water channel built through the middle of the room so that a tributary of the Rio Alcôa could provide a constant source of fresh fish to the monastery – they swam directly into a stone basin. The water was also useful for cooking and washing.

Even now, it's not hard to imagine the scene when Beckford was led here by the abbey's grand priors ('hand in hand, all three together'). He saw:

> 'pastry in vast abundance which a numerous tribe of lay brothers and their attendants were rolling out and puffing up into a hundred different shapes, singing all the while as blithely as larks in a corn field'.

The adjacent refectory, huge and vaulted, is where the monks ate in silence while the Bible was read to them from the pulpit. Opposite the entrance is a 14th-century *lavabo* (bathroom) embellished with a dainty hexagonal fountain. The monks entered through a narrow door on their way to the refectory. Those who could not pass through were forced to fast.

Claustro do Silencio & Sala dos Reis

The beautiful Cloister of Silence dates from two eras. Dom Dinis built the intricate lower storey, with its arches and traceried stone circles, in the 1300s. The upper storey, typically Manueline in style, was added in the 1500s.

Off the northwestern corner of the cloister is the 18th-century Sala dos Reis (Kings' Room), so called because statues of practically all the kings of Portugal line the walls. Below them are *azulejo* friezes depicting stories relevant to the abbey's construction, including the siege of Santarém and the life of St Bernard.

LOVE, POLITICS & REVENGE

As moving as *Romeo and Juliet* – and far more gruesome – is the tragic story of Dom Pedro. The son of Dom Afonso IV, he fell madly in love with his wife's Galician lady-in-waiting, Dona Inês de Castro. Even after the death of his wife, Pedro's father forbade his son from marrying Inês, wary of her Spanish family's potential influence. Various suspicious nobles continued to pressure the king until finally he sanctioned her murder in 1355, unaware that the two lovers had already married in secret.

Two years later, when Pedro succeeded to the throne, he exacted his revenge by ripping out and eating the hearts of Inês' murderers. He then exhumed and crowned her body, and ordered the court to pay homage to his dead queen by kissing her decomposing hand.

MUSEU NACIONAL DO VINHO

This national **wine museum** (☎ 262 582 222; www.ivv.min-agricultura.pt; admission €1.50; 9am-12.30pm & 2-5.30pm Mon-Fri), in an atmospheric old *adega* (winery) 1.2km east of town on the Leiria road, provides a full-bodied portrait of Portugal's wine-making history. You can also sample and buy wine.

RAUL DA BERNARDA MUSEU

The oldest earthenware factory in Alcobaça (established in 1875) is also the only one geared to visitors. Its **museum** (☎ 262 590 600; Ponte D Elias; admission free; 10am-1pm & 3-7pm Tue-Fri, 10am-1pm & 2-7pm Sat), on the northern edge of town, takes you on a journey from traditional blue-and-white earthenware to contemporary multicolour varieties.

Sleeping

Parque de campismo (☎ 262 582 265; Avenida Professor Vieira Natividade; adult/tent/car €2.25/1.50/1.50; Feb-Dec) The small, simple municipal site is 500m north of the bus station. It has some tree shade and disabled access.

Hotel de Santa Maria (☎ 262 590 160; www.hotel.santa.maria.1colony.com; Rua Dr Francisco Zagalo; d €60) This well-appointed, modern place sits just above the square in front of the monastery. The rooms are attractive enough and come with the usual midrange comforts; some have monastery views.

Challet Fonte Nova (☎ 262 598 300; www.challetfontenova.pt; Estrada Fonte Nova; d €110; P) This grand, 19th-century chalet, which would look quite at home on the English seaside, has a lot of charm, with excellent period furnishings in common areas, comfortable doubles of various sizes, decent bathrooms with bathtubs, and a new, whitewashed modern annexe.

Eating & Drinking

Ti Fininho (☎ 262 596 506; Rua Frei António Brandão 34; mains €4-6; lunch & dinner) This ivy-laden place has a snug dining room that serves simple, traditional dishes at good value.

Pensão Restaurante Corações Unidos (☎ /fax 262 582 142; Rua Frei António Brandão 34; mains €5-7.50, tourist menu €10) Near Ti Fininho, the rooms are not particularly good, but the traditional restaurant is renowned for its hearty dishes, including the local speciality, *frango a alcobaça* stewed chicken).

O Telheiro (☎ 262 596 029; Rua da Lavadinha Quinta do Telheiro; mains €12-16; lunch & dinner Sun-Fri) On a lane behind (east of) the monastery complex is the town's best-regarded restaurant, with fine regional fare, from grilled *morcela* to *frango na púcara* (chicken stewed with tomatoes and ham).

Festivals & Events

The **Cistermúsica festival** (☎ 262 580 890), which takes place from mid-May to mid-June, features classical concerts in the monastery and other local venues.

Getting There & Away

BUS

There are about six daily weekday buses (fewer on weekends) to Lisbon (€8.75, two hours). There is also service about hourly to Nazaré (€3.80, 20 minutes), and about eight buses daily to Batalha (€3.20, 40 minutes) and Leiria (€4.10, 50 minutes). Coming from Leiria it's possible to see both Batalha and Alcobaça in a single, carefully timed day.

There is a public car park near the roundabout at the end of Avenida dos Combatentes da Grande Guerra, as you arrive from the EN8 from Leiria.

BATALHA

pop 13,400 / elevation 120m

Like the monastery at Alcobaça, the extraordinary Gothic-Manueline Mosteiro de Santa Maria da Vitória (aka Mosteiro da Batalha) is a greater triumph than the battle it was built to commemorate. Now a World Heritage site, its spiked silhouette bears a striking resemblance to English counterparts in York and Winchester. At once colossal and delicate, it looms over the otherwise unassuming little town. However, the real stars are the cloisters and the off-chapel, with Manueline carving that transforms stone into highly wrought lacework.

Orientation & Information

Buses stop in Largo 14 de Agosto, 200m east of the abbey. Facing the eastern end of the abbey, the **turismo** (☎ 244 765 180; 10am-1pm & 3-7pm May-Sep, 10am-1pm & 2-6pm Oct-Apr) is beside a modern complex of shops and restaurants.

Sights

MOSTEIRO DE SANTA MARIA DA VITÓRIA

This extraordinary **abbey** (admission cloisters & Capelas Imperfeitas adult/child/senior €4.50/2.25/2.25; 9am-2pm Sun free; 9am-6pm Apr-Sep, to 5pm Oct-Mar) was built to commemorate the 1385 Battle of

Aljubarrota (fought 4km south of Batalha), when 6500 Portuguese, commanded by Dom Nuno Álvares Pereira and supported by a few hundred English soldiers, repulsed a 30,000-strong force of Juan I of Castile, who had come claiming the throne of João d'Avis.

João called on the Virgin Mary for help and vowed to build a superb abbey in return for victory, and three years later he made good on his promise as work began on the Dominican abbey.

Most of the monument – the church, Claustro Real, Sala do Capítulo and Capela do Fundador – was completed by 1434 in Flamboyant Gothic, but Manueline exuberance steals the show, thanks to additions made in the 15th and 16th centuries. Work at Batalha only stopped in the mid-16th century when Dom João III turned his attention to expanding the Convento de Cristo in Tomar.

Exterior

The glorious ochre-limestone building bristles with pinnacles and parapets, flying buttresses and balustrades, and Gothic and Flamboyant carved windows, as well as octagonal chapels and massive columns, after the English perpendicular style. The western doorway positively boils over – layers of arches pack in the apostles, various angels, saints and prophets, all topped by Christ and the Evangelists.

Interior

The vast vaulted Gothic interior is plain, long and high like Alcobaça's church, warmed by light from the deep-hued stained-glass windows. To the right as you enter is the intricate **Capela do Fundador** (Founder's Chapel), a beautiful, achingly tall, star-vaulted square room, lit by an octagonal lantern. In the centre is the joint tomb of João I and his English wife, Philippa of Lancaster, whose marriage in 1387 established the cement alliance that still exists between Portugal and England, the world's oldest. The tombs of their four youngest sons line the south wall of the chapel, including that of Henry the Navigator (second from the right).

Claustro Real

Afonso Domingues, the master of works at Batalha during the late 1380s, first built the **Claustro Real** (Royal Cloisters) in a restrained Gothic style, but it's the later Manueline embellishments by the great Diogo de Boitac that really take your breath away. Every arch is a tangle of detailed stone carvings of Manueline symbols, such as armillary spheres and crosses of the Order of Christ, entwined with exotic flowers and marine motifs – ropes, pearls and shells.

Claustro de Dom Afonso V

Anything would seem austere after the Claustro Real, but the simple Gothic **Cloister de Dom Afonso V** is like being plunged into cold water – sobering you up after all that frenzied decadence.

Sala do Capítulo

To the east of the Claustro Real is the early 15th-century **chapterhouse**, containing a beautiful 16th-century stained-glass window. The huge unsupported 19-sq-metre vault was considered so outrageously dangerous to build that only prisoners on death row were employed in its construction. The Sala do Capítulo contains the tomb of the unknown soldiers – one killed in Flanders in WWI, the other in Africa – now watched over by a constant guard of honour.

Capelas Imperfeitas

The roofless **Capelas Imperfeitas** (Unfinished Chapels) at the eastern end of the abbey are perhaps the most astonishing, and certainly the most tantalising, aspect of Batalha. Only accessible from outside the abbey, the octagonal mausoleum with its seven chapels was commissioned by Dom Duarte (João I's eldest son) in 1437. However, the later Manueline additions by the architect Mateus Fernandes overshadow everything else, including the Renaissance upper balcony.

Although Fernandes' original plan for an upper octagon supported by buttresses was never finished, the staggering ornamentation gives a hint of what might have followed, and is all the more dramatic for being open to the sky. Most striking is the 15m-high doorway, a mass of stone-carved thistles, ivy, flowers, snails and all manner of 'scollops and twistifications', as William Beckford noted. Dom Duarte can enjoy it for all eternity; his tomb, and that of his wife, lies opposite the door.

Sleeping & Eating

Pensão Gladius (☎ 244 765 760; fax 244 767 259; Praça Mouzinho de Albuquerque; d €35) In the square right next to the abbey, this is a small, quaint place, loaded with geranium-filled window boxes and offering snug but attractive, spotless and bright modern rooms at excellent value.

Residencial Batalha (☎ 244 767 500; www.hotel-batalha.com; Largo da Igreja; d €50; P) A very good back-up in a modern building close to the abbey, this *residencial* has comfortable, recently redecorated (though slightly lugubrious) rooms; the breakfast room, by contrast, is sunny and boasts great views onto the abbey.

Residencial Casa do Outeiro (☎ 244 765 806; www.casadoouteiro.com; Largo Carvalho do Outeiro 4; d €60; P) This colourful, sunny contemporary place sits just uphill from the abbey, and the best rooms have fine views onto it. All are airy, have been decorated with flair and sport little balconies.

Casa das Febras (☎ 244 765 825; Largo 14 de Agosto; mains €5.50-9; lunch & dinner) In a square behind the abbey, this simple, affordable and dependable eatery serves Portuguese standards.

Getting There & Away

There at least four buses daily to Alcobaça (€2.80, 30 minutes) and Leiria (€2.50, 30 minutes). There is also at least one daily service to Caldas da Rainha (€4.80, 1½ hours). There is no direct service to Lisbon.

There is street parking just east of the abbey, as well as a marked paying public car park a little further on.

LEIRIA

pop 103,500

Set high up on a thickly wooded promontory, Leiria's medieval castle is a commanding presence above the narrow streets and red-tile roofs of the town's compact historic centre. The castle is a reminder that Leiria (lay-*ree*-uh), set amid rich agricultural land, was long one of Portugal's most important towns.

Dom Afonso III convened a *cortes* (parliament) here in 1254; Dom Dinis established his main residence in the castle in the 14th century; and in 1411 the town's sizable Jewish community built Portugal's first paper mill.

These days, life in Leiria is about as unhurried as the waters of the Rio Liz, which loops placidly through town. Still, its bars and cafés tend towards cheerful overcrowding, and back-alleys hide a bevy of shops selling skateboards and club-wear to the town's lively university community.

Leiria makes a convenient base for visiting the region's sites, including Alcobaça, Batalha, Fátima, and the beaches and pine forests of the Pinhal de Leiria. All are easily accessible by bus.

Orientation

The old town is focused on Praça Rodrigues Lobo, with hotels and restaurants nearby. The castle is perched on a wooded hilltop a short walk to the north.

Information

Espaço Internet (Largo de Sant'Ana; 9am-7pm & 8-11pm Mon-Fri, 11am-1.30pm, 2-8pm Sat) Free internet access.

Police station (☎ 244 859 859; Largo Artilharia 4) By the castle.

Post office (Avenida Heróis de Angola 99; 8.30am-6.30pm Mon-Fri, 9am-12.30pm Sat)

St André District Hospital (☎ 244 817 000) About 1.5km east of town in the Olhalvas-Pousos district (follow the signs to the A1 motorway).

Turismo (☎ 244 848 771; 10am-1pm & 3-7pm May-Sep, 10am-1pm & 3-5pm Oct-Apr) Buy the excellent town map (€5) or settle for the free photocopy. Also pick up *Find Us!*, a free bi-monthly multilingual booklet listing events in Leiria and Fátima.

Sights

This long-inhabited clifftop site got its first **castelo** (☎ 244 813 982; castle €1.12, castle & museum adult/child under 12 €2.24/free; 10am-6pm Apr-Sep, 9.30am-5.30pm Oct-Mar) in the time of the Moors. Captured by Afonso Henriques in 1135, it was transformed into a royal residence for Dom Dinis in the 14th century. Inside the walls is a peaceful garden, overgrown with tall trees, and the ruined but still lovely Gothic **Igreja de Nossa Senhora da Penha**, originally built in the 12th century and rebuilt by João I in the early 15th century. It has beautiful leaflike carvings over one arch. The castle's most spectacular feature, however, is a gallery with small corner seats. It provides a fantastic vantage point over the town's red-tiled roofs, though the current structure is largely the result of overeager restoration by early 20th-century Swiss architect Ernesto Korrodi.

The **sé** (cathedral), to the southeast of the castle, was started in the 16th century, and the cloister, sacristy and chapter houses date from 1583 to 1604. It's a plain, cavernous place. Opposite is the wonderfully tiled **Pharmacy Leonardo Paiva** – the beautiful *azulejos* depict Hippocrates, Galen and Socrates. Novelist Eça de Queirós used to live in Rua da Tipografia

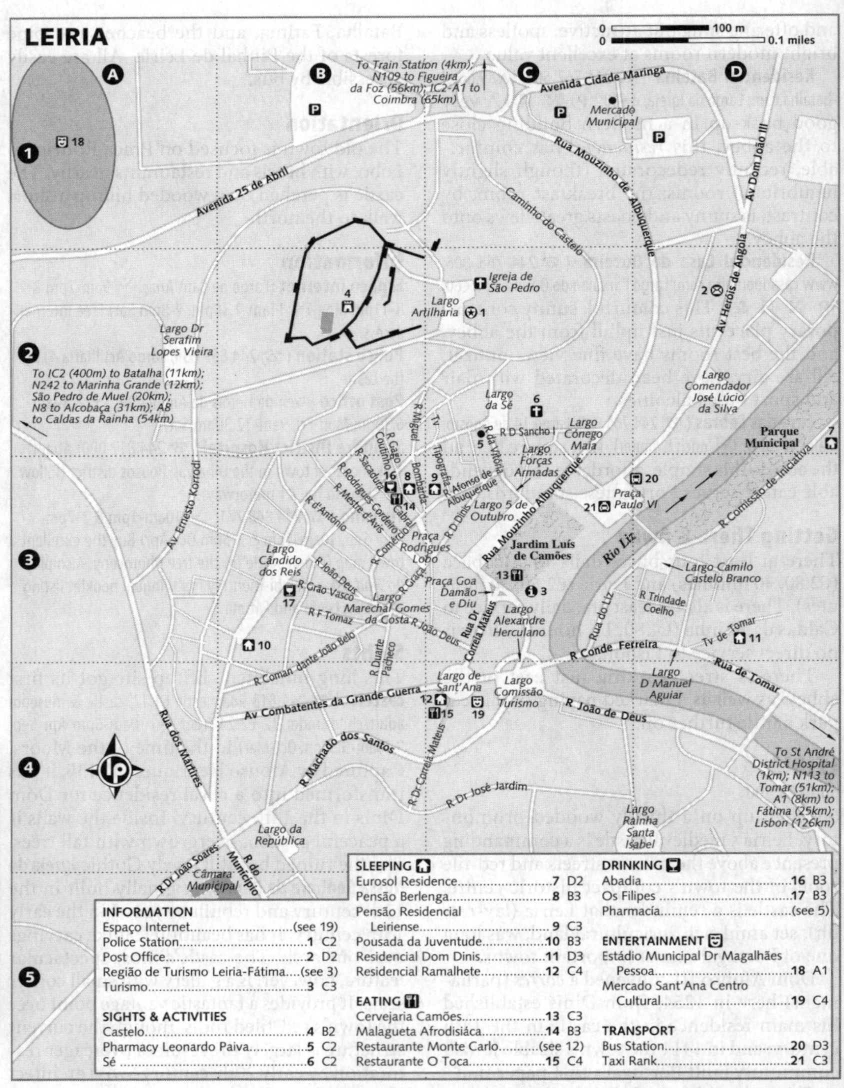

next to the cathedral, and he and his literary group met regularly in the pharmacy. These days, it's a Dutch-owned, Irish-style pub (opposite).

Festivals & Events

Leiria celebrates the joy of eating with the nine-day **Festival de Gastronomia** in early September. Expect folk dancing as well as stalls of mouthwatering traditional food.

Sleeping

Pousada da juventude (☎ 244 831 868; www.movijovem.pt; Largo Cândido dos Reis 9; dm €11, d with shared bathroom €24) In an attractive, 18th-century town house on a charming central square, this friendly hostel offers kitchen and TV privileges, plus high-ceilinged if basic doubles and dorms.

Pensão Berlenga (☎ 962 941 207; Rua Miguel Bombarda 13; d €30) In an old rambling house on a narrow street, this cheapie could do with a lick of paint and some new carpets, though its rock-bottom prices and central location deserve mention.

Residencial Ramalhete (☎ 244 812 802; res.ramalhete@mail.telepac.pt; Rua Dr Correia Mateus 30; d €34; 💻) This clean and efficient if somewhat careworn guesthouse has been cobbled together out of a series of late-Deco apartments with big windows and mostly wooden floors. Some rooms have balconies. Good value.

Residencial Dom Dinis (☎ 244 815 342; fax 244 823 552; Travessa de Tomar 2; s/d €36) Dom Dinis is a friendly, modern *residencial* with small but spotless and mostly bright rooms done up rather tastefully; several have fine views across town to the castle. Another great deal. French is spoken.

Pensão Residencial Leiriense (☎ 244 823 054; fax 244 823 073; Rua Afonso de Albuquerque 6; d €38) Yet another good-value option – this one right in the historic centre on a cobbled street just off Praça Rodriguez Lobo. Rooms are small but all are kept in fine fiddle, and most are surprisingly bright.

Eurosol Residence (☎ 244 860 460; www.eurosol.pt; Rua Commisão da Iniciativa 13; d from €95; P ❄ 💻) A big step up in comfort and Leiria's only luxury option, the Eurosol has attractive, comfortable business-class mini-apartments, many with exceptional views across town to the castle.

Eating & Drinking

Restaurante Monte Carlo (☎ 244 825 406; Rua Dr Correia Mateus 32; mains €3-7, 3-course menu with wine €9; 🕒 lunch & dinner Mon-Sat) Along pedestrianised Rua Dr Correia Mateus are several traditional restaurants, including this family-friendly, no-nonsense spot popular for its great-value menu and filling Portuguese fare.

Restaurante A Toca (Rua Dr Correia Mateus 32; mains €4-10; 🕒 lunch & dinner Sun-Fri) Just next door to Restaurante Monte Carlo is this ever-so-slightly more upmarket place, with a long menu that includes very good meat and fish prepared most nights at a wood grill.

Cervejaria Camões (☎ 244 838 628; Jardim Luís de Camões; mains €6-10; lunch & dinner) In the *jardim* (garden), this contemporary café-restaurant-cum-beerhouse has lots of terrace seating, plus floor-to-ceiling plate-glass windows looking out over the town's little riverside park. Upstairs, Sabor Latino (open from 9pm to 2am) becomes a mainstream disco some nights and a venue for various kinds of Latin dance on other nights.

Malagueta Afrodisiáca (☎ 244 831 607; Rua Gago Coutinho 17; mains €9-13; 🕒 dinner) With aphrodisiac teas and an eclectic fusion of Brazilian, Indian and other ethnic cuisines, this trendy, slinkily decorated place is tucked down a narrow street in the historic centre. A rare deviation from standard Portuguese fare.

Os Filipes (Largo Cândido dos Reis 1a; 🕒 11am-2am Mon-Sat) This simple bar-café has seating on an attractive old square, attracting hosts of students most nights.

Abadia (☎ 244 838 782; Rua Barão de Viamonte 43; 🕒 café 3-9pm, bar 9pm-2am Mon-Sat) A cool bar upstairs plays jazz and electronica during the day for Leiria's intellectual scene. The downstairs bar heats up on weekends when DJs come up from Lisbon.

Pharmácia (Largo Cândido dos Reis 1a; 🕒 8am-2am Mon-Sat) Set inside a marvellous, 19th-century pharmacy you'll find this Dutch-owned, Irish-style bar featuring a mellow vibe and lots imported beers for those sick of Sagres.

Entertainment

Featuring dance, theatre and high-brow cinema, the market-turned-cultural complex **Mercado Sant'Ana Centro Cultural** (☎ 244 815 091; Largo de Sant'Ana) is built around a pleasant courtyard, where you'll find several cafés and an Espaço Internet as well as the theatre.

Leiria hosted some of the 2004 European Football Championships in its 35,000-seat **Estádio Municipal Dr Magalhães Pessoa** (☎ 244 831 774), home ground for local team Unaio de Leiria.

Getting There & Away

Street parking is fairly easy along Rua João de Deus. The train station is 4km northwest of town, with frequent bus connections.

BUS

From the **bus station** (☎ 244 811 507) there are about hourly runs to Batalha (€2.50, 30 minutes), Alcobaça (€4.10, 50 minutes), Fátima (€2.60, 45 minutes), Coimbra (€7.50, 1¼ hours) and Lisbon (€9.20, 1¾ hours). In addition there are about four daily runs to Tomar (€7.40, 50 minutes).

TRAIN

Leiria is on the line that runs from the Mira Sintra-Meclas station (€9.20, 2½) – near Sintra and on the suburban line to Lisbon – to Figueira da Foz (€5.60, 1¼ hours) about three times daily. Buses run frequently from central Leiria's bus station to the train station (€0.90, 15 minutes).

PINHAL DE LEIRIA

First planted by a forward-looking monarch some 700 years ago, the Pinhal de Leiria is a vast forest of towering pines whose fragrance and stippled shade make this one of the most enchanting stretches of Portugal's Atlantic coast. Dom Dinis expanded it significantly as a barrier against encroaching dunes and also as a source of timber for the maritime industry – a great boon during the Age of Discoveries.

Today, the protected forest covers more than 100 sq km along the coast west of Leiria. Narrow roads cut through the serene stands of pine, leading to a number of excellent beaches around the resort towns of **São Pedro de Moel**, **Praia da Vieira** and **Pedrógão**.

Be aware that here as elsewhere on the Atlantic coast, seas and currents can be strong; ask around before venturing into the waters.

Orientation & Information

São Pedro de Moel is 20km west of Leiria. Praia da Vieira and Pedrógão are 16km to the north, along the coastal highway. There are turismos in São Pedro de Moel (☎ 244 599 633) and Praia da Vieira (☎ 244 695 230) that only open in summer.

Sleeping & Eating

SÃO PEDRO DE MOEL

Parque de Campismo Orbitur (☎ 244 599 168; www.orbitur.pt; adult/tent/car €4.80/5.10/4.60;) In among the pine trees yet just 500m from the sea, this well-equipped site includes swimming pool, disabled facilities and playground. You can also rent cabins (four/six people €66/92).

Parque de Campismo Inatel (☎ 244 599 289; adult/tent/car €4.50/3.30/2.20) Just across from the sea, this good if more basic site has smaller, scrubbier trees.

Hotel Mar e Sol (☎ 244 590 000; www.hotelmaresol.com; Avenida da Liberdade 1; d with/without sea views €85/65) A modern, seafront hotel, Mar e Sol was undergoing a needed refurbishing at the time of writing. The midrange rooms are comfortable if uninspired, though many do have grand views over the tussling sea.

Brisamar (☎ 244 599 250; Rua Nicolau Bettencourt 23; mains around €12; lunch & dinner Tue-Sun) Vaguely upmarket if unimpressive at first glance, this place in fact serves some of the best seafood around, including fine swordfish, as well as a variety of good salads.

PRAIA DA VIEIRA & PEDRÓGÃO

Parque de Campismo Praia da Vieira (☎ 244 695 334; adult/tent/car €2/2.20/2.40; Jun-Sep; P) In Praia da Vieira, this site has hot water, adjacent swimming pool, laundry and limited shade. It's also a hop and skip from the beach.

Parque de Campismo Pedrógão (☎ 244 695 403; fax 244 695 447; adult/tent/car €1.90/2.40/2.40; Mar-Nov) In the forest at nearby Pedrógão is this smaller but very good, well-equipped ground with a restaurant, hot water, more shade and air scented sweetly by the surrounding pines.

Hotel Estrela do Mar (☎/fax 244 695 404; Avenida Marginal; d with breakfast €55;) Right on the beach in Praia da Vieira, this place offers good value with decently furnished, neatly kept rooms with tile floors. Angle for a front room with veranda and sea view.

Hotel Cristal (☎ 244 699 060; www.hoteiscristal.pt; Avenida Marginal; d breakfast €90;) This, the most upmarket option in this stretch of coast, has large rooms with midrange comforts, plus a full-service spa for pampering. Almost all rooms have at least a lateral sea view onto Praia da Vieira; an extra €5 gets a frontal sea view.

Solemar (Avenida Marginal; mains €9-12; lunch & dinner Wed-Mon) On the ground floor of the Hotel Estrela do Mar, this place serves up excellent seafood, managing to stay crowded even in the low season with admiring locals.

O Pai dos Frangos (☎ 244 599 158; mains €7-10; lunch & dinner Wed-Mon) At Praia da Velha, 'The Father of Chickens' is a lone restaurant overlooking the beach, with sea views and lots of decorative fishing nets. Specialities include *arroz de marisco* (paella-like rice and seafood stew) and, naturally, grilled chicken.

Getting There & Away

From Leiria there are at least six daily buses to Pedro de Moel (€2.70, 40 minutes). During July and August there are also at least seven daily buses to Praia da Vieira (€2.90, 45 minutes, two daily weekdays). Otherwise, a direct service between Leiria and Praia da Vieira is limited to a couple of school-day buses.

FÁTIMA

pop 10,400 / elevation 320m

Holy and sacrosanct or gaudy and commercial? Your feelings about Fátima will surely depend on the degree of trust you place in its miracles. Whatever your beliefs, you can't help but be impressed by the vast reserves of faith that every year lead as many as six million pilgrims to the glade where, on 13 May 1917, the Virgin Mary is said to have first appeared to three awe-struck peasant children.

The site of the apparition has been given over to huge structures that awe you with their size, though not necessarily their aesthetic merits. The courtyard outside the basilica is twice the size of St Peter's, and a new church is being built with room for 9000 worshippers, due to be finished in 2007. If you like crowds, the best times to visit are 12 and 13 May and 12 and 13 October, when hundreds of thousands of pilgrims arrive to commemorate the 1917 apparitions. Many come on foot, and the highways and byways of Portugal are lined with ramblers in the weeks leading up to the holiest days.

The town itself is a shrine to tat: it's packed with boarding houses and restaurants for the pilgrim masses, and shop windows are crowded with glow-in-the-dark Virgins and unconvincing busts of John Paul II.

Orientation & Information

The focus of the pilgrimages is Cova da Iria, site of the visions, just east of the A1 motorway. Where sheep once grazed there's now a vast 1km-long esplanade dominated by a huge white basilica.

Several major roads ring the area, including Avenida Dom José Alves Correia da Silva to the south, where the bus station is located. To reach the sanctuary, turn right from the bus station and walk 300m, then left along Rua João Paulo II for 500m. The **turismo** (☎ 249 531 139; ⏰ 10am-1pm & 3-7pm May-Sep, 2-6pm Oct-Apr) is also on Avenida Dom José Alves Correia da Silva 300m beyond this turning.

Sights

Dominating the sanctuary is the 1953 **basilica**, a triumphantly sheer-white building with a *praça* and a colonnade that is reminiscent of St Peter's in Rome. It is the focus of intense devotion, and supplicants who have promised penance – for example, in

THE FÁTIMA APPARITION

On 13 May 1917, three children from Fátima – Lúcia, Francisco and Jacinta – claimed to have seen an apparition of the Virgin 'more brilliant than the sun'. Only 10-year-old Lúcia could hear what she said, including her request that the children return on the 13th of each month for the next six months. Word spread and by 13 October some 70,000 devotees had gathered, including agnostic journalists who would go on to write deliriously about what was about to occur: the so-called Miracle of the Sun. Lúcia asked the Virgin for a sign for the gathered masses, and just at that moment rainy skies opened and thousands of pilgrims reported seeing the sun turn into a whirling disc of colours that seemed to shoot its rays down to the very earth. Ophthalmologists have pointed out that these are normal optical phenomena caused by staring at any bright object, but the Vatican, which had hitherto tried to squelch enthusiasm about the appearances, decided it wisest to embrace the events wholeheartedly. The home-grown miracle also proved a great boon to the coming Salazar dictatorship, with its strategic melding of nationalism, Catholicism and fascism.

But the story was not over yet. Lúcia said she had received three secrets from the Holy Mother. First was a vision of hell resulting from 'sins of the flesh,' and a plea to pray heartily and 'make many sacrifices' – standard stuff. Second, the Virgin said that if her request were heeded, 'Russia would be converted and there would be peace.' But the third message was considered too inflammatory to be divulged.

Speculation ended when, during an emotional ceremony in 2000, the visiting Pope John Paul II revealed that the third secret foretold the attempt on his own life in 1981. John Paul's explanation was at odds with the current pope's own 1984 statement that it concerned 'the dangers threatening the faith and the life of the Christian.' Further complicating matters, papal theologian Cardinal Ciappi had written that 'in the Third Secret it is foretold, among other things, that the great apostasy in the Church will begin at the top.' More to be revealed, it seems.

return for helping a loved one who is sick, or to signify a particularly deep conversion – regularly shuffle across the vast esplanade on their knees. The **Capela das Apariçoes** (Chapel of the Apparitions) marks the site where the Virgin appeared. Here devotees also kneel and shuffle, offering flowers and lighting candles. There's a blazing furnace by the chapel where people can throw offerings on the fire. Or you can leave gifts, which are collected at the end of the day and donated to charities.

Inside the basilica are 15 altars dedicated to the 15 mysteries of the rosary. Attention is focused on the tombs of Blessed Francisco (died 1919, aged 11) and Blessed Jacinta (died 1920, aged 10), both victims of the flu epidemic, who were beatified in 2000. Lúcia, the third witness of the apparition, entered a convent in Coimbra in 1928, where she died in 2005.

At the entrance of the sanctuary, to the south of the rectory, is a segment of the **Berlin Wall**, donated by a Portuguese resident of Germany and a tribute to God's part in the fall of communism, as some say was predicted at Fátima.

Eight Masses are held daily in the basilica, and seven daily in the Capela das Apariçoes. (At least two Masses daily are held in English; check at the information booth by the chapel for details.)

The new **Igreja da Santissima Trindade** (Church of the Holy Trinity) will be finished in 2007, and will cost more than €40 million. It's a great disc with a huge walkway through the centre, something like a giant table-tennis paddle, if the architectural projections are to be believed.

The **Museu de Cera de Fátima** (Waxwork Museum; ☎ 249 539 300; www.mucefa.pt; Rua Jacinta Marto; adult/child 6-12 €4.50/2.50; 9.30am-6.30pm Mon-Sat, 9am-6.30pm Sun Apr-Oct, 10am-5pm Nov-Mar) gives a tacky but appealingly blow-by-blow, starry-eyed account of the story of Fátima.

Sleeping

There are dozens of reasonably priced restaurants, *pensões* (guesthouses) and boarding houses, most geared for visiting groups of hundreds and very few with any character.

Plenty of interchangeable pilgrim lodges are in the thick of the shops east of the basilica, including the clean and rather spartan **Casa Poeira** (☎ 249 531 419; Travessa Santo António; d €35).

Hotel Coração de Fátima (☎ 249 531 433; fax 249 531 157; Rua Cônego Formigão; d €60) Next to the post office and not far from the turismo, this popular place offers comfortable, cookie-cutter rooms with midrange comforts and brisk, efficient service.

Getting There & Away

Fátima is a stop on most major north–south bus runs, with at least hourly services between Lisbon (€9.50,1½ hours) and points north such as Coimbra (€9.80, 1½ hours) and Porto (€12.50, two to three hours). Note that Fátima is sometimes referred to as Cova da Iria on bus timetables. There are also at least hourly buses to Leiria (€2.60, 45 minutes).

PORTO DE MÓS

pop 25,200 / elevation 260m

Dominated by a 13th-century hilltop castle, Porto de Mós is an appealing, untouristy town on the little Rio Lena that makes a good base for exploring the mountains and caves of the adjacent Parque Natural das Serras de Aire e Candeeiros. Once the haunt of dinosaurs (see the boxed text, opposite), Porto de Mós became a major Roman settlement whose residents used the Lena to ferry millstones hewn from a nearby quarry and, later, iron from a mine 10km south at Alqueidão da Serra. You can still see the Roman road, which is fantastically cobbled and stretches up into the hills – a great 9km walk.

Orientation & Information

The town spreads out from a cluster of streets just below the castle to a newer area further south around the *mercado municipal* on Avenida Dr Francisco Sá Carneiro, where buses also stop. Walk west from here towards the river and you'll hit Alameda Dom Afonso Henriques, the main road through town. The **turismo** (☎ 244 491 323; 10am-1pm & 3-7pm Tue-Sun May-Sep, 10am-1pm, 2-6pm Tue-Sun Oct-Apr) is at the top of the main road in the *jardim público* (public garden) and offers 15 minutes' free internet access.

Sights

CASTELO

The green-towered **castle** (admission free; 10am-12.30pm & 2-6pm Tue-Sun May-Sep, to 5pm Oct-Apr) was originally a Moorish stronghold that was conquered definitively in 1148 by Dom Afonso Henriques. It was largely rebuilt in 1450 and again after the 1755 earthquake. These days it's too pristine to be convincingly medieval, especially the overneat green tiles of its pitched roof. Still, it's a fine sight and has pleasant views across the valley and into the mountains of the Serras de Aire e Candeeiros.

MUSEU MUNICIPAL

This little **museum** (☎ 244 499 615; Travessa de São Pedro; admission free; ⏰ 10am-12.30pm & 2-5.30pm Tue-Sun), in a pink building beneath the *câmara municipal* (town hall) just off Largo Machado dos Santos, contains a hodgepodge of highly local treasures: dinosaur fossils, Neolithic stones, Palaeolithic flints, Roman columns, *azulejos*, millstones, butterflies, spinning wheels and, just for fun, a few old typewriters.

Sleeping & Eating

Residencial O Filipe (☎ 244 401 455; www.ofilipe.com; Largo do Rossio 41; d with breakfast €40; P) It may be the only *pensão* in town, but this large, pink, recently renovated inn doesn't rest on its laurels, offering 15 trim if slightly grandmotherly rooms, all with telephone.

Quinta de Rio Alcaide (☎ 244 402 124; rioalcaide@mail.telepac.pt; d from €40; P) One kilometre southeast of Porto de Mós, this terrific inn is set in a converted 18th-century paper mill. Rooms and apartments are charming, including one in a former windmill. The grounds, featuring a pool, citrus trees and a cascading stream, are particularly lovely. English spoken.

Canto de Saudade (☎ 244 491 480; Rua da Saudade; mains €6-10; ⏰ lunch & dinner Mon-Sat) Up the hill on the way to the castle, this good traditional restaurant specialises in roast kid and octopus. Offers good-value tourist menus, including soup, main, dessert and drink for around €10.

Esplanada Jardim (⏰ 10am-2am) This pleasant café is in the leafy riverside gardens near the turismo.

Getting There & Away

There are five daily weekday buses to/from Leiria (€2.45, 45 minutes) via Batalha (€1.70, 15 minutes). There are also two daily buses to Alcobaça (€2.25, 35 minutes). You can buy tickets in the municipal market.

PARQUE NATURAL DAS SERRAS DE AIRE E CANDEEIROS

It's not a stretch to imagine dinosaurs roaming this park, with its barren limestone heights that dive down suddenly into deep, rocky depressions. The park is famous for its cathedral-like caves, but above ground it's also scenic, particularly the high Planalto de Santo António (starting 2km south of the Grutas de Santo António). Gorse and olive grove–covered hills are divided by dry-stone walls and threaded by cattle trails, all making for tempting rambles.

Throughout the park there are over a dozen *parques de merendas* (picnic areas). There are also numerous *percursos pedestres* (walking trails), ranging from 2km to 16km, described in Portuguese-language pamphlets available from the park offices.

Information

Ecoteca (☎ 244 491 904; fax 244 403 555; ⏰ 9.30am-12.30pm & 2-6pm Tue-Sun) Main information office in the

DINOSAUR FOOTPRINTS

For years a huge quarry 10km south of Fátima yielded nothing more interesting than chunks of limestone. But when the quarry closed in 1994 a local archaeologist discovered huge footprints embedded in the sloping rock face. These, the oldest and longest sauropod tracks in the world, record a 147m walk in the mud a trifling 175 million years ago.

The sauropods (those nice herbivorous dinosaurs with small heads and long necks and tails) would have been stepping through carbonated mud, later transformed into limestone. As you walk across the slope you can clearly see the large elliptical prints made by the *pes* (feet) and the smaller, half-moon prints made by the *manus* (hands).

Another major dinosaur discovery – a partial skeleton of a flesh-eating *Allosaurus fragilis* – was made in April 1999 at nearby Pombal (26km northeast of Leiria). It proved to be the same species as fossils found in the western USA, throwing into disarray the theory that the Atlantic Ocean opened only during the late Jurassic period.

You can follow in the footsteps of the dinosaurs, through Fátima's **Monumento Natural das Pegadas dos Dinossáurios** (☎ 249 530 160; www.pegadasdedinossaurios.org; adult/child €1.50/0.50; ⏰ 10am-5pm Tue-Sun) at Pedreira do Galinha, 9km east of the N360 running south of Fátima; follow the brown signs marked 'Pegadas da Serra de Aire'.

ESTREMADURA & RIBATEJO

public garden of the turismo in Porto de Mós, where you can pick up information (mostly in Portuguese). Hiking maps are available for €5.

Head office (☎ 243 999 480; www icn.pt in Portuguese; Rua Dr Augusto César da Silva Ferreira) In Rio Maior, at the south of the park.

Sights

MIRA DE AIRE

Portugal's largest **cave system** (☎ 244 440 322; adult/child €4.80/3; 9.30am-8.30pm Jul & Aug, 9.30am-7pm Jun & Sep, 9.30am-6pm Apr & May, 9.30am-5.30pm Oct-Mar, last admission 30min before closing), at Mira de Aire, 14km southeast of Porto de Mós, was discovered in 1947 and opened to the public in 1971. It seems the 45-minute guided tour hasn't changed much since, with groovy psychedelically lit caverns filled with stalactites and stalagmites. The last cavern, 110m down, contains a huge lake with a dramatic fountain display.

There are three buses daily on weekdays from Porto de Mós to Mira de Aire (€2.40, 30 minutes), plus one on Sundays. In July and August there is one additional bus daily.

GRUTAS DE ALVADOS & GRUTAS DE SANTO ANTÓNIO

These **caves** (☎ 244 440 787; adult/child per cave €4.80/3, both caves €8/5; 9.30am-8.30pm Jul & Aug, 9.30am-7pm Jun & Sep, 9.30am-6pm Apr & May, 9.30am-5.30pm Oct-Mar) are about 15km southeast of Porto de Mós, and 2km and 3.5km, respectively, south of the N243 from Porto de Mós to Mira de Aire. They were discovered by workmen in 1964, and are the spiky smaller cousins of Mira de Aire, with similarly disco-flavoured lighting.

There are no direct buses to the Alvados and Santo António caves. Your best bet is to hop off the Porto de Mós–Mira de Aire bus and walk (steeply uphill!) from the N243. A **taxi** (☎ 244 491 351) from Porto de Mós costs about €15 return, including an hour's wait at the caves.

Sleeping

The park operates four rustic *centros de acolhimento* (lodging centres) in its southern section, geared to groups of four to eight and starting at about €60 per night in the high season. This accommodation should be booked at least a week in advance at the park's **ecoteca** (☎ 244 449 700) in Porto de Mós. They are available June through September.

The remote, basic, beautifully set **parque de campismo** (☎ 244 450 555, reservations 244 449 700; adult/tent €2.50/0.75 May-Sep) at Arrimal, 17km south of Porto de Mós, has only 50 pitches, and is accessible by a weekday bus to Porto de Mós (€2.10, 35 minutes).

At the time of writing there was also a youth hostel under construction in Alvados.

RIBATEJO

Literally meaning 'Above the Tejo', Ribatejo is Portugal's heartland – the only province that doesn't border either Spain or the open ocean. A string of Templar's castles are proof of its strategic importance, though these days its clout is economic, thanks both to industry along the Tejo and to rich agricultural plains that spread out from the river's banks. This is also bull country – most of the country's fighters are bred in and around the capital, Santarém.

SANTARÉM

pop 63,100 / elevation 110m

Capital of Ribatejo, old Santarém (sang-tuh-*rayng)* sits on bluffs above a lovely bend in the impressively wide Rio Tejo. Sweeping views of the river and surrounding plains made it a key stronghold of the Moors, and its fall to Portuguese forces marked a turning point in the Reconquista. A group of beautiful Gothic buildings recalls its glory days, though it was quickly eclipsed by Lisbon.

These days, bullfights are the city's claim to fame, though its June agricultural fair is another big draw. A 5000-strong student population keep things lively the rest of the year.

History

Important to the Romans, Santarém became a legendarily impenetrable Moorish stronghold (only the site remains) that Dom Afonso Henriques was finally able to capture in 1147 – perhaps the single most important victory in Portugal's Reconquista. The king built the Mosteiro de Santa Maria de Alcobaça (p281) in thanks for the victory.

Santarém became a favourite royal residence (hunting was the main draw), and its palace served as the meeting place of the *cortes* during the 13th, 14th and 15th centuries. A 400-year royal hiatus ended in 1833 – when Dom Miguel used it as his base during his brief (unsuccessful) war against his brother Pedro.

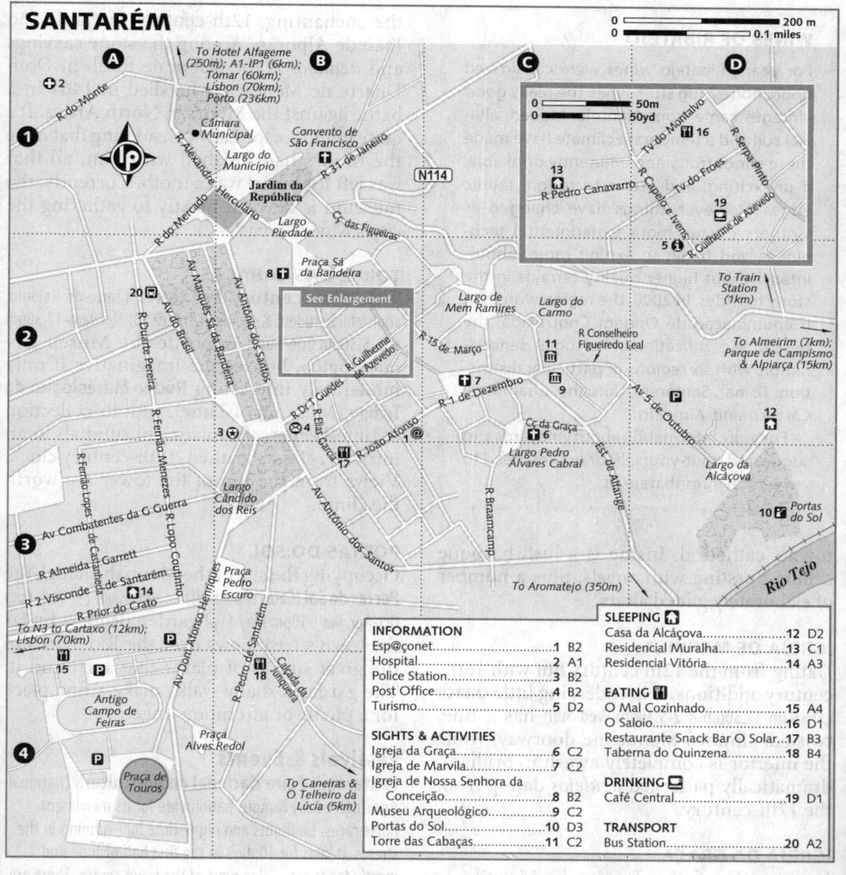

Orientation

At the heart of the old town are the pedestrianised Rua Serpa Pinto and Rua Capelo e Ivens, where you will find the turismo and most of the restaurants, shops and cheap accommodation. Signposts to the Portas do Sol lookout lead visitors on a walk past most of the churches of interest.

Information

Esp@conet (Rua João Afonso 6; 10am-midnight Mon-Sat, 10am-10pm Sun) Free internet access in the upstairs lobby of the Teatro Sá da Bandeira.

Hospital (243 300 200; Avenida Bernardo Santareno Santarém) On the northern edge of town.

Police station (243 322 022; Campo Sá da Bandeira Santarém)

Post office (243 309 730; Rua Dr Teixeira Guedes; 8.30am-6.30pm Mon-Fri, 9am-12.30pm Sat) Has NetPost.

Turismo (243 304 437; fax 243 304 401; Rua Capelo e Ivens 63; 9am-7pm Mon-Fri, 10am-12.30pm & 2.30-5.30pm Sat & Sun) Has a detailed town map with multilingual descriptive text, which describes different thematic routes.

Sights

IGREJA DE NOSSA SENHORA DA CONCEIÇÃO

This baroque, 17th-century Jesuit **church** (9am-12.30pm & 2-5.30pm Wed-Sun), built on the site of the former royal palace, looms over the town's most impressive square, Praça Sá da Bandeira. The church now serves as the

 Book accommodation online at lonelyplanet.com

WINES OF RIBATEJO

For years, Ribatejo wines were considered good, honest jug stuff, while the really good vintages came from Alentejo. Indeed, alluvial soil and a temperate climate have made these wines fruity and eminently drinkable, if unexciting, and prone to rough, tannic edges. However, things have changed as vintners pursue more experimental techniques and begin to exploit more labour-intensive but higher-quality terrains in the stony hillsides. In 2000, the region won DOC (Denominação de Origem Controlada; the best wine certification in Portugal) denomination, with six regions of particular distinction: Tomar, Santarém, Coruche, Chamusca, Cartaxo and Almeirim.

For more information about vineyards and suggested do-it-yourself itineraries, head to www.rotavinhoribatejo.pt.

town's cathedral. Inside is a lush baroque ceiling bursting with angels, plus a number of elaborately gilded altars.

IGREJA DE MARVILA

Dating from the 12th century but with 16th-century additions, this endearing little **church** (9am-12.30pm & 2-5.30pm Wed-Sun) has a fine, twisted, sinuous Manueline doorway, while the interior is completely awash in brilliant, dramatically patterned *azulejos* dating from the 17th-century.

IGREJA DA GRAÇA

Just south of the Igreja de Marvila is Santarém's early 15th-century **church** (9am-12.30pm & 2-5.30pm Wed-Sun), with its delicately carved façade of multilayered arches. Inside, a glorious rose window spills light across the interior, including the tombs of Pedro Álvares Cabral (the 'discoverer' of Brazil, who lived in Santarém) and Dom Pedro de Menezes (the first governor of Ceuta, who died in 1437). The de Menezes family founded the church, which explains why Dom Pedro's funerary monument – supported by a pride of lions – is considerably more ornate than that of the more prominent explorer.

MUSEU ARQUEOLÓGICO

This archaeological **museum** (admission €1; 9am-12.30pm & 2-5.30pm Tue-Sun) is housed in the enchanting, 12th-century Igreja de São João de Alporão. Among the stone carvings and *azulejos* is the elaborate tomb of Dom Duarte de Menezes, who died in 1464 in a battle against the Moors in North Africa. It's quite grand – especially considering that once the Moors had finished with him, all that was left for burial was a tooth. Currently, the museum is devoted mostly to gathering the city's Moorish past.

TORRE DAS CABAÇAS

This 15th-century **bell tower** (Torre do Relógio; adult/child/student & senior €1/free/0.50; 9am-12.30pm & 2-5.30pm Tue-Sun), opposite the Museu Arqueológico, houses the imaginative if only moderately interesting **Núcleo Museológico do Tempo** (Museum of Time), with its collection of time-keepers, from ancient sundials to an intricate, glass-sheathed, 19th-century clock. Views from the top of the tower are worth the climb.

PORTAS DO SOL

Occupying the site of the Moorish citadel, the **Portas do Sol** (Gates of the Sun; free admission; 9am-6pm Oct-Apr, 9am-10pm May-Sep) garden proffers by far the town's best views over the Rio Tejo and the great spread of plains that surround it. The garden's shady walks make a fine place for a picnic or afternoon linger.

Festivals & Events

Santarém's Feira Nacional da Agricultura (National Agriculture Fair) Famous nationwide for its merriment, horse races, bullfights and night-time bull-running in the streets. It lasts for 10 days in the first half of June and mostly takes place 2km west of the town centre. There are lots of associated children's events.

Festival Nacional de Gastronomia Held over a fortnight in October at the Casa do Campino, it encourages you to eat as much traditional Portuguese fare as you can. Stalls sell regional specialities, and selected restaurants from 18 different regions present their finest cuisine.

Sleeping

Pousada da juventude (youth hostel; www.movijovem.pt; Avenida Grupo Forcados Amadores de Santarém) At the time of writing, this cheerful, modern hostel was closed for renovations, set to reopen in 2007.

Parque de Campismo Alpiarça (/fax 243 557 040; adult/tent/car €3.40/3.40/2.20;) The nearest site is at Alpiarça, 15km to the east. It's well equipped and close to a reservoir, with pool, restaurant and some shade.

Residencial Vitória (☎ 243 309 130; Rua 2 Visconde de Santarém 21; d €40; ❄) Tucked away in a quiet area, this night-at-your-great-aunt's-type place is run by Dona Vitória herself, with help from various elderly hangers-on. It has clean, mostly roomy digs and ample street parking.

Residencial Muralha (☎ 243 322 399; Rua Pedro Canavarro 12; d €40) By the old town walls, this simple place offers cheerful, good-value rooms with tiled floors and rather eclectic ornaments. Breakfast is not included.

Hotel Alfageme (☎ 243 377 240; www.hotelalfageme.com; Avenida Bernardo Santareno 38; d €55; ❄) The closest Santarém comes to a business hotel, this white, poured-concrete number offers smallish but comfortable (if unglamorous) plaid-accented rooms.

Casa da Alcáçova (☎ 243 304 030; www.alcacova.com; Largo da Alcáçova; d around €160; P 💻) This 17th-century manor house has an enviable position near Portas do Sol gardens, with the same remarkable vistas. Rooms are impeccable, large, bright, and beautifully furnished, while the handsome, walled garden includes an inviting pool.

Eating & Drinking

As you'd expect of a student-packed agricultural town, Santarém is well off for good-value restaurants.

BUDGET

Restaurante Snack Bar O Solar (☎ 243 322 239; Emilio Infante da Câmara 9; mains €4.50-7; 🕓 lunch & dinner Sun-Fri) With a terracotta floor, exposed brick walls and lace curtains, O Solar is a pleasantly traditional eatery serving Portuguese standards, with a few upmarket touches thrown in.

Café Central (Rua Guilherme de Azevedo 32; 🕓 8am-2am Mon-Sat, 9.30am-5pm Sun) With cool chrome and Art Deco decor, and outside tables for people-watching, this perennially favourite café also serves hot lunches (€5 to €8).

Taberna do Quinzena (☎ 243 322 804; Rua Pedro de Santarém 93; mains around €7; 🕓 lunch & dinner Mon-Sat) Walls plastered with brightly coloured bullfighting posters are a reminder that this place was once a macho refuge, though women are now welcome to join the boys for a simple plate of grilled meats, washed down with a quaffable local Ribatejo wine.

O Saloio (☎ 243 327 656; Travessa do Montalvo 11; mains €2.80-8; 🕓 lunch & dinner Mon-Fri, dinner Sat) This cosy, tiled, family-friendly *tasca* (tavern) has Portuguese standards and inviting outdoor seating.

MIDRANGE

O Telheiro da Lúcia (☎ 243 328 581; mains around €9; 🕓 lunch & dinner) Lúcia is known around town for her version of the regional speciality *fataça na telha* (mullet fish grilled on a tile). Lúcia also bakes her own bread. However, you must call ahead to order your meal one day in advance. Her place is located right on the Tejo in Caneiras, 5km south of town.

Aromatejo (☎ 917 598 861; Travessa do Bairro Falco; mains €9-12; 🕓 dinner Wed-Sun) Overlooking the Tejo, this is a garden restaurant with a fantastic river-and-rural view. It's small inside but has an outside terrace. The menu boasts a lot of aromatically grilled wild game, from partridge to deer to wild boar.

O Mal Cozinhado (☎ 243 323 584; Campo de Feiras; mains €8-14; 🕓 lunch & dinner Mon-Sat, lunch Sun) Near the bullring, this place is worth seeking out for its delicious regional cuisine as well as its smartly rustic interior, which includes white tablecloths, terracotta floors and a plough hanging from the ceiling. Half-portions are available. There are sometimes *fado* performances on Fridays.

Getting There & Away

The train station is 2.4km to the northeast, though there are regular buses to the centre. The **bus station** (Avenida do Brasil) is located right in the centre on a leafy square. There is usually sufficient street parking; there are also a few public car parks near the bullring.

BUS

There are at least hourly buses to Lisbon (€6.40, 1¼ hours) and up to five daily to Coimbra (€10.20, two to three hours) and

CELEBRATING PORTUGUESE HORSEMANSHIP

Located on the banks of the Tejo just downriver from Almourol, Golegã is considered the capital of Portuguese horse country. During the first half of November, the town holds the renowned Feira de São Martinho, with a running of the bulls, bullfights, parades and nightly parties in the attractive town's main square.

Fátima (normal/express €4.80/7.20, 1¾ hours/45 minutes, five daily). There is also at least one daily, local bus to regional destinations such as Alcobaça and Santarém.

TRAIN

Very frequent IC (€9) and IR (€5.60) trains go to Lisbon (50 minutes). Buses run between the town and train station nine times daily (€1.10, 12 minutes), while **taxis** (☎ 243 322 919) charge about €5 for the trip.

CONSTÂNCIA & CASTELO DE ALMOUROL

pop 3800

Spilling down a hillside to the banks of the Tejo, whitewashed Constância makes a fine stop as you head across the Ribatejo plains, though the real reason to come is the neighbouring Castelo de Almourol. Still, Constância has a pleasantly leafy riverfront promenade and gardens, a pretty main square, and a clutch of steep lanes – all worth a gander.

Sights

CASTELO DE ALMOUROL

Like the stuff of legend, the 10-towered Castelo de Almourol seems to have broken away from the land and floated out into the middle of the Rio Tejo. Set on an island that was once the site of a Roman fort, this remarkable sight was built by Gualdim Pais, Grand Master of the Order of the Knights Templar, in 1171. It's no surprise that Almourol has long caught the imagination of excitable poets longing for the Age of Chivalry.

The castelo is 3km from Constância. You can walk, drive, or take the train from Constância's station to Almourol's (€0.95, five minutes). There is almost always someone to ferry you across and back for about €1.

Sleeping & Eating

Casa João Chagas (☎ 249 739 403; vilapoema@mail.telepac.pt; Rua João Chagas, Constância; d €50; ❄) Once the town hall, this 18th-century house offers rather plain but neat, high-ceilinged rooms just off the main square near the river.

Restaurante Esplanada (Constância; mains about €6; ⌚ lunch & dinner Fri-Wed) With a pleasantly leafy esplanade right on the river, this bar-restaurant serves simple Portuguese fare. The bar stays open until 2am Fridays and Saturdays.

Remédio d'Alma (☎ 249 739 405; Largo 5 de Outubro; Constância; mains €10-14; ⌚ dinner Tue, lunch & dinner Wed-Sun) This elegant little place, set in an old house with a lovely garden shaded by orange trees, serves particularly fine regional dishes. It's a short, 200m walk along the waterfront from the main square.

João Chagas also runs O Café da Praça, opposite Casa o Palácio; try the fantastic *queijinhos do Céu* (sweets from heaven), still made by local nuns.

Getting There & Away

The tiny Almourol train station is 1km uphill from the castle. There are four trains daily from Lisbon via Santarém (€2.10, 45 minutes), with a change at Entroncamento.

TOMAR

pop 43,400

In itself, Tomar is a town of great charm, with cobbled streets, whitewashed houses, fine squares and an invitingly leafy riverfront. In addition, the town abuts the lush Mata Nacional dos Sete Montes (Seven Hills National Forest), and the neighbouring countryside is particularly charming, especially alongside the Castelo de Bode reservoir. But what makes Tomar extraordinary – and an inextricable part of Portuguese history – is the Convento de Cristo, the hilltop headquarters of the legendary Knights Templar. A Unesco World Heritage site, this castle-cum-monastery is a rambling concoction of Gothic, Manueline and Renaissance architecture that offers extravagant proof of the vital role the Templars played in the foundation of the Portuguese kingdom.

Orientation

The Rio Nabão neatly divides the town, with new developments largely concentrated on the east bank and the old town to the west. The monastery looks down on it all from a wooded hilltop above the town to the west.

Information

District hospital (☎ 249 320 100; Via da Cintura) A new hospital 1km east of town.

Espaço Internet (☎ 249 312 291; Rua Amorim Rosa; ⌚ 9.30am-8pm Mon-Sat) Free internet access.

Police station (☎ 249 313 444; Rua Dr Sousa)

Post office (☎ 249 310 400; Avenida Marquês de Tomar; ⌚ 8.30am-6pm Mon-Fri, 9am-12.30pm Sat)

Regional turismo (☎ 249 329 000; fax 249 324 322; Rua Serpa Pinto 1; ⌚ 9.30am-12.30pm & 2-6pm Mon-Fri) Head here for information about other places in the region.

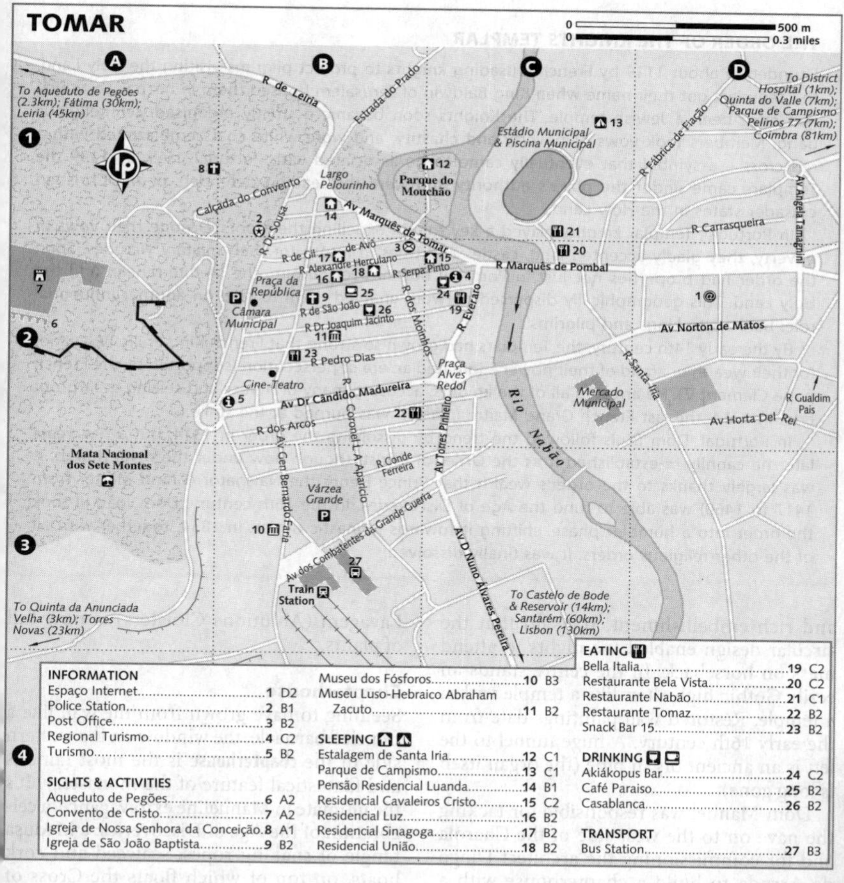

Turismo (☎/fax 249 322 427; Avenida Dr Cândido Madureira; 🕑 10am-1pm & 2-6pm, 10am-7pm Jul & Aug) Offers a good map of the town and an accommodation list with prices. It also has a small 1:5000 map of the adjacent national forest.

Sights

CONVENTO DE CRISTO

Wrapped in equal parts splendour and mystery, the Knights Templar held enormous power in Portugal from the 12th to 16th centuries, and largely bankrolled the Age of Discoveries. Their headquarters, set on wooded slopes above the town and enclosed within 12th-century walls, is a stony expression of magnificence combined with the no-holds-barred theatricality that long lent the order its particular fascination.

The **monastery** (☎ 249 313 481; adult/youth or student €4.50/2, 9am-noon Sun free; 🕑 9am-6.30pm Jun-Sep, 9am-5.30pm Oct-May, last admission 30min before closing) was founded in 1160 by Gualdim Pais, Grand Master of the Templars. It has chapels, cloisters and chapterhouses in widely diverging styles, added over the centuries by successive kings and Grand Masters. You can follow a short route (45 minutes) or take a more comprehensive 90-minute tour.

Charola

This 16-sided Templar **church**, thought to be in imitation of the Church of the Holy Sepulchre in Jerusalem, dominates the complex. The interior is otherworldly in its vast heights – an awesome combination of simple forms

THE ORDER OF THE KNIGHTS TEMPLAR

Founded in about 1119 by French crusading knights to protect pilgrims visiting the Holy Land, the Templars got their name when King Baldwin of Jerusalem housed them in his palace, which had once been a Jewish temple. The Knights soon became a strictly organised, semireligious gang. Members took vows of poverty and chastity, and wore white coats emblazoned with a red cross – a symbol that eventually came to be associated with Portugal itself. By 1139 the Templars came under the pope's authority and were the leading defenders of the Christian crusader states in the Holy Land.

In Portugal, Templar knights played a key role in expelling the Moors. Despite their vows of poverty, they gladly accepted land, castles and titles in return for their military victories. Soon the order had properties not just in Portugal but all over Europe, the Mediterranean and the Holy Land. This geographically dispersed network enabled them to take on another influential role: bankers to kings and pilgrims.

By the early 14th century, the Templars had grown so strong that French King Philip IV – eager for their wealth or afraid of their power – initiated an era of persecution (supported by the French pope Clement V). He arrested all of the knights, accusing many of heresy and seizing their property. In 1314, the last French Grand Maître (Master) was burned at the stake.

In Portugal, Dom Dinis followed the trend by dissolving the order in 1314, but a few years later he cannily re-established it as the Order of Christ, though now under the royal thumb. It was largely thanks to the order's wealth that Prince Henry the Navigator (Grand Master from 1417 to 1460) was able to fund the Age of Discoveries. In the 16th century, Dom João III took the order into a humbler phase, shifting it towards monastic duties. In 1834, together with all of the other religious orders, it was finally dissolved.

and rich embellishment. It's said that the circular design enabled the nights to attend mass on horseback. In the centre stands an eerily Gothic high altar, like a temple within a temple. Restored wall paintings date from the early 16th century. A huge funnel to the left is an ancient organ pipe (the organ itself is long gone).

Dom Manuel was responsible for tacking the nave on to the west side of the Charola and for commissioning the architect Diogo de Arruda to build a chapterhouse with a *coro alto* (choir) above it. The main western doorway into the nave – a splendid example of Spanish plateresque style (named after the ornate work of silversmiths) – is the work of Spanish architect João de Castilho. The same team repeated its success at Belém's Mosteiro dos Jerónimos (p102).

Claustro do Cemitério & Claustro da Lavagem

Two serene, *azulejo*-decorated **cloisters** to the east of the Charola were built during the time when Prince Henry the Navigator was Grand Master of the order in the 15th century. The Claustro do Cemitério (Burial-Ground Cloisters) contains two 16th-century tombs, while the water tanks of the two-storey Claustro da Lavagem (Ablutions Cloisters) is now full of plants.

Chapterhouse

Seeming to have grown from the wall like a frenzied barnacle, the window on the western side of the **chapterhouse** is the most famous and fantastical feature of the monastery. It's the ultimate in Manueline extravagance, a celebration of the Age of Discoveries: a Medusa tangle of snaking ropes, seaweed and cork boats, on top of which floats the Cross of the Order of Christ and the royal arms and armillary spheres of Dom Manuel. These days it's covered in ochre-coloured lichen – appropriate given the seaworthy themes. It's best seen from the roof of the adjacent Claustro de Santa Bárbara. Follow signs to the *janela* (window).

Unfortunately obscured by the Claustro Principal is an almost equivalent window on the southern side of the chapterhouse.

Claustro Principal

The elegant Renaissance **Claustro Principal** (Great Cloisters) stands in striking contrast to the flamboyance of the monastery's Manueline architecture. Commissioned during the reign of João III, the cloisters were probably designed by the Spaniard Diogo de Torralva but completed in 1587 by an Italian, Filippo Terzi. These foreign architects were among several responsible for introducing a delayed Renaissance style into Portugal. The Claustro Principal is arguably the country's finest expression of that style: a sober ensemble of Greek columns and Tuscan pillars, gentle arches and sinuous, spiralling staircases.

The outlines of a second chapterhouse, commissioned by João III but never finished, can be seen from the cloisters' southwest corner.

AQUEDUTO DE PEGÕES

This impressive **aqueduct**, striding towards the monastery from the northwest, was built from 1593 to 1613, to supply water to thirsty monks. Its 180 arches, some of which are double-decker, are thought to have been designed by Italian Filippo Terzi. It's best seen just off the Leiria road, 2.3km from town.

IGREJA DE NOSSA SENHORA DA CONCEIÇÃO

Downhill from the monastery is this strikingly simple, small, pure Renaissance **basilica**, built in the 16th century. It's believed to have been designed by Diogo de Torralva, who is also responsible for the Convento cloisters. At the time of writing it was closed for restoration.

IGREJA DE SÃO JOÃO BAPTISTA

The old town's most striking **church** (admission free; 🕑 10am-7pm Tue-Sun Jun-Sep, 11am-6pm Tue-Sun Oct-May) faces Praça da República, itself an eye-catching ensemble of 17th-century buildings. The newly restored church, now blindingly white, dates mostly from the late 15th century. It has an octagonal spire and richly ornamented Manueline doorways on its northern and western sides. Inside are 16th- and 17th-century *azulejos;* Gregório Lopes, one of 16th-century Portugal's finest artists, painted the six panels hanging inside.

MUSEU LUSO-HEBRAICO ABRAHAM ZACUTO

On a charming cobbled lane in the old town, you'll find the country's best-preserved medieval **synagogue** (Rua Dr Joaquim Jacinto 73; admission free; 🕑 10am-1pm & 2-6pm). Built between 1430 and 1460, it was used for only a few years, until Dom Manuel's convert-or-leave edict of 1496 forced most Jews to do the latter. The synagogue subsequently served as a prison, chapel, hayloft and warehouse until it was classified as a national monument in 1921.

Mostly thanks to the efforts of Luís Vasco (who comes from one of two Jewish families left in Tomar), who is often present, the small, plain building has been remodelled to look something like it would have in the 15th century. It's named after the 15th-century Jewish mathematician and royal astrologer who helped Vasco da Gama plan his voyages. Inside are various tombstones engraved with 13th- and 14th-century Hebraic inscriptions, as well as many touching gifts and contributions from international Jewish visitors. The upturned jars high in the wall were a device to improve acoustics.

MUSEU DOS FÓSFOROS

This **museum** (admission free; 🕑 10am-2pm Jun-Sep, 2-5pm Oct-May), housed in the lovely Convento de São Francisco, contains a collection of over 40,000 matchboxes. The largest collection of its kind in Europe, it was amassed by local 'phillumenist' Aquiles da Mota Lima from the 1950s onwards.

FESTA DOS TABULEIROS

Tomar's Festival of the Trays is a week-long celebration with music, drinking, dancing and fireworks. But the highlight is definitely the procession of about 400 young, white-clad women (traditionally virgins!) bearing headdresses of trays stacked as tall as they are with loaves of bread and ears of wheat, decorated with colourful paper flowers and, finally, topped with a crown, cross or white paper dove. Young male attendants (nonvirgins allowed), dressed in black and white, help the girls balance the load, which can weigh up to 15kg. The following day, bread and wine are blessed by the priest and handed out to local families. The festival is believed to have roots in pagan fertility rites, though officially it's related to the saintly practices of 14th-century Dona Isabel (Dom Dinis' queen).

The festival is held every four years during the first week in July; the next one is scheduled for 30 June to 9 July 2007.

Activities

Via Aventura (☎ 914 998 144; www.via-aventura.com) organises canoe trips on the Rio Nabão as well as to Constância and Castelo de Almourol (around €15 per person).

Festivals & Events

Festa dos Tabuleiros Tomar's most famous event is this tray-toting spectacle (see the boxed text, p299).

Nossa Senhora da Piedade Another important religious festival, this one features a candlelit procession and a parade of floats decorated with paper flowers; it's held on the first Sunday in September.

Sleeping

BUDGET

Parque de Campismo Pelinos 77 (☎ 249 301 814; adult/tent/car €3.30/2.80/1.80; mid-Feb to mid-Oct) This camp site is 7km northeast at Pelinos, just off N110. It is pleasantly remote and small, with simple facilities; bus connections are poor.

Parque de campismo (☎ 249 329 824; adult/tent/car €3.45/3/2.20) Tomar's municipal camp site offers lots of shade, decent facilities, and a great location a short walk from town.

Residencial Luz (☎ 249 312 317; www.residencialluz.com; Rua Serpa Pinto 144; d €33) Very threadbare but central, this place occupies a once-lovely town house on the historic centre's main thoroughfare. Rooms are somewhere between grandmotherly and doleful but clean. No breakfast.

Residencial União (☎ 249 323 161; fax 249 321 299; Rua Serpa Pinto 94; s/d €37) A good budget option in a once-grand town house includes expansive common areas, old-fashioned but large and sprucely maintained rooms, and a bright breakfast room. Reservations recommended in summer.

MIDRANGE

Pensão Residencial Luanda (☎ 249 323 200; Avenida Marquês de Tomar 15; d €45) Run by a particularly jovial owner who lived for a long time in Angola, this simple little establishment has neat, well-maintained rooms in an undistinguished modern building.

Residencial Cavaleiros Cristo (☎ 249 321 203; fax 249 321 067; Rua Alexandre Herculano 7; d €49) In a newer building near the river, this place offers trim rooms with midrange fittings. Forgettable but comfortable and good value.

Residencial Sinagoga (☎ 249 323 083; residencial.sinagoga@clix.pt; Rua de Gil de Avô; d €49) In the centre but removed a little from the action on a quiet residential street, this place offers yet more good-value if undistinguished modern rooms, though this one stands out for its balconies and unrepentantly 1970s furniture.

TOP END

Estalagem de Santa Iria (☎ 249 313 326; www.estalagemiria.com; Mouchão Parque; d €85) Set in lovely, leafy grounds next to the Rio Nabão this slightly kitschy, '40s-style country inn has large comfortable rooms, though they are about due for a refresh. Downstairs are a restaurant and bar with a roaring fireplace in the winter.

Quinta do Valle (☎ 249 381 165; www.quintadovalle.com; 2-/4-person apt €87/105; P) With parts dating back to the 15th century, this manor house together with its outbuildings, has been turned into an upmarket inn, with large grounds chapel and quaint apartments with fireplaces and kitchenettes.

Eating

Snack Bar 15 (☎ 249 324 853; Avenida Infantaria 15; mains from €3.50; 9am-midnight Mon-Sat) Simple but good food at bargain prices served up in a bright, modern café.

Restaurante Tomaz (☎ 249 312 552; Rua dos Arcos 31; mains around €5; lunch & dinner Mon-Sat) A popular bright option, this place offers appealing outdoor seating on a wide, leafy seat, plus simple Portuguese dished such as *bacalhau à brás* (salt-cod fried with onions and potatoes).

Bella Italia (☎ 249 322 996; Rua Everaro 91; mains €5-9; lunch & dinner Wed-Mon) Nondescript but popular, this Italian-owned place serves up pizzas as well as huge portions of pasta.

Restaurante Bela Vista (☎ 249 312 870; Rua Fonte do Choupo 6; mains €6-10; lunch & dinner Tue-Sun) In a handsome old inn with a wisteria-bedecked terrace overlooking the river, Bela Vista serves up excellent regional cuisine at very good value. Recommended.

Restaurante Nabão (☎ 249 313 110; Rua Fonte do Choupo 3; mains €6-10; lunch & dinner Fri-Tue, lunch Wed) Just next door to the Bela Vista, this modern place also has very good, carefully presented regional cuisine, plus large windows looking out onto the river.

Drinking

Café Paraíso (Rua de Serpa Pinto; snacks €1-4; 9.30am-2am Tue, 7.30am-2am Wed-Sat & Mon, 7.30am-8.30pm Sun) This old-fashioned, high-ceilinged Deco café serves as a refuge for the town's alternative scene as well as for anyone in need of a snack and a shot of caffeine or whisky.

Casablanca (Rua de São João 85; 10pm-3am Wed-Sat, to 4am Fri & Sat) Charming side-street bar with movie stills of Bogie.

Akiákopus Bar (Rua de São João 28; 9.30pm-4am) This place looks intimidating because you have to ring the doorbell, but inside it's just a simple, cosy little drinking hole.

Entertainment

Fatias de Cá (☎ 249 314 161; www.fatiasdeca.com) This Tomar-based theatre company presents highly innovative and entertaining performances such as *The Name of the Rose* and *Perfume*, often in amazing locations (eg castles, distilleries or old palaces, including the Convento de Cristo). Performances usually take place on Thursday, Friday and Saturday.

Getting There & Away

From the **bus terminal** (☎ 249 312 738) at least two daily buses go to Fátima (€6.20, one hour) and Batalha (€7.20, 1½ hours), and four to Leiria (€7.40, 50 minutes). Weekday trains run to/from Lisbon's Oriente station (€8, two hours, eight daily) via Santarém (€5.20, one hour).

The bus and train stations are close together, about 500m south of the turismo. You will also find several large car parks here.

The Beiras

From miles-long strands to brooding, granite heights and rolling plains, the Beiras region is like a recapitulation of Portugal itself. The country's history, too, is fully represented. You'll see Roman mosaics and Moorish castles, medieval fortresses built to fend off the Spanish, and baroque churches decked out in Brazilian gold. And for those with gumption, there are the challenging trails of the Parque Natural da Serra da Estrela, home to the country's highest peaks.

Lying along the Atlantic coast, Beira Litoral (Coastal Beira) is dominated by Coimbra, with its ancient hilltop university and labyrinth of medieval streets. Not old enough? Head to Conimbriga, site of some of the Iberian Peninsula's most impressive Roman ruins. For a break from history, the coastline has impressive beaches, most of which remain remarkably undeveloped.

Move inland and the scene changes rapidly as you approach the looming heights of the Serra da Estrela. It's fine terrain for outdoor adventuring year-round, from hiking and biking to white-water rafting. Or come in winter and say you've skied Portugal.

Beyond the mountains, the Planalto (upland plains) of Beira Alta (Upper Beira) and Beira Baixa (Lower Beira) roll all the way to Spain. A region that was for centuries on high alert, it harbours a series of fortress towns set on strategic heights, from imposing Guarda and Castelo Branco to picturesque Sortelha and Monsanto. Moving south, the forbidding high plains of the Beira Alta give way to the hypnotically flat landscapes of the Beira Baixa, with its cork oaks, olive groves and vast agricultural estates.

HIGHLIGHTS

- Studying the medieval lanes and modern mores of **Coimbra** (opposite), Portugal's ancient university town
- Seeking solace in the sacred woods of hilltop **Buçaco** (p316), secret haunt of monks and monarchs
- Distinguishing layers of history in remote **Idanha-a-Velha** (p330), where Roman foundations hold up Moorish arches and Templar towers
- Understanding the threat Spain long posed by penetrating the fortified border towns of **Almeida** (p352), **Trancoso** (p350) and **Sortelha** (p331)
- Contemplating the 360-degree views from **Torre** (p339), Portugal's highest peak

- POPULATION: 2,367,000
- AREA: 22,067 SQ KM

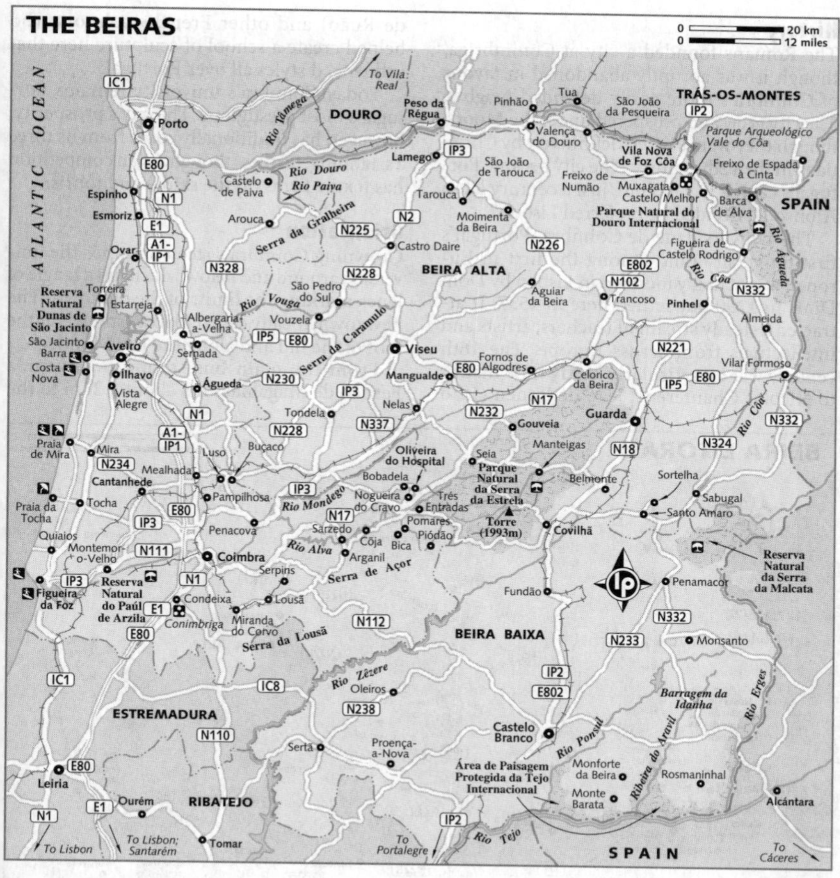

BEIRA LITORAL

COIMBRA

pop 102,000 / elevation 150m

Like a great fortress of learning, Coimbra's ancient university occupies strategic heights above a lazy stretch of the Rio Mondego. Clambering up to the crown of monumental halls and libraries is an absurdly picturesque maze of medieval streets. Yet the whole scene avoids preciousness thanks to an uncommonly raucous student life.

Winding alleyways still channel last-minute dashes to lectures, and cafés buzz with utopian yearnings and, after a certain hour, beery good times.

Founded in 1290, the city's university has a pedigree equal to any European seat of learning, though in fact Coimbra only became its permanent home in 1537. The city was also Portugal's capital in the 12th and 13th centuries, evidenced by a small but remarkable assembly of Romanesque and Gothic buildings. Outside the dense old city, you can also enjoy pleasantly leafy walks along Coimbra's riverfront, shady boulevards, and numerous parks and gardens. The city also makes a fine base for day trips, including mountain excursions or an afternoon wander among the remarkable Roman ruins at Conimbriga (see p315). If you're here in May, throw yourself into Coimbra's boozy student bash, Queima das Fitas (p310).

History

The Romans founded a city at Conimbriga, though it was abruptly abandoned in favour of Coimbra's more easily defended heights. The city grew and prospered under the Moors, though they were evicted definitively by Christians in the 12th century. The city became Portugal's capital in 1145 but, just a century later, Afonso III decided he preferred Lisbon.

The Universidade de Coimbra, Portugal's first university (and among the first in Europe), was actually founded in Lisbon by Dom Dinis in 1290 but settled here in 1537. It attracted a steady stream of teachers, artists and intellectuals from across Europe. The 16th century was a particularly heady time thanks to Nicolas Chanterène, Jean de Rouen (João de Ruão) and other French sculptors who helped create a school of sculpture here that influenced styles all over Portugal.

Today Coimbra's university remains Portugal's most prestigious. The city's prosperity, however, has traditionally come from its three Ts: tanning, textiles (though Asian competition has textile firms on the skids) and tourism.

Orientation

Crowning Coimbra's steep hilltop is the university, around and below which lies a tangle of lanes marking the limits of the old town. The new town, locally called 'Baixa', sprawls at the foot of the hill and along the Rio Mondego.

From the main bus station on Avenida Fernão de Magalhães it's about 1.2km to the

old centre. There are three train stations: Coimbra B (also called *estação velha*, or old station) 2km northwest of the centre; central Coimbra A (also called *estação nova*, or new station, and on timetables called just 'Coimbra'); and Coimbra Parque, south of the centre. Coimbra A and B are linked by a rail shuttle, free for those with an inbound or outbound long-distance ticket.

Pick up a map of the city centre in any of Coimbra's tourist offices.

Information

BOOKSHOPS

There's a cluster of bookshops on Rua Ferreira Borges.

Livraria Bertrand (Map pp308-9; ☎ 239 823 014; Rua Ferreira Borges 11)

CULTURAL CENTRES

British Council (Map pp308-9; ☎ 239 823 549; Rua de Tomar 4; 🕒 library 2.30-8.30pm Tue-Wed, 2.30-7pm Thu & Fri, 10am-12.30pm, 2.30pm-4.30pm Sat, closed Aug) Catch up with British newspapers at the library here.

EMERGENCY

Police station Rua Olímpio Nicolau Rui Fernandes (Map pp308-9; ☎ 239 822 022); Rua Venâncio Rodrigues (☎ 239 828 134; Rua Venâncio Rodrigues 25-31)

INTERNET ACCESS

Casa Municipal da Cultura (Map p306; ☎ 239 702 630; Rua Pedro Monteiro; 🕒 10am-7.30pm Mon-Fri, 2-6.30pm Sat) Limited free access at the public library.

Centro de Juventude (Map p306; ☎ 239 790 600; Rua Pedro Monteiro 73; 🕒 9am-12.30pm & 2-5.30pm Mon-Fri) Free access.

Esp@ço Internet (Map pp308-9; ☎ 239 824 151; Praça 8 de Maio 37; 🕒 10am-8pm Mon-Fri, 10am-10pm Sat & Sun) Free access.

LAUNDRY

Lavandaria Lucira (Map pp308-9; ☎ 239 825 701; Avenida Sá da Bandeira 86; wash & dry per 5kg load €5.90; 🕒 9am-1pm & 3-7pm Mon-Fri, 9am-1pm Sat)

MEDICAL SERVICES

Hospital da Universidade da Coimbra (☎ 239 400 400; Largo Professor Mota Pinto) Located 1.5km northeast of the centre.

POST

Main post office (Map p306; Avenida Fernão de Magalhães 223; 🕒 8.30am-6.30pm Mon-Fri) Best place for poste restante.

Post office Praça da República (Map pp308-9; 🕒 9am-6pm Mon-Fri); Rua Olímpio Nicolau Rui Fernandes (Map pp308-9; 🕒 8.30am-6.30pm Mon-Fri & 9am-12.30pm Sat)

TOURIST INFORMATION

Good town maps as well as a very detailed bimonthly cultural agenda are available from the following tourist offices:

Municipal turismo Largo Dom Dinis (Map pp308-9; ☎ 239 832 591; 🕒 9am-6pm Mon-Fri, 9am-12.30pm & 2-5.30pm Sat & Sun); Rua Olímpio Nicolau Rui Fernandes (Map pp308-9; ☎ 239 834 038; 🕒 9am-6pm Mon-Fri)

Regional turismo (Map pp308-9; ☎ 239 488 120; rtc-coimbra@turismo-centro.pt; Largo da Portagem; 🕒 9.30am-1pm & 2-5.30pm Mon-Fri, 10am-1pm & 2.30-5.30pm Sat & Sun)

TRAVEL AGENCIES

Intervisa (Map pp308-9; ☎ 239 823 873; intervisacoimbra@mail.telepac.pt; Avenida Fernão de Magalhães 11)

Tagus (Map pp308-9; ☎ 239 834 999; www.viagenstagus.pt; Rua Padre António Vieira) In the Associação Acadêmica de Coimbra (AAC); head here for student cards and youth travel discounts.

Top Atlântico (Map pp308-9; ☎ 239 855 970; coimbra.ta@topatlantico.com; Avenida Sá da Bandeira 62)

Sights

Compact Coimbra is best toured on foot. Sights of interest across the river are also accessible on foot via the Ponte de Santa Clara.

Unless otherwise noted, the following sights are all on Map pp308–9.

UPPER TOWN

Long a Moorish stronghold and for a century the seat of Portugal's kings, Coimbra's upper town rises quickly and picturesquely from the banks of the Rio Mondego. The most picturesque way to enter its labyrinth of lanes is via **Arco de Almedina** – the city's heavy-duty Moorish gateway – and up the staggered stairs known as **Rua Quebra-Costas** (Backbreaker). People have been gasping up this hill (and falling down it) for centuries; local legend says it was the 19th-century writer Almeida Garrett who persuaded the mayor to install the stairs.

To the left up Rua Sub Ripas is the grand Manueline doorway of the early-16th-century **Palácio de Sub Ripas**; its Renaissance windows and stone ornaments are the work of Jean de Rouen, whose workshop was nearby.

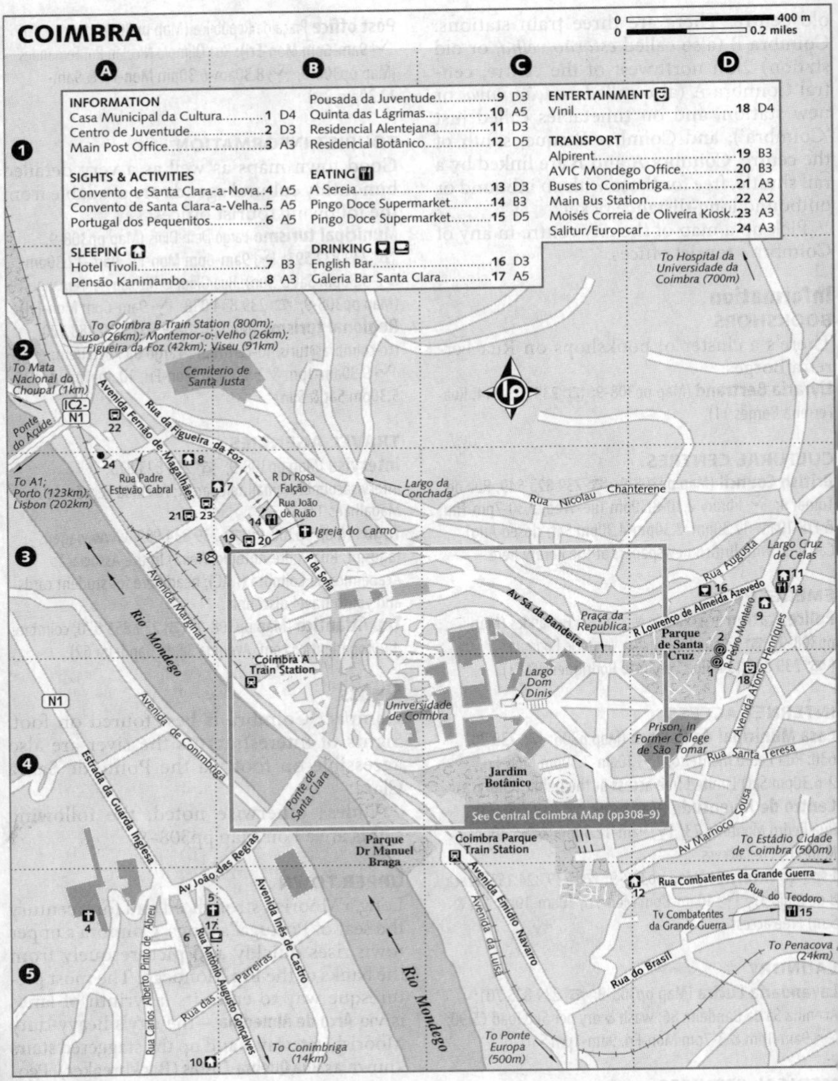

Further on is the **Torre de Anto**, a tower that once formed part of the town walls.

Backtrack and climb via Largo da Sé Velha to the Museu Nacional Machado de Castro and the 'new' campus, much of it founded by the Marquês de Pombal in the 18th century. Dominating Largo da Sé Nova in front of the museum is the severe **Sé Nova** (new cathedral; ☎ 239 823 138; admission free; ⏲ 9.30am-12.30pm & 2-6.30pm Tue-Sat), started by the Jesuits in 1598 but only completed a century later.

Coimbra is adorned with some grand *azulejos* (hand-painted tiles), the finest of them in the former university hospital, now home to the **Museu Acadêmico** (☎ 239 827 396; Colégio de São Jerónimo; adult/student/senior €1/0.50/0.50

🕑 10am-12.30pm & 2-5.30pm Mon-Fri), an otherwise staid and stuffy museum around the corner from Largo Dom Dinis.

For a glimpse of student life, stroll along any of the alleys around the *sé velha* (old cathedral) or below the *sé nova*. Flags and graffiti mark the cramped houses known as *repúblicas,* each housing a dozen or so students from the same region or faculty.

Velha Universidade

In every way the university's high point, the Old University consists of a series of remarkable 16th- to 18th-century buildings, all set around the vast **Patio das Escolas**. You enter the patio by way of the elegant 17th-century **Porta Férrea**, which occupies the same site as the main gate to Coimbra's Moorish stronghold. In the square is a **statue of João III**, who turns his back on a sweeping view of the city and the river. It was he who re-established the university in Coimbra in 1537 and invited big-shot scholars to teach here.

The square's most prominent feature is the much-photographed 18th-century **clock tower**. This tower is nicknamed *a cabra* (the goat) because, when it chimed to mark the end of studies, the first-year undergrads were pounced upon by swaggering elder students and then humiliated without mercy – that is, unless they leapt their way home like mountain goats in order to avoid them.

From the courtyard gate take the stairway on the right up to the rather grand **Sala dos Capelos** (Graduates' Hall), a former examination room hung with dark portraits of Portugal's kings and heavy patchwork, quiltlike decoration. But better yet is a catwalk that leads alongside it with excellent city views.

Back outside, take a peek to the left below the clock tower, where you'll find the entrance to the fanciful **Capela de São Miguel**, an ornate baroque chapel with a brightly painted ceiling and a gilded baroque organ.

However, all else pales before the **Biblioteca Joanina** (João V Library) next door. A gift from João V himself in the early 18th century, it seems far too extravagant and distracting for actual study, with its rosewood, ebony and jacaranda tables, elaborately frescoed ceilings and gilt chinoiserie bookshelves. Its 300,000 books, ancient and leather-bound, deal with law, philosophy and theology, though they might as well be painted onto the walls for all the hands-on study they receive now.

The Capela de São Miguel is free, while admission to both the Biblioteca Joanina and the Sala dos Capelos is €5/2.50/3.50 for adults/seniors/students (or you can visit just one for €3.50/1.75/2.45).

Visitors are only admitted in small numbers and on a timetable (9am to 7pm May to September, to 5pm October to April), and you may find that some rooms are closed during degree ceremonies. Staff at the turismo might urge you to book a few days ahead, but you may still be able to get in if you front up early and are prepared to wait. You can also try to make reservations by emailing a request to reservas@ci.uc.pt. The **ticket office** (☎ 239 859 818) is near the Sala dos Capelos.

Sé Velha

Coimbra's fortresslike **old cathedral** (☎ 239 825 273; Largo da Sé Velha; cloisters adult/under 26/student €1/0.75/0.75; 🕑 10am-1pm & 2-6pm Mon-Thu, 10am-1pm Fri, 10am-7pm Sat) is a reminder of the nation's embattled early days, built in the late 12th century when the Moors were still a threat. Little of the building, fortunately, has changed since; even the 16th-century Renaissance portal in the northern wall is so eroded you hardly notice it. Otherwise, what you see is pure, austere Romanesque, one of the finest Portuguese cathedrals of its time. The interior is equally simple, with the exception of a 16th-century gilded altarpiece.

Museu Nacional Machado de Castro

Housed in a former Bishop's Palace, with a 16th-century loggia overlooking the *sé velha* and the old town, this **museum** (☎ 239 823 727; www.ipmuseus.pt; Largo Dr José Rodrigues) houses one of Portugal's most important collections of 14th- to 16th-century sculpture. Unfortunately, this gem will remain closed for renovations until 2010.

BAIXA & AROUND

Igreja de Santa Cruz

From the trendy shops out on Praça 8 de Maio, this **church** (☎ 239 822 941; adult/student/senior €2.50/1.50/1.50; 🕑 9am-noon & 2-5.45pm Mon-Sat, 4-5.45pm Sun) plunges you back to Manueline and Renaissance times. Step through the Renaissance porch and flamboyant 18th-century arch to find some of the Coimbra School's finest work, including an ornate pulpit and the elaborate tombs (probably carved by Nicolas Chanterène) of Portugal's first kings, Afonso

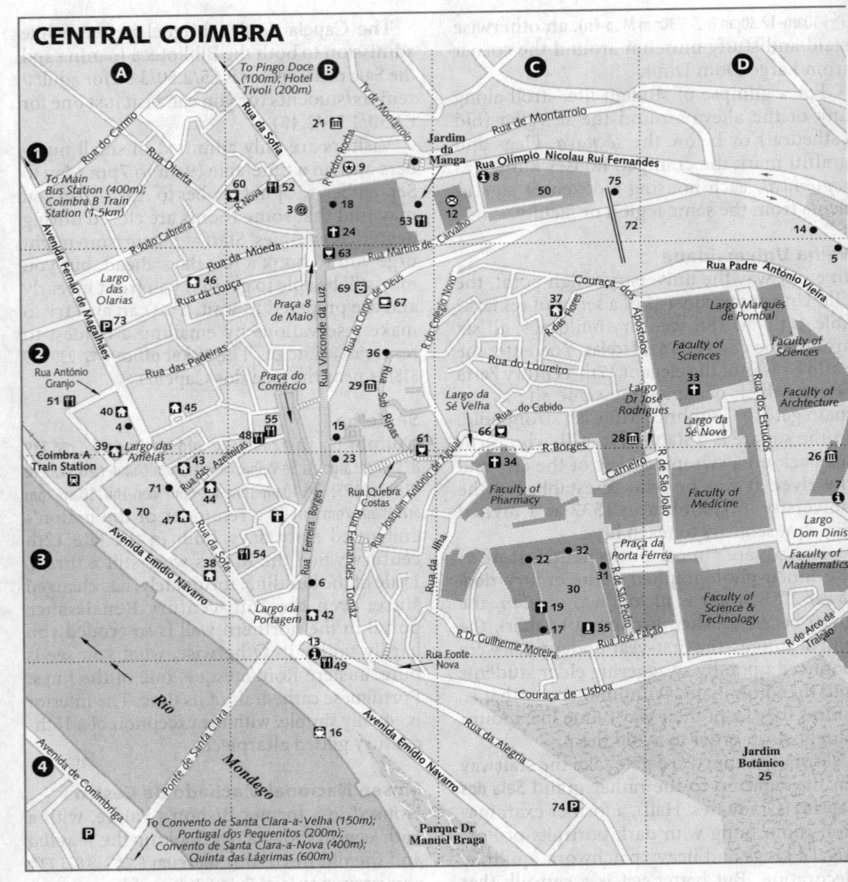

Henriques and Sancho I. The most striking Manueline work is in the restrained 1524 cloister.

Behind the church is the **Jardim da Manga** (once part of the cloister) and its curious fountain: a lemon-yellow, four-buttressed affair.

Edifício Chiado

This sunlit confection of rippling, coiling iron opened in 1910 as a commercial emporium. It now houses a **gallery** (☎ 239 840 754; Rua Ferreira Borges; adult/student/senior €1.50/1/1; 🕑 11am-6pm Mon-Fri, 10am-1pm & 2-6pm Sat & Sun) with a permanent collection of paintings, sculpture, ceramics, furniture and splendid silverware donated by local collector José Carlos Telo de Morais, and temporary exhibitions.

CAV (Centro de Artes Visuais)

This new **museum** (Centre of Visual Arts; ☎ 239 826 178; Pátio da Inquisição; 🕑 2-7pm Tue-Sun) hosts cutting-edge contemporary photographic and video exhibitions within a whitewashed cloister that once served as a prison during the Inquisition. It's hidden in the backstreets west of the *câmara municipal* (town hall).

PRAÇA DA REPÚBLICA & AROUND

Leafy Praça da República is the unofficial student social centre. The surrounding neighbourhood, laid out in the 19th century and still dominated by prim bourgeois homes of the period, is a relaxing break from the high density of both the university and the Baixa area.

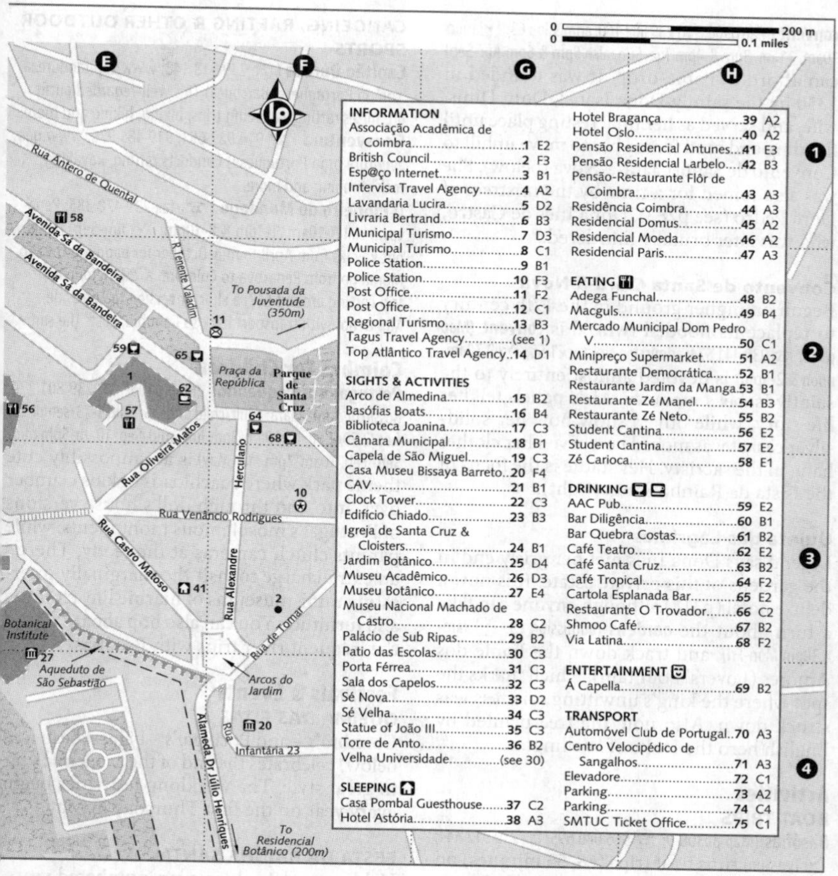

Casa Museu Bissaya Barreto

Bissaya Barreto was a local surgeon, scholar and obsessive hoarder of fine arts, and his handsome, late-19th-century mansion has been turned into a **museum** (☎ 239 853 800; www fbb.pt in Portuguese; Rua da Infantaria 23; admission €2.50; 🕑 3-6pm Tue-Sun Easter-Oct, 3-6pm Tue-Fri Nov-Easter). It's jam-packed with Portuguese sculpture and painting, Chinese porcelain, old *azulejos* and period furniture.

Jardim Botânico

A serene place to catch your breath, the lovely **botanical garden** (☎ 239 855 233; adult/student/senior €1.50/1/1, Mon-Fri free; 🕑 9am-8pm Apr-Sep, 9am-5.30pm Oct-Mar) sits in the shadow of the 16th-century Aqueduto de São Sebastião. Founded by the Marquês de Pombal, the gardens combine formal flowerbeds, meandering paths and elegant fountains. The green-fingered can also visit the lush **greenhouses** (admission €0.50) and the adjacent **Museu Botânico** (Botanical Museum; ☎ 239 855 210; adult/child under 6/student & senior €2/free/1.50; 🕑 9am-noon & 2-5pm Mon-Fri).

ACROSS THE RIVER

In a kind of ecclesiastical counterweight to the university, a cluster of convents, together with several other sights, sits on the far side of the Rio Mondego.

Convento de Santa Clara-a-Velha

Slowly being cleared of the river ooze that has drowned it since the 17th century, this Gothic

convent (Map p306; ☎ 239 801 160; admission €3; ⏲ tours 10am, 11am, 3pm & 4pm Tue-Sun, also 5pm & 6pm Apr-Sep) can afford to name-drop. It was founded in 1330 by the saintly Dona Isabel, Dom Dinis' wife, and served as her final resting place until flooding and mud forced her to move uphill to Convento de Santa Clara-a-Nova (below). She was also joined for a time by the mistress of Dom Pedro (see p282), Dona Inês de Castro, who was later brutally murdered.

Convento de Santa Clara-a-Nova

Begun on higher ground in the 17th century to replace its flooded twin, this **convent** (Map p306; ☎ 239 441 674; admission cloister €1.50; ⏲ 9.30am-noon & 2-5pm) is devoted almost entirely to the saintly Isabel's memory. Aisle panels tell her life story, while others show how her solid-silver casket was moved here. Even her clothes hang in the sacristy. Her statue is the focus of the Festa da Rainha Santa (right).

Quinta das Lágrimas

Legend says Dona Inês met her grisly end in the gardens of this private estate. It is now a deluxe hotel (p312) although anyone can take a turn about the **gardens** (admission €3; ⏲ 9am-4.30pm Mon-Fri), and track down the Fonte dos Amores (Lovers' Fountain), which marks the spot where the king's unwitting mistress was struck down. Also note the tree planted by English hero the Duke of Wellington.

Activities

BOAT TRIPS

Basófias (Map pp308-9; ☎ 966 040 695; fax 239 912 444; ⏲ Tue-Sun) runs boat trips (€8, 55 minutes) on the Rio Mondego. They depart from beside Parque Dr Manuel Braga at 11am, 3pm, 4pm, 5pm and 6pm May to September, and at 3pm and 4pm only from October to April.

CANOEING, RAFTING & OTHER OUTDOOR SPORTS

Capitão Dureza (☎ 239 918 148; www.capitaodureza.com in Portuguese; Barcouça) This well-regarded outfit organises rafting, canoeing trips, biking, hiking and more.

Geoaventura (☎ 914 982 651, 919 485 976; www.geoaventura.pt in Portuguese) Conducts rafting, kayaking, rock-climbing and more.

O Pioneiro do Mondego (☎ /fax 239 478 385; Penacova; call 8-10am, 1-3pm & 8-10pm; ⏲ Jun-Sep) Rents out kayaks from April to mid-October for paddling the Rio Mondego from Penacova to Coimbra, a 25km, four-hour trip costing around €17; a shorter version to Torres de Mondego, with transport back to Coimbra, costs the same.

Coimbra for Children

Portugal dos Pequenitos (Map p306; ☎ 239 801 170; Rossio de Santa Clara; adult/child under 5/child 5-13/senior €5/free/2.50/2.50; ⏲ 9am-8pm Jun–mid-Sep, 10am-5pm mid-Sep–Feb, 10am-7pm Mar-May) is an impossibly cute theme park where coachloads of kids clamber over, into and through doll's house versions of Portugal's most famous monuments, while parents clutch cameras at the ready. There's an extra charge to visit the marginally interesting mini-museums of marine life, clothing and furniture. You can also hop aboard one of the frequent river trips with Basófias.

Festivals & Events

QUEIMA DAS FITAS

Coimbra's – and Portugal's – biggest bash (see below) celebrates the end of the academic year in great style. The weeklong festivities begin every year on the first Thursday in May.

FESTA DA RAINHA SANTA

Held around 4 July in even-numbered years, this large festival commemorates queen-saint Isabel with a Thursday procession, taking her statue from the Convento de Santa Clara-a-

FIRED UP

Beginning on the first Thursday of May, Coimbra marks the end of the academic year with **Queima das Fitas** (www.queimadasfitas.org) – a weeklong party that serves as the country's biggest and best excuse to get roaring drunk. Literally, the name means 'Burning of the Ribbons,' because graduates ritually torch the colour-coded ribbons worn to signify particular courses of study. The calendar includes sports events, private black-tie balls and nightly concerts at the so-called Queimodromo, across the Ponte de Santa Clara. The week peaks during a Tuesday afternoon parade from the hilltop down to Portagem. In their rush to sponsor individual floats, Portuguese breweries provide free beer, which is given out, and drunk, in liberal quantities. Relations between students and police are amazingly friendly, but the strain on local hospitals is heavy, with a strong emphasis on stomach pumping.

Nova to Igreja do Carmo, and another that takes her back on the Sunday. The festival also coincides with the Festa da Cidade (Town Festival), which is all the excuse needed for a proper knees-up – especially in the form of folk music, dancing and fireworks.

OTHER EVENTS

Coimbra hosts international festivals of music in July and magic in mid-September (Coimbra is the home of Luís de Matus, Portugal's most famous magician).

There's folk music and dancing in Praça 8 de Maio and open-air *fado* (traditional Portuguese singing) at the Arco de Almedina and along Rua Quebra Costas from late June to mid-September, usually on Tuesdays and Thursdays.

Sleeping

BUDGET

Pensão Kanimambo (Map p306; ☎ 239 827 151; fax 239 828 408; Avenida Fernão de Magalhães 484; s/d from €14/22; ❄) In a '70s concrete apartment block with décor to match, this cheapie offers clean, basic rooms to rest a weary head just arrived from the nearby bus station.

Pousada da Juventude (Map p306; ☎ 239 822 955; www.movijovem.pt; Rua Dr António Henriques Seco 14; dm €11, d from €24) In a fine old house in a quiet, leafy neighbourhood, this small but pleasant hostel is 500m northeast of Praça da República. There are kitchen facilities and breakfast is served, but there's no restaurant. From Coimbra A station take northbound bus 6, 7 or 29.

Pensão-Restaurante Flôr de Coimbra (Map pp308-9; ☎ 239 823 865; fax 239 821 545; Rua do Poço 5; d with shower & shared/private toilet May-Sep €25/30, Oct-Apr €20/25) In a once-grand, 19th-century building, this creaky guesthouse has received little investment beyond bottles of cleanser and the long-held love of its owner, but it remains clean, cheap and central.

Residencial Paris (Map pp308-9; ☎ 239 822 732; Rua da Sota 41; d with/without bathroom from €30/25) Arguably the best of a number of cheapies near the train station, this place offers small rooms and thin mattresses, but at least it's central and cheap.

Residencial Domus (Map pp308-9; ☎ 239 828 584; residencialdomus@sapo.pt; Rua Adelino Veiga 62; s €25, d from €38; ❄) A great choice, Domus is a welcoming family-run place in a quiet pedestrian shopping zone near Coimbra A. It has snug, plain rooms, some with characterful old furniture.

MIDRANGE

Pensão Residencial Larbelo (Map pp308-9; ☎ 239 829 092; fax 239 829 094; Largo da Portagem 33; d €40; ❄) In a rather grand 19th-century building, Larbelo is bang in the centre and boasts high-ceilinged rooms with wooden-floored rooms, gruff but ultimately friendly staff and a certain old-fashioned charm. Good value.

Residencial Botânico (Map p306; ☎ 239 714 824; fax 239 405 124; Bairro de São Jose 15; d €40; ❄) This large and irreproachably kept guesthouse sits at the bottom of Alameda Dr Júlio Henriques. It has big, elegantly sparse rooms, including a few family suites.

Residencial Moeda (Map pp308-9; ☎ 239 824 784; www.residencialmoeda.web.pt; Rua da Moeda 81; s/d €35/45; ❄) Sitting on a narrow Baixa street above the owner's hole-in-the-wall seashell-and-charms shop near the Igreja de Santa Cruz, this friendly place offers snug but modern, spotless, recently remodelled rooms at good value.

Residencial Alentejana (Map p306; ☎ 239 825 903; www.residencialalentejana.com; Rua António Henriques Seco 1; s/d/tr with breakfast €35/45/60; ❄) Worth the uphill walk, this prominent old town house offers wood-panelled, high-ceilinged older rooms, as well as some less charming but comfortable enough newer ones.

Residência Coimbra (Map pp308-9; ☎ 239 837 996; www.residenciacoimbra.com; Rua das Azeiteiras 55; s/d €30/45; ❄ 💻) In a narrow pedestrian street squeezed full of down-to-earth cafés and restaurants, this well-run place offers a selection of good-value, recently remodelled digs.

Pensão Residencial Antunes (Map pp308-9; ☎ 239 854 720; residencialantunes@mail.pt; Rua Castro Matoso 8; s/d €35/45; Ⓟ) A few steps from the aqueduct and botanical gardens, this large old guesthouse offers long creaky halls, charming, creaky doubles and that Coimbra rarity: free, off-street parking.

our pick **Casa Pombal Guesthouse** (Map pp308-9; ☎ 239 835 175; http://hostalcasapombal.jesdesign.nl; Rua das Flores 18; d with/without bathroom from €58/48; 🕑 closed mid-Dec–mid-Jan) Hidden down a narrow lane near the crown of Coimbra's hilltop university, this winning, Dutch-run guesthouse manages to squeeze a great deal of charm into a narrow space indeed. The price per square metre is high, though for your money you'll get simple, fresh, brightly coloured rooms with wood floors, including a couple of attic eyries with superb views. A fine buffet breakfast is included.

Hotel Oslo (Map pp308-9; ☎ 239 829 071/2/3; www.hotel-oslo.web.pt; Avenida Fernão de Magalhães 25; s/d €55/65; P ✖ 💻) This otherwise bland, modern hotel block redeems itself with well-maintained rooms, plentiful free parking, satellite TV, double-paned windows and a popular 5th-floor bar with views up to the university.

Hotel Bragança (Map pp308-9; ☎ 239 822 171; www.hotel-braganca.com; Largo das Ameias 10; s/d €35/68; ✖) Unpromising on the outside, this '60s concrete hotel has large and rather elegant rooms, all with parquet floors and many with river views. There are also a few small, viewless but otherwise good-value singles.

TOP END

Hotel Astória (Map pp308-9; ☎ 239 853 020; www.almeidahotels.com; Avenida Emídio Navarro 21; s/d €84/101; ✖ 💻) The unmistakable Art Nouveau face of this wedge-shaped hotel contemplates the river and Largo da Portagem. It has bags of personality and professional, spiffy staff, though some of the quiet, plush rooms are a tad dog-eared. The round tower suites (from €105) also score panoramic views from the river up to the university.

Hotel Tivoli (Map p306; ☎ 239 858 300; www.tivolihotels.com; Rua João Machado; d with breakfast €140; P ✖ 💻 🏊) If you require unimpeachable comforts but are willing to give on aesthetics, consider the Tivoli, Coimbra's only true 'business-class' hotel. Although it occupies an ugly modern building in a rather unappealing and trafficky stretch of the Baixa, it has huge rooms with all the expected frills, a pool and a small gym.

Quinta das Lágrimas (Map p306; ☎ 239 802 380; www.quintadaslagrimas.pt; Rua António Augusto Gonçalves; d from €165; P ⊠ ✖ 🏊) This splendid historical palace is now one of Portugal's most enchanting upper-crust hotels. You can choose between richly furnished rooms in the old palace, or Scandinavian-style minimalist rooms in the modern annexe – complete with Jacuzzi. A few of its rooms look out on the garden where Dona Inês de Castro is said to have met her tragic end (see p310).

Eating

BUDGET

During term, there's lots of cheap, filling grub to be had at the university's **student cantinas** (Map pp308-9; meals around €3; 🕒 lunch & dinner), off the courtyard of the **AAC** (Associação Acadêmica de Coimbra; Avenida Sa da Bandeira) – one upstairs at the back (southern) end and one down a flight of steps on the eastern side.

The downstairs restaurant generally has better food but is also more likely to ask to see student ID. There's another cantina nearby on the campus proper, just off Largo Dom Dinis. This one tends to have longer hours and is also most likely to admit nonstudents.

Restaurante Jardim da Manga (Map pp308-9; ☎ 239 829 156; dishes €5-6; 🕒 all day Sun-Fri) A student-friendly place reminiscent of a school canteen but winningly positioned at the back of the Jardim da Manga (p307), this cafeteria-style café-restaurant has a small menu of meaty dishes tailored to tight budgets.

Self-caterers should check out the modern **Mercado Municipal Dom Pedro V** (Map pp308-9; Rua Olímpio Nicolau Rui Fernandes; 🕒 Mon-Sat).

There are a couple of supermarkets:

Minipreço (Map pp308-9; Rua António Granjo 6c; 🕒 9am-8pm Mon-Sat, 9am-1pm & 3-7pm Sun)

Pingo Doce (Map p306; Rua João de Ruão; 🕒 8.30am-8.30pm)

MIDRANGE

Restaurante Democrática (Map pp308-9; ☎ 239 823 784; Rua Nova; mains €5-10; 🕒 lunch & dinner Mon-Sat) If all you're after is a down-to-business, family-friendly place offering good-value standards, this backstreet favourite will fit the bill. It's a Coimbra classic and always filled with hungry students.

our pick **Restaurante Zé Neto** (Map pp308-9; ☎ 239 826 786; Rua das Azeiteiras 8; mains €6-9; 🕒 lunch & dinner Mon-Sat) Marvellous, traditional, family-run place with brusque service but excellent homemade Portuguese fare, including very good *cabrito* (kid). Come in the late morning and you'll catch the elderly owner tapping out the menu on a typewriter of similar vintage.

Adega Funchal (Map pp308-9; ☎ 239 824 137; Rua das Azeiteiras 18; mains €6-10; 🕒 lunch & dinner Sun-Fri) Delicious smells fill the alleyway outside this popular spot. The owners are proud of its *chanfana carne de cabra* (goat stewed in red wine) for two. Service is gruff, however.

Restaurante Zé Manel (Map pp308-9; ☎ 239 823 790; Beco do Forno 12; mains €7-9; 🕒 lunch & dinner Mon-Fri, lunch Sat) Tucked down a nondescript alleyway this little gem, papered with scholarly doodles and scribbled poems, would be easy to miss. Despite its location, it's highly popular so come early or be ready to wait. Try the good *feijoada á leitão* (a stew of beans and suckling pig).

Macguls (Map pp308-9; ☎ 239 842 079; Avenida Emídio Navarro 37; mains €8-12; 🕑 lunch & dinner Mon-Sat) Next to the river, this upmarket Indian place occupies a grand 19th-century dining room, fitted out with deep reds and yellows. Food is not exactly Indian, but it's fresh, fragrant and tasty – and about the only non-Portuguese fare on offer.

A Sereia (Map p306; ☎ 239 824 342; Rua Dr António Henriques Seco 1; mains €8-12; 🕑 lunch & dinner Mon-Fri, lunch Sat) Sit around the large downstairs counter or upstairs in the equally old-fashioned dining room and get some of the best traditional Portuguese fare in town. Nothing fancy, but delicious.

Zé Carioca (Map pp308-9; ☎ 239 835 450; Avenida Sá da Bandeira 89; mains around €11-15; 🕑 lunch & dinner Mon-Sat) Set in a series of colourfully done up rooms in a handsome old town house, this Brazilian eatery is both relaxed and elegant, and the grilled meats are superb. At dinner there's an all-you-can-eat-and-still-waddle-home buffet (including said meats) for €15.90.

Drinking

Praça da República is the epicentre of student nightlife. The big nights are Thursday to Saturday – but during university term time, any night is game.

CAFÉS

Café Teatro (Map pp308-9; Praça da República; 🕑 10am-1am Mon-Fri, 2pm-1am Sat) With huge windows, minimalist décor and a long zinc bar overlooking leafy Praça da República, the café in the upstairs lobby of the university theatre is the place where alternative types get their coffee fix during the day and start out their evenings with a first drink. Ticket-holders only during performances.

Café Santa Cruz (Map pp308-9; ☎ 239 833 617; Praça 8 de Maio; 🕑 Mon-Sat) Scooping the prize for the best people-watching patio in town, Santa Cruz also has one of the most attractive and unusual interiors. It is housed in a vaulted neo-Manueline annexe of the Igreja de Santa Cruz, with creased leather chairs, austere arches and stained glass.

Cartola Esplanada Bar (Map pp308-9; Praça da República) This place has a great plaza-side position and a huge drinks list, making it the ideal place for a spot of student-watching.

Galeria Bar Santa Clara (Map p306; ☎ 239 441 657; Rua António Augusto Gonçalves; 🕑 2pm-3am) Arty tearoom by day and chilled-out bar at night, this terrific place has good art on the walls, a series of sunny rooms and a fine, riverfront terrace.

BARS

Bar Quebra Costas (Map pp308-9; ☎ 239 821 661; Rua Quebra Costas 45-49; 🕑 4pm-4am Mon-Sat, also Sun Jun-Sep) In the perfect position to sip a chilled beer as you watch people puff and pant up the Quebra Costas, this Coimbra classic has a great terrace as well as a recently updated interior with chilled-out electronica and sharp art on the walls.

English Bar (Map p306; Rua Lourenço de Almeida Azevedo 24; 🕑 Mon-Sat) British-style pub that has light meals downstairs and a bar to knock back draught Murphy's upstairs. It has a very popular Latin night on Wednesdays.

Shmoo Café (Map pp308-9; Rua Corpo de Deus 68; 🕑 8.30pm-3am Mon-Sat) This slick bar lays the red light on thick, making for an intimate atmosphere that attracts a chic downtown crowd.

Café Tropical (Map pp308-9; Praça da República; 🕑 10am-2am Mon-Sat) Another bare-bones student place with pleasant outdoor seating, cheap beers and a lively crowds – a favourite place to start out the night.

AAC pub (Map pp308-9; Praça da República) Join the black-cape-clad students at their student-union bar, where beers are under €1 and everyone is welcome. It's a good place to test your *praxe* (student traditions; p314).

CLUBS

Via Latina (Map pp308-9; Rua Almeida Garrett 1; 🕑 midnight-6am Tue-Sat) Students swear by the DJs at this simple, sweaty, excellent dance club. Fridays are particularly good.

Vinil (Map p306; Avenida Afonso Henriques 43; 🕑 midnight-4am Tue-Sat) Another perennial favourite, where a mostly student crowd does the soft shake to predictable pop tunes.

Entertainment

If Lisbon represents the heart of Portuguese *fado* music, Coimbra is its head. The local style is more cerebral than the Lisbon variety, with a greater emphasis on *guitarra*-led instrumental pieces. Its adherents are also staunchly protective: a fracas erupted in Coimbra in 1996 when a woman named Manuela Bravo decided to record a CD of Coimbra *fado*, which is traditionally sung only by men.

The AAC (student union) sometimes sponsors *fado* performances in the Café Santa Cruz

SPEAKING PRAXE *Robert Landon*

When I first visited Coimbra, I noticed many students wearing black suits with dramatic capes. I figured I'd happened upon some kind of midterm graduation party, but my friend Tiago, a recent graduate and former student-body president, explained that at the tradition-bound University of Coimbra, students wear this highfalutin garb year-round just to attend class or down a pint at the student union. 'Try such behaviour at Harvard or Oxford and expect to be razzed out of existence,' I told him. 'Perhaps,' Tiago said, 'but in Coimbra it's actually rather the cool thing to do, and increasingly, other universities around Portugal are adopting the practice'.

Such student traditions – known collectively as *praxe* – are in fact a highly regulated affair, and the student government publishes a long *codigo de praxe* (praxe code) that provides detailed instructions on how to observe rites – some ancient, some modern – from first-year hazing to the annual graduation bash known as the Queima das Fitas (p310).

The black suits may seem elitist today, but Tiago explained that they were invented exactly to create a sense of equality and camaraderie among students of differing classes, since everyone dressed more or less the same. At the same time, capes are made to express each student's individual identity. Nearly everyone sews on *emblemas* – small patches – that reveal their course of study (each represented by its own colour), as well as preferred extracurricular activities (reggae, football, beer drinking, lace-making).

As a traveller you may just find this practice immensely useful. Imagine, for example, that you're in one of the student unions with a (dirt-cheap) pint in your hand and you find there's someone you'd like to get to know better. Now those *emblemas* really come in handy, first to gauge any potential compatibility and then as ready-made conversation starters. I ran this idea by my friend Tiago.

'You're starting to catch on,' he said with a delightfully mischievous grin.

during March, and there's also open-air *fado* to be found at the Arco de Almedina and along Rua Quebra-Costas during summer (p305).

You can listen to *fado* in several *casas de fado* (*fado* houses) on just about any late Friday or Saturday evening.

our pick **Á Capella** (Map pp308-9; ☎ 239 833 985; www.acapella.com.pt; Rua Corpo de Deus; admission €5; ⏲ 10pm-2am) Set superbly in a tiny, atmospheric 14th-century church that has been transformed into a candlelit cocktail lounge, Á Capella regularly hosts the city's most renowned *fado* musicians. As soon as the music starts you'll understand why the impresarios chose this particular chapel: the acoustics are heart-rendingly good, and the place is as intimate as the music itself.

Also recommended:

Bar Diligência (Map pp308-9; ☎ 239 827 667; Rua Nova 30; ⏲ 6pm-2am) This bar usually hosts live *fado* from about 10.30pm.

Restaurante O Trovador (Map pp308-9; ☎ 239 825 475; Largo da Sé Velha 15-17; ⏲ 9am-midnight Mon-Sat) A large and touristy but attractive venue, this restaurant plays host to *fado* performances on Friday and Saturday nights from October to April, and nightly from May to September.

Getting There & Away

BUS

From the **main bus station** (Map p306; Avenida Fernã de Magalhães), **Rede Expressos** (☎ 239 827 081) rur at least a dozen buses daily to Lisbon (€10.8 2½ hours) and to Porto (€10, 1½ hours), an almost as many to Braga (€11.20, 2½ hour and Faro (€19, six to eight hours). In wint there are frequent services to Seia (€8.70, 1 hours), Guarda (€9.20, three hours) and als to other points around the Parque Natural d Serra da Estrela.

Joalto/AVIC (Map p306; ☎ 239 820 141; Rua João Ruão 18; ⏲ 9am-12.30pm, 2-6.30pm Mon-Fri) has bu service to the Roman ruins at nearby Co imbriga (opposite).

CAR

The local branch of the **Automóvel Club de Po tugal** (ACP; Map pp308-9; ☎ 239 852 020; Avenida Emíc Navarro 6) is by Coimbra A.

Various car-rental agencies will drop c the rental car at your hotel, including th following:

Alpirent (Map p306; ☎ 239 821 999; Rua do Carmo 9C

Avis (☎ 239 834 786; Largo das Américas)

Salitur/Europcar (Map p306; ☎ 239 820 594; Edifício Tricana, Rua Padre Estevão Cabral)

TRAIN
Fast intercity (IC) trains usually stop only at Coimbra B, though there are quick, free connections to more central Coimbra A (called just 'Coimbra' on timetables). There's no left-luggage office at either station.

Coimbra is linked by at least five daily *intercidade* (IC) trains to Lisbon (€15, 2¼ hours) and four to Porto (€10.50, 1½ hours). Additional *interregional* (IR) services take at least 30 minutes longer and cost about €2 less. IR trains also run about four times a day to Luso/Buçaco (€1.50, 30 minutes) and at least hourly to Figueira da Foz (€1.70, 70 minutes).

Getting Around
If you come by car, be ready for snarled traffic and scarce parking. You are most likely to find street parking on side streets around Praça da República. If you're willing to pay, look for the blue 'P' signs in the Baixa district, including several car parks each along Avenidas Fernão Magalhães and Ermídio Navarro. If you do decide to park on the street, make sure you're legal – enforcement is strict.

BICYCLE
For mountain bike rental, **Centro Velocipédico de Sangalhos** (☎ 239 824 646; Rua da Sota 23; 🕒 9am-7pm Mon-Fri) charges €7.50 per day.

BUS
Together, buses 27, 28 and 29 run about every half-hour from the main bus station and the Coimbra B train station to Praça da República. Bus 40 makes an anticlockwise loop that takes in the stations as well as the Baixa district.

You can purchase multiuse tickets (three/11 trips €1.70/5.70), also usable on the *elevador* (see right), at the **SMTUC office** (Map pp308-9; ☎ 239 801 100; www.smtuc.pt in Portuguese; Largo do Mercado; 🕒 7.30am-7.30pm Mon-Fri, 8am-1pm Sat) at the foot of the *elevador*, at official kiosks and also at some *tabacarias* (tobacconist/newsagents). Tickets bought on board cost €1.50 per trip.

You may also see *patufinhas* (electric minibuses; also called Linha Azul) crawling around pedestrian areas in the centre of Coimbra, between Baixa and Alta Coimbra and through the medieval heart of the city. You can use the same pre-bought tickets that you would on any other SMTUC buses.

ELEVADOR DO MERCADO
The **elevador** (Map pp308-9; 🕒 7.30am-10pm Mon-Sat, 10am-10pm Sun) – a combination of elevator, walkway and funicular between the market and the university – can save you a tedious walk, though it's slow and fickle. See left for buying tickets, which you punch once for each ascent or descent. You can't buy tickets at the top.

AROUND COIMBRA
Conimbriga
Hidden amid humble olive orchards in the rolling country southwest of Coimbra, Conimbriga boasts the most extensive and best-preserved Roman ruins in Portugal, and ranks with the best-preserved sites in the whole of the Iberian Peninsula. It also tells the poignant tale of a town that, after centuries of security, was first split in two by quickly erected walls and then entirely abandoned as the Roman empire disintegrated.

HISTORY
Though Conimbriga owes its celebrity to the Romans, the site actually dates back to Celtic times (*briga* is a Celtic term for a defended area). However, when the Romans settled here in the 1st century AD, it blossomed into a major city on the route from Lisbon (Olisipo) to Braga (Bracara Augusta). Its prosperity is revealed by well-to-do mansions floored with elaborate mosaics and scattered with fountains.

In the 3rd century the townsfolk, threatened by invading tribes, desperately threw up a huge defensive wall right through the town centre, abandoning the residential area. But this wasn't enough to stop the Suevi seizing the town in 468. Inhabitants fled to nearby Aeminius (Coimbra) – thereby saving Conimbriga from destruction.

SIGHTS
Museum
To get your head around Conimbriga's history, begin at the small but well-organised and informative **museum** (☎ 239 944 100; admission incl ruins adult/child under 14/student, teacher & senior €3/free/1.50, 10am-1pm Sun free; 🕒 10am-1pm & 2-8pm Tue-Sun Mar-Sep, to 6pm Oct-Feb). Displays present every aspect of Roman life from mosaics to medallions. There's a sunny café-restaurant at the back that was being remodelled at the time of writing.

Ruins

The sprawling **Roman ruins** (included in museum admission, same hours; see p315) tell a vivid story. On the one hand, its domesticity is obvious, with elaborate mosaics, heated baths and trickling fountains that evoke delightful, toga-clad dalliances. But smack through the middle of this scene runs a massive defensive wall, splitting and cannibalising nearby buildings in its hasty erection to fend off raids.

It's the disproportionately large wall that will first draw your attention, followed by the patchwork of exceptional mosaic floors below it. Here you'll find the so-called **Casa dos Repuxos** (House of Fountains); though partly destroyed by the wall, it contains cool pond-gardens, fountains and truly extraordinary mosaics showing the four seasons and various hunting scenes.

The site's most important **villa**, on the other side of the wall, is said to have belonged to one Cantaber, whose wife and children were seized by the Suevi in an attack in 465. It's a palace of a place, with baths, pools and a sophisticated underground heating system.

Excavations continue in the outer areas. Eye-catching features include the remains of a 3km-long aqueduct, which led up to a hilltop bathing complex, and a forum, once surrounded by covered porticoes.

GETTING THERE & AWAY

You can catch a bus from Coimbra directly to the site (€1.80, 30 minutes) with **AVIC/Joalto** (☎ 239 823 769) at 9am or 9.35am (only 9.35am at weekends). Buses depart for the return trip at 1pm and 5pm (only 5pm on weekends). It also runs buses to Condeixa (€1.60) about every half-hour (less often on weekends). But note that from Condeixa to the site it's a poorly signposted 2km walk, some of it along the hard shoulder of a high-speed road.

Luso & Mata Nacional do Buçaco

A retreat from the world for almost 2000 years, the slopes of the Serra do Buçaco are now home to the 105-hectare Buçaco (or Bussaco) National Forest. Harbouring an astounding 700 plant species, from huge Mexican cedars to tree-sized ferns, the forest is equally fecund in terms of the poetry it has inspired.

Generations of Coimbra's literary types have enshrined the forest in the national imagination with breathless hymns to its mystical marriage of natural and spiritual beauty. The high stone walls that for centuries have encircled the forest have no doubt helped reinforce its sense of mystery. And in the midst of the forest stands a royal palace completed in 1907; despite the extravagance of its fairy-tale neo-Manueline façade, the dynasty fell just three years later.

Outside the forest walls lies the old-fashioned little spa town of Luso, whose waters are considered a balm for everything from gout to asthma. The forest and spa make an easy day trip from Coimbra. If you want to linger, Luso has a handful of *residenciais* (guesthouses). Those with the wherewithal can stay at the astonishing royal palace, right in the forest.

HISTORY

The Luso and Buçaco area probably served as a Christian refuge as early as the second century AD, although the earliest known hermitage was founded in the 6th century by Benedictine monks. In 1628 Carmelite monks embarked on an extensive programme of forestation. They planted exotic species, laid cobbled paths and enclosed the forest within high stone walls. The forest grew so renowned that in 1643 Pope Urban VIII decreed that anyone damaging the trees would be excommunicated.

The peace was briefly shattered in 1810 when Napoleon's forces under Masséna were soundly beaten here by the Anglo-Portuguese army of the future Duke of Wellington (the battle is re-enacted here every 27 September). In 1834, when religious orders throughout Portugal were abolished, the forest became state property.

ORIENTATION & INFORMATION

From the Luso-Buçaco train station it's a 15-minute walk downhill (east) via Rua Dr António Granjo to the turismo and spa in the centre of Luso. Buses stop on Rua Emídio Navarro, near the turismo. By road the Porta das Ameias, the nearest gate into the forest is 900m east of the turismo. From May to October there's a charge of €5 per car entering the forest, though walkers go in free.

The **turismo** (☎ 231 939 133; jtlb@oninet.pt; Rua Emídio Navarro 136; 🕑 9am-7pm Mon-Fri Jul-Sep, 9.30am-12.30pm & 2-6pm Oct-May, 10am-12.30pm & 2-6pm Sat & Sun year-round) has accommodation information, town and forest maps, and leaflets (in English) detailing flora and points of historical interest. They also offer **internet access** (per hr €5) on a single terminal.

SIGHTS & ACTIVITIES

Forest

The aromatic forest is crisscrossed with trails, dotted with crumbling chapels and graced with ponds and fountains. Some popular trails lead to areas of great beauty, such as the Vale dos Fetos (Valley of Ferns), but you can get enjoyably lost on more overgrown routes. Among several fine viewpoints is **Cruz Alta** (545m), reached by a path called the Via Sacra.

What most visitors come to see is the fairytale **Palace Hotel do Buçaco**. Built in 1907 as a royal summer retreat on the site of a 17th-century Carmelite monastery, this sugary-sweet wedding cake of a building is a fairy-tale conglomeration of turrets and spires, neo-Manueline carving and *azulejos* illustrating scenes from *Os Lusiados* (p44). It's now a deluxe hotel (right), though staff are generally tolerant of gawping nonguests. By road, the hotel is 2.1km from the Portas das Ameias.

Spa

Just the ticket after a long walk in the forest, the **Termas de Luso** (☎ 231 937 910; Rua Alvaro; ⌚ 8am-noon & 4-7pm) welcomes drop-in visitors from May to October – preferably in the afternoon. Therapies for day visitors include a general massage (€16), and a kind of high-velocity shower called *duche de Vichy* followed by a short massage (€15). Or you can fill your bottle for free with spa water at the **Fonte de São João** (fountain), a block east of the turismo.

SLEEPING

Budget

Orbitur Camping Ground (☎ 231 930 916; www.orbitur.pt; Bairro do Comendador Melo Pimenta; adult/car €3.80/3.50, tent €3.80-5.30; ⌚ year-round) This small, lush site is a pleasant, 1.3km walk south of the turismo. Wooden bungalows with kitchen are also available (four-/six-person cabins €58/68).

Residencial Imperial (☎ 231 937 570; www.residencialimperial.com; Rua Emídio Navarro; s/d €30/35; ❄) Trim, attractive and brand new, the Imperial has bright little rooms, all with French windows opening onto small verandas. Great value. Recommended.

Casa de Hóspedes Familiar (☎ 231 939 612; fax 231 939 268; Rua Ernesto Navarro 34; s/d €25/35) Small, simple, cosy rooms are on offer at this handsome, late-Victorian country house just above town. Some rooms have a little veranda with great views. You feel (and are) a guest in someone's family home.

Midrange

Astória (☎ 231 939 182; Rua Emídio Navarro; s/d €35/40; P) Beside the turismo, this homely place feels more like grandma's house than a guesthouse. Its comfortable rooms are filled with frilly décor and various intriguing artefacts.

Central (☎ 231 939 254; Rua Emídio Navarro; s/d €40/45; P) This workaday but comfortable and welcoming, modern *pensão* (guesthouse), has spacious, simply furnished rooms with wooden floors and verandas.

Pensão Alegre (☎ 231 930 256; Rua Emídio Navarro 2; d €50; P ❄ 🏊) This attractive 19th-century town house offers personal service and large doubles filled with plush drapes, decorative plaster ceilings and highly polished period furniture. Plus there's a pretty little vine-draped garden with pool.

Top End

Vila Duparchy (☎ 231 930 790; principe.santos@clix.pt; Rua José Figueiredo; s/d €67/80; P 🏊) Home to French railway engineer Jean Alexis Duparchy while constructing the Beira Alta railway, this rather genteel house is set back from the road on a woody hilltop, 2km outside the centre of Luso off the EN234. English is spoken and meals are available on request.

Palace Hotel do Buçaco (☎ 231 937 970; www.palacehoteldobussaco.com; Mata Nacional do Buçaco; d €175; P ❄) If you can afford it, stay amid all the fuss and finery of this delightfully ostentatious king's palace. Rooms abound in varying degrees of period finery, some of it a touch threadbare. Common areas are stunning and will put you in a royal mood.

EATING

Most *pensões* have reasonable restaurants of their own.

Salão de chá (Praça Fonte São João; ⌚ 10am-8pm) This Art Deco tearoom by the Fonte de São João captures the spa-town atmosphere and is perfect for tea, cakes and other snacks.

Restaurante Imperial (☎ 231 937 570; Rua Emídio Navarro; meals €5-7; ⌚ lunch & dinner Tue-Sun) In the new hotel of the same name, the Imperial serves up simple, delicious grilled meats and other Portuguese fare at great value in a trim, cheerful dining room.

Restaurante Lourenços (☎ 231 939 474; Rua Emídio Navarro; mains €7-10; ⌚ lunch & dinner Thu-Tue) In an uninspired block of shops, this bright, modern place serves surprisingly good regional specialities.

Palace Hotel do Buçaco (☎ 231 937 970; Mata Nacional do Buçaco; 3-course meals incl drinks €45) The royal retreat-turned-hotel offers a blowout three courses, with a menu offering a creative take on regional dishes.

GETTING THERE & AWAY

Buses are the most convenient for a day trip. RBL has five services daily during the week (fewer at the weekend) leaving from Coimbra's main bus station (€2.90, 40 minutes).

IR trains also run about four times a day to Luso/Buçaco (€1.50, 30 minutes).

Reserva Natural do Paúl de Arzila

Bird-watchers and other nature fans may wish to make a detour to the 535-hectare Arzila Marsh Natural Reserve, home to some 120 species of resident and migratory birds, as well as otters. The **on-site centre** (☎ 239 980 500; www.icn.pt) serves as the base for a two-hour interpretive walk.

PIÓDÃO

pop 225 / elevation 690m

Remote Piódão (*pyoh*-down) offers a chance to see rural Portugal at its most pristine. This tiny traditional village clings to a terraced valley in a beautiful, surprisingly remote range of vertiginous ridges, deeply cut valleys, rushing rivers and virgin woodland called the Serra de Açor (Goshawk Mountains).

Until the 1970s you could only reach Piódão on horseback or by foot, and it still feels as though you've slipped into a time warp. The village is a serene, picturesque composition in schist stone and grey slate; note the many doorways with crosses over them, said to offer protection against curses and thunderstorms.

Orientation & Information

Houses descend in terraces to Largo Cônego Manuel Fernandes Nogueira – smaller than its name – and the fairy-tale parish church, the Igreja Nossa Senhora Conceição. You'll also find the village **turismo** (☎ 235 732 787; 🕑 9am-noon & 1-5pm Wed-Sun) here, which has a good booklet on local walks.

Festivals & Events

The area's patron saint, São Pedro do Açor, is honoured with a Mass, religious procession, ball, and a handicrafts fair during the **Santos Populares no Piódão** on the last weekend in June.

Sleeping & Eating

There are *quartos* (private rooms) everywhere, of uneven quality and seriously overpriced at about €25 per person.

Parque de Campismo de Côja (☎ 235 729 666; coja@fpcampismo.pt; Côja; adult/tent & car €3/2.50; 🕑 mid-Mar–mid-Oct) A well-equipped, shady facility near the river, 21km west on the Rio Alva. It also has bungalows from €30 for four people.

Campismo de Ponte de Três Entradas (☎ 238 670 050; ponte3entradas@mail.telepac.pt; adult/tent & car €3.30/2.90; 🕑 Dec-Oct) This shady riverside site 30km from Piódão near Avô also has bungalows from €40 for two.

Casas da Aldeia (☎ 235 731 424; d €25, with toilet, bathroom €40/65) This private house just beyond the centre is kitted out with help from the village-improvement committee. The rooms have kitchenettes.

Estalagem do Piódão (☎ 235 730 100; www.inatel.pt; d €67; P) Run by Inatel, this mammoth caricature of a local schist house looms over everything on a ridge above the village. The hotel has rather luxurious, modern rooms and the town's only decent restaurant.

In the same vein as Casas da Aldeia, village Turihab (Turismo Habitação; scheme for marketing private accommodation) properties with doubles from €35 to €40 (with breakfast) include **Casa da Padaria** (☎ 235 732 773; casa.padaria@sapo.pt) and **Casa Malhadinhas** (☎ 235 731 464).

Cafés around the *largo* (small square) serve pastries and toasted sandwiches. **Restaurante O Fontinha** (☎ 235 731 151; mains €5-8; 🕑 lunch & dinner), one lane back from the *largo*, is cheap but uninspiring.

Getting There & Away

The only transport other than car or bicycle is a bus from Arganil that stops in the *largo* (€2.80, 1¼ hours) twice on Thursday. Buses usually leave at 7.45am and 3pm, returning immediately upon arrival, but check current times with Piódão's tourist office or by calling Arganil's **turismo** (☎ 235 732 787).

The area's breathtaking views, narrow roads and sheer drops are a lethal combination for drivers. Note that side roads marked '4WD' are axle-breakers for ordinary cars.

FIGUEIRA DA FOZ

pop 28,000

Once a fashionable *fin-de-siècle* resort, Figueira da Foz (fi-*guy*-ra da *fosh*), with its candy-striped beach huts and get-rich-quick casino has long been showing its age. Still, the town's original attraction never goes out of fashion: its vast golden beach, one of the longest and widest in the region. Indeed, it takes a five-minute walk across creaky boardwalks simply to reach the sea. Amazingly, all that empty sand fills up with ranks of sizzling bodies in the summer heat. Needless to say, prices rise along with the crowds and the temperatures. Surfers take note: Figueira is a regular surfing championship venue.

Orientation

Just inland from the beach and the 16th-century Forte de Santa Catarina is a knot of streets with the turismo, accommodation and restaurants and the casino. Seafront development continues clear to Buarcos, a former fishing village 3km to the north.

The train station is 1.5km east of the beach, the bus station a tad closer. High-season parking is a headache in the centre, even in the evenings, thanks to the casino. A good bet for street parking is the area between the Jardim Municipal and the train station.

Information

Biblioteca Municipal (Rua Calouste Gulbenkian; 2-7.15pm Mon, 10am-7.15pm Tue-Fri, 2-6.45pm Sat) Free internet.

Main post office (Passeio Infante Dom Henrique; 8.30am-6.30pm Mon-Fri, 9am-12.30pm Sat)

Press Center (Rua Bernardo Lopes 113; 9am-11pm) Newsagent stocking foreign newspapers.

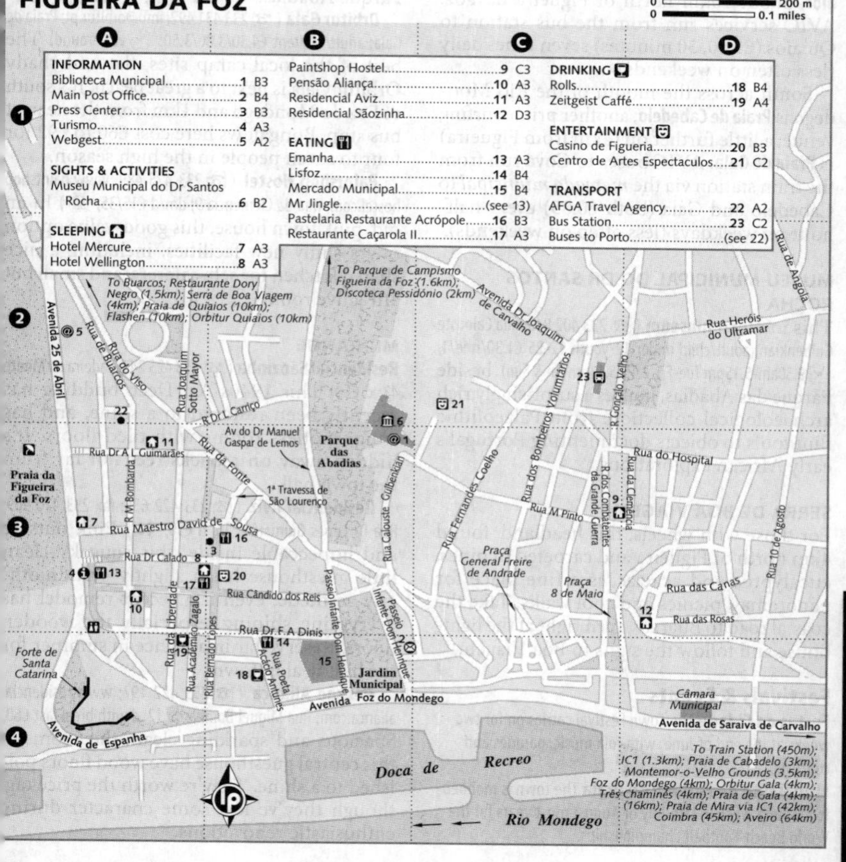

Book accommodation online at lonelyplanet.com

Turismo (☎ 233 422 610; www.figueiraturismo.com; Avenida 25 de Abril; ⏲ 9am-midnight Jul-Sep, 9am-12.30pm & 2-5.30pm Mon-Fri, 10am-12.30pm & 2.30-6.30pm Sat & Sun Oct-May)

Webgest (Avenida 25 de Abril 74; ⏲ 10.30am-11pm) Internet access.

Sights & Activities

BEACHES

Despite its size, the beach is packed in August. For more character and some terrific surf, head north to **Buarcos**. Alfredo Farreca Rodrigues runs buses from the train station via the *mercado municipal* (municipal market) and the turismo to Buarcos (€0.85) every half-hour on weekdays and at least hourly on weekends.

For more seclusion, continue on around the Cabo Mondego headland to **Praia de Quiaios**, about 10km north of Figueira da Foz. AVIC services run from the bus station to Quiaios (€1.80, 30 minutes) seven times daily (less often on weekends).

South across the mouth of the Rio Mondego is **Praia de Cabedelo**, another prime surfing venue; a little further on (4km from Figueira) is **Praia de Gala**. AVIC buses to Cova run from the train station via the *mercado municipal* to Cabedelo and Gala (both €0.85) every half-hour on weekdays (less often on weekends).

MUSEU MUNICIPAL DO DR SANTOS ROCHA

This modern **museum** (☎ 233 402 840; Rua Calouste Gulbenkian; adult/child under 12/youth 12-25 €1.30/free/1; ⏲ 9.30am-5.15pm Tue-Fri, 2.15-5.15pm Sat & Sun), beside Parque das Abadias, houses a surprisingly rich archaeological collection: from Palaeolithic flint tools to objects documenting Portugal's early African explorations.

SERRA DE BOA VIAGEM

For those with wheels, this headland, found 4km north of Figueira and carpeted in pines, eucalyptus and acacias, is a fine place for panoramas, picnics and cool walks. Take the coastal road to Buarcos, turn right at the lighthouse and follow the signs to Boa Viagem.

Festivals & Events

Festas da Cidade The Town Festival carries on for two weeks at the end of June, with folk music, parades and concerts.

Mundialito de Futebol de Praia The town is mobbed for about a week in late July or August most years for the World Beach-Football Championships.

Sleeping

Prices listed are for the high season (July and August). Expect discounts of up to 40% in winter. The turismo has details of a few *quartos* from €25 per double. Touts may approach you at the bus or train stations with their own offers.

BUDGET

Parque de Campismo Figueira da Foz (☎ 233 402 810; www.figueiracamping.com in Portuguese; Estrada de Tavarede; adult/car €3.70/3.20, tent €2.70-3.20; ⏲ year-round) Northeast of the centre and 2km from the beach, this camping ground has a pool, tennis courts and a handy supermarket a mere stone's throw away. To get here, take a Casal de Areia bus (€1, six to 10 daily) from the train station, the *mercado municipal* or Parque Abadias.

Orbitur Gala (☎ 233 431 492; info@orbitur.pt; Praia de Gala; adult/car/tent €4.30/3.80/3.50; ⏲ year-round) The best of the local camp sites, flat and shady Orbitur Gala is next to a great beach. It's south of Foz do Mondego and 1km from the nearest bus stop. Bungalows here cost €60 to €92 for four to seven people in the high season.

Paintshop Hostel (☎ 233 425 489; www.paintshophostel.com; Rua da Clemência 9; dm/d €15/35; 💻) In an old, pink town house, this good-value option offers shiny new facilities, including a nice shared kitchen for self-caterers, and small but attractive rooms.

MIDRANGE

Residencial Sãozinha (☎ 233 425 243; Ladeira do Monte 43; d €50) This 1940s Art Deco building has recently been restored to a shine, and has snug, spotless rooms with tiled floors. It's hidden away on a backstreet not far from the town hall.

Residencial Aviz (☎ 233 422 635; fax 233 420 909; Rua Dr Lopes Guimarães 16; d €50; ❄) Pink outside and impeccable inside, this squeaky-clean little guesthouse has a slightly grandmotherly aesthetic, even if a recent remodel has everything shining, especially the wooden floors. Reserve far in advance in summer for the best deal in town.

Pensão Aliança (☎ 233 422 197; www.residenciaalianca.com; Rua Miguel Bombarda 12; d with breakfast €60) Spacious and sparkling clean, the rooms at this central guesthouse have wood floors polished to a shine. They're worth the price tag though they've lost some character during enthusiastic renovations.

TOP END

Hotel Wellington (☎ 233 426 767/8; www.sabirhoteis.pt; Rua Dr Calado 23-27; s/d €77/88;) Good value but run-of-the-mill hotel near the action; its modern rooms have cable TV. Off-street parking is available at a nearby car park (€4 per night).

Hotel Mercure (☎ 233 403 900; www.mercure.com; Avenida 25 de Abril 22; d with city/ocean view €100/120; P) This is the only four-star hotel in town. Row upon row of balconies boast sweeping views of the vast beach, and rooms offer a welcome touch of comfort.

Eating

Pastelaria Restaurante Acrópole (☎ 233 428 948; Rua Bernardo Lopes 76; dishes €4.50-7; 8am-midnight Wed-Mon) For maximum mileage from your holiday funds, this casual café whips up filling burgers and omelettes for around €5. Tables spilling out onto the street make it great for people-watching.

Restaurante Dory Negro (☎ 233 421 333; Largo Caras Direitas 16, Buarcos; mains €7-10; lunch & dinner Wed-Mon) A slap-up seafood meal is cheaper in Buarcos, and this unassuming restaurant is one of the best spots to indulge. The huge menu includes crab, lobster, shrimp, clams and deep-sea fish. Its scrumptious *arroz de marisco* (€32 for two people), a rich stew of seafood and rice, must be booked at least a day ahead.

Lisfoz (☎ 233 429 203; Rua Dr FA Dinis; mains €7-11; lunch & dinner Tue-Sun) The star dish of this popular glass-sided restaurant is the *sardinha assada* (roasted sardine), though it does plenty of other traditional fish/seafood dishes.

Restaurante Caçarola II (☎ 233 426 930; Rua Bernardo Lopes 85; mains €9-15; lunch & dinner Mon-Sat) A popular, hectic *marisqueira* (seafood restaurant) strewn with fishing tackle and dishing up good-value fish platters that have been translated into intriguing names like 'dog-whelks' or 'frogfish rice'. It also has tables on the pedestrian boulevard outside.

Other options:

Emanha (☎ 233 426 567; Esplanada Silva Guimarães; 8am-midnight) Simple snacks plus 40 flavours of ice cream on a sunny patio overlooking the sprawling beach.

Mercado municipal (Passeio Infante Dom Henrique; Mon-Sat) Opposite the Jardim Municipal.

Drinking

Mr Jingle (Esplanada Silva Guimarães; 2pm-2am Mon-Sat, to 4am in summer) The beachfront patio here is the best spot for a pint at sundown.

Rolls (Rua Poeta Acácio Antunes 1E; daily) Figueira's best bars include Rolls, a grungy, international-style pub that also serves up burgers and Guinness.

Zeitgeist Caffé (Rua Francisco António Dinis 82; 4pm-4am) Near Rolls is the glamorous Zeitgeist, which features lounge, ambient and jazz (plus live music most Sundays).

Entertainment

Discoteca Pessidónio (☎ 233 435 637; Condados, Tavarede; midnight-4am Fri & Sat) Big, popular, and offering standard club music 2km out in Tavarede, Pessidónio is about 400m east of the Parque Municipal de Campismo.

Três Chaminés (☎ 233 407 920; www.3chamines.com in Portuguese; Caceira; midnight-6am Sat, bowling 6pm-1am Mon-Thu, 6pm-3am Fri, 3pm-4am Sat, 3pm-1am Sun) This huge industrial-looking place is 4km east of town on the EN111 towards Coimbra. It encompasses bowling, paintball and a disco on Fridays and Saturdays that largely features Latin-American rhythms.

Casino da Figueira (☎ 233 408 400; www.casinofigueira.pt; Rua Bernardo Lopes; 3pm-3am) Almost glamorous, this casino shimmers in neon and acrylic, and is crawling with cash-laden holidaymakers in search of a quick buck. It has roulette and slot machines, plus a sophisticated piano bar with live music after 11pm most nights. Dress up at night – beach attire, thongs (flip-flops) or sports shoes may keep you out.

Centro de Artes e Espectaculos (☎ 233 407 200; www.cae.pt in Portuguese) Behind the museum, this is the venue for most big-name bands, theatre and art-house cinema. Check the website or pick up a schedule at the turismo.

Getting There & Away

BUS

Figueira's main terminal is served by two long-distance companies. **Moisés Correia de Oliveira** (☎ 233 426 703) has at least hourly service (fewer on weekends) via Montemor-o-Velho to Coimbra (€3.40, 1¼ hours).

Rede Expressos (www.rede-expressos.pt) has buses to Lisbon (€10.80, 2¾ hours, three daily) and to Leiria (€7.20, one hour, two daily). A privately run express bus runs to Porto (€10, two hours) via Aveiro each weekday from the **AFGA travel agency** (☎ 233 402 222; Avenida Miguel Bombarda 79).

For information on transport to local beaches, see opposite.

TRAIN

Train connections to/from Coimbra (€1.70, 70 minutes, hourly) are superior to buses. There are services via Leiria (€4.80, 80 minutes, five to six daily), with continuing service to Sintra, where you can pick up trains to Lisbon. You can also change in Coimbra for frequent connections to Porto and Lisbon.

Getting Around

Joalto (☎ 233 422 648) runs buses (€0.85) from the train station past the *mercado municipal* and turismo to Buarcos.

AROUND FIGUEIRA DA FOZ

Montemor-o-Velho

A stunning hilltop **castle** (admission free; 10am-7pm Tue-Sun Sep-May, 9am-midnight Tue-Sun Jun-Aug) rises like a brooding ghost above marshy fields 16km east of Figueira da Foz, on the N111 to Coimbra. Fortified by both Romans and Moors, it served as a royal retreat in the 14th century. Though forbidding from afar, it's surprisingly tame inside – full of neat lawns and flowerbeds and sheltering the charming Manueline **Igreja de Santa Maria de Alcáçova**. Now there's also a stylishly contemporary café, a fine place to while away an afternoon or evening. Views across the surrounding estuary are impressive, and kids will make a beeline for the unfenced battlements to stage their own battles.

The village itself is small, though there are restaurants and parking beneath the castle's southern and eastern walls. **Residencial Abade João** (☎ 239 687 010; Rua dos Combatentes da Grande Guerra 15; s/d €37.50/42.50) is a beautiful old town house for anyone looking to hang their hat.

Trains between Coimbra (€1.45, 45 minutes) and Figueira da Foz (€1.35, 30 minutes) stop here every hour or two. Moisés Correia de Oliveira buses between Coimbra (€2.75, 55 minutes) and Figueira (€2, 30 minutes) stop five to eight times daily (but just twice on Sunday).

PRAIA DE MIRA

For a few days of sunny, windblown torpor, you couldn't ask for a better stretch of the Atlantic than that between Figueira da Foz and Aveiro. In the 50km of mostly deserted coastline, there are two major access points to the sea, **Praia da Tocha** and **Praia de Mira**. If you fancy seafood, beer and indoor plumbing, go to Praia de Mira.

Sandwiched between a long, clean beach and a canal-fed lagoon, the village of Praia de Mira has little – aside from the candy-striped **Igreja da Nossa Senhora Conceição** on the beachfront – to distract you from the main business in hand: sun, sea and seafood. And plenty of it. You may still glimpse local fishermen hauling in their colourful *xavega* boats in summer, though they're a vanishing species.

Orientation & Information

Praia de Mira is 7km west of Mira on the N109, itself 35km north of Figueira da Foz.

Praia de Mira's axis is Avenida Cidade de Coimbra (also called the N342). The erratic **turismo** (☎ 231 472 566; fax 231 458 185; Avenida da Barrinha; 9am-12.30pm & 2-5.30pm), 450m south of Avenida Cidade de Coimbra beside the lagoon, shares a wooden house with a little ethnographic exhibition.

Sleeping

Rates given here are for the high season (mid-July to August). At other times the rates drop by up to 40%. The town abounds in summer *quartos*, typically €25 to €40 per double. Watch for signs, or ask at the turismo.

Orbitur (☎ 231 471 234; info@orbitur.pt; adult/car €4.40/4, tent €4.60-5.90; Feb-Nov) This well-equipped, shady site is 500m past the municipal camping ground, at the southern end of the lagoon. Four-person bungalows are available from €62; bikes can also be hired.

Pousada da juventude (☎ 231 471 199; www.movijovem.pt; dm €7, d €19; Jun-Aug) Super-cheap but bare-bones – no kitchen or restaurant. It's about 200m from the beach in a pine area south of town. Reception is open from 8am to noon and 6pm to midnight.

Residencial Canadian Star (☎ 231 471 516; Avenida da Barrinha; d with breakfast €45) There is nothing particularly Canadian here, but this place facing the lagoon has modest rates for clean if rather lugubrious and uninspired digs. Balconied rooms with a lagoon view cost €5 more.

Residencial Maçarico (☎ 231 471 114; www.residencial-macarico.com; Avenida Arrais Batista Cêra; d €60) The closest Mira comes to charm, this attractive yellow villa sits back from the beachfront promenade just south of the main street into town. The trim rooms have tiled floors, and for an extra €10 you can get a little balcony with sea views.

Residencial Senhora da Conceição (☎ 231 471 645; www.residencial-sra-conceicao.pt.vu in Portuguese; Avenida Cidade de Coimbra; d €65; P) This new place, on the right just before you cross the lagoon, offers simple but bright and impeccable rooms, a few with lagoon views.

Eating & Drinking

Restaurante Canas (☎ 231 471 296; Avenida da Barrinha; mains €5-9; ⏲ lunch & dinner Mon-Sat) In a no-frills setting opposite the turismo, with some outside seating.

Restaurante Caçanito (☎ 231 472 678; Avenida do Mar; mains €7-10; ⏲ lunch & dinner) Right on the beach, the Caçanito is decorated predictably with rough timber and fishnets, but recompenses with great views and good grilled seafood.

Restaurante A Cozinha (☎ 231 471 190; Avenida da Barrinha 13; mains €8-11; ⏲ lunch & dinner Tue-Sun) This slightly upscale, lagoon-side place, in a modern apartment block about 100m south of the main road, serves up simple, fresh and excellent seafood. Recommended.

Sixties Bar (Travessa Arrais Manuel Patrão; ⏲ 9pm-2am, to 4am Fri & Sat) On the other hand, the Sixties Bar is an old-school Irish-flavoured pub on the first street back from the seafront.

Bar Por do Sol (Rua Raul Brandão; ⏲ 7am-4am Jun-Aug, 1pm-4am Sep-May) Cold beer and late-night internet access near the beach.

Getting There & Away

Joalto runs direct Praia de Mira buses from Aveiro's train station (€3.25, 50 minutes, three to four daily). However, most coastal transport stops inland only at Mira (7km east). There is also service from Figueira da Foz to Mira (€2.90, one hour, about five daily).

Taxis (☎ 231 471 257; Praia de Mira) can ferry you between Mira and Praia de Mira.

AVEIRO

pop 56,500

The Venice of Portugal? OK, that's a stretch, but Aveiro (uh-*vey*-roo) is an intriguing little city set on a series of canals at the mouth of Rio Vouga. A prosperous sea port in the early 16th century, it suffered a ferocious storm in the 1570s that blocked the river mouth, closing it to ocean-going ships and creating fever-breeding marshes. Over the next two centuries, Aveiro's population shrunk by three-quarters. But in 1808 the Barra Canal forged a passage back to the sea, and within a century Aveiro was rich once more, as evidenced by the spate of Art Nouveau houses that still define the town's old centre.

These days, the town's canals and humpback bridges give it a genteel, Dutch feel that make it worth a day's poking around. It also sits amid the Ria – an extraordinary network of wetlands that are rich in birdlife. Consider a ride on a high-prowed *moliceiro* – boats used in harvesting of *molico* (seaweed) for use as fertiliser – which wend their way through the town's canals as well as out into the Ria.

Orientation

From the *azulejo*-clad train station it's a 1km stroll southwest down the main street, Avenida Dr Lourenço Peixinho and Rua Viana do Castelo (together called Avenida by all), to Praça Humberto Delgado, straddling the Canal Central. Nearby are the turismo and a pedestrianised centre dominated by the flashy Forum Aveiro shopping mall.

Information

Aveiro Digital (⏲ 9am-8pm Mon-Fri, 10am-7pm Sat) Free internet.
Hospital (☎ 234 378 300; Avenida Artur Ravada)
Police station (☎ 234 400 290; Praça Marquês de Pombal)
Net7 (internet per hr €2; ⏲ 9.30am-midnight Mon-Sat, 3pm-midnight Sun)
Main post office (Praça Marquês de Pombal; ⏲ 8.30am-6.30pm Mon-Fri, 9am-12.30pm Sat)
Regional turismo (☎ 234 423 680; www.rotadaluz.pt; Rua João Mendonça 8; ⏲ 9am-8pm Jun-Sep, 9am-7pm Oct-May) Very helpful office in an Art Nouveau gem beside the Canal Central.

Sights

MUSEU DE AVEIRO

This fine, if somewhat single-minded, **museum** (☎ 234 423 297; Avenida Santa Joana Princesa; adult/child/youth 14-25 & senior €2/free/1, 10am-2pm Sun free; ⏲ 10am-5.30pm Tue-Sun), in the former Mosteiro de Jesus opposite the Catedral de São Domingos, owes its finest treasures to Princesa (later beatified as Santa) Joana, daughter of Afonso V. In 1472, 11 years after the convent was founded, Joana 'retired' here and, though forbidden to take full vows, she stayed until her death in 1490.

Her tomb, a 17th-century masterpiece of marble mosaic, sits in an equally lavish baroque chancel decorated with *azulejos* depicting her life. The museum's paintings include a late-15th-century portrait of her, attributed to Nuno Gonçalves.

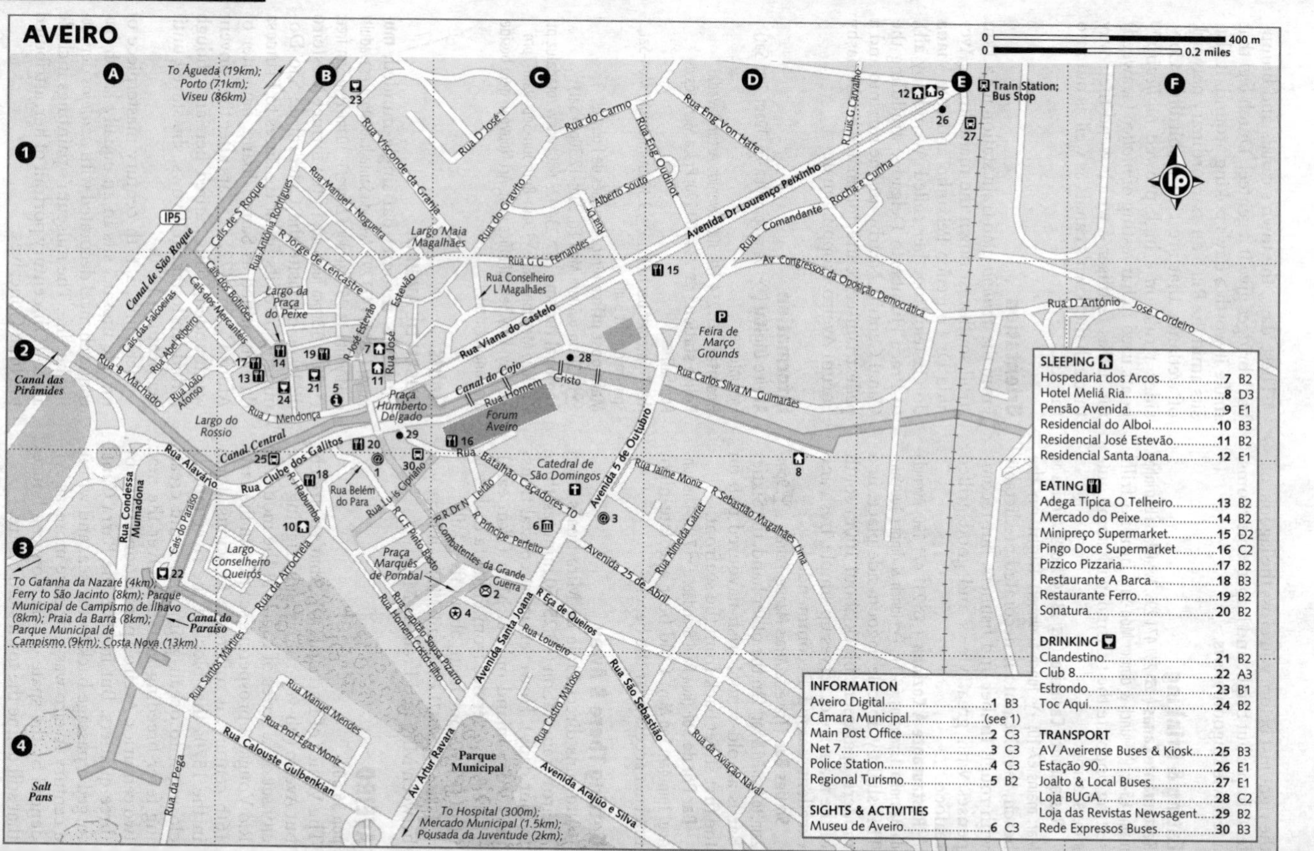
AVEIRO
0 400 m
0 0.2 miles
SLEEPING
Hospedaria dos Arcos 7 B2
Hotel Meliá Ria 8 D3
Pensão Avenida 9 E1
Residencial do Alboi 10 B3
Residencial José Estevão 11 B2
Residencial Santa Joana 12 E1
EATING
Adega Típica O Telheiro 13 B2
Mercado do Peixe 14 B2
Minipreço Supermarket 15 D2
Pingo Doce Supermarket 16 C2
Pizzico Pizzaria 17 B2
Restaurante A Barca 18 B3
Restaurante Ferro 19 B2
Sonatura 20 B2
DRINKING
Clandestino 21 B2
Club 8 22 A3
Estrondo 23 B1
Toc Aqui 24 B2
TRANSPORT
AV Aveirense Buses & Kiosk 25 B3
Estação 90 26 E1
Joalto & Local Buses 27 E1
Loja BUGA 28 C2
Loja das Revistas Newsagent 29 B2
Rede Expressos Buses 30 B3
INFORMATION
Aveiro Digital 1 B3
Câmara Municipal (see 1)
Main Post Office 2 C3
Net 7 3 C3
Police Station 4 C3
Regional Turismo 5 B2
SIGHTS & ACTIVITIES
Museu de Aveiro 6 C3
Train Station; Bus Stop
To Águeda (19km); Porto (71km); Viseu (86km)
To Gafanha da Nazaré (4km); Ferry to São Jacinto (8km); Parque Municipal de Campismo de Ílhavo (8km); Praia da Barra (8km); Parque Municipal de Campismo (9km); Costa Nova (13km)
To Hospital (300m); Mercado Municipal (1.5km); Pousada da Juventude (2km);
Canal das Pirâmides
Canal de São Roque
Canal Central
Canal do Cojo
Canal do Paraíso
Salt Pans
Parque Municipal
Forum Aveiro
Feira de Março Grounds
Catedral de São Domingos
Praça Humberto Delgado
Praça Marquês de Pombal
Largo do Rossio
Largo da Praça do Peixe
Largo Maia Magalhães
Largo Conselheiro Queirós
Avenida Dr Lourenço Peixinho
Avenida 5 de Outubro
Avenida Santa Joana
Avenida 25 de Abril
Avenida Araújo e Silva
Av Artur Ravara
Rua Viana do Castelo
Rua São Sebastião
Rua Calouste Gulbenkian
Rua Condessa Mumadona
Rua Alavário
Rua da Arrochela
Rua Santos Mártires
Rua da Pega
Rua Clube dos Galitos
Rua Eng Von Hafe
Rua Eng Oudinot
Rua do Carmo
Rua Visconde da Granja
Rua D José I
Rua do Gravito
Cristo
Rua Homem
Rua Batalhão Caçadores 10
Rua Carlos Silva M Guimarães
Rua Comandante Rocha e Cunha
Av Congressos da Oposição Democrática
Rua D António José Cordeiro
Rua Jaime Moniz
R Sebastião Magalhães Lima
Rua Almeida Garret
Rua da Aviação Naval
Rua Castro Matoso
Rua Loureiro
R Eça de Queiros
Rua Manuel Mendes
Rua Prof Egas Moniz
Rua Capitão Sousa Pizarro
Rua Homem Costa Filho
R Combatentes da Grande Guerra
R Príncipe Perfeito
R Dr N Leitão
R C F Pinto Basto
Rua Belém do Para
Rua Luís Cipriano
R J Rabumba
Rua J Mendonça
R José Estevão
Rua José Estevão
Rua Conselheiro L Magalhães
Rua G G Fernandes
Alberto Souto
Rua Dr
Rua Manuel L Nogueira
R Jorge de Lencastre
Rua António Rodrigues
Cais de S Roque
Cais dos Botirões
Cais dos Mercantéis
Cais das Falcoeiras
Rua Abel Ribeiro
Rua João Afonso
Rua B Machado
Cais do Paraíso
R Luís G Carvalho
IP5

RESERVA NATURAL DAS DUNAS DE SÃO JACINTO

Stretching north from São Jacinto to Ovar, between the sea and the N327, is an excellent little 6.7-sq-km wooded nature reserve, equipped with trails and bird-watching hides. Entry is via an **interpretive centre** (☎ 234 331 282; http://camarinha.aveiro-digital.net in Portuguese; 9am-noon & 2-5pm Fri-Wed) on the N327. To minimise the impact on wildlife, you can only enter between 9am and 9.30am or between 2pm and 2.30pm for a maximum stay of 2½ hours, and you must book ahead. There's usually a guide on hand to give a free tour, or materials available to help you make the best of a visit on your own.

To get here, take a Forte da Barra bus from the **AV Aveirense kiosk** (☎ 234 423 513; Rua Clube dos Galitos) to the end of the line from where a small passenger ferry crosses to the port of São Jacinto (combined boat-and-bus ticket: adult €2.60, child four to 10 and seniors €1.30). Ask at the turismo for current timetables.

From São Jacinto port the reserve entrance is 1.3km down the Torreira road. Note that by road the entrance is 50km from Aveiro!

Activities

Though not the Costa de Prata's finest beaches, the surfing venues of **Praia da Barra** and **Costa Nova**, 13km west of Aveiro, are good for a day's outing. The prettier Costa Nova has a beach-side street lined with cafés, kitsch gift shops and picturesque candy-striped cottages.

AV Aveirense buses go via Gafanha da Nazaré to Costa Nova (€1.75, hourly) from the kiosk on Rua Clube dos Galitos; the last bus returns at around midnight.

Wilder and more remote is **Praia de São Jacinto**, on the northern side of the lagoon. The vast beach of sand dunes is a 1.5km walk from São Jacinto port, through a residential area at the back of town.

Aveirosub (☎ 919 315 504, 961 409 489; www.aveirosub.com; Avenida José Estevão 724, Gafanha da Nazaré) offers scuba-diving classes (36 50-minute sessions, about half in the sea, for around €400) as well as individual dives (from €18).

One-hour private **moliceiros trips** (adult/child under 6/child 7-12 €8/free/3.80) around the Ria are available subject to passenger numbers; tickets are available at the turismo. Two-hour *moliceiros* trips to São Jacinto may also be on offer in July and August; ask at the turismo.

Festivals & Events

Feira de Março Held from 25 March to 25 April, this festival dates back 5½ centuries. Nowadays it features everything from folk music to rock concerts.

Festa da Ria Aveiro celebrates its canals and *moliceiros* from mid-July to the end of August. Highlights include folk dancing and a *moliceiros* race.

Festas do Município Aveiro sees two weeks of merry-making around 12 May in honour of Santa Joana.

Sleeping

Summer accommodation is even tighter than parking here; consider booking a week or so ahead in peak season.

BUDGET

Parque Municipal de Campismo (☎ /fax 234 331 220; adult/tent & car €2/1; Mar-Nov) The nearest and cheapest camping ground is this city-run and slightly tatty park at São Jacinto, 2.5km from the pier along the Torreira road.

Parque Municipal de Campismo de Ílhavo (☎ 234 369 425; www.campingbarra.com in Portuguese; Rua Diogo Cão, Praia da Barra; adult/car €3.05/2.70, tent €3.30-4.85; year-round) A well-equipped, sandy and flat site next to the beach about 10km from Aveiro.

Orbitur São Jacinto (☎ 234 838 284; info@orbitur.pt; adult/car €3.80/3.60, tent €3.80-5.30; Feb-Nov) Around 2.5km further on, Orbitur is a very nice site with more shade and better facilities (including an ATM) and is close to the sea. There's no bus service along this road; see Reserva Natural das Dunas de São Jacinto (left) for transport details.

Pousada da Juventude (☎ 234 420 536; www.movijovem.pt; Rua das Pombas 182; dm €7, d €19;) Aveiro's youth hostel, 1.5km south of the centre, is basic and rather clinical.

Hospedaria dos Arcos (☎ 234 383 130; Rua José Estevão 47; s/d with breakfast €23/35) This place has a just-like-grandma's-house atmosphere, with several floors of spotless little rooms and a generous breakfast.

MIDRANGE

Pensão Avenida (☎ 234 428 792; Avenida Dr Lourenço Peixinho; d with/without bathroom €40/30) In a handsome Art Nouveau building conveniently just across from the train station, this place offers new management and bright rooms that, at the time of writing, were in the process of being fixed up simply but tastefully.

Residencial Santa Joana (☎ 234 428 604; fax 234 428 602; Avenida Dr Peixinho 227; s/d €30/40) In a modern building very near the train station, this place has mostly remodelled, modern rooms, though expense was definitely spared. Still, it's clean, convenient and good value.

Residencial do Alboi (☎ 234 380 390; www.residencial-alboi.com; Rua da Arrochela 6; s/d €41/55; 💻) Down a quiet lane in the heart of town, this place has attractive if rather standard-issue midrange digs as well as lots of polished granite to lend an air of dignity.

Residencial José Estevão (☎ 234 383 964; Rua João Estevão 23; d €65; ❄) A fine old town house outside and a gleaming new hotel inside, this little place offers up a dozen snug but comfortable, spotless rooms.

TOP END

Hotel Meliá Ria (☎ 234 401 000; www.solmelia.com; Cais da Fonte Nova; s/d €95/105; P ❄ 💻) The city's newest and most chic sleep sits alone along the main canal. Its cubelike exterior is shrouded in intriguing brises-soleil, while inside it's all contemporary lines and business-friendly comforts.

Eating

Sonatura (☎ 234 424 474; Rua Clube dos Galitos 6; set meals €4.75-7; 🕑 lunch Mon-Fri; V) Wholesome, lovingly prepared vegetarian dishes are proffered at the self-service bar here. Even nonvegetarians will love seeing so many vegetables on a Portuguese plate, and at earthy prices.

Pizzico Pizzaria (☎ 234 424 509; Largo da Praça do Peixe 24; pizzas €6-8; 🕑 lunch & dinner) Clean, modern interior and affordable designer pizza draws in the young and hungry.

Restaurante Ferro (☎ 234 422 214; Rua Tenente Resende 30; dishes €7-11; 🕑 lunch & dinner Mon-Sat, lunch Sun) Energetic and popular, this bustling spot is great for a quick lunch stop, with lots of fish and meat dishes, plus omelettes.

Adega Típica O Telheiro (☎ 234 429 473; Largo da Praça do Peixe 20-21; mains €8-13; 🕑 lunch & dinner Sun-Fri) This cosy, popular place has hams hanging from the low wooden ceiling, long tables, red wine by the jug, grilled seafood and reasonable prices. Try the *sopa de mer*, a great, warming seafood chowder. Or just park yourself at the long bar and chew the fat with local barflies.

our pick **Mercado do Peixe** (☎ 234 383 511; Largo da Praça do Peixe; mains €8-18; 🕑 lunch daily, dinner Mon-Sat) Perched above the city's homely fish market is its most upmarket – and best – restaurant. The setting is lovely, with wood-and-metal industrial-chic décor and large windows looking onto the canals and adjacent square. And the seafood is exquisite, from the paella-like *arroz de marisco* to the *ensopado da raia* (ray stew). There are also €5 lunch specials Monday to Friday. Reservations recommended.

Restaurante A Barca (☎ 234 426 024; Rua José Rabumba 5a; mains €9-13; 🕑 lunch & dinner Mon-Fri, lunch Sat) This restaurant has a casual atmosphere and a choice of fish, fish and more fish – all fresh from the nearby market, of course.

Self-caterers can choose from the **mercado municipal** (🕑 Tue-Sat) about 500m further south beyond the Pousada da Juventude, and supermarkets including **Pingo Doce** (🕑 9am-10pm) in the Forum Aveiro mall and **Minipreço** (🕑 9am-8pm Mon-Sat, 9am-1pm & 3-7pm Sun) on the Avenida.

Drinking

With a big student population and a generally party-friendly culture, nightlife is quite raucous in this small city.

Estrondo (☎ 234 383 366; Cais de São Roque 74; 🕑 Mon-Sat) This is a smart wooden-fronted bar for the well-heeled.

Toc Aqui (Largo da Praça do Peixe; 🕑 8pm-2am) This raucous, friendly pub opposite the fish market regularly hosts live music of various types.

Clandestino (Rua do Tenente Resende 35; 🕑 9pm-2am Mon-Sat) Smoky little pub attracting an alternative crowd with chilled-out music and imported DJs.

Club 8 (Cais do Paraíso 19; 🕑 Wed-Sat) The town's all-purpose disco, with varying music and clientele.

Getting There & Away

BUS

Few long-distance buses terminate here – there isn't even a bus station.

Rede Expressos has about three daily services to/from Lisbon (€12.70, four hours) and at least one daily to Coimbra (€5, 45 minutes). Get tickets and timetables at the **Loja das Revistas newsagent** (Praça Humberto Delgado; 🕑 7am-8pm) and catch the bus around the corner.

Joalto goes three to four times a day (fewer at weekends) to Figueira da Foz (€3.70, two hours) from Rua Viana do Castelo and the train station. Several daily buses also serve Praia de Mira (€3.25, 50 minutes).

TRAIN

Aveiro is within Porto's *suburbano* network which means there are commuter trains to/from Porto at least every half-hour (€1.95

40 to 60 minutes); there are slightly faster IC links (€9). There are also at least half-hourly links to Coimbra (€4.80, one hour) and several daily IC trains to Lisbon (€16, 2¾ hours).

Getting Around

Parking is awful and isn't getting any better. Fight your way into the centre, past the turismo to the Largo do Rossio car park, and leave your car there for the duration. The turismo can give you a map showing other car parks.

Local bus routes converge on the Avenida and the train station. A *bilhete de cidade* (city ticket) from a kiosk or *tabacaria* costs €1.20 for two journeys; from the driver they're €1.40 for one trip. The ticket source closest to the train station is a *pastelaria* (pastry or cake shop) called **Estação 90** (Avenida Dr Lourenço Peixinho 352).

Aveiro runs a pioneering free-bike scheme, Bicycleta de Utilização Gratuita de Aveiro (BUGA). Give your ID details at the **Loja BUGA** (🕑 10am-7pm) kiosk beside the Canal do Cojo, take a bike and ride it within the designated town limits, and return it to the kiosk before it shuts, all for free. This system may be changing, though, so check first at the turismo.

BEIRA BAIXA

Beira Baixa closely resembles neighbouring Alentejo, with hospitable locals, fierce summer heat and rolling plains that stretch out to the horizon. It's also home to sprawling agricultural estates, humble farming hamlets and several stunning fortress towns that for centuries guarded the vulnerable plains from Spanish aggression.

CASTELO BRANCO

pop 33,000 / elevation 360m

Just walk up to the remains of Castelo Branco's old fortress and you immediately appreciate its strategic importance – the heights afford sweeping views across the surrounding plains to the Spanish border 20km away. Unfortunately, its position also made it a regular target of aggression, and as a result much of its historic fabric has been destroyed. Still, there are some charming medieval streets clustered around the ruined *castelo* (castle), and the prosperous provincial capital has built itself an attractive series of tree-lined squares and

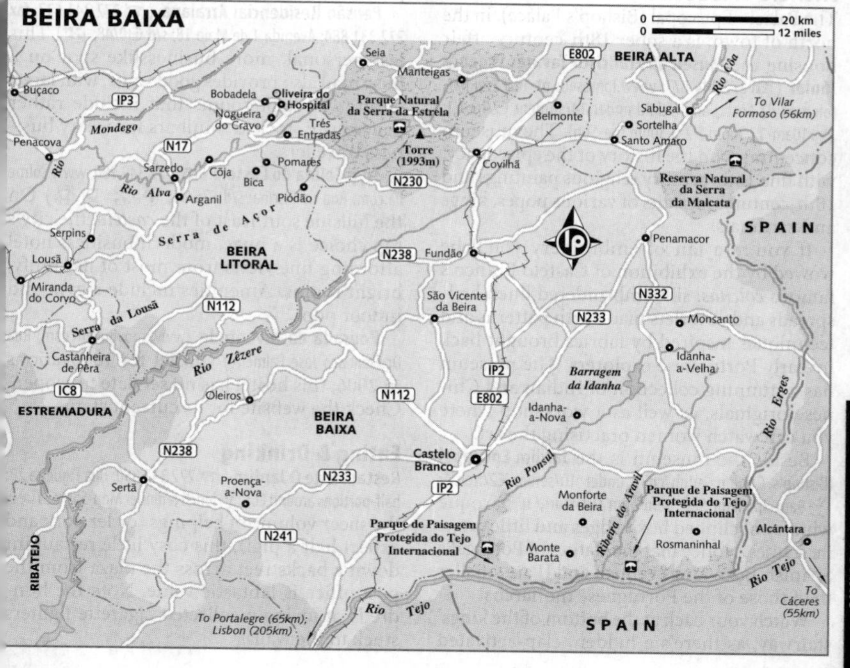

boulevards. It's also a convenient base to visit the ancient village of Monsanto (opposite) and Idanha-a-Velha (p330).

Orientation

From the bus station, turn right down Rua do Saibreiro to central Alameda da Liberdade. From the train station the Alameda is 500m north on Avenida Nuno Álvares.

Information

Cyber Centro Municipal (Praça do Município; internet per hr €1; ⌚ 9am-10pm Mon-Fri) Across the plaza from the turismo in a courtyard behind the yellow façade.

Parque Natural do Tejo Internacional (☎ 272 348 140; www.icn.pt in Portuguese; 3rd fl, Avenida 1 de Maio 99) One block southeast of the turismo.

Post office (Rua da Sé; ⌚ 8.30am-6.30pm Mon-Fri, 9am-12.30pm Sat)

Turismo (☎ 272 330 339; turismo.cmcb@mail.telepac.pt; Alameda da Liberdade; ⌚ 9.30am-7.30pm Mon-Fri, 9.30am-1pm & 2.30-6pm Sat & Sun) Slick, new quarters on the town's main thoroughfare at the southern end of the historic centre.

Sights

PALÁCIO EPISCOPAL

The Palácio Episcopal (Bishop's Palace), in the north of town, is a sober 18th-century affair housing the **Museu de Francisco Tavares Proença Júnior** (☎ 272 344 277; www.ipmuseus.pt; Rua Frei Bartolomeu da Costa; adult/child under 14/student €2/free/1; ⌚ 10am-12.30pm & 2-5.30pm Tue-Sun). The museum concentrates on the history of the episcopacy, with fine 16th-century religious paintings and 18th-century portraits of various popes, kings and cardinals.

If you're a fan of embroidery you'll be wowed by the exhibition of Castelo Branco's famous *colchas:* silk-embroidered linen bedspreads and coverlets made with patterns and techniques inspired by fabrics brought back by early Portuguese explorers. The museum has a stunning collection of Indian and Chinese originals, as well as a workshop where you can watch women practising the art.

Beside the museum is the **Jardim Episcopal** (Bishop's Garden; adult/child under 10/senior €2/free/1; ⌚ 9am-7pm Apr-Sep, 9am-5pm Oct-Mar), a baroque whimsy of clipped box hedges and little granite statues. Notice that the statues of Portugal's Spanish-born kings Felipe I and II are smaller than those of the Portuguese monarchs!

Watch your back at the bottom of the kings' stairway, as there's a hidden, clap-activated fountain. It was built by a loutish 18th-century bishop who liked to surprise maidens by soaking their petticoats. The attendant will show you where to clap.

CASTELO

There's little left of the castle, which was built by the Knights Templar in the 13th century and extended by Dom Dinis. However, the Miradouro de São Gens garden, which has supplanted the walls, offers grand views over town and countryside. The old lanes that lead back down to the town centre are very picturesque.

Sleeping

Parque de Campismo de Castelo Branco (☎ 272 341 615; adult/tent/car €2/1.75/1.75; ⌚ Jan-Nov) About 3km from the centre of town, this dusty site has scattered trees, mostly grassy pitches and basic facilities.

Pensão Império (☎ /fax 272 341 720; Rua Prazeres 20; s/d €22/32; ❄) Best of the budget *pensões,* this friendly, bright, well-kept place can be found in a backstreet near the post office. It's run by chirpy folks who are eager to please, and the plain rooms are good value.

Pensão Residencial Arraiana (☎ 272 341 637; fax 272 331 884; Avenida 1 de Maio 18; s/d €30/48; ❄) This less personal, more businesslike spot on a busy road also provides good value, with large, clean, well-kept rooms that include rather generously stocked minibars for weary business travellers.

Tryp Colina do Castelo (☎ 272 349 280; www.solmelia.com; Rua da Piscina; s/d €75/85; P ❄ 💻 🏊) On the hillside southeast of the *castelo,* the city's top choice is a huge, modern business hotel affording fine views from most of its comfy, bright rooms. Amenities include a gym and indoor pool.

Pousada da Juventude (www.movijovem.com; Rua Dr Francisco José Palmeiro) Closed for renovations in 2006, this hostel has no set date to reopen. Check the website for its current status.

Eating & Drinking

Restaurante O Jardim (☎ 272 342 850; Rua Figueira 29; half-portions around €6; ⌚ lunch & dinner Mon-Sat) Given the sheer volume of helpings (order pork and expect half a pig!), this cosy little restaurant down a backstreet across the plaza from the post office is fantastic value. Note the hundreds of lovingly collected cigarette lighters stuck to the walls.

Kalifa (☎ 272 344 246; Rua Cadetes de Toledo 10; mains €8-13; ⏲ lunch & dinner) Very large, very good, very popular, and very generous with its portions, Kalifa is something of a Castelo Branco institution for hearty, regional fare. There's also a shady, lively patio for coffee or drinks. It's just off Alameda da Liberdade near the turismo.

Praça Velha (☎ 272 328 640; Largo Luís de Camões; dishes €12-18.50; ⏲ lunch & dinner Tue-Sat, lunch Sun; P) For a proper treat, make a beeline here. Praça Velha is in a former Knights Templar abode in the old town and has a low wooden ceiling, stone floors and pillars, and a long buffet table heaped with platters. The menu lives up to its grand setting. Try the *peito de pato flambado com aguardente* (duck-breast flambé) or the fantastic Sunday buffet (€18.50).

Ambienta Café (Alameda da Liberdade; dishes €12-16; ⏲ lunch & dinner 7am-2am Mon-Wed, 7am-4am Thu-Sat, 8am-midnight Sun) This sleek, bright, brand-new café just next to the turismo specialises in fancy teas. It's the place to be seen on warm nights.

Self-caterers can find supplies, including the *queijo de ovelha* (sheep's cheese) for which this region is famous, in the **mercado municipal** (Avenida 1 de Maio) or nearby **Pingo Doce** (Avenida 1 de Maio; ⏲ 8.30am-9pm).

Getting There & Away

BUS

Castelo Branco is served by **Rede Expressos** (☎ 272 340 120; www.rede-expressos.pt), with direct service to Coimbra (€10.60, 2½ hours, about three daily), Lisbon (€10.80, 3½ hours, at least six daily), Guarda (€8.30, 1½ hours, at least six daily), Portalegre (€8.70, 1½ hours, once or twice daily), Covilhã (€4, one hour, at least six daily) and Faro (€18.30, six hours, at least twice daily).

TRAIN

Castelo Branco is on the Lisbon–Guarda line, with six trains daily from Lisbon, including two IC services (€13.50, 2¾ hours), and about four slower regional services (€11.30, 3½ hours).

PARQUE NATURAL DO TEJO INTERNACIONAL

Still one of Portugal's wildest landscapes, this 230-sq-km natural park shadows the Rio Tejo and the watersheds of three of its tributaries: the Rio Ponsul, Ribeira do Aravil and Rio Erges. While not aesthetically remarkable, it shelters some of the country's rarest bird species, including black storks, Bonelli's eagles, royal eagles, Egyptian vultures, black vultures and griffon vultures. The park was established in 2000, after a major push by private environmental organisation Quercus (p66).

Information

The park headquarters are in Castelo Branco (opposite), where you can get a Portuguese-language brochure with good background information and maps of two marked trails that you can hike in about three hours.

For more information, your best bet is **Quercus** (☎ 272 324 272; www.quercus.pt; Travessa da Ferradura 14, Castelo Branco). At Castelo Branco's turismo you can buy Quercus' 250-page *Guia de Percursos Tejo Internacional,* a guide (in Portuguese) to regional geology, climate, flora and fauna, villages, trails and transport.

Quercus runs bird-watching, walking and other programmes. Basic accommodation is available at Rosmaninhal and Monte Barata; for details contact **Paulo Monteiro** (☎ 277 477 463) at Quercus.

MONSANTO

pop 200 / elevation 600m

In 1938 the Salazar dictatorship held a national competition to identify the country's most 'Portuguese' village. Clinging perilously to a rocky promontory far above the Beira Baixa plains, Monsanto is easily the most picturesque, but it feels more Tolkien than typically Portuguese. Still, Monsanto came out on top, and it's easy to understand why.

Cottages, many of which incorporate rough boulders into their walls, seem to grow out of the mountain itself. High above them rises a craggy fortress, parts of which predate even the arrival of the Moors. And views across the plains are, simply put, astonishing. These days, goats and chickens seem to outnumber humans, though elderly women still crochet and kibitz in doorways as tourists labour past them along the village's steeply cobbled lanes.

Orientation & Information

Monsanto is so small that you need only follow the very steep path uphill to reach the castle.

Post office (Largo do Cruzeiro; ⏲ 9-11am Mon-Fri) Near the village entrance.

Turismo (☎ 277 314 642, 968 122 662; Rua Marquês da Gracioça; ⏲ 10am-1pm & 2-6pm May-Sep, 9.30am-1pm, 2-5.30pm Oct-Apr) A little further uphill along the main street.

Sights

VILLAGE

Since being honoured as the most Portuguese village, Monsanto has been largely shielded from modernisation. Several houses near the village entrance are surprisingly grand, some sporting Manueline doorways and stone crests. Halfway to the castle you'll come across the **gruta**, a snug cavern apparently once used as a drinking den – and still used as such, judging by the half-empty glasses of beer inside.

CASTELO

This formidable stone fortress seems almost to have grown out of the boulder-littered hillside that supports it. It's a hauntingly beautiful site, populated by lizards and wildflowers. Immense vistas (marred only by mobile-phone masts) include Spain to the east and the Barragem da Idanha dam to the southwest.

There was probably a fortress here even before the Romans arrived, but after Dom Sancho I booted out the Moors in the 12th century it was beefed up. Dom Dinis refortified it, but after centuries of attacks from across the border it finally fell into ruin.

Just below the entrance is a plaza used for folk dances at festival time. To the right is a ruined Renaissance church and bell tower, as well as five ancient tombs carved into the rock.

Festivals & Events

On 3 May Monsanto comes alive in the **Festa das Cruzes**, commemorating a medieval siege. The story goes that the starving villagers threw their last lonely calf over the walls, taunting their besiegers as if they had plenty to spare. And apparently, their attackers were hoodwinked, because they promptly abandoned the siege. These days, young girls throw baskets of flowers instead, after which there's dancing and singing beside the castle walls.

Sleeping & Eating

Adega Típica O Cruzeiro (☎ 277 314 528; Rua Fernando Namora 4; d €40) In a relatively modern (19th century) building just up from the town entrance, this perennial favourite was under renovations at the time of writing. Rooms are simple but spruce, and a few have amazing views. Downstairs is a rustic but attractive restaurant that serves daily specials (about €6).

Estalagem de Monsanto (☎ 277 314 471; www.estalagemdemonsanto.pt; s/d €75/80) Near the village entrance, this modern inn, built in a somewhat successful effort to mimic the stone houses around it, offers spacious, comfortable digs – a few with grandstand views. There's also a restaurant downstairs (mains €10 to €15). Beware that service can be rather lackadaisical, if good-natured, at both.

Lapa da Moura (☎ 966 150 424; Rua do Castelo 15; mains €6-7; lunch & dinner) Further up the hill near the *gruta*, the small Lapa da Moura doesn't go in much for fixed menus but has good specials; just ask what's available. It has no sign – look for the knife-and-fork symbol outside.

Café Jovem (☎ 277 314 590; Avenida Fernando Ramos Rocha 21; mains €7-9; lunch & dinner) Below the post office right at the town entrance, this humble restaurant cheerfully dishes up good-value Portuguese fare, including a bargain, three-course menu for €10. Closes Monday or Tuesday.

There are also souvenir shops selling homemade honey cakes, some laced with a wicked *aguardente* (alcoholic 'firewater').

Getting There & Away

Without a car, Monsanto can be difficult to reach. **Rede Expressos** (☎ 272 340 120; www.rede-expressos.pt) usally has one bus daily to Castelo Branco, but departure times change often (and can be inconveniently early, usually at 6.30am). There is often additional service during the school year, and an extra afternoon bus on Sundays. Ask at the turismo in either Monsanto or Castelo Branco for the latest schedules.

IDANHA-A-VELHA

While very different from hilltop Monsanto, neighbouring Idanha-a-Velha is just as extraordinary. Nestled in a remote valley of patchwork farms and olive orchards, Idanha-a-Velha was founded as the Roman city of Igaeditânia. Rome's ramparts still define the town, though it only reached its apogee under Visigothic rule. They built a cathedral and made Idanha their regional capital. It's also believed that their legendary King Wamba was born here.

Moors were next on the scene, and the cathedral was turned into a mosque during their tenure. They, in turn, were driven out by the Knights Templar in the 12th century. The mystical knights constructed the town's small but imposing keep, which sits on the remarkably preserved pedestal of a Roman temple.

How has such a tiny village managed to preserve such a grand sweep of history? It's believed that a 15th-century plague virtually wiped out its population, with survivors going on to found Idanha-a-Nova about 30km to the southwest. However, the townspeople's misfortune is our luck, since they left the town virtually intact. A few brave souls eventually returned, and today a small but hardy population of shepherds and farmers live amid the Roman, Visigothic and medieval ruins.

Information

The **turismo** (☎ 277 914 280; Rua da Sé; ⏰ 10am-12.30pm & 2-6.30pm) is built on a see-through floor over ruins of the old settlement. The office is occasionally shut when staff are on guided visits.

There is no accommodation and not even a reliable restaurant in town. Monsanto is the best bet for a hot meal and a place to bed down.

Sights

From the turismo it's a short walk to the 6th-century Visigothic **cathedral**, surrounded by a jigsaw puzzle of scattered archaeological remains; it's undergoing heavy restoration but is accessible with turismo staff. Of the frescoes within, look for the one of São Bartolomeu with what appears to be a teddy bear at his feet.

The nearby **Lagar de Varas** (admission free; ⏰ by request at turismo 10.30am-11.30am & 3-5pm) hosts an impressive olive-oil press made in the traditional way with ruddy great tree trunks providing the crushing power.

The only evidence of the Knights Templar is the **Torre des Templários**, made of massive chunks of stone and now surrounded by clucking hens. It sits on top of what was likely the pedestal of a Roman temple. Wander round the back of the village to see the Roman bridge and walls.

After all this history it's a delight to come across the **Forno Comunitário** (communal bakery; Rua do Castelo) and discover villagers sliding trays of biscuits and enormous loaves of bread into the huge stone oven, blackened from use.

Eating

Café Lafiv (☎ 277 914 180; Rua da Amoreira 1; ⏰ daily) Near the turismo, this is the village's only café, serving sandwiches and smoked sausage.

Getting There & Away

Getting to Idanha-a-Velha by bus can be difficult indeed. On schooldays, there's generally one bus daily to/from Idanha-a-Nova (40 minutes). From here, buses run to Idanha-a-Nova from Castelo Branco (€3.20, 55 minutes, two to three daily).

SORTELHA

pop 800 / elevation 760m

Sortelha is the oldest – and most haunting – of a string of fortresses guarding the frontier east of Guarda and Covilhã. Set on a rocky promontory, its fortified 12th-century castle teeters on the brink of a steep cliff, while immense walls encircle a village of great charms. Laid out in Moorish times, it remains a winning combination of stout stone cottages, sloping cobblestone streets and diminutive orchards.

These days the walled village has only a handful of permanent residents, giving it an eerie silence. A scramble along the ramparts affords views over a landscape of steep valleys and forbidding, boulder-strewn peaks that is just as beautiful and just as haunting as the town itself.

Orientation & Information

'New' Sortelha lines the Santo Amaro–Sabugal road, along which are two restaurants and several Turihab properties. The medieval hilltop fortress is a short drive, or a 10-minute walk, up one of two lanes signposted 'castelo'.

The Liga dos Amigos de Sortelha runs an unofficial turismo and handicrafts shop a block uphill from the castle ruins, but its opening hours are unpredictable.

Sights

The entrance to the fortified old village is a grand, stone Gothic **gate**. From Largo do Corro, just inside the gate, a cobbled lane leads up to the heart of the village, with a *pelourinho* (stone pillory) in front of the remains of a small **castle** to the left and the parish **church** to the right. Higher still is the **bell tower**. Climb it for a view of the entire village (but a sign begs visitors not to ring the bells), or tackle the ramparts around the village (beware precarious sections!).

Sleeping

Sortelha boasts several atmospheric Turihab properties, complete with kitchens, thick stone walls and heating. Calling a week or two ahead is essential in the high season. There is no true budget accommodation.

Casa da Vila (Rua Direita; 1-8 people €35-180) This delightful stone cottage has a privileged place within the village walls. It is owned by the same people that run Casa da Cerca and Casa do Páteo.

Casas do Campanário (☎ 271 388 198; Rua da Mesquita; d €60) Choose between a house for two people and another for up to six; ask at Bar Campanário, at the top of the village just beyond the bell tower.

Casa da Cerca (☎/fax 271 388 113; casadacerca@clix.pt; Largo de Santo António; d €85; P ✖) Just off the main road, this 17th-century house is the town's top choice. Rooms are comfortable and attractive if not luxurious, with wood floors and traditional furnishings. the same owners rent out apartments just across the courtyard in the Casa do Páteo (two/four people with kitchen €60/80).

Eating

Café Restaurante Palmeiras (☎ 271 388 260; mains €4-6) On the main road at the north end of the village, this café has zero atmosphere but lots of cheer and a shortlist of specials.

Restaurante O Celta (☎ 271 388 291; mains €6.50-14; lunch & dinner Wed-Mon) On the main road, this place offers a bigger menu and a smidge more atmosphere. Ask about the two-course menu with wine (€10).

Restaurante Dom Sancho I (☎ 271 388 267; Largo do Corro; mains €12-17; lunch & dinner) The town's top choice sits just inside the main Gothic gates. Prices for the regional cuisine are high, but the food is renowned and the dining room is snug and rustically elegant. For drinks with the local lushes, head to the humbler, downstairs bar.

Getting There & Away

Regional trains on the Covilhã–Guarda line (three to four daily) stop at Belmonte-Manteigas station, 12km to the northwest, where you can catch a local **taxi** (☎ 271 388 182) to Sortelha (around €12). There's no regular bus service.

PARQUE NATURAL DA SERRA DA ESTRELA

When people think of Portugal, they rarely conjure up images of rugged treks through sheer granite peaks. Yet at the country's very heart lies the wildly pristine Serra da Estrela, a glacially scoured plateau that is also mainland Portugal's highest mountain range.

At 1011 sq km, the Serra da Estrela Natural Park is Portugal's largest protected area, straddling both the Beira Alta and Beira Baixa provinces. Though it tops out at a modest 1993m, higher elevations are positively alpine, with rounded peaks, boulder-studded meadows and icy lakes. Lower down, the land furrows into stock trails, terraced fields chopped by drystone walls, and fragrant pine plantations.

The local people are a rare few still living in traditional one-room, stone *casais* (huts) thatched with rye straw, but now mostly concentrated in valley towns. They raise sheep, tend terraced fields, and increasingly churn out traditionally made woollies, bread and distinctive cheeses for souvenir shops.

If you come in winter, expect snow. There's even a modest ski run at Torre and a summer dry run at nearby Manteigas. Every weekend (all week in July and August) Portuguese families drive here in their thousands, creating traffic jams. But for the rest of the week, and off the main road at almost any time, the mountains are blissfully empty and beg to be explored.

Information

There are park offices at Manteigas (headquarters), Seia, Gouveia and Guarda, though not all staff speak English. Turismos at Seia, Gouveia, Manteigas, Covilhã and Guarda also have park information. The park produces a free pamphlet that provides a general introduction in English to the park as well as two suggested walks: a three-hour, 8km loop though the Vale do Rossim just northeast of Torre, and a three-hour, 7km trail between the hamlets of Loriga and Casal do Rei southeast of Torre, following the banks of the little Ribeira de Loriga.

For serious hikers, park offices sometimes have the 1:50,000 topographic map *Carta Turística: Parque Natural da Serra da Estrela* (€5.60), which includes paths, shelters and camp sites. At the time of writing, no copies were available but more were expected. A useful English-language booklet, *Discovering the Region of the Serra da Estrela* (€4.25), has trail profiles, walking times, historic notes and flora and fauna basics.

Flora and fauna details are in the booklet *Estrela: A Natural Approach* (€3.25). There are other books and brochures in English on geography, geology, medicinal plants and archaeology.

Sights & Activities

WILDLIFE

The park harbours many endangered or vulnerable species – especially feathered ones. These include the black stork, Montagu's harrier, chough, turtle dove and 10 species of bats.

Unusual animals also include the mountain gecko, and you may catch a glimpse of more

rare birds such as the peregrine falcon, eagle owl and black-shouldered kite.

The flora, too, is interesting. Popularity as medicinal remedies has put several of the park's plants in the list of endangered or vulnerable species, including mountain thrift *(Armeria transmontana)*, great yellow gentian *(Gentiana lutea)* and juniper *(Juniperus communis)*.

WALKING

Crisp air and immense vistas make this a trekking paradise, with an extensive system of well-marked and mapped trails. Surprisingly few people use them, even in summer. Walkers will feel they have the park to themselves.

While still very chilly and possibly damp, late April has the hillsides bright with wildflowers. The weather is finest from May to October. Winter is harsh, with snow at the higher elevations from November or December to April or May.

Whenever you come, be prepared for extremes: scorching summer days give way to freezing nights, and chilling rainstorms blow through with little warning. Mist is a big hazard not only because it obscures walking routes and landmarks, but because it can also stealthily chill you to the point of hypothermia. You may set out on a warm, cloudless morning and by noon find yourself fogged in and shivering, so always pack for the cold – and the wet, too.

In addition to two three-hour walks, there are three main 'official' routes, as well as branches and alternative trails. T1 runs the length of the park (about 90km), taking in every kind of terrain, including the summit of Torre. T2 and T3 (both around 80km) run respectively along the western and eastern slopes. All of the trails pass through towns and villages, each of which offers some accommodation. Many of the finest walks start around Manteigas (p337).

Within a zone of special protection (which includes almost everything above 1200m altitude), camping and fires are strictly prohibited except at designated sites, all of which are on the main trails. Cutting trees and picking plants are also forbidden.

SKIING

The ski season typically runs from January to March, with the best conditions in February. For a rundown on what's available for skiers, see the listings on Torre (p339) and Manteigas (p337).

BIKING & OTHER ACTIVITIES

Several companies specialise in outdoor activities in the park, including **Adriventura** (☎ 275 325 919, 919 462 183; www.adriventura.com), which organises groups for biking, rock-climbing, hiking and more. **Turistela** (☎ 275 319 120; www.turistela.pt) also organises biking adventures and can offer information about the new **Vodaphone Bike Park** around Torre (half-/full day €15/20). **SkiParque** (p338), east of Manteigas, offers many activities, including paragliding, rock-climbing, canoeing, biking and horse riding.

Sleeping

Useful bases with comfortable accommodations include Seia, Gouveia, Manteigas, Covilhã and Guarda. Whereas camping grounds drop their rates or close in winter, many hotels, *pensões* and *residenciais* actually increase their rates, typically from late December to March.

The park has also begun to rent out basic cabins near Manteigas in **Penhas Douradas** (per 2/4 people €30/60). For reservations, contact the park office in Manteigas (p337).

There are hostels at Penhas da Saúde and Guarda, and at least eight camping grounds near the centre of the park. Turismo Habitação properties, which are concentrated on the western slopes, can be booked through turismos or Adruse in Gouveia (p336).

Getting There & Around

Express buses run daily from Coimbra to Seia, Guarda and Covilhã, and from Aveiro, Porto and Lisbon to Guarda and Covilhã. There are daily IC trains from Lisbon and Coimbra to Guarda (plus IR services calling at Gouveia) and from Lisbon to Covilhã (with IR services on to Guarda). See town listings.

There are regular, though infrequent, bus services around the edges of the park but none directly across it.

Driving can be hairy, thanks to mist and wet or icy roads at high elevations, and stiff winds. The Gouveia–Manteigas N232 road is one of the most tortuous in all of Portugal. Be prepared for traffic jams around Torre on weekends.

SEIA

pop 6000 / elevation 532m

Two kilometres from a main highway and equipped with big shops and comfortable accommodations, Seia is a useful base for weekenders seeking an easy taste of the Serra da Estrela. It's also home to the quaint Museu do Pão (Bread Museum), one of Portugal's most-visited museums. There is little other reason to stop here, though the few square blocks that comprise its historic centre are pleasant enough.

Information

Espaço Internet (🕑 9am-7pm Mon-Fri, 2-6pm Sat) Free internet. You can get here from Avenida dos Combatentes de Grande Guerra (stairs beside the Junta de Freguesia office) or Avenida Luís Vaz de Camões (stairs at left side of Cinema Teatro Jardim).

Parque Natural da Serra da Estrela office (☎ 238 310 440; fax 238 310 441; Praça da República 28; 🕑 9am-12.30pm & 2-5.30pm Mon-Fri)

Post office (Avenida 1 de Maio; 🕑 8.30am-12.30pm & 2-6pm Mon-Fri)

Turismo (☎ 238 317 762; fax 238 317 764; Rua Pintor Lucas Marrão; 🕑 9am-12.30pm & 2-5.30pm Mon-Sat)

Sights & Activities

Museu do Pão (Museum of Bread; ☎ 238 310 760; www.museudopao.pt; admission €2; 🕑 10am-6pm Tue-Sun) has all the information you'll ever need on local bread production. The museum's highlight is the traditional-style shop, which sells local goodies (including freshly ground flour and bread baked on the premises). The museum is 1km northeast of the centre on the road to Sabugueiro.

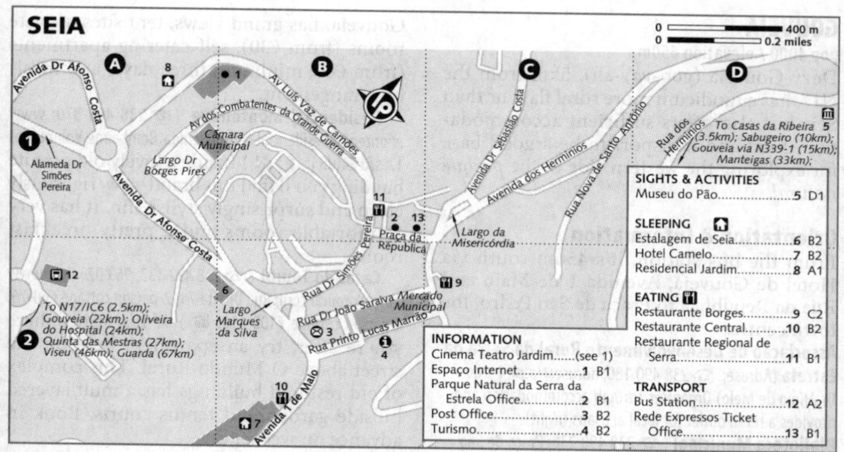

Sleeping

Residencial Jardim (☎ 238 311 414, 966 221 357; fax 238 310 091; Edifício Jardim II, Avenida Luís Vaz de Camões; d €35) Located quirkily in the lower floors of a modern apartment block, this sparsely furnished but squeaky-clean place has some rooms with nice views over the Rio Mondego valley.

Quinta das Mestras (☎ 238 602 988; www.quintadasmestras.com; N510 Nogueira do Cravo-Bobadela road; d with/without bathroom €47.50/40, cabanas with shared facilities €34) With brightly coloured, renovated farmhouse and stables 27km west of Oliveira do Hospital, this rambling farm is split by a stream and surrounded by pine forest. It has snug, peaceful private rooms, two isolated cabanas, and a shared, small kitchen (€10 extra).

Hotel Camelo (☎ 238 310 100; www.eurosol.pt; Avenida 1 de Maio 16; d from €45; P ✗ 💻 🏊) This business-class hotel has large rooms, pink-marble bathrooms, excellent children's play areas, and free off-street parking. All rooms face away from the street and most have views. There is also a very good restaurant (mains €8 to €11).

Estalagem de Seia (☎ 238 315 866; fax 238 315 538; Avenida Dr Afonso Costa; s/d with breakfast €55/58; P ✗ 🏊) The town's oldest building, an elegant 17th-century mansion of thickset stone, has been turned into an inn. The carpeted rooms, despite the antique furniture, are uninspired if plenty comfortable.

Casas da Ribeira (☎ 238 311 221, 919 660 354; www.casasdaribeira.com; Póvoa Velha; 2-/4-person cottages from €60/85) A truly charming collection of vine-draped stone cottages about 5km outside Seia on the road to Sabugueiro – well worth seeking out if you have your own vehicle. There is a two-night minimum, but prices drop significantly for additional nights.

Eating

Restaurante Central (☎ 238 314 433; Avenida 1 de Maio 12b; mains €6-8; 🕑 lunch & dinner) If all you're after is a quick, cheap feed, you'll do well at this plain-faced restaurant, near Hotel Carmelo.

Restaurante Borges (☎ 238 313 010; 1st fl, Travessa do Funchal 7; mains €7.50-14; 🕑 lunch & dinner Fri-Wed) Tucked away in a tight corner off the main street, this country-style place offers large portions of simple Portuguese fare; try its *arroz de feijão* (a stew of beans and rice).

Restaurante Regional de Serra (☎ 238 312 717; Avenida dos Combatentes da Grande Guerra 14; specialities around €9; 🕑 lunch & dinner; P) This trim place is well known for hearty regional specialities, including local cheeses and sausages as well as *chanfana à serrana* (highland goat), plus pricey seafood – some fresh from the tank.

Getting There & Away

Rede Expressos (☎ 238 313 102) has at least one direct bus to Lisbon (€14.50, 4½ hours), as well as direct service to Coimbra (€8.70, 1½ hours) and Guarda (€7.90, 70 minutes). It also has buses to Covilhã on Fridays and Sundays (€10, two hours). Rede Expressos also has a central **ticket office** (Rua da República 52).

Marques (☎ 238 312 858) also has service to Gouveia (€2.10, 25 minutes) and continuing on to Guarda (€4.40, two hours) several times each weekday.

GOUVEIA

pop 4000 / elevation 650m

Dozy Gouveia (goo-*vay*-ah), 5km from the N17, has a modicum more rural flavour than Seia but also offers sufficient accommodation, food and transport to be a good base for exploring the western side of the *parque natural*.

Orientation & Information

From the bus station, it's 450m south via Hotel de Gouveia, Avenida 1 de Maio and Rua da República to Praça de São Pedro, the town centre.

Associação de Desenvolvimento Rural da Serra da Estrela (Adruse; ☎ 238 490 180; adruse@ip.pt; Largo Dr Alípio de Melo) Organises Turihab accommodation and provides a retail outlet for local artisans (right).

Biblioteca Municipal (☎ 238 490 230; Praça de São Pedro 5; 🕒 9.30am-12.30pm & 2-6pm Mon-Fri, 9.30am-12.30pm Sat) Free internet.

Parque Natural da Serra da Estrela office (☎ 238 492 411; fax 238 494 183; Avenida Bombeiros Voluntários 8; 🕒 9am-12.30pm & 2-5.30pm Mon-Fri) A block south of the centre.

Post office (Avenida 1 de Maio 3; 🕒 9am-12.30pm & 2-6pm Mon-Fri) Between Praça de São Pedro and the Hotel de Gouveia.

Turismo (☎ 238 490 243; Avenida 25 de Abril; 🕒 9am-12.30pm & 2-6pm Mon-Sat, 10am-12.30pm & 2-4pm Sun) In a building to the side of the *câmara municipal*. Has leaflets on walks in the area.

Sights

Gouveia's favourite son, Abel Manta (1888–1982), was a painter whose round-faced portraits now fill the former manor house of the Condes de Vinhós, now the **Abel Manta Museu de Arte Moderna** (☎ 238 493 648; Rua Direita 45; admission free; 🕒 9.30am-12.30pm & 2-6pm Tue-Sun), south off Praça de São Pedro. But it's his son João Abel Manta who steals the show, with everything from haunting portraits to cartoons.

Sleeping

Parque de Campismo Curral do Negro (☎ /fax 238 491 008; info@fpcampismo.pt; adult/tent or car €2.70/2.20; 🕒 Jan-Nov; ♿) This grassy camping ground, 3km east on the Folgosinho road, has partial shade and decent facilities.

Quinta das Cegonhas (☎ 238 745 886; www.cegonhas.com; Nabainhos; adult/tent/car €3.40/3.70/2.70, d from €42.50; 🕒 year-round; ♿) Meaning 'House of the Storks', this restored 17th-century *quinta* (country estate), situated 6km northeast of Gouveia, has grand views, tent sites, private rooms (from €30), self-catering apartments (from €60, minimum three days) and meals by arrangement.

Residencial Monteneve (☎ 238 490 370; www.monteneveresidencial.com; Avenida Bombeiros Voluntários 12; s/d €40/55; P ❄) Inside a lovely old granite building you'll find this brand-new, rigorously clean and surprisingly stylish inn. It has very comfortable rooms and a pretty breakfast room.

Casas do Toural (☎ 238 492 132, 963 023 893; www.casasdotoural.com; Rua Direita 74; 2-person cottage €60-75, 4-person cottage €100-110; ♿) If it's atmosphere you're after, try an apartment here on the street above O Mundo Rural. This complex of old restored buildings has a multilayered hillside garden and tennis courts. Book in advance on weekends.

Eating

Restaurante Monteneve (☎ 238 085 480; Avenida Bombeiros Voluntários 12; mains €7; 🕒 lunch & dinner Wed-Sun, lunch Mon) Monteneve is a spruce, new, mostly Italian eatery with huge portions of grilled meats and fish (most mains are enough for two people), as well as good pizzas (from €6 for two people). It's just below the *residencial* of the same name.

Restaurante O Júlio (☎ 238 498 016; Travessa do Loureiro 11a; dishes around €8.50; 🕒 lunch & dinner Wed-Mon) Gouveia's best restaurant, this place has cheerless but faultless service and regional specialities such as *cabrito à serrana* (mountain kid).

Self-caterers will find the **mercado municipal** (🕒 Mon-Fri & Sat morning), opposite O Mundo Rural, at its best on Thursday.

Shopping

O Mundo Rural (☎ 238 490 180; Largo Dr Alípio de Melo; 🕒 10am-12.30pm & 2.30-6.30pm Mon-Sat, 10am-3pm Sun) Housed at Adruse (left), this outlet for regional artisans has fair-priced ceramics, fabrics, cheese, Dão wines, sausages and more.

Getting There & Away

Long-distance coaches stop at the **bus station** (Rua Cidade da Guarda) and in the centre. The main operators are **Rede Expressos** (☎ 238 493 675) and **Marques** (☎ 238 312 858). Marques runs to Seia (€2.10, 25 minutes, five per weekday) and to Guarda (€3.80, 1½ hours). Rede Expressos goes once or twice daily to Coimbra (€10.20, two hours) and twice to Lisbon (€15, 4¾ hours).

Gouveia is on the Beira Alta line from Lisbon to Guarda (the station is 14km north near Ribamondego) – regional trains stop five times a day between Coimbra and Guarda. A taxi between Gouveia and the station will cost around €10.

SABUGUEIRO

pop 700 / elevation 1050m

While pocket-sized Sabugueiro survives largely on tourism, it still has one foot firmly planted in the mountains. Chickens roam the backstreets and a number of sturdy farmer-shepherd families live in granite houses roofed in slate. Attracting tourists from far and wide thanks to its title as Portugal's highest village, Sabugueiro accommodates the influx of sightseers with mostly charm-free *pensões* and souvenir shops on the main road.

Local families manufacture and sell delicious *queijo da serra* (mountain cheese), as well as smoked ham, rye bread and juniper-berry firewater. And for the chilly mountain nights, they make some eminently cosy fleece slippers.

Sleeping & Eating

Prices are for winter months, though you can expect discounts of 25% or more the rest of the year.

Casa do Serrinho (☎ 238 314 304; Largo Nossa Senhora da Fátima; d incl breakfast summer/winter €25/35) At the top of the village, this simple, clean place has a couple of neat rooms with terracotta floors, a shared kitchen and a well-stocked souvenir shop.

You can get closer to local life in one of several dozen restored **stone cottages** (2/4 people from €51/77) that are equipped with a fireplace, kitchenette and bathroom. They fill up fast on weekends and in winter.

You can book accommodation through **Casas do Cruzeiro** (☎ 238 315 872; www.quintadocrestelo.pt). The main office is just off the highway, near the bottom of the hill; just follow the 'Turismo de Aldeia' (Village Tourism) signs. Guests can also use the tennis courts and pool at the nearby Quinta do Crestolo resort.

Getting There & Away

The only public transport is a single bus that runs to/from Seia each Wednesday (Seia's market day), departing from Sabugueiro at about 8am and returning from Seia at about noon. A taxi from Seia will cost around €10.

MANTEIGAS

pop 4000 / elevation 720m

Easily the most picturesque of the Serra towns, Manteigas is set in the glacial Vale do Zêzere, a valley of meadows and pine plantations that ascends to the foot of Torre. From the valley floor, the *serra* (mountain) rises steeply up to craggy heights, with some slopes tamed into terraced meadows and fitted out with both stone *casais* and highly productive beehives.

Manteigas makes an ideal base for exploring the Serra da Estrela: it's centrally and beautifully located and has a parks office, good food and accommodation, and good walks departing in every direction.

There has been a settlement here since at least Moorish times, perhaps because of the hot springs at the nearby spa of Caldas de Manteigas (p338). Manteigas' once-thriving cloth industry has fallen on hard times, but the area has received a boost from the Ski-Parque down the road (p338).

Orientation & Information

From Seia or Gouveia you approach Manteigas down a near vertical switchback, the N232. The bus from Covilhã or Guarda sets you down at the turismo on the N232. The town has no real centre, though you'll find most listings within a few blocks of the Galp petrol station and the nearby turismo.

Parque Natural da Serra da Estrela (☎ 275 980 060; pnse@icn.pt; Rua 1 de Maio 2; 🕒 9am-12.30pm & 2-5.30pm Mon-Fri) Reserve parks accommodation, including camping, here.

Turismo (☎/fax 275 981 129; Rua Dr Esteves de Carvalho; 🕒 9.30am-noon & 2-6pm Tue-Fri, 9.30am-noon & 3-7pm Sat)

Activities

WALKING

You could spend weeks looping in and out of Manteigas. The following are the outlines of a few modest walks. For details and more walks, ask at the turismo or pick up *Discovering the Region of the Serra da Estrela* from the park office.

Poço do Inferno

A 7km, tree-shaded climb takes you to Poço do Inferno (Hell's Well), a waterfall in the craggy gorge of the Ribeira de Leandres. From the turismo go 500m down the N232, turn right and walk for 1km to two bridges. Take the right-hand one across the Rio Zêzere and head downstream. About 200m along, turn right on a forestry track. From here it's 1½ to two hours up to the waterfall, with an elevation change of 400m and fine views northeast.

Return the same way, or head back towards Manteigas down a roughly paved road for about 2.5km to a pine plantation. To the right of the plantation gate, drop down a few steps past a former forestry post, descend to houses by the river, cross the bridge and climb back to Manteigas, for a total walk of about 3½ hours.

Alternatively, carry on past the plantation for a further 3.5km to Caldas de Manteigas, plus 3km along the road back to Manteigas (total 4½ hours).

Penhas Douradas & Vale do Rossim

A more demanding walk goes to Penhas Douradas, a collection of windblown holiday houses. The track climbs northwest out of town via Rua Dr Afonso Costa to join a sealed, switchback forestry road and, briefly, a wide loop of the Seia-bound N232. Branch left off the N232 almost immediately, on another forestry road to the Meteorological Observatory. From there it's a short, gentle ascent to Penhas Douradas.

You're about 700m above Manteigas here, and you mustn't miss the stunning view from a stub of rock called Fragão de Covão; just follow the signs. You can also drive up the N232 just for the view: about 18km from Manteigas, then left at the first turning after the one marked *observatório,* and 1km to the sign for Fragão de Covão. Save your oil-pan and walk the rest of the way.

Walking back the same way makes for a return trip of about 5½ hours. Alternatively, carry on for 3.4km to the Vale do Rossim reservoir and camping ground.

Vale do Zêzere

A long day-walk or a lingering two-day trip takes you through this magnificent, glacier-scoured valley at the foot of Torre. Its only drawback: the trail is shadeless, and baking in clear summer weather. Unfortunately the valley suffered a major forest fire in 2004, and much of the trail now wends through blackened stumps.

Follow the N338 for about 3km to Caldas de Manteigas, leaving the road just below the spa, for the track up the valley. En route are typical stone *casais*. About 9km from Manteigas at Covões (where there's a shelter), a bridge takes you over the Rio Zêzere. Where the huts end, climb up to the N338; a few hundred metres along the road is a crystalline spring. About 3km along the road at a hairpin turn is the Covão da Ametade camp site (opposite), about 3½ hours from Manteigas.

SKIING & OTHER ACTIVITIES

A big dry-ski run 7.5km east of Manteigas, **SkiParque** (☎ 275 982 870; www.skiparque.pt in Portuguese; N232; ⏲ 10am-6pm Sun-Thu, 10am-10pm Fri & Sat) has a lift, gear rental, snowboarding, a café and a camp site (below). Prices for weekday/weekend/night-time skiing start at €10/12/14.50 for two hours, and group lessons are available.

When the weather's good they also organise increasingly popular lessons in **paragliding** at €60 per lesson for first-timers, plus one 15 to 30 minute ride.

To further compensate for the lack of snow in summer, they organise other outdoor activities such as **canoeing**, **rock-climbing**, **biking** and **horse riding** (one-hour lesson €15, horse rental per hour/day €25/150).

HOT SPRINGS

Just south (uphill) from the town centre is the privately run **Caldas de Manteigas** (☎ 275 980 300; www.inatel.pt), where for a €25 consultation with a medical practitioner you can get a prescription for various treatments, from bathing in water from the natural hot springs to massage and other kinds of physiotherapy (€3 to €10). Lodging in the comfortable if slightly workaday hotel costs €46 per person (€61 with full board).

Sleeping

BUDGET

Parque de Campismo Rossio de Valhelhas (☎ 27 487 160; jfvalhelhas@clix.pt; Valhelhas; adult/tent/car €2.45/1.80/1.75; ⏲ May-Sep) A flat, grassy and shady municipal camp site by the N232, about 15km from Manteigas. It also charges €0.5 for hot showers.

Parque de Campismo Vale do Rossim (☎ 27 982 899; www.a-torre.com; N232; adult/car €2.75/1.75, tent €2.50-3; ⏲ 1 Jun-15 Sep) Situated beside a reservoir 23km from Manteigas, with free hot showers, a café-restaurant, a small shop, bikes for rent and a fair amount of shade.

Parque de Campismo Relva da Reboleira (☎ 27 982 870; www.skiparque.pt; adult/car €4/2, tent €2-2.5

year-round) A treeless, functional camp site at the foot of SkiParque. Hot showers cost an extra €0.50.

Two bare-bones, park-run camping grounds that are astonishingly cheap include Covão da Ametade, a popular tents-only site 13km from Manteigas at the head of the Vale do Zêzere, and Covão da Ponte 5.4km up the N232 and 6km along an access road to the Rio Mondego. There are toilets, a snack bar and (at Covão da Ponte) showers, but don't expect electricity or hot water. They're open 15 June to 15 September. Contact the park office in Manteigas for reservations and information (p337).

MIDRANGE

Pensão Serradalto (/fax 275 981 151; Rua 1 de Maio 15; d €45) In a renovated stone house, this fine option offers rooms with wood floors and simple antique furnishings, plus fine valley views from many rooms. It also has a very good restaurant with similar views.

Residencial Estrela (275 981 288; Rua Dr Sobral 5; d with breakfast €45) Estrela provides comfortable, carpeted doubles in a boarding-house atmosphere; a few have fine valley views. The neighbouring church bells go quiet at night, though they're as effective as any alarm clock at 7am. It's located just uphill on the left from the parks office.

Casa de São Roque (275 981 125, 965 357 225; Rua de Santo António 51; d €45) A beautiful, creaky old house that has been lovingly kept with antique furnishings, gauze drapes, cosy lounges and wooden floors. From the turismo take the second left beyond Pensão Serradalto.

TOP END

Casa das Obras (275 981 155; www.casadasobras.pt; Rua Teles de Vasconcelos; d €80; P) Near Residencial Estrela, this 18th-century town house has been carefully renovated to preserve its original grandeur and stonewalled charm. Rooms are snug, well-kept and antique-filled, and breakfast is made from local ingredients, including cheese, honey and jams.

Pousada de São Lourenço (275 980 050; www.pousadas.pt; d €140; P) Pitching for the most stupendous view in the Beiras, this luxurious modern hotel is 13km above and north of town, topping the wiggly switchbacks on the N232: on a clear day, you can see all the way into Spain. Rooms are simple but plush, with a woodsy, alpine feel. The restaurant (open to nonguests) shares the hotel's glorious views.

Eating

Cervejaria Central (275 982 787; grilled dishes €6-7; lunch & dinner) A block back from the park office, this no-nonsense diner is popular with locals for its short, good-value menu, which includes fresh mountain fish, kid, river trout and more.

Restaurante São Januario (275 981 288; mains €7-12; lunch & dinner Tue-Sun) Set just below the Residencial Estrela, this trim restaurant has a culinary whiz in the kitchen and a spare modern design. Its patio is a good spot for coffee or an evening tipple.

Dom Pastor (275 982 920; Travessa Sá da Bandeira; mains €10-15; lunch & dinner Tue-Sun) Set idyllically on the parklike banks of the town's millstream, Manteigas' top-rated restaurant puts fine local ingredients, from cheese and produce to mountain-raised meats, to creative use.

Clube de Compras (Rua 1 de Maio; 9am-1pm & 2-8pm Mon-Fri, 9am-8pm Sat, 9am-6pm Sun) Provides groceries for self-caterers, located just up the street from the parks office.

Getting There & Away

At the time of writing, there was no regularly scheduled bus service to Manteigas, though you may check at the Covilhã and Guarda bus stations for school-day service. It is a fairly easy, 20-minute drive from the IP2, or a more winding 30-minute drive from Covilhã.

TORRE

In winter, Torre's road signs are so blasted by freezing winds that horizontal icicles barb their edges. Portugal's highest peak at 1993m, Torre ('Tower') produces a winter freeze that's so reliable you'll also find the small **Estancia Vodaphone ski resort** (275 319 124; www.turistrela.pt; half-/full day €15/25; 9am-4.30pm during ski season), with three creaky lifts that serve a small set of beginner's slopes. **Ski-gear rental** is also available, including skis, poles and boots (€25 per day) and snowboards (€15 per day).

If you come outside of the snowy season (mid-December to mid-April), Portugal's windy pinnacle is somewhat disappointing – occupied by several ageing golf-ball radar domes, and a sweaty shopping arcade smelling of cheese and smoke. And then there's the 7m-high, neo-Classical obelisk, erected by João VI in the early 19th century so that Portugal could cheekily claim its highest point was exactly 2000m. The complex also has a turismo, though it tends only to be open on weekends and holidays.

There are no bus services to Torre. A taxi costs about €20 to €25 from Covilhã, €25 to €30 from Seia or €15 to €20 from Manteigas.

PENHAS DA SAÚDE

Penhas, the closest spot in which to hunker down near Torre (about 10km from Covilhã on the N339), isn't a town but a weather-beaten collection of chalets at an elevation of about 1900m. It sits just uphill from a burned-out tuberculosis sanatorium and downhill from the Barragem do Viriato dam. Supplies are limited; if you're planning to go walking, do your shopping in Covilhã.

Sleeping & Eating

Pensão O Pastor (☎ 275 322 810; fax 275 314 035; d with breakfast summer/winter €40/50) Above a gift shop, this place has uninspiring, dark, carpeted rooms that are getting past threadbare, though some have fine views.

Pousada da Juventude (☎ 275 335 375; www.movijovem.pt; dm summer/winter €9/16, d €43/25, d with shared bathroom €22/35; year-round; P) Penhas' enormous, first-rate hostel has a communal kitchen and cafeteria, plus a game room with a pool table and table tennis.

Hotel Serra da Estrela (☎ 275 310 300; www.turistrela.pt; d €100; P) This is the top place to stay in Penhas – posh and professional, with handsome rooms as well as woodsy, six-bed chalets (€160) with verandas and great views. The same owners run the resort at Torre. Mountain bikes can be hired for €12.50 per day.

There are several cafés along the N339.

Getting There & Away

At the weekends from mid-July to mid-September and daily during August, local **Transcovilhã** (☎ 275 336 017) buses (€1.70) climb to Penhas from the kiosk on Rua António Augusto d'Aguiar in Covilhã, twice daily. Otherwise, you must take a taxi (€15 to €20), hitch, cycle or walk.

COVILHÃ

pop 35,300 / elevation 700m

Terraced, steeply canted Covilhã is tucked high up in the foothills of the Serra da Estrela, with grandstand views eastward across the plains to Spain. It was once a prosperous textile producer, evidenced by a small historic core of unlikely if modest elegance. Covilhã makes an ideal base from which to steal up into Portugal's highest reaches.

Orientation

From the train and long-distance bus stations, it's a punishing 1.5km climb to Praça do Município, the town centre – for local transport, see p342.

Information

Police station (☎ 275 320 922; Rua António Augusto d'Aguiar)

Post office (8.30am-6.30pm Mon-Fri, 9am-12.30pm Sat)

PostWeb (Rua Comendador Campos Melo 27; per 15min €0.70; 9am-7pm Mon-Fri, 9am-1pm Sat) Internet access.

Regional turismo (☎ 275 319 560; turismo.estrela@mail.telepac.pt; Avenida Frei Heitor Pinto; 9am-5.30pm Mon-Fri, 9am-12.30pm & 2-5.30pm Sat)

Sights

The narrow, winding streets west of Praça do Município have a quiet charm, and in the midst of them is the **Igreja de Santa Maria**, with a startling façade covered in *azulejos*.

Covilhã used to be the centre of one of Europe's biggest wool-producing regions. However, it has fallen on hard times. Stray outside the centre and you'll see the town's ghostly mills standing empty and forlorn.

On the site of the former Real Fábrica de Panos (Royal Textile Factory), founded in 1764 by the Marquês de Pombal, the **Museu de Lanifícios** (Museum of Wool-Making; ☎ 275 319 700, ext 3131; adult/child under 15/youth 15-25 €2/free/1; 9.30am-noon & 2.30-6pm Tue-Sun) looks back at this vanishing local industry. Even if yarn makes you yawn, this is a good little museum – the centrepiece of which is a clutch of giant-sized dyeing vats.

Sleeping

Pião Camping (☎ 275 314 312; fax 275 327 932; adult/tent/car €3/3/2.30; year-round) Some 4km up the N339 towards Penhas da Saúde, you'll find this snug but wooded, well-equipped facility. Bungalows with kitchen facilities are also available (per double from €40).

Pensão Central (☎ 275 322 727; Rua Nuno Álvares Pereira 14; s/d from €10/25) Very creaky and very cheap, this manages to be the only acceptable budget option in town, though you have to share it with those renting by the hour. Ask for a back room with views and no street noise.

Hotel Covilhã Parque (☎ 275 327 518; www.imb-hotels.com in Portuguese; Avenida Frei Heitor Pinto; s/d €42/60;) Ten floors of identical rooms peer over the city from this modern apartment block next to the turismo. Rooms are comfortably uninspired, except that upper floors score fabulous views.

Hotel Solneve (☎ 275 323 001/2; solneve@mail.pt; Rua Visconde da Coriscada 126; d with breakfast €45, Fri & Sat Nov-Mar €65;) This recently refurbished inn has spotless, practically stylish rooms, many with photogenic views of the main square. Plus there's free internet access, a great restaurant and off-street parking (€1.50). An extra €10 to €20 will get you a jet bath and in-room computer. Recommended.

Eating & Drinking

Restaurante Montiel (☎ 275 322 086; Praça do Município 33-37; daily specials around €7; all day) This is a friendly venue for grabbing a caffeine hit, basking in the sun and indulging in flaky Portuguese pastries. The upstairs dining room serves up decent regional cooking: try one of a long list of succulent steaks on offer.

Olvelhita (Largo Infantaria XXI 19; mains €7-10; lunch & dinner Mon-Sat) This newish place on an attractive square serves good regional cuisine, including *cabrito assado* (roast kid) and *leitão* (suckling pig), plus good-value, all-you-can-eat buffet meals with rather generous amounts of vegies (€8 to €11).

Restaurante Solneve (☎ 275 323 001/2; solneve@mail.telepac.pt; Rua Visconde da Coriscada 126; mains €8-11, specials €6; lunch & dinner Mon-Sat, Sun morning) This cavernous eatery sits below street level at the back of Hotel Solneve. Its elegant waiters proffer quality local fare and international dishes from cordon bleu chicken to English roast. Hotel guests get a 10% discount.

Self-caterers will find abundant fruit and vegetables available most mornings at the **mercado municipal** (Rua António Augusto d'Aguiar). There's a big Modelo supermarket a block south of the bus station (both on Eixo TCT).

Faculdade de Cerveja (☎ 919 352 474; Rua Indústria; 5pm-4am Tue-Sat) This gritty DJ bar and club, popular with students, is named the 'Faculty of Beer'. Enough said.

Getting There & Away

From the **bus station** (☎ 275 336 700), Joalto and Rede Expressos run jointly to Guarda (€4.80, 45 minutes, three times daily), and via Castelo Branco (€4, one hour) to Lisbon (€11.60, 3½ hours) about three times a day. There are also multiple daily services to Porto (€12, 4½ to 5½ hours).

Two daily regional (€14.30, 4½ hours) and two IC (€15, four hours) trains run direct from Lisbon via Castelo Branco (€7.50, one hour). There are two regional trains daily to Guarda (€2.80, 1¼ hours).

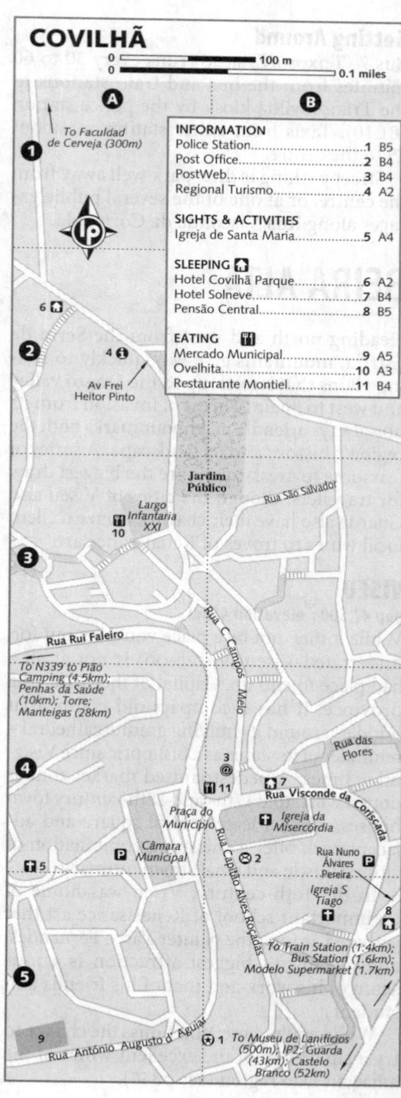

Getting Around

Bus 7 (Teixoso/Estação) runs every 30 to 60 minutes from the bus and train stations to the Transcovilhã kiosk by the police station (€1.10). Taxis from either station are about €5 to the centre.

Street parking is dire; park well away from the centre, or at one of the several public garages along Rua Visconde da Coriscada.

BEIRA ALTA

Heading north and west from the Serra da Estrela, mountains give way quickly to rolling plains that stretch up to the Douro valley and west to Spain. Threat of invasion from its not-always-friendly neighbour marks both the region's history and its landscape. A series of fearsome fortress-towns are the biggest draw for travellers, though the cities of Viseu and Guarda also have their charms, from excellent local wines to troves of Renaissance art.

VISEU

pop 47,500 / elevation 480m

While it may not be a place you'd set out for, underrated Viseu (vi-*zeh*-oo) is not at all a bad place to end up. Capital of the Beira Alta province, it has a compact old centre that huddles around its hulking granite cathedral – reminder of its status as a bishopric since Visigothic times. A pedestrianised market zone is dotted with stoic 17th- and 18th-century town houses, while a leafy central square and adjacent park offer a charming combination of citified bustle and small-town intimacy.

In the 16th-century, Viseu was home of an important school of Renaissance art that gathered around the painter Vasco Fernandes, and the town's biggest attraction is a museum of his work and that of his friends and students.

While you're here, don't miss the chance to try a sip or two of the excellent wines of the adjacent Dão region (see p346).

History

According to legend, Viriato, chief of the Lusitani tribe (p28), took refuge in a cave here before the Romans hunted him down in 139 BC, though there's no sign of a cave now.

The Romans did build a fortified camp just across the Rio Pavia from Viseu, and some well-preserved segments of their roads survive nearby (p345). The town, conquered and reconquered in the struggles between Christians and Moors, was definitively taken by Dom Fernando I in 1057.

Afonso V completed Viseu's sturdy walls in about 1472. The town soon spread beyond them, and grew fat from agriculture and trade. An annual 'free fair' declared by João III in 1510 carries on today as one of the region's biggest agricultural and handicrafts expositions.

Orientation

Viseu sits beside the Rio Pavia, a tributary of the Mondego. In the middle of town is Praça da República, known to all as O Rossio. From here the shopping district stretches east along Rua Formosa and Rua da Paz, and then north into the historic centre along Rua do Comércio and Rua Direita. At the town's highest point and historical heart is the cathedral.

The bus station is 500m northwest of the Rossio along Avenida Dr António José de Almeida.

Information

Bilhares Nortenha (Avenida Alberto Sampaio; internet access €1.50; ⌚ 10am-midnight).

Espaço Internet (Solar dos Condes de Prime, Rua dos Andrades; ⌚ 10am-7pm Mon-Fri, 10am-1pm & 2-7pm Sat, 2-7pm Sun) Free internet.

Main post office (Rua dos Combatentes da Grande Guerra; ⌚ 8.30am-6.30pm Mon-Fri, 9am-12.30pm Sat)

Police station (☎ 232 480 380; Rua Alves Martins)

Regional turismo (☎ 232 420 950; www.rtdaolafoes.com; Avenida Calouste Gulbenkian; ⌚ 9am-12.30pm & 2.30-6pm Mon-Fri, 10am-12.30pm & 2.30-5.30pm Sat & Sun)

São Teotónio Hospital (☎ 232 420 500; Avenida Dom Duarte)

Sights

AROUND THE ROSSIO

At the southern end of Praça da República is the late-18th-century **Igreja dos Terceiros** (admission free), all heavy, gilded baroque but for the luminous *azulejos* portraying the life of St Francis.

Fine modern **azulejos** at the northern end of the Rossio depict scenes from regional life, and beyond these is the *azulejo*-adorned **Museu Almeida Moreira** (☎ 232 423 769; admission free; ⌚ 9am-12.30pm & 2-5.30pm), genteel home to the first director of the Museu de Grão Vasco with fine furnishings and art.

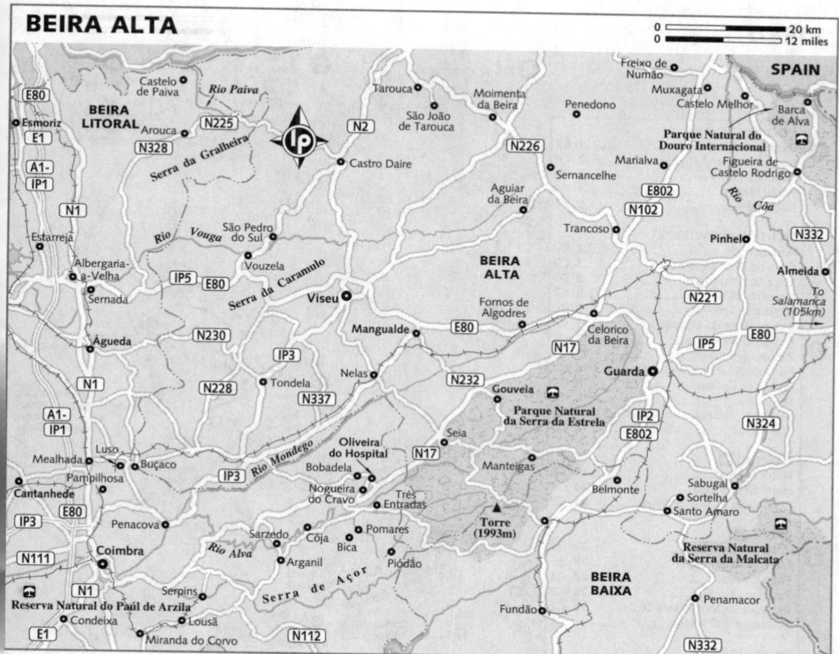

From here the grandest route into the old town is through the **Porta do Soar de Cima**, a gate set into a section of Afonso V's town walls.

SÉ

Resplendent on a rock above the town is the 13th-century granite **cathedral** (admission free; 9am-noon & 2-7pm), of which the gloomy Renaissance façade conceals a splendid 16th-century interior, including an impressive Manueline ceiling.

Stairs in the northern transept climb to the choir and the upper gallery of the **Claustro Jónico** (Ionian Cloister) and the overpriced **Museu de Arte Sacra** (adult/youth 14-26 €2.50/1.25; 9am-noon & 2-5pm Tue-Sat, 2-5pm Sun). However, it's worth paying just to see the side rooms' extraordinary 17th- and 18th-century *azulejos*. They depict such monstrous and comedic scenes as naked men fighting a duel, babies being slaughtered, four-headed beasts on the rampage – and a bevy of nipple-pinching beauties. Hardly the stuff of peaceful contemplation.

The original, lower level of the cloister is one of Portugal's earliest Italian Renaissance structures. Returning to the church you pass through a Romanesque-Gothic portal, rediscovered during restoration work in 1918.

Facing the cathedral is the 1775 **Igreja da Misericórdia** – rococo, symmetrical and blindingly white outside, and neoclassical, severe and rather dull inside.

MUSEU GRÃO VASCO

Adjoining the cathedral is the severe granite box of the Paço de Três Escalões (Palace of Three Steps), probably a contemporary of the cathedral and originally built as the Bishop's Palace. In 1916 it reopened as a splendid **museum** (232 422 049; mgv@ipmuseus.pt; admission €3; 2-6pm Tue, 10am-6pm Wed-Sun) featuring Viseu's own Vasco Fernandes, known as Grão Vasco, 'the Great Vasco' (1480–1543) – one of Portugal's seminal Renaissance painters. It also houses other bright lights of the so-called Viseu School.

Vasco's colleague, collaborator and rival Gaspar Vaz merits special attention. Together they spurred each other on to produce some of the finest artwork ever to come out of Portugal. After five centuries the rich colours and luminous style of their extra-realistic work has lost none of its immediacy.

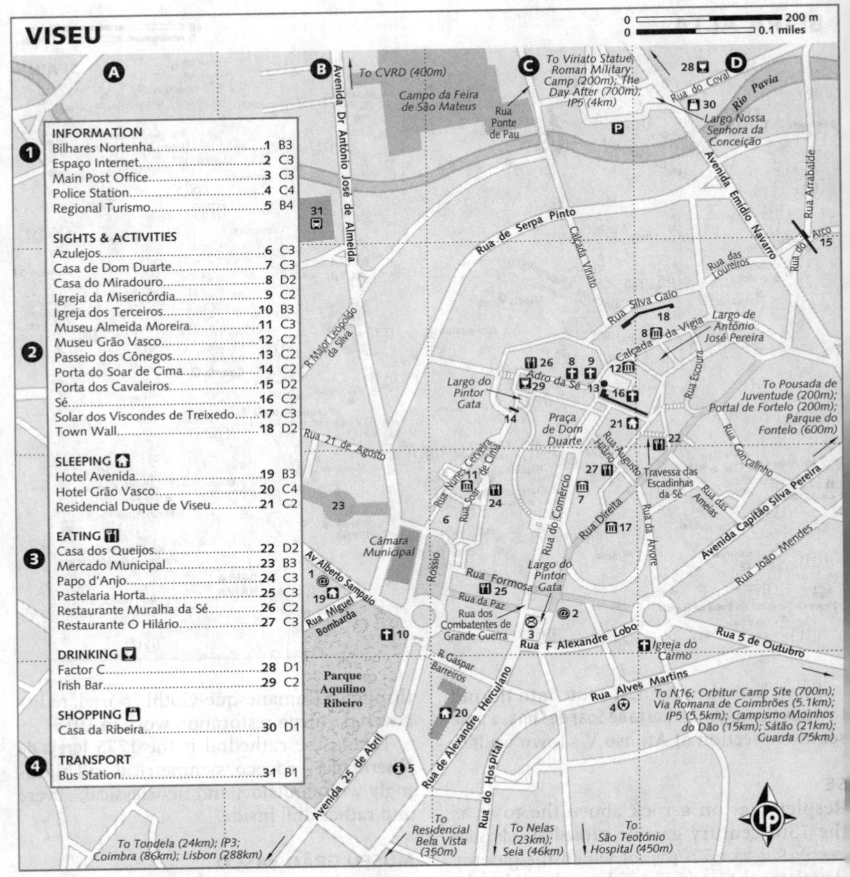

The museum was closed at the time of writing, with no fixed date for reopening.

AROUND THE SÉ

North of the cathedral along Rua Silva Gaio is the longest remaining stretch of the old **town walls**. At the bottom, across Avenida Emídio Navarro, is another old town gate, the **Porta dos Cavaleiros**.

South of the cathedral beneath the Passeio dos Cônegos (Curates Walk, on part of the old wall) is **Praça de Dom Duarte**, named after the Portuguese monarch (brother of Prince Henry the Navigator) who was born in Viseu. Several of the square's old mansions show off their wrought-iron balconies and genteel contours.

Southward is **Casa de Dom Duarte** (Rua Dom Duarte; closed to public), a house with a beautiful Manueline window and traditionally regarded as the king's birthplace.

Rua Augusto Hilário runs southeast through the former **judiaria** (14th- to 16th-century Jewish quarter). **Rua Direita**, Viseu's most appealing street and once the most direct route to the hilltop, is a lively melee of shops, souvenir stands, restaurants and old town houses.

MANSIONS

The most handsome of Viseu's many old town houses is the 18th-century **Solar dos Condes de Prime** (Rua dos Andrades), also called Casa de Cima de Vila, which is currently used by Espaço Internet (p342).

Among other stately homes are the 18th-century **Solar dos Viscondes de Treixedo** (Rua Direita), now a bank, and the 16th-century **Casa do Miradouro** (Calçada da Vigia), just off Largo de António José Pereira. Neither are open to the public.

PARQUE DO FONTELO

A haven of woodland and open space sprawls beyond the Portal do Fontelo. Here are the 16th-century **Antigo Paço Episcopal** (former Bishop's Palace), being refurbished as a Solar do Dão (p346), as well as the once-lovely Renaissance gardens, a stadium and recreation complex.

ROMAN & OTHER SITES

On an embankment north of the centre is a **statue of Viriato**, chief of the Lusitani. Behind it is the site of a **Roman military camp**, though there's little to see.

About 5km southeast of the town centre, off the N16, is the **Via Romana de Coimbrões**, a well-preserved stretch of Roman road. The turismo has a booklet on this and other regional sites of archaeological interest, from the Stone Age to the 19th century.

Festivals & Events

Viseu's biggest annual get-together is the **Feira de São Mateus** (St Matthew's Fair), a jamboree of agriculture and handicrafts from mid-August to mid-September, augmented by folk music, traditional food, amusements and fireworks. This direct descendant of the town's old 'free fair' still takes place on the Campo da Feira de São Mateus, set aside for the event by João III in 1510.

Sleeping

Campismo Moinhos do Dão (☎ 933 011 017; www.portugal-aktief.com; Tibaldinho, 3530 Mangualde; adult/car €3/1.75, tent €1.50-2.50) This camping ground offers something a little different: a no-electricity, no-frills rural place, weedy and relaxed, it was built by Dutch dropouts around several restored water-mills on the Rio Dão, 15km southeast of Viseu. In addition to riverside tent sites, there are various cabins and pretty millhouses available (per week from around €250). To get here, follow the blue camping signs for 6km from exit 19 on the IP5, east of Viseu.

Orbitur (☎ 232 436 146; info@orbitur.pt; adult/car €3.80/3.70, tent €4.10-5.20; Apr-Sep) This friendly and well-forested, well-equipped camping ground is about 1.5km east of the Rossio on the N16. It's on the brink of the large Parque do Fontelo, great for cool woodland walks.

Pousada da Juventude (☎ 232 435 445; www.movijovem.pt; Rua Aristides Sousa Mendes; dm €7, d with/without toilet €19/16; P) A short walk from the centre is this modern, boxy, rather basic hostel. There are no cooking facilities or restaurant.

Residencial Duque de Viseu (☎/fax 232 421 286; Rua das Ameias 22; s/d €20/30;) This snug little place lies in the shadow of the old city walls near the cathedral. It has mostly sunny, spartan rooms, but service is rather lax and the reception is frequently unmanned.

Residencial Bela Vista (☎ 232 422 026; fax 232 428 472; Rua de Alexandre Herculano 510; d €38; P) In a modern apartment block south of the centre, Bela Vista is plain in the extreme, but efficiently run with bright, spick-and-span rooms, some with verandas. Does not accept credit cards.

MIDRANGE

Hotel Avenida (☎ 232 423 432; Avenida Alberto Sampaio 1; s/d €35/45) Standing proudly on a busy corner by the Rossio, this modestly elegant hotel has trim if slightly creaky rooms decorated in regal colours. The breakfast is generous.

TOP END

Hotel Grão Vasco (☎ 232 423 511; www.hotelgraovasco.pt; Rua Gaspar Barreiros; s/d €76/86; P) Top of the scale in central Viseu, this handsome, if slightly pompous, modern granite hotel is set back in leafy grounds above the Rossio. Rooms are properly plush, though a little shy of luxurious.

Eating

Viseu is awash in good food for any budget.

Restaurante O Hilário (☎ 232 436 587; Rua Augusto Hilário 35; mains around €4; lunch & dinner Mon-Sat) This cosy little find has a menu of imaginative meaty dishes, plus righteous prices and attentive service.

Casa dos Queijos (☎ 232 422 643; Travessa das Escadinhas da Sé 7; daily specials around €5, mains €7-9; lunch & dinner Mon-Sat) This stone-walled old place, hidden up narrow stairs, gets top marks for carefully prepared *cozidos* (stews) and grilled salmon. The shop downstairs is stacked high with tempting wines and cheeses.

Restaurante Muralha da Sé (☎ 232 437 777; Adro da Sé 24; mains €11-15; lunch & dinner Tue-Sat, lunch Sun) Go ahead: bust your budget at this unabashedly

WINES OF THE DÃO REGION

The velvety red wines of the Dão region (within the Rio Mondego and tributary Rio Dão, south and east of Viseu) have been cultivated for over 2000 years, and are today among Portugal's best. Vineyards are mostly sheltered in valleys at altitudes of 200m to 900m just west of the Serra da Estrela, thus avoiding the rain of the coast but also the harsh summer heat further inland. This, together with granitic soil, helps the wines retain their natural acidity. They are often called the burgundies of Portugal because they don't overpower but, rather, are subtle and full of finesse.

Some three-dozen Dão vineyards and producers offer multilingual cellar tours and tastings; pick up a list in Viseu's turismo. Many prefer advance bookings, but one vineyard open to drop-in visitors is **Casa da Ínsua** (☎ 232 642 222; Penalva do Castelo), 30km east of Viseu on the IP5 and N329-1. It also has fine grounds and winning 18th-century architecture.

Coordinating them all is the **Comissão Vitivinicola Regional do Dão** (CVRD; ☎ 232 410 060; www.cvrdao.pt; Avenida Capitão Homem Ribeiro 10, Viseu), which at the time of writing was working to open the 16th-century Antigo Paço Episcopal as a posh Solar do Dão in which to sample a range of Dão wines.

White Dão wines are also available, though the full-bodied reds are the best (and the strongest). Also try the sparkling white wines of the separate, small Lafões region, northwest of Viseu.

upper-crust spot under the looming Igreja da Misericórdia. It boasts fine regional cuisine, including excellent ingredients from the nearby Serra da Estrela, plus cathedral views from the terrace seating.

Papo d'Anjo (☎ 232 418 096; Rua Soar de Cima 13; all-you-can-eat buffet €12.50, lunch buffet Mon-Fri €7.50; ⌚ lunch & dinner Mon-Sat, lunch Sun) Both a great value and a real treat, this new eatery serves buffets with wonderful hot dishes, including *cozidos* and grilled meats, as well as fresh salads, sausages and cheeses, and desserts. Heartily recommended.

Pastelaria Horta (Rua Formosa 22; ⌚ 7am-8pm Mon-Sat) The town's best bakery serves traditional sweets made of egg yolk and almonds. There's also outdoor seating on the pleasantly pedestrian Rua Formosa.

Self-caterers will find fruit, vegetables and other goodies at the **Mercado Municipal** (Rua 21 de Agosto; ⌚ Mon-Sat).

Drinking

A clutch of bars near the cathedral overflows onto the streets and makes for a merry atmosphere on summer nights.

Irish Bar (☎ 967 130 270; Largo Pintor Gata 8; ⌚ 9am-2am Mon-Sat, 1pm-2am Sun) Guinness on tap, occasional live Irish music and terrace seating on a charming square.

Factor C (☎ 232 415 808; Largo Nossa Senhora da Conceição 39-43; ⌚ 9pm-2am Mon-Thu, 9pm-4am Fri & Sat) Viseu's trendiest disco, with distinct rooms playing pop, rock and alternative sounds to keep everyone happy.

Day After (☎ 232 450 645; www.thedayafter.pt; ⌚ 11pm-late Tue-Sun) The best visiting DJs and bands invariably play at this warehouse of a disco, with more than half-a-dozen dance halls plus go-karts, a restaurant and more. It's on the N16 west of the Cava de Viriato.

Shopping

Handicrafts here are cheaper than in more touristy towns.

Casa da Ribeira (☎ 232 429 761; Largo Nossa Senhora da Conceição; ⌚ 9am-12.30pm & 2-5.30pm Tue-Sat) Casa da Ribeira is a municipal space where local artisans can work and sell their products. These include lace, ceramics and the region's distinctively black earthenware.

Getting There & Around

Operators at the bus station include **Rede Expressos** (☎ 232 422 822) and **Joalto** (☎ 232 426 093).

Rede Expressos heads to Vila Real (€8.50, 75 minutes, at least two daily), Trancoso (€8.50, 1½ hours, one daily), Coimbra (€7, 75 minutes, six daily), Bragança (€11, 3½ hours, one daily) and Lisbon (€11.50, 3½ hours, one daily).

Joalto heads to Braga (€10.30, three hours, one daily) and Porto (€7.80, two hours, five daily).

Drivers are best advised to avoid the old town, as it is full of harrowing one-way lanes. However, you will find parking just north of the Rio Pavia around the town's fairgrounds.

GUARDA

pop 26,400 / elevation 1056m

Fria, farta, forte e feia (cold, rich, strong and ugly): such is the popular description of Portugal's highest fully fledged city. Set on imposing heights, it was founded in 1197 to guard young Portugal against both Moors and Spaniards (hence the name), and indeed the whole place has distinctly military bearing. Nevertheless this granite-grey district capital and bishopric works a chilly charm on visitors, who come for the looming cathedral, the melancholy lanes of the old Jewish quarter, and the sweeping views of the plains that stretch to Spain. It's also the biggest city within striking distance of the Parque Natural da Serra da Estrela.

Orientation

Old Guarda is perched on a steep hill, a rambling climb from the IP5 or the train station; the latter is 5km northeast of the old centre, linked by a shuttle bus.

From the bus station on Rua Dom Nuno Álvares Pereira, it's 800m northwest to Praça Luís de Camões (also called Praça Velha), heart of the old town. Most accommodation, restaurants and places of interest are near the *praça*.

Information

Á4 (Rua 31 de Janeiro 78; per 30min €1; 8am-9pm Mon-Fri, 8.30am-1pm & 3-6.30pm Sat, 10am-1pm Sun) Internet access.

Mediateca VIII Centenário (271 205 531; Praça Luís de Camões; 9.30am-12.30pm & 2-5.30pm Mon-Fri) Free internet.

Municipal turismo (271 205 530; Praça Luís de Camões; 9am-12.30pm & 2-5.30pm)

Parque Natural da Serra da Estrela office (PNSE; /fax 271 225 454; Rua Dom Sancho I 3; 9am-12.30pm & 2-5.30pm Mon-Fri) Modestly helpful.

Police station (271 222 022; Rua Alves Roçadas 15)

Post office (271 221 754; Largo João de Deus; 8.30am-6pm Mon-Fri, 9am-12.30pm Sat)

Sights

SÉ

Powerful in its sobriety, this Gothic fortress of a **cathedral** (Praça Luís de Camões; 9am-noon & 2-5pm Tue-Sat) squats heavily by a large square in the city centre. The earliest parts date from

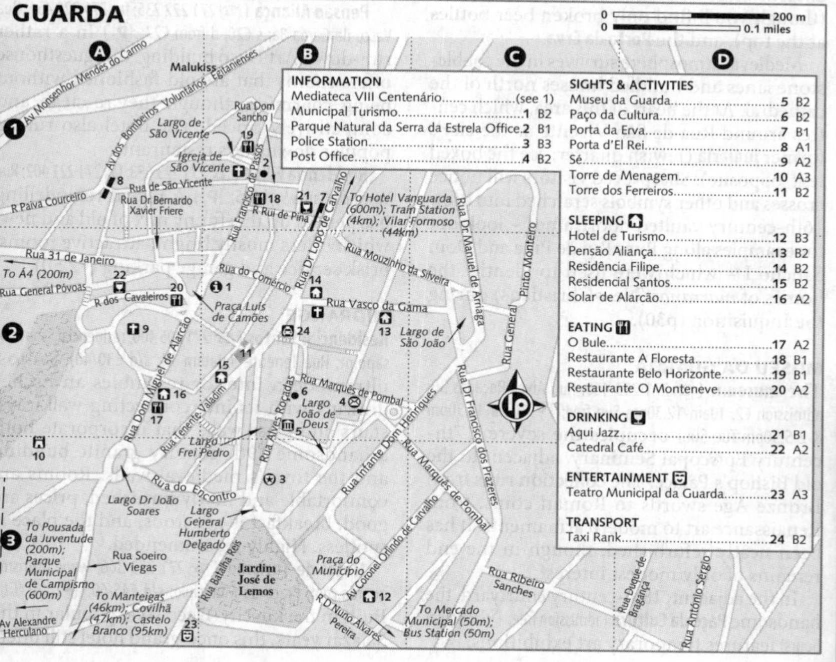

1390 but it took 150 years to finish; it's dotted with Manueline doors and windows and Renaissance ornamentation, while its façade is girded by two handsomely hexagonal bell towers. A recently completed restoration has it looking quite spiffed.

The most striking feature in the immense, granite interior is a four-storey Renaissance altarpiece attributed to Jean de Rouen (João de Ruão), one of a team of 16th-century French artists who founded an influential school of sculpture at Coimbra. Also impressive are the twisted Manueline columns at each transept.

OLD TOWN

With its 16th- to 18th-century **mansions** and overpowering cathedral, Praça Luís de Camões is the town's centrepiece.

Little remains of Guarda's 13th-century castle except the simple **Torre de Menagem** (castle keep; closed to public), on a hilltop above the cathedral. Of the old walls and gates, the stalwart **Torre dos Ferreiros** (Blacksmiths' Tower; Rua Tenente Valadim) is still in good condition. Two other surviving gates are the **Porta d'El Rei**, the ancient steps of which you can still climb (though you'll find only broken beer bottles at the top), and the **Porta da Erva**.

Medieval atmosphere survives in the cobblestone lanes and huddled houses north of the cathedral. At the heart of this area, which centres around Rua de São Vicente, is the city's former **judiaria** (Jewish quarter; see the boxed text, opposite). Sharp-eyed visitors will notice crosses and other symbols scratched into a few 16th-century vaulted doorframes – look out for examples along Ruas Rui de Pina and Dom Sancho I – which were used to identify the homes of *marranos* (New Christians) during the Inquisition (p30).

MUSEU DA GUARDA

The **museum** (☎ 271 213 460; Rua Alves Roçadas 30; admission €2, 10am-12.30pm Sun free; 🕑 10am-12.30pm & 2-5.30pm Tue-Sun) occupies the severe, 17th-century Episcopal Seminary, adjacent to the old Bishop's Palace. The collection runs from Bronze Age swords to Roman coins, from Renaissance art to modern armaments. It has been neatly refurbished, though in the end remains of only modest interest.

In the adjacent, 18th-century courtyard, the handsome **Paço da Cultura** (admission free; 🕑 irregular hours) features temporary art exhibitions.

Festivals & Events

Guarda hosts a jazz festival called **Ciclo de Jazz de Guarda**, with several performances each week from March to May.

The turismo hands out a free calendar of events.

Sleeping

Summer and weekend accommodation gets tight, so try to book ahead. There's no winter high-price season here, though Guarda is almost as close to the snow as the park's other main towns.

BUDGET

Parque Municipal de Campismo (☎ 271 221 200; fax 271 210 025; Rua do Estádio Municipal; adult/tent/car €2/2/1.75; 🕑 year-round) Very close to the town centre and next to a leafy park, this municipal site has hot water and plenty of shade.

Pousada da Juventude (☎ 271 224 482; www.movijovem.pt; Avenida Alexandre Herculano; dm €7, d with/without toilet €19/16; **P**) The modern, rather clinical youth hostel is a short walk to the centre. Reception is open 8am until noon and 6pm until midnight. Some upper rooms have nice vistas.

Pensão Aliança (☎ 271 222 235; fax 271 221 451; Rua Vasco da Gama 8a; s €20, d from €27; **P**) In a rather run-down Art Deco building, this guesthouse offers rooms that are old-fashioned without being charming, though they're clean and competitively priced. The hotel also runs a popular downstairs restaurant.

Residência Filipe (☎ 271 223 658; fax 271 221 402; Rua Vasco da Gama 9; d €35; **P**) A recent remodelling has perked up this funny mix of old and new which offers mostly bright, attractive rooms, brisk service and garage parking (€2.50).

MIDRANGE

Residencial Santos (☎ 271 205 400; residencial_santos@sapo.pt; Rua Tenente Valadim 14; s/d €30/40) Santos' ultramodern interior resembles an Escher drawing with its interconnecting walkways, stairs and glass walls that incorporate both a handsome 19th-century granite building and the town's medieval walls. Rooms are comfortable and newly furnished, prices are good, breakfast is generous, and the place is spotless. Highly recommended.

Hotel de Turismo (☎ 271 223 366; www.hturismoguarda.com; Praça do Município; s/d €45/60; **P** ✖ 💻) Built in the kitschy-Deco style popular in the Salazar years, this once-grand hotel still offers

THE JEWS OF BELMONTE

When the Moors ruled Portugal, it's estimated that 10% of the country's population was Jewish. Jews remained vital to the young Christian state, serving as government ministers and filling key roles in Henry the Navigator's school devoted to overseas exploration. Even the current Duke of Bragança, hereditary king of Portugal, proudly acknowledges his own Jewish parentage.

When Portugal embraced Spain's inquisitorial zeal beginning in the 1490s, thousands of Jews from both Portugal and Spain fled to northeast Portugal, including the Beiras and Trás-os-Montes, where the arm of the inquisitors had not yet reached. Eventually the padres made their presence felt even here, and Jews once again faced conversion, expulsion or death.

However, in the 1980s it was revealed that in the town of Belmonte, 20km south of Guarda, a group of families had been practising Jewish rites in secret since the Inquisition – more than 500 years. While it's believed that many such communities continued in secrecy well into the Inquisition, most slowly died out. But Belmonte's community managed to survive five centuries by meticulously ensuring marriages were arranged only among other Jewish families. The transmission of Jewish tradition was almost exclusively oral and passed not from father to son but from mother to daughter. Each Friday night families descended into basements to pray and celebrate the Sabbath. Now that the community is out in the open, they have embraced male-dominated Orthodox Judaism, though the women elders have not forgotten the secret prayers that have been doggedly transmitted these past 500 years.

The modest **Museu Judaico de Belmonte** (☎ 275 913 505; Rua Portela 4; admission free; 🕒 9.30am-12.30pm & 2-6pm Tue-Sun) tells the story of the Belmonte families and Judaism generally. Ask here about visits to the town's synagogue.

There are frequent daily bus connections between Belmonte and Guarda.

large, bright if slightly dog-eared rooms, plus still-handsome common areas.

Hotel Vanguarda (☎ 213 300 541; www.imb-hotels com; Avenida Monsenhor Mendes do Carmo; d from €75; P ✗ 🖳) This new hotel with a rakishly winglike roof sits just downhill from the centre. It offers good midrange rooms, many with panoramic vistas across the plains to Spain.

Solar de Alarcão (☎ /fax 271 214 392; Rua Dom Miguel de Alarcão 25-27; d €80; P) Easily Guarda's most refined choice, this beautiful 17th-century granite mansion has its own courtyard and loggia, sits within spitting distance of the cathedral, and offers a handful of gorgeous rooms stuffed with antique furniture and drapes.

Eating

Restaurante A Floresta (☎ 271 212 314; Rua Francisco dos Passos 40; mains €7-9; 🕒 lunch & dinner) Just north of the cathedral, this snug and friendly (if well-touristed) place serves up hearty regional cuisine, including the marvellous *chouriçada*: a heaping portion of grilled sausages from the nearby Serra de Estrela.

Restaurante O Monteneve (☎ 271 212 799; Praça Luís de Camões 24; daily specials around €7, mains €7-11; 🕒 lunch & dinner Tue-Sun) Up an old granite staircase opposite the cathedral, this local institution serves up hearty Portuguese fare in an old-fashioned yet bright, spacious dining room.

Pensão Aliança (☎ 271 222 235; Rua Vasco da Gama 8a; specials €6, mains €7.50-10; 🕒 lunch & dinner) This quick-in, quick-out eatery is popular with locals for its grilled meats and good-value lunchtime specials.

Restaurante Belo Horizonte (☎ 271 211 454; Largo de São Vicente 1; mains €8-12; 🕒 lunch & dinner Sun-Fri) Granite-fronted Belo Horizonte packs them in for lunch and dinner, with regional specialities such as *chouriçada* and *cabrito gelada* (grilled kid).

O Bule (☎ 271 211 275; Rua Dom Miguel de Alarcão; 🕒 8am-8pm Mon-Sat, 10am-8pm Sun) This lovely, traditional café near the cathedral specialises in *queijadas*: little cakes made out of sheep's milk.

Self-caterers can head to the *mercado municipal* near the bus station.

Drinking

Guarda has about a dozen central bars – all small and unlikely looking from the outside, but welcoming within. Two central favourites are **Catedral Café** (Rua dos Cavaleiros 18; 🕒 11pm-late), a bar with occasional DJ-and-dancing gigs, and **Aqui Jazz** (Rua Rui de Pinha 29; 🕒 10pm-3am), which attracts alternative and arty types with live jazz.

Entertainment

Teatro Municipal da Guarda (☎ 271 205 240; www.tmg.com.pt; Rua Batalha Reis 12) Like so many Portuguese cities, Guarda too has a boxy, shiny new theatre complex, regularly hosting high-quality theatre, dance and music.

Getting There & Away

BUS

Rede Expressos (☎ 271 221 515) runs services around three times daily via Covilhã (€4.80, 45 minutes) to Castelo Branco (€8.90, 1¾ hours) and Lisbon (€12.60, 5½ hours), and several times daily to Viseu (€7.30, 1½ hours), Porto (€10.20, three hours) and Coimbra (€10.20, three hours).

Marques (☎ 238 312 858) goes daily via Gouveia (€4.40, 1½ hours) to Seia (€4.90, two hours). Rede Expressos also goes to Seia (€7.20, 1¼ hours) once daily Sunday to Friday.

TRAIN

Guarda's train station is served by at least two, fast IC trains lines from Lisbon (€17, four hours). There are also direct trains to Coimbra (€9.10, 2¾ hours). Trains to Porto change at Pampilhosa (€12.60, four hours).

Getting Around

Shuttle buses run between the train station and the bus station (€0.80), with a stop at Rua Marquês de Pombal, every half-hour during the day. Call for a **taxi** (☎ 271 221 863) or board one at the rank on Rua Alves Roçadas. A taxi to/from the train station costs €4.

Parking is competitive in the centre. Try your luck around Largo Dr João Soares.

TRANCOSO

pop 4600 / elevation 870m

A warren of cobbled lanes squeezed within Dom Dinis' 13th-century walls make peaceful, hilltop Trancoso a delightful retreat from the modern world. The town also served as a refuge of Spanish Jews fleeing the Inquisition – until Portugal, too, adopted Spain's persecutory zeal. You can generally spot Jewish houses: most have a pair of doors, a smaller one for the private household and a larger one for a shop or warehouse.

Although it's predominantly a medieval creation, the town's castle also features a rare, intact Moorish tower, while just outside the walls are what are believed to be Visigothic tombs.

Dinis underscored the importance of this border fortress by marrying the saintly Dona Isabel of Aragon here in 1282. But the town's favourite son is Bandarra, a lowly 16th-century shoemaker and fortune-teller who put official noses out of joint by foretelling the end of the Portuguese monarchy.

Sure enough, shortly after Bandarra's death, the young Dom Sebastião died, heirless, in the disastrous Battle of Alcácer-Quibir in 1558. Soon afterwards Portugal fell under Spanish rule.

Information

Espaço Internet (⌚ 3-7pm & 8-10.30pm Mon-Fri, 3-7pm Sat) Free internet.

Police station (Largo Luis Alberquerque; ☎ 271 811 212)

Post office (Estrada de Lamego; ⌚ 9am-12.30pm & 2-6pm Mon-Fri)

Turismo (☎ 271 811 147; turismo@cm-trancoso.pt; ⌚ 9am-12.30pm & 2-5.30pm Mon-Fri, 10am-12.30pm & 2-5.30pm Sat & Sun)

Sights

The **Portas d'El Rei** (King's Gate), surmounted by the town's ancient coat of arms, has always been its principal entrance, and its guillotine-like door has long sealed out unwelcome visitors. The **town walls** run intact for over 1km around the medieval core, which is centred on the main square, Largo Padre Francisco Ferreira (also called Largo do Pelourinho or Largo Dom Dinis). The square, in turn, is anchored by an octagonal **pelourinho** dating from 1510.

Like many northern towns, Trancoso acquired a sizable Jewish community following the expulsion of Jews from Spain at the end of the 15th century.

The **old judiaria** covered roughly the southeast third of the walled town. Among dignified reminders of that time is a former rabbinical residence called the **Casa do Gato Preto** (House of the Black Cat; Largo Luís Albuquerque), decorated with the gates of Jerusalem and other Jewish images. It's now private property.

On a hill in the northeast corner of town is the now-tranquil, 10th- to 13th-century **castelo** (admission free; ⌚ 9am-5.30pm Mon-Fri, 10am-5.30pm Sat & Sun), with its crenellated towers and the distinctively slanted walls of the squat Moorish **Torre de Menagem**.

Across the road from the **Portas do Prado** beside the courthouse, is an untended rock outcrop carved with eerie, body-shaped

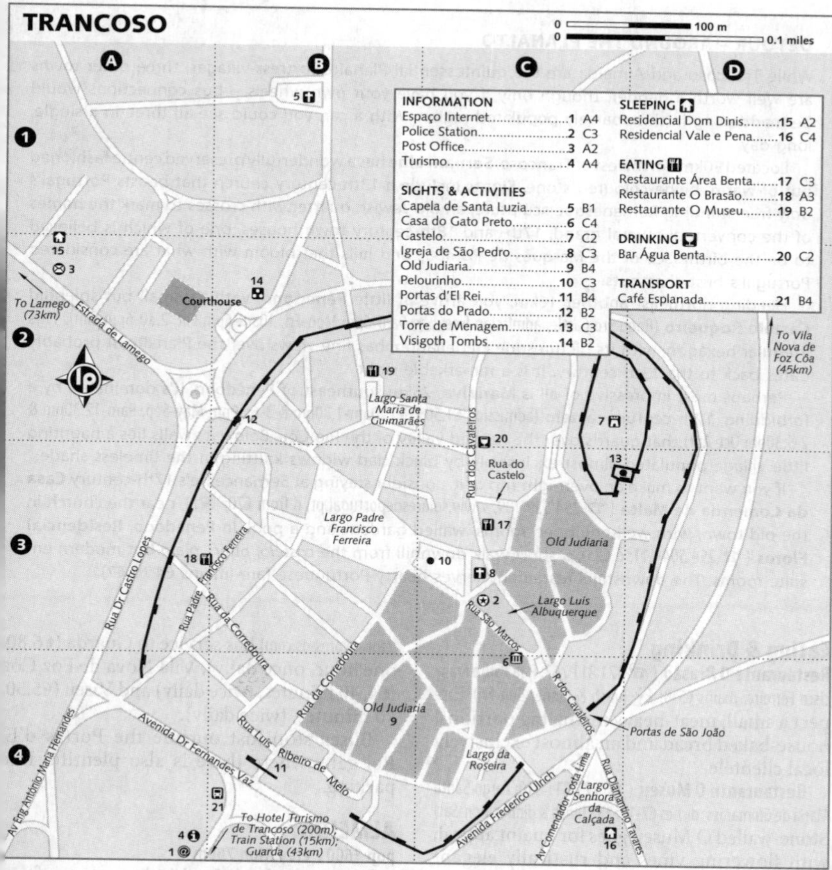

cavities, thought to be **Visigothic tombs** dating back to the 7th or 8th century.

About 150m northward is Trancoso's prettiest church, the 13th-century **Capela de Santa Luzia**, with heavy Romanesque door arches and unadorned dry-stone construction. Trancoso abounds with other churches heavy with baroque make-up, most prominently the **Igreja de São Pedro**, behind the *pelourinho* on Largo Padre Francisco Ferreira.

Sleeping

Ask at the turismo about the possibility of *quartos* for rent.

Residencial Vale a Pena (☎ 271 811 219; Largo Senhora da Calçada; s/d €20/35; P) This simple, friendly place near the Portas de São João offers clean, modern rooms with tile floors and newish furnishings that have a slightly grandmotherly touch.

Residencial Dom Dinis (☎ 271 811 525; fax 271 811 396; Estrada de Lamego; s/d with breakfast €29/39; P) In a rather drab apartment block behind the post office, the Dom Dinis has spotless, if spiritless, carpeted modern rooms and a good little downstairs restaurant (mains around €8). English spoken.

Hotel Turismo de Trancoso (☎ 271 829 200; www.hotel-trancoso.com in Portuguese; Rua Professora Irene Avillez; s/d from €80/100; P) This new, chalk-white and quite stylish monolith offers bright, simply furnished rooms, most with verandas and rural vistas around a semicircular courtyard.

DETOUR – AROUND THE PLANALTO

While Trancoso and Almeida are the quintessential Planalto fortress-villages, three other towns are well worth a gander, though only if you have your own wheels – bus connections would be maddening in this sparsely populated region. With a car, you could see all three in a single, long day.

Located 30km northwest of Trancoso, **Sernancelhe** has a wonderfully preserved centre fashioned out of warm, beige-coloured stone. Sights include a 13th-century church that boasts Portugal's only free-standing Romanesque sculpture; an old Jewish quarter with crosses to mark the homes of the converted; several grand, 17th- and 18th-century town houses, one of which is believed to be the birthplace of the Marquês de Pombal; and hills that bloom with what are considered Portugal's best chestnuts.

Heading northeast another 16km, you arrive at little **Penedono**, with its small but splendid **Castelo Roqueiro** (Roqueiro Castle; admission free; ⏰ 9am-6pm Mon-Fri, 10am-6pm Sat, 2.30-6pm Sun). This irregular hexagon, with its picturesque crenellation, has fine views over the Planalto. It probably dates back to the 13th century. It is a remarkable sight.

Perhaps most impressive of all is **Marialva**, 25km southeast of Penedono. It's dominated by a forbidding, 12th-century **castelo** (admission €1.50; ⏰ 10am-1.30pm & 3-6.30pm May-Sep, 9am-12.30pm & 2-5.30pm Oct-Apr) that guards over the rugged valley of the Rio Côa. Below its walls lies a haunting little village populated almost exclusively by black-clad widows knitting in the timeless shade.

If you want to make an overnight trip of it, consider staying at Sernancelhe's 17th-century **Casa da Comenda de Malta** (☎ 254 559 189; www.solaresdeportugal.pt; d from €70;), near the church in the old town, with well-equipped rooms, walled gardens and a pool. In Penedono, **Residencial Flores** (☎ 254 504 411; d €25), a short walk downhill from the *castelo*, offers plain but modern en-suite rooms. The downstairs restaurant serves hearty Portuguese fare (mains €4 to €7).

Eating & Drinking

Restaurante O Brasão (☎ 271 811 767; Rua Padre Francisco Ferreira; mains €5-8; ⏰ lunch & dinner Sun-Fri) Expect a small, meat-heavy menu, big portions, house-baked bread and an almost exclusively local clientele.

Restaurante O Museu (☎ 271 811 810; Largo Santa Maria de Guimarães; dishes €7-11; ⏰ lunch & dinner Mon-Sat) Stone-walled O Museu goes for quaint appeal, with flowering vines and rustically elegant charm. It has a range of Portuguese standards, as well as pricier seafood (€15 to €50).

Restaurante Área Benta (☎ 271 817 180; Rua dos Cavaleiros 30; mains €7.50-10; ⏰ lunch & dinner Tue-Sat, lunch Sun) This swish, minimalist restaurant in an ancient town house offers very good traditional fare, including *ensopada de borrego* (lamb stew), served with contemporary flair.

Bar Água Benta (Rua dos Cavaleiros 36a; ⏰ noon-3am Sun-Fri, 9pm-4am Sat) Tucked away in the backstreets is this little café-bar, with a cheerful and youthful atmosphere, international beers, and occasional live music and karaoke.

Getting There & Around

Catch buses and buy tickets at **Café Esplanada** (☎ 271 811 188; ⏰ 7am-midnight), right around the corner from the turismo. **Rede Expressos** (www.rede-expressos.com) has service to Guarda (€6.80, one hour, once daily), Vila Nova de Foz Côa (€4, 40 minutes, twice daily) and Viseu (€5.50, 70 minutes, twice daily).

Buses stop just outside the Portas d'El Rei gate, where there is also plentiful free parking.

ALMEIDA

pop 1600 / elevation 760m

After Portugal regained independence from Spain in the 1640s, the country's border regions were on constant high alert. Tiny Almeida, along with Elvas and Valença do Minho, became a principle defence again Spanish incursions. Almeida's vast, star-shaped fortress – completed in 1641 on the site of its medieval predecessor, 15km from Spain – is the least famous but the handsomest of the three.

When its military functions largely suspended in 1927, Almeida settled into weedy obscurity. But the fortress and its old village are now a designated national monument and are in the process of being scrubbed up for tourism. The town may have the disquieting calm of a museum, but it also has enough history and muscular grandeur to set the imagination humming.

Orientation & Information

The fortress is on the northern side of 'new' Almeida. Most visitors arrive via the handsome Portas de São Francisco, consisting of two long tunnel-gates.

The **turismo** (☎ 271 574 204; 9am-12.30pm & 2-5.30pm, from 10am Sat & Sun) is impressively located in an old guard-chamber within the Portas de São Francisco. Here you can get a map of the fortress, though not much else.

Sights

The long arcaded building just inside the Portas de São Francisco is the 18th-century **Quartel das Estradas** (Infantry Barracks), which still serve as military housing.

In a bastion 300m northeast of the turismo are the **casamatas** (casemates or bunkers; 9am-12.30pm & 2-5.30pm Mon-Fri, from 10am Sat & Sun), a warren of 20 underground rooms used for storage, barracks and shelter for up to 5000 troops in times of siege. In the 18th century it also served as a prison.

The fort's **castle** was blown to smithereens during a French siege in 1810, when Britain's and Portugal's own ammunition supplies exploded. You can still see the foundations, 300m northwest of the turismo, from an ugly catwalk. Below the ruins is the former Royal Riding Academy.

Sleeping

Pensão-Restaurante A Muralha (☎ /fax 271 574 357; Bairro de São Pedro; s/d €25/40; P) This functional, modern place sits 250m outside the Portas de São Francisco on the Vilar Formoso road. It has quiet, personality-free rooms and a large restaurant serving unsophisticated, belly-filling platters (mains €6.50 to €9).

Casa Pátio da Figueira (☎ 271 571 133, 271 574 733; lqueiros@mail.telepac.pt; Rua Direita 48; d €80;) At the northern end of the village, this restored 18th-century town house of chunky stone and considerable charm features four elegant double rooms and a lovely garden with a pool.

Pousada Nossa Senhora das Neves (☎ 271 574 283; www.pousadas.pt; d €135; P) Ugly from the outside if entirely respectable on the inside, this modern *pousada* sits on the site of former cavalry quarters near the north bastion. Rooms are large and comfortable and many have balconies, though at the time of writing they were looking rather threadbare.

Eating

4 Esquinas Bar (☎ 271 574 314; Travessa da Pereira 7; breakfast, lunch & dinner) This cosy local café inside the fort serves sandwiches and burgers (around €3).

A Tertúlia (☎ 271 571 134; daily specials €6; lunch & dinner Wed-Mon) In the cluster of modern buildings 250m outside the Portas de São Francisco, on the Vilar Formoso road, you'll find this homey place serving hearty, meat-heavy dishes, including the artery-clogging fried beef in cream sauce.

Restaurante Nossa Senhora das Neves (☎ 271 574 283; mains €15-19; lunch & dinner) For a splurge, try creative takes on regional cuisine in the dining room of the *pousada*. The three-course menu for €28 is a good value. If you're feeling particularly peckish, consider the lamb stew fortified with egg yolks. Save room for pudding made from local almonds.

There are half a dozen small-time snack-bars and café-bars inside the walls.

Getting There & Around

Rede Expressos (www.rede-expressos.pt) has weekday-only service to Celerico Beira, with connections to points onward including Viseu (€8.30, three hours) and Lisbon (€13.80, 7½ hours). There is also Sunday service to Guarda (€7.40, 1½ hours), with onward connections. Unless you come by car you will almost certainly have to stay the night due to limited bus connections.

If you do drive, you're better off parking outside the town and negotiating the inner town on foot.

The Douro

Rising in Spain, the Rio Douro turns suddenly westward, crossing the breadth of Portugal via a stunning series of gorges before reaching the city of Porto and the sea. The world knows the region for its *vinho do porto* (port wine), which has shaped not just its history but the land itself. In Porto, traditional port-wine 'lodges' clamber up the banks of the Douro, while upriver centuries of growers have turned steep hillsides into intricately contrived terraces that blur the distinction between nature and art – and that's before you crack open a bottle of vintage.

However, the Douro valley offers much more than its famous tipple. Thanks to capital from its wine trade, Porto has long been Portugal's economic powerhouse. That energy spills over into its cultural scene, from edgy contemporary architecture to a raucous nightlife. Or you can head into the interior to explore a rich legacy of the region's human presence, from Stone Age petroglyphs and Visigothic churches to the baroque, hillside sanctuary at Lamego. And while you probably wouldn't come for the Atlantic beaches alone, they make a fine diversion, especially as EU regulations help clean up once-iffy waters.

Head upriver if you can. Multiple dams now tame the Rio Douro, allowing you to cruise into the epicentre of port-wine production, around Peso da Régua and Pinhão. Or go by train: tracks stretch almost to Spain. In addition, three narrow-gauge lines climb out of the valley from the main line, offering enchanting diversions to Amarante and into Trás-os-Montes.

Note that this chapter includes a few towns that are technically in the Beira Alta and Trás-os-Montes regions but lie along the Rio Douro.

HIGHLIGHTS

- Savouring the differences between aged tawny, vintage and late-bottled vintage (LBV) port in the historic port-wine lodges of **Vila Nova de Gaia** (p364)
- Testing the acoustics at Porto's **Casa da Música** (p363), Rem Koolhaas' trapezoid-happy, state-of-the-art concert hall
- Negotiating the medieval alleys and river-front promenades of Porto's Unesco-protected **Ribeira district** (p360)
- Heading by **riverboat** (p368) up the Rio Douro's gorges into the extraordinary port-wine country
- Witnessing the past in **Vale do Côa** (p390), home to thousands of Palaeolithic engravings dating back 10,000 years

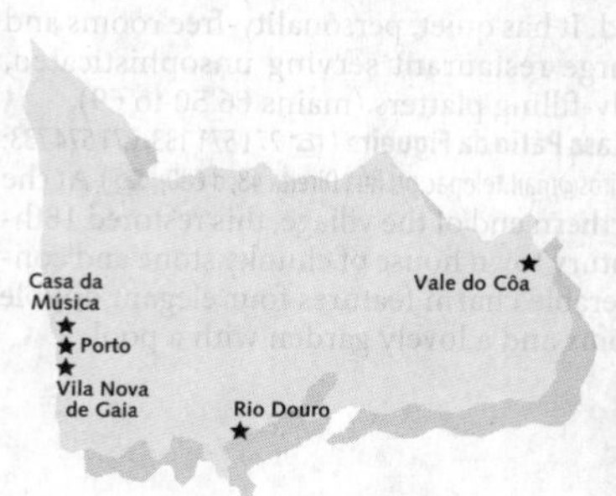

- POPULATION: 1,997,000
- AREA: 3350 SQ KM

PORTO

pop 1,375,000 / elevation 80m

Draped across a series of riverside bluffs, old Porto is a jumble of styles, eras and attitudes: wide Roman ramparts and narrow, medieval alleyways, extravagant baroque churches and prim, Parisian-style squares. And yet the disparate parts add up to an enchanting whole that equally reflects exuberance and melancholy, urbanity and upcountry charm.

Tripeiros (Porto natives), too, are their own peculiar conglomeration. They exhibit a devotion to commerce as well as a certain reserve, both of which are more reminiscent of northern Europe. Proud of their work ethic, they often grumble that Lisbon merely spends what they earn. Yet they don't hesitate to enjoy the fruits of their labours.

The city regularly imports Europe's top DJs, and on warm summer nights the banks of the Douro turn into one long block party. Nor is revelry limited to the young; many nightclubs attract a refreshingly multigenerational clientele.

In the last two decades the city has undergone a remarkable renaissance, expressed in the gleam of its spiffed up squares and monuments and the hum of its new metro system. The crowning glories are two new masterworks – Siza Vieira's Museu de Arte Contemporânea and Rem Koolhaas' Casa da Música (Music Hall) – which have turned the city into a site of pilgrimage for architecture buffs. And yet Porto manages not to feel like simulacrum of itself, as so many prospering European cities do nowadays.

There is still a little too much dog shit in the streets, a few too many unrepentant drunks skulking in the alleys, and a few too many lovely old buildings falling into ruin for anyone to declare that gentrification is complete. We'll drink to that.

Speaking of drinks, we can't forget the town's eponymous tipple. Just across the swift Douro from Porto lies Vila Nova de Gaia (technically another city but included here), where scores of historic port-wine lodges clamber up the far bank.

Every year, vast grape harvests from the Douro valley still make their way here to be matured, blended and bottled – fruity rubies, nuttie tawnies, complex late-bottled vintage port. We'll drink to that, too.

HISTORY

Porto put the 'Portu' in 'Portugal'. The name dates from Roman times, when Lusitanian settlements straddled both sides of the Douro's banks. The area was briefly in the hands of Moors but was reconquered by AD 1000 and reorganised as the county of Portucale, with Porto as its capital. British-born Henri of Burgundy was granted the land in 1095, and it was from here that Henri's son and Portuguese hero Afonso Henriques launched the Reconquista (Christian reconquest), ultimately winning Portugal its status as an independent kingdom.

In 1387 Dom João I married Philippa of Lancaster in Porto, and their most famous son, Henry the Navigator, was born here. While Henry's explorers groped around Africa for a sea route to India, British wine merchants – forbidden to trade with the French – set up shop, and their presence continues to this day, evidenced in port-wine labels such as Taylor's and Graham's.

Over the following centuries Porto acquired a well-earned reputation for rebelliousness. In 1628 a mob of angry women attacked the minister responsible for a tax on linen. A 'tipplers' riot' against the Marquês de Pombal's regulation of the port-wine trade was savagely put down in 1757. And in 1808, as Napoleon's troops occupied the city, Porto citizens arrested the French governor and set up their own, short-lived junta. After the British helped drive out the French, Porto radicals were at it again, leading calls for a new liberal constitution, which they got in 1822. Demonstrations in support of liberals continued to erupt in Porto throughout the 19th century.

Meanwhile, wine profits helped fund the city's industrialisation, which began in earnest in the late 19th century, when elites in the rest of Portugal tended to see trade and manufacturing as vulgar. Today, the city remains the economic capital of northern Portugal and is surpassed only by much-larger Lisbon in terms of economic and social clout.

ORIENTATION

Central Porto sits on a series of bluffs some 5km east of the mouth of the Douro. The city's central axis is Avenida dos Aliados (aka 'Aliados'), a handsome avenue carved out in 1915 in homage to French Art Nouveau. At its northern end are the *câmara municipal* (town hall), the main turismo (tourist office) and the central post office. Just south of the Aliados along the

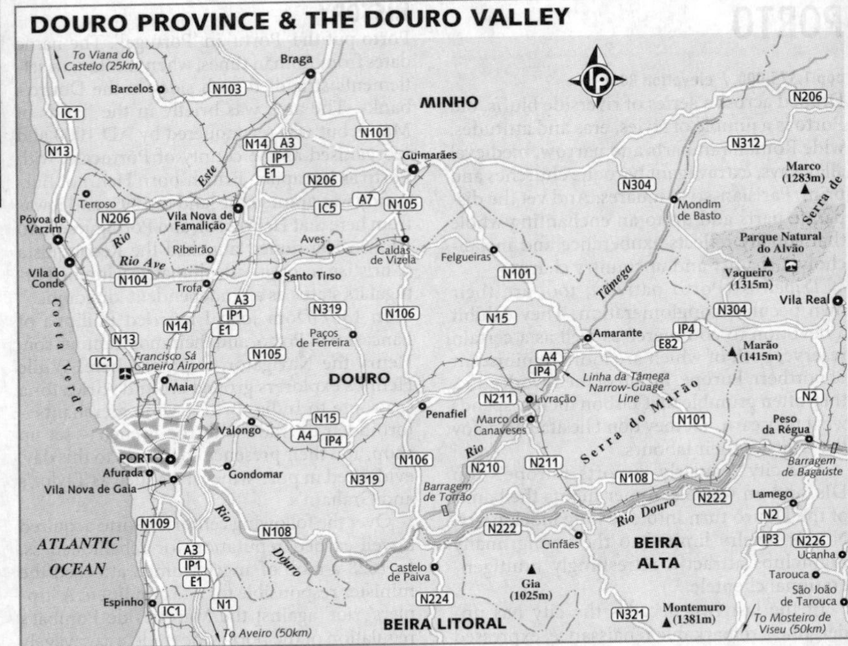

banks of the Douro lies the Ribeira district – the city's historic heart and most picturesque neighbourhood. East of Aliados is a lively shopping area that includes the Mercado do Bolhão (Bolhão Market), Rua Santa Catarina and Praça da Batalha.

'New' Porto sprawls out westward to the sea. It includes the trendy Foz do Douro neighbourhood around the mouth of the Douro and, moving up the coast, the upscale Matosinhos district.

Roughly dividing central Porto from new Porto is the Boavista district. Centred on the giant Praça de Mouzinho de Albuquerque roundabout, it's an area of modern hotels, shopping malls, large office buildings and the new Casa da Música.

Central hubs for city and regional buses include Praça da Liberdade (the southern end of Aliados), the adjacent São Bento train station, and Jardim da Cordoaria about 400m west of Aliados.

Porto's Francisco Sá Carneiro airport lies 19km northwest of the city centre and is connected by the city's newest metro line. There are two train stations: Campanhã, 2km east of the centre, which handles intercity traffic, and central São Bento, which is only for commuter lines. Trindade station, just north of Aliados, is now the hub of Porto's metro system. Intercity bus terminals are scattered all over the city; see p375 for further information.

The World Heritage zone reaches from the Torre dos Clérigos and São Bento station down to the Cais da Ribeira. Also included are the Ponte de Dom Luís I and the Mosteiro da Serra de Pilar in Vila Nova de Gaia.

Parking is competitive in central Porto. Street parking is especially tight, with a two-hour maximum stay on weekdays. There is no limit on weekends and spaces are much more readily available. Most squares now have paying, underground lots – follow the blue Ps. Beware that men may guide you into places and then expect tips. They can be very disagreeable if you don't comply. They also may direct you into an illegal spot – be sure to double-check signs. The Loja de Mobilidade (see p359) provides a map devoted exclusively to parking.

You can pick up free maps of the city, including bus and metro maps, at any of Porto's tourist offices.

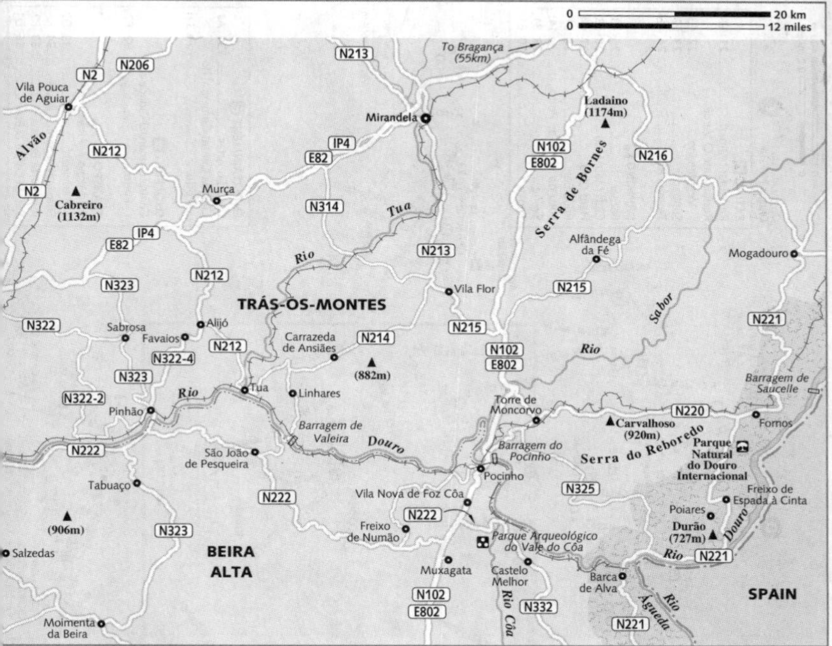

INFORMATION

Bookshops

Newsagents near Aliados and Rua Santa Catarina tend to stock at least a few foreign-language newspapers and periodicals.

Livraria Bertrand (Map p360; ☎ 222 080 638; Centro Comercial Via Catarina, Rua Santa Catarina; 🕑 10am-10pm) Has a selection of travel books and maps.

Livraria Latina Editora (Map p360; ☎ 222 001 294; Rua Santa Catarina 2; 🕑 10am-7pm Mon-Sat) Well-stocked with English-language guidebooks, plus a small selection of foreign novels.

Livraria Lello (Map p360; ☎ 222 002 037; Rua das Carmelitas 144; 🕑 10am-7pm Mon-Sat) Even if you're not after books, don't miss this 1906, neo-Gothic confection stacked to the rafters with new, secondhand and antique books, including foreign-language guidebooks and some literature. Up the curving staircase is a pleasant café.

Cultural Centres

British Council (Map p358; ☎ 222 073 060; Rua do Breiner 155; 🕑 2-8.30pm Mon & Wed, 10am-1pm & 2-8.30pm Tue & Thu, 2-7.30pm Fri, irregular hours Sat mid-Sep–mid-Jun, 2-5.30pm Mon, Wed & Fri, 10am-1pm & 2-5.30pm Tue & Thu mid-Jun–mid-Sep, closed Aug) Has a library full of English-language books and newspapers.

Emergency

Police station (Map p360; ☎ 222 006 821; Rua Augusto Rosa) South of Praça da Batalha.

Tourism police (Map p360; ☎ 222 081 833; Rua Clube dos Fenianos 11; 🕑 8am-2am) Multilingual station beside the main city turismo.

Internet Access

Biblioteca Municipal Almeida Garrett (Map p358; Jardim do Palácio de Cristal; 🕑 2-6pm Mon, 10am-6pm Tue-Sat) Library with free internet access, one-hour slots and long waits.

Laranja Mecânica (Map p360; Rua Santa Catarina 274, Loja V; per hr €1.40; 🕑 10am-midnight Mon-Sat, 2-8pm Sun)

On Web (Map p360; Praça General Humberto Delgado 291; per hr €1.20; 🕑 10am-2am Mon-Sat, 3pm-2am Sun) As little as €0.60 for longer-term users.

Portugal Telecom Office (PT; Map p360; Praça da Liberdade 62; per hr €2.30; 🕑 8am-8pm Mon-Sat, 10am-8pm Sun) The telephone office also has a dozen pricey terminals.

Internet Resources

www.agendadoporto.pt Thorough, day-by-day events guide to the city, in Portuguese.

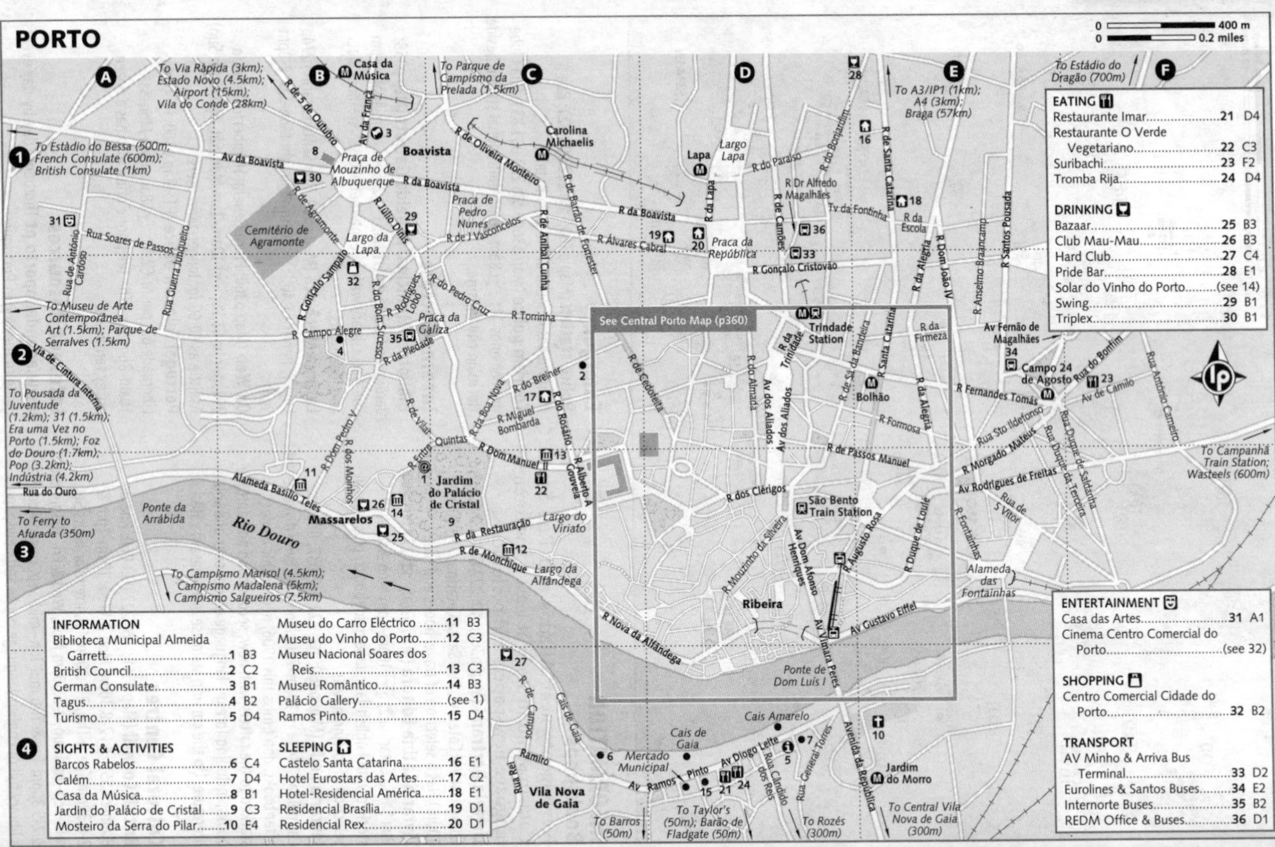
PORTO
0 400 m
0 0.2 miles
A B C D E F
1 2 3 4
To Via Rápida (3km); Estado Novo (4.5km); Airport (15km); Vila do Conde (28km)
To Parque de Campismo da Prelada (1.5km)
To A3/IP1 (1km); A4 (3km); Braga (57km)
To Estádio do Dragão (700m)
To Estádio do Bessa (500m; French Consulate (600m); British Consulate (1km)
To Museu de Arte Contemporânea Art (1.5km); Parque de Serralves (1.5km)
To Pousada da Juventude (1.2km); 31 (1.5km); Era uma Vez no Porto (1.5km); Foz do Douro (1.7km); Pop (3.2km); Indústria (4.2km)
To Ferry to Afurada (350m)
To Campismo Marisol (4.5km); Campismo Madalena (5km); Campismo Salgueiros (7.5km)
To Campanhã Train Station; Wasteels (600m)
To Barros (50m)
To Taylor's (50m); Barão de Fladgate (50m)
To Rozés (300m)
To Central Vila Nova de Gaia (300m)
See Central Porto Map (p360)
Casa da Música
Boavista
Praça de Mouzinho de Albuquerque
Carolina Michaelis
Lapa
Largo Lapa
Praça da República
Trindade Station
Bolhão
São Bento Train Station
Ribeira
Campo 24 de Agosto
Jardim do Palácio de Cristal
Massarelos
Rio Douro
Ponte da Arrábida
Ponte de Dom Luís I
Vila Nova de Gaia
Jardim do Morro
Cemitério de Agramonte
Mercado Municipal
Cais de Gaia
Cais Amarelo
Largo da Lapa
Praça de Pedro Nunes
Praça da Galiza
Largo do Viriato
Largo da Alfândega
Alameda das Fontainhas
Av da Boavista
R da Boavista
R de 5 de Outubro
Av da França
R de Oliveira Monteiro
R de Agramonte
R Júlio Dinis
R de Gonçalo Sampaio
R do Bom Sucesso
R Rodrigues Lobo
R do Pedro Cruz
R da Piedade
R Campo Alegre
R Dom Pedro V
R dos Moinhos
R de Vilar
R Entre Quintas
R Dom Manuel II
R Alberto A Gouveia
R da Restauração
R de Monchique
Alameda Basílio Teles
Rua do Ouro
Rua Soares de Passos
Rua de António Cardoso
Rua Guerra Junqueiro
Via de Cintura Interna
R de Barrão de Forrester
R de Aníbal Cunha
R de J Vasconcelos
R Álvares Cabral
R da Lapa
R do Paraíso
R do Bonjardim
R Dr Alfredo Magalhães
R de Camões
Tv da Fontinha
R de Santa Catarina
R da Escola
R Gonçalo Cristovão
R da Alegria
R Dom João IV
R Anselmo Braamcamp
R Santos Pousada
R Torrinha
R do Breiner
R da Boa Nova
R Miguel Bombarda
R do Rosário
R de Cedofeita
R do Almada
Av dos Aliados
R da Trindade
R de Sá da Bandeira
R Santa Catarina
R da Firmeza
R Formosa
R de Passos Manuel
R dos Clérigos
R Mouzinho da Silveira
Av Dom Afonso Henriques
R Augusto Rosa
R Duque de Loulé
R Nova da Alfândega
Av Vimara Peres
Av Gustavo Eiffel
Av Fernão de Magalhães
R Fernandes Tomás
Rua do Bonfim
Av de Camilo
Rua António Carneiro
Rua Sto Ildefonso
R Morgado Mateus
Rua Duque da Terceira
Rua Duque de Saldanha
Av Rodrigues de Freitas
Rua de S Vitor
R Fontaínhas
Cais de Gaia
R de Campos
Ramiro
Rua Rei
Av Ramos Pinto
Av Diogo Leite
Rua Cândido dos Reis
Rua General Torres
Avenida da República
EATING
Restaurante Imar....21 D4
Restaurante O Verde Vegetariano....22 C3
Suribachi....23 F2
Tromba Rija....24 D4
DRINKING
Bazaar....25 B3
Club Mau-Mau....26 B3
Hard Club....27 C4
Pride Bar....28 E1
Solar do Vinho do Porto....(see 14)
Swing....29 B1
Triplex....30 B1
ENTERTAINMENT
Casa das Artes....31 A1
Cinema Centro Comercial do Porto....(see 32)
SHOPPING
Centro Comercial Cidade do Porto....32 B2
TRANSPORT
AV Minho & Arriva Bus Terminal....33 D2
Eurolines & Santos Buses....34 E2
Internorte Buses....35 B2
REDM Office & Buses....36 D1
INFORMATION
Biblioteca Municipal Almeida Garrett....1 B3
British Council....2 C2
German Consulate....3 B1
Tagus....4 B2
Turismo....5 D4
Museu do Carro Eléctrico....11 B3
Museu do Vinho do Porto....12 C3
Museu Nacional Soares dos Reis....13 C3
Museu Romântico....14 B3
Palácio Gallery....(see 1)
Ramos Pinto....15 D4
SIGHTS & ACTIVITIES
Barcos Rabelos....6 C4
Calém....7 D4
Casa da Música....8 B1
Jardin do Palácio de Cristal....9 C3
Mosteiro da Serra do Pilar....10 E4
SLEEPING
Castelo Santa Catarina....16 E1
Hotel Eurostars das Artes....17 C2
Hotel-Residencial América....18 E1
Residencial Brasília....19 D1
Residencial Rex....20 D1

www.portoturismo.pt Useful & complete guide from the city's tourist office, with English- & Spanish-language versions.

www.portoxxi.com Cultural guide with restaurant listings, including a version in quirky English.

Laundry

Lavandaria São Nicolau (Map p362; ☎ 222 084 621; Rua da Reboleira; 🕑 8.30am-7.30pm Tue-Fri, 8.30am-7pm Sat) Costs €6 to wash and dry a 6kg load. There are also showers in this underground complex.

Medical Services

Hospital Geral de Santo António (Map p360; ☎ 222 077 500; Rua Prof Vicente J Carvalho) Has some English-speaking staff.

Money

There is a currency exchange, open 5am to 1am, as well as several 24-hour ATMs in the airport arrivals hall. If you need a private exchange, consider the following:

Intercontinental (Map p360; ☎ 222 005 557; Rua de Ramalho Ortigão 8; 🕑 9am-noon & 2-6.30pm Mon-Fri, 9am-noon Sat)

Portocâmbios (Map p360; ☎ 222 000 238; Rua Rodrigues Sampaio 193; 🕑 9am-12.30pm & 1.30-6pm Mon-Fri, 9am-12.30pm Sat)

Top Atlântico ((Map p360; ☎ 222 074 020; Praça General Humberto Delgado) Cash your American Express (Amex) travellers cheques here.

Post

Branch post offices Praça da Batalha (Map p360; 🕑 8.30am-6pm Mon-Fri); Rua Ferreira Borges 67 (Map p362; Ribeira; 🕑 8.30am-6pm Mon-Fri)

Main post office (Map p360; ☎ 223 400 200; Avenida dos Aliados; 🕑 8am-9pm Mon-Fri, 9am-6pm Sat, 9am-12.30pm & 2-6pm Sun) Opposite the main city turismo.

Telephone

Post offices, kiosks and newsagents sell Portugal Telecom phonecards, which can be used from most pubic phones.

Portugal Telecom office (PT; Map p360; ☎ 225 001 117; Praça da Liberdade 62; 🕑 8am-8pm Mon-Sat, 10am-8pm Sun) The handiest place for long-distance calls using cardphones or pay-afterward *cabines* (phone boxes). Expect to pay €0.30 to €0.60 per minute for calls to Europe and the US and upwards of €2 for Australia and New Zealand.

Tourist Information

Branch turismos Ribeira (Map p362; ☎ 222 060 412; Rua Infante Dom Henrique 63; 🕑 9am-7pm Jul & Aug, 9am-5.30pm Mon-Fri, 9.30am-4.30pm Sat & Sun Sep-Jun) Run by the city tourist office; Airport (☎ 229 412 534, 229 432 400; 🕑 8am-11pm) Run by ICEP.

ICEP turismo (Map p360; ☎ 222 057 514; Praça Dom João I 43; 🕑 9am-7.30pm Jul & Aug, 9am-7.30pm Mon-Fri, 9.30am-3.30pm Sat & Sun Sep & Apr-Jun, 9am-7pm Mon-Fri, 9.30am-3.30pm Sat & Sun Nov-Mar) For country-wide queries, visit this national turismo.

Main city turismo (Map p360; ☎ 223 393 472; turismo.central@cm-porto.pt; Rua Clube dos Fenianos 25; 🕑 9am-7pm Jul & Aug, 9am-5.30pm Mon-Fri, 9.30am-4.30pm Sat & Sun Sep-Jun) Opposite the *câmara municipal*. This office has a detailed city map, transport map and *Agenda do Porto* cultural calendar. It also houses the **Loja da Mobilidade** (Mobility Store; loja.mobilidade@cm-porto.pt; 🕑 9am-5.30pm Mon-Fri), which dispenses a handy brochure, *Guia de Transportes* (English version available), sells tickets and passes, and can provide details on everything from bus timetables to car parks and metro stations.

Travel Agencies

When booking a tour, see p368 for details of government-run Porto Tours, which acts as impartial intermediary between tour operators and travellers.

Tagus (Map p358; ☎ 226 094 146; www.viagenstagus.pt; Rua Campo Alegre 261; 🕑 9am-6pm Mon-Fri, 10am-1pm Sat) Youth-oriented agency selling discounted tickets, rail passes and international youth and student cards.

Top Atlântico (Map p360; ☎ 222 074 020; Praça General Humberto Delgado) Also Porto's Amex representative.

Wasteels (☎ 225 194 230; www.wasteels.pt; Rua Pinto Bessa 27-29; 🕑 9.30am-12.30pm & 1.45-6pm Mon-Fri) Another youth-oriented agency, near Campanhã train station.

DANGERS & ANNOYANCES

While Porto is generally quite safe, it's worth exercising caution after dark on the side streets of the Ribeira district as well as in the area between the São Bento Station and the cathedral.

Before jumping into the sea at Foz do Douro, ask around about current conditions – pollution has been a problem in the past and doubts have been cast on recent claims of purity. If you have qualms, head to Vila do Conde (26km to the north).

SIGHTS

Most of Porto's sights are found in its compact centre and in easy walking distance of each other, though the city's hills can turn an outing into a vigorous workout.

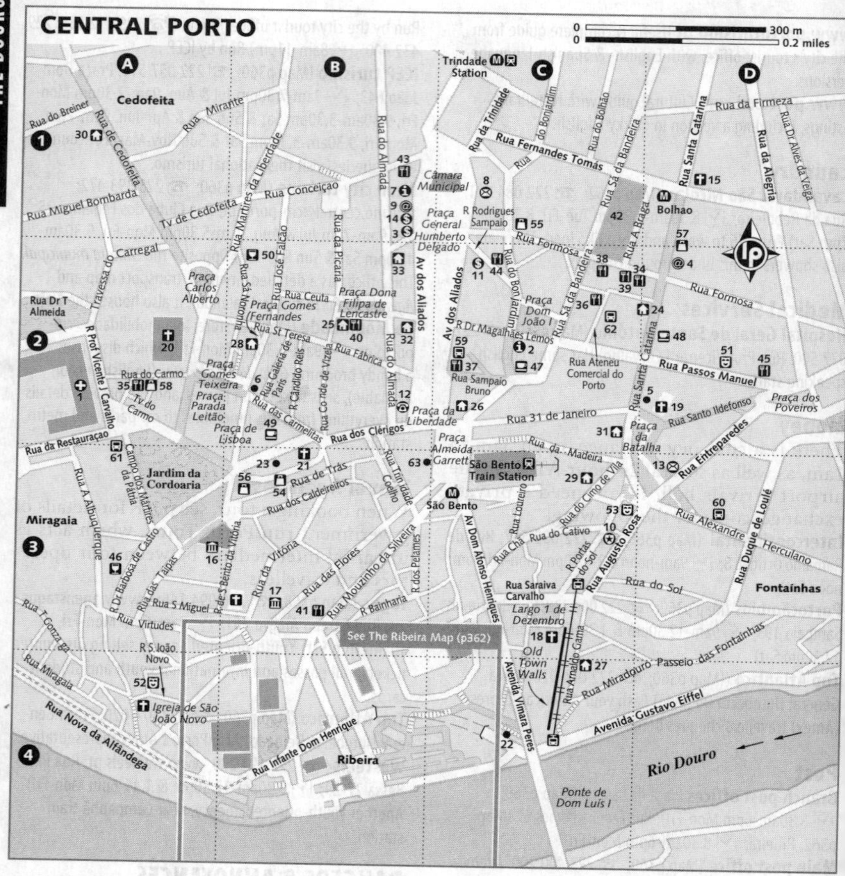

Ribeira

The **Ribeira** district – Porto's riverfront nucleus – is a remarkable window into Porto's history. Perhaps best of all is the riverside promenade, where *barcos rabelos* (the traditional boats used to ferry port wine down the Douro) bob photogenically in the shadow of the glowering Ponte de Dom Luís I. From here you have a fine perspectives of the sea of port-wine lodges across the river in Vila Nova de Gaia. Despite flocks of tourists, the neighbourhood remains easy-going and surprisingly ungentrified.

Just back from the river is the handsomely renovated **Casa do Infante** (Map p362; ☎ 222 060 400; Rua Alfândega 10, Ribeira; adult/senior & under 26 €2/1, Sat & Sun free; ⏲ 10am-noon & 2-5pm Tue-Sat, 2-5pm Sun). It's claimed that Henry the Navigator was born here in 1394, and the house later served as Porto's first customs house and now houses its historical archives. The complex was recently excavated, revealing Roman foundations as well as some remarkable mosaics – all of which are now on display.

Sitting on the nearby Praça Infante Dom Henrique, **Igreja de São Francisco** (Map p362; ☎ 222 062 100; Rua Infante Dom Henrique; adult/student €3/2.50; ⏲ 9am-6pm) looks from the outside to be an austerely Gothic church, but inside hides one of Portugal's most dazzling displays of baroque finery. Hardly an inch escapes unsmothered, as unworldly cherubs and sober monks alike are drowned by nearly 100kg of gold leaf. The church has been deconsecrated, ministering only to tourists greedy to see all that gold.

INFORMATION
Hospital Geral de Santo António...1 A2
ICEP Turismo...2 C2
Intercontinental...3 B1
Laranja Mecânica...4 D2
Livraria Bertrand...(see 57)
Livraria Latina Editora...5 D2
Livraria Lello...6 B2
Main City Turismo...7 B1
Main Post Office...8 C1
On Web...9 B1
Police Station...10 C3
Portocâmbios...11 C2
Portugal Telecom Office...12 B2
Post Office...13 D3
Top Atlântico...14 B1
Tourism Police...(see 7)

SIGHTS & ACTIVITIES
Capela das Almas...15 D1
Centro Português de Fotografia...16 A3
Igreja da Misericórdia...17 B3
Igreja de Santa Clara...18 C3
Igreja de Santo Ildefonso...19 D2
Igreja do Carmo...20 A2
Igreja dos Clérigos...21 B3
Ribeira Negra Mural...22 C4
Torre dos Clérigos...23 B3

SLEEPING
Grande Hotel do Porto...24 D2
Hotel Infante de Sagres...25 B2
Hotel Peninsular...26 C2
Pensão Astória...27 C4
Pensão Duas Nações...28 B2
Pensão Mondariz...29 C3
Pensão-Residencial Estoril...30 A1
Quality Inn Praça da Batalha...31 C2
Residencial dos Aliados...32 B2
Residencial Pão de Açucar...33 B2

EATING
A Pérola do Bolhão...34 C2
A Tasquinha...35 A2
Abadia...36 C2
Café Embaixador...37 C2
Confeitaria do Bolhão...38 C2
Confeitaria do Bolhão Shop...39 C2
Confeitaria Sical...40 B2
Indian Classic...41 B3
Mercado do Bolhão...42 C1
Minipreço...43 B1
Modelo...(see 57)
Pedro dos Frangos...44 C2
Pingo Doce...45 D2

DRINKING
Boys 'R' Us...46 A3
Café A Brasileira...47 C2
Café Ancôra Douro...(see 41)
Café Guarany...(see 32)
Café Majestic...48 D2
Café na Praça...49 B2
Moinho de Vento...50 B2

ENTERTAINMENT
Coliseu do Porto...51 D2
Restaurante O Fado...52 A4
Teatro Nacional São João...53 C3

SHOPPING
Artesanato dos Clérigos...54 B3
Casa Januário...55 C1
Casa Oriental...56 B3
Centro Comercial Via Caterina...57 D1
Garrafeira do Carmo...58 A2

TRANSPORT
AeroBus Terminus...59 C2
Paragem Atlântico Terminal...(see 60)
Rede Expressos...60 D3
Renex Buses...61 A3
Rodonorte Bus Terminal...62 C2
STCP Service Point...63 B3

Next door to the church you'll see another temple – this one dedicated unabashedly to Mammon. The **Palácio da Bolsa** (Stock Exchange; Map p362; ☎ 223 399 000; Rua Ferreira Borges, Ribeira; 9am-6.30pm Apr-Oct, 9am-1pm & 2-5.30pm Nov-Mar) is a splendid neoclassical monument (built from 1842 to 1910) to honour Porto's past-and-present money merchants. Just past the entrance hall is the glass-domed **Pátio das Nações** (Hall of Nations), where the exchange once operated. But this pales in comparison with rooms deeper inside, and to visit these you must join one of the €5 guided tours that set off every 30 minutes, and last for 30 minutes. You can usually join any group; tours are given in any two of Portuguese, English and French. The highlight is a stupendous ballroom called the **Salão Árabe** (Arabian Hall), with stucco walls that have been teased into complex Moorish designs, then gilded with some 18kg of gold.

North of the square on the distinctly Parisian Rua das Flores, you'll find Nicolau Nasoni's rococo façade of the **Igreja da Misericórdia** (Map p360; ☎ 222 074 710; Rua das Flores 15; adult/student €1.50/free; 9.30am-12.30pm & 2-5.30pm Tue-Fri, 9am-noon Sat & Sun). Now a museum, the church shelters the superb, anonymous Renaissance painting known as *Fons Vitae* (Fountain of Life), showing Dom Manuel I and his family around a fountain of blood from the crucified Christ.

Back down by the river, narrow streets open out onto **Praça da Ribeira**, which – with its river views and austerely grand, tiled town houses – is shorthand for Porto itself. From here you have fine views of both the port-wine lodges across the river as well as the monumental, double-decker **Ponte de Dom Luís I**. Completed in 1886 by a student of Gustave Eiffel, the bridge's top deck is now reserved for pedestrians as well as one of the city's metro lines; the lower deck bears regular traffic. Both afford wonderful views. Bringing the art of the *azulejo* (hand-painted tiles) up to date, the modernist, polychromatic **Ribeira Negra** (Map p360) by Júlio Resende is a huge, tiled mural celebrating life in the Ribeira district. Created in 1987, it's located at the mouth of the tunnel to the lower deck of the Ponte de Dom Luís I.

From Praça da Ribeira rises a tangle of medieval alleys and stairways that eventually reach the hulking, hilltop fortress of a **cathedral** (Map p362; ☎ 222 059 028; admission cloister €2; cathedral 8.45am-12.30pm & 2.30-7pm, cloister 9am-12.15pm & 2.30-6pm Mon-Sat, 2.30-6pm Sun, both close 1hr earlier Nov-Mar). Founded in the 12th century, the cathedral was largely rebuilt a century later and then extensively altered in the 18th century. However, you can still make out the church's Romanesque contours. Inside, a rose window and a 14th-century Gothic cloister remain from its early days. Don't miss the upper storey of

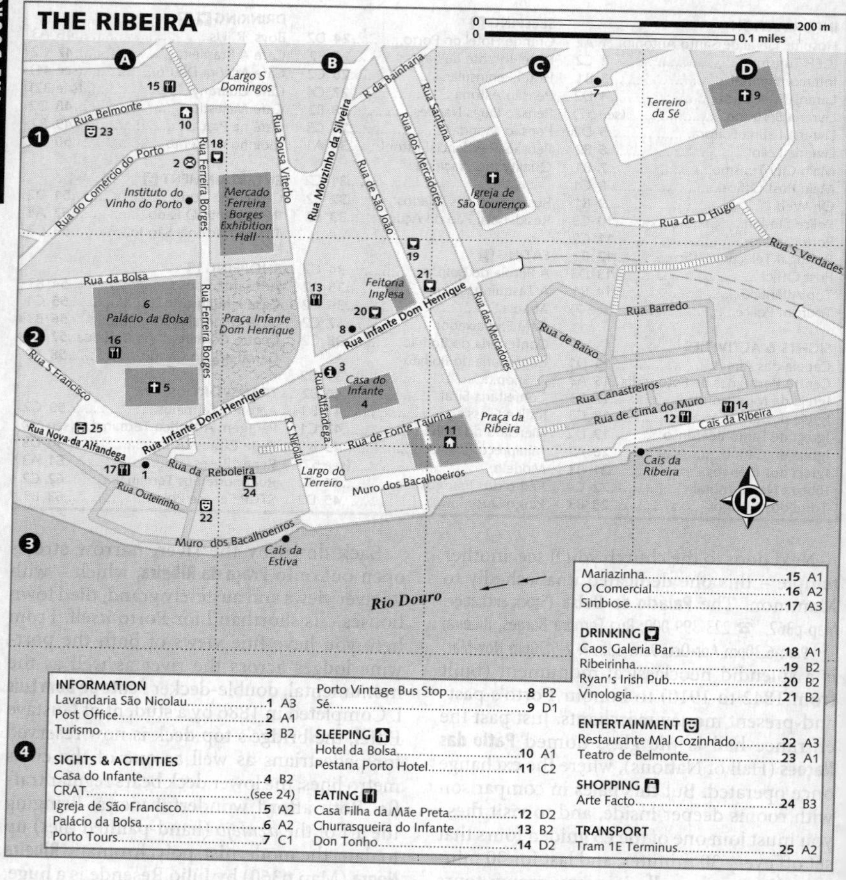

the cloister (reached via a Nasoni-designed stairway), decorated with 18th-century *azulejos* by Vital Rifarto that lavishly illustrate scenes from the Song of Songs.

The **Igreja de Santa Clara** (Map p360; ☎ 222 054 837; Largo 1 de Dezembro; ⏲ 9.30am-11.30am & 3-6pm Mon-Fri), east of the cathedral, was part of another Franciscan convent. Gothic in shape, with a fine Renaissance portal, its interior is also dense with elaborately gilded woodwork.

Aliados, Batalha & Bolhão

With bulging, beaux-arts façades and capped by the grand **câmara municipal**, the short but grand **Avenida dos Aliados** may not be exactly Parisian, but it certainly recalls grand Parisian imitators like Buenos Aires and Budapest. Its central plaza has been recently repaved and spiffed up, and if it weren't for all the buses (this is the city's transport hub) it would be a fine place to linger.

Just uphill from Aliados you can get your bearings and bird's-eye photographs from the vertigo-inducing **Torre dos Clérigos** (Map p360; Rua dos Clérigos; admission €1; ⏲ 10am-1pm & 2-8pm Aug, 9.30am-1pm & 2-7pm Apr-Jul, Sep & Oct, 10am-noon & 2-5pm Nov-Mar). Italian-born baroque master Nicolau Nasoni designed the 76m-high tower in the mid-1700s. To reach the top you must scale its 225-step spiral staircase. Nasoni also designed the adjacent **Igreja dos Clérigos**, with its theatrical façade and unusual, oval-shaped nave.

Just off the Aliados lies **São Bento train station**. Designed by José Marques da Silva and completed in 1903, it seems to have been imported straight from 19th-century Paris, thanks to its mansard roof and imposing stone façade. But the dramatic *azulejos* in the front hall are an entirely Portuguese creation. Completed by Jorge Colaço in 1930, they depict historic battles scenes as well as a history of transport.

Just east of Aliados lies the 19th-century, wrought-iron **Mercado do Bolhão** (Map p360; Rua Formosa; 8am-5pm Mon-Fri, 8am-1pm Sat), where earthy vendors sell fresh produce, including cheeses, olives, smoked meats, fresh flowers and more. Uphill along Rua Formosa are **Confeitaria do Bolhão** (Map p360; Rua Formosa 305) and **A Pérola do Bolhão** (Map p360; Rua Formosa 279) – two Art Nouveau delicatessens stacked high with sausages and cheeses, olives, and dried fruits and nuts.

A little further lies the pedestrianised **Rua Santa Catarina**, the main shopping district in the centre, with its trim boutiques and animated crowds. You won't be able to miss the small but extraordinary façade of the **Capela das Almas** (Map p360; Rua Santa Catarina 428; irregular hours), which is smothered in lustrously blue *azulejos*. Though painted in classic 18th-century style, they actually date back only to the early 20th century.

At its southern end, Rua Santa Catarina opens out onto the lovely, eclectic **Praça da Batalha**. It's anchored at one end by Nasoni's gracefully baroque **Igreja de Santo Ildefonso** (Map p360; 222 004 366; 9.30am-noon & 3-6.30pm Mon-Sat, 9am-12.30pm & 6-7.45pm Sun) and at the other by the lavishly romantic **Teatro Nacional São João** (p374), built in the style of Paris' Opéra-Garnier by the architect of Bento train station.

Cordoaria

Uphill from Aliados and past the Torre dos Clérigos lies the pleasantly leafy **Jardim da Cordoaria** (simply called 'Cordoaria'). Architecture buffs will want to check out the nearby **Hospital Geral de Santo António,** whose neo-Palladian façade recalls an Oxfordshire manor house. Just north of the square, the **Igreja do Carmo** (Map p360; 222 078 400; Praça Gomes Teixeira; 8am-noon, 2-5pm Mon-Fri, 8am-noon Sat) is one of Porto's best examples of rococo architecture; the entrance is via the main door on Rua do Carmo. It features a remarkable, *azulejo*-laden façade, including Silvestre Silvestri's exquisite panel illustrating the legend of the founding of the Carmelite order.

On the south side of Cordoaria is a stately yet muscular building (1796) that once served as a prison and now houses the **Centro Português de Fotografia** (Portuguese Photography Centre; Map p360; 222 076 310; www.cpf.pt; Campo Mártires da Pátria; admission free; exhibition hall 3-6pm Tue-Fri, 3-7pm Sat & Sun). Multiple exhibitions offer a portrait of Porto and Portugal in the age of photography. Note that the rather gloomy lanes south of the museum were once part of Porto's *judiaria* (Jewish quarter).

A short walk west of Cordoaria lands you at **Museu Nacional Soares dos Reis** (Map p358; 223 393 770; www.mnsr-ipmuseus.pt; Rua Dom Manuel II 44; admission €3, 10am-2pm Sun free; 2-6pm Tue, 10am-6pm

MUSIC IN THE HOUSE

Called 'insane' yet 'brilliant' by the *Times* and 'ruthlessly inventive' by the *Guardian*, Porto's new **Casa da Música** (House of Music; Map p358; 220 120 220; www.casadamusica.com; Avenida da Boavista 604) finally opened its doors in 2005 – four years late but every bit worth the wait. Like a gigantic piece of a raw crystal, the cloud-white concrete exterior is at once rigorously geometric and defiantly unsymmetrical. But that monolithic sheathing doesn't prepare you for the surprisingly varied delights inside.

At the building's heart is a classic shoe-box–style concert hall meticulously engineered to accommodate everything from jazz duets to Beethoven's Ninth. It's also home to most of the building's only right angles. The rest of the rooms, from classrooms and practice halls to a light-filled VIP lounge, wind around the central hall in a progression of trapezoids and acute angles. It's as if architect Rem Koolhaas has deliberately crushed and twisted the sombre geometry of high modernism, then added narrative touches such as *azulejos* (hand-painted tiles) and gilded furnishings – though always refracted through his own peculiar vision.

The hall holds concerts most nights of the year, from classical to jazz, *fado* (traditional, melancholic Portuguese singing) to electronica. It also offers guided tours led by students from Porto's highly regarded school of architecture. Tours in English are generally given daily at 11.30am and 4pm, and cost €2.

Wed-Sun). The town's most comprehensive art collection, it ranges from Neolithic carvings to Portugal's take on modernism and is housed in the formidable Palácio das Carrancas. Requisitioned by Napoleonic invaders, the neoclassical palace was abandoned so rapidly that the future Duke of Wellington found an unfinished banquet in the dining hall.

Transformed into a museum of fine and decorative arts in 1940, its best works date from the 19th century, including sculpture by António Soares dos Reis (see especially his famous *O Desterrado*, The Exile) and António Teixeira Lopes, and the naturalistic paintings of Henrique Pousão and António Silva Porto.

Boavista & Western Porto

The vast roundabout at Praça de Mousinho de Albuquerque roughly marks the boundary between 'old' and 'new' Porto. Here you'll find **Casa da Música** (see p363), Porto's extraordinary new concert hall. Three kilometres west, in a leafy, upscale suburb off the grand Avenida Boavista, is Porto's other great work of contemporary architecture.

Designed by eminent, Porto-based architect Álvaro Siza Vieira, the **Museu de Arte Contemporânea** (Fundação de Serralves, Museum of Contemporary Art; ☎ 226 156 500; www.serralves.pt; Rua Dom João de Castro 210; admission museum & park €5, park or museum only €2.50, 10am-2pm Sun free; 10am-7pm Tue, Wed & Fri-Sun, 10am-10pm Thu Oct-Mar, 10am-7pm Tue-Thu, 10am-10pm Fri & Sat, 10am-8pm Sun Apr-Sep) is an arrestingly minimalist construction of vast, whitewashed spaces bathed in natural light.

Most of the museum is devoted to cutting-edge exhibitions, though there's also a fine permanent collection featuring works from the late 1960s to the present by the likes of Gerhard Richter, Ed Ruscha and Georg Baselitz. With a single admission, you can also visit the nearby **Casa de Serralves**, a delightful pink Art Deco mansion (built by a forward-looking nobleman in the 1930s) that also hosts temporary exhibitions.

Both museums are located within the marvellous, 18-hectare **Parque de Serralves**. From lily ponds and formal fountains to a blood-red sculpture of intriguingly oversized pruning sheers, these gardens are well worth a visit in their own right.

The estate and museum are 4km west of the city centre; take bus 78 from Praça da Liberdade or bus 21 from the Casa da Música metro stop.

Palácio de Cristal to Foz do Douro

Sitting atop bluffs just west of Porto's old centre, the leafy **Jardim do Palácio de Cristal** (Map p358; main entrance Rua Dom Manuel II; 8am-9pm Apr-Sep, 8am-7pm Oct-Mar) is home to a striking, domed sports pavilion and pleasant gardens with fantastic river views. But pride of place goes to the new, high-tech **Biblioteca Municipal Almeida Garrett** (p357).

Nestled on the garden's south slopes is the Quinta da Macieirinha, the small but stately home where the exiled king of Sardinia spent his final days holed up in 1843. The upstairs has been turned into the modest **Museu Romântico** (Map p358; ☎ 226 057 033; Rua Entre Quintas 220; admission Tue-Fri €2; 10am-12.30pm & 2-5.30pm Tue-Sat, 2-5.30pm Sun), featuring the king's belongings and dainty period furnishings. Downstairs is the wonderful **Solar do Vinho do Porto** (see p118).

Down by the river in a remodelled warehouse, the modest **Museu do Vinho do Porto** (Port Wine Museum; Map p358; ☎ 222 076 300; Rua do Monchique 45-52; adult/student & senior Tue-Sat €2/1; 11am-7pm Tue-Sun) explores the impact of the famous tipple on the region's history in a series of largely interactive displays, though it doesn't offer much insight into the wine itself.

Down the banks of the Douro is the cavernous **Museu do Carro Eléctrico** (Tram Museum; Map p358; ☎ 226 158 185; http://museu-carro-electrico.stcp.pt; Alameda Basílio Teles 51; admission incl free Andante transport for 4hr €3.50; 9.30am-12.30pm & 2.30-5pm Mon, 9.30am-12.30pm & 2.30-6pm Tue-Fri, 3-7pm Sat & Sun). Housed in a former switching-house, it displays dozens of beautifully restored old trams. See p377 for details of Porto's surviving tramlines, and p376 for information on the Andante card.

Vila Nova de Gaia

While technically its own municipality, Vila Nova de Gaia ('Gaia') sits just across the Douro from Porto and is woven into the city's fabric both by a series of stunning bridges as well as its shared history of port-wine making. Since the mid-18th century, port-wine bottlers and exporters have been obliged to maintain their 'lodges' – basically dressed-up warehouses – here.

Today some 60 of these lodges clamber up the steep riverbank, and at night the entire scene transforms itself into Portugal's version of Las Vegas, with huge neon signs clamouring for the attention of nonexperts and oenophiles alike.

PORT WINE 101

With its intense flavours, silky textures and appealing sweetness, port wine is easy to love, especially when taken with its proper accompaniments – cheese, nuts and dried fruit. Ports are also wonderfully varied, and even nonconnoisseurs can quickly tell an aged tawny from a late-bottled vintage (LBV). For a friendly primer on all things port, head to the convivial **Vinologia** (p373), where learned servers give an enlightening lesson with each glass they pour (English and French spoken). From here, you can head across the Douro to Vila Nova de Gaia to taste the output of particular houses (opposite). Finally, impress friends and loved ones by leading your own tour through the offerings at the remarkable **Solar do Vinho do Porto** (p118).

Until you've become an authority, we've prepared this quick cheat sheet.

History

It was probably Roman soldiers who first planted grapes in the Douro valley some 2000 years ago, but tradition credits the discovery of port itself to 17th-century British merchants. With their country at war with France, they turned to their old ally Portugal to meet their wine habit. The Douro valley was particularly productive, though its wines were dark and astringent. According to legend, the British threw in some brandy with grape juice, both to take off the wine's bite and preserve it for shipment back to England – and port wine was the result. In fact, the method may already have been in use in the region, though what's certain is that the Brits took to the stuff. Their influence in the region has been long and enduring, still evidenced in some of port's most illustrious names, including Taylor's, Graham's, and Cockburn's.

The Grapes

Port wine grapes are born out of adversity. They manage to grow on rocky terraces with hardly any water or even soil, and their roots must reach down as far as 30m, weaving past layers of acidic schist (shalelike stone) to find nourishment. In addition, the vines endure both extreme heat in summer and freezing temperatures in winter. It's believed that these conditions produce intense flavours that stand up to the infusions of brandy. The most common varietals are hardy, dark reds like Touriga, tinto cão and tinto barroca.

The Wine

Grapes are harvested in the autumn and immediately crushed (often still by foot) and allowed to ferment until alcohol levels reach 7% alcohol. At this point, one part brandy is added to every five parts of wine. Fermentation stops immediately, leaving the unfermented sugars that make port sweet. The quality of the grapes, together with the ways the wine is aged and stored, determines the kind of port you get. The most common include:

- Ruby – made from average-quality grapes, and aged at least two years in vats. Rich, red colours and sweet, fruity flavours.
- Tawny – made from average-quality grapes, and aged for two to seven years in wooden casks. Mahogany colours, drier than rubies with nuttier flavours.
- Aged Tawny – selected from higher quality grapes, then aged for many years in wood casks. Subtler and silkier than regular tawny.
- Late-Bottled Vintage (LBV) – made from very select grapes of a single year, aged for around five years in wood casks, then bottled. Similar to vintage, but ready for immediate drinking once bottled. Usually smoother and lighter-bodied than vintage.
- Vintage – made from the finest grape from a single year (and only select years qualify). Aged in barrels two years, then aged in bottles at least 10 years and up to 100 or more. Dark ruby colours, fruity yet extremely subtle and complex.

From Porto's Ribeira district, a short walk across Ponte de Dom Luís I lands you on Gaia's inviting, riverside promenade. Lined with beautiful *barcos rabelos* – flat-bottomed boats specially designed to carry wine down the Douro's once-dangerous rapids – the promenade offers grandstand views of Porto's historic centre. Here you'll find the city's **turismo** (Map p358; ☎ /fax 223 751 902; turismo.vngaia@mail.cm-gaia.pt; Avenida Diogo Leite 242; 🕑 10am-6pm Mon-Sat, 10am-1pm & 2-6pm Sun Jul & Aug, 10am-6pm Mon-Fri, 10am-1pm & 2-6pm Sat Sep-Jun), which dispenses a good town map and a brochure listing all the lodges open for tours.

Most people come here to taste the tipple, of course, and about 20 lodges oblige them. If you come in the high season (June to September), you may feel yourself rushed in the largest lodges. Then again, you won't have to wait long for a tour in your native tongue. Note that more and more large houses are charging for their tours (around €2), though these invariably include free tastings.

Right on the riverfront you can visit the rather grand **Ramos Pinto** (Map p358; ☎ 223 707 000; www.ramospinto.pt; Avenida Ramos Pinto 380; tour & tasting €2; 🕑 10am-6pm Mon-Sat Jun & Sep, 10am-6pm daily Jul & Aug, 9am-1pm & 2-5pm Mon-Fri Oct-May), including its historic offices and ageing cellars. The nearby **Calém** (Map p358; ☎ 223 746 660; Avenida Diogo Leite 26; tour & tasting €2; 🕑 10am-7pm May-Sep, to 6pm Oct-Apr) is a smaller, independent lodge.

Up from the river, British-run **Taylor's** (☎ 223 742 800; www.taylor.pt; Rua do Choupelo 250; tour & tasting free; 🕑 10am-6pm Mon-Fri Sep-Jun, 10am-6pm Mon-Sat Jul-Aug) boasts lovely, oh-so-English grounds with fine views of Porto. Plus its tours are free and even include a tasting of one top-of-the-range (late-bottled vintage) wines – your reward for the short huff uphill.

Barros (☎ 223 752 395; www.porto-barros.pt; Rua Dona Leonor de Freitas; tour & tasting free; 🕑 10am-6pm Jun-Sep, 10am-5.30pm Mon-Fri Oct-May) is also well worth seeking out, with some of the town's oldest surviving cellars and a more in-depth look at the process of making the wine itself.

Watching over the entire scene is the severe, 17th-century hilltop **Mosteiro da Serra de Pilar** (Map p358), with its striking, circular cloister. Requisitioned by the future Duke of Wellington during the Peninsular War (1807–14), it still belongs to the Portuguese military and is closed to the public. The church is open for Mass every Sunday morning from 10am to noon.

Afurada

Technically part of Gaia, Afurada is a picturesque fishing village, near the mouth of the Rio Douro, where many older residents still cling to traditional ways – men fishing and women washing their laundry at communal fonts. Houses are decked with *azulejos* and cafés are redolent with hearty *caldeirada* (seafood stew).

For the most scenic route, take a tram from the Ribeira to the Fluvial I stop just west of the Ponte da Arrábida. From here, catch a small ferry (€0.75) across the river to the village. Hours are not fixed, but if the ferry is not operating, fishing vessels regularly make the crossing and will generally accommodate visitors, so just ask around.

Alternatively, buses 93 and 96 from Cordoaria stop just across the bridge in Vila Nova de Gaia. From here, it's a short walk downhill to Afurada.

WALKING TOUR

Start out with a bird's-eye view of the Ribeira district (and central Porto) from the top of the baroque **Torre de Clérigos** (**1**; p362). Now head down Rua dos Clérigos, passing the foot of **Avenida dos Aliados** (**2**; p362) and pausing to admire the avenue's beaux-arts splendour. Just ahead, you'll see the French-inspired **São Bento train station** (**3**; p362). Check out the tremendous *azulejos* in its main hall. Now cross over to Rua das Flores, a lovely street that seems to have been imported straight from Paris' Montmartre, with some Portuguese customisation.

Near the end of the street is Nicolau Nasoni's baroque masterpiece, the **Igreja da Misericórdia** (**4**; p361). Cross quaint Largo São Domingos to Rua Ferreira Borges, where you will pass the neoclassical **Palácio da Bolsa** (**5**; p361). You can check out its main courtyard – once Porto's stock exchange – for free or stay on for a tour of its elaborate interior. Just next door is the **Igreja de São Francisco** (**6**; p360), with a severe Gothic façade hiding golden splendour inside.

Heading back up Rua Infante Dom Henrique, turn right on Rua da Alfandaga where, just on the left, you'll see the medieval **Casa do Infante** (**7**; p360), the birthplace of Henry the Navigator and the site of some remarkable Roman ruins. Then it's time to go back out, down the narrow, medieval Rua de Fonte Taurina, which gives onto the lovely **Praça**

da Ribeira (**8**; p361). From here, go for a stroll along the waterfront (and perhaps pause in a café for a little refreshment), admiring Vila Nova de Gaia's port-wine lodges across the river. Finally, walk across the Eiffel-inspired **Ponte de Dom Luís bridge** (**9**; p361) to **Gaia's waterfront esplanade** (**10**; p364), where you can gawk at the grandstand views back onto the Ribeira.

WALK FACTS

Start Torre de Clérigos
End Vila Nova de Gaia's riverside esplanade
Distance 2km
Time Two to three hours

COURSES

CRAT (Centro Regional de Artes Tradicionais; Map p362; ☎ 223 320 201; crat@mail.telepac.pt; Rua da Reboleira 37) sometimes runs brief introductory workshops on *azulejo* painting and stamping, aimed at tourists. A lesson costs around €25, and you can usually pick up your freshly fired tiles a few days later.

Madrid-based **Cellar Tours** (☎ 91 521 3939; www.cellartours.com) regularly offers pricey but very good half-day course for five to eight people with one of Porto's top chefs.

PORTO FOR CHILDREN

The best spots to let kids burn off some steam are Porto's numerous parks – the fenced and expansive Parque de Serralves (p364) is

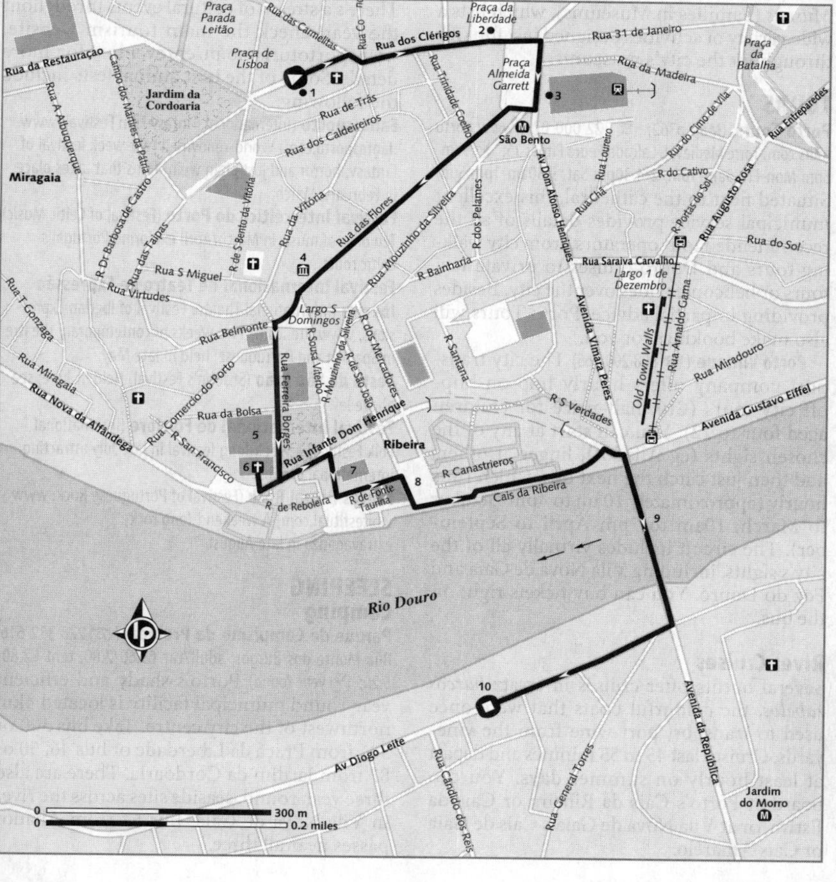

 Book accommodation online at lonelyplanet.com

GET HAMMERED!

Porto's biggest party, Festa de São João (St John's Festival, also called the Festa da Cidade) puts meaning back into the word 'bash'. On the night of 23 June, the city erupts into all manner of merrymaking: music, competitions and riotous parties just for starters. However, the most distinctive custom is for everyone to pound each other on the head with squeaky plastic mallets. In the Ribeira, especially, the streets ring with squeaks and squeals all night long. Everybody's fair game – expect no mercy.

particularly kid-friendly. The tourist office also offers a brochure called *Famílias Nos Museus* (Families in Museums), which lists a wide variety of activities designed just for kids throughout the city's museums.

TOURS

Porto Tours (Map p362; ☎ 222 000 073; www.portotours.com; Torre Medieval, Calçada Pedro Pitões 15; ⏲ 9am-6pm Mon-Fri, 9am-1pm, 2-4.30pm Sat, 9.30am-1pm Sun) Situated next to the cathedral, this excellent municipal service provides details of all the recommended tour operators, from city walking tours and Douro cruises to private taxi tours or helicopter rides over the city. Besides providing impartial advice, Porto Tours will also make bookings for you.

Porto Vintage (☎ 808 200 166) The city transport company offers hourly hop-on-hop-off city tours (€10; half-price for children aged four to 12). You can start at any of the chosen sights (eg Aliados), linger at others and then just catch the next bus, which runs hourly (approximately 10am to 4pm October to March, 10am to 7pm April to September). The circuit includes virtually all of the city's sights, including Vila Nova de Gaia and Foz do Douro. You can buy tickets right on the bus.

River Cruises

Several outfits offer cruises in ersatz *barcos rabelos*, the colourful boats that were once used to transport port wine from the vineyards. Cruises last 45 to 55 minutes and depart at least hourly on summer days. You can board at Porto's Cais da Ribeira or Cais da Estiva, or at Vila Nova de Gaia's Cais de Gaia or Cais Amarelo.

More interesting are full-day cruises that take you into the heart of port-wine country.

Most tours head upriver by boat and return by train or bus (or vice versa), and offer a snack and at least one full meal. Porto–Peso da Régua–Porto costs around €45 to €85, depending on the day of the week and the time of year.

Porto–Pinhão–Porto costs around €85 to €115. For multiday cruises, expect to pay upwards of €120 per day per person based on double occupancy with half-board. By far the largest carrier is **Douro Azul** (☎ 223 402 500; www.douroazul.pt).

For reservations and more information, your best bet is Porto Tours (see left).

FESTIVALS & EVENTS

There's a stream of cultural events throughout the year; check the main tourism website, www.portoturismo.pt/en/eventos, for more details. Some of the best annual fests include the following:

Fantasporto (International Fantasy Film Festival; www.fantasporto.com) World-renowned two-week festival of fantasy, horror and just plain weird films that takes place in February/March.

Festival Intercéltico do Porto (Festival of Celtic Music) Ten days of music in March/April exploring Portugal's Celtic roots.

Festival Internacional de Teatro de Expressão Ibérica (International Theatre Festival of Iberian Expressions; www.fitei.com) Two weeks of contemporary theatre in Spanish and Portuguese; held in late May.

Festa de São João (St John's Festival) Held in June; see above left.

Festival Internacional de Folclore (International Folk Festival) A week-long festival in late July attracting international groups.

Noites Ritual Rock (Festival of Portuguese Rock; www.noitesritual.com) A weekend-long rock extravaganza in late August.

SLEEPING

Camping

Parque de Campismo da Prelada (☎ 228 312 616; Rua Monte dos Burgos; adult/car €3.60/2.80, tent €2.80-5.20; ⏲ year-round) Porto's shady and efficient year-round municipal facility is located 4km northwest of the city centre. Take bus 300 or 301 from Praça da Liberdade or bus 46, 50 or 87 from Jardim da Cordoaria. There are also three year-round, seaside sites across the river in Vila Nova de Gaia. Bus 57 from Aliados passes near all three.

Other camping options:

Campismo Marisol (☎ 227 135 942; fax 227 126 351; Rua Alto das Chaquedas 82, Praia de Canide; adult/tent/car €1.50/3/2.25) Flat, grassy site close to the sea.

Campismo Madalena (☎ 227 122 520; info@orbitur.pt; Rua do Cerro, Praia da Madalena; adult/car €4.30/3.80, tent €3.50-4) Orbitur's well-shaded and sandy option nearer the sea.

Campismo Salgueiros (☎ 227 810 500; canidelo@j-f.org; Rua do Campismo, Praia de Salgueiros; adult/car €1.70/1, tent €1.70-2.30) More basic, packing in campers like sardines.

Ribeira

Hotel da Bolsa (Map p362; ☎ 222 026 768; www.hoteldabolsa.com; Rua Ferreira Borges 101; s/d with satellite TV €65/80; ❄) Large and faultlessly managed three-star hotel behind a handsome façade a few steps above the Instituto do Vinho do Porto. Rooms are smallish and so are windows, making them cosy or dark, depending on your tastes. An extra €15 will get you more light and great views of the Ribeira and the river.

Pestana Porto Hotel (Map p362; ☎ 223 402 300; www.pestana.com; Praça da Ribeira 1; s €120, d from €150; ⊠ ❄ 💻) A clutch of colourfully haphazard buildings have been transformed into what is, hands down, Porto's most sophisticated sleep. Rooms are a fine balance between plush-contemporary and traditional. Be aware that they vary widely in terms of size, light and views (the best face the river). But everyone can tuck into the fine breakfast buffet.

Aliados

Pensão Duas Nações (Map p360; ☎ 222 081 616; www.duasnacoes.com.pt; Praça Gomes Fernandes 59; s with/without bathroom €22.50/13.50, d with/without bathroom €28/21; 💻) Cheap? You'd better believe it. But it's also clean, friendly, centrally located and even has double-glazing to shut out the city din. Rooms are basic but cosy, and the whole affair is packed into a narrow town house that has been modernised in some places and left to its creaky, 19th-century devices in others. No breakfast.

Hotel Peninsular (Map p360; ☎ 222 003 012; Rua Sá da Bandeira 21; s/d with breakfast from €22/34) From a lobby decked out in *azulejos* and polished wood, an ancient lift carries you to a dizzying variety of rooms, architectural styles and pricing schemes that make this place hard to categorise – from poky, dark back rooms to bright, Jacuzzi-endowed, practically deluxe digs. But all offer one thing: value for money.

Residencial Rex (Map p358; ☎ 222 074 590; fax 222 083 882; Praça da República 117; s €35, d from €45; P ❄) Behind a prim, green-tiled façade lies one of Porto's most winning sleeping options. Common areas are full of bourgeois, *belle époque* charms. Quarters are less deluxe but comfortable, with good beds, well-kept carpeting and bathrooms with a distinctly 1970s feel.

Residencial Brasília (Map p358; ☎ 222 006 095; www.residencialbrasiliaporto.com; Rua Álvares Cabral 221; s/d €35/45) With a hodgepodge of pleasant rooms in a rather grand, middle-class town house, the Brasília is a little removed from the action but clean, friendly and good value.

Residencial Pão de Açucar (Map p360; ☎ 222 002 425; www.residencialpaodeacucar.com; Rua do Almada 262; s/d €45/60) Occupying a rather imposing Art Deco building just steps from Aliados, the Pão de Açucar offers two distinct choices: old-fashioned rooms with new beds and polished parquet floors or, for a small premium, modern, top-floor rooms (€75) with huge sliding glass doors onto a wide communal terrace.

Residencial dos Aliados (Map p360; ☎ 222 004 853; www.residencialaliados.com; Rua Elísio de Melo 27; s €45, d with/without air-con €70/60; ❄) One of Aliados' trademark beaux-arts buildings a short walk from the turismo, this guesthouse offers spiff rooms with polished wooden floors, new beds and tasteful if vaguely austere furnishings of dark-stained wood. Beware that street-facing rooms can be noisy. Prices dip dramatically in the low season.

Hotel Infante de Sagres (Map p360; ☎ 223 398 500; www.hotelinfantesagres.pt; Praça Dona Filipa de Lencastre 62; s/d from €160/175; ❄ 💻) An exquisite time warp with liveried doormen, crystal chandeliers, and lavish panelling, this place feels like a royal getaway reconstructed in the heart of the city. Digs are modern but with all the trimmings, though standard rooms are a little careworn; superiors are quite up to scratch.

Batalha & Bolhão

Pensão Mondariz (Map p360; ☎ 222 005 600; Rua do Cimo de Vila 139; s without bathroom €10, d with/without bathroom €30/20) This tatty, backstreet place has creaky beds and thin mattresses, but at least it's central and cheap. There are also a few Art Nouveau touches, and a few higher rooms have pleasant, rooftop views. No breakfast.

our pick **Pensão Astória** (Map p360; ☎ 222 008 175; Rua Arnaldo Gama 56; s with/without bathroom €25/18, d with/without bathroom €32/22) In an austere but elegant town house atop vertiginous stairs that lead down to the Douro, this spotless place has no frills but great charms. Everything here is old-fashioned, from the 1940s (still operational) phone system to the warmth of the mother-daughter team who preside. Rooms vary in size and equipment – only a few have full bathrooms, and even these are oddly distributed. But all are decorated with trim antiques, many have high ceilings, all are clean as whistles, and several have great river and bridge views. Pack flannel jammies in winter, as there's no heating. Reservations recommended.

Hotel-Residencial América (Map p358; ☎ 223 392 930; www.hotel-america.net; Rua Santa Catarina 1018; s/d with breakfast €45/55; P ✱ 🖳) Though a bit out of the way and housed in an uninspired, concrete, '60s-style building, this classic mid-range business hotel has a number of features that make it stand out: rather stylish rooms, a winter garden, cable TV, generous buffet breakfast and free off-street parking.

Castelo Santa Catarina (Map p358; ☎ 225 095 599; www.castelosantacatarina.com.pt; Rua Santa Catarina 1347; s/d from €38/€60; P) And now for something completely different: Castelo Santa Catarina is a whimsical late-19th-century pseudo-Gothic castle, a fabulously over-the-top hideaway in palm-shaded, *azulejo*-smothered gardens complete with its own chapel. Choose between pricier, period-furnished doubles in the castle and smaller rooms in a modern annexe. Reserve well in advance for summer weekends and holidays.

Quality Inn Praça da Batalha (Map p360; ☎ 223 392 300; www.choicehotelseurope.com; Praça da Batalha; r with breakfast €65; ✱ 🖳) It may be a chain, but this place offers attractive, recently remodelled rooms. Many have balconies, and virtually all above the 2nd floor offer fine views.

Grande Hotel do Porto (Map p360; ☎ 222 076 690; www.grandehotelporto.com; Rua Santa Catarina 197; s/d with cable TV €105/115; P ✱) Open since 1880, this proud old institution preserves a good deal of its grandeur, especially its cavernous dining room and gilded parlour. Its rooms are less distinguished but still large and plush.

Cordoaria & Around

Pensão-Residencial Estoril (Map p360; ☎ 222 002 751; www.pensaoestoril.com; Rua de Cedofeita 193; s/d €30/40) Set on a busy pedestrian parade, this dated but cosy family-run place has small but good-value rooms, with new bathrooms. There are also a few doubles without bathroom or window for €20.

Hotel Eurostars das Artes (Map p358; ☎ 222 071 250; www.eurostarshotels.com; Rua do Rosário 160; s/d from €55/€70; P ✱ 🖳) The closest Porto comes to a fashion hotel, this new address offers large rooms with sparkling bathrooms, spare, contemporary furnishings and niceties such as in-room wireless internet access. It's a bit of a walk but great value.

West Porto

Pousada da Juventude (☎ 226 177 257; www.pousadasjuventude.pt; Rua Paulo da Gama 551; dm/d €16/43; 🕑 24hr; P 🖳) In a bright, modern building on bluffs above the Douro, the crown jewel of Portugal's hostels offers basic but handsome doubles with sweeping views of the Douro as well as clean, well-maintained dorms. There's a decent restaurant (meals around €6) and a supermarket across the street (but no open kitchen). One hitch: it's 4km from central Porto. Take bus 207 from Campanhã station or bus 500 from Aliados. Reservations are essential.

Hotel Boa Vista (☎ 225 320 020; www.hotelboavista.com; Esplanada do Castelo 58; s/d from €72/€80) A classic, 19th-century seaside inn outside and a thoroughly modern if somewhat characterless hotel inside, the Boa Vista sits at the mouth of the Douro and one block from the beach in the tiny Foz do Douro neighbourhood.

EATING

You can eat very well in Porto, whatever your budget – even if you don't like to tripe (opposite). Except for a few ethnic and vegetarian eateries, by-the-book Portuguese fare rules the day.

Self-caterers should check out Porto's municipal market, the **Mercado do Bolhão** (p363) plus the nearby grocery-cum-bakery **Confeitaria do Bolhão** (Map p360; Rua Formosa 305) and the Art Nouveau food shop **A Pérola do Bolhão** (Map p360; Rua Formosa 279). Central *supermercados* (supermarkets) include **Minipreço** (Map p360; Rua Conceição; 🕑 9am-8pm Mon-Sat), **Pingo Doce** (Map p360; Rua Passos Manuel 213; 🕑 8.30am-9pm Mon-Sat, 9am-8.30pm Sun) and **Modelo** (Map p360; Centro Comercial Via Catarina, Rua Santa Catarina; 🕑 10am-10pm).

Ribeira

Churrasqueira do Infante (Map p362; ☎ 222 200 885, Praça Infante Dom Henrique; mains around €4; 🕑 lunch & dinner Mon-Sat) This no-frills eatery is popular with students and is the best budget option in the Ribeira, offering tasty, grilled-to-order meats and fish.

Casa Filha da Mãe Preta (Map p362; ☎ 222 055 515; ais da Ribeira 40; half-portions €6-9; ⏲ lunch & dinner ɪon-Sat) Set smack on the Ribeira's riverfront, his is the most congenial of a long line of ouristy riverside restaurants. Go early to bag n upstairs front table for views of the Douro. ɔon't confuse it with the old taverna of the ame name, one street back.

Indian Classic (Map p360; ☎ 222 011 578; Rua Mouzɪho da Silveira 107; mains €7-11; ⏲ lunch & dinner) The ɪnly decent ethnic option in the centre, this heerful eatery cooks up surprisingly good ndian fare, including fragrant lentil soup and xcellent grilled meats and curries. English poken. It's open until midnight.

Simbiose (Map p362; ☎ 222 030 398; Rua Infante Dom enrique 133; mains €9-13; ⏲ lunch & dinner Tue-Sun) On wo floors in an airy, quayside town house, his new spot serves up decent traditional uisine and lovely river views. But the real leal is the very good, weekday lunch buffet €7.50 with drink).

O Comercial (Map p362; ☎ 223 322 019; Palácio da Bolsa, ua Ferreira Borges; mains €12-16; ⏲ lunch & dinner Mon-Fri, inner Sat) Hidden at the back the stock-exchange ɪuilding, this one-of-a-kind restaurant boasts ɔwering arches, old-world service and a stylsh, fireside lounge. At dinner, the food has ɪeen known to disappoint, but the €10, threeourse lunch menu is great value, especially vhen you factor in all that atmosphere.

Don Tonho (Map p362; ☎ 222 004 307; Cais da Ribeira 3-15; mains €12-22; ⏲ lunch & dinner) Built into ncient riverside ramparts, this elegant resaurant serves traditional Portuguese fare preɪared with a contemporary twist. Opened by ʀui Velosa, crown prince of Portuguese pop, : serves up superb seafood, including fine *acalhau* (dried salt-cod), and also boasts one ɪf Porto's most extensive wine lists.

Mariazinha (Map p362; ☎ 222 200 937; Rua Belmonte 2; -course menu with wine around €65; ⏲ Thu-Tue) This nug but rustically elegant eatery, run by an nthusiastic husband-and-wife team, serves reative haute cuisine based on market-fresh ngredients. You must order from the prixixe menu. In fact, each course comes as a urprise, along with a different Portuguese vine. Reservations recommended.

.liados, Batalha & Bolhão

edro dos Frangos (Map p360; ☎ 222 008 522; Rua do onjardim 219; mains from €4; ⏲ all day Wed-Mon) This imple place draws the crowds with its very ood *frango no espeto* (spit-roasted chicken) and other cheap grills, all served with heaps of chips. Join the good old boys for a meal standing at the bar or upstairs in the no-nonsense dining room. There's talk of expanding to a new location across the street.

Confeitaria Sical (Map p360; ☎ 222 056 148; Praça Dona Filipa de Lencastre 29; sandwiches €2-3, mains €5; ⏲ 7am-5.30pm Mon-Fri, 8am-12.30pm Sat) New but already popular with the literary types from the neighbouring publishing houses, this lunchtime joint has a bright interior done up in a clever take on traditional Portuguese tiles.

Café Embaixador (Map p360; ☎ 222 054 329; Rua Sampaio Bruno 5; mains €4-9; ⏲ all day Sun-Fri) A perennial favourite of everyone from suits to construction workers, this double-decker Art Deco restaurant provides good standards at excellent prices. Skip the upstairs buffet – it's overpriced cafeteria fare.

Confeitaria do Bolhão (Map p360; Rua Formosa 339; mains €3.50-9; ⏲ 7am-9pm Sun-Fri, 7am-7.30pm Sat) This cheerful *belle époque* café, popular with everyone but especially ladies of a certain age, serves good food at great prices, including a daily lunch special of soup, main course and fresh-squeezed juice for €5. The front counter serves an irresistible array of local sweets to go.

Suribachi (Map p358; ☎ 225 106 700; Rua do Bonfim 134-140; small dishes €2-6; ⏲ shop 9am-10pm, restaurant lunch & dinner Mon-Sat; Ⓥ) This squeaky-clean restaurant offers decent fare in a contemplative, meat-free atmosphere in the back of a New Age health-food store.

Abadia (Map p360; ☎ 222 008 757; Rua do Ateneu Comercial do Porto 22; mains €7-13; ⏲ lunch & dinner) It's become a little touristy, but this rather cavernous backstreet place serves up very good northern dishes, including excellent *porco preto* (flavourful grilled pork) and *tripas* (stewed tripe).

A LOAD OF TRIPE

It's not what most of us look for on the menu, but many Porto folk can think of nothing finer than a rich stew of tripe (cow's stomach). This affection for *tripas* is said to date back to 1415 when Henry the Navigator was preparing to sail for Ceuta in Morocco. As a sign of their trust and affection, Porto's loyal citizens donated their best meat, keeping the offal for themselves and earning the nickname *tripeiros* (tripe-eaters).

A MEAL WITH A VIEW

Boa Nova Casa-Chá (☎ 229 951 785; Leça da Palmeira; ⏲ noon-10pm Mon-Sat) Designed by famed Portuguese architect Álvaro Siza Vieira and completed in 1963, this cliff-side tea house and restaurant is set alluringly above a crashing sea. Massive boulders frame the white, low-rise building, while inside the Zenlike design continues as light floods the wood and stone interior. The restaurant is 20 minutes north of Porto along the coast. It's also accessible by bus 44 and 76 from Porto.

Cordoaria

Restaurante O Verde Vegetariano (Map p358; ☎ 226 063 886; lower level, Edifício Crystal Park, Rua Dom Manuel II; per kilo €10; ⏲ lunch & dinner Sun-Thu, lunch Fri; Ⓥ) This uncluttered little self-service restaurant has a varied selection of vegetarian dishes and an elegant, minimalist dining area that looks onto a pleasant green space.

A Tasquinha (Map p360; ☎ 223 322 145; Rua do Carmo 23; mains €6-10; ⏲ lunch & dinner Mon-Sat) Tucked inside a rustic house, this touristy but pleasant place offers cask wines, garlicky appetisers and good northern specialities. The €12.50 tourist menu includes three courses, coffee and drink.

Vila Nova de Gaia

Restaurante Imar (Map p358; Avenida Diogo Leite 56; half-portions €3-7.50; ⏲ dinner Mon, lunch & dinner Tue-Sat, lunch Sun) The best deal on Gaia's waterfront, this classic, family-run Portuguese eatery serves up the usual dishes in an unrepentantly old-fashioned dining room.

Barão de Fladgate (☎ 223 742 800; Rua do Choupelo 250; mains €10-14, set meal €26; ⏲ lunch & dinner Mon-Sat, lunch Sun) With excellent food, enviable views, and of course lots and lots of port, the restaurant in Taylor's port-wine lodge is a worthy splurge. The menu is long on seafood, the speciality being (surprise!) *bacalhau*.

Tromba Rija (Map p358; ☎ 223 743 762; Avenida Diogo Leite 102; prix fixe €27.50; ⏲ dinner Mon, lunch & dinner Tue-Sat, lunch Sun) Porto's branch of Leiria's famous eatery offers a huge, soup-to-nuts buffet of classic, well-prepared Portuguese dishes – plus all the wine, port and homemade liqueur you can drink. Tromba Rija is a great introduction Portuguese cuisine – and always festive thanks to all that free booze.

DRINKING

They may have a strong work ethic, but that doesn't stop *portoenses* (Porto locals) from partying – the city has a club scene that is at once sophisticated and largely devoid of status jockeying. The city also boasts a rich theatre and music scene. To keep pace, pick up the *Agenda do Porto*, a monthly cultural events brochure, or consult its site at www.agendadoporto.pt. *Jornal de Notícias* newspaper also has events listings and is available at newsstands.

Cafés

Café Majestic (Map p360; ☎ 222 003 887; Rua Santa Catarina 112; breakfast €15, afternoon tea €9.75; ⏲ 9.30am-midnight Mon-Sat) Porto's best-known tea shop is packed with prancing cherubs, opulently gilded woodwork, leather seats and gold-braided waiters who'll serve you an elegant set breakfast, afternoon tea or any number of snacks and beverages.

Café Ancôra Douro (Map p360; Praça de Parada Leitão 55; ⏲ Mon-Sat) A downmarket counterpoint to Porto's posher cafés, near Cordoaria. It's a cavernous, casual place where students nurse coffees for hours and munch on crepes and light meals.

Café Guarany (Map p360; Avenida dos Aliados 89; ⏲ 9am-midnight) With a sunny, tiled interior marble-top tables, and an Afro-Brazilian mural, this classy affair has attracted business and literary elite since the 1930s. It regularly has live music, and serves full meals.

Café A Brasileira (Map p360; Rua Sá da Bandeira ⏲ 9am-midnight) This beaux-arts treasure is looking a little battered but it's still great to linger amid its bowed windows and Corinthian columns.

Bars & Nightclubs

Porto's clubs usually don't charge admission but do ask you to spend a minimum amount buying drinks: usually between €3.50 and €5 for a bar and €5 to €15 for a club.

RIBEIRA

There are dozens of bars on Praça da Ribeira and along the adjacent quay. On warm nights the outdoor terraces get packed. Hunt out the music and crowd that suits you.

Caos Galeria Bar (Map p362; Rua de Ferreira Borges 86; ⏲ opens midnight) Candlelit and done up in shades of grey, this bar is the hippest central place and regularly holds after-hours parties featuring chilled-out electronica.

GAY & LESBIAN PORTO

Porto's gays and lesbians keep it discreet in the streets, but are more than willing to let loose behind closed doors. Most venues are clustered around Jardim de Cordoaria. Gay Pride festivities take place in the first or second weekend in July. Consult http://portugalgay.pt for listings, events and other information.

Note that while there are no exclusively women's bars or clubs, all the places below are at least somewhat mixed.

- **Café na Praça** (Map p360; ☎ 222 086 498; Clérigos Shopping, Praça de Lisboa; 🕑 10pm-2am) Kick off the night at this attractive café on the ground floor of a small mall near the Torre de Clérigos.
- **Boys 'R' Us** (Map p360; ☎ 917 746 271; Rua Dr Barbosa de Castro 63; 🕑 11pm-4am Wed & Fri-Sun) This long-standing favourite has pumping pop and electronica and raucous drag shows downstairs. Upstairs is a quieter lounge. It's usually best from 1am to 3am.
- **Moinho de Vento** (Map p360; ☎ 222 056 883; Rua Sá Noronha 78; 🕑 10pm-6am Wed-Sun) This small but spiffy bar-disco has a dark room and drag and go-go boys. It usually starts hopping some time after 3am.
- **Pride Bar** (Map p358; Rua Bonjardim 1121; 🕑 midnight-late Fri-Sun) Porto's newest hot spot has live music, drag shows and go-go boys. It's open very late.
- **Swing** (p374) This kitschy, friendly disco draws a mixed gay-straight crowd.

Ryan's Irish Pub (Map p362; ☎ 222 005 366; Rua Infante Dom Henrique 18; 🕑 6pm-4am) Generous drams of whisky with its good ol' Irish tunes. And of course, English is spoken. Follow the Guinness signs.

Ribeirinha (Map p362; ☎ 223 322 572; Rua de São João 70-72; 🕑 10pm-4am Mon-Sat) This intimate, no-frills bar specialises in live rock and metal, but sometimes features DJs spinning reggae and house.

our pick **Vinologia** (Map p362; ☎ 936 057 340; www.vinologia.com; Rua de São João 46; 🕑 2-8pm, 9.30pm-midnight Mon-Sat, 6-8pm, 9.30pm-midnight Sun) One of Porto's real treats, this cosy, casual spot offers a variety of port-wine tastings for beginners as well as experts. It specialises in smaller, independent growers, and friendly and knowledgeable servers provide a brief but cogent lesson with each glass they pour. You can compare different styles of port, such as a ruby, tawny and LBV. Or you can try three within the same style, eg three aged tawnies. If you fall in love with a certain wine, you can usually buy a whole bottle (or even send home a case).

RIVERFRONT TO FOZ DOURO

All the following can be reached via the night-time bus 1M from Aliados.

31 (☎ 226 107 567; www.trintaeum.com; Rua do Passeio Alegre 564; 🕑 club noon-1am Tue-Thu, 3pm-4am Fri & Sat, 3pm-1am Sun) Beguilingly simple place with a large bar, comfortable seating, louche, '70s-inspired décor, dance floor and some of the best DJs from Portugal and around Europe.

Bazaar (Map p358; ☎ 226 062 113; Rua de Monchique 13; 🕑 opens 4pm) The hottest place in Porto at the time of writing, with high-quality house and hundreds of pretty 20- and 30-somethings in their shiny best spread out over three minimalist, whitewashed levels.

Clube Mau-Mau (Map p358; ☎ 226 076 660; Rua do Outeiro 4; club 🕑 11pm-4am Wed-Sat, restaurant 8.30pm-1am Tue-Sat) Formerly Porto's hottest club, this cavernous industrial space has standard R&B and house most nights but still attracts the occasional top guest DJ. Also provides late-night grub. The nearest bus stop is Massarelos.

Era uma Vez no Porto (☎ 226 164 793; Rua do Passeio Alegre 550; 🕑 club noon-1am Tue-Thu, 3pm-4am Fri & Sat, 3pm-1am Sun) Part tearoom, part nightclub, part experimental art gallery and part vintage clothing shop, this place in an airy riverfront town house feels as if you've entered a private party with a cash bar.

Pop (☎ 226 183 959; www.pop-kitchen.com; Rua Padre Luís Cabral 1090; 🕑 midnight-4am Thu-Sat) Dress up and show off in what looks like a nouveau-riche dining room of glass and chandeliers. It caters to a multigenerational crowd, with oldies to please the oldies as well as hipper DJs for the kids.

our pick **Solar do Vinho do Porto** (Map p358; ☎ 226 097 749; Rua Entre Quintas 220; 🕑 2pm-midnight Mon-Sat, closed holidays) The city's swankiest place for a spot of port, this *solar* (manor house) is set in a 19th-century house near the Palácio de Cristal, with a fussy but delightful garden and stunning views of the Douro. Hundreds of ports are available (from €1.20 per glass).

BOAVISTA & WEST PORTO

Swing (Map p358; ☎ 226 090 019; Praceta Engenheiro Amáro da Costa 766; ⌚ midnight-4am) Near Boavista, this is Porto's oldest and most unrepentantly old-school (OK, kitsch) disco, attracting a sociable, mixed gay-and-straight crowd with crowd-pleasing '80s, dance pop, house, and disco. Open Sundays.

Triplex (Map p358; ☎ 226 098 968; Avenida va Boavista 911; ⌚ disco midnight-late Thu-Sat) Set in a pink, three-floor mansion, this louche restaurant-bar-disco attracts pretty people of varying ages. Upmarket but relaxed, it usually pumps out forward house and techno.

Indústria (☎ 226 176 806; Avenida do Brasil 843; ⌚ 11.30pm-4am Thu-Sat) Done up with silver-and-velvet wallpaper and bean-bag chairs, this retro basement club serves up funk, house and, above, all electronica to a crowd that generally skews very young. Take the bus and get off at the Molhe stop.

Via Rápida (☎ 226 109 427; unit 5 Rua Manuel Pinto de Azevedo 567; ⌚ midnight-7am Fri & Sat) This industrial-sized club has an enormous dance floor that reverberates with house, attracting a fairly mainstream younger crowd. The most likely place to catch local starlets.

Estado Novo (☎ 229 385 989; Rua Sousa Aroso 722, Matosinhos; ⌚ midnight-7am Thu-Sat) The Estado Novo's airy, whitewashed interior with slick lighting and rocking sound system attracts teens on some nights, their mums and dads on others. Worth finding out what's on its docket.

VILA NOVA DE GAIA

Just across the river from the gritty Ribeira waterfront, Gaia's esplanade is trendier (though also more mainstream). A string of identical-looking chrome-and-glass bars and nightclubs are surrounded by open-air decks and designer fountains. Poke around until you find your scene.

Hard Club (Map p358; ☎ 223 744 755; www.hard-club.com in Portuguese; Cais de Gaia 1158) Set above the waterfront in an old tannery back, this industrial-inspired club hosts the cream of visiting international and home-grown DJs, plus it boasts a cool rooftop terrace.

ENTERTAINMENT

Cinemas

There are no cinemas in the centre, but you can head by metro to the multiscreen **Cinema Centro Comercial Cidade do Porto** (Map p358; ☎ 226 009 164; Rua Gonçalo Sampaio 350, Boavista).

Fado

Porto has no *fado* tradition of its own, but you can enjoy the Lisbon or Coimbra version of 'Portugal blues' into the wee hours at smoky atmospheric haunts **Restaurante O Fado** (Map p360; ☎ 222 026 937; Largo de São João Novo 16; ⌚ 8.30pm-3.30am Mon-Sat) and **Restaurante Mal Cozinhado** (Map p362; ☎ 222 081 319; Rua Outerinho 11, Ribeira; ⌚ 8.30pm-1am Mon-Sat). The food isn't the main attraction – and in any case is grossly overpriced – but there's a minimum charge, equivalent to a light meal or several drinks.

Theatre & Music

After years of delay, the Casa da Música (p363) finally opened in 2005, quickly becoming the city's premiere music venue, featuring classical and jazz to electronica and *fado*. Other venues:

Teatro Nacional São João (Map p360; ☎ 223 401 900; www.tnsj.pt in Portuguese; Praça da Batalha) Porto's other premiere performing-arts venue, hosting international dance, theatre and music groups.

Coliseu do Porto (Map p360; ☎ 223 324 940; www.coliseudoporto.pt; Rua Passos Manuel 137) Hosts major names in arena-style performances.

Teatro de Belmonte (Map p362; ☎ 222 083 341; www.marionetasdoporto.pt in Portuguese; Rua Belmonte 57) Specialises in puppet shows.

Sport

The flashy, new 52,000-seat Estádio do Dragão, hosted the opening ceremonies and first game of the 2004 European Football Championships. The stadium, home to heroes of the moment **FC Porto** (☎ 808 201 167; www.fcporto.pt), is northeast of the centre, just off the VCI ring road (metro stop Estádio de Dragão).

Porto FC's worthy cross-town rivals are the under-funded **Boavista FC** (☎ 226 071 000; www.boavistafc.pt). The newly spruced-up Estádio do Bessa is their home turf and also hosted several Euro2004 matches. The stadium is west of the centre just off Avenida da Boavista (take bus 3 from Praça da Liberdade).

Check the local editions of *Público* or *Jornal de Notícias* newspapers for upcoming fixtures.

SHOPPING

Porto boasts a diverse shopping scene, from quirky delicatessens to endless *sapatarias* (shoe shops). In addition, there are entire streets specialising in particular items (try Rua Galeria de Paris for fine art or Rua da Fábrica for bookshops). Rua Santa Catarina near Praça da Batalha is another bustling, all-purpose shopping street.

Modern *centros comerciales* (shopping centres) include the central **Cento Comercial Via Catarina** (Map p360; Rua Santa Catarina) and **Centro Comercial Cidade do Porto** (Map p358; Rua Gonçalo Sampaio) in Boavista.

Port & Other Wines

It's great fun buying direct from the warehouses in Vila Nova de Gaia, but you can also try **Garrafeira do Carmo** (Map p360; ☎ 222 003 285; Rua do Carmo 17), specialising in vintage port and high-quality wines at reasonable prices. Other good sources are **Casa Januário** (Map p360; Rua do Bonjardim 352) and the photogenic **Casa Oriental** (Map p360; Campo dos Mártires da Pátria 111).

Handicrafts

Arte Facto (Map p362; Rua da Reboleira 37, Ribeira; 🕑 10am-noon & 1-6pm Mon-Fri) This place sells high-quality handmade crafts, from textiles and toys to puppets and pottery in CRAT's on-site boutique (p367).

Artesanato dos Clérigos (Map p360; ☎ 222 000 257; Rua Assunção 33) A modest shop, this place is stacked high with pottery, tiles, embroidery, copper and pewter.

GETTING THERE & AWAY

Air

The gleaming new **Francisco Sá Carneiro Airport** (☎ 229 432 400; www.ana-aeroportos.pt), ominously named after a beloved politician killed in a plane crash, is 20km northwest of the city centre. Portugália and TAP have multiple daily flights to/from Lisbon. There are also more and more services by low-cost carriers such as Ryanair and Air Berlin. On most days there is nonstop service to London, Madrid, Paris, Frankfurt, Amsterdam and Brussels; see above for details. Note that there is no left-luggage facility.

Bus

Like many Portuguese cities, bus service in Porto is regrettably dispersed. The good news is that there is frequent service to just about everywhere in north Portugal, as well as express service to Coimbra, Lisbon and points south.

DOMESTIC

Renex (Map p360; ☎ 222 003 395; Rua da Restauraçao) is the choice for Lisbon (€15, 3½ hours), with the most direct routes and eight to 12 departures daily, including one continuing to the Algarve. Renex also has frequent service to Braga (€5.20, 1¼ hours).

Rede Expressos (Map p360; ☎ 222 006 954; www.rede-expressos.pt in Portuguese) has service to the entire country from the smoggy **Paragem Atlântico terminal** (Map p360; Rua Alexandre Herculano 370).

For fast Minho connections, mainly on weekdays, three lines run from around Praceta Régulo Magauanha, off Rua Dr Alfredo Magalhães (Map p358). **Transdev-Norte** (☎ 222 003 152) runs chiefly to Braga (€4.40, one hour). **AV Minho** (☎ 222 006 121) goes mainly via Vila do Conde (€2.75, 55 minutes) to Viana do Castelo (€5, 1¼ hours). And **Arriva** (☎ 222 051 383) serves Guimarães (€4.40, 50 minutes).

Rodonorte (Map p360; ☎ 222 005 637; www.rodonorte.pt; Rua Ateneu Comercial do Porto 19) has multiple daily departures (fewer on Saturday) for Amarante (€5.20, one hour), Vila Real (€6.40, 1½ hours) and Bragança (€10.20, 3½ hours).

Santos (Map p358; ☎ 279 652 188; www.santosviagensturismo.pt; Centro Comercial Central Shopping, Campo 24 Agosto; metro: Campo 24 Agosto) has frequent buses to Lisbon (€11.50), Vila Real (€5.50) and Bragança (€8.70).

INTERNATIONAL

There are **Eurolines** (Map p358; ☎ 225 189 299; www.eurolinesportugal.com; Centro Comercial Central Shopping, Campo 24 Agosto; metro: Campo 24 Agosto) services to/from cities all over Europe. Northern Portugal's own international carrier is **Internorte** (Map p358; ☎ 226 052 420; Praça da Galiza 96). Take bus 302 or 501 from Aliados. Most travel agencies can book outbound buses with either operator (p359).

Car & Motorcycle

The Loja da Mobilidade at the main tourist office has a map showing all the car parks in the city. All major European and international rental car companies have offices at the airport as well as in the centre. The best deals include **Budget Castanheira** (☎ 808 252 627; www.budgetportugal.com), **Auto Jardim** (☎ 229 413 661), **Sixt** (☎ 229 483 752; www.e-sixt.com) and **Europcar** (☎ 808 204 050; www.europcar.com in Portuguese).

Train

Porto is the principal rail hub for northern Portugal. Long-distance services start at Campanhã station, 2km east of the centre. Most *suburbano*, regional and *interregional* (IR) trains start from São Bento station, though all these lines also pass through Campanhã.

For destinations on the Braga, Guimarães or Aveiro lines, or up the Douro valley as far as Marco de Canaveses, take one of the frequent *suburbano* trains. Don't spend extra money on *interregional* or *intercidade* (IC) trains to these destinations (eg Porto–Braga costs €1.75 by *suburbano* but €6.50 by IC train).

Second-class IC fares and times for direct journeys from Porto include Coimbra (from €10.50, 1¼ hours, hourly) and Lisbon (€19.50, three hours, hourly).

Information points are at both **São Bento train station** (⌚ 8.30am-8pm) and **Campanhã** (⌚ 9am-7pm). Alternatively, call the toll-free ☎ 808 208 208 or consult www.cp.pt.

GETTING AROUND

To/From the Airport

The metro's new 'violet' line has finally arrived at the airport. A one-way ride to the centre costs €1.30 and takes about 45 minutes. The city-run **AeroBus** (☎ 808 200 166) also connects Aliados and the airport via Boavista every half-hour from 7am to 7pm, taking 40 minutes in good traffic. Buy the €4 ticket on board; it also serves as a free bus and metro pass till midnight of the day you buy it. Arriving TAP passengers who present their boarding pass get this ticket free.

The bus will drop you at any train station, the Parque de Campismo da Prelada, the *pousada da juventude* (youth hostel) or any of about three dozen major hotels. If you're staying at one of these, it will also collect you if you call ☎ 225 071 054 by 7pm the preceding day.

A daytime taxi costs €20 to €25 to/from the centre. Taxis authorised to run *from* the airport are labelled 'Maia' and/or 'Vila Nova de Telha'; the rank is just outside the arrivals hall. Porto city taxis can take passengers *to* the airport but cannot bring any back (some do anyway, and a few overcharge). In peak traffic time, allow an hour or more between the city centre and the airport.

Public Transport

BUS

Porto's transport agency **STCP** (Sociedade de Transportes Colectivos do Porto; Map p360; ☎ information 808 200 166; www.stcp.pt in Portuguese) runs an extensive bus system, with central hubs at Praça da Liberdade (the south end of Avenida dos Aliados), Praça Almeida Garrett (in front of São Bento train station) and Cordoaria. Special all-night lines also run approximately hourly, leaving Aliados on the hour and returning on the half-hour from 1am to 5.30am. City turismos have maps and timetables for day and night routes.

A ticket bought on the bus (one way to anywhere in the STCP system) costs €1.30. But you get steep discounts if you buy multiple tickets in advance from the STCP office or many newsagents and *tabacarias* (tobacconists). For two/10 trips within Porto city limits

ANDANTE CARD

Porto's expanding metro has pushed its transport system to a new level of interconnectivity. You can now purchase a rechargeable **Andante Card** (☎ 808 200 444; www.linhandante.com in Portuguese) that allows you to move smoothly between tram, metro, funicular and many bus lines.

The card itself costs only €0.50 and can be recharged indefinitely. Once you've purchased the card, you must charge it with travel credit according to which zones you will be travelling in. It's not as complicated as it sounds. A Z2 trip covers the whole city centre east to Campanhã train station, south to Vila Nova de Gaia and west to Foz do Douro. And each 'trip' allows you a whole hour to move between different participating methods of transport without additional cost. Your time begins from when you first enter the vehicle or platform: just wave the card in front of a validation machine marked 'Andante'.

You can purchase credit in metro ticket machines and manned TIP booths at central hubs like Casa da Música and Trindade, as well as the STCP office, the funicular, the electric tram museum and a scattering of other authorised sales points.

One/11 'trips' in Z2 (including central Porto, Boavista and Foz do Douro) cost €0.85/8.50. Alternatively, you can choose to roam freely for 24 hours for €3. If you want to go further out than two zones, pick up a map and explanation of zones at any metro station.

you pay €1.55/6.65; those to outlying areas (including Vila Nova de Gaia) cost €2/8.20, and longer trips (including the airport) are €2.30/10.20. Tickets are sold singly or in discounted *cadernetas* (booklets) of 10. Many key lines accept the Andante card (opposite).

Also available is a €2.10 *bilhete diário* (day pass), valid for unlimited trips within the city on buses and the tram.

CAR & MOTORCYCLE

Avoid driving in central Porto if possible. Narrow, one-way streets, construction and heavy traffic can turn 500m into half a morning. See Orientation (p356) for parking details.

FUNICULAR

Long have the people of Porto panted up the steep bank from the Ribeira to the centre of the city. But now a rebuilt **Funicular dos Guindais** (8am-7pm Mon-Fri, until midnight Sat & Sun) once again shuttles up and down a steep incline from Avenida Gustavo Eiffel opposite Ponte de Dom Luís I to Rua Augusto Rosa, near Batalha and the cathedral. The funicular is part of the Andante scheme (opposite).

METRO

Porto's much-anticipated metro system is finally a happy reality. The central hub is Trindade station, a few blocks north of the Aliados corridor. Three lines – Linha A (blue, to Matosinhos), B (red, to Vila do Conde and Povoa de Varzim) and Linha C (green, to Maia) – run from Estádio do Dragão via Campanhã train station through the city centre and then on to far-flung northern and western suburbs. Linha D (yellow) runs north to south from Hospital São João to João de Deus in Vila Nova de Gaia, crossing the upper deck of Ponte Dom Luís I bridge. Key stops include Aliados and São Bento station. And now Linha E (violet) connects via Line B with the airport.

Metro trains run from approximately 6am to 1am daily. For information on prices and tickets, see the boxed text opposite.

TRAM

Porto's trams used to be one of its delights. Only three lines remain, but they're very scenic. The Massarelos stop, on the riverfront near the foot of the Palácio Cristal, is the tram system's hub. From here, line 1 trundles along the river to near Praça Infante Dom Henrique (Ribeira). Line 1E (appears as a crossed-out '1') heads down the river in the opposite direction, towards Foz Douro. And Line 18 heads uphill to the Igreja do Carmo and Jardim do Cordoaria. Trams run approximately every 30 minutes from 9am to 7pm. For fare information see the boxed text, opposite.

Taxi

There are taxi ranks throughout the centre, or you can call a **radio taxi** (☎ 225 073 900). Count on paying around €3 to €5 for trips within the centre during the day, with a 20% surcharge at night. There's an extra charge if you leave the city limits, which includes Vila Nova de Gaia.

AROUND PORTO

VILA DO CONDE

pop 25,900

Though a popular weekend getaway for Porto residents, the town of Vila do Conde – a prime shipbuilding port during the Age of Discoveries – retains much of its salty-dog, historical character. Looming over the town is the immense hilltop Mosteiro de Santa Clara, which, along with surviving segments of a long-legged aqueduct, lends the town an air of unexpected monumentality. At the same time, Vila do Conde's beaches are some of the best north of Porto, and a new metro link makes getting to the beaches an easy afternoon jaunt from downtown Porto. The town is also renowned for its ancient tradition lace-making.

Orientation & Information

Vila do Conde sits on the north side of the Rio Ave where it empties into the sea. From the metro station, look for the aqueduct (about 100m) and follow it towards the large convent (another 300m).

From here it's a few steep blocks downhill to the town's historic centre. From the centre it's another 1.25km via Avenida Dr Artur Cunha Araúja or Avenida Dr João Canavarro to Avenida do Brasil and the 3km-long beach.

Vila do Conde has two **turismos** (☎ 252 248 473; fax 252 248 422; Rua 25 de Abril 103 & Rua 5 de Outubro 207; 9am-6pm Mon-Fri, 9.30am-1pm, 2.30-6pm Sat & Sun), just 150m apart. When one is closed for lunch, the other is open. The one opposite the bus stop shares a space with a small handicrafts gallery.

Book accommodation online at lonelyplanet.com

Sights & Activities

MOSTEIRO DE SANTA CLARA

The stern **Mosteiro de Santa Clara** peers down over the town centre and the Rio Ave. Founded in 1318, it still has a severe-looking Gothic chapel, though the main building is a grand, 18th-century affair. At the time of writing it was a reformatory school for teenage boys, and the entire complex was closed to visitors, but there are plans to transform it into a high-end hotel. If you're lucky, you may find a side door of the church open.

Outside the convent are the poetic remains of a towering **aqueduct** that once brought water to the convent's 100 resident nuns from Terroso, 7km away.

TOWN CENTRE

At the heart of the old town is the Manueline **igreja matriz** (parish church; Rua 25 de Abril; 9am-noon & 2-6pm Tue-Sun), which dates mostly from the early 16th century and has an ornate doorway carved by Basque artist João de Castilho. Outside is a *pelourinho* (stone pillory) topped by the sword-wielding arm of Justice. Inside is the **Museu de Arte Sacra** (252 631 424; admission free; 10am-noon & 2-4pm Jun-Sep, 2-4pm Oct-May), with its modest collection of ecclesiastical art.

It's no accident that seafaring fingers, so deft at making nets, should also be good at lace-making. Vila do Conde is one of the few places in Portugal with an active **school** of the art, founded in 1918. Housed in a typical 18th-century town house in the town centre, the school includes the **Museu das Rendas de Bilros** (Museum of Bobbin Lace; 252 643 070; www.mrbvc.net in Portuguese; Rua São Bento 70; admission free; 9am-noon & 2-7pm Mon-Fri, 3-6pm Sat & Sun), with eye-popping examples of work from Portugal and around the world.

RIVERFRONT

Just south of the centre on the banks of the Rio Ave you'll find the **Museu da Construção Naval** (Museum of Shipbuilding; 252 240 740; Largo da Alfândega; admission free; 9am-6pm Tue-Sun). Shipbuilding has been in Vila do Conde's bones since at least the 13th century; many of the stoutest ships of the Age of Discoveries were made here. The museum is fitted out with an entire ship's prow, earnest exhibits on trade, and interesting displays on the lovingly hand-built *nau* (a sort of pot-bellied caravel once used for cargo and naval operations) that, at the time of writing, was to be moved to a mooring just in front of the museum. The museum occupies the restored Royal Customs House just west of Praça da República.

Nearby is the tiny but striking 17th-century **Capela da Nossa Senhora de Socorro** (Largo da Alfândega; irregular hours), with its crisp, mosquelike dome. The interior is covered in *azulejos* that date back to the church's founding.

BEACHES

The two best beaches, broad Praia da Forno and Praia de Nossa Senhora da Guia, have calm seas suitable for young children, while surfers often ride the swells near the *castelo* (see below). Buses marked 'Vila do Conde' from Póvoa de Varzim stop at the station and then continue out to the beach, about every half-hour all day.

At the river mouth is the 17th-century **Castelo de São João Baptista**, once a castle but now a small deluxe hotel (opposite).

Festivals & Events

Festa de São João The town's biggest religious event takes place on 23 June, with a procession that winds through the streets to the beach.

Feira Nacional de Artesanato (fna.vconde.org) This major fair of Portuguese handicrafts is held during the last week of July and the first week of August.

Sleeping

The turismo has a list of *quartos* (private rooms) and apartments, which get snapped up quickly in summer (most owners prefer long-stay guests).

Parque de Campismo da Árvore (252 633 225; cnm.parque@kqnet.pt; Rua do Cabreiro, Árvore; adult/tent €5/4.50;) Tightly packed and well shaded, this camp site is 3km away from town, right next to Praia da Árvore beach.

Restaurante Le Villageois (/fax 252 631 119; Praça da República 94; d €30) This lively Franco-Portuguese restaurant rents out a handful of humble but comfortable-enough rooms, though breakfast isn't included and they may need a good airing in the low season. Book well ahead in summer.

Residencial O Manco d'Areia (/fax 252 631 748; Praça da República 84; s/d from €35/45) Up an *azulejo*-clad staircase, this thoroughly renovated old town house has fresh and quiet en suite rooms, plus a few triples with shared facilities. Credit cards not accepted.

Pensão Patarata (252 631 894; Cais das Lavandeiras 18; d/tw €35/40) Looking over the river, off the southwest corner of the square, this place has flowery en-suite rooms, a few that are quite large with rivers views and others that are rather dark and poky.

Residencial Bento de Freitas (252 633 557; fax 252 633 077; Avenida Bento de Freitas 398; s/d €50/65;) In a refurbished, 19th-century neo-Gothic town house, this spruce place offers spare but comfortable and spotless rooms done up in period style. There's also a pleasant dining room with exposed stonework and a trim garden.

Estalagem do Brasão (252 642 016; estalagem brazao@netcabo.pt; Avenida Dr João Canavarro; s/d/ste €57/80/97; P) Part modern, part old town house, this welcoming if slightly lugubrious inn has all the comforts – from marble bathroom to cable TV – 200m west of the Rua 25 de Abril turismo.

Hotel Forte São João Baptista (252 240 600; www hotelfortesjoao.com; Avenida Brasil; s/d/ste €125/150/175; P) Hidden within the forbidding, metres-thick stone walls of a 17th-century fort is this small oasis of luxury. The rooms are cosy but plush, and just across the small, pentagonal courtyard is the city's finest restaurant.

Eating & Drinking

Restaurante Le Villageois (/fax 252 631 119; Praça da República 94; mains for 2 €9-20; lunch & dinner Tue-Sun) The popular Villageois offers a huge menu of well-prepared French and Portuguese dishes, a full bar, an airy dining room appointed with *azulejos,* and an appealing sun-drenched patio.

Adega Beira Rio (Cais das Lavandeiras 4; half-portions under €5; lunch & dinner Mon-Sat) At lunchtime this plain-faced family-run place serves good half-portions, and has whistling waiters and canaries competing with the TV.

Ramon (252 631 334; Rua 5 de Outubro 176; mains €9-14; lunch & dinner Wed-Mon) Fresh fish and shellfish as well as *cabrito no forno* (roast kid) are the speciality at this seafood restaurant near the turismo.

Caximar (252 642 492; Avenida Brasil; mains €10-15; lunch & dinner Tue-Sun) For special occasions or a holiday treat tuck into the fine seafood in this simple, bright modern place. It sits directly on the beach, roughly 1km west of Forte São João Baptista.

At the time of writing there were no discos in Vila do Conde, though welcoming bars line the riverside Cais das Lavandeiras near Pensão Patarata.

Shopping

Centro de Artesanato (252 248 473; Rua 5 de Outubro 207; 10am-7pm Mon-Fri, 10am-noon & 1.30-5.30pm Sat) Sharing space with the turismo opposite the bus stop, this is a good place for pottery, wooden toys, basketry, embroidered linen and, of course, lace. Local lace-makers sometimes work here, too.

Getting There & Away

Vila do Conde is 33km from Porto, a straight shot on the IC1 highway. It's now served by Porto's Linha B (red) metro line to Póvoa de Varzim, stopping about 400m from the town centre (see p376). One-way fare from central Porto costs €1.85 and takes about one hour – a little faster if you catch the new, express service.

Buses stop near the turismo on Rua 5 de Outubro. AV Minho express buses stop a dozen times daily (fewer at weekends) en route between Porto (€2.60, 55 minutes) and Viana do Castelo (€3.40, one hour). **Linhares** (252 298 300) also has regular services.

EASTERN DOURO

AMARANTE

pop 11,800 / elevation 150m

Most Portuguese know Amarante as the hometown to São Gonçalo. Portugal's Saint Valentine, he is the object of veneration among lonely hearts who make pilgrimages here in hope of the miraculous – true love. Townsfolk pay homage to their man by exchanging phallus-shaped pastries on his saint's day (13 January) as well as during festivities in early June – no doubt a hold-over from even more ancient, pagan rites.

The town also has charms for the happily settled – or glad-to-be-single. Straddling the Rio Tâmega, the town's old heart is dominated by Gonçalo's namesake church and monastery, which sit theatrically beside a rebuilt medieval bridge that still bears city traffic. The willow-lined riverbanks lend a pastoral charm, as do the balconied houses and switchback lanes that rise quickly from the narrow valley floor.

Surrounded by prized vineyards, Amarante is a something of a foodie Mecca. Besides wine, the region produces excellent cheeses, smoked meats (*fumeiros*), and richly eggy pastries.

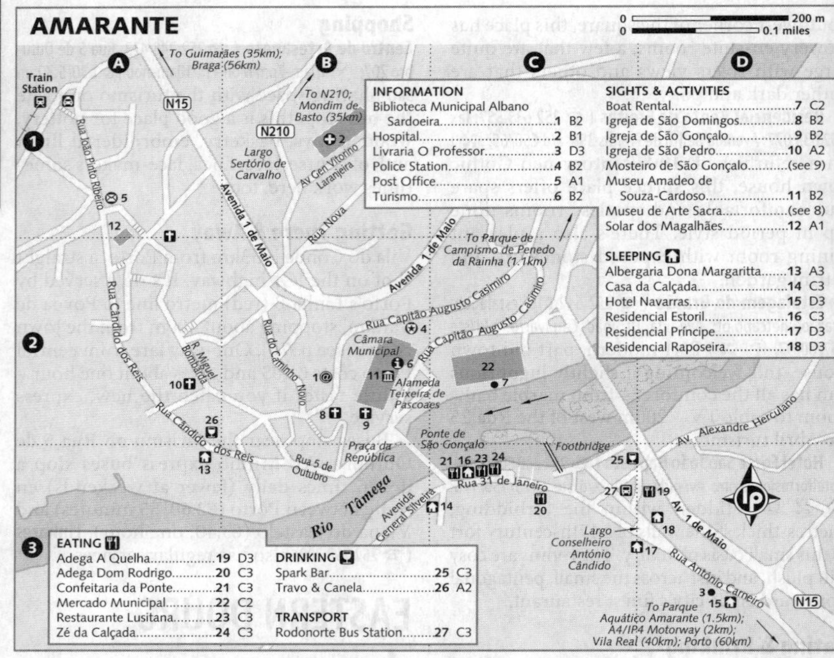

The most appealing way to get here is on the narrow-gauge Linha da Tâmega railway (see p383 for details).

History

The town may date back as far as the 4th century BC, though Gonçalo, a 13th-century hermit, is credited with everything from the founding of the town to the construction of its first bridge.

Amarante's strategically placed bridge (Ponte de São Gonçalo) almost proved to be its undoing in 1809, when the French lost their brief grip on Portugal. Marshal Soult's troops retreated to the northeast after abandoning Porto, plundering as they went. A French detachment arrived here in search of a river crossing, but plucky citizens and troops held them off, allowing residents to escape to the far bank. The French retaliated by burning down much of the town.

Amarante has also suffered frequent natural invasions by the Tâmega. Little *cheia* (high-water level) plaques in Rua 31 de Janeiro and Largo Conselheiro António Cândido tell the harrowing story.

Orientation

The Tâmega flows through the middle of town spanned by the Ponte de São Gonçalo. On th northwest bank is Amarante's showpiece, th Igreja de São Gonçalo. The church's cloisters opposite the market, house the turismo.

The little train station is about 800m south east (and uphill) from the bridge. Nearly a coaches stop in Largo Conselheiro Antóni Cândido, just across the river.

There is free, fairly plentiful parking i front of the turismo.

Information

There are many banks with ATMs along Rua de Outubro and Rua António Carneiro.

Biblioteca Municipal Albano Sardoeira (☎ 255 42 236; Rua Capitão Augusto Casimiro; 🕒 10am-12.30pm & 2-6.30pm Mon-Sat) In the newly refashioned Casa da Cerca; provides free internet access.

Hospital (☎ 255 410 500; Largo Sertório de Carvalho) North of the centre.

Livraria O Professor (☎ 255 432 441; Rua António Carneiro) Stocks foreign-language newspapers.

Police station (☎ 255 432 015; Rua Capitão Augusto Casimiro)

Post office (☎ 255 410 350; Rua João Pinto Ribeiro; 🕑 8.30am-6pm Mon-Fri)

Turismo (☎ 255 420 246; Alameda Teixeira de Pascoaes; 🕑 9am-7pm Jul–mid-Sep, 9am-12.30pm & 2-5.30pm mid-Sep-Jun) In the former cloisters of São Gonçalo.

Sights

PONTE DE SÃO GONÇALO

The granite **Ponte de São Gonçalo** is Amarante's visual centrepiece and symbol of the town's heroic defence against the French (marked by a plaque at the southeastern end). It also offers one of the best views of town. The original bridge, allegedly built at Gonçalo's urging in the 13th century, collapsed in a flood in 1763; this one was completed in 1790.

MOSTEIRO DE SÃO GONÇALO & IGREJA DE SÃO GONÇALO

The **Mosteiro de São Gonçalo** (Monastery of São Gonçalo; ☎ 255 437 425; admission free; 🕑 8am-6pm) and its arresting church, the **Igreja de São Gonçalo**, were founded in 1540 by João III, though only finished in 1620. Beside the church's photogenic, multi-tiered, Italian Renaissance side portal is an arcaded gallery with 17th-century statues of Dom João and the other kings who ruled while the monastery was under construction: Sebastião, Henrique and Felipe I. The bell tower was added in the 18th century.

Within the lofty interior are an impressive gilded baroque altar and pulpits, an organ casing held up by fish-tailed giants, and Gonçalo's tomb in a tiny chapel (left of the altar). Tradition has it that the not-so-young in search of a mate will have their wish granted within a year if they touch the statue above his tomb. And sure enough, its limestone toes, fingers and face have been all but rubbed away by hopefuls.

Through the north portal are a couple of peaceful Renaissance cloisters – one now occupied by the town hall.

MUSEU AMADEO DE SOUZA-CARDOSO

Hidden in one of the monastery's cloisters is the **Museu Amadeo de Souza-Cardoso** (☎ 255 420 233; Alameda Teixeira de Pascoaes; adult/child under 15/student under 26/senior €1/free/0.50/0.50; 🕑 10am-12.30pm & 2-5.30pm Tue-Sun). Its delightfully eclectic collection of modernist and contemporary art is a pleasant surprise in a town this size. The museum is named after Amarante's favourite son, artist Amadeo Souza-Cardoso (1889–1918) – one of the best-known Portuguese artists of the 20th century. He abandoned naturalism for home-grown versions of impressionism and cubism. This museum is full of his sketches, cartoons, portraits and abstracts. But don't overlook the very still portraits and landscapes of António Carneiro, and Jaime Azinheira's touching *Escultura*.

OTHER CHURCHES

Rising beside São Gonçalo are several impressively steep switchbacks topped by the round, 18th-century **Igreja de São Domingos** (admission free), with a tiny, peeling interior and the adjacent **Museu de Arte Sacra** (☎ 255 437 425; admission €1; 🕑 2.30-5.30pm Tue-Fri, Sat 10am-12.30pm & 4.30-6.30pm, Sun 10am-12.30pm & 2-6.30pm). Up on Rua Miguel Bombarda, the baroque-fronted **Igreja de São Pedro** (admission free; 🕑 2-5pm) has a nave decorated with 17th-century blue- and-yellow *azulejos*.

SOLAR DOS MAGALHÃES

This burned-out skeleton of an old **manor house** situated above Rua Cândido dos Reis, near the train station, has been left in ruins – a stark and uncaptioned memento from Napoleon's troops.

Activities

You can potter about on the peaceful Rio Tâmega in a paddle or rowing **boat**. They're for hire in warm weather from the riverbank below the turismo (€5/8 per half-/full hour).

Parque Aquático Amarante (☎ 255 446 648; desporto@tamegaclube.com; A4 exit 15; 🕑 10.30am-7pm Jun-Sep), a water park above the river about 2km southwest of the centre, is a good place for little kids (and big kids) to splash around. It has a choice of three chutes plus swimming pools and sunbathing areas.

Festivals & Events

Held during the first weekend in June, **Festas de Junho** highlights include an all-night drum competition, a livestock fair, a handicrafts market and fireworks, all rounded off with Sunday's procession in honour of the main man – São Gonçalo.

Sleeping

Not surprisingly, accommodation is hard to find during the Festas de Junho, though it's plentiful at other times.

Parque de Campismo de Penedo da Rainha (☎ 255 437 630; ccporto@sapo.pt; Rua Pedro Avelos; adult/car €3/2, tent €2-3; 🕑 Feb-Nov; ♿) This big, shady site cascades down to the river and has a *minimercado* (grocery shop) and bar. It's about 1km upstream (and uphill) from the town centre.

Residencial Príncipe (☎ 255 432 956; Largo Conselheiro António Cândido 78; s with/without bathroom €15/12.50, d without bathroom €30) The furnishings are threadbare and the dogs at reception (which doubles as a café) have been known to bite when provoked, but this old *residencial* (guesthouse) has its advantages, including wood floors, cheap prices and a bit of creaky charm. No breakfast.

Residencial Raposeira (☎ 255 432 221; 1st fl, Largo Conselheiro António Cândido 41; s without bathroom €20, d with/without shower & toilet €30/25) A good value, with small but spotless modern rooms that are, for the price, attractively fitted out. Front-facing rooms are bright and look onto a pretty square. No breakfast.

Residencial Estoril (☎ /fax 255 431 291; Rua 31 de Janeiro 49; d facing street/river €35/40, with balcony €45) Jutting out over the riverbank, this place offers clean, cosy rooms bang in the centre. The real treat are four rooms (two with balcony) with stunning views to São Gonçalo's bridge.

Albergaria Dona Margaritta (☎ 255 432 110; www.albergariadonamargaritta.pa-net.pt in Portuguese; Rua Cândido dos Reis 53; d €40;) This faded but handsome town house has motherly service and is Amarante's most characterful option in its price range. An extra €10 gets you a terrace with river views.

Hotel Navarras (☎ 255 431 036; fax 255 432 991; Rua António Carneiro; s/d €66/83;) Above an unpromisingly common, '70s-style shopping centre, this contemporary place has plenty of comfort and even a dash of style in its newly refurnished, carpeted rooms – some of which have oversized verandas.

Casa da Calçada (☎ 255 410 830; www.casadacalcada.com; Largo do Paço 6; d Sun-Thu €137, Fri & Sat €160; P) Oozing class and boasting every creature comfort, this 16th-century palace rises royally above the Ponte de São Gonçalo. There's huge rooms with marble bathrooms and regal décor, parlours with valuable china and old master paintings, and a fine garden.

Eating

Adega Dom Rodrigo (☎ 255 422 564; Rua 31 de Janeiro; sandwiches €2-3; 9am-8pm) Hung with fine, local meats and cheeses, this cosy shop has a few tables where you can enjoy a sandwich with a *vinho verde* (young, slightly sparkling wine).

Adega A Quelha (☎ 255 425 786; Rua de Olivença; half-portions €5-10; lunch & dinner Tue-Sun, lunch Mon) This chunky, granite-walled place invites you to wash down local cheese and smoked ham with a jug of red wine at the bar, or sit down to some fine local dishes, including a surprising abundance of vegetables.

Restaurante Lusitana (☎ 255 426 720; Rua 31 de Janeiro; mains €7-12; lunch & dinner Wed-Mon) Roasted kid and stewed tripe are house specialities at this traditional Portuguese restaurant with a pretty riverside terrace.

Zé da Calçada (☎ 255 426 814; Rua 31 de Janeiro; mains €14-20; lunch & dinner) Excellent northern cuisine, including a remarkable *posta á marônesa* (grilled local beef), is served in a rustically elegant dining room or on a veranda that juts out over the river.

Confeitaria da Ponte (Rua 31 de Janeiro; mains €14-20; 8am-11pm) With a wonderful, shaded terrace just up from the bridge, this traditional bakery serves up dollops of charm as well as the town's famously eggy sweets.

DETOUR – ROMANCING THE ROMANESQUE

As Christians reconquered northern Portugal from the Moors, Burgundian monks arrived in droves, bringing with them Romanesque architecture – a solid yet graceful style marked by heavy vaulting and rounded arches. The Douro valley has the lion's share of these small, simple yet graceful Reconquista monuments. Most are scattered across the countryside in small villages or hillside retreats, requiring either infinite patience or your own vehicle.

One of the richest spots is the Sousa valley around Penafiel, 35km east of Porto. The town itself has a charming historic centre, and its turismo will mark up a map to indicate the dozen or so Romanesque churches in the area. The most extraordinary is the abbey church in Paço de Sousa, 10km southwest of Penafiel.

The agriculturally rich lands around Amarante also have a number of fine specimens. Amarante's turismo supplies an illustrated map of the sites, including churches in the villages of Travanca, Mancelos and Telões, all within 10km of town.

Finally, there is another extraordinary cluster around Lamego (p386).

You can get picnic fixings at shops along Rua 31 de Janeiro or at the **mercado municipal** (Rua Capitão Augusto Casimiro), whose big days are Wednesday and Saturday.

Drinking

Bars pop up every summer on the riverside promenade along Avenida General Silveira, opposite the monastery.

Spark Bar (Avenida Alexandre Herculano; 12.30pm-4am) This sleekly contemporary, multilevel bar-restaurant turns into a makeshift disco on Friday and Saturday nights.

Travo & Canela (Rua Cândido dos Reis; 1pm-2am) This inviting new wine bar combines trim décor with festive red-and-yellow walls. Try the sandwiches (€2), which are made with local ingredients.

Getting There & Away

BUS

At the busy **Rodonorte bus station** (☎ 255 422 194; www.rodonorte.pt; Largo Conselheiro António Cândido), buses stop at least five times daily from Porto (€4.80, one hour) en route to Vila Real (€5.30, 40 minutes) and Bragança (€10.20, 2¾ hours). Rodonorte also runs daily to Braga (€6.20, 2½ hours), Coimbra (€10.90, 2¾ hours) and Lisbon (€15.50, 5½ hours).

TRAIN

The journey on the narrow-gauge Linha da Tâmega, which runs from the Douro mainline at Livração up to Amarante, takes 25 minutes and costs €1.12 (buy tickets on board). There are six to nine trains a day, most with good connections to Porto.

LAMEGO

pop 9100 / elevation 550m

Most people come to Lamego – a prim, prosperous town 10km south of the Douro – to see (and possibly to climb) the astonishing baroque stairway that zigzags its way up to the Igreja de Nossa Senhora dos Remédios. Connoisseurs also swear by Lamego's *raposeira,* the town's famously fragrant sparkling wine, which provides a fine break between bouts of port.

Lamego is also a natural base for exploring the half-ruined monasteries and chapels in the environs, one of which dates back to the time of the Visigoths. Though technically in the Beira Alta, in spirit Lamego belongs to the Douro region.

History

Lamego was an important centre even in the time of the Visigoths and has had a cathedral since at least the 6th century. The city fell to the Moors in the 8th century and remained in their hands until the 11th century. In 1143 Portugal's first *cortes* (parliament) was convened here to confirm Afonso Henriques as Portugal's first king. The little town grew fat thanks to its position on trading routes between the Douro and the Beiras, and also from its wines, already famous in the 16th century.

Orientation

The town's main axis is Avenida Visconde Guedes Teixeira (known as 'Jardim' and shaded by lime trees) and the wide Avenida Dr Alfredo de Sousa (called 'Avenida' and shaded by chestnut trees).

At the far end of the Avenida the immense stairway ascends to the Igreja de Nossa Senhora dos Remédios, on top of one of the two hills overlooking the town. Northwards, atop a more modest hill, stand the ruins of a 12th-century castle.

Parking can be tight, but there are lots of free, shady spaces around the Jardim (though you must pay along the adjacent Avenida).

Information

C@fenet (Avenida 5 de Outubro 153; internet access per hr €1.50; 8am-midnight)
Hospital (☎ 254 609 980; Lugar da Franzia)
Library (☎ 254 614 013; Rua de Almacave 9; 9.30am-12.30pm & 2-5.30pm Mon-Fri) Provides free internet access in 30-minute chunks.
Police station (☎ 254 612 022; Rua António Osório Mota)
Post office (☎ 254 609 250; Avenida Dr Alfredo de Sousa; 8.30am-6pm Mon-Fri)
Turismo (☎ 254 612 005; douro.turismo@mail.telepac.pt; Avenida Visconde Guedes Teixeira; 10am-12.30pm & 2-6pm Mon-Fri, 10am-12.30pm & 2-5pm Sat & Sun Jul-Sep, 9.30am-12.30pm & 2-5.30pm Mon-Fri, 10am-12.30pm Sat Oct-Jun)

Sights & Activities

IGREJA DE NOSSA SENHORA DOS REMÉDIOS

One of the country's most important pilgrimage sites, the twin-towered 18th-century **church** (admission free; 7.30am-8pm May-Sep, 7.30am-6pm Oct-Apr) is attractive enough, with a blue-and-white stucco interior reminiscent of Wedgwood Jasperware. But it's quite overshadowed by the

zigzagging theatricality of the monumental stairway that lead up to it. The 600-plus steps are resplendent with *azulejos*, urns, fountains and statues, adding up to one of the great works of Portuguese rococo.

It's a dramatic sight at any time, but the action peaks in late summer when thousands of devotees arrive and ascend the steps in search of miracles – or at least a little comfort – during the Festas de Nossa Senhora dos Remédios (opposite).

If you can't face climbing by foot, a road (turn off 1km out on the Viseu road) winds up the hill for about 3km before reaching the top. You can make your way back down through cool winding forest paths on either side of the steps.

SÉ

Lamego's striking **cathedral** (☎ 254 612 766; Largo da Sé; admission free; 🕑 8am-1pm & 3-7pm), which has been declared a National Monument, is older than Portugal itself, though there's little left of the 12th-century original except the base of its square belfry.

The rest of the structure, including the brilliantly carved Flamboyant Gothic triple portal, dates mostly from the 16th and 18th centuries. Arresting biblical frescoes seem to leap off the ceiling. Both these and the high choir stalls are the work of the 18th-century Italian baroque architect Nicolau Nasoni.

With luck you'll find the door open to the peaceful 16th-century cloisters, just around the corner.

IGREJA SANTA MARIA DE ALMACAVE

This unassuming little **church** (☎ 254 612 460; Rua da Almacave; ⌚ 7.30am-noon & 4-7.30pm) is Lamego's oldest surviving building, much of it dating back to the 12th century. The church occupies the site of a Moorish cemetery; some of its grave markers are now in the Museu de Lamego (below). On the south side is a very lovely Romanesque portal.

It's thought that an early version of the *cortes*, Portugal's proto-democratic assembly of nobles and clergy, met here from 1142 to 1144.

MUSEU DE LAMEGO

Occupying a grand, 18th-century episcopal palace, the **Museu de Lamego** (☎ 254 600 230; Largo de Camões; www.ipmuseus.pt; adult/youth 14-25 €2/1, 10am-12.30pm Sun free; ⌚ 10am-12.30pm & 2-5pm Tue-Sun) is one of Portugal's finest regional museums. The collection features some luminous pieces, including five entrancing works by renowned 16th-century Portuguese painter Vasco Fernandes (Grão Vasco), richly worked Brussels tapestries from the same period, and an extraordinarily diverse collection of heavily gilded 17th-century chapels rescued in their entirety from the long-gone Convento das Chagas. Sadly, the museum may require major repairs and is likely to be closed for several years.

CASTELO

Climb the narrow, winding Rua da Olaria to the modest medieval **castle** (Rua do Castelinho; admission by donation; ⌚ 10am-noon & 3-6pm Tue-Sun Jun-Sep, 10am-noon Sun only Oct-May), which is encircled by a clutch of ancient stone houses. What little remains – some walls and a tower – has belonged to the Boy Scouts ever since their mammoth 1970s effort to clear the site after years of use as a glorified rubbish tip. Climb to the roof for spectacular views.

RAPOSEIRA TASTING

At the time of writing, the Caves de Raposeira, which offer informative 20-minute tours and tastings of the local bubbly, were closed. Check with the turismo to see if they have reopened. Or you can call ☎ 254 655 003. They're 1.7km out on the Viseu road (N2).

Festivals & Events

Lamego's biggest shindig, the **Festa de Nossa Senhora dos Remédios**, runs for several weeks from late August to mid-September. In an afternoon procession on 8 September, ox-drawn carts carry religious *tableaux vivants* (scenes represented by a group of silent, motionless people) in the streets, and devotees grit their teeth before slowly ascending the stairway on their knees.

Less-pious events in the run-up include rock concerts, folk dancing, car racing, parades and at least one all-night party.

Sleeping

Parque de Campismo Dr João de Almeida (☎ /fax 254 613 918; Serra das Meadas; adult/car €2.70/2.2, tent €2.70-3.2; ⌚ Jun-Sep) A well-equipped camping facility about 5km west of town. Restaurant, market and some shade.

Residencial São Paulo (☎ 254 613 114; fax 254 612 304; Avenida 5 de Outubro 22; d €35) This clean, good-value sleep is hidden in an uninspired, '70s building with decoration of the same era, including some wild paisley tile-work in some of the bathrooms. Corner rooms have extra windows and verandas, and some rooms have views.

Residencial Solar da Sé (☎ 254 612 060; fax 254 615 928; Avenida Visconde Guedes Teixeira 7; s/d with breakfast €24/39; ❄) Homely but well-equipped rooms, many with French windows and little verandas that look out onto the cathedral's façade – though this also makes them subject to the frequent tolling of its bells.

Residencial Solar do Espírito Santo (☎ /fax 254 655 060; Rua Alexandre Herculano 8; d with breakfast €45; P ❄) Modern place, though with old-world touches like wood floors and *azulejo*-lined common areas. Rooms have had a recent face-lift and are very good value. Breakfast includes fresh-baked goods from the downstairs bakery.

Vila Ferraz (☎ 254 656 956; www.vilaferraz.com in Portuguese; Avenida General Alves Pedrosa; d with breakfast €60; P ❄ 🏊) Just 800m beyond the *castelo*, this converted, 19th-century mansion boasts large rooms decked out in period furniture, plus a huge garden with swimming pool. Every inch is packed with antique character, and no two rooms are alike.

Hotel Parque (☎ 254 609 140; fax 254 615 203; d with breakfast €60; P ❄) With an unrivalled location in a wooded park next to the Igreja de Nossa Senhora dos Remédios, this attractive hotel has tastefully decorated modern rooms with choice craftwork. Best to have your own car; the turn-off for the hotel is 1km out on the Viseu road (N2). Or you can walk up the 600-plus steps if your quads are particularly hearty.

Albergaria Solar dos Pachecos (☎ 254 600 300; www.solar-pachecos.com; Avenida Visconde Guedes Teixeira 27; s/d with breakfast €40/65; ❄) Occupying an impressive, 18th-century nobleman's city home, this central place combines exposed stone walls with bright, modern rooms done up rather stylishly in a crisp white.

Quinta da Timpeira (☎ 254 612 811; www.quintadatimpeira.com; s/d €57/70; P ♿) Surrounded by vineyards, this is an attractive modern place with bright and airy (if smallish) rooms and lovely grounds with pool and tennis courts into the bargain. It's located about 4km out on the Viseu road.

Eating & Drinking

Like most regions that produce good wines, Lamego delivers food to match. Its *fumeiros* – smoked meats – are justly famous. You can eat very well here for very little.

A Lampeão (Rua Virgílio Correia; mains €4-5; 🕑 lunch Sun-Fri) Enjoy simple but fine regional cuisine at rock-bottom prices at this snug, family-run eatery. Try the *febras de porco* (grilled pork steaks dressed with lemon and rosemary). When stars and moods align, they also open for dinner.

Restaurante Trás da Sé (☎ 254 614 075; Rua Virgílio Correia 12; half-portions €5-6; 🕑 lunch & dinner) Congratulations to the chef line the walls at this *adega* (wine cellar)-style place, where the atmosphere is friendly, the menu short and simple, the food good and the *vinho maduro* (wine matured for more than a year) list long.

Adega Matos (Rua Trás da Sé 52; mains around €5; 🕑 lunch & dinner Mon-Sat, lunch Sun) Yet another humble but good cheapie, with *azulejos* on the walls and a friendly owner who speaks some English. Try the strong-tasting *alheiras* (smoked sausages made of poultry, bread and garlic).

The **mercado municipal** (Avenida 5 de Outubro; 🕑 Mon-Fri, morning Sat) and grocery shops on Rua da Olaria sell Lamego's famous hams and wines – perfect picnic food. For more workaday goods, there's **Supermercado Feijoeiro** (Avenida 5 de Outubro 11; 🕑 9am-12.30pm & 2-8pm Mon-Sat).

If you are feeling sociable, consider **Snack Bar Cortilheiro** (Rua Cortes; 🕑 12.30pm-2am Mon-Sat), a youthful *cervejaria* (beer house) under the disapproving shadow of a sombre church and the bishop's palace. Inside the walls of the *castelo* is the atmospheric **Casa do Castelo** (Rua do Castelinho 25; 🕑 noon-2am Tues-Sun), which packs in students on weekend nights. You may even catch a traditional singing contest. English is spoken.

Getting There & Away

The most appealing route to Lamego from anywhere in the Douro valley is by train to Peso da Régua (p388) and by bus or taxi from there. A **taxi** (☎ 254 321 366) from Régua costs about €10 to €12.

From Lamego's bus station, **Joalto/EAVT** (☎ 254 612 116) goes about hourly to Peso da Régua (€1.70, 30 minutes) and daily to Viseu (€6.80, 1¼ hours), Coimbra (€9.80, three hours) and Lisbon (€13.40, 5¾ hours).

Rodonorte (www.rodonorte.pt) also stops here three times each weekday en route between Chaves (€9, 2¼ hours) and Vila Real (€5.20, 55 minutes) to Lisbon (€13.40, 5¾ hours). **Rede Expressos** (www.rede-expressos.pt) stops twice daily en route between Vila Real and Viseu, where you can transfer to other destinations. **Copy Print** (☎ 254 619 447; Avenida Visconde Guedes Teixeira; 🕑 8am-8pm), a newsagent beside the turismo, sells tickets for these services.

Getting Around

A miniature train, the **Circuito Histórico de Lamego** (☎ 936 522 379; 🕑 2-7pm Jun-Sep, 2-7pm Sat & Sun only Oct-May) runs a hop-on-hop-off tour past the major monuments and parks of Lamego for €2.50. It leaves from the roundabout just up from the turismo.

AROUND LAMEGO

Capela de São Pedro de Balsemão

Older than Portugal itself, this extraordinary little **chapel** (admission free; 🕑 10am-12.30pm & 2-5.30pm Wed-Sun, 2-5.30pm Tue, closed 3rd weekend of month) has mysterious origins, but parts were probably built by Visigoths as early as the 7th century. With Corinthian columns, round arches and intriguing symbols etched into the walls, it certainly predates the introduction of even Romanesque architecture to Portugal. Its more ornate 14th-century additions were commissioned by the Bishop of Porto, Afonso Pires, who's buried under a slab in the floor. Check out the ancient casket dominating the entrance chamber: supported by lions and intricately engraved, it depicts the Last Supper.

The chapel is tucked away in the hamlet of Balsemão, 3km southeast of Lamego above the Rio Balsemão. It's a pleasant, downhill walk from Lamego (though a rather steep return trip). From the 17th-century Capela do Desterro at the end of Rua da Santa Cruz head southeast over the river and follow the road to the left.

Mosteiro de São João de Tarouca

The skeletal remains of Portugal's first Cistercian monastery, the **Mosteiro de São João de Tarouca** (☎ 254 678 766; admission free; 🕒 10am-12.30pm & 2-5.30pm Wed-Sun, to 6pm May-Sep), founded in 1124, stand eerily in the wooded Barosa valley below the Serra de Leomil, 15km southeast of Lamego. It fell into ruin after religious orders were abolished in 1834.

Only the church, considerably altered in the 17th century, stands intact among the ghostly ruins of the monks' quarters. Its treasures include the gilded choir stalls, 18th-century *azulejos*, and an imposing 14th-century tomb of the Conde de Barcelos (Dom Dinis' illegitimate son), carved with scenes from a boar hunt. The church's pride and joy is a luminous *São Pedro* painted by Gaspar Vaz, contemporary and colleague of Grão Vasco (p342).

From Lamego, Joalto/EAVT has eight services each weekday (fewer at weekends) to São João de Tarouca (€1.70).

Ponte de Ucanha

Famous for its 12th-century fortified bridge, Ucanha is a lopsided little village 12km south of Lamego, off the N226, just north of Tarouca. A twisted lane leads down from the main road to the chunky Ponte de Ucanha, sitting squatly over the Rio Barosa. The blocky tower was added by the Abbot of Salzedas in the 15th century, probably as a tollgate: look for the stonemasons' initials visible on almost every block. While the medieval stone washing enclosures under the bridge have fallen into disuse, village women still decorate the bridge itself with their laundry.

There are three Joalto/EAVT buses travelling each weekday between Lamego and Ucanha (€2.20).

Mosteiro de Salzedas

Another picturesquely mouldering Cistercian monastery, the **Mosteiro de Salzedas** (admission free; 🕒 9am-12.30pm & 2-5pm Wed-Sun Nov-Apr, 10am-12.30pm & 2-6pm Wed-Sun May-Oct) is about 3km further up the Barosa valley from Ucanha. This was one of the grandest monasteries in the land when it was built in 1168 with funds from Teresa Afonso, governess to Afonso Henriques' five children. The enormous church, extensively remodelled in the 18th century, is black with decay and seems past hope of restoration, though students beaver away each summer, scraping away the moss and mopping up puddles.

From Lamego, Joalto/EAVT runs three buses each weekday to Salzedas (€2).

Parque Biológico da Serra das Meadas

This **biological park** (☎ 254 609 600; www.cm-lamego.pt/parquebio in Portuguese; adult/child under 18/senior €1/0.50/0.50; 🕒 10am-5pm Wed-Thu, 3-6pm Sat & Sun Jun-Sep, 2-5pm Sun Oct-May), in the hills 7km from Lamego, makes a good excursion if you have kids and your own transport. You can see the local fauna, including deer and wild boar, at close quarters, then stroll through the designated walks.

PESO DA RÉGUA

pop 9500 / elevation 125m

Lamego's businesslike alter ego, the sun-bleached town of 'Régua' abuts the Rio Douro at the western edge of the demarcated port-wine region. As the largest regional centre with river access, it grew in the 18th century into a major port-wine entrepôt, though the unofficial title of 'capital of the trade' has now shifted 25km upstream to the prettier village of Pinhão.

Régua remains an important transport junction – thanks in part to the hulking IP3 bridge that soars above the river valley. It makes a convenient base to visit the port-wine country, cruise the Rio Douro and ride the Corgo railway line to Vila Real.

The town itself isn't beautiful, offering little more than an opportunity to learn about (and drink your fill of) port wine. That said, you can stroll along the town's waterside, watch the local fishermen try their luck, and snap a shot or two of the photogenic *barcos rabelos* dotting the river.

Orientation & Information

While the older heart of the city lies further up the sloping riverbank, the main area of interest to traveller is ranged along the riverfront. From the train station or adjacent bus stop bear right at Residencial Império into Rua dos Camilos. Carry on via Rua da Ferreirinha to reach the **turismo** (☎ 254 312 846; fax 254 322 271; Rua da Ferreirinha 505; 🕒 9am-12.30pm & 2-5.30pm Jul–mid-Sep, 9am-12.30pm & 2.30-5.30pm Mon-Fri mid-Sep-Jun), 1km west of the station. For the *cais fluvial* (river terminal) bear left at the Residencial Império.

There is a public car park at the eastern end of the riverfront promenade, a few blocks from the turismo.

Sights & Activities

WINE TASTING

Port-wine enthusiasts can collect an armful of brochures from the **Instituto do Vinho do Porto** (☎ 254 320 130; Rua dos Camilos 90; 8.30am-12.30pm & 2-6pm Mon-Fri). Or for a more hands-on approach, get drinking at the **Solar do Vinho do Porto** (☎ 254 320 960; Rua da Ferreirinha; 11am-8pm Mon-Sat), a new branch of the famous Porto drinking den. Housed in a cavernous 18th-century warehouse, it is full of port-related artefacts and has hundreds wines to choose from.

Not done yet? **Quinta do Castelinho** (☎ 254 320 262; 9am-7pm Jun-Sep, 9am-6pm Mon-Fri Feb-May & Oct-Dec, closed Jan) is the nearest grower to Régua and offers free tours and tastings. It also has a very good restaurant open Tuesday to Sunday. To reach the lodge from the train station, head 600m east on the Vila Real road, turn left and continue for 400m.

TRAIN TRIPS & RIVER CRUISES

Régua is a major stop on the Douro cruise lines (see p368 for more information). Your best bet is to reserve through Porto Tours in Porto (p368). In Regua, you might also try booking at **Rota do Vinho do Porto** (☎ 254 324 774; Largo da Estação; 9am-12.30pm & 2-6pm Feb-Oct, Mon-Fri only Nov-Jan), conveniently located in a converted warehouse right next to the train station.

Also on offer from May to October, if there are enough passengers, are Saturday-only journeys in restored steam trains along the beautiful Linha do Douro line. Trips cost €44, last four hours and leave around 3.35pm. Book with Rota do Vinho do Porto, or call **UVIR** (☎ 211 021 129), a service of the national rail service.

Sleeping

Accommodations are relatively pricey in Peso da Regua.

Dom Quixote (☎ 254 321 151; fax 254 322 802; 1st fl, Avenida Sacadura Cabral 1; d €40; P) Located 800m west of the turismo, the modern Dom Quixote is the closest Régua comes to a decent budget option. It offers comfortable-enough rooms. The real plus is the friendly staff.

Residencial Império (☎ 254 320 120; www.residencialimperio.com; Rua José Vasques Osório 8; d €45; P) Threadbare but acceptable rooms last decorated in the '70s in a faceless high-rise just west of the train station.

Hotel Régua Douro (☎ 254 320 700; www.hotelreguadouro.pt; Largo da Estação; s/d €105; P) This new, industrial-sized hotel sits by the river and is steps from the train station. It has spanking new, carpeted rooms, plus fine river views for just €5 more per night. Expect steep discounts during the week and low season.

Pousada Solar da Rêde (☎ 254 890 130; www.pousadas.pt; Mesão Frio; d from €195; P) This magnificent, 18th-century palace 12km west of Régua sits royally above a particularly stunning bend in the Douro. It preserves all its original glory, including period furnishings and terraced gardens, plus new features like tennis courts and swimming pool. Among Portugal's most regal sleeps.

Eating

Restaurante O Maleiro (☎ 254 313 684; Rua dos Camilos; mains €7-10; lunch & dinner) Situated opposite the post office, this brisk but friendly place offers meaty Portuguese standards prepared with care and served in a simple dining room with *azulejo*-covered walls.

Taberna Zéréré (☎ 254 323 299; Rua Marquês de Pombal 38; mains €8-10; lunch & dinner; P) Excellent Portuguese dishes, including *bacalhau á Zéréré* – dried salt-cod with shrimp, mushroom and spinach – served in a tastefully rustic dining room with a beamed ceiling.

Restaurante Cacho d'Oiro (☎ 254 321 455; Rua Branca Martinho; mains €8-12; lunch & dinner; P) This large cottage-restaurant, 150m west of the turismo, offers a longer menu, a good wine list, a more upmarket atmosphere and some of the best food in town. The *cabrito no churrasco* (grilled kid; €12) is excellent.

Getting There & Away

Joalto buses run hourly to/from Lamego (€1.70, 30 minutes). AV Tâmega runs to Vila Real (€2.60, 40 minutes) about hourly on weekdays and thrice daily on weekends, and Rodonorte goes four times each weekday.

There are around 12 trains daily from Porto (€7.80, two hours); eight go up the valley to Pinhão (€1.30, 25 minutes, nine daily) and Tua (opposite). Around five trains depart daily heading to Vila Real (€1.90, 55 minutes) on the narrow-gauge Corgo line.

THE ALTO DOURO

Heading upriver from Peso da Régua, terraced vineyards wrap around every precipitous hillside. This is a landscape that has been completely refashioned by 2000 years of winemaking. While villages are small and architectural monuments few and far between, it' worth the trip simply for the ride itself (scenic by car but especially by train or boat). If you don't believe us, take it from Unesco, which in 2001 designated the entire Alto Douro wine-growing region a World Heritage site.

As you head towards Spain, the landscape turns drier and harsher – especially during the blisteringly hot summers. Still, the land around Vila Nova de Foz Côa produces fine grapes, nuts and especially olives.

Many port-wine *quintas* offer rural accommodations, though rooms grow scarce in late September and early October during the *vindima* (grape harvest).

Though not technically part of the Douro province, this section of the Douro valley is an integral part of the region and is most easily reached via Porto.

Daily trains run from Porto, with a change at Régua, up to Pinhão, Tua and Pocinho. Travellers with their own wheels can take the river-hugging N222 from Régua to Pinhão, beyond which the roads climb in and out of the valley. For information on river cruises, see p368.

Pinhão

pop 310 / elevation 120m

Encircled by terraced hillsides that produce some of the world's best port, little Pinhão sits on a particularly lovely bend of the Rio Douro, about 25km upriver from Peso da Régua. The scene is dominated by port-wine lodges and their competing signs; even the delightful train station has *azulejos* depicting the wine harvest. The town itself is of little interest but makes a fine base to explore the area's *quintas*.

There are several fine day-trip possibilities for itchy feet, especially by train (below).

ORIENTATION & INFORMATION

The summer-only **turismo** (☎ 254 731 932; Largo do Estação; 🕒 10am-noon & 2-6pm Tue-Sun) is open May to September and is in the train station.

Except on high-season weekends, street parking is straightforward. Look around the train station.

SIGHTS & ACTIVITIES

Train Trips

The most beautiful of Portugal's narrow-gauge lines is the Linha da Tua, running from the sun-blasted backwater of Tua (13km upriver) for 52km up the Tua valley to the pretty market town of Mirandela (p449). The two-hour Pinhão–Mirandela journey (€9.50 return, change at Tua) is feasible as a day trip, departing about 11.30am and leaving Mirandela about 6pm.

Alternatively, take the mainline train for another hour, past dams and vineyards, to the end of the line at Pocinho (single/return €2.50/5), visiting the Pocinho dam and returning the same day, or travelling on up to Vila Nova de Foz Côa (p390).

Wine Tasting

To explore the port *quintas* on your own, you'll need your own vehicle. Ask the tourist office about lodges open to tours and tastings. A 12km digression northeast up the N322-3 to Favaios will also reward you with the discovery of a little-known muscatel wine, one of only two produced in Portugal (the other comes from Setúbal).

SLEEPING & EATING

Residencial Ponto Grande (☎ 254 732 456; Largo do Estação; d €40; ❄) This place just across from the station offers dated but snug rooms above a humble but well-regarded restaurant. Try to snag one of the bright front rooms with river views. Cheapest place in town, though that's not saying much.

Residencial Douro (☎/fax 254 732 404; Largo do Estação; d €50; ❄) This cheery, well-kept guesthouse has several river-facing rooms, other large rooms facing a quiet rear courtyard, and a mini terrace covered with flowering vines.

Quinta de la Rosa (☎ 254 732 254; www.quintadelarosa.com; d from €80; ❄ 🏊) A lovely hillside *quinta* amid terraced vineyards just above the river 2km west of Pinhão, this place is worth seeking out. The higher, airier 'Dona Clara' rooms are worth the extra €10, though all are attractive and with few exceptions have fine river views. Book well ahead.

Vintage House (☎ 254 730 230; www.hotelvintagehouse.com in Portuguese; s/d with breakfast €149/163; P ❄ 💻 🏊) Occupying a string of 19th-century buildings right on the river, this luxurious, though very pricey, sleep is actually very modern once you get past the distinctly English façade (a reminder of the key role Brits played in the port trade).

There are two good riverside restaurant-bars:

Restaurante Veladouro (mains €6-8; 🕒 lunch & dinner Mon-Sat) Simple Portuguese food, such as wood-grilled meats, are served inside this quaint schist building or outside under a canopy of vines. From the train station, turn left and go along the main road for 150m, then left again under a railway bridge, and right at the river.

Restaurante Cais da Foz (mains €6-7; 8am-10pm) A short hop over a footbridge from Restaurante Veladouro, this place offers similar cuisine and prices but in a brighter, more modern building and with unbeatable river views.

GETTING THERE & AWAY

Regional trains go from Peso da Régua (€1.50, 30 minutes, six daily). From Porto you must change at Régua; the quickest links (€7.50, two hours, four daily) are by IC train as far as Régua.

VILA NOVA DE FOZ CÔA

pop 2850 / elevation 420m

Once remote, this whitewashed town in the Douro's *terra quente* (hot country) has been on the map since the discovery in the 1990s of thousands of mysterious Palaeolithic rock engravings in the nearby Rio Côa valley. As it turns out, the region has been popular with human beings ever since, and around 'Foz' you can also find remains of Bronze Age, Roman and Visigothic civilisation.

You may find the climate startlingly Mediterranean if you've just come from the mountains. Indeed, summers are blisteringly hot, temperatures regularly exceeding 45°C. But if you come in late March, you'll be treated to cool temperatures and entire hillsides in blossom thanks to the highest density of flowering almond trees in Portugal.

Orientation

Long-distance coaches stop at the bus station about 150m north of the turismo at Avenida Gago Coutinho. From here the town stretches eastward along Avenida Gago Coutinho, pedestrianised Rua Dr Juiz Moutinho de Andrade, Rua São Miguel and Rua Dr Júlio de Moura to the old town's centre, Praça do Município.

There is usually plenty of free street parking along Avenida Gago Coutinho between the turismo and the park headquarters.

Information

Espaço Internet (Avenida Gago Coutinho; 10am-6pm Mon-Sat) Free internet access behind the tourist office.

Lavandaria Alva Wipp (279 765 317; Rua de São Antonio 35; per kilo €3; Mon-Sat) On a small street off the pedestrian boulevard.

Municipal Turismo (279 760 329; Avenida Gago Coutinho; 9am-12.30pm & 2-5.30pm) Opposite Albergaria Foz Côa.

Parque Arqueológico Office (279 768 260; www.ipa.min-cultura.pt/coa; Avenida Gago Coutinho 19a; 9am-12.30pm & 2-5.30pm Tue-Sun) Staff here are kept busy shuttling visitors out to the rock engravings.

Police station (279 760 500; Rua Dr José Augusto Saraiva de Aguilar) A block behind the park office.

Post office (Avenida Dr Artur de Aguilar 6; 9am-12.30pm & 2-5.30pm Mon-Fri) Three blocks north of the park office via Largo do Rossio.

Sights & Activities

PARQUE ARQUEOLÓGICO VALE DO CÔA

Most visitors to Vila Nova da Foz Côa come for one reason: to see its world-famous gallery of rock art – for more on this see the boxed text opposite.

Although the park is an active research zone, three sites are open to visitors – Canada do Inferno from the **park office** (daily, trips Tue-Sun) in Vila Nova de Foz Côa; Ribeira de Piscos from the **Muxagata visitor centre** (279 764 298; 9am-12.30pm & 2-5.30pm Tue-Sun) on the western side of the valley; and Penascosa from the **Castelo Melhor visitor centre** (279 713 344; 2-5.30pm Tue-Sun) on the eastern side. While Castelo Melhor has some of the most significant etchings, Canada do Inferno – which sits by the half-constructed dam – is the ideal place to understand just how close these aeons-old drawings came to disappearing.

Near Ribeira de Piscos there is also a private site (owned by the Ramos Pinto port-wine lodge) at **Quinta da Ervamoira** (279 759 229; www.ramospinto.pt; Tue-Sun). It has vineyards, wine tastings and a small museum featuring Roman and medieval artefacts. Visits are included in some tours. Times vary; check at the turismo in town.

Because the entire valley is a working archaeological site, all visitors must enter with a guided tour. Visitors gather at the various visitors centres, where they're taken, eight at a time, in the park's own 4WDs, for a guided tour of one of the sites (1½ hours at Canada do Inferno and Penascosa, 2½ hours at Ribeira de Piscos). Visitors with mountain bikes may go on guided bike tours in similar-sized groups. The price in either case is €5 per person.

Visitor numbers are strictly regulated, so from July to September, book a tour well in advance or you may miss out. Likewise, you must book at least a few weeks ahead for

RESCUING PORTUGAL'S ROCK ART

In 1989 researchers were studying the rugged valley of the Rio Côa, 15km from the Spanish frontier, to understand the environmental impact of a planned hydroelectric dam that was to flood the valley. In the course of their work, they made an extraordinary discovery: a number of rock engravings dating back tens of thousands of years.

Yet, it wasn't until 1992, after dam construction was underway, that their discoveries began to snowball. Archaeologists discovered whole clusters of petroglyphs (rock engravings), mostly dating from the Upper Palaeolithic period (10,000 to 40,000 years ago). Then local people joined the search and the inventory of engravings grew into the thousands. Still, Portugal's main power company insisted on completing the dam, only backing down in the face of an international campaign. In 1998 stubborn archaeologists got their ultimate reward when the valley was designated a Unesco World Heritage site.

Today the valley holds the largest-known collection of open-air Palaeolithic art in the world. Archaeologists are still puzzling out what the engravings might signify. Most depict animals: stylised horses, aurochs (extinct ancestors of domesticated cattle) and long-horned ibex (extinct wild goat). Some animals are depicted with multiple heads, while others are drawn so finely that they require artificial light to be seen at all. Later petroglyphs begin to depict human figures as well. And some engravings consists of overlapping layers, some added many thousands of years after the first strokes were applied: a kind of Palaeolithic palimpsest in which generations of hunters worked and reworked the engravings of their forebears.

For more information, pick up the multilingual book (€10.50) sold at the ticket offices.

bicycle trips at any time. You can make bookings through the park office (opposite).

Several private tour operators include park trips in their own programmes; local operators include **Ravinas do Côa** (☎ 279 762 832, 966 746 423; www.ravinasdocoa.lda.pt in Portuguese; Bairro Flor da Rosa 28, Vila Nova de Foz Côa) and **Impactus** (☎ 962 838 261; www.impactus.pt in Portuguese; Rua da Igreja 2, Castelo Rodrigo).

OLD TOWN

Take a leisurely stroll down to Praça do Município to see the impressive granite *pelourinho* topped by an armillary sphere, and the elaborately carved portal of the Manueline-style parish church. Inside, the nave recalls a banqueting hall, with its chandeliers and painted ceiling (supported by perilously pitched columns). Just east off the square is the tiny Capela de Santa Quitéria, once the town's synagogue.

OTHER ATTRACTIONS

Archaeological finds from the Stone Age to the 18th century have been uncovered in the region around Freixo de Numão, 12km west of Vila Nova de Foz Côa. A good little display can be viewed at Freixo de Numão, in the **Museu da Casa Grande** (☎ 279 789 573; www.acdr-freixo.pt; adult/child under 12/under 26 €1.50/0.75/1; 9am-noon & 2-6pm Tue-Sun), a baroque town house with Roman foundations. Some English and French are spoken here. Free with entrance is a leaflet on the museum and the rich Neolithic/Roman/medieval site at Prazo, about 3km west of Freixo de Numão. Guided tours are available by arrangement with the museum.

The turismo in Vila Nova de Foz Côa also offers free brochures for a **self-guided archaeological tour** of the region.

Sleeping

Pousada da Juventude (☎ 279 768 190; www.pousadasjuventude.pt; Caminho Vicinal, Currauteles No 5; dm €11, d with toilet €30; P) This fine new hostel in a modern, pink-brick building is well worth the 800m walk north from the town centre (1.4km by road). Its basic but handsome doubles have views over a rugged valley; four-bed dorms are clean and well-maintained. Amenities include bar, open kitchen, laundry, cafeteria, games room and large patio with sweeping views.

Albergaria Vale do Côa (☎ 279 760 010; www.albergariavaledocoa.net in Portuguese; Avenida Cidade Nova 1a; d €50; P) Offering the only whiff of luxury in town, this modern hotel opposite the tourist office offers comfortable, air-conditioned rooms done up with a modicum of pizzazz.

Quinta do Chão d'Ordem (☎ 279 762 427; www.chaodordem.com; Avenida Cidade Nova 1a; d €60; P) This working farm offers a warm welcome and rather grand rooms in a new wing off the old villa. Breakfasts are wonderful, and amenities include a pool, tennis court, lounge and a remarkable wine cellar in a converted dovecote. The farm is about 6km from Foz Côa, just past Muxagata on the N102 towards Guard. Some English spoken.

Back in town, there are two *residenciais* across from the turismo, both of which offer basic rooms with bathrooms at good prices (but no breakfast):

Residencial Avenida (☎ 279 762 175; Avenida Gago Coutinho 10; d €25) Larger, more attractive rooms, though the welcome is brusque and there can be noise from the downstairs café.

Residencial Marina (☎ 279 762 112, 967 172 231; Avenida Gago Coutinho 2-4; d €25) Friendly hosts, though rooms are small, especially in the stuffy back annexe.

Eating

Restaurante A Marisqueira (☎ 279 762 187; Rua de São Miguel; mains €7-12, daily specials under €5; lunch & dinner Mon-Sat) On a pleasant pedestrian street in the old town, this cheery place serves very good Portuguese meat dishes and just enough *mariscos* (shellfish) to justify the name in a small but bright contemporary dining room.

Rota das Gravuras (☎ 279 760 019; Avenida Gago Coutinho; mains €7-12; lunch & dinner Mon-Sat) Located just across from the Albergaria Vale da Côa, this new place serves high-quality grilled meats in a spacious, modern dining room.

Terrinca (Rua de São Miguel; 7am-7pm, tearoom until midnight) An excellent bakery downstairs and a popular, tricked-up tearoom upstairs.

António & Julia (Rua de São Miguel) Top-quality local hams, sausages, cheese and honey are available for picnics in this charming shop near A Marisqueira and Terrinca.

Getting There & Away

Rede Expressos and Joalto buses each visit daily from Bragança (€6.40, 1¾ hours). Rede Expressos buses come once daily from Miranda do Douro (€5.75, 2½ hours) and three times daily via Trancoso (€4) from Viseu (€7.70, two hours).

Four daily trains run to Pocinho, at the end of the Douro valley line, from Porto (€10.70, four hours) and Peso da Régua (€5.60) through Pinhão (€3.80). A taxi between Pocinho and Vila Nova de Foz Côa costs about €6, and there are infrequent buses, too (€1.15, 10 minutes).

Getting Around

There are no direct buses to Muxagata or Quinta da Ervamoira. However, a twice-daily bus passes the outskirts of Castelo Melhor (€1.50, 15 minutes), from where you can easily walk to the visitor centre. Alternately, there is a taxi stand (☎ 279 762 651) on the square in front of the parks office.

The Minho

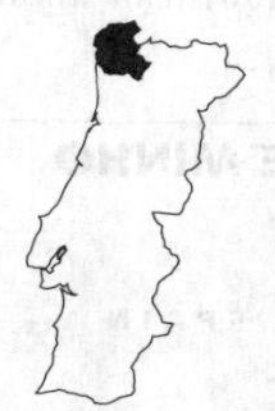

Though it faces the open ocean, Portugal possesses many distinctly Mediterranean qualities – whitewashed towns, baking summer sun, a penchant for olive oil. But the Minho, tucked up in its rainy northeast corner, is very much North Atlantic country. With precipitation levels to rival Ireland's, hillsides stay green into August – long after the rest of Portugal has gone tawny. And speaking of Eire, Celts long dominated Minho along with neighbouring Galicia in Spain. You can see their legacy in impressive archaeological remains, but also in the faces of *minhotos* themselves – often taller and fairer than their countrymen to the south.

For the traveller, green Minho has multiple draws. The southern cities of Braga, Guimarães and Barcelos possess a series of monuments that are a lesson in Portuguese history: Celtic fortresses, Roman roads, Romanesque cathedrals, Baroque sanctuaries. Its Costa Verde, or 'green coast,' is green indeed – though that also implies at least some summer rains. Still, there are fine beaches around the cultured resort town of Viana do Castelo. Inland, the granite peaks, ancient villages and virgin forests of the Parque Nacional da Peneda-Gerês are like a country to themselves. But perhaps most typically *minhoto* are the lush valleys of the Rio Minho and Rio Lima, where sleepy market towns still cluster around medieval bridges.

Despite new superhighways and increasing prosperity, Minho remains one of Europe's most tradition-bound provinces. Its calendar is packed with ancient country markets and fervently observed saints' days; at Easter, Braga – known as Portugal's Rome – puts on a particularly formidable performance. And in the stubbornly poor countryside, you can still see lyre-horned oxen pulling carts and ploughing fields, just as they've done for millennia.

HIGHLIGHTS

- Quaffing chilly glasses of *vinho verde* during a slow meander up the **Rio Minho** (p413)
- Hiking the boulder-strewn peaks and gorse-clad moorlands of the **Parque Nacional de Peneda-Gerês** (p422)
- Strolling across the impressive sweep of the medieval bridge and into the surrounding countryside of **Ponte de Lima** (p416)
- Digging into the Minho's Celtic past at hillside fortress **Citânia de Briteiros** (p408)
- Tapping into the fervour of Easter week in **Braga** (p398)

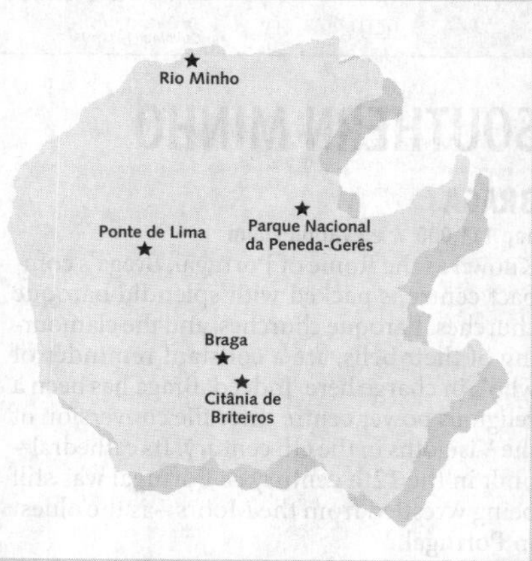

- POPULATION: 1,445,000
- AREA: 5265 SQ KM

THE MINHO

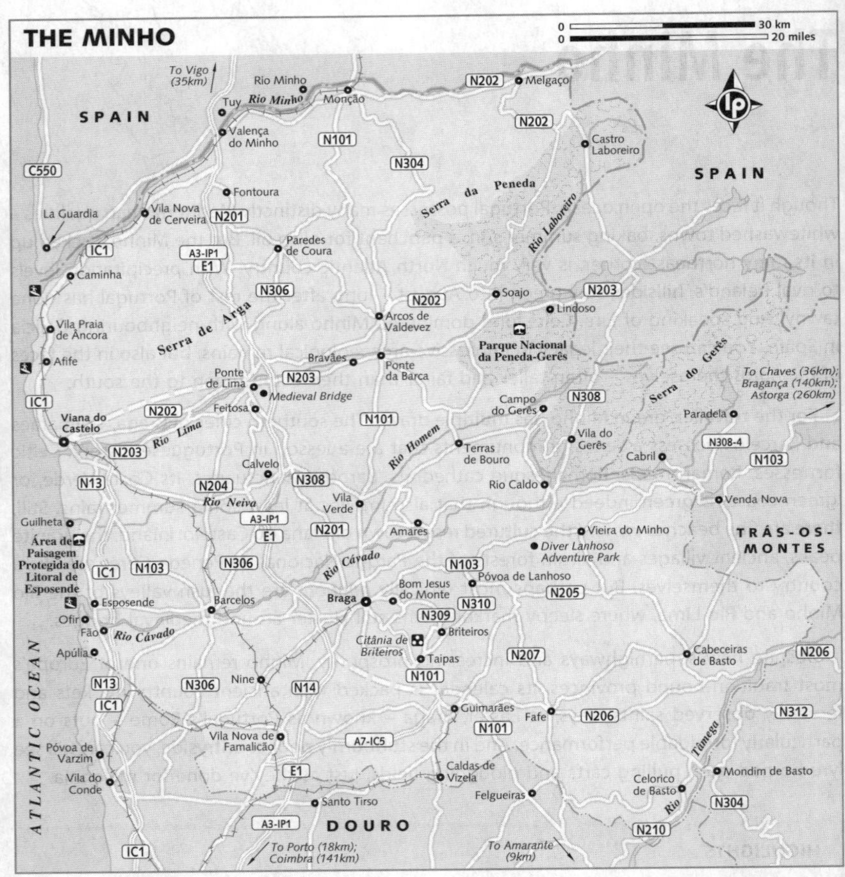

SOUTHERN MINHO

BRAGA

pop 111,000 / elevation 200m

Known as the Rome of Portugal, Braga's compact centre is packed with splendid baroque churches. Baroque churches, and the clamouring of their bells, are a constant reminder of who's in charge here. Indeed, Braga has been a religious power centre since the conversion of the Visigoths in the 6th century. Its cathedral – built in the 12th century as Portugal was still being wrestled from the Moors – is the oldest in Portugal.

The hand of God even extends beyond the city to the area's biggest attraction, the hillside sanctuary of Bom Jesus do Monte (p400), just to the east.

But don't come expecting piety alone: the pedestrian streets of the compact centre are lively with cafés and worldly concerns, and students from the Universidade do Minho add much youthful leavening.

History

Founded by Celts, Braga first attracted Roman attention in 250 BC. The Romans named it Bracara Augusta and made it capital of their province Gallaecia, stretching all the way up into Spain. Braga's position at the intersection of five Roman roads helped it grow fat on trade. Braga fell to the Suevi around AD 410, and was sacked by the Visigoths 60 years later. The

Visigoths' conversion to Christianity in the 6th century and the founding of an archbishopric in the next century put the town atop the Iberian Peninsula's ecclesiastical pecking order.

The Moors moved in around 715, sparking a long-running tug-of-war that ended only when Fernando I, king of Castile and León, definitively reconquered the city in 1040. The archbishopric was restored in 1070, though prelates bickered with their Spanish counterparts for the next 500 years over who was Primate of All Spain. The pope finally ruled in Braga's favour, though the city's resulting good fortune began to wane in the 18th century, when a newly anointed Lisbon archdiocese stole much of its thunder.

Not surprisingly, it was from conservative Braga that Salazar, with his unique blend of Catholicism and fascism, gave the speech that launched his 1926 coup, introducing Portugal to half a century of dictatorship.

Orientation

Praça da República, the city's central square, is a 500m walk south of the bus station, or 1.1km east from the train station. Just east of the *praça* (town square) lie the pedestrianised streets of the historic heart.

Information

Many of the *tabacarias* (tobacconists-cum-newsagents) in the historic centre stock at least a few foreign-language periodicals.

EMERGENCY & MEDICAL SERVICES

Hospital de São Marcos (☎ 253 209 000; Rua 25 Abril) A block west of Avenida da Liberdade.

Police station (☎ 253 200 420; Rua dos Falcões)

INTERNET ACCESS

Casa da Juventude (Instituto Português da Juventude; ☎ 253 204 250; Rua de Santa Margarida; 🕑 9am-6.30pm Mon-Fri) Free internet access at the southern end of the *pousada da juventude* (youth hostel).

Espaço Internet (☎ 253 267 484; Praça Conde de Agrolongo 177; 🕑 9am-7.30pm Mon-Fri, to 1pm Sat) More free access.

Videoteca Municipal (☎ 253 267 793; Rua do Raio; 🕑 10am-12.30pm & 2-6pm Mon-Fri, to 5pm Sat) Yet more free access.

LAUNDRY

Lavandaria Confiança (☎ 253 216 907; Rua Dom Diogo de Sousa 46; per kilo €3; 🕑 9am-1.30pm & 3-8pm Mon-Fri, 9am-2pm Sat)

POST

Post office (Rua Gonçalo Sampaio; 🕑 8.30am-6pm Mon-Fri, 9am-12.30pm Sat) Just off Avenida da Liberdade.

TOURIST INFORMATION

Parque Nacional da Peneda-Gerês (☎ 253 203 480; pnpg@icn.pt; Quinta das Parretas; 🕑 9am-12.50pm & 2-5.30pm Mon-Fri) The park headquarters are 800m west of the town centre and reached via a tunnel under busy Avenida António Macedo.

Turismo (tourist office ☎ 253 262 550; turismo@cm-braga.pt; Praça da República; 🕑 9am-7pm Mon-Fri, 9am-12.30pm & 2pm-5.30pm Sat & Sun Jun-Sep, 9am-12.30pm & 2-6.30pm Mon-Fri, 9am-12.30pm & 2pm-5.30pm Sat Oct-May) Braga's good tourist office is in an Art Deco–style building facing the fountain. Here you'll find a free monthly 'what's-on' brochure, *Braga Cultural*.

TRAVEL AGENCIES

Tagus (☎ 253 215 144; www.viagenstagus.pt; Praça do Município 7; 🕑 9am-6pm Mon-Fri) Sells budget trips and ISIC cards.

Sights

PRAÇA DA REPÚBLICA

A wonderful spot for bench-sitting or coffee-drinking in the sun, this broad **plaza** is the ideal place to start or finish your day. An especially mellow atmosphere descends in the evening, when coloured lights spring up and people of all ages congregate to enjoy the night air.

The square, crenellated tower behind the cafés is the walled-up **Torre de Menagem** (castle keep; Largo Terreiro do Castelo), which is all that survives of a fortified medieval palace.

SÉ

Braga's extraordinary **cathedral** (☎ 253 263 317; Rua Dom Diogo de Sousa; admission free; 🕑 8.30am-6.30pm) is the oldest in Portugal, begun when the archdiocese was restored in 1070 and completed in the following century. It's a rambling complex encompassing a jumble of architectural styles, and architectural buffs could spend half a day happily distinguishing the Romanesque bones from Manueline musculature and baroque frippery. The original Romanesque style is the most interesting and survives in the cathedral's overall shape, the southern entrance and the marvellous west portal, which is carved with scenes from the medieval legend of Reynard the Fox (now sheltered inside a Gothic porch).

The most appealing external features are the filigree Manueline towers and roof – an early work by João de Castilho, who went on

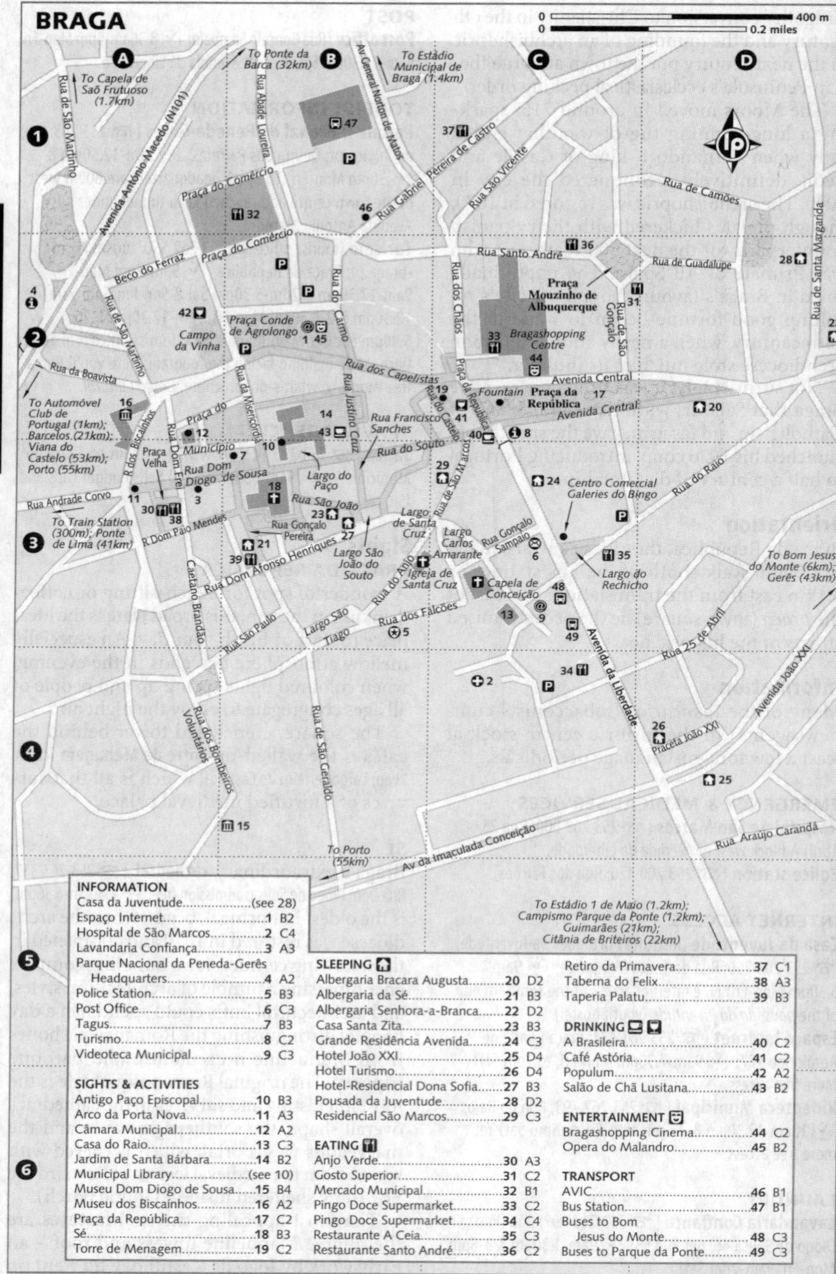
BRAGA
0 400 m
0 0.2 miles
To Capela de Saõ Frutuoso (1.7km)
To Ponte da Barca (32km)
To Estádio Municipal de Braga (1.4km)
To Automóvel Club de Portugal (1km); Barcelos (21km); Viana do Castelo (53km); Porto (55km)
To Train Station (300m); Ponte de Lima (41km)
To Bom Jesus do Monte (6km); Gerês (43km)
To Porto (55km)
To Estádio 1 de Maio (1.2km); Campismo Parque da Ponte (1.2km); Guimarães (21km); Citânia de Briteiros (22km)
Praça Mouzinho de Albuquerque
Bragashopping Centre
Praça da República
Avenida Central
Avenida da Liberdade
Centro Comercial Galeries do Bingo
INFORMATION
Casa da Juventude....(see 28)
Espaço Internet....1 B2
Hospital de São Marcos....2 C4
Lavandaria Confiança....3 A3
Parque Nacional da Peneda-Gerês Headquarters....4 A2
Police Station....5 B3
Post Office....6 C3
Tagus....7 B3
Turismo....8 C2
Videoteca Municipal....9 C3
SIGHTS & ACTIVITIES
Antigo Paço Episcopal....10 B3
Arco da Porta Nova....11 A3
Câmara Municipal....12 A2
Casa do Raio....13 C3
Jardim de Santa Bárbara....14 B2
Municipal Library....(see 10)
Museu Dom Diogo de Sousa....15 B4
Museu dos Biscaínhos....16 A2
Praça da República....17 C2
Sé....18 B3
Torre de Menagem....19 C2
SLEEPING
Albergaria Bracara Augusta....20 D2
Albergaria da Sé....21 B3
Albergaria Senhora-a-Branca....22 D2
Casa Santa Zita....23 B3
Grande Residência Avenida....24 C3
Hotel João XXI....25 D4
Hotel Turismo....26 D4
Hotel-Residencial Dona Sofia....27 B3
Pousada da Juventude....28 D2
Residencial São Marcos....29 C3
EATING
Anjo Verde....30 A3
Gosto Superior....31 C2
Mercado Municipal....32 B1
Pingo Doce Supermarket....33 C2
Pingo Doce Supermarket....34 C4
Restaurante A Ceia....35 C3
Restaurante Santo André....36 C2
Retiro da Primavera....37 C1
Taberna do Felix....38 A3
Taperia Palatu....39 B3
DRINKING
A Brasileira....40 C2
Café Astória....41 C2
Populum....42 A2
Salão de Chã Lusitana....43 B2
ENTERTAINMENT
Bragashopping Cinema....44 C2
Opera do Malandro....45 B2
TRANSPORT
AVIC....46 B1
Bus Station....47 B1
Buses to Bom Jesus do Monte....48 C3
Buses to Parque da Ponte....49 C3

to build Lisbon's Mosteiro dos Jerónimos. In a niche on the east wall is the lovely *Nossa Senhora do Leite* of the Virgin suckling Christ, attributed to 16th-century, expatriate French sculptor Nicolas Chanterène.

You can enter the cathedral through the west portal or via a courtyard and cloister that's lined with Gothic chapels on the north side. The church itself features a fine Manueline carved altarpiece, a tall chapel with *azulejos* (hand-painted tiles) telling the story of Braga's first bishop, and fantastic twin baroque organs held up by formidable satyrs and mermen.

To go upstairs, you must join a snail's-pace tour of the **treasury** (admission choir, chapels & treasury adult/child under 12 €2/free; 9am-noon, 2-6pm) – not surprisingly, a tremendous treasure-trove of ecclesiastical booty, including an iron cross that was used in 1500 to celebrate the very first Mass in Brazil and a flowery pair of high-heeled (10cm) shoes made for a particularly diminutive archbishop.

Then it's on to the choir stalls and an up-close look at the mesmerising organs: this alone is worth the wait – or you can just ask the guide to start here. Then you'll be led downstairs and into the cathedral's showpiece **Capela dos Reis** (Kings' Chapel), home to the tombs of Henri of Burgundy and Dona Teresa, parents of the first king of Portugal, Afonso Henriques. Finally, you arrive at the 14th-century **Capela da Glória**, whose interior was painted in unrepentantly Moorish geometric motifs in the 16th century.

ANTIGO PAÇO EPISCOPAL & AROUND

Facing the cathedral is the severe **Antigo Paço Episcopal** (Archbishop's Palace; admission free; 9am-12.30pm & 2pm-7.30pm Mon-Fri). Begun in the 14th century and enlarged in the 17th and 18th centuries, it's now home to university offices and the municipal library. A heavily carved, painted and gilded ceiling looks down on the library's computer room; this and the *azulejos* lining the main stairway are well worth a peek.

Outside the spiky-topped, medieval north wing is the 17th-century square known as **Jardim de Santa Bárbara**, with narrow paths picking their way through a sea of flowers and topiary. On sunny days, the adjacent pedestrianised streets Rua Justino Cruz and Rua Francisco Sanches fill with buskers and café tables.

At the western end of neighbouring Praça do Município, Braga's **câmara municipal** (town hall) sports one of Portugal's finest baroque façades, designed by André Soares da Silva. A more extrovert Soares work is the **Casa do Raio** (Casa do Mexicano; Rua do Raio), its rococo face covered in *azulejos*. These are both closed to the public, but are still worth seeing from the outside.

ARCO DA PORTA NOVA

West of the old centre on Rua Dom Diogo de Sousa, this diminutive but elegant, 18th-century **arch** once served as the city's main gate. It bears the ostentatious coat of arms of the archbishop who commissioned it, Dom José de Bragança.

MUSEU DOS BISCAÍNHOS

An 18th-century aristocrat's palace is now home to the enthusiastic **municipal museum** (☎ 253 204 650; Rua dos Biscaínhos; adult/child under 14/youth 14-25/senior €2/free/1/1, 10am-2pm Sun free; 10am-12.15pm & 2-5.30pm Tue-Sun), with a nice collection of Roman relics and 17th- to 19th-century pottery and furnishings. The palace itself is the reason to come, with its polychrome, chestnut-panelled ceilings and 18th-century *azulejos* depicting hunting scenes. The ground floor is paved with deeply ribbed flagstones on which carriages would have once rattled through to the stables. The mazelike gardens at the rear also deserve a visit.

MUSEU DOM DIOGO DE SOUSA

This major new **archaeological museum** (☎ 253 273 706; Rua dos Bombeiros Voluntários) was still under construction at the time of writing, with no definite opening date. It's set to house exhibits from the whole of north Portugal, with a particular emphasis on the region around Braga. Check at the tourist office for details.

Festivals & Events

Semana Santa See the boxed text, p398.

Festas de São João A pre-Christian solstice bash dressed up to look like holy days, this festival still bursts with pagan energy. Held on 23 and 24 June, it features medieval folk plays, processions, dancing, bonfires, fireworks – and thousands of little pots of basil. Basil is the symbol of São João (John the Baptist), and traditionally people write poems to loved ones and then conceal them in little pots of the stuff.

Sleeping

Reservations are essential during Semana Santa (Holy Week).

THE MINHO

EASTER IN BRAGA

Braga hosts Portugal's most elaborate Easter bash, which is no surprise in a city where upscale furniture stores hawk blood-spattered, life-size crucifixes alongside sleek leather couches and glass coffee tables. And if you're in need of a crown of thorns, this is your place – they're on prominent display in several shops around the centre.

To help drive out worldly thoughts during **Semana Santa** (Holy Week), Gregorian chants are piped throughout the city centre, and at night streets are ablaze with makeshift, candle-lit altars. The action heats up Holy Thursday's **Procissão do Senhor Ecce Homo**, when barefoot, hooded penitents – members of private Catholic brotherhoods (think Opus Dei) – march through the streets spinning their eerie rattles. The **Good Friday mass** in the cathedral is a remarkable, elaborately staged drama with silk canopies, dirge-like hymns, dozens of frilly-frocked priests, and a weeping congregation. On Saturday evening, the **Easter Vigil mass** begins dourly, the entire cathedral in shadow, only to explode in lights and jubilation. Finally, on Sunday, the people of Braga blanket their thresholds with flowers inviting passing priests to enter and give their home a blessing.

BUDGET

Campismo Parque da Ponte (☎ 253 273 355; adult/tent/car €2.20/1.80/2.00; year-round) On a hillside 1.5km south of the centre, this basic municipal camping ground is little more than a clutch of weedy caravan pitches, but it does have nice vistas of the city. Buses 9, 18 and 56 from Avenida da Liberdade run four services hourly (fewer at weekends) stopping at the camp site (€1.10).

Pousada da juventude (☎ 253 616 163; www.movijovem.pt; Rua de Santa Margarida 6; dm €7, d with/without bathroom €19/16) Braga's rather institutional but lively youth hostel, a 700m walk from the turismo, has frill-free eight-bed dorms as well as very basic en-suite doubles – most with high ceilings and huge windows. Reception is open 8am to noon and 6pm to midnight.

our pick **Casa Santa Zita** (☎ 253 618 331; Rua São João 20; per person with/without bathroom €25/18) A world apart from the youth hostel, this high-ceilinged, impeccably kept pilgrim's lodge (look for the small tile plaque reading 'Sta Zita') has an air of palpable serenity. The sisters offer spotless rooms, nice touches like ironed cotton sheets, and excellent meals in the dining room (€6). Very warmly recommended.

Grande Residência Avenida (☎ 253 609 020; www.residencialavenida.net; 2nd fl, Avenida da Liberdade 738; s €25-35, d €30-40;) Cobbled together from a few big apartments in an Art Deco building, this friendly, family-run place is great value. The carpeted, simply furnished rooms vary widely in size and light; some have verandas. English is spoken.

MIDRANGE

Residencial São Marcos (☎ 253 277 187; fax 253 277 177; Rua de São Marcos 80; s €30, d €45-50;) This welcoming place in a fine old town house has large, comfortable, recently refurbished rooms with high ceilings, parquet floors and a touch of grandeur in the furnishings. Good value.

Albergaria Senhora-a-Branca (☎ 253 269 938; www.albergariasrabranca.pt; Largo da Senhora-a-Branca 58; d €50;) A little removed from the centre, this converted town house has well-kept, carpeted rooms, all with full bathroom and double-glazed windows – and a roaring fire in reception on cold days.

Albergaria da Sé (☎ 253 214 502; www.albergaria-da-se.com.pt; Rua Gonçalo Pereira 39; d €50; P) As the name promises, this simple but attractive guesthouse is within spitting distance of the cathedral. It has wood floors, airy rooms and a scattering of *azulejos* to recommend it. The bright breakfast room and veranda are particularly pleasant.

Hotel João XXI (☎ 253 616 630; reservas@hoteljoaoxxi.com; Avenida João XXI 849; s/d €40/50;) The big smiley face that adorns the welcome desk sets the tone here: keen to find a youthful clientele, the management chose vivid colours and modern art to brighten up an otherwise bland high-rise block. Regular discounts make it a good-value choice.

Hotel-Residencial Dona Sofia (☎ 253 263 160; www.hoteldonasofia.com; Largo São João do Souto 131; s/d €45/60;) On a pretty, central square, prim little Dona Sofia has spotless, carpeted rooms of varying sizes, with all the midrange comforts, including very good beds, plus a generous 'English' breakfast buffet with eggs and sausage.

TOP END

Hotel Turismo (☎ 253 206 000; www.hotelturismobraga.com; Praceta João XXI; d €80; P) All the mod cons but not much more than a hint of character can be found at this big, business-friendly, poured-concrete hotel south of the centre.

Albergaria Bracara Augusta (☎ 253 206 260; www.bracaraaugusta.com; Avenida Central 134; s/d €60/80; ❄) This new, self-consciously upmarket place occupies a grand town house, with rooms that are large and comfortable but rather characterless in comparison with the stylish reception. Suites (€120) have more pizzazz.

Eating

Restaurante Santo André (☎ 253 261 962; Rua Santo André 81; mains from €4; ⏰ lunch & dinner Mon-Sat) With lunch specials from €3, this pleasant if simple-as-sticks, family-run joint serves good Portuguese dishes at a brisk pace and for great prices.

Retiro da Primavera (☎ 253 272 482; Rua Gabriel Pereira de Castro 100; half-portions €4-6; ⏰ 8am-10pm Sun-Fri) Fortifying yourself before your long bus journey? Avoid the bus terminal's café and nip round the corner to this unpretentious place serving a bigger choice of good-value, standard Portuguese fare.

Gosto Superior (☎ 253 217 681; Praça Mousinho de Albuquerque 29; set meal €6; ⏰ lunch Mon-Sat) Keen to prove to the Portuguese that vegetarianism is much more than eating lettuce with their beef, this restaurant serves imaginative, meat-free dishes in a trendy, chilled environment.

Anjo Verde (☎ 253 264 010; Largo da Praça Velha 21; mains €6; ⏰ lunch & dinner Tue-Sat) Two vegetarian places in a small Portuguese city? The newest addition serves up generous, prettily presented food amid a lovely, airy dining room with ancient stone walls splashed with colour.

Restaurante A Ceia (☎ 253 263 932; Largo do Rechicho 331; half/full portions around €5-7; ⏰ lunch & dinner Tue-Sun) This locally popular, easy-going *adega* (wine cellar) has highly recommended Minho specialities such as *alheira*, a light, garlicky sausage of poultry or game.

Taberna do Felix (☎ 253 617 701; Praça Velha 17; dishes €7-10; ⏰ dinner Mon-Sat) Situated near the Arco da Porta Nova, this very attractive country-style tavern prepares unusual Franco-Portuguese dishes; try the tapas or delicious *pataiscas* (fish fritters; €7).

Taperia Palatu (☎ 253 279 772; Rua Dom Afonso Henrique 35; small dishes €8-12; ⏰ lunch & dinner Mon-Sat) A Spanish-Portuguese couple serves up some of the best food in northern Portugal in a pleasantly minimalist dining room with communal tables. The menu combines classic Spanish tapas with Galician and Portuguese influences. The *lulas grelhadas* (grilled calamari) are addictive.

The **mercado municipal** (municipal market; Praça do Comércio; 8am-3pm Mon-Fri, 6am-1pm Sat) buzzes on weekdays and Saturday mornings. There are Pingo Doce supermarkets in the **Bragashopping centre** (⏰ 10am-11pm) and on Avenida da Liberdade (open 9am to 9pm). Several fruit-and-vegetable shops are open during the day along Rua São Marcos.

Drinking & Entertainment

CAFÉS

Salão de Chá Lusitana (Rua Justino Cruz 119; ⏰ 8am-8pm) Next to sweet-smelling Jardim de Santa Bárbara, this sunny, well-preserved Art Deco teashop is a local favourite with all walks, but especially ladies who lunch.

A Brasileira (☎ 253 273 944; Largo Barão de São Marinho; ⏰ 7am-8pm Mon-Sat) Another classic, bright old café that has seen better days – which is the point.

BARS & CLUBS

Opera do Malandro (☎ 963 619 816; Praça Conde Agrolongo; ⏰ 10pm-2am Mon-Sat) Buried in a kind of bunker in the middle of an old square, this new jazz bar has a contemporary-lounge feel and live jazz and bossa nova as well as jazz-themed musical theatre.

Café Astória (☎ 253 273 944; Praça da República; ⏰ 8am-2am Mon-Sat, 10am-2am Sun) This once-genteel coffee house under a grand old portico has now been slicked up and painted blood red. It's crowded most nights after 10pm.

Populum (☎ 253 610 966; Campo da Vinha 115; ⏰ 10pm-5am Thu-Sat) Populum delivers up standard pop, house and other club fare on Thursday and Saturday, while Friday is devoted to Latin dance.

CINEMA

Bragashopping Cinema (☎ 253 217 819; Avenida Central) has the usual Hollywood fare, with the occasional art film.

SPORT

Now home to Braga's football team, Sporting Clube de Braga, the city's new 30,000-seat Estádio Municipal de Braga was built to host the European Football Championships (Euro2004). It's 2km north of the centre off the northbound EN 101; you can buy match tickets at the **team shop** (☎ 253 271 320; Avenida da Liberdade; ⏲ 10am-1pm & 2.30-7pm Mon-Fri, 10am-1pm Sat) in the Centro Comercial Galeries do Bingo.

Getting There & Away

Because of one-way and pedestrian-only streets, driving in central Braga is difficult and parking maddening. There is a large, paying lot under Praça da República. You might also try side streets east of Avenida da Liberdade.

BUS

Braga has a centralised bus station that serves as a major regional hub. Within the Minho, **Transdev Norte/Arriva** (☎ 253 209 401) has at least eight buses per day to Viana do Castelo (€3.60, 1½ hours), Barcelos (€2, one hour), Guimarães (€2.50, 50 minutes), and Porto (€4, one hour), plus four per day to Campo do Gerês (€3, 1½ hours). Service drops by half at weekends.

Rede Expressos (☎ 253 209 401) has a service to Viseu (€10.60, three hours) and on to Lisbon (€14.50, 4½ hours).

Empresa Hoteleira do Gerês (☎ 253 262 033) also serves Rio Caldo (€3.30, 1¼ hours) and Campo do Gerês (€3.50, 1½ hours) about hourly during the week and six times Saturday and Sunday.

CAR & MOTORCYCLE

Braga has a branch of the **Automóvel Club de Portugal** (ACP; ☎ 253 217 051; Avenida Conde Dom Henrique 72), and **AVIC** (☎ 253 270 302; Rua Gabriel Pereira de Castro; ⏲ 9am-6pm Mon-Fri) is an agent for several car-rental companies.

The A3/IP1 motorway makes Braga an easy day trip from Porto. However, the N101 from Braga to Guimarães is more congested and poorly signposted.

TRAIN

Braga is at the end of a branch line from Nine and also within Porto's *suburbano* network, which means commuter trains travel every hour or so from Porto (€1.95, about one hour); don't waste €12.50 on an *intercidade* (IC) train. Useful IC links include Coimbra (€15.50, two hours, two to three daily) and Lisbon (€26, four hours, two to three daily).

AROUND BRAGA

Bom Jesus do Monte

The goal of legions of penitent pilgrims every year, Bom Jesus is one of the country's most recognisable icons. Lying 5km east of central Braga just off the N103, this sober neoclassical church, completed in 1811, stands atop a forested hill that offers grand sunset views across Braga. However, most people don't come for the church or even the view. They come to see what lies below: the extraordinary baroque staircase, **Escadaria do Bom Jesus**.

The photogenic climb is made up of various tiered staircases, dating from different decades of the 18th century. The lowest is lined with chapels representing the Stations of the Cross and eerily lifelike terracotta figurines. **Escadaria dos Cinco Sentidos** (The Stairway of the Five Senses) features allegorical fountains and over-the-top Old Testament figures. Highest is the **Escadaria das Três Virtudes** (Stairway of the Three Virtues), with chapels and fountains representing Faith, Hope and Charity.

The area around the church has become something of a resort, with sumptuous hotels, tennis courts and flower gardens. It's choked with tourists on summer weekends.

SLEEPING & EATING

Accommodation here is splendid, pricey and – in summer – usually full.

Hotel do Elevador (☎ 253 603 400; www.hoteisbomjesus.web.pt; Bom Jesus do Monte; d €90; P) This modern hotel offers fairly plush rooms, many with gorgeous mountain views, and also has a restaurant (set meal €17.50) with similar views.

Hotel do Parque (☎ 253 603 470; Bom Jesus do Monte; d €90; P) Run by the same company as the Hotel do Elevador, this *fin-de-siècle* hotel has modernised rooms, though decorated in period style.

Hotel do Templo (☎ 253 603 610; Bom Jesus do Monte; d €90; P) The same group has also opened this hotel, which features more contemporary rooms, some with great views over the church. At the time of writing, a large pool was in the works for guests of all three hotels. All three are within steps of the main sanctuary, at the top of the steps.

Castello Bom Jesus (☎ 253 676 566; www.armilaworldusa.com; N103; d from €100; P) The neo-Gothic castle is really a dream of a place, with whimsical gardens, gazebos, grottoes, pools and peacocks – all overlooking grandstand views of Braga and surrounding mountains. The grand rooms, most with views, are a worthy splurge.

GETTING THERE & AWAY

City bus 2 runs from Braga's Avenida da Liberdade to the bottom of the Bom Jesus steps (€1.20, 20 minutes) – the end of the line – every half-hour all day (hourly on Sunday). From here you have to hoof it up the steps, as the funicular, built in 1882, had at writing been put out to pasture. A taxi from central Braga to the top of the steps costs around €12.

BARCELOS

pop 20,800 / elevation 100m

The Minho is famous for its sprawling outdoor markets, but the largest, oldest and most celebrated is the Feira de Barcelos, held every Thursday in this ancient town on the banks of the Rio Cávado. Tourist buses now arrive by the dozen, spilling their contents into the already brimming marketplace. Even if you don't come on a Thursday you'll find Barcelos has a pleasant medieval core, as well as an ancient but still-thriving pottery tradition.

Orientation

From the train station and bus stations it's about 1km walk southwest to Campo da República (Campo da Feira), an immense shady square where the market is held. The medieval town is on the slopes above the river, just southwest of the Campo.

Information

Hospital Santa Maria Maior (☎ 253 809 200; Campo da República)

Police station (☎ 253 802 570; Avenida Dr Sidónio País)

Post office (☎ 253 811 711; Avenida Dr Sidónio País; 8.30am-6.30pm Mon-Fri, 9am-12.30pm Sat)

Turismo (☎ 253 811 882; turismo@cm-barcelos.pt; Largo Dr Jose Novais 8; 9.30am-6pm Mon-Fri, 10am-1pm & 2-5pm Sat, 10am-1pm & 2-4pm Sun Mar-Sep, 9.30am-5.30pm Mon-Fri, 10am-1pm & 2-5pm Sat Oct-Feb)

Vog@Net (☎ 253 812 799; Rua Francisco Torres; per hour €1.50; 9am-midnight) A backstreet games hall with internet access.

Sights

FEIRA DE BARCELOS

You'll need at least a couple of hours to eyeball all the goods in this sprawling market. Despite attracting travellers, the **fair** (Campo da República) retains its rural soul. Villagers hawk everything from scrawny chickens to hand-embroidered linen, and Roma women bellow for business in the clothes section. Snack on sausages and homemade bread as you wander among the brass cowbells, hand-woven baskets and carved ox yokes.

Pottery is what outsiders come to see, especially the yellow-dotted *louça de Barcelos* ware and the gaudy figurines à la Rosa Ramalho, a local potter (known as the Grandma Moses of Portuguese pottery) whose work put Barcelos on the map in the 1950s. The trademark Barcelos cockerel motif (see the boxed text, above) is everywhere.

Get there early: tour buses arrive by midmorning and the whole scene winds down after midday.

PLAYING CHICKEN

His colourful crest adorns a thousand souvenir stalls, but just how and why did the proud Portuguese cockerel become a national icon? It seems that a humble pilgrim, plodding his way to Santiago de Compostela in the 16th (some say 14th) century, stopped to rest in Barcelos, only to find himself wrongfully accused of theft and then swiftly condemned to be hanged. The outraged pilgrim told the judge that the roast on the judge's dinner table would affirm the pilgrim's innocence. As it would happen, just as the judge was about to tuck in, the cooked cock commenced to crow throatily. The pilgrim, needless to say, was set free.

MUSEU ARQUEOLÓGICO & AROUND

On a ledge above Barcelos' 14th-century bridge over the Rio Cávado are the roofless ruins of the former palace of the counts of Barcelos and dukes of Bragança. Practically obliterated by the 1755 earthquake, it now serves as an alfresco **archaeological museum** (admission free; 9am-5.30pm).

Among the mysterious phallic stones, Roman columns and medieval caskets, you'll find a 14th-century stone cross, the Crucifix O Senhor do Galo, depicting the gentleman of the cockerel story and said to have been commissioned by the lucky pilgrim himself. Near the entrance is a late Gothic *pelourinho* (stone pillory) topped by a granite lantern.

Eastwards along the bluffs is a remnant of the medieval **town walls**.

Peek inside the **igreja matriz** (10am-5.30pm Tue-Fri, 9.30am-11.45pm & 3.30-7.30pm Sat & Sun), the

stocky Gothic parish church behind the Museu Arqueológico, to see its 18th-century *azulejos* and gilded baroque chapels.

MUSEU DE OLARIA

This good **pottery museum** (☎ 253 824 741; Rua Cônego Joaquim Gaiolas; adult/child under 14/under 26/senior €1.40/free/0.70/0.70, Sun morning free; 🕑 10am-12.30pm & 2-5.30pm Tue-Sun) features ceramics in many of Portugal's regional styles, from Azores pots to Barcelos, Estremoz and Miranda do Corvo figurines, plus striking pewterware.

IGREJA DO SENHOR BOM JESUS DA CRUZ

On a corner of the Campo, this arresting **octagonal church** (Templo do Bom Jesus; admission free; 🕑 8.30am-noon & 2-5.30pm Wed-Mon), built in 1704, overlooks a garden of obelisks. Its baroque interior includes some bright *azulejos* and a grand gilded altarpiece.

IGREJA DO TERÇO

Smothering the walls of this deceptively plain **church** (Avenida dos Combatentes da Grande Guerra; admission free; 🕑 10am-noon & 2-4pm), once part of a Benedictine monastery, is an overwhelming display of *azulejos* on the life of St Benedict by the 18th-century master António de Oliveira Bernardes. In what little space escapes the *azulejos*, a carved, gilded pulpit and a ceiling with other saintly scenes compete for attention.

Festivals & Events

Festa das Cruzes (Festival of the Crosses) For one week, in the first week of May, this festival turns Barcelos into a fairground of flags, flowers, coloured lights, and open-air concerts. The biggest days are generally 1 to 3 May.

Festival de Folclore This celebration of folk song and dance in this tradition-loving town takes place on the last weekend in July or the first weekend in August.

Sleeping

Accommodation is always tight on Wednesday and Thursday in the run-up to the fair.

Residencial Solar da Estação (☎ 253 811 741; Largo Marechal Gomes da Costa 1; s/d incl breakfast €15/30) Conveniently located opposite the train station this recently refurbished pink confection offers terrific value with its spotless, frilly rooms with handsome wood furniture and small but sparkling bathrooms. There's no breakfast, but there is a friendly café on the ground floor.

Albergaria do Terço (☎ 253 808 380; www.arterco.com; Edifício do Terço; s €37, d €40-45; P ✠) Opened in 2004, this ultra-modern midrange option sits atop its namesake shopping centre (take the lift round the back). The stylish, squeaky-clean rooms could have come straight out of an Ikea catalogue, while the bar earns brownie points with its comfy leather couches. Parking costs €2 per day. Breakfast buffet is €5 per person.

Residencial Arantes (☎/fax 253 811 326; Avenida da Liberdade 35; d incl breakfast & with/without bathroom €45/30) Fronting Campo da República, this friendly, family-run favourite offers a mixed bag of well-kept, carpeted rooms distributed over a pair of old town houses.

Hotel Bagoeira (☎ 253 809 500; www.bagoeira.com; Avenida Dr Sidónio Pais 495; d €75) Brand new, business-class hotel just across from the fairgrounds, with tastefully done-up, contemporary digs with shiny new bathrooms. Expect significant discounts outside July and August.

Quinta do Convento da Franqueira (☎ 253 831 606; www.quintadafranqueira.com; s/d €70/100; ⏲ May-Oct; P) Six kilometres from Barcelos, south off the N205, lies this remarkable 16th-century convent turned vineyard and upscale inn. The complex includes cloisters, a bell tower and gatehouse (now a self-catering apartment). Rooms are prim, antique affairs, and all have garden views, while the surrounding property yields a fine *vinho verde* (a young, slightly sparkling white or red wine).

Eating

Restaurante Dom António (☎ 253 812 285; Rua Dom António Barroso 85; mains around €8; ⏲ lunch & dinner) Down a short passageway from the busy pedestrianised street outside, this locally popular choice has lots of good half-portions for under €5. House specialities include roast kid and grilled game meat, including wild boar and deer.

Restaurante Arantes (☎ 253 811 645; Avenida da Liberdade 33; €6-12; ⏲ lunch & dinner Wed-Mon) Here you'll find speedy service and regional specialities such as *rojões á moda do Minho* (a casserole of marinated pork). The neighbouring *confeitaria* (patisserie or confectionary shop) of the same name makes its own mouthwatering pastries; try a custard-filled *sonho* (dream) drenched in syrup or sugar.

Restaurante Bagoeira (☎ 253 811 236; Avenida Dr Sidónio Pais 495; dishes €7-15; ⏲ lunch & dinner) With an open kitchen and attractive dining room, this place serves regional specialities made with the best, fresh ingredients, including very good grilled meats and fish. The staff deal admirably with the jovial chaos of market day.

Two stops for self-caterers are the **mercado municipal** (Largo da Madalena; ⏲ 7am-7pm Mon-Fri, to 1pm Sat) and a nearby **Pingo Doce** (Rua Filipa Borges 223) supermarket.

Drinking

Barcelos has little nightlife to speak of, but you could while away summer evenings on the picturesque, riverside patio of **Turismo Bar** (Rua Duques de Bragança; ⏲ 11.30am-3am).

Getting There & Away

Parking is very tight on Thursdays, so avoid driving if you can. Other days, look for spots around Campo da República.

BUS

There's a new, centralised bus terminal 1km east of the centre. **Transdev Norte/Arriva** (☎ 253 209 401) has at least eight buses to Braga (€2, one hour) on weekdays, and about four on weekends. It also has service to Ponte de Lima (€2.75, one hour).

Linhares (☎ 253 811 571) has a service every hour or two to Braga and Porto (€3.50, two hours) daily, and to Viana do Castelo (€2.75, one hour). Service drops to about four daily on weekends.

TRAIN

Barcelos station is on the Porto–Valença line. There are two daily direct Intercity trains a day to/from Porto (€5.60, 50 minutes), though there are commuter trains every hour or two that change at Nine (€3, one hour). There is similar service to Braga (€2.40, 45 minutes).

AROUND BARCELOS

Parque Natural do Litoral Norte

Embracing the Braga district's entire 18km of seashore, this protected area was set aside to safeguard its unstable sand dunes, delicate vegetation and the remnants of an ancient way of life – symbolised by the Minho's photogenic if decrepit coastal windmills.

The partnership of land and sea is illustrated by the area's agricultural fields immediately behind the dunes, watered by ocean spray and fertilised with algae and crustaceans from the sea. However, it's an area that continues to be nibbled away by the sea on one side and by humans on the other.

THE MINHO

 Book accommodation online at lonelyplanet.com

Attempts are being made to stabilise the dunes with fencing and plants, and access is largely restricted to elevated walkways. For more information, contact the **area office** (☎ 253 965 830; pnln@icn.pt; Rua 1 de Dezembro 65, Esposende; Mon-Fri 9am-12.30pm & 2-5.30pm).

SLEEPING

Basic accommodation is available at Esposende, some 15km west of Barcelos, and at Ofir and Apúlia.

At Fafão, 3km south of Esposende, there's a level, shaded **camping ground** (☎ 253 981 777; cccb@esoterica.pt; Rua São João de Deus; adult/car €3.20/2.55, tent €2.80-3.50; year-round) with hot showers, laundry, services for the disabled, and a bar-restaurant. There's also an attractive pink villa-turned-**pousada da juventude** (☎ 253 981 790; www.movijovem.pt; Alameda Bom Jesus; d/d with toilet/apt for 4 €11/30/70; P) that boasts bikes for hire, a grassy garden, proximity to the beach, and an outdoor pool. Reserve well in advance during summers and holidays.

GETTING THERE & AWAY

AV Minho has four daily weekday buses and one daily bus on the weekend that run to/from Porto (€2.70, one hour) on their way to Viana do Castelo (€2.40, 40 minutes) and on to Valença (1½ hours) and Monção (1¾ hours).

GUIMARÃES

pop 53,400 / elevation 400m

The Portuguese kingdom was born in Guimarães – a fact the town's eager signage won't let you forget. Still, the claim is fair enough. Afonso Henriques, the first independent king of Portugal, was born here in 1110 and later used the city to launch the main thrust of the Reconquista against the Moors.

Happily, Guimarães preserves much of its illustrious history. Its medieval centre has a labyrinthine charm, plus a pair of winning squares, while on an adjacent hill stands a 1000-year-old keep and, next to it, the bristling, massive 'modern' palace built by the first duke of Bragança in the 15th century. No accident, then, that Unesco added Guimarães to its list of World Heritage sites in 2001.

But it's not all dusty treasures and national history. Guimarães also knows how to party as required; this is a university town, and its lively atmosphere explodes into full-scale revelry during the Festas de Cidade e Gualterianas (p407).

History

Guimarães caught the royal eye as early as AD 840 when Alfonso II of León convened a council of bishops here, but it only started to grow in the 10th century after the powerful Countess Mumadona Dias, widowed aunt of another king of León, gave it her attention, founding a monastery and building a castle built to protect it. Henri of Burgundy chose Guimarães for his court, as did his son Afonso Henriques until he shifted the capital to Coimbra in 1143.

Orientation

Old Guimarães is in the northeast of the modern city. Most points of interest lie within a demarcated tourist zone stretching south from the castle to an arc of public gardens at Alameda de São Dâmaso. Guimarães' commercial heart is Largo do Toural.

The main turismo is a 600m walk north up Avenida Dom Afonso Henriques from the train station. It is a 1km slog up Avenida Conde de Margaride from the main bus station, which is beneath the Centro Comercial Guimarães Shopping.

Information

Espaço Internet (☎ 253 590 371; Rua Egas Moniz 29/33; 11am-1pm & 2-10pm Mon-Sat, 10am-1pm & 2-6pm Sun) Free internet access.

Hospital (☎ 253 512 612; Rua dos Cotileros, Creixomil) Opposite the bus station.

Livraria Ideal (☎ 253 422 750; Rua da Rainha 34; 9am-1pm & 3-7pm Mon-Fri, 9am-1pm Sat) The city's best bookshop.

Police station (☎ 253 519 598; Avenida Dr Alfredo Pimenta)

Post office (Largo Navarros de Andrade 27; 8.30am-6.30pm Mon-Fri, 9am-12.30pm Sat)

Turismo (☎ 253 518 790; Praça de Santiago; 9.30am-6.30pm Mon-Fri, 10am-6pm Sat, 10am-1pm Sun)

Sights

PAÇO DOS DUQUES

Recognisable by its forest of brick chimney the **Paço dos Duques** (Ducal Palace; ☎ 253 412 27 adult/child under 14/under 26/senior €3/free/1.50/1.5 9am-12.30pm Sun free; 9.30am-7pm Jul-Sep, 9.30am 12.30pm & 2-5pm Oct-Jun) has pushed its way int the foreground on Guimarães' hilltop. Bui in 1401 by a later and equally famous Afons (the future first Duke of Bragança), it fell int ruin after his powerful family upped stick

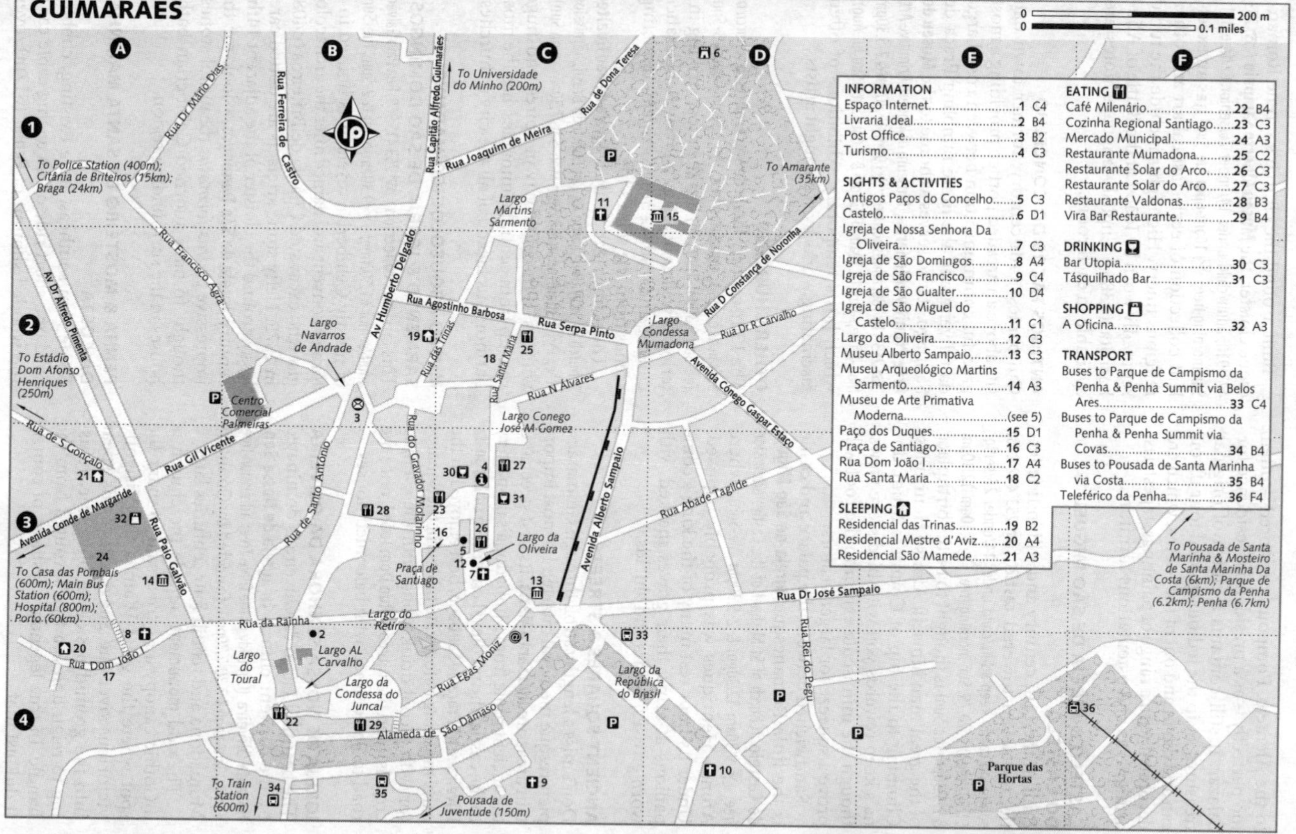
GUIMARÃES
0 200 m
0 0.1 miles
INFORMATION
Espaço Internet 1 C4
Livraria Ideal 2 B4
Post Office 3 B2
Turismo 4 C3
SIGHTS & ACTIVITIES
Antigos Paços do Concelho 5 C3
Castelo 6 D1
Igreja de Nossa Senhora Da Oliveira 7 C3
Igreja de São Domingos 8 A4
Igreja de São Francisco 9 C4
Igreja de São Gualter 10 D4
Igreja de São Miguel do Castelo 11 C1
Largo da Oliveira 12 C3
Museu Alberto Sampaio 13 C3
Museu Arqueológico Martins Sarmento 14 A3
Museu de Arte Primativa Moderna (see 5)
Paço dos Duques 15 D1
Praça de Santiago 16 C3
Rua Dom João I 17 A4
Rua Santa Maria 18 C2
SLEEPING
Residencial das Trinas 19 B2
Residencial Mestre d'Aviz 20 A4
Residencial São Mamede 21 A3
EATING
Café Milenário 22 B4
Cozinha Regional Santiago 23 C3
Mercado Municipal 24 A3
Restaurante Mumadona 25 C2
Restaurante Solar do Arco 26 C3
Restaurante Solar do Arco 27 C3
Restaurante Valdonas 28 B3
Vira Bar Restaurante 29 B4
DRINKING
Bar Utopia 30 C3
Tásquilhado Bar 31 C3
SHOPPING
A Oficina 32 A3
TRANSPORT
Buses to Parque de Campismo da Penha & Penha Summit via Belos Ares 33 C4
Buses to Parque de Campismo da Penha & Penha Summit via Covas 34 B4
Buses to Pousada de Santa Marinha via Costa 35 B4
Teleférico da Penha 36 F4
To Police Station (400m); Citânia de Briteiros (15km); Braga (24km)
To Estádio Dom Afonso Henriques (250m)
To Casa das Pombais (600m); Main Bus Station (600m); Hospital (800m); Porto (60km)
To Train Station (600m)
Pousada de Juventude (150m)
To Universidade do Minho (200m)
To Amarante (35km)
To Pousada de Santa Marinha & Mosteiro de Santa Marinha Da Costa (6km); Parque de Campismo da Penha (6.2km); Penha (6.7km)
Av Dr Alfredo Pimenta
Rua Paio Galvão
Avenida Conde de Margaride
Rua de S Gonçalo
Rua Gil Vicente
Rua Francisco Agra
Rua Dr Mário Dias
Rua Ferreira de Castro
Av Humberto Delgado
Rua Capitão Alfredo Guimarães
Rua Joaquim de Meira
Rua de Dona Teresa
Rua D Constança de Noronha
Rua Dr R Carvalho
Avenida Cónego Gaspar Estaço
Rua Serpa Pinto
Rua Agostinho Barbosa
Rua das Trinas
Rua Santa Maria
Rua N Alvares
Avenida Alberto Sampaio
Rua Abade Tagilde
Rua Dr José Sampaio
Rua Rei do Pegu
Rua do Gravador Molarinho
Rua de Santo António
Rua da Rainha
Rua Egas Moniz
Alameda de São Dâmaso
Rua Dom João I
Largo Martins Sarmento
Largo Condessa Mumadona
Largo Conego José M Gomez
Largo da Oliveira
Praça de Santiago
Largo do Retiro
Largo AL Carvalho
Largo da Condessa do Juncal
Largo do Toural
Largo Navarros de Andrade
Centro Comercial Palmeiras
Largo da República do Brasil
Parque das Hortas

THE MINHO

to the Alentejo. Pompously restored – often too perfectly – as a presidential residence for Salazar, it still contains a clutch of original treasures. Skip the tedious guided tour if you can and dip in and out of the rooms, which are decorated with a range of paintings, tapestries, armaments and ostentatious furniture.

CASTELO & IGREJA DE SÃO MIGUEL DO CASTELO

Built in the 11th century and still in fine fettle, the seven-towered **castle** (☎ 253 412 273; admission castle keep adult/child under 14/under 26/senior €1.50/free/0.75/0.75, Sun morning free; 9.30am-12.30pm & 2-5.30pm Tue-Sun) is thought to be the birthplace of the great man himself, Afonso Henriques. Climbing to the top of Countess Mumadona's keep rewards you with bird's-eye views, though the minuscule exit onto the roof will prove a squeeze for larger visitors.

Sandwiched between the palace and castle is the little Romanesque **Igreja de São Miguel do Castelo** (Church of St Michael of the Castle; admission free; 9.30am-12.30pm & 2-5.30pm Tue-Sun), where Afonso Henriques was probably baptised. Under its floor rest many of the king's companions-at-arms, their graves marked with worn crosses, spears and shields.

ANCIENT SQUARES & STREETS

Don't miss a lengthy stroll through Guimarães' picturesque medieval quarter. Its most important areas are **Rua Santa Maria**, its first street and the ancient route from Mumadona's monastery to the castle; the medieval ensemble of **Largo da Oliveira** and **Praça de Santiago**, best enjoyed in the early morning before café tables fill the squares (or with a cool drink along with the evening crowds); and the narrow **Rua Dom João I**, once the road to Porto, lined with balconied houses.

IGREJA DE NOSSA SENHORA DA OLIVEIRA

The beautiful Largo da Oliveira is dominated by the convent church of **Igreja de Nossa Senhora da Oliveira** (Our Lady of the Olive Tree; admission free; 7.15am-noon & 3.30-7.30pm), founded by Countess Mumadona and rebuilt four centuries later.

The odd **monument** outside the church is a Gothic canopy and cross said to mark the spot where the great Wamba the Visigoth, victorious over the Suevi, drove his spear into the ground beside an olive tree, refusing to reign unless a tree sprouted from the handle. In true legendary fashion, of course, it did just that.

Built around the church's serene Romanesque cloister, the **Museu Alberto Sampaio** (☎ 253 423 910; adult/child under 14/under 26/senior €2/free/1/1, Sun morning free; 10am-6pm Tue-Sun) has an excellent collection of ecclesiastical art and other religious finery. Highlights include the tunic reputedly worn by João I at the Battle of Aljubarrota (1385). English-language notes are available in each room.

ANTIGOS PAÇOS DO CONCELHO

Guimarães' 14th-century, former town hall sits above an arcaded portico providing a most graceful communication between cosy Largo da Oliveira and the more rambling Praça de Santiago. It also serves as home to the **Museu de Arte Primitiva Moderna** (Museum of Modern Primitive Art; ☎ 253 414 186; admission free; 9am-12.30pm & 2-5.30pm Mon-Fri Sep-Jun, 10.30am-12.30pm & 3-6pm Sat & Sun Jul-Aug), which hosts temporary exhibitions of often fascinating works by self-taught artists.

OTHER CHURCHES

The 13th-century **Igreja de São Francisco** (Church of St Francis of Assisi; admission free; 9.30am-noon & 3-5pm Tue-Sat, 9.30am-1pm Sun) has the most striking interior as well as boasting a lovely Renaissance cloister and 18th-century *azulejos* depicting scenes from the saint's life.

The skinny 18th-century **Igreja de São Gualter** (Church of St Walter; Largo da República do Brasil; admission free; 7.30am-noon & 3-5pm Mon-Sat, 7.30am-noon Sun), with its 19th-century twin spires and huge run-up from central Guimarães, has the most harmonious façade of all the city's churches.

MUSEU ARQUEOLÓGICO MARTINS SARMENTO & IGREJA DE SÃO DOMINGOS

This curious **collection** (☎ 253 415 969; Rua Paio Galvão; adult/senior €1.50/free; 9.30am-noon & 2-5pm Tue-Sun) of mostly Celtiberian artefacts is housed in a former convent and named after the archaeologist who excavated Citânia de Briteiros (p408) in 1875. Hefty stone artefacts are dotted carelessly around the cloister of the adjacent 14th-century **Igreja de São Domingos** – look for the impressive *pedras formosas* (beautiful stones), thought to have adorned Celtiberian bathhouses in the surrounding region.

PENHA & MOSTEIRO DE SANTA MARINHA DA COSTA

Some 7km southeast up a twisting, cobbled road or a short ride on an ageing cable car is the wooded summit of **Penha** (617m), over looking Guimarães and the highest point for miles. Its cool woods make it a wonderful escape from the city and summer heat. Kids love losing themselves amid the massive boulders, many cut with steps, crowned with flowers and crosses, or hiding secret grottoes.

On the lower slopes of the hill lies the **Mosteiro de Santa Marinha da Costa**, 1.5km east of the centre. It dates from 1154 when Dona Mafalda, wife of Afonso Henriques, commissioned it to honour a vow she made to the patron saint of pregnant women. Rebuilt in the 18th century, it's now a flagship Pousada de Portugal (right). Nonguests can still snoop around the chapel and gardens.

The easiest route to the monastery is on municipal bus 51 or 52 to São Roque (€1.10, every half-hour Monday to Saturday, hourly on Sunday), which departs from the south side of the public gardens; get off at Costa. But the finest way to the top is on the **Teleférico da Penha** (cable car; ☎ 253 515 085; each way €1.50; ⌚ 10.30am-6.30pm Mon-Fri, to 7.30pm Sat, Sun & holidays May-Sep, 10am-5pm Fri-Sun Oct-Apr), which starts from Parque das Hortas, 600m east of the old centre.

Festivals & Events

Festas de Cidade e Gualterianas (www.aoficina.pt) Marked by a free fair (held in Guimarães since 1452 to honour its patron saint), this festival also features folk dancing, rock concerts, bullfights, fireworks and parades. It takes place in the first weekend in August.

Encontros de Primavera This series of classical and early music concerts is held at historical venues in late May and June.

Jazz Festival One of the country's top festivals, this jazz extravaganza runs for about three weeks in November.

Sleeping

BUDGET

Parque de Campismo da Penha (☎ 253 515 912; www.turipenha.pt; adult/car €2/1.65, tent €1.65-3; ⌚ Apr-Oct) With a terrific position near the top of Penha, this is a well-equipped and densely wooded municipal camping ground. It has an outdoor pool for hot days and a TV room with a fireplace for cool nights. Take the *teleférico* (☎ 253 515 085; each way €1.50) to get there.

Pousada de Juventude (☎ 253 421 380; www.movijovem.pt; Largo da Cidade; dm €13, d €36, apt for 4 €70; ♿) This terrific new hostel in the home of a prosperous factory owner has hardwood floors, clean, bright dorms and doubles that are downright stylish. It also has kitchen and laundry facilities, and wheelchair-accessible rooms.

MIDRANGE

Residencial das Trinas (☎ 253 517 358; www.residencialtrinas.com; Rua das Trinas 29; s/d incl breakfast €25/35; ❄) This renovated house in the historical zone offers likeable little rooms with double glazing, satellite TV, and patterned ceramic-tile floors. You won't get a better position for the price.

Residencial Mestre d'Aviz (☎ 253 422 770; r_mestre_aviz@iol.pt; Rua Dom João I 40; d incl breakfast €40; ❄) Fronted by curlicue ironwork, this handsomely renovated town house is Guimarães' best midrange bargain. It has slick modern touches, a stone-slab bar and minimal street traffic on the narrow old lane outside. Upper (hotter) floors have air-con.

Residencial São Mamede (☎ 253 513 092; www.residencial-smamede.com; Rua São Gonçalo; d €45; ❄) Sitting in a high-rise above the city's traffic-jam central is this good-value, modern guesthouse. The cable TV can always help drown out the traffic noise.

TOP END

Pousada de Santa Marinha (☎ 253 511 249; www.pousadas.pt; d from €165; P ❄ 🏊) This is the real deal: history, beauty and an unbeatable location. A restored former monastery overlooking the city from the slopes of Penha, the *pousada* (upmarket inn) is now a far cry from past frugality. Guests may wander round the cloister past dribbling fountains and masterful *azulejos*, and sleep in now-luxurious converted monks' cells. For transport information, see opposite.

Eating

Restaurante Mumadona (☎ 253 416 111; Rua Serpa Pinto 260; half-portions €4.50-7.50; ⌚ lunch & dinner Mon-Sat) Snug and family-friendly, this place packs in a remarkable amount of people for its size. The menu is weighted heavily towards *bacalhau* (dried salt-cod) and includes good-value half-portions at lunch.

Cozinha Regional Santiago (☎ 253 516 669; Praça de Santiago 16; half-portions €5-8; ⌚ lunch & dinner Mon-Sat) An enviable location plum in the central *praça* (town square) hasn't stopped this good little restaurant from offering fair prices. You can relax in the sunny square without, or hole up in the stone-walled dining room within.

Vira Bar Restaurant (☎ 253 518 427; Largo Condessa do Juncal 27; mains €8-12; ⌚ lunch & dinner Mon-Sat) This genteel venue features vaulted ceiling and stained-glass windows. Specialities include wood-grilled meat and fish and *sopa de nabos* (turnip soup).

Restaurante Valdonas (☎ 253 511 411; Rua Val de Donas 4; mains €10-12; ⌚ lunch & dinner Mon-Sat, lunch Sun; ✱) A long wine list, chalk-white minimalist decor, and a changing menu based on market-fresh availability have generated buzz at Guimarães' newest restaurant, situated in a 17th-century manor house.

Restaurante Solar do Arco (☎ 253 513 072; Rua de Santa Maria 50; mains around €17-22; ⌚ lunch & dinner Mon-Sat, lunch Sun; ✱) With a handsomely panelled dining room and enviable terrace seating under a graceful arcade, this is the top central choice. Attentive service and Portuguese classics made with straight-from-the-market ingredients round out the happy picture.

Café Milenário (Largo do Toural; ⌚ 7am-1am) The quintessential after-work venue, this large, open corner café pulls in a crowd of all ages to banter over bar food, light meals and drinks.

Self-caterers will like the **mercado municipal** (Rua Paio Galvão; ⌚ Mon-Sat morning).

Drinking & Entertainment

One of a swathe of bar-hopping venues in the historic centre, the cosy, ever-popular **Tásquilhado Bar** (Rua de Santa Maria 42; ⌚ 9.30pm-2am Wed-Sat) plays alternative sounds and has happy hour on Wednesday and Thursday lasting till midnight. Another bar with a more mainstream pop-and-rock bias is **Bar Utopia** (Praça de Santiago; ⌚ to 2am Mon-Sat).

Shopping

Today, as in medieval times, Guimarães is renowned for its linen. Other crafts contributing to its prosperity are embroidery, worked gold and silver, and pottery. For quality work by Guimarães artisans, visit the municipal outlet **A Oficina** (☎ 253 515 250; Rua Paio Galvão 11; ⌚ 9am-6pm Mon-Sat).

A big flea market takes over Praça de Santiago and Largo da Oliveira on the first Saturday of each month.

Getting There & Away

There is street parking in front of the Convento do Carmo at the foot of the Paço dos Duques.

BUS

REDM/Arriva (☎ 253 516 229) has eight weekday and four weekend links to Braga (€2.40, 50 minutes). It also goes to Porto (€3.90, 50 minutes) about hourly on weekdays but less often at weekends, and to Lisbon (€13.90, five hours) daily. **Rodonorte** (☎ 253 514 476) heads for Amarante (€5.40, 50 minutes), Vila Real (€6.40, 1½ hours) and Bragança (€12.20, four hours) two or three times daily Sunday to Friday.

TRAIN

Guimarães is the terminus of a branch of Porto's wide *suburbano* network. Commuter trains potter out to Guimarães from Porto (€1.95, one hour) about 11 times daily Monday to Friday and eight daily at weekends. Try to avoid the once-daily Intercidades train, which costs €10.

AROUND GUIMARÃES

Citânia de Briteiros

One of the most evocative archaeological sites in Portugal, **Citânia de Briteiros**, 15km north of Guimarães, is the largest of a liberal scattering of northern Celtic hill settlements, called *citânias,* dating back at least 2500 years. It's also likely that this sprawling 3.8-hectare **site** (admission incl museum €2; ⌚ 9am-6pm), inhabited from about 300 BC to AD 300, was the Celtiberians' last stronghold against the invading Romans.

When archaeologist Dr Martins Sarmento excavated the site in 1875, he discovered the foundations and ruins of more than 150 rectangular, circular and elliptical stone huts, linked by paved paths and a water distribution system, all cocooned by multiple protective walls. Highlights include two reconstructed huts that evoke what it was like to live in the settlement, and – further back down the hill – a bathhouse with a strikingly patterned stone doorway.

Ask at the entrance for a detailed plan (€0.25), keyed to markers around the site, with information in French and English.

Some artefacts are on display in the Museu Arqueológico Martins Sarmento in Guimarães (p406), but the new **Museu da Cultura Castreja** (Museum on Pre-Roman Culture; ☎ 253 478 952; Solar da Ponte, Briteiros Salvador; ⌚ 9.30am-12.30pm & 2-6pm Tue-Sun) also has important artefacts from various sites in Sarmento's 18th- and 19th-century manor house. It's about 2km back down the hill towards Guimarães in the village of Briteiros Salvador.

GETTING THERE & AWAY

From Guimarães, **REDM/Arriva** (☎ 253 516 229) has about six weekday buses that pass within 1km of the site; get off between the towns of Briteiros and Santa Leocádia. Check with the Guimarães Turismo (p404) or at the bus station for current schedule information.

COASTAL & NORTHERN MINHO

VIANA DO CASTELO

pop 36,800

While Portugal's coastal resorts tend to be either souped-up fishing villages or long-tatty Victorian numbers, Viana do Castelo's charms seem downright sophisticated, from its flowery, 19th-century thoroughfares to its narrow lanes crowded with Manueline manors and rococo palaces. It's also the place where conservative Minho comes to let its hair down, with raucous traditional festivals complemented by a few slick nightclubs. The town's setting by the Rio Lima estuary means it's a short hop from some excellent beaches, and it also makes a handy base for exploring the lower Lima valley.

History

There are remains of Celtic hill settlements on Monte de Santa Luzia, overlooking the contemporary town centre, while Rome's only lasting mark was to call their settlement Diana, which, over the years, evolved into Viana.

Manueline mansions and monasteries attest to Viana's 16th-century prosperity as a major port for codfishing off Newfoundland. By the mid-17th century it had become Portugal's biggest port, with merchants trading as far afield as Russia.

More riches arrived in the 18th century, with the advent of the Brazilian sugar and gold trade. But with Brazil's independence and the rising importance of Porto, Viana's golden age stuttered and faded. These days it is still a deep-sea-fishing centre, though it earns much of its living as the Minho's favourite resort town.

Orientation

From the adjoining train and bus station, the main axis down to the river is Avenida dos Combatentes da Grande Guerra (often just called 'Avenida'). East of here is the old town, centred on Praça da República. West lies the old fishing quarter.

Information

Foreign-language newspapers are available at many of the *tabacarias* around the centre.

EMERGENCY & MEDICAL SERVICES

Hospital (☎ 258 829 081; Estrada de Santa Luzia) North of the train station.

Police station (☎ 258 822 022; Rua de Aveiro)

INTERNET ACCESS

Esp@ço.net (Rua General Luis do Rego 21; per hour €1; 🕒 9am-7pm Mon-Fri, until 6pm Sat)

Instituto Português da Juventude (Rua do Poço 16-26; 🕒 9am-5.30pm Mon-Fri) Free access.

POST

Post office (Avenida dos Combatentes; 🕒 8.30am-6pm Mon-Fri, 9am-12.30pm Sat)

TOURIST INFORMATION

Regional turismo (☎ 258 822 620; fax 258 827 873; Rua Hospital Velho; 🕒 9am-12.30pm & 2-5.30pm Mon-Fri, 9.30am-1pm & 2-5.30pm Sat, 9.30am-1pm Sun Oct-Apr, 9am-12.30pm & 2.30-6pm Mon-Fri, 9.30am-1pm & 2-6pm Sat, 9.30am-1pm Sun May-Jul & Sep, 9am-7pm daily Aug) Housed in a 15th-century inn.

Sights & Activities

PRAÇA DA REPÚBLICA & AROUND

The fine Praça da República is at the heart of the old town's well-preserved zone of mansions and monuments – the city's most picturesque quarter. Especially elegant is the *praça*'s **Chafariz**, a Renaissance fountain built in 1554 by João Lopes the Elder. It's topped with Manueline motifs of an armillary sphere and the cross of the Order of Christ. The fortresslike **Antigos Paços do Concelho** is the old town hall – another 16th-century creation.

At right angles to this is the striking former **Misericórdia** almshouse, designed in 1589 by João Lopes the Younger, its loggias supported by monster caryatids. Adjoining the almshouse is the **Igreja de Misericórdia** (admission free; 🕒 10am-12.30pm & 2-5pm Mon-Fri Aug, 11am-12.30pm Sun year-round), which was rebuilt in 1714 and is adorned with some of Portugal's finest *azulejos* by the master António de Oliveira Bernardes and his son Policarpo.

IGREJA MATRIZ

This elegant **parish church** (admission free; Rua da Aurora do Lima; 🕒 irregular hours) – also known as the *sé* – dates back to the 15th century, although it has since been through several reincarnations. Check out its unusually sculpted Romanesque towers and Gothic doorway, carved with figures of Christ and the Evangelists.

MUSEU MUNICIPAL

The 18th-century **Palacete Barbosa Maciel** (☎ 258 820 377; Largo de São Domingos; admission €2; ⏲ 9am-noon & 2-5pm Tue-Sun) bears witness to Viana's affluent past. It is home to a very impressive collection of 17th- and 18th-century ceramics (especially blue Portuguese china), *azulejos* and furniture. There are also plans to open an annexe devoted to linen and other traditional handicrafts; entrance will be included in the same ticket.

CASTELO DE SÃO TIAGO DA BARRA

You can still scoot around the ramparts of this squat castle (⏲ 9am-5pm Mon-Fri), a short walk west of the centre, which began in the 15th century as a smallish fort. It was integrated into a larger fort, commissioned by Felipe II o Spain (Felipe I of Portugal) in 1592, to guar the prosperous port against pirates.

MONTE DE SANTA LUZIA

There are two good reasons to visit Viana' 228m, eucalyptus-clad hill. One is the god's eye **view** down the coast and up the Lima val ley. The other is the fabulously over-the-top 20th-century neo-Byzantine **Templo do Sagrad Coração de Jesus** (Temple of the Sacred Heart of Jesu ☎ 258 823 173; admission free; ⏲ 8am-7pm Apr-Se 8am-5pm Oct-Mar). You can get a little closer t heaven on its windy, graffiti-covered roof, vi an elbow-scrapingly tight stairway (€0.50 take the entrance marked *zimbório* (dome or the lift (€0.80).

There's an over-the-top Pousada de Portugal (Pousada do Monte de Santa Luzia; p412) up here, too, behind and above the basilica. Behind that is another attraction, the poorly maintained ruins of a Celtiberian **citânia** from around the 4th century BC, though these remained closed for redevelopment at the time of writing. You can also make the short walk onwards to the summit.

You can get up the mountain by car or taxi (3.5km) or on foot – an often steep, 2km climb only for the fit and/or penitent. The road starts by the hospital, and the steps begin about 200m up the road. An old funicular to the top has been growing rusty from disuse.

GIL EANNES

Demanding attention on the waterfront near Largo 5 de Outubro is this pioneering naval hospital ship, the *Gil Eannes* (zheel *yan*-ish). The **ship** (☎ 258 809 710; adult/child under 6 €1.50/free; 🕑 2-7pm Mon-Fri Jul-Sep, 9am-noon & 2-7pm Sat, Sun & holidays Apr-Sep, 9am-noon & 2-5.30pm Sat, Sun & holidays Oct-Mar) once provided on-the-job care for those fishing off the coast of Newfoundland. Now restored, visitors can clamber around the steep decks and cabins, though a scattering of old clinical equipment may make your hair stand on end.

It even houses a novel – if cramped – youth hostel (see Our Pick, p412).

BEACHES

Viana's enormous arcing beach, **Praia do Cabedelo**, is one of the Minho's best, with little development to spoil its charm. It's across the river from town, and one way to get there is by passenger ferry from the pier south of Largo 5 de Outubro. The five-minute trip costs about €0.85 one way, and the ferry goes about hourly between 8.15am and 7.30pm daily from May to September, and often later in July and August

Alternatively, **TransCunha** (☎ 258 821 392) have multiple daily buses to Cabedelo (€0.75) from the bus station. Check at the station or turismo for current schedules.

There's a string of fine beaches north of Viana for 25km to Caminha, including good **surfing** at **Afife**. Four daily regional trains (€1.15, 15 minutes) make their way up the coast to Afife.

RIVER TRIPS

If there are enough passengers, boats run up and down the Rio Lima daily in summer, from the pier south of Largo 5 de Outubro. The most common trip takes 45 minutes (€5), but longer excursions, with lunch, are available in midsummer. For details call **Portela & Filhos** (☎ 258 842 290) or check at the pier.

Festivals & Events

Viana has a knack for celebrations. The **Romaria de Nossa Senhora d'Agonia** (www.festas-agonia.com), held in August, is the region's biggest annual bash (see the boxed text, below), and **Carnaval** festivities here are considered northern Portugal's best. The town also goes a little nuts in mid-May during **Semana Acadêmica** (or Queima das Fitas), a week of student end-of-term madness similar to Coimbra's.

And that's not all. Almost every Saturday from May to September sees traditional dancing and a photogenic food market on Praça da República.

The turismo has details of other annual events, which include the following:

Encontros de Viana A week-long festival of documentaries and short films; held in the first half of May.

Festival Maio A national folk-dance extravaganza that takes place at the end of May.

Sleeping

Accommodation can be tight in summer, particularly August. Prices listed are for July and August, but discounts of around 30 percent are common outside high season. The turismo keeps a list of trustworthy *quartos* (private rooms); expect to pay at least €30 for a double in summer. It also has details of several nearby cottages and manor houses (around €65 to 90), though most will require your own wheels.

WHO'S SORRY NOW?

Streets decorated with coloured sawdust. Women decked out in traditional finery of scarlet and gold. Men drinking like bawdy fish. Viana's Romaria de Nossa Senhora d'Agonia (Our Lady of Sorrows) is one of the Minho's most spectacular festivals. Expect everything from emotive religious processions to upbeat parades with deafening drums and lumbering carnival *gigantones* (giants) and *cabeçudos* (big heads). The festival takes place for three or four days around 20 August. Accommodation is very tight at this time, so book well ahead.

THE MINHO

BUDGET

Orbitur (☎ 258 322 167; info@orbitur.pt; Praia do Cabedelo; adult/car €4.30/3.80, tent €3.50-5.90; year-round;) This beach-side site is within walking distance of the ferry pier on the Cabedelo side, and also has four-person bungalows (€75). It heaves with holidaymakers in summer.

our pick **Pousada da Juventude Gil Eannes** (☎ 258 821 582; www.movijovem.pt; Gil Eannes; dm €8, d with/without air-con €22/15) Ever slept in the oily bowels of a huge, creaky hospital ship? No? In Viana you can make this long-held dream a reality aboard this unusual *pousada da juventude*. It scores well for novelty but don't expect easy access, luxury or more natural light than fits through a few portholes. While discouraged for fusses and claustrophobics, it's certainly memorable for the rest of us. Reception is open from 8am to noon and 6pm to midnight only.

Pousada da juventude (☎ 258 800 260; www.movijovem.pt; Rua da Argaçosa; dm €13, d with toilet €36; P) For landlubbers and other claustrophobics, Viana has a second hostel 1km east of the town centre, with neat dorms and doubles, some with balconies overlooking the marina.

MIDRANGE

Pensão-Restaurante Dolce Vita (☎ 258 824 860; pizzaria.dolcevita@iol.pt; Rua do Poço 44; d incl breakfast €40-55;) The snug rooms at Dolce Vita are faultlessly spick-and-span, each with shower, toilet and TV. It's good value for being in the town centre. Expect hunger-inducing smells from the pizzeria below.

Residencial Viana Mar (☎/fax 258 828 962; Avenida dos Combatentes 215; d with/without bathroom €50/35) A friendly older couple run this congenial place, which has a small bar and four floors of well-worn, carpeted but largely shipshape rooms on the town's main street. Angle for one of the bright back rooms with balconies.

Residencial Jardim (☎ 258 828 915; www.residencialjardim.com.sapo.pt; Largo 5 de Outubro 68; d €50;) In a stately, 19th-century town house, this quirky place has cosy carpeted rooms that are ready for a refresh, though most are at least bright. Several have delightful views of the riverfront, while others look onto the historic centre.

Residencial Laranjeira (☎ 258 822 261; www.residencialaranjeira.com; Rua General Luís do Rego 45; d €55; P) This well-managed place has comfortable rooms with décor inherited from various bygone decades, though there are plans for a major remodel. Off-street parking costs €5 per day.

Margarida da Praça (☎ 258 809 630; www.margaridadapraca.com; Largo 5 de Outubro 58; d €60;) At the highest end of the midrange options, this hotel offers remodelled rooms in a handsome town house with a great riverfront location. The rooms are showing wear quickly and the reception can be rather lacklustre, but still decent value.

TOP END

Pousada do Monte de Santa Luzia (Pousada de Viana do Castelo; ☎ 258 800 370; www.pousadas.pt; d with/without sea view from €215/180; P) This regal, 1918 hotel sits squarely atop Monte de Santa Luzia, peering down at the basilica's backside and beyond it to some of the best coastal views in Portugal. Common areas are splendid, while the rooms themselves are bright and luxurious if less inspired than the views.

Eating

Estação Biológica (☎ 258 100 082; Estação Viana Shopping, 2nd fl; mains €5; lunch & dinner; V) This natural-products shop in, of all places, a shopping mall food court, does quite good all-veggie meals.

Pensão-Restaurante Dolce Vita (☎ 258 824 860; Rua do Poço 44; mains & pizzas around €5; lunch & dinner) This no-frills place is popular with locals for its big menu of good-value pizza and pasta dishes.

A Gruta Snack Bar (☎ 258 820 214; Rua Grande 87; mains €4-8; lunch & dinner Mon-Sat) This stone-walled little bistro has an economical lunch menu, including wine, soup, *bacalhau* and coffee for €9.

Restaurante O Garfo (☎ 258 829 415; Largo 5 de Outubro 28; mains €6-9; lunch & dinner) Hunkering down in the arches that face the docks, O Garfo is a solid, unpretentious eatery offering lots of very fresh fish dishes and more. There are tables outside in summer.

Restaurant O Pescador (☎ 258 826 039; Largo de São Domingos 35; mains €8-13; lunch & dinner Tue-Sun) A simple, friendly, family-run restaurant admired by locals for its for its excellent seafood.

Taberna do Valentim (☎ 258 827 505; Rua Monsignor Daniel Machado 180; mains €10-18; lunch & dinner Mon-Sat) Hidden among the humble abodes of the old fishermen's neighbourhood you'll find this fantastic seafood restaurant, easily one of the best in northern Portugal. The rich, red seafood stew is the house speciality – and quite heavenly.

The **mercado municipal** (Avenida Capitão Gaspar de Castro; Mon-Sat morning) is just northeast of the centre. Rua Grande and its eastward extension have numerous small food shops.

Drinking & Entertainment

A rather pretentious restaurant until 10pm, a hip bar until midnight, and a disco playing commercial house and pop until the wee hours, **Glamour** (Rua da Bandeira 179-185; 7.30pm-4am Mon-Sat) is Viana's longest-running disco. Admission varies depending on the season/night of week/special event.

But now it has challengers in a new complex of chic bars and restaurants on the waterfront across from the Jardim Marginal. Among them is **Caffe del Rio** (258 822 963; Rua da Bandeira 179-185; 1pm-2am Sun-Thu, to 4am Fri & Sat), which at writing is the hottest club north of Porto, with imported DJs spinning house, electronica and hip-hop as well as pop and R&B. The sleek, glass and chrome, '60s-style bar upstairs has great river views.

Or to drink and be merry in the open air, consider the greenhouse-like **Café Girassol** (8am-8pm, to midnight Jun-Sep) in the Jardim Marginal, with tables spilling out into the park.

Getting There & Away

Parking can be a challenge. Try along Avenida dos Combatentes da Grande Guerra or at the riverfront lot at its foot.

BUS

Long-distance *expresso* buses operate from the new, centralised bus station, which is now just across the tracks from the train station.

AV Minho (258 800 341) runs a line from Porto (€5.50, 2¼ hours) four times during the week, passing through Esposende (€2.40, 45 minutes) and on to Valença (€3.20, 1¼ hours) and Monção (€3.60, 1½ hours). Service drops to one or two runs on weekends.

Transdev Norte (253 209 410) has at least eight weekday and four weekend runs to Braga (€3.60, 1½ hours).

AV Cura/Transcolvia (258 800 340) runs up the Lima valley to Ponte de Lima (€2.60, 50 minutes), Ponte da Barca (€3.30, 1½ hours) and Arcos de Valdevez (€3.50, 1½ hours) at least hourly weekdays (fewer at weekends).

TRAIN

Daily direct services from Porto include three IR/international trains (€6.80, 1½ hours) and five regional services (€6.40, 1¾ hours). For Braga (€3.80, from 1½ hours, 12 daily), change at Nine. There are also at least eight daily trains to Valença (€2.80, 45 minutes to one hour) during the week.

VALENÇA DO MINHO

pop 5100

Occupying strategic heights above the picturesque Rio Minho, Valença do Minho (Valença) sits just a cannon-ball shot from Spain. Its impressive pair of bastions long served as the Minho's first line of defence against the Spanish aggression. But history insists on repeating itself, and these days the town is regularly overrun by Spanish hordes. They come armed with wallets and make away with volumes of towels and linens that are stacked high along the cobbled streets of the fortresses. Indeed tourist brochures have rechristened the mighty citadel as 'the Shopping Fortress.' Ah, progress!

The good news is that on even the busiest days, you can sidestep the towel touts and discover that these two interconnected forts also contain a fully functioning village where locals shop, eat, drink and gossip among pretty squares and narrow, medieval lanes. And when in the evening the weary troops retreat back to Spain with their loot, the empty watchtowers return once again to the silent contemplation of their ancient enemy – the glowering Spanish fortress just across the river.

Orientation & Information

An uninspiring new town sprawls at the foot of the fortress. From the bus station it's 800m north via Avenida Miguel Dantas (the N13) and the Largo da Trapicheira roundabout (aka Largo da Esplanada) to the **turismo** (/fax 251 823 374; Avenida de Espanha; 9.30am-12.30pm & 2-5.30pm Mon-Sat year-round). The train station is just east of Avenida Miguel Dantas.

The fortress has its own **post office** (Travessa do Eirado; 9am-12.30pm & 2pm-5.30pm Mon-Fri). **Espaço Internet** (251 809 588; 10am-12.30pm & 2-6.30pm Mon-Fri), by the bus station, has free internet access.

Sights

There are in fact two **fortresses**, bristling with bastions, watchtowers, massive gateways and defensive bulwarks, and connected by a single bridge. The old churches and Manueline mansions inside testify to the success of the fortifications against several sieges, some as late as the 19th century. The earliest fortifications date from the 13th-century reign of Dom Afonso III, though largely what you see today was built in 17th century, its design inspired by the French military architect Vauban.

Press on through the gift shops and towel merchants along the cobbled lanes to the far end of the larger northern fortress, which incorporates Dom Afonso's original stronghold and contains almost everything that's of interest.

From Praça da República bear right, then left, into Rua Guilherme José da Silva. On the left, opposite the post office, is the **Casa da Eira**, with a handsome Manueline window. The 14th-century **Igreja de Santo Estevão**, with its neoclassical façade, is at the end of the street. Nearby is a 1st-century **Roman milestone** from the old Braga–Astorga road.

From the milestone continue north to the end of Rua José Rodrigues and the now decrepit Romanesque parish church, **Igreja de Santa Maria dos Anjos** (St Mary of the Angels), dating from 1276. At the back is a tiny **chapel** with leering carved faces and Romano-Gothic inscriptions on the outside, though this is in an appalling state of disrepair and closed to the public.

To the left of the parish church is the **Capela da Misericórdia** and beyond it the Pousada de São Teotónio (right). All around this area there are picturesque ramparts and sweeping views to Tuy.

Turn right by the *pousada* and descend the atmospheric lane through one of the 13th-century **original gates**, with a trickling stream running below and an impressive echo. Keep going and you'll pass through several thick onion-skin fortress layers to the outside world.

Sleeping

Most accommodation is near the fortresses in the new town, though the two top choices are within the fortress walls. There are no true budget options.

Residencial Rio Minho (☎ 251 809 240; fax 251 809 248; Largo da Estação; d incl breakfast €40) Staggering out of the train station and can't wait to drop your kit? Well you won't do much better than this guesthouse-restaurant. Bonuses include a vine-covered terrace, double-paned windows, and a number of airy, high-ceilinged rooms with views of a leafy square; back rooms are pokier.

Val Flores (☎ 251 824 106; fax 251 824 129; Centro Comercial Val Flores; d incl breakfast €40) This friendly, spotless but plain *residencial* (guesthouse), in a concrete box on the road looking up at the fortress walls, offers decent value, with rooms that are clean if threadbare.

Hotel Lara (☎ 251 824 348; www.hotellara.com; Avenida Dos Bombeiros; d incl breakfast €65;) A very comfortable if lacklustre business hotel in a modern low-rise. Most of the carpeted rooms have been recently remodelled, and many have verandas.

Casa da Eira (☎ 251 921 905; www.casaeira.net; Laços; d incl breakfast €75; P) Occupying an 18th century farmhouse with lustrous wood floors, this place offers handsomely furnished rooms with sparkling, tiled bathrooms, plus a grassy garden with pool. It's 8km east of Valença towards Monção. Turn off the N101 towards Laços and follow the signs.

Casa do Poço (☎ 251 825 235; www.casadopoco.fr.fm; Travessa da Gaviarra 4; ste from €120) For a personal touch, head to this gorgeously restored 17th-century house, which once formed part of the Misericórdia hospital. It now cares for wealthy tourists, with contemporary European art, a library, billiard room and six antique-appointed, silk-wallpapered suites.

Pousada de São Teotónio (☎ 251 800 260; www.pousadas.pt; Rua de Baluarte do Socorro; d €155; P) Perched on the outermost post of the fortress and surrounded by green ramparts, this bright, modern *pousada* has large, rather luxurious rooms, most with prime views overlooking the walls and river to Spain; a few have winning verandas.

Eating

Grabbing a bite in the fortress alongside Spanish tour groups almost guarantees a jolly atmosphere.

Solar do Bacalhau (☎ 251 822 161; mains for two €8-18; lunch & dinner Tue-Sun) The newest restaurant in the fortresses has clean, contemporary lines and serves very good *bacalhau* in dozens of forms, as well as other Portuguese fare.

Restaurante Fortaleza de Valença (☎ 251 823 146; mains for two €10-19; Rua Apolinário da Fonesca 5; lunch & dinner Wed-Mon) On a little plaza between the two castle, this pleasant and traditional if well-touristed place offers outdoor seating and specialities such as *arroz de marisco* (rice and seafood stew) and *cabrito assado* (roast kid).

Restaurante Mané (☎ 251 823 402; mains €10-15; Avenida Miguel Dantas 5; lunch Tue-Thu, lunch & dinner Fri & Sat) Hidden in a rather ugly modern building you'll find Valença's top choice, which rustles up the best, freshest ingredients to deliver classic Minho specialities, including the seasonal, eel-like *lampreia*. They also have a popular bar-café downstairs that serves cut-above snacks.

Getting There & Away

There is free parking in lots just west of the fortresses, though they can fill to capacity at weekends.

BUS

AV Minho (☎ 251 652 917) has two daily weekday and one daily weekend runs that begin in Monção (€1.70, 20 minutes) and goes all the way to Porto (€6.80, 3½ hours) via Viana do Castelo (€3.20, 1¼ hours).

TRAIN

Five IR/international trains run daily to Valença from Porto (€8 to €9.20, two to 2½ hours), two of which continue on as far as Vigo in Spain.

MONÇÃO

pop 2600

Lacking Valença's strategic heights, neighbouring Monção (mohng-*sowng*) is a more modest, but in many ways more charming, affair. The town survives on its natural spa, a particularly fine local *vinho verde* and the lashings of charm of its old historic centre, which is girdled by remains of a 14th-century fortress.

It's said that during a siege by Castilian soldiers in 1368, a local townswoman named Deu-la-Deu Martins managed to scrabble together enough flour from starving citizens to make a few loaves of bread, and in a brazen show of plenty tossed them to the enemy with the message, 'if you need any more, just let us know'. The disheartened Spaniards immediately withdrew.

Orientation

From the bus station it's 600m east to the defunct train station, then another two blocks north up Rua General Pimenta de Castro to the first of the town's two main squares, Praça da República. Praça Deu-la-Deu and the heart of the old town lie just one block further on.

Information

Post office (Praça da República; 9am-12.30pm & 2-5.30pm Mon-Fri)

Turismo (☎ 251 652 757; Praça Deu-la-Deu; 9.30am-12.30pm & 2-6pm Mon-Sat)

Sights & Activities

OLD MONÇÃO

In chestnut-shaded Praça Deu-la-Deu, a hand-on-breast statue of its namesake tops a **fountain** and looks hungrily down over the surrounding cafés. The Senhora da Vista bastion at the northern end offers a gentle view across the Rio Minho into Spain – a mere slingshot's throw away. The **Capela da Misericórdia** at the square's southern end has a coffered ceiling painted with cherubs.

East of the square is the snug, cobbled old quarter. Two blocks along Rua da Glória is the pretty little Romanesque **igreja matriz**, where Deu-la-Deu is buried.

WINE-TASTING

Alvarinho is a delicious, full-bodied variety of white *vinho verde* produced around Monção and neighbouring Melgaço. If you'd like a free

GOING GREEN IN VINHO VERDE COUNTRY

Outside Portugal, *vinho verde* (literally, 'green wine') gets a bum wrap, but often for good reason – exports tend to sit on shelves far too long. The stuff is made to be drunk 'green' – that is, while it is still very young, preferably less than one year old.

While the wine is made from fully ripe rather than still-green grapes as is sometimes believed, the straw-coloured whites can indeed achieve greenish tints – a visual reminder of the green landscape from which they come. Served well chilled on a hot summer day, its fruity nose, fine bubbles and acidic bite make it one of the great delights of travelling in northern Portugal. Try it with seafood or grilled pork for maximum effect.

Vinho verde is grown in a strictly demarcated region that occupies the coastal lowlands between the Douro River and the Spanish border. Traditionally, the vines are trained high both to conserve land and save the grapes from rot, and you can still see great walls of green in the summer months. Like German wines, *vinho verde* tends to be aromatic, light-bodied and low in alcohol. There are red *vinho verdes*, though you may find them chalky and more of an acquired taste. White is both the most common and the easiest to appreciate.

For more information about the wine, its history and visiting particular regions and vineyards, check out www.vinhoverde.pt.

tasting, either contact the **Adega Cooperativa de Monção** (☎ 251 652 167; fax 251 651 108), 1.8km south of Monção on the N101 to Arcos de Valdevez.

Otherwise, the clutch of bars around Monção's principal squares will be only too happy to oblige.

Festivals & Events

Festa da Nossa Senhora das Dores (Our Lady of Sorrows) A big five-day celebration in the third week of August headed by a pious procession.

Festa do Corpo de Deus The town's biggest party, held on Corpus Christi (the ninth Thursday after Easter). Events include a religious procession and medieval fair, with a re-enactment of St George battling the dragon.

Sleeping

Croissanteria Raiano (☎ 251 653 534; raiano4950@hotmail.com; Praça Deu-la-Deu 34; s/d €25/35) A few of the small but cheerful rooms above this chirpy café have limited views across to Spain. The waste-not-want-not décor uses the same chintzy material on bedspreads, tablecloths and curtains. Very good value.

Hospedaria Beco da Matriz(☎ 251 651 909; Beco da Matriz; d €35) Just left of the façade of the *igreja matriz* (main church), this place offers simple but impeccable rooms, including a few with lovely views over the adjacent ramparts to Spain. The unsmiling but ultimately kind host can be found in the cosy, good-ole-boy bar around back.

Residencial Esteves (☎ 251 652 386; Rua General Pimenta de Castro; d around €35) Though not particularly old itself, this *residencial* has a certain old-fashioned cosiness, with decent if dated rooms and a friendly welcome from the two accommodating old dears that run it. No breakfast.

Near town are two manor houses on estates producing Alvarinho wine grapes:

Casa de Rodas (☎ 251 652 105; rodas@solaresdeportugal.pt; Lugar de Rodas; d €80; P) One kilometre south of the town centre is this elongated, 17th-century manor house offers mostly large, antique-appointed room, with breakfast served in a fine dining room around a common table. English and French are spoken.

Solar de Serrade (☎ 251 654 008; www.solardeserrade pt; Mazedo; d €65-95; P) A few kilometres further on from Casa de Rodas, the rather magnificent, 17th-century mansion has whimsical gardens and a few suites with elaborately furnished digs good for romantic getaways.

Eating

The pick of local specialities is fresh shad, salmon and trout from the Rio Minho, and lamprey eels in spring.

Croissanteria Raiano (☎ 251 653 534; Praça Deu-la-Deu 34; lunch about €4-7; lunch Mon-Fri) A few doors from the turismo, this place has a few modest lunch-time specials (with vegetables, hurray!) and snacks into the evening.

Deu-La-Deu (☎ 251 652 137; Praça da República; mains €6-9; lunch & dinner) This typical local joint sees the most lunch-time traffic. It does good regional dishes such as *cabrito à Monção* (stewed kid).

Sete á Sete (☎ 251 652 577; Rua João da Cunha; mains €12-15; lunch & dinner Tue-Sat) About 1km out of town on the road to the bridge to Spain, this new place is worth seeking out. Top-notch *bacalhau* as well as Minho specialities, made with the finest, freshest ingredients.

Getting There & Away

You'll find street parking around Praça da República.

Salvador/Renex (☎ 251 653 881) makes six weekday and one weekend run to Arcos de Valdevez (€3.20, 45 minutes), plus four weekday and one weekend run to Braga (€5.20, two hours). **AV Minho** (☎ 251 652 917) operates one weekend and two weekday runs that begin in Monção and go all the way to Porto (€7.40, four hours) via Viana do Castelo (€3.60, 1½ hours).

PONTE DE LIMA

pop 2800 / elevation 175m

This photogenic town by the Rio Lima springs to life every other Monday, when a vast market sprawls along the riverbank, offering farm-fresh fruit and cheese, farm tools, wine barrels and – these days – made-in-China electronics. And it all takes place in the shadow of Portugal's finest medieval bridge.

When a Roman regiment first passed through here, soldiers were convinced that the Rio Lima was Lethe itself – the mythical 'river of oblivion.' Alas, no such luck. Decimus Junius Brutus forced his men to plunge ahead, and yet they still remembered all their sins upon reaching the far side. The impressive Ponte Romana (Roman Bridge) – part of the Roman road from Braga to Astorga in Spain and the town's namesake – supposedly marks their crossing. Though largely rebuilt in medieval times, it still contains traces of its Roman antecedent.

DETOUR – MELGAÇO & INTO GALÍCIA

In the most northerly nook of Portugal, the town of **Melgaço** shares the same green, vine-rich valley as Monção and Valença. If less picturesque, it's more doggedly countrified, especially during the Friday market when farmers set up shop along the town's old walls.

Just outside town there are two Romanesque churches worth seeing, **Paderne** (3km west of town towards Monção) and **Nossa Senhora da Orada** (1km east on the road towards Spain) – reminders that you're in the cradle of the kingdom of Portugal. And four kilometres west on the road to Monção and above a lovely stretch of the Rio Minho, the town Peso has a parklike **spa** (☎ 251 402 647; ⏲ May-Oct), where you can take the waters as well as other specialised treatments.

You might also consider a day trip across the Spanish border into two classically Galician towns. On the banks of the Minho near Spain's A-52 highway lies **Ribadavia**, which is famous for its Ribeiro red wines and also has a well-preserved medieval core. **Celanova** is dominated by fine, baroque monastery, which also encompasses a pre-Romanesque chapel that is one of the oldest in Spain. Both are within a couple of hours winding, country drive from Melgaço.

In Melgaço, you can stay at the **Quinta da Calçada** (☎ 251 402 547; d €75), a 17th-century manor house with pool, formal grounds and rooms fitted out with rustic antiques. It's 1km east of the turismo on the road towards São Gregorio.

There is at least one daily bus service to/from Monção and Valença on to Porto.

The carefully restored town and bridge are worth an afternoon's gander. This is the heartland of Turismo de Habitação (p456), and the surrounding countryside is packed with appealing manor houses for those who want to linger.

Orientation

The bus station is 800m uphill from the town centre, though all long-distance buses loop down to within a block of the turismo on Praça da República. Most places of interest are located in the short strip between the turismo and the riverbank.

Information

Biblioteca municipal (☎ 258 900 411; Largo da Matriz; ⏲ 10am-12.30pm & 2-6.30pm Mon-Fri) Provides free internet access.

Espaço Internet (☎ 258 900 400 ext 415; Avenida António Feijó; ⏲ 1-8pm Mon-Fri, 10am-8pm Sat) More free internet access.

Hospital (☎ 258 909 500; Rua Conde de Bertiandos)

Police station (☎ 258 941 113; Rua Dr Luís da Cunha Nogueira)

Post office (Praça da República; ⏲ 8.30am-5.30pm Mon-Fri)

Turismo (☎ 258 942 335; Praça do Marquês; ⏲ 9.30am-12.30pm & 2-6pm Mon-Sat, 9.30am-12.30pm Sun Jun-Aug, 9.30am-12.30pm & 2-5.30pm Mon-Sat, 9.30am-12.30pm Sun Sep-May) This well-organised tourist office shares an old tower with a small handicrafts gallery. The lower floor has glass walkways over the excavated layers of an ancient tower.

Sights

PONTE ROMANA & ARCOZELO

The city's *pièce de résistance,* this elegant, 31-arched bridge across the Rio Lima is now limited to foot traffic. Most of it dates from the 14th century, though the segment on the north bank by the village of **Arcozelo** is bona fide Roman.

In down-at-heel Arcozelo you'll find the extremely photogenic little **Igreja Santo António** and the kitsch **Parque do Arnado** (admission free; ⏲ 10am-7pm), an architecturally themed park that crams in styles from all around the world.

In Ponte de Lima, **Largo de Camões**, with a fountain resembling a giant bonbon dish, makes a fine spot to watch the sun set over the bridge.

MUSEU DOS TERCEIROS & AROUND

Down river, the 18th-century Igreja de São Francisco dos Terceiros is now a rambling **museum** (☎ 258 942 563) full of ecclesiastical and folk treasures, although the highlight is the church itself, with its gilded baroque interior. The Renaissance-style **Igreja de Santo António dos Frades**, once a convent church, is adjacent to the museum. However, both church and museum were shut for renovations at the time of writing with no set date to reopen.

Behind the museum, on Rua Agostinho José Taveira, stands Ponte de Lima's pride, the galleried **Teatro Diogo Bernardes** (☎ 258 900 414), built in 1893. It regularly hosts interesting music and theatre performances.

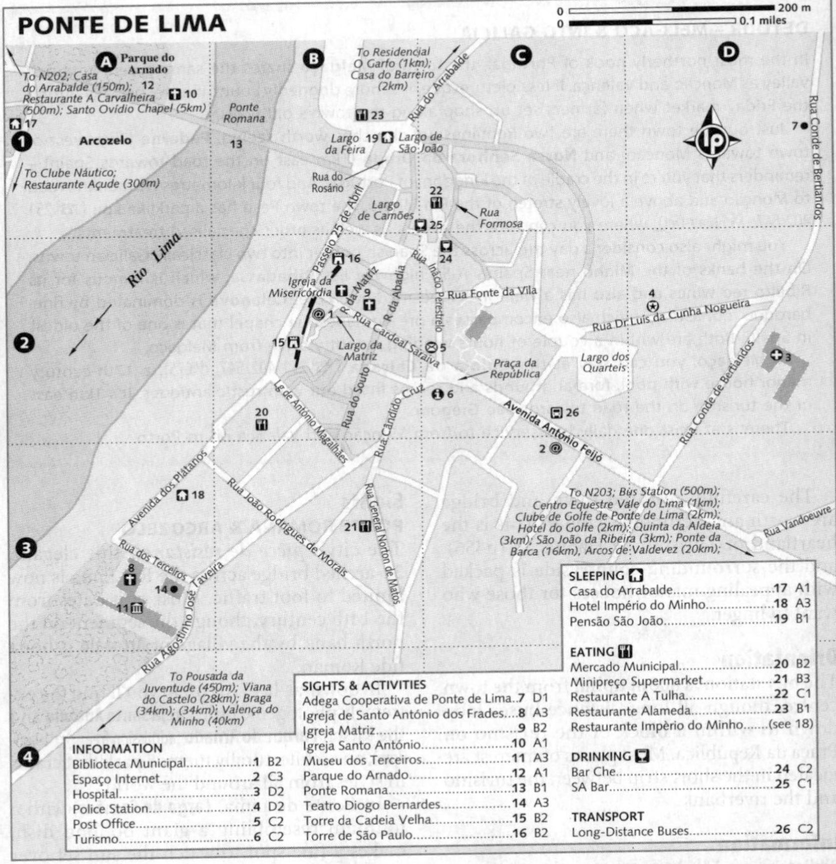

TOWN WALLS & TOWERS

Two crenellated towers (part of the 14th-century fortifications) face the river at the end of Rua Cardeal Saraiva. The **Torre da Cadeia Velha** (Old Prison Tower; admission free; 2-6pm Tue-Sun) now houses temporary art exhibitions, plus a host of nesting pigeons on its window ledges.

Fragments of the walls survive behind and between this and the other tower, the **Torre de São Paulo**. Note the somewhat bizarre *azulejo* image on its front wall, entitled *Cabras são Senhor!* (They're goats m'lord!) – a reference to a local story in which Dom Afonso Henriques almost attacked a herd of goats, apparently mistaking them for Moors!

Behind the tower is the rather staid, mostly 15th-century **igreja matriz** (Rua Cardeal Saraiva; admission free; daily), sporting a pretty Romanesque doorway.

Activities

WALKING

There are charming walks all round the area – through the countryside, past ancient monuments and along cobbled lanes trellised with vines. The turismo has descriptions of walks ranging from 5km to 14km. Pack water and a picnic – cafés and restaurants are rare.

A steep climb north of Arcozelo yields panoramic views up and down the Lima valley. A steep climb up a hill north, about 5km from Ponte de Lima, is a tiny and bizarre **chapel** (open irregular hours) dedicated to Santo Ovídio, patron saint of ears. Yes, you read that right. The interior is covered with ear-shaped votive candles offered in hopes of, or as thanks for, the cure of an ear affliction. You can also drive up; the turning off the N202 is about 2.5km upstream of the N201 bridge.

BOATING

The **Clube Náutico** (☎ 258 944 499; ⌚ 10am-1pm & 2.30-7pm Jul-Sep, 10am-1pm & 3-7pm Sat & Sun Oct-Jun), across the river and 400m downstream by the N201 bridge (you can walk via Arcozelo), rents canoes and plastic kayaks for tootling around on the river, for €3 per person for 1½ hours.

GOLF

Clube de Golfe de Ponte de Lima (☎ 258 743 414; www.golfe-pontedelima.com; Feitosa) is 2km south of Ponte de Lima near the intersection of the N201 and the N536. The 18-hole course covers the wooded slopes above town, commanding grand views, and is open to nonmembers for around €50 (less if you're staying in a Turihab property).

HORSE RIDING

You can hire horses (from around €15 per hour) at the **Centro Equestre Vale do Lima** (☎ 258 743 620), about 1km south of Ponte de Lima off the N201.

WINE-TASTING

For a taste of both red and white varieties of *vinho verde*, as well as two brands of *aguardente* (firewater) at their source, head to the **Adega Cooperativa de Ponte de Lima** (☎ 258 909 700; Rua Conde de Bertiandos; ⌚ 9.30am-noon & 2-4.30pm Mon-Fri).

Festivals & Events

Feiras Novas (New Fairs) Held here since 1125, this is one of Portugal's most ancient ongoing events. Stretching over three days in the third week in September, it centres on the riverfront, with a massive market and fair, and features folk dances, fireworks, brass bands and all manner of merrymaking. Book accommodation well ahead.

Vaca das Cordas & Corpus Christi Another tradition that probably dates back at least to Roman times, and possibly with Phoenician origins. Held on the ninth Wednesday and Thursday after Easter, it features a kind of bull-running in which young men goad a hapless bull (restrained by a long rope) as it runs through the town. It's followed the next day by the more pious Festa do Corpo de Deus, with religious processions and flowers carpeting the streets.

Sleeping

There are dozens of Turihab properties in the Ponte de Lima area, from humble farmhouses to enormous mansions: pick up a list at the turismo (p417).

Pousada da Juventude (☎ 258 943 797; pontelima@movijovem.pt; Rua Agostinho José Taveira; dm/d €11/30; P 💻) Built of glass, metal and pink stone, this new, contemporary youth hostel is a pleasant 800m walk from the centre of town along the river. Facilities are limited, but the rooms are clean and attractive. Reception is open from 8am to noon and 6pm to midnight.

Pensão São João (☎/fax 258 941 288; Largo de São João; d with/without toilet & shower €30/25) This is the town's best lower-end choice, with clean, serviceable and mostly bright rooms (no TV) and parquet floors that rattle a little underfoot. Ask at the restaurant on the ground floor.

Hotel Império do Minho (☎ 258 741 510; hotelimperio@sapo.pt; Avenida dos Plátanos; d incl breakfast €70; P ❄ 🏊) In a gracelessly modern building by the river, this place manages to be pleasant thanks to well-equipped rooms, all with parquet floors and balconies and many with river views. There is also an outdoor pool.

Casa do Barreiro (☎ 258 948 137; www.casadobarreiro.com; Quinta de Pias, Fornelos; d €70, 2-bedroom cottage €120; P 🏊) Particularly elegant, this 17th-century manor house features original details, including stone mantles and *azulejos*. Rooms are spare but lovely, and the walled garden has pool and tennis courts.

our pick Casa do Arrabalde (☎ 258 742 442; www.casadoarrabalde.com; d €80, 2-bedroom cottage €130; P 🏊) This terrific option sits conveniently just across the Ponte Romana in Arcozelo. The main quarters are still inhabited by the family who built the place in the 18th century. Rooms are grand and furnished with period antiques; cottages are more contemporary. There are huge grounds and an inviting pool.

Eating

Restaurante Alameda (☎ 258 941 630; Largo da Feira; dishes €5-8; ⌚ lunch & dinner Tue-Sun) This cosy, jovial place packs in locals and tourists alike with meaty regional specialities at bargain prices.

Restaurante Império do Minho (Largo da Feira; dishes €6-10; ⌚ lunch & dinner Tue-Sun) In the hotel of the same name, this place serves no-nonsense Portuguese fare. The tourist menu available from Monday to Wednesday offers soup, main, dessert and drink for an unbeatable €7.

Restaurante A Tulha (☎ 258 942 879; Rua Formosa; half-portions €6-10; lunch & dinner Tue-Sun;) All dark wood, stone and terracotta tiles inside, this restaurant serves excellent meat and fish dishes with plenty of vegetables. Try the *medalhão á Tulha* – a deliciously thick steak wrapped in bacon.

Restaurante A Carvalheira (☎ 258 742 316; N202; mains €12-18; lunch & dinner Tue-Sun; P) On the N202 at the northern end of Arcozelo, country-style A Carvalheira is generally agreed to serve the area's best food. Order ahead if you want the regional favourite – *arroz de sarrabulho* (stewed rice with pork and pork blood).

Restaurante Açude (☎ 258 944 158; Arcozelo; mains €14-18; lunch & dinner Tue-Sun; P) Beside the Clube Náutico, this place has lots of knotty-pine floors and walls and big windows onto the river. Try the fresh fish or *bacalhau com broa* (dried salt-cod in cornbread).

Self-caterers can try the **Minipreço supermarket** (Rua General Norton de Matos; 9am-8pm Mon-Sat, 9am-1pm & 3-7pm Sun). The recently rebuilt **mercado municipal** (Avenida dos Plátanos; 7am-7pm Mon-Fri, 7am-2pm Sat) has fresh fruit, veggies and other regional goodies.

Drinking

At **Bar Che** (Rua Formosa; 4pm-2am), images of the bar's namesake revolutionary decorate this cosy place that attracts alternative types.

Spitting distance away, **SA Bar** (Rua Formosa; 1pm-2am) has a pleasant terrace and snug indoor bar that pulls in an eager, younger crowd most nights – especially when there's a big football match.

Getting There & Away

There is street parking uphill from Praça da República; higher up, it's free.

Board long-distance buses on Avenida António Feijó (buy tickets on board) or at the bus station. All services thin out on Sunday.

AV Cura/Transcolvia (☎ 258 800 340) has a service to Viana do Castelo (€2.60, 50 minutes). **Rede Expressos** (☎ 258 942 870) has one daily run to Braga (€6.20, 30 minutes), Valença (€5.60, 25 minutes) and Lisboa (€16.50, 6½ hours) via Porto (€10.40, 70 minutes).

PONTE DA BARCA

pop 2100 / elevation 178m

Peaceful Ponte da Barca, named after the *barca* (barge) that once ferried pilgrims and others across the Rio Lima, has an idyllic, willow-shaded riverfront, a handsome 16th-century bridge, a tiny old centre and appealing walks in the surrounding countryside. It's also the home of the best source of information on the Parque Nacional de Peneda-Gerês.

The town erupts in activity every other Wednesday (alternating with Arcos de Valdevez), when a large market spreads along the riverside.

Orientation

The old town, just east of the bridge, is packed into narrow lanes on both sides of the main road, Rua Conselheiro Rocha Peixoto. Uphill and away from the river, where the main road becomes Rua António José Pereira and Rua Dr Joaquim Moreira de Barros (and eventually the N101 to Braga), is the less picturesque new town.

Information

Adere-PG (Parque Nacional da Peneda-Gerês Regional Development Association) Park information (p423).

Post office (☎ Rua das Fontaínhas; 9am-12.30pm & 2-5.30pm Mon-Fri)

Turismo (☎ /fax 258 452 899; Rua Dom Manuel I; 9.30am-12.30pm & 2.30-5.30pm Mon-Sat) The tourist office is about 750m east of the bridge down a small street, and has a town map and accommodation information. The adjacent shop has local wine, honey and jam.

Sights & Activities

You'll remember the town for its riverfront. Take a romantic stroll beneath the picturesque weeping willows lining the banks of the Rio Lima, and admire the lovely, 10-arched **ponte** (bridge), which originally dates from the 1540s.

Beside it is the old arcaded marketplace and little garden, **Jardim dos Poetas**, dedicated to two 16th-century poet brothers, Diogo Bernardes and Agostinho da Cruz, born in Ponte da Barca.

The turismo has a booklet on **hikes** in the surrounding valley (€3), some of them punctuated with ancient sites.

You could take a simple stroll westwards for 4km to Bravães, a village famous for its lovely, small Romanesque **Igreja de São Salvador**, once part of a Benedictine monastery. Its west portal is adorned with intricate carved animals, birds and human figures; its interior shelters simple frescoes of the Virgin and of the Crucifixion.

Festivals & Events

The **Festa de São Bartolomeu**, held from 19 to 24 August, sees folk music and dancing aplenty, not to mention parades and fireworks.

Sleeping

Parque de Campismo de Entre Ambos-os-Rios (☎ 258 588 361; Entre Ambos-os-Rios; adult/car €2.15/2.40, tent €1.90-2.40; mid-May–Sep) This basic, pine-shaded, riverside site is 11km upriver from town. It can be booked through Adere-PG (p423). Take any Lindoso-bound bus to reach it (p425).

Pensão Restaurante Gomes (☎ 258 452 288, 258 454 016; Rua Conselheiro Rocha Peixoto 13; d with shared bathroom €18) A bargain with bags of creaky old character to boot, this guesthouse has homely old rooms, many with sloping roofs and quaint old-fashioned furnishings (stuffy in summer); they and the rooftop terrace offer privileged views of the river and bridge. Warmly recommended.

Residencial San Fernando (☎ 258 452 580; Rua Heróis da India; d incl breakfast €35; P) At the very top of the new town, about 800m beyond Pensão Gomes, this more modern, businesslike *residencial* has smart, bright rooms with more up-to-date comforts. Very good value.

Casa do Correio Mor (☎ 258 452 129; www.laceme.com; Rua Trás do Forno 1; d €65-110; P) Lovingly restored, this 17th-century manor house on the street above the town hall offers 10 graceful old rooms, some with four-poster beds, that are well worth the price tag. Bonuses include a Jacuzzi, steam bath and sauna.

There are four more Turismo Rural properties within 5km of town, including the red-tiled and whitewashed villa **Quinta da Prova** (☎ 258 452 163; http://members.xoom.com/quintaprova/; 2-/4-bed ste €60/100) just across the old bridge. Guests stay in new buildings that are undistinguished, though they have fireplaces, kitchenettes, and little patios with the town's finest views.

Eating

Pensão Restaurant Gomes (☎ 258 452 288; Rua Conselheiro Rocha Peixoto 13; mains about €7-12; lunch & dinner) The sleepy service at this large place doesn't stop them serving up tasty regional fare, including the wonderful *truta á Rio Lima* (River Lima trout).

Restaurante O Moinho (☎ 258 452 035; Largo do Cûrro; mains about €9-14; lunch & dinner Tue-Sat) About the best restaurant in town, even if it's not fancy, this place specialises in two of Portugal's best meat treats: *posta de barrosã* (grilled steak of locally raised veal) and *porco preto* (Alentejan pork).

Entertainment

You'll find a number of bars dotted around the pretty little riverside Jardim dos Poetas. The newest and most sensational of these is the Danish-owned **Belião Bar** (☎ 258 454 195; www.beliao.com; Sun-Thu 2pm-2am, until 4am Fri-Sun), with its Cirque-du-Soleil interior and music that ranges from electronica to kitsch. The owners are currently planning to open a restaurant on the premises, as well as a hostel nearby.

Getting There & Away

You'll find free parking in the shady square at the western end of the bridge.

AV Cura buses run to Arcos de Valdevez (€0.80, 10 minutes), Ponte de Lima (€2.10, 40 minutes) and Viana do Castelo (€3.40, 1½ hours) four to five times daily from Monday to Friday, and once or twice a day on weekends.

Salvador buses travel through Ponte da Barca twice a day Monday to Friday on their way from Arco de Valdevez to Soajo (€2.10, 45 minutes) and Lindoso (€2.20, one hour) in Parque Nacional de Peneda-Gerês. Buses stop in front of Pensão Restaurant Gomes, just west of the old bridge. Inquire at the turismo for information on the current schedule.

ARCOS DE VALDEVEZ

pop 2300 / elevation 200m

Drowsy little Arcos is home to a couple of interesting old churches and several stately homes in a small, almost tourist-free old centre. It also has a winning, willow-shaded riverfront, though minus the ancient bridges of its more illustrious neighbours. While it doesn't merit a special trip, it's a handy gateway to the northern Parque Nacional da Peneda-Gerês.

The bus station is almost 1km north of the town centre, but regional buses will stop on request in front of the **turismo** (☎ 258 510 260; Campo do Transladário; 9.30am-12pm & 2.30-6pm Mon-Sat), which is on the N101 just north of where it crosses the river.

The **national park office** (☎ 258 515 338; Rua Padre Himalaya; 9am-12.30pm & 2-5.30pm Mon-Fri), uphill

Book accommodation online at lonelyplanet.com

on the right about two blocks west of the riverfront fountain, sells books and maps for the park.

Sleeping & Eating

Residencial Dona Isabel (☎ 258 520 380; fax 258 520 389; Rua Mário Júlio Almeida Costa; d incl breakfast €40;) A short hop from the tourist office and near the town bridge, Dona Isabel has simple but spruce, modern rooms, irreproachable bathrooms and a bright breezy restaurant that's also open to nonguests.

Hotel Ribeira (☎ 258 510 240; hotelribeira@sapo.pt; Largo dos Milagres; d incl breakfast €55; P) Except for its picturesque fairy-pink façade, this early 1900s town house has, unfortunately, been largely gutted of its original character, but it does have spotless, comfortable rooms and an excellent position by the river. One room has been adapted for wheelchair access and use.

Casa de Cortinhas (☎ 258 522 190; mpulrich@hotmail.com; d €65; P) Just off road to Ponte Barca, 1km south of town, this pink manor house looks out on a classic, green Minho landscape and offers rather grand rooms. It also has a winning parlour with a fireplace and original fittings.

Restaurante Minho Verde (☎ 258 516 296; Rua Mário Júlio Almeida Costa 37; mains €6-12; lunch & dinner Mon-Sat) Arcos de Valdevez' finest restaurant is in an unlikely location in an ugly block down the waterfront from the turismo. However, it serves excellent Minho specialities, ranging from *posta de vitela* (veal steak) to *arroz de sarrabulho*.

Doçaria Central (☎ 258 515 215; Rua General Norton de Matos 47; 9am-5.30pm) Founded in 1830, this confectioners stocks the town's favourite sweet – *rebuçados dos arcos* (enormous, jawbreaking, hard-boiled sweets). To get there take the street to the right of the tourist office, past the post office.

Getting There & Away

AV Cura buses run to Ponte de Barca (€0.80, 10 minutes), Ponte de Lima (€2.60, 40 minutes) and Viana do Castelo (€3.70, 1½ hours) four to five times daily Monday to Friday, and once or twice at weekends.

Salvador buses head at least twice on weekdays to Soajo and Lindoso (€2.40, one hour) in Parque Nacional de Peneda-Gerês. At the time of writing Salvador had no weekend service.

PARQUE NACIONAL DA PENEDA-GERÊS

Spread across four impressive granite massifs in Portugal's northernmost reaches, this 703-sq-km park encompasses boulder-strewn peaks, precipitous valleys, gorse-clad moorlands and lush forests of oak and fragrant pine. It also shelters more than 100 granite villages that, in many ways, have changed little since Portugal's founding in the 12th century. Established in 1971, Peneda-Gerês – Portugal's first and most important national park – has helped preserve not just a unique set of ecosystems but also a highly endangered way of life.

The horseshoe-shaped park is blessed (or cursed) with more rain than anywhere else in Portugal, swelling its rivers and five sizable reservoirs. Within the southern park in particular, you'll find exceptional hiking through forests and over high plateaus dotted with beehives and archaeological sites. The northwest is known for its idyllic rural accommodation in far-flung cottages and stone shelters.

Villages are dwindling as young residents leave for the cities, but so far they're still able to offer a glimpse into a vanishing way of life. Meanwhile, the heights close to the Spanish border (especially in the Serra do Gerês, where several peaks rise over 1500m), are almost free of human activity, other than the shifting of livestock to high pastures in summer.

The park shares 80km of frontier with Spain and embraces a corresponding Spanish reserve. The main base is spa town Vila do Gerês. Portuguese day-trippers swarm up here on summer weekends, but if you go beyond the main camping areas you'll quickly give crowds the slip.

Many of the park's oldest villages remain in a time warp, with oxen trundled down cobbled streets by black-clad widows, and horses shod in smoky blacksmith shops. The practice of moving livestock, and even entire villages, to high pasture for up to five months still goes on in the Serra da Peneda and Serra do Gerês.

Despite joint governmental and private initiatives, this rustic scene is fading away as young people head for the cities. Village populations are shrinking, and an astonishing 75% of local people are over 65.

Information

An EU-assisted consultancy formed to spur development in the region, **Adere-PG** (Parque Nacional da Peneda-Gerês Regional Development Association; ☎ 258 452 250; www.adere-pg.pt; Largo da Misericórdia 10, Ponte da Barca; 9am-12.30pm & 2.30-6pm Mon-Fri), is the best resource on the park. Materials available include pamphlets on the park's natural, architectural and human landscapes; village-to-village walks on marked trails; and a booklet on accommodation.

Adere-PG is also the booking agent for many camping grounds, shelters and rural houses located in the park. You can also book online as well as see pictures of, and read about, accommodations (in Portuguese) at www.adere-pg.pt.

Somewhat less user-friendly are the park information centres at Braga (p395, Arcos de Valdevez (p421) and Montalegre (p430). However, they should have pamphlets and brochures available.

It's best to buy topographical maps at home or in Lisbon (p461).

Environment

WILDLIFE

The Serra da Peneda gets more rain than anywhere else in Portugal – so it's little wonder that it supports a rich diversity of flora and fauna.

In the more remote areas a few wolves still roam, as do wild boar, badgers, polecats and otters. With luck, you may catch a quick

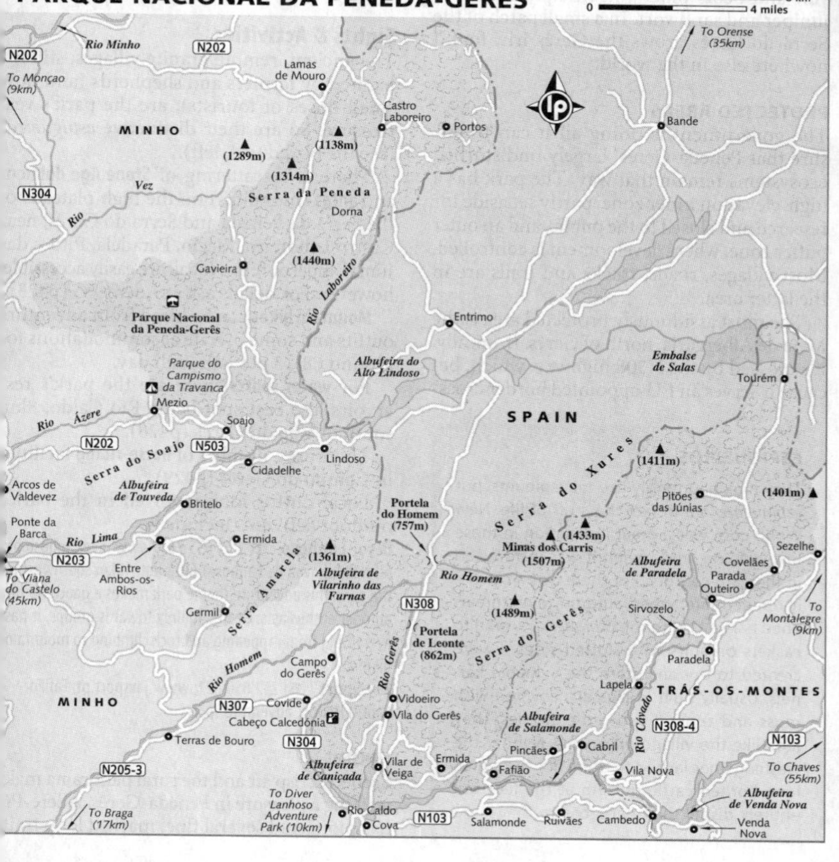

glimpse of roe deer and a few wild ponies. Closer to the ground are grass snakes and the very occasional venomous black viper. Bird-fanciers can also be on the lookout for red kites, buzzards, goshawks, golden eagles and several species of owl.

But it's not just the wild animals that get all the glory here; the park's domestic animals are also of interest – and don't tend to run away so fast. In particular, primitive local breeds of long-horned cattle (the mahogany-coloured *barrosã* and darker *cachena*), goats, sheep, and the huge, sturdy Castro Laboreiro sheepdog are all unique to the area.

In terms of flora, sheltered valleys hold stands of white oak, arbutus, laurel and cork oak. Forests of black oak, English oak and holly give way at higher elevations to birch, yew and Scots pine, and in alpine areas to juniper and sandwort. In a small patch of the Serra do Gerês grows the Gerês iris, found nowhere else in the world.

PROTECTED AREAS

The government is doing all it can to ensure that Peneda-Gerês' largely undisturbed ecosystems remain that way. The park has a high-elevation inner zone, partly set aside for research and closed to the public, and an outer buffer zone, where development is controlled. Most villages, roads, tracks and trails are in the latter area.

The most assiduously protected area is the Mata de Albergaria, north of Gerês. Ironically, it's crossed by the N308 highway, which, because it serves an EU-appointed border crossing, cannot simply be closed. Motorised traffi is tolerated on a 6km stretch of road abov Gerês but forbidden to linger. At checkpoin at either end, drivers during July and Augu get time-stamped tickets and have 15 minut to turn them in at the other end. This stretc is patrolled daily from July to September an at weekends the rest of the year. Two sid roads are also no-go areas for nonresident southwest down the Rio Homem valley an east from Portela do Homem into the hig Serra do Gerês.

Campers must use designated sites or ris the wrath of park rangers. There are als restrictions on the type of boats in the park *albufeiras* (reservoirs), and no boats at a are allowed on the Vilarinho das Furnas an Paradela. Even swimming is prohibited i Vilarinho das Furnas.

ESPIGUEIROS

They look hauntingly like mausoleums, but *espigueiros* are in fact the stuff of life. New World corn was a great innovation in these low-yielding lands when it was introduced in the 18th century. But there was a catch – it ripened late, when autumn rains threatened harvests with rot. *Espigueiros* – granite caskets on stilts with slotted sides – were created to dry and store the valuable kernels. Usually built in clusters, covered with moss and topped with little crosses, they look like the village graveyard. Neither the washing lines lashed to them nor the squat, long-horned cattle grazing at the feet can entirely dispel their eerie charm.

Sights & Activities

The ancient, remote granite villages, still in habited by farmers and shepherds (and no small doses of tourists), are the park's rea treasure. So are their distinctive *espigueiro* (see the boxed text, left).

There is a scattering of **Stone Age dolmen** and **antas** (megaliths) on the high plateaus c the Serra da Peneda and Serra do Gerês, nea Castro Laboreiro, Mezio, Paradela, Pitões da Júnias and Tourém. Not all are easily accessible however. For details ask at Adere-PG (p423).

Mountain bikes can be hired from adventur outfits and some private accommodations fo around €8/13 per half-/full day.

For **water sports** there are the park's res ervoirs, the best spot being Rio Caldo, 8km south of Vila do Gerês (p428).

There are a number of **horse-riding** facilitie in Campo do Gerês (p429).

Local outfits long involved in the park' outdoor activities include:

Diver Lanhoso (☎ 253 635 763; www.diverlanhoso.pt; off N103, Póvoa de Lanhoso) Although 10km southwest of the park, this adventure theme park makes a good trip for outdoor enthusiasts. Geared mainly towards groups, it has everything from rappelling and rock climbing to mountain biking.

Jav Sport (☎ 252 850 621; www.javsport.pt; Fafião, Cabril) Hiking, adventure sports.

HIKING

Scenery, crisp air and the rural panorama mak walking a pleasure in Peneda-Gerês. Adere-PC has pioneered several fine, marked loop trail from 4km to 9km, described in free, illustrated foldout maps available at park offices.

Day walks around Vila do Gerês are popular but crowded (see p427 for details).

Elsewhere in the park there's a certain amount of dead reckoning involved, although tracks of some kind (animal or vehicle) are everywhere in the populated buffer zone, nearly all within a half-day's walk of a settlement or a main road.

Sleeping

Camping grounds include basic, park-run sites at Entre Ambos-os-Rios (p421), Lamas de Mouro and Vidoeiro (open from mid-May to September). There are also private sites at Campo do Gerês (p429) and Cabril (p430).

You can book restored rural houses in Soajo and Lindoso under a programme called Turismo de Aldeia, or around Arcos de Valdevez and Ponte da Barca under Adere-PG's Casas Antigas e Rústicas programme (p423). Prices for two start at about €45 per night and cost up to €180 for 8-person cottages. Most also include some kind of cooking facilities for self-catering. Adere-PG also manages 10 rustic, self-catering *casas de abrigo* (shelter houses) with four double rooms in each. They're great value at €65 per night (minimum of two nights), but must be rented in full, so they're impractical for individuals. You can now book online and read about the houses (in Portuguese) at www.adere-pg.pt.

There is also a rustic **youth hostel** in Campo do Gerês (p429).

Vila do Gerês has many mainstream *pensões* (guesthouses), though they overflow in summer.

Shopping

Local honey is on sale everywhere. The best – unpasteurised, unadulterated and with a faint piney taste – is from small dealers; look for signs on private homes.

Getting There & Around

BUS

Empresa Hoteleira do Gerês (☎ 253 262 033) buses go from Braga to Vila do Gerês (€3.50, 1½ hours) hourly during the week and six times Saturday and Sunday.

Salvador buses pass through Ponte da Barca twice on weekdays on their way from Arco de Valdevez to Soajo and Lindoso (€2.20, one hour) in Parque Nacional de Peneda-Gerês.

CAR & MOTORCYCLE

Note that the back roads can be axle-breakers, even when maps suggest otherwise. There's no practical way to travel between the Peneda and Gerês sections of the park, except from outside of it – most conveniently via Spain, or back through Braga.

SOAJO

pop 500 / elevation 300m

Sturdy, remote Soajo (soo-*ahzh*-oo), high above the upper Rio Lima, is best known for its photogenic *espigueiros* (stone granaries; see the boxed text, opposite). Thanks to village enterprise and the Turismo de Aldeia, you can stay in one of Soajo's restored stone houses and look out onto a vanishing way of life. The programme has succeeded: it fills up in summer.

Orientation & Information

Soajo is 21km northeast of Ponte da Barca on the N203 and N530, or the same distance from Arcos de Valdevez via the scenic N202 and N304. Buses stop by Restaurante Videira at the intersection of these two roads. A few hundred metres down the N530 towards Lindoso are Soajo's trademark *espigueiros*.

Soajo's small main square, Largo do Eiró – with a *pelourinho* (stone pillory) topped by what can only be described as an ancient smiley face – is down a lane in the opposite direction from the bus stop. There's an ATM below the parish council office, off the far side of the square.

The **Turismo de Aldeia office** (Adere-Soajo; ☎ 258 576 427; Largo da Cardeira, Bairros; 9am-noon & 2-7pm Mon-Fri, 9am-1pm Sat) is the village's de facto turismo; follow the signs west from the bus stop for 150m. Here you can book a room, get tips on good walks and pick up a basic map of the region.

Activities

Soajo is filled with the sound of rushing water, a resource that has been painstakingly managed over the centuries. A steep **walk** above Soajo shows just how important these streams once were.

On the N304, 250m north of the bus stop, is a roofed pool for communal laundry. At a 'T' on the track directly behind it, turn left and immediately right. A path paved with immense stones and grooved by centuries of ox-cart traffic climbs though a landscape shaped by agriculture, taking in granite cottages, *espigueiros* and superb views.

Further up are three derelict **water mills** for grinding corn, stone channels that once funnelled the stream from one mill to the next, and the reservoir that fed them. This much of the walk takes half an hour.

Above here a network of paths, often overgrown, leads to more mills and the abandoned **Branda da Portelinha**. (A *branda* was a settlement of summerhouses for villagers, who drove their livestock to high pastures and lived with them all summer.)

Another walk, a steep two-hour round trip, takes you down to the **Ponte da Ladeira**, a simple medieval bridge. The path drops down to the right from the Lindoso road, about 150m down from the *espigueiros*, then forks to the right further down.

Sleeping

Village houses (for 2- to 8-person cottages €40-160) About a dozen houses are available for tourist accommodation under the Turismo de Aldeia scheme. Each has a fireplace or stove (with firewood in winter) and a kitchen stocked with breakfast food, including fresh bread on the doorstep each morning. Stays of more than one night are preferred at the weekend. You can book through Adere-PG in Ponte da Barca (p420).

Casa do Adro (☎/fax 258 576 327; www.casadoadroturismorural.com; r incl breakfast €47; P 💻) This manor house (rather than a cottage), located off Largo do Eiró by the parish church, dates to the 18th century. Rooms are old-fashioned and modest but comfortable. There is a minimum three-night stay in July and August.

The basic camping facility at Travanca was closed at the time of writing, but there were plans to reopen it.

Eating

There are two good restaurants in town.

Restaurante Videira (☎ 258 576 205; mains €7-10; 🕑 lunch Thu-Tue Jul-Sep, Sat & Sun only Oct-Jun) Situated by the bus stop, Videira serves authentic regional snacks such as ham, sausage, cheese and other *pataiscas* (snacks).

Restaurante Espigueiro de Soajo (mains €8-10, half-portions from €5; 🕑 lunch & dinner Tue-Sun) A cosy if modern place about 200m north of the centre on the N304, with good regional food, including the hearty *arroz de frango caseiro* (stewed rice with chicken).

Soajo also has several cafés and a *mini-mercado* (small grocery shop), all found near the bus stop.

Getting There & Away

Weekdays there are two Salvador buses from Arco de Valdevez (€2.20, 45 minutes) via Ponte de Barca (€2.10, 35 minutes). A taxi from Arcos or Ponte de Barca costs about €15 to 20.

LINDOSO

pop 500 / elevation 380m

Across the deep valley cut by the upper Rio Lima lies Lindoso (leen-*doze*-oo). This hardscrabble town offers a glimpse of what Soajo may have looked like before the tourist money started rolling in, with stone houses in an unsteady state, chickens pecking on the paths, black-clad women washing at communal fonts, and untethered cows grazing amid the *espigueiros* (p424). Crowning all this atmosphere is a small, hilltop fortress that has guarded the strategic Lima valley pass since medieval times.

Sights

The village and a cluster of *espigueiros* sit at the foot of a small, restored **castle** (adult/child under 11 €1/free; 🕑 at least 9am-12.30pm & 2-5.30pm Tue-Sun, closes 30-60min earlier Oct-Mar). First built in the 13th century by Afonso III, it was beefed up by Dom Dinis, occupied by the Spanish in 1662 to 1664, and used as a military garrison until 1895. Now it's occupied by the national park, with a tiny exhibition on the castle and the village.

Sleeping & Eating

Lindoso has at least half a dozen restored village houses, with prices similar to those in Soajo. These must be booked through Adere-PG in Ponte da Barca (p420).

Casa do Destro (☎ 258 577 534; d €45; ❄) The first building after the turn-off into the village, this modern *pensão* has a good restaurant downstairs (mains for two €10 to €15; open lunch and dinner Thursday to Tuesday) with *cabrito serrano assado* (grilled mountain kid) as the house speciality. Upstairs are prim spotless little rooms, most with fine views.

Restaurante Lindoverde (☎ 258 578 010; mains for 2 €10-15 🕑 lunch & dinner Sat-Thu, lunch Fri) On the N304-1, about 900m east of the turning to the village Lindoverde doubles as a restaurant serving standard Portuguese fare and an early-bird bar (open till midnight Saturday to Thursday).

Getting There & Away

Weekdays there are two Salvador buses from Arco de Valdevez (€2.40, one hour) via Ponte de Barca (€2.20, 50 minutes). A taxi from Arcos or Ponte de Barca costs about €20.

VILA DO GERÊS

pop 800 / elevation 350m

If the southern branch of the national park has a 'capital', it's Vila do Gerês – also known as Caldas do Gerês (*caldas* means hot springs) or, to confuse matters further, simply as Gerês. Sandwiched tightly into the wooded valley of the Rio Gerês, this spa town a has small and rather charming *fin-de-siècle* core surrounded by a ring of less appealing, modern *pensões*. Many accommodations close from October to April, as does the spa itself. By the same token, it's packed to the brim in July and August.

Orientation

The town is built on an elongated, one-way loop of road, with the *balneário* (spa centre) in the pink buildings in the middle. The original hot spring, some baths and the turismo are in the staid colonnade at the northern end. Buses stop at a traffic circle just south of the loop.

Information

Espaço Internet (🕑 9am-12.30pm & 2pm-5.30pm Mon-Fri) Free internet access up the stairs across from Hotel Universal.

Park office (☎ 253 390 110; Centro de Educação Ambiental do Vidoeiro; 🕑 9am-noon & 2-5.30pm Mon-Fri) About 1km north of the village on the track leading to the camping ground.

Post office (🕑 9am-12.30pm & 2pm-5.30pm Mon-Fri) By the roundabout at the southern end of the village.

Turismo (☎ 253 391 133; fax 253 391 282; 🕑 9.30am-12.30pm & 2.30-6pm Mon-Wed & Fri-Sat) Located in the colonnade.

Sights & Activities

WALKING

Miradouro Walk

About 1km up the N308 is a picnic site, which is the start of a short, popular stroll with good views to the south.

Gerês Valley

A park-maintained loop trail, the **Trilho da Preguiça**, starts on the N308 about 3km above Gerês, by a lone white house, the Casa da Preguiça. For 5km it rollercoasts through the valley's oak forests. A leaflet about the walk is available from the park office (€0.60). You can also carry on – or hitch – to the **Portela de Leonte**, 6km north of Gerês.

Further on, where the Rio Homem crosses the road (10km above Gerês), a walk east up the river takes you to a picturesque **waterfall**. (See p424, for driving and parking restrictions in the Mata de Albergaria.)

An 8km walk heads southwest from the Mata de Albergaria along the Rio Homem and the Albufeira de Vilarinho das Furnas to Campo do Gerês. This route takes you along part of an ancient **Roman road** that once stretched 320km between Braga and Astorga (in Spain), and now has World Heritage status. Milestones – inscribed with the name of the emperor during whose rule they were erected – remain at miles XXIX, XXX and XXXI; the nearest to Campo do Gerês is 1km above the camping ground. Others have been haphazardly collected at the Portela do Homem border post, 13km from Gerês.

Trilho da Calcedónia

A narrow, sealed road snakes over the ridge from Vila do Gerês to Campo do Gerês, offering short but spectacular, high-elevation walks from just about anywhere along its upper reaches. One of these walks is an easy, Adere PG-signposted, 3km (two-hour) loop that climbs a 912m **viewpoint** called the Cabeço Calcedónia, with views to knock your socks off.

The road is easy to find from Campo but trickier from Gerês; the turning is about 700m up the old Portelo do Homem road from Pensão Adelaide.

BALNEÁRIO

After a long hike, finish the day by soaking away aches and pains in the **spa** (☎ 253 391 113; www.aguasdogeres.pt; 🕑 8am-noon & 3.20-6pm Mon-Sat May-Oct). These days you need a doctor's prescription to enjoy its benefits, though this can be arranged easily enough on the premises.

WATER SPORTS

Gerês looks down on a stunning pair of reservoirs in Rio Caldo, 8km to the south, where you can swim and also engage in other waters sports (p428).

Sleeping

Private rooms are available in summer from around €30 per double; owners often approach travellers at the bus stop. Gerês also has plenty of *pensões*, though in summer you may find some are block-booked for spa patients and other visitors. Outside July and August, on the other hand, prices plummet and bargaining is in order.

BUDGET

Parque de Campismo de Vidoeiro (☎ 253 391 289; www.adere-pg.pt; adult/car €2.25/2.50, tent €2-2.50; ⏲ mid-May–Sep) This cool and shady hillside park-run facility is next to the river, about 1km north of Vila do Gerês. Book ahead through Adere-PG (p423).

Pensão Flôr de Moçambique (☎ 253 391 119; fax 253 392 042; d €35) The best budget option in town, this guesthourse offers modern rooms, most with verandas and nice vistas. However, they're small and beds are readying themselves for replacement.

MIDRANGE

Pensão Adelaide (☎ 253 390 020; www.pensaoadelaide.com.pt; d incl breakfast & with/without veranda €50/45; ⏲ year-round;) This big lemon-yellow, modern place wins for value. Rooms have nice tiled floors and new beds, some with valley views. Guests also have access to a great outdoor pool at Quinta Souto-Linho. It's uphill from the southern end of the town loop.

Pensão Baltazar (☎ 253 392 058; www.pensaobaltazar.com; N308; d from €40) In a fine old granite building, this ultra-friendly, family-run place just up from the turismo has well-kept if not deluxe rooms, many of which look out onto a pleasant wooded scene. The downstairs restaurant (right) is good value.

Quinta Souto-Linho (☎ 253 392 000; souto_linho@yahoo.com; d incl breakfast €60; P) This delightful little Victorian manor house has been simply but tastefully remodelled into the town's one genuinely nonbland option. Rooms are cosy and spotless and have hardwood floors; some also have views. And there's now a large swimming pool with fine vistas.

Hotel Universal (☎ 253 390 220; www.ehgeres.com; Avenida Manuel F Costa; d incl breakfast €70; P) Grandly *fin-de-siècle* on the outside and rather uninspired if comfortable inside, this place has one grace note – its bright central atrium.

TOP END

Hotel Águas do Gerês (☎ 253 390 190; www.aguasdogeres.pt; Avenida Manuel Francisco Costa; d 80; P) At the top of the luxury ladder, this newly fitted-out hotel is, like the rest, built for volume business, though its rooms are attractiv enough and certainly the best equipped. Th hotel also runs the *termas* (hot springs) an offers special packages. Optional full boar costs an extra €29 per person per day.

Eating

Restaurants crowded at 11.30am and again a 6.30pm, with customers washing down thei meals with water not wine? In Portugal? It' only because they're all spa patients, on strict, if temporary, regimen.

Churrasqueira Geresino (Lugar de Brufe; mains €6-1 ⏲ lunch & dinner) Grilled meats are the specialit at this family-run place about 1km uphill fron the turismo in a little mall. The three-cours tourist menu for €11.50 isn't a bad deal. If yo need a break from pork and beef, they do pretty mean *frango* (chicken).

Pensão Baltazar (N308; mains €7-11; ⏲ lunch & dinne Gerês' best-value restaurant, this family-ru place is always brimming with customers. It small menu always includes one daily regiona special, plus lots of beef dishes such as famou *posta de barrosã* (grilled veal steak). Helping are wholesome, vegetable-heavy and hug (probably good for two).

Getting There & Away

Ten buses a day (and at least five on weekends operate through **Empresa Hoteleira do Gerê** (☎ 253 615 896) from Braga to Gerês (€3.50 1½ hours).

RIO CALDO

pop 1000 / elevation 160m

Just below Vila do Gerês, this tiny town sit on the backs of the stunning Albufeira d Caniçada reservoir, making it the park's cen tre of for water sports.

English-run **AML** (Água Montanha e Lazer; ☎ 25 391 779, 968 021 142; www.aguamontanha.com; Lugar d Paredes, Rio Caldo) rents single/double kayaks fo €3/5 for the first hour, plus pedal boats, row ing boats and small motorboats. They'll als take you water-skiing or water-boarding (€2 per 20 minutes). Inquire here, too, about kay aking the Albufeira de Salamonde. The sho is 100m from the N304 roundabout, but a weekends and on most summer days you'r more likely to find them by the water on th other side of the bridge to Vila do Gerês.

AML also has several local houses for ren for up to nine people (see the website fo details and prices).

ERMIDA & FAFIÃO

From the picnic site above Vila do Gerês, a newly paved and impossibly scenic road runs 11km southeast to Ermida, a village of smallholdings and sturdy stone houses that cling to the steep hillsides.

Casa do Criado (☎ 253 391 390; Ermida; d incl breakfast €25, with full board €60) is a modern building in a bucolic spot, with chirpy hosts, six homely rooms (book ahead) and a simple restaurant (mains €6 to €10). The village also has a few **private rooms** (around €20), several cafés and a *minimercado*.

You can also continue east for 6km to Fafião, another village surrounded by terraced farms with rooms and a café or two.

CAMPO DO GERÊS

pop 150 / elevation 690m

Campo do Gerês (called São João do Campo on some maps, and just Campo by most) was once a humble hamlet in the middle of a wide, grassy basin. These days it's got more tourists than shepherds once the weather turns warm, which makes sense since it's a good base for hikes into the surrounding peaks.

Orientation & Information

Arriving from Vila do Gerês, you first arrive at a little traffic circle and, adjacent, the town's museum. The old village centre is another 1.5km straight on, while the youth hostel is 1km up the road to the left.

Sights

The neighbouring village of **Vilarinho das Furnas** was for centuries a remarkably democratic and fiercely independent village with a well-organised system of shared property and decision-making. But the entire town was submerged by the building of a dam in 1972. In anticipation of the end of their old way of life, villagers collected stories, and objects for a moving memorial that has been fashioned into the **Museu Etnográfico** (☎ 253 351 888; adult/child under 16/student €2/free/1; 10am-noon & 2-5pm Tue-Sun). All exhibit explanations are in Portuguese.

In late summer and autumn when the reservoir level falls, the empty village walls rise like spectres from the water. You can visit the spooky remains about 2.5km beyond the dam, which is a comfortable three-hour return hike.

Activities

The Parque Campismo de Cerdeira (just below) has marked three, looped **hiking** trails around Campo do Gerês, lasting from two to five hours. They sell walking and orienteering maps (€1.50). They may also have a few military topographical sheets (€7.50). Among its activities are interpretive walks, traditional games, a mountain-fitness circuit and orienteering competitions.

There are also several outfits that provide horse riding, including **Equi Campo** (☎ 253 357 022, equicampo@sapo.pt), located on the right just before you arrive in town (hour/two hours/day €15/25/75).

Sleeping & Eating

Parque Campismo de Cerdeira (☎ 253 351 005; www.parquecerdeira.com; adult/car €4.30/3.90, tent €3.40-4.90, 2-/4-person bungalows with kitchenette €57.50/77.50; year-round; P) This privately run facility has oak-shaded sites, laundry, pool, *minimercado,* tennis, a particularly good restaurant (open to public) and bikes to hire. Booking ahead is definitely recommended, especially in August. Look for the turn-off just before you reach the village.

Pousada da Juventude de Vilarinho das Furnas (☎ 253 351 339; www.movijovem.pt; d with/without toilet €30/25) Campo's woodland hostel began life as a temporary dam-workers' camp and now offers a good clutch of spartan doubles (no dorms).

Albergaria Stop (☎ 253 350 040; www.albergariastop.eol.pt; d incl breakfast €50; P) This peremptorily named modern guesthouse, complete with tennis courts, spotless and comfy rooms with verandas, pleasant common areas and nice little touches (heated towel racks for one), is located just before the village. It also has a modest restaurant (mains around €7 to €10).

The road to Cerdeira is lined with signs advertising **houses** (for 4 people €40 to €55) for rent.

our pick **O Abocanhado** (☎ 253 352 944; www.abocanhado.com; mains around €15) This new restaurant is an odd and wonderful thing – a sleekly contemporary restaurant stuck out in just about the humblest, remotest spot in the Iberian peninsula. The dining room is a handsome combination of granite, wood and glass, with panoramic mountain views. And the kitchen is a temple to the finest ingredients that the surrounding countryside has to offer, including wild *javeli* (wild boar), *veado* (venison) and *coelho* (rabbit) as well as beef and goat raised in the adjacent fields. Finish with *requeijão* – a soft goat's cheese so fresh it's actually sweet.

Getting There & Away

From Braga, REDM has three daily buses (€3.40, 1½ hours; fewer at weekends), stopping at the museum crossroad and the village centre.

EASTERN PENEDA-GERÊS

Cabril, on the eastern limb of the national park, and Montalegre, just outside it, are actually in Trás-os-Montes, but you're unlikely to visit unless you're coming in or out of the park.

Cabril

pop 700 / elevation 400m

Although it hardly looks the part, peaceful Cabril – set with its outlying hamlets in a wide, fertile bowl – is the administrative centre of Portugal's biggest *freguesia* (parish), stretching up to the Spanish border. Your best reference point is **Largo do Cruzeiro**, with its old *pelourinho*. To one side is the little **Igreja de São Lourenço**, said to have been moved five centuries ago, brick by brick, by villagers of nearby São Lourenço. Some 400m southwest is a bridge over an arm of the Albufeira de Salamonde.

SLEEPING & EATING

Parque de Campismo Outeiro Alto (☎ 253 659 860; www.geocities.com/campingouteiroalto; Eiredo; adult/car €3/1, tent €3-4.50; ⏰ year-round) This hilly woodland facility over the bridge and 800m up the Pincães road has 48 tent sites and a patch for caravans, plus a lovely old granite café-bar with fine views from its stone terrace.

Café Águia Real (☎ 253 659 752, 962 935 691; d €20) Plain and cosy, this is 300m up the Paradela road. It's often booked well ahead of time. The café (open 7am to midnight) does light meal and carries on in the evening as a bar.

Restaurante Ponte Nova (☎ 253 659 752; half portions from €4; ⏰ 7am-midnight) At a picturesqu spot next the bridge, this place does good rive trout and, if you order ahead, *cabrito* (kid) o *vitela assada* (roast veal).

GETTING THERE & AWAY

There are no buses to Cabril, but you coul take any Braga–Montalegre or Braga–Chave bus and get off the Ruivães bus stop, then hik the last 4km.

Drivers can cross into the park from th N103 via the Salamonde dam; a longer but fa more scenic route is via the Venda Nova dam 14km east of Salamonde at Cambedo.

Montalegre

pop 2000 / elevation 1000m

Technically in Trás-os-Montes, Montalegr is the park's eastern gateway. Presiding ove the town and the surrounding plains is a smal but particularly striking castle (closed to th public), part of Dom Dinis' 14th-centur ring of frontier outposts. The future Duke o Wellington made use of it in his drive to ri Portugal of Napoleon's troops in 1809.

ORIENTATION

From the bus station it's 500m uphill on Ru General Humberto Delgado to a five-wa roundabout, beside which you'll find the tow hall and turismo.

INFORMATION

Espaço Internet (☎ 276 518 050; Rua Vitor Branco; ⏰ 10am-noon & 2-6pm Mon-Fri) Free internet access.

Park information office (☎ 276 518 320; Rua do Reigoso 17; ⏰ 9am-12.30pm & 2-5.30pm Mon-Fri) This gruff office is two blocks north beyond the town hall (on Rua Direita), then right at the *pelourinho*.

DETOUR: PITÕES DE JÚNIAS

A stunning, 40-km drive northeast of Cabril takes you into fine walking country, including an easy loop that leads to one of the remotest sights in Portugal – the ruins of the 13th-century Romanesque **Mosteiro de Santa Maria das Júnias**. In just 3.5km, you take in a perfectly preserved mountain village, waterfalls, mountain vistas, and the haunting, lichen-covered ruins that date to the very foundation of Portugal.

You can get a helpful pamphlet on the walk from any national park (p423). About halfway between Cabril and Pitões de Junias in the unrepentantly old-fashioned town of Outeiro, you'll find **Hospedaria Rocha** (☎ 276 566 147) with its fine regional cuisine served in a rustic dining room (meals around €10), plus simple, en-suite rooms upstairs in the old granite farmhouse.

Post office (9am-12.30pm & 2-5.30pm Mon-Fri) is 400m northeast of the roundabout down Avenida Dom Nuno Álvares Pereira.

Turismo (276 511 010; fax 276 510 201; 9am-12.30pm & 2-5.30pm Mon-Fri, 10am-5.30pm Sat, 10am-4pm Sun Jul-Aug, 9am-12.30pm & 2-5.30pm Mon-Fri Sep-Jun). Just off the roundabout at the top of town.

SLEEPING & EATING

Casa Zé Maria (276 512 457; Rua Dr Victor Branco 10; d €40; P) This rustic, 19th-century granite manse was recently converted into a rather old-fashioned inn with hardwood floors and large, lace-accented rooms at good value. Located just down the street opposite the turismo.

Quality Inn Montalegre (276 510 220; www.choicehotelsportugal.com; Rua do Avelar 2; d incl breakfast from €70; P) Just southwest of the roundabout at the top of town, this somewhat out-of-place business hotel has high-quality rooms with satellite TV. It also features a relaxing and tropically heated indoor swimming pool, sauna and gym. Oh, and did we mention that it used to be a political prison during Salazar's reign?

At the end of Rua Dr Victor Branco, **Pizzaria Cantinho** (276 511 095; lunch & dinner) has decent, individual-sized pizzas for €4 to €5. For simple but high-quality, generously portioned regional dishes, try **Restaurante Terra Fria** (276 512 101; lunch & dinner; mains €8-10), on the same corner.

GETTING THERE & AWAY

REDM/AV Tâmega (276 512 131) buses stop at Montalegre between Braga (€5.20, 2½ hours) and Chaves (€4.20, 1¼ hours) four times daily Monday to Friday; they run less frequently on weekends. Change at Chaves for Bragança or Vila Real.

Trás-os-Montes

Separated from the rest of Portugal by a series of rugged ranges, Trás-os-Montes (literally 'beyond the mountains') is in many ways a world apart. It's a place where fields are still ploughed by oxen, and the people are equal parts bawdy humour and uncommon bonhomie. The rest of Portugal looks on the region with raised eyebrows, considering it backwards – even pagan. Indeed, remote towns still harbour mysterious practices, many of which predate even Roman rule. Cable TV and superhighways are making rapid inroads on ancient ways, but so far *trasmontanos* have held firmly to their tradition of robust hospitality, expressed in the phrase *'entre quem é'*, meaning 'come on in, whoever you may be'.

While the entire province is ruggedly beautiful, Trás-os-Montes can be divided neatly into two distinct zones. The higher altitudes, generally in the north and west, are known as *terra fria* (cold land), where winter temperatures can drop to freezing for months at a time. By contrast, the lower altitudes, generally in the south and east along the Alto Douro, are known as the *terra quente* (hot land), where Mediterranean summers ripen olives, almonds, chestnuts and the port-wine grapes of the Douro and Tua valleys.

The province is blessed with three natural parks – each very different but all extraordinary. Safeguarding the deep canyons of the upper Rio Douro that define the border with Spain, the Parque Natural do Douro Internacional is renowned for its birds of prey and ancient Celtic customs. Parque Natural do Alvão, near Vila Real, harbours traditional mountain villages, fine hiking and remarkable alpine vistas. And the heather-clad hills of the Parque Natural do Montesinho, near Bragança, are home to some of the most traditional settlements in Western Europe.

HIGHLIGHTS

- Strolling the picture-perfect gardens of **Palácio de Mateus** (p434), a baroque masterpiece and Portugal's most elegant country seat
- Spotting endangered raptors amid the towering canyon walls of the **Parque Natural do Douro Internacional** (p453)
- Hiking with the shepherds along the peaks of **Parque Natural do Alvão** (p436)
- Riding horseback between the ancient villages of **Parque Natural de Montesinho** (p446)
- Crossing **Ponte Romana** (p440), Chaves' Roman bridge, 1900 years old and still bearing city traffic

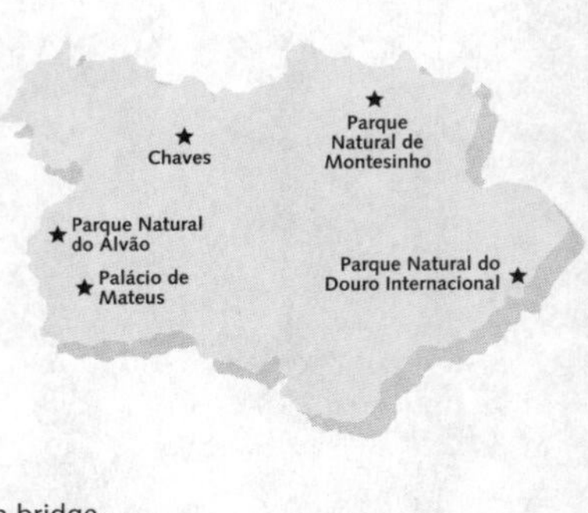

- POPULATION: 273,100
- AREA: 11,772 SQ KM

TRÁS-OS-MONTES

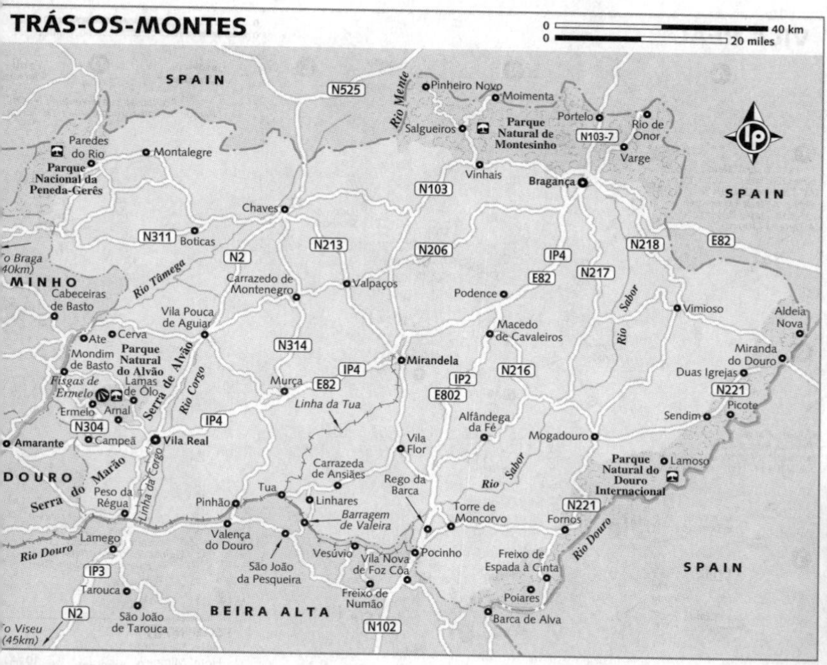

'WESTERN 'RÁS-OS-MONTES

'ILA REAL

'p 24,500 / elevation 445m

'erched at the confluence of the Rio Corgo 'nd Rio Cabril, Vila Real is as close as Trás-os-'ontes gets to a big city, though in fact it's little 'ore than a placid college town and county 'at. Besides a handful of churches, pleasant, 'ee-lined streets and a pretty river gorge, there 'little to see in the town itself. But just outside 'es the resplendent Palácio de Mateus, one of 'urope's most elegant country houses.

Vila Real is a regional transport hub and 'good base for visiting the adjacent Parque 'atural do Alvão.

'rientation

'ccommodation and food options cluster 'ound the axis of Avenida Carvalho Araújo. 'ne train station is about 1km across the Rio 'orgo from the turismo (tourist office); the 'odonorte bus station is 300m northwest on Rua Dom Pedro de Castro. The bus stand for AV Tâmega, Rede Expressos and Santos buses is about a further 100m northwest.

Information

Espaço Internet (Avenida 1 de Maio; 🕓 10am-2pm & 4-7pm Mon-Fri) Free internet in a booth near Hotel Miracorgo.

Hospital de São Pedro (☎ 259 300 500; Lordelo)

Parque Natural do Alvão office (☎ 259 302 830; pnal@icn.pt; Largo dos Freitas; 🕓 9am-12.30pm & 2-5.30pm Mon-Fri)

Police station (☎ 259 330 240; Largo Conde de Amarante)

Post office (Avenida Carvalho Araújo; 🕓 8.30am-6pm Mon-Fri, 9am-12.30pm Sat)

Regional Turismo (☎ 259 322 819; turismarao@mail.telepac.pt; Avenida Carvalho Araújo 94; 🕓 9.30am-12.30pm & 2-6pm Mon-Sat Oct-May, 9.30am-7pm Mon-Fri, 9.30am-12.30pm & 2-6pm Sat & Sun Jun-Sep) Located in a Manueline house in the town centre.

Sights

AROUND THE CENTRE

Once part of a 15th-century Dominican monastery, the Gothic **sé** (cathedral; Igreja de São Domingos; Travessa de São Domingos) has just been

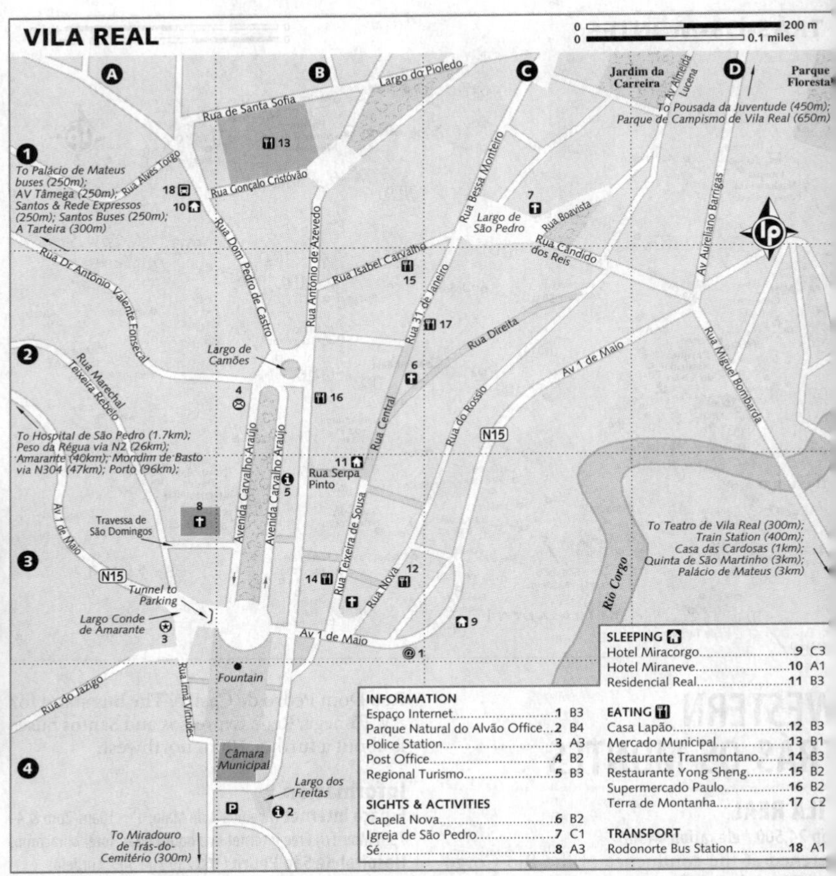

given a lengthy face-lift that has restored the 15th-century grandeur of its rather spare interior.

Northeast of the cathedral is the magnificently over-the-top baroque façade of the 17th-century **Capela Nova** (Igreja dos Clérigos; irregular hours). Inside are fine, 18th-century *azulejos* (tiles) and large-headed cherubs with teddy-boy coifs.

More baroque, and more *azulejos*, are on view at the **Igreja de São Pedro** (Largo de São Pedro; admission free), one block north of Capela Nova.

For a fine view across the gorge of the Rio Corgo and Rio Cabril, walk south to the **Miradouro de Trás-do-Cemitério**, just beyond a small cemetery and chapel.

PALÁCIO DE MATEUS

Famously depicted on bottles of Mateus ros the 18th-century **Palácio de Mateus** (Solar de Mateu 259 323 121; admission palace & gardens/gardens or €6.50/3.70; 9am-7.30pm Jun-Sep, 9am-1pm & 2-6p Mar-May & Oct, 10am-1pm & 2-5pm Nov-Feb) is one Portugal's great baroque masterpieces – prob ably the work of Italian-born architect Nic lau Nasoni.

Its granite wings ('advancing lobster-lik towards you,' wrote English critic Sachever Sitwell) shelter a lichen-en crusted forecou dominated by an ornate stairway and guarde by rooftop statues. Surrounding the palace is fantasy of a garden, with tiny boxwood hedge prim statues and a fragrant cypress tunn that's blissfully cool on even the hottest day

Guided tours of the interior (in English, French, Spanish and German) take you through the main quarters, which combine rusticity with restrained grandeur. The library contains one of the first editions of Luís Vaz de Camões' *Os Lusiados* (p44, Portugal's most important epic poem, and one room houses a unintentionally droll collection of religious bric-a-brac, including 50 macabre relics bought from the Vatican in the 18th-century: a bit of holy fingernail, a saintly set of eyeballs, and the inevitable piece of Christ's cross – each with the Vatican's 'proof' of authentication.

The palace is 3.8km east of the town centre. The local Corgobus bus 1 to Lordelo (€1, 20 minutes) runs about every half-hour from the centre from 7.30am to 8pm, with fewer buses on weekends; ask at the turismo for the latest timetable and nearest stop. If you ask for 'Mateus' the bus driver will set you down about 250m from the palace (if you don't ask, he may not stop).

Sleeping

BUDGET

Parque de Campismo de Vila Real (☎ 259 325 625; Rua Dr Manuel Cardona; adult/car/tent €3.40/2.40/2.10; ⏲ Mar-Nov) This simple, shady hillside camp site above the Rio Corgo, 1.2km northeast of the centre, has a small restaurant and pool nearby.

Pousada da Juventude (☎ 259 373 193; www.movijovem.pt; Rua Dr Manuel Cardona; dm/d €10/27) Situated at the rear of a building 200m before the camping ground, this isn't one of the country's better-equipped hostels. Quarters are basic and rather dreary. No meals are available, but you can use the kitchen, and the dull, high-rise residential neighbourhood does have a few cafés.

Residencial Real (☎ 259 325 879; fax 259 324 613; Rua Central 5; s/d incl breakfast €25/35) Nicely positioned in the middle of a pedestrian zone, above a popular *pastelaria* (pastry shop), this family-run place offers bright, neatly kept rooms, some with high ceilings and French windows. Good value.

MIDRANGE

Vila Real has a number of fine semirural guesthouses that are reasonably priced, close to town and very charming.

Hotel Miraneve (☎ 259 323 153; Rua Dom Pedro de Castro 17; s/d €45/65; P ❄) Though blandly modern, this hotel offers well-kept rooms with verandas, some with mountain views. Lower, front-facing rooms can cop noise from the busy bus station below.

Casa Agrícola da Levada (☎ 259 322 190; www.casadalevada.com; Timpeira; d/4-person apt €65/120; P ❄) At the end of a long, shady drive lies this little gem of an inn. Rooms in the main house are large, dark and low-ceilinged, while the brighter, more contemporary quarters in the outbuildings are more inviting.

GHOST TOWNS: THE TRASMONTANA EXODUS

Along with Greece and Ireland, Portugal is one of the few European countries to experience mass emigration well into the 20th century. In the 1970s alone, it's estimated that 775,000 people left the country – nearly 10% of the total population.

With difficult agricultural conditions and little industry, it's little surprise that Trás-os-Montes (along with the neighbouring Minho) contributed more than its share to the exodus. The region's population shrank by nearly 29% between 1960 and 1991. To give an idea of the kinds of conditions they were fleeing, consider this: 60% of the region's workforce was engaged in agriculture into the 1990s – a figure higher than many developing nations.

At the turn of the 20th century, the lion's share of emigrants headed to Brazil, which was undergoing a coffee boom. Later, many left for Portugal's African possessions, which received increased investment and interest during Salazar's regime. Then as Europe's postwar economy heated up in the 1960s and '70s, *transmontanas* began to stick closer to home, finding work as labourers in Germany, Belgium and especially France.

The effect of this exodus is still visible, especially in rural areas. Many villages have been abandoned wholesale, left to a few widows and a clutch of chickens. Around others you will find a ring of modern construction, almost always paid for not by the fruit of the land but money earned abroad. And don't be surprised to meet a villager, scythe in hand and oxen in tow, who speaks to you in perfect Parisian argot.

Quinta de São Martinho (☎ 259 323 986; www.quintasaomartinho.com; Lugar de São Martinho, Mateus; s/d €60/70; P) Fashioned out of a rambling granite farmhouse and surrounded by pretty gardens, this little inn sits just 400m from the Palácio de Mateus. Rooms aren't fancy but have wood-beamed ceilings and are traditionally furnished. The adjacent restaurant (three-course meals around €15; reservations essential) is also well regarded.

Hotel Miracorgo (☎ 259 325 001; www.hotelmiracorgo.com; Avenida 1 de Maio 78; s/d €49/71; P) As close as Vila Real gets to luxury, this modern midrise business hotel has well-appointed, if unexciting rooms, all with large verandas. Rooms in back also have fine views of the Rio Corgo canyon.

Casa das Cardosas (☎/fax 259 331 487; fax 259 331 487; Rua Central, Folhadela; s/d €55/60; P) Yet another great guesthouse in a semirural setting, this 18th-century farmhouse has traditionally kitted-up rooms, fine gardens and views. It's 600m south of the train station.

Eating

A Tarteira (☎ 259 328 063; Rua Dr Pedro Serra, 1st fl, Shop 12; 2-course set meal & drink €6; lunch & dinner Mon-Fri, lunch Sat; V) This natural-products shop, opposite a big fountain, about 500m west of the centre, also serves up organic vegetarian lunches.

Restaurante Yong Sheng (☎ 259 323 540; Rua Isabel Carvalho 30; mains €4-8; lunch & dinner) Tired of *bacalhau* (dried salt cod) and roast kid? This friendly Chinese restaurant serves decent fare, especially the *tai-ban* (sizzling platters). And you get a free shot of fruity liqueur on your way out.

Restaurante Transmontano (☎ 259 323 540; Rua Teixeira de Sousa; mains €6-10; lunch & dinner) A plain-faced, family-run place serving delicious, belly-filling regional dishes that attract the lion's share of locals.

Terra de Montanha (☎ 259 372 075; Rua 31 de Janeiro 16-18; mains €10-16; lunch & dinner Mon-Sat) From the black crockery to the halved wine casks that serve as booths, everything here is rigorously *transmontana* – including the hearty but fine cuisine, from *posta barrosã* (grilled veal steak) to regional wines and cheeses.

Casa Lapão (Rua Nova 51; breakfast, lunch & dinner) This spruce new tearoom specialises in traditional local sweets, including *cristas de galo* (almond and egg paste in a buttery pastry dough).

Self-caterers can stock up on rural produce at the **mercado municipal** (municipal market; Rua de Santa Sofia; Mon-Sat), and pick up other goods at **Supermercado Paulo** (☎ 259 378 780; Rua António de Azevedo 84; 9am-8pm Mon-Sat).

Drinking & Entertainment

The slick, new, boxlike **Teatro de Vila Real** (☎ 259 320 000; www.teatrodevilareal.com; Alameda de Grasse), in a parklike area across the Corgo from the city centre, has high-quality live performances most nights. In the back of the building there's a bright café overlooking the Corgo that has become the favourite of Vila Real's beau monde.

Getting There & Around

Parking along Avenida Carvalho Araújo is generally not difficult. Alternatively, there is a paying lot at the top avenue, behind the *câmara municipal* (town hall).

BUS

There are several bus lines serving Vila Real. **AV Tâmega** (☎ 259 322 928; www.avtamega.pt) and **Rede Expressos** (☎ 962 060 655; www.rede-expressos.pt) leave from a lot at the corner of Rua Dr António Valente Fonseca and Avenida Cidade de Ourense. **Santos/Rodonorte** (☎ 259 340 710; www.rodonorte.pt) buses leave from the station below Hotel Miraneve on Rua Dom Pedro de Castro.

Within Tras-os-Montes, all three serve Chaves (€5.90, 1¼ hours) and Bragança (€8.50 to €9.50, two hours). Rodonorte leaves early weekday mornings for Miranda do Douro (€9.20, three to four hours)

Rodonorte and Rede Expressos have frequent services to Porto (€6.50, 1½ hours) as well as to Lamego (€5.20, one hour) and Lisbon (€16, 5½ hours).

TRAIN

Vila Real is at the end of the narrow-gauge Linha da Corgo from Peso da Régua (€2, 5? minutes), with connections to Porto (€8, 3½ to four hours). A taxi between the train station and town centre costs €4.

PARQUE NATURAL DO ALVÃO

Straddling the central ridgeline of the Serra do Alvão just west of Vila Real, this small (72 sq km) but extraordinary park is one of the best-kept secrets in northern Portugal. The mountains, which reach more than 1300m, occupy a transition zone between the humid coast and the dry interior, blessing the region wit a remarkable variety of flora and fauna. Most fascinating, though, are the highest elevations, where hardscrabble mountain villages eke out a living amid the barren, granite peaks.

The Rio Ôlo, a tributary of the Rio Tâmega, rises in the park's broad granite basin. A 300m drop above Ermelo gives rise to the spectacular Fisgas de Ermelo waterfalls, the park's major tourist attraction.

Exploring the park on your own is not simple, as both maps and public transport are limited. Whether you plan to hike or drive in the park, it's worth visiting one of the park offices for bus schedules and hiking maps.

Information

There are park offices in Vila Real (p433) and Mondim de Basto (p438). Both sell leaflets, with English-language inserts, on local products (including linen cloth and smoked sausages), land use and wildlife. Mondim de Basto's turismo is another good source of park information.

Sights

ERMELO

The 800-year-old town of Ermelo is famous for its schist cottages capped with fairy-tale slate roofs that seem to have been constructed from broken blackboards. Once the capital, as it were, of the region, it boasts traditional *espigueiros* (stone granaries; see p424), an ancient chapel, a sturdy granite *pelourinho* (pillory), a workshop that still practises the ancient local art of linen-making, and **Ponte de Várzea** – a Roman bridge rebuilt in medieval times.

The Ermelo turn-off is about 16km south of Mondim de Basto on the N304. The heart of town is about 1km uphill. Ask at the Mondim de Basto turismo (p438) about school-year bus services via Rodonorte/Mondinense.

FISGAS DE ERMELO

About 1.3km closer to Mondim de Basto on the N304 is a turn-off to the dramatic Fisgas de Ermelo waterfalls. It is a shadeless 4km climb to the falls; take water and snacks. To get here by bus, check current schedules at Mondim de Basto's turismo (p438).

LAMAS DE ÔLO

Set in a wide, verdant valley some 1000m above sea level, the somnolent Lamas de Ôlo is known for its photogenically thatched roofs as well as a mill above the village that was long driven by water from a crude aqueduct.

Activities

There are a number of fine hikes in the park. For a three-hour jaunt around the southern village of **Arnal**, get hold of *Guia do Percurso Pedestre* (€0.40), a park leaflet with an English-language insert. The hike delivers views east beyond Vila Real to the Serra do Marão. While you're in Arnal, track down the slate-roofed centre for traditional handicraft techniques.

Some other walks, ranging from 2.5km to 11.5km, are outlined in a Portuguese-language booklet, *Percurso Pedestre: Mondim de Basto/Parque Natural do Alvão* (€0.60), with a rough, 1:50,000 trail map.

Basto Radical (☎ 962 715 121, 965 302 294; www.basto-radical.pt in Portuguese) is a local outfit arranging hiking, rock climbing and mountain biking (and bike rental), and – outside summer season – rafting trips, with English- or French-speaking guides.

Sleeping & Eating

Accommodation in the park is scarce, but you can also make Vila Real or Mondim de Basto your base.

Café Albina de Ôlo (☎ 250 341 950; d €25) In Lamas de Ôlo, this café is run by the laconic but kind Albina herself and offers a pair of basic rooms with fine views. The café is steps from the town bus stop. Reservations are highly recommended at weekends and in summer.

Restaurante A Cabana (☎ 259 341 745) About 2km south of Lamas de Ôlo, and sitting all alone, is this pine-shaded restaurant. It's known for its trout dishes, and has one double room for rent.

Ermelo has no restaurants or hotels but there are several cafés, where you can also inquire about private rooms.

Getting There & Away

Rodonorte operates three buses between Lamas de Ôlo and Vila Real (€1.75, 30 minutes) on school days only. There were no other regularly scheduled buses at the time of writing, but it's worth checking at park offices for other school-year services.

MONDIM DE BASTO

pop 8500 / elevation 200m

Sitting in the Támega valley at the intersections of the Douro, Minho and Trás-os-Montes regions, the low-lying Mondim de Basto has no compelling sights beyond a few flowery squares, but does make an attractive

 Book accommodation online at lonelyplanet.com

base from which to explore the heights of the Parque Natural do Alvão. A fine bonus is the *vinho verde* (semisparkling young wine; p415) that its vineyards yield.

Orientation & Information

Buses stop behind the *mercado municipal*, 150m west of the **turismo** (☎ 255 389 370; Praça 9 de Abril; 9am-9pm Jul–mid-Sep, 9am-12.30pm & 2-5.30pm Mon-Fri mid-Sep-Jun) and what remains of the old town.

About 700m west of the turismo is the **Parque Natural do Alvão office** (☎/fax 255 381 209; pnal@icn.pt; Lugar do Barrio; 9am-12.30pm & 2-5.30pm Mon-Fri).

There is street parking along Avenida Augusto Brito.

Activities

HIKING

Hikers wanting to feel a little burn in their thighs should consider the long haul up to the 18th-century Capela de Senhora da Graça on the summit of pine-clad **Monte Farinha** (996m). It takes two to three hours to reach the top. The path starts east of town on the N312 (the turismo has a rough map). By car, turn off the N312 3.5km from Mondim towards Cerva; from there it's a twisting 9.5km to the top.

SWIMMING

At Senhora da Ponte, 2km south of town on the N304, there's a rocky swimming spot by a disused water mill on the Rio Cabril. Follow signs to the Parque de Campismo de Mondim de Basto and then take the track to the right.

WINE-TASTING

The refreshing local 'Basto' *vinho verde* is produced nearby at Quinta do Fundo (below). The turismo has details of further-flung wineries.

Sleeping

Parque de Campismo de Mondim de Basto (☎/fax 255 381 650; mondim.basto@fpcampismo.com; adult/car €2.90/2.10, tent €2.40-3.90) This shady, well-run facility is about 1km south of town on hard ground beside the Rio Cabril. The river offers a cool plunge on hot summer days and there's a snack bar (but no restaurant).

Residencial Carvalho (☎ 255 381 057; Avenida Dr Augusto Brito; s/d incl breakfast €20/30; P) These plain rooms are in a graceless, modern building west of the turismo, next to a petrol station. Still, the price is right, and some rooms have air-conditioning.

Casa das Mourôas (☎ 255 381 394; Rua José Carvalho Camões; d incl breakfast from €50; P) Occupying an old stone house on the same flower-filled square as the turismo, this little place has three humble but neat rooms ranged around a delightful, vine-covered terrace. English is spoken. Reservations are recommended on weekends and in summer.

Quinta do Fundo (☎ 255 381 291; www.quintadofundo.com; Vilar de Viando; d/ste incl breakfast €50/75; P) An idyll of calm, this handsome property – 2km south on the N304 – has decent rooms, fine mountain vistas, a tennis court and a swimming pool. The quinta also produces its own *vinho verde* – as testified by the vineyards surrounding the house.

Casa do Campo (☎ 255 361 231; www.casadocampo.pt; Molares, Celorico de Basto; d €75; P) If you have wheels and funds, consider this antique-packed, 17th-century manor house complete with chapel and extravagant if weedy topiary gardens. Rooms are modest but pleasant, with wood floors and plain country furnishings. It's 7km west of Mondim.

Eating

Adega Sete Condes (☎ 255 382 342; Rua Velha; half-portions €4-6, mains €6-10; lunch & dinner Tue-Sun, lunch Mon) Tucked into a tiny corner behind the turismo, this rustic, granite-walled spot has a small menu of well-prepared traditional dishes, including *bacalhau* and a very tasty *feijoada* (pork and bean casserole).

Adega São Tiago (☎ 255 386 957; Rua Velha; mains €6-10; lunch & dinner Fri-Wed, lunch Thu) Very similar to Adega Sete Condes, this restaurant is just up the street.

Getting There & Away

Auto Mondinense/Transcovizela (☎ 259 381 296) has eight weekday and three to four weekend buses to Porto via Guimarães (€7.80, 2½ hours) as well as daily service to Lisboa (€16, six hours).

CHAVES

pop 14,300 / elevation 340m

Literally meaning 'keys', Chaves (*shahv*-sh) probably derives its name from its strategic importance in controlling the small but fertile plain that surrounds it. Romans built a key garrison here, and it was subsequently contested by the Visigoths and Moors, French and Spanish alike. It saw particularly fierce fighting during the Napoleonic invasion, when

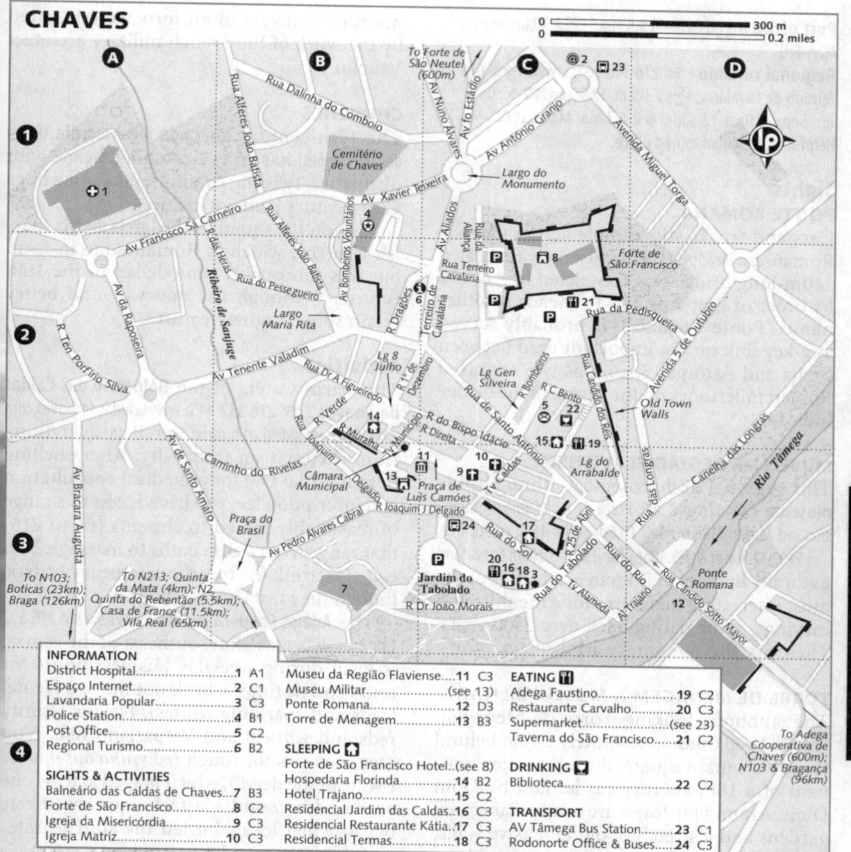

it was at the forefront of resistance against French domination.

These days, fortunately, Chaves is a most placid backwater – a place where the Portuguese come not to defend the national honour but to pamper themselves in the natural hot springs that bubble up in the city's heart. The city also has an appealing historic core, consisting of narrow lanes radiating out from a fine central square. But its real claim to fame is a 16-arched Roman bridge, which has straddled the Rio Tâmega these past 19 centuries.

Orientation

Chaves' town centre is a 700m walk southwest of the AV Tâmega bus station, and a few blocks northeast of the Rodonorte bus stop on Rua Joaquim J Delgado. The backbone of the old town is Rua de Santo António, which eventually leads to the Roman bridge. The spa is near the river, just south of the centre.

There is paying public parking near the river in and around Jardim do Tabolado.

Information

District hospital (☎ 276 300 900; Avenida Francisco Sá Carneiro) Northwest of the centre.
Espaço Internet (🕑 9am-7pm Mon-Fri) Free internet.
Lavandaria Popular (☎ 276 332 621; Rua do Tabolado; 🕑 9am-1pm & 3-7pm Mon-Fri, 9am-1pm Sat) Will do your laundry for €2.50.
Police station (☎ 276 323 125; Avenida Bombeiros Voluntários)

Post office (Largo General Silveira; 8.30am-6pm Mon-Fri)

Regional turismo (276 340 660; www.rt-atb.pt; Terreiro de Cavalaria; 9.30am-12.30pm & 2-5.30pm Jun-Sep, 9.30am-12.30pm & 2-5.30pm Mon-Sat Oct-May) Helpful multilingual tourist office.

Sights

PONTE ROMANA

Cars and trucks still rumble across Chaves' Roman-era bridge. The handsomely rusticated 140m-long bridge was completed in AD 104 by order of Emperor Trajan (hence its other name, 'Ponte Trajano'). It probably served as a key link on the important road between Braga and Astorga (Spain), as two engraved Roman milestones on the centre of the bridge indicate.

MUSEU DA REGIÃO FLAVIENSE

This regional archaeological-ethnographic **museum** (276 340 500; Praça de Luís Camões; admission incl Museu Militar adult €0.50, under 18 & senior free; 9am-12.30pm & 2-5.30pm Tue-Fri, 2-5.30pm Sat & Sun) naturally has lots of Roman artefacts, but the most interesting items are stone menhirs and carvings, some dating back over 2500 years. There are also temporary art displays.

TORRE DE MENAGEM & MUSEU MILITAR

The stubborn-looking Torre de Menagem (castle keep) stands resolutely alone behind the town's main square, the only major remnant of a 14th-century castle built by Dom Dinis. Around the tower are neatly manicured gardens and a stretch of old defensive walls, with views over the town and countryside.

The *torre* now houses a motley collection of military gear in the **Museu Militar** (admission incl Museu da Região Flaviense adult €0.50, under 18 & senior free; 9am-12.30pm & 2-5.30pm Tue-Fri, 2-5.30pm Sat & Sun) and you can climb a series of creaky stairs to emerge onto the roof (usually busy with smooching couples).

FORTE DE SÃO FRANCISCO & FORTE DE SÃO NEUTEL

With impressively thick walls that overlook the old town, Forte de São Francisco was completed in 1658 around a 16th-century Franciscan convent. These days it's a top-end hotel, though nobody minds if you snoop around inside the walls. The smaller, 17th-century Forte de São Neutel, 1.2km northeast of the centre, is open only for occasional summertime concerts. Both forts were inspire by the work of the French military archite Vauban.

CHURCHES

The 17th-century **Igreja da Misericórdia** (Pra de Luís Camões) has an eye-catching façade wit distinctive, twisting columns, plus some hug 18th-century *azulejos* inside.

Also on the square is the **igreja matriz** (pa ish church), which is Romanesque in forr but was thoroughly remodelled in the 16t century – though the doorway and belfr retain some original features.

Activities

The warm waters of the **Balneário das Calda de Chaves** (276 332 445; www.caldasdechaves.co .pt; Largo das Caldas) are said to relieve everythin from rheumatism to obesity. After shellin out an initial €60 for a medical consultatio and inscription fee, you have access to a rang of reasonably priced treatments (€4 to €16 that range from steam baths to massage. Yo can also drink the bicarbonate-heavy waters though they taste pretty awful.

The **Adega Cooperativa de Chaves** (276 32 183; Avenida Duarte), 1km southeast of the centre is open during weekday business hours fo tours and tastings. Check out the São Neute (reds and sparkling whites), Flavius (sturd reds and whites) and Vespasiano reds. Yo may even risk the rough red *vinho dos morto* ('wine of the dead'), which is aged at least on year underground – a technique that likel began when locals buried the stuff to safe guard it from invading Napoleonic troops.

Sleeping

Try to book ahead in summer, when the spa i in full swing. Most places offer big discount from September to May.

BUDGET

Quinta do Rebentão (/fax 276 322 733; Vila Nova d Veiga; adult/car €2.50/2.70, tent €2-4; Jan-Nov) Just of the N2 6km southwest of Chaves is this grassy partly shaded, suburban camping facility with free hot showers, pool access and basic sup plies. Bikes rentals are also available.

Residencial Termas (276 333 280; fax 276 333 19(Rua do Tabolado; d €30;) This place has smallish workaday rooms with souped-up linoleum floors, but decent beds and private bathroom make it the best budget option in town.

Residencial Restaurante Kátia (☎ 276 324 446; Rua do Sol 28; d incl breakfast €35) Sometimes the family in charge here seems to have forgotten that it is running a guesthouse (so service may be a bit lackadaisical), but it still manages to offer small, prim, spotless rooms – some with verandas. Reservations are essential in summer.

MIDRANGE

Hospedaria Florinda (☎/fax 276 333 392; Rua dos Açougues; s/d €20/40;) In an older building on a narrow street in the centre, Florinda offers small, spotless, refurbished rooms with floral prints and a tiny dining room that serves top-notch regional meals (mains €6 to €10); reservations are essential in summer. The lady of the house is a paragon of *transmontana* hospitality. Recommended.

Residencial Jardim das Caldas (☎ 276 331 189; www.residencialjardimdascaldas.com; Jardim do Tabolado 5; d €40) In a modern building facing Chaves' riverside park, this guesthouse has tidy and well-kept if rather institutional rooms. If no-one is at reception, ask at the restaurant on the ground floor.

Casa de France (☎ 276 965 453; www.geocities.com/casadefrance; N314; d incl breakfast €50; P) This *transmontana* country house in the village of France, 12km south of Chaves, has been converted into an attractive inn. The poolside garden has vistas of the fertile plains around Chaves.

Hotel Trajano (☎ 276 301 640; www.hoteltrajano.com; Travessa Cândido dos Reis; d from €55;) Though a slightly pretentious, modern eyesore from the outside, this '70s-style hotel (with décor to match) offers solid comforts and good views from the higher rooms.

TOP END

Quinta da Mata (☎ 276 340 030; quintadamata@mail.telepac.pt; Solares de Portugal, Nantes; d €80; P) If you've got wheels and the wherewithal, consider this isolated country haven, a lovingly restored 17th-century manor house 4.5km southeast off the N213, with tennis courts and sauna. It's a family-friendly place, bathed in beautiful, flower-filled gardens on the lush hills looking down on the city.

Forte de São Francisco Hotel (☎ 276 333 700; www.forte-s-francisco-hoteis.pt; d Sun-Thu €125, Fri & Sat €140; P) Rare-bird aviary? Check. Private chapel? Check. This is an extraordinary blend of four-star hotel and national monument, with faultless rooms, tennis courts and sauna inside a 16th-century convent that is in turn within the walls of a 17th-century fort. It also has an upscale restaurant and bar (mains around €20), open for lunch and dinner.

Eating

Chaves is known for its delicious smoked *presunto* (ham) and sausages.

Adega Faustino (☎ 276 322 142; Travessa Cândido dos Reis; dishes €3-7; lunch & dinner Mon-Sat) Resembling a fire station from the outside, this cavernous ex-winery offers a long list of carefully prepared regional meals, from *salpicão* (small rounds of smoked ham) to pig's ear in vinaigrette sauce. There's also a good selection of quaffable local wines.

Taverna do São Francisco (Forte de São Francisco; small dishes €5-8; lunch & dinner Tue-Sat) Set in the guard's quarters, right inside the fort's thick walls, this atmospheric joint serves light regional dishes, including the dozens of hams and cheeses hanging from the ceiling.

Restaurante Carvalho (☎ 276 321 727; Jardim do Tabolado; dishes around €8-13; lunch & dinner Fri-Wed) You get more here than you'd expect from its position amid boisterous parkside cafés and a forest of plastic chairs: the regional dishes are top-notch at this award-winning spot.

Self-caterers must settle for the supermarket upstairs from the AV Tâmega bus station.

TRÁS-OS-MONTES

PIG MYSTERIES

Golden calves are one thing, but stone-carved pigs? Hundreds of crudely carved granite pigs or boars known as *berrões* (singular: *berrão*) are still scattered around remoter parts of Trás-os-Montes and over into Spain. Some date back more than 2000 years, others to the 2nd or 3rd century AD. No-one knows for sure what purpose the statues served, but theories abound: fertility or prosperity symbols, grave guardians, offerings to Iron Age gods or simply property markers. You can see these mysterious pigs in museums in Bragança, Chaves and Miranda do Douro, or *in situ* in Bragança's citadel, where there's a rather weather-beaten example pinioned by his Iron Age pillory. However, the best-preserved example sits heavily atop a pedestal in the central square of tiny Murça, 30km northeast of Vila Real.

Drinking

The bar-cum-disco **Biblioteca** (Travessa Cândido dos Reis), with a name meaning 'library,' attracts a raucous and decidedly non-literary younger crowd.

More upmarket is the bar and sometime disco at the at Forte de São Francisco Hotel.

Getting There & Away

On weekdays, **REDM/AV Tâmega** (☎ 276 332 384) has services via Montalegre (€4.20, 80 minutes) to Braga (€9.50, 3½ hours) six times daily; to Vila Real (€5.30, 1¼ hours) three times daily; via Porto (€10.20, 2½ hours) to Coimbra (€11.50, 5½ hours) and Lisbon (€17, seven hours) daily; and to Bragança (€8.80, 2¼ hours) twice daily. All services drop off at weekends, especially Saturday.

Rodonorte (☎ 276 333 491; Rua Joaquim J Delgado) runs via Vila Real and Amarante (€8.50, two hours) to Porto (€10.20, three hours) eight times per weekday, but far less often at the weekend.

AV Tâmega also has four local services each weekday to the border at Feces de Abaixo (€1.70, 20 minutes), where you can pick up Spanish buses to Orense.

EASTERN TRÁS-OS-MONTES

BRAGANÇA

pop 20,500 / elevation 650m

Still guarded by its looming citadel, Bragança has long been a symbol of national grit and determination. The city became the seat of a newly established duchy in the 14th century, reminding the predatory Spaniards that this was Portuguese land, thank you very much. When the duke of Bragança ascended to the Portuguese throne in 1640, the city's illustrious name was assured.

Yet the reality on the ground has been very different. Mountains, bad roads and poor communications kept the city isolated from the rest of the country until the 1990s, when an EU-funded motorway suddenly brought the world to Bragança. Even now, the city's roots are in the hardscrabble farms that surround it.

While sights are limited to the bristling castle and the warren of medieval streets they enclose, Bragança possesses a certain earthy charm, and also makes a fine base for day trips into the underrated Parque Natural de Montesinho.

History

Established by Celts, fortified by Roman and repeatedly savaged during a long tu of war between Moors and Christians, Bragança came into its own when Dom João determined to beat off the Spanish threa assumed direct control and declared his ba tard son Afonso the first Duke of Braganç The House of Bragança grew into one the country's wealthiest and most powerf families, though they spent most of the time and money in Lisbon.

In 1640, following 60 years of Spanish rul the eighth Duke of Bragança reluctantly too the Portuguese throne as João IV.

Orientation

The town centre is Praça da Sé, the square i front of the old cathedral: from here one roa runs to the citadel, one to Spain and one t the rest of Portugal.

The main axis is Avenida João da Cru Rua Almirante Reis and Rua Combatente da Grande Guerra (commonly called Ru Direita).

The defunct train station at the top of Ave nida João da Cruz now serves as the centra bus station.

Parking is generally not difficult. Ther are lots of spots in the square just south o the Sé.

Information

Cyber Centro Bragança (☎ 273 331 932; 1st fl, Mercado Municipal; internet access per hour €0.75; 🕑 10am-11pm Mon-Sat, 2-8pm Sun)

District Hospital (☎ 273 310 800; Avenida Abade de Baçal) West of the centre.

Lavandaria Brasiliera (☎ 273 322 425; Rua do Paço 22; per kilo €2.50; 🕑 9am-7pm Mon-Fri, to 1pm Sat) Leave your dirty socks at this place, which has a next-day service.

Parque Natural de Montesinho office (☎ 273 300 400; pnm@icn.pt; Rua Cónego Albano Falcão 5; 🕑 9am-12.30pm & 2-5.30pm Mon-Fri) The headquarters are northeast of the turismo; a free schematic park map is available.

Police station (☎ 273 303 400; Rua Dr Manuel Bento) Just north of the *câmara municipal*.

Post/telephone office (🕑 8.30am-5.30pm Mon-Fri, 9am-12.30pm Sat) Doubles as a telephone office.

Turismo (☎ 273 381 273; Avenida Cidade de Zamora; 🕑 9am-12.30pm & 2-5pm Mon-Fri, 10am-12.30pm Sat) Helpful office provides bus schedules for the park. Occasionally open Sundays in summer.

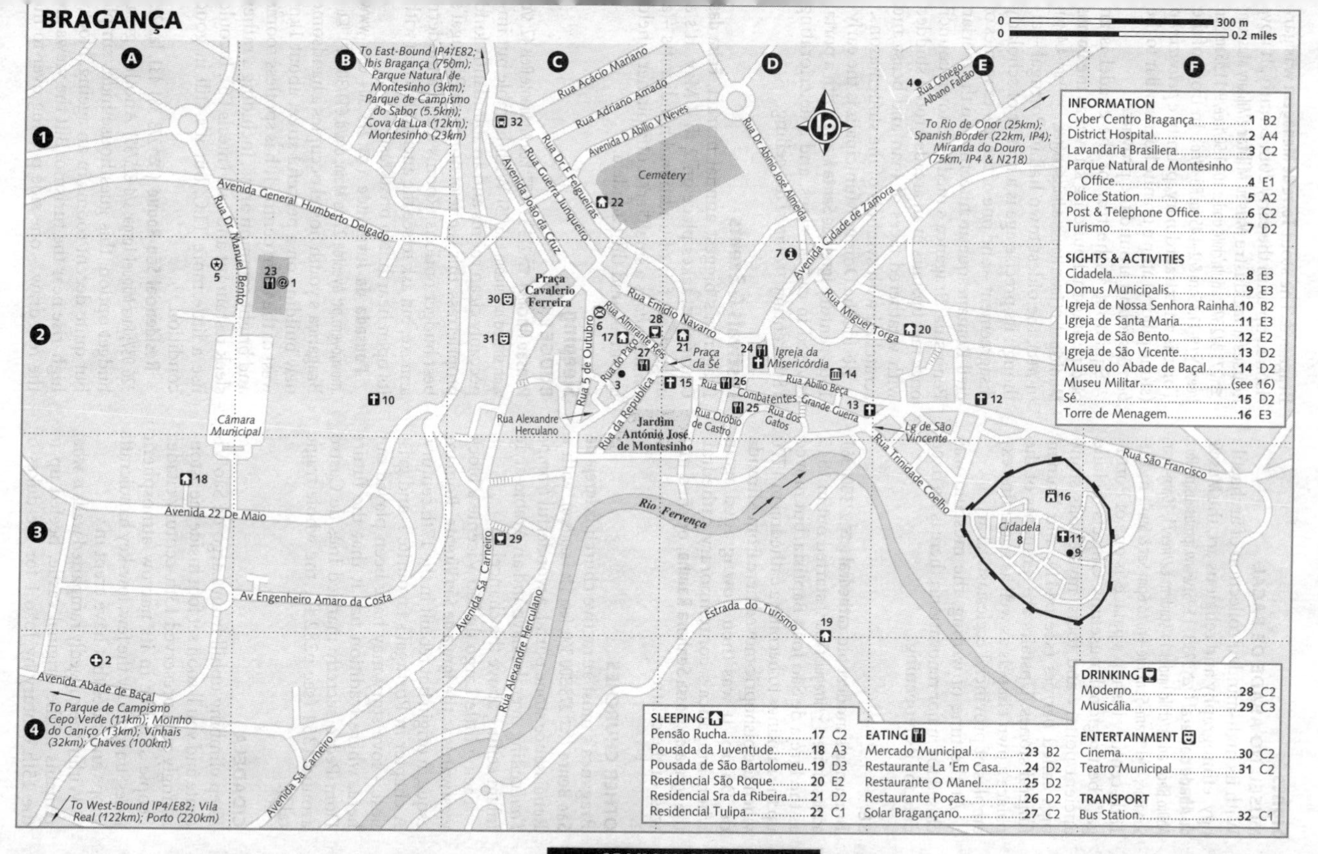
BRAGANÇA
0 300 m
0 0.2 miles
To East-Bound IP4/E82; Ibis Bragança (750m); Parque Natural de Montesinho (3km); Parque de Campismo do Sabor (5.5km); Cova da Lua (12km); Montesinho (23km)
To Rio de Onor (25km); Spanish Border (22km, IP4); Miranda do Douro (75km, IP4 & N218)
To Parque de Campismo Cepo Verde (11km); Moinho do Caniço (13km); Vinhais (32km); Chaves (100km)
To West-Bound IP4/E82; Vila Real (122km); Porto (220km)
Rua Acácio Mariano
Rua Adriano Amado
Avenida D Abílio V Neves
Rua Dr Abílio José Almeida
Rua Cónego Albano Falcão
Avenida General Humberto Delgado
Rua Dr Manuel Bento
Rua Dr F Felgueiras
Rua Guerra Junqueiro
Avenida João da Cruz
Cemetery
Avenida Cidade de Zamora
Rua Miguel Torga
Praça Cavalerio Ferreira
Rua Emídio Navarro
Rua Almirante Reis
Rua do Paço
Rua 5 de Outubro
Praça da Sé
Igreja da Misericórdia
Rua Abílio Beça
Rua Combatentes Grande Guerra
Rua dos Gatos
Rua Oróbio de Castro
Rua da República
Rua Alexandre Herculano
Jardim António José de Montesinho
Lg de São Vincente
Rua Trinidade Coelho
Rua São Francisco
Cidadela
Câmara Municipal
Avenida 22 De Maio
Av Engenheiro Amaro da Costa
Avenida Sá Carneiro
Rio Fervença
Estrada do Turismo
Avenida Abade de Baçal
INFORMATION
Cyber Centro Bragança 1 B2
District Hospital 2 A4
Lavandaria Brasiliera 3 C2
Parque Natural de Montesinho Office 4 E1
Police Station 5 A2
Post & Telephone Office 6 C2
Turismo 7 D2
SIGHTS & ACTIVITIES
Cidadela 8 E3
Domus Municipalis 9 E3
Igreja de Nossa Senhora Rainha 10 B2
Igreja de Santa Maria 11 E3
Igreja de São Bento 12 E2
Igreja de São Vicente 13 D2
Museu do Abade de Baçal 14 D2
Museu Militar (see 16)
Sé 15 D2
Torre de Menagem 16 E3
DRINKING
Moderno 28 C2
Musicália 29 C3
ENTERTAINMENT
Cinema 30 C2
Teatro Municipal 31 C2
TRANSPORT
Bus Station 32 C1
SLEEPING
Pensão Rucha 17 C2
Pousada da Juventude 18 A3
Pousada de São Bartolomeu 19 D3
Residencial São Roque 20 E2
Residencial Sra da Ribeira 21 D2
Residencial Tulipa 22 C1
EATING
Mercado Municipal 23 B2
Restaurante La 'Em Casa 24 D2
Restaurante O Manel 25 D2
Restaurante Poças 26 D2
Solar Bragançano 27 C2

Book accommodation online at lonelyplanet.com

Sights

MUSEU DO ABADE DE BAÇAL

With its high-minded collection of archaeology, ethnography and religious art, the **Museu do Abade de Baçal** (☎ 273 331 595; www.ipmuseus.pt; Rua Abílio Beça; adult/child under 14/student €2/free/1, 10am-2pm Sun free; ⏲ 10am-5pm Tue-Fri, to 6pm Sat & Sun), in the 18th-century bishop's palace, is one of Portugal's best regional museums. Objects include ancient pottery and tools, mysterious stone pigs called *berrões* (see p441), and Roman funeral stones. Upstairs are remnants of the palace's own chapels as well as some fine examples of provincial ecclesiastical art.

At the time of writing, the museum was closed for major renovations; there is no fixed date for its reopening.

SÉ

Bragança's modest old **cathedral** (☎ 273 300 360; admission free; ⏲ irregular hours) started out in 1545 as the Igreja de São João Baptista, but moved up the rankings to become a cathedral in 1770 when the bishopric moved here from Miranda do Douro. It was then downgraded again when Bragança's contemporary cathedral, the **Igreja de Nossa Senhora Rainha**, opened just west of the centre.

OTHER CHURCHES

Bragança's most attractive church is **Igreja de São Bento** (☎ 273 300 360; Rua São Francisco), with a Renaissance stone portal, a wonderful *trompe l'œil* ceiling over the nave and an Arabic-style inlaid ceiling above the chancel.

Facing little Largo de São Vicente a block westwards is the **Igreja de São Vicente**, Romanesque in origin but rebuilt in the 17th century. A chapter in Portugal's favourite – and grisliest – love story may have been played out here, where tradition has it that the future Dom Pedro secretly married Inês de Castro around 1354 (see p282 for the whole tragic tale).

CIDADELA

Keep climbing uphill from Largo de São Vicente and you'll soon set foot inside the astonishingly well-preserved 13th-century citadel. People still live in its narrow atmospheric lanes, unspoilt by the few, low-key handicrafts shops and cafés that have crept in.

Within the ruggedly ramparted walls is what remains of the original castle, beefed up in the 15th century by João I for the dukes of Bragança. The stout **Torre de Menagem** was garrisoned up until the early 20th century. It now houses a lacklustre **Museu Militar** (Military Museum; ☎ 273 322 378; adult/child under 10 €1.50/free, 9-11.45am Sun free; ⏲ 9-11.45am & 2-4.45pm Fri-Wed). In front of the Torre is an extraordinary, primitive *pelourinho* (stone pillory) atop a granite boar similar to the *berrões* found around the province.

Squatting at the rear of the citadel is an odd pentagonal building known as the **Domus Municipalis** (Town House; admission free; ⏲ 9am-4.45pm Fri-Wed), the oldest town hall in Portugal – although its precise age is a matter of scholarly disagreement – and one of the few examples of civil Romanesque architecture on the Iberian Peninsula. Bragança's medieval town council once met upstairs in an arcaded room studded with weathered faces of man and beast and scratched with symbols of the stonemasons.

Beside the Domus Municipalis is the early-16th-century **Igreja de Santa Maria**, with a portal covered in carved vines, and a deteriorating 18th-century *trompe l'œil* ceiling.

Festivals & Events

Bragança's biggest annual market, **Feira das Cantarinhas**, takes place on 2 to 4 May. It's a huge street fair of traditional handicrafts – a *cantarinha* is a small terracotta pitcher – held in and around the Cidadela.

Sleeping

BUDGET

Pensão Rucha (☎ 273 331 672; Rua Almirante Reis 42; s/d with shared bathroom €15/25) With humble but impeccably clean rooms and an abundantly kind proprietress, this is one of northern Portugal's best budget options. Rooms are in a modern annexe, but ask to see the ancient kitchen with its open hearth. No breakfast.

Pousada da Juventude (☎ 273 304 600; www.movijovem.pt; Avenida 22 de Maio; dm/d €11/30; P 💻) Bragança's youth hostel occupies a handsome new building on a peaceful street about 1km west of the town centre. It has spotless rooms and bright common areas, including a rather sleek restaurant and café (meals €6). It could use a little more TLC, but it's still in good condition.

Residencial São Roque (☎ 273 381 481, fax 273 326 937; Rua Miguel Torga; s/d €25/35) Another great budget option, this guesthouse hides simple but quite decent rooms in an ageing, blocky high-rise near the turismo. But the views are the real draw – one side peering over to the hilltop citadel, and the other commanding a privileged sweep of the Parque Natural de Montesinho.

Residencial Sra da Ribeira (/fax 273 300 555; Travessa da Misericórdia; d €35;) Hidden away in an easy-to-miss alleyway, this attractive, modern guesthouse has small but colour-coordinated rooms and new renovated bathrooms.

There are also two camping grounds in the nearby Parque Natural de Montesinho – the Parque de Campismo do Sabor and Parque de Campismo Cepo Verde (p448).

MIDRANGE

Residencial Tulipa (273 331 675; tulipaturismo@iol .pt; Rua Dr Francisco Felgueiras 8-10; d €40; P) The uniformly spotless, unfussy modern rooms are great value for money, and the service is courteous. One room has been adapted for disabled visitors. Some have castle views.

Ibis Bragança (273 302 520; www.ibishotel.com; Rotunda do Lavrador Transmontana; d €44;) Not as cold and box-like as most Ibis hotels, Bragança's newest sleep is a bland chain affair but not bad if you need business services like wi-fi.

Moinho do Caniço (273 323 577; www.bragancanet pt/moinho; Castrelos; up to 4 people €100; P) This refurbished, schist water mill – complete with centuries-old kitchen and open fireplace – is on the banks of the Rio Baceiro, 13km west of Bragança on the N103. The stone-floored cottages have fireplaces and are rustically furnished.

TOP END

Pousada de São Bartolomeu (273 331 493; recepcao sbartolomeu@pousadas.pt; Estrada do Turismo; d Sun-Thu €134, Fri & Sat €144; P) This whitewashed modern affair may not, in itself, be the most arresting *pousada* (upmarket inn) in Portugal, but its views over the citadela and countryside are way up there. It sits proudly alone, on a hilltop 1.5km southeast of the centre, and boasts lots of creature comforts, including bright contemporary rooms with balconies and a great breakfast buffet.

Eating

Restaurante Poças (273 331 428; Rua Combatentes de Grande Guerra 200; dishes €5-8; lunch & dinner) Despite the touristy, multilingual menus, Restaurante Poças serves very good regional food at non-touristy prices. The fresh *truta* (trout), stuffed with ham, is recommended, as is the delicious *chouriço* (pork sausage).

Restaurante Lá Em Casa (273 322 111; Rua Marquês de Pombal; mains €6-10; lunch & dinner) This place serves heaping platters of excellent, wood-grilled local meats in a slightly melancholic, pine-panelled dining room. The veal and lamb are especially savoury.

Restaurante O Manel (273 322 480; Rua Oróbio de Castro 27-29; dishes €7-11; lunch & dinner Mon-Sat;) O Manel offers excellent food in a bright, simple dining room. Specialities include *ossinhos de porco á transmontana*: marinated pork chops served with fried egg.

Solar Bragançano (274 323 875; Praça da Sé 34; mains €9-14; lunch & dinner) Upstairs in a manor house opposite the cathedral square, this is the centre's only top-end choice. It boasts oak-panelled rooms, a small garden and a seasonal menu weighted towards local game such as boar and pheasant, best finished with a plate of creamy goat's cheese.

Pousada de São Bartolomeu (left) This inn has a very good upmarket restaurant, with less atmosphere but better views than Solar Bragançano; cuisine and prices are similar.

Self-caterers will find numerous *minimercados* (grocery shops) in the backstreets. It's a longish walk to the new, rather antiseptic **mercado municipal** (8am-7pm Mon-Sat), behind the *câmara municipal*.

Drinking

Moderno (273 327 766; Rua Almirante Reis; midnight-4am) This is the city's principle disco, with DJs spinning everything from electronica to *tuna* (Portuguese brand of alternative rock).

Musicália (Avenida Sá Carneiro 121; 5pm-2am Mon-Sat, 8pm-2am Sun) The stylish Musicália serves up varied live music, from rock to jazz to *fado* (a traditional Portuguese singing style), plus Guinness on tap.

There are also atmospheric bars in the Cidadela where you can down shots of cherry liqueur with Bragança's version of good ole boys.

Entertainment

The boxy new **Teatro Municipal** (273 302 740; Praça Cavaleiro Ferreira) has given the city's cultural life a great boost, hosting high-quality music, theatre and dance performances most nights.

There's also a multiscreen **cinema** (707 220 220; Forum Theatrum) featuring mostly standard Hollywood fare in the shopping centre next door.

Getting There & Away

Bragança's centralised and centrally located bus station is served by both **Rede Expressos** (☎ 966 482 215; www.rede-expressos.pt) and **Rodonorte/Santos** (☎ 273 326 552; www.rodonorte.pt). Station offices tend to be open only at departure times.

Santos offers direct service to Miranda do Douro (€7.50, 2¾ hours) via Mogadouro (€6.50, 1¾ hours) on weekdays only. There is also daily service via Guimarães to Braga (€12.50, four to five hours).

Rede Expressos goes daily to Vila Nova de Foz Côa (€6.40, 1¾ hours), Trancoso (€8.80), Viseu (€10.20, 3½ hours) and points south all the way to Lisbon (€16, 7½ hours). Rede Expressos also heads daily to Porto (€10.20, three hours).

Remember that service drops off significantly at weekends, especially Saturdays.

PARQUE NATURAL DE MONTESINHO

Spread across a pair of granite massifs in Portugal's extreme northeastern corner, this 750-sq-km park was established to protect its 88 lean villages as much as its deciduous forests and undulating grasslands. This harsh, remote *terra fria* inspired early Portuguese rulers to establish a system of collective land tenure and then leave the villages to their own devices, allowing for a remarkably democratic, communal culture that still persists today.

Unfortunately, remote villages continue to be deserted by their young, and many have not a single resident under the age of 60. However, these settlements – mostly just small clusters of granite houses roofed in slate and sheltering in deep valleys – retain an irresistible charm, especially in late April, when cherry and chestnut trees are in flower. In some towns, the government has helped preserve traditional slate-roofed stone houses as well as churches, forges, mills and the characteristic, charming *pombals* (dovecotes).

Villages that retain lashings of character include Pinheiro Novo, Sernande, Edroso, Santalha, Moimenta and Dine in the west, and Donai, Varge, Rio de Onor and Guadramil in the east.

The natural base from which to explore the park is Bragança. There's some accommodation at villages within the park, though public transport is dire.

Information

There are park offices at Bragança (p442) and **Vinhais** (☎ 273 771 416; Casa do Povo, Rua Dr Álvaro Leite; 🕑 9am-12.30pm & 2-5.30pm Mon-Fri). A free schematic park map is available from both offices. Brochures on flora, archaeology and handicrafts and a booklet on park walks are in Portuguese, although English-speaking staff at Bragança are more than willing to answer questions.

Sights

The most famous inhabitant of the eastern Serra de Montesinho is the rust-coloured Iberian wolf (p62). Indeed, this natural park and the adjoining Spanish park together form the last major refuge for this seriously endangered animal. Other threatened species include the royal eagle and the black stork.

In vast forests of Iberian oak and chestnut, and among riverside alders, willows, poplars and hazel, there are also roe deer, otter and wild boar; in the grasslands are partridge, kite and kestrel. Above 900m the otherwise barren ground is carpeted in heather and broom in spring.

RIO DE ONOR

This lovely little town of 70 souls in the eastern half of the park is entirely unfazed by the Spanish–Portuguese border splicing it down the middle. It's interesting not just for its rustic stone buildings but also its staunch maintenance of the communal lifestyle once typical of the region – though its youngest practitioners are now well into their senior years. The twinned village also has one other claim to fame – a hybrid Portuguese-Spanish dialect known as *rionorês*.

The border itself runs smack through the middle of the village, while the Rio de Onor trickles along perpendicular to it. The road from Bragança branches left to cross the border and right to cross the river on an old stone bridge, to the prettiest part of the village.

STUB bus No 5 (€1.10) heads to Rio de Onor via Varge at least twice daily. A taxi from Bragança costs around €20/40 (one way/return) with an hour's wait.

MONTESINHO

Hidden literally at the end of the road in narrow valley wedged between forbidding granite heights, this tiny village in the eastern half is one of the park's best-preserved thank

to a programme to restore old dwellings and stop construction of new ones. The village is also the jumping-off point for a hiking trail through the rugged hills to a nearby dam. There is no bus service to Montesinho. A taxi from Bragança costs under €20.

DINE & MOIMENTA

A new road has finally connected Dine and Moimenta, two of the loveliest villages in the western half of park – both a stone's throw from the Spanish border. In well-preserved Dine, you can visit a tiny **archaeological museum** that documents the 1984 find by a Danish diplomat of Iron Age remains in a nearby cave. The museum is usually locked, but just ask around and someone will rustle up the French-speaking caretaker, who may also lead you around to the cave itself – pointing out wild-growing medicinal herbs on the way.

The beautiful drive between Dine and Moimenta takes you past a remarkably well-preserved **medieval bridge**, with a single impressive arch. Moimenta has a lovely core of granite houses roofed in terracotta, plus a small baroque church – a rare dose of luxury in these thin lands. However, a ring of modern construction keeps Moimenta from being as pristine as Dine.

Activities

There are plenty of opportunities for biking and hiking. Park offices offer two maps with **biking trails**, one around Moimenta and the other in the Sabor valley. They also have excellent, detailed guides to six **hiking trails**. At the time of writing, all these guides were being translated into English.

Park-run stables in França offer **horse riding**, including guides and lessons (per hour/day from €10/40). You must reserve with the park offices.

If you come in summer, you can always cool off in the park's plentiful if chilly rivers and streams.

For other adventure activities, including climbing, kayaking and archery, contact **Montesinho Aventura** (☎ 273 326 080; montesinhoaventura@mac.com; Rua do Meio – Montesinho) in Bragança.

Sleeping & Eating

For a more complete list of sleeping options in the area, pick up a free *Turismo no Espaço Rural* booklet from Bragança's tourist office.

EASTERN PARK

Parque de Campismo do Sabor (☎ 273 331 535; N103-7 Estrada de Rabal; adult/car €1.50/2, tent €2-2.50; ⏲ May-Sep) Bragança's flat, featureless but shady and quiet municipal camping ground is 6km north of Bragança by the Rio Sabor. Facilities include bikes for hire, a café and a *minimercado*. From Bragança take STUB bus Linha 7.

Rio de Onor has set up a bare-bones **camping ground** (⏲ Apr-Sep) off the main road just as you arrive in town. Inquire at the town's café (across the Rio de Onor) for the town 'presidente' to negotiate your stay. From Bragança take STUB bus Linha 5 (€1.10, two daily).

TRÁS-OS-MONTES

KINDNESS OF STRANGERS *Robert Landon*

The people of Portugal are, in my book, the least ego-driven in Europe. That is not to say they're saints immune to concerns of status or always perfectly patient or generous. However, they value amiability above all things, and since 'attitude' is an impediment to this, it's considered not a show of power but very poor form. Travels in Portugal's former colonies have only confirmed this impression. Brazil vs Argentina, Guinea-Bissau vs Senegal, Macau vs Hong Kong – every time, the former Portuguese colony come out on top, at least in terms of easy sociability.

In the hills of the Parque Natural de Montesinho, I encountered the logical extension of my theory. As I stepped out of my car in a town whose main road had only recently been paved, an old man greeted me and asked what I was doing in his town. 'What business is it of his?' I thought. 'Why is he trying to make me feel unwelcome?' Within half an hour, I was, happily, proven so very wrong as he poured me glasses of port, then homemade cherry hooch (it was April and the hills all around us were in high bloom with next year's batch). His wife arrived, scythe in hand, and encouraged me to take pictures of her goats. 'They're so beautiful,' she said. At one point, she pointed at her wrist, where there was no watch. 'We don't have to worry about that here'.

As we stood there together, it dawned on me that this man had asked what I was doing not to mark his territory (as would have been the case in my country) but merely so he could help me find whatever it was that I'd been seeking. I'd had no idea that what I wanted above all was simply to spend this moment with him and his wife and then his neighbours who, as the shadows lengthened, were returning from their fields and soon joining us with their hoes and staffs, pleased to have a stranger among them.

There are a number of self-catering studios in stone cottages in the village of Montesinho. Note that rooms book up in July and August.

Café Montesinho (☎ 273 919 219, 936 272 876; Montesinho; up to 4 people €50) Serving snacks and drinks, Café Montesinho also rents an upstairs two-bedroom apartment with a pleasant veranda overlooking the village. The kind couple in charge can also fix you meals for an extra fee.

Dona Maria Rita (☎ 273 919 229; Montesinho; 2/4 people €35/60; P) This place has a few cosy rooms and a kitchen complete with an old stone oven, plus a tiny but charming cottage at the edge of the village.

Senhor Antero Pires (☎ 273 919 248; Montesinho; d with/without kitchen from €60/40) This place features a handful of rooms.

A Lagosta Perdida (☎ 273 919 031; www.lagostaperdida.com; Montesinho; d incl breakfast & dinner €90; P) For a little more luxury, the delightful A Lagosta Perdida, run by an Anglo-Dutch couple, offers tasteful en-suite rooms, a heated pool and a vegetarian-friendly kitchen, all in a lovingly restored schist farmhouse. There is no bus service to Montesinho. A taxi from Bragança to Montesinho will cost under €20.

Dom Roberto (☎ 273 302 510; www.amontesinho.pt; Gimonde; mains around €15; lunch & dinner) In the town of Gimonde, on the southern border of the park just east of Bragança, this award-winning and widely admired restaurant seeks out the best local ingredients and serves them up in a charmingly rustic dining room. Roberto also rents out three handsomely restored cottages, all with en-suite rooms (doubles €45), air-conditioning and shared kitchen privileges.

In Rio de Onor, there is a little café where you can get snacks and drinks. You can also ask here about the possibility of renting rooms in town.

WESTERN PARK

Parque de Campismo Cepo Verde (☎ 273 999 37… adult/tent/car €3/1.80/1.80; Apr-Sep) This medium-sized rural facility is 12km west of Bragança near the village of Gondesende and comes equipped with a café, shade and pool. STUB bus Linha 4 to/from Bragança passes near the site.

Abrigo de Montanha da Senhora da Hera (☎ 27… 999 414; Cova da Lua; d €50; Feb-Dec; P) In Cova da Lua, this modern, simple inn serves breakfast and has a pool to cool off in. There's also a little restaurant where, with advance notice you can get simple meals including soup, main, wine and coffee for €6.

Casa dos Marrões (☎ 273 999 550; www.casadosmarroes.com; Vilarinho; d incl breakfast €50; P ✕) Just up the road in Vilarinho and easily the most tasteful of the self-catering options, with beamed ceilings and exposed-stone wall.

The tiny schist village of Gondesende on the park's southern border has two self-catering, converted schist cottage options: **Casa da Bica** (☎ 273 999 454; www.bragancanet.pt/casadabica; d €40) and the more charming **Casa do Passal** (☎ 273 323 506; www.casadopassal.no.sapo.pt; Gondesende; up to 4 people €80).

Just north in Espinhosela, **Casa d'Ó Poço** (☎ 273 325 135; d €50) offers similar digs. STUB bus Linha 4 serves both towns.

Moimenta has a café-snack bar where you can ask about accommodations.

Note that at the time of writing there was no bus service to Cova da Lua, Vilarinho or Moimenta.

Getting Around

Exploring the park is difficult without a car, a bike or sturdy feet. The park's new map clearly indicates which roads are paved – unpaved roads can be dicey both during and after rains.

Only parts of the park are served by STUB, Bragança's municipal bus company. However, there is more daily service than in the past. The tourist office in Bragança supplies updated schedules. Each trip costs €1.10 and most take 30 minutes or less.

MIRANDELA

pop 10,700 / elevation 270m

Sitting in the centre of Trás-os-Montes' agricultural heartland, Mirandela is a down-to-business market town and transport junction. As a tourist you're most likely to scoot through en route to/from the Alto Douro via the lovely, narrow-gauge Linha da Tua (p450). But consider taking a quick stroll beside the Rio Tua to see its remarkable, flower-bedecked medieval bridge, then stop to admire shop windows hung with the region's renowned sausages and smoked hams.

Orientation

Rua Dom Afonso III runs in front of the newly combined train and bus stations. Take it to the right, then right again (north) along the river, to the town's medieval bridge and an adjacent new one. By the old bridge you can either carry on along Rua da República to the turismo and market (about 800m from the train station), or turn right and uphill on Rua Dom Manuel I to the *câmara municipal* and the old town.

Information

District hospital (☎ 278 260 500; Avenida Nossa Senhora do Amparo) Just across the old bridge.

Espaço Internet (☎ 278 261 924; Mercado Municipal, 1st fl; 9am-7pm Mon-Fri, to 1pm Sat) Free internet; bring a photocopy of your ID.

Police station (☎ 278 265 814; Praça 5 de Outubro) Four blocks north of the post office.

Post office (☎ 278 200 450; Rua Dom Manuel I; 8.30am-12.30pm & 1.30-6pm Mon-Fri) Just below the *câmara municipal*.

Turismo (☎ 278 203 143; Praça de Cocheira; 9.30am-12.30pm & 2-6pm Mon-Fri, 9.30am-1pm Sat) Just off Rua da República near the *mercado municipal*.

Sights

The medieval, 15th-century **Ponte Românica** (Romanesque bridge), featuring 20 uniquely proportioned arches, has been put out to pasture as Portugal's most elegant footbridge.

Old Mirandela is centred on the *câmara municipal*, in the splendiferous **Palácio dos Távoras** (Praça do Município), built in the 17th century for António Luiz de Távora, patron of one of northeast Portugal's powerful aristocratic families. The adjacent Praça de Outubro has a church and several palaces from the same period.

Sleeping

Parque de Campismo des Três Rios (☎ 278 263 177; Maravilha; adult/tent/car €3.50/3/3, 2-/4-person bungalows €50/65;) This flat, shady, riverside camping ground is 3km north of the centre on the N15. It has a restaurant and *minimercado*.

Pensão Praia (☎ 278 262 497; Largo 1 de Janeiro 6; s/d from €15/25) This creaky old place near the new bridge has small, rickety rooms (mostly with shared bathroom) around a skylit atrium. Some rooms have French windows facing a small square, though these can be noisy. No breakfast.

Hotel Mira-Tua (☎ 278 200 140; fax 278 200 143; Rua da República 42; d incl breakfast €50; ✕) This modern '70s hotel has smallish (but comfortable), carpeted midrange rooms – they've seen some wear but are kept in good trim. A few have verandas, although these overlook a busy street.

TRÁS-OS-MONTES

 Book accommodation online at lonelyplanet.com

Hotel Dom Dinis (☎ 278 260 100; www.hoteis-arco.com; Avenida Nossa Senhora do Amparo; s €69, d from €84; P ⊠ ✱ □ ☎) Oversized and out of place, this charmless but comfortable business hotel sits right at the far end of the medieval bridge. The rooms may be bland but they're huge, many sporting balconies and fine views of the bridge and river.

Eating

Lots of photogenic delicatessens sell the local speciality, *alheira de Mirandela*, a smokey, garlicky sausage of poultry or game. Also keep an eye out for fresh fish dishes from the Rio Tua.

Pizzaria Diablo (Rua Vasco da Gama; mains €8-12.50; ⏲ lunch & dinner Tue-Sun) Just uphill from the train station on the right, this anonymous-looking pizzeria serves excellent, piping-hot pizza straight from the wood-burning oven. It's a great break from sometimes heavy Portuguese fare.

Flor de Sal (☎ 912 583 982; Parque de José Gama; mains around €15; ⏲ lunch & dinner) Across the river and just next to the new bridge, this new, upmarket restaurant is a sleek take on the schist cottage. It's also won high praise for its creative, beautifully presented regional dishes. And the riverside terrace is a fine place to while away an afternoon or evening with a cool drink.

The *mercado municipal* hums along every morning except Sunday, trailing off into the afternoon.

Getting There & Away

BUS

Rede Expressos (☎ 278 265 805) and **Santos/Rodonorte** (☎ 278 262 541) buses go to Bragança (around €5.80, one hour) and to Vila Real (€5.50, one hour), with Rede Expressos continuing on to Porto (€9.20, 2½ hours).

Santos/Rodonorte buses also head to Miranda do Douro from Monday to Friday (€7.60, 2½ hours).

TRAIN

From Mirandela, two daily trains take the slow and scenic, narrow-gauge Linha da Tua down to Tua (€4.80, 1½ hours) in the Douro valley; check at the turismo, the station or www.cp.pt for current schedules. The journey to Porto (€14, 4½ hours, twice daily) requires a change of trains at Tua and possibly Peso da Régua.

MIRANDA DO DOURO

pop 2000 / elevation 560m

Looming above a spectacular river gorge that also serves as the border with Spain, Miranda do Douro is a classic frontier town with fortified walls that testify to the threat Spain long posed. Besides beautiful canyon views, the old town is handsome in its own right, with ruins of a medieval castle watching over a charming cluster of whitewashed buildings and cobbled lanes.

The town's beautifully hulking, 16th-century church may seem all out of proportion to the rest of the town, but it once served as cathedral for the entire region. And don't miss the ethnographic museum, which sheds light on the region's border culture, including ancient rites such as the 'stick dancing' of the *pauliteiros* (p452).

It's possible to see everything in a couple of hours, but the vagaries of public transport make it almost essential for nondrivers to stay longer. Avoid Mondays, when both the museum and the cathedral are shut.

History

Miranda was a vital bulwark during Portugal's first centuries of independence, and the Castilians had to be chucked out at least twice: in the early days by Dom João I, and again in 1710 during the Wars of the Spanish Succession. In 1545, perhaps as a snub to the increasingly powerful House of Bragança, a diocese was created here – hence the oversized cathedral.

During a siege by French and Spanish troops in 1762, the castle's powder magazine exploded, pulverising most of the castle and killing some 400 people. Twenty years later, shattered Miranda lost its diocese to Bragança. No one paid much attention to Miranda again until the nearby dam was built on the Douro in the 1950s.

Orientation

Buses stop just past Largo do Menino Jesus da Cartolina, a roundabout that roughly divides the old and new town. The turismo is just off the roundabout in a large, glass kiosk.

Uphill (southwest) from the roundabout past the old walls and castle ruins, are the old town and what was once the citadel. The main axis is Rua da Alfândega (also called Rua Mouzinho da Albuquerque), which runs into central Praça de Dom João III and, a little further on, Largo da Sé and the cathedral.

SPEAKING MIRANDÊS

France has Provençal, Britain has Welsh and Scottish, and Italy has dozens of distinct regional dialects. Portugal, by contrast, is one of Europe's most linguistically monolithic countries, thanks both to its long-stable borders (unchanged since 13th century) and the fact that it was conquered and consolidated within a very short period of time (less than 200 years).

The region around Miranda is a significant exception. Because of its proximity to Spain and long isolation from the rest of Portugal, the towns and villages around Miranda do Douro still speak what linguists have now recognised as an entirely distinct language. Closely related to Astur-Leonese – the regional language of the adjacent Spanish province – Mirandês is in fact closer to Iberian Latin, the language spoken during the Roman period, than it is to either Portuguese or Spanish.

While Mirandês has largely died out in the city of Miranda do Douro itself, it's still the first language of some 10,000 people in the surrounding villages. The Portuguese government officially recognised it as a second language in 1998, and increasingly the region's road signs are bilingual.

In 1882 Portuguese linguist José Leite de Vasconcelos described Mirandês as 'the language of the farms, of work, of home and love'. The same is true today.

Information

There are plans to open a free internet facility in the new bus station just past Largo do Menino Jesus da Cartolina.

Parque Natural do Douro Internacional office (☎/fax 273 431 457; Palácio da Justiça, Rua do Convento; 🕑 9am-12.30pm & 2-5.30pm Mon-Fri) Around the block from the cathedral and across a baroque church that has been converted into a public library.

Post office (Largo da Sé; 🕑 9am-12.30pm & 2-5.30pm Mon-Fri)

Turismo (☎ 273 430 025; Largo do Menino Jesus da Cartolina; 🕑 9am-12.30pm & 2-5.30pm Mon-Sat, to 7pm Jul-Aug)

Sights & Activities

MUSEU DE TERRA DE MIRANDA

In a handsome, 17th-century building and former city hall, this modest **museum** (☎ 273 431 164; www.ipmuseus.pt; Praça de Dom João III; adult/youth 14-25/senior €1.50/0.75/0.75, 9.30-12.30pm Sun free; 🕑 9.30am-12.30pm & 2-6pm Wed-Sun, 2.30-6pm Tue Apr-Oct; 9am-12.30pm & 2-5.30pm Wed-Sun, 2-5.30pm Tue Nov-Mar) houses a fascinating collection of local artefacts: pots and pans, local textiles and clothing, musical instruments and (almost) tribal masks. It may be laid out like a school project, but the museum sheds light on a unique culture that has preserved millennial traditions into the 21st century.

OLD TOWN

The back streets in the old town hide some dignified 15th-century **façades** on Rua da Costanilha (which runs west off Praça Dom João III) and a **Gothic gate** at the end of it.

Inside the right transept of the handsomely severe 16th-century **sé** (cathedral; admission free), look for the doll-like Menino Jesus da Cartolinha, a Christ child in a becoming top hat whose wardrobe rivals Imelda Marcos', thanks to deft local devotees. It's open the same hours as the Museu de Terra de Miranda.

BARRAGEM DE MIRANDA & RIVER CRUISES

A road crawls across this 80m-high dam about 1km east of town, and on to Zamora, 55km away in Spain. Even dammed, the gorge is dramatic.

You can take a one-hour boat trip through the gorge with **Europarques** (☎ 273 432 396; per person €12; 🕑 4pm Mon-Fri, 11am & 4pm Sat & Sun). Boats leave from beside the dam on the Portuguese side. Outside August, call in advance to check that there are enough passengers (minimum 20). In August there are 11am trips during the week as well.

Sleeping

Parque de Campismo de Santa Luzia (☎ 273 431 273; Rua do Parque de Campismo; adult/car/tent €1.70/2.25/2.25; 🕑 Jun-Sep) This modest municipal camp site is at the end of a residential street, 1.8km west of Largo da Moagem across the Rio Fresno.

Pensão Vista Bela (☎/fax 273 431 054; Rua do Mercado 63; d incl breakfast from €35) Spotless if unspectacular rooms in a modern building with cork-lined floors in the new town; rooms tend to be gloomy but some have terrific views over the gorge.

TRÁS-OS-MONTES

THE HILLS ARE ALIVE: STRANGE WAYS IN TRÁS-OS-MONTES

For centuries, the remoteness of Trás-os-Montes has insulated it from central authority, helping its people preserve nonconforming ways that sometimes still raise eyebrows in other parts of Portugal.

A number of licentious – and blatantly pagan – traditions still survive in the countryside. Witness the antics of the Caretos of Podence (near Macedo de Cavaleiros) – gangs of young men in *caretos* (leering masks) and vividly striped costumes who invade the town centre, bent on cheerfully humiliating everyone in sight. Prime targets are young women, at whom they thrust their hips and wave the cowbells hanging from their belts. Similar figures are to be seen in Varge, in the Parque Natural de Montesinho.

Saturnalian high jinks also take place in many villages around Christmas or Twelfth Night during the so-called Festa dos Rapazes (Festival of the Lads), when unmarried boys over 16 light all-night bonfires and rampage around in robes of rags and masks of brass or wood. Unchristian indeed!

Then there are the *pauliteiros* (stick dancers) of the Miranda do Douro region, who look and dance very much like England's Morris dancers. Local men deck themselves out in kilts and smocks, black waistcoats, bright flapping shawls, and black hats covered in flowers and ribbons, and do a rhythmic dance to the complex clacking of *paulitos* (short wooden sticks) – a practice that likely survives from Celtic times. The best time to see *pauliteiros* in Miranda is during the Festas de Santa Bárbara (also called Festas da Cidade, or City Festival) on the third weekend in August.

Finally, there are the region's so-called crypto-Jews. During the inquisition, Jews from Spain and Portugal found that they could evade ecclesiastical authorities here. Many families secretly observed Jewish practices – often without realising that they were in fact Jewish – well into the 20th century (see p349).

Pensão Santa Cruz (☎ 273 431 374; Rua Abade de Baçal 61; s/d incl breakfast €20/35; ☒) In the old town off the *largo* (small square) by the castle ruins, this family-run spot has primly pretty little rooms with new furnishings, recently refitted bathrooms and a small but impressive collection of soft-focus kitty paintings.

Hotel Turismo (☎ 273 438 030; fax 273 438 031; Rua 1 de Maio 5; s/d €25/40; ☒) With common areas that glisten with black granite, this newer place opposite the turismo offers large, spotless rooms with cable TV and great marble bathrooms. Front rooms have large windows with views across to the castle ruins.

Estalagem Santa Catarina (☎ 273 431 005; www.estalagemsantacatarina.pt; Largo da Pousada; d from €102; P ☒ ☐) Every guest gets a private veranda with spectacular views of the gorge at this luxurious, modern hotel perched on the canyon's edge. Rooms are a handsome mix of traditional and contemporary, with hardwood floors and large marble bathrooms. The restaurant (mains €12 to €17) is the most upmarket in town.

Eating

Restaurante-Pizzeria O Moinho (☎ 273 431 116; Rua do Mercado 47d; individual pizza from €4, mains €7-10; ⏲ lunch & dinner) New-town spot serving up glorious Douro views plus a large selection of pizzas, salads and Portuguese standards.

Restaurante São Pedro (☎ 273 431 321; Rua Mouzinho de Albuquerque; mains €6-10; ⏲ lunch & dinner; ☒) This spacious restaurant, just in from the main old-town gate, serves up a fine *posta á São Pedro* – delicious grilled veal steak dressed with garlic and olive oil. The €12.50 tourist menu comes with soup, main, dessert and wine.

Capa d'Honras (☎ 273 432 699; Travessa do Castelo 1; mains €10-15; ⏲ lunch & dinner; ☒) Named after the sinister-looking cape that is traditional to the region, this more upmarket place serves local specialities like *posta* (veal steak) as well as very good *bacalhau*.

Drinking

Atalaia Bar (☎ 919 029 545; Largo do Castelo; ⏲ 1.30pm-4am Mon-Sat, 3pm-1am Sun) Miranda's neon-lit old-school disco serves up pop and dance standards.

Bar Rochedo (☎ 912 184 311; ⏲ 1pm-4am) This trendy new video bar becomes a makeshift disco on Saturday and Sunday after midnight.

Getting There & Around

Santos/Rodonorte (☎ 273 432 667) has weekday service to Bragança (€5.90, 1¾ hours), Moga douro (€3.50, 50 minutes), and Vila Nova de Foz Côa (€6.40, 2¼ hours) via the train station at Pocinho (€6.90, two hours). Santos also goes via Mogadouro to Mirandela (€7.60, 2½ hours), Vila Real (€9.20, 3¼ hours) and Porto (€10.80, five hours) daily except Saturday.

By car, the quickest road from Bragança is the N218 and N218-2, a winding 80km trip. The 80km route (N216/N221) from Macedo de Cavaleiros via Mogadouro is one of the loveliest – and curviest – in Portugal. It crosses a *planalto* (high plain) dotted with olive, almond and chestnut groves, with a dramatic descent into the Rio Sabor valley.

Look for parking around Largo do Menino Jesus da Cartolina.

PARQUE NATURAL DO DOURO INTERNACIONAL

Tucked into Portugal's far northeast corner, this 852-sq-km, Chile-shaped park runs for 120km along the Rio Douro and the monumental canyon it has carved along the border with Spain. The canyon's towering, granite cliffs are the habitat for several threatened bird species, including black storks, Egyptian vultures, griffon vultures, peregrine falcons, golden eagles and Bonelli's eagles.

The human habitat is equally fragile. In the undulating plains that run right up to the canyon lip, there are some 35 villages, many still inhabited by descendents of banished medieval convicts as well as Jews fleeing the Inquisition. The region's isolation has enabled its people to preserve even more ancient roots, such as the Celtic *dança dos paulitos* (opposite). And many villagers still speak Mirandês, a language distinct from both Spanish and Portuguese that linguists believe descends directly from Iberian Latin (p451).

As you move south along the river, the terrain gains a distinctly Mediterranean air, with rolling orchards of olives and chestnuts and, in the southernmost reaches, land demarcated for port-wine grapes.

Orientation & Information

The park's headquarters are in **Mogadouro** (☎ 279 340 030; pndi@icn.pt; Rua de Santa Marinha 4; 🕑 9am-12.30pm & 2-5.30pm Mon-Fri) with smaller park offices in **Miranda do Douro** (☎/fax 273 431 457; Palácio da Justiça, Rua do Convento), **Figueira de Castelo Rodrigo** (☎ 271 313 382; Rua Artur Costa 1) and **Freixo de Espada à Cinta** (☎ 279 658 130; Largo do Outeiro).

Offices offer a detailed park map (€3.40), four leaflets (€0.50) on nature trails within the park, and a Portuguese-language booklet on the Egyptian vulture (€2.50).

Miranda do Douro and Mogadouro are the best places from which to explore the park.

Sights & Activities

There are four marked **hiking** trails in the park. One of the most convenient – and most beautiful – is an 18km loop from Miranda do Douro that includes striking vistas of the river at São Joao. There is also the multiday, 62km trail that travels for much of the length of the park. In addition there are sturdy **viewing platforms** at (north to south, with the nearest village in parentheses): São João das Arribas (Aldeia Nova), Fraga do Puio (Picote), Carrascalinho (Fornos), Penedo Durão (Poiares) and Santo André (Almofala).

In Miranda do Douro you can also take an hour-long cruise along the Douro (p451).

Based in Torre de Moncorvo, **Sabor Douro e Aventura** (☎ 279 258 270; www.sabordouro.com) offers guided hikes as well as canoeing and rafting.

Sleeping & Eating

Miranda do Douro is the most attractive base for the park.

Restaurante-Residencial A Lareira (☎ 279 342 363; Avenida Nossa Senhora do Caminho 58, Mogadouro; s/d €17.50/30) This place has small, spotless, well-equipped rooms that are excellent value. The downstairs restaurant (mains €7 to €12) offers outstanding local beef and veal grilled on an open fireplace by the French-trained proprietor. Warmly recommended.

Solar dos Marcos (☎ 279 570 010; www.solar-dos-marcos.com; Rua Santa Cruz, Mogadouro; d €75; P) About 12km northeast of Mogadouro in the ramshackle village of Bemposta, this place is the most upmarket option in the region. The reception is in an 18th-century manor house, while the comfortable rooms are in a modern annexe at the back.

Getting There & Around

There is a regular bus service to Miranda do Douro and Mogadouro via **Santos/Rodonorte** (www.rodonorte.pt). However, public transport to villages is extremely limited, mostly designed to serve school children. Schedules change, so it's best to check with the park offices or the turismo in Miranda do Douro for current schedule information.

TRÁS-OS-MONTES

Directory

CONTENTS

ACCOMMODATION

There's an excellent range of good-value, inviting accommodation in Portugal. Budget places provide some of Europe's cheapest rooms, while you'll find atmospheric, charming, peaceful accommodation in farms, palaces, castles, mansions and rustic town houses – usually giving incredibly good mileage for your euro.

In tourist resorts, prices rise and fall with the seasons. July to mid-September are firmly high season (book ahead); May to June and mid-September to October are midseason; and other times low season, when you can get some really good deals. Outside the resorts, prices don't vary much.

Note that in some tourist areas, there are four or five different prices used throughout the year. In the big Algarve resorts, you'll pay the highest premium from mid-July to the end of August, with slightly lower prices from June to mid-July and all of September, and substantially less (as much as 50% less) if you travel between November and April. For example, a room that's listed as €120 in July, may cost €160 in August, €100 in June and September, €85 in May and October and €70 the rest of the year. Note that a handful of places close in the winter.

We list July prices throughout this book. Listings are in order from least to most expensive (budget to top end), starting with bare-bones camping grounds and ending with glammy *pousadas* (upmarket inns); rooms are en suite unless otherwise indicated.

We categorise hotels or guesthouses costing less than €40 for a double room as budget accommodation, and include camping grounds and hostels in this category. In some budget places, you might have to share a bathroom.

In the middle range, a double room runs from €40 to €80. For this you'll almost always get an en-suite bathroom, TV (sometimes satellite), often air conditioning and telephone.

In the top end of the lodging category you'll pay anywhere from €80 to €300, with the odd stratospheric place where you can chill by the pool with visiting royals or football stars.

We list rack rates for midrange and top-end places in this book, but often you won't be charged the full whack – ask about special deals and packages. The websites on p20 also sometimes feature special offers. Most *pousadas* are cheaper during the week; they have lots of discount deals and prices.

Your bargaining power depends on what season it is and how much choice you have. If it's low season or echoingly empty, people will usually drop prices without you even needing to ask. If you plan to stay more than a few days, it's always worth inquiring whether lower rates are available for longer stays. If you're looking for somewhere cheaper than the room you have been shown just say so; frequently the management will show you the cheaper rooms they previously forgot to mention.

Turismos (tourist offices) hold lists of accommodation and *quartos* (private rooms), but they overlook anywhere not registered with them – which can mean the cheapest options. The government grades accommodation with a star system that's bewildering and best ignored.

Some good sites for sizing up charismatic accommodation options are www.manor-houses.com or www.innsofportugal.com.

Camping & Caravan Parks

Camping is massive in Portugal, with countless excellent camping grounds, often in good locations and near beaches. Prices usually range from about €3 to €4 per adult, around €4 per tent and €3 to €4 per car.

The swishest places are run by **Orbitur** (www.orbitur.pt) but there are lots of other good companies, such as **Inatel** (www.inatel.pt). Most towns have municipal sites, which vary in quality.

To be a really happy camper, or at least a well-informed one, pick up the **Roteiro Campista** (www.roteiro-campista.pt; €5.50) sold at *turismos* and bookshops. It has details of most Portuguese camping grounds with maps and directions.

The Camping Card International (CCI) can be presented instead of your passport at camping grounds affiliated to the Federation Internationale de Camping et de Caravanning (FICC). It guarantees third-party insurance for any damage you may cause and can be good for discounts.

Sometimes certain camp sites run by local camping clubs may be used by foreigners *only* if they have a CCI, so don't forget to pick one up before you travel.

The CCI is available to members of most national automobile clubs, except those in the USA; the RAC in the UK charges members £6.50 for a card. It is also issued by FICC affiliates such as the UK's **Camping & Caravanning Club** (☎ 0845 130 7632; www.campingandcaravanningclub.co.uk) and the **Federação de Campismo e Montanhismo de Portugal** (Map pp84-5; ☎ 218 126 890; www.fcmportugal.com in Portuguese; Avenida Coronel Eduardo Galhardo 24D, 1199-007 Lisbon).

Guesthouses

Government-graded guesthouses are small-scale budget or midrange accommodation, with the personal feel that can be lacking in larger hotels. The best ones are often better than the cheapest hotels. High-season *pensão* (guest-house) rates are €35 to €65 for a double.

Residenciais may be more expensive, and usually include breakfast. The title *residenciais* means the guesthouse hasn't received the official approval that a *pensão* has, but this doesn't mean that it's a bad place to stay. *Hospedarias* and *casas de hóspedes* are usually cheaper, with shared bathrooms.

PRACTICALITIES

- Portugal uses the metric system for weights and measures. (See the inside front cover for a metric conversions chart.) Decimals are indicated by commas, thousands by points.
- The electrical current is 220V, 50HZ. Plugs are rounded with two prongs (sometimes with a third middle prong), as used elsewhere in Continental Europe.
- Portugal uses the PAL video system, incompatible with both the French SECAM system and the North American NTSC system.
- Main newspapers include *Diário de Noticias, Público, Jornal de Noticias* and the tabloid best-seller *Correio da Manhã*.
- English-language media mostly comprises Algarve offerings: the *APN*, the *Portugal News* (www.the-news.net), *Algarve Resident* (www.portugalresident.com).
- TV channels include Rádio Televisão Portuguesa (RTP-1 and RTP-2), Sociedade Independente (SIC) and TV Independente (TV1), with RTP-2 providing the best selection of foreign films and world-news coverage. Other stations fill the airwaves with a mix of Portuguese and Brazilian soaps, game shows and dubbed or subtitled foreign movies.
- Radio stations consist of state-owned Rádiodifusão Portuguesa (RDP), which runs Antena 1, 2 and 3 and plays Portuguese broadcasts and evening music. For English-language radio there's the BBC World Service and Voice of America (VOA) or a few Algarve-based stations, such as Kiss.

Hostels

Portugal's 36 or so *pousadas da juventude* (youth hostels) are all affiliated with HI. Although the accommodation is basic, hostels offer excellent value and are often in lovely settings or historic buildings.

High-season beds cost €11 to €16. Most also offer bare doubles and some have small apartments. Bed linen and breakfast are included in the price. Many have kitchens, cafés and internet access, and some have swimming pools, such as those in Alcoutim and Portimão.

In summer you'll need to reserve, especially for doubles. Contact **Movijovem** (Map p90; ☎ 707 203 030; www.pousadasjuventude.pt; Avenida Duque d'Ávila 137, Lisbon).

If you don't have a Hostelling International (HI) card, you can get a guest card, which requires six stamps (€2 per time) – one from each hostel you stay at – after which you have paid for your membership.

Most hostels open 8am to midnight. Some (Almada, Braga, Bragança, Foz Côa, Foz do Cávado, Lagos, Lisbon, Porto and Viana do Castelo) are open 24 hours. Staff will usually let you stash your bags and return at check-in time (usually 8am to noon and 6pm to midnight).

Portugal has a small number of private hostels as well, which offer similar services at similar prices.

Pousadas

In 1942 the government started the **pousadas scheme** (☎ 218 442 001; www.pousadas.pt), turning castles, monasteries and palaces into luxurious hotels, roughly divided into rural and historic options. July prices range from €130 to €210; prices in August cost €10 to €15 more. You can pick up a comprehensive booklet listing all the *pousadas*, with photos, at any of the group. You may be able to take advantage of frequent and ongoing special offers, such as reduced prices for the over 60s, or for the 18 to 30s.

Private Rooms

In coastal resorts, mostly in summer, you can often rent a private room or *quarto* in a private house. These usually have a shared bathroom, and are cheap, clean and might remind you of a stay with an elderly aunt. If you're not approached by an eager owner or don't spot a sign (*se aluga quarto*), try the local *turismo* – they usually have a list. You will find that prices are generally from €25 to €35 per double.

Rental Accommodation

Plenty of villas and cottages are available for rent. The site www.chooseportugal.com lists hundreds of private houses and apartments for rent, with the majority found in the Algarve. You'll find characterful houses in the north on www.casasnocampo.net.

Turihab Properties

These charming properties are part of a government scheme, either Turismo de Habitação, Turismo Rural or Agroturismo, through which you can stay in a farmhouse, manor house, country estate or rustic cottage as the owner's guest.

Divided into historic, heritage or rustic categories, these properties provide some of the best bargains in Portugal. Though they are more expensive than some other options, you'll usually be staying in splendid surroundings. A high-season double ranges from €60 to €100. Many have swimming pools and usually include breakfast (often with fresh local produce).

Turismos keep detailed information of Turihab properties in the area. You can also look them up online at www.turihab.pt or www.solaresdeportugal.pt.

ACTIVITIES

In Portugal there are many ways to spend a sun-drenched afternoon. Surfing, biking, hiking, bird-watching and horse riding are among the best ways to enjoy the country's fine climate and geography. See p67 for details.

BUSINESS HOURS

Most shops open from 9.30am to noon and 3pm to 7pm. Many close Saturday afternoon (except at Christmas) and Sunday. Malls open around 10am to 10pm daily. Banks open from 8.30am to 3pm and government offices from 9am to noon and 2pm to 5pm or 5.30pm Monday to Friday. Post offices keep similar hours, though some may stay open at lunchtime. Museums usually close on Monday, and open from around 10am to 12.30pm and 2pm to 5pm or 6pm Tuesday to Saturday. If Monday is a holiday, they'll often close on the Tuesday too.

CHILDREN

The great thing about Portugal for children is its manageable size and the range of sights and activities on offer. There's so much to explore and to catch the imagination, even for those with very short attention spans.

The Algarve has to be the best kid-pleasing lestination in Portugal, with endless beaches, oos, water parks, horse riding and boat trips. Kids will also be happy in Lisbon and its outlying provinces. There are trams, puppet shows, huge aquarium, a toy museum, horse-drawn arriages, castles, parks and playgrounds.

As for fairy-tale places, Portugal has these in pades. Some children enjoy visiting churches, specially if they get to light a candle. They'll njoy the make-believe of the Knights Templar buildings at Almourol (p296) and Tomar p297), and can explore castles in Sintra (p129), Castelo de Vide (p247) and Elvas (p240).

Near Fátima, north of Lisbon, thrill the kids with the sight of dinosaur footprints; visit the xtraordinary Monumento Natural das Pegadas los Dinossáurios (p291) with huge dinosaur lents. Special kid-pitched tours are available.

In towns, hop-on hop-off tours are good for aving small legs, and miniature resort trains often cause more excitement than you would have thought possible.

Kids will like Portugal almost as much as hey like sweets, and they are welcome just about everywhere. They can even get literary: Nobel Prize winner José Saramago, the great Portuguese novelist, has written a charming children's fable *The Tale of the Unknown Island*, available in English. For an entertaining guide packed with information and tips, turn to Lonely Planet's *Travel with Children*.

Turismos can often recommend local childcare, and branches of the youth-network **Instituto Portuguese da Juventude** (IPJ; Map p90; ☎ 707 203 030; Avenida da Liberdade 194, Lisbon) sometimes advertise baby-sitting.

Several travel operators offer specially tailored family tours, including these UK-based outfits:

Cosmos (☎ 0870 44 35 285; www.cosmos-holidays.co.uk)

JMC (☎ 0870 750 5711; www.jmc.com)

Powder Byrne (☎ 020 8246 5300; www.powderbyrne.com)

CLIMATE CHARTS

Portugal has a warm and sunny climate, with mild winters. Summer temperatures in the Algarve can top 30°C, and the mercury climbs in the Alentejo and Alto Douro too, with temperatures recorded as high as 47°C in the Alentejo. In the northwest weather is milder and damper, so bring an umbrella. Up to 2000mm of rain can fall annually (the national average is 1100mm).

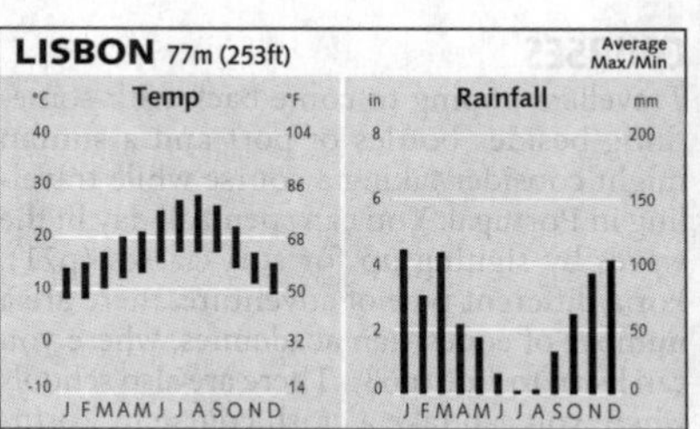

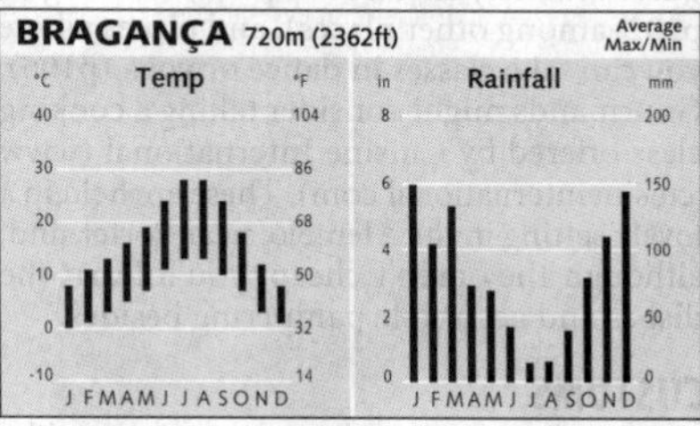

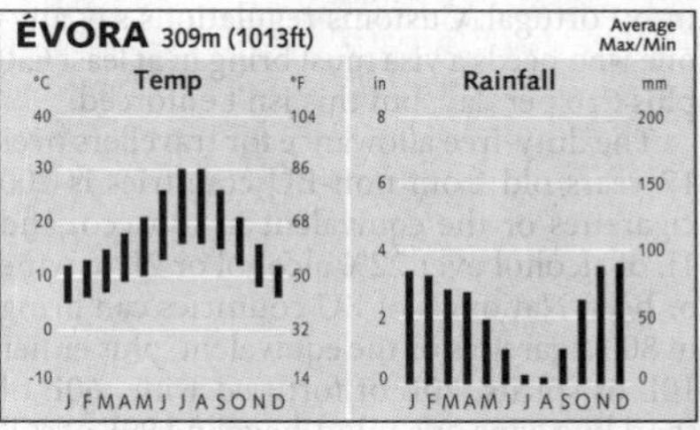

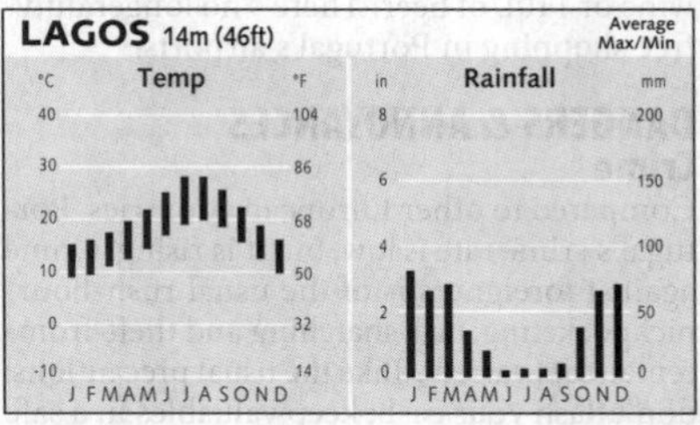

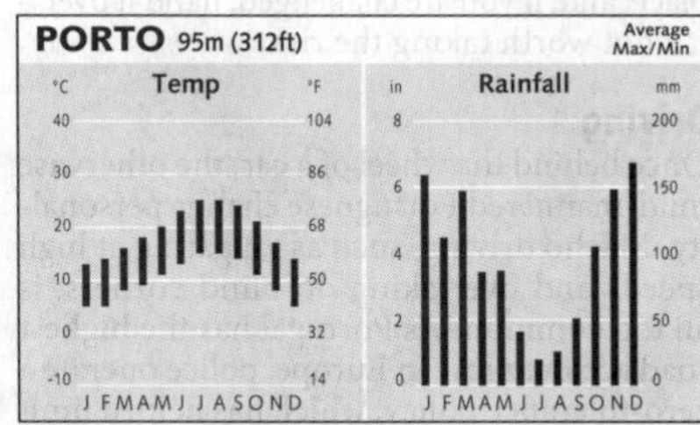

COURSES

Travellers hoping to come back with something besides bottles of port and a suntan might consider taking a course while travelling in Portugal. You can spend all day in the waves by signing up for surf classes (p71). For a different type of adventure, there are a number of equestrian academies, where you can learn to ride (p68). There are also schools where you can take a crash course in Portuguese (namely in Lisbon, p106, and Lagos, p202), among other places), and places where you can take classes in dance or yoga (p106). Gourmands might consider taking a cooking class offered by Cuisine International (www.cuisineinternational.com). These are held in a lovely setting in the Alentejo, near Portel, and, although they aren't cheap, you'll learn the dishes and get ample pampering besides.

CUSTOMS

You can bring as much currency as you like into Portugal. Customs regulations say anyone who needs a visa must bring in at least €50 plus €10 per day, but this isn't enforced.

The duty-free allowance for travellers over 17 years old from non-EU countries is 200 cigarettes or the equivalent in tobacco, and 1L of alcohol over 22% alcohol or 2L of wine or beer. Nationals of EU countries can bring in 800 cigarettes or the equivalent, plus either 10L of spirits, 20L of fortified wine, 60L of sparkling wine or a mind-boggling 90L of still wine or 110L of beer! There's no longer duty-free shopping in Portugal's airports.

DANGERS & ANNOYANCES

Crime

Compared to other European countries, Portugal's crime rate is low, but it is rising. Crime against foreigners is of the usual rush-hour-pickpocketing, bag-snatching and theft-from-rental-cars variety. Take the usual precautions: don't flash your cash; keep valuables in a safe place; and, if you are challenged, hand it over – it's not worth taking the risk.

Driving

Once behind the wheel of a car, the otherwise mild-mannered Portuguese change personality. Macho driving, such as tailgating at high speeds and overtaking on blind corners, is all too common. As Portugal has the highest road accident rate in Europe, police operate a zero-tolerance policy, which has helped limit the damage on formerly nightmare routes such as on the cheerfully named 'highway of death' from Salamanca in Spain.

Nightclub Violence

In the last decade or so, there have been some fatal attacks in Portugal nightclubs. In 1997 an arson attack in Amarante left 13 dead. Seven were killed in Lisbon's Luanda club in 2000 after tear-gas canisters were released. In March 2001 at Kremlin in Lisbon, three people opened fire after being refused entry. Although this sounds like a catalogue of incidents, in the main clubs are peaceful places.

Smoking

Smoking is prevalent in Portugal, and at the moment very few restaurants have nonsmoking sections; there are certainly none in any bars. Despite a recent poll showing that 90% of Portuguese support a smoking ban in public indoor areas – bars, restaurants and the workplace – the government has proven ineffective at introducing antismoking legislation.

DISCOUNT CARDS

Portugal's network *pousadas da juventude* (p456), is part of the HI network. An HI card from your hostelling association at home entitles you to the standard cheap rates.

A student card will get you reduced admission to almost all sights. Likewise, those over 65 with proof of age will save cash.

The Lisboa Card (p95) allows discounts or free admission to many attractions and free travel on public transport in Lisbon.

EMBASSIES & CONSULATES

Portuguese Embassies & Consulates

Portuguese embassies and consulates abroad include the following:

Australia Canberra (☎ 02-6290 1733; www.consulportugalsydney.org.au; 23 Culgoa Circuit, O'Malley, ACT 2606); Sydney (☎ 02-9262 2199; Level 9, 30 Clarence St, Sydney, NSW 2000)

Canada Ottawa (☎ 613-729 0883; www.embportugal-ottawa.org; 645 Island Park Drive, Ottawa, ON K1Y 0B8); Vancouver (☎ 604-688 6514; 700 West Pender St, Vancouver, BC V6C 1G8) Also in Montreal and Toronto.

France Paris (☎ 01 47 27 35 29; www.embaixada-portugal-fr.org; 3 rue de Noisiel, 75116 Paris); Lyon (☎ 04 78 17 34 40; 71 rue Crillon, 69458 Lyon) Also in Bayonne, Bordeaux, Marseille, Strasbourg and Toulouse.

Germany Berlin (☎ 030-590 06 35 00; Zimmerstrasse 56, 10117 Berlin); Düsseldorf (☎ 0211-13 87 80; Graf-Adolf-

Strasse 16, 4000 Düsseldorf) Also in Stuttgart, Frankfurt-am-Main and Hamburg.

Ireland Dublin (☎ 01-289 4416; Knock Sinna House, Knock Sinna, Fox Rock, Dublin 18)

Morocco Rabat (☎ 07-756 446; 5 rue Thami Lamdouar, Souissi, Rabat)

The Netherlands The Hague (☎ 070-363 02 17; ambportugal@wxs.nl; Bazarstraat 21, 2518 AG The Hague); Rotterdam (☎ 010-411 15 40; Willemskade 18, 3016 DL Rotterdam)

New Zealand Auckland (☎ 09-309 1454; daniel@silva.co.nz; PO Box 305, 33 Garfield St, Parnell, Auckland)

Spain Madrid (☎ 91 782 49 60; embaportugal@telefonica.net; Calle Pinar 1, 28006 Madrid); Barcelona (☎ 93 318 81 50; Ronda San Pedro 7, 08010 Barcelona) Also in Seville and Vigo.

UK London – Belgrave Sq (☎ 020-7235 5331; london@portembassy.co.uk; 11 Belgrave Sq, London SWIX 8PP); London – Brompton Rd (☎ 020-7581 8722; 62 Brompton Rd, London SW3 1BJ)

USA Washington DC (☎ 202-328 8610; www.portugal emb.org; 2125 Kalorama Rd NW, Washington DC 20008); New York (☎ 212-765 2980; Suite 801, 630 Fifth Ave, New York, NY 10111) Also in Boston & San Francisco.

Embassies & Consulates in Portugal

Your embassy or consulate is the best first stop in any emergency. Most can provide lists of reliable local doctors, lawyers and interpreters. If your money or documents have been stolen, your embassy might help you get a new passport or advise you on how to have funds transferred, but a free ticket home or a loan for onward travel is vastly unlikely. Most embassies no longer have mail-holding services or reading rooms with home newspapers. Foreign embassies and consulates in Portugal include the following:

Australia Lisbon (Map p90; ☎ 213 101 500; portugal.embassy.gov.au; 2nd fl, Avenida da Liberdade 200, 1250-147 Lisbon)

Canada Lisbon (Map p90; ☎ 213 164 600; lisbon@dfait-maeci.gc.ca; 3rd fl, Avenida da Liberdade 196, 1269-121 Lisbon); Faro (☎ 289 803 757; Rua Frei Lourenço de Santa Maria 1, 8000-352 Faro)

France Lisbon (Map p89; ☎ 213 939 100; ambafrance@hotmail.com; Rua de Santos-o-Velho 5, 1249-079 Lisbon); Porto (☎ 226 094 805; Rua Eugénio de Castro 352, 4100-225 Porto)

Germany Lisbon (Map p90; ☎ 218 810 210; embaixada.alemanha@clix.pt; Campo dos Mártires da Pátria 38, 1169-043 Lisbon); Porto (Map p358; ☎ 226 052 810; 6th fl, Avenida de França 20, 4050-275 Porto) Also in Faro.

Ireland (Map p89; ☎ 213 929 440; Rua da Imprensa, Estrela, 1200-684 Lisbon)

Morocco Lisbon (Map pp84-5; ☎ 213 010 842; Rua Alto do Duque 21, 1400-099 Lisbon)

The Netherlands Lisbon (Map p89; ☎ 213 914 900; nlgovlis@mail.telepac.pt; Avenida Infante Santo 43, 1399-011 Lisbon); Porto (☎/fax 222 080 061; Rua da Reboleira 7, 4050-492 Porto) Also in Faro.

New Zealand Lisbon (☎ 213 509 690; 9am-1pm Mon-Fri) There's no New Zealand embassy in Portugal. In emergencies, New Zealand citizens can call the honorary consul at this number. The nearest New Zealand embassy is Rome (☎ 06 441 71 71; nzemb.rom@flashnet.it).

Spain Lisbon (Map p90; ☎ 213 472 792; edu.lisb.es@mail.telepac.pt; Rua do Salitre 1, 1269-052 Lisbon); Porto (☎ 225 101 685; consulado.porto@oninet.pt; Rua de Dom João IV 341, 4000-302 Porto; also in Valença do Minho & Vila Real de Santo António)

UK Lisbon (Map p89; ☎ 213 961 191; Rua de São Bernardo 33, 1249-082 Lisbon); Porto (☎ 226 184 789; consular@oporto.mail.fco.gov.uk; Avenida da Boavista 3072, 4100-120 Porto) Also in Portimão.

USA Lisbon (Map p90; ☎ 217 273 300; www.american-embassy.pt; Avenida das Forças Armadas, 1600-081 Lisbon); Porto (☎ 226 172 384; Rua Marechal Saldanha 454, 4150-652 Porto)

FESTIVALS & EVENTS

As a Catholic country that likes to party, Portugal has some thrilling festivals and events, mostly centred on something religious, and which have often grown out of previously pagan events. Here are some of the best:

February/March

Carnaval Sequins, feather, floats – biggest in Loulé (p186), Nazaré (p280), Ovar and Viana do Castelo (p411).

March

Ovibeja Beja's huge Alentejan agricultural fair (p258).

March/April

Senhor Ecce Homo Braga's grand, pathos-packed Semana Santa (p398).

May

Fátima Romaris Huge pilgrimage to commemorate the apparition of the Virgin in 1917 (p289).

Festa das Cruzes In Barcelos, the folksy festival of the crosses is good for handicrafts and processions (p402).

June

Corpo de Deus Corpus Christi and time for big parties and processions in the north.

Feira Nacional da Agricultura Santarém shows its best bulls, in a livestock fair with lots of regional song and dance (p294).

Festa de Santo António Knees up for Lisbon's favourite saint (p107).
Festa de São João Porto (p368) and Braga (p397) go crazy for a week.

July

Festa dos Tabuleiros Bread-laden trays on virgins' heads in Tomar every four years (p299), including 2007.

August

Romaria e Festa da Nossa Senhora da Agonia Pilgrimage, parades, folk art and fireworks in Viana do Castelo (p411).
Festival do Sudoeste The Alentejan Glastonbury, near Zambujeira, with music (previous years have included Oasis and Fatboy Slim) and food stalls. Held in early August (p266).

September

Feiras Novas Fairs, folk and a vast riverside market on the banks of the Rio Lima, this Ponte de Lima bash dates back to the 12th century (p419).

October

Fátima Part two of the May festival.

November

Feira de São Martinho Horse parades, bullfights and hearty feasts in Golegá Ribatejo (p295.

FOOD

In this book, budget-designated places are those with snacks or mains costing less than €6, midrange costs around €6 to €12, and top end is about €12 and up. For more tasty nuggets, see p74.

GAY & LESBIAN TRAVELLERS

How out you can be depends on where you are in Portugal. In Lisbon, Porto and the Algarve, acceptance has increased, whereas in most other areas, same-sex couples would be met with incomprehension. In this conservative Catholic country, homosexuality is still outside the norm. And while homophobic violence is pretty much unknown, discrimination has been reported in schools and workplaces.

Lisbon has the country's best gay and lesbian network and nightlife (p121). Lisbon, Porto and Leiria hold Gay Pride marches, but outside these events the gay community keeps a discreet profile. When you go to a gay bar or club, you'll usually have to ring a doorbell for admission.

HOLIDAYS

Banks, offices, department stores and some shops close on the following public holidays. On New Year's Day, Easter Sunday, Labour Day and Christmas Day, even *turismos* close.

New Year's Day 1 January
Carnaval Tuesday February/March – the day before Ash Wednesday
Good Friday March/April
Liberty Day 25 April – celebrating 1974 revolution
Labour Day 1 May
Corpus Christi May/June – ninth Thursday after Easter
Portugal Day 10 June – also known as Camões and the Communities Day
Feast of the Assumption 15 August
Republic Day 5 October – commemorating 1910 declaration of Portuguese Republic
All Saints' Day 1 November
Independence Day 1 December – commemorating 1640 restoration of independence from Spain
Feast of the Immaculate Conception 8 December
Christmas Day 25 December

INSURANCE

Don't leave home without a travel-insurance policy to cover theft, loss and medical problems. You should get insurance for the worst-case scenario, for example, an accident or illness requiring hospitalisation and a flight home.

If you can't afford insurance, you certainly can't afford to deal with a medical emergency abroad. There are loads of policies available; the international policies handled by youth and student travel agencies are good value.

Check the small print, as some policies specifically exclude 'dangerous activities' such as scuba diving, motorcycling or even trekking. If these activities are in your sights, either find another policy or ask about an amendment (usually available for an extra premium) that includes them.

Make sure you keep all documentation for any claims later on. Some policies ask you to call back (reverse charges) to a centre in your home country where an immediate assessment of your problem is made.

Citizens of the EU are eligible for free emergency medical treatment if they have a European Health Insurance Card (EHIC), which replaces the no-longer valid E111 certificate. In the UK, you can apply for this card online (www.ehic.org.uk) or pick up an application at a post office.

INTERNET ACCESS

Free internet access is more and more prevalent in Portugal. Try local branches of the Instituto Português da Juventude (IPJ), some of which are attached to IPJ hostels; at the *biblioteca municipal* (library); or at a growing number of municipal **Espaços Internet** (www.espacosinternet.pt in Portuguese). Usually you have to show some ID and then get 30 minutes free time (unless there's no-one waiting). Cybercafés, common in cities and towns, charge from around €2 per hour. Some post offices have terminals for NetPost, an internet facility payable with a special card, but these are often out of order.

If you have your own laptop and a global modem, and your ISP offers global roaming, you may be able to log in from your hotel room, however, only midrange and top-end hotels will have room phone sockets. Most telephone sockets in Portugal are US (RJ-II); for those that aren't you'll need an adaptor. One problem is the faint beeps measuring calling time, which can interfere with a connection. The solution is an in-line filter. Such accessories are available from **Teleadapt** (www.teleadapt.com).

Wireless access is still a rarity in Portugal, though you will find wi-fi hotspots at Lisbon airport, a few high-end hotels and some McDonald's restaurants scattered around the country. For a complete list, visit www.wi-fihotspotlist.com.

LEGAL MATTERS

Fines for illegal parking are common. If you're parked illegally you'll be towed and will have to pay around €100 to get your car back. Be aware of local road rules, as fines for other transgressions will also be enforced.

Narcotic drugs were decriminalised in 2001 in an attempt to clear up the public-health problems among drug users, and to address the issue as a social rather than a criminal one. You may be brought before a commission and subject to fines or treatment if you are caught with up to 10 doses of a drug. Drug dealing is still a serious offence and suspects may be held for up to 18 months before coming to trial. Bail is at the court's discretion.

LEGAL AGES

- Drinking: no minimum age
- Driving: 17
- Sex (hetero/homosexual): 14/16

MAPS

Lonely Planet publishes the well-indexed, full-colour *Portugal Road Atlas* at 1:400,000.

Most current, though not indexed, is the 1:350,000 *Mapa das Estradas*, updated every June by the Automóvel Club de Portugal (p473). More or less equivalent is Michelin's 1:400,000 *Portugal, Madeira*, No 940.

Two government-mapping agencies exist: the military **Instituto Geográfico do Exército** (IGeoE; Army Geographic Institute; Map pp84-5; ☎ 218 520 063; www.igeoe.pt in Portuguese; Avenida Dr Alfredo Bensaúde, Lisbon), which is located in the middle of nowhere, 2km northwest of Gare do Oriente station; and the civilian **Instituto Geográfico Português** (IGP; Portuguese Geographic Institute; Map p90 ☎ 213 819 600; fax 213 819 699; Rua Artilharia Um 107, Lisbon). IGeoE publishes 1:25,000 topographic sheets covering the entire country, plus less useful 1:50,000 and 1:250,000 series, including *Portugal Continental Mapa de Estradas*, which is precise, but not always up to date. IGP's 1:50,000 maps tend to be more current, but lack the precision of the military publications. Both agencies sell maps from their Lisbon headquarters.

National and natural park offices usually have simple park maps, though these are of little use for trekking or cycling. Other local sources for topographic maps are noted in the text. The following offer a good range of maps:

Maps Worldwide (☎ 012 2570 7004, www.mapsworldwide.co.uk; Datum House, Lancaster Rd, Melksham, UK)

Omni Resources (☎ 336-227 8300, www.omnimap.com; 1004 South Mebane St, Burlington, NC, USA)

Stanfords (☎ 020-7836 1321, www.stanfords.co.uk; 12-14 Long Acre, Covent Garden, London, UK)

MONEY

Since 1 January 2002 Portugal has used the euro, along with Austria, Belgium, Finland, France, Germany, Greece, Ireland, Italy, Luxembourg, the Netherlands and Spain. Prices jumped, but the easy conversion (100 escudos equalled €0.50) made the changeover less painful than in other countries. Some people still talk in escudos.

Banks and bureaux de change are free to set their own rates and commissions, so a low commission might mean a skewed exchange rate.

ATMs & Credit Cards

The most convenient way to get your money is from an ATM. Most banks have a Multibanco ATM, complete with annoying animated graphics, accepting Visa, Access, Mastercard, Cirrus and so on. You just need your card and PIN. Your home bank will usually charge around 1.5% per transaction. But it's wise to have a back-up source of money; sometimes ATMs temporarily stop accepting a certain type of card, usually a hiatus lasting a day or so. You'll be asked for a six-digit PIN, but it still works fine if yours is only four digits.

Credit cards are accepted at smarter hotels and restaurants and in larger towns, but won't be any use to pay for things in the budget arena or in rural outposts.

Travellers Cheques

These are a safe way to carry money as they will be replaced if lost or stolen, but are less convenient than the card-in-machine method. Amex, Thomas Cook or Visa are most widely recognised. It's best to get cheques in euros, and keep a record of the ones you've cashed in case you do mislay them. However, although travellers cheques are easily exchanged, with better rates than for cash, they are poor value because commission is so high.

Tipping

If you're satisfied with the service, tip 5% to 10%. Bills at pricier restaurants may already include *serviço* (service charge). After a snack at a bar or café, some shrapnel is enough. Taxi drivers are not generally tipped, but 10% for good service would be appreciated.

POST

Post offices are called **CCT** (www.ctt.pt). *Correio normal* (ordinary mail) goes in the red letter boxes, *correio azul* (airmail) goes in the blue box. Postcards and letters up to 20g cost €0.75/0.60/0.34 outside Europe/within Europe/local. International *correio azul* costs €1.85 for a 20g letter. Post to Europe takes up to five working days, and the rest of the world up to seven. Economy mail (or surface airlift) is about a third cheaper, but takes a week or so longer.

You can send mail to poste restante in main post offices of cities and large towns.

Many post offices have NetPost for internet access, but the machines are frequently out of order. If they do work, it costs €2.50 per hour, with cards costing €5.50.

SHOPPING

Home of ceramics, port, wine, lace and crazy cockerel mascots, Portugal is a splendid place to shop, not least because it moves at a relaxed pace that's ideal for browsing and window-shopping. Its low prices also mean more gain for less pain.

Port, Wine & Food

Port is Portugal's best-known export, and is easy to find. To hunt it to its source, visit port wine lodges at Vila Nova de Gaia (p364), across the river from Porto, or pop into a supermarket where you'll find a good range. Lisbon, Porto and other cities have specialist shops. In Lisbon or Porto you can visit port-tasting places, then note down your favourite to buy later.

Buying wine is also popular, with some excellent drops at affordable prices. There's a wine route you can follow in the Alentejo (p224), visiting wineries, tasting and buying. Other areas to try are Estremadura and near Setúbal; Dão also has some excellent lodges where you can tour and taste.

Olive oil and honey are also good buys all over the country. Try Mértola and Serpa in Alentejo, or Parque Nacional da Peneda-Gerês in the Minho.

Linen, Cotton & Lace

Hand-embroidered linen and cotton, traditional costumes, and lacework (a speciality of coastal fishing towns) are sold at modest prices all over the country, but especially in seaside resorts such as Nazaré and Viana do Castelo. Guimarães has been famous for its linen since medieval times, so it must be doing something right. Castelo Branco is a hot spot for embroidered bed covers. Bobbin lace comes from Vila do Conde, Peniche and the eastern Algarve. There are also several speciality shops in Lisbon selling lacework and linen.

Music

Take home a tragic stoic soundtrack for those dramatic moments. Try the good speciality music shops, *turismos* and the *fado* museum (p98) in Lisbon. Most towns have a selection of small music shops, all of which will have some fado. To help you choose, see p47.

Ceramics

Portugal produces beautiful ceramics, from refined tiling to rustic bowls, all bursting with brilliant colours. See p123 for where to buy th best ceramics in the capital. Caldas da Rainha is a ceramics centre, with museums devoted to its masters, and many artisan workshops and shops. Also try São Pedro do Corval, with around 30 businesses producing brightly coloured rustic ceramics. Nearby, Reguengoz de Monsaraz has some cutting-edge and traditional ceramics at a local co-op, Tear (p232).

Estremoz in the Alentejo produces unique, charming figurines – mainly saints with flowing robes that look like they've been caught in a wind machine. The town has several small shops and a wonderful workshop selling these (and other crafts), as well as a fantastically thriving Saturday market where you can combine your figurine-shopping with purchasing a goat.

Rugs, Jewellery & Leather

Portugal's finest carpets are produced in Arraiolos in the Alentejo; they are hand-stitched and prices reflect this. More rustic *mantas* (woollen rugs and blankets) are a speciality of Regenguoz de Monsaraz and Mértola in the Alentejo.

In the Algarve, Loulé's Saturday market (p186) is a great place to buy all sorts of crafts, from brass to basketware to leather goods and every sort of souvenir.

The exquisite gold and silver filigree jewellery of the Porto area is expensive, but good value. Leather goods, especially shoes and bags, are also good buys.

Icons

If you're interested in religious icons or out-and-out kitsch, Fátima rivals Disney in the merchandise stakes, with candles, miniature saints and all sort of shepherds-and-vision tableaux.

Other Handicrafts

Rush, palm and wicker basketwork pieces are appealing and cheap. They're best found in municipal markets all over the country. Trás-os-Montes is good for woven handicrafts and tapestries and, with Beira Alta and Beira Baixa, for wrought-iron work.

In the Alentejo you can buy lovely traditional hand-painted wooden furniture, such as you will see in many local hotel rooms. Monchique sells unique small wooden scissor stools.

Lisbon and Porto are also good places to buy traditional crafts from all over the country; see p123 and p375 for details.

TOP FIVE BIZARRE SOUVENIRS

- Umbrellas, baseball caps and aprons made of cork
- Barcelos Cockerel (p401)
- Port bottles shaped like shoes, swords or ships
- Beautifully wrapped canned fish (p124)
- Glow-in-the-dark Virgin Marys (p289)

Bargaining

Bargaining is only really done at markets, although you may sometimes be able to bargain down accommodation prices when things are quiet.

SOLO TRAVELLERS

The Portuguese tend to be friendly and welcoming, and with lots of other travellers on the road, you're unlikely to feel lonely if you're on your own. In rural areas it's odd to see a woman travelling alone, but this is likely to be put down to foreign weirdness, and unlikely to provoke anything more than a little curiosity.

Single rooms usually cost about two-thirds of the double-room price, so it's more expensive to travel alone. Youth hostels are a good bet if you're on a budget; not only are they cheap, but they are also really good places to meet other travellers.

TELEPHONE

To call Portugal from abroad, dial the **international access code** (☎ 00), then Portugal's **country code** (☎ 351), then the number. All domestic numbers have nine digits, and there are no area codes. On a public phone, it's easiest to call from a card-operated phone, as coin-operated telephones have an annoying habit of munching your money. You can also make calls from booths in Portugal Telecom offices and some post offices – pay when your call is finished.

Calls from public card-operated phones (Credifone) are charged per number of *impulsos* (beeps or time units) used. The price per beep is fixed (€0.06) with a phonecard, but the length of time between beeps depends on destination, time of day and type of call. Coin telephones cost €0.07 per beep; hotel and café phones rack up three to six times the charges. It costs two/three beeps extra to make a domestic/international connection.

All but local calls are cheaper 9pm to 9am weekdays, all weekend and on holidays.

Local, Regional & National Calls

The cheapest way to call within Portugal is with a Portugal Telecom *cartão telefónico* (phonecard). These are available for €3/6/9 (50/100/150 beeps) from post and telephone offices and many newsagents. A youth or student card should get you a 10% discount.

A beep lasts three minutes for any local call. It last 46 seconds for a regional call (under about 50km) and 30 seconds for a national call, and lasts twice as long during the previously mentioned economy periods. Numbers starting with 800 (*linha verde;* green line) are toll free. Those starting with 808 (*linha azul;* blue line) are charged at local rates from anywhere in the country.

International Calls & Card

From Portugal Telecom, you can get a Hello CardPT or PT Card Europe, both costing €5. You call an access number then key in the code on the back of the card. This is a cheaper way of making international calls. There are lots of competing cards offering much the same service. Note that peak and off-peak periods vary from company to company.

Directory Inquiries

Portugal's directory inquiries number is ☎ 118; operators will search by address as well as by name. The international directory inquiries operator is ☎ 177. Two independent inquiry services, charged at local call rates, are **Telelista** (☎ 707 222 707; www.telelista.iol.pt in Portuguese) and **Páginas Amarelas** (Yellow Pages; ☎ 707 202 222; www.paginasamarelas.pt in Portuguese).

To make a *pagar no destino* (reverse-charge call) with the help of a multilingual operator, dial ☎ 171.

Mobile Phones

Mobile phone usage is widespread in Portugal, with extensive coverage in all but the most rural areas. The main domestic operators are Vodafone (www.vodafone.pt), Optimus and TMN. All sell prepaid SIM cards that you can insert inside a GSM mobile phone and use as long as the phone is not locked by the company providing you service. If you need a phone, you can often buy one at the airport and shops throughout the country with a package of minutes for under €100. This is generally cheaper than renting a phone. Note that mobile numbers usually begin with a '9'. It's illegal in Portugal to drive while talking on a mobile phone.

TIME

Portugal, like Britain, is on GMT/UTC in winter and GMT/UTC plus one hour in summer. This puts it an hour earlier than Spain year-round (a strange thought when you are crossing the border). Clocks are set forward by an hour on the last Sunday in March and back on the last Sunday in October.

TOURIST INFORMATION

Portugal's umbrella tourism organisation is **Investimentos, Comércio e Turismo de Portugal (ICEP)**. Lisbon is the **head office** (Map pp84-5; ☎ 21 909 500; www.visitportugal.com; Avenida 5 de Outubro 10, Lisbon), and there are branches in **Porto** (Map p36; ☎ 222 057 514; Praça Dom João I 43) and at **Porto airport** (☎ 229 412 534, 229 432 400).

Locally managed *postos de turismo* (tourist offices, usually signposted 'turismo') are everywhere, offering brochures and varying degrees of help with sights and accommodation. ICEP maintains a *regiões de turismo* (regional office) in the main town of each of its regions, and information desks at Lisbon, Porto and Faro airports. Lisbon, Porto, Coimbra and a few other towns have municipal and ICEP turismos.

Multilingual staff at the toll-free tourist helpline **Linha Verde do Turista** (☎ 800 296 29; 9am-9pm) can provide basic – though not uniformly accurate – information on accommodation, sightseeing and so on.

There are various regional tourist offices:

Alentejo Serra de São Mamede (☎ 245 300 770; www.rtsm.pt; Região de Turismo de São Mamede, Estrada de Santana 25, Portalegre); Planície Dourada (☎ 284 310 150; www.rt-planiciedourada.pt; Praça da República, Beja)

Beiras Coimbra (☎ 239 488 120; rtc-coimbra@turismo-centro.pt; Largo da Portagem); Aveiro (☎ 234 423 680; aveiro.rotadaluz@inovanet.pt; Rua João Mendonça 8); Covilhã (☎ 275 319 560; turismo.estrela@mail.telepac.pt; Avenida Frei Heitor Pinto); Viseu (☎ 232 420 950; turismo@rt-dao-lafoes.com; Avenida Calouste Gulbenkian)

Douro Lamego (☎ 254 612 005; douro.turismo@mail.telepac.pt; Avenida Visconde Guedes Teixeira)

Minho Viana do Castelo (☎ 258 822 620; fax 258 827 87; Rua Hospital Velho); Bairros (Adere-Soajo; ☎ /fax 258 576 427; turismo.adere-soajo@sapo.pt; Turismo de Aldeia, Largo da Cardeira)

rás-os-Montes Vila Real (☎ 259 322 819; rismarao@mail.telepac.pt; Avenida Carvalho Araújo 94); ıaves (☎ 276 340 660; rturismoatb@mail.telepac t; Terreiro de Cavalaria; 9.30am-12.30pm & 2-6pm n-Sep, Mon-Sat Oct-May)

RAVELLERS WITH DISABILITIES

he term *deficientes* (Portuguese for disabled) ives some indication of the limited awareness f disabled needs. Although public offices and gencies are required to provide access and ıcilities for disabled people, private busiesses are not.

Lisbon airport is wheelchair-accessible, hile Porto and Faro airports have disabled ɔilets. The useful website www.allgohere om has information on facilities offered by ll airlines.

Disabled parking spaces are allotted in ıany places but are frequently occupied. The U parking card entitles visitors to the same reet parking concessions given to disabled esidents. If you're in the UK, contact the **epartment for Transport** (☎ 020-7944 6800; www ıobility-unit.dft.gov.uk).

Most camping grounds have disabled toilets ıoted in the text). Newer and larger hotels nd to have some adapted rooms, though the isabled facilities may not be up to scratch; ask the local *turismo*. Those hostels at Abrantes, lcoutim, Almada, Almograve, Aveiro, Braança, Catalazete, Coimbra, Foz Côa, Guarda, agos, Leiria, Lisbon, Ovar, Penhas da Saúde, ortimão, Porto, Santarém, Viana do Castelo ıd Viseu have disabled facilities.

Lisbon, with its cobbled streets and hills, difficult for the disabled, but not imposble. The Baixa's flat grid and Belém are ne, and all the sights at Parque das Nações re accessible.

For more details, contact the following:

ccessible Portugal (☎ 919 195 680; www.accessible rtugal.com; Almeida Garrett 2, Lisbon) This Lisbon-based ur agency offers a wide range of itineraries and can range accommodation, transfers, overnight trips and tdoor activities such as tandem skydiving and hot-air ılloon trips.

ɔoperatia Nacional Apoio Deficientes (CNAD; Map 84-5; ☎ 218 595 332; Praça Dr Fernando Amado, Lote 6-E, 1900 Lisbon) This is a private organisation that can lp with travel needs.

ial-a-ride Disabled Bus Service Lisbon (☎ 217 585 6); Porto (☎ 226 006 353)

ecretariado Nacional de Rehabilitação (Map 0; ☎ 217 929 500; www.snripd.pt; Avenida Conde de Valbom, 63-1069-178 Lisbon) The national governmental organisation representing the disabled supplies information and provides links to useful operations and publishes guides (in Portuguese) that advise on barrier-free accommodation, transport, shops, restaurants and sights.

Taxi Services for Disabled Persons Braga (☎ 253 684 081); Coimbra (☎ 239 484 522).

Wheeling Around the Algarve (☎ 289 393 636; www.player.pt; Rua Casa do Povo, 1, Almancil) Another private set-up, with great advice on accommodation, transport, care hire, sport and leisure facilities, and equipment.

VISAS

Nationals of EU countries don't need a visa for any length of stay in Portugal. Those from Canada, New Zealand, the USA and (by temporary agreement) Australia can stay for up to 90 days in any half-year without a visa. Others, including nationals of South Africa, need a visa unless they're the spouse or child of an EU citizen.

The general requirements for entry into Portugal also apply to citizens of other signatories of the 1990 Schengen Convention (Austria, Belgium, Denmark, Finland, France, Germany, Greece, Iceland, Italy, Luxembourg, the Netherlands, Norway, Spain and Sweden). A visa issued by one Schengen country is generally valid for travel in all the others, but unless you're a citizen of the UK, Ireland or a Schengen country, you should check visa regulations with the consulate of each Schengen country you plan to visit. You must apply for any Schengen visa in your country of residence.

To extend a visa or 90-day period of stay after arriving in Portugal, contact the **Foreigners' Registration Service** (Serviço de Estrangeiros e Fronteiras; Map p90; ☎ 213 585 545; Rua São Sebastião da Pedreira 15, Lisbon; 9am-3pm Mon-Fri); major tourist towns also have branches. As entry regulations are already liberal, you'll need convincing proof of employment or financial independence, or a pretty good story, if you want to stay longer.

WOMEN TRAVELLERS

Women travelling alone in Portugal report few serious problems. As when travelling anywhere, women should take care – be cautious about where you walk after dark and don't hitch.

If you're travelling with a male partner, people will expect him to do all the talking and ordering, and pay the bill. In some conservative pockets of the north, unmarried couples will save hassle by saying they're married.

CLIMATE CHANGE & TRAVEL

Climate change is a serious threat to the ecosystems that humans rely upon, and air travel is the fastest-growing contributor to the problem. Lonely Planet regards travel, overall, as a global benefit, but believes we all have a responsibility to limit our personal impact on global warming.

Flying & Climate Change

Pretty much every form of motor transport generates CO_2 (the main cause of human-induced climate change) but planes are far and away the worst offenders, not just because of the sheer distances they allow us to travel, but because they release greenhouse gases high into the atmosphere. The statistics are frightening: two people taking a return flight between Europe and the US will contribute as much to climate change as an average household's gas and electricity consumption over a whole year.

Carbon Offset Schemes

Climatecare.org and other websites use 'carbon calculators' that allow travellers to offset the greenhouse gases they are responsible for with contributions to energy-saving projects and other climate-friendly initiatives in the developing world – including projects in India, Honduras, Kazakhstan and Uganda.

Lonely Planet, together with Rough Guides and other concerned partners in the travel industry, supports the carbon offset scheme run by climatecare.org. Lonely Planet offsets all of its staff and author travel.

For more information check out our website: lonelyplanet.com.

If you're a victim of rape or violence while you're in Portugal, you can contact the following organisations:

Associação Portuguesa de Apoio à Vítima (Portuguese Association for Victim Support; APAV; ☎ 218 884 732; www.apav.pt) Can offer assistance for rape victims.

Comissão para a Igualdade e para os Direitos das Mulheres (Commission for the Equality & Rights of Women; Map p90; ☎ 217 983 000; www.cidm.madbug.com in Portuguese; Avenida da República 32, Lisbon) There's no specific rape-crisis hotline, but the commission operates the toll-free number for victims of violence.

WORK

The most likely kind of work you will be abl to find is teaching English, if you have Teach ing English as a Foreign Language (TEFL certification. If you're in the UK, contact th British Council, or get in touch with languag schools in the area where you want to teacl as possible avenues of work.

Bar work is a possibility on the Algarve particularly in Lagos; ask around. You ca also try looking in the local English press fo job ads (p455).

ransport

ONTENTS

ETTING THERE & AWAY

NTERING THE COUNTRY

oming from within Europe, you'll have no roblems entering Portugal by land, sea or r. However, if you're arriving from further ield, check p465 to see if you'll need to seıre a visa before arrival.

IR

irports & Airlines

ortugal has international airports at **Lisbon** irport code LIS; Map pp84-5; ☎ 218 413 500;), **Porto** irport code OPO; ☎ 229 412 534) and **Faro** (Airport code); ☎ 289 800 800). For more information, see ww.ana-aeroportos.pt. Portugal's flagship ternational airline is TAP Air Portugal. The ain domestic airline – but with a growing enu of European connections – is PGA ortugália Airlines. Following are details of ajor carriers serving Portugal:

r Lingus (airline code EI; ☎ 217 220 511; www rlingus.ie)
r Berlin (airline code AB; ☎ 289 800 832; www rberlin.com)
r France (airline code AF; ☎ 808 202 800; www rfrance.fr)
r Luxor (airline code LK; ☎ 707 500 505; www rluxor.com)

THINGS CHANGE

The information in this chapter is particularly vulnerable to change: Prices for international travel are volatile, routes are introduced and cancelled, schedules change, special deals come and go, and rules and visa requirements are amended. You should check directly with the airline or a travel agent to make sure you understand how a fare (and ticket you may buy) works and be aware of the security requirements for international travel.

The upshot of this is that you should get opinions, quotes and advice from as many airlines and travel agents as possible before you part with your hard-earned cash. The details given in this chapter should be regarded as pointers and are not a substitute for your own careful, up-to-date research.

Alitalia (airline code AZ; ☎ 800 307 300; www.alitalia.com)
British Airways (airline code BA; ☎ 808 200 125; www.britishairways.com)
British Midland/BMIbaby (airline code BD; www.bmibaby.com)
Continental Airlines (airline code CO; ☎ 808 200 079; www.flycontinental.com)
Delta (airline code DL; ☎ 213 139 860; www.delta.com)
Finnair (airline code AY; ☎ 213 522 689; www.finnair.fi)
GBAirways (☎ 289 800 771; www.gbairways.com)
Go/easyJet Airways (airline code U2; www.easyjet.com)
Grupo SATA (airport code S4; ☎ 707 227 282; www.sata.pt)
Iberia (airline code IB; ☎ 808 261 261; www.iberia.com)
KLM (airline code KL; ☎ 204 747 747; www.klm.nl)
Lufthansa (airline code LH; ☎ 214 245 155; www.lufthansa.com)
Monarch Airlines (airline code ZB; ☎ 289 889 475; www.flymonarch.com)
PGA Portugália Airlines (airline code NI; ☎ 707 789 090; www.flypga.com)
Regional Air Lines (airline code FN; ☎ 218 425 559; www.regional.com)
Ryan Air (airline code FR; ☎ 289 889 407; www.ryanair.com)
Swiss International Air Lines (airline code LX; ☎ 808 200 487; www.swiss.com)

DEPARTURE TAX

International airport taxes, normally levied by countries of both origin and destination, are invariably included in the price of your ticket, either scheduled or charter.

TRANSPORT

TAP Air Portugal (airline code TP; ☎ 707 205 700; www.tap.pt)
Transavia Airlines (airline code HV; ☎ 218 925 454; www.transavia.com)
Tunisair (airline code TU; ☎ 218 496 350; www.tunisair.com.tn)
Varig (airline code RG; ☎ 214 245 170; www.varig.com.br)
Virgin Express (airline code VS; ☎ 808 208 082; www.virgin-express.com)

Continental Europe

FRANCE

Carriers with multiple daily Paris–Lisbon and Paris–Porto connections include Air France, Portugália and TAP. Direct connections to Lisbon from elsewhere in France also include those from Bordeaux, Nice, Lyon and Toulouse. More expensive flights to Porto go daily from Bordeaux, and weekly from Nice. Flights to Faro are less easy to come by.

Agencies with branches around Portugal:
Nouvelles Frontières (☎ 08 25 00 07 47; www.nouvelles-frontieres.fr)
OTU Voyages (☎ 08 20 81 78 17; www.otu.fr)
Voyages Wasteels (☎ 08 25 88 70 70; www.wasteels.fr).
Voyageurs du Monde (☎ 08 92 23 56 56; www.vdm.com).

SPAIN

Carriers with daily Madrid–Lisbon connections include Iberia, Portugália and TAP. Portugália, TAP and Iberia also fly Barcelona–Lisbon. Portugália also has affordable smaller aircraft flying direct to Lisbon from Bilbao, La Coruña, Málaga and Valencia.

For Porto, Portugália has daily direct flights from Madrid and Barcelona.

Reliable Madrid-based air-fare specialists with offices throughout Spain include **Barceló Viajes** (☎ 902 116 226; www.barceloviajes.es).

ELSEWHERE IN CONTINENTAL EUROPE

An air-fare specialist with branches around Germany is **STA Travel** (☎ 01805-456 422; www.statravel.de). In Belgium go to **Usit Connections** (☎ 070-23-33-13; www.connections.be). In the Netherlands, try Amsterdam-based **Air Fair** (☎ 020-62 5121; www.airfair.nl).

The major links from Germany are Frankfurt, Berlin and Munich to Lisbon, and Frankfurt to Porto. Other direct connections t Lisbon are from Cologne, Hamburg and Stuttgart; and to Faro from Frankfurt. German also has busy charter traffic to Portugal.

From Amsterdam, there are daily flights t Lisbon and Porto, and several weekly to Far Charter specialist **Transavia** (☎ 020-406 04 06; ww.transavia.nl) also offers scheduled flights fror Amsterdam to Porto, and Rotterdam to Far

For a similar fare, there are multiple dail flights from Brussels to Lisbon and weeken connections to Faro.

UK & Ireland

Thanks to the UK's long love affair with Portugal and its 'bucket-shop' tradition, bargair are plentiful. The UK's best-known bargai agencies and internet-based dealers:
Expedia (www.expedia.co.uk)
Flight Centre (www.flightcentre.co.uk)
Lastminute (www.lastminute.com)
STA Travel (☎ 0870-160 0599; www.statravel.co.uk)
Trailfinders (☎ 0845-050 5891; www.trailfinders.co.u

Reliable sources in Ireland:
Trailfinders (☎ 01-677 7888; www.trailfinders.ie)
Usit (☎ 0818-200 020; www.usit.ie)

Scheduled direct flights go daily to Lisbo from London Heathrow, Gatwick and Manchester. Porto flights also leave daily fro Heathrow and Manchester, and less frequent from Gatwick. There's also a veritable banc wagon of flights to Faro. At the time of wri ing, 'no-frills' carriers to Portugal include Go/easyJet (London, Bristol and East Mi lands to Faro), BMIbaby (East Midlands Faro), Monarch (London to Lisbon and Far Manchester to Faro) and Ryanair (Dubli and Shannon to Faro; Dublin, Liverpool ar London Stansted to Porto).

Charters operate from all over the UI mostly to Faro. A reliable charter-flight clea ing house is **Destination Portugal** (www.destinati-portugal.co.uk).

USA & Canada

The only direct air links are to Lisbon: dai from New York JFK, Newark and Los Angel and less frequently from Boston. There are direct flights between Canada and Portugal. If you don't mind connecting flights, return fares start at around US$700 from New York or US$1100 from Los Angeles.

Circle the Planet (☎ 800 799 8888; www.circletheplanet.com) is a leading consolidator, and you can always try your luck with **Orbitz** (www.orbitz.com) or **Hotwire** (www.hotwire.com). A big air-fare specialist in the USA is **STA Travel** (☎ 800 781 4040; www.statravel.com). Canada's best bargain-ticket agency is **Travel CUTS** (☎ 866 246 9762; www.travelcuts.com).

LAND

Bicycle

Bicycles can be taken on aeroplanes, but check this with the airline well in advance. Let some of the air out of the tyres to prevent them from bursting in the low-pressure baggage hold. Bikes are not allowed as baggage on Eurolines buses. For information on cycling in Portugal, see p472.

Bus

Buses are slower and less comfortable than trains, but they're cheaper, especially if you qualify for an under-26, student or senior discount. The major long-distance carriers that serve European destinations are Eurolines and Busabout, neither of which have services in Portugal (you'll have to go to Spain first). Eurohop services Spain and two Portugal destinations.

EUROLINES

Eurolines (www.eurolines.com) is a consortium of coach operators forming Europe's largest network. A Eurolines Pass gives you unlimited travel among 35 European cities, although Madrid is currently the closest city to Portugal covered by the pass. High-season prices range from €329/279 (adult/under 26) for a 15-day pass to €439/359 for a 30-day pass; low-season prices are 20% to 25% lower.

Eurolines' main Portugal offices are in **Lisbon** (Map pp84-5; ☎ 218 957 398; Loja 203, Gare do Oriente) and in **Porto** (Map p358; ☎ 225 189 299; Centro Comercial Central Shopping, Campo 24 de Agosto 125). For some European routes, Eurolines is affiliated with the three big Portuguese operators **Intercentro** (Map p90; ☎ 213 571 745; Rua Engenheiro Vieira Silva 55, Lisbon), **Internorte** (Map p358; ☎ 226 052 420; www.internorte.pt in Portuguese; Praça da Galiza 96, Porto) and **Eva Transportes** (☎ 289 899 700; www.eva-bus.com).

BUSABOUT

Busabout (www.busabout.com) is a hop-on hop-off network linking 36 cities in Europe. Buses run from May to October, and travellers can move freely around one of three networks. The bus picks up and drops off near select hostels and camp sites.

Passes range from UK£275 to UK£575, giving you from two weeks to up to six months to complete your journey. Youth (under 26) and student-card holders pay about 10% less. The nearest stops to Portugal are in Spain (Madrid, Barcelona and San Sebastian).

EUROHOP

Eurohop (www.eurohop.es) is a hop-on hop-off network linking nine cities in Spain and two in Portugal (Lagos and Lisbon). Buses run from June to September, and travellers can move freely around the network, with buses leaving from each city every two days. Depending on your itinerary, prices run from €88 to a whopping €345. The bus picks up and drops off near select hostels.

CONTINENTAL EUROPE

France

Eurolines offers regular connections from Paris to all over Portugal, including Porto (25 hours), Lisbon (26 hours) and less often to Faro (29 hours). Expect to pay €88 to €95. Hefty surcharges apply to one-way or return tickets for most departures from July to mid-August and also on Saturday year round.

Spain

UK–Portugal and France–Portugal Eurolines services cross to Portugal via northwest Spain. Sample fares to Lisbon include €33 from Salamanca.

From Madrid, Eurolines/Internorte runs daily via Guarda to Porto (€41 one way, 8½ hours) and also via Badajoz and Évora to Lisbon (€41, eight hours); twice weekly, the Lisbon service starts from Barcelona (€84, 18 hours). The Spanish lines **AutoRes** (☎ 902 02 09 99; www.auto-res.net) and **Alsa** (☎ 913 27 05 40; www.alsa.es) each have regular Madrid–Lisbon services (€38).

From Seville, Alsa/Eurolines goes five to six times weekly via Badajoz and Évora to Lisbon (€38, seven hours).

The Portuguese carrier **Eva** (☎ 289 899 700; www.eva-bus.com) and the Spanish line **Damas** (☎ 95 925 69 00; www.damas-sa.es) operate a joint

TRANSPORT

service three times weekly from Seville to Lisbon (€33 to €38, 4½ hours); with connecting buses to other cities at Ficalho.

Eurolines affiliate **Intersul** (☎ 289 899 770; Loja A, Terminal Rodoviário, Faro) runs from Seville to Lagos regularly in summer, and Eva/Damas runs a twice-daily service from Seville to Faro (€14, four to five hours), Albufeira and Lagos (€17, 4½ hours) via Huelva.

Elsewhere in Continental Europe

Eurolines has services to Portugal from destinations across Europe, typically about twice a week. Sample one-way fares from Hamburg are around €158/167/188 to Porto/Lisbon/Faro. Fares from Amsterdam or Brussels are around €140 to Lisbon or Faro.

UK

Eurolines runs several services to Portugal from Victoria coach station in London, with a stopover and change of bus in France and sometimes Spain. These include two buses a week to Viana do Castelo (34 hours), five to Porto (33 hours), five via Coimbra to Lisbon (35 hours) and two via Faro to Lagos (38 hours). These services cost around UK£152 return.

Car & Motorcycle

Of more than 30 roads that cross the Portugal–Spain border, the best and biggest do so near Valença do Minho (E01/A3), Chaves (N532), Bragança (E82/IP4), Guarda/Vilar Formoso (E80/IP5), Elvas (E90/A6/IP7), Serpa (N260) and Vila Real de Santo António (E1/IP1). There are no longer any border controls.

INSURANCE & DOCUMENTS

Nationals of EU countries need only their home driving licences to operate a car or motorcycle in Portugal, although holders of the UK's old, pre-EU green licences should also carry an International Driving Permit (IDP). Portugal also accepts licences issued in Brazil and the USA. Others should get an IDP through an automobile licensing department or automobile club in their home country (or at some post offices in the UK).

If you're driving your own car or motorcycle into Portugal, you'll also need vehicle registration (proof of ownership) and insurance documents. If these are in order you should be able to keep the vehicle in Portugal for up to six months.

Motor vehicle insurance with at least third-party cover is compulsory throughout the EU. Your home policy may or may not be extendable to Portugal, and the coverage of some comprehensive policies automatically drops to third-party only outside your home country unless the insurer is notified. Though it's not a legal requirement, it's wise to carry written confirmation from your home insurer that you have the correct coverage.

If you hire a car, the rental firm will provide you with registration and insurance papers, plus a rental contract.

UK

The quickest driving route from the UK to Portugal is by car ferry to northern Spain with **P&O Portsmouth** (☎ 0870 520 2020; www.poferries.com) from Portsmouth to Bilbao (35 hours, twice weekly mid-March to mid-December), or **Brittany Ferries** (☎ 0870 366 5333; www.brittany-ferries.com) from Plymouth to Santander (18 hours, twice weekly from March to November). From Bilbao or Santander it's roughly 1000km to Lisbon, 800km to Porto or 1300km to Faro. Fares are wildly seasonal. A standard weekday, high-season, return ticket for a car/motorcycle with driver and one passenger (with cabin accommodation) starts at about UK£660/420, but you can usually beat this with special offers.

An alternative is to catch a ferry across the Channel (or the Eurotunnel vehicle train beneath it) to France and motor down the coast.

Train

Trains are a popular way to get around Europe – comfortable, frequent and generally on time. But unless you have a rail pass the cost can be higher than flying.

There are two standard long-distance rail journeys into Portugal. Both take the *TGV Atlantique* from Paris to Irún (in Spain), where you must change trains. From there the *Sud-Expresso* crosses into Portugal at Vilar Formoso (Fuentes de Oñoro in Spain) continuing to Coimbra and Lisbon; change at Pampilhosa for Porto. The other journey runs from Irún to Madrid, with a change to the *Talgo Lusitânia*, crossing into Portugal at Marvão-Beirã and on to Lisbon. For trips to the south of Portugal, change at Lisbon.

Two other important Spain–Portugal crossings are at Valença do Minho and at Caia (Caya in Spain), near Elvas.

You'll have few problems buying long-distance tickets as little as a day or two ahead, even in summer. For those intending to do a lot of European rail travel, the exhaustive *Thomas Cook European Timetable* is updated monthly and is available from **Thomas Cook Publishing** (☎ 01733-416477; www.thomascooktimetables.com) for UK£11.50 online, plus postage.

TRAIN PASSES

Many of the following passes are available through **Rail Europe** (www.raileurope.co.uk); most travel agencies also sell them, though you'll save a little by buying directly from the issuing authority. Note that even with a pass you must still pay for seat and couchette reservations and express-train supplements.

The **Inter-Rail Pass** (www.interrail.com) divides Europe into zones; zone F is Spain, Portugal and Morocco). One-zone passes are good for 16 consecutive days; the 2nd-class adult/under-26 price is £206/140. Two-zone passes are also available for 22 consecutive days (£285/198). Better-value multizone passes, good for a month, cost £393/277.

The **EuroDomino Pass** (www.eurodomino.co.uk) is good for a number of consecutive days within a specified month, in a specified country. For 2nd-class adult/under-26 travel in Portugal the cost is from €75/52 for three days to €135/115 for eight days. There's also a 1st-class option.

Both Inter-Rail and EuroDomino passes Both are available to anyone resident in Europe for six months before starting their travels. You cannot use either one in your home country.

The **Eurailpass** and the **Eurail Selectpass** (www.eurail.com), both for non-European residents, are meant to be purchased from your home country but are available at a higher price from some European locations. The Eurailpass is valid for unlimited travel (1st/2nd class for those over/under 26) in 18 European countries, including Portugal. It's valid for 15 days (US$605/394) to up to three months (US$1702/1108); various 'flexi' versions allow a chosen number of travel days over a longer period. The Eurail Selectpass allows you to travel between three, four or five of your chosen Eurail countries (they must be directly connected by Eurail transport). You can choose from five to 10 travelling days (or up to 15 for five countries), which can be taken at any point within a two-month period. Three countries cost US$382/249 for five days, and up to US$580/375 for 10 days, while five countries cost US$472/306 for five days up to an increased total of fifteen days for US$850/552. For both these passes, there is also a 'saver' option for those travelling in groups (two people qualify as a group).

The Iberic Rail Pass (found on www.europeanrailguide.com), available only to non-European residents, is also valid for a specified period of 1st-class travel in Spain and Portugal during a two-month period, from three days (adult/saver US$249/219) to 10 days (US$494/429).

CONTINENTAL EUROPE

France

The daily train journey from Paris (Gare d'Austerlitz) to Lisbon takes 20 hours. An adult, 2nd-class (Apex), under-26 ticket costs around €240 return for a couchette on the overnight Irún–Lisbon section. You can book directly with French railway **SNCF** (www.voyages-sncf.com).

Spain

The daily Paris–Lisbon train goes via Vitória, Burgos, Valladolid and Salamanca, entering Portugal at Vila Formoso. A 2nd-class one-way reserved seat from Salamanca to Lisbon costs €56.

The main Spain–Portugal rail route is from Madrid to Lisbon via Cáceres and the border station of Marvão-Beirã. The nightly journey on the *Talgo Lusitânia* takes 10½ hours. A 2nd-class one-way reserved seat costs €109; add on €82 for a berth in a four-person compartment or €102 in a two-person compartment.

The Badajoz–Caia–Elvas–Lisbon route (€18, five hours), with two regional trains a day and a change at Entroncamento, is tedious, though the scenery through the Serra de Marvão is grand. Onward Seville–Badajoz connections are by bus.

In the south, trains run west from Seville only as far as Huelva, followed by bus connections. You're better off on a bus.

UK

The fastest and most convenient route to Portugal is with Eurostar from London Waterloo to Paris via the Channel Tunnel, and then onward by TGV.

SEA

There are no scheduled seagoing ferries to Portugal, but many to Spain. For details on those from the UK to Spain, see p470.

The closest North African ferry connections are from Morocco to Spain; contact **Transmediterranea** (www.trasmediterranea.net), **Euro Ferrys** (www.euroferrys.com), and **FerriMaroc** (www.ferrimaroc.com) for details. Car ferries also run from Tangier to Gibraltar.

Car ferries cross the Rio Guadiana border from Ayamonte in Spain to Vila Real de Santo António in the Algarve every 40 minutes from 8.20am to 7pm Monday to Saturday, 9.15am to 5.40pm on Sundays; buy tickets from the waterfront office (€1.30/4.40/0.65 per person/car/bike).

TRANSPORT

GETTING AROUND

A helpful website for schedules and prices to assist with your trip planning is www.transpor.pt.

AIR

Airlines in Portugal

Flights within mainland Portugal are expensive, and for the short distances involved, not really worth considering. Nonetheless, **PGA Portugália Airlines** (☎ 218 425 559; www.flypga.com) and **TAP Air Portugal** (☎ 707 205 700; www.tap.pt) both have multiple daily Lisbon–Porto and Lisbon–Faro flights (taking less than one hour) year round. For Porto to Faro, change in Lisbon.

BICYCLE

Mountain biking is hugely popular in Portugal, even though there are few dedicated bicycle paths. Possible itineraries are numerous in the mountainous national/natural parks of the north (especially Parque Nacional da Peneda-Gerês), along the coast or across the Alentejo plains. Coastal trips are easiest from north to south, with the prevailing winds. More demanding is the Serra da Estrela (which serves as the Tour de Portugal's 'mountain run'). You could also try the Serra do Marão between Amarante and Vila Real.

Local bike clubs organise regular Passeio BTT trips; check their flyers at rental agencies, bike shops and turismos (tourist offices). Guided trips are often available in popular tourist destinations. For jaunts arranged from abroad, see p67.

Cobbled roads in some old-town centres may jar your teeth loose if your tyres aren't fat enough; they should be at least 38mm in diameter.

Documents

If you're cycling around Portugal on your own bike, proof of ownership and a written description and photograph of it will help police in case it's stolen.

Hire

There are numerous places to rent bikes, especially in the Algarve and other touristy areas. Prices range from €8 to €20 per day. Rental outfits are noted in the text.

Information

For listings of events and bike shops, buy the bimonthly Portuguese-language *Bike Magazine,* available from larger newsagents.

For its members, the UK-based **Cyclists' Touring Club** (CTC; ☎ 0870 873 0060; www.ctc.org.uk) publishes useful and free information on cycling in Portugal, plus notes for half a dozen routes around the country. It also offers tips, maps, topoguides and other publications by mail order.

Transporting Your Bicycle

Boxed-up or bagged-up bicycles can be taken free on all *regional* and *interregional* trains as accompanied baggage. They can also go, unboxed, on a few suburban services on weekends or for a small charge outside the rush hour. Most domestic bus lines won't accept bikes.

BOAT

Other than river cruises along the Rio Douro from Porto (p388) and the Rio Tejo from Lisbon (p106), Portugal's only remaining waterborne transport is cross-river ferries. Commuter ferries include those across the Rio Tejo to/from Lisbon (p124), and across the mouth of the Rio Sado (p151).

BUS

A host of small private bus operators, most amalgamated into regional companies, run a dense network of services across the country. Among the largest companies are **Rede Expressos** (☎ 707 223 344; www.rede-expressos.pt), **Rodonorte** (www.rodonorte.pt) and the Algarve line **Eva** (☎ 289 899 760; www.eva-bus.com).

Bus services are of three general types: *expressos* are comfortable, fast buses between major cities, *rápidas* are quick regional buses, and *carreiras*, marked CR, stop at every crossroad (never mind that *carreiras* means something like 'in a hurry' in Portuguese). Some companies also offer a fast deluxe category called *alta qualidade*.

Even in summer you'll have little problem booking an *expresso* ticket for the same or next day. A Lisbon–Faro express bus takes four hours and costs €15; Lisbon–Porto takes 3½ hours for €13.50 or more. By contrast, local services, can thin out to almost nothing on weekends, especially in summer when school is out.

An under-26 card should get you a discount of around 20%, at least on the long-distance services. Senior travellers can often get up to 50% off.

Don't rely on turismos for accurate timetable information. Most bus-station ticket desks will give you a little computer print-out of fares and all services.

CAR & MOTORCYCLE

Portugal's modest network of *estradas* (highways) is gradually spreading across the country. Main roads are sealed and generally in good condition. And if you choose to pootle around on lesser routes you'll find most of the roads empty.

The downside is your fellow drivers. A leading Swedish road-safety investigator was quoted as saying the Portuguese 'drive like car thieves' and the prime minister described what happens on Portugal's major highways as 'civil war'. The country's per-capita death rate from road accidents has long been one of Europe's highest, and drinking, driving and dying are hot political potatoes.

A tough law in 2001 dropped the legal blood-alcohol level to the equivalent of a single glass of wine. But the law was suspended months later following intense pressure from – you guessed it – Portugal's wine producers. Even the present limit of 0.5g/L is pretty stringent, plus there are fines up to €2500.

The good news is that recent years have seen a 10% decline in road-death rates thanks to a zero-tolerance police crackdown on accident-prone routes and alcohol limits. Along those lines, it's also illegal in Portugal to drive while talking on a mobile phone.

Driving can be tricky in Portugal's small walled towns, where roads may taper down to donkey-cart size before you know it, and fiendish one-way systems can force you out of your way.

PARKING

Parking is often metered within city centres, but is free Saturday evening and Sunday. Central Lisbon has car parks, and these cost around €10 per day. For more details on driving and parking in Lisbon see p126. In towns where parking is difficult we've included parking information in the Getting There & Around or Getting Around sections.

A common sight in larger towns is the down-and-outers who lurk around squares and car parks, wave you into the parking space you've just found for yourself, and ask for payment for this service. Of course it's a racket and of course there's no need to give them anything, but the Portuguese often do, and €0.50 might keep your car out of trouble.

For information on what to bring in the way of documents, see p470.

Accidents

If you are involved in a minor 'fender-bender' with no injuries, the easiest way for drivers to sort things out with their insurance companies is to fill out a Constat Aimable (the English version is called a European Accident Statement). There's no risk in signing this: it's just a way to exchange the relevant information and there's usually one included in rental-car documents. Make sure it includes any details that may help you prove that the accident was not your fault. To alert the police, dial ☎ 112.

Assistance

Automóvel Club de Portugal (ACP; Map p90; ☎ 808 502 502; www.acp.pt in Portuguese; Rua Rosa Araújo 24, Lisbon; ⏲ 8am-8pm Mon-Fri), Portugal's national auto club, provides medical, legal and breakdown assistance for its members. Road information and maps are available to anyone at ACP offices, including the head office in Lisbon and branches in Aveiro, Braga, Bragança, Coimbra, Évora, Faro, Porto and elsewhere.

If your national auto club belongs to the Fédération Internationale de l'Automobile or the Alliance Internationale de Tourisme, you can also use ACP's emergency services and get discounts on maps and other products.

TRANSPORT

ROAD DISTANCES (KM)

	Aveiro	Beja	Braga	Bragança	Castelo Branco	Coimbra	Évora	Faro	Guarda	Leiria	Lisbon	Portalegre	Porto	Santarém	Setúbal	Viana do Castelo	Vila Real	Viseu
Aveiro	---																	
Beja	383	---																
Braga	129	504	---															
Bragança	287	566	185	---														
Castelo Branco	239	271	366	299	---													
Coimbra	60	329	178	314	191	---												
Évora	305	78	426	488	191	251	---											
Faro	522	166	643	732	437	468	244	---										
Guarda	163	369	260	197	102	161	291	535	---									
Leiria	126	273	244	402	179	72	195	412	233	---								
Lisbon	256	183	372	530	264	202	138	296	402	146	---							
Portalegre	276	178	403	390	93	222	100	344	193	172	219	---						
Porto	71	446	58	216	308	123	368	585	202	189	317	339	---					
Santarém	188	195	309	464	181	134	117	346	295	78	80	147	251	---				
Setúbal	299	143	420	575	316	246	105	256	406	189	47	186	362	123	---			
Viana do Castelo	144	519	56	241	382	191	441	658	275	262	387	412	73	324	435	---		
Vila Real	169	528	94	120	261	199	450	683	159	282	412	352	98	349	460	150	---	
Viseu	86	415	185	228	177	86	366	554	75	158	288	268	127	220	331	241	113	---

Among clubs that qualify are the AA and RAC in the UK, and the Australian, New Zealand, Canadian and American automobile associations.

The 24-hour emergency help number is ☎ 707 509 510.

Fuel

Fuel is expensive – about €1.39 (and rising) for a litre of *sem chumbo* (unleaded petrol) at the time of writing. There are plenty of self-service stations, and credit cards are accepted at most.

Highways & Toll Roads

Top of the range are *auto-estradas* (motorways), all of them *portagens* (toll roads); the longest of these are Lisbon–Porto and Lisbon–Algarve. Toll roads charge cars and motorcycles around €0.06 per kilometre (eg a total of €18.15 for Lisbon–Porto, €6.60 for Lisbon–Setúbal and €17.75 for Lisbon to the Algarve).

Nomenclature can be baffling. Motorway numbers prefixed with an E are Europe-wide designations. Portugal's toll roads are prefixed with an A. Highways in the country's main network are prefixed IP *(itinerário principa* and subsidiary ones IC *(itinerário complemen tar)*. Some highways have several designation and numbers that change in mid-flow.

Numbers for the main two-lane *estrad nacionais* (national roads) have no prefix le ter on some road maps, whereas on othe maps, they're prefixed by N. If you want t get off the big roads, consider going for th really small ones, which tend to be pretti and more peaceful.

Hire

To rent a car in Portugal you must be at lea 25 years old and have held your driving l cence for more than a year (some compani allow younger drivers at higher rates). Th widest choice of car-hire companies is at Li bon, Porto and Faro airports. Competition h driven Algarve rates lower than elsewhere.

Some of the best advance-booking rat are offered by internet-based brokers such **Holiday Autos** (www.holidayautos.com). Other bargai come as part of 'fly-drive' packages. The wor deals tend to be those done with internation firms on arrival, though their prepaid prom ional rates are competitive. Book at least a few ays ahead in high season. For on-the-spot ental, domestic firms such as **Auto Jardim** (www uto-jardim.com) have some of the best rates.

Renting the smallest and cheapest available ar for a week in the high-season costs as little s €135 (with tax, insurance and unlimited nileage) if booked from abroad, and a similar mount through a Portuguese firm. It can cost p to €400 if you book through Portuguese ranches of international firms such as Hertz, uropcar and Avis.

For an additional fee you can get personal nsurance through the rental company, un- ss you're covered by your home policy (see 470). A minimum of third-party coverage is ompulsory in the EU.

Rental cars are especially at risk of break- ns or petty theft in larger towns, so don't eave anything of value visible in the car. If ou can unscrew the radio antenna, leave inside the car at night; and put the wheel overs (hubcaps) in the boot (trunk) for the uration of your trip.

Motorcycles and scooters can be rented in rger cities, and all over coastal Algarve. Ex- ect to pay from €30/60 per day for a scooter/ notorcycle.

lotorail

aminhos de Ferro Portugueses (CP; ☎ 808 208 208; ww.cp.pt; 7am-11pm), which is the state rail- ay company, offers car transport by rail ith certain services on the Lisbon–Porto, isbon–Guarda, Lisbon–Castelo Branco and orto–Faro lines.

oad Rules

ou may not believe it after seeing the antics f Portuguese drivers, but there are rules. To egin with, driving is on the right, overtaking on the left and most signs use international ymbols. An important rule to remember is nat traffic from the right usually has prior- y. Portugal has lots of ambiguously marked ntersections, so this is more important than ou might think.

Except when marked otherwise, speed lim- s for cars (without a trailer) and motorcycles without a sidecar) are 50km/h in towns and illages, 90km/h outside built-up areas and 20km/h on motorways. By law, car safety elts must be worn in the front and back seats, nd children under 12 years may not ride in ne front. Motorcyclists and their passengers must wear helmets, and motorcycles must have their headlights on day and night.

The police can impose steep on-the-spot fines for speeding and parking offences, so save yourself a big hassle and remember to toe the line.

HITCHING

Hitching is never entirely safe anywhere, and we don't recommend it. In any case it isn't an easy option in Portugal. Almost nobody stops on major highways, and on smaller roads drivers tend to be going short distances so you may only advance from one field to the next.

LOCAL TRANSPORT

Bus

Except in Lisbon or Porto there's little reason to take municipal buses, as most attractions are within walking distance. Most areas have regional bus services, for better or worse (see p472).

Metro

Both Lisbon and Porto have ambitious un- derground systems that are still growing; see p127 and p377.

Taxi

Taxis offer pretty good value over short dis- tances, and are plentiful in large towns and cities. Ordinary taxis are usually marked A (which stands for *aluguer,* for hire) on the door, number plate or elsewhere. They use meters and are available on the street and at taxi ranks, or by telephone for a surcharge of €0.75.

The fare on weekdays during daylight hours is about €1.90 *bandeirada* (flag fall) plus around €0.50 per kilometre, and a bit more for periods spent idling in traffic. A fare of €4 will usually get you across bigger towns. It's best to insist on the meter, although it's possible to negotiate a flat fare. If you have a sizable load of luggage you'll pay a further €1.50.

Rates are about 20% higher at night (9pm to 6am), on weekends and holidays. Once a taxi leaves the city limits you also pay a sur- charge or higher rate.

In larger cities, including Lisbon and Porto, meterless taxis marked T (for turismo) can be hired from private companies for excur- sions. Rates for these are higher, but standard- ised; drivers are honest and polite, and speak foreign languages.

To La Coruña
SPAIN
Vigo
Tuy
Valença do Minho
Viana do Castelo
Vila Nova de Famalição
Braga
Nine
Guimarães
Linha da Tâmega (Narrow Gauge)
Póvoa de Varzim
Trofa
Ermesinde
Porto
Amarante
Livração
Vila Real
Linha da Corgo (Narrow Gauge)
Mirandela
Linha da Tua (Narrow Gauge)
Tua
Peso da Régua
Pocinho
Espinho
Oliveira de Azeméis
ATLANTIC OCEAN
Aveiro
Mangualde
Vilar Formoso
Guarda
Fuentes de Oñoro
Ciudad Rodrigo
Salamanca
To Madrid; Irún; Par
Pampilhosa
Figueira da Foz
Coimbra
Serpins
Alfarelos
Lousã
Covilhã
Leiria
Fátima
Tomar
Castelo Branco
Lamarosa
Caldas da Rainha
Entroncamento
Abrantes
To Madri
Torre das Vargens
Marvão-Beirã
Valencia de Alcántara
Cáceres
Santarém
Setil
Sintra
Cacém
Cascais
Estoril
Lisbon
Barreiro
Pinhal Novo
Vendas Novas
Elvas
Badajoz
Caia (Portugal) Caya (Spain)
Mérida
Setúbal
Évora
Casa Branca
SPAIN
To Madri
Zafra
Beja
Funcheira
To Córdob
Lagos
Portimão
Tunes
Vila Real de Santo António
Ayamonte
Huelva
Seville
Faro
Tavira

Trams

Enthusiasts of stately progress shouldn't miss the trams of Lisbon (p126) and Porto (p377) – an endangered species.

TOURS

Lisbon-based **Cityrama** (☎ 213 191 090; www.city rama.pt), Viana do Castelo's **AVIC** (☎ 258 806 180; www.avic.pt), Porto's **Diana Tours** (☎ 223 771 230; www.dianatours.pt), and the Algarve's **Megatur** (☎ 289 807 485; www.megatur.pt) all run bus tours.

Caminhos de Ferro Portugueses (CP; ☎ 808 208 208, www.cp.pt; 7am-11pm), the state railway company, organises weekend day trips up the Douro valley during almond-blossom time.

If you prefer to assemble your own holiday, Portugal specialist **Destination Portugal** (www destination-portugal.co.uk) will tell you all you need to know and can help with flights, car hire and accommodation, separately or together.

Locally run adventure tours are noted in individual town listings; activity-based tours are listed in Portugal Outdoors (p67); or try the following for special-interest tours:

Arblaster & Clarke (☎ 01730-893344; www.arblaster andclarke.com) Offers wine tours in the Douro.

Martin Randall Travel (☎ 020-8742 3355; www martinrandall.com) Cultural specialist that arranges first-rate escorted art and architecture tours.

Naturetrek (☎ 01962-733051; www.naturetrek.co.uk) Specialist in bird-watching and botanical tours, runs an eight-day excursion around southern Portugal.

TRAIN

If you can match your itinerary to a regional service, travelling with **Caminhos de Ferro Portugueses** (CP; ☎ 808 208 208; www.cp.pt), the state railway company, is cheaper than by bus. Trains tend to be slower than long-distance buses, however.

Since the recent completion of main-line tracks to Pinhal Novo, there is now a direct rail link from Lisbon to the south of Portugal.

Three of the most appealing old railway lines, on narrow-gauge tracks climbing out of the Douro valley, survive in truncated form: the Linha da Tâmega from Livração to Amarante (p383); the Linha da Corgo from Peso da Régua to Vila Real (p436); and the beautiful Linha da Tua from Tua to Mirandela (p450).

Discounts

Children under four travel free; those aged four to 12 go for half-price. A youth card issued by Euro26 member countries gets you 30% discount on *regional* and *interregional* services on any day, and on *intercidade* (express) services from Monday noon to Friday noon. Travellers aged 65 and over can get 50% off any service by showing some ID.

Information & Reservations

Get timetable and fare info at all stations and from **CP** (www.cp.pt). You can book *intercidade* and Alfa Pendular tickets up to 30 days ahead, though you'll have little trouble booking for the next or even the same day. Other services can only be booked 24 hours in advance. A seat reservation is mandatory on most *intercidade* and Alfa trains; the booking fee is included in the price.

Types & Classes of Service

There are three main types of long-distance service: *regional* trains (marked R on timetables), which stop everywhere; reasonably fast *interregional* (IR) trains; and express trains, called *rápido* or *intercidade* (IC). Alfa Pendular is a deluxe, marginally faster and pricier IC service on the Lisbon–Coimbra–Porto main line. International services are marked IN on timetables.

Lisbon and Porto have their own *suburbano* (suburban) train networks. Lisbon's network extends predictably to Sintra, Cascais, Setúbal and up the lower Tejo valley. Porto's network takes the definition of 'suburban' to new lengths, running all the way to Braga, Guimarães and Aveiro. *Suburbano* services also travel between Coimbra and Figueira da Foz. The distinction matters where long-distance services parallel the more convenient, plentiful, and considerably cheaper, *suburbanos*.

Only the Faro–Porto *Comboio Azul* and international trains like *Sud-Expresso* and *Talgo Lusitânia* have restaurant cars, though all IC and Alfa trains have aisle service and most have bars. There's a nonsmoking section somewhere on every CP train.

Train Passes

The Portuguese Railpass (US$135) gives you unlimited 1st-class travel on any four days out of 15. It's only available to travellers from outside Europe, and must be purchased before you arrive; contact **Rail Europe** (www.raileurope.com).

Special CP *bilhetes turísticos* (tourist tickets), valid for unlimited travel during seven/14/21 consecutive days, cost €118/196/288 (half-price for those under 12 or over 65), and are on sale at major stations. For other rail passes, see p471.

Health

Dr Caroline Evans

CONTENTS

BEFORE YOU GO

Prevention is the key to staying healthy while abroad. A little planning before departure, particularly for pre-existing illnesses, will save trouble later. See your dentist before a long trip, carry a spare pair of contact lenses and glasses, and take your optical prescription with you. Bring medications in their original, clearly labelled, containers. A signed and dated letter from your physician describing your medical conditions and medications, including generic names, is also a good idea. If carrying syringes or needles, be sure to have a physician's letter documenting their medical necessity.

INSURANCE

If you're an EU citizen, be sure to get the EHIC (European Health Insurance Card), which replaces the no-longer valid E111 certificate. You can apply for this card online (www.ehic.org.uk) or pick up an application at any British post office. The EHIC will not cover you for nonemergencies or emergency repatriation. Citizens from other countries should find out if there is a reciprocal arrangement for free medical care between their country and Portugal. If you do need health insurance, strongly consider a policy that covers you for the worst possible scenario, such as an accident requiring an emergency flight home. Find out in advance if your insurance plan will make payments directly to providers or reimburse you later for overseas healt expenditures. The former option is generall preferable, as it doesn't require you to pay ou of pocket in a foreign country.

> **TRAVEL HEALTH WEBSITES**
>
> It's usually a good idea to consult your government's travel health website before departure, if one is available:
>
> **Australia** (www.smartraveller.gov.au)
> **Canada** (www.hc-sc.gc.ca/english/index.html)
> **UK** (www.doh.gov.uk)
> **United States** (www.cdc.gov/travel)

RECOMMENDED VACCINATIONS

The WHO recommends that all traveller should be covered for diphtheria, tetanus measles, mumps, rubella and polio, regardles of their destination. Since most vaccines don produce immunity until at least two week after they're given, visit a physician at leas six weeks before departure.

INTERNET RESOURCES

The WHO's publication *International Trav and Health* is revised annually and is avail able on line at www.who.int/ith. Other usef websites include www.mdtravelhealth.co (travel health recommendations for ever country; updated daily), www.fitfortrav .scot.nhs.uk (general travel advice for the lay person), www.ageconcern.org.uk (advice o travel for the elderly) and www.mariestope org.uk (information on women's health an contraception).

IN PORTUGAL

AVAILABILITY & COST OF HEALTH CARE

Good health care is readily available and fo minor illnesses pharmacists can give valuab advice and sell over-the-counter medicatio Most pharmacists speak some English. The can also advise when more specialised help equired and point you in the right direction. The standard of dental care is usually good, ut it is sensible to have a dental check-up efore a long trip.

'RAVELLER'S DIARRHOEA

f you develop diarrhoea, be sure to drink lenty of fluids, preferably an oral rehydration olution (eg Dioralyte). A few loose stools on't require treatment, but if you start having nore than four or five stools a day, you should tart taking an antibiotic (usually a quinolone rug) and an antidiarrhoeal agent (such as operamide). If diarrhoea is bloody, persists or more than 72 hours or is accompanied by ever, shaking, chills or severe abdominal pain ou should seek medical attention.

NVIRONMENTAL HAZARDS

leat Exhaustion & Heat Stroke

Ieat exhaustion occurs following excessive uid loss with inadequate replacement of fluids and salt. Symptoms include headache, dizziness and tiredness. Dehydration is already appening by the time you feel thirsty – aim to rink sufficient water to produce pale, diluted rine. To treat heat exhaustion, replace lost uids by drinking water and/or fruit juice or n oral rehydration solution, such as Dioralyte, and cool the body with cold water and ans. Treat salt loss with salty fluids such as oup or Bovril, or add a little more table salt o foods than usual.

Heat stroke is much more serious, resulting n irrational and hyperactive behaviour and ventually loss of consciousness and death. apid cooling by spraying the body with water nd fanning is ideal. Emergency fluid and lectrolyte replacement by intravenous drip recommended.

nsect Bites & Stings

Iosquitoes are found in most parts of Europe. hey may not carry malaria but can cause irtation and infected bites. Use a DEET-based sect repellent.

Bees and wasps cause real problems only those with a severe allergy (anaphylaxis). you do have a severe allergy to bee or wasp ings, carry an 'epipen' or similar adrenaline ijection.

Sand flies are found around Mediterranean eaches. They usually cause only a nasty itchy ite but can carry a rare skin disorder called utaneous leishmaniasis.

Bed bugs lead to very itchy, lumpy bites. Spraying the mattress with crawling insect killer after changing the bedding will get rid of them.

Scabies are tiny mites that live in the skin, particularly between the fingers. They cause an intensely itchy rash. Scabies is easily treated with lotion from a pharmacy; other members of the household also need treating to avoid spreading scabies between asymptomatic carriers.

Snakes & Scorpions

Avoid getting bitten by snakes – don't walk barefoot or stick your hand into holes or cracks. Half of those bitten by venomous snakes are not injected with poison (envenomed). If bitten by a snake, don't panic. Immobilise the bitten limb with a splint (eg a stick) and apply a bandage over the site firmly, similar to a bandage over a sprain. Do not apply a tourniquet, or cut or suck the bite. Get medical help as soon as possible so that antivenin can be administered if necessary.

Scorpions are found in Portugal and their sting can be extremely painful but is not considered fatal.

Jellyfish, Sea Urchins & Weever Fish

Stings from jellyfish are painful but not dangerous. Douse the wound in vinegar to deactivate any stingers that haven't 'fired'. Applying calamine lotion, antihistamines or analgesics may reduce the reaction and relieve the pain.

Watch for sea urchins around rocky beaches. If you get their needles embedded in your skin, immerse the limb in hot water to relieve the pain. But to avoid infection visit a doctor and have the needles removed.

Thankfully, it is very rare to find the dangerous weever fish that inhabit shallow tidal zones along the Atlantic coast. They bury themselves in the sand with only their spines protruding and inject a powerful toxin if trodden upon. Soaking your foot in very hot water breaks down the poison, but you should seek medical advice in any event, since in rare cases this can cause permanent local paralysis.

Rabies, though rare in Portugal, is a risk, and transmittable via the bite of an infected animal. It can also be transmitted if the animal's saliva comes in contact with an open wound. If you've been bitten by a wild animal, a treatment of shots must begin at once.

TRAVELLING WITH CHILDREN

All travellers with small children should know how to treat minor ailments and when to seek medical treatment. Make sure the children are up to date with routine vaccinations, and discuss possible travel vaccines with your doctor well before departure as some vaccines are not suitable for children under a year.

In hot moist climates any wound or break in the skin is likely to let in infection. The area should be cleaned and kept dry.

Remember to avoid contaminated food and water. If your child has vomiting or diarrhoea, lost fluid and salts must be replaced. It may be helpful to take rehydration powders for reconstituting with boiled water.

Children should be encouraged to avoid and mistrust any dogs or other mammals because of the risk of rabies and other diseases. Any bite, scratch or lick from a warm blooded, furry animal should immediately be thoroughly cleaned. If there is any possibility that the animal is infected with rabies, immediate medical assistance should be sought.

WOMEN'S HEALTH

Travelling during pregnancy is usually possible but always consult your doctor before planning your trip. The most risky times for travel are during the first 12 weeks of pregnancy and after 30 weeks.

SEXUAL HEALTH

Emergency contraception is most effective if taken within 24 hours after unprotected sex. The **International Planned Parent Federation** (www.ippf.org) can advise about the availability of contraception in different countries.

When buying condoms, look for a European CE mark, which means they have been rigorously tested, and then store them in a cool and dry place or they may crack and perish.

Abortion is still illegal in Portugal.

Language

CONTENTS

Portuguese is the language spoken by 10 million Portuguese and 180 million Brazilians, and is the official language of the African nations of Angola, Mozambique, Cape Verde, Guinea-Bissau, and São Tomé e Príncipe. In Asia you'll hear it in the former Portuguese territories of Macau and East Timor, and in enclaves around Malaka, Goa, Damão and Diu.

As you travel through Portugal, the use of a few Portuguese words and phrases (such as greetings, the essentials of getting a room ordering a meal, catching a bus or train, timetable basics, 'please', 'thank you', 'yes' and 'no') can transform people's willingness to welcome and help you. For useful culinary language, see p80, and for information on institutes that offer language courses within Portugal, see p106 and p202.

Nearly all turismo (tourist office) staff in Portugal speak some English. In Lisbon, Porto, most of the Algarve and other big tourist destinations it's fairly easy to find English speakers, especially among younger people. Some in the service industry, like waiters and baristas, may insist on showing off their English skills, despite your attempts to stick to Portuguese. Among older folk and in the countryside, English speakers are rare. In the Minho and other areas where local emigrant workers have spent time abroad, you may find people able to speak French or German.

If you'd like a more detailed guide to Portuguese in a compact and easy-to-use form, get yourself a copy of Lonely Planet's *Portuguese Phrasebook*.

LANGUAGE HISTORY

Like French, Italian, Romanian and Spanish, Portuguese is a Romance language derived from Latin. Its pronunciation is quite different to other Romance languages, but the similarities are clear when you see it in the written form.

The pre-Roman inhabitants of the Iberian Peninsula were responsible for Portuguese's most striking traits, but the influence of the vulgar Latin of Roman merchants and soldiers gradually took over from indigenous languages and caused a strong neo-Latin character to evolve.

After the Arab invasion in AD 711, Arabic became the prestige cultural language in the Peninsula and exerted a strong influence on the Portuguese language. This connection was significantly weakened when the Moors were expelled in 1249.

Portuguese underwent several changes during the Middle Ages, mostly influenced by French and Provençal (another Romance language). In the 16th and 17th centuries, Italian and Spanish were responsible for innovations in vocabulary.

PRONUNCIATION

Most sounds in Portuguese are also found in English, with the most difficult ones being nasal vowels and diphthongs (explained on p483). The letter **ç** is pronounced like an English 's' and the letter **x** sounds like the 'sh' in 'ship' – *criança* is said 'kree-*an*-sa' and *Baixe Alentejo* 'baysh a-leng-*te*-zho'. The letter **h** is silent, but when combined to form **lh** it's pronounced like the 'lli' in 'million' and in **nh** it's like the 'ny' in 'canyon'. A circumflex (eg **ê**) or an acute accent (eg **é**) or a over a vowel marks word stress.

Vowels

In this pronunciation guide, we've used the following symbols for vowel sounds.

a	as the 'u' in 'run'
ai	as in 'aisle'
aw	as in 'saw'
ay	as in 'day'
e	as in 'bet'
ee	as in 'bee'
o	as in 'go'
oo	as in 'moon'
ow	as in 'how'
oy	as in 'boy'

Nasal Sounds

A characteristic feature of Portuguese is the use of nasal vowels and diphthongs (vowel combinations). Pronounce them as if you're trying to make the sound through your nose rather than your mouth. English also has nasal vowels to some extent – when you say 'sing' in English, the 'i' is nasalized by the 'ng'. In Portuguese, written vowels that have a nasal consonant after them (**m** or **n**), or a tilde over them (eg **ã**), will be nasal. In our pronunciation guide, we've used 'ng' to indicate a nasal sound.

Consonants

These symbols represent the trickier consonant sounds in Portuguese.

ly	as the 'lli' in 'million'
ny	as in 'canyon'
r	as in 'run'
rr	as in 'run' but stronger and rolled
zh	as the 's' in 'pleasure'

Word Stress

Stress generally falls on the second last syllable of a word, though there are exceptions. When a word ends in **-r** or is pronounced with a nasalized vowel, the stress falls on the last syllable. Vowels marked with an accent are always stressed.

In our transliteration system, the stressed syllable is shown in italics.

GENDER

Portuguese has masculine and feminine forms of nouns and adjectives. Alternative endings appear separated by a slash with the masculine form first. Generally, a word ending in **o** is masculine and one ending in **a** is feminine.

ACCOMMODATION

I'm looking for a ...
Procuro ... proo·*koo*·roo·...

Where's a ...?
Onde é ...? ongd e ...

bed and breakfast
um turismo de habitação oong too·*reezh*·moo de a·bee·ta·*sowng*

camping ground
um parque de campismo oong park·de kang·*peezh*·moo

guesthouse
uma pensão *oo*·ma peng·*sowng*

hotel
um hotel oong oo·*tel*

youth hostel
um pousada da juventude oong po·*za*·da da zhoo·*veng*·tood

room
um quarto oong *kwarr*·too

I'd like a ... room.
Queria um quarto de ... *kree*·a oong *kwarr*·too de ...

Do you have a ... room?
Tem um quarto de ...? teng oong *kwarr*·too de ...

double
casal ka·*zal*

single
individual ing·dee·vee·*dwal*

twin
duplo *doo*·ploo

For (three) nights.
Para (três) noites. *pa*·ra (trezh) noytsh

Does it include breakfast?
Inclui pequeno almoço? eeng·kloo·*ee* pee·*ke*·noo al·*mo*·soo

May I see it?
Posso ver? *po*·soo verr

I'll take the room.
Fico com ele. *fee*·koo kom *e*·lee

I don't like it.
Não gosto. nowng *gos*·too

I'm leaving now.
Estou indo embora agora. shto *een*·doo em·*bo*·ra a·*go*·ra

How much is it per ...?
Quanto custa por ...? *kwang*·too *koos*·ta porr ...

night
uma noite *oo*·ma noyt

person
pessoa *pso*·a

week
uma semana *oo*·ma se·*ma*·na

MAKING A RESERVATION
(for phone or written requests)

To ...	*Para ...*
From ...	*De ...*
Date	*Data*
I'd like to book ...	*Queria fazer uma reserva ...* (see the list under 'Accommodation' for bed/room options)
in the name of ...	*no nome de ...*
for the nights of ...	*para os dias ...*
from ... to ...	*de ... até ...*
credit card ...	*cartão de credito ...*
number	*número*
expiry date	*data de vencimento*

Please confirm availability/price.
Por favor confirme a disponibilidade/o preço.

CONVERSATION & ESSENTIALS

Hello.
Bom dia. bong *dee*·a
Hi.
Olá. o·*la*
Good day.
Bom dia. bong *dee*·a
Good evening.
Boa noite. *bo*·a noyt
See you later.
Até logo. a·*te lo*·goo
Goodbye.
Adeus. a·*dyoos*
How are you?
Como está? *ko*·moo shta
Fine, and you?
Tudo bem, e tu? *too*·doo beng e too
I'm pleased to meet you.
Prazer em conhecê-lo/-la. (m/f) pra·*zerr* eng ko·nye·*se*·loo/la
Yes.
Sim. seeng
No.
Não. nowng
Please.
Faz favor. fash fa·*vorr*
Thank you (very much).
(Muito) Obrigado/a. (m/f) (*mweeng*·too) o·bree·*ga*·doo/da
You're welcome.
De nada. de *na*·da
Excuse me. (to get past)
Com licença. kong lee·*seng*·sa
Excuse me. (before asking a question/making a request)
Desculpe. des·*koolp*
What's your name?
Como se chama? *ko*·moo se *sha*·ma
My name is ...
Chamo-me ... *sha*·moo·me ...
Where are you from?
De onde é? de *ong*·de e
I'm from ...
Sou (da/do/de) ... so (da/do/de) ...
May I take a photo of you?
Posso tirar-lhe uma foto? *po*·soo tee·*rarr*·lye oo·ma *fo*·too

DIRECTIONS

Where's ...?
Onde fica ...? ongd *fee*·ka ...
Can you show me (on the map)?
Pode mostrar-me (no mapa)? pod moos·*trarrm* (noo *ma*·pa)
What's the address?
Qual é a morada? kwal e a moo·*ra*·da
How far is it?
Qual a distância daqui? kwal a dees·*tan*·see·a da·*kee*
How do I get there?
Como é que eu chego ali? *ko*·moo e ke e·oo *she*·goo a·*lee*

SIGNS

Posto de Polícia	Police Station
Pronto Socorro	Emergency Department
Aberto	Open
Encerrado	Closed
Fechado	Closed
Entrada	Entrance
Saída	Exit
Não Fumadores	No Smoking
Lavabos/WC	Toilet
Homens (H)	Men
Senhoras (S)	Women

Turn ...	*Vire ...*	veer ...
at the corner	*na esquina*	na *skee*·na
at the traffic lights	*no semáforo*	noo *sma*·foo·roo
left	*à esquerda*	a *skerr*·da
right	*à direita*	a dee·*ray*·ta

here	*aqui*	a·*kee*
there	*ali*	a·*lee*
near ...	*perto ...*	*perr*·too ...
straight ahead	*em frente*	eng frengt

LANGUAGE

north	*norte*	nort
south	*sul*	sool
east	*este*	esht
west	*oeste*	oo·*esht*

EMERGENCIES

Help!
Socorro! soo·*ko*·rroo
It's an emergency.
É uma emergência. e *oo*·ma e·merr·*zheng*·sya
I'm lost.
Estou perdido/a. (m/f) shto perr·*dee*·doo/da
Where are the toilets?
Onde ficam os lavabos? ong·de *fee*·kam oos la·*va*·boos
Go away!
Vai-te embora! vai·te eng·*bo*·ra

Call ...!
Chame ...! *sham ...*
a doctor
um médico oong *me*·dee·koo
an ambulance
uma ambulância *oo*·ma am·boo·*lan*·sya
the police
a policía a poo·lee·*see*·a

HEALTH

I'm ill.
Estou doente. shto doo·*engt*
I need a doctor (who speaks English).
Preciso de um médico (que fale inglês). pre·*see*·zoo de oong *me*·dee·koo (ke fal eeng·*glesh*)
It hurts here.
Aqui dói. a·*kee* doy
I've been vomiting.
Tenho estado a vomitar. *ta*·nyo *shta*·doo a voo·mee·*tarr*
(I think) I'm pregnant.
(Acho que) Estou grávida. (*a*·shoo ke) shto *gra*·vee·da

Where's the nearest ...?
Onde fica ...is perto? *on*·de *fee*·ka ... mais *perr*·to
dentist
o dentista oo deng·*teesh*·ta
doctor
o médico oo *me*·dee·koo
hospital
o hospital oo osh·pee·*tal*
medical centre
a clínica médica a *klee*·nee·ka *me*·dee·ka
(night) phramacist
a farmácia (de serviço) a farr·*ma*·see·a (der ser·*vee*·soo)

I feel ...
Estou ... shto ...
dizzy
com tonturas kong tong·*too*·ras
nauseous
com naúseas kong *now*·shas

asthma	*asma*	*azh*·ma
diarrhea	*diarréia*	dee·a·*ray*·a
fever	*febre*	febr
pain	*dores*	dorsh

I'm allergic to ...
Sou alérgico/a à ... so a·lerr·*zhee*·koo/ka a ...
antibiotics
antibióticos ang·tee·*byo*·tee·koos
aspirin
aspirina ash·pee·*ree*·na
bees
abelhas a·*be*·lyas
peanuts
amendoins a·meng·*doyngs*
penicillin
penicilina pnee·see·*lee*·na

antiseptic
antiséptico an·tee·*sep*·tee·koo
contraceptives
anticoncepcional an·tee·kon·*sep*·syoo·nal
painkillers
analgésicos a·nal·*zhe*·zee·koos

LANGUAGE DIFFICULTIES

Do you speak English?
Fala inglês? *fa*·la eeng·*glesh*
Does anyone here speak English?
Alguém aqui fala inglês? al·*geng* a·*kee* *fa*·la eeng·*glesh*
Do you understand?
Entende? eng·*tengd*
I (don't) understand.
(Não) Entendo. (nowng) eng·*teng*·doo

Could you please ...?
Pode por favor ...? *po*·de·porr fa·*vorr* ...
repeat that
repetir isso rrpe·*teerr* *ees*·soo
speak more slowly
falar mais devagar fa·*larr* maizh dva·*garr*
write it down
escrever num papel es·kre·*verr* noom pa·*pel*

NUMBERS

0	*zero*	*ze*·roo
1	*um/uma* (m/f)	oong/*oo*·ma

2	*dois/duas* (m/f)	doys/dwash
3	*três*	tresh
4	*quatro*	*kwa*·troo
5	*cinco*	*seeng*·koo
6	*seis*	saysh
7	*sete*	set
8	*oito*	*oy*·too
9	*nove*	nov
10	*dez*	desh
11	*onze*	ongz
12	*doze*	doz
13	*treze*	trez
14	*quatorze*	ka·*torrz*
15	*quinze*	keengz
16	*dezesseis*	dze·*saysh*
17	*dezesete*	dze·*set*
18	*dezoito*	*dzoy*·too
19	*dezenove*	dze·*nov*
20	*vinte*	veengt
21	*vinte e um*	veengt e oong
22	*vinte e dois*	veengt e doysh
30	*trinta*	*treeng*·ta
40	*quarenta*	kwa·*reng*·ta
50	*cinquenta*	seeng·*kweng*·ta
60	*sessenta*	se·*seng*·ta
70	*setenta*	*steng*·ta
80	*oitenta*	oy·*teng*·ta
90	*noventa*	noo·*veng*·ta
100	*cem*	sang
200	*duzentos*	doo·*zeng*·toosh
1000	*mil*	*meel*

QUESTION WORDS

Who?
Quem? keng

What?
(O) Quê? (oo) ke

When?
Quando? *kwang*·doo

Where?
Onde? *ong*·de

Why?
Porque? porr·*ke*

Which/What?
Qual/Quais? (sg/pl) kwal/kwais

SHOPPING & SERVICES

What time does ... open?
A que horas abre ...? a ke *o*·ras abr ...

I'd like to buy ...
Queria comprar ... *kree*·rya kom·*prarr* ...

I'm just looking.
Estou só a olhar. shto so a ol·*yar*

May I look at it?
Posso vê-lo/la? (m/f) *po*·soo *ve*·loo/la

How much is it?
Quanto é? *kwang*·too e

That's too expensive.
É muito caro. e *mweeng*·too *ka*·roo

Can you lower the price?
Pode baixar o preço? *po*·de ba·*sharr* oo *pre*·soo

Do you have something cheaper?
Tem uma coisa mais barata? teng *oo*·ma *koy*·za maizh ba·*ra*·ta

I'll give you (five euros).
Dou (cinco euros). do (*seeng*·koo *yoo*·roos)

I don't like it.
Não gosto deste. nowng *gosh*·too desht

I'll take it.
Vou levar isso. vo le·*var* *ee*·soo

Where is ...?
Onde fica ...? *ong*·de *fee*·ka ...

an ATM	*um multibanco*	oom mool·tee·*bang*·koo
a bank	*o banco*	oo *ban*·koo
a bookstore	*uma livraria*	*oo*·ma lee·vra·*rya*
the ... embassy	*a embaixada do/da ...*	a eng·bai·*sha*·da doo/da ...
a foreign-exchange office	*uma loja de câmbio*	*oo*·ma *lo*·zha de *kam*·byoo
a laundrette	*uma lavandaria*	*oo*·ma la·vang·*dree*·a
a market	*o mercado*	oo merr·*ka*·doo
a pharmacy/chemist	*uma farmácia*	*oo*·ma far·*ma*·sya
the police station	*o posto de polícia*	oo *pos*·too·de poo·*lee*·see·a
the post office	*o correio*	oo coo·*ray*·oo
a supermarket	*o supermercado*	oo soo·perr·merr·*ka*·doo

Can I pay ...?
Posso pagar com ...? *po*·soo pa·*garr* kom ...

by credit card	*cartão de crédito*	karr·*towng* de *kre*·dee·too
by travellers cheque	*traveler cheque*	*tra*·ve·ler *she*·kee

less	*menos*	*me*·noos
more	*mais*	maizh
large	*grande*	grangd
small	*pequeno/a* (m/f)	*pke*·noo/na

LANGUAGE

I want to buy ...
Quero comprar ... ke·roo kom·*prarr* ...
a phone card
um cartão telefónico oong kar·*towng* te·le·*fo*·nee·koo
stamps
selos *se*·loosh

Where can I ...?
Onde posso ...? *on*·de *po*·soo ...
change a travellers cheque
trocar traveler cheques troo·*karr* tra·ve·*ler she*·kes
change money
trocar dinheiro troo·*kar* dee·*nyay*·roo
check my email
ver o meu e-mail ver oo *me*·oo e·mail
get Internet access
aceder à internet a·se·*der* a een·terr·*net*

TIME & DATES

What time is it?
Que horas são? ke *o*·ras sowng
It's (ten) o'clock.
São (dez) horas. sowng (desh) *o*·ras

now	*agora*	a·*go*·ra
this morning	*esta manhã*	*esh*·ta ma·*nyang*
this afternoon	*esta tarde*	*esh*·ta *tard*
today	*hoje*	ozh
tonight	*esta noite*	*esh*·ta noyt
tomorrow	*amanhã*	a·ma·*nyang*
yesterday	*ontem*	*on*·teng

Monday	*segunda-feira*	sgoon·da·*fay*·ra
Tuesday	*terça-feira*	terr·sa·*fay*·ra
Wednesday	*quarta-feira*	kwarr·ta·*fay*·ra
Thursday	*quinta-feira*	keeng·ta·*fay*·ra
Friday	*sexta-feira*	saysh·ta·*fay*·ra
Saturday	*sábado*	*sa*·ba·doo
Sunday	*domingo*	doo·*meeng*·goo

January	*Janeiro*	zha·*nay*·roo
February	*Fevereiro*	fe·*vray*·roo
March	*Março*	*marr*·soo
April	*Abril*	a·*breel*
May	*Maio*	*ma*·yoo
June	*Junho*	*zhoo*·nyoo
July	*Julho*	*zhoo*·lyoo
August	*Agosto*	a·*gosh*·too
September	*Setembro*	*steng*·broo
October	*Outubro*	o·*too*·bro
November	*Novembro*	noo·*veng*·broo
December	*Dezembro*	*dzeng*·broo

ROAD SIGNS

Ceda a Vez	Give Way
Entrada	Entrance
Portagem	Toll
Proibido Entrar	No Entry
Rua Sem Saída	Dead End
Saída	Freeway Exit
Sentido Único	One-way

TRANSPORT

Public Transport

Which ... goes to Lisbon?	*Qual o ... que vai para Lisboa?*	kwal oo ... ke vai *pa*·ra leezh·*bo*·a
boat	*barco*	*barr*·koo
intercity bus	*camionetes*	kam·yoo·*ne*·tesh
local bus	*autocarro*	ow·too·*ka*·rroo
ferry	*ferry*	*fe*·ree
plane	*avião*	a·vee·*owng*
train	*comboio*	kom·*boy*·oo

When's the ... (bus)?	*Quando sai o ... (autocarro)?*	*kwang*·doo sai oo ... (ow·too·*ka*·rroo)
first	*primeiro*	pree·*may*·roo
next	*próximo*	*pro*·see·moo
last	*último*	*ool*·tee·moo

Is this the (bus) to ...?
Este (autocarro) vai para ...? esht (ow·to·*ka*·rroo) vai *pa*·ra ...?
What time does it leave?
Que horas sai? ke *o*·ras sai
What time does it get to ...?
Que horas chega a ...? ke *o*·ras *she*·ga a ...
Do I need to change?
Tenho de mudar de linha? te·nyoo de moo·*darr* de *lee*·nya

A ... ticket to (...)	*Um bilhete de ... para (...)*	oong bee·*lyet* de ... *pa*·ra (...)
1st-class	*primeira classe*	pree·*may*·ra klas
2nd-class	*segunda classe*	se·*goon*·da klas
one-way	*ida*	*ee*·da
return	*ida e volta*	*ee*·da e *vol*·ta

the luggage check room
o balcão de guarda volume oo bal·*kowng* de *gwarr*·da voo·*loo*·me
a luggage locker
um cacifo de bagagem oong ka·*see*·foo de ba·*ga*·zheng

Is this taxi available?
Este táxi está livre? *esht tak*·see shta leevr
How much is it to ...?
Quanto custa ir a ...? *kwang*·too *koos*·ta eerr a ...

lease put the meter on.
Por favor ligue o taxímetro.
porr fa·*vorr lee*·ge oo tak·*see*·me·troo

lease take me to (this address).
Leve-me para (esta morada), por favor.
le·ve·me *pa*·ra (*esh*·ta moo·*ra*·da) porr fa·*vorr*

'rivate Transport

d like to hire a/an ...
ueria alugar ...
ə·rya a·loo·*garr* ...

4WD		
um quatro por quatro	oom *kwa*·troo por *kwa*·troo	
bicycle		
uma bicicleta	*oo*·ma bee·see·*kle*·ta	
car		
um carro	oong *ka*·rroo	
motorbike		
uma motocicleta	*oo*·ma mo·too·see·*kle*·ta	

: this the road to ...?
Esta é a estrada para ...?
esh·ta e a es·*tra*·da *pa*·ra ...

How long) Can I park here?
(Quanto tempo) Posso estacionar aqui?
(*kwang*·too *teng*·poo) *po*·soo es·ta·shyoo·*narr* a·*kee*

Where's a gas/petrol station?
Onde fica um posto de gasolina?
on·de *fee*·ka oong *pos*·too de ga·zoo·*lee*·na

lease fill it up.
Enche o depósito, por favor.
en·she oo de·*po*·see·too porr fa·*vorr*

d like ... litres.
Meta ... litros.
me·ta ... *lee*·troosh

iesel	*diesel*	*dee*·sel
PG	*gás*	gash
nleaded	*gasolina sem chumbo*	ga·zoo·*lee*·na seng *shoom*·bo

Also available from Lonely Planet:
Portuguese Phrasebook

The (car/motorbike) has broken down at ...
(O carro/A motocicleta) avariou em ...
(oo *ka*·rroo/a moo·too·see·*kle*·ta) a·*va*·ryo eng ...

The car won't start.
O carro não pega.
o *ka*·ho nowng *pe*·ga

I need a mechanic.
Preciso de um mecânico.
pre·*see*·soo de oong me·*ka*·nee·koo

I've run out of gas/petrol.
Fiquei sem gasolina.
fee·*kay* seng ga·zoo·*lee*·na

I've had an accident.
Sofri um aciden te.
soo·*free* oong a·see·*dent*

TRAVEL WITH CHILDREN

I need (a/an) ...
Preciso de ...
pre·*see*·zoo de ...

Do you have (a/an) ...?
Aqui tem ...?
a·*kee* teng ...

baby change room
uma sala para mudar o bebé
oo·ma *sa*·la *pa*·ra moo·*darr* o be·*be*

baby seat
um assento de criança
oong a·*seng*·too de kree·*an*·sa

child-minding service
um serviço de ama
oong serr·*vee*·soo de *a*·ma

children's menu
um cardápio para criança
oong kar·*da*·pyo *pa*·ra kree·*an*·sa

(disposable) nappies/diapers
fraldas (descartáveis)
fral·das (des·karr·*ta*·vays)

(English-speaking) baby-sitter
uma ama (que fale ingles)
oo·ma *a*·ma (ke *fa*·le eeng·*glesh*)

formula (milk)
leite em pó (para bebé)
layt eng po (pa·ra be·*be*)

highchair
uma cadeira de criança
oo·ma ka·*day*·ra de kree·*an*·sa

Do you mind if I breastfeed here?
Importa-se que eu amamente aqui?
een·*porr*·ta·se ke eu a·ma·*meng*·te a·*kee*

Are children allowed?
É permitida a entrada de crianças?
e perr·mee·*tee*·da a eng·*tra*·da de kree·*an*·sas

Glossary

For food and drink terms, see the Food & Drink Glossary (p80), and for general terms see the Language chapter (p481).

aberto – open
adegas – wineries
Age of Discoveries – the period during the 15th and 16th centuries when Portuguese sailors explored the coast of Africa and finally charted a sea route to India
aluguer – for hire
albergaria – upmarket inn
albufeira – reservoir, lagoon
aldeia – village
alta – upper
alta qualidade – fast deluxe bus
anta – see *dolmen*
arco – arch
armazém – warehouse
armillary sphere – celestial sphere used by early astronomers and navigators to chart the stars; a decorative motif in Manueline architecture and atop *pelourinhos*
arrabalde – outskirts, environs
arrayal, arraiais (pl) – street party
artesanato – handicrafts shop
auto-estradas – motorways
avenida – avenue
aviação – airline
azulejo – hand-painted tile, typically blue and white, used to decorate buildings

bagagem – left-luggage office
bairro – town district
baixa – lower
balneário – health resort, spa
bandarilha – spears
bandeirada – flag fall
barcos rabelos – colourful boats once used to transport port wine from vineyards
barragem – dam
beco – cul de sac
berrão, berrões (pl) – ancient stone monument shaped like a pig, found mainly in Trás-os-Montes and the adjacent part of Spain
biblioteca – library
bicyclete tudo terrano (BTT) – mountain bike
bilhete de cidade – city ticket
bilhete diário/turístico – day pass/tourist ticket

cabines – phone boxes
câmara municipal – city or town hall
caderneta – booklet of tickets (train)
cais fluvial – river terminal
caldas – hot springs
cantarinha – small terracotta pitcher
Carnaval – Carnival; festival that takes place just before Lent
carreiras (CR) – stop at every crossroad (never mind that *carreiras* means something like 'in a hurry' in Portuguese)
cartão telefónico – plastic card used in *Credifone* telephones
casa de abrigo – shelter house (eg for staff and/or the public in a national or natural park)
casa de banho – toilet (literally bathroom)
casa de fado – *fado* house; a place (usually a café or restaurant) where people gather to hear *fado* music
casa de hóspedes – boarding house, usually with shared showers and toilets
casa de povo – village common house
casais – huts
castelo – castle
castro – fortified hill town
cavaleiro – horseman
CCI – Camping Card International
Celtiberians – descendants of Celts who arrived in the Iberian Peninsula around 600 BC
centro de comércio – shopping centre
centro de saúde – state-administered medical centre
centros de acolhimento – lodging centres
chegada – arrival (of bus, train etc)
cidade – town or city
cidadela – fortress
citânia – Celtic fortified village
claustro – cloisters
concelho – municipality, council
conta – bill (in a restaurant)
coro alto – choir stalls overlooking the nave in a church
correios – post office
cortes – Portugal's early parliament
couvert – cover charge added to restaurant bills to pay for sundries
CP – Caminhos de Ferro Portugueses (the Portuguese sta[illegible] railway company)
Credifone – card-operated public telephone
cromeleque – circle of prehistoric standing stones
cruz – cross

direita – right; abbreviated as D, dir or Dta
distrito – district
dolmen – Neolithic stone tomb (*anta* in Portuguese)

om, Dona – honorific titles (like Sir, Madam) given to
oyalty, nobility and landowners; now used more generally
s a very polite form of address
ormidas – sign indicating a rooming house
uplo – room with twin beds

levador – lift (elevator), funicular
menta – menu
ncerrado – closed or shut down (eg for repairs)
ntrada – entrée/starter or entrance
spigueiros – stone granaries
splanada – terrace, seafront promenade
squerda – left; abbreviated as E, esq or Esqa
stação – station (usually train station)
stacionamento – parking
stalagem – inn; more expensive than an *albergaria*
stradas nacionais – main two-lane national roads
xpressos – comfortable, fast buses between major cities
stradas – highways

adista – singer of *fado*
ado – traditional, melancholic Portuguese style of singing
armácia – pharmacy
echado – closed (eg for the day/weekend or holiday)
eira – fair
érias – holidays, vacation
esta – festival
ICC – Fédération Internationale de Camping et de
aravanning (International Camping & Caravanning
ederation)
orcados – young men who face a bull barehanded
ortaleza – fortress
PCC – Federação Portuguesa de Campismo e Caravanismo
Portuguese Camping & Caravanning Federation)
reguesia – parish

NR – Guarda Nacional Republicana, the national guard
he acting police force in rural towns without PSP police)
uitarra – guitar
ruta – cave

ipermercado – hypermarket
orários – timetables
ospedaria – see *casa de hóspedes*

C (intercidade) – express intercity train
CEP – Investimentos, Comércio e Turismo de Portugal,
he government's umbrella organisation for tourism
DD – International Direct Dial
greja – church
greja matriz – parish church
ha – island
nfantário – children's daycare centre
R (interregional) – fairly fast train that doesn't make
oo many stops

itinerário complementar (IC) – subsidiary highways
itinerário principal (IP) – highways in the country's main network
IVA – Imposto sobre Valor Acrescentado, or VAT (value-added tax)

jardim – garden
jardim municipal – town garden
jardim público – public garden
judiaria – quarter in a town where Jews were once segregated
junta de turismo – see *turismo*

largo – small square
latifúndios – Roman system of large farming estates
lavabo – toilet
lavandaria – laundry
lista – see *ementa*
litoral – coastal
livraria – bookshop
Lisboêtas – Lisbon dweller
loggia – covered area or porch on the side of a building
lugar – neighbourhood, place

Manueline – elaborate late Gothic/Renaissance style of art and architecture that emerged during the reign of Dom Manuel I in the 16th century
mantas alentejanas – handwoven woollen blankets
marranos – 'New Christians,' ie Jews who converted during the Inquisition
menir – menhir, a standing stone monument typical of the late Neolithic Age
mercado municipal – municipal market
mesa – table
MFA – Movimento das Forças Armadas, the military group that led the Revolution of the Carnations in 1974
minimercado – grocery shop or small supermarket
miradouro – viewpoint
Misericórdia – derived from Santa Casa da Misericórdia (Holy House of Mercy), a charitable institution founded in the 15th century to care for the poor and the sick; it usually designates an old building that was founded by this organisation
moliceiro – high-prowed, shallow-draft boats traditionally used for harvesting seaweed in the estuaries of Beira Litoral
mosteiro – monastery
mouraria – the quarter where Moors were segregated during and after the Christian *Reconquista*
mudéjar – originally a Muslim under Christian rule; also used as an adjective to describe the art and architecture of the mudéjars
museu – museum
música popular – modern folk-music scene

paço – palace
paisagens protegidas – protected landscape areas
parque de campismo – camping ground
parque de merenda – picnic area
parque infantil – playground
parque nacional – national park
parque natural – natural park
partida – departure (of bus, train etc)
pauliteiro – stick dancer
pega – second phase of a bullfight
pelourinho – stone pillory, often ornately carved; erected in the 13th to 18th centuries as symbols of justice and sometimes as places where criminals were punished
pensão, pensões (pl) – guesthouse, the Portuguese equivalent of a bed and breakfast (B&B), though breakfast is not always served
peões de brega – footmen
percurso pedestre – walking trail
planalto – high plain
pombal – dovecote, a structure for housing pigeons
ponte – bridge
portagem – toll road
posto de turismo – see *turismo*
pousada or Pousada de Portugal – government-run scheme of upmarket inns, often in converted castles, convents or palaces
pousada da juventude – youth hostel; usually with kitchen, common rooms and sometimes rooms with private bathroom
praça – square
praça de touros – bullring
praia – beach
pré-pagamento – prepayment required (as in some café-restaurants)
PSP – Polícia de Segurança Pública, the local police force

quarto de casal – room with a double bed
quarto individual – single room
quarto particular – room in a private house
quinta – country estate or villa; in the Douro wine-growing region it often refers to a wine lodge's property

rápidas – quick regional buses
R (regional) – slow train
Reconquista – Christian reconquest of Portugal (718–1249)
recreio infantil – playground
rés do chão – ground floor (abbreviated as R/C)
reservas naturais – nature reserves
residencial, residenciais (pl) – guesthouse; slightly more expensive than a *pensão* and usually serving breakfast
retornados – refugees
ribeiro – stream
rio – river
romaria – religious pilgrimage
rua – street

sanitários – public toilets
sapataria – shoe shop
saudade – melancholic longing for better times
sé – cathedral
selos – stamps
sem chumbo – unleaded (petrol)
senhor – man
senhora – woman
senhora dona – elderly or respected woman
serra – mountain, mountain range
solar – manor house
supermercado – supermarket

tabacaria – tobacconist-cum-newsagent
talha dourada – gilded woodwork
tasca – tavern
termas – spas, hot springs
terra fria – cold country
terra quente – hot country
torre de menagem – castle tower, keep
tourada – bullfight
troco – change
Turihab – short for Turismo Habitação, a scheme for marketing private accommodation (particularly in northern Portugal) in cottages, historic buildings and manor houses
turismo – tourist office

vila – town
vovó – grandma

Behind the Scenes

THIS BOOK

'or this, the 6th edition of *Portugal*, Regis St Louis vas the coordinating author, assisted by co-author Robert Landon. Abigail Hole, Charlotte Beech and Richard Sterling wrote the 5th edition of the guide and John King and Julia Wilkinson wrote the first our editions. The Health chapter was written by Dr Caroline Evans. This guidebook was commissioned n Lonely Planet's London office, and produced by he following:

Commissioning Editor Sally Schafer
Coordinating Editors Adrienne Costanzo, iz Heynes, Jeanette Wall
Coordinating Cartographers Csanad Csutoros, Matthew Kelly
Coordinating Layout Designers Pablo Gastar, ara Smith
Managing Editor Suzannah Shwer
Senior Editor Katie Lynch
Managing Cartographer Mark Griffiths
Assisting Editors Gennifer Ciavarra, Melissa Faulkner, oanne Newell, Simon Sellars
Assisting Cartographers Julie Dodkins, Tony Fankhauser, oshua Geoghegan, Valentina Kremenchutskaya
Cover Designer Mary Nelson-Parker
Project Manager Kate McLeod
Language Content Coordinator Quentin Frayne

Thanks to Sally Darmody, Kate McDonald, Darren O'Connell, Trent Paton, Celia Wood. Thanks also to Teresa Ventura at the Portuguese Tourist Office in London.

THANKS

REGIS ST LOUIS

Many thanks to Sally Schafer for inviting me on board, Christian Simms for his fine company in Lisbon, Rita for the excellent insider tour around the Alfama, and Cassandra for a sunshine-filled trip in the Algarve. I'd like to thank the numerous readers who wrote in and shared some worthwhile tips and suggestions. I also owe a big thanks to the many Portuguese who helped along the way; your guidance was invaluable.

ROBERT LANDON

Thanks to: Sally for hiring and shadowing; Paulo for his birthday company; Carlos and Susi for fresh eyes in Belmonte; Tiago for his version of Coimbra; Manuel, who manages to be thanked in all my books; Mom for her mutual love of travel and writing; and the open, ready, kind people of Portugal, too numerous to mention.

OUR READERS

Many thanks to the travellers who used the last edition and wrote to us with helpful hints, useful advice and interesting anecdotes:

A Palmer Acheson **B** Margaret Bahr, Alan Benfield, Robert Best, Frédéric Bettosinie, Helen Blöchlinger, Esther Bloemenkamp, Claire Brousse, Damon Burn, Nellie Butler **C** Michele Campbell, David Cantrell, Luis Carvalho, Stephanie Chang, Rodolfo Coceancig, Elizabeth Coleman, Natalia Cooper, Joe & Laura Crapanzano, Bev Crawford **D** Margarida da Silva, Caroline Dahlem,

THE LONELY PLANET STORY

The story begins with a classic travel adventure: Tony and Maureen Wheeler's 1972 journey across Europe and Asia to Australia. There was no useful information about the overland trail then, so Tony and Maureen published the first Lonely Planet guidebook to meet a growing need.

From a kitchen table, Lonely Planet has grown to become the largest independent travel publisher in the world, with offices in Melbourne (Australia), Oakland (USA) and London (UK). Today Lonely Planet guidebooks cover the globe. There is an ever-growing list of books and information in a variety of media. Some things haven't changed. The main aim is still to make it possible for adventurous travellers to get out there – to explore and better understand the world.

At Lonely Planet we believe travellers can make a positive contribution to the countries they visit – if they respect their host communities and spend their money wisely. Every year 5% of company profit is donated to charities around the world.

Magdalena del Pedregal, Raul Diniz-Inacio, Nelson Duarte, Amanda Dube **F** Hannah Fellehner, Emmanoel Ferreira, Claude Forestier-Walker, Victor Fraser, Anders Fredriksson, Yonnie Fung **G** Hellena Gallant, Victor Gallant, Suzel Gary, Jodie Geissler, Diana Gill **H** Peter Hallier, Andrew Hammett, René Hansen, Guillermo Herrero, Frank Hilarius, Annie Hubert **J** Hamish Jackson, Nicola James **K** Sheila Kane, Marian Kelly, Irma Kennaway, Joy Kennedy, Marjie King, Lizzie Kinross, Martina Kubaniova **L** Tony Lake, Stephen Lee, Robert Leger, David Littlewood, Sharon Livingstone, Catarina Lopez **M** Claudia Maran, Sabine Mark, Robert Maule, Desmond Murphy **P** Joanne Parker, Frieda Pruim, Anna Ptaszynska **R** Nuno Raposo, Nalini Reimer, Ydun Ritz, Rick Ross **S** Vahan Sardaryan, Debra & Alan Sayles, Carrie Schaffner, Martin Shankeman, Eduardo Soares, John Spurway, Hope Stenton, Geoff Stone, Tak Suizu **T** Pam & Eric Tremont **U** Alexander Unwin **V** Diego Valdes, Luke Valentine, Mannis van Oven, Joao Varela, Andrew & Marilyn Vasilevich, Carla Veríssimo, Stella Voutta **W** Paul Wagner, Haydn Walker, Nathan Walker, Judith Weibrecht **Z** Azriel Zaiden

SEND US YOUR FEEDBACK

We love to hear from travellers – your comments keep us on our toes and help make our books better. Our well-travelled team reads every word on what you loved or loathed about this book. Although we cannot reply individually to postal submissions, we always guarantee that your feedback goes straight to the appropriate authors, in time for the next edition. Each person who sends us information is thanked in the next edition – and the most useful submissions are rewarded with a free book.

To send us your updates – and find out about Lonely Planet events, newsletters and travel news – visit our award-winning website: **lonelyplanet.com/contact**.

Note: we may edit, reproduce and incorporate your comments in Lonely Planet products such as guidebooks, websites and digital products, so let us know if you don't want your comments reproduced or your name acknowledged. For a copy of our privacy policy visit www.lonelyplanet.com/privacy.

Index

ABBREVIATIONS
PN Parque Natural
RN Reserva Natural

000 Map pages
000 Photograph pages

000 Map pages
000 Photograph pages

INDEX

Q

R

S

INDEX

12am
1am
2am
3am
4am
5am
6am
7am
8am
9am
10am
11am
12pm
Mon
Sun
International Date Line
ARCTIC OCEAN
Queen Elizabeth Is (Can)
Ellesmere Is (Can)
GREENLAND SEA
9am
Greenland (Denmark)
CHUKCHI SEA
BEAUFORT SEA
Banks Is (Can)
Victoria Is (Can)
BAFFIN BAY
11am
NORWEGIAN SEA
Russia
Alaska (US)
5am
4am
3am
Baffin Is (Can)
Iceland
NORTH SEA
BERING SEA
HUDSON BAY
United Kingdom
GULF OF ALASKA
Canada
LABRADOR SEA
2am
6am
8am
Ireland
NORTH ATLANTIC OCEAN
7am
8.30am
Azores (Port)
United States
Spain
Portugal
NORTH PACIFIC OCEAN
Bermuda (UK)
1am
Midway Is (US)
Morocco
Canary Is (Sp)
Mexico
GULF OF MEXICO
The Bahamas
Cuba
Haiti
Eastern Caribbean Islands
Mauritania
Mali
Hawaii (US)
12pm
Cape Verde
CARIBBEAN SEA
Guatemala
Senegal
Burkina Faso
Nicaragua
Guinea
Panama
Venezuela
Guyana
Liberia
Ghana
Colombia
Suriname
Galapagos Is (Ecuador)
GULF OF GUINEA
EQUATOR
Ecuador
Kiribati
8am
Ascension (UK)
Samoa
2.30am
Peru
Brazil
9am
7am
Tahiti
French Polynesia (Fr)
Bolivia
SOUTH ATLANTIC OCEAN
Tonga
Cook Is (NZ)
2am
12am
1am
Pitcairn Is (UK)
3.30am
Easter Is (Chile)
Paraguay
Uruguay
Chile
New Zealand
Argentina
Tristan da Cunha (UK)
12.45am
Gough Is (UK)
SOUTH PACIFIC OCEAN
Chatham Is (NZ)
Falkland Is (UK)
South Georgia & South Sandwich Is (UK)
Bouvet Is (Norway)
12am
1am
2am
3am
4am
5am
6am
7am
8am
9am
10am
11am
12pm

12pm 1pm 2pm 3pm 4pm 5pm 6pm 7pm 8pm 9pm 10pm 11pm 12am

Svalbard (Norway)
Zemlya Frantsa-Iosifa (Russia)
Severnaya Zemlya (Russia)
Mon | Sun
International Date Line
KARA SEA
Novaya Zemlya (Russia)
BARENTS SEA
LAPTEV SEA
Novosibirskie Ostrovo (Russia)
EAST SIBERIAN SEA
Sweden 1pm
2pm Finland
Norway
3pm
7pm
9pm
11pm
12am
4pm
5pm
Russia
10pm
Denmark
Latvia
Belarus
Poland
Germany
France
Austria
Ukraine
Romania
4pm
6pm
Kazakhstan
Mongolia
SEA OF OKHOTSK
BERING SEA
3am
2am
Italy
Uzbekistan
4pm
Kyrgyzstan
Greece
Turkey
Turkmenistan
North Korea
Tunisia
MEDITERRANEAN SEA
Syria
Iraq
Iran 3.30pm
Afghanistan 4.30pm
China
South Korea
Japan
NORTH PACIFIC OCEAN
Tibet (China)
8pm
Algeria
2pm
Libya
Egypt
5pm
Pakistan
Nepal 5.45 pm
Saudi Arabia
India
6.30 pm
EAST CHINA SEA
Taiwan
1pm
4pm
Oman
5.30 pm
Myanmar
Northern Mariana Is (US)
Niger
6pm
9pm
Marshall Is (US)
Chad
Sudan
Eritrea
Yemen
Thailand
ARABIAN SEA
BAY OF BENGAL
Philippines
12am
Nigeria
Ethiopia
5.30pm
Vietnam
Central African Republic
3pm
Sri Lanka
Palau
Federated States of Micronesia 11am
Kiribati
Somalia
Congo
Kenya
Maldives
Malaysia
Gabon
1pm
Congo (Zaire)
Indonesia
Nauru EQUATOR
Papua New Guinea
Tanzania
SOUTH PACIFIC OCEAN
Seychelles 4pm
6.30 pm
Solomon Is
Angola
East Timor
Malawi
Cocos (Keeling) Is (Aust)
Zambia
Vanuatu
Madagascar
Fiji
Namibia
Zimbabwe
Mauritius
INDIAN OCEAN
Botswana
Mozambique
Reunion (Fr)
9.30 pm
New Caledonia (Fr)
Australia
11.30 pm
10.30 pm
Norfolk Is (Aust)
South Africa
Lord Howe Is (Aust)
New Zealand
Prince Edward Is (S. Africa)
French Southern & Antarctic Territories (Fr)
TASMAN SEA
SOUTHERN OCEAN
Heard & McDonald Is (Aust)

12pm 1pm 2pm 3pm 4pm 5pm 6pm 7pm 8pm 9pm 10pm 11pm 12am

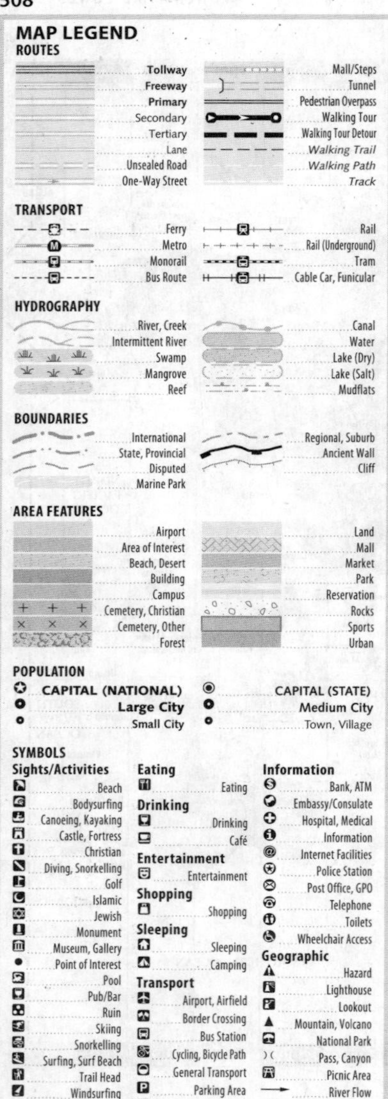

R.C.L.

SEP. 2007

G

LONELY PLANET OFFICES

Australia
Head Office
Locked Bag 1, Footscray, Victoria 3011
☎ 03 8379 8000, fax 03 8379 8111
talk2us@lonelyplanet.com.au

USA
150 Linden St, Oakland, CA 94607
☎ 510 893 8555, toll free 800 275 8555
fax 510 893 8572
info@lonelyplanet.com

UK
72–82 Rosebery Ave,
Clerkenwell, London EC1R 4RW
☎ 020 7841 9000, fax 020 7841 9001
go@lonelyplanet.co.uk

Published by Lonely Planet Publications Pty Ltd
ABN 36 005 607 983

© Lonely Planet Publications Pty Ltd 2007

© photographers as indicated 2007

Cover photograph: Nazaré, Portugal, Jürgen Wackenhut/Photolibrary. Many of the images in this guide are available for licensing from Lonely Planet Images: www.lonelyplanetimages.com.

All rights reserved. No part of this publication may be copied, stored in a retrieval system, or transmitted in any form by any means, electronic, mechanical, recording or otherwise, except brief extracts for the purpose of review, and no part of this publication may be sold or hired, without the written permission of the publisher.

Printed by SNP Security Printing Pte Ltd, Singapore

Lonely Planet and the Lonely Planet logo are trademarks of Lonely Planet and are registered in the US Patent and Trademark Office and in other countries.

Lonely Planet does not allow its name or logo to be appropriated by commercial establishments, such as retailers, restaurants or hotels. Please let us know of any misuses: www.lonelyplanet.com/ip.

Although the authors and Lonely Planet have taken all reasonable care in preparing this book, we make no warranty about the accuracy or completeness of its content and, to the maximum extent permitted, disclaim all liability arising from its use.